A Review of the Events of 1980

The 1981 World Book Year Book

The Annual Supplement to The World Book Encyclopedia

World Book–Childcraft International, Inc.
A subsidiary of The Scott & Fetzer Company
Chicago London Paris Sydney Tokyo Toronto

Staff

Editorial Director
William H. Nault

Editorial Staff
Executive Editor
Wayne Wille

Managing Editor
Paul C. Tullier

Chief Copy Editor
Joseph P. Spohn

Senior Editors
Patricia Dragisic
Marsha F. Goldsmith
Beverly Merz
Jay Myers
Edward G. Nash

Copy Editor
Irene B. Keller

Chief Statistical Editor
Robert Gauron

Index Editor
Claire Bolton

Editorial Assistant
Lettie Zinnamon

Executive Editor,
The World Book Encyclopedia
A. Richard Harmet

Art Staff
Executive Art Director
William Dobias

Senior Art Director
William Hammond

Art Director
Roberta Dimmer

Senior Artist
Margaret Smith

Artists
Karen Forch
Margot McMahon

Photography Director
John S. Marshall

Photographer
Stephen Hale

Senior Photographs Editors
Carol A. Parden
Paul Quirico

Photographs Editors
Karen Koblik
Jo Anne Martinkus

Assistant Photographs Editors
Sandra Ozanick
Kathleen Kase

Research and Services
Director of Editorial Services
Susan C. Kilburg

Head, Editorial Research
Lenore Glanz

Senior Researcher
Robert Hamm

Head, Research Library
Indrani Embar

Head, Cartographic Services
H. George Stoll

Product Production
Executive Director
Philip B. Hall

Director of Manufacturing
Joseph C. LaCount

Director of Pre-Press
J. J. Stack

Production Control Managers
Sandra Grebenar
Barbara Podczerwinski

Assistant Product Manager
Madelyn Krzak

Composition Manager
John Babrick

Film Separations Manager
Alfred J. Mozdzen

Film Separations Assistant Managers
Ann Eriksen
Barbara J. McDonald

Manager, Research and Development
Henry Koval

Printed in the United States of America
ISBN 0-7166-0481-7
Library of Congress Catalog Card Number: 62-4818

Preface

Late one afternoon in November 1980, as the YEAR BOOK Board of Editors' annual meeting was ending, Harrison Brown remarked that the day would not be complete without some reference to the remarkable achievement of the *Voyager 1* spacecraft. "When you look at those pictures," he said, "not only of Saturn this year, but of Jupiter earlier, it is just a breathtaking performance, a continuing demonstration of our technical genius. It says something about our civilization, about our culture, that I think is very important."

Indeed it does. In a frustrating time of economic and political problems, *Voyager 1*'s technical achievements remind us that humankind is capable of great accomplishments. It is also somehow reassuring to discover that usually reserved scientists are capable of being amazed. When the spacecraft revealed that two of Saturn's rings appear to be kinked and braided, in defiance of known laws of nature, scientists termed the finding "mind-boggling" and "raving mad." Again we realize how little we know, compared with what is still to be known — and understood — not only about the solar system, but also about our existence on Earth. That may be the most important lesson. WAYNE WILLE

Voyager 1 made and sent back to Earth in November this photograph of the planet Saturn and two of its moons, Tethys, above, and Dione.

Contents

4

A tear-out page of cross-reference tabs for insertion in THE WORLD
BOOK ENCYCLOPEDIA appears after page 16.

Contributors

Adachi, Ken, M.A.; Literary Editor, *The Toronto Star.* [LITERATURE, CANADIAN]

Alexiou, Arthur G., M.S., E.E.; Associate Director, Office of Sea Grant. [OCEAN]

Alsop, Ronald J., B.A.; Reporter, *The Wall Street Journal.* [Special Report: THE INFLATION RATE, THE COST OF LIVING. . . AND YOU]

Anderson, Leo S., B.A.; Editor, *Telephony Magazine.* [COMMUNICATIONS]

Anderson, Virginia E., B.A., M.S.W.; Free-Lance Writer. [COMMUNITY ORGANIZATIONS; HANDICAPPED; NATIONAL PTA (NATIONAL CONGRESS OF PARENTS AND TEACHERS); SOCIAL SECURITY; WELFARE; YOUTH ORGANIZATIONS]

Araujo, Paul E., Ph.D.; Assistant Professor of Human Nutrition, University of Florida. [NUTRITION]

Banovetz, James M., Ph.D.; Chairman, Department of Political Science, Northern Illinois University. [CITY; City Articles; HOUSING]

Barabba, Vincent P., M.B.A.; Director, U.S. Bureau of the Census. [CENSUS]

Barber, Margaret, B.A., M.L.S.; Director, Public Information Office, American Library Association. [AMERICAN LIBRARY ASSOCIATION]

Bass, Dan M., B.S., M.S., Ph.D.; Head, Petroleum Engineering Department, Colorado School of Mines. [WORLD BOOK SUPPLEMENT: PETROLEUM]

Beaumont, Lynn, Member, Tourism Advisory Board, New School for Social Research. [TRAVEL]

Beckwith, David C., J.D.; Managing Editor, *Legal Times of Washington.* [COURTS AND LAWS; CRIME; PRISON; SUPREME COURT]

Benson, Barbara N., A.B., M.S., Ph.D.; Assistant Professor, Biology, Cedar Crest College. [BOTANY; ZOOLOGY]

Berkwitt, George J., B.S.J.; Chief Editor, *Industrial Distribution Magazine.* [MANUFACTURING]

Bornstein, Leon, B.A., M.A.; Labor Economist, U.S. Dept. of Labor. [LABOR]

Boyarsky, Bill, B.A.; City-County Bureau Chief, *Los Angeles Times.* [WORLD BOOK SUPPLEMENT: REAGAN, RONALD WILSON]

Boyum, Joy Gould, Ph.D.; Professor of English, New York University. [MOTION PICTURES]

Bradsher, Henry S., A.B., B.J.; Foreign Affairs Writer, *Washington Star.* [Asian Country Articles]

Brody, Jane E., B.S., M.S.; Science Writer and Personal Health Columnist, *The New York Times.* [Special Report: CAN AN ASPIRIN A DAY HELP KEEP THE DOCTOR AWAY?]

Brown, Kenneth, Editor, *United Kingdom Press Gazette.* [EUROPE and European Country Articles]

Cain, Charles C., III, B.A.; former Automotive Editor, Associated Press. [AUTOMOBILE]

Callaway, John D., Director of News and Current Affairs, WTTW Chicago Public Television. [Special Report: WALTER CRONKITE WRAPS IT UP]

Carlson, Eric D., Ph.D.; Senior Astronomer, Adler Planetarium. [ASTRONOMY]

Clark, Phil, B.A.; Free-Lance Garden and Botanical Writer. [GARDENING]

Cromie, William J., B.S.; Executive Director, Council for the Advancement of Science Writing. [BUILDING AND CONSTRUCTION; SPACE EXPLORATION]

Csida, June Bundy, former Radio-TV Editor, *Billboard* Magazine. [RADIO; TELEVISION]

Cuscaden, Rob, Editor, *Home Improvement Contractor Magazine.* [ARCHITECTURE]

Cviic, Chris, B.A., B.Sc.; Editorial Staff, *The Economist.* [DEATHS OF NOTABLE PERSONS (Close-Up); Eastern European Country Articles; EUROPE (Close-Up)]

Dale, Edwin L., Jr., B.A.; Writer, Business Analyst. [INTERNATIONAL TRADE AND FINANCE]

Datre, Donna M., B.A.; Consumer Affairs Manager, Toy Manufacturers of America, Inc. [GAMES, MODELS, AND TOYS]

Deffeyes, Kenneth S., M.S.E., Ph.D.; Professor of Geology, Princeton University. [GEOLOGY]

DeFrank, Thomas J., B.A., M.A.; White House Correspondent, *Newsweek.* [ARMED FORCES]

Delaune, Lynn de Grummond, M.A.; Assistant Professor, College of William and Mary; Author. [LITERATURE FOR CHILDREN]

Dewey, Russell A., Ph.D.; Asst. Professor of Psychology, Georgia Southern College. [PSYCHOLOGY]

Dixon, Gloria Ricks, B.A.; Vice-President for Public Affairs and Education, Magazine Publishers Association. [MAGAZINE]

Eaton, William J., B.S.J., M.S.J.; Washington Correspondent, *Los Angeles Times.* [U.S. Political Articles]

Epstein, George, B.S., M.S., Ph.D.; Professor, Computer Science Department, Indiana University. [WORLD BOOK SUPPLEMENT: COMPUTER]

Esseks, J. Dixon, Ph.D.; Associate Professor of Political Science, Northern Illinois University. [AFRICA and African Country Articles]

Farr, David M. L., D.Phil.; Professor of History and Director, Paterson Centre for International Programs, Carleton University, Ottawa. [CANADA; CANADA (Close-Up); Canadian Province Articles; SCHREYER, EDWARD RICHARD; TRUDEAU, PIERRE ELLIOTT]

Feather, Leonard, Author, Broadcaster, Composer. [MUSIC, POPULAR; RECORDINGS]

Fox, Michael W., D.Sc., Ph.D., B. Vet. Med., M.R.C.V.S.; Director, Institute for the Study of Animal Problems. [Special Report: WHAT IS YOUR PET TRYING TO TELL YOU?]

French, Charles E., Ph.D.; Study Director, President's Reorganization·Project. [FARM AND FARMING]

Gayn, Mark, B.S.; Member, Editorial Board, *The Toronto Star;* Author. [ASIA and Asian Country Articles]

Goldner, Nancy, B.A.; Critic, *Dance News, The Nation,* and *Christian Science Monitor.* [DANCING]

Goldstein, Jane, B.A.; Publicity Director, Santa Anita Park. [HORSE RACING]

Graham, Jarlath J., B.A.; Director of Editorial Development, *Advertising Age.* [ADVERTISING]

Griffin, Alice, Ph.D.; Professor of English, Lehman College, City University of New York. [THEATER]

Hales, Dianne, B.A., M.S.; Editor/Writer. [HEALTH AND DISEASE; HOSPITAL; MEDICINE; MENTAL HEALTH; PUBLIC HEALTH]

Hamilton, Lawrence S., P.Sc.F., M.S., Ph.D.; Research Associate, Environment and Policy Institute of the East-West Center, Honolulu, Hawaii. [Special Report: PONDERING THE FATE OF THE FORESTS]

Haverstock, Nathan A., Director, The Latin American Service. [LATIN AMERICA and Latin American Country Articles]

Hechinger, Fred M., B.A.; Vice-President, *The New York Times* Company Foundation, Inc. [EDUCATION]

Huenergard, Celeste, B.A., M.A.; Midwest Editor, *Editor & Publisher* Magazine. [NEWSPAPER; PUBLISHING]

Hummel, Dean L., B.S., M.A., Ph.D.; Professor of Counselor Education, Virginia Polytechnic Institute and State University. [Special Report: WHAT SHOULD I BE WHEN I GROW UP?]

Jacobi, Peter P., B.S.J., M.S.J.; former Professor, Medill School of Journalism, Northwestern University. [MUSIC, CLASSICAL]

Jessup, Mary E., B.A.; former News Editor, *Civil Engineering* Magazine. [DRUGS; STEEL]

Joseph, Lou, B.A.; Manager, Media Relations, American Dental Association. [DENTISTRY]

Kaiman, Arnold G., M.A., D.D.; Rabbi, Congregation Kol Ami. [JEWS AND JUDAISM]

Karr, Albert R., M.S.; Reporter, *The Wall Street Journal.* [TRANSPORTATION and Transportation Articles]

Kind, Joshua B., Ph.D.; Associate Professor of Art History, Northern Illinois University; Author, *Rouault;* Contributing Editor, *New Art Examiner.* [VISUAL ARTS]

Kisor, Henry, B.A., M.S.J.; Book Editor, *Chicago Sun-Times.* [LITERATURE]

Kitchen, Paul, B.A., B.L.S.; Executive Director, Canadian Library Association. [CANADIAN LIBRARY ASSOCIATION]

Knapp, Elaine Stuart, B.A.; Editor, *State Government News,* Council of State Governments. [STATE GOVERNMENT]

Koenig, Louis W., Ph.D., L.H.D.; Professor of Government, New York University; Author, *Bryan: A Political Biography of William Jennings Bryah.* [CIVIL RIGHTS]

Langdon, Robert, Executive Officer, Pacific Manuscripts Bureau, Australian National University. [PACIFIC ISLANDS; WORLD BOOK SUPPLEMENT: KIRIBATI, TARAWA]

Larsen, Paul A., P.E., B.S., Ch.E.; Member: American Philatelic Society; Collectors Club of Chicago; Royal Philatelic Society, London. Past President, British Caribbean Philatelic Study Group. [STAMP COLLECTING]

Levy, Emanuel, B.A.; Editor, *Insurance Advocate.* [INSURANCE]

Litsky, Frank, B.S.; Assistant Sports Editor, *The New York Times.* [Sports Articles]

Maki, John M., Ph.D.; Professor of Political Science, University of Massachusetts. [JAPAN]

Marty, Martin E., Ph.D.; Fairfax M. Cone Distinguished Service Professor, University of Chicago. [PROTESTANTISM; RELIGION]

Mather, Ian, M.A.; Defense and Diplomatic Correspondent, *The Observer* (London). [GREAT BRITAIN; IRELAND; NORTHERN IRELAND]

Mathews, Thomas G., B.A., M.A., Ph.D.; Research Professor, Institute of Caribbean Studies, University of Puerto Rico. [WORLD BOOK SUPPLEMENT: KINGSTOWN; SAINT VINCENT AND THE GRENADINES]

Miller, J.D.B., M.Ec.; Professor of International Relations, Australian National University. [AUSTRALIA]

Miller, Julie Ann, Ph.D.; Life Sciences Editor, *Science News.* [BIOCHEMISTRY; BIOLOGY]

Mullen, Frances A., Ph.D.; Secretary General, International Council of Psychologists, Inc. [CHILD WELFARE]

Murray, G.E., M.A.; Poetry Columnist; Free-Lance Writer. [POETRY]

Newman, Andrew L., M.A.; Information Officer, U.S. Department of the Interior. [CONSERVATION; ENVIRONMENT; FISHING; FISHING INDUSTRY; FOREST AND FOREST PRODUCTS; HUNTING; INDIAN, AMERICAN; WATER]

Oatis, William N., United Nations Correspondent, The Associated Press. [UNITED NATIONS]

O'Leary, Theodore M., B.A.; Special Correspondent, *Sports Illustrated* Magazine. [BRIDGE, CONTRACT; CAT; DOG; HOBBIES]

Pearl, Edward W., Meteorologist, Geophysical Research and Development Corporation. [WEATHER]

Poli, Kenneth, Editor, *Popular Photography.* [PHOTOGRAPHY]

Price, Frederick C., B.S., Ch.E.; Free-Lance Writer. [CHEMICAL INDUSTRY]

Prochaska, Peter, B.A.; Associate Director, U.S. Chess Federation. [CHESS]

Rabb, George B., Ph.D.; Director, Chicago Zoological Park. [ZOOS AND AQUARIUMS]

Rowse, Arthur E., I.A., M.B.A.; President, Consumer News, Inc. [CONSUMER AFFAIRS]

Schmemann, Alexander, S.T.D., D.D., LL.D., Th.D.; Dean, St. Vladimir's Orthodox Theological Seminary, New York. [EASTERN ORTHODOX CHURCHES]

Shand, David A. B.C.A., B.C.M.; Senior Lecturer, Australian National University. [NEW ZEALAND]

Shaw, Robert James, B.S., B.A.; former Editor, *Library Technology Reports,* American Library Association. [LIBRARY]

Shearer, Warren W., Ph.D., J.D.; former Chairman, Department of Economics, Wabash College. [ECONOMICS]

Sheerin, John B., C.S.P., A.B., M.A., LL.D., J.D.; General Consultor, American Bishops' Secretariat for Catholic-Jewish Relations. [ROMAN CATHOLIC CHURCH]

Shelton, Patricia, B.A.; Fashion Editor, *Chicago Sun-Times.* [FASHION]

Spencer, William, Ph.D.; Professor of Middle East History, Florida State University; Author, *Land and People of Algeria.* [IRAN (Close-Up); MIDDLE EAST; Middle Eastern Country Articles; North Africa Country Articles]

Stockwell, Foster P., B.A.; Free-Lance Writer. [NOBEL PRIZES; SAFETY; SCIENCE AND RESEARCH]

Summers, Larry V., Ph.D.; Agricultural Economist, U.S. Department of Agriculture. [FOOD]

Swanton, Donald, B.S., M.S., Ph.D., M.B.A.; Chairman, Department of Finance, Roosevelt University. [Finance Articles]

Thompson, Carol L., M.A.; Editor, *Current History* Magazine. [U.S. Government Articles]

Thompson, Ida, Ph.D.; Assistant Professor, Department of Geological and Geophysical Sciences, Princeton University. [PALEONTOLOGY]

Tiegel, Eliot, B.A.; Managing Editor, *Billboard Magazine.* [MUSIC, POPULAR; RECORDINGS]

Vallee, Frank G., Ph.D., F.R.S.C.; Professor of Anthropology and Sociology, Carleton University, Ottawa, Canada. [ANTHROPOLOGY]

Verbit, Lawrence, Ph.D.; Professor of Chemistry, State University of New York. [CHEMISTRY]

Walker, Gerald M., A.B.; Managing Editor, News, *Electronics* Magazine. [ELECTRONICS]

White, Thomas O., Ph.D.; Lecturer in Physics, Cambridge University, Cambridge, England. [PHYSICS]

Woods, Michael, B.S.; Science Editor, *The Toledo Blade.* [COAL; ENERGY; MINES AND MINING; PETROLEUM AND GAS]

Zimansky, Paul E., Ph.D.; Adjunct Assistant Professor, Department of History, State University of New York at Stony Brook. [ARCHAEOLOGY]

Chronology

1975
1977
1978
1979
1980

A month-by-month listing presents highlights of some of the significant events of 1980.

See September 22, page 18.

Jan. 28

Jan. 3-6

January

		1	2	3	4	5
6	7	8	9	10	11	12
13	14	15	16	17	18	19
20	21	22	23	24	25	26
27	28	29	30	31		

1-3 **Iranian officials discuss** release of the United States hostages, held since Nov. 4, 1979, with United Nations (UN) Secretary-General Kurt Waldheim.

3 **Francisco Sa Carneiro** is sworn in as Portugal's prime minister.
Cleveland teachers end 11-week strike.

3-6 **Indira Gandhi wins** control of India's lower house in national elections. She is sworn in as prime minister on January 14.

4 **President Jimmy Carter** cuts grain sales to Russia after invasion of Afghanistan.

7 **Chrysler aid bill** granting $1.5 billion in loan guarantees to auto company is signed by President Carter.

10 **George Meany dies** at 85. He had been president of the American Federation of Labor and Congress of Industrial Organizations (AFL-CIO) for 25 years.

14 **UN General Assembly demands** that Russian troops withdraw from Afghanistan.

16 **Scientists announce laboratory production of interferon,** a disease-fighting protein.

18 **Gold soars to** $835 per troy ounce (31 grams), up $311 since Dec. 31, 1979. Silver hits an all-time high of $50.35 per ounce three days later.

19 **China cancels talks** on improving relations with Russia because of Soviet invasion of Afghanistan.
Justice William O. Douglas, 81, who served on the Supreme Court of the United States for a record 36 years, dies.

20 **Boycott Moscow Olympics,** President Carter urges, unless Russian troops leave Afghanistan.

21 **Pittsburgh Steelers win** Super Bowl XIV, defeating the Los Angeles Rams 31-19.

22 **Russia exiles** physicist Andrei D. Sakharov in the industrial city of Gorki.

23 **State of the Union message** by President Carter warns Russia that the United States would use military force to keep the Persian Gulf open.

24-27 **Nine earthquakes** shake area near San Francisco in northern California.

25 **Abol Hasan Bani-Sadr** is elected president of Iran.
The Department of Labor reports that the U.S. Consumer Price Index rose 13.3 per cent in 1979 – the highest inflation rate since 1946.

28 **Canadian diplomats help** six U.S. Embassy employees escape from Iran.
Carter presents a $615.8-billion "prudent and responsible" budget to Congress.

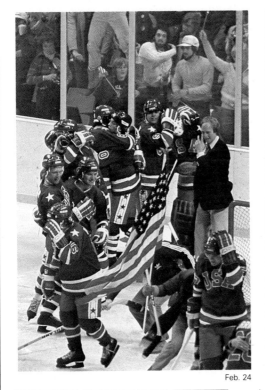

Feb. 18

Feb. 24

Feb. 27

February

					1	2
3	4	5	6	7	8	9
10	11	12	13	14	15	16
17	18	19	20	21	22	23
24	25	26	27	28	29	

2 **Abscam probe** of bribery and corruption by Federal Bureau of Investigation (FBI) reports evidence against some members of Congress.

2-3 **New Mexico prison riot** leaves 33 dead after 36-hour rampage of murder and vandalism.

4 **U.S. dietary guidelines** recommend avoiding excessive fats, cholesterol, sugar, salt, and alcohol.

5 **China attends** disarmament conference in Geneva, Switzerland, for the first time.

8 **Carter announces draft registration** plan that would sign up 19- and 20-year-old men and women.
Gunnar Thoroddsen becomes Iceland's prime minister as head of a center-left coalition.

11 **Economic reforms** are announced by the civilian-military junta ruling El Salvador.
Chicago schools reopen after two-week strike by teachers protesting overdue pay and proposals to lay off 1,600 teachers.

12 **Environmental protection** restricting commercial development is extended to 40 million acres (16.1 million hectares) of federal land in Alaska for 20 years by Secretary of the Interior Cecil D. Andrus.

12-24 **The Winter Olympics** are held in Lake Placid, N.Y. East German athletes win total of 23 medals; Russians win 22; and U.S. athletes, 12. U.S. speed skater Eric Heiden becomes the first athlete to win five individual gold medals. U.S. hockey team defeats heavily favored Russia on February 22, takes gold medal by defeating Finland two days later, as shown above.

13-22 **Storms kill 26** persons and leave thousands homeless in southern California.

18 **Pierre Elliott Trudeau** returns as Canada's prime minister, ending nine months of rule by Charles Joseph (Joe) Clark. Liberal Party wins firm majority in House of Commons.

21-26 **Afghans stage** general strike in Kabul, their capital. Violence erupts and spreads to other cities.

23 **UN commission investigating** the rule of Shah Mohammad Reza Pahlavi arrives in Iran.

25 **Surinam army sergeants overthrow** Prime Minister Henck A. E. Arron.

26 **President Carter, Ronald Reagan** win the New Hampshire presidential primary, first of the 1980 campaign.

27 **Leftist guerrillas** seize the Dominican Republic Embassy in Bogotá, Colombia.

28 **Great Britain's Conservative government** survives a no-confidence vote in Parliament.

March 23

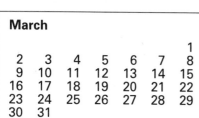

March 4

March 30

March

						1
2	3	4	5	6	7	8
9	10	11	12	13	14	15
16	17	18	19	20	21	22
23	24	25	26	27	28	29
30	31					

1   **UN Security Council** unanimously demands that Israel dismantle its West Bank and Gaza Strip settlements, but President Carter says two days later the U.S. vote was cast in error because of a communications problem.

4   **Robert Mugabe,** a former guerrilla leader, is declared winner of a three-day national election for a new government in Zimbabwe Rhodesia.
Senator Edward M. Kennedy wins the Democratic presidential primary in Massachusetts, but Carter wins in Vermont. George H. W. Bush narrowly defeats Congressman John B. Anderson (R., Ill.) in the Massachusetts Republican primary, and Ronald Reagan wins in Vermont.

5   **Senator Howard H. Baker, Jr.** (R., Tenn.), drops out of the Republican presidential race.

6   **Proposal to register women** for the draft loses in the House Armed Services military personnel subcommittee.

8   **Chicago fire fighters** end a 23-day strike and agree to turn issues over to a fact-finding panel.

9   **John B. Connally** quits Republican presidential campaign after Reagan beats him in South Carolina primary.

11   **Papua New Guinea's** Prime Minister Michael Thomas Somare loses a confidence vote and is succeeded by opposition leader Julius Chan.

13   **Ford Motor Company** is found not guilty of reckless homicide by an Indiana jury in connection with three deaths in the fiery 1978 crash of a Pinto automobile.
John Wayne Gacy is sentenced to death in Chicago for the murders of 33 young men.

15   **Senator Robert J. Dole** of Kansas withdraws from the Republican presidential race.

19   **Italian Premier Francesco Cossiga** resigns after Socialists join Communists in opposition to government.

22   **Antidraft rally** in Washington, D.C., draws 30,000 persons.

23   **Shah of Iran moves** from Panama to Egypt and enters Cairo hospital.
Swedish voters approve use of nuclear power in a referendum.

24   **Technicians cap Ixtoc I** offshore oil well that blew out off Mexico's Yucatán Peninsula on June 3, 1979.

26   **Mount Saint Helens erupts** in Washington, hurling volcanic ash and dust 15,000 feet (4,600 meters) into the air and causing mud slides and avalanches.

27   **Floating oil platform capsizes** in the North Sea, killing 123 persons.

29   **Iran-Iraq** border skirmishes break out.

30   **Bombs and gunfire** at the funeral of Archbishop Oscar Arnulfo Romero, assassinated in El Salvador on March 24, cause a stampede that kills some 30 persons.

April 26

April 18

April 25

April 30

April

		1	2	3	4	5
6	7	8	9	10	11	12
13	14	15	16	17	18	19
20	21	22	23	24	25	26
27	28	29	30			

1   **Workers end 13-week strike** against the state-owned British Steel Corporation.

1-6   **About 7,000 Cubans** gather inside the Peruvian Embassy compound in Havana, seeking safe passage out of the country.

1-11   **Transit workers strike** in New York City.

2   **Carter signs** the Crude Oil Windfall Profit Tax Act of 1980.

7   **U.S. breaks** diplomatic relations with Iran and ends exports to that country.

9-14   **Israeli troops occupy** a small strip of land in southern Lebanon in retaliation for a Palestinian terrorist attack on a kibbutz.

10   **A controversial film,** *Death of a Princess*, is shown on British television, straining relations between Great Britain and Saudi Arabia.

12   **Liberia's President** William R. Tolbert, Jr., is killed in a coup d'état by army enlisted men. Master Sergeant Samuel K. Doe takes over.
U.S. Olympic Committee votes to boycott the 1980 Summer Olympics.

14   *Kramer vs. Kramer,* a film about a child-custody battle, wins Oscar as the best picture. Best actor and actress awards go to Dustin Hoffman and Sally Field.

18   **Zimbabwe Rhodesia** becomes the independent nation of Zimbabwe at a ceremony conducted by Prince Charles of Great Britain.

21   **About 50 U.S. fishing boats** sail to Mariel, Cuba, to bring refugees to the United States. The number of boats swells to 600 by April 24.
Bill Rodgers wins third straight Boston Marathon. Rosie Ruiz' apparent victory is disputed, and race officials award the women's title to Jacqueline Garreau on April 29.

24   **John B. Anderson announces** that he will run for President as an Independent.

25   **U.S. hostage rescue attempt** is called off in an Iranian desert. Eight crewmen die when a helicopter hits a transport plane.

26   **Cyrus R. Vance resigns** as U.S. secretary of state. Senator Edmund S. Muskie (D., Me.), shown above, succeeds him on April 29.

27   **The 61-day occupation** of the Dominican Republic Embassy in Bogotá, Colombia, ends peacefully as the leftist captors are allowed to fly to Havana.

28   **New York state sues** Occidental Petroleum Corporation and its Hooker Chemical unit for $635 million for dumping poisonous chemicals in the Love Canal area near Niagara Falls.

30   **Princess Beatrix** becomes queen of the Netherlands. She succeeds her mother, Queen Juliana.
Federal grand jury acquits former U.S. Budget Director T. Bertram Lance of nine counts of bank fraud.

May 18

May 17-19

				1	2	3
4	5	6	7	8	9	10
11	12	13	14	15	16	17
18	19	20	21	22	23	24
25	26	27	28	29	30	31

1-11 **Strikes, lockouts** idle one-fourth of labor force in Sweden.

2-12 **Pope John Paul II** visits Africa.

3 **Israel deports three** Palestinian West Bank leaders. The UN Security Council condemns this act five days later.

4 **President Josip Broz Tito dies** in Yugoslavia.

5 **Greek voters elect** Prime Minister Constantine Caramanlis president. George Rallis becomes prime minister on May 8.

British commandos storm the Iranian Embassy in London and free 19 persons held captive since April 30.

11 **Army group ousts** Uganda's President Godfrey Lukogwa Binaisa.

14 **Carter announces** a five-point plan for managing the influx of Cuban refugees. Some 88,000 enter the United States by May 29.

16 **Japan's government loses** a no-confidence vote, schedules general elections.

Los Angeles Lakers win the National Basketball Association championship, defeating Philadelphia by four games to two.

17-19 **Miami race riots** leave 14 persons dead and cause $100 million in damage after an all-white jury acquits four white police officers who were charged in fatal beating of a black man.

18 **Mount Saint Helens erupts,** killing at least 31 persons and hurling steam and ash 60,000 feet (18,000 meters) into the sky. Hot rocks and gas flatten trees in a 120-square-mile (310-square-kilometer) area.

South Korea's Prime Minister Hyon Hwack Shin resigns two days after imposing total martial law.

Peruvian voters elect Fernando Belaunde Terry president.

European Community (EC or Common Market) nations vote for limited economic sanctions against Iran.

20 **Reagan's delegate count** tops the number needed for nomination after gains in the Michigan and Oregon primaries. George Bush, his last opponent, quits on May 26.

Quebec voters reject separation of the province from Canada.

21-28 **Women graduate** from U.S. military academies for the first time.

24 **Iran ignores** International Court of Justice order to release the U.S. hostages.

29 **A sniper shoots** black civil rights leader Vernon E. Jordan, Jr., in Fort Wayne, Ind.

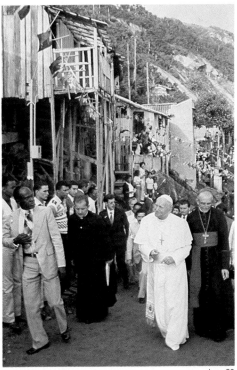

June 22

June 30

June

1	2	3	4	5	6	7
8	9	10	11	12	13	14
15	16	17	18	19	20	21
22	23	24	25	26	27	28
29	30					

3   **U.S. air defense computer error** causes a false signal of a Russian attack – the third such error in seven months.

5-6   **Congress overrides Carter** veto of a resolution blocking an oil-import fee that would have raised gasoline prices 10 cents per gallon (3.8 liters).

7   **Lebanon's Prime Minister** Salim Ahmad al-Huss resigns.

9-10   **Oil's base price** is hiked to $32 per barrel by the Organization of Petroleum Exporting Countries (OPEC).

10   **Swedish dockworkers** end a strike that began on May 2.

12   **Japan's Prime Minister** Masayoshi Ohira, 70, dies of a heart attack.

13   **EC backs Palestinians,** and opposes Israel's occupation of the West Bank and Gaza Strip.
A record $1.8 billion is awarded to MCI, Incorporated, in an antitrust case against the American Telephone & Telegraph Company.

16   **Biological organisms can be patented,** the U.S. Supreme Court rules.

19   **Carter approves the sale** of 38 short tons (35 metric tons) of enriched uranium to India, overruling the Nuclear Regulatory Commission.

22   **Economic summit** vows to develop alternatives to oil and denounces Russia's invasion of Afghanistan. Leaders of Canada, France, Great Britain, Italy, Japan, the United States, and West Germany meet in Venice, Italy.

23   **Vietnamese troops** enter Thailand, clash with Thai troops.

26   **France has tested a neutron bomb,** President Valéry Giscard d'Estaing announces.
Muslim extremist's grenade wounds Syria's President Hafiz al-Assad.

27   **Parliament picks "O Canada"** as Canada's official national anthem.

28   **Venting of radioactive gas** begins at the Three Mile Island nuclear reactor in Pennsylvania, where an accident occurred in March 1979.

30   **Pope John Paul II** begins a 12-day visit to Brazil.
Government-funded abortions are not required by the Constitution, the U.S. Supreme Court rules.
Synthetic fuels bill is signed by President Carter.
Sioux Indian nation wins $122.5 million in compensation and interest for the federal government's illegal seizure of their Black Hills land in 1877.

July 11

July 19

July 16

July 17

July

		1	2	3	4	5
6	7	8	9	10	11	12
13	14	15	16	17	18	19
20	21	22	23	24	25	26
27	28	29	30	31		

1   **Carter signs** a bill that substantially deregulates the trucking industry.

2   **Italy approves** measures to curb inflation, strengthen the currency, and decrease the balance of payments deficit.
U.S. Supreme Court rules that Congress may impose racial quotas in granting contracts.
New home rule plan for Northern Ireland is outlined by Great Britain.

4-6   **Bjorn Borg and Evonne Goolagong Cawley** win Wimbledon tennis titles.

7-9   **Lebanon's Falangist Party** defeats rival Christian group, the National Liberal Party, in fighting in the Beirut area.

9-15   **South Korea purges** 232 high government officials, 4,760 lesser officials, and 431 employees on such charges as corruption and incompetence.

11   **Iran frees U.S. hostage** Richard I. Queen, who has multiple sclerosis.

13   **Botswana's president** dies of cancer. Sir Seretse M. Khama is succeeded by Vice-President Quett Masire.

14   **Billy Carter registers** as agent of the Libyan government.

14-30   **Women from more than 100 countries** attend the second conference of the United Nations Decade for Women in Copenhagen, Denmark.

16-17   **Republicans nominate** Ronald Reagan for President and George H. W. Bush for Vice-President.

17   **Zenko Suzuki is elected** prime minister of Japan.
Bolivia's armed forces take over the government.

19   **The XXII Olympic Games** begin in Moscow. Athletes from some 81 nations participate, but many countries boycott the games to protest Russia's invasion of Afghanistan.

20   **Honduras military junta** turns the government over to an elected Assembly.

21   **First U.S. draft registration** since 1975 begins.

22-24   **Racial violence** breaks out in Chattanooga, Tenn., after the acquittal of two members of the Ku Klux Klan charged in the shooting of four black women.

27   **The shah of Iran dies** in a military hospital in Egypt.

29   **UN General Assembly** calls for the establishment of a Palestinian state and Israeli withdrawal from all occupied lands.
New Hebrides Islands become the nation of Vanuatu, ending joint British and French rule.

30   **Israel's *Knesset* (parliament) declares** that all of Jerusalem is the nation's capital.

Oct. 21

Oct. 18

October

			1	2	3	4
5	6	7	8	9	10	11
12	13	14	15	16	17	18
19	20	21	22	23	24	25
26	27	28	29	30	31	

2 **U.S. House of Representatives expels** Michael Myers (D., Pa.) who had been convicted of taking an Abscam bribe.
Larry Holmes whips Muhammad Ali to remain the World Boxing Council heavyweight champion.

3 **Bomb explodes** outside a synagogue in Paris, killing four persons and injuring 12, following a wave of attacks on Jewish targets.
Solidarity, Poland's independent union, stages a one-hour nationwide strike protesting the government's delay in providing promised wage hikes.

5 **West German Chancellor** Helmut Schmidt and Portugal's Prime Minister Francisco Sa Carneiro increase their parliamentary majorities in national elections.

7 **Congressman John W. Jenrette, Jr.** (D., S.C.), is convicted of taking an Abscam bribe.

8 **Russia and Syria** sign a 20-year friendship pact that calls for military cooperation.

9 **East Germany tightens** currency-exchange rules for visitors from the West.

10 **Two tremendous earthquakes** strike El Asnam, Algeria, killing thousands of persons.

11 **New space endurance record** is set by Russian cosmonauts Valery Ryumin and Leonid Popov, who land after 185 days in orbit.

14 **Nearly 40,000 Canadian** federal employees end a 15-day strike.
U.S. railroad deregulation bill is signed into law by President Carter.

18 **Australians re-elect** Prime Minister Malcolm Fraser.
Arnaldo Forlani becomes Italy's prime minister, succeeding Francesco Cossiga.

20 **Greece rejoins** the military wing of the North Atlantic Treaty Organization (NATO) after a six-year absence.

21 **Philadelphia Phillies** win the World Series, defeating the Kansas City Royals, four games to two. Phillies' relief pitcher Tug McGraw (pictured above) wins one game, saves two.

23 **Aleksey N. Kosygin resigns** as chairman of Russia's Council of Ministers. First Deputy Chairman Nikolay A. Tikhonov succeeds him.

25 **Month-long World Synod** of Roman Catholic Bishops ends in Vatican City after reaffirming traditional teachings on abortion, birth control, and other family issues.

28 **Carter and Reagan** debate on national television.
Ford Motor Company announces a $595-million loss for the third quarter.

30 **Jamaican voters elect** Laborite Edward Seaga prime minister, rejecting Socialist incumbent Michael N. Manley.

Nov. 4

Nov. 21

Nov. 23

November

						1
2	3	4	5	6	7	8
9	10	11	12	13	14	15
16	17	18	19	20	21	22
23	24	25	26	27	28	29
30						

1   **Egypt recognizes** Iran's revolutionary regime.
2   **Australia's Prime Minister** Malcolm Fraser shakes up Cabinet. Two ministers exchange portfolios, and five others are replaced.
Iran's parliament approves a four-point plan for releasing the U.S. hostages.
4   **Ronald Reagan is elected** President of the United States with 51 per cent of the popular vote. Republicans also pick up 33 House seats and gain a Senate majority.
5   **New York Stock Exchange** reacts to Reagan victory with sharp price gains as a record 84 million shares change hands.
10   **Michael Foot is elected** leader of Great Britain's Labour Party, succeeding James Callaghan.
Auto import curbs would not be justified, the U.S. International Trade Commission rules.
Poland's Supreme Court declares that Solidarity's charter need not assert the Communist Party's supremacy. The decision averts the threat of a major strike.
U.S. officials respond to Iran's hostage terms through Algerian intermediaries.

11   **A 35-nation meeting** to review the 1975 Helsinki accords on European security and cooperation opens in Madrid, Spain.
12   **Voyager 1 spacecraft** passes within 77,000 miles (124,000 kilometers) of Saturn's clouds as it transmits spectacular photographs of that planet, its rings, and satellites to earth. Major discoveries include peculiar braided rings.
South Korea bans 811 politicians from all political activities.
14   **Poland stops** almost all food exports to counteract shortages.
Some 24 million acres (9.7 million hectares) of land in the western United States are designated as potential wilderness areas by the U.S. Department of the Interior's Bureau of Land Management.
15   **Pope John Paul II** begins a five-day tour of West Germany.
20   **China's "Gang of Four"** and six other defendants go on trial in Peking (Beijing).
21   **Fire in MGM Grand Hotel** in Las Vegas, Nev., kills 84 persons.
23   **Tremendous earthquakes** in southern Italy, Europe's worst since 1915, kill about 3,000 persons and drive 250,000 from their homes.
24   **Polish rail workers strike** for two hours in Warsaw and Gdańsk.
25   **Southern California fires** force tens of thousands of persons to evacuate their homes.

Dec. 8

December

```
        1   2   3   4   5   6
7   8   9  10  11  12  13
14  15  16  17  18  19  20
21  22  23  24  25  26  27
28  29  30  31
```

1 **Russia's new five-year plan** indicates an economic slowdown through 1985.

2 **Carter warns Russia** against invading Poland.
Poland dismisses four members of its ruling Politburo.
President Carter signs a bill protecting more than 100 million acres (40 million hectares) of Alaska wilderness from development.

3 **Fugitive radical leader** Bernardine Dohrn surrenders in Chicago.
Abscam defendants Representatives Frank Thompson, Jr. (D., N.J.), and John M. Murphy (D., N.Y.) are convicted. Representative Richard Kelly (R., Fla.) goes on trial the next day.

4 **Portugal's Prime Minister** Francisco Sa Carneiro dies in an airplane crash.
Black "homeland" of Ciskei votes for independence from South Africa.

8 **John Lennon of the Beatles** (shown at top left in the early photo above) is shot to death in New York City.

13 **El Salvador's junta** is shaken up as Jose Napoleon Duarte becomes president.

Apollo Milton Obote is declared winner of Uganda's presidential election.

14 **Polish farmers meet** in Warsaw to discuss forming a union.

15 **Dave Winfield signs** the richest contract in sports history. The New York Yankees will pay the 29-year-old outfielder an estimated $25-million over eight to 10 years.

16 **OPEC approves** an oil price hike up to $41 per barrel.
Call for reconciliation is issued by Poland's Communist Party, church officials, and independent labor leaders at a memorial service in Gdańsk.

17 **Chrysler Corporation** says that its 1980 deficit will be about $1.7 billion.

18 **Aleksey N. Kosygin,** former chairman of Russia's Council of Ministers, dies at age 76.
Seven Irish prisoners end a 7½-week hunger strike in Belfast, Northern Ireland.
Israel's Labor Party selects Shimon Peres as its candidate for prime minister in 1981 elections.

20 **U.S. banks** raise their prime rate to a record 21.5 per cent.

21 **Iran demands** $24 billion in "guarantees" for shah's wealth and return of its frozen assets in exchange for release of U.S. hostages.

23 **Consumer Price Index** is 12.6 per cent higher than a year earlier, the U.S. Bureau of Labor Statistics reports.

27 **Iran proposes** to negotiate a financial settlement with the United States while it continues holding the hostages.

The Year in Focus

1975
1977
1978
1979
1980

The meaning of some of the important events and trends of 1980 is discussed by the members of THE YEAR BOOK Board of Editors:

Harrison Brown, Director, the East-West Resource Systems Institute, the East-West Center, Honolulu, Hawaii.
Lawrence A. Cremin, President, Teachers College, Columbia University.
James J. Kilpatrick, columnist for the Universal Press Syndicate.
Sylvia Porter, columnist for the Field Newspaper Syndicate; author of *Sylvia Porter's New Money Book for the 80s*.
Carl T. Rowan, columnist for the Field Newspaper Syndicate.

Seated: Brown, Porter; standing, left to right: Kilpatrick, Cremin, Rowan.

Harrison Brown

Lawrence A. Cremin

James J. Kilpatrick

Sylvia Porter

A Mandate?
Perhaps.
A Change?
Definitely.

American voters sent a new government to Washington, D.C., on November 4. Did they also send a political message?

On Nov. 4, 1980, for the first time since 1932, United States voters rejected a President they had elected four years earlier. Was the election of Ronald Reagan an "anti" vote, a repudiation of Jimmy Carter, or was it a positive statement of conservative principles by the electorate? Did Ronald Reagan receive a mandate from the voters? If so, what was it? And, looking beyond the election, should we improve the process by which Presidents are selected? These were some of the questions asked when the YEAR BOOK Board of Editors met at Teachers College, Columbia University, in New York City in mid-November 1980. Joining the discussion were William H. Nault, editorial director of World Book – Childcraft International, Incorporated, and Wayne Wille, executive editor of THE YEAR BOOK.

Carl T. Rowan

William H. Nault

Wayne Wille

William H. Nault: During last year's meeting we spent a good deal of time discussing that elusive quality — leadership. We talked about a crisis in leadership that we all sensed in the United States. And since that meeting, some 12 months ago, we find that inflation, for example, continues unabated in double digits, and unemployment has increased. Russia has occupied Afghanistan, and we are concerned about what its objectives are and what we are capable of doing in response. We also now have a war between Iran and Iraq in the Persian Gulf area, and that could threaten oil supplies. Iran is still holding the U.S. hostages, adding to our frustrations. With all this as background, the voters on November 4 spoke with what many people would call a clarion voice in repudiating President Jimmy Carter. I'd like to begin today, Jack, by asking if you feel that the United States has now found the leader we talked about a year ago.

James J. Kilpatrick: I'm not sure we found *the* leader, but we certainly have undertaken a change. I think that is mainly what this election was all about. It was our desire for change. It was a repudiation of Jimmy Carter, and also a repudiation of the programs with which Carter and the Democratic Party have been identified.

It might be helpful to put the election in perspective. It was, of course, a landslide victory for Ronald Reagan by a margin of more than 8 million popular votes. Reagan carried 44 states, with 489 electoral votes. Carter took only six states and the District of Columbia, with 49 electoral votes. We have had other landslides in this century, including 1932, the year with which this 1980 election has frequently been compared. Herbert Hoover carried only six states in 1932, which is about what Jimmy Carter carried. We have had a great deal of discussion about this question of leadership, and about whether Reagan is to be equated in 1980 with Franklin D. Roosevelt in 1932, in both similarities and dissimilarities. Because history is mostly biography, it is useful to know that when Roosevelt came in in 1933, he was 51 years old. Reagan will be nearly 70 when he takes office in January 1981, a big difference. At the time Roosevelt was elected, he was still in the governor's mansion in New York; Reagan is now five years out of the governor's mansion in California. Roosevelt came into office with a tremendous majority in both houses of Congress — a majority of 23 in the Senate and, of course, about 200 in the House of Representatives. Reagan, by contrast, has a lesser majority in the Senate, and his party is 50 votes out in the House. So, while there are some reasons to compare Reagan and Roosevelt, I doubt that there are that many, mainly because the conditions were so unlike. At the time Roosevelt came in, the country was in a serious depression, and the remedy seemed to call for greater governmental intervention. This time around, we are in economic trouble, but not a depression, and the call is not for more government, but for much less government.

Carl T. Rowan: Jack and I probably differ to a substantial degree in terms of how we view this election and how we interpret what happened. We are in agreement that it was a repudiation of Jimmy

Carter. Carter came to Washington, D.C., in 1977 as an outsider, and he remained an outsider, to the point of his defeat. Carter never won over the kinds of friends in the Congress that a President has to have to be successful. He also lacked the forcefulness to make people in Congress do certain things he wanted them to do. I think the American public perceived him as a weak man in a great many respects, and I think they perceived this particularly in the last few days before the election. But there was something else involved in that election other than the repudiation of Carter. Now, here is where Jack and I differ.

I don't think it was as much a repudiation of the Democratic Party, and the policies and programs that that party stands for, as it was a repudiation of certain aspects of that policy. I think what we saw was an incredible coalescing of frustrations. Where, for example, the middle-class American sits there believing he is being taxed out of all proportion to fairness — forced to pay for the follies of the rich and the laziness of the poor. So a lot of people said, "Look, if you are talking about cutting my taxes 30 per cent, I will take it," without much thought about what the consequences might be. You had a situation where the votes of union members no longer could be controlled by the union bosses, because the blue-collar workers were feeling the brunt of inflation. They believed that the policies followed by Jimmy Carter were eating up their paychecks, and they wanted change — even if that change might produce things they won't like in the course of the next four years.

You had farmers unhappy with Carter because he cut off their sales

Kilpatrick: "This election was a repudiation of Jimmy Carter, and also a repudiation of the programs with which Carter and the Democratic Party have been identified."

of grain to the Soviet Union after the invasion of Afghanistan. They believed he was hurting them in the pocketbook. So, a lot of them voted against him, without giving an awful lot of thought to some of the other things that would come along with this change. Many Jews believed that Carter had pressured the Israeli government unfairly. Some felt that if Carter got back in, he would really be hard on Israel because he wouldn't have to worry about being re-elected. So, while American Jews did not run to Reagan, some 20 per cent of them defected from the Democrats and voted for John Anderson, the Independent.

Kilpatrick: Are you suggesting that it was entirely an "anti" vote?

Rowan: I am suggesting that it was much more an "anti" vote than it was a pro-Reagan vote. I believe that many Americans didn't want any of those candidates, including Anderson. They wanted some *change*. Now, you can take any one of those groups I mentioned, and they would say, "Yes, not all change is progress, but there can't be any progress without change, so I am voting for change." And then the day after the election they might say, "Yes, but I didn't really mean to give control of the Senate to the Republicans." Now, there might be some in those groups who did intend that, but I will venture to say that those groups as a whole got a lot more change than they bargained for.

Wayne Wille: On this matter of an "anti" vote and a landslide, the statistics seem to indicate that it was an anti-Carter landslide in the popular vote, where he won only 41 per cent of the votes. I'm not sure you can call it a pro-Reagan landslide, since he took only 51 per cent, a slim majority. The Reagan landslide shows up in the electoral votes. Beyond the presidential race, of course, there did seem to be a conservative Republican landslide in the Senate races.

Kilpatrick: "You have only to look at which senators lost to see the pattern that emerged. Only three conservatives were defeated, all of them Democrats . . . in each case the loser was replaced by a still more conservative candidate."

Harrison Brown: That major change in the Senate bears some looking at. There is always, of course, the coattail effect. That is well known. Whoever is at the top of the ticket determines the level of voting for the other people on that ticket and carries a good many of them into office with him. But added to that this year some very interesting things happened. First of all, an enormous amount of campaign money was put into certain congressional races by the largest collection of political action committees from industry and from labor that has ever been seen in American politics. Superimposed upon that, several liberal senators were targeted for defeat by ultraconservatives, the Moral Majority, and so forth.

Kilpatrick: That certainly had some effect, no question about it.

Sylvia Porter: It would be difficult to overstress that the election was held against one of the worst economic backgrounds that we have had in this country in the half-century since Hoover. When we went to the polls on November 4, the annual rate of inflation was back into double digits and was eating away the buying power of our dollars at a pace that most Americans could hardly believe. No one could go into a grocery store with a 10-dollar bill and come out with much of a bag of groceries.

At the same time, unemployment had taken a big, big jump early in this economic turndown. And in this century, the only times that a

sitting political party lost the White House were times when unemployment was rising. Now, this economic background is not to be downgraded. In no way is it to be shrugged off. The people voted on November 4 against Carter's disastrous economic policies, his shilly-shallying, his inability to develop sound economic policies that made sense and to stick to them. The advisers with whom he surrounded himself seemed progressively less knowledgeable and consistent. He himself seemed to be progressively less able to describe what he was doing or why.

Kilpatrick: I certainly would agree that economic factors were very great in this election, but I want to go back to what Harrison was saying about the Senate elections. I think we are plainly seeing the reflection of a philosophical tilt. This was a conservative landslide. You have only to look at which senators lost to see the pattern that emerged. Only three conservatives were defeated – all of them Democrats – Herman Talmadge of Georgia, Richard Stone of Florida, and Robert Morgan of North Carolina – and in each case the loser was replaced by a still more conservative candidate.

The Committee on Political Education [COPE] of the AFL-CIO [American Federation of Labor and Congress of Industrial Organizations] gave 100 per cent ratings to eight senators. Of them, Abraham Ribicoff of Connecticut stepped aside and didn't run for re-election, but Birch Bayh of Indiana, John Culver of Iowa, and Mike Gravel of Alaska were all defeated. Going on down the list, Warren Magnuson of Washington rated 94 with COPE; he went down. George McGovern, South Dakota, also 94; he was defeated. Gaylord Nelson of Wisconsin, 88 with COPE; down he went. Jacob Javits of New York, a Republican, of course, but a 78 rating; he was defeated. John Durkin, in New Hampshire, with a 76 rating; down he went. Donald Stewart of Alabama, 69 per cent; down he went. Frank Church of Idaho, rated at 65; down he went. The Senate races tell a clear story. The conservatives simply took over. That was what it was about.

Brown: It is important, though, to recognize that while to some extent it was a conservative take-over, the coattail effect, I suspect, was substantial. Some of those newly elected conservatives just rode in along with Reagan.

Was it a mandate?

Nault: Soon after the election, *The Wall Street Journal* carried a lead editorial that said the election was a clear mandate for change. Yet there were other newspaper columns, other commentators, who said the election was no mandate. Was it?

Rowan: I think what I am about to say speaks to that point. I would agree with Jack that there was a conservative mood swing involved in all of this. I would not underestimate the impact of the state of the economy either, Sylvia. I think Carter made a colossal mistake in that televised debate with Reagan, telling the American people that the most important thing was to stop nuclear proliferation. That is

Porter: "The people voted on November 4 against Carter's disastrous economic policies, his shilly-shallying, his inability to develop sound economic policies that made sense and to stick with them."

important, obviously, but those people out there who couldn't balance their budgets were saying, "Nuclear proliferation is not the most important thing to me."

Now, beyond that, we had this great spectacle of the Iranians twisting Jimmy Carter like a top with the hostage situation on the eve of the election. Would they release them or wouldn't they? And this enhanced that mood, that feeling of frustration, regarding America's position in the world – the belief that the Iranians were toying with us, that the Soviets were pushing us around, that the United States had lost respect abroad. I think this was a big factor in that great shift in voter preference that the public opinion polls showed in the week before the election. I think it had a lot to do with the magnitude of Reagan's victory.

So, what is the mandate there? I think the American people were saying that this is a mandate to do something stronger, to regain our place in the world. Now, Reagan may find out that it is a lot more difficult to do than it is to talk about.

New cast of characters or new philosophy?

Lawrence A. Cremin: I think this mandate question is a very important one. In one sense, we can determine the meaning of the election only by looking at the way in which the issues were defined. We talked last year about leadership, and I think all of us agreed that one very important function of leadership in a democratic society is to define issues in such a way that once the vote has been taken, one can impose meaning on what has happened. Well, I think if we look at the way in which the candidates for the presidency and for the Senate and the House defined the issues this year, we find that it is very difficult to talk about any mandate. Last year we talked about how political parties mean less today than they formerly did, so November 4 was not a rejection of the Democratic Party. Jack says it was really a statement of conservatism. I would say that if you look at the way certain liberal senators and congressmen were targeted, it may be far more a mere change of particular individuals than a pure statement of conservative philosophy by the electorate.

Carl went down a list of frustrated interest groups – ranging from farmers to Jews to union members. As he did so, I made a note that it was not party, it was not ideology, it was a shift in the cast of characters in an election that, I think, did less well in defining issues for the American people than any election in the past 20 years. And it was very much because of the way in which television was used in this election and the way in which money was spent. If I'm right that the most important thing the election did was to change the cast of characters, then we impute any larger meaning at great risk.

Kilpatrick: I would have to disagree. The most important thing the election did was to change the cast of certain characters in a certain way, to wit: the Senate. By giving the Republican Party, as a party, a decisive majority in the Senate, the voters swept out committee

Porter: "The annual rate of inflation was back into double digits . . . You just couldn't go into a grocery store with a 10-dollar bill and come out with much of a bag of groceries."

chairmen; they swept out Democratic-dominated staffs; they made a conspicuous party change. It wasn't just the individual senators who were changed. As for the coattail effect that Harrison mentioned, where you had two very conservative candidates, almost equally conservative, the voters took the Republican. I think there was a demand to get the kind of change, not merely of characters, but of parties, that resulted in the new Senate.

Brown: This is a very iffy matter, because after all, Reagan was elected by only a bare majority of the popular vote, and until Bill Nault used it in his question, nobody had uttered the word *mandate*. I don't like to use the word.

Kilpatrick: Yes. Even though there are areas in which you could put that interpretation on the election, such as increased defense spending, I am as wary as Harrison about this word *mandate*. I have seen many slim mandates, I've seen vanishing mandates, I've seen all kinds of mandates.

Nault: But if, just for the sake of discussion, we accept the proposition that it was a mandate, what *was* the mandate?

Kilpatrick: There were several. There was a mandate to increase defense spending. There was a mandate to build up the image of the United States, generally speaking, in foreign affairs. I think there was a mandate to get government off our backs in all kinds of areas. There may have been a mandate to reduce taxes.

Brown: And a mandate to get closer to a balanced federal budget.

Porter: Yes. For the first time in my memory, the voter was showing a consciousness of the size of the federal budget deficit. Nobody can really understand what a million dollars is, and you certainly can't understand a billion. But when we start building budget deficits running into tens of billions year after year, even the person who can't comprehend these statistics realizes that something is out of kilter.

The word *mandate?* I would go along with the idea that the election expressed some orders and some wishes: I, for one, want my country back in a position where I can be proud to be called an American instead of being spit on. I want my country back in a position where the dollar is sound again. I want my country back to the point where the government is off my back.

Cremin: I think the voters found that rhetoric more persuasive than the rhetoric on the losing side. I think the election was fought in such a way that the voters do not know what particular set of programs they bought, and what they will have to do without if some of those programs are achieved. Again, I would make the distinction between a campaign with a rhetoric of promises and one with a real debate over programs and priorities. I don't think there was a real debate. The people bought the rhetoric, but they didn't know what they were buying as far as the consequences of the programs. And they will reject many of those consequences when the effort is made to embody the rhetoric in legislative action.

Rowan: If we must talk about a mandate, I think it was a very vague one. The mandate was — "do something different and make me feel

Porter: "It would be difficult to overstress that this election was held against one of the worst economic backgrounds that we have had in this country in the half-century since Herbert Hoover. Unemployment had taken a big, big jump early in this economic downturn."

economically secure and internationally secure." But I don't think many of those votes really turned on specifics. For example, a farmer may have accepted the rhetoric of having the government get off of his back, but he sure wasn't for an end to federal price supports for farm goods.

Cremin: Yes. My point exactly, and you make it well.

Rowan: You have a whole host of groups in this country which say, "Get government off of my back, but don't let government do away with this program that benefits me." Now, you take this business of feeling ashamed that we are trampled on abroad. I think a lot of Americans really want to believe that if we had had more military forces, the Iranians would never have seized those hostages. That is nonsense. The people who seized the hostages are virtually crazy; they are fanatics. Americans don't want to face the reality of the kind of decision they have got to make if they say, "Don't let them kick Uncle Sam in the shin." We would have to make, first of all, the hard decision that the fate of those 52 hostages does not come first, that those hostages must die like good soldiers, in the interest of the United States image abroad, and the United States reputation. And that means going in militarily, letting the hostages get killed by way of saying to the rest of the world, "Don't mess with us." Now, I'll bet you that most Americans don't want to make that specific decision with regard to the 52 hostages.

Cremin: You are going to have to do that without draft registration, too.

Rowan: That is right. When young people are out in the streets protesting when all anybody wants to do is register them, you know that there is no great enthusiasm for going to the Persian Gulf area to fight what might be a wider war once we get into Iran.

The great dilemma

Brown: I like Carl's enunciation of this in broad terms. Do you call it a mandate if the voters simply told Reagan, "We want you to create a more secure economy, to create a more militarily secure nation"? Is that really a mandate?

Rowan: If you had to sum up what most Americans were saying, that would be it. But I don't think they were going into all the specifics about how Reagan is to bring this about. And that is the great dilemma. This is what is probably troubling for him, because he may have that broad mandate to deliver something that nobody on earth can deliver. As we were asking a year ago, is there anybody out there who can meet all of the requirements that Americans are looking for in terms of leadership?

Kilpatrick: There may have been a subjective kind of mandate out there dealing with traditional American values. In certain sections of the country, the so-called Moral Majority, the evangelicals, the fundamentalists, played a conspicuous role in this election. And they were expressing some sort of desire to get back to old values of family

Brown: "I personally favor having a nation that is militarily secure. But national security today far transcends the purely military aspects of the problem."

and morality, and to get away from such things as pornography, promiscuity, abortion. Now, I don't know how much of a factor this was in the election, but it was there. And in some specific races it may have been a very decisive factor.

Wille: Could we focus on one aspect of this mandate? National security received quite a bit of attention during the campaign. Reagan promised to strengthen our armed forces, to give the United States a stronger defense. Harrison, you said that that was one of the things the voters were saying – that they wanted a more militarily secure nation. Could you expand on that?

More than just counting missiles

Brown: It's a very complex matter of both defense spending and foreign policy, obviously. Unfortunately, too many people look upon this in a very simplistic way. They count the number of intercontinental ballistic missiles on each side, and the nuclear weapons on each side, and if it looks as though the Soviet Union has more than we do, then they say we have to do something to beef up ours. Now, I personally favor having a nation that is militarily secure. But national security far transcends the purely military aspects of the problem. For example, we have to take into account that in 1973 and 1974, oil was used for the first time as a major weapon of war during the Arab oil embargo, and used very effectively. Today it is again being used very effectively as a weapon of war, in that we are hamstrung as to what we are going to do or not do with respect to certain problems in the Middle East. We are truly hamstrung by the oil situation, and by what Saudi Arabia, for example, is going to think of what we do about this or about that.

Rowan: "The question is, does Reagan have the forcefulness of personality, or whatever it takes, to tighten the Western alliance, to make our allies understand that their security is involved with ours?"

I don't think that the problems of the Middle East are going to be solved in a military way by the United States. I think having a military presence is important. But the United States is dealing with an enormously complex array of factors that we have got to come to grips with, not militarily but in other ways, though we do need the military backup to show that we mean business.

In the world today, a world of some 160 sovereign states, we have what amounts to a four-cornered, three-dimensional pyramid. In one corner we have the industrial democracies, many with internal problems and all of them having trouble with one another as well – trade problems, for example. In another corner we have the Eastern European nations. In still another corner, we have OPEC – the Organization of Petroleum Exporting Countries – which interacts with both the industrial democracies and Eastern Europe. And then at the fourth corner of the pyramid are the lesser-developed countries. As a result of rapid population growth, a relatively low rate of economic growth, and vastly increased expenditures for imported oil, most of these countries are now going through an extraordinary economic period that – unless something can be done about it – is going to spawn far more chaos.

These are the kinds of problems that the Reagan Administration is going to have to come to grips with. And it should not consider the military problems as isolated from them.

Cremin: I'd like to add one point to this discussion of the military problem. It is a point that the military themselves were debating in the latter part of the year, and that is the readiness of the men and women who make up our military forces.

We can talk about the enormous technical capabilities that have to do with nuclear submarines and intercontinental ballistic missiles, and so on, but we cannot ignore the quality of the men and women in the services, and of their leaders. We have an all-volunteer armed force. There has been considerable complaint about their readiness, about their education. The armed forces themselves invest enormous resources in technical and general training. A colleague of mine, who works with the Navy, said that 1 naval person in 4 is in a classroom each day in some kind of educational program. The people you need for modern peacekeeping must have enormous technical capability. It throws us back to the question of whether our schools and colleges are producing these capabilities, and how we maintain them in an all-volunteer force.

Kilpatrick: The great problem in our armed forces is attrition of these young men and women after they have gone through the training you mentioned. The Navy is so short of experienced petty officers that some of its ships can't put out to sea. The Air Force doesn't have enough mechanics to maintain its airplanes. We also have all kinds of sophisticated weapons, and relatively few persons able to maintain them. The reason is that the incentives to join and remain in the armed services are very poor. The pay scales are way down. Many of the wives of servicemen have to work; a lot of them are on food stamps. Until we do something about these incentives to remain in, to sign up for a second or third or fourth enlistment, we are going to continue to have this problem.

Brown: We need a core of extremely competent professional military personnel, with the kind of incentives Jack is talking about to keep them in the services. But beyond that, though I hate to come to this conclusion, I don't see any way out other than to go to the traditional European type of system — a conscription system where every youth spends one or two years in the military, just as a part of his or her life.

Cremin: Either in the military or in some other form of universal national service. That is an issue that hasn't been debated in this country. It is an issue that raises tremendous problems of cost and commitment. I am not going to argue that we ought to choose one way rather than another. I would say that it hasn't been debated before the American people.

Kilpatrick: I don't buy universal national service; I don't buy it. A wartime draft, of course, is entirely different. In a free society, in peacetime, it would be absolutely a disgrace for the government to reach in and command these young people to serve for one or two years in some capacity. I am not ready to buy that.

Rowan: "I think a lot of Americans really want to believe
that if we had more military forces, the Iranians would
never have seized those hostages. That is nonsense."

Cremin: "I think [Carter] was a completely different candidate in this election from the candidate he was four years ago. The issues aside, his style was quite different. He was much more the creature of his advisers."

Cremin: Are you ready to have it debated?

Kilpatrick: Yes.

Rowan: One of the real questions is whether the American people really want to pay enough to provide the incentives to keep people in the services, and still also pay for new generations of weapons. The Russians, of course, are in a totalitarian society where they can deny all sorts of things to their people in order to pay for new weapons.

Brown: They already are doing exactly that.

Rowan: Yes, and to an extent that Americans so far have been unwilling to tolerate. So the question, in my mind, is where are we going? Because I can tell you, fear is the force here. And if you tell Americans that the Soviet Union is gaining dominance, they are going to say, "Spend the money on arms." They are going to say, "Well, I would rather make the mistake of having too many weapons than to have too little." So, where does the cost spiral go? I don't know.

Brown: I think there is a very serious danger there. If we don't handle arms-limitation talks with the Soviet Union well, we are going to find ourselves in another full-scale arms race in which new technologies are introduced, making the old ones obsolete. You have to pay all the money to put the new weapons in place, then the next thing you know there are still other new technologies, and you must pay for them.

Porter: The cost spiral is a very real question. We have to consider what all the costs of keeping our armed forces up to date or superior to Russia's would do to our economy. Every single suggestion you have made, Larry – or you, Carl, or you, Jack – every single suggestion has set my mind reeling with dollar signs. But they don't come out just dollars, they come out billions of dollars. And they don't come out billions, they come out disaster. Interest rates would be pushed through the roof as corporations that were given the job of turning out these new weapons borrowed money to finance their effort. What would happen to interest rates and the consumer price index – the cost of living – is horrendous to contemplate. That is another fact Americans will have to think about when they start looking at some of the specifics involved in carrying out the broad mandate for making our nation militarily sound.

Rowan: There is one aspect of national security we all ought to remember, and it goes far beyond the question of how strong our military forces are. We can have a tremendously powerful military, but we cannot sit in isolation. Even the most powerful nation in the world needs allies. As Harrison said, we need allies who are willing to let us have their petroleum. Reagan has the opportunity to do great things in this area, but there are some potential pitfalls.

For example, when we imposed sanctions on the Soviet Union after they invaded Afghanistan, Japan went along with us. The U.S. and Japan had been negotiating with the Soviets on a $350-million steel plant. But as soon as Japan and America said to the Soviets, "Absolutely not; this is out as long as your troops are in Afghanistan," the French moved right in and negotiated with the Soviets about that steel plant. Now, the question is, does Reagan have the

Rowan: "Reagan . . . may have that broad mandate to deliver something that nobody on earth can deliver. As we were asking a year ago, is there anybody out there who can meet all the requirements Americans are looking for in terms of leadership?"

forcefulness of personality, or whatever it takes, to tighten the Western alliance, to make our allies understand that their security is involved with ours? That if they don't do certain things, or if they keep undercutting the alliance, there will be consequences to pay? That is one side of the deal.

Then there is a diplomatic side. Our second biggest provider of petroleum, after Saudi Arabia, is Nigeria. The Nigerians were terribly unhappy with our policies in southern Africa before the Carter Administration came along. Now, though, we have some marvelous relationships with the Nigerians because they like the way Carter stood up in the Rhodesia-Zimbabwe situation. We hear a lot of talk about another tilt to South Africa in the Reagan Administration, which could get us into tremendous difficulties with Nigeria, perhaps back to the point where we run the risk of losing that particular supply of petroleum. These are the kinds of things Americans also have to think about in terms of how secure we are.

Brown: I agree with Carl, and I would like to go one step further. Something like 35 per cent of the oil produced in the world today is produced in the Middle East. This places the industrial democracies, almost all of which are oil importers, in a very precarious position. The Middle East is explosive, and not only because of the Iran-Iraq war. Look at the Israeli-Palestinian situation. Look at the Libyan situation, with respect to Egypt. Look at the internal instability of Saudi Arabia and of some other countries in that region. These are problems that we cannot easily resolve in a military way, as I have stressed. It is good to have a military strength visible and available, but we are not going to solve these problems that way. They can be solved, I suspect, only through negotiations. And not just by looking at them as OPEC always sees these problems – in terms of raising or not raising the price of petroleum – but by looking at them with respect to the world economy, with respect to the lesser-developed nations, and so forth.

Nault: Let's shift gears slightly, away from the discussion of what the election meant, whether it was a mandate, and what problems the new President will have to face. Let's look at the election as a process by which the American people get – or don't get – educated about the issues. Let's also look at some ways by which the process might be improved. Larry, you expressed concern earlier about the electorate's not having the issues defined well.

Cremin: It's something I feel strongly about. I teach courses in the history of education. And one of the things I frequently do with the students is turn to *The Federalist* papers – that series of essays written during the debate over ratification of the U.S. Constitution in the 1780s – and study them as an example of a widespread process of public education. Look at the level at which Alexander Hamilton and James Madison and John Jay addressed their fellow Americans about the issues in that Constitution. If you compare that with the level at which the American people in our time have been addressed about issues equally as profound, you see the cynicism with which candidates today approach the question of winning votes and of informing the electorate.

There has been some speculation about whether the tremendous shift to television journalism and television news, away from print journalism and print news, has changed the mode by which we carry on our electoral debates. One scholar has remarked that printed news tends to lead to divergent thinking. That when you get a news article in print, or when you get columns of opinion, they tend to set the issue out. Even if the journalist comes to a conclusion, the reader is left to reflect on it. But television news, even where there is a debate, tends to wrap it up, so to speak, tends to seek convergence in thinking. Maybe it is the nature of the medium – maybe it is the nature of the style with which we have learned to use the medium.

However that may be, the great shift to television has meant that you get rapid-fire statements of code words and key words, but you do not get the opportunity and the leisure you need to talk about consequences and circumstances and, really, to set alternative ideas before people. I would make one other point with respect to that: To

the extent that the candidates are in the hands of advisers who want them to make maximum use of the time available, to achieve certain changes in public attitude, they are less and less themselves. They are more and more the creations of advisers who create and present images – not issues. Take Carter. I think he was a completely different candidate in this election from the candidate he was four years ago. The issues aside, his style was quite different. He was much more the creature of his advisers, I believe, than he was in 1976.

We have entered a situation where one quality of leadership that I think is required in a democracy – namely, the ability to explicate the issues and open them up in a mature way before the electorate – has been lacking, with the result that the electorate is less informed. This is particularly true regarding younger voters, who are less informed and, I believe, tend to participate less in the electoral process.

Rowan: I'd like to raise the question of whether the American public really wants to be educated on some of these issues, and whether there really is a way to do it sufficiently. Let's take, for example, one of the major issues in this particular campaign. It's one we have been talking about – military posture, defense posture: How do we make America look strong to the world again? There were a lot of frustrated Americans who, I am sure, did not want to be bothered with all of the statistics about how many ballistic missiles we have and how many the Soviet Union has. They were inclined to say simply, "I want the man who comes across as the guy who is really going to make us look tough again." And that is just about all they want to take in mind when they try to decide how to vote. Can you ever get Americans to listen to facts and figures?

Kilpatrick: Probably not. I start out, Larry, with the homely observation that you can lead a horse to water, but in a true sense you can't make him drink. My impression of this recent campaign is that tremendous quantities of information were spread out before the American people. The television coverage was often superficial, I grant you that, but there was some television that did explore the issues, and there were editorials in the newspapers, columns of opinion, news articles, enormous amounts of information spread out. And yet, we talk about how uninformed the people were. I think it was that they just didn't want to pick it up.

Let me make this point: You draw the comparisons between *The Federalist* papers and today. Hamilton, Madison, and Jay were, after all, addressing a very tiny audience. They weren't even talking to women, they weren't talking to blacks. They were talking to white male Americans – and the relatively few of those who elected the delegates to the ratifying conventions of 1787 and 1788. So they had a highly selective audience. Today there is the problem that you are talking to men and women, blacks and other minorities, the 18-year-olds on up. Your political audience is so much larger.

Cremin: I agree; it is a larger audience now. Quite right, they did not address themselves to women or to blacks. But they did address themselves to a much broader portion of the male population than we

Brown: "The United States is dealing with an enormously complex array of factors that we have got to come to grips with, not militarily but in other ways, though we do need the military backup to show we mean business."

Brown: "In one corner we have the industrial democracies, many with internal problems and all of them having trouble with each other as well — trade problems, for example."

have heretofore thought. That was a highly literate population. American white males at the time of the debates over the Constitution were probably more literate than any white males anywhere in the world. But given universal public education today, given the extent to which the electorate is literate, I believe we undervalue their ability to partake of the system. I think it is the job of the leadership to be so persuasive as to the meaning of the issues, granted their complexity, that — to borrow your observation — when the horse comes to the water, the horse drinks and partakes. A good leader, a good teacher, has to do that.

Wille: There was a very widespread feeling that one of television's efforts to present the issues during the campaign, the so-called debate between Reagan and Carter, was a significant factor in the election. What did the electorate get out of that, and what effect did it have on the election?

Kilpatrick: I got the impression from the debate that Ronald Reagan was not the saber-rattling gunslinger that Carter tried to characterize him as. That was the main impression, as I understand it, that was derived from that debate. Reagan had been picked on by Carter as a racist, as a warmonger. And here came this grandfatherly fellow with an "aw shucks" look on his face, saying, "Mr. Carter, oh there you go again." He was reassuring, and he seemed to be sincere. That was the big thing. I don't think the issues mattered very much.

Rowan: I think also they got the impression there was something lacking — they couldn't say what it was — something lacking about a President who tells you how his daughter told him that nuclear proliferation was the biggest issue of the day. And I think that lost Carter a considerable number of votes, because he opened himself up to ridicule. I think the debate was significant in that respect.

Kilpatrick: Perception is almost always more important in politics than reality. How was Carter perceived? How was Reagan perceived? Carter is a very intelligent man. He was — he is, I am sure — deeply concerned about this nuclear issue, but he was perceived badly when he made that unfortunate remark about his daughter.

Porter: I have more optimism about the American public's ability and willingness to absorb information than I think most of you have — except, perhaps, Larry — because I have lived through an era in which the public has taken to the dismal art — the dismal trade, really — of economics. The public has taken to it because ordinary men and women can see how it has affected their paychecks, the bills they pay. And the public has absorbed knowledge to a point way beyond consumer economics, to a point where people want to know: What is the American economic system? What is the importance of an interest rate? Why does it go up and down? Why does the consumer price index do what it is doing? These people are asking questions. They are ordinary American people of all ages — young, middle-aged, elderly — and they certainly will turn on television shows on economic issues if the television people will just put them on. A big portion of the blame must fall on the directors of the television shows who insist that the shows reach for the lowest level instead of giving the shows a chance now and then to reach the highest level that they can reach. I will never forget the time one of the biggest television stars in the country phoned me late one afternoon and said his show was in a terrible spot, and he wanted me to define devaluation of the dollar. He wanted me to do it in 15 seconds — 15 seconds! That is sad. People want to know. The American public is willing to be educated.

Rowan: I don't know if anybody knows the answer to this, but one of the problems we have here is the extent to which the public is turned off — or doesn't want to hear too much about some of these issues during the election — because they think that none of the politicians is any good. We heard it said so often in this election: "Is that all the choice we get?" Now, I don't know whether that is an alibi lots of Americans make for not reading about the issues and for not voting, or whether it is really true that they are turned off by the way we pick our candidates, by the way we nominate them. But it is a factor.

Reforming the process

Nault: This seems like the right time to raise the matter of the process by which we select a President. What are some of the problems with the way it is done now, and are there any useful new approaches?

Rowan: For one thing, I think there very definitely ought to be some *reforms* of the Democratic Party's reforms of a few years ago. In their zeal to get away from the smoke-filled rooms where a few insiders determined the candidate — an effort I applauded — the reformers went so far that very few senators showed up at the Democratic National Convention this year; very few governors were there, very few mayors. They reformed out of the nominee-selecting process an awful lot of people who should have been in it. There has to be a place for the political pros, the people who run government, who handle budgets, who have dealt with these problems.

Wille: Do all reforms tend to go too far?

Cremin: I suspect that is a truism that you could document. They either go too far or they result in new problems in new times that those who instituted the reforms could not foresee.

Kilpatrick: I agree with Carl. I would like to see the nominating conventions have an honest function again. We have seen that they have lost their main function, which is to nominate. They have been reduced to nullities by all these primary elections that stretch out for months and essentially sew up the nomination for a candidate long before the convention is held.

Rowan: The primary season runs far too long, and it is front-end loaded. The guy who wins the early ones has something of an advantage immediately. He tilts the results of the upcoming primaries because the news media are giving all of this publicity: So-and-so killed them in Iowa, so-and-so killed them in New Hampshire. I swear, all the primaries have convinced me that there ought to be a national primary.

Porter: "I have more optimism about the American public's ability and willingness to absorb information than I think most of you have . . . . People want to know. The American public is willing to be educated."

Kilpatrick: They haven't convinced me. I would be very much opposed to a national primary. I think it would nullify the national conventions. Under the principle of federalism, we now operate by states, and a national primary would go absolutely away from that fundamental principle of our political process.

Rowan: But we have to do something to get away from the business where a Jimmy Carter, with some money and a lot of time on his hands, can run around tinkering with the system to the point where all of a sudden he wins the nomination of the Democratic Party, to which he is not really beholden; to the point where he is disavowing most of the people who run things in Washington and the states. My point is that Americans who have sat around and complained about the choices on the ballot had better go back and look at the primaries and at ward and precinct politics. The American intellectuals and the supersophisticates who have been crying about what they got would not be caught dead at a political party's ward or precinct meeting or in a primary campaign. They had better get in there, though, because those are the beginnings of the selection of our presidential candidates.

Kilpatrick: Would you be with me in forbidding open primaries? They make a travesty of party primaries. When just anybody can come in and vote in a Democratic primary, how does it become a Democratic primary? It is anybody's primary.

Rowan: That is right. There I would go along with you; I would cut out the crossovers.

A role for the party pro's

Kilpatrick: Then, if we could have just a few regional primaries, say between the middle of March and the middle of May, in order to shorten the campaign period and open it up to candidates who don't have the time or the money for the present lengthy primary schedule, I think we would be on our way to something useful. Then, going back to something you said, Carl, if there were some way that you could build into the conventions a role for the governors, the senators, the members of the House, the mayors, the other party professionals, I think the nominating conventions might have some real role again.

Brown: I remember that when I first moved to Chicago during World War II, the first person to pay a social call on me was our local party professional, the Democratic Party precinct captain. He welcomed me to Chicago, and he said, "Now, if there is anything I can do, if a street light is casting too much light into your apartment, or something like that, I can get that fixed for you. Just don't hesitate to call me." Then came the first election. He paid a call just to make sure I knew who the candidates were, and so forth. I went to vote on election day, and there he was, standing the legal distance from the polling place. He smiled as I went in, and then as I came out he walked over to me and shook my hand. He said, "Thank you very much," as though I had voted just for him. I would have voted without him, of course, but that

Cremin: "I know of no school district in this country that has a successful program of getting youngsters involved in political activities of a constructive sort in the community. We need more of it."

Kilpatrick: "Perception is almost always more important in politics than reality. How was Carter perceived? How was Reagan perceived?"

precinct captain was just the kind of person we've been talking about. He does the grass-roots party work, and he ought to have more of a voice in his party's affairs.

Kilpatrick: I would like to extend this discussion of reforms a bit, to the question of some fundamental constitutional changes that might be worth considering. Lloyd Cutler, Jimmy Carter's counsel, recently wrote a provocative article for *Foreign Affairs* magazine. He analyzed the structure of our political system and tossed out a few intriguing proposals for discussion. Cutler isn't ready for us to adopt Great Britain's parliamentary system, but what if we gave the President the power to dissolve Congress and to call for new elections in midterm? What if, for its part, Congress could order a new presidential election? These are radical proposals. I'm not sure I like them. I don't think our country is ready for party discipline of the kind that they have in Great Britain. I don't think we are ready, but all my instincts say we have to start strengthening our two-party system toward party accountability. There is almost none now.

Still, as I say, the changes Cutler proposes are so radical that I kind of want to creep up on them. His idea, if I understand it correctly, is to bring everything into government in a package. You would have a President serving for six years and senators and representatives also serving for six years simultaneously. We would have to vote for it all as a package — all Democrats or all Republicans. You would have a

party elected to power and held accountable. If the party failed to win a vote of confidence, there would be a new election.

It is a radical proposal, but it might cure some of the ills that I see in our political system, which is absent of any accountability. Nobody is in charge of the store now. The President has diminishing powers; he is almost out of the political process in all kinds of ways. The process increasingly is run by the entrenched bureaucracy and the lobbies of various interest groups, and the President, no matter who he is, sits in the White House in lonely grandeur, having relatively little to do with what really is happening. Perhaps we ought to think about some improvements.

Nault: One improvement might be to get our young people, who, after all, represent the future of our country, involved more deeply in the political process. Larry, what can be done about it?

Cremin: As in many areas of life, the school has taught young people the facts and tried to teach them attitudes, but it has not helped initiate them into the realities of political life. A number of reports that came out in the mid-1970s said, basically, that our high schools have to stop attempting to provide the entire education of their students in the school building, and have to broker a series of relationships with local businesses, with labor unions, with communi- ty-service agencies, with political parties — to give the youngsters a firsthand chance to participate actively in the realities of community life. And then – because I do not believe that active participation always brings education – the students have to take the experience back to the school, reflect on it, and connect it with the formal education in the classroom. I know of no school district in the country that has a successful program of getting youngsters involved in political activities of a constructive sort in the community. We need more of it.

Porter: I think there is more to it than just looking at failures of institutions or of teachers. You must look inside the youngsters themselves. You can get a real turnout of young voters on the question of nuclear power, for example. You can really bring them out for an issue they are concerned about. But I think there has been a tremendous feeling of rebellion, rejection, even disgust since the Watergate affair. I believe we have gone through a period during which the youngsters of this country were fed up with the morals of the older generation. I think that accounts for a great deal. But I think the youngsters are tuning back in. Looking at the university campuses, you see kids studying today who used to say, "I can't change anything; I'm not going out and vote; I'm going to stay home and play my guitar, and a pox on both your houses." Now these college students are studying again, returning to traditional values of education and involvement.

Cremin: I see them studying more than I see them tuning in.

Kilpatrick: Taking up Sylvia's point – maybe in this election we recently held there was no issue that really concerned young people deeply. They are not so subject to the rigors of the economy and the

Cremin: "I think that students will . . . become active in politics when they realize that there is not going to be some cataclysmic change because of this vote or that vote and when they begin to look at the more limited goals of improvement in politics."

inflation and unemployment as older groups are. There was no war in Vietnam to inflame them. The question of draft registration, really, has subsided. And I don't think the abortion issue engaged them very much, either. I don't think there was any issue this time around that deeply aroused our youngsters. I wish that they had turned out in greater numbers on election day, but the figures are depressing. What is it – half of them registered to vote, but fewer than half of those who registered actually voted.

Brown: There is another important point here, when we talk about young people and the difficulty of getting them to vote or participate in politics. My generation was young during World War II, and at the end of the war most of us had not been involved in the political process except to vote in the 1940 election. But at the end of the war, the powers that be just got us mad. We'd been working on the atomic bomb project, and a bill was proposed in Congress that would have vested all the control over atomic energy in the military. We just got very mad at that; we thought it was terribly wrong. And we tried to use friendly persuasion with some of the powers that be, and failed. So we went to Washington, and we lobbied, and we defeated the bill. When you can do something like that, you feel that you have an influence on things. That marked my entrance into politics, and I continued to be active. What kept me going was, in part, the feeling that we were accomplishing things. The really important thing, though, was that I recognized that there is a political process and that you have to use it in order to get things done. I think that so often our young people have no sense of involvement because they don't think that anything can be accomplished.

Cremin: With respect to that, I think that students will join the electorate and become active in politics when they, perhaps, realize that there is not going to be some cataclysmic change because of this vote or that vote and when they begin to look at the more limited goals of improvement in politics.

Nault: Well, our time has about run out, and we seem to have come full circle in our discussion. We began the day by looking at the recent election and the process that produced the upcoming change in government from Jimmy Carter to Ronald Reagan, and we have ended by looking ahead to future elections and ways in which the United States political process might be improved. I think we have given our readers a good many ideas to ponder, and I want to thank all of you for your participation today.

For further reading:

Numerous articles in THE WORLD BOOK ENCYCLOPEDIA provide background information on some of the matters discussed by THE YEAR BOOK Board of Editors in this Focus article. These articles include ELECTION; ELECTION CAMPAIGN; ELECTORAL COLLEGE; GREAT BRITAIN (Government); NATIONAL DEFENSE; POLITICAL CONVENTION; POLITICAL PARTY; PRESIDENT OF THE UNITED STATES (How a President Is Elected); PRIMARY ELECTION; UNITED STATES, GOVERNMENT OF THE; and VOTING.

Special Reports

1975 1976 1977 1978 1979 1980

Six articles give special treatment to subjects of current importance and lasting interest.

See "What Should I Be When I Grow Up?" page 106.

Walter Cronkite Wraps It Up

An interview with
Walter Cronkite,
conducted by John Callaway

Soon to retire as anchorman of "The CBS Evening News," the renowned newsman talks about how television and journalism mix

He held a power not available to any president or prime minister. Every weeknight, his words and his image were transmitted to tens of millions of Americans, bearing the bad news and sometimes the good. He steered us through every national and global crisis and triumph of the past two decades.

When our leaders were assassinated, he spoke to us through tears. When our men reached the moon, he shouted with glee. We wept with him, and we shouted with him. When the world appeared sometimes to be coming apart, he kept a steady course, strong at the center. When the country held its 200th birthday celebration, he was our national cheerleader.

In an age of cynicism and despair, he remains an enduring hero. "Uncle Walter" has almost replaced "Uncle Sam" as our symbol of trust in the United States of America.

Uncle Walter, of course, is Walter Cronkite, the correspondent whose "CBS Evening News with Walter Cronkite" has dominated American broadcast journalism for the past 18 years. If anyone ever deserved the title of "anchor man," it is Cronkite. Few Americans can remember any national or international event of significance in this generation without associating it with the calming, reasoned voice of Walter Cronkite.

In an age of celebrities and superstars, he remains a down-to-earth working journalist who prides his position as managing editor of the "CBS Evening News" more than he does the title of anchor man.

Cronkite was born in St. Joseph, Mo., on Nov. 4, 1916. His father and a grandfather were dentists, but it was clear soon after his family moved to Houston when he was 10 years old that Cronkite wanted to perform on a bigger stage. He worked on school papers – the *Purple Pup* and the *Campus Cub* – at the University of Texas and then was campus correspondent for the *Houston Post*. Cronkite dropped out of the University of Texas during his junior year to take a full-time job with the *Houston Press*. By 1937, he had moved to Kansas City, Mo., where he began an 11-year career with United Press. During World War II, he covered the Allied invasions of North Africa and Normandy; flew with bombing missions; and crash-landed in a glider during the Battle of the Bulge in 1944. He joined CBS News in Washington, D.C., in 1950.

THE WORLD BOOK YEAR BOOK talked with Cronkite one morning late in November 1980, a few months before his scheduled retirement from his nightly news duties. The interview took place on West 57th Street in New York City at the CBS Broadcast Center, a converted dairy known to its inhabitants as "the cow barn." Cronkite's tiny office, located next to the CBS newsroom, is a working newsman's cubicle, cluttered with books, magazines, *Facts On File*, and Emmy trophies. The no-nonsense atmosphere is set off by a *Mad* magazine "Alfred E. Neuman for President" poster.

He is dressed in a blue pinstriped suit and vest and is wearing black-rimmed glasses. He is hoarse with a cold and pops throat lozenges into his mouth from time to time. He says he is going to make his own recording of our conversation for reference if, and when, he gets around to writing his autobiography, which he calls "that book."

The author:
John Callaway is director of news and current affairs at WTTW-TV in Chicago. His show, "John Callaway Interviews," appears on many public television stations in the United States.

John Callaway: Is it true that when you were a boy, you thought about some career other than journalism?
Walter Cronkite: Yes, it is indeed. I thought about mining engineering for a while. There was a magazine called *American Boy*. It had a marvelous series of short stories, fictionalized versions of what various careers, professions, and businesses were like: a young hero going through his daily routine as a mining engineer, of being caught in a mine or whatever; a journalist; and things of that kind.

The two that really struck my fancy were journalism and mining engineering. But the mining engineering didn't last very long. That

Two giants of broadcast journalism, Edward R. Murrow, left, and Lowell Thomas, right, appear with Cronkite in a panel discussion in the 1950s.

was a very youthful thing. It was really just the next step from wanting to be a fireman or a policeman, both honorable professions but not ones that a lot of us think of very long in life. They are glamorous to smaller kids. Then you realize how much work and danger there is and you decide you want to do something else.

Callaway: But you decided on journalism. Why, as you look back on it now, did you choose journalism?

Cronkite: I don't really think there was any question of it in my mind. I was editor of the high school paper, and working summers at the *Houston Post*.

From the time I was cognizant of what the business really meant, what I would be faced with in trying to be a success in it and what the challenges were in it, it was always journalism that I wanted to be in.

Callaway: What is it that journalism meant to you?

Cronkite: I think what it meant mostly was being on the inside of everything. I think I always had a kind of a generalist's interest in life. Everybody's occupation interests me. Everybody else's work interests me. Always has. My wife says that I am the only person she knows that could spend a whole evening talking to a shoe clerk about his business. But I can. I find it fascinating that all those boxes are there and how do they know what model is in each one of those boxes, and don't they have to learn an awful lot to know what those numbers all mean and to find the shoes. I found that I could make a business of other people's business.

Callaway: Very early in your career, you ended up in very dangerous situations: flying with bombing missions over Germany in World War II. Were you prepared for that kind of journalism?

Cronkite: Oh, I think so. Yes, that was part of the glamour of the business, that one might be in dangerous situations.

Callaway: Did it end up being glamorous when you got to do it?

Cronkite: Sure. I can't deny that. Frightening, terrifying. I don't pretend for one minute to be brave about it. Each assignment scared me to death. On the other hand, there was a great exhilaration over having accomplished the assignment, and living through it.

Callaway: When you were covering World War II for United Press, the late Edward R. Murrow offered you a job with the great CBS news staff that was being developed in Europe, and you turned it down, even though he offered you more money. Why?

Cronkite: Well, that goes back quite a long way, really. I had dipped into radio from time to time in my early career. It looked interesting. It looked like a new frontier of journalistic enterprise, and it paid better than newspaper work did.

But every time I got into it, I was disappointed with it. It did not seem totally serious or professional to me. It seemed to be all right on the air. But when I got into it, it was, I thought, terribly superficial [and] run by people who were not professional journalists. They were people who came from other businesses into this new area of show business, some of them from show business, theater management, and things of that kind. They weren't keyed to journalism.

Yet they thought they could be, because everybody thinks they can edit a newspaper or write a piece or broadcast it or run a news organization better than the people who run them. We are probably the most underrated business as far as the complexities of running it and the public's opinion of it.

I had great respect for Ed Murrow in London and for the team of people he had assembled there — Charles Collingwood and Eric Sevareid and Richard Hottelet and others whom I thought very highly of as journalists. So when he offered me the job, I was very impressed and thought, well, this was an organization I could work for.

Then, after accepting the job, I went back to the United Press and got such a vote of confidence from UP that I settled there for considerably less than I would have made at CBS.

Callaway: Then you did later on accept another invitation from him, did you not, to join CBS?

Cronkite: Yes [after working for a group of Middle Western radio stations and toying with the idea of becoming a station manager]. You see, I never really saw myself as a performer, and I don't now. That is not the interesting part of this business to me. It has been something you do, and that is where the money is, but it is not the reason for being in the business. The thing I like about this job now is being managing editor of the broadcast.

Callaway: Which means?

Cronkite: Selecting the items that go into the broadcast, editing the copy that comes from the correspondents, writing and editing my own copy, getting the best we can out of this raw material which is the day's flow of news, taking those items and putting them into the short form we need in television to get the maximum information in the minimum amount of time. This is the challenge. It is no particular challenge to sit up there in front of the camera and recite the news after the material is prepared.

It is more of a challenge to do an ad lib broadcast such as election night, conventions, spaceshots, assassinations. Stories of that nature are far more difficult, and therefore far more interesting, than any other aspect of this business. But on the daily news, the thing that I like is the editing of the news.

Callaway: Isn't the business of television journalism going more in the direction of performance as opposed to those other values?

Cronkite: You mean why people are hired, qualifications they are looking for?

Callaway: Particularly at the local level.

Cronkite: Yes, I am afraid that is so, and it worries me greatly. I think this is very unfortunate and it could even be said to be a dangerous trend, dangerous from two standpoints. One, it is another case of the public not getting quite what it believes it is getting. There is too much of that going on today in all aspects of life.

In television journalism, when they present an individual as a news authority and that person is not a news authority but merely a performer, this is fraudulent in an area where fraud is terribly dangerous. If people can't believe what they are given in the news, then there is very little they can believe and little they can depend upon. They have got to have faith that we are doing our best in all areas of the news to be forthright, honest, unprejudiced, unbiased. We ought to be what we seem and present ourselves to be.

Second, more and more people are getting all or most of their news from television. We already have a very serious problem in discharging the responsibility that is loaded upon us.

We can't totally discharge that responsibility in the time given us. As a matter of fact, we probably could not discharge it if we had the whole day's schedule, because people's tolerance for sitting in front of a set and watching a visual and an audio presentation of the news is limited. I don't know what that limit is, but I suspect it is not a great deal more than what we are doing right now.

Now if we have got that responsibility, then we have to do our very best to try to discharge it with the very best product we can put forward. In the local news market particularly, there is not an adequate attempt to cover the serious news of the area. A lack of dedication to the job is indicated when the local manager thinks that the way to get an audience for the news is to present a good-looking broadcaster instead of presenting a full news broadcast.

I don't blame those pretty faces that are out there. They are filling a vacuum in a job market which is very attractive. I can understand why they want to do it. But it does concern me. I am afraid there are young people going through, quote, communications schools, un-quote, today that are not journalism schools. Their desire in life is to be a performer, not a journalist. They don't start out with the same gut feelings of what a reporter is all about, what an editor is all about. They start out with the kind of gut feeling that an actor has who wants to go to acting school and be on in front of the public, performing. That is not what the business is about.

Callaway: Do you have any advice for young people who might read this about what a good education is for somebody who wants to go into television journalism?

Cronkite: I can say that it starts with the broadest-based education the individual can get. You have to start out, if you want to be a journalist, to be a generalist first – that is, know as much as you can about everything. Then if you wish to specialize after you have got that basic knowledge, go out and take postgraduate courses in science or economics or business management, whatever field you wish.

I think that a journalism course, some journalism courses, as you get along much further in your education, are a good idea. In high school, a journalism course is a very good idea, fairly early on in high school, a basic journalism course. With that knowledge, you can work on the high school paper, maybe even be a high school campus correspondent for a local paper or a radio station or television station, write as much as you can.

Callaway: Print experience is good before you go into television?

Cronkite: I would require it. If I were the boss of CBS News, we would not hire anybody without it – with maybe a rare exception. Of course, there are always exceptions. But the basic rule would be a minimum of three years print experience. And if one of those years was spent in a press service, so much the better.

There are very good reasons for that, to my mind. Television does not have the economic structure to put reporters on the beat – the police beat for eight hours a day five days a week, on city hall, county courts, the education beat, PTA and the school board, the places

Cronkite's show is far from a one-man operation. In a typical scene, the program's director, a writer, and others discuss late changes with Sanford Socolow, executive producer of the "CBS Evening News."

A newsman's clutter covers Cronkite's desk. His book-lined shelves hold a few reminders of his love for boats, and a single political poster.

where the most essential news affecting the citizen is made. They don't have anybody like that because the economics of the business don't support it.

So we don't have a training ground in television to learn how that beat is really organized, where those stories really are, what the importance of the various sources are, which sources can be believed and cannot be believed, which ones are self-serving or not self-serving, where the story may be buried.

Callaway: So you need years of that?

Cronkite: It takes years. Two years are not nearly enough for that experience in the city hall, the county courts. But at least the rudiments, the fundamentals of that kind of reporting and digging and source development are there. And there is none of that here.

Callaway: How do you feel about the radio-TV major as a major?

Cronkite: My inclination is to paint with a very broad brush and condemn it, but I can't do that because I don't know that much about it. I don't know that every college is as bad as some that I have had a look at and dislike. The curriculum in the radio-TV course in many colleges is far too heavy with technique and far too short on journalism substance.

Callaway: Is this any business for somebody who wants to be a good parent and a good husband or a good wife? Can you have the good, rich personal life still?

Cronkite: Nobody has asked me that before. I don't know the answer. I am not sure anybody has the answer. That means an awful lot of personal magic between two people as to whether it works or not.

This is a very demanding profession, demanding of a great deal of understanding on the part of the spouse, whether male or female.

The day's news is gathered in the CBS newsroom, *above,* put into broadcast form by the writers flanking Cronkite's semicircular desk, *top,* and then given a final polish by the managing editor himself, *opposite page, top.*

There are ways to make a career in journalism, certainly, without disrupting the normal kind of schedule of home life. You can be a copy editor with Newspaper Guild hours, put in five days, eight-hour days — now seven-hour days in many places. You could be a broadcaster and not go out on assignments, not respond to every fire bell.

If you are going to live what I would think is even the glamorous life of the young reporter — the ones whose legs are still strong — and are going to answer the fire bells, then you are going to have to have an arrangement and a wife or a husband who is understanding.

Callaway: So you better think about it in advance?

Cronkite: Yes. The divorce rate is very high in the network television news business. It is very high. Home life is quite disrupted.

Callaway: How do you think historians will judge the performance of network television journalism, say, in its first 30 or so years, on the question of helping viewers anticipate international crises or wars that would envelop their lives?

Cronkite: I think the historians will not judge us too favorably. But I think when they make that judgment, they are going to be doing what academics frequently do, and that is take a very narrow, tunneled look at a situation and not see any of the peripheral parts or problems of it. It is certainly true that we are not alerting people to danger spots around the world before they arise.

Sometimes we don't know about it. Sometimes the background journalism isn't there. But I must make note that sometimes the CIA doesn't know and the State Department and the Defense Department don't know.

Certainly Iran, the blowup in Iran, the revolution in Iran, I think the press was probably making more of that in the early days with [Ayatollah Ruhollah] Khomeini's statements out of Paris than even the State Department was acknowledging. Frequently the press has been ahead of official recognition of the situation.

Modern minicameras and sensitive sound equipment capture the news events, *above,* and an artist prepares an explanatory graphic display, *right.* Then CBS videotape editor Mike McGuire, *below,* edits and blends the sights and the sounds of the day's happenings for the "Evening News."

On the other hand, we don't belabor these things. The historians are likely to criticize that. We should have kept the focus on these things, constantly alerting people. Well, we are not built to do that. That is not our function, it is not our role.

We are a daily news service. We are not a journal of opinion. We are not a journal of academe. We are not the *Foreign Policy Quarterly*. We are not *Harper's*. We are not even *Time* magazine or *Newsweek*. We are a daily news service with a half-hour, trying to give people the headlines and the clues to their day, that day in history, that day in news, not what may be coming six months from now or two years from now. We are there to report that day's events as they occurred, and that is all we can be charged with doing in that 23 minutes that we have left after the commercials.

But beyond that, what the historians with their tunnel vision may not choose to see is that we have done so much more. We give people a picture of the places where news is made that they could never get through any other medium. We give them a good look at the people who make their news in a way that they would never have. They get to know their leaders in a way they have never gotten to know them before, which may have some bearing on why our leaders don't seem to be quite the heroic figures that they once seemed to be.

We do background on the news as it occurs. We raise occasionally a warning flag when we can crowd it into the day's heavy schedule. We have a bank of those pieces. We are constantly looking for them and doing them.

Cronkite, Socolow, and newswriter Sandor Polster discuss the best way to handle a news story.

I think we were absolutely out at the cutting edge of that big burst of awareness of ecology and environment that began in 1970. I think

Writer John Mosedale checks facts in a story with a staff researcher.

we led the way, I believe right on this broadcast, with the series "Can the World Be Saved?"

But it is not our first responsibility. If they start trying to lay that responsibility on us, I think they are missing the point.

Callaway: Let's say that the historian recognizes that he can't lay that responsibility on the Walter Cronkite evening news itself. But he says to the people who run the networks that, considering all the hours available, the right programming focus just wasn't there and that the success of "60 Minutes" proves that if you go with a quality hour of television, it will be watched in prime time – in short, that they could have had prime-time television journalism for years. Would that be a fair criticism of the networks themselves?

Cronkite: I would agree with that completely, absolutely. I think television has done fairly well, but not well enough. We have done some fine documentaries that have had great impact and have been important warning flags. But certainly not to the degree we should have.

Callaway: How do you think television has done in the first 30 years?

Cronkite: I think there is no question that it has been 95 per cent escapism, perhaps 5 per cent enlightenment. That is a wild number picked out of the hat. But I think it is perfectly clear you could take the evening prime-time program schedule and do a comparative analysis on it – what has been truly cultural, what has been informational, and what has been popular pap – and come up with numbers something like those.

There is a question – of quality control, I guess – in the intellectual sphere. I don't think that television has done badly by that comparison. I would bet that television's percentage on network prime time of substantive material, either cultural – good plays, good shows, good music – or informational material, is higher than the percentage of worthwhile book titles or magazine articles.

Callaway: What impact do you think television is having on the political process in this country and what do you think of that impact?

Cronkite: It has a major impact, just like movable type had a major impact. Any new means of communication that is as profound a change as television is over print is bound to have an effect.

It affects the political process in many ways. The first way is that the political leaders are far better known to the public than they have ever been known before. Their personalities become important, where they did not become quite so obvious before in print.

Second, I think that the people are far more aware today because problems are brought to them in a far more dramatic manner through television than they ever were before. People are more sensitive to them and, therefore, to the performance of their leaders than they ever were before on a day-to-day basis.

The third point is that the leaders can communicate to the people. I am thinking now of the President of the United States. He can now mobilize the people or address the people everywhere in a fashion that was never possible before.

One of the reasons why I do not think that we should put down as either a problem or as a handicap the fact that we now may select a leader on his television capabilities is that the man who can use that medium well, very well might be the best leader, if all other qualifications are the same.

Callaway: Ah, but that is the rub. Doesn't that get back to your comment on the tendency to have local anchor men who are more

As air time approaches, Cronkite times his lead story to the second and weighs last-minute changes. The on-screen Cronkite is monitored in the control room.

interested in performance? What I think people are scared of is that we are developing a kind of marketing of politicians, people who enjoy running for office but don't have that gut feeling for government the way you have that gut feeling for journalism.

Cronkite: I think there is some danger in that. I think the public, however, is too discerning to let that happen. I think that the politician can't really go over the heads of the entire political process and appeal to the people simply because he is an actor.

I guess we are going to have to watch that simile, now that it has happened to an actor. But Ronald Reagan did his work in the political process. He became governor of California, proved that he could be an administrator of a major state. He went out and did his work on the hustings with the other candidates, supporting them, helping them, building up his I.O.U.'s. I don't think he was a marketed candidate.

In fact, we have seen some heavily marketed candidates who tried to campaign solely with the use of television advertising, slick expensive advertising, and the campaigns fell right on their faces.

Callaway: Are you concerned that there might be a really good-quality journalist who had long exposure on television and would then use it to run for high office?

Cronkite: I worry about that.

Callaway: If Ronald Reagan can come out of movies and be a quality politician, why couldn't a television journalist run for office?

Cronkite: Because of a much different set of circumstances. If the public begins to get the feeling that anchor people on television are editing the news and presenting the news in such a way as to lay a political base for themselves, that this might be the ultimate goal of an anchor person, I think it would destroy the public's confidence in television news, and properly so. I would be very worried if I thought that the person I was watching on the evening news was being careful to avoid offending leaders to whom he or she might some day want to appeal for a high office. I think that would be dangerous.

Callaway: You yourself have been offered high position, have you not?

Cronkite: Oh, my gosh, practically all of them–from various people and groups who are serious, and a lot who aren't very serious. I get a lot of letters that I ought to be a senator, President even. And those are nice, I appreciate them, people feeling that way about it. But I have had some far more serious than that. Delegations call upon me and ask me to run for this office or that office.

In most cases, when the delegations are made up of powerful political figures, I have found that I am a little disturbed because they rarely ask me what I stand for. They are trying to buy prominence. They are trying to cash in, in other words, on what they consider to be a popularity quotient of a high number.

I wonder whether they feel that they will be able to control me once I get into office, whether they are that confident of their own political muscle and that demeaning in their consideration of what I am about, or whether they are so cynical that they don't care what I stand for.

Callaway: Talking about what you stand for, you have been quite careful over the years not to dot your broadcast with opinions. But in 1968 you finally came out against the war in Vietnam, and some observers have said that is really when President Lyndon Baines Johnson understood that if he couldn't get Cronkite, he couldn't get the American people behind the war. Do you agree with that?

Cronkite: Metaphorically, possibly. If he meant by that, "If I can't get Cronkite and John Chancellor and Harry Reasoner, if I can't get the kind of middle-American leaders in that sense behind me, then I can't get middle America behind me," I would suppose that there is some justice in that, yes. I accept that.

Callaway: Will we hear more of your opinions and what you believe in now that you are going to be off the nightly anchor position?

Cronkite: I would suppose so, simply because I wouldn't find any reason to suppress them any longer. I imagine they will pop up from time to time. I am not going to write a manifesto and go out and preach it to the countryside.

Callaway: I have read that you are interested in doing something that will make people better consumers of news. Is that of interest?

Cronkite: It is. I feel that we ought to have courses in high school and probably earlier, junior high school, and a refresher course maybe in high school, maybe as part of a civics course or something, and something in college. Sort of a journalism for consumers, teaching journalism to people that have no intention of using it. As consumers of journalism, I think the people need to know what the handicaps and restrictions are for each area of journalism.

They ought to know why the "CBS Evening News" is limited in its capacity to deliver all the news that they need. They need to know that they cannot get all the news they need from the "CBS Evening News" or "NBC Nightly News" or ABC. They need to know what good reporting can be, what it should be.

To mark Cronkite's coming retirement from the "Evening News," CBS News President William Leonard presents him with the microphone he used at the 1952 Democratic National Convention, his first.

After nearly 20 years of reporting the day's news to the nation, America's most trusted man wonders about the way it will be.

They have got to know what their newspapers and the news magazines can and can't do. They have to know what the deadline problems are. They should know how news magazines work in researching a story, and that one person writes it and somebody else rewrites it and edits it. They should know all the input and who makes the decisions.

If they knew that, they would first of all be far more discriminating customers. They would demand better products. Second, they could not be misled by demagogues who, at a time of crisis, wish to turn them against the media.

Callaway: Some summing-up questions. What is your reading of this civilization? Are we going to make it or are we in a decline?

Cronkite: I am an eternal optimist, I guess, in the face of all the evidence to the contrary. I guess we will make it. I cannot come to the belief that man is as insensitive as he seems to be. I don't believe that we can go on killing each other and tolerating killing and still maintain that we are civilized. Therefore, I have to be an optimist. But I certainly see problems that can bring us down in fairly short order, problems we are failing to address today with the urgency and the intensity that are required.

I think we have the four horsemen of the modern apocalypse riding down on us. Any one of them can do us in. Population, which we cannot seem to bring under control. That is the base problem. The others in a sense stem from that: pollution, depletion of natural resources, and atomic proliferation. Any one of these four could do us in. Yet we worry about today's problems of the economy and inflation, unemployment, import quotas, and other things which are important, of course, and have a great deal to do with the strength of the nation and the economy. But I don't see anybody really terribly concerned about any of these major issues.

Callaway: Right, we tend to wonder about our own fire department.

Cronkite: Yes. But we *have* to worry about that, that's the problem. We have an awful lot to do. That is the reason why democracy is always a difficult way to operate. The citizen has to go out and make a living, take care of his family and simply see that they are fed, clothed, housed, and get to school on time, and he has to get to work on time, he has to buy the automobile that gets him there, and a few things like that. He is also expected to worry about how the fire department is being run, and how the police are being run.

He has to worry about the purity of the water and waste disposal in the plant 30 miles away. He has to worry about air pollution. He has to worry about Brezhnev and the Soviet Union's invasion of Afghanistan and whether his own boys will have to go in the military and serve over in Afghanistan. And he has to worry about the hostages in Iran and the national honor. My gosh, where does this end? No one person can worry about all these things every day, or our suicide rate would be the fifth horseman of the apocalypse.

So we have to unload problems on other groups. Then we have to trust their judgment. That is where the press comes in. That is really what press freedom is all about. We have to then say, all right, you selected these people to make your decision on air pollution, but let us tell you that they are not doing the job. Or that they *are* doing the job, but when they are done it may cost you your job, and you have to accept that the group that you selected says that your job has to go because what you are doing — no fault of yours — but what you are doing is endangering your whole neighborhood, or maybe a neighborhood 3,000 miles away. It is hard for people to accept.

Callaway: What are you going to do after you get off the nightly news?

Cronkite: I am probably going to sign up for a long term at CBS doing documentaries, specials, advisory to a certain extent in news, and be around and helpful.

Callaway: One last question. I don't mean to retire you early, but how do you want to be remembered?

Cronkite: I guess with fondness. I would like to be remembered as one who brought journalistic professionalism to television or worked to preserve that professionalism in a business that could easily be show business. I think that is what I would like to be remembered for most.

One leaves with the impression that we will be hearing much, much more from Walter Cronkite in the years to come. We won't see him nightly with the familiar benediction of "And that's the way it is," but we may see a Cronkite who finally will share with us his passions, insights, and opinions based on his 40 years of reporting and reflection. And that's the way it should be.

The Inflation Rate, the Cost of Living . . . and You

By Ronald J. Alsop

While inflation shrinks the buying power of the dollar, economists wonder how to control it, and how to measure it

Inflation, which nagged consumers in the United States throughout the 1970s, became almost an obsession as the 1980s began. People bought and bought, seemingly despite the cost, because they thought that prices could only soar higher. Buying slowed down, but only for a few months, after President Jimmy Carter announced temporary restrictions on credit cards in March 1980. Public opinion polls repeatedly indicated that inflation was considered the greatest problem in the United States. Bumper stickers, often an accurate barometer of public sentiment, appeared in many areas, urging, "Honk if you hate inflation!"

Not surprisingly, then, much attention was focused on the Consumer Price Index (CPI), the statistic prepared by the Bureau of Labor Statistics (BLS) that measures changes in the prices of products and services from month to month. The CPI serves as a gauge of inflation for government and business, as well as for the average consumer. But as the CPI claimed more of the spotlight, it became controversial. Aside from the problem of how to slow inflation, measuring it accurately seemed to be a problem in itself.

Many economists and political leaders think that the CPI over-states increases in the cost of living. They say that it fails to take changes in consumer buying habits into account and that it puts too much emphasis on housing costs, including mortgage rates.

"The CPI is a very poor measure of the cost of living and should be used only as a very loose indicator of inflation," says Charles Reeder, chief economist at E. I. du Pont de Nemours & Company, a giant chemical manufacturer. "The CPI has a notorious upward bias," Reeder adds. That is, it magnifies the true inflation rate.

The BLS is not disturbed by such criticism. Agency officials point out that the index is not intended to be a precise measure of the cost of living. Rather, the CPI measures price changes each month for a specific group of items — called a fixed market basket of goods. The selected items are grouped in seven major categories: food and beverages, housing, apparel and its upkeep, transportation, medical care, entertainment, and other — mainly education, personal care, and tobacco. Prices vary by city and region, so local indexes are compiled along with the national CPI.

The CPI does not attempt to total all the money spent on the seven major categories. Nor does it attempt to total all the money spent on all goods and services. Instead, the CPI tracks only price *changes* for the market basket items from a reference date — 1967 for most items. The 1967 CPI is said to equal 100. By measuring today's index number against 100, you can see how much prices have changed. At the end of 1979, for example, the overall CPI stood at 229.9, meaning it cost $229.90 then to buy the same market basket items that cost $100 in 1967. Critics of the CPI worry that the details of how the CPI is compiled are poorly understood. Most consumers, they say, notice only that the CPI is going up and panic about their own cost of living.

The CPI is in reality a composite of certain items and should be used only as a rule of thumb by the individual consumer. "The official CPI is totally unrepresentative of any single individual," says Reeder. "Everybody has his own CPI."

The author:
Ronald J. Alsop is a reporter for the *Wall Street Journal's* Philadelphia bureau.

Illustrations by William Petersen

You and your family may not buy the specific items that are checked to compile the CPI. The CPI measures prices, as its name implies. However, it does so only on that limited list, or market basket, of items — not all the items that Americans actually buy. Nor does it measure how Americans divide up the dollars they spend among the major categories — the actual cost of living.

Nonetheless, "The CPI is the best measure of purchasing power we have," says Janet L. Norwood, who, as commissioner of labor statistics, is in charge of compiling the CPI. Some observers agree that the CPI does what it was meant to do — measure the price change of a fixed basket of goods and services — quite well. The problem, they contend, lies in how the CPI is used and interpreted by some economists, labor unions, and news media.

The Congress of the United States has tied some major benefit programs directly to the CPI, linking regular payment hikes to CPI increases. For example, Social Security benefits have been tied to the CPI since 1975. Each year on July 1, retired people receive an increase that is based on the CPI, to help them cope with inflation. On July 1, 1980, an increase of 14.3 per cent went to the more than 35 million Social Security recipients. Another 2.6 million persons on federal civil service and military pensions get semiannual increases when the CPI goes up.

As many as 6 million labor union members may be covered by contracts that have cost-of-living adjustment (COLA) clauses tied to the CPI. When the CPI goes up, their wages go up automatically — generally on a yearly basis, but in some cases every three or six months. Many unions that do not have COLA protection nevertheless use the CPI in their bargaining sessions, pointing to CPI increases to justify their wage demands.

Even the federal grants for school lunch programs are affected by the CPI. In fact, so many types of payments in government, business, and industry are tied to the CPI that the BLS does not know how many people are included under the CPI's umbrella. As much as half of the population of the United States might be affected.

The CPI is also important for other reasons. It is used as a guide for government economic policy, and it reflects the success or failure of that policy. As the CPI rises, pressure increases on administration leaders in Washington, D.C., to take steps to curb inflation.

Perhaps the strongest criticism of the CPI is directed at its treatment of homeownership costs. Although mortgage interest rates rose as high as 17.5 per cent in March 1980 and prices for new houses were at record levels, many economists contend that the CPI overstated the true inflation rate by overemphasizing these dramatic changes. The CPI counts the entire cost of a house, plus all the interest you will pay on your mortgage, as your housing cost for the year in which you buy the house. Most Americans did not buy a new house in 1979 or 1980, so they were not directly hurt by the high mortgage rates and home prices. And yet the CPI, recording the price swing in housing just like that of other items in the market basket, rose by a shocking 13.3 per cent in 1979, the largest annual jump since 1946.

House prices and mortgage rates contributed 4.1 percentage points to the 1979 increase, which means that the rise in the CPI exclusive of housing was 9.2 per cent. The seven categories used to calculate the CPI are not weighted equally in the total. Prices for all housing costs including utilities make up fully 45 per cent of the overall CPI figure for any month. The monthly CPI for July 1980 showed clearly how this weighting can distort the real inflation picture. For the first time in 13 years, the monthly CPI did not increase because housing costs

Housing
Most heavily weighted of seven categories in the Consumer Price Index (CPI), housing includes the cost of a new house; mortgage costs, including interest; maintenance and repairs; and rent. The CPI for housing rose dramatically from 1969 to July 1980.

Transportation
The costs of new and used cars, other private transportation, gasoline, repairs, and public transit make up this category. Much of the increase in transportation prices from 1969 to July 1980 shown in graph results from the jump in gasoline prices.

Food and Beverages
Major divisions in the food category include food you buy to cook and eat at home, food eaten in restaurants, and alcoholic beverages. The graph shows how food and drink prices increased from 1969 to July 1980.

Apparel and Upkeep
Prices for such items as clothing and shoes for men, women, and children — along with such apparel services as dry cleaning — rose moderately from 1969 to July 1980.

The pie chart shows: HOUSING 45.0%, FOOD & BEV. 18.7%, TRANSPORTATION 18.6%, MEDICAL 4.8%, MISCELLANEOUS 4.1%, ENTERTAINMENT 3.7%, CLOTHING 5.1%

Medical Care

This category takes in such services as physicians' fees, hospital rooms, drugs, and other medical supplies. Medical-care prices rose sharply from 1969 to July 1980.

Entertainment

This category includes such diverse items as books, magazines, newspapers, sports equipment, toys, games, hobby supplies, and pet supplies. Also included are tickets to sporting events, motion pictures, plays, and other events. The graph shows how entertainment prices increased from 1969 to July 1980.

Miscellaneous

The category "other goods and services" includes tobacco products; such personal-care items as haircuts, hairbrushes, and cosmetics; school tuition and fees; and schoolbooks and supplies. The rise in such miscellaneous prices between 1969 and July 1980 is shown on this graph.

Parts of the Whole

The seven categories of the CPI are weighted in the overall figure, with housing making up the lion's share. The CPI-W was used here for all seven categories.

decreased. But all other categories of the CPI rose, so price inflation actually was still proceeding apace.

In addition to housing's weight in the overall CPI, some critics dislike the way the housing figures are compiled. "The current concept of homeownership treats houses like any other goods — that is, as though they were consumed in the year they were bought," says Lawrence E. DeMilner, chief of the Congressional Budget Office's inflation impact unit. "In fact, the services rendered by a house are consumed over its entire lifetime." DeMilner and other economists stress that a house is not only a place to live, but also an asset that you invest in and resell later to yield a profit.

Some observers believe it might be preferable to treat homeownership costs more like rent. "This alternative treats the homeowner as though he were an investor who rents out the use of the house to himself," says DeMilner. In this way, the BLS could measure the value of the house as a source of shelter, he explains.

Many critics have attacked the homeownership component of the CPI for another reason — because few people buy homes in any given year. "Costs of homeownership are calculated as if all consumers face the same change in house prices as those entering the housing market each month," members of the House Budget Committee declared in a February 1980 letter urging President Carter to revise the CPI.

A leading labor union economist, however, believes the current treatment of homeownership costs is just fine. Because many unions have COLA protection, a higher CPI brings their members higher wages. "We do not find very realistic the notion of the family's house as strictly a financial instrument, as if the alternative were the use of the same funds in the stock or credit markets," asserts Rudy Oswald, who serves as director of the department of economic research for the American Federation of Labor and Congress of Industrial Organizations (AFL-CIO).

The BLS in 1980 began publishing and testing five alternative methods of calculating homeownership costs, with an eye toward changing the housing component. But Norwood stresses that these indexes are at present still only experimental: "We have one official Consumer Price Index, and we will continue to have one official Consumer Price Index."

The CPI may also overstate inflation because it does not take account of the adjustments and substitutions that consumers make in their buying to minimize the misery of inflation. Because inflation has persisted for so long, virtually all consumers have made these adjustments — for example, cutting back on higher-priced foods, buying clothes only on sale, or spending less on entertainment.

Richard Ruggles, an economics professor at Yale University, calls the "constant market basket" concept — the idea that people will always keep buying the same items no matter how high the price — "a distortion of reality."

"Unless you're the dumbest creature in the world, you shouldn't experience as high an inflation rate as the Consumer Price Index assumes," says Audrey Freedman, a senior research associate for the Conference Board, an economic research organization. "People are constantly making choices and adjustments, but the CPI doesn't reflect when you switch to chicken breasts from T-bone steaks."

The Morrisseys, a Columbus, Ohio, couple, provide an example of the kind of adjustments that families make to keep down their personal inflation rate. Gail Morrissey, a young businesswoman, has reduced her apparel bill by doing part-time work for a local clothing store that gives her a 50 per cent discount on purchases. She also models for a beauticians' class in exchange for free haircuts and permanents. Doug Morrissey, an auto distributor, used to eat lunch at a restaurant but now eats soup in his office and avoids the 11.4 per cent increase in 1979 on food eaten away from home. The Morrisseys subscribe to a cable-television station that shows recent movies for a monthly fee of $12, substituting for movie tickets at $4 apiece. While the CPI for entertainment admissions, or tickets, rose 7.5 per cent in 1979, the Morrisseys cut their costs. "Constant cutbacks and adjustments are just a reality today," Doug Morrissey says without a trace of bitterness.

If the Morrisseys had children, they might be forced to make even more crucial trade-offs. Many families with young children are squeezed particularly hard by the rising costs of food, medical care, and clothing. They resort to trading outgrown clothing with other families, buying shoes for their children instead of clothing for themselves, and getting loans to finance school tuition or fees. Services are especially costly, so many parents cut their children's hair, launder by hand clothes that should be dry-cleaned, and repair their appliances — all to save money for essentials.

The BLS believes there is merit in not reflecting this kind of adjustment in the CPI. "Because a market basket change could amount to a change in living standards, those whose income payments are adjusted by the CPI would not be assured that their living standards would remain at the same level," maintains Norwood. "If, in adjusting to higher prices, a family decides to forego its weekly restaurant dinner, the family is both changing its market basket and lowering its satisfaction or standard of living."

Critics also say that the CPI uses an outdated market basket of goods and services, based on a survey of consumer spending in 1972 and 1973. Although the CPI does not claim to measure exact spending patterns, price information is useful only for products and services that many people buy. Thus, buggy whips and barbershop shaves are no longer included because they are outmoded. Such products as microwave ovens, handheld calculators, and birth-control pills were added to the survey in the 1970s. But new products continually surface in this technologically oriented society, and the

CPI does not yet include such products as the home video recorder and such fast-growing services as pay-TV.

The CPI is also said to be outdated on gasoline prices. It includes the many price increases of recent months, but the index is weighted on the basis of how much gasoline drivers used in 1973. Many consumers have curtailed their driving and gasoline purchases since then as prices have risen.

The creators of the CPI surely never dreamed it would become so important and so controversial. The CPI was developed in 1917 to set fair wage levels in the shipbuilding industry during World War I. Since then, it has gradually been revised to reflect the entire U.S. population as well as changes in buying habits.

In all, the government has made five major revisions of the CPI. The most recent and thorough revision, in 1978, created a stir by producing two national CPI figures. A new index, CPI-U, covers all urban consumers, or about 80 per cent of the U.S. population. The CPI-U is now the most widely quoted index. The BLS also kept the original index for urban wage earners and clerical workers, CPI-W, which covers about 40 per cent of the U.S. population and overlaps with the group included in CPI-U. When the latest CPI is reported in the newspaper or on TV, the "U" or "W" is often omitted; in such a case, the CPI-U is the index quoted.

The CPI-W was retained because labor unions feared that their members' living costs might not be reflected accurately in the all-urban-consumer index. To date, however, the figures compiled for the two measures have been almost exactly the same.

Almost as soon as a major revision is completed, the BLS begins the lengthy process of gathering data on consumer buying habits for its next big revision, according to Patrick Jackman, a BLS economist. "I expect the revision in about four years," Jackman says. "At that time, a different measure of housing might also be adopted."

In addition to the two national indexes, the bureau also compiles individual CPI's for 28 major U.S. urban areas and four regions, to provide for local variations (see maps on facing page).

The job of collecting the data for the CPI is an exhaustive process. Workers for the BLS gather information on housing costs and the prices of food and other CPI items by contacting more than 18,000 tenants in rental units, 18,000 homeowners, and about 24,000 establishments — for example, hospitals, grocery and department stores, and gas stations — in 85 urban areas in the United States. Field representatives make personal visits to obtain most of the prices. However, mail questionnaires are used to survey utility rates, some fuel prices, and other items.

The seven major categories of the CPI are divided into subcategories, and most are broken down again. For example, the food and beverages category is divided into food eaten at home, food eaten away from home, and alcoholic beverages. Food eaten at home is

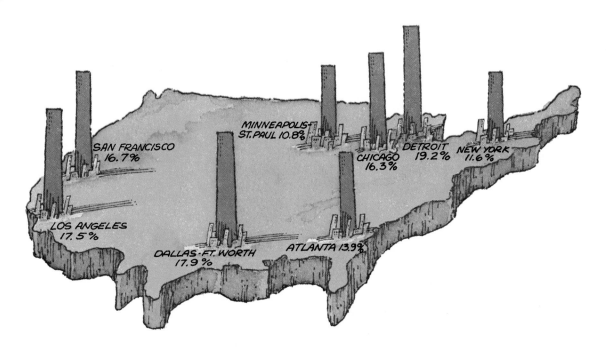

The U.S. Bureau of Labor Statistics compiles an individual CPI for each of 28 major metropolitan areas so that residents can compare their costs with those in other cities. Each region has its own CPI, too. A few examples show how much the CPI increased in selected metropolitan areas from June 1979 to June 1980. The average increase for all cities in the survey was 14.3 per cent, ranging from a high of 19.2 to a low of 10.8.

broken down into narrower categories, such as fruits and vegetables, and these into such specifics as potatoes.

Housing is broken down to reflect rents, other rental costs, home-purchase costs, financing, and maintenance and repairs. Fuel and other utilities are broken down to include fuel oil, coal, bottled gas, piped gas, electricity, and other utilities. Apparel and upkeep is made up of men's and boys' clothing, women's and girls' clothing, infants' clothing, shoes, and such apparel services as dry cleaning and laundry. Transportation includes the cost of new cars, used cars, gasoline, oil, automobile maintenance and repair, other private transportation, and public transit.

Medical care is composed of commodities – prescription drugs, nonprescription drugs, eyeglasses, and such supplies as thermometers – and medical services. Hospital rooms, one of the fastest-growing prices, are also included. Entertainment includes price changes for commodities such as reading materials, sporting goods, toys, hobbies, and games, and for services, mainly tickets for sports contests and other entertainment events. The category "other goods and services" includes tobacco products, personal-care items such as cosmetics and wigs, personal-care services such as haircuts, and educational expenses such as tuition, books, and supplies.

Some people, including those receiving Social Security benefits and military pensions, are sheltered from inflation to some extent because their payments are linked to increases in the CPI. They get periodic increases to compensate for CPI rises.

The CPI excludes income taxes and personal property taxes. But it does measure changes in real estate and sales taxes.

Some critics condemn the CPI not only because they consider it a faulty yardstick of inflation, but also because they believe it fuels our already spiraling inflation. Because so many wage contracts, pension benefits, and government subsidy programs are tied to the CPI and rise along with it, economists and government officials worry about all the money pumped unnecessarily into the economy if the CPI is overstated by even one percentage point.

The Labor Department estimates that an increase of one percentage point in the CPI triggers a $1-billion increase in federal payments. But U.S. Representative Paul Simon (D., Ill.), citing a Congressional Budget Office estimate, says that figure may be low and that an increase of one percentage point in the CPI triggers a $2-billion increase in expenditures for Social Security and other federal programs. And even that figure does not include the union and other private-sector wage increases tied to the CPI. Reducing such hefty government outlays would help balance the federal budget, a move that many economists favor to slow inflation.

Besides its direct financial impact, the CPI exerts indirect psychological effects that feed inflation. Experts say that consumers kept

buying at a lively pace during 1979 partly because they felt they should buy now and escape the next round of inflation – the TV set that was expensive in 1979 would only be more costly in 1980. Increased demand for goods usually leads to inflation in prices. Reports of large CPI increases also create a psychology that results in enormous wage demands. Many economists think that big wage increases without a corresponding increase in productivity – the actual goods or services turned out by a worker in a given time period – also feed inflation.

The recession that started in 1979 began the slow task of cooling the inflation rate. During the first three months of 1980, the CPI rose at an 18.1 per cent annual rate, but it had slowed to a 12.2 per cent annual rate by the end of October. Some economists regard recession as the lesser of two evils. They believe that a high inflation rate is more destructive than the temporarily high unemployment a recession causes. Rising unemployment generally results in less spending, particularly for items such as appliances, entertainment, personal services, and luxuries.

Amid all the calls for improvements in the CPI, this measuring system still has its vocal defenders. Revising the CPI so that it rises more slowly would hurt those whose wages and retirement benefits depend on the index. For that reason, most labor unions and groups representing retired people strongly support the CPI as it is. "As far as we're concerned, the CPI accurately measures price changes" and reflects the actual cost-of-living increases experienced by Americans, says Steve Clem, research director of the United Rubber Workers of America union.

"Labor unions pressure the Bureau of Labor Statistics against changing the CPI because they don't want their sacred cow tampered with," Robert Gordon, an economics professor at Northwestern University in Evanston, Ill., complains. "They like the errors because they tend to boost union wages."

Federal, state, and local income taxes are not included in the CPI. Proposals have been made to compute these taxes in the CPI, since they are part of the burden carried by consumers.

Most consumers have been forced to adjust their standard of living to cope with inflation. Few have switched from limousine to chauffeured bicycle, but many have turned to chicken instead of steak.

Some observers advocate specialized consumer price indexes, especially one for older people that could be used as a base for Social Security and pension adjustments. Whether such an index would be higher or lower than the overall CPI, it would undoubtedly be different. Older people buy fewer houses and use less gasoline than younger people, but they have heftier medical bills.

While some persons think the CPI errs on the high side and others think it's just right, some critics think that it understates inflation's bite for some individuals. The National Center for Economic Alternatives in Washington, D.C., maintains that low-income people bear the brunt of inflation, because almost all of their money is spent on necessities. Economist Jeff Faux, co-director of the center, points out that food, shelter, energy, and medical care costs rose a seasonally adjusted 17.6 per cent in 1979, while the overall increase in the CPI was 13.3 per cent.

"Poor people live from paycheck to paycheck and can't try to beat inflation by buying meat on sale and keeping it in the freezer," says Faux. "I can go from steak to hamburger, but it's hard to go from dog food to nothing."

People at the other end of the income scale also complain that the CPI understates inflation. Their gripe is that the index does not include federal, state, or city personal income taxes, or Social Security taxes. When middle- and upper-income families receive pay increases to help them cope with inflation, they also face higher taxes — and the more they earn, the higher their tax rate. They would like to see income tax rates, as well as wages and retirement benefits, adjusted for inflation.

For instance, consider the case of Charles Schulze, a Cincinnati, Ohio, telephone company executive. Despite healthy wage increases, Schulze says that his disposable income has shrunk as he has moved into higher tax brackets. He complains that his income rose 40 per cent from 1975 to 1979, but his Social Security and income taxes climbed 69 per cent. "Despite good promotions and raises, I feel like I'm treading water," he says. While he can make adjustments to curb his high food and energy costs, he notes, "There's no alternative to paying taxes except going to jail."

With the CPI in wide disfavor, some economists and government officials are taking a close look at another inflation measure – the price deflator for personal consumption expenditures (PCE) issued by the U.S. Department of Commerce. The Commerce Department compiles the PCE in the process of computing the gross national product (GNP). The dollar value of all goods and services produced in the United States in a year is totaled for the GNP, then compared with the total for the previous year. The government statisticians then attempt to calculate how much of the annual change – usually an increase – results from an increase in real value, and how much represents inflation.

The PCE's advantage over the CPI is that it is adjusted regularly for changes in consumer buying habits. It also treats housing costs in such a way that skyrocketing mortgage rates and house prices do not distort it. The PCE for 1979 rose about 9 per cent over the 1978 figure, as opposed to the 13.3 per cent CPI increase.

"If you're interested in how your cost of living is going up, the PCE is better than the CPI," declares Arnold H. Packer, assistant secretary of labor for policy, evaluation, and research. But he cautions against too much trust in either index. "It's futile to look for a perfect cost-of-living measure, but I think we could do better than what we have," Packer says. "Somewhere between the CPI and PCE deflator would be better."

Some observers think that arguing over which index is better is pointless. "No matter which measure you look at, we have horrible inflation," says Lawrence Chimerine, chairman and chief economist at Chase Econometrics of Bala-Cynwyd, Pa. "Everyone is getting sidetracked from the main issue, that there's much too much inflation." According to the BLS, a 1967 dollar would have been worth 40.4 cents in 1980 – and that is inflation.

Some observers think that the CPI controversy accelerated in 1980 for political reasons. They speculate that elected officials, handicapped by double-digit inflation in an election year, wanted to distract the voters' attention from the key issue of controlling inflation and hoped to convince them that inflation was not nearly so bad as the CPI let on. Some commentators likened this technique to the ancient practice of blaming the messenger – in this case, the CPI – for bringing the bad news.

While economists and politicians bicker about the CPI, consumers are finally most concerned about what is happening to their standard of living: Is life still as satisfying as it was? A basic part of "the

American dream" has always been economic — making a good living, making life more comfortable over the years, and ensuring an even better standard of living for our children and grandchildren.

With persistent inflation, many families now believe that they are not even holding their own on the standard of living — much less improving it. Older people worry whether their savings, carefully accumulated over many years, will see them through retirement. Parents worry about how they will squeeze the money from an already tight budget to send their children to college. Those with savings accounts in a bank worry about inflation draining the money from their passbooks. These concerns are very real and cannot be wiped out by jiggling the CPI a bit in either direction.

A related issue is the quality of goods and services available today. Are the items that now cost you more the same in quality? Or are they better or shoddier than the goods you used to buy? The CPI basically ignores changes in the quality of goods and services, except for automobiles. But many people are convinced that they are receiving less quality, as well as less quantity. In that case, the CPI would be understating inflation. The poorer quality of some clothing items available today, for example, is mentioned by many people concerned about this issue.

On the other hand, to the extent that products have been improved, the CPI overstates inflation. For example, if a color-TV set costs more this year than last, that is clearly inflation. But if the TV set produces a better picture and lasts longer, you get more for your money, so the price boost is not entirely due to inflation.

The quality issue is a complex one. It is difficult to imagine, for example, how you would draw up objective quality standards for goods and services — standards that could be agreed upon by the buying public, business and industry, workers, and government observers. Still, if people believe that the quality of goods and services has been declining steadily, they conclude that their standard of living has gone down.

Debate about the CPI is healthy if it helps focus attention on crucial questions — starting with the most basic question: What is the CPI and what does it measure? Also, does the widespread linking to the CPI of government and business payments fuel inflation? Even broader questions are being aired in the CPI debate: How can inflation be slowed down? What kind of economic future can we look forward to?

For further reading:

The Consumer Price Index: Concepts and Content Over the Years. U.S. Department of Labor, 1977.
"Inflation's COLA Cure," *Time,* July 28, 1980.
"Make a Budget for Your Inflation Rate," *Changing Times,* August 1980.
Mitchell, Daniel J. B. "Does the CPI Exaggerate or Understate Inflation?" *Monthly Labor Review,* May 1980.

Pondering the Fate of the Forests

By Lawrence S. Hamilton

The future of wooded lands hangs in the balance as developing nations weigh sound forest management against their people's need for food and fuel

Concern about the world's forests, especially the tropical and subtropical forests of the developing countries, accelerated in international importance in 1980. The International Union for the Conservation of Nature and Natural Resources, together with the World Wildlife Fund and the United Nations (UN) Environment Program, released their report on *The World Conservation Strategy* in March. Among other topics, it stressed the urgent need for more conservative treatment of the earth's forests. The National Research Council of the United States National Academy of Sciences commissioned a study of the rate of disappearance of tropical forests, and issued its findings on *Conversion of Tropical Moist Forests* in April. The U.S. Department of State in May released *The World's Tropical Forests: A Policy, Strategy and Program for the United States*, which recognized the important American stake in these forests and our responsibility for their welfare. *The Global 2000 Report* in July, which examined the earth's ability to supply resources over the next 20 years, painted a gloomy picture in the area of forest resources, and earlier in the year, an international group of tropical forest scientists, convened by the UN in Nairobi, Kenya, expressed concern about the lack of management and the deterioration of forests in many parts of the world.

I talked throughout 1980 with foresters and conservationists from many countries and can attest that widespread concern exists. In September and October, I visited the Philippines, Malaysia, Indonesia, Papua New Guinea, Australia, and Fiji. Earlier in the year, I traveled to Puerto Rico, Trinidad, and Venezuela. Although I found much to generate despair, I saw some glimmers of hope. In spite of tremendous pressures for destructive cutting and forest clearing, foresters, ecologists, and environmentalists around the world are starting to make some headway in altering prevailing practices. They need and merit greater support from the rest of us. During the time that I was writing this article, I met with foresters from Sri Lanka, India, Malaysia, Thailand, South Korea, the Philippines, Papua New Guinea, Bangladesh, and the United States. We worked on developing ways to present rational forest policies in new packages. Our hope is that this approach may sway the governments and other people who are deciding the fate of the forests of Asia and the Pacific Islands.

The forests of the world are extremely varied. While it is difficult to describe the different types simply, they may be broadly categorized as follows. *Rain forests* have no extended dry periods, and range from the exuberant tropical lowland rain forest to cloud forests on mountains and hilltops to temperate rain forests such as the coastal redwoods of California. *Seasonal forests* show fluctuating annual growth patterns, either because of alternating cold and warm conditions, as in the temperate, leaf-dropping forests of eastern North America, Europe, and eastern Asia, or because of alternating wet and dry periods in the tropics and subtropics, such as in the monsoon forests of east Asia. *Open forests,* or woodlands, occur in the tropics and subtropics (for example, the open eucalyptus forests of Australia); on the Mediterranean coast and coastal California; and as a woodland of sparse trees in the Far North. An unusual kind of salt-tolerant forest – the mangroves – grows in the intertidal zone of coastlines of the tropics and subtropics.

The author:
Lawrence S. Hamilton is a research associate in the Environment and Policy Institute of the East-West Center in Honolulu, Hawaii.

The most obviously useful product of every type of forest is wood. Wood was the first fuel known to our ancient ancestors, and it has continued to supply much of the world's need for heating and cooking fuel despite the discovery of fossil fuels and hydroelectric power. In a 1979 report to the Worldwatch Institute in Washington, D.C., conservationist and senior research ecologist Erik Eckholm called attention to the startling fact that "for one-third of the world's people, the energy crisis does not mean the dwindling resources and high

Forests mean different things to different people.
Hikers on Sourdough Ridge in Oregon's Cascade
Mountains, *above,* enjoy nature's green expanse.
A worker picks nutmeg for a living in an Indian
forest, *below.* Loggers in Washington fell trees,
right, to make paper for books like this one.

Blazing autumn foliage in an Adirondack forest stages a colorful farewell. But unseen tree roots absorb water from the soil and store minerals, and leaves appear in the spring, feeding the trees and converting carbon dioxide to oxygen.

prices of petroleum. It means something much more basic – the daily scramble to find the wood needed to cook dinner. The search for wood was once a simple chore. But now as forests recede, it requires long hours – in some areas a day's labor.''

A 1979 UN Food and Agriculture Organization study indicated that 1.5 billion persons use wood for cooking and heating and that 80 per cent of all energy, other than human and animal, used in rural areas of developing countries comes from wood. The impact is heaviest on tropical and subtropical open woodlands and seasonal forests.

In East Africa, these forests are being cut down to make charcoal, much of it for export to Middle Eastern countries. Heavy cutting in such forests for wood fuel is common in China. South Korean forests have been so largely destroyed that many rural people must collect leaves, grass, and crop and animal wastes for fuel. In countries such as India and Bangladesh where people burn animal waste, further economic problems are triggered because it is needed for fertilizer.

In many parts of the world, trees literally hold the land together. Their roots keep the earth from drying up and blowing away or being washed down into watercourses. Nowhere are the adverse effects of the assault on forests for firewood more evident than in mountainous Nepal, where 87 per cent of the energy consumed comes from forests. Ground-protecting trees in Nepal and similar areas in the Himalaya are disappearing rapidly as the population increases. As the trees disappear, the soil is being washed down into the Ganges, Indus, and Brahmaputra rivers, which carry it to the plains of India, Bangladesh, and Pakistan. There it pollutes drinking water, kills food fish, and silts up reservoirs, thus lowering the generating potential for hydropower, reducing irrigation-water storage, and decreasing flood-control capacity. For example, the Mangla Reservoir in Pakistan, completed in 1967, was designed to last for 100 years. However, about 100 million short tons (90.7 million metric tons) of sediment now collect in it yearly. At this rate, the reservoir probably will lose its capacity in 50 years.

A shortage of wood for cooking also plagues people who live in areas bordering on deserts, and removing the few trees that grow there speeds the spread of arid areas. "Desertification is the most pressing, the most frightening problem facing people of the Sahel," Edward C. White, a representative of the UN Development Program in Mauritania, said in September 1980. In these countries – Senegal, Mauritania, Mali, Upper Volta, Niger, Chad, Gambia, and the Sudan – continued cutting and overgrazing have removed the trees and turned the area into more desert. The UN is now using space satellites to monitor the movements of spreading sand dunes, and scientists are devising ways to halt them. One project calls for planting acacia trees, in the hope of stabilizing the dunes.

The stepped-up search for firewood has also begun in the past few years in the Northern United States and Canada. The high cost of such fossil fuels as gas and oil or electricity for heating has caused thousands of people to put wood-burning stoves or heaters into their homes. There are probably 5 million households with wood-burning stoves in the United States. Some large power-generating plants in the Northeastern states are now fueled with wood chips.

If harvested with care, the cool temperate leaf-dropping forests, containing such trees as ash, oak, birch, and pine, could sustain substantial cutting for wood fuel. While use of firewood will not end our heavy dependence on fossil fuels, it will help many people.

The intensity of the firewood problem illustrates how dependent many people still are on the world's forests. We who live in the developed countries value forests as vast expanses of wooded lands we can turn to for mental revival, rather than physical survival, as in the wood-hungry nations. The United States has organized a National Wilderness System, containing vast areas of public forests, for recreation and for scientific study. But some of us are beginning to realize that our ability to maintain wilderness areas depends on other nations' willingness to part with theirs.

However, even if a country is eager to sacrifice its forests for economic gain, the well-being of the rest of the world may dictate that it should not do so. The fact is, we need forests. Forests are energy systems fueled by the sun. They take in carbon dioxide from the atmosphere and nutrient-bearing moisture from the soil and produce vegetable material of great use to people and other animals. In the process, they contribute to the oxygen supply, without which life as we know it would be impossible.

Forests are parts of larger natural systems and complex biological and chemical cycles that sustain all life on the earth. The loss of forests may contribute to the increasing concentration of carbon dioxide that has aroused worldwide scientific concern because it could cause undesirable changes in the earth's climate. Forests, especially those in the tropics, also play an important role in the world's heat budget. When large areas of forests are replaced by other land uses, such as farming, more heat radiates from the earth's surface, and this increase could shift world wind patterns and rainfall. Forests are part of the world's hydrologic cycle, or "water budget," and play a significant role in maintaining and timing water discharge so that flood peaks are reduced. Moreover, they retard snowmelt, thus reducing snowmelt floods and providing water further into the dry season, when it may be needed for water supply or irrigation.

Forests are a pollution-control device, working to maintain a healthy environment for living things. The crowns of trees in a forest act as a physical filter, partially cleansing air of the particulate matter it carries as it passes through the leaves. The leaves are then washed off by rains, and the particulates become part of the forest floor debris. Unless overloaded by high concentrations, forests can remove and safely store other air contaminants. For example, U.S. Forest

Service scientists at the Hubbard Brook Experimental Forest in the White Mountains of New Hampshire found that rain and snow falling on the forest contained lead concentrations above safe public health limits. However, water flowing from the forest contained scarcely detectable quantities of lead.

A complete list of forest products would be almost impossible to compile. Scientists are still discovering new drugs, resins, fibers, foods, and other plant materials in this rich treasure-trove of the forests. Products from the forest range from rubber in Malaysia to cork in Portugal, from pulpwood for paper to a host of organic chemical compounds that are of great importance as medicines. Varieties of fig, palm, pine, and other trees beautify homes and public places around the world. And, of course, for many people Christmas wouldn't be Christmas without a tree.

Amazingly rich in color and form, the canopy of the Amazon rain forest contains more different species of plants and animals than any similar area on earth.

This exquisite new orchid, first reported in 1965 by a botanist exploring the Sierra San Luis cloud forest in Venezuela, suggests that other species await discovery in remote areas.

The Christmas tree tradition began in Europe, and perhaps this love and reverence for trees helps explain why European forests have remained relatively stable for the past 200 years. Population has increased relatively slowly, and European farmers have had plenty of time to sort out the best farmland. Although the forest area is diminishing slowly because of population growth, there has been no drastic change in land use. The two World Wars that ravaged Europe caused serious overcutting and physical damage, but the cool temperate seasonal forests are resilient, and they have largely recovered. Intensive forest management is responsible in part for this recovery and stability. Europe is the cradle of scientific forestry, and such forestry practices as controlled harvesting and reproduction, fertilization, tree breeding, reforestation, and protection from pests have maintained forest productivity.

By and large, North American forests, whose trees were respected by native Americans for ages before they were aggressively removed by the early colonists, are emerging from a history of exploitation in relatively good shape. The assault on the forests of the Northeastern United States and southern Canada began in earnest only about 175 years ago. With a huge influx of immigrants from Europe, many of them experienced farmers, the rural economy boomed and lands were cleared at an amazing rate. Trees were felled with ax and crosscut saw, and the pioneers burned what they could not use, much like the slash-and-burn methods people use in the tropics even today. However, the settlers intended their clearings to be permanent and their agriculture stable, as in Europe, rather than shifting, as in the tropics. Pioneer businessmen also developed a sawmill industry that prospered as long as there were readily accessible, large, high-quality trees to cut down. A pulpwood and paper industry that used smaller trees followed. All of this activity had substantial impact on the forests. New York state was typical. By 1880, 74 per cent of its land had been cleared for farming, and much of the remaining forest had been logged over.

However, following the logging, the forest grew again, even where fire had followed the cutting. Also, land no longer competitive with

Disappearance of forests in Africa means that women in Lesotho spend more time searching for firewood than their ancestors did.

more productive farmland in the West or not suitable for the improving agricultural technology was returned to forest. This happened both naturally and by planting with *conifer* (evergreen) trees. From a low of 26 per cent forest in 1880, New York state almost doubled its forestland in 100 years and is now more than 50 per cent forested. Much the same story holds true in other Northeastern states and in southern Canada. Moreover, the world lost few if any species of plants or animals in this process because the eastern North American seasonal forest is so resilient. This is not the case with the land clearing and logging currently taking its toll in the forests of the developing countries of the tropics and subtropics.

The tropical rain forest extends in a belt on both sides of the equator that encompasses about 70 countries. However, more than 80 per cent of the tropical rain forest lies in nine countries — Bolivia, Brazil, Colombia, Peru, and Venezuela in South America; Indonesia and Malaysia in Southeast Asia; and Gabon and Zaire in Africa.

Lowland tropical rain forests boast the most diverse and least known collection of land plant and animal life on the earth. These masses of trees, flowers, vines, shrubs, mosses, ferns, and herbaceous plants harbor within their lush interiors new species that are continually being discovered. The interior of the forest is dark and cathedral-like, but spectacular colors — in the form of flowers and myriads of birds — flash in the treetops. Biologists estimate that the Malay

Rice is harvested from vast fields cleared of rain forest in Brazil's Amazon River Basin, *left,* in industrialist Daniel K. Ludwig's vast Jari River planting project. Many trees were destroyed in the West Coast rain forest on Mount Rainier in Washington, *below left,* when fire took its toll (foreground) and logging followed on upper slope.

Slash-and-burn is the typical method of clearing land for farming in developing countries. After removing all trees valuable for timber and pulpwood, growers replant with cash crops and fast-growing trees.

Peninsula alone may have 2,500 species of trees. While a rich and varied forest in the Eastern United States may have a maximum of 60 tree species per hectare (2.4 acres), and in Europe or Central Asia a maximum of 25, a rich tropical rain forest in Central or South America, in Africa or India, in Papua New Guinea or Indonesia, may have 220 species per hectare.

The forest does not teem with grazing or browsing mammals, as do many tropical grasslands and *savannas* (treeless plains). But the abundant animal life — insects, birds, monkeys, lemurs, and many others — lives in the treetops along with the flowers and birds. Although many different species may live in a given area, there usually are few individuals of any one species. Thus, both plant and animal species may be easily eliminated from the forest. Diversity but rarity is the rule in the rain forest, and many of the world's endangered species live there. In Colombia and Venezuela alone, destruction of forest habitat has put the jaguar, ocelot, three-toed sloth, tapir, quetzal, silky anteater, Andean spectacled bear, and cock of the rock in danger of extinction. Destroying these forests can result in degraded and unproductive land, an altered global heat budget, an increase in flash floods, and an irreplaceable loss of species. It can also strongly affect the traditional lives of the people who live in the rain forest. Understanding how they use forest plants and animals might contribute to their welfare — and to ours.

In some tropical and subtropical countries, forest-dwelling natives depend totally on the forest, its wildlife, and the fish in its streams for their livelihood. These are true hunter-gatherers. Also, in all developing countries, forest farmers practice slash-and-burn shifting agriculture within the forest. They depend on the forest to renew the productivity of their abandoned plots so that the sites may be cleared and farmed again.

Forest farmers have used this system for thousands of years in the tropics. They cleared small patches of forest, burned the wood, and planted crops for two to four years. When yields declined, the farmers abandoned the plot and let it lie fallow. Wild forest returned and renewed soil fertility and eliminated unwanted weeds. Meanwhile, they would start a new plot. As long as the fallow period lasted long enough for soil fertility to return naturally — as much as seven years in some places — the forest farmer could keep repeating the process in the same small area. Also, as long as only gently sloping land was tilled, the torrential tropical rains would not wash away the soil.

But various factors have now upset this stable system. Rapid population growth has forced the people to try to produce more food by reducing the fallow period, farming larger plots, and opening up new lands on steeper slopes. This new pattern is not only destroying the forest but is also reducing the productivity of large areas of the tropical developing world.

For example, world agricultural survey scientists estimate that forest farmers in Central America and such Asian countries as Indonesia, the Philippines, and Thailand are clearing a forest area as large as Great Britain for cultivation each year. Although the immediate results may be impressive, the April report from the National Research Council made it clear that many tropical soils do not remain productive for long without heavy fertilization. "Consequently," the report went on, "the likelihood of instability, both ecological and human, is increased dramatically as the forests are altered and eliminated."

A similar problem has surfaced in the Amazon region, Brazil's vast rain forest. There, great swaths of forest have been cleared for cattle grazing. Many ranches become unprofitable in less than 10 years because the new grasslands are not self-sustaining, and then ranchers simply clear more land. It is profitable for them to remove the forest because the beef they export to developed countries brings high prices, and the trees they clear off the land meet a growing demand for timber. If such use could be sustained, this would be a rational process for a developing country. However, the problem is to identify appropriate sites through adequate land-resource surveys — a task that has too often been ignored.

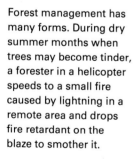

Forest management has many forms. During dry summer months when trees may become tinder, a forester in a helicopter speeds to a small fire caused by lightning in a remote area and drops fire retardant on the blaze to smother it.

Replanting goes on come rain or come shine in Jari River area cleared of rain forest, *left,* where plantation worker sets out Caribbean pine seedlings on a damp day. Better weather prevails under greenhouse glass in Oregon, *below,* as miniature Douglas firs stretch toward the sun.

Each forest denizen fits its niche.
Counterclockwise from right:
An oyster on a Florida mangrove;
a harlequin beetle in Trinidad;
lichens in California's Muir Woods;
Central American red-eyed tree
frogs; and an endangered species,
the three-toed sloth in Colombia,
typify the creatures that make
their homes in the world's forests.

Until recently, logging in the rain forest and seasonal forest of the tropics and subtropics was very selective. Only a few commercially valuable trees, such as mahogany, teak, and rosewood, were taken. However, the high-technology, bring-on-the-bulldozers logging begun in the developed world is now underway all over. Moreover, because any and all trees can now be used for wood-chip production, loggers are clear-cutting – removing all the trees in an area. This drastically alters wildlife habitat, species are more easily lost, and watershed-protection values are impaired. The logging roads and clear-cutting also encourage land-hungry squatters to move in and begin their shifting agriculture. Thus, a forest that is renewable, that could yield repeated harvests of trees and other products, is being altered irreparably.

Because the future of forests worldwide is so precarious, many local, national, and international agencies have become involved with planning to use them more rationally. One of the most ambitious of these programs is the UN Educational, Scientific, and Cultural Organization's (UNESCO) Man and the Biosphere (MAB) Program, which started in 1971. Through research, the MAB program

is trying to assemble the scientific information needed by land managers and government planners. Here are some of the projects underway in just one kind of forest — the tropical rain forest:

- Ecologists from Venezuela, West Germany, and the United States in 1975 began to study how a tropical lowland forest ecosystem works in the part of the Amazon region that lies in Venezuela. They have been conducting research at San Carlos de Rio Negro on the soils, climate, forest structure and productivity, zoology, and nutrient cycling and on how the forest system responds to natural and human disturbance.
- In Indonesia, University of Mulawarman faculty members and students are looking into the relationship of people and forests in East Kalimantan (Borneo). They are studying such things as the environmental effects of different kinds of land use and how timber camps affect the economics of established villages.
- In the Tai Forest of Africa's Ivory Coast, 40 scientists from the host country, France, Italy, and Switzerland are comparing the structure and function of natural forest ecosystems with areas that are being managed for timber production or planted to produce cocoa and coffee.

Other major MAB research projects are underway in the Gogol Valley of Papua New Guinea; Puerto Galera, Philippines; Sakaerat, Thailand; Jalapa, Mexico; and many other sites. All of them are aimed at learning how best to use the world's tropical rain forests for long-term human well-being.

While human beings throughout history have been cutters of trees, they have also been planters of trees. However, for most of our history such activity has usually gone no further than setting out individual trees or small groups of trees to provide shade, protect from wind, or enhance beauty. Reforestation, the planting of large plots of open land with both native and imported species of trees, is a fairly recent development. Beginning in Europe about 200 years ago, it slowly spread throughout the industrialized world as an activity designed to restore the productivity of open and somewhat degraded lands, usually land that was released from agriculture. It has been a major land-use activity in the United States since the 1930s.

In the past 10 years, the major focus of reforestation activity has shifted to rehabilitation of the once-forested lands of the developing countries. It was prompted by a need to restore denuded, steep, upper watershed slopes that were ill-advisedly cleared and by the desire to put lands that had been degraded by the clearing-and-burning process back into some kind of production.

The dwindling firewood supply has given new impetus to such programs. Many plantations are being established as energy sources in developing countries. They are largely devoted to growing foreign, fast-maturing trees. The major testing ground for this practice has been New Zealand. Very large areas of a single foreign species have also been successfully established in Australia and South Africa over the past 30 years. One of the most useful trees in these plantings has been the Monterey pine, from coastal California.

Forest scientists have stepped up their search for new fast-growing species. They have undertaken artificial tree breeding to produce hybrids that grow rapidly and have other desirable properties. The search is also on for multipurpose trees, such as *Leucaena*. This tree grows very fast, and also helps improve the soil, because of its nitrogen-fixing ability — that is, its roots contain bacteria that turn atmospheric nitrogen into a chemical form that fertilizes the soil. Its leaves are good cattle fodder, and its wood is useful as fuel and pulp. This tree is being widely planted in the Philippines, where it is known as *ipil-ipil*.

The governments of China and South Korea have undertaken large-scale reforestation programs. Similar large-scale efforts are also needed in the tropics, and they might be used in Nepal and India to rehabilitate the deteriorated watersheds and in North Africa to restore unproductive lands.

One fascinating, if somewhat controversial, private large-scale reforestation program is being conducted by American industrialist Daniel K. Ludwig in an area as large as Connecticut along the Jari River in Brazil's Amazon Basin. Instead of planting open land, Ludwig is felling rain forests and planting fast-growing foreign trees. The practice of felling native forests and replanting them with foreign trees is a subject of hot debate in some countries. Timber producers and environmentalists are at loggerheads in Australia and New Zealand, and the governments are hammering out new policies. Large-scale plantings, particularly of a single introduced species, always run ecological risks of being wiped out by major pest invasions. Many foresters prefer using native species and mixtures in order to avoid that danger, even though there may be less short-run potential payoff in fast growth.

Whether the impetus comes from government or private individuals, whether native trees are saved or foreign plants are introduced, whether people are prompted by concern for their fellow beings or by the thought of one day waking up in a wasteland, it is clear that we must handle our forests more rationally — more conservatively. We have come part of the way, but we are not yet out of the woods.

For further reading:

Eckholm, Eric. *Losing Ground: Environmental Stress and World Food Prospects.* Norton, 1976.

Emmel, Thomas and Hofmann, Lieselotte (editors). *Global Perspectives on Ecology.* Mayfield Publishing Company, 1977.

Hamilton, Lawrence S. *Man and the Humid Tropics. Programme on Man and the Biosphere.* (Booklet and slide/tape program) UNESCO, 1980.

UNESCO. *Tropical Forest Ecosystems: a state of knowledge report prepared by UNESCO/UNEP/FAO.* Natural Resources Research No. 14, 1978.

What Should I Be When I Grow Up?

By Dean L. Hummel

How parents and children can get a head start in preparing for one of life's most important and difficult decisions — choosing a career

"**I** wish I could have had more to say about my career." "If I had known then what I know today, I wouldn't be in this dead-end job." "With a little reliable help and accurate information, I could have prepared for and entered a career that I really would be happy in." "The decision I made several years ago closed out later chances to make other decisions about my career." "I wish I knew how to help my child avoid the mistakes I made."

How many times have you heard such remarks? In more than 25 years as a career counselor, I have heard them from hundreds of people who look back on their lives with regret.

Many of these unhappy people could have avoided such disappointment if they had only known how to plan effectively and make decisions based on accurate information about themselves and their career opportunities. However, there is now ample evidence that most of today's parents are determined to help their children avoid the mistakes they themselves might have made. Helping their children plan and make decisions about a career was listed as a high-priority concern among parents in the 12th annual Gallup Poll on education, conducted in 1980.

I believe that the search for identity is a major struggle in each of our lives. In the United States, as elsewhere, personal identity is shaped by the kind of work we do, our life style, and our leisure activities. We are largely responsible for establishing our own identity. The Great American Dream is founded upon the belief in equal opportunity and freedom of choice. For most of us, the dream is possible; the opportunities exist, and we can learn how to make an intelligent choice in deciding on a career. However, we may need a little help in finding that information and using it properly.

From the time a child learns to talk, parents and others ask, "What are you going to be when you grow up?" In fact, many parents develop dreams and plans for their children. But, beyond dreams and plans, many parents become frustrated when they try to help their children plan careers. Some of them feel that they simply do not understand their children well enough to assess their interests and abilities realistically. Many parents are unaware of the wealth of information and resources that is available, facts that can be so helpful in career development. Nevertheless, studies show that children turn first to their parents for advice when they begin to think about a career. They are wise to do so. I believe parents provide the greatest amount of help in planning for their children's careers — when they know how to help.

To provide the proper guidance for their children, parents must learn how to use career-information resources. They must work as partners with counselors and teachers to help their children to develop their potential.

The author:
Dean L. Hummel is professor of counselor education at Virginia Polytechnic Institute and State University and co-author of *How to Help Your Child Plan a Career.*

The Schells were typical of the many families I have counseled. They wanted to establish this type of partnership. Frank Schell is an ophthalmologist who diagnoses and treats eye diseases in a large Eastern city. His wife, Christine, is a graphic artist with an advertising agency. Their son, Mark, is a junior high school student. I based my session with the Schells — one Thursday afternoon in October — around questions designed to help parents develop a better career-planning partnership with their children.

I began by asking Mark if he had shared his dreams about what he wanted to become with his parents. Mark replied that he had told his parents that he wanted to be a building contractor. The parents then described how Mark's interest had evolved from his preschool days, when he had spent hours playing with blocks, to his recent construction of a derby-winning soapbox racer. It was obvious that the Schells were well aware of their son's developing career preference.

I asked the Schells if they accepted Mark's weaknesses as well as his strengths. Frank Schell admitted that he had been upset that Mark had a low attention span in school and preferred working with his hands to studying academic subjects. He conceded that Mark would probably show a greater interest in high school work when he could study such subjects as mechanical drawing and drafting.

My next question took the Schells by surprise. I asked Mark if he had ever played games in which he acted out his job fantasies. He said that when the Schell house was renovated five years ago, he had played with the tools that the carpenters left in the house overnight. I asked his parents if they had joined in these fantasies — perhaps as workers under "foreman Mark's" supervision. Both admitted that they had been too preoccupied with the remodeling project and their own careers to pay much attention to Mark's games. This was unfortunate. Parents can learn much about their children's potential career interests by participating in such games.

"Do you relate to jobs and things Mark likes to do," I asked the elder Schells, "even if you have no experience in those fields?" Both parents acknowledged that they had little interest in the building trades. I suggested that Christine Schell, as a designer, might enjoy looking at books and magazines on architecture with Mark. Frank Schell then suggested that he could take Mark on a tour of a new wing being built at the hospital at which he practiced.

Then I asked all the Schells if Mark had access to books, magazines, and games that could give him an idea of the basic concerns, values, and skills associated with the building trades. Mark volunteered that he had assembled several cars from model kits and had always spent most of his allowance on small tools and materials for projects like the soapbox racer and a tree house he had built the previous summer. I suggested that he might want to supplement these practical activities by reading some of the trade magazines, such as *Professional Builder,* that would give him a better feel for responsibilities involved in the business end of the construction industry.

The Schells scored high on this question: "Do you serve as a career model and introduce your child to other vocations outside your field of work?" Both parents had taken Mark to work with them several times. They had also taken pains to explain exactly what their friends and neighbors did for a living. Recently, Christine had taken Mark to a community Careers Fair at a nearby junior college.

The Schells had already answered my next question, "Has Mark tried out work experiences, even though you, Frank and Christine, are not necessarily interested in construction?" From his answers to my previous questions, I knew Mark had pursued his interest through building car models, a tree house, and a soapbox racer. The Schells

also said they wanted to help Mark find a summer job in construction work when he was 16.

The Schells had also partially answered my next question: "Do you find and use job information in trying to learn more about specific occupations?" They had obviously taken advantage of firsthand sources such as friends, neighbors, and institutional programs like the college Careers Fair. However, they had not yet used the wealth of materials available from the public library, the federal government, and building-trades associations.

The Schells answered my question – "Do you support the school's efforts in career education?" – affirmatively. Both Frank and Christine had discussed their professions at junior high school programs. In addition, Frank had arranged for Mark's class to tour the hospital and observe people working there in a variety of jobs. The students saw people engaged in more than 20 occupations, ranging from maintenance work to radiation therapy.

Children in primary grades are already starting to form an idea of what they want to be when they grow up. They may express their fantasies through self-portraits or through such games as "store," and develop a sense of responsibility by doing chores. Parents and teachers can encourage children to explore special interests by providing related books, toys, and trips and, most importantly, by offering a helping hand.

Frank and Christine Schell also did very well on the last question — one I consider very important. "Do you permit your child to explore interests in nontraditional occupations regardless of sex, or social and economic background?" When Christine made the appointment for our counseling session, she had indicated that both she and Frank were somewhat dismayed that Mark had shown little interest in going to college and wanted to enter a blue-collar trade. However, they had decided that if Mark was truly interested in the building trades they would do all they could to help him find his place in that field.

I had failed that question myself several years ago when I tried to dissuade my daughter Gretchen from abandoning her graduate studies in my field, counseling psychology, and entering law school. I pointed out to her that there were more than 400,000 attorneys in this overcrowded field. She countered that fewer than 7 per cent of them were women. Last spring, Gretchen graduated from law school and is now working in the Ohio state attorney general's office.

CAR WASH $1.00

The junior high school student may begin to show a decided aptitude for a specific subject, such as art. Parents and teachers can help preteens to develop their interests by assisting with extracurricular activities — perhaps scout work, nature walks, museum visits, or music lessons. Some activities, such as running a car wash as a fund-raising project, can help students learn to handle job responsibilities.

In writing *How to Help Your Child Plan a Career* in 1979, my co-author, Carl McDaniels, and I worked out a practical approach to career decision-making for young people. We use the acronym *SWING* for this decision-making process. The process has five major steps: *s*tudy self; *w*in awareness; *i*dentify information; *n*egotiate plans; and *g*ain experiences.

How other people respond to us determines how we deal with the world, according to educational psychologist William W. Purkey of the University of North Carolina at Greensboro. Children who feel good about themselves are more likely to study themselves—to explore all aspects of their personalities without worrying about what they might discover. Parents, of course, are the most influential "other people" in a child's life. To a large extent, the relationship between the child and the parents determines the child's degree of self-confidence. I have found that children who are secure tend to have parents who are sensitive to their needs and have established a bond of trust. These children can depend on their parents to respond to their dreams and hopes positively, yet objectively.

I emphasize to the families I counsel that young people must become aware of their strengths and weaknesses, as well as their interests, before they can make sound career decisions. Parents can help children assess their interests, abilities, aptitudes, and personality traits by showing interest in the evaluations and testing, and by helping them to interpret their test results realistically. For example, everyone is involved in one way or another with job activities that relate either to people, data, or things. A child who enjoys being with other children, playing with dolls, or watching television, is likely to be "people-oriented." The data-oriented child might be more of a loner who prefers reading or visiting museums. A child is "things-oriented" if he or she plays with gadgets and takes things apart but does not care very much about being with other children.

Of course, a child's interests may span more than one of these three areas. A child who is both people- and data-oriented might be interested in becoming a teacher or an investment counselor; one who is data- and things-oriented may choose a career as a technical writer.

Parents can use such cues to provide the child with the appropriate playthings. For example, if I saw that my child was interested in building things, I might bring home some cardboard boxes that he or she could play with. Parents need to reinforce the youngster's feelings of self-worth and help the child test potential skills. By translating youthful interests into career areas, parents can help their children explore and learn about careers that interest them.

How do children and parents interested in career development begin to identify and obtain information? Using the people-data-things concept to categorize interests can be especially helpful, because more than 20,000 jobs in the United States are classified in this way in the *Dictionary of Occupational Titles*. Another valuable

By planning their courses wisely, high school students can learn skills like drafting that can be useful later in life. Counselors can help students evaluate their interests and abilities and can offer them a wide range of career information — from college catalogs to military recruitment pamphlets. Part-time work and activities such as sports and drama can accustom them to some of the demands of a job.

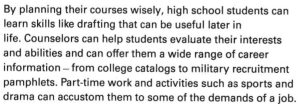

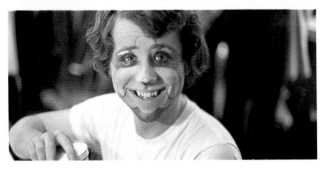

source of occupational information is the *Occupational Outlook Handbook*. Both books are found in most libraries and school counselors' offices. Of course, there are many other career-information resources: printed materials, people at work, and courses in career education. (See the list of suggested reading at the end of this article for a broad sampling of these resources.)

How important and reliable are tests in studying self, becoming aware, and identifying appropriate information? During the elementary grades, standardized achievement tests and teacher's grades are good, though not foolproof, indicators of potential skills, especially the basics needed to succeed in many careers. Aptitude tests can also provide important data because they are designed to predict how a person compares with others interested in a given field. Interest tests can pinpoint an individual's likes and dislikes, but they do not indicate what a person is or will be good at. Most standardized tests are scientifically developed, but an individual's test results should be interpreted very carefully.

Darryl Laramore, in his book *Careers: A Guide for Parents and Counselors*, points out that a carefully devised plan is essential for those who expect to control their own career development and life growth. Parents can support and aid their child by helping to weigh all the factors related to the child's self-concept and potential. Once the child's career plans have been made, they can be evaluated against actual experiences as the child puts the plan into action. Although it may be difficult, parents should avoid pressuring their child to think only of career activities favored by the parents. They should, however, help the child to weigh the pros and cons when a career direction seems impractical. In such cases, parents can help the child pursue an interest in a closely related occupation in the field. For example, the desire to be a professional musician might lead to a career in composing, lyric writing, teaching, or managing musicians.

We know that experience is often the best teacher. And such experience can begin at home with work around the house, in prevocational school courses, or in part-time or summer jobs. All too often, children are left to themselves to find such activities without parental interest or help. These experiences are too important to be left to chance. Parents and children should discuss how certain jobs can relate to their career plans, provide more career information, or help youngsters decide if they are fitted for such careers.

In addition to the basic questions I ask each family I counsel, I urge children to get career-related experience in school — take elective and prevocational courses, join clubs and extracurricular activities, try athletics, and go to summer school and camps. Each of these activities provides children with a different type of experience. I feel that the broader their experiences and the more they are able to try out their abilities, the better prepared children will be to decide what they want to do for a living.

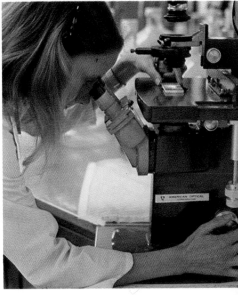

College affords a wealth of career experiences and opportunities. Many students gain professional experience through extra work — making architectural models, for example. If they have chosen such specialized fields of study as biochemistry, they may want to enter graduate school. Activities like varsity sports can be very demanding, but may also lead to a career. As they enter the job market, students must be able to describe their abilities and goals in résumés and interviews. College graduates who have used all of the resources at their disposal will be ready for one of life's most important decisions — choosing a career.

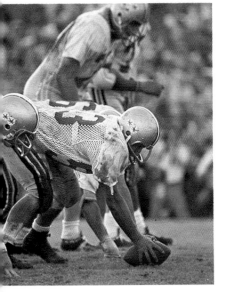

Part-time jobs are especially valuable because they give children an idea of the responsibilities involved in working regularly. If they are fortunate enough to find work in a field that they plan to enter, they can gain a better feeling for that particular type of work, perhaps if only to decide that it is not for them. For example, I once knew a high school newspaper editor who felt that she wanted to work as a reporter on a large metropolitan daily newspaper. After a summer as a copy clerk on such a paper, she concluded she did not want to live under the constant pressure of daily deadlines. She changed her college course of study from journalism to English literature and is now a professor of creative writing at a small Eastern college.

Sometimes, even the most carefully planned careers do not work out. The parents may have been sensitive and responsive to their children's needs — providing materials and activities to nurture their developing interests. The children may have chosen their school courses carefully, participated in extracurricular activities, and held part-time jobs. They may have done well in high school and graduated from college, ready to begin their chosen careers, only to find that these particular careers — the ones they had planned for and worked toward for so many years — are not the answer. They may find that their fields have become crowded; that salary levels are lower than they had expected; or that the work itself is simply not satisfying.

Such cases are all too common. Every year in the United States, some 30 million people between the ages of 25 and 60 consider changing their careers. That is why I feel that it is essential for a person to remain flexible — to realize that, whatever his or her age or circumstance — there are still a number of career options open. Changing careers may involve retracing some of the SWING steps to re-evaluate one's interests and abilities, to acquire more education or experience, or to re-evaluate the job market.

In many instances, persons changing careers can draw upon their own experiences. They may turn their hobbies into new careers, as did the magazine editor who used his Oriental rug collection as the basis of a successful carpet business. They may develop skills or interests in one line of work that can lead them into more satisfying professions. For example, a lawyer who represented an architectural firm became so intrigued with building problems that she abandoned her thriving legal practice to return to school in pursuit of a graduate degree in architecture.

Career decision-making, whether it involves choosing or changing one's job, is an important process. Most people spend more than 100,000 hours — or one-sixth of their lives — at work. As Charles F. Kettering, the inventor and engineer, once said, "The future is all we are interested in, because we are going to spend the rest of our lives there." Obviously, anything that takes up so much of our lives should be carefully planned — to ensure a career directed by choice rather than chance.

Career-Search Resources

General Career Planning

Barth, George F. *Your Attitudes: You Do Best What You Are Fitted To Do*. Lathrop, 1974.

Bolles, Richard N. *The Three Boxes of Life*. Ten Speed Press, 1978.

Bolles, Richard N. *What Color is Your Parachute?* Ten Speed Press, 1978.

Buskirk, Richard. *Your Career: How to Plan It, Manage It, Change It*. New American Library, 1976.

Chapman, Elwood N. *Career Search: A Personal Pursuit*. Science Research Associates, 1976.

Dictionary of Occupational Titles. United States Department of Labor, 1977.

Hopke, W. E. *The Encyclopedia of Careers and Vocational Guidance*. Doubleday & Co., 1978.

Hummel, Dean L. and McDaniels, Carl. *How to Help Your Child Plan a Career*. Acropolis Books Ltd., 1979.

Karlin, Muriel S. *Solving Your Career Mystery*. Richards Rosen Press, 1975.

Keefe, John and Stein, Stanley J. *The Joy of Work*. Richards Rosen Press, 1974.

Laramore, Darryl. *Careers: A Guide for Parents and Counselors*. Brigham Young Press, 1978.

Lembeck, Ruth. *1001 Job Ideas for Today's Woman*. Prentice-Hall, 1976.

Lobb, Charlotte. *Exploring Careers Through Part-Time and Summer Employment*. Richards Rosen Press, 1977.

Lobb, Charlotte. *Exploring Careers Through Volunteerism*. Richards Rosen Press, 1976.

Occupational Outlook Handbook. United States Department of Labor, 1980.

Raskin, A. H. "The Job in Your Future," *The 1978 World Book Year Book*. World Book – Childcraft International, Inc., 1978.

Splaver, Sarah. *Nontraditional Careers for Women*. Julian Messner, 1973.

Vocational School and College Guides

Accredited Institutions of Post-Secondary Education 1980-81. American Council on Education, 1980.

Cass, James and Birnbaum, Max. *Comparative Guide to Two-Year Colleges and Career Programs*. Harper & Row, 1976.

The College Blue Book. Macmillan, 1977.

Education Directory, Colleges and Universities 1979-1980. National Center for Education Statistics, 1980.

Lovejoy, Clarence E. *Lovejoy's Career and Vocational School Guide*. Simon and Schuster, 1978.

Lovejoy, Clarence E. *Lovejoy's College Guide*. Simon and Schuster, 1976.

The National Guidance Handbook: A Guide to Vocational Educational Programs. Science Research Associates, 1975.

Searching for Jobs, Writing Résumés, and Interviewing

Bolles, Richard N. *Tea Leaves: A New Look at Résumés*. Ten Speed Press, 1976.

Bostwick, Burdette E. *Résumé Writing*. Capitol Publications, Inc., 1976.

Garrison, Clifford et al. *Finding a Job You Feel Good About*. Argus Communications, 1977.

Gelinas, Robert P. and Gelinas, Paul J. *How Teenagers Can Get Good Jobs*. Richards Rosen Press, 1971.

Haldane, Bernard, et al. *Job Power Now!* Acropolis Books, 1977.

Keefe, John. *Coping with the Interview*. Richards Rosen Press, 1979.

How to Complete Job Application Forms. American Personnel and Guidance Association, 1975.

McDaniels, Carl. *Finding Your First Job*. Time Share, 1975.

Sweet, D. H. *The Job Hunters' Manual*. Addison-Wesley, 1975.

What Is Your Pet Trying To Tell You?

By Michael W. Fox

**By learning to interpret your cat's or dog's
rich vocabulary of body-language signals, you
can better understand its wants and needs**

When I come home from work in the evening, I sometimes like to relax by playing my flute while my dog, Benji, and wolf, Tiny, enjoy a good howl. Neighbors who might glimpse me harmonizing with my companions sometimes smile patronizingly. Few know that, by joining in this canine duet, I am actually communicating with my animals and deepening my friendship with them. For, although our dogs and cats share our homes and affections, most of us know very little about communicating with them.

As a veterinarian trained in animal psychology, I have studied cats and dogs for almost 20 years, trying to learn how they communicate, to better understand their wants and needs. I am convinced that we could respond to their needs more readily and could control them more successfully if, by learning to recognize and interpret their expressions and postures, we could learn how to communicate with them more effectively. In short, we could develop deeper, more satisfying relationships with them.

When I graduated from the Royal Veterinary College in London in 1962, I set out to study brain disorders in dogs. However, I soon realized that my schooling had omitted a study of how animals develop and behave. Before I could determine if a dog's behavior stemmed from some abnormality in the nervous system, I had to know how a dog's brain and behavior develops normally. Therefore, I jumped at a chance to join the staff at Jackson Laboratory in Bar Harbor, Me., and conduct research directed at determining how dogs develop reflexes. Doing this research, I was struck with the similarities between canines and humans — not only in body signals, but also in expressions of emotion.

I broadened my research to include cats when I moved to the Galesburg (Ill.) State Research Hospital in 1964. I discovered that, though cats react and communicate differently from dogs, they too have a rich and varied vocabulary of body signals and facial expressions to call into play.

To understand the psychology and behavior of animals, we need to know how they perceive the world around them. Both dogs and cats have specialized sensory organs. Their whiskers are highly sensitive touch organs attached to nerves in the skin that transmit signals to the brain. The whiskers help them negotiate their way through narrow spaces, protect their eyes, and tell them the direction that the wind is blowing.

Neither cats nor dogs see as well as human beings. Both animals are thought to be color-blind, though cats are somewhat sensitive to red and green. Their eyes are more acutely sensitive to movement than to brightness or shape. Perhaps to compensate for poor color sensitivity, both animals have exquisitely sensitive hearing that can pick up high-frequency sounds inaudible to humans.

Both cats and dogs have a keen sense of smell aided by a second scent organ that is located behind their upper front teeth. This organ is connected to the parts of the brain that regulate sexual, aggressive, and territorial behavior — the animal's instinctive need to protect its turf. It may be responsible for the profound effect that certain odors, such as catnip or musk, can have on our pets' behavior.

Our pets respond to the information they take in through their senses with a wide assortment of body-language signals called *displays*. I can tell a lot about the moods of my pets just by looking at them. When my dog, Benji, or my cats, Mocha and Sam, stand upright and alert or stretch out long and low, they are feeling assertive, aggressive, confident, or playful. When they crouch or contract their bodies, they are literally shrinking in fear or submission. Of course some pets, like some people, tend to adopt certain postures as part of their personalities. Benji is habitually confident and playful, while Mike, a neighbor's dog, is naturally submissive. Mike is a constant embarrassment to his owners, who fear that other people might interpret Mike's cowering as a sign of mistreatment.

The author:
Michael W. Fox, director of the Institute for the Study of Animal Problems in Washington, D.C., enjoys a quiet moment with his dog, Benji.

I have seen Benji move from his characteristically alert posture, with tail and ears erect, through a variety of positions as his emotional reactions change. When another dog moves into Benji's territory, he may respond with a stiff wag of the tail, a direct stare, and an aggressive snarl. If he is afraid of the dog, however, Benji shifts his body weight backward and lowers his tail in what we have come to recognize as a fearful or defensive type of aggression. If Benji feels extremely threatened, he might even curl up with his ears flattened against his head and remain still or cowed in a display of complete submission. I have seen other dogs roll over and urinate submissively, very much like young puppies. Dogs use this same vocabulary of displays to communicate aggressive or submissive feelings to people. Dog owners who do not understand that such urination is a sign of deference frequently make the mistake of disciplining their dogs for it.

The cats, Mocha and Sam, have a more limited, but no less effective, vocabulary of body signals than Benji has. Their displays also communicate mood shifts as they vary the position of their heads and the angle of their bodies. Sam, a male Abyssinian, usually takes the dominant role, standing upright with his head held low, as though ready to attack, when challenging Mocha, our female Burmese. Mocha may then assume a defensive crouch. Cats do not roll over onto one side to display submission as dogs do. Instead, they may arch their backs with their fur standing on end. This is one way of increasing their apparent size — a kind of illusory trick. This "Halloween cat" posture is not meant as a threat, as some people assume, but is actually a defensive display that indicates intense fear.

Both cats and dogs use definite, though different, signals to announce that they want to play. A cat rolls or flops over on one side and may squirm. A dog bows, wags its tail, and may raise a front paw in a friendly gesture.

The play bow may stem from the dog's habit of yawning and stretching to communicate his relaxed behavior to another dog or a person. It establishes a relaxed mood, signaling that what comes next, such as a seemingly aggressive snap or lunge, is all in fun. The play bow is one type of body language that people can use to communicate with their dog. I encourage children to mimic the dog's play bow to show that they want to play.

A cat's tail is a good barometer of its intentions. An excited or aggressively aroused cat will whip its entire tail back and forth. When I talk to Sam, he holds up his end of the conversation by occasionally flicking the tip of his tail. Mother cats move their tails back and forth to invite their kittens to play. A kitten raises its tail perpendicularly to beg for attention; older cats may do so to beg for food. When your cat holds its tail aloft while crisscrossing in front of you, it is trying to say, "Follow me" — usually to the kitchen, or more precisely, to the refrigerator. Unfortunately, many cats have lost their tails in refrigerator doors as a consequence.

Pets use a variety of expansive expressions and postures to communicate friendly intentions. A cat may roll over and gaze invitingly, asking you to play. A dog may perk its ears and break into a toothy grin to express pleasure.

In contrast to their expansive friendly postures, cats and dogs contract
in fear or aggression. The cat arches its back defensively, its
fur standing on end. The dog pulls its lip back in a warning snarl.

A cat's expression changes with its mood. Its eyes, half-closed in relaxed contentment, *above left,* widen quickly as the cat is alerted to potential danger, *center,* and remain open as the cat responds with a defensive hiss, *right.*

A cat will also raise its tail in a vertical position when it is being petted. This may have evolved from the kitten's natural response as its mother cleans its hind end. Adult cats may also respond to petting with other perfectly natural regressions to kittenish behavior, such as drooling, pushing with the head as though trying to nurse, and kneading with the front paws.

I have noticed that Sam sometimes asserts dominance by mounting Mocha and grasping the scruff of her neck. This is often misinterpreted as sexual behavior, but it is usually just a highly effective wrestling tactic. Seizing a cat by the scruff of the neck immobilizes the animal and as such is a very effective way of gaining control over a cat that may be difficult to handle.

When two cats confront each other, eye contact also plays a very important role. The dominant cat will stare at the subordinate one. When the dominant cat breaks eye contact, the subordinate cat is then allowed to move away. The subordinate cat usually moves slowly, because if it were to run, the dominant cat might attack it.

During social encounters, cats touch noses frequently, possibly checking each other's odors. A familiar odor usually ensures acceptance. However, even cats who know each other well may fight if one of them smells of a strange cat, or returns from the veterinary hospital smelling quite different.

If you have ever watched a meeting between two suspicious cats, you may have witnessed the full array of facial expressions that indicate a cat's emotions and intentions. The dominant cat keeps a cool front, showing little or no expression when facing up to its rival. Its face is a model of passive indifference with upright ears, straight whiskers, and eyes directed fearlessly ahead. It may even close its eyes. The fearful cat will flatten its ears and hiss. Its eyes are open wide and the pupils are clearly enlarged. If the cat is torn between flight and attack, it will twist its ears sideways and stare almost cross-eyed with moderately enlarged pupils. In another reaction, a cat may gape with its eyes half-closed, as if drugged, when it has sniffed some strange odor or the urine of another cat.

The facial expressions of dogs are even richer and more varied than those of cats. In fact, a dog can express more than one emotion at one

The smile it shares with its human companion is only one of the dog's many and varied facial expressions.

time, like a human. For example, it may combine an aggressive snarl or sneer with a submissive grin to indicate both aggression and fear. Dogs also have an open-mouthed "play-face" expression, often accompanied by panting — the canine equivalent of laughter. I sometimes get down on all fours and pant at Benji. This is one way of talking "dog" and saying to him, "Let's play." Usually Benji will reciprocate by mimicking my grin. While some people may misinterpret this type of toothy display as an aggressive signal, the dog is doing nothing more than trying to imitate the friendly smile of its human companions.

Friendly face-licking behavior originates when hungry pups solicit food that the mother would normally regurgitate for them. The theory is that such food-soliciting behavior carries over into maturity as face licking. Cats do not "face-kiss" like dogs do, probably because mother cats do not regurgitate food.

Interaction between two dogs may begin with the get-acquainted ritual of circling and sniffing, *left.* If one dog is clearly dominant, the other may roll over in submission, *below left;* if not, they may fight for supremacy, *below.* In an established canine friendship, a grin is an invitation to play, *bottom.*

Cats rely heavily on body language to define relationships. Affectionate grooming is often a sign of deep friendship, *top,* while a threatening hiss warns a stranger to come no closer, *above.* Even friends fight for dominance at times, however, *right.*

I have also been fascinated by the way animals "square off" when they meet. As you may have noticed, dogs and cats approach each other from the side and frequently circle each other before one animal stands still and allows the other to sniff it. Strange animals generally avoid a frontal or face-to-face approach. Dogs face each other directly only when they know each other, regardless of whether they are friends or rivals. Humans should also observe this respectful canine gesture by approaching a strange dog from the side and avoiding direct eye contact. I have seen judges at dog shows bitten because they approached a strange dog from the front.

A direct stare between two dogs or cats — or any animal and a human being — can be a challenge and can intimidate an animal into behaving submissively and passively. But if you know the animal or are confident about handling it, a direct stare followed by a verbal command can be a very effective form of control. When Sam leaps up to the table to join the family dinner, I need only look him in the eye and say, "No!" and he is back on the floor in an instant. But it is wise to avoid challenging an animal you do not know with a direct stare because it could respond in one of two ways — by attacking or by becoming very fearful of you.

While the dominant animal usually responds to a direct stare by staring back, it may also avoid eye contact, as a sign of indifference. In this case, the animal behaves like a person who responds to a friendly "hello" by avoiding eye contact and giving you the cold shoulder. Humans can also use the cold shoulder technique on an unfriendly dog to avert an attack, by turning away and pretending that the dog is not there. The dog might well interpret your avoiding eye contact as a sign of confidence and psychological superiority. However, backing away from the dog while avoiding eye contact indicates to the dog that the person is afraid.

Sometimes when two cats are facing up to each other, there is some hesitation while they determine which is dominant. One of the cats

A drowsy pup snuggles against its master, symbolizing the strong bonds that can form between pets and their human companions.

The dog's gentle expression and the cat's relaxed pose indicate that their wrestling match is a friendly one.

may pause in the midst of an aggressive confrontation to lick a paw, sniff the ground, or groom itself. Any such inappropriate behavior in a tense situation is called *displacement behavior*. It is apparently the cat's attempt to relax its rival or to gain time while it assesses the situation more completely.

Many people say that you can tell when a storm is coming because your cat will engage in bouts of rather intense displacement grooming. Such behavior could mean that the cat is feeling tense and anxious because of the change in barometric pressure or in the electric charge of the air prior to a storm. Animals are more sensitive to these changes than humans are. Cats also often groom themselves briefly after a reprimand — such as being told to get off the table — perhaps as a sign of embarrassment. Some dogs also scratch or lick themselves when frustrated or embarrassed.

The vocal repertoire of dogs, like their facial expressions, resembles our own. They growl in anger, whine for attention, howl (or cry) when they are lonely or distressed, and yelp or scream when they are hurt or afraid. Barking serves many purposes. A barking dog may be seeking attention, or threatening, or warning of an intruder, or it may simply be excited. And dogs can combine certain sounds, producing a yelp-bark of excitement or a growl-bark of threat and warning. Many dogs howl when they hear an ambulance or police siren or a musical

Cats and dogs never outgrow the need to play. It may be a solitary swipe at a spider plant, *right,* or it may be a romp on the beach, *below,* with the dog's mistress mimicking its play bow to show that she, too, wants to play.

Scent-marking is the pet's way of leaving its calling card. A cat labels a chair with oils from glands in its head, *above left.* By sniffing a fire hydrant, *above,* a dog can identify previous canine visitors.

instrument. This is, I believe, an instinctive response, much like one wolf calling to another or a wolf pack engaging in a group howl. Try howling with your dog or playing a musical instrument to get him to howl – you might both enjoy it. But do respect your neighbors' rights and avoid holding your duets in the backyard – barking dogs are one of the most common public nuisances in urban areas today.

Cats also use a rich variety of vocal sounds to communicate their moods, intentions, and desires – the hiss and growl of fear and anger; the meow for attention; the purr for contact and grooming or petting; the "chirp" call, or chattering when eying birds; the loud, deep meow call when in heat; and the howling caterwauling when cats congregate outdoors at night. These sounds vary with age and sex and also with breed and individual temperament. Siamese are quite "talkative," while other cats rarely make noise. Some cats have a mouselike squeak instead of the customary meow. Why cats purr is still a mystery, but I believe it may be a way of maintaining friendly contact and even "grooming" a companion from a distance.

In addition to direct communication with body-language displays, facial expressions, and vocal sounds, cats and dogs make scent-markings to leave messages. Cats mark furniture and their companions – people and other cats alike – to give them a familiar odor. For example, they brush their tails, which have scent glands under the skin, across pieces of furniture. They have additional scent glands on the temples in front of the ears, under the chin, and on each side of the lips. Cats regard those who smell the same as friends, so it is logical for cats to engage in a good deal of reciprocal marking.

Cats have another – and less pleasant – way of scent-marking. Sometimes they spray objects with their urine. More males than

Dogs need more attention than cats and must go outdoors for exercise in all kinds of weather, so cats may soon become the favored pet of urban apartment dwellers.

females use this form of marking, but females and castrated males may spray when they believe they must defend their territory. The presence of a rival cat spraying outdoors or a change in the social relationship within the cat's home – the arrival of a new cat or a new person, or the prolonged absence of its owner, for instance – can make it feel insecure and therefore more likely to mark or spray within the house.

For dogs, however, marking trees and fire hydrants with their urine is an important social communication ritual. I believe that most dogs mark trees and other vertical objects to leave a calling card rather than to stake out their territory. We should give a dog on the leash plenty of time to sniff these scent posts because they tell the animal exactly which other dogs have been there. To a dog, sniffing a scent post is as important as reading a newspaper is to a human being. Dogs who live together, especially males and females, will carefully mark over spots where their companions have marked. Unfortunately, this social ritual can have a significant environmental impact in cities, where the dog population is very dense, and it may contribute to the death of many young trees. It is also a serious health hazard because it spreads communicable canine diseases, particularly canine hepatitis and leptospirosis, a form of jaundice. When a dog has finished marking, it will often scrape the ground with its paws to add a visual mark as well, much as a leopard rakes a tree with its claws after spraying.

Much to its owner's dismay, a dog seems to be in heaven when it finds some foul-smelling material. Dogs love to roll in manure, rotten meat, and other decaying organic materials, perhaps because of their highly developed sense of smell, which may be a million times more acute than ours. I believe that dogs like to "wear" such odors much as we humans, a more visual species, like to wear bright clothes. Nor does a pet's appreciation of odors stop at the obnoxious. They react to certain perfumes and other toiletries, especially those that contain musk. I know of cats that have attacked their musk-wearing owners as though they were intruding strangers, and of dogs who have become sexually aroused at a whiff of certain perfumes.

Cats and dogs of all ages enjoy playing. I love to watch a cat playing with a leaf, a ball of wool, or its own tail. This indicates to me that kittens have imagination. Sometimes they chase after an imaginary object and "catch" it between their front paws. Other times they leap up and bat at a fleck or mark on the wall as though it were a fly. Puppies are no less playful, but, like many cats, they tend to lose their playfulness as they grow up.

Animals and people who play together stay together because play not only is good physical exercise, but also brings owner and pet closer together. Both dogs and cats enjoy such games as play-fighting, wrestling, chasing, retrieving, stalking, and games of ambush and "scare me." Dogs enjoy a tug of war with an old towel or a stick. Cats play "scare me" by walking up to a wall mirror, arching their backs, and then running away as though terrified. You can play with your cat by scaring it, then playing hide-and-seek.

Cats and dogs also communicate their needs indirectly, when they behave undesirably or unusually. Some cats develop behavior problems out of boredom — excessive licking, self-sucking, or chewing various things in the house, for example. Because cats need social play, it is better to keep two cats rather than one at home, especially if you are gone all day at school or at work.

Dogs suffer even more than cats if they are left alone during the working day. In fact, they may become so frustrated and lonely that they abandon their house-training, bark excessively, and chew up furniture and drapes.

Because dogs need more attention, I believe the cat is destined to become our most popular companion animal. Unlike a dog, it does not need to be housebroken, will willingly use a litter tray, does not need to go outdoors for exercise, and adapts extremely well to a life lived entirely indoors.

When a cat refuses to use the litter tray and defecates in various places in the house, it may mean that the animal is upset because of some social change — especially if there is more than one other cat in the home. Perhaps the cat feels insecure and has a greater urge to mark its territory. There are many other circumstances – such as an aversion to the litter material – that can cause cats to act in this way. Constipation and pain in passing hard stools can make them dislike the litter tray and refuse to use it. And a cat suffering from cystitis, a painful bladder infection, may urinate in various places in the house, sometimes even at the owner's feet, as though to signal that it is sick and needs help.

When a leashed dog is out walking with its owner, it may be more aggressive toward other dogs because it considers the owner part of its territory. When I am walking Benji on a leash and a strange dog approaches, I know that if I were to start shouting and pulling on Benji's leash, he might attack the other dog. Instead, I allow the other dog to sniff and investigate Benji. Then it is Benji's turn to investigate the other dog. If I were to pull Benji away, I might disrupt this getting-acquainted ritual.

Even when Benji is not with me, I remain quite still when a strange dog approaches and allow the dog to sniff and investigate me. This is part of good "dog manners" and if more people realized it, fewer would be bitten by dogs. A sudden movement can provoke a dog to attack; the worst thing that a person can do is move suddenly or try to run away when confronted by an aggressive dog. If the dog is clearly

Our pets look to us to satisfy their wants and needs. The better we understand their behavior, emotions, and intentions, the better we will be able to provide for them.

aggressive, the person has four options: call the dog's bluff with a direct stare; ignore it because indifference is a form of dominance; talk to it in a gentle voice; or sternly command it to "sit," "stay," or "go home." The most important thing to remember is that most dog attacks can be avoided if the person does, above all, not move and does not panic.

An estimated 1 million persons are bitten by dogs in the United States each year. I believe that many of these people are bitten because they do not understand dog body language and do not know how to behave toward a strange dog. But there are also dogs that are not raised to regard people as dominant leaders as well as loving "parents." It is our responsibility to provide proper training for our puppies so that they do not grow up to be social delinquents with no qualms about biting anybody.

Once we have learned something about communicating with our pets, how far should we go in making them adapt to our ideas about "proper" behavior? As director of the Institute for the Study of Animal Problems in Washington, D.C., I have seen far too many instances of unnecessary animal surgery – cats declawed, dogs that have had ears *cropped* (cut short) or have been *debarked* (had vocal cords altered so that they cannot bark). I do not believe that we should mutilate animals merely for cosmetic reasons or to make them conform to our life styles. Cat owners should encourage their cats to use scratching posts rather than having them declawed because cats enjoy scratching and use it as a social display and a way of marking territory. Scratching posts can be "spiced" with a little catnip to make them more attractive. Neutering dogs or cats of either sex has no adverse psychological effects. In fact, by removing the need to seek out a mate, it may help a pet adapt to life indoors, and it also helps to reduce the pet overpopulation problem.

As you can see, the body language and facial expressions of dogs and cats are remarkably similar to those of humans, and they depict a similar range of emotions. The more we understand our pets' behavior, emotions, and intentions, the better our relationships with them will be. Above all, through understanding their ways, we can better appreciate them as sensitive, intelligent beings. We can then treat them with the respect that all of the creatures great and small under our stewardship deserve.

For further reading:

Fox, Michael W. *Understanding Your Dog.* Bantam Books, 1977.
Fox, Michael W. *Understanding Your Cat.* Bantam Books, 1977.
Gates, Wende D. and Fox, Michael W. *What Is Your Dog Saying?* Coward, McCann & Geoghegan, Inc., 1976.
Gates, Wende D. and Fox, Michael W. *What Is Your Cat Saying?* Coward, McCann & Geoghegan, Inc., 1981.
McGinnis, Terri. *The Well Cat Book.* Random House, 1975.
McGinnis, Terri. *The Well Dog Book.* Random House, 1974.
Monks of New Skete. *How to Be Your Dog's Best Friend.* Little, Brown & Co., 1978.

Can an Aspirin a Day Help Keep the Doctor Away?

By Jane E. Brody

A talented "miracle drug" that has stood the test of time, aspirin is being studied for use in preventing strokes and heart attacks

Every day, Sidney takes one aspirin tablet, though he rarely has aches or pains or suffers the miseries of any ailment for which aspirin is widely recommended. In fact, despite a heart attack several years ago, Sidney is in excellent health. He takes the aspirin in the hope that he will stay that way. Sidney has heard that aspirin can prevent blood clots and thus might protect him from another heart attack.

Sidney's heart specialist told him that aspirin's benefit to heart patients was by no means proven, but that one tablet per day might help him. The doctor warned Sidney about aspirin's side effects and advised him to stick to a low-fat diet and exercise program rather than relying on aspirin alone to keep him healthy.

Sidney is one of millions of people throughout the world who may benefit from recent discoveries that are extending aspirin's already long list of medical uses. Aspirin's ability to relieve pain and reduce

*Salix alba
a species
of willow*

Headache

Aspirin

Thermometer

fever and inflammation is well known. It is now under study as a potential lifesaver in preventing strokes, heart attacks, and other disorders caused by blood clots.

Aspirin has already shown that it can ward off serious strokes and prevent dangerous blood clots in susceptible patients. Physicians who prescribe aspirin for their patients for such purposes are turning one of the drug's side effects — its tendency to cause bleeding — to medical advantage.

Researchers must conduct carefully controlled studies of aspirin's anticlotting role to determine the ideal dosage and to find out which kinds of patients are most likely to benefit. But aspirin is clearly a more versatile and respected drug today than it was when it was introduced more than 80 years ago.

Aspirin does not cure any disease, but it comes closer to being a universal medicine than any other substance. Every day, human beings swallow tons of these pills — there are more than 1,000 aspirin-based products on the market to fight pain, fever, and inflammation. Aspirin remains popular despite the fact that it can cause such side effects as ulcers, internal bleeding, prolonged bleeding time, gastric irritation, ringing in the ears, temporary hearing loss, kidney failure, liver damage, and, in a small percentage of individuals, allergic reactions that threaten life. Most people taking a one- or two-tablet dose of aspirin three or four times a day will lose about two-fifths of a teaspoon (2 milliliters) of blood from the stomach.

Researchers have developed several anti-inflammation drugs in recent years, but aspirin is still usually the doctor's first treatment for the crippling, painful inflammation of rheumatoid arthritis. It is by far the first-choice remedy for fever, and it has outperformed many prescription drugs, including the narcotic codeine, in relieving mild to moderate pain. Other pain-reliever drugs have had little impact on aspirin's popularity. Aspirin is still the leading drug to treat headache, muscular aches and pains, and menstrual cramps. In fact, aspirin is the main active ingredient in most of the over-the-counter drugs that claim to be its superiors. It is indeed "the pain-reliever doctors recommend most." Aspirin's leading nonaspirin competitor, acetaminophen, does not cause bleeding, but it lacks aspirin's ability to reduce inflammation, a common cause of aches and pains.

Sidney would be amazed to learn about some of the other benefits recently claimed for aspirin. Some people use it to relieve anxiety and help them sleep. Taken soon after exposure to harsh sunlight, aspirin has reduced the severity of sunburn. It has also been used to prevent rejections of transplanted organs, to counter dehydration in children with gastrointestinal infections, and to reduce the incidence of cold sores in some patients.

"When you think of things that have absolutely revolutionized medicine, you have to put aspirin up there with antibiotics, general anesthesia, and digitalis," says J. Richard Crout, director of the

The author:
Jane E. Brody is a science writer for The New York Times.

United States Food and Drug Administration's (FDA) Bureau of Drugs, who is not normally given to expansive comments about drugs. Joseph C. Fratantoni of FDA's division of blood and blood products echoes Crout's enthusiastic sentiments: "If there's one drug we could name as the wonder drug, it's aspirin," he said in an interview with *Medical World News*. "Aspirin is an incredibly safe drug, given its potency."

Aspirin is far from a recent discovery. Even ancient healers knew about some of its benefits. Aspirin is acetylsalicylic acid, and salicylates—the basic substances from which acetylsalicylic acid comes—are found in willow trees and other plants that have been used therapeutically for thousands of years. More than 2,000 years ago in Greece, Hippocrates, the father of modern medicine, recommended the chewing of willow leaves or bark to relieve the pain of childbirth and post-childbirth fever. Pliny the Elder, an ancient Roman historian and lawyer who died in A.D. 79, described the use of poplar bark, which also contains a salicylate, to counter sciatica—a nerve pain felt in the hip, thigh, and leg. Long before the Pilgrims

An American Indian medicine man of the 1600s mixes a brew of willow bark, which, his ancestors discovered, reduces fever. Brewing the willow bark extracts salicin, a close chemical cousin of acetylsalicylic acid—or plain aspirin.

Algonkian shaman making medicine

Felix Hofmann develops commercial process

German chemist Felix Hofmann worked in the early 1890s on ways of making acetylsalicylic acid, which had been discovered in 1853. He developed a method of producing commercial amounts of the substance inexpensively in 1893.

landed at Plymouth Rock, American Indians used a brew of willow bark to reduce fever. In Africa, the Hottentots prepared a similar brew to relieve rheumatic pains.

Aspirin found its way into Sidney's medicine cabinet through a strange twist of logic fashionable in English medical circles in the 1700s. Prevailing opinion held that nature provides remedies for specific ailments in the areas of the countryside where those ailments occur most frequently. This theory indicated that a remedy for the *ague* (chills and fever) could be found in wet areas. Sure enough, Edward Stone, a minister, reported to the Royal Society of London for Improving Natural Knowledge in 1763 that he had found the bark of the willow — a tree that grows near water — to be beneficial to people afflicted with the ague. Stone explained his discovery this way: "As this tree delights in a moist or wet soil, where agues chiefly abound, the general maxim that many natural maladies carry their cures along with them or that their remedies lie not far from the causes was so very apposite [appropriate] to this particular case that I could not help applying it; and that this might be the intention of Providence here, I must own, had some little weight with me."

Nevertheless, aspirin's ancestral compounds remained in the realm of folk medicine until the 1800s. French pharmacist Henri Leroux isolated willow bark's active ingredient in 1829 and named it *salicin*, for the genus name of the willow, *Salix*. During the next 20 years, researchers converted salicin to salicylic acid. One plant used was spiraea, from which came the name *aspirin*.

In 1853, French chemist Charles Gerhardt prepared a chemical cousin of salicylic acid — acetylsalicylic acid, or aspirin — but this compound was not used in treatment until 40 years later. Meanwhile, people used salicylic acid and salicylates to treat such ailments as fever, gout, rheumatism, diabetes, and infection, but both substances irritated the stomach too much and tasted too vile to become popular.

Finally, in 1893, German chemist Felix Hofmann — responding to the desperate pleas of his rheumatic father, who could not tolerate salicylates — developed a commercial method for making acetylsalicylic acid. Hofmann's colleague at Friedrich Bayer and Company, Heinrich Dreser, then tested acetylsalicylic acid and proved that it was far less toxic and provided greater relief of pain than did salicylic acid and salicylates. With Dreser's recommendation, Bayer put powdered aspirin on the market in 1899.

Somewhere along the way, the product got its original trademark name, aspirin. This trademark probably was an invention of Hof-

Aspirin powder was available in the early 1900s, but was seldom used. After World War I, however, an American company learned how to mass-produce aspirin tablets cheaply and began to market them.

The First Aspirin containers

Making Aspirin Tablets
The process of making
aspirin tablets begins
with a chemical reaction,
top left, that produces
pure aspirin powder.
A machine, *top right,*
then compresses a
mixture of the powder
and starch into tablets.
Then, *at right, from left
to right,* the aspirins leave
the compressing machine
and are counted and
bottled, while samples
are tested chemically
for purity and measured.

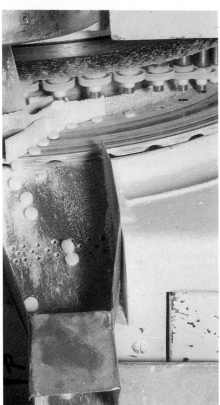

mann, Dreser, and Bayer's chief chemist, Arthur Eichengrun. According to one story, the three scientists considered shortening "acetylsalicylic acid" to "a-salicylic," then to "a-salicin," from the salicylate first found in the willow tree. One of the men then recalled that the spirea plant also yielded salicin. It was a short step to coining the name "a-spirea" and, finally, "aspirin."

After World War I, a U.S. firm, Sterling Products Incorporated, produced aspirin in the tablet form that we all know by binding the powder with starch. It quickly became the nation's leading drug. The U.S. pharmaceutical industry now produces 12,000 short tons (10,800 metric tons) of aspirin per year for domestic consumption.

Yet, despite aspirin's diverse and growing uses over many decades, scientists did not know how it worked until 1970. Then pharmacologist John R. Vane and his colleagues at Great Britain's Royal College of Surgeons' Institute of Basic Medical Sciences in London discovered that aspirin slows the production of hormonelike substances called prostaglandins. Cells throughout the body produce prostaglandins when infections develop. Prostaglandins can induce redness, fever, swelling, and pain; when injected into the blood, they cause headache and fever. Some prostaglandins cause blood vessels to constrict; others cause them to expand. One type of prostaglandin inhibits blood clotting; another makes it easier for clots to form. By slowing the production of prostaglandins, aspirin can cause a wide range of effects, depending in part on how much aspirin reaches the bloodstream and at what stage of prostaglandin formation it gets there.

The body forms prostaglandins from a fatty acid called arachidonic acid. An *enzyme* (a protein that alters other molecules in the body) converts this acid to substances called endoperoxides. Other enzymes change endoperoxides into various prostaglandins, including those that cause pain, fever, and inflammation. Aspirin throws a monkey wrench into the prostaglandin machinery by adding an assembly of atoms called an acetyl group to the enzyme that forms endoperoxides. This group inactivates the enzyme, and the prostaglandins cannot be formed. The result is a reduction in pain, fever, and inflammation.

When it comes to clotting action, however, the aspirin-prostaglandin story is more complex (see drawing on pages 148 and 149). Aspirin slows the formation of two prostaglandins: prostacyclin, which is secreted by cells in the blood vessel walls; and thromboxane, secreted by platelets, the blood cells central to clot formation. Prostacyclin keeps platelets from clumping together and thereby inhibits clotting. It also expands blood vessels, so that they are less likely to be blocked by a clot. By slowing prostacyclin formation, aspirin acts as a clot promoter.

Thromboxane, on the other hand, causes platelets to gather in clumps. It also constricts blood vessels, increasing the likelihood that a clot will cut off the flow of blood. Thus, by blocking thromboxane formation, aspirin inhibits clotting.

The fact that aspirin causes bleeding strongly suggests that aspirin is better at preventing the formation of thromboxane than it is at blocking prostacyclin. Studies show that aspirin's effect on a blood-vessel cell that produces prostacyclin wears off when the cell uses up the aspirin, and the cell begins to produce prostacyclin again. But aspirin's effect on a platelet never wears off. Once aspirin blocks a platelet's ability to produce thromboxane, the platelet can never produce that substance during its weeklong life. However, the body continues to form new platelets whose thromboxane production must be blocked, so a continuous supply of aspirin must be administered. But thromboxane blocking requires one aspirin tablet a day or less, a much smaller dose of aspirin than is needed to block prostacyclin. This indicates that very low doses of aspirin act strictly as a clot inhibitor. Based on this finding, blood specialist Aaron J. Marcus of Cornell University Medical College in New York City says, "We currently recommend no more than a single 325-milligram [5-grain] aspirin tablet daily" to prevent blood clots.

California physician Lawrence L. Craven noted aspirin's potential as a clot inhibitor in 1953, after studying heart attacks among his older patients. Physicians had known that heart attacks usually result from a clot that blocks a major artery feeding the heart. Craven noted that no heart attacks occurred over a period of several years among 1,400 overweight, sedentary, middle-aged men under his care who took one or two aspirin tablets per day. However, Craven's study included no control group—a group of men of similar age and circumstances who did not take aspirin—with which to compare the experience of the aspirin-treated group. Because of this, Craven's findings were dismissed by the medical profession as meaningless.

Researchers who test the effects of a medication on human volunteers set up their programs so that they can accurately compare the results of taking the medicine with the consequences of going without it. Scientists usually do this by dividing the volunteers into two groups. One group receives the medication while the other, called the control group, gets a *placebo*—a preparation that resembles the medication but has no active ingredient. The volunteers do not know whether they are receiving the medication or the placebo, and they are all treated in the same way. Some tests go a step further. Neither the volunteers nor the people dispensing the two substances and examining the volunteers know who is receiving which substance. Only the researchers administering the tests know who receives medication.

At the same time that Craven was revealing his findings, researchers at Harvard University in Cambridge, Mass., found that rheumatoid arthritis patients who took aspirin were less likely to suffer fatal heart attacks than would be expected on the basis of average death rates among such patients.

Twenty years later, a chance rediscovery of aspirin's possible effect on heart attacks started the current wave of studies and is responsible

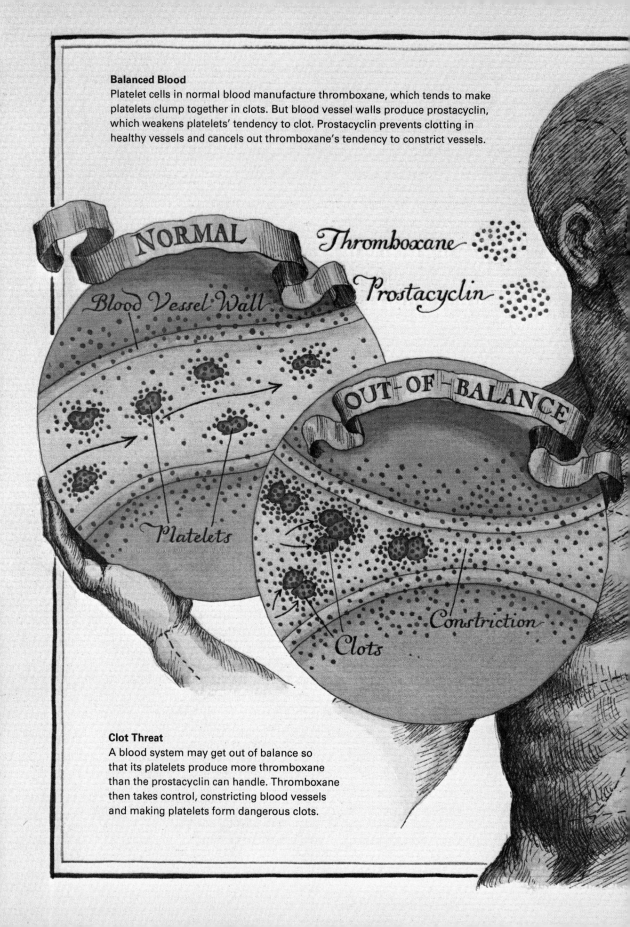

Balanced Blood

Platelet cells in normal blood manufacture thromboxane, which tends to make platelets clump together in clots. But blood vessel walls produce prostacyclin, which weakens platelets' tendency to clot. Prostacyclin prevents clotting in healthy vessels and cancels out thromboxane's tendency to constrict vessels.

NORMAL

Thromboxane

Prostacyclin

Blood Vessel Wall

Platelets

OUT-OF-BALANCE

Clots

Constriction

Clot Threat

A blood system may get out of balance so that its platelets produce more thromboxane than the prostacyclin can handle. Thromboxane then takes control, constricting blood vessels and making platelets form dangerous clots.

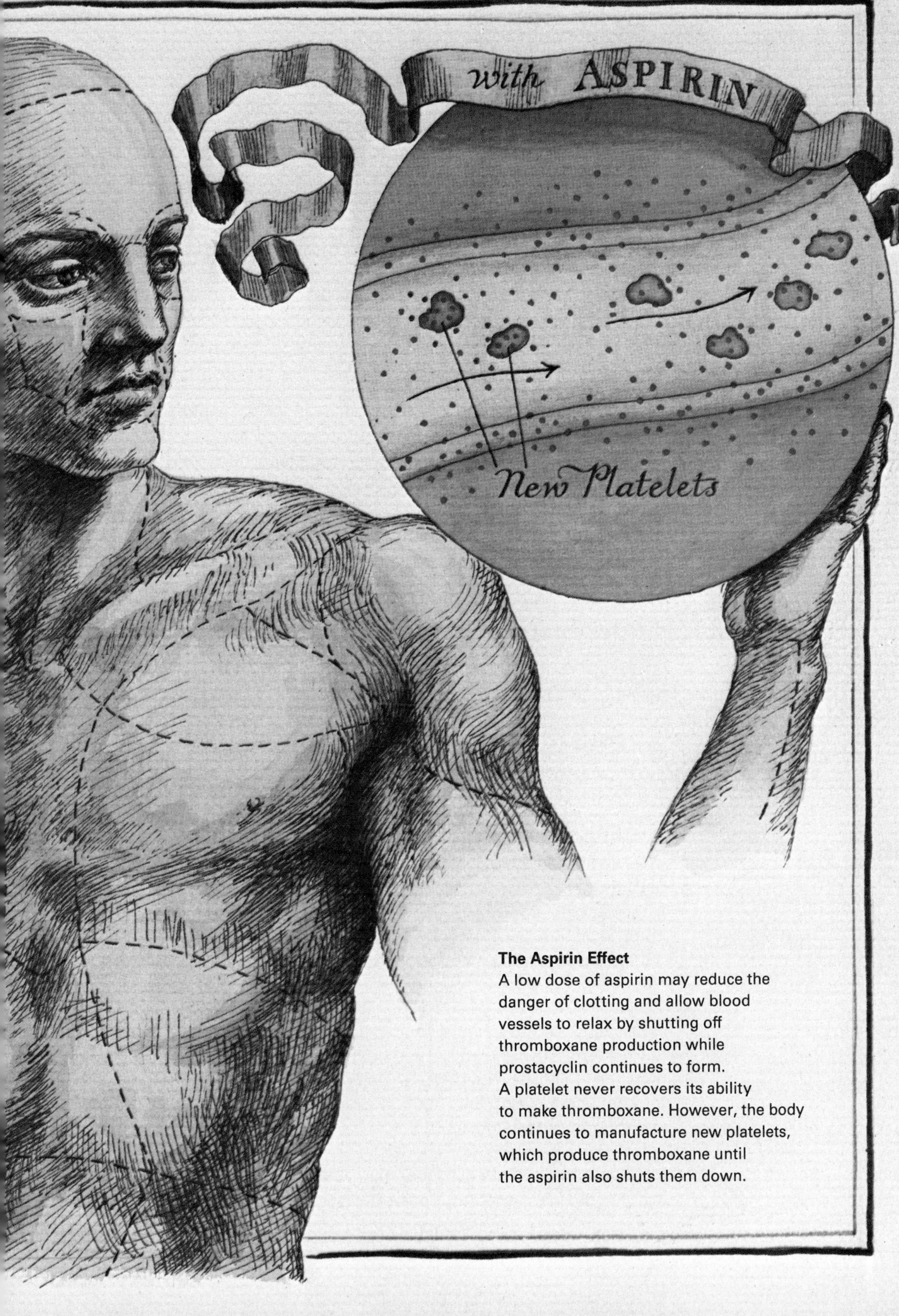

with ASPIRIN

New Platelets

The Aspirin Effect
A low dose of aspirin may reduce the
danger of clotting and allow blood
vessels to relax by shutting off
thromboxane production while
prostacyclin continues to form.
A platelet never recovers its ability
to make thromboxane. However, the body
continues to manufacture new platelets,
which produce thromboxane until
the aspirin also shuts them down.

for Sidney's daily dosage. In 1974, the Boston Collaborative Drug Surveillance Program, a continuing cooperative research project set up to uncover the adverse effects of drugs, detected instead a potential drug benefit. The researchers asked 776 patients who were hospitalized for heart attack what drugs they were taking, then examined their medical histories. They found that significantly fewer nonfatal heart attacks occurred among persons who used aspirin regularly than among those who did not.

Also in 1974, a team headed by Peter C. Elwood, a specialist in epidemic diseases at the Medical Research Council Epidemiological Unit in Cardiff, Wales, reported that it found 24 per cent fewer heart attack deaths among 1,233 study participants who had been treated for a year with 300 milligrams of aspirin once a day. In 1976, the U.S. Coronary Drug Project, a study conducted by the National Heart, Lung, and Blood Institute (NHLBI), reported 30 per cent fewer cardiac deaths than the average among 1,529 males who used aspirin. And a 1977 European study of 626 men who received aspirin or a placebo showed that fatal heart attacks among those who took aspirin were 42 per cent below the average. However, because of the relatively small number of people involved in each study, none of these findings established what scientists call a statistically significant difference in death rates. That is, researchers could not be sure that the results were not caused by chance. So they were not certain that aspirin provided the apparent benefit.

In 1979, Elwood published the results of a second study of 1,682 men and women. He found that heart attacks were 28 per cent below the average and heart attack deaths were down 22 per cent when a dose of 300 milligrams of aspirin was given three times a day. Again, the findings were not statistically significant.

The growing enthusiasm for aspirin as a heart-attack preventive was apparently stifled in 1980 by the long-awaited findings from NHLBI's three-year Aspirin Myocardial Infarction Study (AMIS) involving 4,524 persons treated at 30 U.S. medical centers. All the participants had already suffered one heart attack, and aspirin was being tested as a means of preventing a second attack. AMIS found fewer nonfatal heart attacks and strokes among those given 500 milligrams of aspirin twice a day for three years than among those who took a placebo, but slightly more fatal heart attacks occurred in the aspirin-treated group. Here again, the differences were not statistically significant. The researchers concluded that their results did not support the use of aspirin to prevent heart attacks. Furthermore, the aspirin-treated group suffered considerably more gastrointestinal side effects, including symptoms of peptic ulcer, gastritis, and erosion of the stomach lining.

However, even before the AMIS researchers had analyzed their findings, some experts predicted that AMIS would not show meaningful results because the aspirin dosage used in the study was too large. Scientists discovered aspirin's dual effect on clotting — inhibiting it at low doses but possibly promoting it at higher doses — while AMIS was in progress, too late to change the dosage used in the study. So researchers still must determine whether a very low dose, such as Sidney's one 325-milligram tablet or less per day, can ward off fatal and nonfatal heart attacks in enough people to justify its routine use.

Meanwhile, three studies have suggested that aspirin could prevent other types of life-threatening clots. Most strokes occur when a clot blocks an artery that feeds blood to a certain part of the brain. Before suffering a stroke, 3 out of 4 victims experience a series of transient ischemic attacks (TIA's), mini-strokes that are, in effect, warning signs of an impending stroke. Nerve specialist William S. Fields of the University of Texas Health Sciences Center in Houston studied aspirin treatment among 307 TIA patients in 1977. Fields's research showed that four tablets a day could decrease the frequency of second attacks. A similar study completed in 1978 in Canada showed that men who took four aspirins a day had many fewer mini-strokes, half as many strokes, and half as many fatal strokes as did men given placebos. For unknown reasons, however, no benefit from aspirin was found among the women studied.

Blood clots that form in veins after surgery can travel to the lungs, where they can cause death. Between 50,000 and 150,000 Americans die from such pulmonary embolisms each year. In 1977, a medical team from Massachusetts General Hospital, Beth Israel Hospital, and Harvard Medical School in Boston tested aspirin's ability to prevent clots from forming in veins in men and women who had undergone hip-replacement surgery. Again, benefit was apparent only in men — only four of 23 men given aspirin developed clots in their veins after surgery, compared with 14 of 25 men receiving a placebo. The aspirin-treated group received the equivalent of nearly four tablets per day for two weeks, starting on the day before surgery.

A 1979 study at Washington University School of Medicine in St. Louis tested the ability of just half a tablet per day to prevent clotting in patients undergoing kidney dialysis. Many of these patients develop clots in the shunt tube that directs their blood to the kidney machine where it is cleansed of wastes. The aspirin-treated group developed less than half as many clots as the control group. Furthermore, the scientists noted that this low dosage of aspirin produced no toxic side effects.

The St. Louis researchers concluded that most of the previous studies, including AMIS, used too much aspirin. They maintain that one tablet per day is enough to stop production of thromboxane, the clot-promoting prostaglandin. A larger dose may block clot-inhibiting prostacyclin and cancel out part of the benefit gained by blocking thromboxane production. Higher doses also cause more side effects and therefore diminish the ratio of benefit to risk.

Consumers can choose from a wide variety of aspirin tablets, pain relievers that are chemically similar to aspirin, and products that contain aspirin and other ingredients.

So researchers will have to conduct new tests to determine whether a lower dose, such as one tablet or less per day, or less frequent administration – one tablet every other day, for example – produces more anticlotting benefits and fewer undesirable side effects when tested in a large enough group of people. The researchers will try to determine a dosage that blocks thromboxane but not prostacyclin.

More research is needed to settle these points, but if your physician believes that aspirin may be helpful in your case, an effective medication is available from among the vast array of brand-name drugs that compete with aspirin in a market that brings in more than $700 million per year in the United States alone. Most competing drugs – such as Anacin, Bufferin, and Excedrin – contain aspirin as their main and most effective ingredient. Products that also contain caffeine offer no particular benefit, except possibly for persons suffering from a caffeine-withdrawal headache, because caffeine does not relieve pain. Tablets that have several pain-relieving ingredients increase the likelihood of unpleasant side effects, yet do not necessarily offer greater relief of symptoms.

Several products that proclaim "extra strength" simply contain larger amounts of aspirin per tablet than does the standard 325-milligram aspirin tablet. You can duplicate the potency of these products at lower cost by taking a somewhat larger dose of plain aspirin. Brand-name aspirin tablets cost more than store brands, but they may be of higher quality. Do not accept a bottle that contains broken tablets or tablets that look yellow or smell vinegary, because the acetylsalicylic acid may be deteriorating and turning into acetic acid, thus losing its potency.

Some studies have shown that buffered aspirin tablets, containing an antacid, may prevent the stomach irritation in some people who cannot tolerate plain aspirin, but they do not reduce the stomach bleeding. Aspirin taken on an empty stomach is more likely to cause gastrointestinal upset than aspirin taken after a meal.

Another alternative is the most expensive form of aspirin — enteric-coated aspirin tablets. Their coating prevents them from dissolving until they reach the small intestine. Plain aspirin dissolves in the stomach. Enteric-coated aspirin tablets are especially useful for arthritis patients and for other persons with pain caused by inflammation who cannot tolerate plain aspirin's gastric irritation. However, the body absorbs the coated aspirin more slowly than plain aspirin. Consequently, relief is somewhat delayed.

Aspirin's leading competitor, acetaminophen — sold under such brand names as Tylenol, Datril, Anacin-3, and Bayer Acetaminophen — does not cause gastric irritation, erosion, or bleeding, so it is a useful pain reliever for people with ulcers. Acetaminophen's ability to relieve pain is comparable to that of aspirin, but it lacks aspirin's ability to reduce inflammation — in arthritic joints or injured muscles, for example. It has no effect on blood platelets and would not be useful as an anticlotting agent. However, it is a good substitute for plain aspirin as a pain reliever for those who have bleeding disorders or who take anticoagulants.

Acetaminophen has long had an advantage over aspirin in treating very young children who cannot swallow pills. It is stable in liquid form and can be administered by dropper or spoon, while aspirin must be used as a tablet, powder, or suppository. However, West Virginia University scientists in Morgantown in 1980 patented a liquid form of aspirin stabilized by a new solvent called DMI. If this product becomes commercially available, it could mean faster absorption, and therefore faster relief, possibly at a lower dosage and with fewer side effects.

Aspirin's future appears to be at least as bright as its past. Perhaps like Sidney, millions of people throughout the world will one day use aspirin to help ward off a second heart attack or a second stroke — or to prevent the first one.

A Year in Perspective

1875
1877
1878
1879
1880

THE YEAR BOOK casts a backward glance at the furors, fancies, and follies of yesteryear. The coincidences of history that are revealed offer substantial proof that the physical world may continually change, but human nature — with all its inventiveness, amiability, and even perversity — remains fairly constant, for better or worse, throughout the years.

See page 163.

The Passing Scene —Then and Now

By Paul C. Tullier

A foreign power ruled in Afghanistan, and the U.S. experienced an unpopular census and a malicious presidential campaign

In December, most of the nation's newspapers analyzed the significance of the passing year's most newsworthy events. Some surveyed the national scene. Others viewed the world at large. The New York *Post* was in the latter group, and the editors concluded that the world was in a woeful state. "We are no longer a world of congenial nations striving to accommodate the needs of our fellow man," the editorial declared. "Rather we are individual tribes selfishly harvesting for our [respective countries] the rewards that accrue from greed and avarice. Hunger and despair are the daily lot of the earth's poor for whom there is no surcease from plunder . . . by the rich [ones]."

Based on the international developments of 1880, the editorial's conclusions seemed logical. Africa had become fair game for aggres-

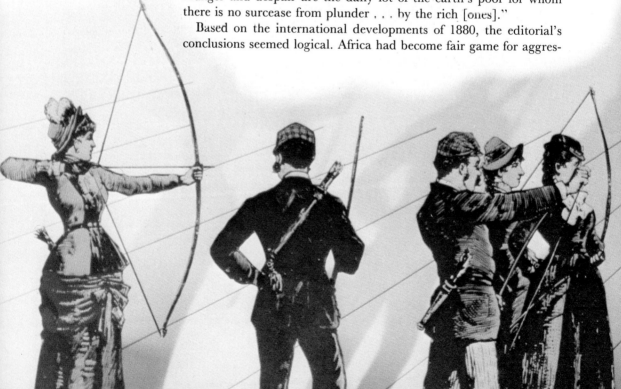

The year 1880 sees the opening of the St. Gotthard Tunnel; the first elephant to be born in the United States; Oberammergau's Passion Play; the Metropolitan Museum's first exhibit in its new home; and the new popularity of archery.

sive European powers bent on territorial aggrandizement. Italy had staked out a Red Sea colony on Africa's east coast. Belgium's King Leopold II had proclaimed himself sovereign of the ore- and mineral-rich Congo, while along the North African coast France and Italy were squabbling over territorial rights to the fertile coastal plains of Tunisia. In Transvaal (South Africa), the British were waging war against the uncompromising Boers, who were determined to secure their independence of Great Britain.

In Europe, Russia's grip on Poland was brutally firm. Within Russia, turmoil reigned. After an attempt to assassinate the czar and his family failed, the government established a new secret police force, *Okhrana*. In Germany, a controversy had arisen over an alleged anti-Semitic version of Oberammergau's Passion Play. Turkish brigands had captured and were holding for ransom British Consul William Synge, his wife, and a military attaché. In France, the royalists provoked Republican fury by belittling a government decree officially designating July 14 as "The Fall of the Bastille" day. However, both groups approved France's annexation of Tahiti and the Society Islands as French colonies in the Pacific Ocean.

In the Middle East, the British government had stopped short of annexing Afghanistan, whose rebellious tribes had finally been subdued by British troops. Although Great Britain granted Abdur Rahman Khan the title of supreme emir of Kabul, it retained full control of Afghanistan's foreign policy and was restructuring the Afghan government to conform with its own views. India and Persia (Iran) were competing fiercely for the larger share of the opium trade with China. India was exporting 90,000 "chests" of opium annually. The Persians were shipping 70,000 chests annually but had stepped up opium production at Shiraz, Yazd, and Isfahan. The *Post* editorial noted disapprovingly that the "proliferation of poppy farms has caused serious curtailment of food production on a million acres of cropland in both countries" and that a "famine is inevitable." But it was restrained in its comments on an increasingly tense situation in Palestine, where Jewish refugees, fleeing from persecution in Europe, were resettling in large numbers among resentful Arabs. "The Jews have made progress in Palestine [as is] especially evident in the erection of many new buildings in Jerusalem. Outside the town, entirely new suburbs have sprung up. Inside, the Jews have formed among themselves building societies which have erected long barrackslike buildings adapted for several families . . . The improvements reflect a regeneration of Jewish hopes for a permanent reaffixment to their land of origin."

In the Western Hemisphere, bits and pieces of the problems in Europe, Africa, and the Middle East were reflected in Central and South America. A boundary dispute had erupted into war between Peru and Bolivia; Venezuela's agitation to regain its lost province of Panama was roiling Central America; religious persecution of Roman

The author:
Paul C. Tullier is Managing Editor of THE WORLD BOOK YEAR BOOK.

Catholics in El Salvador, Costa Rica, and Mexico kept the region in turmoil. Few American newspapers gave these Latin American — or neighboring Canada's — affairs more than passing mention. Some did note that a language problem was sowing the seeds of disharmony in Canada, but few reported that the government of English-speaking Manitoba had been "reconstituted to include one representative of the French-speaking population."

In the United States, year-end newspaper reviews either ignored or commented only briefly and warily on such matters as nudism being practiced as a health measure in California; the increase in child abuse; the lowly status of women; and the militant activities of an antivivisection movement. A rare few acknowledged the increase in health-food faddism, including wild-fern diets, or the peculiar practices of religious sects that had withdrawn from the American mainstream to found self-sufficient colonies. Some inquiring minds were trying to determine if plants had "feelings," but these endeavors were largely ignored, as was a cause célèbre reported from Watsonville, Calif., concerning the death of one Charles Parkhurst. Parkhurst was a stagecoach driver and a farmer, and his good disposition had endeared him to the grieving town. Grief gave way to disbelief when the embalmer revealed that the deceased was a woman.

These omissions were understandable. But no year-end summary would have been complete without some acknowledgment of the role weather played in American lives in 1880. The respected *Farmer's Almanac,* in an earlier edition, had assured its readers that a simple explanation for many human aberrations could be found in the weather patterns. "Weather," it quoted Benjamin Franklin as saying, "is as critical to the human disposition as it is to a farmer's crops. Mankind blooms or withers accordingly." In January and February, Americans from California to the Carolinas withered before the onslaught of a phenomenal cold wave. In the Great Lakes region, arctic-cold gales swept the icecapped waters with devastating force. Fleets of tugs and scows were wrecked. Shoreline installations, such as cranes, were destroyed. On Lake Ontario alone, 19 lives were lost in a single week's time. There was no letup even in the spring, when heavy snowfalls hit Georgia and northern Florida. And although summer brought a respite from the withering cold, Americans now wilted as a heat wave blanketed the nation. On June 28, 186 deaths from "heat prostration" were reported in the Southwest. The next day, another 212 were recorded in the Midwest.

It was no wonder that crops were ruined and people grew crotchety with aches and pains, fancied or otherwise. Nothing could be done for the crops, but panaceas were at hand for the grumblers. Dr. Pearson's Extract of celery and camomile offered soothing relief for nervous irritation, sick headaches, and nasal obstructions. "Electric" belts were recommended in advertisements as a perfect remedy for relaxing tense muscles, curing stomachaches, and even halting any tendencies to premature debility, a euphemism for "loss of manhood." The London Galvanic Generator promised to relieve neuralgia and a weak back.

For the weather-dazed who had become slightly unhinged, there was Adams Nervine Asylum, a newly opened institution in Boston offering "occupational therapy for the dispirited." For the overspirited, so to speak, Leslie E. Keeley had opened the Keeley Institute in Dwight, Ill. A Civil War physician, Keeley had developed a legitimate, medically accepted treatment for alcoholics and drug addicts that would become world famous as the Keeley Cure.

Alcoholism was indeed a prevalent if stubbornly unacknowledged problem in the United States and one not likely to be mentioned in year-end reports. But it existed, and Kansas took the devil by the horns in 1880 by adopting a liquor-prohibition law – the first Midwestern state to do so. Rescuing victims from the evils of drink was also a major goal of the Great Britain-based Salvation Army, which established its New York City headquarters in 1880 in "Harry Hills Variety," a music hall on the Bowery. On March 14, the army launched its first drive in the United States. The following day, a somewhat puzzled New York *World* reported the event under a headline that read "A Peculiar People Among Queer Surroundings." (The army found itself in other new surroundings in 1880 when it also expanded its operation to Australia.)

The entire Salvation Army contingent in New York City consisted of only one man and seven women, the latter soon to be known affectionately as Army Lasses. Their tied-under-the-chin black straw bonnets and shaking tambourines would become familiar sights and sounds in and around the Bowery. But their presence in such a tough neighborhood disturbed the city's more prudish males, who expected females to function in more genteel surroundings while performing more ladylike tasks.

One institution that met both requirements was the Philadelphia School of Design for Women, which, early in the year, moved into the spacious old Edwin Forrest mansion at Broad and Masters streets in Philadelphia. Student enrollment stood at an all-time high of 40. Because the minimal tuition fees barely supported the school, income was supplemented by a $3,000 contribution from the state of Pennsylvania. The students "composed" designs for fabrics and wallpaper, among other things, but decorating china was the school's specialty. "Porcelain art" it was called. Mary Cassatt, a Philadelphia heiress-turned-painter, had given it a brief try but rejected it. She had shocked society in 1868 by moving to Paris against her father's wishes to pursue "real" art studies. In 1880, she became the first American female to be invited to exhibit with the French impressionists.

Neither Cassatt nor the impressionists would have found any works remotely resembling their own in the staid Metropolitan Museum of Art, which in 1880 moved to new, larger quarters in New York City's

Central Park. Among its main attractions were plaster casts of Greek and Roman sculpture "tastefully conmingled" with reproductions of Egyptian pharaohs. (Coincident with the Metropolitan's opening was the arrival in New York City of Cleopatra's Needle, an ancient obelisk sent as a gift by the Egyptian government to the American people.) The Metropolitan's new quarters, however, left much to be desired: Knowledgeable visitors complained that "thousands of interesting objects are stored away out of sight for want of room to properly display them." Maintenance costs were also a source of discontent, particularly to the board of trustees, whose wealth had made the Metropolitan possible. "To keep the museum's doors open year round costs the sum of $20,553," groused one trustee, "an exorbitant sum that warrants changing from a *free*-admission to a *fee*-admission policy."

Maintenance costs seemingly posed no problem for William Wilson Corcoran, a banker and philanthropist, who was the sole founder and principal patron of the Corcoran Gallery of Art in Washington, D.C. Lack of space, however, was a problem he shared with the Metropolitan. But his efforts to solve it by purchasing a plot of land adjacent to his gallery were rebuffed by the notoriously crusty landowner, Admiral S. P. Lee, a nephew of the Confederacy's redoubtable General Robert E. Lee. A space problem of a different sort affected Germany's massive Cologne Cathedral. Begun in the 13th century, it was officially completed in 1880. But its soaring Gothic-arched ceiling still looked down on acres of wall space whose bare niches were not yet filled with appropriate sculpture.

Detailed descriptions of the Cologne Cathedral's impressive architectural proportions as well as the elaborate dedication services were featured in a unique but short-lived monthly magazine called *Pallette and Chisel*, subsidized by Abner Doubleday. It was only one of a wide variety of magazines introduced that year to capitalize on the public's growing appetite for more specialized reading material. Most popular — and long lived — among the

In 1880, electricity first lights up New York City's Broadway; a Paris hospital installs an anesthetic gas machine; Panama Canal builder De Lesseps seeks funds.

new ones were *The Dial,* a sedate monthly magazine of literary criticism, and *The Musical Courier,* a weekly journal of musical events at home and abroad. A third magazine, *Science,* made its appearance on July 3, 1880. It was financed jointly by inventor Thomas A. Edison and John Michels, an obscure New York City journalist who served as editor, writer, and subscription agency.

Book publishers were also becoming increasingly aware of a potential and profitable market for works other than novels or belles-lettres. Two such books that did well in 1880 were *A Practical Treatise on Nervous Exhaustion* – a book on neurasthenia by B. M. Beard – and *Bacteria,* a textbook by A. Magnin. By and large, however, fiction still dominated the publishers' lists. In 1880, the flow of books from Europe included two outstanding works from England: Francis Thompson's *The City of Dreadful Night* and Benjamin Disraeli's *Endymion.* From Russia came Fyodor Dostoevsky's *The Brothers Karamazov.* The French press contributed Guy de Maupassant's *Ball-of-Fat* and Émile Zola's *Nana.* For American readers who

Left to right, from opposite page: Russia's secret police seize an underground printing plant; fireworks mark France's Bastille Day celebration; British troops escort deposed ruler of Afghanistan into exile; English land agent Boycott and his family, shunned by Irish farmers, have to harvest their own crops.

preferred home-grown authors there were Henry Wadsworth Longfellow's *Ultima Thule*, Lew Wallace's *Ben-Hur: A Tale of the Christ*, and Joel Chandler Harris' *Uncle Remus: His Songs and His Sayings* — a collection of pieces that Harris had written for the *Atlanta Constitution*. Soft-cover books continued to win a large share of the market, the best seller in 1880 being a tear-jerker titled *To The Very Dregs* by Mrs. M. V. Victor. Purchasers were given a free plate to hang on the wall showing two children cowering in fear before a drunken father's wrath. The paperback cost 30 cents.

The heartache-and-despair theme in literature found its mirror image in the popular songs of the day; many were mournful in both melody and verse. "Why Did They Dig Ma's Grave So Deep?" queried one. "Cradle's Empty, Baby's Gone" grieved another. What lighter fare was available often originated in the burlesque theaters, with the irrepressible comedy team of Harrigan and Hart contributing the hit of the year: "Never Take the Horse Shoe from the Door." An unexpected sheet-music sellout was "Funiculi-Funicula," a song in Neapolitan dialect by Luigi Denza.

At the moment, most Americans probably preferred popular music to symphonic classics, but for devotees of the latter the year's crop of new works was bountiful. From Russia's Peter Ilich Tchaikovsky came the thunderous "1812" overture and the *Italian Capriccio;* Germany's Johannes Brahms produced his *Tragic Overture.* From Czech composer Antonín Dvořák came his *Symphony "No. 1" in D;* for the vocalist's repertoire, he provided *Songs My Mother Taught Me.* In Paris, the Opéra staged the first European performance of *Aida.* Adelina Patti sang the title role, with composer Giuseppe Verdi conducting in the orchestra pit. French critics lauded Verdi for his conducting as well as his music. British critics were less kind, however, to German composer Max Bruch, whose appointment as conductor of the Liverpool Philharmonic Society orchestra caused a number of vigorous protests in English journals. In Russia, performances of Modest Mussorgsky's opera *Boris Godunov* were banned as being politically offensive.

Fortunately, American theater audiences faced no such governmental bans, though the threat of a raid by the ever-vigilant Society for the Suppression of Vice remained constant. Theatrical producers, aware of such a possibility, kept firm reins on their creative talent. Many warily awaited the much-anticipated U. S. debut of Sarah Bernhardt, whose stage roles ranged from fallen women to murderous wives. On November 8, Bernhardt opened at Booth's Theatre in New York City in *Adrienne Lecouvrier*. She followed this, seven days later, in Alexandre Dumas the Younger's *The Lady of the Camellias*. No untoward incidents occurred, to the relief of all.

Earlier in the year, the Madison Square Theatre, New York City's newest and most lavish, opened its doors with Steele Mackaye's *Hazel Kirke*. An instant success, it played to capacity audiences until May 1881, for a then-astounding total of 486 performances. Rivaling *Hazel Kirke* in popularity was Bret Harte's *M'Liss,* a dramatization of his short story "The Work on Red Mountain." A few weeks earlier, the Park Theatre staged *The Wedding March*, a farcical comedy by William Gilbert, who was librettist to operetta composer Arthur Sullivan. Anticipating demand, the management proudly announced that reserved seats could be ordered by telephone. It was an innovation not adaptable to the uses of the nearby Cooper and Bailey Circus, which was the proud owner of the first elephant born in the United States. The infant was named Little Hebe.

Theater ticket prices varied according to the attraction, the least expensive being the vaudeville houses, which charged 10, 20, or 30 cents according to seat location. Prices for most goods and services in 1880 were relatively inexpensive by today's standards. A five-course dinner cost $1.80, and perhaps included terrapin soup. Men's linen shirts cost $2; men's suits from Rogers Peet or Brooks Bros. cost, at the most, $18. Ladies' lace shawls cost 65 cents; silk dress fabric from Wanamakers cost $1.95 a yard. Travel was encouraged by the low fares offered as inducements. A train ride from New York City to Washington, D.C., cost $2; the New York-Chicago run cost 25 cents more. The Inman Royal Mail Steamers line offered first-class one-way passage from New York City to Southampton, England, for $80. Inman and other lines charged slightly more for passage to Hamburg, Germany; Le Havre, France; or Naples, Italy. Steerage passage was considerably less, and standard, on all lines – $28.

Few Americans deigned to travel in steerage, but it was the only accommodation within the financial reach of the hordes of immigrants flooding into the United States in 1880 from England, Ireland, Germany, and Scandinavia. Although shiploads arrived at New Orleans, Galveston, and Baltimore, the main port of entry was New York City. Nearly 176,000 immigrants had landed at the Battery in 1879; in 1880, the number soared to over 200,000. Confronted by this human avalanche, many Americans turned against all foreigners. "We may do well to speculate," began an editorial in *Leslie's Illustrated Weekly*, "as to what will be the characteristics of the resulting composite race which will inhabit our broad domain a hundred years from now." It would not be long before factories in the East, with plenty of cheap labor available, would post signs at their gates advising would-be applicants that "no dogs or Irishmen need apply."

Resentment of the immigrants was further heightened in 1880 – the year of the census – by their frequent moves from state to state in search of work or congenial surroundings. On June 1, some 12,000 enumerators under the direction of 150 supervisors fanned out over the United States. (The enumerators received $4 pay per day; the supervisors received a flat fee of $500.) To cover the overall cost of the census, Congress had appropriated $3 million and had allocated two weeks to complete the task. To everyone's dismay, a seemingly easy job turned formidable. "The enumerators," said *Leslie's*, "are more prone to play the peeping Tom than to proceed with propriety . . . the impertinence of the enumerators' questions is exceeded only by the impropriety of their behaviour." In the weeks that followed, complaints multiplied. "Heretofore," said the *World*, "the enumerators have had a single day, namely the 1st of June every 10th year [to complete their work]. Now it has been extended over a period of five months. The consequence has been that many persons through their migration from place to place have been counted twice while others have not been counted at all." Comments in *The St. Louis Post-Dispatch* went to the heart of the matter: "The miscounting may appear to be mere inconsequential errors of arithmetic. It will appear differently when congressional seats are reapportioned on the basis of that erroneous count." The carping notwithstanding, the census was completed, its figures accepted, and by year's end Americans knew that their population had soared above the 50-million mark – 50,155,783 to be exact – including 2,812,195 immigrants. Reapportionment, however, was minimal.

Only a relatively small percentage of the burgeoning population would go beyond the eighth grade in elementary school. For that relatively small percentage who would eventually reach college, a wider choice of study courses was being offered. Matthew and John G. Vassar announced plans to erect a $10,000 science laboratory at Vassar College. New Jersey physician Joseph A. Taylor pledged his large estate as a site for a college specifically dedicated to women's educational needs. His generosity, coupled with the ardor of The Religious Society of Friends, also known as Quakers, would make Bryn Mawr College possible. In Cleveland, Leonard Case left property valued at $1 million to establish a school of applied science in that city. Johns Hopkins College inaugurated a seaside laboratory at Beaufort, S.C., "to provide a suitable undistracted scene for discussions of scientific matters pertaining to the ocean flora and fauna." Educational opportunities remained limited for blacks. Only a few colleges admitted a small number of them. Among those so fortunate had been Samuel Lowery. The son of slaves, Lowery had received his law degree in the 1870s. On Feb. 2, 1880, he was admitted to practice before the Supreme Court of the United States — the first of his race to be accorded the privilege. At his request, Lowery took his oath in front of a niche containing the bust of Chief Justice Roger B. Taney, author of the Dred Scott decision, which said in 1857 that no Negro could claim U. S. citizenship.

Unlimited opportunities awaited the college graduate in 1880, according to an article in *Harper's Weekly Magazine* encouraging young men to specialize in "the natural sciences." The facts justified the article's premise. In Greece, archaeologists were excavating sites on Mount Olympus; in Egypt, a team of engineers were surveying the Sahara with a view to constructing a railway across that desert. In Switzerland, engineers scored a breakthrough, literally, when they opened the St. Gotthard Tunnel through the Alps. Two Americans were participating in an international meteorological conference in Sydney, Australia, where the establishment of a uniform system of weather telegraphy for remote Australian towns and settlements was under consideration. French engineer Ferdinand de Lesseps was in

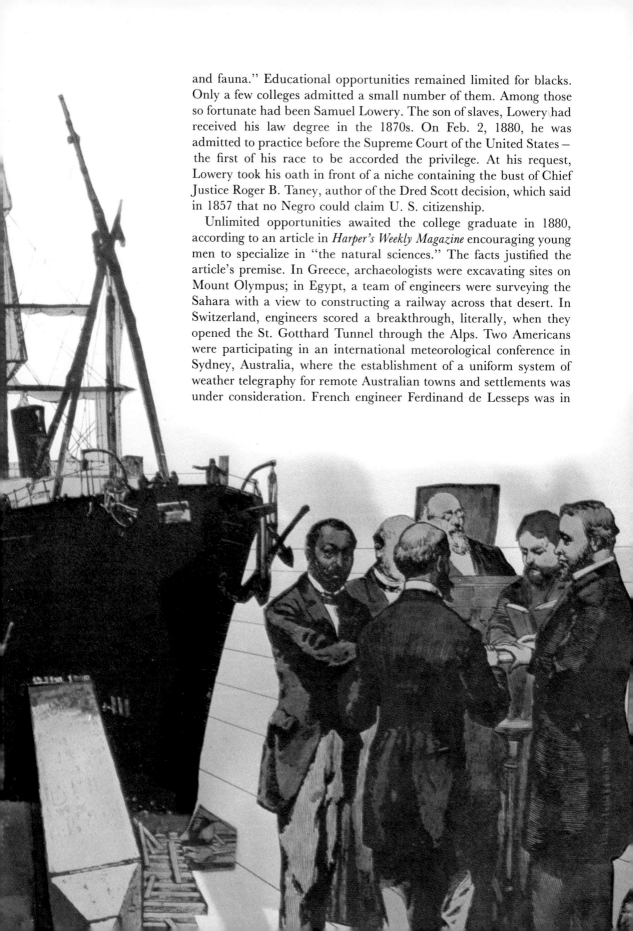

the United States raising funds and recruiting engineers for the construction of a canal across the Isthmus of Panama. College-trained mechanical designers saw new frontiers opening up for their skills with the installation of an anesthetic gas-producing machine in a Paris hospital.

Opportunities abounded for men of skill and imagination. Designs for a revolutionary flour-rolling mill were patented by John Stevens of Neenah, Wis. Another Wisconsinite, John F. Appleby, announced he had applied for a patent on an automatic twinbinding harvester. Pittsburgh celebrated the completion of Andrew Carnegie's first large steel furnace. But it was electricity and its uses that captured Americans' attention in 1880. In March, Wabash, Ind., became the first U. S. municipality to put in operation – albeit on a small scale – an electric street-lighting system. In June, electric lighting helped speed construction of the Rockaway Beach Hotel on Long Island, N.Y. It was the first time construction work had been carried out on a 24-hour basis. In December, the Brush Electric Light Company illuminated 1 mile (1.6 kilometers) of New York City's Broadway, from 14th to 34th streets, with 22 arc lamps, two to each block. (A reporter covering the dazzling spectacle suggested that Broadway be renamed Whiteway. It eventually became known as

Left to right, from opposite page: Egyptian workers load obelisk for shipment to the United States; the first black lawyer is admitted to practice before U.S. Supreme Court; a family greets unwelcome census taker with hostility; U.S. officials check papers of anxious European immigrants.

The Great White Way.) To be first in using electricity in some new way aroused keen competition, even among homeowners; department-store proprietor Marshall Field eventually claimed the honor for his elegant mansion located on Chicago's Prairie Avenue.

Competition was esteemed as a healthy attribute by Americans. No form of it was more healthful to the participants – or more pleasurable to the spectators – than sports. On May 1, the League of American Wheelmen held its first national meeting at Newport, R. I. There, 160 bicyclists representing 31 clubs from all over the United States held a three-day series of races culminating in a grand parade. The participants wore red, white, and blue racing caps with ties and armbands to match. In September, sports lovers witnessed the first national tennis tournament at New Brighton on New York City's Staten Island, where 23 players entered the singles competition. A $100 silver cup from Tiffany's was the prize. In November, the National Rifle Association voted an honorary membership to one G. Ligowsky of Cincinnati, Ohio; he had patented a device that catapulted clay pigeon targets skyward.

Bullfighting was introduced in the United States as a sport on August 14. About 3,000 persons assembled at what is now 116th Street and Sixth Avenue in New York City to watch six colorfully clad matadors bait the bulls. The venture was later dropped, however, because of a lack of customers and adverse reactions from both the press and the pulpit. Ministers thundered against the sport, deploring it as displaying a "love of cruelty inherent in the human race." Henry Ward Beecher, a Protestant minister, quoted France's Duc de La Rochefoucauld in one of his sermons: "There is something in the misfortunes of others," the duke had written, "that is not entirely displeasing to us. Cruel words, like cruel deeds, satisfy the secret malice in us all."

Cruel words, cruel deeds, and especially malice might be said to have characterized the U. S. presidential race in 1880. Scandalous rumors sul-

The Democratic Party convenes in Cincinnati in 1880; Republican presidential nominee Garfield greets voters; Verdi conducts Aida in Paris Opéra house.

lied the reputations of both major party candidates. A forged letter, allegedly written by Republican Party nominee James A. Garfield, in favor of the importation of cheap Chinese labor was widely circulated in the Democratic Party press. It was an explosive issue. Garfield denied authorship. An attempt was made to link him to the recent Credit Mobilier financial scandal, but it too failed. The Democratic Party candidate, General Winfield Scott Hancock, fared no better. Stories circulated that he had been holding two black female house-servants in virtual peonage for years. The servants refuted the charges. Nor did the candidates of the lesser political parties escape. The Prohibition Party candidate—Joshua N. Osgood—allegedly drank two bottles of Kentucky rye whiskey every day. Ludicrous charges flew, including a Democratic Party charge that federal officeholders were being assessed by the incumbent Republicans to contribute to the Republican Party's campaign funds.

The press maintained, for the most part, a pox-on-both-your-houses attitude. "The country is called to witness today," editorial-ized *Leslie's,* "the extraordinary spectacle of [a Republican] party which has lost the art of administering free government by the methods which commend themselves to popular approval and [a Democratic] party which has lost the art of educating the people into a ripeness for the measures seen to be essential for a restoration of civil concord, of financial security, and of economical justice. Hence it is that the politics of the hour revolve so largely in the sphere of negations." Garfield emerged the winner, with 214 electoral votes to 155 for Hancock.

In post-election interviews, two of the defeated candidates—Hancock and Osgood—cried foul. They blamed their defeats on prejudicial reporting by the press, whose news columns reflected "a serious falling off in the authenticity of the news they purvey to their readers and reflect the biased opinions of the editors and their acceptance as gospel truth of the most scurrilous assumptions." *Leslie's* acknowledged the charges, but it insisted that although "the power of the press may sometimes be abused it is more often beneficial in redressing wrongs." One such benefice in 1880 involved the case of a rent-gouging English land agent representing an absentee landlord in Ireland's County Mayo. On September 24, the Irish Land League ordered its members in Mayo to refuse to perform any services or even sell any goods to the agent—Captain Charles Boycott. British newspapers reported the story; *Leslie's* and other U.S. newspapers reprinted it. More stories followed. By year's end, a local affair had become an international cause célèbre. Boycott's name was known throughout the English-speaking world.

A hundred years later, the names of the losing presidential candi-dates had become the dust of history. But the word *boycott* and its power to redress wrongs was an enduring tribute to the power of the press, which had created it in 1880.

The Year
on File

1975
1976
1977
1978
1979
1980

Contributors to THE WORLD BOOK YEAR BOOK report on the major developments of 1980. The contributors' names appear at the end of the articles they have written, and a complete roster of contributors, listing their professional affiliations and the articles they have written, is on pages 6 and 7.

Articles in this section are arranged alphabetically by subject matter. In most cases, the article titles are the same as those of the articles in THE WORLD BOOK ENCYCLOPEDIA that they update. The numerous cross references (in **bold type**) guide the reader to a subject or information that may be in some other article or that may appear under an alternative title. "See" and "See also" cross references appear within and at the end of articles to direct the reader to related information elsewhere in THE YEAR BOOK. "In WORLD BOOK, see" references point the reader to articles in the encyclopedia that provide background information to the year's events reported in THE YEAR BOOK.

See "Dog," page 287.

ADVERTISING

ADVERTISING played a role in and was affected by the biggest news topics of 1980 — recession, inflation, and the United States presidential election. The recession was less severe than some economists had predicted, and wholesale cuts in advertising budgets were few and far between. Inflation added to the cost of advertising, as it did to the cost of everything else. And the election required that presidential candidates and others spend enormous amounts of money for advertising in all media, particularly in television.

Despite the recession, final advertising expenditures in the United States in 1979 amounted to an estimated $55 billion, up more than 10 per cent over 1978, according to the annual study that Robert J. Coen, senior vice-president of McCann-Erickson Worldwide, conducts. World advertising expenditures matched the U.S. figure for the first time, also totaling $55 billion.

Advertising Agencies, both in the United States and abroad, generally had a good year in 1979. Agencies in the United States reported to *Advertising Age* that their gross income was up 18.5 per cent to $4.1 billion. The leader once again was J. Walter Thompson Company in New York City, with $253.9 million in gross worldwide income, followed by McCann-Erickson, with $250.4 million, and Young and Rubicam Incorporated, with $247.6-

million. American advertising agencies continued to expand into other parts of the world, particularly Latin America and the Far East, including the People's Republic of China.

The 100 largest U.S. advertisers boosted their advertising spending in 1980 by 11.5 per cent to a record $11.7 billion. The leader again was Procter and Gamble Company, with $614.9 million.

The Cable News Network, which offered 24-hour satellite-beamed news coverage, went into operation on June 1. Its owner, Ted Turner, best known as a yachtsman and owner of the Atlanta Braves baseball team and the Atlanta Hawks basketball team, invested more than $30 million in the project. Cable television was much in the news all year as more and more U.S. homes were equipped to receive cable programs. Some cable systems carried advertising or planned to carry it, while others hoped to make their income from monthly subscription fees.

Fall Television Fare changed drastically in 1980 because of a strike by members of the Screen Actors Guild and the American Federation of Television and Radio Artists. The unions called the strike when only a few of the fall shows had been produced, so instead of a "new season," viewers saw reruns and a few specials. The strike was settled on September 25, and by mid-November

Billboard advertising of once-forbidden beauty products blossoms in Peking, China, in March. The English text is meant to attract foreign business.

172

most of the postponed programs were airing their season premières (see TELEVISION).

According to a survey by *Advertising Age*, the television shows that charged the highest advertising rates were "M*A*S*H," "60 Minutes," and "Dallas," all of which cost an advertiser approximately $150,000 per 30-second commercial. After piquing interest with preseason publicity, CBS Inc. raised its asking price to $200,000 or more per spot for the November 21 "Dallas" episode, on which viewers learned who really shot J.R.

The New York Times, *The Washington Post*, and nine other newspapers joined an electronic news service in June. Each evening, the newspapers supplied their entire editorial content to a computerized information service in Columbus, Ohio. Persons owning a Videotex system, a television set, and a telephone could receive the service electronically for a time-sharing fee of about $5 per hour.

Callbacks and Giveaways. The Procter and Gamble Company abruptly halted all advertising for its Rely tampons in September after the U.S. Centers for Disease Control in Atlanta, Ga., released a study linking Rely to a sometimes fatal bacterial infection called *toxic shock syndrome*. In addition to halting all advertising for the product, the manufacturer ran a four-week print and broadcast ad campaign urging women to return Rely tampons for a refund. Tampax Incorporated, another maker of feminine hygiene products, also used ads to educate consumers about toxic shock syndrome and its link to tampons. Other manufacturers attached cautionary labels to packages of their tampons.

United Airlines, the major U.S. air carrier, suffered along with smaller airlines in 1980. Soaring fuel costs led to ever-increasing fare hikes, and competition for passengers became so fierce that it brought on a new merchandising age of sweepstakes, giveaways, and other promotional efforts. The battle began in April when United offered 10,000 free trips to passengers who played its "Take-Off" game.

Seductive Advertising became more outspoken than ever. In what *The Wall Street Journal* called "the year of the leer," purveyors of products ranging from avocados to designer jeans turned to leggy young women in suggestive poses to entice buyers. Men, too, appeared as "sex objects" on Americans' home screens, notably in an ad for a men's cologne that, its manufacturers admitted, would not have been shown even five years ago. Occasionally, the public decided it had had enough. For example, the Regional Transportation Authority in Chicago received so many complaints in September about ads for jeans that were plastered on its buses that the offending ads went back into the corporate closet.   Jarlath J. Graham

In WORLD BOOK, see ADVERTISING.

AFGHANISTAN. The Russian invasion in December 1979 to support the government of Revolutionary Council President and Prime Minister Babrak Karmal brought all-out war to Afghanistan in 1980 on a scale unequaled in the world since the Vietnam War (see Close-Up). As the Soviet build-up reached 80,000 to 90,000 troops, supported by tanks, jet aircraft, and deadly helicopter gunships, upwards of 100 Afghan groups waged fierce guerrilla warfare against the invaders. More than half of the 85,000-man Afghan Army defected, helping the guerrilla cause, as did the rugged terrain.

Despite their enormous superiority in numbers and modern equipment, the Russians were able to control only the main roads and major cities. Soviet casualties averaged hundreds a week, reaching 6,000 by November, though the Afghan government's ban on foreign correspondents and the exaggerated claims of the guerrillas made it difficult to get an accurate assessment.

What did become clear was the effect of the invasion on the civilian population. Soviet bomb and rocket attacks on villages suspected of aiding the guerrillas caused heavy casualties. With their villages in ruins, hundreds of thousands of Afghans fled to neighboring Pakistan. By May, 800,000 refugees were crammed into 80 tent cities hastily set up by the United Nations (UN).

With weapons as varied as their clothing,
a band of Afghan guerrillas assembles near
Herat, Afghanistan's third largest city.

Russia Moves South

While invading Russian soldiers fanned out over Afghanistan's rugged countryside on Jan. 1, 1980, an Afghan government broadcast on Radio Kabul harshly condemned "the present aggressive actions of the enemies of Afghanistan." But the broadcast did not refer to the Russians. It was directed against Afghan tribesmen who were resisting the invaders as they had resisted the pro-Russian government since it took power in April 1978.

The army had set up a Revolutionary Council to govern the country and chose a Marxist civilian, Noor Mohammad Taraki, as president and prime minister. But Muslim tribal groups opposed Taraki's leftist views, which clashed with their religious beliefs and tribal customs, and they resented his close cooperation with Russia. So groups of Afghan tribesmen began fighting the Taraki regime from a base in Pakistan, 25 miles (40 kilometers) from historic Khyber Pass on Afghanistan's eastern border. The tribesmen's fierce independence prevented them from organizing under one leader, but it sustained them in battles against the 85,000-man Afghan army.

The Revolutionary Council further antagonized the tribesmen in March 1979 by appointing Foreign Minister Hafizullah Amin as prime minister, with Taraki remaining as president. An ardent Marxist, Amin carried out unpopular land-reform and literacy programs.

Rebel forces picked away at the army, and by June, the Afghan army was crumbling. Russian diplomats advised the government to slow the pace of leftist reform in order to increase its popularity. But Taraki was ousted on September 16, and the radical Amin assumed complete control. By October, rebel forces operated freely in half of the country.

Then 6,000 Russian troops were flown into Afghanistan on December 27, and Amin was executed. Installed in his place was Babrak Karmal, who had been living in exile in eastern Europe. Amin and Taraki had been members of the *Khalq* (Masses) Party, while Karmal was in the rival *Parcham* (Flag) group.

United States President Jimmy Carter said on Jan. 4, 1980, that an Afghanistan occupied by the Russians "threatens both Iran and Pakistan and is a stepping stone to possible control over much of the world's oil supplies."

Carter halted shipment of 18.7 million short tons (17 million metric tons) of grain to Russia, suspended the sale to Russia of high-technology equipment, and announced that the United States would boycott the 1980 Summer Olympics in Moscow.

The United States also offered to help Pakistan by providing $400 million in economic aid and defensive weapons. Pakistan refused the offer.

The European Community (Common Market) suspended export subsidies and stopped selling grain and dairy products to Russia. Canada and Australia said that they would not make up any grain-import shortfall that resulted from the U.S. embargo, Great Britain announced that it would allow a credit agreement to lapse, and New Zealand reduced the number of Russian boats permitted to fish in its waters.

In February, Carter issued a draft-registration plan. "Our objective is plain," he declared. "To deter Russian aggression." Russia, however, insisted that its troops were not aggressors but were in Afghanistan to support a legitimate revolutionary government, and that the rebels and those who helped them were the aggressors.

By February, there were 70,000 Russian troops in Afghanistan. By mid-May, about 800,000 Afghans had fled to Pakistan and another 100,000 were in Iran. Russians were operating Afghan government offices and utilities, and were doing most of the fighting. More than half of the Afghan army had defected.

Karmal tightened his control in July by dismissing members of the Khalq faction from government posts in favor of his Parcham allies. By the end of 1980, Karmal was in firm control. Tribesmen continued to harass the Russians, but Radio Kabul could report that 1980 had been a bad year for the "enemies of Afghanistan."　　　Jay Myers

Russian soldier

Civilian resistance was strong in the cities. Strikes and demonstrations hit Kabul, the capital, in February and again in May, and were suppressed by Russian shows of force. Most Afghans opposed the invaders, and widespread murders made even cities unsafe for Russians.

The Afghan guerrilla groups received little outside aid despite international condemnation of the Soviet invasion, which culminated in a resolution of censure in the UN General Assembly, approved on January 14 by a 104-18 vote. Pakistan provided refugee aid and moral support, while a trickle of arms flowed in from other sources.

Rebel Disunity posed the major problem for the guerrillas. The only thing many of the guerrillas had in common was their hatred of the atheistic Russians. An agreement among the six major groups to form an Islamic Alliance for the Liberation of Afghanistan, reached in January in Peshawar, Pakistan, produced little coordination.

A more positive step toward unity was taken in May with the convening in Peshawar of a *Loya Jirga*, the traditional Afghan tribal assembly. Some 1,000 delegates – representing the various Afghan tribes, ethnic groups, and urban and rural leaders – agreed to form an Afghan government-in-exile. Its goals were the overthrow of the Karmal regime and establishment of an Islamic republic.

The presence of many *mullahs* (religious leaders) and *pirs* (holy men) lent an air of Islamic sanctity. A Revolution Council dominated by the two major factions, the Liberation Front and the United Islamic Revolution Front, was established.

The Karmal Government tried in a number of ways to shed its Communist image and win popular support. The red Afghan flag was changed to one predominantly green, the color of Islam, in January. Karmal's radio broadcasts and speeches were given in Dari, the language of the Tajiks, second-largest Afghan ethnic group. Socialist slogans and photographs of public leaders were removed from public buildings in accordance with the Islamic prohibition on public images. But the regime remained committed to building a socialist state. The 1980-1984 five-year plan, introduced in March, was modeled on Russian plans.

Internal Quarrels damaged what little credibility the government held with the people. Violent rivalry between the *Khalq* (Masses) faction and Karmal's *Parcham* (Flag) faction of the ruling Peoples' Democratic Party led to the murder of 70 to 75 officials of both factions. Karmal reorganized the government on July 22, replacing Khalq ministers with his own appointees.   William Spencer

See also ASIA (Facts in Brief Table). In WORLD BOOK, see AFGHANISTAN.

Jet cargo planes from the Soviet Union unload military supplies at Kabul airport as Russia flies in materiel to support the Afghan invasion.

AFRICA

The end of the colonial era drew closer as Zimbabwe, formerly Rhodesia, became independent on April 18, 1980. Only one African territory – Namibia (South West Africa), administered by South Africa – remained a colony. Although the progress of African states toward self-determination had often seemed long and halting, it had been fairly swift when viewed through a historical perspective. Some 40 African nations had gained political independence within 20 years.

Strong ethnic and religious rivalries were still very much in evidence in 1980, however, fueling civil strife and coups d'état. Armed rebellions turned parts of Angola, Chad, and Ethiopia into war zones, and military leaders toppled governments in Guinea-Bissau, Liberia, and Upper Volta.

Political and economic problems seemed interrelated as young African governments struggled to raise their nations' standards of living and to develop favorable balances of trade. Even oil-rich Nigeria encountered difficulties (see NIGERIA).

Independence for Zimbabwe. The nation's long struggle for independence under black-majority rule came to an end on April 18, when Great Britain handed over power to a government headed by Robert Mugabe. As Rhodesia, it had known a form of independence once before, when leaders of its white-minority government had unilaterally declared the territory independent of Great Britain in November 1965. However, black nationalists within the country and most other governments refused to accept the white-minority government.

Black guerrillas began armed opposition in 1972, and by the end of 1979, at least 25,000 persons had been killed in civil war. With the help of Great Britain and other foreign mediators, black and white Zimbabwean leaders agreed in December 1979 to a cease-fire, a temporary resumption of British rule, and parliamentary elections. In the parliamentary elections, held from Feb. 27 to 29, 1980, guerrilla leader Mugabe's party won a majority of the seats, and he became prime minister. See ZIMBABWE.

Namibia's Quest. In Namibia also, whites are in the minority, comprising only about 10 per cent of the population. Black nationalists fear that South Africa is attempting to turn power over to an independent government dominated by whites. Those fears were strengthened on July 1 when

Zimbabwe's prime minister, Robert Mugabe, and President Canaan Banana embrace during ceremonies marking the nation's independence in April.

South Africa permitted a white-led coalition of parties to form a Council of Ministers for the territory, taking over some administrative responsibilities formerly held by South African government departments.

The United Nations (UN) and Western governments continued efforts to achieve a form of independence for Namibia preceded by fair elections in which all major political parties participate. Namibia's most important black nationalist party, the South West Africa People's Organization (SWAPO), refused to take part in elections unless they were supervised by the UN. South Africa balked at that condition, objecting in August that the UN was likely to favor SWAPO in its supervision of elections. See NAMIBIA.

In South Africa, a white minority comprising about 17 per cent of the population controls the government and most of the country's economy. About 71 per cent of the people are black, while the remaining 12 per cent are of Asian or mixed-race backgrounds. The white government announced policy changes to improve conditions for blacks in 1980. For the first time, public education will be compulsory for all black children, and blacks working in cities will have greater freedom of movement. However, many black leaders continued to work for more fundamental changes, including the elimination of *apartheid*, the country's system of racial segregation.

The white government also conceded the need to consult formally with nonwhites on constitutional changes. It proposed a council representing whites, Asians, and persons of mixed race to deliberate on proposals to change the country's Constitution. Plans for a separate council for blacks were dropped after blacks protested being excluded from the first group. See SOUTH AFRICA.

Civil Wars persisted in Angola, Chad, and Ethiopia. In Angola, the rebel National Union for the Total Independence of Angola (UNITA) movement continued to control much of the countryside in the southeastern section of the country. It drew most of its support from the Ovimbundu people who live in that region and comprise about 40 per cent of Angola's population. The Marxist central government has been supported militarily by Communist bloc countries, especially Russia and Cuba. As of mid-1980, an estimated 20,000 Cuban troops were stationed in Angola. See ANGOLA.

In Chad, Christian groups fought against Muslim government forces. Neighboring Libya intervened militarily in November on behalf of the government, capturing the capital city and forcing a cease-fire. See CHAD.

Secessionist rebellions persisted in two regions of Ethiopia – Eritrea along the Red Sea in the north and the Ogaden area bordering on Somalia in the southeast. The 18-year-old Eritrean struggle to

Facts in Brief on African Political Units

Country	Population	Government	Monetary Unit*	Foreign Trade (million U.S. $) Exports†	Imports†
Algeria	20,315,000	President Chadli Bendjedid; Prime Minister Mohamed Ben Ahmed Abdelghani	dinar (3.7 = $1)	6,316	8,682
Angola	6,925,000	President Jose Eduardo dos Santos	kwanza (52.7 = $1)	382	464
Benin	3,656,000	President Mathieu Kerekou	CFA franc (205 = $1)	26	267
Bophuthatswana	1,719,000	President Lucas J. K. Mangope	rand (1 = $1.33)	no statistics available	
Botswana	799,000	President Quett K. J. Masire	pula (1 = $1.32)	448	531
Burundi	4,380,000	President Jean-Baptiste Bagaza	franc (83 = $1)	105	153
Cameroon	8,498,000	President Ahmadou Ahidjo; Prime Minister Paul Biya	CFA franc (205 = $1)	1,129	1,271
Cape Verde	330,000	President Aristides Pereira; Prime Minister Pedro Pires	escudo (52.7 = $1)	2	25
Central African Republic	2,512,000	President David Dacko; Prime Minister Jean-Pierre Le Bouder	CFA franc (205 = $1)	72	57
Chad	4,561,000	President Goukouni Weddeye	CFA franc (205 = $1)	59	118
Comoros	418,000	President Ahmed Abdallah; Prime Minister Salim Ben Ali	CFA franc (205 = $1)	9	11
Congo	1,602,000	President Denis Sassou-Nguesso; Prime Minister Louis-Sylvain Goma	CFA franc (205 = $1)	139	261
Djibouti	250,000	President Hassan Gouled Aptidon; Prime Minister Barkat Gourad Hamadou	franc (166 = $1)	5	72
Egypt	42,636,000	President & Prime Minister Anwar el-Sadat; Vice-President Mohamed Hosni Moubarek	pound (1 = $1.45)	1,840	3,837
Equatorial Guinea	346,000	President Obiang Nguema Mbasogo	ekuele (67 = $1)	36	12
Ethiopia	31,679,000	Provisional Military Government Chairman Mengistu Haile-Mariam	birr (2.1 = $1)	423	576
Gabon	1,048,000	President Omar Bongo; Prime Minister Leon Mebiame	CFA franc (205 = $1)	1,307	589
Gambia	613,000	President Sir Dawda Kairaba Jawara	dalasi (1.6 = $1)	58	141
Ghana	11,698,000	President Hilla Limann	cedi (2.7 = $1)	965	1,398
Guinea	5,128,000	President Ahmed Sekou Toure; Prime Minister Lansana Beavogui	syli (15.8 = $1)	334	272
Guinea-Bissau	580,000	Revolutionary Council President Joao Bernardo Vieira; Vice-President Victor Saude Maria	peso (33.5 = $1)	11	50
Ivory Coast	7,768,000	President Felix Houphouet-Boigny	CFA franc (205 = $1)	2,516	2,488
Kenya	16,516,000	President Daniel T. arap Moi	shilling (7.2 = $1)	1,062	1,535
Lesotho	1,348,000	King Moshoeshoe II; Prime Minister Leabua Jonathan	rand (1 = $1.33)	35	270
Liberia	1,879,000	Head of State Samuel K. Doe	dollar (1 = $1)	537	507
Libya	3,052,000	Leader of the Revolution Muammar Muhammad al-Qadhafi; General People's Congress Secretary General Abd al-Ati al-Ubaydi; General People's Committee Chairman (Prime Minister) Jadallah Azzuz al-Talhi	dinar (1 = $3.42)	9,907	4,602
Madagascar	9,589,000	President Didier Ratsiraka; Prime Minister Desire Rakotoarijaona	franc (205 = $1)	386	443

Country	Population	Government	Monetary Unit*	Foreign Trade (million U.S. $) Exports†	Imports†
Malawi	6,268,000	President H. Kamuzu Banda	kwacha (1 = $1.26)	233	400
Mali	6,541,000	President Moussa Traore	franc (410 = $1)	107	219
Mauritania	1,647,000	President & Prime Minister Mohamed Khouna Ould Haidalla	ouguiya (45.9 = $1)	148	259
Mauritius	957,000	Governor General Sir Dayendranath Burrenchobay; Prime Minister Sir Seewoosagur Ramgoolam	rupee (7.6 = $1)	326	501
Morocco	20,368,000	King Hassan II; Prime Minister Maati Bouabid	dirham (4 = $1)	1,925	3,807
Mozambique	10,600,000	President Samora Moises Machel	metical (52.7 = $1)	150	495
Namibia (South West Africa)	1,027,000	Administrator-General D. J. Hough	rand (1 = $1.33)	no statistics available	
Niger	5,405,000	Supreme Military Council President Seyni Kountche	CFA franc (205 = $1)	128	122
Nigeria	74,409,000	President Shehu Shagari	naira (1 = $1.96)	9,483	12,857
Rwanda	4,975,000	President Juvenal Habyarimana	franc (88.5 = $1)	70	179
São Tomé & Príncipe	87,000	President Manuel Pinto da Costa	dobra (34.5 = $1)	23	14
Senegal	5,743,000	President Abdou Diouf; Prime Minister Habib Thiam	CFA franc (205 = $1)	623	762
Seychelles	69,000	President France Albert Rene	rupee (6.4 = $1)	13	51
Sierra Leone	3,845,000	President Siaka Stevens	leone (1 = $1)	161	278
Somalia	3,731,000	President Mohamed Siad Barre	shilling (6.8 = $1)	107	241
South Africa	29,563,000	President Marais Viljoen; Prime Minister Pieter Willem Botha	rand (1 = $1.33)	10,385	6,382
Sudan	19,152,000	President & Prime Minister Gaafar Mohamed Nimeiri	pound (1 = $2.02)	533	1,198
Swaziland	546,000	King Sobhuza II; Prime Minister Prince Mabandla Dlamini	lilangeni (1 = $1.34)	197	312
Tanzania	17,950,000	President Julius K. Nyerere; Prime Minister Cleopa David Msuya	shilling (8.1 = $1)	457	1,117
Togo	2,602,000	President Gnassingbe Eyadema	CFA franc (205 = $1)	241	448
Transkei	5,916,000	President Kaiser Matanzima	rand (1 = $1.33)	no statistics available	
Tunisia	6,912,000	President Habib Bourguiba; Prime Minister Mohamed Mzali	dinar (1 = $2.49)	1,690	2,830
Uganda	14,121,000	President Milton Obote	shilling (7.3 = $1)	350	187
Upper Volta	7,084,000	Chief of State Saye Zerbo	CFA franc (205 = $1)	42	191
Venda	320,000	President Patrick Mphephu	rand (1 = $1.33)	no statistics available	
Zaire	29,501,000	President Mobutu Sese Seko; Prime Minister Nguza Karl-I-Bond	zaire (2.8 = $1)	1,171	523
Zambia	6,610,000	President Kenneth David Kaunda; Prime Minister Daniel Lisulo	kwacha (1 = $1.33)	853	630
Zimbabwe	7,734,000	President Canaan Banana; Prime Minister Robert Mugabe	dollar (1 = $1.60)	1,154	937

*Exchange rates as of Dec. 1, 1980. †Latest available data.

establish a Muslim state, separate from Christian Ethiopia, was hampered by neighboring Sudan's decision to close Eritrean rebel bases within its borders. Sudanese President and Prime Minister Gaafar Mohamed Nimeiri favored negotiations rather than a continuation of the civil war. See SUDAN.

Somali-speaking rebels in the Ogaden fought to detach their area from Ethiopia and to join it to neighboring Somalia. They were aided by Somalian military supplies and troops. See SOMALIA.

An estimated 13,000 Cuban troops and about 1,000 Russian military advisers assisted Ethiopia in the conflict. Large numbers of Soviet and Cuban forces had been in Ethiopia since late 1977.

Military Coups deposed governments in Liberia, Guinea-Bissau, and Upper Volta. On April 12, a group of noncommissioned officers led by Master Sergeant Samuel K. Doe killed Liberia's President William R. Tolbert, Jr., and established a new military government. The coup ended the long reign of the True Whig Party, which had controlled Liberia's government for more than 100 years. Despite protests from other African nations, Doe's government tried and executed 13 ousted officials. See LIBERIA.

In Guinea-Bissau, military officers overthrew the government of President Luis de Almeida

Cabral on November 14. Cabral had headed that country since it became independent from Portugal in 1974. He and several of his aides were reported to be under arrest. The new government was headed by Major Joao Bernardo Vieira, prime minister under Cabral.

Upper Volta's President Aboubakar Sangoule Lamizana was deposed on November 25. One of Africa's few presidents to be chosen in a contested election, Lamizana was ousted by military units led by Colonel Saye Zerbo, a former foreign minister and the commander of armed forces stationed in the capital.

Peaceful Transitions. In contrast, leadership changed peacefully in both Botswana and Tanzania. Botswana's president, Sir Seretse M. Khama, who had led Botswana since it gained its independence from Britain in 1966, died of cancer on July 13. The National Assembly chose Vice-President Quett K. J. Masire as his successor.

Tanzania held parliamentary and presidential elections on October 26. More than half of the incumbent legislators were defeated. President Julius K. Nyerere, re-elected to a fourth 5-year term, announced that he would not seek a fifth term. Ivory Coast also held peaceful elections in November. President Leopold Sedar Senghor of Senegal resigned on December 31, after 20 years in office.

In a symbolic meeting of two cultures, tribal dancers welcome Pope John Paul II to Zaire as he begins a six-nation good-will tour of Africa in May.

Military Pacts. The United States concluded military-base agreements with two African nations. In August, the United States pledged to provide at least $40 million in military aid and $5 million in economic aid to Somalia in exchange for the use of two naval and air bases strategically located on the Indian Ocean and the Gulf of Aden.

On June 24, the United States concluded an agreement allowing the use of a military base in Kenya. Kenya agreed to permit the United States to have greater access to air and naval facilities at the Indian Ocean port of Mombasa.

Both accords provide for the United States to use existing facilities rather than build new bases. The United States was expected to use them for refueling and resupplying ships in the Indian Ocean and for planes stationed at the U.S. base on the island of Diego Garcia, southwest of Sri Lanka.

OAU Summit. The 17th annual summit meeting of the Organization of African Unity (OAU) was held from July 1 to 4 in Freetown, Sierra Leone. Delegates to this meeting passed a resolution calling on the United States to hand over the island of Diego Garcia to Mauritius. The United States leased the island from Great Britain in 1976 and is developing a major military base there. However, Mauritius, an island nation in the Indian Ocean, claims Diego Garcia. The OAU resolution termed the U.S. base "a threat to Africa and the concept of a zone of peace in the Indian Ocean."

The OAU meeting failed to agree on the Western Sahara issue. The territory, formerly a colony of Spain known as the Spanish Sahara, is claimed by Morocco. However, the Saharan People's Independence Movement (Polisario), a nationalist movement, wants to establish an independent country to be known as the Sahara Arab Democratic Republic (SADR). Polisario, which receives arms support from Libya and Algeria, asked the OAU to accept the SADR as the organization's 51st member state. Despite the backing of 26 nations, action was postponed because some members, including Morocco, Senegal, and Zaire, threatened to withdraw from the OAU if the SADR was admitted. The members adopted a compromise resolution calling for further OAU mediation between Morocco and the Polisario.

Famine and Refugees. According to the UN World Food Conference, famine conditions occurred in 17 African countries during 1980. Drought afflicted East Africa, killing cattle and damaging crops in Djibouti, Ethiopia, Sudan, Uganda, Kenya, Somalia, and Tanzania. Breakdowns in the distribution of food worsened the situation. Bandits pillaged scarce food supplies in Kenya, and rebellious soldiers attacked convoys bearing emergency rations in Uganda. Among the hardest-hit areas was the Karamoja district of northern Uganda. By June, about 400,000 persons were threatened with starvation, with an estimated 400 dying each day from starvation or related diseases. The Sahel, an area along the Sahara stretching from Mauritania and Senegal on the west to Chad on the east, was also affected by drought and famine.

More than 1.5 million refugees from the civil war in southeastern Ethiopia fled to neighboring Somalia. In October, more than 840,000 were being cared for in refugee camps there. However, food supplies were inadequate, in part because of a shortage of vehicle fuel needed to truck food to the camps. Relief organizations reported difficulties in raising money for emergency work in Somalia and other parts of East Africa. The public response was not as generous as in the case of the Vietnamese "boat people" and the Cambodian refugees.

Pope John Paul II visited six African countries – Zaire, the Congo, Ghana, Ivory Coast, Upper Volta, and Kenya – in a 10-day tour that began on May 2. He spoke against racial discrimination and the abuse of governmental authority.   J. Dixon Esseks

In WORLD BOOK, see AFRICA.

AGRICULTURE. See FARM AND FARMING.

AIR FORCE. See ARMED FORCES.

AIR POLLUTION. See ENVIRONMENT.

AIRPORT. See AVIATION.

ALABAMA. See STATE GOVERNMENT.

ALASKA. See STATE GOVERNMENT.

ALBANIA improved economic relations with Yugoslavia in 1980 but strongly condemned Russia's invasion of Afghanistan as unwarranted aggression and as a possible precedent for a thrust into the Balkans. The Communist Party daily newspaper *Zeri i Popullit* (*Voice of the People*) said in January that if Yugoslavia's independence were threatened, Albania and Yugoslavia would fight side by side as they had against Germany during World War II.

Albania's Foreign Trade Minister Nedin Hoxha visited Yugoslavia in July to sign a long-term trade agreement. The visit was the first by a senior Albanian official in more than 30 years. Trade with Yugoslavia grew from $53.6 million to more than $80 million in 1980, and was expected to reach $720 million in the five-year period ending in 1985.

Zeri i Popullit criticized China in September for adopting certain features of Yugoslavia's political system. Albania also charged that the strikes in Poland were "inspired and manipulated" by the West, the Roman Catholic Church, and "internal reactionaries."

Albania launched a five-year plan in June that called for an increase of 40 per cent in industrial production. The plan gave priority to mining and oil drilling and projected a 41 per cent boost in agricultural output.   Chris Cviic

See also EUROPE (Facts in Brief Table). In WORLD BOOK, see ALBANIA.

ALBERTA. Canada's largest oil-producing province armed itself in 1980 for another round in the struggle with the federal government in Ottawa, Ont., over the price and taxation of its vast oil resources. The Alberta legislature approved a law on May 23 permitting the cabinet to set maximum monthly production levels from provincially owned oil reserves, which hold about 85 per cent of Alberta's oil. Thus, the provincial cabinet could decide to leave Alberta's oil in the ground if it could not manage to reach agreement with Ottawa on a price.

Western Canada's largest compressor station, at Brooks, which pumped 3 billion cubic feet (85 million cubic meters) of gas per day into the Transcanada Pipelines long-distance network, was destroyed by explosion and fire on February 26. An experimental greenhouse was also destroyed.

Record spending and conservative estimates of revenue from oil royalties did not prevent Alberta from registering further budget surpluses in 1980. A surplus of $3.1 billion in the general revenue fund was projected when the budget was presented on April 2. It would add to accumulations from previous years, as well as to the March 1981 sum of $8.7 billion in the Alberta Heritage Savings Trust Fund, a public endowment that receives 30 per cent of provincial resource revenues.   David M. L. Farr

See also CANADA. In WORLD BOOK, see ALBERTA.

The 13-member Organization of Petroleum Exporting Countries, meeting in Algiers in June, sets a new $37-per-barrel oil ceiling.

ALGERIA. President Chadli Bendjedid cemented his authority as Algeria's leader and began to shape new policies of his own during 1980, his second year in office. A special congress of the ruling National Liberation Front (FLN) in June approved his appointees for a new FLN political bureau. The bureau included representatives of factions whose rivalries had hampered government efficiency since the death of President Houari Boumediene in December 1978. In July, Bendjedid named a new Cabinet for day-to-day government operations. It was dominated by senior army commanders. The actions signaled the end of factionalism and the revival of army influence to a degree not seen since the 1965 revolution that brought Boumediene to power.

In October, Bendjedid pardoned former President Ahmed ben Bella, who had been in prison or under house arrest since 1965.

Ethnic Violence flared for the first time in the Boumediene-Bendjedid era. In January, Arabic-speaking students at Algiers University went on strike, alleging favoritism for French-speaking students. The government agreed to give both groups equal treatment.

A more serious situation developed in April in the Berber-speaking region of Kabylia. Students protesting a ban on Berber poetry and cultural programs at Tizi Ouzou University clashed violently with police on April 19, causing hundreds of casualties. Army units were called in to restore order after strikes shut down the entire region. A military court sentenced 21 students to six-month jail terms for sedition.

Economic Policy was changed in June, when the FLN congress approved Bendjedid's new program designed to reduce Algeria's dependence on Western aid and imports and to concentrate on domestic development. The program was incorporated into the 1980-1984 five-year plan approved by the National Assembly at the same time. The program emphasizes development of alternative energy resources and improvement of transportation, housing, agricultural education, and public health. As a beginning, on July 1 Algeria raised its oil price to $33 per barrel and reduced oil production by 3 per cent with a further 10 per cent cut introduced on October 1. The 1980 budget of $13 billion included an increase in the daily minimum wages for agricultural workers.

On October 10, two earthquakes devastated the city of El Asnam, 100 miles (160 kilometers) southwest of Algiers. At least 3,000 persons died, and about 400,000 were left homeless. William Spencer

See also AFRICA (Facts in Brief Table). In WORLD BOOK, see ALGERIA.

AMERICAN LEGION. See COMMUNITY ORGANIZATIONS.

AMERICAN LIBRARY ASSOCIATION (ALA). More than 14,500 librarians, publishers, and friends of libraries met in New York City in June 1980 for the ALA's 99th annual conference, the largest in its history. Preceding the conference, Newton N. Minow, former chairman of the Public Broadcasting Service, moderated a two-day meeting at New York University's Bobst Library on "An Information Agenda for the 1980's." Minow led a group of information scholars, administrators, and scientists in exchanging ideas about how to manage the many challenges implicit in today's technology explosion.

Gene F. Jankowski, president of the CBS Inc. Broadcast Group, addressed the opening session on "Books and Television: A Complementary Relationship." Peggy Sullivan, assistant commissioner for Extension Services at the Chicago Public Library, took office as ALA president. She announced that the theme for her term will be "Libraries and the Pursuit of Happiness."

School Librarians. The American Association of School Librarians held its first national conference in 1980. More than 2,000 school media specialists met in Louisville, Ky., to discuss legislation and funding, education and accountability, and networking and resource sharing. The Public Library Association published *Planning Process for Public Libraries*, a manual to aid libraries in developing services tailored to meet community needs.

National Awards. The Intellectual Freedom Committee won the 1980 Bailey K. Howard-World Book Encyclopedia-ALA Goals Award to finance a national meeting of educators who will study ways to understand censorship problems and strengthen intellectual freedom in the schools. The Committee on the Status of Women in Librarianship and the Office for Library Personnel Advisory Committees won the 1980 J. Morris Jones-World Book Encyclopedia-ALA Goals Award. The award will fund a study of library workers to find salary inequities.

Joan W. Blos, the author of *A Gathering of Days, A New England Girl's Journal 1830-32*, won the 1980 Newbery Medal for the most distinguished contribution to American literature for children. Barbara Cooney, illustrator of *Ox-Cart Man*, won the 1980 Caldecott Medal for the most distinguished American picture book for children. Theodor Geisel, known to millions of children as Dr. Seuss, won the 1980 Laura Ingalls Wilder Award. The award is given every three years to an author or illustrator whose books have made a substantial and lasting contribution to children's literature in the United States.   Margaret Barber

See also CANADIAN LIBRARY ASSOCIATION (CLA); LIBRARY; LITERATURE FOR CHILDREN. In WORLD BOOK, see AMERICAN LIBRARY ASSN.

Theodor Geisel, better known as Dr. Seuss, accepts the Laura Ingalls Wilder Award for his lasting contributions to children's literature.

ANDERSON, JOHN BAYARD (1922-   ), a Republican congressman from Illinois since 1961, became an Independent candidate for President of the United States on April 24, 1980. Anderson withdrew as a Republican presidential candidate after a surprisingly good showing against Ronald Reagan and other party candidates in the early primaries. Anderson received 5.6 million votes, or 7 per cent of those cast, in the November 4 general election. His showing qualified him for a minimum of $4.2-million in federal campaign aid.

Anderson was born in Rockford, Ill., on Feb. 15, 1922. He graduated from the University of Illinois in 1942 and received a law degree from that university in 1946. He earned a master of law degree from Harvard University in 1949. He returned to Rockford to practice law, then joined the United States Foreign Service in 1952, serving with that agency until 1955.

Anderson was elected to Congress in 1960. Initially a staunch conservative, he became an advocate of many traditionally liberal causes. His liberal views in part prompted his break with the basically conservative Republican Party. He chose a Democrat, former Wisconsin Governor Patrick J. Lucey, as his vice-presidential running mate.

Anderson married Keke Machakos in 1953. They have five children.   Beverly Merz

ANDORRA. See EUROPE.

ANGOLA. The government of President Jose Eduardo dos Santos continued its five-year struggle against the National Union for the Total Independence of Angola (UNITA), a political-military movement led by Jonas Savimbi, throughout 1980. Although some 15,000 to 20,000 Cuban troops assisted the government, UNITA guerrilla attacks kept the Benguela railway, the country's most important transportation line, closed most of the year. UNITA forces also waged war in urban areas, including the major cities of Lobito and Huambo, and captured the southern border town of Cuango on April 14.

Angola also came under siege from some 3,000 South African military forces in June in a three-week raid designed to capture arms and destroy bases used by guerrillas fighting against South African rule in neighboring Namibia. The Angolan press reported that South African forces killed more than 300 civilians and wounded more than 250 civilians in this foray. South Africa denied these charges, claiming that soldiers had warned civilians prior to their attacks. However, the United Nations Security Council censured South Africa for aggression. See NAMIBIA.　　　J. Dixon Esseks

See also AFRICA (Facts in Brief Table). In WORLD BOOK, see ANGOLA.

ANIMAL. See CAT; CONSERVATION; DOG; ZOOLOGY; ZOOS AND AQUARIUMS.

ANTHROPOLOGY. An ancient ape that lived 30 million years ago may have been the ancestor of apes and man, according to anthropologists Elwyn L. Simons and Richard Kay of Duke University in Durham, N.C. They reported in February 1980 on how they reconstructed *Aegyptopithecus zeuxis* (connecting ape of Egypt). Simons said that *Aegyptopithecus* had a long tail and weighed about 12 pounds (5.5 kilograms).

Simons first found some bone fragments in the 1960s in the Al Fayyum area of Egypt and said they represented ancient apes. But now he has assembled enough bone fragments to provide a comprehensive portrait of what the animal looked like and how it lived. Kay believes that the animal was a vegetarian, eating mostly fruit. Simons and Kay think that *Aegyptopithecus* came just before *Dryopithecus*, which came just before apes and humans.

African Ancestors. A 120,000-year-old cranium – a skull with the jaw missing – from the Laetoli area of Tanzania belonged to a species that may have been a link between *Homo sapiens* – modern man – and older *Homo* species. Physical anthropologists Michael H. Day and C. Magori of St. Thomas Medical School, London, and Mary N. Leakey reported in March that the cranium has a rounded back of the skull, like modern skulls, but also has a thick braincase and prominent ridges over the brows, like more primitive skulls.

In his book *Paleoanthropology* (1980), anthropologist Milford H. Wolpoff of the University of Michigan attempts to produce an overall synthesis of various theories of *hominid* (human) origins. He traces the evolutionary process through several stages.

During the Miocene Epoch, between 14 and 26 million years ago, a drastic environmental change saw the shrinking of East African forests and the emergence of grasslands. Wolpoff says the advantage went to creatures that could handle the powerful chewing required for a diet of seeds, roots, and tubers. The apelike *Ramapithecus*, one of the successful creatures, spread from Africa into Greece, India, and Asia and became diversified.

Wolpoff argues that one line of the *Ramapithecus* species then evolved into the *Australopithecus* species, to include species found in recent years in the Laetoli area by Mary N. Leakey and at Afar, in Ethiopia, by physical anthropologist Donald C. Johanson of the Cleveland Museum of Natural History. Wolpoff acknowledged that this link-up is the most controversial one in his scheme.

By the early Pleistocene Epoch, about 1.75 million years ago, at least two forms of Australopithecines existed. One became increasingly robust and apelike. The other, probably a small form, turned away from eating seeds and roots and began

A sketch shows what anthropologists think *Aegyptopithecus zeuxis* (connecting ape of Egypt) looked like; it lived 30 million years ago.

to get meat in daytime hunting when other predators were resting. Wolpoff says that this *Australopithecus* line led to *Homo erectus*, the first truly human form. Wolpoff's provocative theories should help fuel anthropology's running debate on humanity's origins.

Sex Roles. A number of articles and books on sex roles in societies around the world appeared in 1980. Many such studies challenge traditional theories that label biology as the overwhelming influence in shaping and limiting female roles. They point instead to cultural and historical factors in explaining the status of women.

For example, anthropologists Mona Etienne and Eleanor Leacock maintain that colonization of primitive societies was often responsible for the subjugation of women. In their book *Woman and Colonization: Anthropological Perspectives* (1980), they argue that some early societies featured sexual equality. But when a more developed society conquered a primitive society, men would be commandeered for the military and various forms of hard labor and then gradually take on a superior role. Other anthropologists disagree, however, arguing that some discrimination against women has existed in every society.   Frank G. Vallee

See also ARCHAEOLOGY. In WORLD BOOK, see ANTHROPOLOGY; PREHISTORIC MAN.

AQUARIUM. See ZOOS AND AQUARIUMS.

ARCHAEOLOGY. It seemed clear in 1980 that opportunities for making scientific advances in archaeology are both created and limited by politics, technology, and economic conditions. For example, the political climate in Israel apparently fostered a new and intensive investigation of the remains of ancient Jerusalem. Digging outside the walls of the Old City in an area known as the City of David, a team of Israeli archaeologists led by Yigal Shiloh of the Hebrew University Institute of Archaeology found a large public building that may have been the palace of King Solomon or King David around 1000 B.C.

Researchers long knew about one wall of the building but did not excavate it because they thought it was a fortification wall from a more recent period. But exact dates and relationships to Bible history are not yet available.

This major effort runs counter to the general trend of Near East archaeology, because an influx of oil money and associated increases in labor costs have all but brought to an end the era of great expeditions in the area. Instead, the rapid economic development has spurred new concern for salvage, as archaeologists turn their attention to sites in danger of being destroyed by construction.

In Iraq, for example, teams from eight nations worked hurriedly in an area about to be flooded when a new dam on the Diyala River goes into operation. At several sites, they discovered circular, fortresslike buildings dating to around 3000 B.C. that contribute to our understanding of Mesopotamian architecture. The best-preserved building was unearthed by a joint Danish-United States expedition led by McGuire Gibson of the University of Chicago at Uch Tepe, about halfway between Baghdad and Kirkuk. The walls were preserved to a height of about 10 feet (3 meters) and formed a vault. Such an early example of an arch is remarkable because the ancient Mesopotamians used unbaked mud brick for their buildings, a material thought to be too weak to support an arch.

However, all work in Iraq came to an abrupt halt in September when war broke out between Iran and Iraq. Archaeology in Iran had been more or less stalled since the revolution in January 1979.

Stefano De Caro, resident archaeologist in Pompeii, Italy, reported that the historic excavated city suffered serious damage in the major earthquake that struck southern Italy on November 23. Pompeii, buried by a volcanic eruption in A.D. 79, suffered about 100 major cracks and cave-ins in the quake and was closed to the public.

Mayan Canals. Technology contributed one of the year's most intriguing discoveries. A sophisticated radar imaging system designed for mapping the surface of Venus located an elaborate network of canals in Guatemala. A complex pattern of markings showed up when the radar system was tested for the space program in 1977 and 1978. After interpreting the information on the radar photographs, archaeologists Richard E. W. Adams of Cambridge University in England and Patrick Culbert of the University of Arizona explored the area — now in a dense rain forest — by car and boat. Their observations confirmed that the canals had been dug between 250 B.C. and A.D. 900.

This means that the Maya developed large-scale irrigation works, as did other early complex societies. Impressive irrigation projects were associated with such other early regions as Mesopotamia, Egypt, the Indus Valley, China, and coastal Peru. But until the canals were discovered in Guatemala, archaeologists thought that the Maya stood apart. Their only known irrigation works were modest projects in some highland areas.

The *Pinta* Found? The wreck of a ship off Key West, Fla., may have been the *Pinta*, one of three vessels in Christopher Columbus' expedition to the New World in 1492, according to a document found in October. Treasure hunters found the wreck in 1977, and a newly discovered tax record from Spain linked the ship to Columbus. Archaeologists planned to study the wreck in detail, though it seemed certain that many artifacts had been removed in the three years since the ship was found.   Paul E. Zimansky

In WORLD BOOK, see ARCHAEOLOGY.

ARCHITECTURE

ARCHITECTURE. The American Institute of Architects (AIA) emphasized the crucial importance of energy-saving buildings at its annual meeting in Cincinnati, Ohio, from June 1 to 4, 1980. AIA members heard that because buildings currently consume about 35 per cent of the nation's energy, efficiently designed structural and mechanical systems can improve energy conservation.

United States Secretary of Energy Charles W. Duncan, Jr., told a seminar that he was grateful that AIA supports the department's proposed building energy performance standards. Duncan underscored the belief of many architects when he said that energy conservation "is the cheapest environmentally safe way of getting more energy. Saving energy in buildings should be accomplished by design, not by decree."

One of America's most famous architectural clients, J. Irwin Miller, chairman of the Cummins Engine Company in Columbus, Ind., received a standing ovation following his address to the AIA. Miller has made Columbus a showcase of contemporary architecture by paying the architectural fees for many buildings erected in that town. Without Miller's intervention, the buildings' owners might not have chosen designs by such adventuresome architects as Eero Saarinen and Harry Weese or the firms of Skidmore, Owings & Merrill and Venturi & Rauch.

Miller said the architect actually has just two real clients: the users of the building and the architect's own critical self. Acknowledging the legendary tug of war over design between clients and architects, Miller asserted that the client who pays the bills should be relegated to a secondary position. He asked his AIA audience to consider such questions as: "If you are designing a factory, what kind of place will it be for a worker laboring at one machine for eight hours a day?"

Pittsburgh Renaissance II. Despite the economy's slump, downtown construction in many of the larger U.S. cities, such as Los Angeles, Houston, Chicago, and New York City, boomed during 1980. Pittsburgh was in the midst of a four-year, $1-billion construction splurge, with work underway on three giant, multiuse high-rises and a $480-million subway system. Pittsburgh Mayor Richard S. Caliguiri dubbed the development construction "Renaissance II," a sequel to the city's creation of the Golden Triangle development in the 1950s.

The buildings under construction typify a new wave of downtown commercial high-rise architecture. This generation of structural giants is attempting to accommodate the many shops and restaurants at street level they have invariably displaced. The 54-story, 1.7-million-square-foot (158,000-square-meter) Dravo Building, designed by Welton Beckett Associates, will emphasize retail facilities on its three-block site. The 46-story,

The interior, *top,* and patio, *above,* of a home in Mexico City exemplify the eloquent geometry of Pritzker Architecture Prizewinner Luis Barragán.

1-million-square-foot (92,000-square-meter) One Oxford Centre, designed by Hellmuth, Obata & Kassabaum, will have a five-story base housing various facilities. PPG Industries' 40-story, 1.5-million-square-foot (139,000-square-meter) headquarters building, spread over 5 acres (2 hectares), is to be part of a six-building complex.

Like other cities, Pittsburgh is taking a hard look at some of the other urban-design principles that have prevailed for the past 20 years. For instance, Mayor Caliguiri said the city's recently constructed pedestrian mall would be removed because it had "destroyed" certain retail businesses.

Pritzker Prize. The $100,000 Pritzker Architecture Prize was awarded to Luis Barragán of Mexico City. "We are honoring Barragán for his commitment to architecture as a sublime act of the poetic imagination," said Jay A. Pritzker, chairman of the Chicago-based Hyatt Corporation and president of Hyatt Foundation, which funds the prize. Philip Johnson in 1979 won the first such award, often referred to as the "Nobel Prize of architecture."

The 78-year-old Barragán's designs feature clean, flat, angular walls drenched in vivid colors — reds, blues, pinks, and magentas. His houses are very private, the largest windows always facing quiet, interior gardens. Something of a mystic, Barragán has said, "The concepts of serenity, silence, intimacy, and amazement have nestled in my soul."

Notable New Buildings. The $13-million Helen G. Bonfils Theatre Complex, dedicated on January 7, completes the Denver Center for the Performing Arts. The concrete and glass structure, designed by Connecticut-based architects Kevin Roche and John Dinkeloo, contains three stages and a cinema. A glass-roofed galleria 80 feet (24 meters) high links this building with the 1907 Auditorium Theater and the 1978 Boettcher Concert Hall.

The 48-story Wells Fargo Building in downtown Los Angeles, under construction since February and slated for completion in autumn 1981, was designed by the city's Albert C. Martin & Associates. Its facade, sheathed in metal and reflective blue-green glass, steps back every 11 floors. Canary Island palm trees will shade a street-level plaza, and the building will have a roof heliport.

Architect Helmut Jahn of C. F. Murphy Associates had two large projects underway in downtown Chicago by late autumn. His 40-story One South Wacker Building has a two-tone gray-and-silver glass-curtain wall and six 3-story atriums. Jahn said the design is "reminiscent of the classic architectural style and elegance of the 1920s." The $115-million, 17-story State of Illinois Center is a wedge-shaped structure that features a huge arc slanting inward in a series of three setbacks on its southern face.   Rob Cuscaden

In WORLD BOOK, see ARCHITECTURE.

ARGENTINA. The military government of President Jorge Rafael Videla, irked by United States criticism of its human-rights violations, turned toward Russia in 1980 in developing its trade. Russia became the principal purchaser of Argentine meat. In defiance of the U.S. grain embargo imposed on Russia after the Soviet invasion of Afghanistan, Argentina agreed to supply Russia with 20 million short tons (18 million metric tons) of grain over the next five years and 500,000 short tons (450,000 metric tons) of soybeans.

Among the irritants cited by Argentine officials was a report by the U.S. Department of State in February alleging widespread arbitrary arrests, torture, and summary executions in Argentina since the 1976 military coup brought Videla to power. Two months later, a report by the Organization of American States, prepared with the cooperation of the Argentine government, concluded that "thousands of detainees who have disappeared [in Argentina] . . . may be presumed dead."

International Pressure. With U.S. support, an international campaign to pressure Argentina into ending its harsh handling of dissidents gained momentum. Amnesty International, a human-rights organization, called for an end to repression. A further boost for human rights came when the Nobel Prize for Peace was awarded to Adolfo Pérez Esquivel, a 48-year-old Argentine architect who is head of the Service for Peace and Justice in Latin America. Pérez Esquivel said that his $212,000 in prize money would be used to fight injustice and poverty in Latin America.

The Economy. Meanwhile, the military government continued to follow an economic plan aimed at reducing the role of the state and enhancing the participation of a private sector that was increasingly competitive in international trade.

Major investments made to develop the nation's natural gas reserves included a pipeline across the Strait of Magellan that would bring gas from Tierra del Fuego, at the southern tip of Argentina, to the mainland. There were also sizable new investments in farming and cattle raising, and plans to reclaim a wide green belt around Buenos Aires, which had been lost to farming through haphazard urban growth.

Inflation continued to take its toll. The buying power of the average salary decreased 25 per cent in real terms during the eight months ending in April, while government-decreed wage increases took up only 15 per cent of the slack. The government announced a 20 per cent value-added tax to begin in September to help reduce a growing budget deficit.   Nathan A. Haverstock

See also LATIN AMERICA (Facts in Brief Table).

In WORLD BOOK, see ARGENTINA.

ARIZONA. See STATE GOVERNMENT.

ARKANSAS. See STATE GOVERNMENT.

ARMED FORCES. In the first combat action by United States troops since the 1975 *Mayaguez* incident, U.S. Army and Marine commandos landed in the Iranian desert on April 24, 1980, on a dramatic mission to rescue 52 Americans held hostage for nearly six months in Teheran. Mechanical failures on five of the eight helicopters involved forced cancellation of the operation at the desert rendezvous, however, and the mission failed. In the ensuing withdrawal, eight U.S. servicemen were killed when a helicopter collided with a C-130 cargo plane.

The secret operation, code-named Eagle's Claw, had been planned for months, after diplomatic negotiations to free the hostages had collapsed. It called for a force of 90 specially trained troops to land in the desert and be driven into Teheran by American agents for an assault on the U.S. Embassy.

In an unusually critical assessment of the mission released on August 23, a special Pentagon review panel cited major deficiencies in planning and execution, including poor communications and lines of authority, lack of sufficient helicopters, and a failure by mission planners to submit their plans to cross-examination by senior defense officials. See IRAN; PRESIDENT OF THE UNITED STATES.

Rubble surrounds the gaping, gutted silo of a Titan II missile after an explosion destroyed the missile and damaged its nuclear warhead.

Strategic Developments. The Russian invasion of Afghanistan in December 1979 prompted President Jimmy Carter to ask Congress to postpone consideration of the Strategic Arms Limitations Treaty (SALT II) signed in 1979. Carter pledged to abide by the terms of the treaty if the Russians reciprocated, but the United States continued work on new strategic weapons. Development proceeded on the M-X land-based missile system and the Trident submarine-launched intercontinental ballistic missile (ICBM), and a prime contractor was chosen for the air-launched cruise missile.

The Congress of the United States ordered the Pentagon to develop a new strategic bomber by 1987. In a major refinement of U.S. nuclear strategy, defense officials revealed in August that targeting priority was being shifted from Russian population centers to military bases in hopes of providing a greater deterrent to a Russian first strike.

In conventional weapons developments, the Army ordered full production of the Abrams main battle tank in March. Pentagon officials confirmed published reports in August that the Air Force had secretly developed and successfully flown a "stealth" aircraft that was virtually immune to Soviet air defenses. Secretary of Defense Harold Brown hailed the experimental plane as "a major technological advance" that "alters the military balance significantly." Critics said Brown's announcement, coming during the presidential election campaign, was politically motivated.

Indian Ocean Build-Up. The seizure of American hostages by Iran and Russia's invasion of Afghanistan prompted a massive build-up of U.S. military power in the Indian Ocean and Persian Gulf region. By May 1, U.S. strength in the area had reached 37 warships and 34,000 men and, by the end of the year, two aircraft carrier battle groups were in the Indian Ocean. To underscore long-term U.S. interest in the region, the Carter Administration negotiated naval- and air-basing rights with Oman, Kenya, and Somalia.

The Pentagon accelerated a $9-billion, five-year plan to create a Rapid Deployment Force of Marine and airborne troops to be airlifted on short notice anywhere in the world. Major elements of the plan included the development of a fleet of giant cargo jets and the purchase of 15 merchant ships to be stocked with military equipment and supplies and positioned throughout the world for use in crises.

Military Strength. United States troop strength was up slightly in 1980. On Sept. 30, 1980, troop strength stood at 2,050,357, an increase of 23,000 from the previous year. More than 488,700 troops were stationed overseas, including 244,300 in West Germany and West Berlin, 46,000 in Japan and Okinawa, 38,800 in South Korea, 13,400 in the Philippines, and 59,400 at sea.

Defense Budget. President Carter submitted a Department of Defense budget request to Congress for fiscal 1981 (Oct. 1, 1980, to Sept. 30, 1981) on January 28. It asked for $142.7 billion, $15.3-billion more than the previous year's request and a 3.3 per cent increase after inflation. Congress approved $160.1 billion on December 7.

The budget supported a military establishment of 16 Army and 3 Marine divisions, 26 Air Force tactical wings, 12 Navy and 3 Marine air wings, 17 strategic airlift squadrons, and a Navy fleet of 544 ships. Strategic forces included 450 Minuteman II and 550 Minuteman III missiles; 54 Titan II missiles; and 160 Polaris, 432 Poseidon, and 64 Trident I submarine-launched missiles. An estimated $12 billion was allocated for strategic forces, $58 billion for general purpose forces, $14 billion for research and development, and $10.7 billion for military intelligence and communications. The Navy was to receive $44.5 billion; the Air Force, $40.3 billion; and the Army, $34.9 billion.

The Navy asked for $2.1 billion for the Trident nuclear submarine and ballistic missile, $1.8 billion for 48 F-18 Hornet carrier-based jet fighters, and $1.6 billion for two guided-missile cruisers. The Air Force requested $1.9 billion for 180 F-16 jet fighters, $1.6 billion for the M-X missile, and $869.7 million for 30 F-15 Eagle jet fighters. The Army asked for $1.2 billion for 569 Abrams main battle tanks, $541.6 million for 183 Patriot air-defense missiles, and $538.4 million for 400 armored fighting vehicles.

Readiness Problems. While spending for weaponry continued to escalate, the Pentagon was beset with maintenance and manpower problems to the point that congressional and other critics charged the U.S. defense establishment was no longer a sufficiently credible deterrent to aggression.

The manpower shortage in the volunteer army was eased when the economic downturn sent thousands of unemployed streaming into recruitment centers. As a result, Army recruiters exceeded their quotas after several years of declining enlistments.

All three services reported severe shortages of skilled personnel. The Air Force was short several thousand experienced pilots, and the Navy was short 20,000 petty officers.

As a result, the combat readiness of some units was called into question. Because of personnel shortages and lack of spare parts, nearly half of the Navy's F-14 squadrons and the Air Force's F-15 squadrons and six of the Army's 10 U.S. divisions were rated as unprepared for combat.

As if to underscore concerns about U.S. defenses and personnel, a Titan ICBM exploded in its silo near Damascus, Ark., on September 19, killing one Air Force technician and injuring 21 others. The explosion was caused when a maintenance technician dropped a wrench socket that fell 70 feet (21

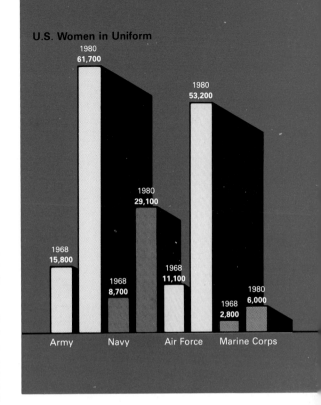

U.S. Women in Uniform

meters) and struck the missile, rupturing a fuel tank. The blast hurled the missile's nuclear warhead some 600 feet (180 meters) from the site. The Air Force said the warhead was slightly damaged but was never in danger of detonating.

New Draft? The Pentagon's manpower problems intensified pressure to resume the draft, but Administration officials continued to resist a return to conscription. However, Carter on January 23 urged a resumption of draft registration to enable the Selective Service System to mobilize quickly, and, after congressional approval, 19- and 20-year-old males began registering on July 21. Carter had recommended that women be required to register, but the proposal was rejected by Congress.

Command Changes. Despite opposition from conservative congressmen claiming he had become less a spokesman for the military than a political agent of the White House, General David C. Jones was confirmed by the U.S. Senate for a second 2-year term as chairman of the Joint Chiefs of Staff in June. Hazel W. Johnson was named chief of the Army Nurse Corps, becoming the first black woman general in the U.S. Army. Thomas M. DeFrank

In WORLD BOOK, see DISARMAMENT and articles on the service branches.

ARMY. See ARMED FORCES.

ART. See ARCHITECTURE; DANCING; LITERATURE; MUSIC, CLASSICAL; POETRY; VISUAL ARTS.

ASIA

Boom and bust rubbed elbows on this vast continent in 1980. War and race riots brought death to thousands, and poverty remained the general condition.

Political rivals were eliminated by gun or show trials. Dictators, in or out of uniform, ruled most countries, and even the nations that could not feed their people spent billions in cash or on credit to expand their armies. A dozen nations had to put off whatever development plans they had because available funds were diverted to pay the ever-rising prices demanded by the oil producers. And not far beyond the horizon loomed the specter of nuclear mushroom clouds from bombs that at least two Asian nations were putting together.

The Soviet presence in Afghanistan created problems and deep uneasiness for its Asian neighbors. Russia invaded Afghanistan in December 1979, kept up to 85,000 troops there throughout 1980, and fought more or less continual battles with Afghan guerrillas. Fighting spilled over the border into Pakistan on several occasions as thousands of Afghani refugees — armed and otherwise — fled to that nation. See AFGHANISTAN (Close-Up).

Russia Dominant. For East Asians, the dominant strategic fact of 1980 was that Russia had replaced the United States as master of the Pacific Ocean. Asian observers believed Russia had become powerful enough to challenge the U.S., cut its supply routes, and, if need be, attack the West Coast.

United States dominance in the western Pacific had ended in 1975 with the withdrawal of the last U.S. troops from Vietnam. Even the powerful U.S. Seventh Fleet, once unchallenged in the seas of Southeast Asia, was reduced to a skeleton with the transfer of its strongest units to the Middle East.

But as U.S. naval strength declined, that of the Soviet Pacific fleet grew, with an estimated 130 submarines, some aged but about 20 known to be new and nuclear powered. Japan received a startling reminder of this when a Russian nuclear-powered submarine caught fire east of Okinawa on August 21 and drifted while Japanese officials worried about radiation leaks. The Russian ship *Minsk*, a new helicopter carrier designed for antisubmarine warfare, roamed the seas between Vladivostok and Vietnam, and Soviet bombers made regular runs along the coast of Japan, thus demonstrating that country's vulnerability.

Other Asians, too, felt threatened. The Philippines protested the incursion of Soviet aircraft based in Vietnam. Thailand's borders were under pressure from the Vietnamese troops in Cambodia, and Viet raiders crossed the line in June. Thailand

also protested the incursions of Soviet warships into the Gulf of Thailand.

Nations that felt themselves endangered built up their armaments. The five members of the Association of Southeast Asian Nations (ASEAN) — Malaysia, Indonesia, Thailand, Singapore, and the Philippines — spent $5 billion for defense, 45 per cent more than in 1979. Despite their growing anxiety, the five were not yet ready for a military alliance. But each increased its military spending — Thailand allotting nearly 25 per cent of its budget for this purpose, and Malaysia boosting its defense and security expenditures by 140 per cent. About $645 million of this was spent on a huge base in northeast Malaysia, an hour's flight from

Cambodian refugees flee deeper into Thailand
from border camps during June attacks
by Vietnamese troops based in Cambodia.

Ho Chi Minh City (formerly Saigon), Vietnam. It was widely assumed that the base would be put at the disposal of U.S. bombers in an emergency.

But Southeast Asia was not alone in its anxieties — and its rearmament. In the northeast, Japan steadily expanded its armed strength, not as rapidly as Washington urged, but enough to give it the world's eighth largest defense budget.

Other Nations Arm. Although China cut its military spending $2 billion to $12.8 billion in 1980, it too was modernizing its war establishment. China announced on May 18 that it had conducted successful tests of an intercontinental ballistic missile, but this was only a small part of the effort. Chinese buyers traveled across western Europe, from Sweden to Italy, in search of military hardware. After prolonged negotiations, the United States in September approved more than 400 export licenses for sales to China of electronic gear, a sophisticated computer system, and military support equipment. In exchange, China agreed to sell to the United States the scarce heat-resistant metals titanium, tantalum, and vanadium.

India also continued to develop its armaments industry. In May, it signed a deal by which Russia

Facts in Brief on the Asian Countries

Country	Population	Government	Monetary Unit*	Foreign Trade (million U.S. $) Exports†	Imports†
Afghanistan	22,450,000	Revolutionary Council President & Prime Minister Babrak Karmal	afghani (44.5 = $1)	431	326
Australia	14,860,000	Governor General Sir Zelman Cowen; Prime Minister John Malcolm Fraser	dollar (1 = $1.16)	18,473	16,432
Bangladesh	92,908,000	President Ziaur Rahman; Prime Minister Azizur Rahman	taka (14.1 = $1)	669	2,110
Bhutan	1,344,000	King Jigme Singye Wangchuck	Indian rupee	1	1
Burma	35,138,000	President U Ne Win; Prime Minister U Maung Maung Kha	kyat (6.3 = $1)	363	319
Cambodia (Kampuchea)	9,649,000	President & Prime Minister Khieu Samphan	no currency in use	1	20
China	951,580,000	Communist Party Chairman Hua Guofeng; Premier Zhao Ziyang	yuan (1.5 = $1)	10,100	11,100
India	697,616,000	President Neelam Sanjiva Reddy; Prime Minister Indira Gandhi	rupee (7.8 = $1)	6,440	8,150
Indonesia	159,546,000	President Suharto; Vice-President Adam Malik	rupiah (625 = $1)	15,578	7,225
Iran	37,989,000	President Abol Hasan Bani-Sadr; Prime Minister Mohammad Ali Rajai	rial (70.4 = $1)	19,307	7,261
Japan	119,900,000	Emperor Hirohito; Prime Minister Zenko Suzuki	yen (217.7 = $1)	103,045	110,670
Korea, North	19,619,000	President Kim Il-song; Premier Yi Chong-ok	won (1.8 = $1)	967	902
Korea, South	40,550,000	President Chun Doo Hwan; Prime Minister Nam Duck Woo	won (656.3 = $1)	15,055	20,339
Laos	3,794,000	President Souphanouvong; Prime Minister Kayson Phomvihan	kip (400 = $1)	15	80
Malaysia	14,072,000	Paramount Ruler Ahmad Shah Ibni Al-Marhum Sultan Abu Bakar; Prime Minister Datuk Hussein Onn	ringgit (2.2 = $1)	11,008	7,805
Maldives	150,000	President Maumoon Abdul Gayoom	rupee (7.6 = $1)	4	9
Mongolia	1,721,000	People's Revolutionary Party First Secretary & Presidium Chairman Yumjaagiyn Tsedenbal; Council of Ministers Chairman Jambyn Batmonh	tughrik (2.9 = $1)	258	336
Nepal	14,550,000	King Birendra Bir Bikram Shah Dev; Prime Minister Surya Bahadur Thapa	rupee (12 = $1)	91	241
New Zealand	3,346,000	Governor General Sir David Stuart Beattie; Prime Minister Robert D. Muldoon	dollar (1.1 = $1)	4,694	4,542
Pakistan	85,386,000	President Mohammad Zia-ul-Haq	rupee (9.8 = $1)	2,056	4,061
Papua New Guinea	3,183,000	Governor General Sir Tore Lokoloko; Prime Minister Sir Julius Chan	kina (1 = $1.51)	963	810
Philippines	50,483,000	President Ferdinand E. Marcos	peso (7.5 = $1)	4,601	6,142
Russia	268,380,000	Communist Party General Secretary & Supreme Soviet Presidium Chairman Leonid Ilich Brezhnev; Council of Ministers Chairman Nikolay Aleksandrovich Tikhonov	ruble (1 = $1.56)	64,762	57,773
Singapore	2,450,000	President Benjamin Henry Sheares; Prime Minister Lee Kuan Yew	dollar (2.1 = $1)	14,233	17,635
Sri Lanka	15,027,000	President J. R. Jayewardene; Prime Minister R. Premadasa	rupee (16 = $1)	890	1,441
Taiwan	18,051,000	President Chiang Ching-kuo; Premier Sun Yun-hsuan	new Taiwan dollar (36 = $1)	12,700	11,000
Thailand	49,182,000	King Bhumibol Adulyadej; Prime Minister Prem Tinsulanonda	baht (20 = $1)	5,308	7,156
Vietnam	54,918,000	Acting President Nguyen Huu Tho; Prime Minister Pham Van Dong	dong (2.2 = $1)	300	900

*Exchange rates as of Dec. 1, 1980. †Latest available data.

agreed to supply $1.6 billion in artillery, planes, missiles, and other equipment. Pakistan moved apace with its Project 706, the creation of what has been called an Islamic nuclear bomb. The United States strove to prevent it by keeping down aid levels despite Pakistan's persistent requests for $3-billion to deal with the Afghan border crisis. Pakistan got help with its nuclear project from Libya, so the United States expected a test explosion as early as 1982.

Iraq, with French assistance, might also be preparing to build a nuclear bomb. Its secret nuclear research center near Baghdad was bombed in September, presumably by Iran.

For most Asians, two other developments were worrisome. One was the seeming attempt to convert Southeast Asia into a major Sino-Soviet battlefield, with Cambodia as principal casualty. The other was the growing closeness among China, Japan, and the United States. The relationship was still informal and limited to exchanges of information and technology, but Moscow was already denouncing it as the "Peking-Tokyo-Washington axis."

The Asian Economy presented a patchy picture. Japan and the five ASEAN countries were in better condition than the great industrial nations of the West, with an annual growth rate of 5 to 7 per cent. But, at the other extreme, countries such as Bangladesh, Laos, and Pakistan survived only with foreign aid, and Cambodia remained on the edge of starvation.

But for the well-to-do and the impoverished alike, soaring oil prices remained a catastrophe – except for Indonesia, a major oil producer. South Korea's oil bill doubled in 1980 to $6 billion, and Thailand's oil bill rose from $1.6 billion to $2.5-billion. From Japan to Vietnam to Pakistan, nations engaged in a feverish search for oil, often with World Bank help but usually with only indifferent success. Malaysia's successful oil strikes were the exception.

The high cost of oil drained national treasuries, slowed down development programs, and sent prices and inflation rates soaring. Even in China, with its controlled economy, the inflation rate rose by 7 to 10 per cent. As oil prices rose, real incomes declined, leading to social unrest in much of Asia.

Nuclear Power Boom. The rising oil prices made the building of nuclear power plants one of Asia's booming industries. Except for the poorest and smallest, most Asian countries were building nuclear plants in 1980, and Japan was second only to the United States in its use of nuclear power. India, which launched its program in 1960, had at least three more nuclear power plants under construction. After 15 months of delay caused by poor planning, the Philippines resumed work on a plant near Manila in September.

Japan's Emperor Hirohito, right, toasts China's Communist Party Chairman Hua Kuo-feng (Hua Guofeng) during Hua's visit to Japan in May.

Taiwan, where nuclear plants provided 17 per cent of total power capacity in 1980, expected that figure to rise to 45 per cent in 1982, when four other generators would be completed. Taiwan expects to add six more generators by 1991. South Korea, with two nuclear power plants completed and three under construction, hoped to have a dozen or more such plants operating by 1990. China agreed to buy two French power plants. A panel of 100 Chinese nuclear scientists and energy experts in November proposed the construction of six nuclear power plants in the nation's southeast and east, where industry is chronically short of electric power.

The Green Revolution provided one of the brighter spots in the Asian economy. With constantly improved seed, the yield kept rising, enabling grain importers to become net exporters. Pakistan exported wheat in 1980, and the Philippines sold 300,000 metric tons (330,000 short tons) of rice abroad; Indonesia had by far the largest rice crop in its history. But 1980 studies also indicated that the rich crops often magnified economic inequity. For example, in Malaysia's rice bowl more and more land apparently has been falling into the hands of rich farmers able to use machinery, while the poor till ever-smaller holdings, and the sharecroppers – some 30 per cent of all farmers – are squeezed out.

Human Rights were largely honored in the breach. Ignored in Communist countries, they were also crudely violated by military or martial-law regimes from Pakistan to South Korea. Thousands of political prisoners filled the jails, free speech was denied, "undesirables" were deprived of their livelihood, and law books were doctored to add to the curbs on freedom. See CIVIL RIGHTS.

Overpopulation remained a crucial problem, with most family-planning programs ineffective. China was the only Asian country in which the birth control campaign made gains in 1980. Through a system of rewards and harsh penalties, a new family was allowed to have only one or, rarely, two children. Parents with three were penalized in pay, bonuses, promotion, and even schooling and milk for their offspring.

In Szechwan (Sichuan) province, which has 10 per cent of China's people, officials vowed to "start this year putting an end to having a third child, and ensure that over 50 per cent of couples of childbearing age have only one child instead of two." China's birth rate has been reduced by such means from 33.59 births per 1,000 persons in 1970 to 26 per 1,000 in 1980. Through these policies, China hoped to achieve zero population growth by the year 2000.   Mark Gayn

See also the various Asian country articles. In WORLD BOOK, see ASIA.

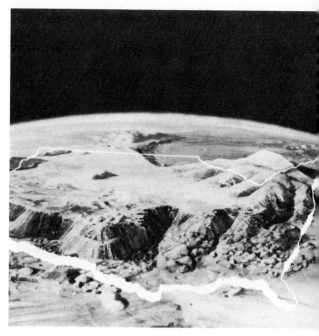

The first scientifically accurate painting of the varied terrain on Venus comes from radar data sent to Earth by *Pioneer* orbiter in May.

ASTRONOMY achieved another "first" on Nov. 12, 1980, when *Voyager 1* passed within 124,000 kilometers (77,000 miles) of Saturn's cloud tops. For several weeks before and after that date, the spacecraft surveyed Saturn's changing cloud patterns, ring system, and moons, and sent its findings back to Earth across nearly 1.6 billion kilometers (1 billion miles) of space. Among the sights that astounded astronomers were close-up views of the planet's cloud belts, several new moons, and unexpected complexities in the ring system.

Saturn's clouds show the same banded structure seen on Jupiter, but Saturn has many more of the alternating bright zones and darker colorful belts. Extremely high winds of nearly 1,450 kilometers (900 miles) per hour occur in the middle of some of Saturn's dark belts. In addition, Saturn has many swirling, brownish, oval-shaped "storms" that resemble the white oval storms on Jupiter, but none are as large as Jupiter's Great Red Spot, which may also be a storm.

The *Voyager* observations established the existence of a D ring of material orbiting between the cloud tops and the C ring. The three major rings are designated A, B, and C. The D ring had been seen from Earth but was not detected by the *Pioneer* probe on its September 1979 fly-by. *Voyager* showed that Saturn's main ring system consists of hundreds of smaller "ringlets." And some ringlets

were clearly elliptical in shape, rather than round as astronomers expected. Nor could scientists explain the strange dark, fingerlike "spokes" they found in the B ring. The narrow F ring of material orbiting just outside the A ring is only 100 kilometers (60 miles) across and seems to be made up of three ringlets twisted in a "braid," also an unexplained phenomenon. The distant E ring extends 480,000 kilometers (298,000 miles) from Saturn, beyond the moon Dione.

Astronomers monitoring radio emissions detected by the two *Voyager* spacecraft on their way to Saturn revised their estimates of the planet's rotation period from 10 hours 14 minutes to 10 hours 39.4 minutes. The radio noise from Saturn is emitted from regions below the visible clouds and is therefore a truer indicator of the planet's rotation period than the shifting clouds.

Earth-based observations revealed in March that the long-disputed 10th moon of Saturn does not exist. Instead, there are two moons in nearly identical orbits — the 10th and 11th moons of the planet that has so many followers. They orbit about 156,000 kilometers (97,000 miles) from Saturn's center. Astronomers also learned in March that a small 12th moon of Saturn travels just ahead of Dione, in the same orbit. Three additional moons were discovered during the November fly-by, bringing the known total to 15. Two of them flank the F ring, and one orbits just outside the A ring.

Early *Voyager 1* observations showed that the nine previously known moons of Saturn are heavily cratered. Rhea and Dione show bright, wispy markings, and Tethys is split by a huge trench. Mimas has a 130-kilometer (80-mile) wide crater with a raised rim 9,000 meters (30,000 feet) high. The crater stretches across one-fourth of the moon's diameter. Enceladus is relatively smooth.

The atmosphere on Titan, the largest of Saturn's moons, consists mainly of nitrogen, like that on Earth. It also has some hydrocarbons that give it a hazy orange appearance that obscures its surface. The atmospheric pressure on Titan may be almost three times that on Earth. Titan's diameter at the bottom of its atmosphere is less than 5,150 kilometers (3,200 miles). *Voyager* recorded temperatures of $-185°C$ ($-300°F$.), which appeared to put an end to speculation that life might have evolved on Titan.

Venus. Astronomers also got their first detailed "look" at most of the surface of Venus in 1980, despite the planet's perpetual cloud cover. The United States National Aeronautics and Space Administration's (NASA) *Pioneer* orbiter relayed to Earth radar data that were then transformed into facts about the altitudes on Venus that were accurate to 200 meters (660 feet). Scientists carefully timed radar pulses from the spacecraft as they penetrated Venus' clouds, bounced off the surface features, then returned to the spacecraft. The researchers used these data to determine the distance between the surface of Venus and the spacecraft. Then, through computer processing, they produced topographic maps of Venus and simulated views of the terrain, complete with artificial shadows, from various angles. *Pioneer's* orbit permitted it to view 93 per cent of the planet's surface. It missed only small areas over each pole.

The radar views revealed that most of the planet is covered by low, rolling plains that are generally so flat that they vary less than 900 meters (3,000 feet) in altitude all across Venus. A few basins dip below this level. Atalanta Planitia, the largest of these, is about as big as the North Atlantic Ocean Basin but is only 2,800 meters (9,000 feet) deep. The basins on Venus are completely dry because the surface heat is so intense and because there is scarcely any water vapor in the atmosphere.

Mars. Only one *Viking* spacecraft was still operating in 1980. The lone survivor of the original fleet of two orbiters and two landers, the *Viking 1* lander, continued to return data from the Chryse Basin and was expected to continue its mission until December 1994. The *Viking 2* lander ended its career in April 1980 and was followed into silence in August by the *Viking 1* orbiter. The *Viking 2* orbiter shut down in 1978.

Jupiter. Planetary astronomer Stephen P. Sinnott of the NASA *Voyager* optical navigation team reported that he had discovered the 15th and 16th moons of Jupiter. The 15th moon, which was discovered in March and is about 80 kilometers (50 miles) in diameter, orbits between the moons Amalthea and Io once every 16 hours 11 minutes 21 seconds at 151,000 kilometers (93,900 miles) above Jupiter's cloud tops. The 16th moon, first seen in July, has a diameter of about 40 kilometers (25 miles) and orbits just outside Jupiter's ring of dust particles every 7 hours 4½ minutes. It is about 56,200 kilometers (34,900 miles) above the clouds.

Pluto. Astronomer Uwe Fink of the University of Arizona in Tucson reported in October that he had discovered a thin atmosphere of methane on Pluto. Fink said that Pluto's atmosphere may be frozen during much of its 248-year orbital period, changing to gas only when the planet is closest to the Sun. The thinness of Pluto's atmosphere may be inferred by comparing it with that of Earth and Mars. If the atmosphere of each planet were compressed to a constant standard pressure and temperature from the ground up, the air on Earth would be 8,000 meters (26,000 feet) deep; on Mars, 80 meters (260 feet) deep; and on Pluto, 30 meters (100 feet) deep. Eric D. Carlson

See also SPACE EXPLORATION. In WORLD BOOK, see ASTRONOMY; articles on the planets.

AUSTRALIA held its first general election since 1977 on Oct. 18, 1980, and voters re-elected the Liberal-National Country Party government headed by Prime Minister Malcolm Fraser. Although the government's majority in the House of Representatives was cut in half, it remained substantial. However, its position in the Senate deteriorated somewhat. The opposition Australian Labor Party gained votes at the expense of minor parties.

Ian Sinclair, the federal minister for primary industries, resigned in 1979 after an investigation of alleged forgery and misappropriation of funds in connection with family companies. He returned to his post and to leadership of the House of Representatives on August 19 after being acquitted of all charges against him. After the elections, Prime Minister Fraser reduced the size of his ministry slightly and appointed five new junior ministers. Andrew Peacock, the minister for foreign affairs for five years who is considered a possible successor to Fraser, moved to the domestic portfolio of industrial relations. Bill Hayden retained leadership of the Labor Party, and Bob Hawke, former president of the Australian Council of Trade Unions who was elected to Parliament from Wills, Victoria, did not challenge him for the position.

New Buildings. Richard Thorp, an Australian-born New York City architect, won the design competition for a new Parliament House in Canberra in June. Queen Elizabeth II opened the permanent home of the High Court of Australia on May 26. The building is next to Lake Burley Griffin in Canberra. The new Parliament House will be erected on a hill overlooking the lake.

Several disputes about Aborigines' land rights arose in 1980, especially with respect to mining and oil drilling on Aboriginal reserves and areas regarded as sacred by the Aborigines. Controversy reached a peak in August over the Western Australian state government's determination to drill at Noonkanbah, which Aborigines said was sacred.

Foreign and Defense Policies were much affected by events in Iran and Afghanistan in 1980. The government decided not to break off diplomatic relations with Iran over the detention of American hostages taken in November 1979, but cut off all exports to that country except food and medical supplies. Growing conflict in and near the Persian Gulf led Australia to increase its defense spending and to extend its cooperation with the United States. The government allowed U.S. B-52 strategic bombers based on Guam to fly training missions over the north of Australia, and in September announced that it would give the U.S. Air Force staging facilities for training and surveillance. Fraser also offered in March to provide home-port facilities in Western Australia for the U.S. Navy.

Grain Embargo. The government responded vigorously to the Russian invasion of Afghanistan. The prime minister on January 9 announced an embargo on increased sales of grain, and suspended various projects and cooperation agreements with the Soviet Union. He also asked the Australian Olympic Federation (AOF) to boycott the Olympic Summer Games in Moscow if Russian troops remained in Afghanistan. However, the AOF decided in June to participate.

The Economy. Inflation continued at about a 10 per cent rate, and the unemployment level was about 6 per cent. A widespread drought reduced farmers' expectations of high incomes, and there were fresh developments in the resource and energy fields. The policy of import parity pricing for Australian crude oil caused major increases in gasoline prices and domestic airfares, but there was also a drop of 5 per cent in total oil use.

Encouraging signs of new oil discoveries surfaced in South Australia. The Rundle oil shale project in Queensland was launched to develop reserves estimated at about equal to known crude oil reserves. Developers pushed forward schemes for producing ethanol. They also launched a massive natural gas project on the Northwest shelf.

The manufacturing industry showed a 3 per cent growth in jobs for the first time in five years.

Six judges, including famed architect I. M. Pei, at far left, choose Richard Thorp's plan as the winning design for Canberra's new Parliament House.

Problems occurred in the automobile industry early in 1980, but new-vehicle registrations increased by the end of the year, and car manufacturers planned new investments. The clothing, textile, and footwear industries, which had been hurt by imports, received a fresh lease on life when the government announced on August 15 that it would begin a seven-year assistance program to those industries in 1982.

Other Developments. Multicultural television became a reality in Australia on October 24 with the opening of new channels in Sydney and Melbourne that presented programs for ethnic groups. These government-funded programs, from nations all over the world, were presented in the originating nations' language with English subtitles.

Immigration continued to be an important subject. Minister for Immigration and Ethnic Affairs Ian McPhee said on June 5 that 19,500 refugees and 2,000 other persons would be admitted to Australia under humanitarian programs in 1980 and 1981. He also expected many more people to enter the country in order to find jobs and to join their relatives. McPhee also announced in June a Regularization of Status Program that would grant amnesty to illegal immigrants who declared their status. J. D. B. Miller

See also ASIA (Facts in Brief Table). In WORLD BOOK, see AUSTRALIA.

AUSTRIA celebrated the 25th anniversary of its liberation from Allied occupation on May 15, 1980. Austria was "annexed" by Germany in 1938 and was occupied by the Allies from the end of World War II until 1955, when Russia, the United States, Great Britain, and France signed the treaty of independence. President Rudolf Kirchschlaeger stressed Austria's neutral role at the observance.

Kirchschlaeger was elected to a second term as president on May 18, receiving 80 per cent of the vote. The main opposition, the People's Party, declined to put up a candidate against the popular Kirchschlaeger, but the neo-Nazi National Democratic Party's chairman, Norbert Burger, polled 3.2 per cent of the vote.

Foreign Affairs. Austria angered Israel on March 13 when Chancellor Bruno Kreisky confirmed that the government had recognized the Palestine Liberation Organization. Kreisky led an international fact-finding mission to Teheran, Iran, in May to investigate the holding of United States hostages since Nov. 4, 1979.

In a June 15 referendum, 60 per cent of the population of the western province of Vorarlberg voted to negotiate with the central government for more self-government. They demanded the right to make more policy decisions and to set taxes.

Austria almost escaped the recession that disturbed its neighbors. The schilling remained among the world's strongest currencies. Inflation held at about 5 per cent and unemployment at 2 per cent. But Austria feared that imported energy products would increase its trade deficit.

Censure Move. Parliament was recalled on August 21 to debate a no-confidence motion against the government and Finance Minister Hannes Androsch over a scandal involving a Vienna hospital project. The 2,100-bed hospital's cost had spiraled upward, and there were allegations of bribery. Several people were arrested, and a parliamentary commission said hospital money had been sidetracked into political party funds. When completed in 1986, the hospital will have cost $4.6-billion. Parliament defeated the motion. Kreisky threatened to resign if Androsch's powers were not curtailed, and presented a program that would limit the finance ministry's duties. Androsch resigned on December 11, but the ruling Socialist Party asked him to stay through January 1981.

Atomic Energy supporters in November gathered more than the 200,000 signatures necessary for Parliament to reconsider a ban on nuclear power. An antinuclear group gathered 100,000 signatures on a petition to maintain the ban. Austrian voters narrowly rejected a plan to open a nuclear power plant in 1978. Kenneth Brown

See also EUROPE (Facts in Brief Table). In WORLD BOOK, see AUSTRIA.

AUTOMOBILE manufacturers in the United States found the going rough in 1980, with Chrysler Corporation's financial woes continuing to be the industry's number-one headache. Inflation, high interest rates, rising fuel costs, and competition from imported cars all contributed to Detroit's problems, and set the stage for record industry losses. On October 27, General Motors Corporation (GM) announced that it had lost $567 million in the third quarter of 1980 alone. The next day, Ford Motor Company said that it lost $595 million during the same three months. American Motors Corporation lost $155.7 million during the year ending on September 30, and Chrysler Corporation was expected to lose a thumping $1.7 billion by year's end, the largest yearly loss in United States history.

United States auto production fell to an estimated 6.5 million cars for the year, the lowest total since the 5,522,404 built in 1961. Total sales, including imports, were 8.95 million, the lowest since 1975 and down 15.2 per cent from 1975. United States manufacturers reported sales of 6.58 million autos, the lowest number since 1961 and a 20 per cent drop from the previous year. The falling sales resulted in long-term layoffs of more than 200,000 auto workers.

Sales of imports, strong all year, continued in November when 171,000 cars, about 24 per cent of

Chrysler Chairman Lee A. Iacocca steps into the first of the new
K cars he hopes will boost sales and revive the ailing auto firm.

the market and up 8 per cent over November 1979, were sold. However, Robert M. McElwaine, president of the American Imported Automobile Dealers Association, predicted that import car sales in the United States would total 2.1 million for 1980 and drop to about 2 million in 1981. He noted that sales of import cars dropped from 27 per cent of the market to 21 per cent shortly after new American small cars were introduced.

Prices Go Up. In a typical example of 1981 model pricing, GM raised its basic car prices $176, or 1.9 per cent, in mid-August. Five days after the new cars went on sale, it posted a second round of price hikes averaging $238, or 2.5 per cent. The two price hikes placed the price of a GM 1981 passenger car with average equipment at about $9,450. Among the imports, the average 1981 Toyota went up $310, or 5.2 per cent.

GM declined to join Ford Motor Company and the United Auto Workers (UAW) in seeking restrictions on automotive imports. Ford and the UAW petitioned the U.S. International Trade Commission to curb Japanese sales in the United States, but the agency turned down the request on November 10. GM's Chairman Thomas A. Murphy said, however, that increasing Japanese auto exports to the United States are a problem that the new Administration of President Ronald Reagan would soon have to deal with. Henry Ford II,

retired Ford board chairman, said Japanese auto imports into the United States were causing "an economic Pearl Harbor."

The Smaller Car with better mileage figures was the trend in the American domestic auto market. Ford pinned high hopes on its new Escort and Lynx, and Chrysler relied on its K cars in 1980. GM was already in the marketplace with its front-wheel-drive (FWD) small cars.

Chrysler, explaining what it considered the advantages of FWD, said that mounting the engine crosswise up front over the drive wheels provides more interior room for people and luggage. Power is transmitted to the front wheels, eliminating the drive shaft, differential, rear axle, and the hump down the middle of the floor.

Chrysler Fights for Life. Chrysler took drastic steps in late December as Board Chairman Lee A. Iacocca tried to save what had been the nation's third largest automotive company – ranked behind GM and Ford. Iacocca disclosed that Chrysler, which had been granted $1.5 billion in bailout money by the Congress of the United States in 1979, had already received $800 million of that amount and would seek $400 million more.

Iacocca laid the blame for the company's woes on rising interest rates and on federal monetary policies that he called "madness." He centered much of his fire on the increase in the prime interest rate. He had previously said Chrysler might make it into the black in the final quarter of 1980, but abandoned that belief as the prime rate climbed to 20 per cent on December 10 for the second time in 1980 — and then went on to a record 21 per cent on December 16.

To boost its new car sales, Chrysler began a rebate program. Effective from Dec. 5, 1980, to Jan. 20, 1981, when the Reagan Administration took office, the new plan linked cost rebates on 1981 Chrysler·cars, except for Imperials, to changes in the prime rate. The amount of the rebate, paid only to the 70 per cent of Chrysler customers who bought on credit, went up or down as the prime rate charged by banks fluctuated.

Ford offered a somewhat similar plan to bolster sagging sales. Under its plan, credit buyers purchased their cars in the usual manner and then received benefits ranging from $500 to $1,000 in direct interest subsidies to buyers of certain slower-selling models.

Chrysler Cutbacks. The ailing auto firm came up with a drastic belt-tightening program in late 1980, designed to cut $650 million from its operating expenses in the first year. The UAW was asked to freeze its members' wages — $17.31 per hour for base wages and fringes — for 21 months and to forego a scheduled 1980 cost-of-living adjustment.

An electric van that can travel 150 miles (240 kilometers) on a charge and reach speeds of 55 miles (88 kilometers) per hour is demonstrated.

UAW President Douglas Fraser, a member of the Chrysler board of directors, indicated that the union would investigate thoroughly before accepting any wage freeze or other cutbacks. Chrysler said the freeze could save $600 million. The company planned to ask 20,000 supplier firms to freeze prices or roll them back by 5 per cent in 1981. The firm reportedly asked 25 banks to convert $572-million in uninsured loans to Chrysler into preferred stock, saving $100 million in interest payments in 1981. It also ordered a 5 per cent across-the-board cut in internal operating expenses.

There were industry rumors that Chrysler was working on a possible merger with the French auto firm P.S.A. Peugeot-Citroen or with Japan's Mitsubishi Motor Corporation. There had been earlier, unconfirmed reports about similar talks between Chrysler and Volkswagen. American Motors Corporation stockholders voted on December 16 to give control of the company to the French automaker Renault.

An Indiana jury acquitted Ford Motor Company on March 13 on three charges of reckless homicide in connection with the fiery deaths of three women in the August 1978 crash of a 1973 Ford Pinto. As the first criminal case involving alleged product defects, the case received national attention.   Charles C. Cain III

In WORLD BOOK, see AUTOMOBILE.

AUTOMOBILE RACING. Alan Jones of Australia narrowly defeated Nelson Piquet of Brazil to become the 1980 world drivers' champion. But their battle on the track was overshadowed by off-the-track disputes involving control of Formula One racing, the safety of the tiny roadsters, and the desirability of racing them at Watkins Glen, N.Y.

The world drivers' series consisted of 14 Grand Prix races in 13 nations (the United States had two races). Jones won five races in his Williams-Ford and Piquet three in a Brabham-Ford.

Piquet captured the U. S. Grand Prix West on March 30 in Long Beach, Calif. Jones became champion by winning the last two races — the Canadian Grand Prix on September 28 in Montreal, and the U.S. Grand Prix East on October 5 in Watkins Glen. Renault of France won three races in revolutionary turbocharged cars. Renault's 1.5-liter V-6 engines generated more horsepower than the 3-liter engines of most other cars.

A 15th Grand Prix race was run without sanction on June 1 in Madrid, Spain, because of a dispute between the International Auto Sport Federation, which controlled Formula One racing, and most car owners. Citing safety, the federation banned ground-hugging lateral "skirts," which allowed cars to take corners faster, for 1981 and legislated tire changes for 1982. Most car owners opposed the ban.

Safety was a factor at Watkins Glen. The federation was dissatisfied with the track surface, paddock, press facilities, pits, working area, and spectator behavior. It threatened to cancel the Grand Prix, but the track obtained the $500,000 needed for improvements a month before race day.

USAC and CART. Administrators and car owners battled for control of oval-track racing for Indianapolis-type cars. Speed was a factor here, too, as the major car owners, banded together in Championship Auto Racing Teams (CART), wanted faster cars. The U.S. Auto Club (USAC) wanted to restrict the speed of the turbocharged Cosworth engines so that smaller teams could stay competitive using less costly stock-block engines.

CART contended that restricting speed would be dangerous because drivers would lack extra power to carry them out of tight quarters. It cited the world's richest race, the $1,505,425 Indianapolis 500 on May 25. Johnny Rutherford of Fort Worth, Tex., won in a Chaparral-Cosworth and averaged 142.862 miles (229.914 kilometers) per hour, slowest time since 1962. Rutherford also won CART's season series.

NASCAR. Dale Earnhardt of Kannapolis, N.C., and Cale Yarborough of Timmonsville, S.C., excelled in the National Association for Stock Car Auto Racing's (NASCAR) 31-race series for late-model sedans. Earnhardt narrowly defeated Yarborough for the series title. Both drove Chevrolets in most races and Oldsmobiles in others. Yarborough set a record by being fastest qualifier for 14 races. In all, Yarborough won six races, Earnhardt and Darrell Waltrip of Owensboro, Ky., won five each, and Bobby Allison of Hueytown, Ala., four.

The most lucrative race of the $6-million series was the $663,250 Daytona 500 on February 17 in Daytona Beach, Fla. Buddy Baker of Charlotte, N.C., in an Oldsmobile, won on a gamble. Running out of gas near the finish, he made a pit stop, took on one can of gas rather than two, and was back on the track in six seconds. After the race, his crew put in more gas to reach Victory Lane.

Other Racing. In endurance competition, Lancia won the World Manufacturers Championship series, and John Paul, Sr., and John Paul, Jr., of Lawrenceville, Ga., in a turbocharged Porsche, took the World Challenge for Endurance Drivers. On June 15, Jean Rondeau of France became the first driver to win the 24 Hours of Le Mans in France in a car he built himself.

In sports-car competition, Lola introduced the T350 for the 10-race Can-Am series. Patrick Tambay of France, who won the series in a Lola in 1977, won again. His Chaparral stock-block engine generated almost 600 horsepower. Frank Litsky

In WORLD BOOK, see AUTOMOBILE RACING.

Alan Jones of Australia clinches the world drivers' championship by winning the Grand Prix of Canada on September 28 in Montreal.

AVIATION companies in the United States saw traffic slump, fuel costs climb, and profits disappear in 1980. United States airlines lost nearly $200 million, the worst loss in U.S. airline history, according to George W. James, the U.S. airline industry's chief economist. Commercial airline service between the United States and China resumed in December for the first time since 1949.

United States domestic-airline passenger traffic through September was down 4.8 per cent from the first nine months of 1979, air freight slipped 1.8 per cent, but international air freight rose 2.9 per cent. The International Air Transport Association said scheduled airlines carried 5.7 per cent more paying passengers on North Atlantic routes in the first six months of 1980 than in the same period in 1979, and cargo was up 5 per cent. International traffic carried by U.S. airlines edged downward by 0.9 per cent through October.

China Pact. The United States and China signed an agreement in September that sanctioned scheduled airline service between the two nations. The U.S. Civil Aeronautics Board (CAB) on October 17 named Pan American World Airways (PanAm) over four other contenders as the U.S. carrier on the U.S.-China flights.

The United States and Great Britain agreed in March to expand air service between the two countries. Some 13 additional U.S. cities could have direct flights to and from London by 1984.

In January, the CAB limited U.S.-Moscow flights by Aeroflot, the Russian state airline, to protest against Russia's invasion of Afghanistan. The CAB curbed Aeroflot charter flights in March.

Climbing Fares. The CAB permitted basic fare increases of more than 20 per cent on international routes and allowed airlines to raise fares by another 5 to 15 per cent above the basic fare level in 1980. It even allowed unlimited increases in some instances. The board granted domestic fare hikes of more than 11 per cent.

In May, the CAB began to allow carriers to push up fares for long-haul routes by 30 per cent of the basic maximum, medium-distance fares by 50 per cent, and fares for short-haul routes by an unlimited amount. After 11 U.S. senators complained that the policy discriminated against people who used small-town airports served by short-haul flights, the CAB changed its policy in September to allow airlines to impose on all routes an additional charge of $15 plus up to 30 per cent of the basic charge.

Airlines hiked fares substantially and cut some discounts, but a fare war broke out on transcontinental routes. In April, World Airways offered a one-way fare of $139.99 for flights from Newark, N.J., or Baltimore to Hawaii, and made cheaper fares available for short periods. Eastern Air Lines invaded the New York City-Los Angeles and New York City-San Francisco markets with a $99 fare briefly in June, forcing other carriers to come down from much higher levels.

Eastern announced on November 12 that it would virtually double its bargain coast-to-coast round-trip fares on Jan. 1, 1981. But Trans World Airlines (TWA) then set its lowest round-trip coast-to-coast fare for 1981 at $298 for night flights and $338 for daytime trips, lower than Eastern's fares. American Airlines, Eastern, and United Airlines matched this rate on November 21.

Mixed Fortunes. Some carriers, such as regional airlines, did well in 1980, the second year of deregulation, but other carriers suffered. Losses, flight cutbacks, and layoffs were common. Braniff International cut back operations sharply.

The CAB approved mergers of the two largest U.S. air-cargo carriers – Tiger International, Incorporated, and Seaboard World Airlines, Incorporated – and of Republic Airlines with Hughes Air West. Continental Air Lines and Western said in August that they would try again to merge, contending that increased airline competition should ease CAB fears that their consolidation would reduce competition too much. The CAB had refused to allow the two airlines to merge in 1979.

Air Safety. The National Transportation Safety Board reported that no airline-crash fatality oc-

curred in the United States in 1980. In 1979, 279 persons died in airline accidents.

Commuter airline safety came under closer scrutiny. The number of commuter flights had increased sharply since deregulation began in 1978, and crashes became more frequent. As a result, the Federal Aviation Administration (FAA) issued tougher flight-experience regulations for commuter-airline pilots in February, and in June proposed new safety standards for airports that serve mostly commuter airlines.

A National Research Council panel studying air safety reported in June that the FAA should improve its safety-regulation practices. The panel said that the FAA should review its aircraft-certification methods and that the FAA's engineering competence had fallen behind that of the aircraft industry. But the panel also said that the U.S. air safety system was still "the standard of the world." The panel had been formed after the worst airline disaster in U.S. history, the 1979 crash of an American Airlines DC-10 shortly after take-off in Chicago that killed 274 persons. The FAA blamed the crash on a crack in the DC-10's engine-mount assembly. The crash occurred when the engine and assembly came off the aircraft and severed control and stall-warning lines. The FAA said that an American Airlines maintenance procedure caused the crack. The procedure deviated from a recommendation by McDonnell Douglas Corporation, the manufacturer.

In January 1980, the FAA ordered airlines to modify their DC-10s so that each would have two independently powered computers to monitor wing-slat positions, and so that both the pilot and co-pilot would have a device to warn them when the plane was about to stall. The FAA ordered some changes in the engine-mount design in May, to make it less susceptible to damage during maintenance work.

The DC-9 Super 80, a larger version of the McDonnell Douglas DC-9, was certified on August 25 by the FAA for safe flight. The Super 80 had experienced two accidents during hard test landings. The tail section broke off in a May accident at Edwards Air Force Base in California. In June, the jet veered off the runway at Yuma, Ariz. FAA Administrator Langhorne M. Bond said that the first accident was caused by pilot error and that the second occurred when the plane was being tested to meet stiffer requirements than those laid down by the FAA.

Hartsfield International Airport in Atlanta, Ga., opened a huge, $500-million terminal in September. The terminal is the world's largest in floor area – 2.2 million square feet (204,000 square meters) – and in number of gates, 138. Albert R. Karr

See also TRANSPORTATION. In WORLD BOOK, see AVIATION.

AWARDS AND PRIZES presented in 1980 included the following:

Arts Awards

Academy of Motion Picture Arts and Sciences. *"Oscar" Awards:* **Best Picture,** *Kramer vs. Kramer,* Columbia, Stanley R. Jaffe, producer. **Best Actor,** Dustin Hoffman, *Kramer vs. Kramer.* **Best Actress,** Sally Field, *Norma Rae.* **Best Supporting Actor,** Melvyn Douglas, *Being There.* **Best Supporting Actress,** Meryl Streep, *Kramer vs. Kramer.* **Best Director,** Robert Benton, *Kramer vs. Kramer.* **Best Original Screenplay,** Steven Tesich, *Breaking Away.* **Best Screenplay Based on Material from Another Medium,** Robert Benton, *Kramer vs. Kramer.* **Best Cinematography,** Vittorio Storaro, *Apocalypse Now.* **Best Film Editing,** Alan Heim, *All That Jazz.* **Best Original Musical Score,** George Delerue, *A Little Romance.* **Best Original Song,** "It Goes Like It Goes," from *Norma Rae,* music by David Shire, lyrics by Norman Gimbel. **Best Visual Effects,** *Alien,* H. R. Giger, Carlo Rambaldi, Brian Johnson, Nick Allder, Denys Ayling. **Best Foreign Language Film,** *The Tin Drum,* West Germany. **Best Documentary Feature,** *Best Boy,* Ira Wohl, producer. **Best Documentary Short Subject,** *Paul Robeson: Tribute to an Artist,* Janus Films. See FIELD, SALLY; HOFFMAN, DUSTIN.

American Academy and Institute of Arts and Letters. *Awards:* sculptor Howard Newman; painters Richard Anuskiewicz, Edward Dugmore, Marion Lerner Levine, and Charmion von Wiegand. *Richard and Hinda Rosenthal Award,* Dolores Milmoe. *Marjorie Peabody Waite Award,* Sidney Laufman.

American Institute of Architects. *Architectural Firm Award,* Edward Larrabee Barnes, architect, FAIA, New York City. *Award for Excellence in Architectural Education,* Serge Ivan Chermayoff, New York City. *The Twenty-Five Year Award,* for a significant building at least 25 years old, to Lever House, New York City, designed by Skidmore, Owings, and Merrill.

Antoinette Perry (Tony) Awards. *Drama:* **Best Play,** *Children of a Lesser God,* by Mark Medoff. **Best Actor,** John Rubinstein, *Children of a Lesser God.* **Best Actress,** Phyllis Frelich, *Children of a Lesser God.* **Best Director,** Vivian Matalon, *Morning's at Seven.* *Musical:* **Best Musical,** *Evita,* directed by Harold Prince. **Best Actor,** Jim Dale, *Barnum.* **Best Actress,** Patti LuPone, *Evita.* **Best Director,** Harold Prince, *Evita.* **Best Choreography,** Tommy Tune and Thommie Walsh, *A Day in Hollywood, A Night in the Ukraine.* **Best Musical Score,** Tim Rice, Andrew Lloyd Webber, *Evita.* **Best Musical Book,** Tim Rice, *Evita.* *Lawrence Langer Award,* Helen Hayes, for "distinguished lifetime achievement in American theater."

Cannes International Film Festival. *Golden Palm Grand Prize,* *All That Jazz* (U.S.A.) and *Kagemusha* (Japan). *Special Jury Prize,* Alain Resnais, for *Mon Oncle d'Amerique* (France). **Best Actor,** Michel Piccoli, *Salto nel Vuoto* (Italy). **Best Actress,** Anouk Aimée, *Salto nel Vuoto.* **Best Director,** Krzystof Zanussi, *Constans* (Poland).

Capezio Dance Foundation. *Capezio Dance Award,* Walter Terry, dance critic, for "his role as crusader for the dance throughout the United States and the world."

Hyatt Foundation. *Pritzker Architecture Prize,* Luis Barragán, Mexico, for creating "some of our most unforgettable gardens, plazas, and fountains, all magical places for meditation and companionship."

John F. Kennedy Center for the Performing Arts. *Honors,* "for artistic achievement," Leonard Bernstein, composer, conductor, and pianist; James Cagney, actor; Agnes de Mille, choreographer; Lynn Fontanne, actress; and Leontyne Price, singer.

National Academy of Recording Arts and Sciences. *Grammy Awards:* **Record of the Year,** "What a Fool Believes," the Doobie Brothers. **Album of the Year,** "52nd Street," Billy Joel. **Song of the Year,** "What a Fool Believes," Michael McDonald and Kenny Loggins. **Best New Artist of the Year,** Rickie Lee Jones. **Best Jazz Vocal Performance,** Ella Fitzgerald, "Fine and Mellow." **Best Jazz Performance, Solo,** "Jousts," Oscar Peterson. **Group,** "Duet," Gary Burton and Chick Corea. **Big Band,** "At Fargo, 1940 Live," Duke Ellington. **Best Pop Vocal Performance, Female,** "I'll Never Love This Way Again," Dionne Warwick. **Male,** "52nd Street," Billy Joel. **Duo, Group, or Chorus,** "Minute by Minute," the Doobie Brothers. **Best Pop Instrumental Performance,** "Rise," Herb Alpert. **Best Rhythm and Blues Vocal Performance, Female,** "Déjà Vu," Dionne Warwick. **Male,** "Don't Stop Till You Get Enough," Michael Jackson. **Instrumental,** "Boogie Wonderland," Earth, Wind, and Fire. **Duo, Group, or Chorus,** "After the Love Has Gone," Earth, Wind, and Fire. **Best Country Vocal Performance, Female,** "Blue Kentucky Girl," Emmylou Harris. **Male,** "The Gambler," Kenny Rogers. **Duo, Group, or Chorus,** "The Devil Went Down to Georgia," Charlie Daniels Band. **Instrumental,** "Big Sandy-Leather Britches," Doc and Merle Watson. **Best Country Song,** "You Decorated My Life," written by Bob Morrison and Debbie Hupp. **Best Rock Vocal Performance, Female,** "Hot Stuff," Donna Summer. **Male,** "Gotta Serve Somebody," Bob Dylan. **Duo, Group, or Chorus,** "Heartache Tonight," the Eagles. **Instrumental,** *Rockestra Theme,* Wings. **Best Album, Original Score for Motion Picture or Television Special,** *Superman,* John Williams. **Best Original Cast Album,** *Sweeney Todd,* Stephen Sondheim. **Album of the Year, Classical,** Brahms: *Complete Symphonies,* Chicago Symphony Orchestra, Sir George Solti, conductor. **Best Classical Orchestral Performance,** Brahms: *Complete Symphonies,* Chicago Symphony Orchestra, Sir George Solti, conductor. **Best Opera,** Benjamin Britten: *Peter Grimes,* Royal Opera House, Covent Garden, Colin Davis, conductor. **Best Classical Choral Performance,** Brahms: *A German Requiem,* Chicago Symphony Orchestra, Sir George Solti, conductor. **Best Chamber Music Performance,** Copland: *Appalachian Spring,* St. Paul Chamber Orchestra, Dennis Russel Davies, conductor. **Best Instrumental Solo Performance with Orchestra,** Bartok: *Piano Concertos, Nos. 1 and 2,* Maurizio Pollini, Chicago Symphony Orchestra, Claudio Abbado, conductor. **Best Instrumental Solo Performance,** *The Horowitz Concerts 1978/79,* Vladimir Horowitz. **Best Classical Vocal Solo Performance,** *O Solo Mio (Favorite Neapolitan Songs),* Luciano Pavarotti.

National Academy of Television Arts and Sciences. *Emmy Awards:* **Best Comedy Series,** "Taxi." **Leading Actress in a Comedy Series,** Cathryn Damon, "Soap." **Leading Actor in a Comedy Series,** Richard Mulligan, "Soap." **Best Drama Series,** "Lou Grant." **Lead Actress in a Dramatic Series,** Barbara Bel Geddes, in "Dallas." **Lead Actor in a Dramatic Series,** Ed Asner in "Lou Grant." **Best Limited Series or Special,** "Edward and Mrs. Simpson." **Best Actress, Limited Series or Special,** Patty Duke Astin in *The Miracle Worker.* **Best Actor, Limited Series or Special,** Powers Boothe in "Guyana Tragedy: The Story of Jim Jones." **Best Classical Performing Arts Program,** "Live from Studio 8H: A Tribute to Toscanini." **Best Informational Program,** "The Body Human: The Magic Sense."

New York Drama Critics Circle Awards. **Best Play,** *Talley's Folly,* by Lanford Wilson. **Best Musical,** *Evita,* lyrics by Tim Rice and music by Andrew Lloyd Webber. **Best Foreign Play,** *Betrayal,* by Harold Pinter.

Outer Critics Circle Awards. **Best Play,** *Children of a Lesser God,* by Mark Medoff. **Best Musical,** *Barnum,* music by Cy Coleman, lyrics by Michael Stewart. **Contributions to the Theater,** The Ensemble Studio Theater, Curt Dempster, director. *The John Gassner Playwriting Medallion,* to Samm-Art Williams for *Home.*

Journalism Awards

American Society of Magazine Editors. *National Magazine Awards:* **Public Service,** *Texas Monthly.* **Specialized Journal-**

ism, *IEEE Spectrum.* **Design,** *GEO.* **Essays and Criticism,** *Natural History.* **Fiction,** *Antaeus.* **Reporting,** *Mother Jones.* **Service to the Individual,** *Saturday Review.* **Single-Topic Issue,** *Scientific American.*

Alfred I. DuPont-Columbia University Awards in Broadcast Journalism, to KCTS-TV, Seattle, for *Do I Look Like I Want To Die?,* a nuclear power debate; KDFW-TV, Dallas, for reporting on aliens and children; KUTV, Salt Lake City, Utah, for *Clouds of Doubt,* a documentary on atomic testing; KXL Radio, Portland, Ore., for "The Air Space – How Safe?" a 25-part series; WGBH-TV, Boston, for *World/Inside Europe: F-16 Sale of the Century,* on world arms sales; WHA-TV, Madison, Wis., Catalyst Films, and the Wisconsin Educational Television Network for *An American Ism: Joe McCarthy;* ABC News, for *Close-Up – Arson: Fire for Hire!;* ABC News, for *World News Tonight – Second to None,* on the arms-limitation treaty debate; CBS News for "60 Minutes"; Bill D. Moyers, for outstanding reporting on CBS News and WNET-TV.

Long Island University. George Polk Memorial Awards. News Photography, United Press International, for pictures of Kurdish rebels and police officers of deposed Shah Mohammad Reza Pahlavi's regime being executed in Iran. **Foreign Reporting,** John Kifner, *The New York Times,* for his coverage of Iranian affairs from November 1979 to mid-January 1980. **National Reporting,** Brian Donovan, Bob Wyrick, and Stuart Desmond, *Newsday,* Long Island, N.Y., for coverage of the gas shortage in the summer of 1979. **Local Reporting,** Ed Petykiewicz, *The Saginaw* (Mich.) *News,* for a series on the Saginaw County justice system. **Regional Reporting,** Jim Adams and Jim Detjen, *The Louisville Courier-Journal,* for exposing illegal dumping of chemical wastes in Brooks, Ky. **Metropolitan Reporting,** Walt Bogdanich and Walter Johns, Jr., *The Cleveland Press,* for exposing corruption at a suburban hospital. **Special Interest Reporting,** Wilbert Rideau and Billy Sinclair, the *Angolite,* Angola State Prison, Louisiana. **Foreign Television Reporting,** Ed Bradley, CBS News, for reporting on Cambodian refugees. **National Television Reporting,** WRC-TV, Washington, D.C., for an investigation on the discharge of asbestos from some hair dryers. **Film Documentary,** Jack Willis and Saul Landau, New Time Films, for a study of a reporter's crusade against atomic test health hazards. **Book,** William Shawcross, for *Sideshow: Kissinger, Nixon, and the Destruction of Cambodia.* **Commentary,** the Notes and Comment section of *The New Yorker* magazine. **Special Award,** Alden Whitman, retired obituary writer for *The New York Times,* for "new standards of excellence in what had been considered a routine assignment."

The Newspaper Guild. Heywood Broun Award, Gene Miller, Carl Hiaasen, Patrick Malone, and William Montalbano, *The Miami* (Fla.) *Herald,* for a series of articles on "dangerous doctors" – alcoholics, drug addicts, incompetents, and psychopaths – who practice medicine in Florida. The series resulted in a reconstituted state medical board and new state medical-practice legislation.

The Society of Professional Journalists, Sigma Delta Chi. Newspaper Awards: General Reporting, Gene Miller, Carl Hiaasen, Patrick Malone, and William Montalbano, *The Miami* (Fla.) *Herald,* for "Dangerous Doctors: A Medical Dilemma." **Editorial Writing,** Rick Sinding, *Hackensack* (N.J.) *Record,* for a series of six editorials on the New Jersey state legislature, focusing on its problems. **Washington Correspondence,** Gordon Eliot White, *Deseret News,* Salt Lake City, Utah, for articles on the dangers of radioactive fallout caused by atomic testing in Nevada. **Foreign Correspondence,** Karen DeYoung, *The Washington Post,* for her coverage of the Nicaraguan revolution that ended the Somoza dictatorship. **News Photography,** Eddie Adams, the Associated Press, for a collection of photos, "The World's Homeless," showing the plight of the more than 10 million refugees in the world today.

Editorial Cartooning, John P. Trever, *Albuquerque* (N. Mex.) *Journal,* for cartoons on a variety of subjects. **Public Service in Journalism,** *The Miami Herald,* for its series "Police Brutality: The Violent Few," an in-depth study that is now required reading in the Miami police training program, though it was initially resisted by the department. **Magazine Awards: Reporting,** Michael W. Vargo, *Pennsylvania Illustrated,* for his article "Innocence Lost," on the reactions of the people of Middletown, Pa., to the Three Mile Island nuclear accident. **Public Service in Magazine Journalism,** *The National Geographic,* for its study, "The Promise and Peril of Nuclear Energy," presenting both the positive and negative aspects of atomic energy. **Radio Journalism: Reporting,** ABC Radio News, for its coverage of the Iran hostage crisis. **Public Service in Radio Journalism,** WJR Radio, Detroit, for a series on the multimillion-dollar credit life insurance industry. **Editorializing on Radio,** WTLC Radio, Indianapolis, for a series of editorials on "Abuse of Police Power." **Television Journalism: Reporting,** ABC-TV News and Bob Dyk, for their coverage of the Iran hostage crisis. **Public Service in Television Journalism,** KXAS-TV, Fort Worth/Dallas, for its study of an illegal immigrant, "Life Is Good, But For Whom?" **Television Editorializing,** KPTX-TV, San Francisco, for its broadcast "Save The Babies," about the high infant death rate in Oakland, Calif. **Research in Journalism,** Lloyd Wendt, Sarasota, Fla., for his history of "one of the most vigorous newspapers in the country," *Chicago Tribune: The Rise of a Great American Newspaper.*

Writers Guild of America. Award, Spot News Writing, Gilbert A. J. Longin, ABC Radio News.

Literature Awards

Academy of the American Book Awards. The American Book Awards, Autobiography, *By Myself,* by Lauren Bacall. **Biography,** *The Rise of Theodore Roosevelt,* by Edmund Morris. **Fiction,** *Sophie's Choice,* by William Styron. **General Nonfiction,** *The Right Stuff,* by Tom Wolfe. **History,** *White House Years,* by Henry Kissinger. **Religion,** *The Gnostic Gospels,* by Elaine Pagels. **Science,** *Gödel, Escher, Bach: An Eternal Golden Braid,* by Douglas R. Hofstadter. **Translation,** Jane Gary Harris and Constance Link, for *The Complete Critical Prose and Letters* of Osip E. Mandelstam. **National Medal of Literature,** Eudora Welty, for the "excellence of her past and continuing contribution to literature."

Academy of American Poets. Lamont Poetry Selection Award, Michael Van Walleghen, for his book *More Trouble with the Obvious.* **Walt Whitman Award,** Jared Carter, for his book of poems, *Work, for the Night Is Coming.* **Harold Morton Landon Award for Translation,** Saralyn R. Daly, for her translation from medieval Spanish of *The Book of True Love,* by Juan Ruiz; and Edmund Keeley, for his translation of poems by the Greek poet Yannis Ritsos, *Ritsos in Parentheses.*

American Library Association (ALA). Bailey K. Howard – World Book Encyclopedia – ALA Goals Award, to the Intellectual Freedom Committee of the ALA. **Joseph W. Lippincott Award,** E. J. Josey, Bureau of Specialist Library Services, State Educational Department, Albany, N.Y. **Melvil Dewey Medal,** Robert D. Stueart, dean and professor of the Graduate School of Library Science and Information Science, Simmons College, Boston. **Newbery Medal,** for the most distinguished contribution to children's literature, Joan W. Blos, for *A Gathering of Days, a New England Girl's Journal, 1830-32.* **Caldecott Medal,** for illustration, to Barbara Cooney, illustrator of *Ox-Cart Man,* text by Donald Hall.

Public Service Awards

Albert Einstein Peace Prize Foundation. The Albert Einstein Peace Prize, Alva Reimer Myrdal, former Swedish ambassador to India, for "her prolific writing and activities on behalf of social justice, women's rights, peace, and disarmament."

The Anti-Defamation League of B'nai B'rith. *American Heritage Award,* Henry Ford II, for "his genius in building America and his consummate sense of responsibility for the welfare of his fellow man."

The Templeton Foundation. *Templeton Prize,* Ralph W. Burhoe, theologian, for being "instrumental in widening man's knowledge of God."

U.S. Government. *Medal of Freedom,* for contributions to world peace, the security of national interest, or in cultural or other significant public or private endeavors: Ansel Adams, photographer; Lucia Chase, director of the American Ballet Theater; Archbishop Iakovos, head of the Greek Orthodox Church of North and South America; Clarence Mitchell, Jr., retired director of the Washington, D.C., office of the National Association for the Advancement of Colored People; Roger Tory Peterson, ornithologist and author; Eudora Welty, author; and Tennessee Williams, playwright. Posthumous awards: Lyndon B. Johnson, John Wayne, Hubert H. Humphrey, and Rachel Carson.

Pulitzer Prizes

Journalism. *Public Service,* The Gannett News Service, for a series of articles by John M. Hanchette, William F. Schmick, and Carlton Sherwood on the questionable use of donated funds by the Pauline Fathers, a Roman Catholic religious community. *General Local Reporting,* *The Philadelphia Inquirer,* for its coverage of the Three Mile Island nuclear mishap. *Special Local Reporting,* Nils J. A. Bruzelius, Alexander B. Hawes, Jr., Stephen A. Kurkjian, and Joan Vennochi, *The Boston Globe,* for reporting on the mismanagement in the Boston transit system. *National Reporting,* Bette Swenson Orsini and Charles Stafford, *The St. Petersburg* (Fla.) *Times,* for an investigation of the Church of Scientology. *International Reporting,* Joel Brinkley (reporter) and Jay Mather (photographer), *The Louisville* (Ky.) *Courier-Journal,* for reports on Cambodia. *Editorial Writing,* Robert I. Bartley, *The Wall Street Journal,* for a range of topics. *Spot News Photography,* name withheld, United Press International, for a photograph of a firing squad at work in Iran. The photographer's name was withheld because unsettled conditions in Iran could place him in danger. *Feature Photography,* Erwin H. Hagler, *The Dallas* (Tex.) *Times Herald,* for photographs of modern cowboys. *Editorial Cartooning,* Don Wright, *The Miami* (Fla.) *News,* for a variety of cartoons. *Distinguished Commentary,* Ellen H. Goodman, *The Boston Globe,* for her syndicated column. *Distinguished Criticism,* William A. Henry III, *The Boston Globe,* for his television criticism. *Feature Writing,* Madeleine Blais, *The Miami* (Fla.) *Herald.*

Letters. *Biography,* Edmund Morris, for *The Rise of Theodore Roosevelt.* *Drama,* Lanford Wilson, for *Talley's Folly.* *Fiction,* Norman Mailer, for *The Executioner's Song.* *General Nonfiction,* Douglas R. Hofstadter, for *Gödel, Escher, Bach: An Eternal Golden Braid.* *History,* Leon F. Litwack, for *Been in the Storm So Long.* *Music,* David Del Tredici, for "In Memory of a Summer Day." *Poetry,* Donald Rodney Justice, for *Selected Poems.*

Science and Technology Awards

American Association for the Advancement of Science (AAAS). *AAAS Socio-Psychological Prize,* Ronald S. Wilson, director, the Louisville Twin Study, School of Medicine, University of Louisville. *AAAS-Newcomb Cleveland Prize,* Stanton J. Peale, University of California, Santa Barbara; and Patrick M. Cassen and Ray T. Reynolds, Ames Research Center, National Aeronautics and Space Administration.

American Chemical Society. *Arthur C. Cope Award,* Gilbert Storck, Columbia University, New York City.

Priestley Medal, Milton Harris, Washington, D.C.

American Geophysical Union. *William Bowie Medal,* Charles Whitten, retired, U.S. Coast and Geodetic Survey. *Maurice Ewing Medal,* J. Tuzo Wilson, director general, the Ontario Science Centre, Canada.

American Institute of Physics. *Dannie Heinemann Prize for Mathematical Physics,* James Gilbert Glimm, Rockefeller University; and Arthur Michael Jaffe, Harvard University.

Columbia University. *Louisa Gross Horwitz Prize,* Cesar Milstein, molecular biologist and immunologist, Medical Research Council, University of Cambridge, England.

The Franklin Institute. *The Franklin Medal,* G. Evelyn Hutchinson, professor emeritus of zoology, Yale University.

Gairdner Foundation. *Gairdner International Awards,* for outstanding contributions to medical science, James W. Black, Wellcome Research Laboratories, Kent, England; George F. Cahill, Jr., Harvard Medical School, Boston; Walter Gilbert, Harvard University, Cambridge, Mass.; Elwood V. Jensen, University of Chicago; Frederick Sanger, Medical Research Council of Molecular Biology, University of Cambridge; and Charles R. Scriver, McGill University-Montreal Children's Hospital Research Centre, Montreal, Canada.

Geological Society of America. *Penrose Medal,* Hollis D. Hedberg, professor emeritus of geology, Princeton University. *Arthur L. Day Medal,* Harry G. Thode, McMaster University, Hamilton, Canada.

Albert and Mary Lasker Foundation. *Albert Lasker Basic Medical Research Award,* Paul Berg, Stanley N. Cohen, and A. Dale Kaiser, Stanford University, and Herbert W. Boyer, University of California, San Francisco, for contributions to recombinant-DNA research.

National Medal of Science, Robert H. Burris, professor of biochemistry, University of Wisconsin; Elizabeth C. Crosby, professor of anatomy, University of Michigan; Joseph L. Doob, professor of mathematics, University of Illinois, Urbana; Richard R. Feynman, professor of physics, California Institute of Technology; Donald E. Knuth, professor of computer science, Stanford University; Arthur Kornberg, professor of biochemistry, Stanford; Emmett N. Leith, professor of electrical engineering, University of Michigan; Herman F. Mark, professor of chemistry, Polytechnic Institute of New York, Brooklyn; Raymond D. Mindlin, professor of applied science, Columbia University; Robert N. Noyce, chairman, Intel Corporation, Santa Clara, Calif.; Severo Ochoa, Roche Institute of Molecular Biology, Nutley, N.J.; Earl R. Parker, professor of metallurgy, University of California, Berkeley; Edward M. Purcell, professor of physics, Harvard University; Simon Ramo, vice-chairman of the board, TRW, Incorporated, Redondo Beach, Calif.; John H. Sinfelt, scientific adviser, Exxon Corporate Research Laboratories, Linden, N.J.; Lyman Spitzer, Jr., professor of astronomy, Princeton University; Earl R. Stadtman, chief, laboratory of biochemistry, National Heart, Lung, and Blood Institute, National Institutes of Health, Bethesda, Md.; George L. Stebbins, Jr., professor of genetics, University of California, Davis; Paul A. Weiss, professor of biology, Rockefeller University; Victor F. Weisskopf, professor of physics, Massachusetts Institute of Technology.

Society of Chemical Industry. *Perkin Medal,* Herman F. Mark, Polytechnic Institute of New York.

Wolf Foundation. *Wolf Prize,* in physics, Michael E. Fisher and Kenneth G. Wilson, Cornell University, and Leo P. Kadanoff, University of Chicago.   Edward G. Nash

BAHAMAS. See LATIN AMERICA (Facts in Brief Table).

BAHRAIN. See MIDDLE EAST.

BALLET. See DANCING.

BANGLADESH endured harsh tests in 1980, as in the preceding eight years of its existence. Summer floods, which usually inundate one-third of the country, covered more than half, taking at least 350 lives, killing countless farm animals, and washing away thousands of homes. Wells became polluted, and cholera broke out. Coming on the heels of a crippling drought in 1979, the floods increased the need for imported grain from 1.3 million metric tons (1.4 million short tons) to 3 million metric tons (3.3 million short tons).

The economy remained depressed. About 40 per cent of the labor force was unemployed, and – in a land with the world's third lowest per-capita income – 84 per cent of the people lived below the poverty line. The inflation rate was estimated at about 35 per cent. Although foreign aid continued to flow in, an estimated $1.4 billion in 1980, it was not enough. The second five-year plan, launched in July, called for $9.5 billion in foreign aid. The United States remained the largest single donor.

Zia's "Revolution." In the face of adverse developments, President Ziaur (Zia) Rahman displayed impressive political understanding. His "revolution" in the countryside – promised in late 1979 – translated into moves to increase food production, reduce illiteracy (affecting about 80 per cent of the people), and cut down the birth rate. Bangladesh

expected the population to rise from 92.9 million in 1980 to 98 million in 1985. Zia predicted that the grain output, 13 million metric tons (14 million short tons) in 1980, would be doubled by 1985. With the president shuttling from village to village in a helicopter to encourage them, local farmers had dug 300 miles (480 kilometers) of canals by March. The plans provided for another 400 miles (640 kilometers) by year's end, to irrigate 2 million acres (800,000 hectares). Zia also moved to increase the energy output, signing an agreement with France in August for a nuclear power plant, to be built in northern Bangladesh with French aid.

While impressed, World Bank officials, who managed the aid program, remained skeptical. They doubted the claimed successes of the family-planning program; in the 1970s, the increase in the population growth rate was nearly double that of grain production. Another disturbing fact was the emergence of a well-to-do class living in luxury, while 60 per cent of the people were suffering from malnutrition.

Unrest Continued. A general strike in February erupted into violence, and two persons were killed. Opposition political parties called the strike to protest the killing of three prisoners in a Rajshahi jail during a demonstration.   Mark Gayn

See also ASIA (Facts in Brief Table). In WORLD BOOK, see BANGLADESH.

BANI-SADR, ABOL HASAN (1933-), was elected the first president of the Islamic Republic of Iran on Jan. 25, 1980. He had been dismissed as acting foreign minister in late November 1979, apparently because he favored United Nations mediation on the question of the United States hostages held in Iran. He is considered a moderate and the leading theoretician of the Iranian revolution. See IRAN.

Bani-Sadr was born in Hamadan in western Iran, the son of an *ayatollah* (religious leader). He had a strict Islamic upbringing. He attended Teheran University, becoming involved in the student nationalist movement in 1951. In 1953, he joined an anti-shah underground group.

After several arrests by Savak, Shah Mohammad Reza Pahlavi's secret police, Bani-Sadr served a short prison term, then went into exile in France in 1964, studying and later teaching at the University of Paris. He wrote three books and dozens of articles attacking the shah and advocating revolution. When Ayatollah Ruhollah Khomeini went to live in France in 1978, Bani-Sadr became an active supporter. He returned to Iran with Khomeini in early 1979 and became president of the secret Revolutionary Council, which led the revolution and effectively governed Iran for months, though it did not formally replace the Iranian government until early in November 1979.   Edward G. Nash

Bangladesh President Ziaur Rahman greets residents of Chandpur during a tour promoting population control and greater farm output.

BANKS AND BANKING

BANKS AND BANKING. Interest rates and the conditions under which banks in the United States do business underwent more drastic changes in 1980 than in any year since the Civil War ended in 1865. After a long period of *stagflation* – a muddled, stagnant economy afflicted with a high inflation rate – the United States fell into a sharp recession in 1980 and painfully began to find its way out. Three major federal policy moves affected the banking industry during the year.

Tight Money Policy. In January, the financial markets were still learning to live with the Federal Reserve Board (Fed) decision of October 1979 to let interest rates float and concentrate on controlling the growth rate of the money supply. Federal Reserve policy had been to control the federal funds rate – the rate of interest at which banks lend one another reserves. When this rate rose above the Fed's allowable range, the Fed would pump more money into the banking system by buying U.S. Treasury securities, enabling banks to make more loans and temporarily driving down the price of credit. However, driving down the price of credit by expanding the money supply relative to the supply of goods and services also meant driving prices up. So, the Fed, feeling that controlling inflation was of paramount importance, refrained from buying Treasury securities.

Bankers immediately expected tighter credit conditions, and interest rates rose. The 90-day Treasury bill (T-bill) rate rose from 10.2 per cent to more than 12 per cent and held at about 12 per cent until the second week in February. The federal-funds rate jumped to 15.7 per cent early in November 1979, but fluctuated between 13 and 14 per cent until mid-February. The longer-term, five-year Treasury security rate rose only to slightly more than 11 per cent in November 1979, indicating that the market expected a lower inflation rate. Long-maturity interest rates that are lower than short-term rates indicate that lenders expect the inflation rate to fall.

Thus, the Fed's move appeared at first to work. The rate of increase in the money supply went down. The money supply in its narrowest definition, called M1A, includes currency in the hands of the public and checking-account balances in banks (excluding interbank and government deposits). The M1A had been rising at 5.3 per cent annually early in 1979 and rose at only 4.7 per cent annually from November 1979 to March 1980. M1B, which includes M1A and checking-type deposits in savings and loans (S&L's), credit unions, and similar institutions, had been growing at 7.3 per cent annually in mid-1979 and grew at only 5.6 per cent from November 1979 to March 1980. The new, more broadly defined money supply, M2, slowed its growth rate from 9.8 to 7 per cent over the same period. M2 adds all savings-account balances and

Britain's giant Midland Bank bought Crocker National Corporation of California in the biggest foreign take-over of a U.S. bank.

small certificates of deposit in all institutions, as well as money-market-fund accounts and some other balances.

But the inflation rate continued to rise – from 13.9 per cent at the end of 1979 to 16.3 per cent for the first half of 1980 as measured by the Consumer Price Index (CPI). (In the Special Reports section, see THE INFLATION RATE, THE COST OF LIVING . . . AND YOU.) This increase produced fears that consumers would continue to expand their borrowing and reduce their saving. The saving rate – historically about 6 per cent – had dropped in the fourth quarter of 1979 to 3.5 per cent, and consumer installment credit had risen to a high of $311-billion at the end of 1979 as consumers borrowed to buy durable goods before prices went up more.

Clamps on Credit. These fears prompted President Jimmy Carter to announce consumer credit restrictions on March 14 and say that he would use his powers under the Credit Control Act of 1969 to restrict banks' ability to make loans. But consumer credit by this time was already falling at an annual rate of 7 per cent, and business loans from large commercial banks had peaked in January.

The program required financial institutions to set aside non-earning reserves equal to 15 per cent of certain managed liabilities of banks – mostly large certificates of deposit – and of new balances on credit cards and increases in money-market-fund account balances. This effectively increased the cost of funds to lenders and immediately sent interest rates to unprecedented highs.

Interest Rates Rocket. Conventional mortgage rates exceeded 16 per cent in April, the federal-funds rate hit 19.2 per cent, and the *prime rate* – the rate banks charge their best corporate customers – rose to 20 per cent on April 2. As another result, money-market funds, which normally lend money to banks by purchasing large certificates of deposit and to corporations by buying commercial paper (short-term notes), dried up as a source of new loans when managers refused to accept new accounts. The total invested in money-market funds had risen from $12 billion in January 1979 to $61-billion in March 1980 as high interest rates caused investors to pull deposits from banks and S&L's, whose interest rates paid on savings were held under 6 per cent by the Fed's Regulation Q.

The credit-restraint program was short-lived. Demand for consumer credit and business loans was falling as a result of the recession, and some provisions of the program were withdrawn even before going into effect. The last controls were withdrawn by August 11.

Interest rates fell quickly. By May 28, the prime rate fell to 12 per cent. By the middle of June, the federal-funds rate had dropped more than 10 percentage points, and the 90-day T-bill rate was below 7 per cent. The inflation rate also dropped to below 7 per cent between June and September, including the month of July when the CPI rose from 247.6 to 247.8 (1967 prices=100), the smallest increase since 1963.

The Economy Edges Up. By July, the economy was beginning to expand slowly, a process that continued for the rest of the year. Business loans from large commercial banks, which had fallen to $158 billion in June, began to expand again at an annual rate of 18 per cent. Checking-account balances in banks, which represent money about to be spent, rose at a 12 per cent rate.

Interest rates began to rise again as they usually do in an expansion. The 90-day T-bill rate was above 12 per cent and rising in November, the prime rate was above 14 per cent, and the five-year Treasury security rate, which had been below 9 per cent in June, was above 12 per cent. These increases indicated a greater demand for credit due to the recovery and greater expectations of inflation as the money supply began to grow rapidly.

The narrowly defined M1B fell by $5 billion to $382 billion from March to the end of April, but it resumed its climb at a 14 per cent rate for the rest of the year. The more widely defined M2 grew from May on at over 17 per cent annually. Year's end saw an expanding economy, continued double-digit inflation, and a prime rate that reached a record 21.5 per cent on December 20.

Banking Deregulated. President Carter signed the Depository Institutions Deregulation and Monetary Control Act of 1980 on March 31. The two major effects of this act were to blur the distinctions between commercial banks and other depository institutions by removing restrictions on the services that they may offer and ending *disintermediation*, the periodic flow of funds out of those institutions whenever market rates rise above official interest ceilings.

Beginning on Jan. 1, 1981, the act provides, banks, S&L's, credit unions, and mutual savings banks may offer interest-bearing checking accounts. S&L's will be able to offer automobile loans as well as mortgages.

Two of the act's provisions dealt with interest rates. Regulation Q, which limits the interest that depository institutions may pay for deposits, will be phased out over the next six years. Interest-rate ceilings will be lifted gradually until they meet market rates and will then be abolished. This will end the disintermediation that threatens the ability of banks and S&L's to make new loans. On the other hand, the act also suspends all state usury laws that put ceilings on the interest rates that banks may charge for loans.   Donald W. Swanton

See also ECONOMICS. In WORLD BOOK, see BANKS AND BANKING.

BARBADOS. See WEST INDIES.

BASEBALL. The Philadelphia Phillies won baseball's top prize after an exciting 1980 season followed by thrilling play-offs and World Series. The Phillies defeated the Kansas City Royals, 4 games to 2, in a World Series between two virtual strangers to that fall competition.

The Phillies, who started playing in 1883, had won only two previous pennants – in 1915 and 1950 – and had never won a World Series. This was the first World Series for the Royals in their 12-year history.

The Royals led the American League's Western Division by 20 games on September 1 and won the division by 14 games over the surprising Oakland A's. Of the three other major-league division races, two were decided on the next-to-last day of the regular season and the other the day after the season was scheduled to end.

More excitement came from George Brett's assault on a .400 batting average, last achieved in the major leagues when Ted Williams of the Boston Red Sox hit .406 in 1941. The Kansas City third baseman, hampered by injuries all season, finished with .390, the highest in the major leagues since Williams' big year.

National League. At the start of September, Philadelphia, the Montreal Expos, and the Pittsburgh Pirates were virtually tied for first place in the Eastern Division, and the Houston Astros led the Los Angeles Dodgers by a half-game in the West. Pittsburgh, slowed by knee injuries to Willie Stargell and Dave Parker, its leading sluggers, was eliminated with a week remaining in the season. The other races were decided in head-to-head series – Philadelphia at Montreal and Houston at Los Angeles – that closed the regular season.

Philadelphia won the division title on the night before the season ended on Mike Schmidt's 11th-inning home run. Los Angeles had to win three straight games from Houston to end the season tied for first place, and it did. The next day – in a one-game division play-off in Los Angeles – Houston won, 7-1, on Joe Niekro's six-hit pitching.

The pennant play-off between Philadelphia and Houston went the full five games, the last four requiring extra innings. Philadelphia won the deciding game, 8-7 in 10 innings, in a series so entertaining that the spectators in the Houston Astrodome stood after the final out and applauded both teams.

The Astros had other problems. Although they attracted almost 2.5 million spectators and came within six outs of their first pennant, Tal Smith, the club president, was fired for lack of success. And J. R. Richard, their star pitcher, suffered a stroke on July 30 that endangered his baseball career and, for a while, his life.

American League. The Yankees won the Eastern Division title by three games over the Baltimore Orioles. The Yankees finished the season strongly after dissipating a large lead, and George Steinbrenner, their principal owner, frequently criticized his players and manager Dick Howser, who finally resigned in November under pressure.

The surprising team of the season was Oakland, which climbed from a won-lost record of 54-108 and last place in 1979 to 83-79 and second place. Billy Martin had become Oakland's 10th manager in 11 years, and he emphasized speed, bunting, stealing, hit and run, and starting pitchers who seldom needed relief.

No one threatened Kansas City during the regular season or the play-offs. The Royals won their division title easily and then swept by the Yankees in three straight play-off games, 7-2, 3-2, and 4-2.

World Series. Philadelphia and Kansas City had much in common. Each had won its fourth division title in five years, but only its first pennant in that time. Each had a manager serving his first full season – Dallas Green for Philadelphia and Jim Frey for Kansas City. Each club also had batting and pitching balance.

The key players for Philadelphia were third baseman Mike Schmidt and pitcher Steve Carlton. Schmidt led the major leagues in home runs (48)

Final Standings in Major League Baseball

American League

Eastern Division	W.	L.	Pct.	GB.
New York	103	59	.636	
Baltimore	100	62	.617	3
Milwaukee	86	76	.531	17
Boston	83	77	.519	19
Detroit	84	78	.519	19
Cleveland	79	81	.494	23
Toronto	67	95	.414	36

Western Division

	W.	L.	Pct.	GB.
Kansas City	97	65	.599	
Oakland	83	79	.512	14
Minnesota	77	84	.478	19½
Texas	76	85	.472	20½
Chicago	70	90	.438	26
California	65	95	.406	31
Seattle	59	103	.364	38

Offensive Leaders

Batting Average – George Brett, Kansas City	.390
Runs – Willie Wilson, Kansas City	134
Home Runs – Reggie Jackson, New York; Ben Oglivie, Milwaukee (tie)	41
Runs Batted In – Cecil Cooper, Milwaukee	122
Hits – Willie Wilson, Kansas City	230
Stolen Bases – Rickey Henderson, Oakland	100

Leading Pitchers

Games Won – Steve Stone, Baltimore	25
Win Average – Steve Stone, Baltimore (25-7) (162 or more innings)	.781
Earned-Run Average – Rudy May, New York	2.46
Strikeouts – Len Barker, Cleveland	187
Saves – Rich Gossage, New York; Dan Quisenberry, Kansas City (tie)	33

Awards

*Most Valuable Player – George Brett, Kansas City
*Cy Young – Steve Stone, Baltimore
*Rookie of the Year – Joe Charboneau, Cleveland

National League

Eastern Division	W.	L.	Pct.	GB.
Philadelphia	91	71	.562	
Montreal	90	72	.556	1
Pittsburgh	83	79	.512	8
St. Louis	74	88	.457	17
New York	67	95	.414	24
Chicago	64	98	.395	27

Western Division

	W.	L.	Pct.	GB.
*Houston	93	70	.571	
Los Angeles	92	71	.564	1
Cincinnati	81	73	.549	3½
Atlanta	81	80	.503	11
San Francisco	75	86	.466	17
San Diego	73	89	.451	19½

*Won division play-off game, 7-1

Offensive Leaders

Batting Average – Bill Buckner, Chicago	.324
Runs – Keith Hernandez, St. Louis	111
Home Runs – Mike Schmidt, Philadelphia	48
Runs Batted In – Mike Schmidt, Philadelphia	121
Hits – Steve Garvey, Los Angeles	200
Stolen Bases – Ron LeFlore, Montreal	97

Leading Pitchers

Games Won – Steve Carlton, Philadelphia	24
Win Average – Jim Bibby, Pittsburgh (19-6) (162 or more innings)	.760
Earned-Run Average – Don Sutton, Los Angeles	2.20
Strikeouts – Steve Carlton, Philadelphia	286
Saves – Bruce Sutter, Chicago	28

Awards

*Most Valuable Player – Mike Schmidt, Philadelphia
*Cy Young – Steve Carlton, Philadelphia
*Rookie of the Year – Steve Howe, Los Angeles
†Manager of the Year – Bill Virdon, Houston
*Selected by Baseball Writers Association of America.
†Selected by *The Sporting News.*

Mike Schmidt leaps happily onto a pile of celebrating Phillies teammates after they won decisive sixth World Series game.

contract created the free-agent system that escalated salaries. The owners insisted that the new contract require clubs that signed free agents to compensate the players' former clubs with established major-leaguers rather than amateur draft choices. The players said that such a requirement would effectively destroy the system.

On April 1, with no agreement reached, the players, in effect, canceled the remaining preseason exhibition games. They would start the regular season on schedule, eight days hence, but would strike if no contract was agreed on by May 22. Less than 10 hours before the deadline, agreement was reached on the other issues and the free-agent problem was deferred until January 1981.

Hall of Fame. Outfielders Al Kaline, who spent his 22 major-league seasons with the Detroit Tigers, and Edwin (Duke) Snider, who spent 16 of his 18 National League seasons with the Brooklyn and Los Angeles Dodgers, were voted into the National Baseball Hall of Fame. It was Kaline's first year and Snider's 11th year on the ballot.

Chuck Klein, a National League outfielder for 16 years, and Tom Yawkey, who owned the Red Sox for 43 years, were posthumously voted in by a veterans' committee. The committee was limited to two selections. Third in its voting was first baseman Johnny Mize.   Frank Litsky

In WORLD BOOK, see BASEBALL.

and the National League in runs batted in (121). The left-handed Carlton led the major leagues in innings pitched (304) and strikeouts (286).

Kansas City's leading players were Brett, Willie Wilson, and Dan Quisenberry. The 27-year-old Brett missed 44 games with bruises, a torn ankle ligament, and tendinitis, and his World Series play was hampered until minor hemorrhoid surgery after the second game. Wilson, an outfielder, batted .326, stole 79 bases, and led the American League in hits (230) and runs scored (134). Quisenberry, a relief pitcher, saved 33 games, tying him with Rich Gossage of the Yankees for the major-league lead.

The Phillies won the first two World Series games, the Royals the next two, the Phillies the last two. Schmidt, with eight hits, seven runs batted in, two home runs, and a .381 average, was voted Most Valuable Player. Carlton won two games, and relief pitcher Frank (Tug) McGraw saved two.

Willie Aikens hit four home runs and Amos Otis three for Kansas City. However, Wilson batted only .154 and struck out 12 times, a World Series record, in 26 at-bats. Frank White, the second baseman, who hit .545 in the play-offs, batted only .080 — two hits in 25 at-bats.

Player Relations. The four-year contract between club owners and the Major League Baseball Players Association expired on Dec. 31, 1979. The old

BASKETBALL. The Los Angeles Lakers won the National Basketball Association (NBA) 1979-1980 championship, and the University of Louisville captured the National Collegiate Athletic Association (NCAA) title. However, much of the excitement was provided by the Boston Celtics and the University of California, Los Angeles (UCLA), two teams that almost climbed back to the very top.

During the previous season, the Celtics finished with a 29-53 won-lost record, the poorest in their division. This time, the revitalized Celtics had a new coach in Bill Fitch and the Rookie of the Year in Larry Bird, a power forward who was College Player of the Year in 1978-1979.

The NBA's 22 teams played 82 games from early October 1979 to late March 1980. The Celtics (61-21) had the best record. The Lakers, Atlanta Hawks, and Milwaukee Bucks won the other division titles.

The Lakers were led by Kareem Abdul-Jabbar and Earvin (Magic) Johnson. Abdul-Jabbar, the 7-foot 2-inch (218-centimeter) center, was named the NBA's Most Valuable Player for the sixth time in his 11 pro seasons. Johnson, the 6-foot 8-inch (203-centimeter) guard who had been the number-one choice in the annual draft of college seniors, became an instant pro star.

Jack McKinney started the season as Laker coach. After 14 games, he suffered severe head injuries in a bicycling accident, and Paul West-head, the assistant coach, took over. Under West-head, the Laker record was 50-18 for the rest of the regular season and 12-4 in the play-offs.

McKinney asked to return in mid-March, but Lakers owner Jerry Buss refused to break up a winning combination. After the season, Buss signed Westhead to a four-year, $1.1-million contract as head coach. McKinney became coach of the Indiana Pacers.

The Play-Offs. In the conference finals, the Lakers eliminated the defending champion Seattle SuperSonics, 4 games to 1, and the Philadelphia 76ers beat the Celtics, 4-1. The Lakers won the championship finals in six games, and the last game, played on May 16 in Philadelphia, was a memorable one.

Abdul-Jabbar had sprained his left ankle severely while scoring 40 points in the previous game and could not play. His substitute was Johnson, who gave away height, weight, strength, and experience to Darryl Dawkins, the 76ers' 6-foot 11½-inch (212-centimeter), 252-pound (114-kilogram) center. Johnson played 47 of the 48 minutes, scored 42 points, and collected 15 rebounds and 7 assists. The Lakers won, 123-107, and Johnson was voted Most Valuable Player in the play-offs.

George Gervin of the San Antonio Spurs won his third straight scoring title, averaging 33.1 points per game. Michael Ray Richardson of the New

National Basketball Association Final Standings

Eastern Conference

Atlantic Division	W.	L.	Pct.
Boston	61	21	.744
Philadelphia	59	23	.720
Washington	39	43	.476
New York	39	43	.476
New Jersey	34	48	.415

Central Division	W.	L.	Pct.
Atlanta	50	32	.610
Houston	41	41	.500
San Antonio	41	41	.500
Cleveland	37	45	.451
Indiana	37	45	.451
Detroit	16	66	.195

Western Conference

Midwest Division	W.	L.	Pct.
Milwaukee	49	33	.598
Kansas City	47	35	.573
Chicago	30	52	.366
Denver	30	52	.366
Utah	24	58	.293

Pacific Division	W.	L.	Pct.
Los Angeles	60	22	.732
Seattle	56	26	.683
Phoenix	55	27	.671
Portland	38	44	.463
San Diego	35	47	.427
Golden State	24	58	.293

Leading Scorers	G.	FG.	FT.	Pts.	Avg.
Gervin, San Antonio	78	1,024	505	2,585	33.1
Free, San Diego	68	737	572	2,055	30.2
Dantley, Utah	68	730	443	1,903	28.0
Erving, Philadelphia	78	838	420	2,100	26.9
Malone, Houston	82	778	563	2,119	25.8
Abdul-Jabbar, Los Angeles	82	835	364	2,034	24.8
Issel, Denver	82	715	517	1,951	23.8
Hayes, Washington	81	761	334	1,859	23.0
Birdsong, Kansas City	82	781	286	1,858	22.7
Mitchell, Cleveland	82	775	270	1,820	22.2

College Champions

College Tournament Champions
NCAA Division I: Louisville
NCAA Division II: Virginia Union
NCAA Division III: North Park College
NAIA: Cameron
NIT: Virginia
AIAW (Women) Division I: Old Dominion
AIAW Division II: Dayton
AIAW Division III: Worcester State

Conference	School
Atlantic Coast	Maryland (regular season)
	Duke (ACC tournament)
Big East	Georgetown-St. John's-Syracuse (tie)
	Georgetown (Big E tournament)
Big Eight	Missouri (regular season)
	Kansas State (Big 8 tournament)
Big Sky	Weber State
Big Ten	Indiana
East Coast	St. Joseph's (regular season)
	La Salle (EC tournament)
Eastern 8	Duquesne-Rutgers-Villanova (tie)
	Villanova (E-8 tournament)
Ivy League	Pennsylvania-Princeton (tie)
	Pennsylvania (play-off)
Metro Seven	Louisville
Mid-American	Toledo
Midwestern City	Loyola (Chicago) (regular season)
	Oral Roberts (MC tournament)
Missouri Valley	Bradley
Ohio Valley	Western Kentucky-Murray State (tie)
	Western Kentucky (OV tournament)
Pacific Coast Athletic	Utah State (regular season)
	San Jose State (PCAA tournament)
Pacific Ten	Oregon State
Southern	Furman
Southeastern	Kentucky (regular season)
	Louisiana State (SEC tournament)
Southland	Lamar
Southwest	Texas A. & M.
Southwestern Athletic	Alcorn State
Sun Belt	South Alabama (regular season)
	Virginia Commonwealth (SB tournament)
Trans America Athletic	Northeast Louisiana
West Coast Athletic	San Francisco
Western Athletic	Brigham Young

Women's Professional Basketball League

Eastern Division	W.	L.	Pct.
New York	28	7	.800
New Orleans	22	12	.647
New Jersey	19	17	.528
St. Louis	15	21	.417

Midwest Division			
Iowa	24	12	.667
Minnesota	22	12	.647
Chicago	17	19	.472
Milwaukee	10	24	.294

Western Division			
Houston	19	14	.576
San Francisco	18	18	.500
California	11	18	.379
Dallas	7	28	.200

Guard Darrell Griffith of Louisville drives past UCLA defenders in NCAA championship game and leads his team to the college title.

teams, finished only fourth in the Pacific 10 Conference, and was trying to regain its glory with a new coach in Larry Brown and four freshmen in key positions. Its nine defeats were its most in 17 years.

Louisville won the Metro Conference title and finished the regular season with a 28-3 record. In the NCAA national semifinals on March 22 at Indianapolis, Louisville beat Iowa, 80-72, and UCLA eliminated Purdue, 67-62.

In the championship final on March 24 at Indianapolis, UCLA led Louisville, 54-50, with 4 minutes 32 seconds remaining. Then Darrell Griffith led a Louisville rally, UCLA made mistakes, and Louisville won, 59-54. Griffith, a 6-foot 4-inch (193-centimeter) guard, was chosen as the tournament's Most Valuable Player.

Mark Aguirre, a De Paul forward; Michael Brooks, a La Salle forward; and Griffith were named players of the year in various polls. Others chosen for all-American teams included Joe Barry Carroll, Purdue's 7-foot 1-inch (216-centimeter) center; Mike Gminski of Duke; Albert King of Maryland; and Kyle Macy of Kentucky.

Old Dominion University of Norfolk, Va., won the Association for Intercollegiate Athletics for Women championship for the second straight year. It defeated Tennessee, 68-53, on March 23 at Mount Pleasant, Mich., in the final.   Frank Litsky

In WORLD BOOK, see BASKETBALL.

York Knickerbockers led the league in assists (10.1 per game) and steals (3.23 per game).

The all-star team consisted of Abdul-Jabbar at center, Julius Erving of Philadelphia and Bird at forward, and Paul Westphal of Phoenix and Gervin at guard. After the season, Westphal was traded to Seattle for guard Dennis Johnson.

The Women's Professional Basketball League started its second season with 14 teams, but Philadelphia and Washington dropped out in December 1979. The New York Stars defeated the Iowa Cornets, 3 games to 1, in the play-off finals.

Ann Meyers of the New Jersey Gems and Molly Bolin of Iowa shared the season's Most Valuable Player award. Meyers was the leading scorer with a 32.8-point average after she failed in a highly publicized tryout with Indiana of the NBA.

The Colleges. No one seemed to want the top ranking among colleges. Kentucky, number one in the preseason polls, was upset by Duke in the first game of the season. Indiana was then number one until forward Mike Woodson was injured. Duke was then number one until it returned from a Christmas trip to London and was upset. De Paul was then number one until it lost to UCLA in the second round of the NCAA championships.

The NCAA tournament was expanded to 48 teams from 40. UCLA was one of the last two teams invited. It was not ranked among the top 20

BEATRIX (1938-   ) became queen of the Netherlands on April 30, 1980. She succeeded her mother, Queen Juliana, who abdicated on that day – her 71st birthday. Queen Juliana had announced her intention to abdicate on January 31, Beatrix' birthday.

Beatrix Wilhelmina Armgard was born on Jan. 31, 1938, the first child of Queen Juliana and Prince Bernhard. During the German occupation in World War II, the royal family lived in exile in Great Britain and Canada. When they returned to the Netherlands in 1945, Beatrix received as normal an upbringing as her parents could provide. For example, her weekly allowance was reportedly $1.50 per week until her 18th birthday.

Princess Beatrix studied sociology, parliamentary history, and law at the University of Leyden. She earned a doctor's degree in law there in 1961.

In 1965, she became engaged to Claus von Amsberg, a German diplomat. The engagement aroused controversy because he had been a member of the Hitler Youth and served in the German Army during World War II. But a denazification court cleared him after the war. The two were married in 1966, and they have three sons.

Queen Beatrix enjoys horseback riding, skiing, tennis, and sailing, and she is interested in sculpture, painting, drama, and ballet.   Jay Myers

See also NETHERLANDS.

BELAUNDE TERRY, FERNANDO (1912-), was inaugurated president of Peru on July 28, 1980, after a May election that gave him 43 per cent of the popular vote in a field of 15 candidates. Belaunde, who has a large following among the poor, served as president from 1963 to 1968, when he was ousted by a military coup d'état. His re-election marked the return of civilian rule. See PERU.

Fernando Belaunde Terry was born on Oct. 7, 1912, in Lima, into an aristocratic family that had long been involved in Peruvian politics. His father, Rafael Belaunde Diez Canesco, had served as prime minister and as ambassador to Mexico and Chile. Belaunde was educated and worked as an architect and urban planner in France and the United States during the years of exile when his father was at odds with the ruling Peruvian regime.

Belaunde entered politics in 1944 and was elected to the Chamber of Deputies in 1945. In 1948, he became dean of the National School of Architecture. He ran unsuccessfully for the presidency in 1956 and 1962, before winning in 1963. After his 1968 ouster, he lived in exile in the United States for seven years, teaching at such universities as Harvard, Columbia, and Johns Hopkins. Belaunde has written extensively on Peruvian history and culture. He is married to Violeta Correa, his former secretary.   Edward G. Nash

BELGIUM endured three threats to the center-left coalition government of Christian Democrat Prime Minister Wilfried Martens early in 1980, then saw the government collapse in April and October. The first threat started in January with a 15-day strike of doctors, dentists, and pharmacists, who opposed plans for British-style socialized medicine. An emergency bill would have cut $184 million from their fees, but Parliament rejected it.

French-speaking parties threatened to pull out of Martens' five-party coalition on January 8 in opposition to his plan to end the rivalry between Dutch-speaking Flemings in the north and French-speaking Walloons in the south. Martens wanted to grant some autonomy to the two groups, but he shelved his plans after the pullout threat. Nevertheless, the French-speaking Democratic Front (FDF) of Brussels withdrew from the coalition on January 16, depriving the government of the two-thirds majority needed to pass reform measures. But Martens struggled on. Rioting on March 8 and 9 posed a new threat. Shots were fired between Walloon and Flemish militants fighting in the eastern district of Fourons.

A Party Revolt involving Christian Democrats toppled the coalition on April 9. The Flemish wing objected to proposals for a new system of regional administration. They demanded equal representa-

Flemish militants close ranks in a cemetery while fighting against their ethnic rivals, the Walloons, during March riots.

tion in the 19 borough councils of Brussels and in the city's administration, though most Brussels residents speak French. King Baudouin I persuaded Martens to patch together his old coalition, so he promised to shelve the question of Brussels' status until 1982. A new six-party government was sworn in on May 18.

Parliament passed by 156 votes to 19 a bill granting partial autonomy to Flanders and Wallonia on August 5. Brussels remains temporarily under central control. Wallonia, with a population of about 3.1 million, and Flanders, which has 5.5 million persons, will have their own legislatures and executives to handle local issues. Wallonia's parliament was installed on October 15 in Namur.

The Second Fall came on October 4 when the coalition disagreed on methods of financing the social security system's $1.2-billion deficit. The government wanted to limit unemployment compensation and medical insurance, but trade unions and Socialists in the coalition opposed it. King Baudouin asked Martens to form a new government on October 7. Martens assembled a coalition on October 22. Kenneth Brown

See also EUROPE (Facts in Brief Table). In WORLD BOOK, see BELGIUM; FLANDERS.

BELIZE. See LATIN AMERICA.

BENIN. See AFRICA.

BHUTAN. See ASIA.

BIOCHEMISTRY. Two approaches to genetic remodeling of mammals moved selected genes into living animals in 1980. Martin J. Cline of the University of California, Los Angeles, a specialist in blood disorders, transplanted a gene from the bone marrow cells of one set of mice into cells that subsequently populated bone marrow of other mice.

Bone-forming tissue is suitable for gene replacement in adult animals because it grows very rapidly throughout life. Cline used bone marrow cells of mice susceptible to the toxic drug methotrexate, used in the treatment of cancer. He let those cells take up genetic material from cells of mice resistant to the drug. A group of mice susceptible to methotrexate were treated with radiation to destroy their own bone marrow cells and then injected with the foreign cells, some of which had picked up the resistance genes. Cline gave the mice methotrexate to encourage growth of the drug-resistant cells. Within a month, resistant cells predominated in the bone marrow, and the mice could tolerate high doses of the drug. Cline predicted such a technique eventually could be used to transfer genes for drug resistance into the blood cells of human patients receiving anticancer drugs.

Cline said in October that he had used a similar gene-remodeling technique on human patients in Israel and Italy in July. He transplanted genes to step up hemoglobin production into the bone marrow of two women suffering from thalassemia, a blood disease. It was still not known by year-end if the treatment was effective. Scientists have not yet used gene remodeling on human patients in the United States.

Another Method of introducing a gene into adult mice was to slip it into the embryo and let it reproduce as the embryo developed. Using a glass needle finer than a human hair, a team of scientists led by cell biologist Francis H. Ruddle of Yale University injected into newly fertilized mouse eggs about 1,000 copies of two viral genes. The eggs were then implanted in foster mothers. The researchers extracted the genetic material from the mice just after birth and in several cases found evidence that the viral gene had been distributed to most, if not all, of the mouse cells. But Ruddle could not determine whether the viral genes functioned in any mouse cell.

Pure Human Antibody. Scientists at Stanford University in Palo Alto, Calif., developed a technique to produce large amounts of human monoclonal antibodies – exact copies of one specific antibody – which may be useful in studying and treating human diseases. The advance built on the method developed five years earlier by British scientists, who combined two types of mouse cells into hybrid cells that grow indefinitely in the laboratory and produce monoclonal antibodies.

Physicians Lennart Olsson and Henry S. Kaplan of Stanford reported in July that they had fused two types of human cell – cancerous bone marrow cells, chosen for their ability to grow under laboratory conditions, and spleen cells that produce antibodies. The spleen cells were taken from organs removed during clinical evaluation of patients with Hodgkin's disease. All descendants of each hybrid cell growing in laboratory culture are alike, producing the same specific antibody.

The human body responds to an invading microorganism with a complex mix of antibodies aimed at different parts of the intruder. Pure human material from laboratory-grown cells may be useful for diagnosing infections, cancers, and heart disease; making vaccines; bolstering the immune system; and carrying drugs to specific sites in the body.

Recombinant-DNA techniques, which use gene-splicing on bacteria to produce valuable mammalian materials, moved closer to commercial application in 1980. The small companies that sprang up in the 1970s to employ recombinant-DNA techniques, as well as large corporations such as the drug manufacturer Eli Lilly and Company, increased the scale of their operations.

The National Institutes of Health (NIH) gave researchers case-by-case permission to grow batches of bacteria containing specific foreign genetic material in pilot plant facilities. Lilly began growing insulin-producing bacteria in 2,000-liter (2,100-quart) batches. The NIH also issued permission for stepped-up production of human growth hormone, human hormone somatostatin, and the hormone thymosin alpha-1, which stimulates the human immune system.

Lilly on July 14 began the first human tests of a bacterial product altered with recombinant-DNA techniques. Eight nondiabetic, healthy subjects received human insulin made by bacteria, and preliminary results showed the hormone to be as effective as naturally produced insulin.

Human Proteins. Using gene-splicing techniques on bacteria, scientists produced an impressive array of human proteins. Probably the greatest excitement was generated by the announcement on January 16 that scientists working for Biogen S.A., a small company based in Geneva, Switzerland, had created bacteria able to make active human interferon. Interferon is a substance that animal cells produce to fight viral infection. Previous experiments with very limited amounts of interferon available from humans had indicated that it might be useful for fighting hepatitis, other viral infections, and some forms of cancer. Other laboratories soon reported bacterial production of interferon. Julie Ann Miller

In WORLD BOOK, see BIOCHEMISTRY; CELL.

BIOLOGY. The Supreme Court of the United States ruled on June 16, 1980, that life forms—specifically, bacteria—can be patented. The court decided that microbiologist Ananda M. Chakrabarty could receive a patent on a *Pseudomonas* bacterium that he crossbred and fused from existing strains. He developed the bacterium, which breaks down crude oil and therefore could be used to clean up oil spills, about eight years ago in research for the General Electric Company. The court said the bacterium is not nature's handiwork, but Chakrabarty's, and therefore is patentable.

The decision opens up the possibility that the many researchers who are altering microorganisms with genetic-engineering techniques may obtain patents. After the Supreme Court decision, a spokesman for the U.S. Patent and Trademark Office told reporters it had more than 100 applications on file for patents on microorganisms and would begin processing them. Bacteria that manufacture human insulin, human growth hormone, and human interferon are among those that promise to be commercially valuable. The People's Business Commission, a citizens' group that has warned of dangers of genetic engineering, said the decision lays the groundwork for corporations to own the processes of life.

Patents have been available for new breeds of plants under special congressional acts passed in 1930 and 1970. Whether the Supreme Court's June decision will apply eventually to animals altered by genetic engineering remained an open question.

Birds, Bees, and Mice. A tree-climbing mouse is the animal responsible for pollinating an air plant in a tropical forest in Costa Rica. Botanists Cecile Lumer and Ghillean T. Prance of the New York Botanical Garden described the first documented case of a nonflying mammal pollinating a plant. Previously, scientists had observed bats, birds, and bees pollinating flowers. Using red light to observe the blossoms at night, Lumer saw mice climb tree trunks and suck the nectar of *epiphyte* (air plants) flowers hanging above their perches. The mice carried pollen dust on their noses to other flowers.

Historic Habitat. A living coral reef, with more than 200 species of plants and animals, went on display at the Smithsonian Institution's National Museum of Natural History in Washington, D.C., on October 15. Smithsonian scientists were the first to sustain the complex ecological system of a reef away from the ocean. The behavioral patterns, community interrelationships, and energy economics of the museum reef operate much as they do in nature, said marine biologist Walter H. Adey, developer of the system. The novel techniques used in the system were expected to be applicable to other aquatic communities. Because scientists can

Marine biologists in Florida study the giant sea roach, a crustacean, for insight into life at ocean depths of 4,000 feet (1,200 meters).

make more extensive observations of plants and animals in a model system than in the ocean, such miniature systems are expected to dramatically advance learning in marine biology and ecology.

Innovations in the reef system include use of metal halide lamps that simulate the intensity of spectrum of tropical sunlight. They provide sufficient light to nourish at least 35 species of algae, the base of the community's food chain.

A wave generator is another unusual feature of the reef system. Two large buckets periodically add surges of water to prevent stagnation of the main tank's 3,000-gallon (11,400-liter) water supply and to wash sediment from the reef plants and animals. Water from the main tank circulates through several other tanks in the system.

The water flows through "scrubbers," lawns of threadlike algae grown on a light-dark cycle opposite that of the main tank. The scrubbers are there to maintain the optimal balance of chemical elements in the system. But Adey found that the harvest of algae from the scrubbers was so great — with only low levels of nutrients and no fertilizer — that he thinks floating platforms of algae in the ocean could provide biomass to be converted to alcohol or methane fuel.   Julie Ann Miller

In WORLD BOOK, see BIOCHEMISTRY; CORAL.

BIRTHS. See CENSUS; POPULATION.

BLINDNESS. See HANDICAPPED.

BOATING. Other nations have challenged the United States 24 times without success since 1851, when the yacht *America* won the America's Cup. The latest challenge came in 1980 when *Freedom,* a year-old sloop sailed by Dennis Conner of San Diego, defeated *Australia,* 4 races to 1.

Three yachts competed for the role of defender — *Freedom; Courageous,* the defender in 1974 and 1977; and the new yacht *Independence. Courageous* was sailed by Ted Turner, owner of the Atlanta Braves baseball team and Atlanta Hawks basketball team. *Independence* was sailed by Russell Long, at 24 the youngest helmsman ever in the trials.

Conner, a drapery manufacturer, had spent more than 1,000 hours in practice. His campaign cost $2.1 million, put up by 300 donors. His aluminum craft gained speed from sails made of a revolutionary sailcloth of Mylar and Kevlar.

Three sets of American trials were held from June to August. *Freedom* won 43 of 47 races and was chosen as defender. At the same time, *Australia, France 3, Sverige* of Sweden, and *Lionheart* of Great Britain held an elimination series to determine the challenger. *Australia,* sailed by Jim Hardy, won, as it did in 1977.

The Challenge Races were held from September 16 to 25 off Newport, R.I., for the 30-short-ton (27-metric-ton) yachts. *Australia* used a radical new bendable mast, the top 15 feet (5 meters) made of

The yacht *Freedom* sails to victory in the final race of the America's Cup competition. *Freedom* won four of five races with *Australia.*

fiberglass, that allowed it to carry an extra 250 square feet (23 square meters) of sail. But when the wind blew hard, *Australia* was no match for *Freedom*.

In January and February, Turner's 61-foot (19-meter) sloop *Tenacious* won its class in the Southern Ocean Racing Conference's important six-race series off Florida and the Bahamas. *Acadia*, a new 42-foot (13-meter) sloop owned by Burt Keenan of New Orleans, was overall winner.

Powerboats. Bill Elswick, a 32-year-old boatbuilder from Fort Lauderdale, Fla., had spectacular success. The national offshore championship was decided in nine races from March to October. He won three races and the title in *Long Shot*, a new 39-foot (12-meter) Halter-Cigarette powered by twin 640-horsepower Rahilly-Grady engines. The Harmsworth Trophy was offered for the first time since 1961, and Elswick won that, too.

The national unlimited-hydroplane series of 10 races ran from June to September. Dean Chenoweth, 43, of Tallahassee, Fla., won the title in a new *Miss Budweiser*.

Chenoweth was sidelined briefly after an August 7 accident in which he broke seven ribs and a shoulder blade. Ten months before, he suffered eight broken ribs, a broken pelvis, and lung contusions when he flipped over at 215 miles (346 kilometers) per hour.   Frank Litsky

In WORLD BOOK, see BOATING; SAILING.

BOLIVIA. A military junta, headed by General Luis Garcia Meza Tejada, seized control of the government on July 17, 1980. The coup d'état successfully prevented Congress from convening as scheduled on August 4 to certify the nation's next president, Hernan Siles Zuazo, head of the left-of-center Democratic and Popular Union Party. Zuazo, a former president, had won the popular vote in general elections held on June 29.

Internal resistance to the coup was widespread. The coup was also denounced by Bolivia's partners in the Andean group as well as by the United States. The United States halted all drug-enforcement assistance to Bolivia and reduced its embassy staff by half. The main reason was the allegation that Meza and members of his administration have been involved in the narcotics trade.

The Bolivian economy was precarious. The country was mired in a deepening economic crisis, and unable to control inflation. Bolivia's mining industry was in a recession, with tin production expected to be at a 20-year low.   Nathan A. Haverstock

See also LATIN AMERICA (Facts in Brief Table). In WORLD BOOK, see BOLIVIA.

BONDS. See STOCKS AND BONDS.

BOOKS. See CANADIAN LITERATURE; LITERATURE; LITERATURE FOR CHILDREN; POETRY; PUBLISHING.

BOPHUTHATSWANA. See AFRICA.

BOTANY. Acid rain — precipitation that picks up chemicals polluting the air and deposits them on the ground — has had a dramatic impact on bodies of water in North America and Europe, producing significant changes in plant and animal life within the waters. Several 1980 studies have shown that organisms on land are also affected by acid rain.

For example, botanists Lance S. Evans and Christine A. Conway of Manhattan College in New York City reported that acid solutions apparently affect the sexual reproduction of the fern *Pteridium aquilinum*. In the sexual reproduction of ferns, spores produced on the undersurfaces of fern leaves fall to the ground and develop into small heart-shaped structures called prothallia. The egg and sperm are produced on the prothallium, and the sperm swims to the egg to fertilize it. A new fern plant grows from the fertilized egg.

Acidity Effects. Evans and Conway found that fern sperm are less able to make the crucial swim after they have been exposed to acid solutions that simulate the pH measurement of acid rains. Scientists measure acidity in pH units, a measurement of hydrogen ion concentration. The pH scale runs from 14 (highly basic) to 0 (highly acidic). When *Pteridium aquilinum* sperm were exposed to a solution of pH6.1 for one minute, 25 per cent were completely immobilized. But responses varied considerably. One group of fern sperm became immobilized at relatively moderate pH levels — 5.6 to 6.1 — and then showed some recovery. Another group did not succumb until a much more acid level of pH was reached and then did not recover. The fern sperm was more acid sensitive than the other tissues of the plant.

Evans and Conway also evaluated how well fertilization took place under various pH levels, in the laboratory and in Petri dishes under a forest canopy. In both situations, fertilization at pH levels of 4.5 to 3.6 was 50 per cent lower than at pH6.1 levels. At pH3.0, fertilization was only 10 to 20 per cent as successful as at pH6.1 levels. Thus, tracking the fertilization of this fern might serve as a "bioindicator" of rain-water contamination.

Plant Converters. Science may be closer to using green plants to convert the sun's radiant energy into fuels such as hydrogen gas. A team of biochemists led by Hideo Ochiai of Shimane University in Japan intercepted electrons from the photosynthesis process — used by plants to make food — in blue-green algae. The scientists produced an electric current from blue-green algae coated with gel and undergoing photosynthesis in artificial light. Other researchers have done this with spinach, but not for so long a period of time — the current was generated for 20 days.   Barbara N. Benson

See also BIOLOGY; ZOOLOGY. In WORLD BOOK, see BOTANY; FERN; PHOTOSYNTHESIS.

BOTSWANA. See AFRICA.

BOWLING. The 22-year-old Wayne Webb of Akron, Ohio, and 21-year-old Steve Martin of Kingsport, Tenn., taught their elders a few bowling lessons in 1980. Webb won three tournaments, including the richest of the year – the $150,000 Firestone Tournament of Champions, held from April 15 to 19 in Akron. He led in tour earnings with $115,080 to $101,660 for Mark Roth of Little Silver, N.J.

Martin had to beat the four other finalists in the five-man stepladder finals of the $131,000 United States Open in March in Windsor Locks, Conn., and he did by rolling 32 strikes in 46 attempts. In the Tournament of Champions finals, Webb rolled 15 consecutive strikes and 27 strikes in 34 attempts.

The PBA Tour. The Professional Bowlers Association (PBA) tour comprised 34 tournaments from January to November carrying $3.3 million in purses. The three major tournaments – the United States Open, PBA championship, and Tournament of Champions – were crammed into five weeks.

Johnny Petraglia, 33, of Staten Island, N.Y., won the PBA championship in March in Sterling Heights, Mich., the 14th tour title of his career. Neil Burton of St. Louis, 34, and Ernie Schlegel of Vancouver, Wash., 37, won their first titles.

Burton's victory came in the $116,000 American Bowling Congress Masters tournament in May in Louisville. He defeated his better-known brother,

Nelson Burton, Jr., 205-191, in his next-to-last match and Roth, 204-182, in the final.

Schlegel, a 12-year tour veteran, captured the King Louie Open in April in Overland Park, Kans., with nine strikes on his last 10 rolls. He took the City of Roses Open in June in Portland, Ore., with a strike on his last ball.

Costly Kick. Marshall Holman of Medford, Ore., talented but temperamental, paid a high price for his temper. In the televised final match of the Showboat Doubles Classic on June 6 in Las Vegas, Nev., the 25-year-old Holman made a bad shot, then kicked the foul-line light and broke it. Holman already was on probation for three outbursts in previous tournaments. The latest incident prompted Commissioner Joe Antenora to levy the strongest disciplinary action in PBA history – a 10-week suspension and a $2,500 fine. Holman said, "I just kicked. That's where my foot went."

On the shorter, less-affluent Women's PBA tour, Pat Costello of Union City, Calif., won the United States Open; Donna Adamek of Duarte, Calif., the Women's International Bowling Congress (WIBC) Queens tournament; and Betty Morris of Stockton, Calif., the WIBC open title. In a three-week span starting with the U.S. Open, Shinobu Saitoh of Japan finished second, third, and first in three American tournaments.   Frank Litsky

In WORLD BOOK, see BOWLING.

BOXING. Even in defeat, a 38-year-old, worn-out Muhammad Ali attracted more attention in 1980 than Larry Holmes, who beat him, or Roberto Duran and Sugar Ray Leonard, who waged a memorable welterweight war.

Ali last fought in 1978, when he outpointed Leon Spinks, won the heavyweight title for a record third time, and retired. He returned in 1980 and fought the 31-year-old Holmes of Easton, Pa., the World Boxing Council (WBC) champion.

It seemed folly. Ali had not looked impressive since his memorable 1975 knockout of Joe Frazier in Manila, the Philippines. By the time he resumed training, his weight had ballooned.

Contract negotiations shifted from day to day. He was going to fight John Tate or Scott LeDoux or Bernardo Mercado or Holmes in Taiwan or Rio de Janeiro or Cairo or Las Vegas. Finally, the Holmes fight was set for October 2 in Las Vegas, Nev.

Holmes was seven years younger, fitter, and stronger, and he battered Ali until the fight was stopped between the 10th and 11th rounds. It was recorded as an 11th-round knockout. It marked the first time Ali had been knocked out.

Ali said he had been weakened by too much medication. He said nothing about the 91°F. (33°C) heat or the lack of punching that helped make his performance, according to Red Smith of *The New York Times,* "an unappetizing charade."

Left-handed Pam Buckner shows the smooth delivery that helped her win a women's professional bowling tournament in June.

World Champion Boxers			
Division	Champion	Country	Year Won
Heavyweight	†Larry Holmes	U.S.A.	1978
	*Mike Weaver	U.S.A.	1980
Cruiserweight	†Carlos DeLeon	Puerto Rico	1980
	*No champion		
Light-heavyweight	†Matthew Saad Muhammad	U.S.A.	1979
	*Eddie Mustafa Muhammad	U.S.A.	1980
Middleweight	Marvin Hagler	U.S.A.	1980
Junior-middleweight	†Maurice Hope	England	1979
	*Ayub Kalule	Uganda	1979
Welterweight	†Ray Leonard	U.S.A.	1980
	*Thomas Hearns	U.S.A.	1980
Junior-welterweight	†Saoul Mamby	U.S.A.	1980
	*Aaron Pryor	U.S.A.	1980
Lightweight	†Jim Watt	Scotland	1979
	*Hilmer Kenty	U.S.A.	1980
Junior-lightweight	†Rafael Limon	Mexico	1980
	*Yatsutsune Uehara	Japan	1980
Featherweight	*Eusebio Pedroza	Panama	1978
	†Salvador Sanchez	Mexico	1980
Junior-featherweight	†Wilfredo Gomez	Puerto Rico	1977
	*Sergio Palma	Argentina	1980
Bantamweight	*Jeff Chandler	U.S.A.	1980
	†Lupe Pintor	Mexico	1979
Junior-bantamweight	†Rafael Orono	Venezuela	1980
	*No champion		
Flyweight	*Peter Mathebula	South Africa	1980
	†Shoji Oguma	Japan	1980
Junior-flyweight	*Yoko Gushiken	Japan	1976
	†Hilario Zapata	Panama	1980

†Recognized by World Boxing Council.
*Recognized by World Boxing Association.

BRAZIL. The political liberalization process pledged by President Joao Baptista de Oliveira Figueiredo at his inauguration in March 1979, and designed eventually to return the nation to democracy, continued during 1980. Brazil's jails were emptied of political prisoners. People exiled for opposing military rule were allowed to return to the country. The government was once again criticized by the nation's news media. Television programs on which ordinary citizens aired their grievances against the bureaucracy enjoyed unprecedented popularity.

To reduce its near-total dependence on imported oil, Brazil had announced late in 1979 an ambitious program to produce 2 million alcohol-powered cars by 1985. Owing to an 11-day strike begun on April 1 involving the automotive industry, however, the government had to move the date to 1988. Despite the setback, the country expected to produce 100,000 such cars in 1980, with priority assigned to taxis and vehicles for government agency fleets.

Oil Shortage. Brazil's worst fears over its energy dependence were realized when war between Iran and Iraq broke out on September 22. The sudden cutoff of oil imports from Iraq and Iran, which supply about 50 per cent of Brazil's needs, sent Brazilian diplomats scrambling for alternate

The title fight was the fourth of the year for the undefeated Holmes. He knocked out Lorenzo Zanon of Italy in six rounds on February 3 in Las Vegas; Leroy Jones of Chicago in eight on March 31 in Las Vegas; and Scott LeDoux of Anoka, Minn., in seven on July 7 in Bloomington, Minn.

Other Bouts. There were two World Boxing Association (WBA) heavyweight title fights. Unbeaten John Tate of Knoxville, Tenn., was 45 seconds away from keeping the title when Mike Weaver of Pomona, Calif., knocked him out on March 31 in Knoxville. Weaver then knocked out Gerrie Coetzee of South Africa in 13 rounds on October 25 in Bophuthatswana.

Ali's $8-million purse was the third highest in boxing history. The highest was the $9.5 million earned by the 24-year-old Leonard of Palmer Park, Md., when he defended the WBC welterweight title against Duran on June 20 in Montreal, Canada. The unbeaten Leonard lost a decision to the 29-year-old Duran, former world lightweight champion from Panama, in a classic fight. For their return fight in New Orleans on November 25, Duran made $9.5 million and Leonard, $6 million. But Duran quit in the eighth round, complaining of cramps. Frank Litsky

In WORLD BOOK, see BOXING.
BOY SCOUTS. See YOUTH ORGANIZATIONS.
BOYS' CLUBS. See YOUTH ORGANIZATIONS.

Joao Baptista de Oliveira Figueiredo
addresses political rally during
Brazil's presidential race in 1980.

Miners carry heavily loaded sacks of ore-bearing earth from the slopes of Bald Mountain, site of the biggest gold rush in Brazil's history.

sources. The loss of Iraqi oil was especially painful because Brazil had invested some $180 million in the development of two oil fields in Iraq in return for guarantees of Iraqi crude oil.

To make up for a shortfall estimated at about 400,000 barrels per day, Brazil turned to two Western Hemisphere producers. Venezuela promised to double its exports to Brazil in 1981, and Mexico was reportedly willing to help, too.

Brazil cultivated closer relations with Argentina, its traditional rival, in 1980. On May 15, Brazil's President Figueiredo met with Argentina's President Jorge Rafael Videla in Buenos Aires. It was the first time in 30 years that a Brazilian president had paid an official call on Argentina. At the end of the three-day meeting, a joint communiqué was issued announcing agreements designed to make the two economies complementary. Provisions were made for cooperation in science and technology as well as in the joint development of nuclear reactors to produce atomic power. Brazil's first nuclear power plant was scheduled to begin operating in late 1980, and four more plants were under construction.

The Economy. Brazil was suffering from an astronomically high rate of inflation, about 106.8 per cent in the year ending on June 1, 1980. The nation's growing foreign debt, which stood at about $50 billion in March, also gave cause for concern. However, Brazilians remained confident that financially astute Planning Minister Antonio Delfim Netto would resolve a pending crisis by negotiating extended credit agreements as well as new loans through the International Monetary Fund and the World Bank.

Brazilians living in cities were troubled by a sharp rise in street crime, attributed by some of the nation's Roman Catholic Church leaders to the persisting wide gap between rich and poor.

Polio Drive. There was also grave concern — and controversy — over an alleged resurgence of polio in Brazil. In February, Albert B. Sabin, who developed the oral polio vaccine, visited Brazil at the government's invitation to devise programs to wipe out polio among children. His conclusion that polio cases in Brazil had actually risen rather than declined angered Brazilian health officials who had reported an 86 per cent decline in the disease to the World Health Organization.

Brazilians of all classes accorded a tumultuous welcome to Pope John Paul II, who arrived on June 30 for a 12-day pilgrimage. Millions hailed the first pontiff to visit the most populous Roman Catholic country as he rode into Rio de Janeiro. See ROMAN CATHOLIC CHURCH. Nathan A. Haverstock

See also LATIN AMERICA (Facts in Brief Table). In WORLD BOOK, see BRAZIL.

BRIDGE. See BUILDING AND CONSTRUCTION.

BRIDGE, CONTRACT. France won the world contract bridge championship in a competition among 58 countries that ended on Oct. 11, 1980, in Valkenburg, the Netherlands. Playing against a United States team, France went into the final day trailing by 21 international match points but won by 20. The world women's championship went to a United States team consisting of Jacqui Mitchell, Gail Moss, and Dorothy H. Truscott, all of New York City; Emma Jean Hawes of Fort Worth, Tex.; Marilyn Johnson of Houston; and Mary Jane Farell of Los Angeles.

A team characterized by its youth won the Harold A. Vanderbilt knockout team championship at the American Contract Bridge League (ACBL) spring championships in March in Fresno, Calif. The team included three students in their early 20s: Bobby Levin of Miami, Fla.; Jeff Meckstroth of Reynoldsburg, Ohio; and Eric Rodwell of Lafayette, Ind. Playing with them were Bud Reinhold and Russ Arnold, both of Miami.

The Spingold knockout team title at the ACBL summer nationals held in Chicago in July went to Michael Becker, Ron Rubin, Peter Weichsel, and Alan Sontag of New York City; Ron von der Porten of San Francisco; and Kyle Larsen of Walnut Creek, Calif. Theodore M. O'Leary

In WORLD BOOK, see BRIDGE, CONTRACT.

BRITISH COLUMBIA increased its exports of coal to Japan in 1980, and Japanese Prime Minister Masayoshi Ohira studied future prospects when he visited the Pacific province on May 6. Ohira learned that a large coalfield to be developed in the northeastern part of the province will be linked to the existing rail system by a 70-mile (115-kilometer) branch of the British Columbia Railway. Plans were announced to build a new port for the coal and grain trade on Ridley Island near Prince Rupert, and expand the Roberts Bank deepwater port, south of Vancouver, to handle rapidly rising coal exports. At least two more terminal sites will be created.

Premier William R. Bennett imposed a seven-year moratorium on uranium exploration and mining on February 27. Environmentalists were jubilant when a project to develop a 10.5-million-pound (4.7-million-kilogram) deposit of uranium oxide near Kelowna was shelved indefinitely. On December 20, Energy Minister Robert H. McClelland said he had told two provincially owned companies not to pay a new excise tax on sales of natural gas. The tax had been imposed, effective November 1, to increase the federal government's share of oil and gas revenues. David M. L. Farr

See also CANADA. In WORLD BOOK, see BRITISH COLUMBIA.

Hundreds of card players bid for prizes at the American Contract Bridge League's spring championships in Fresno, Calif., in March.

Switzerland's new St. Gotthard Tunnel, opened on September 5, enables cars to drive through the Alps from Göschenen in north to Airolo in south.

BUILDING AND CONSTRUCTION. Home builders in the United States experienced their worst year in 1980 since the recession of 1973-1974. Housing starts dropped in 1980 to an estimated 1.22 million, down from 1.75 million in 1979. High interest rates prepared contractors for the slump, and they countered it by reducing inventories early in the year. When interest rates began to fall in April 1980, they resumed construction.

Housing starts peaked in June, rising to an annual rate of 1.9 million units as average interest rates for conventional mortgages on single-family houses fell to 11.2 per cent. Interest rates began to climb again, and construction starts declined in July to a level 12 per cent below that of July 1979. Contractors who completed houses faced the prospect of finding buyers in an economy characterized by high interest rates and high unemployment.

Those who could afford to buy found that prices did not increase as much as in previous years. The median price of a single-family house reached an estimated $68,800 in 1980, up from $66,000 in 1979. The National Association of Home Builders predicted that high interest rates would keep 1981 housing starts at or below the 1.5 million level.

Construction Spending fell an estimated 8.1 per cent in 1980. The annual rate totaled $212.9 billion in August, down from $231.6 billion in 1979. Commercial and industrial construction dropped from $40.3 billion to $39.7 billion. Heavy construction — including transportation, highways, and sewers — decreased from $42.8 billion to $42.2-billion. Construction spending by federal, state, and local governments dipped from $52 billion to $49.6 billion. Residential construction plunged from $98.9 billion to $79 billion.

Construction unemployment reflected the building slump. The October unemployment rate reached 14.3 per cent, compared with 9.9 per cent in 1979. The August 1980 rate in the construction industry soared to 18.5 per cent, while the general rate was 7.6 per cent. Construction employment rose by 45,000 jobs in September to 4.4 million, but it remained lower than the 1979 level of 4.5 million. At the same time, construction union wages escalated faster than at any time since early 1976, according to the United States Department of Labor. Wages increased an average of 7.8 per cent and wages and benefits an average of 7.6 per cent in fiscal year 1980. Wages and benefits for electricians totaled $16.80 per hour at the end of the fiscal year, and painters received $14.25 per hour.

New Techniques. Covington Brothers Technologies Corporation of Fullerton, Calif., developed a method of erecting walls made from polystyrene, the plastic foam used for picnic coolers, then spraying the walls inside and outside with Portland cement to reduce labor and material costs. The

221

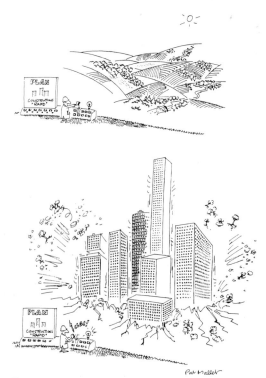

Mallet in *Pourquoi Pas*, Brussels. *World Press Review.*

houses Covington builds cost $50,000, about half the average cost of a conventionally built, single-family house in California.

An aluminum dome 70 feet (21 meters) tall and 320 feet (98 meters) in diameter was built from the top down in southern California's Mojave Desert. The contractor, Tencor Domes, hung the center of the dome from a 170-foot (52-meter) erection tower and construction proceeded from the center outward. Workers at ground level added a section of struts to the outside of the umbrella-shaped structure, then the dome was raised on the tower. Plans called for the frame of the $1.3-million structure to be covered with triangular aluminum panels. The 80,400-square-foot (7,236-square-meter) dome will protect a limestone storage area at a cement plant.

Codes and Specifications. Experts and organizations, including the Council on Wage and Price Stability, continued to contest federal building energy-performance standards (BEPS). No one questioned the underlying intent of BEPS—to ensure that energy economy is designed into new buildings. They doubted whether the standards will work and can be enforced. In contrast, Standard 90-75 of the American Society of Heating, Refrigerating, and Air Conditioning Engineers has been adopted by three-fourths of the states.

California's strict energy standards, similar to BEPS, also came under strong criticism that sug-gested the kinds of problems BEPS might face. Although they went into effect in 1978, one of the biggest problems facing the regulations was the lack of awareness of them. In addition, local officials did not have the resources to enforce them properly. After complaints about the workings of the California energy-conservation plan arose in local hearings on the BEPS, the state energy agency began to review building plans and to check construction sites to determine whether the work follows approved plans.

Dams. Engineers in the Soviet Union attempted to stop the lowering of the Caspian Sea's level with a dam 250 feet (70 meters) wide and 20 feet (6 meters) high. The water level has dropped 7 feet (2.1 meters) since the 1930s, making it difficult for ships to reach port and increasing salinity so much that many fish cannot survive. The water was lost when it flowed through a narrow strait on the eastern shore of the Caspian Sea into Kara-Bogaz-Gol, a shallow gulf, and evaporated in the hot desert air.

The U. S. Army Corps of Engineers inspected 4,906 nonfederal dams and found that 32 per cent of them were unsafe. When all inspections are completed in fiscal 1981, federal officials estimate, about 2,600 dams may be declared unsafe and a serious hazard. The nation's 50,000 nonfederal dams may include 14,500 that require repairs. It has not been decided whether the federal or state governments, or the public and private dam owners, will pay the repair bill, which may be as high as $7.5 billion.

Bridges. A Venezuelan-Panamanian combine received a $100-million contract to design and build a suspension bridge across the Panama Canal. The four-lane structure, scheduled for completion in 1983, will be located at the Miraflores Locks near the Pacific Ocean end of the canal. Plans call for a 4,265-foot (1,300-meter) bridge with a 1,995-foot (608-meter) main span that clears the canal by 220 feet (67 meters). The bridge is expected to speed Pan American Highway traffic through the Panama City area.

Tunnels. A new bore through the Alps provides the shortest highway route between Paris and Rome. The 8-mile (13-kilometer), $296-million Frejus Tunnel links the industrial areas of Lyon, France, and Turin, Italy. It replaced the treacherous, often snowbound, Mount Cenis Pass. The tunnel, located at an altitude of 4,300 feet (1,311 meters), took six years to complete.

Workmen finished the first tunnel under the Suez Canal in April. The 3-mile (4.8-kilometer)-long bore connects mainland Egypt with the Sinai Peninsula and includes a 1-mile (1.6-kilometer) stretch under the waterway.   William J. Cromie

In WORLD BOOK, see BRIDGE; BUILDING CONSTRUCTION; DAM; TUNNEL.

BULGARIA remained a loyal ally of Russia in 1980 but continued to develop economic links with both the East and the West. Relations with Yugoslavia improved after a renewed quarrel over Macedonia in January.

Bulgaria patched up its quarrel with Iraq over factional struggles among the 700 Iraqi students in Sofia after Foreign Minister Petŭr Mladenov visited Baghdad in April and State Council Chairman Todor Zhivkov went there in May. Iraq promised in July to supply Bulgaria with additional oil. Zhivkov discussed oil policy while in Libya in March, and, while no oil agreement was announced, Bulgaria agreed to a joint venture that called for Bulgaria to use 4,500 of its trucks to carry equipment for Libyan farm projects and to transport farm goods to Libya's neighbors.

Zhivkov signed economic cooperation agreements in Syria in April. He met Palestine Liberation Organization leader Yasir Arafat during the visit and then publicly condemned United States policy in the Middle East.

Ethiopia's Provisional Military Government Chairman Mengistu Haile-Mariam visited Bulgaria in July and signed a treaty of friendship and cooperation that also provided for military cooperation. Zambia's President Kenneth David Kaunda and Mozambique's President Samora Moises Machel visited Sofia in September and signed agreements on economic, scientific, and technological cooperation.

Joint Ventures. In March, Bulgaria enacted a law that allowed foreign companies to set up joint ventures with state firms on Bulgarian soil, let foreign businesses hold stock majorities in such ventures, and granted foreign partners special tax concessions. In May, Bulgaria signed a long-term agreement with Shell International on joint research, prospecting, and production of mineral reserves, chemical products, and metals to be sold in other countries.

Bulgaria set up a commission on energy and raw-material problems in May to supervise the country's energy policy. A Japanese firm, Toshiba, received a $40-million contract in May to build a power station in Bulgaria with a capacity of 864,000 kilowatts.

Industrial production increased by 4.5 per cent in the first six months of the year. However, the state economic plan had projected a 6.3 per cent increase, which was already scaled down from the original target of 8.6 per cent. Delays were reported in completing power, chemical, iron and steel, and mining industry projects. Bulgaria spent $2.8 billion on capital investment in the first half of 1980, including $1.3 billion for modernization and expansion.   Chris Cviic

See also EUROPE (Facts in Brief Table). In WORLD BOOK, see BULGARIA.

BURMA. President U Ne Win proclaimed amnesty in May 1980 for political opponents who had fled abroad. The most eminent among the returning exiles was 73-year-old former Prime Minister U Nu, who in the 1970s led an unsuccessful armed insurrection. U Nu returned from India in July. The government also said that about 2,000 armed rebels in the hills had answered its offer of amnesty, but the claim was thought to be exaggerated. The amnesty was widely regarded as a sign that Ne Win was easing his heavy-handed rule.

But the country was endangered — especially in the north — by rebel armies that financed their gun purchases with opium and heroin, as well as aid from China. Reports from other countries in August estimated that at least 4,000 government troops had died since November 1979.

After long self-isolation, Burma cautiously opened its doors to outside investors, who remained wary. Foreign loans totaled just over $200-million, and the United States resumed foreign aid on a modest scale. Despite slight improvement in the economy, Burma remained one of Asia's most troubled and poorest nations, with an annual per capita income of less than $140.   Mark Gayn

See also ASIA (Facts in Brief Table). In WORLD BOOK, see BURMA.

BURUNDI. See AFRICA.

BUS. See TRANSIT; TRANSPORTATION.

BUSH, GEORGE H. W. (1924-   ), was elected Vice-President of the United States on Nov. 4, 1980, as the running mate of Ronald Reagan. Bush had withdrawn as a contender for the presidential nomination on May 26, the last of Reagan's opponents to do so. See REPUBLICAN PARTY.

Bush was born on June 12, 1924, in Milton, Mass., the son of a Republican senator. After graduating from Phillips Academy in Andover, Mass., in 1942, he enlisted in the U.S. Navy. He completed his active duty in 1945 and entered Yale University, graduating in 1948.

Bush entered the oil business in Midland, Tex., shortly after graduation, founding a drilling company there in 1954. He moved to Houston in 1959 and became active in Republican politics. Bush ran unsuccessfully for the U.S. Senate in 1964 and 1970, but was elected to the U.S. House of Representatives in 1966 and 1968.

He served as U.S. ambassador to the United Nations in 1971 and envoy to the People's Republic of China in 1974. He directed the Central Intelligence Agency from January 1976 until January 1977, when he resigned to become chairman of the First National Bank of Houston.

Bush married Barbara Pierce in 1945. They have four sons and a daughter.   Beverly Merz

BUSINESS. See ECONOMICS; LABOR; MANUFACTURING.

CABINET, UNITED STATES. President Jimmy Carter made one change and one addition to the Cabinet in 1980. After the election of Ronald Reagan as President on November 4, Carter's Cabinet was relegated to lame-duck status, and attention turned to Reagan's Cabinet choices.

The Carter Cabinet. Cyrus R. Vance on April 28 became the first secretary of state since 1915 to resign as a result of a policy dispute, stating that he could not support the President's attempt to rescue the American hostages in Iran. Carter appointed Senator Edmund S. Muskie (D., Me.) to the office on April 29 (see MUSKIE, EDMUND S.).

The Carter Cabinet's ranks increased as the Department of Health, Education, and Welfare (HEW) split into the Department of Health and Human Services (HHS) and the Department of Education on May 4. Shirley M. Hufstedler, a former appeals court judge, became secretary of education, and HEW secretary Patricia Roberts Harris became HHS secretary.

The Reagan Cabinet. After a highly publicized talent search, Reagan on December 11 announced his first Cabinet appointments. Donald T. Regan, chairman of Merrill Lynch & Company, Incorporated, was named secretary of the treasury; Caspar W. Weinberger, former HEW secretary, secretary of defense; William French Smith, Reagan's personal attorney, attorney general; Senator Richard S. Schweiker (R., Pa.), secretary of HHS; industrialist Malcolm Baldrige, secretary of commerce; and Andrew L. Lewis, Jr., management consultant, secretary of transportation.

In subsequent announcements, Reagan named Alexander M. Haig, Jr., chief of staff during part of the Administration of Richard M. Nixon, as secretary of state; Raymond J. Donovan, a New Jersey contractor, secretary of labor; conservative public interest lawyer James G. Watt, secretary of the interior; Illinois agriculture director John R. Block, secretary of agriculture; New York City lawyer Samuel R. Pierce, Jr., secretary of housing and urban development; South Carolina oral surgeon James B. Edwards, secretary of energy; and Utah's commissioner of higher education, Terrel H. Bell, secretary of education. All appointments required Senate approval, and hearings began on Jan. 6, 1981.

Other High-Level Posts. Reagan also announced the appointments of three others to Cabinet-level posts. Political science professor Jeane Jordan Kirkpatrick was named chief U.S. delegate to the United Nations; Representative David A. Stockman (R., Mich.), director of the Office of Management and Budget; and William J. Casey, manager of Reagan's presidential campaign, director of the Central Intelligence Agency.   Beverly Merz

In WORLD BOOK, see CABINET.

CALIFORNIA. See LOS ANGELES; STATE GOV'T.

CAMBODIA (Kampuchea) was racked by guerrilla war and hunger throughout 1980, with little relief in sight. The fighting was primarily between 200,000 Vietnamese troops and guerrilla forces of the former Khmer Rouge regime, which the Vietnamese forced out of Phnom Penh, the capital, in January 1979. Khmer Rouge forces were based on the Thailand-Cambodia border, and the fighting sometimes involved Thai ground and air forces. See ASIA; THAILAND; VIETNAM.

Pol Pot, the Khmer Rouge regime's Communist leader, turned over the premiership of his exiled government on Dec. 27, 1979, to Khieu Samphan, but he retained command of the guerrillas. The change seemed intended mainly to improve world opinion of the group that had been responsible for wholesale numbers of murders from 1975 to 1979. China was the only strong supporter of the Khmer Rouge.

UN Actions. Although widely denounced for its atrocities, the Khmer Rouge group again won Cambodia's United Nations (UN) seat over the claims of the regime installed in Phnom Penh by the Vietnamese Army. The UN General Assembly voted 74-35, with 32 abstentions, on October 13 to retain Khmer Rouge representatives. The General Assembly voted on October 22 to call for withdrawal of Vietnamese troops from Cambodia, an international conference on Cambodia's problems, and UN-supervised elections there. Vietnam rejected the call.

India on July 7 became the first non-Communist country to recognize the Vietnamese-backed government of President Heng Samrin. This move drew praise from Russia, mutual friend of Vietnam and India, but criticism from the Association of Southeast Asian Nations. Heng Samrin was overshadowed during 1980 by Vice-President Pen Souvan, also the defense minister and Phnom Penh's army commander.

Other Developments. Prince Norodom Sihanouk, the former ruler of Cambodia, visited Morocco and the United States in February seeking support for a neutral third force. But, he said in Washington, D.C., he found "much sympathy but little concrete support." Returning to exile in North Korea, he announced once again his withdrawal from politics.

Western and Communist countries spent an estimated $730 million by the end of 1980 to try to prevent starvation in Cambodia. Food distribution was generally difficult, however, and Phnom Penh used much of the supply of food that it received to pay officials rather than to feed the country's hungry villagers.   Henry S. Bradsher

See also ASIA (Facts in Brief Table). In WORLD BOOK, see CAMBODIA.

CAMEROON. See AFRICA.

CAMP FIRE GIRLS. See YOUTH ORGANIZATIONS.

CANADA

Changes in the Canadian constitution are the topic as Prime Minister Pierre Trudeau and the 10 provincial premiers confer in Ottawa, Ont.

Pierre Elliott Trudeau returned to dominate Canadian political life in 1980. Out of office for nine months, the 61-year-old Trudeau regained power as prime minister after his Liberal Party won the election of February 18, gaining a solid majority in Parliament. Following the defeat of separatism in the Quebec referendum on May 20, Trudeau made constitutional reform his top priority (see Close-Up). When he was unable to obtain agreement from Canada's 10 provinces on his proposals for

change, he took the package to the federal Parliament for action. A new federal budget in October showed the federal government's determination to manage oil and gas production in Canada. The resulting conflict on two fronts placed new strains on Canada's 113-year-old federal system.

The Election. The minority Conservative administration of Joseph (Joe) Clark, who took office in May 1979, faced the challenge of a general election as 1980 opened, because of the unexpected

225

defeat of the Clark government's first budget in Parliament on Dec. 13, 1979. The event persuaded Trudeau, who had announced in November that he was stepping down as Liberal leader, to reconsider and guide the party through his fifth general election. Trudeau began the campaign knowing that public opinion polls had turned against the Clark government. Clark had come to power in 1979 because of the widespread feeling outside Quebec that Trudeau and the Liberals had been in office too long. However, in Clark's nine months as head of the government he had failed to establish confidence in his administration.

The Conservatives saw their support fall away on election day all across the country except in their stronghold, the West. In the Atlantic Provinces, the two parties reversed their position from the 1979 election, with the Liberals taking 19 seats to the Progressive Conservatives' 13. Quebec gave the Liberals an unparalleled victory, dropping the Conservatives to one seat and leaving the once-formidable Social Credit party without a seat. The federalist Liberals took 74 seats. In Ontario, the Liberals won an additional 20 seats over their 1979 showing, ending up with 52 of the province's 95 representatives. West of Ontario, the Liberals collapsed. They won only two seats in Manitoba and lost the one they had held in British Columbia. The prairie West returned 33 Conservatives, with an additional 16 elected from British Columbia.

The Liberals elected a total of 147 in 1980, and 103 Conservatives won seats. Four Conservative Cabinet ministers were defeated. The socialist New Democratic Party (NDP) took the remainder of the 282 seats in the House of Commons, 32, for the best showing in its history. In the popular vote, the Liberals polled 44 per cent, a gain of 4 per cent from 1979, while the Conservatives dropped 3 per cent to 33. The NDP polled 20 per cent.

Clark stepped down on March 3 after 272 days as prime minister, ending the shortest elected administration in Canadian history. Trudeau entered office with a 33-member Cabinet that was a mixture of old and new faces. He included 17 former ministers, brought in 13 new ones, and dropped 5 from the last Liberal administration.

The top posts went to Allan J. MacEachen of Nova Scotia, a 27-year veteran who had served in the Cabinet of Prime Minister Lester B. Pearson. MacEachen was given the sensitive portfolio of minister of finance and made deputy prime minister. Trudeau selected two of his Quebec confidantes for important posts. He named Marc Lalonde to head the energy ministry and Jean Chrétien to head the justice ministry. The chief surprise was the choice of Mark MacGuigan, a Windsor, Ont., law professor, as minister for external affairs. One of the two Western Liberals elected was made a minister, and three appointed Liberal senators were given Cabinet posts to provide Western representation. Jeanne Sauvé, a former Cabinet minister, was chosen as the first woman Speaker of the House of Commons (see SAUVÉ, JEANNE).

Federal-Provincial Problems. The Quebec referendum on May 20, in which voters rejected the independence option, strengthened Trudeau's position as the spokesman for federal power in Canada. He met the 10 provincial premiers in Ottawa, Ont., on June 9 to resume the difficult task of "renewing" the federal system. The group drew up a list of 12 items for priority attention and turned it over to later gatherings of officials and ministers. Discussions went on all summer, but officials could not agree on the next steps to be taken. Therefore, the

Federal Spending in Canada

Estimated Budget for Fiscal 1981*

	Billions of Dollars
Health and welfare	18.512
Public debt	10.275
Economic development and support	7.604
Defense	6.071
Transportation and communications	3.549
Fiscal transfer payments to provinces	3.446
General government services	2.523
Education assistance	1.949
Internal overhead expenses	1.672
Foreign affairs	1.131
Culture and recreation	1.130
Total	57.862

*April 1, 1980, to March 31, 1981

Spending Since 1975

Billions of dollars

Fiscal Year: 1975-'76 '76-'77 '77-'78 '78-'79 '79-'80 '80-'81

Source: Treasury Board of Canada

Quebec Opts for Canada

Premier René Lévesque

Quebec residents voted decisively to stay in Canada in a dramatic referendum that took place on May 20, 1980. About 85 per cent of the province's 4.3 million eligible voters cast their ballots, and they turned down Premier René Lévesque's call for an independent Quebec. Sixty per cent of them voted for Canadian Prime Minister Pierre Elliott Trudeau's vision of a Quebec fulfilling its destiny within a renewed Canadian federal state.

Ever since the separatist Parti Québécois (PQ) came to power in November 1976, it had held out the promise of a vote on Quebec's future. Impassioned oratory resounded throughout the province for years, but it all came down to one consideration. By late 1979, the PQ was ready to ask the electorate a carefully worded question: Would you give the government a mandate to negotiate a new relationship of sovereignty-association with the rest of Canada?

This was the "soft question" that Lévesque hoped would attract the support of those outside his party who favored changes short of independence. Under the new status, Quebec would have the power to enact its own laws, levy its own taxes, and establish contacts abroad. Quebec would have an economic union with Canada, including a common currency. If this relationship could be negotiated, another referendum would be held before the province committed itself to leaving the federation of Canada.

The referendum campaign, so eloquent and emotional that it occasionally divided families, lasted 35 days. Debate took place not just among politicians, but also wherever voters gathered. One large Montreal law firm banned all discussion among its partners. Other employers forbade workers to wear "Yes" or "No" campaign buttons, called "cookies" in Quebec slang.

Leading the "No" forces were the provincial Liberals, led by former newspaper editor Claude Ryan, a committed federalist who issued his own plan for constitutional reform on the eve of the referendum campaign.

Many federal ministers campaigned with Ryan, most notably Trudeau, who was back in power in Ottawa after the February 18 general election. Sovereignty-association represented the denial of all his hopes for his native Quebec. In addition, the premiers of the other provinces had made it plain that sovereignty-association was unacceptable to the rest of Canada. Quebecers would have to decide whether they put Canada or Quebec first in their thoughts.

Some 2.1 million voters or 59.6 per cent said "No" to Lévesque's question, and 1.4 million or 40.4 per cent said "Yes." Among French-speaking voters, an estimated 48 per cent voted "Yes." Only in the rugged Saguenay-Lac St.-Jean region, north of the St. Lawrence River, did a majority favor independence. Elsewhere – in large cities and small towns, in farming communities and industrial centers, on all economic levels, and in all ethnic groups – the answer was a resounding "Yes" to Canada.

Lévesque accepted the results with good grace. The people had given their verdict, and it was his duty – and his party's – to accept it. At a conference on October 5, the Parti Québécois decided not to hold another referendum on sovereignty-association during its second term of office, if it succeeded in winning the provincial election that was bound to be held within a year of the May 20 referendum.

As the year ended, Canadians debated constitutional change, but it was change that would affect the whole country. Sovereignty-association seemed to be a doubtful prospect because Quebec had decided that it wanted to continue as part of the Canadian family. The pressing task now was to rebuild the family home, not only to make Quebec more comfortable, but also to satisfy the desires and needs of other parts of the federation. This was the challenge that Trudeau faced in his constitutional proposals of October 2. The coming months would gauge his success and establish his place in Canadian history.   David M. L. Farr

Reporters question Canadian Ambassador to
Iran Kenneth Taylor in Paris after he helped
six U.S. Embassy employees escape from Teheran.

premiers were pessimistic when they gathered in Ottawa for a conference on September 8.

Their opening statements revealed deep differences in their visions of Canada. The discussion of the control of natural resources and offshore mineral rights, two topics vital to the provinces, continued this impression.

Trudeau showed the confidence his strong electoral position had given him by presenting a charter of rights that he insisted should be made part of the new Canadian constitution. His package included basic freedoms such as speech, religion, and the press; minority-language and language-education rights; and the right to pursue a livelihood anywhere in Canada. These rights, he declared, were "non-negotiable." He also demanded powers to strengthen Canada as an "economic union."

Seven provinces vigorously opposed the charter of rights. Some saw it as encroaching on provincial powers, and others objected to it being enforced by the courts and not directly by the legislatures. The provinces retired to put together their list of demands, which included provincial control of offshore resources, a provincially appointed upper house to replace the federally chosen Senate, and stronger powers in interprovincial trade, natural resources, fisheries, and communications. They rejected the prime minister's entrenched charter of rights. On September 12, Trudeau turned down

the provincial proposal, claiming that it represented a simple listing of the maximum demands of each province. The meeting broke up the next day.

On October 2, just before Parliament resumed for the autumn session, Trudeau announced that he intended to ask for a joint House of Commons-Senate resolution requesting the British Parliament to enact certain changes in Canada's constitution, the 1867 British North America Act. One change would make the constitution amendable in Canada, which it had never been, because Canadians could not agree on an amending formula after more than 50 years of intermittent discussion. Thus the act, as a statute of the British Parliament, can be changed only in London. Trudeau proposed to bring the constitution to Canada. He said it should include his charter of rights, which would be binding on the provinces and the federal government.

Trudeau presented his constitutional proposals to Parliament when it resumed on October 6. They were hotly attacked by Clark and the Conservative opposition. Later, even after the Liberals had made concessions in the proposals to guarantee provincial control over resources, only three premiers supported the Trudeau package—those of Ontario, New Brunswick, and Saskatchewan. The depth of feeling aroused by Trudeau's unilateral attempt to change the Canadian federal system made it clear that more battles lay ahead.

The Economy marked time in 1980. Real growth in the gross national product (GNP) was projected at only 0.5 per cent. Several key indicators, including housing starts, level of inventories, manufacturing, and the trade balance, showed weakness. A shrinking United States demand for Canadian products, such as automobiles and lumber, affected the economy. Fortunately the wheat crop was better than expected, in spite of a severe drought.

Another round of double-digit inflation seemed in prospect as the consumer price index rose to an annual rate of 10.7 per cent in September. Even food prices, which normally fall in September, increased. But unemployment remained relatively stable at the seasonally adjusted rate of 7.4 per cent, compared with 7.1 per cent a year earlier.

Canada moved on March 10 to a floating bank rate, which was designed to give the central bank more flexibility in controlling interest rates and defending the exchange value of the dollar. The rate was set in relation to the interest yield at the weekly auction of 91-day federal treasury bills. The Canadian dollar hovered between 87 and 85 cents (U.S.) throughout the year.

Alberta Oil Issue. Finance Minister MacEachen presented his first budget on October 28, after months of fruitless discussion between the federal government and the oil-rich province of Alberta over a suitable price for oil and gas and an acceptable sharing of petroleum revenues. The

Jeanne Sauvé, House of Commons' first woman speaker, is escorted to her seat by Prime Minister Trudeau, right, and Opposition Leader Clark.

Alberta government contended that it must recover maximum prices for a declining resource, in terms of conventional reserves. The federal government insisted it had a responsibility to act for those parts of the country that lacked domestic petroleum reserves. Complicating the issue was the effect of oil and gas price levels upon the pace of frontier discovery and the exploitation of resources in the tar sands and in heavy oils.

MacEachen met the issue by authorizing an immediate oil price increase of 80 cents per barrel, bringing the total rise in 1980 to $3.80. In the long run, Canadian oil prices would not be allowed to exceed 85 per cent of world prices. The compensation now being paid Eastern Canadian users of higher-priced imported oil, which cost the federal treasury about $3 billion in 1980, would be shifted to consumers over the next three years through a refining tax to be paid by all Canadians.

The federal government proposed to siphon off a larger share of the revenues from higher energy prices in the future. There would be a new tax on all natural gas and liquid gas sold in Canada or exported. The government also imposed an 8 per cent production tax on the net operating revenues of oil and gas companies. The long-term result of these taxes would be to change the distribution of oil and gas revenues. The provincial share, now 45 per cent, would drop to 43 per cent; industry's share would fall from 45 to 33 per cent; and the federal portion would rise from 10 to 24 per cent.

Premier Peter Lougheed of Alberta reacted angrily to MacEachen's budget statement on October 30. He said he would cut his province's oil production by 15 per cent, or 180,000 barrels per day, within nine months, and would suspend the order only if Eastern Canada suffered a serious oil shortage. The Alberta government would press a court challenge to the federal tax on natural gas and would hold off on erecting $8 billion worth of oil tar sands plants while it reassessed its royalty arrangements. Later, Trudeau and Lougheed agreed to talks on an oil-pricing agreement.

U.S. Relations were marked by a series of disagreements in 1980. Faced with difficult economic conditions, both countries seemed to be more interested in protecting their positions than in cooperating. For example, a treaty negotiated in 1979 to set quotas for fish stocks in common North Atlantic waters and to define a maritime boundary in the Gulf of Maine was held up in the United States Senate throughout 1980. Canadian authorities feared that overfishing in the disputed area would lead to serious depletion of fish stocks and to clashes among fishermen.

Acid rain was another source of difficulty as the United States moved to force its Northeastern power plants to use coal rather than oil to generate

229

The Ministry of Canada*
In order of precedence

Pierre Elliott Trudeau, prime minister

Allan Joseph MacEachen, deputy prime minister and minister of finance

Jean-Luc Pepin, minister of transport

Jean Chrétien, minister of justice and attorney general of Canada and minister of state for social development

John Munro, minister of Indian affairs and northern development

H. A. Olson, minister of state for economic development

Eugene Francis Whelan, minister of agriculture

Herbert Gray, minister of industry, trade, and commerce

André Ouellet, minister of consumer and corporate affairs and postmaster general

Marc Lalonde, minister of energy, mines and resources

Raymond Joseph Perrault, leader of the government in the Senate

Roméo LeBlanc, minister of fisheries and oceans

John Roberts, minister of state for science and technology and minister of the environment

Monique Bégin, minister of health and welfare

Jean-Jacques Blais, minister of supply and services and receiver general of Canada

Francis Fox, secretary of state of Canada and minister of communications

Gilles Lamontagne, minister of national defence and acting minister of veterans affairs

Pierre De Bané, minister of regional economic expansion

Hazen Argue, minister of state for the Canadian Wheat Board

Gerald Regan, minister of labor and sports

Mark MacGuigan, secretary of state for external affairs

Robert Kaplan, solicitor general of Canada

James Fleming, minister of state for multiculturalism

William Rompkey, minister of national revenue

Pierre Bussières, minister of state for finance

Charles Lapointe, minister of state for small business

Edward Lumley, minister of state for trade

Yvon Pinard, president of the queen's privy council for Canada and government house leader

Donald Johnston, president of the Treasury Board

Lloyd Axworthy, minister of employment and immigration and minister of state for status of women

Paul Cosgrove, minister of public works with responsibility for Canada Mortgage and Housing Corporation

Judy Erola, minister of state for mines

*As of Dec. 31, 1980.

Premiers of Canadian Provinces

Province	Premier
Alberta	Peter Lougheed
British Columbia	William R. Bennett
Manitoba	Sterling R. Lyon
New Brunswick	Richard B. Hatfield
Newfoundland	Brian Peckford
Nova Scotia	John Buchanan
Ontario	William G. Davis
Prince Edward Island	Angus MacLean
Quebec	René Lévesque
Saskatchewan	Allan Blakeney

Commissioners of Territories

Northwest Territories	John H. Parker
Yukon Territory	Douglas Bell, Administrator

electricity. Sulfur and nitrogen oxides emitted when coal is burned combine with falling rain to form weak sulfuric acid that pollutes water surfaces and may threaten the growth of plants and trees. While the elimination of acid rain is technically possible, industry estimated that it would cost staggering sums over the next 20 years. Still, the two countries made some progress in preparing for negotiations to control the transboundary movement of acid rain.

There were disagreements in the commercial field, too. Canada was concerned about the growing number of "buy American" laws in the U.S. that gave preference to domestic suppliers. For their part, Americans were disturbed by the 1976 Canadian tax act that prevented Canadian companies from claiming tax deductions when they advertised on U.S.-border broadcasting stations.

A welcome show of cooperation occurred when the two countries moved to push the delayed Alaska Highway natural gas pipeline. The United States cleared away most of the remaining legal hurdles to the project while Canada decided to allow the southern "prebuild portion" to be constructed before the main route. Approved by the Canadian Cabinet on July 17, the southern portion would allow Canadian gas to flow to the Northern United States by 1981, thus providing revenue that could be used for building the main line to Alaska.

Canada announced on April 10 that it would purchase 137 F-18A Hornet fighter aircraft for its forces in North America and Europe. The government gave the McDonnell Douglas Corporation of St. Louis a $2.7-billion order for aircraft to be delivered between 1982 and 1989. Another U.S. aircraft, the long-range Aurora patrol plane built by Lockheed Aircraft Corporation, began to arrive in Canada during 1980 as part of a large procurement program.

In World Affairs, Canada and the United States tended to adopt similar poses. Canadian governments headed by both Clark and Trudeau showed their disapproval of Russia's invasion of Afghanistan. Canada boycotted the Olympic Summer Games held in Moscow. Canadian wheat sales were held to traditional levels, and the government promised to compensate farmers for the ensuing drop in prices. Canada cut off trade and investment with Iran. Kenneth Taylor, the Canadian ambassador in Teheran, Iran, aided in sheltering six U.S. diplomats for three months after the U.S. mission was seized in November 1979 and then, in January 1980, helped them to escape from Iran. For this resourceful act, Taylor was honored by the Congress of the United States and by his own country. He was later appointed Canadian consul-general in New York City.

President Jose Lopez Portillo of Mexico visited Canada in May and was given the honor of ad-

Canada and Provinces
Population Estimates

	1979	1980
Alberta	2,012,500	2,068,800
British Columbia	2,569,900	2,626,400
Manitoba	1,032,000	1,027,100
New Brunswick	700,900	705,700
Newfoundland	573,700	578,200
Northwest Territories	43,400	42,800
Nova Scotia	847,700	851,600
Ontario	8,503,300	8,558,200
Prince Edward Island	123,000	124,000
Quebec	6,283,700	6,298,000
Saskatchewan	959,000	967,400
Yukon	21,700	21,400
Canada	**23,670,700**	**23,869,700**

City and Metropolitan
Population Estimates

	Metropolitan Area June 1, 1979 estimate	City 1976 Census
Toronto	2,864,700	633,300
Montreal	2,818,300	1,080,500
Vancouver	1,175,200	410,200
Ottawa-Hull	738,600	304,500
Edmonton	594,900	461,400
Winnipeg	590,300	560,900
Quebec	559,100	177,100
Hamilton	538,600	312,000
Calgary	522,700	469,900
St. Catherines-Niagara	307,300	123,400
Kitchener	283,500	131,900
London	275,300	240,400
Halifax	273,200	117,900
Windsor	245,400	196,500
Victoria	224,800	62,600
Regina	163,700	149,600
Sudbury	153,400	97,600
St. John's	147,900	86,600
Saskatoon	141,600	133,800
Oshawa	141,300	107,000
Chicoutimi-Jonquiere	130,000	60,700
Thunder Bay	121,200	111,500
Saint John	118,700	86,000

dressing the Canadian Parliament. He agreed that Mexico would sell Canada 50,000 barrels of crude oil per day starting in October. The two countries also signed a pact on industrial cooperation.

Facts in Brief: Population: 24,552,000. Government: Governor General Edward Richard Schreyer; Prime Minister Pierre Elliott Trudeau. Monetary unit: the Canadian dollar. Foreign trade: exports, $68,134,000,000; and imports, $66,544,000,000.   David M. L. Farr

See also Canadian provinces articles; CANADIAN LIBRARY ASSOCIATION (CLA); CANADIAN LITERATURE; SCHREYER, EDWARD RICHARD; TRUDEAU, PIERRE ELLIOTT. In WORLD BOOK, see CANADA; CANADA, GOVERNMENT OF.

CANADIAN LIBRARY ASSOCIATION (CLA) received the final report in October 1980 on Project: Progress, the $110,000 national study on the future of public libraries. The study provided a listing of some 2,400 libraries and other permanent service locations, the most complete ever compiled.

The report pointed out growing competition from private providers of information, the need to use high technology in meeting the information demands of a better educated public, and the effects of increasing unionization of library workers. Information for the report came from questionnaires sent to all public libraries; interviews with library administrators, public officials, and elected representatives; and a national telephone survey.

Fighting Censorship. CLA continued its financial and organizational efforts in opposing censorship of the printed word, particularly at libraries. Contributions from individual members boosted the size of CLA's intellectual freedom fund to $20,000 in 1980, and CLA appointed a voluntary intellectual freedom officer and a legal adviser.

In November 1980, CLA sent the federal government its official response to the proposed master plan of the National Library of Canada, which had been published in December 1979 under the title *The Future of the National Library of Canada.*

Some 1,720 delegates attended CLA's 35th annual conference in Vancouver, B. C., from June 11 through 17. The conference urged the federal government to give financial aid to *Owl*, a children's magazine that needs promotional funding, and to provide financial incentives for preparing a multiple-volume Canadian encyclopedia.

Awards. CLA's Outstanding Service to Librarianship Award went to Jessie B. Mifflen, who was instrumental in developing regional library services in Newfoundland until she retired in 1972. Onésime Tremblay, secretary of the Catholic Separate School Board, Sudbury, Ont., received the Distinguished Service Award for School Administrators; Beryl L. Anderson of the National Library, Ottawa, Ont., received the Award for Special Librarianship; and N. Ray Wight of the Newfoundland Public Library Board, St. John's, the Canadian Library Trustees Merit Award.

CLA awarded the Howard V. Phalin-World Book Graduate Scholarship in Library Science to Monika Langer, Montreal; the H. W. Wilson Education Foundation Scholarship to Hana Cipris, Hamilton, Ont.; and the Elizabeth Dafoe Scholarship to Heather M. Kirkpatrick, Saskatoon, Sask.

CLA presented the Book of the Year for Children Award to James Houston for *River Runners; a Tale of Hardship and Bravery* (McClelland and Stewart); and the Amelia Frances Howard-Gibbon Illustrator's Award to Laszlo Gal for *The Twelve Dancing Princesses* (Methuen).   Paul Kitchen

In WORLD BOOK, see CANADIAN LIBRARY ASSN.

CANADIAN LITERATURE suffered from economic hardship in 1980. Many major publishers cut back their staffs and published fewer works, while the small literary presses were relatively inactive. Nevertheless, some outstanding books – particularly Mordecai Richler's novel *Joshua Then and Now* and Phyllis Grosskurth's biography of Havelock Ellis – showed that serious writing in Canada was as fine as ever.

Fiction. Richler's book was the highlight of the year – an intricate, witty, satiric chronicle of a Jewish writer who tries to come to terms with his unsettled present and the ghosts of his past. Hugh MacLennan contributed *Voices in Time*, a brooding tale of an old man recalling the destruction of civilization by a nuclear war. Ian McLachlan, whose *The Seventh Hexagram* gained unusually spirited praise for a first novel in 1976, produced *Helen in Exile*, which mixed ancient myth and the suspension of civil liberties in Canada in 1970.

Ruby Wiebe's fondness for writing about real-life heroes among the ranks of the dispossessed and disinherited was visible again in *The Mad Trapper*. This is the story of Albert Johnson, who was killed in 1931 by the Royal Canadian Mounted Police after a two-month manhunt in the Arctic. Other noteworthy novels included *Kowalski's Last Chance* by Leo Simpson, *Basic Black with Pearls* by Helen Weinzweig, *The Charcoal Burners* by Susan Musgrave, *The Emperor's Virgin* by Sylvia Fraser, *Contract with the World* by Jane Rule, *Final Things* by Richard Wright, and *General Ludd* by John Metcalf. The best collection of short stories was W. P. Kinsella's *Shoeless Joe Jackson Comes to Iowa*.

Tim Wynne-Jones's *Odds End*, a psychological thriller, won the third annual $50,000 Seal Books first-novel competition. Silver Donald Cameron's *Dragon Lady* and Richard Rohmer's *Periscope Red* capitalized on interest in international intrigue. *The Third Temptation*, Charles Templeton's semiautobiographical chronicle of a big-time evangelist who loses his faith, aroused wide interest. So did *A Right Honourable Lady* by Judy LaMarsh, the former Cabinet minister-turned-novelist who died in October.

Biographies of influential figures provided insights into Canadian politics. William Lyon Mackenzie King, who served as prime minister for 21 years, was the subject of Joy Esberey's *Knight of the Holy Spirit*. Richard Gwyn's *The Northern Magus* examined the career of Pierre Elliott Trudeau, who regained his post as prime minister of Canada in 1980 after briefly losing it to Charles Joseph (Joe) Clark. Warner Troyer analyzed Clark's government in *Joe Clark in Power*, as did Jeffrey Simpson in *Discipline of Power*.

Canadian author Margaret Atwood chats with a fan at an autograph session for *Life Before Man,* her 1980 novel about an unsuccessful marriage.

Drapeau by Brian McKenna and Susan Purcell looked at the almost legendary career of Jean Drapeau, the Montreal, Que., mayor who combined a showman's flair with what critics saw as a poor grasp of financial realities in launching Expo 67 and the 1976 Olympic Games. None of these books, however, matched University of Toronto Professor Phyllis Grosskurth's *Havelock Ellis*, a sympathetic and entertaining biography of the pioneer in the psychology of sex.

Most prominent among a cluster of intriguing memoirs was *Confessions*, a controversial book by Barbara Amiel, a Toronto, Ont., journalist widely known for her neoconservative attitudes. Austin Clarke, whose novels are based on the experience of black Caribbean immigrants in Toronto's often unwelcoming white society, charted the years of his struggling youth in Barbados in *Growing Up Stupid Under the Union Jack*. The posthumously published *Someone with Me* by painter William Kurelek is a vivid memoir that includes a harrowing account of his four years in an English insane asylum. In *Daddy's Girl*, novelist Charlotte Vale Allen revealed her incestuous relationship with her father.

History. Pierre Berton continued to popularize Canada's past in *The Invasion of Canada 1812-1813*, the first of a two-volume series on the War of 1812. Peter Stursburg's oral history, *Lester Pearson and the American Dilemma*, told the story of that Canadian prime minister's role in international affairs.

John Fraser's *The Chinese* was a sensitive, anecdotal account of two years spent in China as a newspaper correspondent and as an innocent in Chinese customs, rituals, and language. Ted Ferguson's *Desperate Siege* told about two Canadian battalions that reinforced the British garrison in Hong Kong just before it fell to the Japanese army in 1941. Most of the survivors spent the rest of World War II in prisoner-of-war camps. Another powerful memoir of combat in World War II was Canadian essayist and novelist Farley Mowat's *And No Birds Sang*. More than 21,000 Canadians of Japanese ancestry spent the war in camps in Canada — the subject of Takeo Nakano's poetic *Within the Barbed Wire Fence*. *Deemed Suspect* by Eric Koch added another interesting sidelight on history — the incarceration of 2,290 refugees, most of them Jewish — behind Canadian barbed wire during the early years of World War II. Kenneth Bagnell's *The Little Immigrants* described Canada's treatment of another group of foreigners, the 80,000 homeless children, mainly under 14, who were shipped as indentured laborers from British slums to Canadian farms and homes from 1889 until the early 1930s.

Poetry collections by Ralph Gustafson, Irving Layton, Marilyn Bowering, Robert Finch, Fred Cogswell, and Raymond Souster demonstrated the diversity of Canadian writers. Tom Marshall completed an ambitious quartet of books on philosophical themes with *The Elements*.

Governor General's Literary Awards for books published in 1979 went to Jack Hodgins for *The Resurrection of Joseph Bourne* (English fiction); Maria Tippett for *Emily Carr* (English nonfiction); Michael Ondaatje for *There's a Trick with a Knife I'm Learning To Do* (English poetry); Marie-Claire Blais for *Le sourd dans la ville* (French fiction); Dominique Clift and Sheila McLeod for *Le fait anglais au Quebec* (French nonfiction); and Robert Mélançon for *Peinture aveugle* (French poetry). Tippett's biography also won the Sir John A. Macdonald Prize for the most significant contribution toward understanding Canada's past.

The Canada Council Translation Prize went to Allan Van Meer for his English translation of three plays — Renald Tremblay's *La céleste Gréta*, Claude Roussin's *Une job*, and Serge Mercier's *Encore une peu* — and to Collette Tonge, for her French translation of Alice Munro's *Dance of the Happy Shades*.

Donald Jack won the Stephen Leacock Memorial Award for humor with his novel *Me Bandy, You Cissie*. The Prix Goncourt, French literary prize, went to Antonine Maillet for her novel *Pélagie-la-charrette*.   Ken Adachi

See also LITERATURE. In WORLD BOOK, see CANADIAN LITERATURE.

CAPE VERDE. See AFRICA.

CARAMANLIS, CONSTANTINE E. (1907-   ), prime minister and leader of the New Democracy Party, was elected president of Greece on May 5, 1980. Members of Parliament chose him to succeed 81-year-old Constantine Tsatsos (see GREECE). Caramanlis had returned from an 11-year self-imposed exile to become prime minister on July 24, 1974, one day after the military junta that had ruled Greece for seven years resigned.

Caramanlis, also spelled Karamanlis, was born on Feb. 23, 1907, in the village of Prote, Macedonia. He received a law degree in 1932 from the University of Athens, was elected to Parliament in 1935, and became a Cabinet minister in 1946. He was appointed prime minister by King Paul on Oct. 6, 1955, to fill a vacancy and was elected prime minister on Feb. 19, 1956.

A staunch anti-Communist, Caramanlis enjoyed friendly relations with the United States, which assisted him in implementing progressive domestic programs that produced an economic boom. Reelected in 1958, he tried to solve the Cyprus question through agreements with Turkey and Great Britain guaranteeing Cypriot independence. He also brought Greece into the European Community (Common Market) as an associate member. Caramanlis resigned and left the country in 1963 after a dispute with King Paul, then the head of state.   Marsha F. Goldsmith

President Jimmy Carter is amused at grandson Jason's attempt to block out helicopter noise as the Carter family returns from a weekend at Camp David.

CARTER, JAMES EARL, JR. (1924-   ), 39th President of the United States, struggled through the last year of his presidency in 1980, trying to deal with a host of international and domestic problems. On the world scene, he had to cope with the Russian invasion and occupation of Afghanistan, a flood of Cuban and Haitian refugees, continuing turmoil in the Middle East, and the captivity of American hostages in Iran. At home, he faced the vexing problems of inflation, rising unemployment, and accelerating interest rates.

Despite a generally unfriendly press, Carter held more news conferences than any previous President and made a number of televised addresses to the American people. But instead of providing inspiration and leadership, he often lectured Americans about their spiritual uneasiness, and asked them to make sacrifices to conserve energy, to accept delays in dealing with Iran's militants, and to recognize that the United States must play a new, less dominant role in a changing world.

Popularity Sinks. As many Americans came to view the Carter Administration as inept, his popularity sank lower than any other President since the advent of public opinion polls. After defeating Senator Edward M. Kennedy (D., Mass.) in the race for the Democratic presidential nomination, Jimmy Carter waged a lackluster campaign, failing to unify the Democratic Party. Nor did he score a victory against Republican presidential candidate Ronald Reagan in their televised debate on October 28.

Thus, on November 4, Carter and his party lost the White House and a Senate majority in a Republican victory that was predicted by Carter's pollsters the previous evening. Even before the polls closed on the West Coast, Jimmy Carter conceded defeat. In a graceful concession speech, he extended hope of an orderly transition to the Reagan Administration.

Policy Blunders. Several unfortunate decisions eroded Carter's image in 1980. The aborted effort in April to free the hostages in Iran by force drew sharp criticism and ridicule at home and overseas. His verbal attack on Secretary of State Cyrus R. Vance following Vance's resignation in protest of the rescue attempt was widely regarded as evidence of a "mean streak." His failure to attend the funeral of Yugoslavia's President Josip Broz Tito in May was viewed as a diplomatic error, and his refusal to leave the White House to campaign against Kennedy early in the presidential primary campaigns was considered a political ploy.

Income and Finances. According to a statement released on April 15, Carter lost his status as a millionaire in 1979. Due to losses in the family peanut business, his net worth, as reported on his 1979 personal income tax return, had declined to

Billy Carter ponders a question as he testifies before a Senate Judiciary subcommittee on his financial dealings with the Libyan government.

CAT. The Cat Fanciers' Association selected Gr. Ch. Kyina Patience of Oakway, a tortoise-shell Persian female owned by Judy Sturm and Anne and Amanda Bright of Oakville, Ont., Canada, as Best Cat of the Year in 1980.

Kitten of the Year was Gr. Ch. Corsica's Wouldn't You Know About It, a red Persian male owned by George and Diana West of Ontario, Calif. Best Alter cat was Gr. Pr. & Ch. Helium's Spitfire, owned by Jeanette Walder of Chicago.

A city ordinance requiring cat owners in Charlotte, N.C., to have their pets vaccinated against rabies at a cost of $8 and licensed for $5 went into effect in August. Less than a week after the ordinance was passed, 224 cats had been abandoned and had to be destroyed by animal control officers.

The Internal Revenue Service (IRS) ruled in September that a taxpayer could deduct the cost of maintaining a cat to alert a deaf person to possible dangers. The decision extended an earlier ruling that permitted tax deductions for watchdogs.

Two 1980 surveys yielded different figures for the United States cat population – a pet-food industry census, 38 million; and a United States Humane Society census, 23 million.   Theodore M. O'Leary

In the Special Reports section, see WHAT IS YOUR PET TRYING TO TELL YOU? In WORLD BOOK, see CAT.

$893,304.35. His income included his presidential salary and expense allowance of $237,499.98, as well as $22,670.53 in interest on investments. Because of an $80,000 business loss, Carter and his wife, Rosalynn, were scheduled to receive a tax refund of $16,703.59. His total tax was $64,944.81.

After leaving office on Jan. 20, 1981, Carter was to receive an annual pension of $69,630; $150,000 a year for his office staff; and up to $1 million to share with Vice-President Walter F. Mondale to cover the expense of winding up his Administration's affairs. Like all former Presidents, Carter will also have Secret Service protection for life.

Brother Billy. Billy Carter's acceptance of a $220,000 loan from the government of Libya and his subsequent role as an intermediary to Libya in an attempt to negotiate the release of the hostages in Iran provoked a Senate subcommittee investigation. In a report to the subcommittee on August 4, the President denied that his brother had influenced U.S. policy toward Libya. The subcommittee concluded that, though Billy Carter had not acted illegally or influenced policy, President Carter, members of his family, and some Cabinet and staff officials had exercised bad judgment in handling information concerning Billy Carter and his relationship with Libya.   Carol L. Thompson

See also PRESIDENT OF THE UNITED STATES. In WORLD BOOK, see CARTER, JAMES EARL, JR.

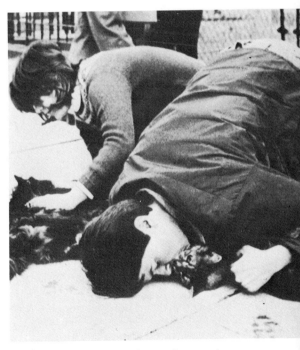

Cats overcome by smoke receive mouth-to-mouth resuscitation and other emergency aid after their rescue from a Boston residential fire.

CENSUS. The 20th Decennial Census of Population and Housing in 1980 was the most controversial in the history of the United States census, which dates to 1790. The Bureau of the Census also termed it the most complete and accurate census.

The estimated population of the United States on census day, April 1, was 221,672,000 and the number of housing units was 86 million. However, because of intensive publicity and better census techniques, 4.8 million additional persons and 2 million more housing units were counted, bringing the actual 1980 U.S. population total to more than 226 million and the number of housing units to 88 million.

The Official Count. Using the 1970 census figure of 203,235,298 as a base, and adding estimates made since 1970, the Census Bureau made the estimate for April 1, 1980, of 221,672,000. The difference between the two figures reflected the number of births during the 10 years (33,238,000); the number of deaths (19,275,000); and net immigration (4,475,000). The addition of an estimate of 4.5 million persons not counted in 1970 brought the estimated 1980 population to 226 million.

The final 1980 census count, released on December 31, was 226,504,825. Based on this result, the national undercount estimate for 1980 will probably be about 0.5 per cent of the population – about 1 million persons – or less. It may even approach zero, as opposed to the estimated 2.5 per cent undercount in 1970.

The Bureau's Task was to count all residents of the United States, Puerto Rico, the Virgin Islands, Guam, American Samoa, and the Trust Territories of the Pacific Islands. Data were compiled for 3,200 counties; 20,000 incorporated villages, towns, and cities; 37,000 county subdivisions; 45,000 census tracts; 300,000 enumeration districts and block groups; and 2,500,000 city blocks.

Planning for the 1980 census started nine years earlier, shortly after the 1970 census was completed. The work gradually built in intensity until actual counting started.

The Bureau of the Census also instituted major coverage improvements to improve the 1980 census accuracy. One of these was a local review program that gave local officials an opportunity to check early population and housing figures before the temporary offices that had been set up throughout the United States were closed and the counts became final. Local review helped to pinpoint such major problems as clusters of missed housing units, geographic mistakes, and incorrectly located local boundaries.

Households across the country received census questionnaires in the mail on March 28, 1980, and 90 per cent of the households were asked to fill out and mail back completed forms. Census takers picked up the remaining 10 per cent, sent primarily to households in sparsely settled areas.

About 4 out of 5 households answered 19 basic questions on the "short form." The remaining households filled in a longer questionnaire with 46 additional socioeconomic questions.

A temporary work force of more than 300,000 persons checked returned questionnaires for completeness, completed personal interviews where necessary, and handled a wide variety of clerical tasks. The census employees worked out of 409 temporary district offices containing 4 million square feet (370,000 square meters) of space.

Questionnaires were checked in the district offices, then shipped to processing centers in Indiana, Louisiana, and California. After processing through high-speed microfilming equipment there, the data were transmitted to computers at Census Bureau headquarters in Suitland, Md.

Reaching Minorities. Minority populations were the most undercounted in the 1960 and 1970 censuses, and the Bureau of the Census set out to remedy this defect in the 1980 count. A Minority Statistics Program was developed early in the 1970s, aimed at improving the initial count and all statistics on blacks, Hispanic Americans, Asian and Pacific Americans, and American Indians, Eskimos, and Aleuts. A National Services Program worked across the country to inform minorities

Population of the United States 1790-1980

Millions of people

225
200
175
150
125
100
75
50
25
0

1790 1820 1850 1880 1910 1940 1970 1980

Census workers at cardboard desks in makeshift quarters in a vacant Elizabeth, N.J., store make preparations for the 1980 national count.

through hundreds of exhibits, workshops, and meetings. A Community Services Program, employing about 200 specialists, worked in minority neighborhoods and with city, state, and regional organizations explaining the census workers' task and promoting cooperation.

Added to these programs was a nationwide promotional campaign to gain the support of minority media organizations and national groups such as the National Association for the Advancement of Colored People. Also, brochures, pamphlets, and articles prepared in English and 13 other languages were distributed in minority communities to inform residents about the census.

A massive advertising campaign preceded the 1980 census. The nonprofit Advertising Council coordinated a volunteer national media campaign whose message was "Answer the Census. We're Counting on You." As a result, the 1980 census campaign received the equivalent of almost $38-million in time and space in newspapers, on radio and television, and in other media.

Congressional Shifts. The Census Bureau was legally obligated to provide President Jimmy Carter with census population totals for each state by Dec. 31, 1980. On December 16, the bureau released figures for 49 of the 50 states. The numbers for New York state were delayed by a fire in a local census office.

The count showed that Nevada, with a 64 per cent increase since 1970, was the fastest-growing state. Arizona, Florida, Wyoming, Utah, Alaska, Idaho, Colorado, New Mexico, Texas, Hawaii, and Oregon followed, all up by at least 25 per cent. See STATE GOVERNMENT (Table).

The President then forwarded the population figures to the clerk of the United States House of Representatives, who notified the 50 state governors of the number of House seats apportioned to their respective states. The figures showed that 17 seats in the House of Representatives would shift as a result of population changes during the decade. As a result of the Sun Belt population growth, Florida gained four House seats, Texas gained three seats, and California gained two. One additional seat each went to Arizona, Colorado, Nevada, New Mexico, Oregon, Tennessee, Utah, and Washington.

Losses of population in Northern states meant a loss of five seats for New York; two seats each for Illinois, Pennsylvania, and Ohio; and one seat each for Indiana, Missouri, Michigan, South Dakota, Massachusetts, and New Jersey. The congressional changes will affect the 98th Congress, which will be elected in 1982.

The Census Bureau must also provide the 50 states with statewide population breakdowns by April 1, 1981, to assist in state legislative redistrict-

I AM FROM THE CENSUS, MADAM. WE ARE TRYING TO FIND OUT HOW MANY PEOPLE LIVE IN THE UNITED STATES

OH, HAVE **YOU** COME TO THE WRONG PLACE! I DON'T HAVE THE FAINTEST IDEA

Clarence Brown in *Saturday Review*

ing. Population shifts since 1970 have created a need within many states to redraw their congressional election district boundaries so that each state representative serves approximately the same number of constituents. Many municipalities, too, were scheduled to use 1980 population figures to redraw the local election district boundaries for such offices as city council and county township supervisor.

Because so much political and economic power, including congressional reapportionment and the distribution of $50 billion each year in federal funds, rides on census results, many big cities and organizations chose to challenge the census counts in court, and redistricting may be delayed.

The Illegal Alien. A suit brought by the Federation for American Immigration Reform (FAIR) and 28 members of Congress challenged the traditional inclusion of all U.S. residents in the official population total used for reapportionment. FAIR argued that the apportionment count would include several million unlawful residents, and this would deprive the plaintiffs of certain constitutional rights, privileges, and protections. The suit was dismissed on February 26 in Washington, D.C. The district court ruling in favor of the bureau was appealed by FAIR, but the Supreme Court of the United States on March 17 rejected FAIR's plea for postponement of the census.

The Big City Challenge. Although the Census Bureau has been warning for years that big cities were losing population, an unprecedented number of suits concerning the 1980 census were brought by cities. The most widely publicized came from Detroit, which started proceedings on April 2, claiming that a census undercount of Detroit's minority population would cost the area political representation and millions of dollars in federal funds for its community programs.

A federal district court ruled in September in favor of Detroit. The U.S. Department of Justice appealed the decision, partly on the grounds that there is no practical and statistically sound method to measure the census undercount in jurisdictions smaller than states. The decision was temporarily suspended by the Supreme Court on December 24.

Other court actions taken against the Census Bureau included those by New York City and state; Cook County, Illinois; Pontiac, Mich.; Newark, N.J.; Philadelphia; Duluth, Minn.; Atlanta, Ga.; Denver; Chester, Pa.; the state of New Mexico; Doña Ana County, New Mexico; and the Chicago Spanish Coalition for Jobs. Suits filed by Cincinnati, Ohio, and Baltimore were dismissed. On December 30, the Supreme Court set aside an order by a New York City federal judge, clearing the way for the census count to be official. Various other lawsuits were still in process at year's end.

The Privacy Question. Names, addresses, and telephone numbers on questionnaires were deleted as the forms were transmitted to the computers. The original forms were destroyed after the tabulation was completed, another step in ensuring confidentiality. Social Security numbers were not requested by the census. No information gathered by the Census Bureau concerning any individual may be released to anyone other than that individual, even if requested by the President of the United States or other government agencies. In the history of the Census Bureau, no census employee has ever been charged with a breach of this confidentiality. However, a federal district court order was issued in October 1980 requiring the Census Bureau to turn over 1980 census address lists to the city and state of New York. The bureau director refused to comply with the order because federal statutory law prohibits disclosure of information in these lists. Furthermore, the bureau claimed that such disclosure would seriously hurt the historic guarantee of confidentiality and undermine public confidence in the privacy of census information.

Other Census Bureau Findings released in 1980 included the following:
■ The number of husbandless women heading families has soared nearly 50 per cent since 1970 to more than 8 million.
■ The traditional family household of mother, father, and one or more children now accounts for

less than 33 per cent of U.S. households, the lowest percentage ever.

■ The number of unmarried couples sharing a household has more than doubled in 10 years.

■ Young people are postponing marriage, and couples are postponing parenthood.

■ The number of singles living alone rose by nearly 60 per cent, including young adults (18 to 34) and the elderly (65 and over), the two fastest-growing groups in the 1970s.

■ In 1970, the average household had 3.1 persons. In 1979, it had 2.8 persons.

■ Both husband and wife had earned income in about 50 per cent of the 48 million husband-wife families in the United States, a new high.

■ The median age of the population reached 30 in 1979, compared with 28.1 in 1970.

■ For the first time since World War II, more women than men were enrolled in U.S. colleges and universities in 1979. Of the 11.4 million college students, 5.9 million were women.

Many of these findings help explain the tremendous increase in the number of U.S. housing units, despite a substantial decrease in the population in many areas. Vincent P. Barabba

See also POPULATION. In WORLD BOOK, see CENSUS; POPULATION.

CENTRAL AFRICAN REPUBLIC. See AFRICA.

CEYLON. See SRI LANKA.

CHAD was wracked by civil war in 1980 as fighting between factions led by President Goukouni Weddeye and former Defense Minister Hissene Habre continued. A November 1979 peace agreement involving the two major and nine minor political factions fell apart in March 1980. The agreement provided for a coalition government; withdrawal of rival military forces from N'Djamena, the capital, by February 5; and installation of an inter-African peacekeeping force.

The first peacekeeping force – 400 Congolese troops – arrived on January 18, but Chadian military factions ignored the deadline and remained in N'Djamena. Heavy fighting broke out among rival Chadian factions on March 22 and continued into April, taking about 700 lives.

Peacekeeping forces made no attempt to suppress the violence, and some 1,100 French troops stationed at the N'Djamena airport were withdrawn from the country in May after evacuating Europeans. Congolese troops remained as the only African peacekeeping forces. Togo's President Gnassingbe Eyadema flew to N'Djamena on April 5 and negotiated a truce, but hostilities resumed the next day. In November Libya intervened, capturing N'Djamena in mid-December and forcing Habre to agree to a cease-fire. J. Dixon Esseks

See also AFRICA (Facts in Brief Table). In WORLD BOOK, see CHAD.

CHEMICAL INDUSTRY sales in the United States started well in 1980, tailed off by midyear, but began to recover near the end of the year. Capital spending on new plants and equipment had been expected to rise, but slumped somewhat.

McGraw-Hill Publications Company's Department of Economics had reported in 1979 that the industry expected to invest $11.6 billion during 1980, up 17 per cent from 1979. This level held up during the first quarter, but by midyear, spending was running only about 15 per cent ahead of 1979. Late estimates indicated that spending for the year ran about 12 per cent ahead. About half of the 1980 spending went for plants and equipment that the industry expected would increase productive capacity by about 4 per cent.

Cyclic Business. Strong activity in chemicals and allied products carried over from the fourth quarter of 1979 into 1980, but the year was a study in contrasts. First-quarter sales were up about 18 per cent, outpacing the rest of the economy. But sales of some major items dropped by 25 to 40 per cent in the second quarter. Sales rebounded midway through the third quarter, with shipments just below the January peak. Increasing sales also enabled chemical producers to trim inventories. Final-quarter sales continued strong because of increases in the automobile, housing, defense, and consumer-goods industries.

Benzene Revisited. The Supreme Court of the United States on July 2 upheld a lower court ruling that invalidated stringent federal regulations limiting workers' exposure to benzene. The Department of Labor's Occupational Safety and Health Administration (OSHA) had set rules in 1978 that reduced the permissible limits of benzene, which was suspected of causing leukemia, from 10 parts per million (ppm) to 1 ppm. The Supreme Court said that OSHA must provide more justification for its job safety and health rules than it did in writing the 1978 benzene rules.

Of the five justices who ruled against OSHA, only one accepted the lower court's reasoning that OSHA was required to determine that the economic effects of its standards bear a reasonable relationship to the expected benefits. The other four supported the lower court ruling on another basis – that OSHA had not obtained any actual evidence that exposure to benzene at or below 10 ppm had ever caused leukemia.

Environmental Events. The Environmental Protection Agency (EPA) issued more than 2,000 pages of documents in June on tracking and disposing of hazardous wastes. The rules are designed to prevent companies that handle such wastes from piling up tons of unidentified dangerous chemicals that could leak into nearby areas. EPA estimated that the massive and complex regulations will cost industry about $1 billion per year.

Fire burns in an Elizabeth, N.J., chemical storage area. Toxic fumes from the April fire forced school closings in Elizabeth and Staten Island.

The Congress of the United States passed a bill in December that would create a chemical-industry superfund of $1.6 billion to clean up chemical spills and toxic-waste sites such as the abandoned Love Canal dump in Niagara Falls, N.Y. (see ENVIRONMENT [Close-Up]). Chemical companies would provide most of the money. President Jimmy Carter signed the bill in December.

Worker Safety. OSHA in August issued a list of 107 substances used in industrial plants that may cause cancer in workers, in order to stimulate public discussion of scientific data. Companies and organized labor responded by sending OSHA large amounts of toxicological and epidemiologic data to try to influence the agency's decisions on a list that it will issue in early 1981.

EPA proposed on Dec. 31, 1979, that companies be required to submit unpublished data concerning the health and environmental effects of various substances. OSHA adopted regulations in May that give employees, their representatives, and the agency itself access to company medical and exposure records. Many companies believe that giving labor unions, OSHA, and other third parties access to these records would be an invasion of privacy. Employers also said that granting access to information about chemicals in the workplace might jeopardize trade secrets.　　Frederick C. Price

In WORLD BOOK, see CHEMICAL INDUSTRY.

CHEMISTRY. A potentially important drug in the treatment of cancer was synthesized in the laboratory for the first time in October 1980 by a team of chemists led by Elias J. Corey of Harvard University in Cambridge, Mass. The researchers made maytansine, an organic compound that kills about 100 times more cancer cells than normal cells. Most cancer drugs destroy only slightly more cancer cells than normal cells. Corey and his team – Leland O. Weigel, A. Richard Chamberlin, Hidetsura Cho, and Duy H. Hua – took five years to synthesize maytansine, found in nature in the fruit of the Ethiopian shrub *Maytenus ovatus*.

Maytansine is a complex molecule that has 35 carbon atoms, 46 hydrogens, 10 oxygens, 3 nitrogens, and 1 chlorine atom. Nineteen of the carbon atoms are linked together to form a ring. In addition, maytansine contains several optically active carbon atoms. These are carbons whose four attached groups of atoms are arranged in only one of two possible orientations.

The Harvard chemists started their synthesis by putting together the carbon framework of maytansine. Then they carried out reactions to form the correct orientations of the optically active carbons and removed groups of atoms that they had placed on certain parts of the molecule to prevent main groups from changing during reaction steps carried out on other parts of the molecule.

The synthesis required 19 main reactions. The scientists had to perform as many as 25 experiments in order to find the right conditions for some of the main reactions. Now chemists can synthesize maytansine and related compounds that might not occur naturally and study their effectiveness in treating cancer.

Carbynes Found. Research that may provide new clues about the origin of the solar system was reported in 1980. Three teams of chemists working together found that samples of two meteorites contained carbyne, an unusual form of carbon. Carbynes are composed of units of two carbon atoms joined by a triple bond – two carbons sharing three pairs of electrons.

Team members A. Greenville Whittaker and Ethel J. Watts of Aerospace Corporation in El Segundo, Calif.; Roy S. Lewis and Enward Anders of the University of Chicago; and Ryoichi Hayatsu, Robert G. Scott, and Martin H. Studier of Argonne National Laboratory near Chicago found that heating a meteorite sample to 250° to 330°C (480° to 625°F.) released carbynes containing from one to five triply bonded carbon units.

Knowing the temperatures at which carbynes form helps to determine a meteorite's history. The researchers found that they could form carbynes by heating carbon monoxide and hydrogen with a chromite catalyst to 300°C (570°F.).

This information, together with the concentrations of various isotopes of neon and xenon – two gases found in the meteorites – led the scientists to conclude that one meteorite contained material that condensed from the forming solar system at relatively low temperatures, about 300°C (570°F.). The other meteorite sample had much different gas concentrations. The researchers concluded that it had condensed from material formed before the birth of the solar system.

Nobel and Priestley Prizes. Paul Berg, 54, of Stanford University in California won half of the 1980 Nobel Prize for Chemistry for his research on nucleic acids, the genetic material found in the nucleus of all cells. Walter Gilbert, 48, of Harvard University, and Frederick Sanger, 62, of Cambridge University in England shared the other half for determining the sequence of the organic acids in nucleic acids. Sanger had won the 1958 Nobel Prize for Chemistry for identifying the amino acid components of the important protein, insulin.

Herbert C. Brown, 68, of Purdue University in West Lafayette, Ind., won the 1981 Priestley Medal of the American Chemical Society, highest honor in United States chemistry. Brown was co-winner of the 1979 Nobel Prize for Chemistry for applying boron compounds to organic synthesis, making possible mass production at reasonable cost of many important chemicals.   Lawrence Verbit

In WORLD BOOK, see CHEMISTRY.

CHESS. Viktor Korchnoi, a Russian now living in Switzerland, and Robert Hübner of West Germany survived competition featuring eight grandmasters in 1980, and played for the right to meet titleholder Anatoly Karpov of Russia in 1981 for the world championship. The Korchnoi-Hübner match began in Merano, Italy, on December 20.

The quarterfinal matches, held in March and April, saw Korchnoi defeat Tigran Petrosian of Russia, 5½-3½, in Velden, Austria; and Hübner defeat Hungarian Andras Andorjan, 5½-4½, in Bad Lauderberg, West Germany. Lev Polugaevsky surprised the chess world by upsetting fellow Russian Mikhail Tal, 5½-2½, in Alma Alta, the Soviet Union. Another Russian, Boris Spassky, and Lajos Portisch of Hungary were tied after their 10 quarterfinal games in Mexico City. Two additional sets of two games each did not break the tie, so Portisch was declared the winner because he had won more games with the black pieces. Korchnoi defeated Polugaevsky, 7½-6½, in their semifinal in Argentina, and Hübner beat Portisch, 6½-4½, in Italy.

Chess Olympics. Russia won both the men's and women's Chess Olympics in Malta in November and December. Hungary was second in both events. The United States men's team finished a solid fourth behind Yugoslavia. The U.S. women finished 15th.

U.S. Chess Championship tournament, held in June at Thiel College in Greenville, Pa., produced three cochampions – grandmasters Walter Browne of Berkeley, Calif., Larry Christiansen of Modesto, Calif., and Larry Evans of Reno, Nev. International master John Fedorowicz of Clearwater, Fla., and grandmaster Florin Gheorghiu of Romania won the U.S. Open championship in August in Atlanta. New York City's Joel Benjamin won the 1980 U.S. Junior championship in July in Hollywood, Calif.

Other Tournaments. The World Open drew about 900 players to Philadelphia over the July 4 weekend. Winners were grandmasters Christiansen, Roman Dzindzihashvili of Israel, Gheorghiu, Anthony Miles of Great Britain, and international master Lawrence Day of Toronto, Canada. The 1980 American Open was held over Thanksgiving weekend in Santa Monica, Calif., and was won by Browne, international master John Grefe of Ashland, Ore., and fide master David Strauss of Dana Point, Calif. Dzindzihashvili took a clear first at the 1980 Louis Statham Tournament in March in Lone Pine, Calif. Gary Kasparov of Russia won the 1980 World Junior championship.

Karpov won the 1980 Bugojno Tournament in May in Yugoslavia, which was one of the strongest tournaments in recent years. The International Association of Chess Journalists awarded Karpov the Chess Oscar as the outstanding player of 1979. It was his record sixth Oscar.   Peter C. Prochaska

In WORLD BOOK, see CHESS; HOBBY.

Chicago Mayor Jane M. Byrne chastises fire fighters, on strike for the first time in the city's history, for ignoring back-to-work orders.

CHICAGO weathered a number of crises in 1980, emerging in surprisingly good condition at year-end. The city's school system came near bankruptcy; its credit rating dropped; and teachers and fire fighters struck. Nonetheless, financial advisers produced a budget for fiscal 1981 that, for the first time in years, accounted for all city funds, wiped out old deficits, and was in balance.

A budget deficit of nearly $500 million forced the Chicago Board of Education to miss two consecutive paydays in December 1979 and January 1980 before the state of Illinois and the city government on January 5 announced an $875-million financing package designed to keep the schools solvent through the 1979-1980 school year. The plan also called for the creation of a five-member Chicago School Finance Authority to oversee school spending, a January budget cut of more than $60 million, and a $51-million cut for the next school year.

Financial Trouble. To protest cuts and the projected layoff of some 2,000 school district employees, teachers conducted a two-week walkout ending on February 11. In the strike settlement, teacher layoffs were greatly reduced.

The school crisis and a city budget deficit of about $80 million shook the financial community's faith in Chicago's fiscal health. On January 31, Moody's Investors Service Incorporated lowered the city's bond rating from Aa to A; Standard and Poor's Corporation dropped its rating from A+ to A−. However, Mayor Jane M. Byrne's chief financial adviser, Edwin H. Yeo, set up a cash-management program, froze city hiring, and arranged a series of short-term loans. When he presented a $2.7-billion 1981 budget in November, he forecast a slight surplus.

Police and Fire Fighters. Chicago's fire fighters walked off the job for the first time in city history on February 14 in a dispute over collective bargaining. During the 23-day strike, nonunion fire fighters – about 10 per cent of the force – and 700 recruits provided fire protection.

Chicago police voted on November 11 to unionize, designating the Fraternal Order of Police (FOP) as bargaining agent for more than 10,000 officers. The election followed an October 16 vote to determine which, if any, of five organizations would represent the police in future contract negotiations. The FOP and "no union representation" were top vote-getters, necessitating a runoff.

Desegregation. The U.S. Department of Justice agreed on September 24 to a Chicago schools desegregation program that was less stringent than a federal plan rejected by the school system in 1979. In a March 31 agreement with the Justice Department, the city also agreed to promote more black and Hispanic fire fighters.   James M. Banovetz

See also CITY. In WORLD BOOK, see CHICAGO.

CHILD WELFARE. The U.S. Department of Health, Education, and Welfare became the Department of Health and Human Services (HHS) on May 4, 1980, when a separate Department of Education was set up under Secretary of Education Shirley M. Hufstedler. The new HHS, headed by Patricia Roberts Harris, includes the Administration for Children, Youth, and Families (ACYF), which contains three major bureaus: Head Start, the Children's Bureau, and the Youth Development Bureau. John A. Calhoun, former commissioner of youth services in Massachusetts, was appointed commissioner of the ACYF.

Legislation. Little improvement in federal support for children and families or local services to aid them was expected in 1980, and less was attained. Legislators gave priority to defense, inflation, energy, and unemployment problems.

Even the Adoption Assistance Child Welfare Act, which was signed into law in June, was no exception. The legislation requires states to provide assistance to families who adopt children with special needs, such as the handicapped, minorities, refugees, and others who are difficult to place. The states receive matching federal grants, and costs are minimal, because many of these children would otherwise require foster care or placement in institutions at greater expense. Cuts in the Aid to Families with Dependent Children program and other federal projects were tacked on to the bill, making the total impact one of cost-cutting. President Jimmy Carter on January 10 announced plans for a $2-billion youth training and employment program to increase opportunities for basic skills training of unemployed youths and to encourage industry to provide jobs for beginners.

Family Problems. A June 1980 report by social researcher Trude W. Lash and colleagues at New York City's Foundation for Child Development said that 5,567 cases of child abuse and neglect in that city were confirmed in 1978. This was an increase of 1,000 cases over 1977.

Responsibility for the welfare of a minor child was always presumed to rest with the parents if they were not obviously abusive. But the complicated case of 12-year-old Walter Polovchak, who left home not because he was abused but because he did not want to leave Chicago and return with his parents to Russia's Ukraine, may set a legal precedent. An Illinois judge ruled in August that Walter should be placed in a "neutral" foster home until the question of his civil rights could be decided. See CIVIL RIGHTS.   Frances A. Mullen

In WORLD BOOK, see CHILD WELFARE.

CHILDREN'S BOOKS. See LITERATURE FOR CHILDREN.

Sophia Loren, head of an alliance to prevent child abuse, and President Jimmy Carter greet guests at a White House reception for the group.

CHILE. In a national plebiscite held on Sept. 11, 1980, Chileans approved by a 2-to-1 margin a new constitution and the continuance of military rule until the constitution becomes effective in 1989. The referendum, which had been announced less than four weeks before the balloting, provided for continued authoritarian rule, allowing President Augusto Pinochet Ugarte to hold power for eight more years beginning on March 11, 1981. Popular elections or political activity would be prohibited before 1989.

The plebiscite was denounced as a farce both at home and abroad. Former President Eduardo Frei Montalva called it a fraud, and urged the immediate formation of a joint civilian-military government to return Chile to democracy in two or three years. Editorials in newspapers in other countries condemned the plebiscite on several grounds, including the short interval between its announcement and the voting, which did not leave adequate time for public debate.

Tax Cuts. Shortly before the plebiscite, the government announced tax cuts that freed an estimated 1 million persons at the bottom of the economic ladder from paying any taxes. There were also reductions for those in higher tax brackets, lower taxes on real estate and automobile purchases, and a 15 per cent reduction in taxes on electricity and gasoline. All of these were designed to appeal to the voters.

As the plebiscite approached, the country's economy was thriving. Foreign reserves stood at an all-time record $2.2 billion. Because of favorable prices for copper exports, Chile's foreign trade during the first half of 1980 was 50 per cent higher than during the comparable period in 1979. Moreover, the military leadership was permitting greater personal freedom, and human rights violations appeared to be diminishing.

Get-Tough Policy. However, the liberalization trend was overshadowed early in the year when the government reinstated many of the harsh police-state measures that had characterized the early years of the Pinochet regime. The state-of-emergency rules under which Chile is ruled were tightened in May because of a resurgence of outlawed leftist political groups that had flourished under the Marxist government of President Salvador Allende Gossens. In March, 17 students accused of antigovernment activities were exiled to remote villages and forced to support themselves. Later, seven labor lawyers charged that secret police seized them and questioned them for a day about alleged leftist connections. The lawyers also produced documents concerning other illegal interrogations that included electric shocks and other torture tactics.   Nathan A. Haverstock

See also LATIN AMERICA (Facts in Brief Table). In WORLD BOOK, see CHILE.

CHINA, PEOPLE'S REPUBLIC OF. The year 1980 turned out to be one of startling change – like 1966, when the late Communist Party Chairman Mao Tse-tung (Mao Zedong in the phonetic Pinyin alphabet) launched his Cultural Revolution. Under the pragmatic Old Revolutionary leader Deputy Premier Teng Hsiao-p'ing (Deng Xiaoping), the new ruling group confirmed the vast changes in ideals, goals, and methods at the top that it has been making since Mao's death on Sept. 9, 1976, and the roundup of the "Gang of Four" and other radicals.

Perhaps the most significant change was the abandonment of Mao's cardinal tenets, such as "better Red than expert," and the campaign to prove him fallible, errant, and – in his last years – manipulated by his lieutenants, including his wife, Chiang Ching (Jiang Qing). All but one of Mao's portraits in Tien An Men Square in the heart of Peking (Beijing) were removed in July and August. "The East Is Red," a song of musical praise for Mao, was attacked for promoting his cult.

The current leadership began to describe the Cultural Revolution as "the 10 catastrophic years," and its victims were numbered at 100 million. The "Four Modernizations" – of industry, agriculture, defense, and science – were reaffirmed as the nation's supreme goal. The educational system, all but wrecked between 1966 and 1976, was rebuilt, and thousands of students were sent to Japan and the West to refill the depleted ranks of experts. Intellectuals, hounded during the last years of Mao's life, were restored to high status.

Muckraking Grows. Much of the process of reshaping the people's minds was achieved through exposés of myths, leaders, and institutions glorified in Mao's last decade. Under Mao, the nation was enjoined to "learn from Dachai," the commune in barren Shansi (Shanxi) Province that supposedly made its way to prosperity and true socialism through hard work and Maoist discipline. However, exposés that began in June tended to show the commune as a gigantic fraud. It was not hard work that made Dachai (Dazhai) China's showplace, but the vast amounts of money spent on it by the government and the diversion of county funds to benefit Dachai at the expense of other communes. Ch'en Yung-Kuei (Chen Yonggui), who rose under Mao's patronage from Dachai brigade chairman to membership in the ruling Politburo, was accused of a variety of crimes, including torture and murder.

Another one of the hundreds of exposés showed the much publicized rolling mills in Wu-han (Wuhan), completed by Japanese and West German suppliers in 1977, to have been a $450-million boondoggle. The mills were still unused in 1980.

The Trial of the Gang of Four opened on November 20, providing a milestone in the history of the republic and of de-Maoization. The four – Chiang

The National People's Congress, meeting in Peking (Beijing) in September, approves the leadership's appointment of Zhao Ziyang as China's premier.

Ching and her three allies from Shanghai, Chang Chun-chiao (Zhang Chunqiao), Yao Wen-yuan (Yao Wenyuan), and Wang Hung-wen (Wang Hongwen) – were arrested in October 1976 after demanding key party and government posts. Interrogated often during the next four years, they were finally ordered in September to stand trial.

To general surprise, their trial was linked with that of five generals associated with Mao's onetime heir-designate, Defense Minister Lin Piao (Lin Biao), who, according to the official version, died in September 1971 while fleeing to Russia. This was ironic, because the Gang of Four had led a heated campaign against Lin Piao in the 1970s. A still greater surprise was the inclusion among the accused of Chen Po-ta (Chen Poda), who was Mao's secretary and ghost writer and field commander of the Cultural Revolution from 1966 to 1971.

The chief prosecutor announced on September 27 that the 10 defendants were charged with sedition, conspiracy to overthrow the government, persecution of officials, armed rebellion, and plotting to assassinate Mao. The civilians and the military were to be tried in separate courts.

The trials were postponed repeatedly, leading to speculation that Chiang Ching still refused to make the required confession, attributing her actions to Mao's direction. Others believed the delays were caused by the reluctance of some leaders, including some older army marshals, to see Mao blamed for the excesses.

General Wu Faxian, one of the five military defendants, testified on November 23 that he was responsible for "unimaginable damage" to China's air force and that he participated in the unsuccessful plot to kill Mao. In early sessions, Chiang Ching insisted she was innocent of all charges, but on December 3 she admitted – reportedly with a show of emotion – that she had led a plot to unseat Liu Shao-chi (Liu Shaoqi), then chief of state. On December 29, a prosecutor demanded the death penalty for Chiang Ching. She denounced her judges as fascists, and she was forcibly removed from the courtroom. The verdict was put off until January 1981.

Crucial Decisions. The course to be followed in the 1980s was charted at a party Central Committee session in February. The first order of business was to sweep the remaining four Maoists out of the Politburo and install two key Teng lieutenants in the ruling seven-man inner circle. As general secretary of the Central Committee, Hu Yao-pang (Hu Yaobang), 65, took over the day-to-day running of the party machine. Zhao Ziyang, 61, who had been boss of Szechwan (Sichuan) Province, was appointed to the Politburo. With ringing rhetoric, the session rehabilitated Liu, who, sick and maltreated, had died in a provincial prison in 1969.

In a move that disturbed many, the session also decided to delete the so-called Four Greats from the nation's Constitution – the rights to "speak out freely, air views fully, hold great debates, and write big-character posters." The Central Committee said "the masses have the full right and opportunity to express their views," but the Four Greats were "not a good way to achieve this." In September, *Jintian (Today)*, the last of 30 dissident magazines that sprang up in late 1978, was declared illegal.

More Changes. Some of the party decisions made in February were made public in September by the National People's Congress, a rubber-stamp institution normally used to inform the nation of new policies and leaders. But this congress, attended by 3,000 delegates, turned out to be rich in news. Thus, Communist Party Chairman Hua Kuo-feng (Hua Guofeng) announced on September 7 that he was giving up his post as premier to Teng's choice, Zhao, whom he called "a suitable choice and worthy of trust" (see ZHAO ZIYANG). This was widely seen as the beginning of Hua's decline in the party hierarchy and there were reports in December that he would resign as chairman in January 1981. Also important was the September announcement that Teng, 76, and five other aged vice-premiers would retire from their government – but not party – posts. Teng had thus

Portrait of Mao Tse-tung (Mao Zedong) is removed from a building in Peking (Beijing) during drive to de-emphasize the late leader.

achieved what Mao never could – the orderly transfer of power to younger heirs.

The Economy. The congress confirmed what was already long known. China's extravagant modernization plans, nurtured in 1977-1978 and then formally downgraded in 1979, were being trimmed anew. The badly flawed 10-year plan that was to end in 1985 was replaced by new five-year and 10-year plans to take the country through the 1980s. China was simply too poor to make its dreams of 1977-1978 come true.

In a private speech in January, Teng said the annual per capita income of $200 in China compared unfavorably with $2,000 for Hong Kong and $3,000 for Singapore. He noted that Japan produced about a ton of steel per year per capita; the United States, 0.5 ton; and China, 0.06 ton.

A severe drought cut the grain yield by 15 million short tons (13.6 million metric tons) below that of 1979. Officials announced a "famine" in Hopeh (Hebei) Province. As a result, the United States and China signed a four-year contract on October 22 providing for the delivery of at least 6.6 million short tons (6 million metric tons) of U.S. grain annually. There were also grain purchases from Canada and Australia. A major problem was the continuing severe unemployment, with industry unable to provide enough jobs for young people leaving school, the millions of urban youths returning from exile in the countryside, and those formerly employed in factories that were closed as inefficient.

Foreign and Military Affairs. Relations with the United States grew increasingly closer, with Washington relaxing some restrictions on the sale of strategically important items – excluding weapons. By September, the United States had approved more than 400 export licenses for the sale of such items as helicopters, radar systems, and sophisticated computers. In return, Peking agreed to sell to the United States titanium, vanadium, and tantalum, badly needed by the U.S. aircraft industry.

United States Secretary of Defense Harold Brown visited Peking for military talks in January. Chairman Hua and President Jimmy Carter met in July in Tokyo, where both attended memorial services for Japan's Prime Minister Masayoshi Ohira, and Carter noted their mutual concern over Russia's invasion of Afghanistan.

Between May 18 and 21, China successfully launched two 3-stage intercontinental ballistic missiles from somewhere in the country's north to a target area in the South Pacific, about 6,000 miles (9,600 kilometers) away. It also set off a nuclear explosion in the atmosphere on October 16. A tentative deal was made with France to purchase two nuclear reactors.   Mark Gayn

See also ASIA (Facts in Brief Table); TAIWAN. In WORLD BOOK, see CHINA.

CHRONOLOGY. See pages 8 through 21.

CHUN DOO HWAN (1931-   ), who came to power in a shoot-out, was elected the fifth president of South Korea on Aug. 27, 1980, by the country's electoral college. Chun was unopposed and planned his victory celebration before having the election ballots printed. But he quickly appointed several distinguished civilian experts to his first Cabinet – to forestall any impression that he might be running a military government.

An army major general, Chun won a power struggle that began with the assassination of President Chung Hee Park on Oct. 26, 1979. Chun led a gun battle in December 1979 to arrest General Seung Hwa Chung, the country's martial law commander. Already head of the Defense Security Command, Chun consolidated his power in April by becoming head of Korea's Central Intelligence Agency.

Chun was born on Jan. 18, 1931, in the village of Hapchongun. He graduated from Korea's national military academy with honors in 1955, then received U.S. Army special forces training in the United States.

Chun is married and has three sons and one daughter. He maintains a childhood interest in herbal medicine.   Patricia Dragisic

CHURCHES. See EASTERN ORTHODOX CHURCHES; JEWS AND JUDAISM; PROTESTANTISM; RELIGION; ROMAN CATHOLIC CHURCH.

CITY. Financial problems persisting from the mid-1970s continued to plague the cities of the United States in 1980. Tax bases continued to shrink as unemployment rose and city dwellers moved to the suburbs and beyond. Moreover, a number of federal aid-to-cities programs were cut out in congressional budget-cutting maneuvers. To compound these woes, preliminary figures from the 1980 United States census showed population losses for most older cities, bringing the threat of reductions in congressional representation and federal funds.

Preliminary census figures showed that the nation's cities lost an estimated 4 per cent of their population during the 1970s, while suburban populations increased 14 per cent and nonmetropolitan populations rose 11 per cent. The major population losses occurred in older Midwest and Northeast cities. St. Louis suffered a decline of almost 28 per cent; Washington, D.C., 16 per cent; and Baltimore and Philadelphia, each 14 per cent. Cities in the so-called "Sun Belt" of the South and West – such as Houston, Phoenix, and Los Angeles – registered population gains, however.

Census Controversy. Preliminary census figures provoked charges of undercounting. Chicago; Detroit; Newark, N.J.; New York City; and Philadelphia filed lawsuits to demand recounts.

U.S. District Court Judge Horace W. Gilmore of Detroit ruled on September 25 that the Bureau of the Census seriously undercounted the nation's population, particularly its minorities, and that the 1980 figures must be adjusted before they could be used for reapportioning congressional seats or distributing federal funds. Gilmore's ruling was suspended on December 24. See CENSUS.

Urban populations in the United States deviated sharply from the world picture, however. The United Nations (UN) Conference on Population and the Urban Future, meeting in Rome in September, was warned that the world's urban population was growing so rapidly that it would present serious, if not critical, problems in food, supplies, energy, and employment unless brought under control. Predictions voiced at the conference indicated that the world's urban population – currently estimated at 1.8 billion persons – would expand to 3.2 billion by the year 2000, with most of the growth occurring in the developing countries.

Urban Policy. In his revised 1981 budget released in late March, President Jimmy Carter recommended cutting or eliminating a number of existing programs, including antirecession aid to cities, revenue sharing for the states, jobs under the Comprehensive Education and Training Act (CETA), and Law Enforcement Assistance Administration grants. The proposed cuts brought an angry reaction from big-city mayors. The U.S. Conference of Mayors' meeting in Seattle in June called for "an antirecession package of spending and tax programs which will create jobs, contribute positively to urban development efforts and, at the same time, combat inflation." Nonetheless, the final $632.4-billion budget approved on November 20 sharply limited outlays for social programs to the cities.

The Carter Administration announced on June 30 that it was redirecting $96 million to create 32,000 summer jobs in the 31 cities hardest hit by the economic recession. The jobs were allocated to students and other young people and were primarily in city parks and public-works agencies. President Carter reported to the Congress of the United States on September 23 that he planned to strengthen and extend his national urban policy in an effort to halt the migration of poverty from rural to urban areas.

Eighteen big-city mayors met in Chicago on November 13 to map strategy for dealing with the incoming Administration of President-elect Ronald Reagan. The group sent a party of four, headed by Gary Mayor Richard G. Hatcher, president of the U.S. Conference of Mayors, to Washington, D.C., for meetings with congressional leaders and members of the Reagan transition team. The mayors resolved to renew their pleas for continuing revenue sharing and urban-employment programs.

Fiscal Stress. A survey released on April 10 by the Joint Economic Committee of Congress re-

50 Largest Cities in the United States

Rank	City	Population (a)	Per cent change in population since 1970 census	Mayor or City Manager (b)
1.	New York	7,015,608	− 11.1	Edward I. Koch (D, 1/82)
2.	Chicago	2,969,570	− 11.9	Jane M. Byrne (D, 4/83)
3.	Los Angeles	2,950,010	+ 4.9	Tom Bradley (NP, 6/81)
4.	Philadelphia	1,680,235	− 13.8	William J. Green (D, 1/84)
5.	Houston	1,554,992	+ 26.1	Jim McConn (NP, 1/82)
6.	Detroit	1,192,222	− 21.3	Coleman A. Young (D, 1/82)
7.	Dallas	901,450	+ 6.8	*George R. Schrader (1973)
8.	San Diego	870,006	+ 24.7	*Ray Blair (1978)
9.	Baltimore	783,320	− 13.5	William Donald Schaefer (D, 12/83)
10.	San Antonio	783,296	+ 19.7	*Thomas E. Huebner (1977)
11.	Phoenix	781,443	+ 33.7	*Marvin A. Andrews (1976)
12.	Indianapolis	695,040	− 4.8	William H. Hudnut III (R, 12/83)
13.	San Francisco	674,063	− 5.8	Dianne Feinstein (ND, 1/84)
14.	Memphis	644,838	+ 3.3	Wyeth Chandler (I, 12/83)
15.	Washington, D.C.	635,233	− 16.0	Marion S. Barry, Jr. (D, 1/83)
16.	Milwaukee	632,989	− 11.8	Henry W. Maier (D, 4/84)
17.	San Jose	625,763	+ 36.1	*James A. Alloway (1979)
18.	Cleveland	572,532	− 23.8	George V. Voinovich (D, 11/81)
19.	Boston	562,118	− 12.3	Kevin H. White (D, 1/84)
20.	Columbus, Ohio	561,943	+ 4.1	Tom Moody (R, 12/83)
21.	New Orleans	556,913	− 6.2	Ernest N. Morial (D, 5/82)
22.	Jacksonville, Fla.	541,269	+ 7.3	Jake M. Godbold (D, 7/83)
23.	Seattle	491,897	− 7.3	Charles Royer (NP, 1/82)
24.	Denver	488,765	− 5.0	William H. McNichols, Jr. (D, 6/83)
25.	St. Louis	448,640	− 27.9	James Conway (D, 4/81)
26.	Kansas City, Mo.	446,562	− 12.0	*Robert A. Kipp (1974)
27.	Nashville-Davidson	439,599	+ 3.2	Richard H. Fulton (D, 9/83)
28.	El Paso	424,522	+ 31.7	Thomas Westfall (NP, 4/81)
29.	Pittsburgh	423,962	− 18.5	Richard S. Caliguiri (D, 1/82)
30.	Atlanta	422,293	− 14.7	Maynard Jackson (D, 1/82)
31.	Cincinnati	399,072	− 12.0	*Sylvester Murray (1979)
32.	Buffalo	378,617	− 18.2	James D. Griffin (D, 12/81)
33.	Oklahoma City	372,690	+ 1.2	*James J. Cook (1976)
34.	Omaha	368,347	+ 2.8	Al Veys (NP, 6/81)
35.	Fort Worth	367,432	− 6.6	*Robert L. Herchert (1978)
36.	Portland, Ore.	364,735	− 4.6	Francis J. Ivancie (D, 1984)
37.	Minneapolis	353,992	− 18.4	Donald M. Fraser (D, 1/82)
38.	Toledo	351,686	− 8.2	*J. Michael Porter (1979)
39.	Miami	347,862	+ 3.9	*Joseph R. Grassie (1976)
40.	Long Beach	339,629	− 6.0	*John E. Dever (1977)
41.	Oakland	332,247	− 8.1	*David A. Self (1978)
42.	Tulsa	328,684	− 0.5	James M. Inhofe (R, 5/82)
43.	Austin	319,194	+ 23.3	*Dan H. Davidson (1972)
44.	Louisville	317,503	− 12.2	William B. Stansbury (D, 12/81)
45.	Newark	314,412	− 17.7	Kenneth A. Gibson (D, 7/82)
46.	Baton Rouge	311,053	+ 15.2	J. Patrick Screen, Jr. (D, 12/84)
47.	Tucson	301,875	+ 12.9	*Joel D. Valdez (1974)
48.	Charlotte	299,444	+ 4.2	*David A. Burkhalter (1971)
49.	Albuquerque	295,150	+ 20.7	David Rusk (D, 12/81)
50.	Norfolk, Va.	280,568	− 8.9	Vincent J. Thomas (NP, 6/82)

Sources
(a) Ranks 1–30, preliminary results, 1980 census; Ranks 31–50, 1978 estimates (U.S. Bureau of the Census).
(b) *Asterisk before name denotes city manager (as of September 1978, *Municipal Year Book, 1979*, International City Management Association); all others are mayors (as of June 1978, National League of Cities). Dates are those of expiration of term for mayors and dates of appointment for city managers.
D—Democrat, R—Republican, NP—Nonpartisan, I—Independent.

Average cost of living (family of 4) (c)	Unemployment rate (d)	Revenue (e)	Gross debt outstanding (e)	Per capita income (f)	Sales tax rate (g)
$23,856	7.3	$15,970,970	$14,343,134	$8,852	8%
20,564	8.5	1,661,495	1,309,551	9,493	6%
19,871	7.0	2,345,246	2,718,165	9,399	6%
21,436	7.2	1,424,982	1,555,074	8,162	6%
19,025	4.8	576,648	917,843	9,398	5%
20,821	n/a	1,112,743	685,195	9,512	4%
18,301	5.3	372,234	485,744	8,756	5%
20,088	7.5	346,264	139,750	7,947	6%
20,316	8.2	1,136,355	493,281	7,905	5%
n/a	8.2	506,895	714,743	6,648	5%
n/a	7.0	321,028	545,426	8,170	5%
n/a	8.7	350,108	283,685	8,342	4%
21,478	5.8	1,059,344	656,955	10,492	6%
n/a	7.0	755,333	732,733	7,231	6%
22,206	4.6	1,791,328	1,581,177	10,259	6%
21,387	6.4	350,637	285,283	8,786	4%
n/a	6.0	227,213	145,719	9,771	6%
20,868	6.4	378,437	478,011	9,204	5½%
24,381	5.9	851,693	599,006	8,306	5%
n/a	9.0	240,035	340,126	7,602	4%
n/a	6.5	371,120	371,621	7,649	6%
n/a	6.4	463,095	643,472	7,140	4%
20,719	8.5	384,970	516,225	9,582	6.3%
20,468	5.5	437,467	441,921	9,080	6%
19,963	9.0	364,910	151,832	8,251	4⅝%
19,618	7.2	307,092	307,241	8,524	4⅛%
n/a	6.6	559,020	552,361	7,601	6%
n/a	10.0	110,295	59,449	5,639	5%
19,890	7.7	186,820	137,666	8,307	6%
18,821	6.6	290,436	911,213	8,328	4%
20,287	8.2	301,206	203,854	8,064	4½%
21,806	10.0	404,826	318,279	7,628	7%
n/a	4.0	191,741	408,732	7,903	4%
n/a	5.9	136,192	115,877	7,676	4½%
n/a	5.3	159,522	195,754	8,756	5%
n/a	n/a	180,984	109,426	9,140	—
21,426	5.2	231,569	307,736	8,921	4%
n/a	11.8	140,809	153,911	8,090	4½%
n/a	6.5	127,659	133,720	8,567	4%
19,871	7.0	245,734	85,110	9,399	6%
21,478	5.8	211,982	157,405	10,492	6%
n/a	4.1	157,808	327,897	8,195	4%
n/a	4.0	259,751	532,483	7,270	5%
n/a	8.6	234,155	340,129	8,058	5%
n/a	8.0	385,951	168,696	9,487	5%
n/a	7.3	133,677	289,553	7,526	6%
n/a	6.6	135,994	178,167	6,973	6%
n/a	5.7	134,748	165,717	7,815	4%
n/a	8.6	136,588	125,638	7,405	4¼%
n/a	7.1	226,363	199,545	6,890	4%, 7%

(c) Estimates for autumn, 1979, for Standard Metropolitan Statistical Areas (U.S. Bureau of Labor Statistics). n/a—not available.
(d) June 1980 preliminary figures for Standard Metropolitan Statistical Areas (U.S. Bureau of Labor Statistics).
(e) 1977–78 figures in thousands (U.S. Bureau of the Census).
(f) 1978 figures for Standard Metropolitan Statistical Areas (U.S. Bureau of Economic Analysis).
(g) Total sales tax rate, including state, county, city, school district, and special district taxes (The Tax Foundation).

vealed that many cities operated with a budget deficit in 1978 and 1979, and that more were expected to do so in 1980. The survey polled officials in 300 cities varying in population from 10,000 to over 250,000. It found deficit spending on the increase in cities of all types and sizes and in every region of the United States. Some of these deficits were discovered only recently. New administrations in Chicago, Philadelphia, and Washington, D.C., uncovered municipal debts that had been masked by questionable accounting procedures. These deficits were attributed to shrinking tax bases, a decline in federal aid, and high bond rates. They persisted despite decreases in capital expenditures and bargaining that kept average municipal pay increases below the inflation rate.

Boston, which relies heavily on property-tax revenues, typified this situation. When funds to operate the Metropolitan Transit Authority (MTA) ran out, Massachusetts Governor Edward J. King issued an emergency proclamation putting the MTA under state control on November 25, and the system kept running until a court order terminated King's authority on December 5. Service halted on December 6 but the state legislature, in an emergency session, granted the MTA $41 million in operating funds, and service resumed on December 7. Nonetheless, a proposition that placed a ceiling on property taxes, passed on November 4, threatened to curtail transit funds in 1981.

Some chronically distressed cities made significant progress in solving their fiscal problems in 1980. Cleveland emerged from default on November 18 after the City Council on October 8 approved an agreement between Mayor George V. Voinovich and eight banks to refinance $36.2 million in debts, including $10.5 million of the $14-million in notes that the city had been unable to pay since December 1978. A mandatory 40-day waiting period followed the agreement. New York City; Wayne County (Detroit), Michigan; and Chicago also moved toward economic solutions.

Strikes and Walkouts. Fiscal uncertainty provoked tension in some cities, and municipal employees struck, demanding increased pay and benefits. Chicago experienced the first fire-fighters' strike in its history in February; police in South Bend, Ind., called in sick on June 8 in a contract dispute; and New York City narrowly averted a strike by police and fire fighters in July. Uniformed employees also walked off the job in Mobile, Ala.; Nashville, Tenn.; and Youngstown, Ohio.

A six-day strike by fire fighters in Kansas City, Mo., ended on March 22 when a judge ordered the reinstatement of 42 fire fighters dismissed during a work slowdown in December 1979. The city had begun firing the fire fighters on the second day of the strike, and 72 had been jailed for refusing to obey a back-to-work order.

50 Largest Cities in the World

Rank	City	Population
1.	Shanghai, China	10,820,000
2.	Mexico City, Mexico	9,233,770
3.	Tokyo, Japan	8,219,888
4.	Moscow, Russia	7,831,000
5.	Peking (Beijing), China	7,570,000
6.	São Paulo, Brazil	7,198,608
7.	London, England	7,028,200
8.	New York City, N.Y., U.S.A.	7,015,608
9.	Seoul, South Korea	6,879,464
10.	Cairo, Egypt	6,133,000
11.	Bombay, India	5,970,575
12.	Jakarta, Indonesia	5,490,000
13.	Hong Kong	4,867,000
14.	Rio de Janeiro, Brazil	4,857,716
15.	Bangkok, Thailand	4,835,000
16.	Teheran, Iran	4,716,000
17.	Tientsin (Tianjin), China	4,280,000
18.	Leningrad, Russia	4,073,000
19.	Karachi, Pakistan	3,515,402
20.	Ho Chi Minh City, Vietnam	3,460,000
21.	Santiago, Chile	3,448,700
22.	Delhi, India	3,287,883
23.	Madrid, Spain	3,201,234
24.	Calcutta, India	3,148,746
25.	Berlin (East & West), East & West Germany	3,038,689
26.	Buenos Aires, Argentina	2,972,453
27.	Chicago, Ill., U.S.A.	2,969,570
28.	Baghdad, Iraq	2,969,000
29.	Los Angeles, Calif., U.S.A.	2,950,010
30.	Lima, Peru	2,941,473
31.	Rome, Italy	2,868,248
32.	Bogotá, Colombia	2,850,000
33.	Sydney, Australia	2,765,040
34.	Yokohama, Japan	2,723,940
35.	Osaka, Japan	2,600,001
36.	Istanbul, Turkey	2,534,839
37.	Pyongyang, North Korea	2,500,000
38.	Melbourne, Australia	2,479,442
39.	Madras, India	2,469,449
40.	Pusan, South Korea	2,450,125
41.	Shen-yang (Shenyang), China	2,411,000
42.	Alexandria, Egypt	2,320,000
43.	Paris, France	2,299,830
44.	Rangoon, Burma	2,276,000
45.	Singapore, Singapore	2,234,400
46.	Lahore, Pakistan	2,169,742
47.	Wu-han (Wuhan), China	2,146,000
48.	Kiev, Russia	2,144,000
49.	Chung-ch'ing (Chongqing)	2,121,000
50.	Budapest, Hungary	2,093,187

Sources: 1980 Bureau of the Census preliminary results for cities of the United States; censuses and estimates from governments or UN *Demographic Yearbook, 1978* for cities of other countries.

The Republican National Convention was held in Detroit in July amid a public employee strike, and Los Angeles experienced the second such strike in its history in November. Transit workers struck in New York City in April, as did public-works employees in Boston in August.

Court Rulings. Two decisions by the Supreme Court of the United States broadened city liability for personal damages. The court ruled 5-4 on April 16 that cities are liable for actions by city officials that violate an individual's constitutional rights. The court said that although a city has common-law immunity for making "discretionary" judgments for the public's general interest, it "has no 'discretion' to violate the federal Constitution." The court broadened this doctrine on June 25 when it ruled, by a 6-3 vote, that individuals can use an 1871 civil rights law to collect damages when an act passed by a local government violates a legal right given by Congress. The court ruled unanimously in the cities' favor on June 10 that municipalities may preserve open space by restricting development of private property.

A federal court ruling forced Cairo, Ill., to change from a system of at-large representation to one of aldermanic ward representatives on its City Council. The ruling, handed down on March 11 by U.S. District Court Judge James L. Foreman, divided the city into five wards, two of which are composed primarily of black residents, in a plan to assure minority representation on the council.

School Integration. The Supreme Court on April 28 upheld a lower court order consolidating 10 New Castle County school districts with the predominantly black Wilmington, Del., school district for integration purposes. The court on January 21 let stand a lower-court ruling that raised doubts about the legality of a Dallas desegregation plan relying on voluntary pupil transfers.

A two-year, 14-city study released on November 16 reported that metropolitan school desegregation is the most effective means of breaking up segregated housing patterns. The study predicted that metropolitan-wide busing would produce housing integration, which, in turn, would eliminate the need for busing. Cleveland and Los Angeles both instituted major new busing programs during the year. Federal courts also ordered busing for 9,000 schoolchildren in the Indianapolis metropolitan area and for 13,500 students in Austin, Tex.

Racial Violence occurred in Chattanooga, Tenn.; Oceanside, Calif.; Wichita, Kans.; and Miami and Orlando, Fla. The U.S. Department of Justice on April 22 signed an unprecedented agreement with Memphis, under which the city's police department pledged an investigation of police-misconduct charges. See CIVIL RIGHTS.   James M. Banovetz

See also city articles. In WORLD BOOK, see CITY and articles on cities.

CIVIL RIGHTS. Citizens in several nations ruled by governments that had previously allowed few civil liberties received greater civil rights in 1980. After 12 years of military rule, Peru returned to a democratic form of government with the inauguration on July 28 of President Fernando Belaunde Terry for a five-year term.

Probably the severest test of democratic elections occurred in Zimbabwe, formerly Rhodesia, on March 11 when Marxist guerrilla leader Robert Mugabe was elected prime minister. Mugabe tried to dispel the white population's fear of black reprisals, declaring that there was a place for everyone in the new Zimbabwe.

In contrast, however, other developments abroad eroded existing civil rights. South Korea's brief progress toward democracy was halted when martial law was imposed following student demonstrations in May. Chun Doo Hwan, an army general who resigned his military post on August 22, was elected president on August 27. Military judges on September 17 sentenced Dae Jung Kim, opposition leader, to death for sedition.

In the Philippines, President Ferdinand E. Marcos continued to use heavy-handed tactics against his opponents. In July, arrest warrants were issued for 85 persons accused of subverting the Marcos regime. In September, eight labor leaders were arrested, and military authorities issued warrants to arrest others as discontent grew following the government's refusal to grant wage increases.

In Taiwan, a military court on April 18 convicted eight dissidents of sedition for using their magazine, *Formosa*, to subvert the government. The defendants, who were given long prison sentences, countercharged that police interrogators had coerced confessions by denying them sleep and by composing statements for them to sign.

European Setbacks. The Russian government announced on January 22 that physicist and dissident leader Andrei D. Sakharov had been banished from Moscow to Gorki, a city closed to foreigners. Sakharov won the 1975 Nobel Prize for Peace.

Fearful of growing street crime, France's National Assembly passed the Security and Freedom Act on June 21. The act, which must also be passed by the Senate to become effective, would allow police to stop anyone at any time and demand identification, increase the penalties for some infractions, and speed judicial processes. Critics said the act would dangerously expand police power.

In Great Britain, an appeals court ruled in May that television journalists who broadcast information based on confidential documents discrediting the nationalized steel industry must reveal their sources or face possible imprisonment. The House of Lords upheld the decision on July 30.

Riots exploded in May in Liberty City, a Miami neighborhood suffering depression-level unemployment, high crime rates, and smoldering resentment against police. Hostilities erupted after an all-white jury on May 17 set free four policemen who, as part of a larger group of policemen, had beaten a black insurance man to death after chasing him down for a traffic violation. Florida National Guard troops brought the violence under control by May 19, and U.S. Attorney General Benjamin R. Civiletti pledged to investigate Miami abuses.

Officials withdrew all police patrols from the Alton Park section of Chattanooga, Tenn., and turned over security to volunteer patrols of black leaders after violence erupted in July. The riots began on July 22 after an all-white jury acquitted two members of the Ku Klux Klan charged with shooting four black women.

Court Decisions. A California Superior Court judge on May 19 ordered the Los Angeles Unified School District to start a busing program designed to desegregate the school system. The busing program went into effect on September 16.

The Supreme Court of the United States ruled on April 16 that local governments cannot limit private civil rights suits against them on the grounds that city employees acted in good faith or committed civil rights violations unintentionally. The court handed down a decision in favor of affirmative action in July, in upholding a public

works program that set aside 10 per cent of federal construction grants for companies owned by members of minority groups. The ruling allowed Congress to award federal benefits on the basis of race.

The Supreme Court backtracked from a controversial 1979 ruling in which it had refused to find a public right to attend criminal trials in the Sixth Amendment. The court ruled on July 2 that the First Amendment's guarantees of free speech and free press give the press and the public an all but absolute right to attend criminal trials.

In other civil liberties decisions, the Supreme Court ruled on June 9 that states can require the owners of private shopping centers to provide access to individuals wishing to circulate petitions or otherwise exercise their right of free speech.

Women in the United States gained additional rights through administrative and court action. The U.S. Department of Justice obtained a consent order on July 15 requiring the city of Philadelphia to hire women to comprise 30 per cent of its police officers. A federal district judge on May 20 awarded an estimated $6 million in back pay and $10-million in increased future earnings to women bindery workers in the U.S. Government Printing Office, ruling that they had been victims of sex discrimination. However, the Supreme Court ruled on June 30 that Congress may refuse to finance abortions for women, except in pregnancies that resulted from incest or rape, or if the life of the mother would be endangered.

Press Relations continued to be a sensitive and controversial civil rights topic in 1980. In Boise, Ida., law officers on July 26 raided a television station and seized copies of news videotape made inside the Idaho State Penitentiary during a riot a few days earlier. A federal appeals court on October 2 gave television stations permission to broadcast videotapes from the Abscam trial of U.S. Representative Michael Myers (D., Pa.) (see CONGRESS OF THE UNITED STATES).

Children's Rights. A suit challenging a Texas law restricting free public education to citizens and "legally admitted aliens" was initiated in March on behalf of children of illegal aliens who were either barred from Texas public schools or charged tuition. In August, an Illinois judge ordered that a 12-year-old boy, Walter Polovchak, who came to Chicago from the Soviet Union's Ukraine republic with his parents, be turned over to a "neutral" foster home pending further determination of his future. Walter left his parents in July so that he would not have to return to Russia with them. In effect, the court substituted itself and the state for Walter's parents.   Louis W. Koenig

See also articles on individual countries; COURTS AND LAWS; SUPREME COURT OF THE UNITED STATES. In WORLD BOOK, see CIVIL RIGHTS.
CLOTHING. See FASHION.

Walter Polovchak, a 12-year-old who refused to return to Russia with his parents, was granted political asylum in the United States in July.

COAL. The United States, with 31 per cent of the world's economically recoverable coal, could become the "Saudi Arabia of coal," an international study of world coal resources concluded in May 1980. The study was directed by engineer Carroll L. Wilson of the Massachusetts Institute of Technology in Cambridge. It urged a massive international effort to expand facilities for the production, transport, and use of coal. By tripling production and increasing exports of steam coal 10 to 15 times, coal-rich nations could end the energy crisis and sustain world economic growth for decades. The report concluded that the coal needed by the world to ease dependence on petroleum could be mined, transported, and burned economically without endangering human health or the environment.

According to the study, the United States has by far the greatest potential for exporting coal, with a capacity to ship more than 350 million metric tons (385 million short tons) per year. Australia is next, with an export capacity of 200 million metric tons (220 million short tons), followed by South Africa, with a capacity of 100 million metric tons (110 million short tons). United States overseas exports totaled 46 million metric tons (51 million short tons) in 1979. Another 19 million metric tons (21 million short tons) were sold to Canada.

Another report on coal's future prospects came from the President's Commission on Coal. The commission warned in March that the 1980s would be a decade of "dangerous energy vulnerability" unless use of coal is increased.

Slump Continues. Despite such optimism, the U.S. coal industry remained in a slump that officials blamed on federal regulations, poor economic conditions, and inadequate dock facilities for coal exports. About 20,000 coal miners were out of work for much of the year. The industry was faced with about 90 million metric tons (100 million short tons) of excess capacity – coal that could have been mined but was left in the ground because there was no market. And, although foreign demand for U.S. coal increased, orders could not be filled because of inadequate facilities at East Coast ports.

The National Coal Association estimated that domestic coal production would reach about 750 million metric tons (825 million short tons) during 1980, up 6.3 per cent from 1979. Much of the growth was due to the increased demand from electric utilities using coal instead of costly imported oil. Coal's share of total electricity generation rose to 50.3 per cent during the first six months of 1980. But the sharpest increase in coal demand came from foreign buyers – particularly members of the European Community – who turned to U.S. coal as a replacement for Persian Gulf oil. Overseas coal exports rose 43 per cent in 1980, to 65 million metric tons (72 million short tons).

Port Loading Capacity, not demand, limited overseas shipments in 1980. Plans for construction of major coal-exporting facilities in Savannah, Ga., and Portsmouth, Va., were announced in September and October, respectively. The Savannah facility would cost $60 million, be completed by 1985, and have the capacity to ship 11 million to 14 million metric tons (12 million to 15 million short tons) of coal per year. The Portsmouth facility, scheduled for completion in 1983 at a cost of $60-million to $100 million, would be able to handle 18 million metric tons (20 million short tons) of coal per year. On March 6, President Jimmy Carter proposed a $10-billion program to help the electric utility industry convert plants now burning oil and natural gas to coal. The program would save 600,000 barrels of oil per day by 1990.

Russia disclosed on September 1 that it is developing a major new coal-mining and electricity-generating complex in northeast Kazakhstan. The complex is scheduled to produce 170 million metric tons (187 million short tons) of coal per year by the late 1980s. The leaders of West Germany, Great Britain, France, Canada, Italy, Japan, and the United States met in Venice, Italy, in June, and pledged to reduce oil consumption and double consumption of coal during the 1980s. Michael Woods

See also ENERGY; MINES AND MINING. In WORLD BOOK, see COAL.

COIN COLLECTING. The auction of the third of four groups of coins in the famed John W. Garrett collection in New York City on Oct. 1 and 2, 1980, brought unprecedented prices for relatively "minor" coins, producing total sales of just under $4-million. The 572 lots of coins in the second Garrett group had sold for $11.7 million in March, compared with total sales of $7.1 million for the 621 lots in the first group, which were sold in November 1979. While the first two groups of coins were sold to investors, coins in the third group were purchased almost exclusively by collectors. The Garrett collection, formed in the late 1800s by railroad executive T. Harrison Garrett, had been bequeathed to Johns Hopkins University.

Highest price paid at the March auction was $500,000 by coin dealer Donald H. Kagin of Des Moines, Iowa, for an 1851 Augustus Humbert $50 slug, a California gold piece. Pullen & Hanks – an El Paso, Tex., coin dealer – paid $190,000 for an 1887 quarter and $400,000 for an 1804 silver dollar, the most ever paid for what has been called "the king of American coins." The firm sold the coin to Sam Colavita of Trenton, N.J., in April for a price reported to be about $500,000.

Gold and Silver. The Department of the Treasury on July 15 began taking orders for gold medallions weighing 1 troy ounce (31.10 grams) and 0.5 troy ounce (15.55 grams) to be sold at a price pegged to the previous day's gold price on the New York Commodity Exchange. Initially, each purchaser was limited to three medallions of each size. The Treasury planned to offer 10 different medallions over the next five years, each honoring a different American artist. The first to be so commemorated were painter Grant Wood on the 1-troy-ounce medallion and singer Marian Anderson on the 0.5-troy-ounce medallion.

The General Services Administration began in February to sell the last of the Carson City silver dollars minted from 1879 to 1891. Deborah Duke Swan, project manager for the sale, reported an "overwhelming" avalanche of orders for the 923,287 available coins. Prices for the dollars ranged from $45 to $65.

Popular and Unpopular Coins. The U.S. Bureau of the Mint reported in June that it had received orders since June 1979 for about 500,000 medals commemorating motion-picture actor John Wayne.

The mint stopped producing Susan B. Anthony dollars on March 31. Issued in 1979, the coin proved unpopular, largely because it was so easily confused with the U.S. quarter. Mint officials said in July they would conduct a test run of the dollars using a new alloy that would give the Anthony dollar a brassy look, making it more easily distinguishable. Theodore M. O'Leary

In WORLD BOOK, see COIN COLLECTING.

Helmeted police rescue fellow lawman wounded in shoot-out with guerrillas holding hostages in Dominican Embassy in Bogotá, Colombia.

COLOMBIA. On Feb. 11, 1980, 16 heavily armed members of the terrorist group Movement of April 19, also known as M-19, seized the Embassy of the Dominican Republic in Bogotá while a diplomatic reception was being held. Among the 80 hostages captured were representatives of 17 nations, including Diego C. Asencio, the United States ambassador to Colombia.

World attention was focused on the fate of the hostages for 61 days. Some women and children, as well as "hardship" cases, were released during the negotiations, but the terrorists held firm to their demand that the Colombian government free all political prisoners, including 311 who were supposedly M-19 members. The group also demanded a $50-million ransom.

By mid-April, negotiations had reached an impasse. However, mediation by Cuba and the Inter-American Human Rights Commission of the Organization of American States ultimately resolved the impasse. Reportedly, the release had been facilitated by the payment of a $2.5-million ransom by two Colombians. On April 27, the terrorists and 12 of their remaining captives were flown to Cuba under a flag of truce. The terrorists remained there.

The embassy seizure overshadowed the release in February of Richard Starr, a U.S. Peace Corps volunteer who had been held captive by guerrillas for almost three years. A $250,000 ransom, raised through public subscription in the United States, was paid to his captors.

By-Elections were held on March 9 to fill 8,617 seats on municipal councils and 406 seats in departmental legislatures. About 37,000 candidates were involved in the various races. During the voting, in which less than 25 per cent of the nation's 13.8 million registered voters went to the polls, the army provided tight security.

Tensions created by the presence of the M-19 group in the embassy and fears that other members of the group might provoke anti-election street violence kept most voters away from the polls.

Late in the year, President Julio Cesar Turbay Ayala proposed that a qualified amnesty be offered to an estimated 2,000 guerrillas active in the country. If the guerrillas could be persuaded to lay down their arms, the state of siege that had prevailed for almost 30 years could be lifted. The appeal went unanswered, however, while kidnappings for ransom continued. The country's huge traffic in drugs flourished. Estimates indicated that revenues from the marijuana and cocaine trade exceeded the value of Colombian coffee exports, the mainstay of the economy. Nathan A. Haverstock

See also LATIN AMERICA (Facts in Brief Table). In WORLD BOOK, see COLOMBIA.

COLORADO. See STATE GOVERNMENT.
COMMON MARKET. See EUROPE.

COMMUNICATIONS leaders had expected that legislation giving the United States a cohesive communications policy would be passed in 1980. Two major bills were introduced – one in the House of Representatives and one in the Senate – but both died in committee, leaving the 97th Congress to deal with the matter when it convened in 1981.

However, changing patterns in the structure of the international telephone, telegraph, and telex industries already have emerged without benefit of legislation. They have resulted from rulings by the Federal Communications Commission (FCC), the chief federal agency that regulates communications, and from court rulings.

Competition will be the keynote of future communications systems. Customers will have the right to buy their own telephones, switchboards, and other terminal devices not only from the telephone companies, but also from the so-called "interconnect" companies that have formed to compete with the telephone companies.

The FCC on October 9 issued a series of proposals specifically designed to spur competition among five of the largest U.S. communications companies for overseas markets and so force down high rates. The American Telephone and Telegraph Company (A.T. & T.), the parent company of the Bell System, which now monopolizes overseas telephone markets, would have to permit four international carriers to compete for those markets. In turn, A.T. & T. would be allowed to provide overseas telegraph and telex service, which is now dominated by the International Telephone and Telegraph Corporation, RCA Global Communications Incorporated, Western Union International, and the TRT Telecommunications Corporation.

In June, A.T. & T. lost an antitrust suit to MCI Communications Corporation and faced paying a $1.8-billion penalty. However, A.T. & T. said it would appeal the verdict, carrying on the fight against MCI, a small competitor in the long-distance telephone business.

Reorganization abounded in the communications field as the major established telephone companies, including the Bell System and all of the larger independent telephone companies, rearranged themselves to be ready for whatever changes may be decreed by federal agencies or by new legislation. The main thrust of these actions was to set up the companies to quickly establish separate subsidiaries to handle competitive areas of marketing and to rearrange the businesses on a market-oriented rather than function-oriented basis. Many of the telephone companies have branched out into such fields as consulting, cable television, data processing, and burglar-alarm services.

Technological Innovations and the accelerating convergence of communications and data processing were important trends in 1980. New devices appeared that promised business communicators better control of costs through least-cost routing and precise call records.

While United States telecommunications companies have long looked upon themselves as the world leaders in the field, they have begun to discover that other countries can also score noteworthy advances. In midsummer, A.T. & T. began a test in Coral Gables, Fla., of an interactive computer-based home information system that allows people to call up on their television sets about 15,000 "pages" of information – everything from restaurant menus to used-car-lot offerings. Similar systems have been in operation in Great Britain and West Germany for several years. The system, known as viewdata, was developed by the British Post Office.

At least 12 French companies, at the urging of the French telecommunications authority, prepared to offer a number of technologically advanced telecommunications products and systems for sale in the United States. One of the most promising is a telephone directory that will do away with paper directories. Each telephone subscriber will have a small screen on which other subscribers' numbers will appear.   Leo S. Anderson

In WORLD BOOK, see COMMUNICATIONS; TELEPHONE.

The Scribophon system, featuring an electronic writing tablet and TV screen connected to a telephone, may help deaf persons communicate.

COMMUNITY ORGANIZATIONS. American Red Cross volunteers and staff organized a relay system to handle the anxious inquiries of Italian Americans about friends and relatives in southern Italy, after the disastrous earthquake there on Nov. 23, 1980. They also assisted the International Committee of the Red Cross and the League of Red Cross Societies in helping Cambodian refugees in Thailand and Vietnamese "boat people" in various Southeast Asian countries.

The Salvation Army celebrated its American and Australian centennials in 1980. "A Century in America, Serving God and Man," was the U.S. centennial theme. More than 12,000 members from 50 states and 20 countries attended the centennial congress held in Kansas City, Mo., in June.

The Young Men's Christian Association (YMCA). The largest voluntary, youth-serving, human-care organization in the non-Communist world, the United States YMCA had some 10.7 million members and registered participants in 1980. Many YMCA's focused on preventive health care through their fitness programs.

The Young Women's Christian Association (YWCA), with more than 2.5 million members and participants in 1980, represented women and girls in 49 states and was at work in 5,000 locations. The YWCA was involved in programs on health, juvenile justice, employment of women and teens, sex and age discrimination, and affirmative action.

Service Organizations. Kiwanis International reported its 1980 membership at more than 300,000 in 7,900 clubs in 72 nations. Merald T. Enstad, a Fergus Falls, Minn., real estate and insurance executive, was elected president and announced a program aimed at combating communication disabilities of all types among young people.

Lions Clubs International elected William C. Chandler of Montgomery, Ala., as president in July. He chose as his theme "Touch a Life with Hope," and called on Lions to extend services to more of the needy. Membership stood at 1.3 million in 33,500 clubs.

Rotary International had more than 18,800 clubs, with more than 875,000 members in 154 countries in 1980. The Rotary Foundation granted more than 1,000 international scholarships for 1980-1981, at a cost of $12.8 million.

Veterans' Organizations. The Veterans Administration (VA) marked its 50th anniversary in July. With a budget of $21 billion and a work force of 218,000, it served more than 30 million veterans and 60 million veterans' dependents and survivors.

The controversy over the effects of "Agent Orange," a herbicide containing dioxin that was used to defoliate forests during the Vietnam War, continued unabated. The VA, the Department of Health and Human Services, and the Department of Defense claimed that research was inconclusive and that there was no proof that the defoliant caused cancer, genetic defects, and various neurological diseases in soldiers exposed to it, though tests showed it causes cancer in animals. A government task force set up to coordinate research on Agent Orange called for further research in late July. On November 24, a federal appeals court dismissed a class-action suit by hundreds of veterans against five chemical companies, saying it had no jurisdiction in the matter.

At a ceremony in the White House Rose Garden on July 1, President Jimmy Carter signed a bill providing for construction in Washington, D.C., of a memorial to the 2.7 million Americans who served in the Vietnam War. The memorial will be located in Constitution Gardens near the Lincoln Memorial and will include the names of the 57,000 Americans who died in that war. The memorial's $2.5-million cost will be raised through donations. The government provided the land. Virginia E. Anderson

In WORLD BOOK, see articles on the various community organizations.

COMOROS. See AFRICA.

COMPUTER. See WORLD BOOK SUPPLEMENT section.

CONGO (BRAZZAVILLE). See AFRICA.

CONGO (KINSHASA). See ZAIRE.

Members celebrate the Salvation Army's first 100 years in the United States at their national convention in Kansas City, Mo.

CONGRESS OF THE UNITED STATES. The second session of the 96th Congress of the United States convened for business on Jan. 21, 1980. With all seats in the House and one-third in the Senate being contested on November 4, the approaching elections cast a shadow over Congress, which adjourned on October 2. It reconvened on November 12 following a sweeping Republican victory — the first lame-duck Congress in 10 years. The session usually ends before election day.

This was a penny-wise Congress, much aware of the energy crisis, unemployment, and the prevailing belief that taxes were too high and federal spending too loose. Thus, the 96th Congress dealt cautiously with economic measures, paring many and letting others expire as the session ended.

Congressional Leaders. Vice-President Walter F. Mondale served in his constitutional role as president of the Senate. West Virginia Democrat Robert C. Byrd was majority leader; California's Alan Cranston, majority whip; and Washington's Warren G. Magnuson, president pro tem. Howard H. Baker, Jr., of Tennessee was minority leader, and Theodore F. Stevens of Alaska, minority whip.

Thomas P. (Tip) O'Neill, Jr., a Massachusetts Democrat, was speaker of the House; James C. Wright, Jr., of Texas was majority leader; John Brademas of Indiana was majority whip. John J. Rhodes of Arizona was minority leader, and Robert H. Michel of Illinois, minority whip.

The State of the Union. President Jimmy Carter sent his third State of the Union message to Congress on January 21. In the 75-page document, the President asked Congress to pass the legislation left pending in its first session; to grant military aid to Pakistan; and to provide for new youth-training programs. Carter promised to reduce the budget deficit and to slow inflation.

The President delivered a 32-minute televised State of the Union address to Congress on January 23. Speaking soberly of Russia's December 1979 invasion of Afghanistan and the crisis in Iran, the President called for the revival of Selective Service registration and warned that the United States would use "any means necessary" to repel an attack on the Persian Gulf.

The Budget. On January 28, Carter sent Congress his proposed budget for the 1981 fiscal year, which began on Oct. 1, 1980. Described by the President as "prudent and responsible," the budget projected receipts of $600 billion, outlays of $615.8 billion, and a deficit of $15.8 billion — 60 per cent less than the deficit written into the 1980 budget. The defense budget was set at $142.7-billion — a $20-billion increase — and automatic new expenditures of $34.4 billion were allocated for welfare, Social Security, and other transfer payments, with cuts proposed for health care, veterans' benefits, and welfare programs.

According to legislation passed in 1974 to reform the budgetary process, Congress must propose its own budget totals by September 15 of each fiscal year before acting on specific appropriations. The Joint Economic Committee of Congress on February 28 recommended a series of budget cuts and a $25-billion federal tax cut by the summer of 1981. The President on March 31 sent Congress a revised fiscal 1981 budget projecting receipts of $628 billion and outlays of $611.5 billion.

The President and Congress encounter one major difficulty in paring federal expenditures — so-called uncontrollable items, including Social Security payments, Medicare, and interest on the national debt, none of which are part of the appropriation process. In fiscal 1981, these items represented more than 76 per cent of outlays.

Congress agreed on June 26 to raise the temporary federal debt ceiling to $925 billion from $879-billion effective until Feb. 28, 1981. Yet when Congress adjourned for its election recess on October 2, it had not agreed on a revised final budget ceiling, and, for the second consecutive year, the new fiscal year began without a budget. However, both houses of Congress on October 1 approved a bill allowing federal agencies to continue spending at the fiscal 1980 rate until December 15, and approved by a narrow margin a controversial

Representative Charles C. Diggs, Jr., resigned from Congress in June after the Supreme Court refused to review his 1978 mail fraud conviction.

Representative Michael Myers, the first member of the House to be expelled since the Civil War, was disciplined for his Abscam bribery conviction.

provision that, with few exceptions, federal funds could not be used to finance an abortion. The final budget, passed on November 20 during the lame-duck session, established a spending ceiling of $632.4 billion.

The Energy Program. Congress approved a great deal of President Carter's energy program in 1980. The House on March 13 and the Senate on March 27 passed a bill taxing the so-called windfall profits of oil companies, those profits arising from the decontrol of prices on oil produced after March 1, 1980. The tax is expected to yield $227.3 billion in revenue over the next 10 years. President Carter signed the act on April 2.

On June 19, after almost a year of discussion in Congress, the Senate voted 78 to 12 to provide $20 billion for a federally owned United States Synthetic Fuels Corporation to develop fuels to replace petroleum. The House approved the measure 317 to 93 on June 26, and the President signed it into law as the Energy Security Act on June 30. President Carter signed a bill on July 1 authorizing $426 million in operating funds for the Nuclear Regulatory Commission. The bill stiffened safety standards for nuclear power plants. On October 7, the President signed the Magnetic Fusion Engineering Act, providing for research and development of nuclear fusion as an energy source. See ENERGY.

The President was unable to persuade Congress to approve his proposed tax on imported oil, though the revenue would have helped to balance the federal budget. On June 4, the House voted 367 to 30 and the Senate voted 73 to 16 to repeal the fee of $4.62 per barrel on imported oil imposed by the President, who planned to pass the fee on to consumers as a surcharge of 10 cents per gallon (3.8 liters) on gasoline prices. After the President vetoed the bill on June 5, the House and Senate voted overwhelmingly to override his veto.

Deregulating the Economy. The President signed the Depository Institutions Deregulation and Monetary Control Act on March 31, allowing banks to raise the interest they pay on small savings deposits. The act also authorized banks to pay interest on checking accounts, and increased to $100,000 the ceiling on bank savings insured by the federal government.

Carter on July 1 signed legislation that substantially deregulated the trucking industry. The new law, which eliminates regulations restricting service and makes it easier for new companies to enter trucking, is expected to increase competition and lower rates, saving consumers an estimated $8-billion a year. See TRUCK AND TRUCKING.

On October 14, the President signed legislation allowing the nation's railroads more flexibility in setting their own rates without the approval of the Interstate Commerce Commission. This was the last measure in Carter's three-part program to deregulate the nation's transportation industry.

The Senate and the House approved by voice vote on May 22 a measure authorizing $750 million for passenger rail service improvements on the high-speed Northeast Corridor that links Boston and Washington, D.C. The action authorized $90-million in aid to the bankrupt Chicago, Rock Island, and Pacific Railroad. See RAILROAD.

Defense Appropriations. Acting at President Carter's request, the House voted 234 to 168 on June 25 to approve funds needed to register men born in 1960 and 1961 for possible military service. The Senate had approved the measure on June 12 by a vote of 58 to 34. The President signed it on June 27. Some 4 million men were to sign up at their post offices during a two-week period beginning July 21 at an estimated cost of $13.3 million. Carter's original plan to require both men and women to register for the draft, which was presented to Congress on February 8, was defeated on April 22 when the House refused to fund the registration of women.

The House voted 360 to 49 and the Senate voted 78 to 2 on August 26 to approve a $52.8-billion authorization for military pay; weapons, procurement, and research and development in fiscal 1981. Provisions included $1.6 billion to develop the M-X missile and an 11.7 per cent pay raise for

Members of the United States Senate

The Senate of the first session of the 97th Congress consisted of 53 Republicans, 46 Democrats, and 1 Independent, when it convened in January 1981. Senators shown starting their term in 1981 were elected for the first time in the Nov. 4, 1980, elections. Those shown ending their current terms in 1987 were re-elected to the Senate in the same balloting. The second date in each listing shows when the term of a previously elected senator expires. For organizational purposes, the one Independent will line up with Democrats.

State	Term
Alabama	
Howell T. Heflin, D.	1979—1985
Jeremiah Denton, R.	1981—1987
Alaska	
Theodore F. Stevens, R.	1968—1985
Frank H. Murkowski, R.	1981—1987
Arizona	
Barry Goldwater, R.	1969—1987
Dennis DeConcini, D.	1977—1983
Arkansas	
Dale Bumpers, D.	1975—1987
David H. Pryor, D.	1979—1985
California	
Alan Cranston, D.	1969—1987
S. I. Hayakawa, R.	1977—1983
Colorado	
Gary Hart, D.	1975—1987
William L. Armstrong, R.	1979—1985
Connecticut	
Lowell P. Weicker, Jr., R.	1971—1983
Christopher J. Dodd, D.	1981—1987
Delaware	
William V. Roth, Jr., R.	1971—1983
Joseph R. Biden, Jr., D.	1973—1985
Florida	
Lawton Chiles, D.	1971—1983
Paula Hawkins, R.	1981—1987
Georgia	
Sam Nunn, D.	1972—1985
Mack Mattingly, R.	1981—1987
Hawaii	
Daniel K. Inouye, D.	1963—1987
Spark M. Matsunaga, D.	1977—1983
Idaho	
James A. McClure, R.	1973—1985
Steven D. Symms, R.	1981—1987
Illinois	
Charles H. Percy, R.	1967—1985
Alan J. Dixon, D.	1981—1987
Indiana	
Richard G. Lugar, R.	1977—1983
J. Danforth Quayle, R.	1981—1987
Iowa	
Roger W. Jepsen, R.	1979—1985
Charles E. Grassley, R.	1981—1987
Kansas	
Robert J. Dole, R.	1969—1987
Nancy Landon Kassebaum, R.	1979—1985
Kentucky	
Walter Huddleston, D.	1973—1985
Wendell H. Ford, D.	1975—1987

State	Term
Louisiana	
Russell B. Long, D.	1948—1987
J. Bennett Johnston, Jr., D.	1972—1985
Maine	
William S. Cohen, R.	1979—1985
George J. Mitchell, D.	1980—1983
Maryland	
Charles McC. Mathias, Jr., R.	1969—1987
Paul S. Sarbanes, D.	1977—1983
Massachusetts	
Edward M. Kennedy, D.	1962—1983
Paul E. Tsongas, D.	1979—1985
Michigan	
Donald W. Riegle, Jr., D.	1977—1983
Carl M. Levin, D.	1979—1985
Minnesota	
David F. Durenberger, R.	1978—1983
Rudolph E. Boschwitz, R.	1979—1985
Mississippi	
John C. Stennis, D.	1947—1983
Thad Cochran, R.	1979—1985
Missouri	
Thomas F. Eagleton, D.	1968—1987
John C. Danforth, R.	1977—1983
Montana	
John Melcher, D.	1977—1983
Max Baucus, D.	1979—1985
Nebraska	
Edward Zorinsky, D.	1977—1983
J. James Exon, D.	1979—1985
Nevada	
Howard W. Cannon, D.	1959—1983
Paul Laxalt, R.	1975—1987
New Hampshire	
Gordon J. Humphrey, R.	1979—1985
Warren B. Rudman, R.	1981—1987
New Jersey	
Harrison A. Williams, Jr., D.	1959—1983
Bill Bradley, D.	1979—1985
New Mexico	
Pete V. Domenici, R.	1973—1985
Harrison H. Schmitt, R.	1977—1983
New York	
Daniel P. Moynihan, D.	1977—1983
Alfonse M. D'Amato, R.	1981—1987
North Carolina	
Jesse A. Helms, R.	1973—1985
John P. East, R.	1981—1987
North Dakota	
Quentin N. Burdick, D.	1960—1983
Mark Andrews, R.	1981—1987

State	Term
Ohio	
John H. Glenn, D.	1975—1987
Howard M. Metzenbaum, D.	1977—1983
Oklahoma	
David L. Boren, D.	1979—1985
Donald L. Nickles, R.	1981—1987
Oregon	
Mark O. Hatfield, R.	1967—1985
Robert W. Packwood, R.	1969—1987
Pennsylvania	
H. John Heinz III, R.	1977—1983
Arlen Specter, R.	1981—1987
Rhode Island	
Claiborne Pell, D.	1961—1985
John H. Chafee, R.	1977—1983
South Carolina	
Strom Thurmond, R.	1956—1985
Ernest F. Hollings, D.	1966—1987
South Dakota	
Larry Pressler, R.	1979—1985
James Abdnor, R.	1981—1987
Tennessee	
Howard H. Baker, Jr., R.	1967—1985
James R. Sasser, D.	1977—1983
Texas	
John G. Tower, R.	1961—1985
Lloyd M. Bentsen, D.	1971—1983
Utah	
Edwin Jacob Garn, R.	1975—1987
Orrin G. Hatch, R.	1977—1983
Vermont	
Robert T. Stafford, R.	1971—1983
Patrick J. Leahy, D.	1975—1987
Virginia	
Harry F. Byrd, Jr., Ind.	1965—1983
John W. Warner, R.	1979—1985
Washington	
Henry M. Jackson, D.	1953—1983
Slade Gorton, R.	1981—1987
West Virginia	
Jennings Randolph, D.	1958—1985
Robert C. Byrd, D.	1959—1983
Wisconsin	
William Proxmire, D.	1957—1983
Robert W. Kasten, Jr., R.	1981—1987
Wyoming	
Malcolm Wallop, R.	1977—1983
Alan K. Simpson, R.	1979—1985

Members of the United States House

The House of Representatives of the first session of the 97th Congress consisted of 242 Democrats, 192 Republicans, and 1 Independent (not including representatives from American Samoa, the District of Columbia, Guam, Puerto Rico, and the Virgin Islands) when it convened in January 1981, compared with 273 Democrats and 159 Republicans, with 3 seats vacant, when the second session of the 96th Congress adjourned. This table shows congressional district, legislator, and party affiliation. Asterisk (*) denotes those who served in the 96th Congress; dagger (†) denotes "at large."

Alabama
1. Jack Edwards, R.*
2. William L. Dickinson, R.*
3. William Nichols, D.*
4. Tom Bevill, D.*
5. Ronnie G. Flippo, D.*
6. Albert Smith, R.
7. Richard C. Shelby, D.*

Alaska
† Don Young, R.*

Arizona
1. John J. Rhodes, R.*
2. Morris K. Udall, D.*
3. Bob Stump, D.*
4. Eldon Rudd, R.*

Arkansas
1. Bill Alexander, D.*
2. Ed Bethune, R.*
3. John Paul Hammerschmidt, R.*
4. Beryl F. Anthony, Jr., D.*

California
1. Eugene A. Chappie, R.
2. Don H. Clausen, R.*
3. Robert T. Matsui, D.*
4. Vic Fazio, D.*
5. John L. Burton, D.*
6. Phillip Burton, D.*
7. George Miller, D.*
8. Ronald V. Dellums, D.*
9. Fortney H. Stark, D.*
10. Don Edwards, D.*
11. Tom Lantos, D.
12. Paul N. McCloskey, Jr., R.*
13. Norman Y. Mineta, D.*
14. Norman D. Shumway, R.*
15. Tony Coelho, D.*
16. Leon E. Panetta, D.*
17. Charles Pashayan, Jr., R.*
18. William M. Thomas, R.*
19. Robert J. Lagomarsino, R.*
20. Barry M. Goldwater, Jr., R.*
21. Bobbi Fiedler, R.
22. Carlos J. Moorhead, R.*
23. Anthony C. Beilenson, D.*
24. Henry A. Waxman, D.*
25. Edward R. Roybal, D.*
26. John H. Rousselot, R.*
27. Robert K. Dornan, R.*
28. Julian C. Dixon, D.*
29. Augustus F. Hawkins, D.*
30. George E. Danielson, D.*
31. Mervyn M. Dymally, D.
32. Glenn M. Anderson, D.*
33. Wayne R. Grisham, R.*
34. Dan Lungren, R.*
35. David Dreier, R.
36. George E. Brown, Jr., D.*
37. Jerry Lewis, R.*
38. Jerry M. Patterson, D.*
39. William E. Dannemeyer, R.*
40. Robert E. Badham, R.*
41. Bill Lowery, R.
42. Duncan L. Hunter, R.
43. Clair W. Burgener, R.*

Colorado
1. Patricia Schroeder, D.*
2. Timothy E. Wirth, D.*
3. Ray Kogovsek, D.*
4. Hank Brown, R.
5. Ken Kramer, R.*

Connecticut
1. William R. Cotter, D.*
2. Samuel Gejdenson, D.
3. Lawrence J. DeNardis, R.
4. Stewart B. McKinney, R.*
5. William R. Ratchford, D.*
6. Toby Moffett, D.*

Delaware
† Thomas B. Evans, Jr., R.*

Florida
1. Earl D. Hutto, D.*
2. Don Fuqua, D.*
3. Charles E. Bennett, D.*
4. William V. Chappell, Jr., D.*
5. Bill McCollum, R.
6. C. W. Young, R.*
7. Sam M. Gibbons, D.*
8. Andy Ireland, D.*
9. Bill Nelson, D.*
10. L. A. Bafalis, R.*
11. Dan Mica, D.*
12. Clay Shaw, R.
13. William Lehman, D.*
14. Claude D. Pepper, D.*
15. Dante B. Fascell, D.*

Georgia
1. Ronald Ginn, D.*
2. Charles F. Hatcher, D.
3. Jack T. Brinkley, D.*
4. Elliott H. Levitas, D.*
5. Wyche Fowler, Jr., D.*
6. Newt Gingrich, R.*
7. Lawrence P. McDonald, D.*
8. Billy Lee Evans, D.*
9. Ed Jenkins, D.*
10. Doug Barnard, D.*

Hawaii
1. Cecil Heftel, D.*
2. Daniel K. Akaka, D.*

Idaho
1. Larry Craig, R.
2. George Hansen, R.*

Illinois
1. Harold Washington, D.
2. Gus Savage, D.
3. Martin A. Russo, D.*
4. Edward J. Derwinski, R.*
5. John G. Fary, D.*
6. Henry J. Hyde, R.*
7. Cardiss Collins, D.*
8. Dan Rostenkowski, D.*
9. Sidney R. Yates, D.*
10. John Edward Porter, R.*
11. Frank Annunzio, D.*
12. Philip M. Crane, R.*
13. Robert McClory, R.*
14. John N. Erlenborn, R.*
15. Tom Corcoran, R.*
16. Lynn Martin, R.
17. George M. O'Brien, R.*
18. Robert H. Michel, R.*
19. Thomas F. Railsback, R.*
20. Paul Findley, R.*
21. Edward R. Madigan, R.*
22. Daniel B. Crane, R.*
23. Charles Melvin Price, D.*
24. Paul Simon, D.*

Indiana
1. Adam Benjamin, Jr., D.*
2. Floyd J. Fithian, D.*
3. John P. Hiler, R.
4. Daniel R. Coats, R.
5. Elwood H. Hillis, R.*
6. David W. Evans, D.*
7. John T. Myers, R.*
8. H. Joel Deckard, R.*
9. Lee H. Hamilton, D.*
10. Philip R. Sharp, D.*
11. Andrew Jacobs, Jr., D.*

Iowa
1. James Leach, R.*
2. Thomas J. Tauke, R.*
3. Cooper Evans, R.
4. Neal Smith, D.*
5. Tom Harkin, D.*
6. Berkley Bedell, D.*

Kansas
1. Pat Roberts, R.
2. James E. Jeffries, R.*
3. Larry Winn, Jr., R.*
4. Dan Glickman, D.*
5. Robert Whittaker, R.*

Kentucky
1. Carroll Hubbard, Jr., D.*
2. William H. Natcher, D.*
3. Romano L. Mazzoli, D.*
4. Marion Gene Snyder, R.*
5. Harold Rogers, R.
6. Larry J. Hopkins, R.*
7. Carl D. Perkins, D.*

Louisiana
1. Robert L. Livingston, R.*
2. Lindy Boggs, D.*
3. Billy Tauzin, D.*
4. Charles Roemer, D.
5. Jerry Huckaby, D.*
6. W. Henson Moore, R.*
7. John B. Breaux, D.*
8. Gillis W. Long, D.*

Maine
1. David F. Emery, R.*
2. Olympia J. Snowe, R.*

Maryland
1. Roy Dyson, D.
2. Clarence D. Long, D.*
3. Barbara A. Mikulski, D.*
4. Marjorie S. Holt, R.*
5. Gladys N. Spellman, D.*
6. Beverly Butcher Byron, D.*
7. Parren J. Mitchell, D.*
8. Michael D. Barnes, D.*

Massachusetts
1. Silvio O. Conte, R.*
2. Edward P. Boland, D.*
3. Joseph D. Early, D.*
4. Barney Frank, D.
5. James M. Shannon, D.*
6. Nicholas Mavroules, D.*
7. Edward J. Markey, D.*
8. Thomas P. O'Neill, Jr., D.*
9. John J. Moakley, D.*
10. Margaret M. Heckler, R.*
11. Brian J. Donnelly, D.*
12. Gerry E. Studds, D.*

Michigan
1. John Conyers, Jr., D.*
2. Carl D. Pursell, R.*
3. Howard E. Wolpe, D.*
4. David Stockman, R.*
5. Harold S. Sawyer, R.*
6. Jim Dunn, R.
7. Dale E. Kildee, D.*
8. Bob Traxler, D.*
9. Guy Vander Jagt, R.*
10. Donald J. Albosta, D.*
11. Robert W. Davis, R.*
12. David E. Bonior, D.*
13. George W. Crockett, Jr., D.
14. Dennis M. Hertel, D.
15. William D. Ford, D.*
16. John D. Dingell, D.*
17. William M. Brodhead, D.*
18. James J. Blanchard, D.*
19. William S. Broomfield, R.*

Minnesota
1. Arlen Erdahl, R.*
2. Thomas M. Hagedorn, R.*
3. Bill Frenzel, R.*
4. Bruce F. Vento, D.*
5. Martin O. Sabo, D.*
6. Vin Weber, R.
7. Arlan Stangeland, R.*
8. James L. Oberstar, D.*

Mississippi
1. Jamie L. Whitten, D.*
2. David R. Bowen, D.*
3. G. V. Montgomery, D.*
4. Jon Hinson, R.*
5. Trent Lott, R.*

Missouri
1. William L. Clay, D.*
2. Robert A. Young, D.*
3. Richard A. Gephardt, D.*
4. Ike Skelton, D.*
5. Richard Bolling, D.*
6. E. Thomas Coleman, R.*
7. Gene Taylor, R.*
8. Wendell Bailey, R.
9. Harold L. Volkmer, D.*
10. Bill Emerson, R.

Montana
1. Pat Williams, D.*
2. Ron Marlenee, R.*

Nebraska
1. Douglas K. Bereuter, R.*
2. Hal Daub, R.
3. Virginia Smith, R.*

Nevada
† James Santini, D.*

New Hampshire
1. Norman E. D'Amours, D.*
2. Judd Gregg, R.

New Jersey
1. James J. Florio, D.*
2. William J. Hughes, D.*
3. James J. Howard, D.*
4. Christopher H. Smith, R.
5. Millicent Fenwick, R.*
6. Edwin B. Forsythe, R.*
7. Marge S. Roukema, R.
8. Robert A. Roe, D.*
9. Harold C. Hollenbeck, R.*
10. Peter W. Rodino, Jr., D.*
11. Joseph G. Minish, D.*
12. Matthew J. Rinaldo, R.*
13. James A. Courter, R.*
14. Frank J. Guarini, D.*
15. Bernard J. Dwyer, D.

New Mexico
1. Manuel Lujan, Jr., R.*
2. Joe Skeen, R.

New York
1. William Carney, R.*
2. Thomas J. Downey, D.*
3. Gregory W. Carman, R.
4. Norman F. Lent, R.*
5. Raymond McGrath, R.
6. John LeBoutillier, R.
7. Joseph P. Addabbo, D.*
8. Benjamin S. Rosenthal, D.*
9. Geraldine A. Ferraro, D.*
10. Mario Biaggi, D.*
11. James H. Scheuer, D.*
12. Shirley Chisholm, D.*
13. Stephen J. Solarz, D.*
14. Frederick W. Richmond, D.*
15. Leo C. Zeferetti, D.*
16. Charles Schumer, D.
17. Guy Molinari, R.
18. S. William Green, R.*
19. Charles B. Rangel, D.*
20. Ted Weiss, D.*
21. Robert Garcia, D.*
22. Jonathan B. Bingham, D.*

23. Peter A. Peyser, D.*
24. Richard L. Ottinger, D.*
25. Hamilton Fish, Jr., R.*
26. Benjamin A. Gilman, R.*
27. Matthew F. McHugh, D.*
28. Samuel S. Stratton, D.*
29. Gerald B. Solomon, R.*
30. David Martin, R.
31. Donald J. Mitchell, R.*
32. George Wortley, R.
33. Gary A. Lee, R.*
34. Frank Horton, R.*
35. Barber B. Conable, Jr., R.*
36. John J. LaFalce, D.*
37. Henry J. Nowak, D.*
38. Jack F. Kemp, R.*
39. Stanley N. Lundine, D.*

North Carolina
1. Walter B. Jones, D.*
2. L. H. Fountain, D.*
3. Charles Whitley, D.*
4. Ike F. Andrews, D.*
5. Stephen L. Neal, D.*
6. Eugene Johnston, R.
7. Charles Rose, D.*
8. W. G. Hefner, D.*
9. James G. Martin, R.*
10. James T. Broyhill, R.*
11. William M. Hendon, R.

North Dakota
† Byron L. Dorgan, D.

Ohio
1. Willis D. Gradison, Jr., R.*
2. Thomas A. Luken, D.*
3. Tony P. Hall, D.*
4. Tennyson Guyer, R.*
5. Delbert L. Latta, R.*
6. Bob McEwen, R.
7. Clarence J. Brown, R.*
8. Thomas N. Kindness, R.*
9. Ed Weber, R.
10. Clarence E. Miller, R.*
11. J. William Stanton, R.*
12. Bob Shamansky, D.
13. Donald J. Pease, D.*
14. John F. Seiberling, D.*
15. Chalmers P. Wylie, R.*
16. Ralph S. Regula, R.*
17. John M. Ashbrook, R.*
18. Douglas Applegate, D.*
19. Lyle Williams, R.*
20. Mary Rose Oakar, D.*
21. Louis Stokes, D.*
22. Dennis E. Eckart, D.
23. Ronald M. Mottl, D.*

Oklahoma
1. James R. Jones, D.*
2. Michael L. Synar, D.*
3. Wes Watkins, D.*
4. Dave McCurdy, D.
5. Mickey Edwards, R.*
6. Glenn English, D.*

Oregon
1. Les AuCoin, D.*
2. Denny Smith, R.
3. Ron Wyden, D.
4. James Weaver, D.*

Pennsylvania
1. Thomas M. Foglietta, Ind.
2. William H. Gray III, D.*
3. Raymond F. Lederer, D.*
4. Charles F. Dougherty, R.*
5. Richard T. Schulze, R.*
6. Gus Yatron, D.*
7. Robert W. Edgar, D.*
8. James K. Coyne, R.
9. Bud Shuster, R.*
10. Joseph M. McDade, R.*
11. James Nelligan, R.
12. John P. Murtha, D.*
13. Lawrence Coughlin, R.*
14. William J. Coyne, D.
15. Donald L. Ritter, R.*
16. Robert S. Walker, R.*
17. Allen E. Ertel, D.*
18. Doug Walgren, D.*
19. William F. Goodling, R.*
20. Joseph M. Gaydos, D.*
21. Don Bailey, D.*
22. Austin J. Murphy, D.*
23. William F. Clinger, Jr., R.*
24. Marc L. Marks, R.*
25. Eugene V. Atkinson, D.*

Rhode Island
1. Fernand J. St. Germain, D.*
2. Claudine Schneider, R.

South Carolina
1. Thomas F. Hartnett, R.
2. Floyd D. Spence, R.*
3. Butler C. Derrick, Jr., D.*
4. Carroll A. Campbell, Jr., R.*
5. Ken Holland, D.*
6. John L. Napier, R.

South Dakota
1. Thomas A. Daschle, D.*
2. Clint Roberts, R.

Tennessee
1. James H. Quillen, R.*
2. John J. Duncan, R.*
3. Marilyn Lloyd Bouquard, D.*
4. Albert Gore, Jr., D.*
5. William H. Boner, D.*
6. Robin L. Beard, Jr., R.*
7. Ed Jones, D.*
8. Harold E. Ford, D.*

Texas
1. Sam B. Hall, Jr., D.*
2. Charles Wilson, D.*
3. James M. Collins, R.*
4. Ralph M. Hall, D.
5. James Mattox, D.*
6. Phil Gramm, D.*
7. Bill Archer, R.*
8. Jack Fields, R.
9. Jack Brooks, D.*
10. J. J. Pickle, D.*
11. Marvin Leath, D.*
12. James C. Wright, Jr., D.*
13. Jack Hightower, D.*
14. William Patman, D.
15. Eligio de la Garza, D.*
16. Richard C. White, D.*
17. Charles W. Stenholm, D.*
18. Mickey Leland, D.*
19. Kent Hance, D.*

20. Henry B. Gonzalez, D.*
21. Thomas G. Loeffler, R.*
22. Ronald E. Paul, R.*
23. Abraham Kazen, Jr., D.*
24. Martin Frost, D.*

Utah
1. James V. Hansen, R.
2. Dan Marriott, R.*

Vermont
† James M. Jeffords, R.*

Virginia
1. Paul S. Trible, Jr., R.*
2. G. William Whitehurst, R.*
3. Thomas J. Bliley, Jr., R.
4. Robert W. Daniel, Jr., R.*
5. Dan Daniel, D.*
6. M. Caldwell Butler, R.*
7. J. Kenneth Robinson, R.*
8. Stanford E. Parris, R.
9. William C. Wampler, R.*
10. Frank R. Wolf, R.

Washington
1. Joel Pritchard, R.*
2. Al Swift, D.*
3. Don Bonker, D.*
4. Sid Morrison, R.
5. Thomas S. Foley, D.*
6. Norman D. Dicks, D.*
7. Mike Lowry, D.*

West Virginia
1. Robert H. Mollohan, D.*
2. Cleve Benedict, R.
3. Mick Staton, R.
4. Nick J. Rahall, D.*

Wisconsin
1. Les Aspin, D.*
2. Robert W. Kastenmeier, D.*
3. Steven Gunderson, R.
4. Clement J. Zablocki, D.*
5. Henry S. Reuss, D.*
6. Thomas E. Petri, R.*
7. David R. Obey, D.*
8. Toby Roth, R.*
9. F. James Sensenbrenner; Jr., R.*

Wyoming
† Richard B. Cheney, R.*

Nonvoting Representatives

American Samoa
Fofo Sunia, D.

District of Columbia
Walter E. Fauntroy, D.*

Guam
Antonio Won Pat, D.*

Puerto Rico
Baltasar Corrada, D.*

Virgin Islands
Ron de Lugo, D.

active military personnel. Carter signed the legislation on September 8. See ARMED FORCES.

Education. The House approved a $48.4-billion higher-education program by voice vote on September 18, and the Senate approved the measure 83 to 6 on September 25. The legislation increased interest charges from 7 to 9 per cent on federally guaranteed student-loan interest rates. The President signed the measure on October 3.

In Other Action, the Senate on January 24 and the House on January 29 passed a resolution approving President Carter's proposed boycott of the 1980 Olympic Summer Games in Moscow (see OLYMPIC GAMES). The 96th Congress also increased the number of refugees that can be admitted to the United States annually and empowered the President to raise the number further during an emergency; approved interim funding for the food-stamp program; passed the Central Idaho Wilderness Act adding 2.3 million acres (900,000 hectares) to the national wilderness system; established a commission to investigate injustices to Japanese-Americans during World War II; raised benefits paid to survivors of military personnel; approved an act limiting the surprise search of newsrooms; approved an act to reorganize federal programs for mental health services; expanded programs for low- and middle-income housing; and approved a $12-billion appropriation bill for energy and water projects.

The Lame-Duck Session. The Democrats lost 12 Senate seats in the November 4 election, giving the Republicans a majority with 53 seats. There were 46 Democrats and 1 Independent (who lines up with the Democrats). The election also narrowed the Democratic majority in the House from 117 to 50 (see ELECTIONS). When Congress reconvened on November 12, several bills were given top priority.

In its final days, Congress passed the revised budget; the Alaska Wilderness Act, which protected 104.3 million acres (42 million hectares) of Alaskan land; a $1.6-billion appropriation for toxic-waste cleanup; and a $9.1-billion appropriation for the departments of State, Justice, and Commerce.

Investigations and Reprimands. A Senate subcommittee investigated charges that the President's brother, Billy Carter, used his influence at the White House to obtain $220,000 in loans from the Libyan government. The President and his wife, Rosalynn, and several federal officials were implicated in using Billy Carter as an intermediary to Libya in an attempt to negotiate the release of the hostages in Iran. On October 2, the Senate subcommittee reported that no illegal or unethical actions had occurred, but it declared that the President and some members of his White House staff had exercised "bad judgment."

Congressional ethics committees also investigated members of Congress implicated in the Abscam operation in which a Federal Bureau of Investigation agent posing as an Arab millionaire offered lawmakers bribes in return for favors. In the first such action since 1861, the House on October 2 expelled Michael Myers (D., Pa.) following his bribery conviction in August. Action was dropped against another representative, John W. Jenrette, Jr. (D., S.C.), convicted of the same charge, after he failed to win re-election. He resigned from Congress on December 10. Representatives Frank Thompson, Jr. (D., N.J.), and John M. Murphy (D., N.Y.) were convicted of bribery and conspiracy, respectively, on December 3, and three other congressmen—Representatives Raymond F. Lederer (D., Pa.) and Richard Kelly (R., Fla.) and Senator Harrison A. Williams, Jr. (D., N.J.)—were indicted

Two other representatives resigned from Congress. Daniel J. Flood (D., Pa.) pleaded guilty to a charge of conspiracy to violate federal campaign laws. Charles C. Diggs, Jr. (D., Mich.), was convicted on charges of mail fraud and salary kickbacks.

Carol L. Thompson

See also PRESIDENT OF THE UNITED STATES; UNITED STATES, GOVERNMENT OF THE. In WORLD BOOK, see CONGRESS OF THE UNITED STATES.

CONNECTICUT. See STATE GOVERNMENT.

CONSERVATION. The Congress of the United States approved legislation on Nov. 12, 1980, to protect more than 100 million acres (40 million hectares) of icy wilderness in Alaska from development. President Jimmy Carter, who signed the legislation on December 2, called the action, which ended more than 20 years of conflict, "one of the most important pieces of conservation legislation in the history of our country."

In 1979, the House of Representatives had approved a bill that set aside 128 million acres (52 million hectares) of federal land in Alaska for parks, wildlife refuges, and forests. On Aug. 19, 1980, the Senate approved legislation to protect about 104 million acres (42 million hectares).

Environmentalists preferred the House bill because it barred more land from development and banned oil and gas exploration and development in the William O. Douglas Wildlife Range near the Prudhoe Bay oil field in northeastern Alaska. Conservationists contended that oil development in the range would harm the 120,000 porcupine caribou that use the range as a calving ground. The oil industry argued that the range should not be "locked up." The House finally accepted the Senate version, including provisions that would allow seismic exploration of the range, and called for a congressional decision in five years on whether to allow drilling.

The Sagebrush Rebellion, a movement to gain more state control of federally owned lands in western states, gained support. Arizona, New Mexico, Utah, and Wyoming passed legislation supporting Nevada's 1979 bill that asserts state ownership of federal land within its borders. Some 21 U.S. congressmen sponsored a sagebrush-rebellion bill that was introduced in the House on July 25.

But there were signs of growing opposition to the movement. Critics charged that the rebellion was a massive land grab inspired by mining, timber, and cattle interests. A sagebrush bill was defeated in Idaho, and Governor Edmund G. Brown, Jr., vetoed sagebrush legislation in California. At their national convention, Republicans defeated a proposed campaign platform plank that supported the rebellion because they feared it would be misinterpreted in the East. The U.S. Department of the Interior's Bureau of Land Management on November 14 designated 24 million acres (9.7 million hectares) of public lands in Western states for study as potential wilderness areas and released 150 million acres (60 million hectares) from further consideration.

Strip Mining. The Senate passed legislation to weaken federal enforcement of the 1977 strip-mining reclamation law on August 22. The measure passed as an amendment to a bill that the House had already passed. The Senate bill would have allowed states to set their own regulations to enforce most provisions of the 1977 act. Environmental groups charged it was designed to permit a return to pre-1977 mining practices with minimal land reclamation. House and Senate conferees finally dropped the amendment from the bill.

M-X Missile. Plans to deploy the M-X mobile missile system in Western states moved ahead despite increased opposition from conservation groups. The $33.8-billion system would be the largest public-works project in United States history. Some 200 missiles would shuttle among 4,600 shelters built along a track in order to reduce the missiles' vulnerability to Russian attack.

The United States Senate Armed Services Committee authorized $1.5 billion on June 11 to begin work on the system under a compromise that would allow some shelters to be built outside Utah and Nevada. Key decisions were expected to come in 1981 when Congress was to approve land withdrawals covering 30,000 square miles (78,000 square kilometers) for the shelters and roads.

Nuclear Power opponents suffered setbacks but continued to criticize the industry as unsafe. On September 23, Maine voters rejected by a 3-to-2 margin a proposal that would have banned nuclear power in the state. The voters decided not to close the Maine Yankee power plant, the state's only such facility. It was the first time voters decided on whether to close an operating nuclear plant.

Cowboy and helicopter team up to move burros from Grand Canyon to a corral for safekeeping. The burro herd was threatening canyon wildlife.

Sweden voted in a referendum on March 23 to continue using nuclear power beyond the year 2000.

The U.S. National Academy of Sciences (NAS) reported on January 14 that the only chance for the United States to meet its electricity demands over the next 30 years lay in burning coal and building nuclear plants. The NAS report was based on a four-year study that drew from the work of more than 250 economists, scientists, engineers, and industrialists.

No Whale Moratorium. The International Whaling Commission (IWC) concluded its annual meeting in Brighton, England, on September 26 without adopting a moratorium on commercial whaling. IWC measures helped to reduce the take of great whales from 34,000 in 1975 to 14,500 in 1981, but some observers predicted that commercial whaling would end throughout the world by 1985. U.S. Whaling Commissioner Richard A. Frank pledged that the United States would continue to press for a moratorium.

The IWC set a three-year quota on the take of bowhead whales – 45 landed or 65 struck – by Alaskan Eskimos. The U.S. Department of the Interior asked the Eskimo whalers to end their fall subsistence hunt on September 19 after reports that they had exceeded the 1980 quota. But the Alaska Eskimo Whaling Commission refused to accept the IWC quota, contending instead that the IWC had underestimated the number of bowheads in existence.

Endangered Sea Turtles. Representatives of 40 nations had concluded after a 1979 conference convened by the U.S. Department of State that commercial exploitation had brought six of the seven species of sea turtles close to extinction. Many valuable products come from sea turtles, ranging from tortoise shells and flipper skins to turtle eggs and turtle meat.

The Pacific ridley turtle was put on the endangered species list by the U.S. Fish and Wildlife Service in 1978 because its population dwindled from 10 million to 400,000 in a 10-year period. A federal grand jury in Miami, Fla., indicted four men and six corporations on Aug. 7, 1980, for importing 45 short tons (41 metric tons) of Pacific ridley meat into the United States.

Barrier Islands. An unusually long period of light damage by storms along the coasts of the Atlantic Ocean and the Gulf of Mexico had lulled Americans into developing the shifting sands of the barrier islands along those coasts at twice the rate of development in the nation as a whole. Conservationists argued against underwriting development of these islands through road and sewer projects and then paying for hurricane damage in the built-up areas.

Legislation was introduced in the Senate that would limit federal disaster aid and reduce programs to subsidize bridges and other developments on many of the 300 barrier islands. Representative Phillip Burton (D., Calif.) proposed a bill that would add land on about 100 barrier islands to the National Park System. But the legislation was held up by arguments that states were already acting.

Other Developments. The Forest Service, an agency of the U.S. Department of Agriculture, and the Interior Department's National Park Service began studies to help them decide whether they should recommend that Congress set aside as a national park or recreation area part of the land ravaged by the May 18 eruption of Mount Saint Helens in Washington.

Conservationists praised the May 1 appointment of Russell E. Dickenson, a 33-year veteran of the National Park Service, to head the agency. Dickenson succeeded William J. Whalen, who was dismissed after drawing sharp criticism from conservation groups.

Dickenson faced a host of difficult problems. Overcrowding had led to pressures to limit the number of visitors to some parks. In addition, Congress had not appropriated enough money to hire full staffs to administer the more than 150 areas added to the National Park System since World War II.   Andrew L. Newman

See also ENVIRONMENT. In WORLD BOOK, see CONSERVATION; NATIONAL PARK SYSTEM.

CONSTITUTION OF THE UNITED STATES. A constitutional amendment requiring a balanced federal budget was rejected by the Senate Judiciary Committee on March 18, 1980, eliminating it from Senate consideration. The Constitution specifies that a proposed amendment must be passed by both houses of Congress or drafted by a convention and then adopted by three-fourths of the states – 38 states – to become law. A drive to call a convention to draft the budget amendment was also stalemated. At year-end, only 30 of the necessary 34 states had passed resolutions calling for a constitutional convention, but none did so in 1980.

The Equal Rights Amendment (ERA), which would prohibit discrimination on the basis of sex, also failed to gain any ground in 1980, remaining three states short of ratification. The ERA was once again a campaign issue, however. The Democratic Party supported the amendment, but the Republican Party withdrew its support.

Two additional states ratified and one state rejected an amendment to secure voting representation for District of Columbia residents. Nebraska rejected the amendment on February 11; Maryland and Hawaii ratified it on March 17 and April 17, respectively. At year-end, nine states had approved it and 11 states had rejected it. Beverly Merz

In WORLD BOOK, see CONSTITUTION OF THE UNITED STATES.

CONSUMER PROTECTION. Inflation continued to be the worst problem facing consumers in the United States in 1980. But the rate of increase in the government's Consumer Price Index (CPI) moderated from an 18.1 per cent annual rate in the first three months of the year to just over 12 per cent after the first 10 months. By September, the annual rates of increases in the CPI were 10.1 for food, 11.0 for medical care, 14.1 for housing, and 23.9 for gasoline. In the Special Reports section, see THE INFLATION RATE, THE COST OF LIVING . . . AND YOU.

An anticonsumer atmosphere became strong in the Congress of the United States during the year. For the first time in six years, there was no attempt to win legislative approval for a separate federal consumer agency, in addition to the Office of Consumer Affairs in the White House complex and the Department of Health and Human Services (formerly the Department of Health, Education, and Welfare). Consumer leaders not only gave up trying to get major legislative changes, but also found themselves spending most of their time fighting to keep earlier gains from being lost.

Deregulation became the dominant theme, particularly at federal levels. The Administration of President Jimmy Carter responded to criticism of government regulations by relaxing laws and rules governing the banking, airline, trucking, rail, and communications industries.

The net effect was a loss of numerous consumer programs and protections. One of the biggest changes was the gradual phase-out of traditional fixed-rate mortgages in favor of renegotiated rate mortgages (RRM's), which permit financial institutions to raise or lower interest rates as they change in the financial market place. The Federal Home Loan Bank Board gave its approval to RRM's on April 3. Another change was a set of stiff new penalties for withdrawing savings certificates before maturity. The penalties, authorized in June, can mean loss of principal as well as interest. They require deduction of three months' interest if a certificate with a maturity of one year or less is cashed prematurely, and deduction of six months' interest for premature cashing of a certificate with a maturity of more than one year, regardless of how soon withdrawal occurs after purchase.

Consumers won a benefit, however, from another change, which permitted banks and savings and loan associations to offer interest-bearing checking accounts beginning Jan. 1, 1981. The introduction of the new Negotiable Order for Withdrawal accounts was expected to stimulate competition for the checking dollar, giving consumers a wider choice of terms. See BANKS AND BANKING.

Esther Peterson, a federal consumer official, waves to the crowd at the opening of the National Consumer Cooperative Bank in Washington, D.C.

Individual borrowers and credit purchasers found little to be happy about in 1980, however, as interest rates began soaring again in the fall after recovering from record heights reached earlier in the year. Mortgage rates rose above 15 per cent and the prime rate to above 20 per cent in December, putting a new damper on the auto- and home-buying plans of many people. The prime rate is that charged by banks to their best commercial customers. In an effort to dampen the fires of inflation in March, the Carter Administration established a system of credit controls. In response, many retailers and credit-card firms raised minimum payments, lowered credit limits, and imposed higher interest rates.

Other Changes. Responding to political pressure, federal agencies competed with one another in relaxing rules and regulations along other fronts. In July, President Carter announced elimination of some auto-pollution standards and told the auto industry that the government would not issue "any major safety rules" during the rest of the year.

Many cattle farmers apparently simply ignored a Department of Agriculture (DOA) rule prohibiting the use of diethylstilbestrol (DES), a cancer-causing synthetic hormone, to speed the fattening process in cattle. The DOA estimated in April that more than 400,000 animals in 20 states had been fed DES. It threatened violators with "immediate action . . . including criminal charges." But when politically powerful farm groups objected and said most of the DES-fed animals had already been consumed, the DOA backed down without bringing any charges.

Curbs on the FTC. Hardest hit by the antiregulatory mood was the Federal Trade Commission (FTC), the country's chief consumer-protection agency. Congress was adamant about slashing the agency's powers, largely because of complaints from businesses that had been targets of FTC actions. It forced the agency to shut down twice for brief periods because of insufficient funds while legislators chipped away at the FTC's broad authority over the market place.

Final legislation imposed severe restrictions, such as a curb on further investigation of the insurance industry, a ban on completing an investigation of pricing practices of agricultural cooperatives, a prohibition against requiring used-car dealers to provide a warranty to buyers, relaxation of proposed regulations governing funeral practices, discontinuance of action seeking to repeal trademarks that have become common terms, and elimination of any action against advertising on the grounds of unfairness. In addition, Congress set up a legislative veto allowing both the House of Representatives and the Senate to reject any FTC rule within 90 days. It was the first such veto imposed on a regulatory agency.

Other Legislation. Congress also passed a law completely revamping rules regarding the household moving industry, a frequent source of consumer complaints. Legislation wiped out more than 30 years of regulations, including 45,000 pending charges against 45 firms for alleged violations of federal rules of the Interstate Commerce Commission. The new law encourages competition by permitting truckers to charge different rates and make binding estimates. It also encourages – but does not require – companies to set up arbitration systems for settling disputes.

Another new law, signed in June by President Carter, gives the government new powers to police abuses in the selling of so-called Medigap insurance policies, which say they provide benefits not covered by Medicare. The measure authorizes the government to establish a voluntary certification program for such policies by July 1, 1982, in every state that fails to set up an equivalent or stronger program. The legislation also prohibits sellers of such policies from making false statements, knowingly selling duplicate coverage, and representing themselves as working for the government.

Court Decisions. The Supreme Court of the United States in January upheld the conviction of six Maryland real estate firms for conspiring to raise sales commissions from 6 to 7 per cent in

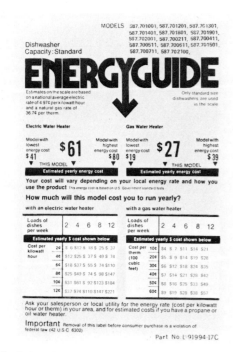

The Federal Trade Commission requires that manufacturers of eight types of appliances include a label detailing the energy costs of operating them.

1974. The ruling was expected to make a greater variety of rates available to homeowners in all states.

In October, the U.S. Supreme Court came to the rescue of people made ill by products whose manufacturers are not known to the victims. The case involved a suit by mothers whose daughters got vaginal cancer after puberty allegedly because the mothers had taken DES during pregnancy. The plaintiffs did not know the specific drug manufacturers and sued the five major firms. California courts rejected the case, but the Supreme Court sent it back for trial, saying the women did not need to single out any specific company to seek damages.

Corporate Progress. Consumers made some inroads in corporate offices and board rooms. The Society of Consumer Affairs Professionals, which started with 100 members in 1973, counted 2,000 members in 18 chapters in 1980. Many members were consumer "advocates" or "representatives" at the vice-presidential level.

At the same time, a growing number of business firms were calling on individual consumers to serve on their boards of directors. An organization for such people, the Association of Outside Directors, celebrated its third birthday in 1980. Arthur E. Rowse

In WORLD BOOK, see CONSUMER PROTECTION; CREDIT; MORTGAGE.

COSSIGA, FRANCESCO (1928-   ), Christian Democratic prime minister of Italy since August 1979, weathered two major political storms in 1980, but was swept away by a third. His minority coalition with the Social Democrats and Liberals collapsed in March when the Communists and Socialists voted against it. But Cossiga then formed a majority government with the Socialists and the small Republican Party on April 4.

Cossiga was also the object of the first attempt to impeach an Italian prime minister since the republic was formed in 1947. But Parliament on July 27 voted down a charge that Cossiga gave government secrets to a colleague whose fugitive son was a suspected terrorist.

Cossiga's new coalition fell apart on September 27 when Parliament rejected his economic plans. Christian Democrat Party leader Arnaldo Forlani succeeded him as prime minister on October 18. See FORLANI, ARNALDO.

Francesco Cossiga was born on July 26, 1928, in Sassari on the island of Sardinia. He has been in Parliament since 1958 and served as undersecretary of defense from 1966 until 1970. Cossiga became minister for public administration in 1974. In this post, he negotiated with public employees' labor unions. Jay Myers

See also ITALY.

COSTA RICA. See LATIN AMERICA.

COURTS AND LAWS. The rule of law among nations experienced a mixed year during 1980. Several countries flouted the judgment of international tribunals when that course suited their self-interest. Libya continued to defy a 1978 ruling by the United Nations (UN) International Court of Justice at The Hague, the Netherlands, on territorial water boundaries in the Mediterranean Sea. Libya used a show of naval force in August to stop an apparently legal oil-drilling expedition licensed by neighboring Malta. Iran ignored a formal order on May 24 from the court demanding the release of 53 American hostages taken in 1979 and holding Iran liable for reparations in the matter. The 15-member court, in a rare unanimous opinion, ordered the hostages freed and cautioned Iran not to put them on trial. The court had made a preliminary ruling in December 1979 ordering the hostages' release.

In broader international law, however, there were major breakthroughs. Following a two-week conference in Canberra, Australia, 15 nations, including the United States and Russia, signed an agreement on May 20 designed to prevent overfishing and to protect animal life in the Antarctic. A six-year, 150-nation effort by the UN Law of the Sea Conference to draft a worldwide treaty finally produced tentative agreement during a midsummer session in Geneva, Switzerland, leading to hopes for a final Law of the Sea treaty in March 1981. The draft treaty, which contains more than 300 articles, sets up mechanisms to control disputes over deep-sea fishing, mining, coastal boundaries, and environmental problems. United States delegate Elliot L. Richardson suggested the Geneva session was "the most significant single development of the rule of law since the founding of the UN itself" (see OCEAN).

Legal Ethics. The U.S. legal profession struggled with attempts to improve the administration of justice. Chief Justice Warren E. Burger of the United States took lawyers to task on February 3 at the midwinter convention of the American Bar Association (ABA) in Chicago, for their rapidly escalating fees and their failure to address ethical problems adequately.

An ABA commission chaired by Omaha, Nebr., attorney Robert J. Kutak on January 30 unveiled a proposed revision of the ABA's model code of ethics, but it immediately ran into trouble. Some lawyers faulted the format of the proposal. Others criticized portions that would require attorneys to disclose certain illegal conduct by their clients and require lawyers to devote an unspecified number of hours annually to unpaid public interest service.

The U.S. News Media figured in several courtroom controversies during the year. The U.S. Judicial Conference in June issued a revised set of guidelines for civil suits that allows trial judges

Former U.S. budget director T. Bertram Lance leaves the courtroom in April after a jury cleared him of nine counts of bank fraud.

civil rights activities, and they had been named "political prisoners" by Amnesty International.

Following a 15-week trial, T. Bertram Lance, former director of the Office of Management and Budget and a powerful figure in President Jimmy Carter's Administration, and three co-defendants were cleared of nine counts of bank fraud by a federal jury in Atlanta, Ga., on April 30. The jurors, who deliberated eight days, were unable to agree on three other similar charges, but a federal judge dismissed all counts on June 9.

An all-white jury in Tampa, Fla., acquitted four Miami policemen – since dismissed from the force – on May 17 of charges stemming from the fatal beating of a black insurance executive who had been stopped for a traffic violation. The verdict prompted racial rioting in Miami.

Ford Motor Company, the first company in U.S. history to stand trial on criminal charges for allegedly selling defective products, was declared not guilty by a Winamac, Ind., jury on March 13. Ford was accused of reckless homicide in the 1978 deaths of three girls who burned to death when the gas tank of their 1973 Ford Pinto exploded following a rear-end collision with a van. The prosecution maintained that Ford knew the Pinto's gas tank was defective.   David C. Beckwith

See also CRIME. In WORLD BOOK, see COURT; LAW.

to waive the filing of deposition papers and discovery material – often bulky, therefore costly to reproduce – with federal court clerks. News organizations opposed the move but failed to persuade Congress to overturn the revision. In an apparent turnabout from a 1979 ruling, the Supreme Court of the United States voted 7 to 1 on July 2 that the press and public cannot be excluded from criminal trials except in extraordinary circumstances (see SUPREME COURT OF THE UNITED STATES).

A nationwide storm of protest during the year succeeded in sharply curtailing the strip-searching at U.S. police stations of women arrested for minor violations. News accounts in Chicago exposed the practice in 1979. On March 26, the city of Chicago agreed to pay $69,500 in damages to 191 women subjected to strip and body-cavity searches in previous years. Most of the women had been stopped for traffic offenses.

Court Verdicts. A Chicago jury sentenced John Wayne Gacy to death on March 13 for murdering 33 young men in one of the worst mass murder cases in U.S. history. Appeal of the sentence was pending before the Illinois Supreme Court at the end of 1980. A federal court in December overturned the 1972 convictions of the "Wilmington 10," nine blacks and a white, for the firebombing of a grocery store in Wilmington, N.C. The 10 maintained they had been framed because of their

CRIME. Increasing use of murder, bombing, and kidnapping as political devices continued to unsettle governments in 1980. North America, Northern Ireland, Western Europe, and the Middle East were particularly hard-hit.

The U.S. Central Intelligence Agency (CIA) reported on May 11 that terrorists killed 587 persons throughout the world in 1979, the highest total since the CIA began keeping records in 1968. By year's end, however, it was clear that the 1980 figure would be much higher.

The year's bloodiest incident occurred in Bologna, Italy, on August 2. A bomb exploded in the second-class waiting room at the central train station, killing 80 persons and injuring about 180. On August 27, Rome police arrested 22 persons in connection with the bombing. All were right wing extremists or sympathizers.

Frustration with the slow resettlement of 120,000 newly arrived Cuban refugees led to a sharp resurgence in aircraft hijackings in the United States. Eleven domestic airliners were diverted to Havana during the five weeks starting on August 10, at least eight of the hijackings by homesick refugees. Cuban authorities then stopped the outbreak by returning hijackers to the United States immediately to face criminal charges.

Abscam Scandal. The crime story of the year in the United States broke on February 2 and 3, when news media reported that several members of the U.S. Congress had been videotaped taking bribes from a Federal Bureau of Investigation (FBI) agent masquerading as a wealthy Arab. The disclosures came after a two-year probe code-named Abscam.

Senator Harrison A. Williams, Jr. (D., N.J.); and Representatives John W. Jenrette, Jr. (D., S.C.); Richard Kelly (R., Fla.); Raymond F. Lederer (D., Pa.); John M. Murphy (D., N.Y.); Michael Myers (D., Pa.); and Frank Thompson, Jr. (D., N.J.), were indicted on bribery charges along with Mayor Angelo J. Errichetti of Camden, N.J., three Philadelphia city councilmen, and seven others. Myers and three co-defendants were convicted in a Brooklyn federal court on August 31 for receiving a $50,000 bribe. Jenrette and a co-defendant were convicted on October 8 in Washington, D.C., for taking $50,000. On December 3, Thompson was convicted of bribery and conspiracy and Murphy was found guilty of conspiracy, conflict of interest, and receiving an unlawful gratuity. Two Philadelphia men were also found guilty, but their convictions were overturned on grounds of entrapment.

During 1980, all major crime in the United States increased for the second year in a row. Violent crime – murder, robbery, forcible rape, and aggravated assault – increased 11 per cent during the first nine months of 1980, compared with the same period in 1979. Reported incidence of more numerous property crimes – burglary, larceny-theft, and motor-vehicle theft – jumped by 10 per cent.

Crimes of Violence. In July and August, police arrested three men from the Los Angeles area and a former area resident in connection with the murder of at least 21 young male hitchhikers over the past 10 years. These killings, and more than 20 others, were known as the "Freeway Murders" because many of the victims were abandoned along freeways.

On November 2, Atlanta authorities identified the skeleton of the 15th black child abducted and found dead in 16 months.

Rock musician John Lennon was shot to death on December 8 in New York City. Police arrested Mark David Chapman, 25, and charged him with murdering the ex-Beatle. See Music, Popular (Close-Up).

The year's most lucrative heist occurred on August 15. A part-time Brink's, Incorporated, security guard drove away from San Francisco International Airport with an armored truck containing $1.8 million in cash. David C. Beckwith

See also Courts and Laws. In World Book, see Crime; Terrorism.

Federal agents search Columbia River bank in Oregon in February after cash was found that had been taken in a 1971 air hijacking by "D. B. Cooper."

CUBA. In one of the most remarkable exoduses of modern times, some 125,000 Cubans fled their homeland in 1980 and sought refuge in the United States and elsewhere. The mass departure was triggered on April 4 when about 25 Cubans sought political asylum in the Peruvian Embassy in Havana. Within days, their number multiplied, and by mid-April, when Cuba began granting exit visas, the crowd had swollen to nearly 11,000.

The Boat-Lift. Other embassies became equally swamped. Some countries – such as Spain, Costa Rica, and Venezuela – began evacuating the refugees by plane. In the United States, Cuban-American boat owners and others formed flotillas to head for various Cuban ports. For weeks, the nearly 100-mile (160-kilometer) stretch of water between Cuba and Florida was speckled with boats.

U.S. President Jimmy Carter, caught off guard as the influx into the United States reached massive proportions, quickly adjusted U.S. policy. He switched from a position threatening legal action against those operating the refugee boat-lift, to an offer of government assistance in mounting an orderly transfer of the disaffected Cubans. Moreover, the U.S. government took a leading role in ensuring a welcome for the refugees in 18 other nations that offered refuge. President Fidel Castro took advantage of the boat-lift operation to empty jails of hardened criminals and forcibly deport homosexuals and the insane. He unilaterally ended the boat-lift on September 26.

Castro's behavior seemed to foreclose for the time being any improvement in United States-Cuban relations. Relations were further chilled by Cuba's involvement in fomenting rebellion elsewhere in Latin America and in Africa and the Middle East. For Russia, the cost of maintaining Cuba as a satellite and its representative in developing countries rose sharply in 1980 to an estimated $6 million to $8 million per day.

The Cuban Economy was in a shambles, according to a secret report made by Castro on Dec. 27, 1979, to Cuba's leadership. The Cuban ruler reshuffled his Cabinet on January 11, and took over the management of key ministries. He also continued his quest for Third World leadership. While in Managua, Nicaragua, in July for ceremonies marking the triumph of that nation's revolution, Castro warned against the consequences of a victory by Republican Ronald Reagan in the U.S. presidential elections. Seemingly to help re-elect Carter, he freed 30 Americans from Cuban jails shortly before the November elections.   Nathan A. Haverstock

See also LATIN AMERICA (Facts in Brief Table).
CYPRUS. See EUROPE.

Thousands of unhappy Cubans, waiting for a chance to leave the country, crowd into the grounds of the Peruvian Embassy in Havana in April.

CZECHOSLOVAKIA maintained its hard-line ideological and political posture in 1980, but allowed experiments with the economy. Communist Party General Secretary and President Gustav Husak was re-elected to another five-year term on May 22. Foreign Minister Bohuslav Chňoupek visited Afghanistan in July. Czechoslovakia delivered $21-million worth of trucks and spare parts to Afghanistan in 1980, under a special credit arrangement, and provided $90 million worth of equipment for cement, chemical, and food-processing factories.

The Czechoslovak Communist Party took a hard line toward "anti-socialist" forces in Poland when strikes swept that country (see POLAND). Party Presidium member Vasil Bil'ak attacked these forces in September and October. He compared events in Poland with those in Czechoslovakia in 1968, when Warsaw Pact troops invaded Czechoslovakia to suppress the liberal regime of Alexander Dubček.

Arrest of Dissidents. The government cracked down on dissidents throughout the year. Police arrested 15 signers of the Charter 77 human rights declarations in June. Others were arrested in September in connection with a solidarity statement that Charter 77 supporters had sent to the Polish strikers. But on September 26, Czechoslovakia released former Charter 77 spokeswoman Ota Bednarova from prison because of illness after she had served only one year of her three-year sentence. Dissident philosopher Julius Tomin was allowed a year's stay in England in September, but earlier in the year his unofficial philosophy seminar was repeatedly disrupted, and several Western scholars were expelled for attending it.

Economic Experiments. The party Presidium—Czechoslovakia's policymaking body—announced in March that it would expand the economic experiments begun in 150 factories in 1978. The experiment would spread to the whole economy in 1981. Factories would no longer be judged solely according to the amounts of goods that they produced, but also on productivity increases and the quality of their products. Czechoslovakia planned to employ material incentives and to link prices to rising world prices of energy and raw materials.

Industrial output increased by 3.8 per cent in the first half of 1980, but more than one-third of the country's engineering enterprises failed to meet their output targets. Construction of two nuclear power stations was delayed. The grain harvest was poor, so Czechoslovakia announced that it would import grain again in 1980. In 1979, the country imported 2.5 million short tons (2.3 metric tons) of grain and other foods.   Chris Cviic

See also EUROPE (Facts in Brief Table). In WORLD BOOK, see CZECHOSLOVAKIA.

DAIRYING. See FARM AND FARMING.

DAM. See BUILDING AND CONSTRUCTION.

DANCING. Mikhail Baryshnikov's ascent to artistic director of the American Ballet Theater (ABT) on September 1 was the most significant of several administrative changes in the dance world in 1980. Lucia Chase had directed the ABT since she co-founded the company in 1940. Never before has an American dance organization undergone such radical changing of the guard, and the results will probably not be seen for some time.

However, a trend toward an international repertory of choreographic importance could be predicted from Baryshnikov's plans for the 1980-1981 season. Among 10 new productions were works by George Balanchine, Sir Frederick Ashton, Paul Taylor, and Vaslav Nijinsky. A full evening of *divertissements* (short ballets) created by Marius Petipa, the great exponent of Russian classicism in the 1800s, was also scheduled. ABT's first performances under its new director began at the Kennedy Center for the Performing Arts in Washington, D.C., on December 10. Principal dancers Gelsey Kirkland and Patrick Bissell did not perform that night as scheduled. ABT had fired them for failing to attend a dress rehearsal on December 9.

E. Virginia Williams, founder and sole director of the Boston Ballet, began sharing artistic control of the company in September with Violette Verdy, former principal dancer of the New York City Ballet and director of the Paris Opera Ballet. Many observers expected Verdy to inject new life into the company. However, Williams' reign ended with a bang. In June, the Boston Ballet became the first United States ballet troupe to perform in China. They appeared in Canton (Guangzhou), Peking (Beijing), and Shanghai. The Milwaukee Ballet also underwent administrative upheaval when director Jean-Paul Comelin's contract was not renewed in April. He was replaced by former Pennsylvania Ballet and ABT dancer Ted Kivitt.

Other Companies. While some older companies changed their profiles, two new ones emerged. Natalia Makarova formed Makarova and Company, which debuted at the Uris Theater in New York City on October 7 for a month-long run. Surrounding herself with such guest artists as Anthony Dowell, Fernando Bujones, and Cynthia Gregory and an ensemble of 30 accomplished student dancers, Makarova commissioned new works as well as producing a revival of divertissements from Petipa's *Paquita*.

Maria Tallchief, one of the New York City Ballet's greatest dancers in the 1950s, announced in January that she would become director of the reorganized Chicago City Ballet. The troupe, formerly the Lyric Opera Ballet, expected to give its first performance in 1981.

The Joffrey Ballet was reborn in May. After an eight-month layoff caused by financial difficulties, the company resumed touring and performed in

Dancer-choreographer Twyla Tharp, second from left, and members of her troupe première her dance-drama *When We Were Very Young* in March.

Chicago; Seattle, Wash.; and San Francisco; and at various summer arts festivals until August. The Joffrey then opened for a month's run at the New York City Center on October 28, its first appearance in New York City in two years. Two of the ballets added to the repertory were especially noteworthy. *Postcards*, a new work by Robert Joffrey, was unveiled on June 10 in Seattle, and celebrated avant-gardist Laura Dean's *Night*, her first ballet work, premièred on October 29.

Other New Works. The most welcome of the many ballets introduced in 1980 were those by George Balanchine. *Ballade*, first seen on May 8, and *Davidsbundlertanze*, which premièred on June 19, were his first works for the New York City Ballet since 1978. Although both are in a romantic vein, they are completely different. *Ballade*, danced to music by French composer Gabriel Fauré, explored the inherent qualities of the music. Balanchine created the piece for ballerina Merrill Ashley and Ib Andersen, a Royal Danish Ballet star who joined the New York City Ballet at the opening of its spring season on April 29 at the New York State Theater in Lincoln Center. *Davidsbundlertanze* was an overtly dramatic allegory based on the life and

Auditorium in Washington, D.C. But few agreed on whether it was comic or tragic, or whether Taylor had succeeded in living up to the formidable history of the music by Russian composer Igor Stravinsky and original choreography by Nijinsky.

The biggest ballet spectacle of 1980, Makarova's staging of the full-length *La Bayadère* by Petipa, also invited questions. The production premièred on May 21 during ABT's 10-week season at New York City's Metropolitan Opera House in Lincoln Center. Commentary centered on whether the piece was a hopeless war horse or workable today, whether classic Russian ballet should be modernized as Makarova had done, whether ABT should be spending so much money on a single production, and whether the thrust of ABT should be focused on the past or on the contemporary scene.

Other Events. However, revivals of works by another choreographer famous in the 1800s, August Bournonville, a Dane, drew unanimous acclaim. The fourth annual International Dance Festival, held in Chicago from June 12 to 19, featured the Royal Danish Ballet in a weeklong celebration of full-length Bournonville ballets. Historians of Danish ballet also participated in the festival's lectures and panel discussions.

The most novel of the many other foreign troupes that visited the United States was the Shanghai Acrobatic Theater. The skill with which the Chinese acrobats tumbled and balanced objects, as well as the imaginative staging, transcended the usual circus format and appeared as a true art form. The company opened in New York City on March 25, then visited Philadelphia; Washington, D.C.; Chicago; Minneapolis, Minn.; and the West Coast.

The much-anticipated spring visit of the Paris Opera Ballet to the United States was canceled because the Parisian dancers objected to having Rudolf Nureyev imposed upon them as guest artist. But a bit of France and a bit of Nureyev turned up anyway. Nureyev performed with the Martha Graham Dance Company at the Metropolitan Opera House from April 23 to May 3. And in August and September, Roland Petit's Ballet de Marseille danced on the West Coast and in New York City in programs featuring Zizi Jeanmaire.

***Dance Magazine* Awards,** on the 25th occasion of their presentation, went to Patricia McBride, Paul Taylor, and Ruth Page at a ceremony in New York City on March 31. McBride has been a principal dancer with the New York City Ballet since 1961. Taylor has been called "one of the handful of truly extraordinary choreographers in American modern dance." Page, who celebrated her 80th birthday on March 22 and still runs a dance school in Chicago, was hailed as a pioneer of dance in America. Nancy Goldner

In WORLD BOOK, see BALLET; DANCING.

the artistic circle of German composer Robert Schumann. Many critics considered the work to be a milestone in Balanchine's career because of its somewhat mysterious, private source of emotion.

Other new works proved to be controversial, if not so mysterious. Twyla Tharp clearly set out to conquer new territory when she collaborated with playwright Thomas Babe and composer John Simon for her dance, *When We Were Very Young*. Premièred during her company's Broadway season from March 24 to April 12, this dance-drama revived the old argument about whether fusion of dance and words is possible. Most critics were fascinated by Paul Taylor's *Le Sacre du Printemps* (*The Rehearsal*), first seen in January at Lisner

DEATHS OF NOTABLE PERSONS in 1980 included those listed below. An asterisk (*) indicates the person is the subject of a biography in THE WORLD BOOK ENCYCLOPEDIA. Those listed were Americans unless otherwise indicated.

Adamson, Joy (1910-Jan. 3), Czech-born Austrian author of *Born Free* (1960), the story of the lioness she raised from a cub.

Allon, Yigal (1918-Feb. 29), Israeli military and political leader, a hero of the Jewish struggle for independence.

Ardrey, Robert (1908-Jan. 14), author whose controversial books on anthropology included *African Genesis* (1961) and *The Territorial Imperative* (1966).

Arnold, Elliot (1912-May 13), novelist whose books included the acclaimed *Broken Arrow* (1954).

Ashford, Emmett L. (1914-March 1), first major-league black umpire, who served in the American League from 1966 to 1970.

Bailey, Jack (1908-Feb. 1), actor who hosted the "Queen for a Day" television and radio show for 20 years.

Ballantrae, Lord (Bernard Edward Fergusson) (1911-Nov. 28), governor of New Zealand from 1962 to 1967.

Barthes, Roland (1915-March 25), French critic and theorist. His books include *A Lover's Discourse*.

Beaton, Sir Cecil (1904-Jan. 18), British portrait photographer and designer of stage sets and costumes for more than 20 shows including *My Fair Lady*.

Belcher, Page (1899-Aug. 2), Republican congressman from Oklahoma from 1950 to 1972.

Alice Roosevelt
Longworth, celebrity.

William O. Douglas,
Supreme Court justice.

Jesse Owens,
Olympic champion.

Jean-Paul Sartre,
French philosopher.

Bigard, Barney (1906-June 27), a noted jazz clarinetist with Duke Ellington, Louis Armstrong, and other bands.

Blanshard, Paul (1892-Jan. 27), writer, noted for his attacks on the Roman Catholic Church in such books as *American Freedom and Catholic Power* (1949).

Bonham, John H. (1949-Sept. 24), British rock star, drummer for the Led Zeppelin group.

Britton, Barbara (1920-Jan. 17), film and TV actress who played in the TV series "Mr. and Mrs. North."

Brook, Alexander (1896-Feb. 26), artist noted for his still lifes and landscapes.

Bullard, Sir Edward C. (1907-April 3), British geophysicist who pioneered the theory that the continents were once joined together as a single supercontinent.

Burpee, David (1893-June 24), seed merchant whose catalogs spelled spring to millions.

Byrd, Henry (Professor Longhair) (1918-Jan. 30), New Orleans singer and pianist who helped transform rhythm and blues into rock and roll.

Caetano, Marcello (1906-Oct. 26), prime minister of Portugal from 1968 to 1974.

Champion, Gower (1921-Aug. 25), one of Broadway's leading musical directors and choreographers. His shows included the acclaimed *Bye Bye Birdie* and *Hello, Dolly!*

*****Cochran, Jacqueline** (1912-Aug. 9), pioneer pilot and the first woman to break the sound barrier. She served as director of the Women's Air Force Service Pilots during World War II.

Collier, John (1901-April 6), British-born writer, best known for his collection of macabre short stories *Fancies and Goodnights*.

*****Connelly, Marc** (1890-Dec. 21), playwright whose *The Green Pastures* won a Pulitzer Prize in 1930.

Darlington, Gilbert (1892-May 30), Episcopal clergyman who published 360 million volumes of Scriptures as American Bible Society treasurer from 1920 to 1958.

*****D'Aulaire, Ingri** (1905-Oct. 24), author of many children's books.

Day, Dorothy (1897-Nov. 29), Roman Catholic social worker, a founder of the Catholic Worker Movement.

De Moraes, Vinicius (1914-July 9), Brazilian poet who wrote the lyrics for the bossa nova hit song "The Girl from Ipanema."

Deutsch, Adolph (1898-Jan. 1), British-born composer-arranger who won Academy Awards for the motion-picture scores of *Annie Get Your Gun, Seven Brides for Seven Brothers*, and *Oklahoma!*

*****Doenitz, Karl** (1891-Dec. 24), admiral who commanded Germany's submarine fleet in World War II.

Dornberger, Walter (1895-reported July 2), German-born aeronautical engineer and physicist who headed Nazi Germany's V-2 flying-bomb project during World War II. He later worked in the U.S. missile industry.

Douglas, Helen Gahagan (1900-June 28), Democratic congresswoman from California from 1944 to 1950. She was defeated in 1950 in a bitter campaign for a California U.S. Senate seat that pitched Richard M. Nixon into national prominence.

*****Douglas, William O.** (1899-Jan. 19), renowned justice who served on the Supreme Court of the United States for 36 years, longer than any other justice.

Dragonette, Jessica (1905-March 18), India-born soprano whose performances in operetta and semiclassical music made her one of radio's most popular singers.

*****Durante, Jimmy (James Francis)** (1893-Jan. 29), gifted comic singer and pianist who parlayed a rasping voice and a long nose into a lifelong career. "There's a million good-lookin' guys," he often said, "but I'm a novelty."

*****Duvoisin, Roger A.** (1904-June 30), artist, illustrator of children's books who won the Caldecott Medal for *White Snow, Bright Snow*.

Evans, Bill (1929-Sept. 15), jazz pianist noted for his lyricism and harmonic structure.

Fallon, George (1902-March 21), Democratic congressman from Maryland from 1945 to 1971.

Farago, Ladislas (1906-Oct. 15), Hungarian-born author whose many books include *Patton: The Ordeal and Triumph* (1964).

Fernandez, Royes (1929-March 3), principal dancer with the American Ballet Theater from 1950 to 1972.

Fischetti, John (1916-Nov. 18), political cartoonist noted for his wit and his compassion for the underdog. He won the Pulitzer Prize in 1969 and worked with the *Chicago Daily News* and *Sun-Times* since 1967.

Fogarty, Anne (1919-Jan. 15), fashion designer noted for her youthfully feminine and light-hearted clothes.

Fouche, Jacobus J. (1898-Sept. 23), president of South Africa from 1968 to 1975.

Fox, Virgil (1912-Oct. 25), organist whose impeccable style helped establish the modern organ as a concert instrument.

Frank, Morris (1908-Nov. 22), a founder in 1929 of The Seeing Eye Incorporated, a guide-dog training center for the blind. He was blinded in a boxing accident at 16.

Frank, Otto (1889-Aug. 19), German-born Jewish businessman whose teen-age daughter, Anne, described two years of hiding from the Nazis in the acclaimed *Diary of Anne Frank* (1947).

Froman, Jane (1907-April 22), actress and singer whose heroic comeback from injuries suffered in a plane crash was portrayed in the film *With a Song in My Heart* (1952).

*****Fromm, Erich** (1900-March 18), German-born psychiatrist who called love the only "sane and satisfactory answer to the problem of human existence." His many books include *The Art of Loving* (1956).

Galindez, Victor (1949-Oct. 26), World Boxing Association light-heavyweight champion from 1974 to 1978.

Gandhi, Sanjay (1946-June 23), Indian politician, son of Prime Minister Indira Gandhi.

Gardiner, Reginald (1903-July 7), British-born character actor in nearly 100 films. He also charmed theater audiences with his imitations of inanimate objects such as French wallpaper and wastebaskets.

Garrett, Ray D., Jr. (1920-Feb. 3), chairman of the Securities and Exchange Commission from 1973 to 1975.

Gary, Romain (1914-Dec. 2), Russian-born French writer whose many books included *The Dance of Genghis Cohn* (1968) and *Your Ticket Is No Longer Valid* (1977).

*****Giri, Varahagiri V.** (1894-June 24), president of India from 1969 to 1974.

Glueck, Sheldon (1896-March 10), Polish-born criminologist who developed controversial "prediction tables" for detecting potential delinquents.

Goldman, Richard F. (1910-Jan. 19), composer, conductor of the Goldman Band from 1955 to 1979. The band's unusual program included both symphonic music and traditional band numbers.

Gorman, Patrick E. (1892-Sept. 3), head of the Amalgamated Meat Cutters and Butcher Workmen of North America for more than 50 years.

Griffin, John H. (1920-Sept. 9), author, best known for *Black Like Me* (1961), a book based on his travels posing as a black.

Griffith, Hugh (1912-May 14), British actor, best known for his role as the lusty squire in the film *Tom Jones* (1963). He won an Oscar in 1959 for his performance in *Ben-Hur*.

Halberstam, Michael J. (1932-Dec. 5), cardiologist and editor of *Modern Medicine* magazine.

Hall, Paul (1914-June 22), head of the Seafarers International Union for almost 25 years.

Haymes, Dick (1918-March 28), popular singer in the 1940s with the bands of Tommy Dorsey, Harry James, and Benny Goodman.

*****Hitchcock, Alfred J.** (1899-April 29), British-born filmmaker noted for such psychological thrillers as *The 39 Steps* (1935) and *Psycho* (1960).

Hoeven, Charles B. (1895-Nov. 10), Republican congressman from Iowa from 1943 to 1965.

Hoskins, Allen C. (1920-July 16), actor who played Farina in Our Gang comedy films of the 1930s.

Howard, Elston (1929-Dec. 14), a star catcher and first black to play for the New York Yankees. He won the American League's Most Valuable Player award in 1963, the first black player so honored.

Hurley, Ruby (1909-Aug. 9), "the queen of civil rights," known for her courageous investigations of racial violence and the struggle to gain entrance for blacks to universities in the South.

*****Iturbi, José** (1895-June 28), Spanish-born concert pianist and conductor who appeared in several films, including *A Song to Remember* and *Anchors Aweigh*.

Janssen, David (David Harold Meyer) (1930-Feb. 13), actor who appeared in more than 100 feature and TV films, including the TV series "The Fugitive"; "Richard Diamond, Private Detective"; and "Harry O."

Johnson, Willie (1913-May 3), a gospel-music innovator credited with developing the rhythm-and-blues syncopation and vocal style that led to rock-and-roll music.

Kaminska, Ida (1899-May 21), Polish actress who reigned for decades as the queen of classic Yiddish theater. She played the Jewish shopkeeper in the acclaimed Czech film *The Shop on Main Street* (1966).

Kendrick, Pearl L. (1890-Oct. 8), microbiologist who helped develop a whooping cough vaccine.

Khama, Sir Seretse M. (1921-July 13), president of Botswana since 1966.

Mohammad Reza Pahlavi, shah of Iran.

David Janssen, a popular actor.

C. P. Snow, a noted British writer.

Jimmy Durante, comedian and actor.

*Kokoschka, Oskar (1886-Feb. 22), Austrian-born painter, a key figure in the expressionist movement.

Kostelanetz, André (1901-Jan. 13), popular Russian-born composer and conductor with the New York Philharmonic from 1952 to 1979.

*Kosygin, Aleksey N. (1904-Dec. 18), chairman of Russia's Council of Ministers from 1964 until he resigned because of ill health on Oct. 23, 1980.

*Krumgold, Joseph (1908-July 10), writer, winner of the Newbery Medal for his books . . . And Now Miguel (1954) and Onion John (1960).

LaMarsh, Julia V. (1924-Oct. 27), Canadian lawyer and politician, minister of health and welfare in Prime Minister Lester B. Pearson's Cabinet.

Lauck, Chester A. (1902-Feb. 21), actor who played Lum on the "Lum 'n' Abner" radio show.

*Léger, Jules (1913-Nov. 22), governor general of Canada from 1974 to 1979.

Lennon, John (1940-Dec. 8), British musician and composer who was a member of the Beatles. See MUSIC, POPULAR (Close-Up).

Lesage, Jean (1912-Dec. 11), Canadian lawyer and politician, premier of Quebec from 1960 to 1966.

Levene, Sam (1905-Dec. 28), Russian-born actor who created the role of Nathan Detroit in Guys and Dolls.

Levenson, Sam (1911-Aug. 27), humorist, former Brooklyn schoolteacher whose humorous and touching tales of immigrant family life entertained millions.

*Libby, Willard F. (1908-Sept. 8), chemist who won the 1960 Nobel Prize for Chemistry.

Linge, Heinz (1913-March 17), butler to Adolf Hitler. He claimed to be the last person to have seen Hitler alive.

Loden, Barbara (1932-Sept. 22), actress and director, first woman to write, direct, and star in her own feature film — Wanda (1970).

Longley, James B. (1924-Aug. 16), Independent governor of Maine from 1975 to 1979.

Longworth, Alice Roosevelt (1884-Feb. 20), last surviving child of President Theodore Roosevelt. Noted for her wit and beauty, she was a prominent figure in Washington society for 80 years.

Lowenstein, Allard K. (1929-March 14), a leader of the anti-Vietnam War movement in 1968 that opposed President Lyndon B. Johnson. He was a New York congressman from 1969 to 1971.

Mackey, Bernard (1910-March 5), singer, an original member of The Ink Spots quartet in the 1930s. Their hit records included "Do I Worry?" and "If I Didn't Care."

Malik, Yakov A. (1906-Feb. 11), Russian diplomat, delegate to the United Nations from 1948 to 1952 and from 1968 to 1976.

Mann, Marty (1904-July 22), founder of the National Council on Alcoholism and the first woman to become a member of Alcoholics Anonymous. Her book New Primer on Alcoholism is considered a classic.

Mantovani, Annunzio P. (1905-March 29), Italian-born British conductor whose recordings of string-filled harmonies such as "Charmaine" sold in the millions.

Margolis, Sidney (1911-Jan. 31), pioneer reporter on consumer affairs.

Marini, Marino (1901-Aug. 6), Italian sculptor and painter, known for his portrayals of hefty nudes and men on horseback.

Marquard, Rube (Richard) (1889-June 1), pitcher who won 19 consecutive victories for the New York Giants baseball club in 1912.

Martin, Pete (1901-Oct. 13), journalist with The Saturday Evening Post from 1926 to 1963, noted for his celebrity interviews.

Martinez, Maria Povera (1887-July 20), San Ildefonso Pueblo Indian known as Maria the Potter whose black-on-black pottery is in museums throughout the world.

Mathieu, Simone (1908-Jan. 7), France's leading woman tennis player from 1928 to 1940.

Matthias, Bernd T. (1918-Oct. 27), German-born physicist, said to have discovered more elements and compounds with superconducting properties than any other scientist.

Mauchly, John W. (1907-Jan. 8), physicist and engineer who invented the first practical electronic digital computer, ENIAC.

McCarty, Mary (1923-April 5), brassy-voiced character actress who played Nurse Starch in the TV series "Trapper John, M.D."

*McCormack, John W. (1891-Nov. 22), speaker of the U.S. House of Representatives from 1962 to 1971. He served as Democratic congressman from Massachusetts from 1928 to 1971.

McDonnell, James S. (1899-Aug. 22), aeronautical engineer, chairman of McDonnell Douglas Corporation and a pioneer in spacecraft.

McFarlane, William D. (1894-Feb. 18), Democratic congressman from Texas from 1933 to 1939.

McKelway, St. Clair (1905-Jan. 10), writer, former managing editor of The New Yorker magazine, noted for his elegant prose and dry wit.

*McLuhan, Marshall (1911-Dec. 31), Canadian educator, writer, and communications theorist who coined the phrase "the medium is the message."

McQueen, Steve (1930-Nov. 7), film actor whose portrayals of the tough loner in such films as The Great Escape (1963) and Bullitt (1968) made him one of America's most popular stars.

Alfred J. Hitchcock, master of suspense.

Masayoshi Ohira, prime minister of Japan.

Luis Muñoz Marín, Puerto Rican leader.

Katherine Anne Porter, a noted writer.

McWilliams, Carey (1905-June 27), editor of *The Nation* from 1955 to 1975 and a long-time crusader for the underprivileged.

*Meany, George (1894-Jan. 10), president of the American Federation of Labor and Congress of Industrial Organizations since 1955 (see LABOR [Close-Up]).

*Miller, Henry (1891-June 7), writer who advocated glorifying the self and the senses. His controversial bawdy book *Tropic of Cancer* (1934) was banned in the United States until 1961.

Medford, Kay (1920-April 10), comic actress best known for her Broadway portrayals of doting Jewish mothers in *Don't Drink the Water* and *Funny Girl*.

Milestone, Lewis (1895-Sept. 25), Russian-born film director who won Oscars for *Two Arabian Knights* (1928) and *All Quiet on the Western Front* (1930).

*Mohammad Reza Pahlavi (1919-July 27), shah of Iran from 1941 to 1979.

Monroney, A. S. (Mike) (1902-Feb. 13), Democratic senator from Oklahoma from 1950 to 1968. He served as congressman from 1939 to 1950.

Morgenthau, Hans J. (1904-July 19), German-born political scientist, noted for his opposition to U.S. involvement in Vietnam in the 1960s.

Mosley, Sir Oswald (1896-Dec. 3), British fascist who led a 1930s blackshirt movement in support of Adolf Hitler.

Muhlenberg, Frederick A. (1887-Jan. 19), Republican congressman from Pennsylvania from 1946 to 1948.

*Muñoz Marín, Luis (1898-April 29), first elected governor of Puerto Rico, who served from 1948 to 1964.

Nenni, Pietro (1891-Jan. 1), leader of Italy's Socialist Party from 1949 to 1969.

Nielsen, Arthur C. (1897-June 1), president of A. C. Nielsen Company from 1923 to 1957. He developed the Nielsen Survey, which checks what the television audience watches and influences radio and TV programming.

Niles, John Jacob (1892-March 1), folklorist, folk singer, and collector of ballads and carols for 80 years. He composed the *Niles-Merton Song Cycles* (1972) with noted Trappist monk and philosopher Thomas Merton.

Nugent, Elliott (1896-Aug. 9), playwright and actor who co-authored and starred in *The Voice of the Turtle*. His books include *Events Leading Up to the Comedy*.

O'Hara, Mary (Mary O'Hara Alsop Sture-Vasa) (1885-Oct. 15), writer whose novels included the best-selling *My Friend Flicka* (1941) and *Thunderhead* (1943).

Ohira, Masayoshi (1910-June 12), prime minister of Japan since 1978.

Okun, Arthur M. (1928-March 23), economist who developed "Okun's Law," a mathematical theory correlating unemployment and productivity.

*Owens, Jesse (1913-March 31), track star who won the 100-meter dash, 200-meter dash, and broad jump and led the winning U.S. 400-meter relay team in the 1936 Olympic Games.

Page, Joe (1917-April 21), ace relief pitcher for the New York Yankees in the 1940s.

Pal, George (1908-May 2), Hungarian-born film director who won eight Oscars for such films as *When Worlds Collide, War of the Worlds*, and *The Time Machine*.

Patterson, William L. (1890-March 5), lawyer and writer who was active in human rights issues and the American Communist Party for more than 50 years.

*Piaget, Jean (1896-Sept. 17), Swiss psychologist noted for his study of the thought processes of children.

Popovic, Cvjetko (1896-June 9), last surviving member of the Yugoslavian Young Bosnia group that plotted the assassination of Archduke Franz Ferdinand of Austria in 1914, which sparked World War I.

*Porter, Katherine Anne (1890-Sept. 18), writer acclaimed for her short fiction. Her only novel was *Ship of Fools* (1962).

Powers, John A. (Shorty) (1923-Jan. 1), pilot who became the "voice of the astronauts" in the early 1960s and coined the term *A-OK*.

Raft, George (1895-Nov. 24), Hollywood actor whose poker-faced style in gangster films made him a hit in the 1930s and 1940s.

Randolph, Lillian (1915-Sept. 12), actress who played Madame Queen in the "Amos 'n' Andy" TV series.

Reed, Stanley F. (1884-April 3), justice of the U.S. Supreme Court from 1938 to 1957.

Renaldo, Duncan (1904-Sept. 3), Romanian-born film actor who played The Cisco Kid in the 1950s TV series.

Rhine, Joseph B. (1895-Feb. 20), psychologist who pioneered in studies of clairvoyance and mental telepathy. He coined the term *extrasensory perception* (*ESP*).

Robbins, Gale (1921-Feb. 18), actress and singer, a popular pin-up girl during World War II.

Roberts, Rachel (1927-Nov. 26), Welsh-born actress noted for her performances in *Saturday Night and Sunday Morning* (1960) and *Yanks* (1980).

Rosenstein, Nettie (1890-March 13), Austrian-born dress designer whose name was synonymous with understated chic.

Roth, Lillian (1910-May 12), actress and singer whose struggle against alcoholism was told in her best-selling book *I'll Cry Tomorrow*.

Rubin, Morris H. (1911-Aug. 8), editor and publisher of *The Progressive* magazine from 1940 to 1973. *The Progressive* was among the first journals to investigate the tactics of Senator Joseph McCarthy in 1954.

Peter Sellers, a
gifted comic actor.

Helen Gahagan Douglas,
congresswoman.

Jules Léger,
Canadian governor general.

Aleksey N. Kosygin,
Russian leader.

Tito's Dubious Bequest

Yugoslavia's President Josip Broz Tito had a profound impact on European history as a wartime guerrilla leader, as a rebel against Russian domination of world Communism, and as the man who guided his country down its independent "road to Socialism." But when he died on May 4, 1980, there were doubts about the quality of his accomplishments and the value and permanence of the institutions he established.

Even the role of Tito's guerrilla fighters in Axis-occupied Yugoslavia during World War II remains controversial. Some observers dispute the widely held view that Tito's Partisans held down large Axis forces practically alone. Some claim that the other resistance force—Colonel Draža Mihailovich's royalist Chetniks—would have done even better against the Axis had the Allies not switched their support to Tito in 1943. Tito's political flair helped the Partisans win Allied recognition and international legitimacy for their postwar rule.

Tito's defiance of Russia's dictator Joseph Stalin in 1948 was a milestone in the history of world Communism. It resulted in Yugoslavia's expulsion from the Cominform, predecessor of the Warsaw Pact, but it encouraged other Eastern European countries that wanted greater independence from Russia. Paradoxically, Tito was not sorry when Russia intervened in Hungary in 1956. In his view, Hungary had gone too far toward political pluralism at home and pro-Western neutrality abroad.

Tito helped found an international organization in 1961 in order to give a third choice to countries that did not wish to align themselves politically with the Eastern or Western bloc. Member nations of this *nonaligned movement* met regularly to chart a careful course between the two superpower groupings. But Tito saw the movement abandon its original purpose by issuing a strongly pro-Russian final document at its 1979 conference in Havana, Cuba.

Tito attracted a huge following during World War II with his idea of ruling Yugoslavia through a federal system—creating semiautonomous political subdivisions for the country's many ethnic groups. After the war, Tito divided the country into six republics—Bosnia and Hercegovina, Croatia, Macedonia, Montenegro, Serbia, and Slovenia—and two self-governing provinces, Kosovo and Vojvodina. The system worked well for many years, but ethnic rivalries began to grow in the 1970s. Tito's purge of Croatian officials in 1971 and a 1972 Serbian purge removed some of the talented leaders that Yugoslavia would need during the post-Tito years.

Tito guided Yugoslavia's system of worker control over factories when it emerged in the late 1940s, but the system could not cope with Yugoslavia's complex economic problems. Tito strengthened this management system in 1956 by decentralizing industry and de-emphasizing central economic planning. He also stopped subsidizing nonessential businesses that were unprofitable, devalued the currency, and boosted consumer-goods prices sharply in 1956. Even so, the attractiveness of the Yugoslav model in Eastern Europe had diminished greatly by the time of his death. Yugoslavia struggled with economic difficulties, including high unemployment, inflation, and shortages, and still had not resolved problems of social inequalities among workers, managers, and party officials.

In the political sphere, Tito left his successors a system of rotating, supposedly equally capable, leaders. An eight-member State Presidency—made up of one representative from each republic and self-governing province—runs the country, and a similar group directs the Communist Party. Leadership rotates among the members, who preside for one year.

Tito devised this system to avoid struggles for supremacy among ethnic groups and individual leaders, and it worked well during the months following Tito's death. However, it did not seem to give these leaders a chance to achieve one major goal that had eluded Tito—the establishment of a national Yugoslavian identity.

Chris Cviic

Josip Broz Tito (1892-1980)

Rukeyser, Muriel (1913-Feb. 12), poet, noted for her powerful poems of social protest. Her book, *The Collected Poems of Muriel Rukeyser* (1979), mirrors U.S. history from the Great Depression to the Vietnam War.

Runnels, Harold L. (1924-Aug. 5), Democratic congressman from New Mexico since 1971.

Sa Carneiro, Francisco (1934-Dec. 4), prime minister of Portugal since January 1980.

Sanders, Colonel Harland (1890-Dec. 16), white-haired Kentucky colonel who founded the Kentucky Fried Chicken fast-food franchise.

*__Sartre, Jean-Paul__ (1905-April 15), French philosopher and playwright whose writings on existentialism influenced two generations of intellectuals.

Schary, Dore (1905-July 7), playwright and film producer who wrote *Sunrise at Campobello* and the Oscar-winning *Boys Town* (1938).

Sellers, Peter (1925-July 24), British film actor whose roles ranged from a duchess in *The Mouse That Roared* to a mad nuclear expert in *Dr. Strangelove or How I Stopped Worrying and Learned to Love the Bomb*.

Sharaf, Abdul H. (1939-July 3), prime minister of Jordan since 1979.

Shea, George E. (1902-April 27), financial editor of *The Wall Street Journal*.

Sherrill, Bishop Henry K. (1890-May 11), theologian, presiding bishop of the Episcopal Church from 1946 to 1958, and a leader in the ecumenical movement.

Shukairy, Ahmed (1908-Feb. 26), leader of the Palestine Liberation Organization from 1964 to 1967.

Silverheels, Jay (1920-March 5), Mohawk Indian actor, Canadian-born, who played Tonto in "The Lone Ranger" TV series.

Slack, John M., Jr. (1915-March 17), Democratic congressman from Virginia since 1959.

*__Snow, C. P. (Lord Charles P.)__ (1905-July 1), British novelist, playwright, and physicist who wrote 25 books, including the 11-volume series *Strangers and Brothers*.

*__Somoza Debayle, Anastasio__ (1925-Sept. 17), ruler of Nicaragua from 1967 to 1972 and 1974 to 1979.

Stein, William H. (1911-Feb. 2), biochemist, co-winner of the 1972 Nobel Prize for Chemistry.

Stewart, Donald Ogden (1895-Aug. 2), Hollywood screenwriter and humorist who wrote the award-winning script for *The Philadelphia Story*.

*__Still, Clyfford__ (1904-June 23), painter, a leading member of the abstract expressionist movement.

Stone, Milburn (1904-June 12), actor who played the crusty but lovable Doc Adams in the TV series "Gunsmoke" for 20 years.

Summerskill, Baroness Edith C. (1901-Feb. 4), British gynecologist who fought for women's rights as a Labour member of Parliament and a Cabinet minister.

Sutherland, Graham (1903-Feb. 17), British artist whose portrait of Sir Winston Churchill was destroyed by Lady Spencer-Churchill because she did not like it.

Sutton, Willie (Willie the Actor) (1901-Nov. 2), bank robber and escape artist who stole close to $2 million in a 35-year crime career and spent 33 years in prison.

Tarnower, Herman (1910-March 10), cardiologist who achieved worldwide fame on the basis of one book — *The Complete Scarsdale Medical Diet* (1979).

Teale, Edwin W. (1899-Oct. 18), naturalist and writer, whose lyrical books on the four seasons included the Pulitzer prizewinning *Wandering Through Winter* (1966).

*__Tito, Josip Broz__ (1892-May 4), president of Yugoslavia since 1963 (see Close-Up).

Tobias, George (1901-Feb. 27), character actor, best known for his role as neighbor Abner Kravitz in the "Bewitched" TV series.

Tolbert, William R., Jr. (1913-April 12), president of Liberia since 1971.

Ton Duc Thang (1888-March 30), president of Vietnam since 1969.

John W. McCormack, speaker of the House.

Willard F. Libby, Nobel laureate for Chemistry.

Steve McQueen, actor, top-ranking movie star.

Gower Champion, choreographer.

Tynan, Kenneth P. (1927-July 26), British playwright and drama critic known for his controversial reviews. His play *Oh Calcutta!* opened on Broadway in 1969.

Van, Bobby (Robert King) (1933-July 31), actor, comedian, and dancer.

Walsh, Raoul (1887-Dec. 31), veteran director of such films as *What Price Glory?*, *They Died With Their Boots On*, and *High Sierra*.

West, Mae (1893-Nov. 22), Hollywood's original Diamond Lil. She parlayed sultry innuendoes into a million-dollar career that spanned six decades.

Westheimer, Irvin F. (1879-Dec. 30), investment banker who founded the Big Brothers organization.

Whitaker, Frederic (1881-March 9), artist whose watercolors and landscapes are displayed in numerous museums and galleries.

Wilder, Alec (1907-Dec. 23), composer of such songs as "I'll Be Around" and "While We're Young." He also wrote operas, choral works, and chamber music.

Williams, Paul R. (1894-Jan. 23), first black member of the American Institute of Architects.

Wright, James A. (1927-March 25), Pulitzer Prize-winning poet noted for his lyric poems about poverty and his native Middle West.

Yahya Khan, General Agha Mohammad (1917-Aug. 8), Pakistan's military ruler from 1969 to 1971.

Yellow Bird, Jo Ann (1948-July 7), a Sioux Indian activist who won a $300,000 civil rights judgment against the city of Gordon, Nebr., in 1979.   Irene B. Keller

DELAWARE. See STATE GOVERNMENT.

DEMOCRATIC PARTY. The general election on Nov. 4, 1980, was a "disaster for the Democrats," in the blunt appraisal of Speaker of the House Thomas P. (Tip) O'Neill, Jr., of Massachusetts, who was slated to become the highest-ranking Democrat in the new Administration. President Jimmy Carter and Vice-President Walter F. Mondale were routed by the landslide triumph of Republican challenger Ronald Reagan and his running mate, George H. W. Bush. Republicans wrested control of the Senate from Democrats for the first time in 26 years; picked up 33 seats in the House to shrink the Democrats' once-huge majority in that chamber; added four governors; and gained more than 200 seats in state legislatures.

The scope of Carter's defeat was staggering. He lost most of his native South, all of the West except Hawaii, and nearly all of the Midwest and East. The first elected President to be turned out of office since Republican Herbert Hoover's defeat in 1932, he carried only six states and the District of Columbia for a total of 49 electoral votes. Reagan, however, cracked the traditional Democratic coalition of blue-collar workers, ethnic groups, and city residents, to sweep 44 states and 489 electoral votes. In the popular vote, Reagan got 43,899,248 votes, or 51 per cent of the total cast, to 35,481,435, or 41 per cent, for Carter. Independent candidate John B. Anderson received 5,719,437 votes, or 7 per cent, and was not a factor in the outcome.

Carter was hurt by the economic situation at home – inflation running at an annual pace of 12.6 per cent on election day and recession-level unemployment of 7.6 per cent. His inability to gain the release of the American hostages in Iran also made him look weak.

Party Rift. Carter's candidacy was also seriously damaged by the long battle for the Democratic presidential nomination waged by Senator Edward M. Kennedy of Massachusetts. Although Kennedy made consistently poor showings in public opinion polls and won only a few primaries, he had the support of several prominent Democrats and went to the Democratic convention on August 8 with 1,200 delegates to President Carter's 2,000.

Only when Kennedy's plan for an "open convention" – the release of all committed delegates to vote for any candidate they wished – was defeated on August 10 did he concede to Carter. Nonetheless, he continued to dominate the convention. On August 12, he delivered a stirring call to Democrats to "renew the party's commitment to economic justice." His speech, which was followed by 35 minutes of applause and demonstration, received far more attention than Carter's acceptance speech.

Jimmy Carter appears with Senator Edward Kennedy, *above,* and Vice-President Walter F. Mondale, *right,* to accept the Democratic presidential nomination.

Although Kennedy and other Democrats regrouped behind Carter, the few weeks remaining in the campaign did not provide enough time to heal party rifts. In addition, the Democrats, who have historically profited from a large voter turnout, were hurt when only 54 per cent of the nation's 160.5 million eligible voters cast ballots.

Congressional Losses. The scope of Carter's defeat extended to Democrats running for the Senate and House. Republicans gained 12 seats in the Senate, ousting seven liberal Democrats, producing a line-up of 53 Republicans, 46 Democrats, and 1 Independent for the 97th Congress, compared with 58 Democrats, 41 Republicans, and 1 Independent in the previous Congress.

The Democratic losers included such notables as Senator George S. McGovern of South Dakota, the party's presidential nominee of 1972, and six-term Senator Warren G. Magnuson of Washington state. Other defeated liberals, who were succeeded primarily by conservative Republicans, were: Birch Bayh of Indiana, Frank Church of Idaho, John C. Culver of Iowa, John A. Durkin of New Hampshire, and Gaylord Nelson of Wisconsin.

However, Democrats managed to retain control in the House. The Republicans picked up 33 seats, producing a line-up of 242 Democrats, 192 Republicans, and 1 Independent in the 97th Congress, compared with 276 Democrats and 159 Republicans at the beginning of the 96th Congress. Many veteran Democrats, including House Whip John Brademas of Indiana, were defeated. Casualties of the conservative tidal wave also included Al Ullman of Oregon, chairman of the Ways and Means Committee; Harold T. Johnson of California, chairman of the Public Works Committee; and Thomas L. Ashley of Ohio, a 26-year veteran.

At the State Level, Democrats suffered a net loss of four governors, reducing their total to 27. Losers included Arkansas Governor Bill Clinton, at 34 the youngest governor in the United States; Missouri Governor Joseph P. Teasdale; North Dakota Governor Arthur A. Link; and Democratic contender James A. McDermott in Washington state.

Democratic governors were re-elected in five states. West Virginia Governor John D. (Jay) Rockefeller IV reportedly spent $9 million to win a second term. Other incumbents returned to office were Hugh J. Gallen, New Hampshire; James B. Hunt, Jr., North Carolina; J. Joseph Garrahy, Rhode Island; and Scott M. Matheson of Utah.

Democrats also lost control of state legislative chambers in Illinois, Ohio, and Pennsylvania. Overall, Democrats lost more than 200 state legislative seats. William J. Eaton

See also ELECTIONS. In World Book, see DEMOCRATIC PARTY.

DENMARK struggled in 1980 to shore up its sagging economy. The country has the highest standard of living in the European Community (Common Market), but its payments deficit almost doubled to $2.9 billion from 1978 to 1979. Foreign debts represented almost one-fourth of the gross domestic product.

Prime Minister Anker Henrik Jorgensen's minority Social Democratic government submitted an economic austerity package to the *Folketing* (parliament) on April 10 calling for a $1.3-billion tax hike and an $830-million cut in government spending. But the Liberals said that the program did not redress Denmark's economic problems, while the Conservatives declared that the tax hike would be too high and the spending cut too low. So Jorgensen proposed a plan on May 5 that would ease taxes by about $900 million and decrease spending by $1.4 billion in 1981. He estimated that the new plan would eliminate half of the deficit by 1984.

Jorgensen did not get Liberal and Conservative support for his new package in the beginning. But after he warned that unemployment would rise from 6.5 to 8 per cent in 1981 and inflation would increase from 9.5 per cent at midyear to 11.5 per cent unless the measures passed, the Folketing passed the bill in May. Liberals and Conservatives finally consented when Jorgensen dropped plans to impose a temporary state tax on property, increase road taxes, and make pensioners prove that they needed certain payments.

Nuclear Power. On January 26, the government postponed indefinitely Folketing action on nuclear power. The government had wanted to decide in 1980 and hold a public referendum in 1981, so that the first nuclear power stations would be in use by 1991. But the March 1979 accident at the Three Mile Island nuclear reactor in Pennsylvania reinforced doubts about nuclear power's safety, environmental impact, and economy. The government also said that it could not solve the problem of how to dispose of reactor waste.

Undersea Link. Denmark began talks with Norway on piping gas from Norwegian fields under the North Sea. Denmark already plans to supply more than one-third of its energy needs from its own North Sea oil and gas fields by the mid-1980s. Norway said that it would consider Denmark's additional needs before the spring of 1981, the deadline for deciding on piping gas to other countries. Denmark pressed Norway to link up with a Danish pipeline that would run from the North Sea fields over Jutland Peninsula and the island of Fyn to Sjaelland island on which Copenhagen stands, and possibly on to Sweden.   Kenneth Brown

See also EUROPE (Facts in Brief Table). In WORLD BOOK, see DENMARK.

DENTISTRY. Acarbose, an experimental chemical to combat obesity, may turn out to be a potent weapon against tooth decay. Dental researcher Ernest Newbrun of the University of California, San Francisco, reported in March 1980 that studies show that acarbose, which is produced by bacteria, is effective in preventing decay.

Acarbose was originally isolated by German scientists in the late 1970s. Initial studies showed that it can curb weight gain by blocking the action of enzymes that break food starches into small forms of sugar that the body absorbs. Sugars that are not broken down pass through the body without being absorbed.

Newbrun told the American Association for Dental Research meeting in Los Angeles that the chemical also blocks the action of another enzyme, glucosyl-transferase (GTF). GTF uses sugars in the mouth to create a sort of glue that helps decay-causing bacteria to stick to teeth. Without the glue, most bacteria are washed away through salivation or drinking liquids. Newbrun emphasized, however, that he has so far studied the effects of acarbose only in the laboratory.

Wisdom Tooth Removal. Many patients who balk at their dentist's suggestion to extract wisdom teeth or third molars when they are not causing pain or other problems may later face more difficult oral surgery, with greater postoperative discomfort,

new studies have disclosed. "Our observation . . . is that younger patients will have an easier operative and postoperative course than older patients following third-molar surgery," said dental researcher Robert A. Bruce of the University of Michigan School of Dentistry at Ann Arbor in August. Postoperative problems ranged from excessive pain and swelling to prolonged healing time.

Fluoride Mouth Rinses, now available without a prescription, can give users added protection against tooth decay, according to the American Dental Association (ADA). In July, the ADA Council on Dental Therapeutics gave its Seal of Acceptance to two national brands of fluoride mouth rinse, attesting that the products – Fluorigard and StanCare – are safe and effective.

The ADA action supports statements by a Food and Drug Administration advisory panel that fluoride mouth rinses and gels are effective in preventing tooth decay. The ADA also urged that the product labels carry the recommendation that the rinses be used regularly in conjunction with a fluoride toothpaste. In addition, it recommended that the rinses not be used by children under 6. "For years we have stressed brushing and flossing," said Edgar W. Mitchell, secretary of the Council on Dental Therapeutics. "Now it will probably be brushing, flossing, and rinsing."   Lou Joseph

In WORLD BOOK, see DENTISTRY; TEETH.

DETROIT struggled with fiscal crisis throughout 1980 as city officials tried to stretch a budget of $1.46 billion – a sum smaller than the previous year's – to cover expenses and meet pay-raise demands. The city's financial slump was directly related to the decline in automobile sales that affected its largest employers, Chrysler Corporation and General Motors Corporation. Plant cutbacks reduced revenues from personal and corporate taxes and left 20 per cent of the work force jobless.

Moreover, the state of Michigan, upon which Detroit depends heavily for financial support, had a $90-million deficit. Under Michigan law, that deficit and Detroit's $70-million deficit are illegal.

Strikes and Layoffs. Some 9,000 municipal workers walked off the job on July 1, demanding higher wages. The strike, waged by the American Federation of State, County, and Municipal Employees, involved one-third of the city's workers. The strike ended on July 12 in a settlement that granted an average wage increase of $3,229 over three years.

In an effort to pare $27.6 million from the city budget, Mayor Coleman A. Young on September 5 ordered the layoff of 690 police officers – 18 per cent of the city's patrol force – damaging an affirmative action program that had placed significant proportions of blacks and women on the force. Of the officers laid off, 44.4 per cent were black men;

The Joe Louis Arena, foreground, played host to some 20,000 delegates and journalists attending the Republican National Convention in Detroit in July.

29.8 per cent, black women; 16 per cent, white men; and 9.4 per cent, white women.

Bright Spots. Detroit had recovered from the municipal employees' strike sufficiently to present an image of bustling efficiency to delegates attending the Republican Party's National Convention in the Joe Louis Arena from July 14 to July 17. Although 80 per cent of the delegates polled before the convention said they would prefer meeting in another city, 95 per cent of those polled after the convention reported that Detroit was better than they had expected.

U.S. District Judge Horace W. Gilmore ruled on September 25 that the U.S. Bureau of the Census had seriously undercounted Detroit's population. In a suit against the bureau, the city claimed that the census had missed some 67,000 residents and, as a result, had deprived Detroit of more than $50-million in federal aid. See CENSUS.

Voters in Wayne County, which includes Detroit and some of its suburbs, approved a referendum on August 5 to reorganize the government. The vote established a commission that will offer for voter approval two forms of government — one headed by an elected county executive and the other headed by an appointed county manager.   James M. Banovetz

See also CITY. In WORLD BOOK, see DETROIT.

DICTIONARY. See DICTIONARY SUPPLEMENT.

DISARMAMENT. See ARMED FORCES.

DISASTERS. About 3,000 persons were killed and more than 250,000 left homeless by a devastating earthquake in southern Italy on Nov. 23, 1980. The quake, which destroyed entire towns, centered on Potenza, near Naples. About a month earlier, on October 10, two earthquakes struck El Asnam, Algeria, killing about 3,000 persons.

At least 34 persons died in a very rare disaster, the eruption of a volcano within the 48 contiguous United States. Mount Saint Helens in Washington erupted repeatedly during the year, with the deaths occurring in a major explosion on May 18. See GEOLOGY (Close-Up).

One of the worst air disasters in history occurred on August 19 near Riyadh, Saudi Arabia, when a Saudi Arabian jet caught fire and burned, killing 301 persons. A passenger on the jet apparently touched off the blaze when he lighted a portable stove to make tea. Twenty-two American amateur boxers, their coaches, and U.S. amateur boxing officials were among 87 persons killed on March 14 when a Polish jet en route from New York City crashed and exploded while attempting an emergency landing near Warsaw, Poland.

Disasters that resulted in 10 or more deaths in 1980 included the following:

Aircraft Crashes

Jan. 21 – Northern Iran. An Iran Air Boeing 727 jet crashed in heavy fog, killing all 128 persons on board.

A section of the Sunshine Skyway Bridge lies in Tampa Bay after the bridge was rammed by the freighter *Summit Venture*. At least 35 died.

Jan. 24 – Near Mandalay, Burma. A Burmese military transport plane crashed, killing 42 of the 44 persons on board.

Feb. 21 – Sydney, Australia. An Australian Beechcraft twin-engine commuter plane crashed while attempting an emergency landing, killing all 13 persons on board. The plane just missed hitting a Boeing 727 jetliner that had landed seconds before.

Feb. 22 – Agra, India. An Indian air force plane crashed shortly after take-off when a fuel tank exploded and 46 of the 47 persons on board died.

March 14 – Warsaw, Poland. A Polish Ilyushin 62 jet crashed, killing all 87 persons on board – including 22 Americans.

March 14 – Turkey. A U.S. Air Force C-130 Hercules transport plane based in Turkey crashed in the Taurus Mountains, killing all 18 persons on board.

April 12 – Florianópolis, Brazil. A Brazilian Boeing 727 crashed while landing in a rainstorm, and 54 persons died.

April 25 – Canary Islands. A British Boeing 727 crowded with vacationers crashed in the mountains on Tenerife, killing all 146 persons on board.

April 27 – Bangkok, Thailand. A Thai Hawker Siddeley 748 turboprop airliner crashed as it approached an airport runway. Forty of the 57 persons on board died.

June 12 – Near Omaha, Nebr. An Air Wisconsin plane en route from Minneapolis, Minn., to Lincoln, Nebr., crashed during a thunderstorm, killing 12 persons.

June 28 – Tyrrhenian Sea, off Italy. An Italian DC-9 jetliner crashed, apparently after an explosion. There were no survivors among the 81 persons aboard.

July 7 – Alma-Ata, Russia. A Soviet TU-154 airliner crashed on take-off, killing at least 163 persons.

Aug. 9 – Gulf of Mexico, off Louisiana. A helicopter evacuating offshore oil workers from a platform crashed in Hurricane Allen, killing 13 persons.

Aug. 19 – Riyadh, Saudi Arabia. A fire on board a Saudi Arabian Lockheed L-1011 jet just after takeoff engulfed the cabin, killing 301 persons.

Aug. 26 – Jakarta, Indonesia. An Indonesian Viscount turboprop airplane crashed, killing all 31 persons on board.

Sept. 14 – Near Medina, Saudi Arabia. A Saudi Hercules C-130 troop transport plane crashed, killing all 89 persons on board.

Nov. 13 – Near Cairo, Egypt. A U.S. Air Force C-141 transport plane crashed, killing all 13 persons on board.

Nov. 19 – Seoul, South Korea. A Korean Air Lines Boeing 747 crashed on approach to an airport, killing at least 13 persons.

Dec. 21 – Colombia. A Colombian jetliner crashed in a desert, killing all 68 persons on board.

Bus and Truck Crashes

April 7 – Near Culiacán, Mexico. A bus plunged off a bridge onto a riverbank, killing 46 persons.

June 5 – Near Jasper, Ark. A chartered bus crashed after veering off a steep mountain road, killing 20 Texas tourists and injuring 13.

June 7 – Near Durban, South Africa. At least 45 passengers died when their bus was hit by a speeding train.

June 7 – Near Orkney, South Africa. A truck crashed into a tractor-trailer, killing 17 persons.

June 15 – Java, Indonesia. A bus skidded off a road and caught fire; 21 persons died.

June 25 – Central India. A bus plunged into a flooded culvert, killing nearly 100 persons.

June 29 – Near Rawalpindi, Pakistan. About 90 persons were killed when a bus veered off a road and plunged into a canal.

Sept. 21 – Near Lahore, Pakistan. A bus fell into a canal, killing about 50 persons.

Nov. 1 – Near Cairo, Egypt. A collision involving a bus and two trucks killed at least 30 persons.

Earthquakes

Jan. 1 – Azores. An earthquake measuring 7.0 on the Richter scale hit these islands in the Atlantic Ocean, killing at least 52 persons and injuring about 300.

Oct. 10 – El Asnam, Algeria. Two earthquakes measuring 6.5 and 7.5 on the Richter scale killed about 3,000 persons and left 400,000 homeless.

Oct. 24 – Southern Mexico. At least 40 persons were killed in an earthquake registering 6.5 on the Richter scale.

Nov. 23 – Southern Italy. An earthquake measuring 6.8 on the Richter scale and followed by unusually strong shocks killed about 3,000 persons, left 250,000 homeless, and wreaked major destruction in Potenza, Naples, Salerno, and Pompeii.

Dec. 19 – Central Iran. Two earthquakes, measuring 5.7 and 5.9 on the Richter scale, killed 26 persons.

Explosions and Fires

Jan. 22 – China. An explosion and fire on a passenger train killed more than 20 persons, causing Chinese authorities to step up their campaign against carrying firecrackers and other combustible items on trains.

May 9 – Pakistan. A fire destroyed a small village, killing 18 persons and demolishing 50 homes.

May 20 – Kingston, Jamaica. At least 157 poor and elderly women died when fire destroyed a home for women.

July 7 – Bohai Bay, China. A Japanese news service reported that an explosion in an underwater oil rig had killed about 70 workers.

July 14 – Mississauga, Canada. A fire in a nursing home killed at least 21 persons, most of them patients in the wing for chronically ill.

July 26 – Bradley Beach, N.J. A fire in a boarding house killed 24 of the 37 residents, most of them elderly or mentally retarded.

Aug. 19 – Khuzistan Plain, Iran. About 90 persons were killed when an explosives plant blew up.

Oct. 23 – Ortuella, Spain. An explosion destroyed a school, killing at least 64 persons, most of them children.

Oct. 28 – Mecca, Saudi Arabia. A fire killed at least 20 persons in a lodging house for Muslim pilgrims.

Nov. 1 – Gorna Grupa, Poland. About 50 persons died when fire swept a mental hospital.

Nov. 16 – Bangkok, Thailand. An explosion in a munitions factory killed at least 60 persons and injured about 400.

Nov. 19 – Kawaji, Japan. At least 42 persons died when fire swept a resort hotel in northern Japan.

Nov. 21 – Las Vegas, Nev. A fire in the luxury MGM Grand Hotel killed 84 persons. Hundreds of others escaped to the roof, where they were picked up by helicopters.

Nov. 24 – Near Ankara, Turkey. At least 97 women died when a faulty light fixture exploded and started a fire at a crowded engagement party.

Dec. 4 – White Plains, N.Y. A fire in the Stouffer's Inn hotel killed at least 26 persons.

Floods

March 31 – Turkey. About 75 persons were killed in four days of flooding and mud slides in a fertile farming area.

April 21 – Peru. About 160 persons died in two weeks of flooding and mud slides in central Peru.

Sept. 1 – Arandas, Mexico. At least 24 persons died in a flood that started when a dam broke.

Sept. 9 – Northern India and Bangladesh. Flooding and mud slides caused by monsoon rains killed almost 1,500 persons in three months and caused extensive crop losses.

Sept. 25 – Caracas, Venezuela. Torrential rains caused floods and mud slides, killing 20 persons in a week.

Oct. 21 – Colombia. At least 40 persons were dead and 50 missing in one day of heavy rains and flooding in the north and west.

Hurricanes, Tornadoes, and Other Storms

Feb. 18 – California, Arizona, and Mexico. A storm that blew in from the Pacific Ocean killed at least 24 persons in six days. Many residents were evacuated from homes in the Los Angeles area, where damage was estimated at $20 million.

March 3 – Southern and Eastern United States. At least 36 persons died in a severe winter storm that blanketed much of the East. North Carolina, especially hard-hit with 13 deaths, and other Southern states were largely unprepared for the cold and snow.

March 27 – North Sea, off Norway. The floating oil-field platform *Alexander L. Keilland* capsized in a storm that featured winds up to 65 mph (105 kph), drowning 123 workers.

June – China. A severe storm killed 151 persons, injured 262, and caused extensive damage in Chekiang (Zhejiang) Province.

Aug. 5-12 – Central America and Southeastern United States. Hurricane Allen killed at least 273 persons on its sweep through Haiti, Louisiana, and Texas. Damage in Texas alone was estimated at $600 million.

Mine Disasters

March 27 – Orkney, South Africa. Thirty-one miners were killed in the world's largest gold mine when an elevator cable broke, plunging them about 1.2 miles (2 kilometers) to their deaths.

Oct. 1 – Near Johannesburg, South Africa. Fourteen miners died in an elevator accident in a gold mine.

Shipwrecks

Jan. 28 – Tampa Bay, Gulf of Mexico. The oil tanker *Texas Capricorn* and the U.S. Coast Guard buoy tender *Blackthorn* collided, sinking the *Blackthorn* and drowning 23 of its crew members.

April 20 – Bangladesh. At least 230 persons drowned when a ferryboat designed to carry 60 passengers, but carrying about 300, capsized in the Padma River.

April 22 – Tablas Strait, Philippines. The Philippine oil tanker *Tacloban City* rammed the passenger ship *Don Juan*, which sank; 116 persons died.

Aug. 24 – Off Carmen, Mexico. A ferryboat sank in the Gulf of Mexico, killing at least 50 persons.

Sept. 8 – Nepal. A boat capsized on the Narayani River, drowning 86 persons.

Oct. 23 – Andhra Pradesh state, India. A boat sank, killing about 100 of the farm workers on board.

Train Wrecks

June 2 – Near Borlänge, Sweden. Two trains collided head-on, killing at least 12 persons and injuring 50.

July 15 – Spain. An express train en route from Madrid to Barcelona jumped the track, killing 16 persons and injuring at least 60.

Aug. 1 – County Cork, Ireland. An express passenger train derailed, and 18 persons were killed.

Aug. 19 – Poland. The head-on collision of a freight train and a passenger train killed at least 69 persons.

Other Disasters

Jan. 7 – Java, Indonesia. Eighteen persons died of food poisoning and 95 others were hospitalized after eating pollution-tainted soybean cakes.

Jan. 16 – Bihar state, India. A cold wave killed at least 79 persons who lacked sufficient food and clothing to cope with temperatures of about 32°F. (0°C).

Entire villages were destroyed in the earthquake that devastated southern Italy on November 23; about 3,000 persons died.

Jan. 21 – Sincelejo, Colombia. Bleachers collapsed at a bullfight, killing 222 persons and injuring an estimated 500 others.

April 29 – Northern India. At least 50 persons perished in a heat wave lasting two weeks – as the temperature reached 112°F. (44°C).

May 9 – Tampa Bay, Florida. The freighter *Summit Venture* rammed the Sunshine Skyway Bridge, causing a section of the bridge to collapse. At least 35 persons died after a bus, a truck, and several automobiles plunged into the water.

May 18 – Mount Saint Helens, Washington. At least 34 persons died when the Mount Saint Helens volcano erupted.

May 30 – Near Bombay, India. A four-story apartment building collapsed, killing at least 29 persons.

June-August – Southwestern and Midwestern Plains States. A prolonged heat wave, with temperatures regularly exceeding 100°F. (38°C), killed about 1,265 persons and caused losses of nearly $20 billion. Missouri was hit hardest, with more than 300 deaths.

June 25 – Himalaya, India. A landslide swept away a small village, killing at least 50 persons.

July 6 – China. Officials reported a recent accident in which an oil-drilling rig collapsed off Tientsin (Tianjin), killing about 70 persons.

Aug. 9 – Nepal. About 45 persons died from eating poisonous wild mushrooms and berries during a food shortage.

Aug. 14 – Mount Fuji, Japan. A rockslide on Japan's highest peak killed 12 mountain climbers and injured at least 30 others.

Oct. 2 – Persian Gulf, off Saudi Arabia. A blowout in a United States-owned oil rig released toxic gas that killed 19 workers.   Patricia Dragisic

DJIBOUTI. See AFRICA.

DOE, SAMUEL KANYON (1952-   ), became head of the government of Liberia on April 12, 1980, after reportedly assassinating President William R. Tolbert, Jr., during a military coup d'état. Doe proclaimed himself chairman of the People's Redemption Council, a 15-member unit of military men that he installed as the supreme governing body of Liberia. See LIBERIA.

Doe was born on May 6, 1952, in Tuzon in southern Liberia, the son of a teacher. He dropped out of school in the 11th grade and enlisted in the Liberian National Guard, where he gained a reputation as a skilled sharpshooter and an expert in hand-to-hand combat. He rose to the rank of master sergeant and was selected for special training in a program conducted by a United States Special Forces team.

Like many of his fellow Krahn tribesmen, Doe resented the economic and political advantages that Americo-Liberians, descendants of the freed American slaves who founded the nation in 1847, kept for themselves. Doe condemned the Tolbert government's failure to respond to the needs of the poor, and promised his countrymen "a new society in which there is human justice, dignity, and fair treatment for all."

Doe is married and has two children. For recreation, he prefers such solitary sports as swimming and running.   Beverly Merz

DOG. A Siberian husky, Ch. Innisfree's Sierra Cinnar, owned by Kathleen Kanzler of Accokeek, Md., was selected best-in-show at the Westminster Kennel Club show in New York City on Feb. 12, 1980. It was the first time a husky had taken top honors. The judge of the event, E. Irving Eldredge of Middleburg, Va., disregarded the fact that Cinnar was missing the tip of an ear, which had been bitten off in a fight with a kennel mate in 1978. The show drew 2,769 entries.

According to figures released in March, more poodles were registered with the American Kennel Club (AKC) in 1979 than any other breed. Poodles have led in AKC registrations since 1960. Following them were Doberman pinschers, cocker spaniels, German shepherds, Labrador retrievers, golden retrievers, beagles, dachshunds, miniature schnauzers, and Shetland sheepdogs.

Canine *parvovirus*, a serious intestinal disease, killed thousands of dogs in 1980. A vaccine was available to combat the virus, but demand for it far exceeded the supply.   Theodore M. O'Leary

In the Special Reports section, see WHAT IS YOUR PET TRYING TO TELL YOU? In WORLD BOOK, see DOG.

DOMINICAN REPUBLIC. See LATIN AMERICA.

DRAMA. See THEATER.

DROUGHT. See WATER; WEATHER.

Rats, a decorated and twice-wounded member of the 1st Battalion Welsh Guards, stands in line as he is retired from military service on April 9.

DRUGS. The East Coast of the United States saw a massive increase in heroin use and heroin-caused deaths in 1980, according to Manhattan District Attorney Robert M. Morgenthau, Jr. Morgenthau said on September 22 that heroin was being smuggled into New York City and several other Eastern cities primarily from Iran, Pakistan, Afghanistan, and Turkey, rather than from Mexico as before. The drugs came through European cities.

West Germany was the source of Quaaludes, addictive nonbarbiturate sedatives, which were flooding into East Coast cities in ever-increasing numbers in 1980. Congressman Lester L. Wolff (D., N.Y.), chairman of the House Select Committee on Narcotics, told a Senate hearing that by midyear, officials in Miami, Fla., had seized 10 million Quaalude tablets and enough methaqualone to make another 10.5 million.

Julius B. Richmond, surgeon general of the United States, announced on September 30 that physicians specializing in the treatment of cancer may apply for licenses to prescribe synthetic marijuana pills to cancer patients to relieve the nausea and vomiting caused by chemotherapy. When marijuana was found to relieve nausea, synthetic preparations were made for medical use.

Tranquilizers. J. Richard Crout, director of the Bureau of Drugs at the Food and Drug Administration (FDA), in September reported a sharp drop in the number of tranquilizers, sedatives, painkillers, and other psychoactive drugs prescribed by U.S. physicians. He cited figures compiled by the National Prescription Audit showing that legally filled tranquilizer prescriptions dropped from 88.3 million in 1975 to 62.3 million in 1979. The greatest decrease was recorded in the prescription of Valium, the most widely used tranquilizer. Several major drug manufacturers announced in July they had agreed with the FDA to warn physicians that tranquilizers should not be prescribed for "the stress of everyday life."

New Drugs. Five major arthritic diseases, including osteoarthritis, may be relieved by sulindac, a drug approved by the FDA that has fewer side effects than aspirin. Sulindac apparently reduces the chance of stomach upsets and ulcers because it does not become effective until after it is absorbed by the digestive system. The nonsteroidal, anti-inflammatory drug is available by prescription.

The drug sulfinpyrasone lowered the incidence of sudden death among heart attack victims by 74 per cent in the first seven months following coronaries, according to an international study reported in January. The study, sponsored by the Ciba-Geigy Corporation of Summit, N.J., which markets the product, involved 1,558 patients in the United States and Canada.

Controversial Drugs. The Supreme Court of the United States ruled in October that terminal cancer patients do not have a constitutional right to use Laetrile, an apricot-pit derivative. Dimethyl sulfoxide (DMSO), a chemical legally available as a veterinary drug but not as a human drug, was being applied externally by thousands of persons to treat pain not relieved by legal drugs. The U.S. Department of Justice began investigating FDA testing of DMSO after televised reports bared a controversy over possible DMSO benefits.

Other Developments. Daughters of women who took diethylstilbestrol (DES) during pregnancy received more bad news in 1980. Three separate medical studies confirmed that DES daughters who became pregnant faced an increased risk of miscarrying or delivering a premature infant. Research in the 1970s had shown that DES daughters developed cancers because their mothers had taken the drug.

President Jimmy Carter in June signed into law a bill blocking any government ban of the artificial sweetener saccharin until after June 30, 1981. Studies by the American Health Foundation, Harvard University, and the National Cancer Institute showed no evidence of a link between saccharin use and human cancers.   Mary E. Jessup

In the Special Reports section, see CAN AN ASPIRIN A DAY HELP KEEP THE DOCTOR AWAY? In WORLD BOOK, see DRUG.

EARTHQUAKE. See DISASTERS.

EASTERN ORTHODOX CHURCHES. The first meeting of a newly formed international Roman Catholic-Eastern Orthodox Theological Commission began in May 1980 on the Greek islands of Patmos and Rhodes. Orthodox commission members stated that the discussions revealed deep and persistent disagreements between the two groups. The commission was appointed after Pope John Paul II's meeting with Ecumenical Patriarch Demetrius in Turkey in November 1979.

The Ecumenical Patriarch Demetrius in February invited the five so-called Non-Chalcedonian or Monophysite churches — the Coptic Church of Egypt, the Armenian Church, the Syrian Jacobite Church, the Malabar Church in India, and the Ethiopian Church — to form a joint commission for dialogue with Orthodoxy. At year-end, preparations for such a dialogue were still going on.

Russian Arrests. The Soviet government took decisive steps to eliminate religious dissent. Leaders of the Christian Committee for the Defense of Believers' Rights, including Lev Regelson, Gleb Yakunin, and Victor Kapitanchuk, were arrested in January, as were leaders and members of the Christian Seminar on Problems of Religious Renaissance. Regelson and Kapitanchuk pleaded guilty and escaped prison terms. Yakunin, a Russian Orthodox priest and an active dissenter since the 1960s, was the only member of the group not to

Russian Orthodox clergy and lay people demonstrate in New York City to protest the arrest of their co-believers in Russia.

plead guilty. The 46-year-old co-founder of the Christian Committee declared in court that his activities were "my religious duty as a priest." He was convicted of "anti-Soviet activities" in August and sentenced to five years in prison and five additional years of internal exile.

The arrest of Dimitri Dudko, a Russian Orthodox priest, was also reported in January. His books denouncing Russian persecution of Orthodoxy are well known, and he has served eight years in Russian labor camps for dissent. His arrest provoked protests and demonstrations in several Western countries. Dudko recanted his "anti-Soviet activities" in a nationally televised speech on June 20 and was released from jail the next day. This recantation was considered a decisive blow to the circle of outspoken religious dissenters.

American Anniversary. The Orthodox Church in America, at its sixth All-American Council in Detroit in November, marked the 10th anniversary of its *autocephaly* — the administrative independence granted by the Moscow Patriarchate in April 1970. By an amendment to church statutes, the council abolished the statute that prevented women from being elected delegates or alternates to the All-American Council, the highest governing body of the church.   Alexander Schmemann

See also RELIGION. In WORLD BOOK, see EASTERN ORTHODOX CHURCHES.

ECONOMICS. The United States economy finally experienced the recession in 1980 that economists had expected for nearly a year. The slump was unexpectedly sharp and surprisingly brief, if indicators late in the year were to be believed.

The U.S. gross national product (GNP) – the total of all the goods and services the economy produces – showed a slight gain during the first quarter of 1980 and a decline of almost 10 per cent in the second quarter, both computed as an annual rate adjusted for inflation. However, recovery apparently began during the third quarter, which showed a 1 per cent increase in the GNP that continued into the fourth quarter. The total GNP expressed in current dollars was approximately $2.53 trillion, compared with $2.37 trillion in 1979. When these figures were adjusted for inflation, using 1972 dollars as the standard, the actual output declined from $1.43 trillion in 1979 to less than $1.40 trillion in 1980.

The Unemployment Rate was high, but the total number of persons employed in the United States was only slightly lower than it had been during 1979. Although the rate of unemployment at the end of 1980 was about 8 per cent, which meant that about 8 million persons were out of work, these figures concealed different effects on particular segments of the population.

The civilian labor force is measured by those persons actively employed, those who have lost jobs, and those who are actively seeking employment but who may or may not have ever had a job. In addition, there is a fourth group, called "discouraged workers," who are not seeking a job because they think they cannot find one and who are included neither in the labor force nor among the unemployed. Although the Department of Labor sets this figure at about 5 million, only about 700,000 of these persons state as their reason for not seeking work that there are no jobs available. School attendance, poor health, and miscellaneous other reasons keep the remainder out of the job market. Therefore, economic conditions would appear to be only a minor source of "discouraged workers." Even if these persons were counted as unemployed, the unemployment rate would increase by less than 0.7 per cent.

These data, however, also conceal much that is important to know. The unemployment rate among all teen-agers was nearly 19 per cent in late 1980, but it was more than 40 per cent among black teen-agers. This statistic goes far to explain the growing unrest in many large cities in the United States. Another important fact is the duration of unemployment. Although the average was about 13 weeks at the end of 1980, almost one-third

With Japanese and other imports capturing about one-fourth of the market, U.S. automakers introduced new compact, fuel-efficient models.

of all unemployed persons had been out of work for 15 weeks or more; another one-third had been idle for less than five weeks; and the remaining one-third, from five to 14 weeks. Almost 1 million workers had experienced 27 or more weeks of unemployment.

The data make it clear that a most important task facing the United States is to provide jobs for teen-agers, especially blacks and Hispanics, and for the long-term unemployed. For the teen-agers, the task is primarily to open up opportunities for a first job. But for the long-term unemployed, the task may be to train them to do a different job than they have previously done.

The Inflation Problem was the major one facing the United States. The most commonly cited measure, the Consumer Price Index (CPI), showed an increase at the end of the year of about 13 per cent above December 1979 levels. The more broadly based index known as the GNP deflator rose slightly less, but still at the alarming rate of about 10 per cent. With consumer prices rising rapidly, wage earners found themselves unable to maintain their real purchasing power in spite of healthy wage increases, which averaged about 9.5 per cent in 1980. They suffered nearly a 4 per cent decline in purchasing power even before considering the effect of income taxes, which took deeper and deeper bites out of gross income as families rose into higher tax brackets.

During the election campaign, both President Jimmy Carter and Republican Ronald Reagan identified inflation as the number-one U.S. problem. There is little doubt that the Carter Administration's failure to bring inflation under control was a major cause contributing to his defeat in November. However, most economists doubt that rising prices can be brought under control quickly. The problem is complicated by the fact that, as a candidate, Reagan promised tax cuts when he took office, as well as increases in defense expenditures. This combination would seem to promise a budget deficit in the neighborhood of $40 billion to $60 billion even if nondefense items in the federal budget can be reduced substantially.

There is a minority school of thought headed by Arthur Laffer, professor of business economics at the University of Southern California in Los Angeles, which argues that a tax cut may actually produce more revenues than are apparently lost because of it. Proponents of this view maintain that a certain rate of tax exists that will produce the maximum amount of revenue. If rates rise above this level, then revenues will decline as people work less hard, and a smaller tax base results. Thus, if taxes today have already exceeded the level at which this phenomenon occurs, a tax cut might so increase the tax base, by stimulating productivity, as to produce even more revenues than the existing

tax does. Whatever the validity of this argument — and it has not been proved — even its proponents admit that the effect of the tax cut on increasing productivity may take time to become evident. In any short period, such as a year, government revenues might well be reduced.

A slightly different form of the Laffer argument suggests that reducing corporate income tax rates and substantially increasing depreciation allowances would increase the after-tax return on new investment enough to encourage increased productivity. Such increased productivity would serve to increase the tax base and would also help to control inflation, which has been aggravated by slow productivity gains of less than 1 per cent for the past two or three years. Of course, these increases would not be evident immediately.

Fluctuating Interest. The Federal Reserve Board announced in October 1979 that in the future it would try to control the money supply by controlling the monetary base, and would pay less attention to maintaining stable interest rates. The board warned that this new policy might lead to much greater fluctuations in interest rates than had been permitted, and proof was not long in coming. From a level of about 13.5 per cent at the time of the announcement, the *prime rate* — the rate at which banks lend to their most creditworthy corporate customers — rose to an unprecedented 20 per cent on April 18, 1980. It then dropped sharply as the money supply expanded, but began to rise again in August. On December 20, it rose to a new peak of 21.5 per cent.

Monetary analysts feared that the renewed rise in interest rates would choke off the recovery that seemed to start in the third quarter. The automobile and housing industries are particularly sensitive to the pressures applied by interest rates. Almost all house purchasers and most car buyers borrow money to finance their purchases, and the higher interest rates rise, the larger their monthly payments become. Large increases place such purchases beyond the capacity of many buyers, and a decline in production results. For example, new housing starts in May dropped to an annual rate of less than 1 million, about 65 per cent lower than in 1979 and the lowest in five years.

Similarly threatened is the automotive industry, which produced and sold about 25 per cent fewer cars in 1980 than in 1979, itself a substandard year. Near the close of 1980, more than 180,000 workers were on indefinite layoff in the auto industry, and temporary closings to adjust inventories to less-than-robust sales of new models were announced almost every week. The automobile industry was also plagued by the steadily increasing gasoline prices. Fewer drivers were willing to buy the gas-guzzling larger models that were Detroit's major output for so many years. See AUTOMOBILE.

Selected Key U.S. Economic Indicators

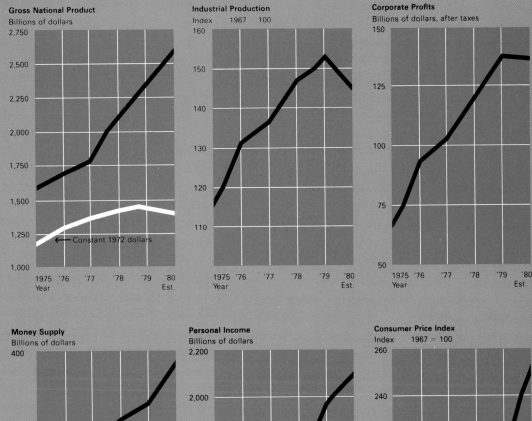

Gross National Product
Billions of dollars

← Constant 1972 dollars

1975 '76 '77 '78 '79 '80
Year   Est.

Industrial Production
Index   1967   100

1975 '76 '77 '78 '79 '80
Year   Est.

Corporate Profits
Billions of dollars, after taxes

1975 '76 '77 '78 '79 '80
Year   Est.

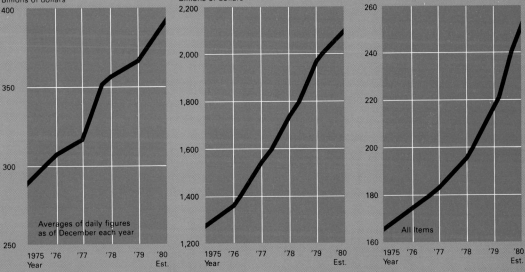

Money Supply
Billions of dollars

Averages of daily figures
as of December each year

1975 '76 '77 '78 '79 '80
Year   Est.

Personal Income
Billions of dollars

1975 '76 '77 '78 '79 '80
Year   Est.

Consumer Price Index
Index   1967 = 100

All Items

1975 '76 '77 '78 '79 '80
Year   Est.

The most comprehensive measure of the nation's total output of goods and services is the *Gross National Product* (GNP). The GNP represents the dollar value in current prices of all goods and services plus the estimated value of certain imputed outputs, such as the rental value of owner-occupied dwellings. *Industrial Production* is a monthly measure of the physical output of manufacturing, mining, and utility industries. *Corporate Profits* are quarterly profit samplings from major industries.

Money Supply measures the total amount of money in the economy in coin, currency, and demand deposits. *Personal Income* is current income received by persons (including nonprofit institutions and private trust funds) before personal taxes. *Consumer Price Index* (CPI) is a monthly measure of changes in the prices of goods and services consumed by urban families and individuals. CPI includes selected goods and services. All 1980 figures are *Year Book* estimates.

Profits and Income. Not surprisingly, corporate profits were down by about 10 per cent on both before-tax and after-tax bases. In light of this fact, it was surprising that spending for plants and equipment rose by about 10 per cent. Farmers also felt the impact of inflation as they saw their costs rise faster than agricultural prices. As a result, net income from farm operations was down by 25 per cent (see FARM AND FARMING).

Stock market prices did not reflect the economy's decrease in profitability, however. The Dow Jones industrial average stood at 963.99 at the end of 1980 – almost a 15 per cent increase over the 1979 year-end figure of 838.74. Money market followers confidently predicted that the Dow would go to record highs in 1981, perhaps even to 1,500, but more cautious analysts warned that until profit expectations improved and the rate of inflation was reduced, markedly higher stock prices would be difficult to sustain. See STOCKS AND BONDS.

Total personal income continued to rise, however, thanks largely to substantially increased transfer payments. These were mainly social insurance benefits and other government payments that reflect cost-of-living increases, along with greatly increased personal-interest income stemming from the high interest rates available to consumers on a variety of investment instruments.

The gap between government revenues and expenditures widened substantially during the year. The increase in the deficit was not unexpected because revenues were lower than they would have been had the economy been operating at its full capacity, and expenditures were higher because of the increased transfer payments, which were a result both of the recession and of the adjustment of these payments to increases in the cost of living. It was apparent, however, that the federal budget was, as many have claimed, "out of control," inasmuch as purchases of goods and services increased by an alarming 18 per cent – far above the rate of inflation. Although budget deficits may not be the primary cause of inflation, they do add fuel to the flames.

International Inflation was also apparent. Among the industrialized countries, only Japan and West Germany managed to keep the rise in consumer prices under 10 per cent. In Great Britain, the rate approached 20 per cent and threatened to go even higher. At the same time, the British were suffering from the most severe unemployment in almost 50 years. Industrial output showed substantial gains only in Japan, where the rate of growth was about 11 per cent. France, West Germany, and Italy all managed to show slight gains.

The Communist Countries showed some of the most interesting developments. Russia experienced another bad crop year, and President Carter imposed a grain embargo after Soviet troops invaded Afghanistan in December 1979. The grain embargo had no apparent immediate impact, but by the end of 1980 the threat of reduced 1981 meat supplies in Russia was clear. Russia's persistent failure to increase agricultural productivity is the most extreme example of its failure to meet economic targets. Continued heavy military spending, which amounts to about 10 per cent of total output – almost double the percentage in the United States – unquestionably contributed to the failure to meet planned targets. However, it would appear that the inefficiencies in the Soviet economy are as much the result of socialism as of anything else. For example, most economists agree that the heavy losses of nationalized industries in Great Britain, which has a partially socialist economy, and their consequent demands for greater government support, contribute to inflation.

The most interesting development within the Soviet sphere was the formation of a free labor union in Poland, demanded by strikers in the heavily industrialized city of Gdańsk. The government yielded to their demands, and in late November the proportion of Polish workers enrolled in the new Solidarity movement was estimated to be higher than union membership anywhere else in the world. Westerners watched with considerable interest and concern at year-end to see how Russia

Federal Reserve Chairman Paul A. Volcker, third from left, meets with congressional leaders to discuss proposed cuts in the federal budget.

would react to this distinct rebuff to the inefficiencies of Communist government.

In China, it appeared that government constraints on industrial and agricultural production had distinctly been loosened. The trial of the "Gang of Four" and six associates and other events indicated that Chinese leaders were preparing to make changes in the country's economic policy.

World Prospects for 1981 were uncertain. It seemed almost a foregone conclusion that food and oil prices would rise. The Organization of Petroleum Exporting Countries raised crude oil prices by 10 per cent on December 16, to as high as $41 per barrel. Meat production in the United States would be hard put to keep up with rising demand, and agricultural experts predicted that food prices would rise by 10 to 15 per cent in 1981. Meanwhile, the rest of the industrial world, except Japan, seemed to be headed for at least a mild recession, though Great Britain hoped for some improvement in its situation. Whether an arms race, which would vastly complicate the worldwide economic outlook, could be avoided, was another major uncertainty. Warren W. Shearer

See also INTERNATIONAL TRADE AND FINANCE and individual country articles. In the Special Reports section, see THE INFLATION RATE, THE COST OF LIVING . . . AND YOU. In WORLD BOOK, see ECONOMICS; GROSS NATIONAL PRODUCT.

ECUADOR. President Jaime Roldos Aguilera threatened to resign in April 1980 because of the personal feud that had developed between himself and Assad Bucaram, the leader of Congress. Ironically, Bucaram had been Roldos' political mentor.

Between his inauguration on Aug. 10, 1979, and April 11, 1980, Roldos vetoed 48 of 70 bills sent to him by the Bucaram-dominated Congress, which took little or no action on the president's own legislative program. To resolve the impasse, Roldos had proposed a legislative reform that, among other things, would have empowered the president to dissolve the 69-seat legislature once in his five-year term and call new legislative elections within 60 days. When his plan was defeated by Congress on April 10, Roldos announced that he would call a plebiscite on constitutional reform.

Support for Roldos. However, the president reconsidered on May 19 and canceled plans for the plebiscite In the interval, congressmen had heard from their constituents, and a majority of the legislators signed a petition promising to support his administration. It was only in mid-1980 that Roldos was able to move on his own program. A key element in it was an economic offensive aimed at using a substantial portion of the nation's oil earnings to modernize agriculture and build a network of roads and communications to expand the nation's industrial base.

Roldos' five-year plan called for the investment of $800 million in rural development. Some 3 million acres (1.2 million hectares) of coastal, highland, and Amazonian farmland would be brought into production within 17 target areas. The Agrarian Reform Institute hoped to distribute nearly 2 million acres (800,000 hectares) to land-hungry Ecuadoreans by 1984.

Other Programs. To make his administration popular, President Roldos has insisted on keeping interest rates low on development loans by subsidizing interest rates with government funds. A 40-hour work week was scheduled to go into effect in October. The government's literacy program had reportedly reached about 200,000 Spanish-speaking Ecuadoreans and 20,000 Quechua-speaking Indians, who are now literate in their own language. Low-cost housing projects in the squalid slums of such major cities as Quito and Guayaquil have proved welcome.

The nation's state-run oil corporation took a prominent part in pushing for the opening of new oil fields, particularly in the northeast. Their output could be tied directly into the trans-Ecuador pipeline that moves oil from the lowland Amazonian region over the Andes to tankers docking at west coast ports. Nathan A. Haverstock

See also LATIN AMERICA (Facts in Brief Table). In WORLD BOOK, see ECUADOR.

EDUCATION. The Department of Education (DOE), approved by the Congress of the United States in September 1979, began operations on May 4, 1980, with Shirley M. Hufstedler, a former federal judge, as the first secretary of education. The new department had a staff of 17,000 and an initial budget of $14 billion.

The nation's organized teaching profession entered fully into a presidential campaign for the first time in 1980. The National Education Association (NEA), with a membership of 1.8 million, campaigned actively for President Jimmy Carter, who made good on his 1976 promise to create a separate Department of Education, one of NEA's top demands. The rival 500,000-member American Federation of Teachers (AFT) strongly endorsed Senator Edward M. Kennedy (D., Mass.), Carter's opponent in the Democratic primaries. Following Carter's nomination, however, the AFT joined the NEA in supporting Carter's unsuccessful re-election bid.

Total Enrollment in U.S. schools and colleges declined for the eighth consecutive year in 1980. The National Center for Education Statistics reported that an estimated 57.8 million persons were expected to enroll in formal educational programs from kindergarten through graduate school in the 1980-1981 academic year. This was a decline of nearly 1.3 per cent from the previous year, when enrollments stood at 58.4 million. Nevertheless, the number of Americans engaged directly in education, as teachers or students, remained at 61.4 million, representing nearly 3 out of every 10 persons in the United States.

Elementary grades enrolled 31.2 million children, and of those, 27.4 million were in public schools. This was a decline of 1.4 per cent, continuing a downward trend that began in 1970. For the first time in many years, enrollment in nonpublic schools showed a slight increase – about 30,000.

High schools were expected to enroll 14.9 million students, down 2.8 per cent from 1979's 15.3 million. Further declines are expected throughout the 1980s. The number of students enrolled in public high schools in 1980 was expected to be 13.3 million.

An increase of 1 per cent, from 11.6 million in 1979 to 11.7 million in 1980, was expected to bring the enrollment in institutions of higher learning to another record high. However, all signs indicate that college enrollments are near their peak, with a decrease expected after 1981 (see Close-Up). Public institutions accounted for 9.1 million of the total, up from about 9 million in 1979. Enrollment in private institutions increased by only 17,000 to 2.6 million.

The Graduates. High school graduates had totaled 3.1 million annually for five years, and the graduating class of 1981 was also expected to exceed 3 million. Colleges and universities were expected to award 952,000 bachelor's degrees, 316,000 master's, 33,000 doctorates, and 70,000 first professional degrees in 1980-1981. The figures for bachelor's and first professionals were near the all-time highs, while the master's and doctor's degrees were down slightly from peaks reached in 1977 and 1973, respectively.

The Bureau of the Census reported that there were approximately 110 million high school graduates in the United States in 1980. Nearly 24 million of these had also completed four or more years of college. The median number of school years completed by persons 25 years and over was 12.5, compared with nine years in 1949. The number of adults with less than five years of schooling decreased about 54 per cent in the last 30 years, from 9.446 million to 4.324 million.

School Desegregation. Public school busing to integrate schools in St. Louis began peacefully in September. The program, involving some 16,000 students, ended an eight-year court battle. In Chicago, a federal judge approved an agreement to desegregate city schools before the 1981-1982 school year. The agreement, which resolved a civil law suit filed by the U.S. Department of Justice, did not specify how the Chicago system, which is 80 per cent black, Hispanic, and other minority groups, could achieve integration.

The Teachers. An estimated 2.5 million elementary- and secondary-school teachers were involved in classroom instruction, and 300,000 worked as superintendents, principals, supervisors, and other staff members. In addition, there were 830,000 college-level teachers.

As the 1980-1981 school year got underway, there were 119 strikes, down from the previous year, which had a record 242. Many of the stoppages hit Michigan (27) and Illinois (21). Some strikes also affected colleges.

Union Setback. The Supreme Court of the United States ruled on February 20 that faculty members at private universities are "managerial" employees and that federal labor laws do not protect their efforts to unionize. The decision, which referred specifically to the refusal of Yeshiva University in New York City to bargain with a faculty union, was seen as a major setback to union efforts in all private institutions of higher education. It does not affect teacher unions at public colleges and universities.

The American Association of University Professors reported that average faculty salaries increased by 7.1 per cent, the largest rise in the past decade. But professors still suffered a loss in purchasing power in the same period – a result of double-digit inflation. Average salary for full-time faculty of all ranks at all types of institutions was $21,620.

Education Expenditures at all levels for the 1980-1981 school year were estimated by DOE at $181-billion, 9 per cent over the outlay of $166 billion in 1979-1980. Most of the increase was due to inflation. Higher education was to receive $65 billion, with the elementary and secondary schools' total set at about $116 billion. Of the total expenditures, about $34 billion was slated for private schools, colleges, and universities, an increase of $5 billion.

Federal government funds continued to grow at all levels. Federal grants for educational purposes, including grants to individuals, increased nearly threefold over the past 10 years, from $8.7 billion to $24.4 billion. State governments contributed about 36 per cent; local governments, 28 per cent; the federal government, 12 per cent; and nongovernmental sources, about 24 per cent. Total expenditures for education from all sources amounted to about 7 per cent of the gross national product, a decline of about 1 per cent.

Student Achievement continued to cause concern. A report prepared by the DOE and the National Science Foundation warned in October that most Americans are headed "toward virtual scientific and technological illiteracy" because of a decline in elementary and secondary science and mathematics programs. The study called for new federal support for science education, particularly for students not majoring in science.

The Coming Campus Crunch

For college and university students in the United States, the next 20 years could be a golden age. For their teachers, however, the future looks grim. The years remaining in this century will present problems and opportunities that will radically change the educational environment in the United States.

These conclusions are drawn from a far-reaching 1980 report, "Three Thousand Futures: The Next 20 Years for Higher Education." The report, by the Carnegie Council on Policy Studies in Higher Education, assesses the coming changes.

The basic problem is one of numbers. Total enrollment in U.S. schools and colleges has been declining. So the U.S. educational system — expanded over the past 35 years to take care of millions of veterans of World War II and the Korean War and then their children, the "baby boom" that came to college in the late 1960s and early 1970s — must now sell itself to a shrinking pool of prospective students.

The resulting increased competition for students will put them in a "seller's market." The report predicts that students will "be recruited more actively, admitted more readily, retained more assiduously, counseled more attentively . . . financed more adequately, taught more conscientiously. . . . They will seldom, if ever, have had it so good."

As the student population declines, its makeup will change. By the year 2000, the council predicts, more than half of those attending colleges and universities will be women, and one-fourth will be members of minority groups. Nearly half will be part-time students.

United States colleges and universities will encounter this challenging new world burdened with the fixed or rising costs of large physical plants and faculty members who are protected from ouster by tenure.

Inevitably, the shrinking national student body will force some colleges and universities to close. Those most vulnerable are less prestigious liberal arts colleges and private junior colleges. The big universities with substantial research programs, the most-respected liberal arts colleges, and public junior colleges will best be able to survive the academic shakeout. The council cautions against too much government interference in this weeding-out process. Curriculum changes and the mergers and closings of schools are best left to market-place choices by students.

Teachers stand to lose the most in the next two decades. Their salaries will probably fail to keep up with inflation, some positions will be eliminated, and competition for jobs will be fierce. Compounding the problem is the large number of relatively young teachers already protected by tenure on U.S. faculties. In a static market, these jobs can open up only through faculty deaths, retirements, or transfers.

A far-reaching side effect of this faculty logjam is the potential harm to research as new minds and ideas are locked out of the academic world. To ease this, the council suggests that the federal government absorb "all, or part, of the cost of some existing tenured positions," enabling institutions to hire new teachers.

Since the late 1950s, the federal government has assumed an increasing role in higher education through research grants, student loans, and educational policy. In the future, perhaps state governments should take more responsibility, because the negative effects of a declining student population will vary from region to region. The council proposes that current state per-capita financial contributions to higher education be maintained, despite the drop in the student population, and that the percentage of federal research and development funds allocated to colleges and universities — from 12 to 13 per cent — should also remain unchanged.

United States higher education, according to the council's report, "offers access to more of the population and finds talent more adequately than in any other nation, and it offers students more range of choice." With good sense and good will, this dynamic and varied system — both public and private — has the capacity to improve itself even as enrollment declines.   Edward G. Nash

Classroom

Secretary of Education Hufstedler unveils a sign in Washington, D.C., to inaugurate the new Cabinet-level Department of Education.

The College Entrance Examination Board in October reported another decline in Scholastic Aptitude Test (SAT) scores. From 1979 to 1980, scores declined one point on the mathematics section and three points on the verbal section. A perfect score on the tests is 800. Average scores on the two-part, standardized test fell from 502 to 466 in mathematics and from 478 to 424 in verbal skills between 1962 and 1980.

The tests themselves came under twofold attack. The California legislature, following New York's lead, enacted a "truth-in-testing" law that would require annual publication of the test questions and permit students to see their scored answers. Similar bills were introduced in 20 other states, and hearings concerning the matter were held in Congress. The board that administers the tests announced it will voluntarily allow students to see their answer sheets, but will not publish the questions. This policy is intended to deal with the issue of wrong scoring without exposing the tests to public scrutiny, which would require a costly annual production of entirely new questions, according to the board.

The other attack on testing came in January from consumer advocate Ralph Nader and his associates in a critical report on the nation's largest testing organization, the Educational Testing Service, which compiles the SAT tests. The 550-page report, "The Reign of ETS: The Corporation That Makes Up Minds," charged that the tests do not accurately predict success in college and that they favor the children of affluent parents. The test makers rejected both charges, claiming that the tests make college admission criteria more objective and give colleges a better comparative yardstick by which to judge the standards of some 20,000 high schools.

Minimum Competency tests to determine high school students' capacity in the basic skills of reading, writing, and mathematics have been introduced in 36 states. They have been opposed by the NEA but supported by the AFT. The most serious question raised by opponents is whether it is fair to administer the tests in the students' junior or senior year in high school, leaving too little time for them to correct their deficiencies.

Public Attitudes toward the schools, which for many years had been highly critical, improved for the first time in 10 years. The percentage of respondents who gave the schools an A rating had slipped steadily from 18 per cent in 1974 to 8 per cent in 1979, but climbed to 10 per cent in 1980, according to a study by the Gallup Poll and the Charles F. Kettering Foundation. The poll also indicated that schools rank second only to churches on the list of U.S. institutions in which people have a "great deal" of confidence. Of those polled, 28 per cent put schools ahead of courts and local government, with 19 per cent; state government, 17 per cent; federal government, 14 per cent; and big business, 13 per cent.

Higher Education's Cost continued to increase. The average tuition at private, four-year colleges went up 10.1 per cent in 1980-1981 to $3,279. The average hike at public institutions was $706, an increase of 4.4 per cent. Average total costs, including board, supplies, and other expenses were $6,082 at private colleges and $3,409 at public institutions.

Gifts to higher education set a record, with a 1979 total of $3.2 billion, an increase of 6.3 per cent. Gifts from alumni stood at $785 million, and foundations contributed $701 million. Most of the remainder was given by corporations.

Television was used increasingly as a means of instruction. More than 60 per cent of all colleges and universities used television for credit or noncredit courses. The National University Consortium of 11 colleges and public TV stations began offering undergraduate degrees via television.

The U.S. Congress approved a $48.4-million higher-education bill in September that included extensive direct aid and loans for college students. Interest rates for guaranteed student loans were raised from 7 to 9 per cent, starting with loans for the 1981-1982 school year.   Fred M. Hechinger

In WORLD BOOK, see EDUCATION.

EGYPT. The normalization of relations with Israel continued in 1980 with the opening of their common border in January and the establishment of formal diplomatic relations in February. Egypt's first ambassador to Israel took up his post in February. In October, President Yitzhak Navon became the first Israeli head of state to pay an official visit to Egypt. Israeli newspapers appeared on Cairo newsstands, and, in July, freighter service began between the Israeli port of Haifa and Alexandria, Egypt.

There was little internal opposition to President Anwar el-Sadat's peace moves. The opposition's main concern was Palestinian rights to self-determination and Israeli withdrawal from occupied Arab territories according to United Nations (UN) Resolution 242, goals with which Sadat's government was in full agreement, though negotiations with Israel on these matters was deadlocked.

Domestic Focus. Sadat played host to Iran's exiled Shah Mohammad Reza Pahlavi during the shah's last illness – he died in an army hospital near Cairo on July 27 – and expelled Russian technicians and 43 members of the Soviet Embassy staff in Egypt to protest Russia's invasion of Afghanistan. But his government devoted most of its attention to the country's urgent domestic economic and social problems.

A major concern was the growing militancy of Islamic fundamentalists, as violence was directed at the Coptic Christian minority. Attacks on Christians and church bombings caused the Coptic patriarch to cancel traditional Easter celebrations. Fundamentalist opposition to the peace treaty with Israel and to the secularization of Egyptian life led to riots in several cities.

Dissatisfied with the slow pace of economic and social change, Sadat staged a massive government shakeup in May. Prime Minister Mustafa Khalil resigned on May 15, and Sadat took over the post. The Cabinet was reduced in size, and new provincial governors were appointed to supervise provincial development. Sadat also reduced prices on staple commodities and increased the minimum wage 25 per cent.

Some Economic Pluses. The Suez Canal was widened and deepened to handle 150,000-ton supertankers in October. New oil strikes brought Egyptian oil production to 605,000 barrels per day. Remittances from Egyptian workers abroad increased. A major consequence of good relations with the United States was a flow of aid and technical help equal to post-World War II levels, including $335 million in basic food imports subsidies.   William Spencer

See also MIDDLE EAST (Facts in Brief Table). In WORLD BOOK, see EGYPT.

ELECTIONS. Voters on Nov. 4, 1980, elected Republican Ronald Reagan President of the United States by a surprising and spectacular margin, splintering the traditional Democratic coalition and sending President Jimmy Carter back to his Plains, Ga., home after one term in the White House. The Reagan landslide was, in part, attributed to crossover voting by disaffected Democrats. Republicans gained control of the Senate for the first time in 26 years, and picked up 33 seats in the U.S. House of Representatives.

Reagan swept 44 states with 489 electoral votes and received 43,899,248 popular votes – 51 per cent of the ballots cast. Carter, in contrast, received 35,481,435 votes – 41 per cent – carrying only his native Georgia, Hawaii, Maryland, Minnesota, Rhode Island, West Virginia, and the District of Columbia for 49 electoral votes. Independent candidate John B. Anderson received 5,719,437 votes – 7 per cent of the popular vote – not enough to affect the election's outcome.

A Republican Majority. The breadth of Reagan's support caused some GOP leaders to revive hopes of a permanent Republican majority, ending almost 50 years as the minority party. "This could be the break-point election in bringing about a party realignment," said Republican National Chairman William E. Brock III. "In this election, we have brought together the elements of a new coalition.

On an artillery caisson, the body of Iran's Shah Mohammad Reza Pahlavi is borne with full military honors to his tomb in a Cairo mosque.

The cementing of that coalition depends on our performance in office."

Reagan did get far more than the historic share of the vote from union members, Roman Catholics, Jews, Southerners, and big-city residents who traditionally vote Democratic. Many analysts interpreted the results more as a repudiation of Carter, however, than as a watershed event that would change the course of American politics. This view was bolstered by pre-election polls indicating a close contest, with the shift toward Reagan apparently occurring in the final days of the campaign.

Carter's Handicap. Carter said he did not believe that the results represented a "personal turning against me." Yet many voters blamed him for the double-digit inflation, recession-level unemployment, and near-record interest rates that prevailed during the last half of his term.

Carter told reporters after the election that voters' frustrations over the detention of the American hostages in Iran had cost him the presidency. Throughout the campaign, Reagan had termed the continued imprisonment of the hostages "a humiliation and a disgrace" for the United States, but he did not say how he would secure the hostages' release. The issue took on added importance when Iran issued new conditions for the hostages' release on November 2 and Carter broke off campaigning in Chicago. The hopes raised by Iran's unexpected move were dashed again, however, and the hos-

Election winners include, *clockwise from above*, John D. Rockefeller IV, West Virginia governor; Mervyn M. Dymally, new House member from California; Lynn Martin, replacing John B. Anderson in the House; Christopher J. Dodd, new senator from Connecticut; Jeremiah Denton, new Alabama senator; and Paula Hawkins, new senator from Florida.

tages remained in Iran on November 4, the first anniversary of their captivity.

Reagan's campaign was strengthened when the last of his Republican primary opponents dropped out of the race in May, producing a unified party at the GOP convention in Detroit in July. In contrast, Carter's renomination was strongly contested by Senator Edward M. Kennedy (D., Mass.), who mounted an aggressive challenge for nearly nine months, until it became apparent at the Democratic National Convention in New York City in August that he did not have sufficient support. Kennedy's subsequent lukewarm declaration of support for Carter was not sufficient to heal political wounds. Nor was Carter's principal campaign theme that Reagan was a dangerous reactionary who might lead the nation into war effective. Public opinion polls indicated that voters perceived Reagan as "presidential" after he and Carter met in Cleveland on October 28 in a nationally televised debate.

Carter's defeat was magnified for the Democrats by loss of control of the Senate. The new Senate line-up had 53 Republicans, 46 Democrats, and 1 Independent, compared with 41 Republicans, 58 Democrats and 1 Independent in the previous Senate. The turn-about was significant because, in several instances, conservative GOP candidates defeated staunch Democratic liberals.

The Democratic Casualties included George S. McGovern of South Dakota, the party's 1972 presidential candidate, and such other well-entrenched liberals as Frank Church of Idaho, Birch Bayh of Indiana, Warren G. Magnuson of Washington, Gaylord Nelson of Wisconsin, and John C. Culver of Iowa. In some instances, the Republican victors had been conservative members of the House. Representative James Abdnor beat McGovern; Bayh lost to Representative J. Danforth Quayle; Culver was defeated by Representative Charles E. Grassley. Robert W. Kasten, Jr., ousted Nelson. Washington Attorney General Slade Gorton defeated Magnuson, and Steven D. Symms defeated Church.

In other Democratic setbacks, John A. Durkin of New Hampshire lost to Warren B. Rudman; Robert Morgan of North Carolina lost to John P. East, and Herman E. Talmadge of Georgia was upset by Mack Mattingly, former GOP state chairman.

The Republican Party also retained most of the seats it had held in the previous Senate. Incumbent Republican senators returned to office were: Barry Goldwater of Arizona; Robert J. Dole of Kansas; Charles McC. Mathias, Jr., of Maryland; Paul Laxalt of Nevada; Robert W. Packwood of Oregon; and Edwin Jacob Garn of Utah. One prominent Republican, Jacob K. Javits, of New York, ran on the Liberal Party ticket after losing a primary fight to Alphonse M. D'Amato, who won the general election. Mark Andrews of North Dakota, Donald L. Nickles of Oklahoma, and Arlen Specter of Pennsylvania also won seats previously held by other Republicans.

Three Democratic senators who lost primary elections had their seats captured by Republicans. Richard B. Stone of Florida was replaced by Paula Hawkins, a public service commissioner; Donald W. Stewart of Alabama was succeeded by Jeremiah Denton, former prisoner of war in Vietnam; and in Alaska, Mike Gravel's seat was taken by Frank H. Murkowski, a banker.

Democratic senators retaining their seats were Dale Bumpers of Arkansas, Alan Cranston of California, Gary Hart of Colorado, Daniel K. Inouye of Hawaii, Wendell H. Ford of Kentucky, Russell B. Long of Louisiana, Thomas F. Eagleton of Missouri, John H. Glenn of Ohio, Ernest F. Hollings of South Carolina, and Patrick J. Leahy of Vermont. Two new Democratic senators were chosen. Christopher J. Dodd replaced retiring Senator Abraham A. Ribicoff of Connecticut, and Alan J. Dixon succeeded retiring Senator Adlai E. Stevenson III of Illinois.

In the House, the damage to Democratic ranks was almost as severe. Republicans picked up 33 seats, producing a line-up of 242 Democrats, 192 Republicans, and 1 Independent compared with 276 Democrats and 159 Republicans elected to the preceding Congress. The new members who were elected were overwhelmingly conservative and, as in the Senate, replaced many liberal Democrats, shifting the power balance in the House sharply to the right.

The Democrats lost their whip, John Brademas of Indiana, as well as Al Ullman of Oregon, chairman of the Ways and Means Committee. Other veteran Democrats who were defeated included Thomas L. Ashley of Ohio; Bob Eckhardt of Texas; and James C. Corman, Harold T. Johnson, and Lionel Van Deerlin of California. There was but one upset of a House GOP leader – the defeat of Samuel L. Devine of Ohio, the third-ranking Republican. Robert E. Bauman of Maryland, who was convicted of a sex offense, was also defeated.

In Governors' Races, the Republicans gained four statehouses. Arkansas Governor Bill Clinton was defeated by Frank D. White; Missouri Governor Joseph P. Teasdale was beaten by former Governor Christopher S. Bond, North Dakota Governor Arthur A. Link was replaced by Allen I. Olson, and John Spellman, a Seattle county executive, was elected governor of Washington, replacing Dixy Lee Ray. In legislative contests, the Republicans gained more than 200 seats and won control of the Illinois House of Representatives, the Ohio Senate, and the Pennsylvania House. The election raised the number of legislative chambers under GOP command from 26 to 30 of the 98 partisan state chambers.

Other Issues. Voters also decided a wide variety of issues on November 4. Massachusetts voters approved a 40 per cent reduction in property taxes by passing Proposition 2½, which would roll back these taxes to 2.5 per cent of assessed valuation. The measure was expected to cripple transportation systems and public services that rely on property tax revenues.

Missouri and South Dakota voters rejected restrictions on nuclear power plants, while Montana voters turned down a measure that would severely limit uranium mining. Washington state voters approved strong limits on nuclear-waste storage, however, and Oregon voters barred construction of nuclear plants without federally licensed dump sites for radioactive waste.

California voters rejected a proposal to set up smoking and nonsmoking sections in public areas. Iowans rejected a state equal-rights amendment. In a controversial referendum, voters in Dade County, Florida, halted six years of bilingualism by banning mandatory government use of Spanish or any language other than English.   William J. Eaton

See also DEMOCRATIC PARTY; REPUBLICAN PARTY. In WORLD BOOK, see ELECTION.

ELECTRIC POWER. See ENERGY.

ELECTRONICS manufacturers increased the capacity and cut the prices of microelectronic devices in 1980. Semiconductor technology continued to provide more processing and memory capability in a wide range of products, from large computers that carry out 10 million instructions per second to handheld games that simulate baseball action.

Talking Machines. The most striking innovation in semiconductor technology was voice synthesis – using just two or three tiny chips to make sounds that closely resemble the human voice. Also under development in 1980 were voice-recognition devices that convert spoken words and phrases into computer signals, enabling electronic and mechanical devices to obey spoken instructions or to print the spoken words.

The most popular speech synthesizers are in teaching aids such as Speak & Spell, made by Texas Instruments Incorporated, in Dallas. However, other semiconductor firms in the United States and Japan are also manufacturing synthesis chips, so more consumer appliances, toys, and industrial equipment will be chattering away.

Design by Computer. Another major 1980 trend was putting the equivalent of proven computers and minicomputers on very-large-scale integrated circuits. A dramatic example was International Business Machines Corporation's (IBM) very-

The 1980 Electoral College Vote

large-scale integration of the processor portion of its popular System 370 computer, announced in October. The integrated processor was not a commercial product, but the research, conducted by IBM's Data Systems Division in East Fishkill, N.Y., proved that computer-aided design (CAD) programs can be used to map the complex interconnections necessary to pack more than 5,000 circuits on a slice of silicon measuring 7 millimeters (0.3 inch) on a side.

As semiconductor devices increased in density, designers focused more attention on CAD. The process of designing chips that contain some 100,000 transistors is impossibly slow without the help of a computer. As a result, a number of universities and computer manufacturers have developed a new way to lay out and interconnect the cells that make up large-scale integrated circuits. Designers have switched from drawing boards to computer-driven cathode-ray tube displays for preparing intricate circuit patterns. The computer can spot an error in design as it is made.

Memory Experts. Manufacturers of commercial one-chip microcomputers added increased memory and other important features to their products. Motorola Semiconductor Corporation in Phoenix; Zilog Corporation in Cupertino, Calif.; and Intel Corporation in Santa Clara, Calif., used a new technique to connect an external erasable, programmable, read-only memory (EPROM) to a single-chip processor. A read-only memory (ROM) stores data in the computer until it is deliberately erased. An EPROM can be erased and reprogrammed repeatedly by the computer user. The company that buys the processor is not limited to a program built in by the chip manufacturer.

Major manufacturers continued to develop the random access memory (RAM), a memory device in which successive individual pieces of information are accessible to the computer's processor in any order. By the end of 1980, 11 United States, 5 Japanese, and 2 European companies had announced 64K RAMs – the conventional term for devices that can store 65,536 bits. (A *bit* is the basic unit of information in digital computers.)

For the Consumer. Matsushita Electric Industrial Company of America in Secaucus, N.J., introduced a 14-ounce (390-gram) handheld computer capable of hooking up to a variety of peripheral machines such as a converter for telephone transmission, a printer, and a cassette tape drive. Tandy's Radio Shack in Dallas introduced a computer that weighs 6 ounces (170 grams).

Ohio Scientific Incorporated in Aurora, Ohio, announced Challenger 8P-HD, a new tabletop computer designed primarily for handling home security. The company offers both speech synthesis and voice recognition as options.   Gerald M. Walker

In WORLD BOOK, see ELECTRONICS.

EL SALVADOR. Fear stalked the streets of San Salvador, the capital, in 1980 while frequent terrorist killings and confrontations between leftists and rightists were reported in the countryside. By October, what amounted to an intermittent civil war had left 6,000 dead.

The violence resulted from a classic struggle: too little land to satisfy need, a widening gap between rich and poor, and a sharp split of the population into two camps, extremes of right and left. In January, the tense situation erupted in violence. Fighting during an antigovernment march by 3,000 leftists in San Salvador left 20 dead and 27 wounded. The reformist junta blamed the killing on right wing extremists.

Government Reforms. Then, under pressures from the United States, the junta announced broad and sudden reforms in February, trying to nullify the left's appeal. It nationalized the banks, put the government in control of the country's foreign trade, and mounted an ambitious agrarian reform program that included breaking up farms of more than 125 acres (50 hectares).

But even these far-reaching reforms were not enough to calm a situation approaching anarchy, in which the extreme left saw its chance of obtaining total victory. It was widely feared that the March 24 assassination of Roman Catholic Archbishop Oscar Arnulfo Romero, one of Latin America's most outspoken and respected clerics, might touch off a final conflagration. The archbishop was killed as he was celebrating Mass in the chapel of a hospital for terminally ill cancer patients.

Romero's widely denounced murder touched off a wave of violence. Before dawn the following day, 30 bombs exploded in various parts of the nation, causing heavy damage to bank buildings and business establishments. There was more violence at the archbishop's funeral on March 30. A crowd estimated at 75,000 converged on the plaza fronting the Metropolitan Cathedral. During a homily to the slain prelate, explosions and gunfire set off a stampede. About 30 persons were killed and hundreds wounded. The murder of three American nuns and a social worker on December 2 prompted the United States to suspend $25 million in military and economic aid and to send representatives to investigate the crime.

On December 10, military and civilian leaders replaced the junta with a president, Jose Napoleon Duarte, a Christian Democratic politician and junta member. Earlier, the junta had announced that an assembly to draft a new constitution would be elected in 1982.   Nathan A. Haverstock

See also LATIN AMERICA (Facts in Brief Table). In WORLD BOOK, see EL SALVADOR.

EMPLOYMENT. See ECONOMICS; EDUCATION; LABOR; SOCIAL SECURITY; WELFARE.

ENDANGERED SPECIES. See CONSERVATION.

ENERGY. Calling it the keystone of United States energy policy, President Jimmy Carter signed the Energy Security Act of 1980 on June 30, creating a multibillion-dollar government corporation that will foster development of a domestic synthetic-fuels (synfuels) industry. The bill established a Synthetic Fuels Corporation with authority to use loan guarantees, price guarantees, and other financial incentives to induce private firms to begin making synthetic oil and gas from coal, oil shale, and other abundant domestic energy resources.

The Congress of the United States gave the corporation authority to spend $20 billion during the next five years on projects that will produce oil at the equivalent of 500,000 barrels per day (bpd) by 1987. The corporation's long-range goal is to boost synfuel production to the equivalent of 2 million bpd by 1992. This could require expenditure of an additional $68 billion. Carter named John C. Sawhill, deputy assistant secretary of energy, as chairman and chief executive officer of the corporation. The government moved swiftly to implement the legislation, funding $200 million worth of synfuel projects in July and another $270-million in December.

Other Provisions. The Energy Security Act was actually an omnibus energy bill that included a number of other provisions intended to decrease U.S. dependence on foreign oil. One such provision required the federal government to resume filling the Strategic Petroleum Reserve, a series of salt domes along the Gulf Coast that will eventually store 750 million barrels of crude oil. The Carter Administration stopped buying oil for the reserve in October 1978, when the Iranian revolution tightened world oil supplies. The reserve then contained about 90 million barrels of oil.

Other sections of the Energy Security Act create a "solar bank" that will use credits, loan guarantees, and subsidies to stimulate development of renewable energy sources, and a "conservation bank" in the Department of Housing and Urban Development that will underwrite low-interest homeowner loans for insulation and other energy-conservation measures. There also will be financial aid for factories producing fuel-grade alcohol from grain. The alcohol will be used in the 90 per cent gasoline and 10 per cent alcohol mixture now being marketed on a limited basis as "gasohol."

The energy security bill was one of three major pieces of legislation proposed by Carter in 1979 in the midst of the Iranian oil cutoff. Congress killed legislation on June 27 that would have established an energy mobilization board to speed new energy projects through the maze of government regulation and bureaucracy. It imposed the Crude Oil Windfall Profit Tax Act on the oil industry, believed to be the largest tax ever levied on any American industry. Carter signed the tax bill on

April 2, declaring it "a victory for every American citizen." The tax is expected to raise $227 billion by 1990. It is designed to recover, for public use, some of the estimated $1 trillion that oil companies will reap in extra profits during the 1980s as a result of government decontrol of crude oil prices.

U.S. Energy Consumption totaled 39.2 quadrillion British Thermal Units (B.T.U.'s) during the first half of 1980, the Department of Energy (DOE) reported in October. The total was 3.1 per cent less than during the same period in 1979, mainly because the consumption of petroleum products dropped 8.4 per cent – equivalent to 1.4 million bpd. There was also a 10.5 per cent drop in the consumption of electricity generated with nuclear power. But the average daily consumption of coal, hydroelectric power, and natural gas all increased. Coal consumption was up 3.7 per cent; hydroelectric 1.1 per cent; and natural gas 0.3 per cent.

Energy production grew by 3.5 per cent, with the biggest increase – 9.9 per cent – in coal. There was a 2 per cent increase in the daily average rate of crude oil production, a 1.1 per cent increase in hydroelectric production, and a 0.9 per cent increase in natural gas production.

Record Summer Heat parched the South, Southwest, and other parts of the United States, causing sharp increases in the use of air conditioning. The result was a record consumption of electricity during 1980. The Edison Electric Institute reported that consumption reached 52.6 billion kilowatt hours during the week ending July 19. The previous record – 49.5 billion kilowatt hours, set in August 1979 – was exceeded every week between July 19 and August 16.

Consumers paid more for electricity in 1980 than in any previous year. The nationwide average cost of one kilowatt hour was more than 4.3 cents, up from 3.97 cents in 1979. In 1970, it was 1.67 cents.

Two U.S. Government Studies of the 1979 gasoline shortage that caused long lines at service stations found the major oil companies blameless in precipitating the crisis. The studies, ordered by President Carter to investigate possible illegal activity by the oil industry, were conducted by DOE and the U.S. Department of Justice. Both agencies concluded on July 17 that the shortage resulted from declining domestic oil production, the Iranian oil cutoff, and, ironically, the federal government's own complex and cumbersome regulations on gasoline pricing and allocation.

Fuel Projects. DOE announced plans to award $56 million for 44 proposed alcohol fuels projects that would have a combined capacity of 1 billion gallons (3.8 billion liters) per year. About $21-million was slated for feasibility studies on 42 plants, and the rest will help pay construction and preconstruction costs on two fuel alcohol facilities. One is a $52.4-million project in Southport, Ohio, that will produce about 60 million gallons (230 million liters) of ethyl alcohol, or ethanol, each year from corn. The other, a $53-million plant in Franklin, Ky., will produce 21 million gallons (80 million liters) of ethanol from corn. Both plants will use coal to fuel the process. Carter set a national goal of 500 million gallons (1.9 billion liters) of ethanol production capacity by the end of 1981. This would be enough alcohol to meet 10 per cent of the projected demand for gasoline. Current fuel alcohol production totals about 100 million gallons (380 million liters) per year.

World Energy. The World Bank said in August that it is considering establishing a special energy affiliate to help developing countries make maximum use of their energy resources. The bank, an international lending agency, said that developing countries could face a devastating bill of $110 billion for imported energy in 1990 if they do not tap domestic energy resources. The bank estimated the countries would need between $450-billion and $500 billion during the 1980s to do so.

In its exhaustive study of global energy policy, the bank expressed special concern about the widespread deforestation that is producing "immense" energy problems in villages that depend on firewood for fuel. Villagers who once could quickly obtain ample fuel wood near their homes must now spend half a day or more searching for it. The study cautioned that if developing countries were forced to switch from wood to kerosene, the demand for oil in these countries could rise by as much as 20 per cent. The bank urged a major effort to plant new trees and make more efficient use of existing wood resources. In the Special Reports section, see PONDERING THE FATE OF THE FORESTS.

Drought in Mexico forced the country's Federal Electricity Commission to cut its power supplies to industry by as much as 33 per cent. The commission also ordered blackouts of up to two hours per day for domestic and municipal electricity users. The cutbacks came in August, after drought threatened to cripple Mexico's hydroelectric generating stations. Hydroelectric power supplies about 30 per cent of Mexico's electricity.

Japanese Prime Minister Masayoshi Ohira announced in January a package of energy conservation measures designed to reduce oil consumption by 7 per cent. Included were proposals that would require all television transmissions to end at midnight; set maximum city and expressway speed limits; and keep wintertime temperatures in homes, offices, and stores at a maximum of 64°F. (18°C). Japan has virtually no domestic sources of petroleum, and faced an oil import bill estimated at $35 billion in 1979. Michael Woods

See also COAL; PETROLEUM AND GAS. In WORLD BOOK, see ENERGY; ENERGY SUPPLY.
ENGINEERING. See BUILDING & CONSTRUCTION.

ENVIRONMENT. Many environmental leaders in the United States feared that the victory of Ronald Reagan in the 1980 presidential election, Republican control of the Senate, and the election of a more conservative Congress might set back the environmental movement. They expected the Reagan Administration to impose a moratorium on new environmental initiatives and to relax environmental regulations viewed as impeding economic growth. However, some observers noted that Reagan's environmental record as governor of California from 1967 to 1975 generally reflected a willingness to compromise, rather than to take a doctrinaire approach to conservation issues.

Although environmentalists were disappointed by some of President Jimmy Carter's decisions, 22 conservation leaders endorsed Carter on September 10. Environmental issues that had been in the background of the campaign received front-page attention on October 8 when Reagan said that federal environmental officials are "no growth" advocates and that, if elected, he would invite the coal and steel industries to rewrite clean air rules. He also said air pollution has already been "substantially controlled."

Global 2000 Report. In an authoritative report to President Carter on July 23, the Council on Environmental Quality and the Department of State warned that present trends indicate the potential for global environmental problems of "alarming proportions by the year 2000."

"The Global 2000 Report to the President" resulted from a study begun in 1977. "Environmental, resource, and population stresses are intensifying and will increasingly determine the quality of human life on our planet," the report declared.

Gus Speth, chairman of the Council on Environmental Quality, said that the report's conclusions are not new, but that many U.S. decision-makers do not yet believe them. Among the most striking conclusions of the report:
- A world population of 6.35 billion by 2000, compared with about 4 billion in 1975, will be the foremost problem compounding all others. The number of malnourished people is likely to triple from today's estimated 400 million.
- The most serious problems over the next 20 years will be "an accelerating deterioration and loss of resources essential for agriculture."
- At least 500,000 plant and animal species will be extinct in 20 years.
- Deforestation will result in the loss of virtually all the physically accessible forests in the less developed countries. In the Special Reports section, see PONDERING THE FATE OF THE FORESTS.

Earth Day Reassessments. The United States celebrated the 10th anniversary of Earth Day on April 22 with assessments lauding the gains that

Love Canal's Toxic Legacy

When President Jimmy Carter declared a state of emergency in Love Canal, a tidy residential neighborhood in Niagara Falls, N.Y., on May 21, 1980, the area was neither in a state of civil unrest nor weathering one of nature's onslaughts. Rather, it was suffering an increasingly common consequence of our industrialized society – toxic-waste pollution. In this case, the pollutant was a malodorous sludge composed of 82 chemicals, including 12 suspected carcinogens.

The Love Canal emergency did not occur overnight. Its roots can be traced to the early 1900s when entrepreneur William T. Love began digging a channel to connect the upper and lower levels of the Niagara River. The water would produce electricity for a planned model city.

However, an economic recession destroyed Love's dream, and in 1910 he abandoned the 3,000-foot (900-meter) trench he had dug. The canal served as a community swimming hole until 1942, when Hooker Electrochemical Corporation gained permission to dump chemical wastes there. Hooker bought the property in 1947, and by 1953 had poured 21,000 short tons (19,000 metric tons) of toxic wastes into the canal.

Hooker closed the site in 1953 and deeded the property to the Niagara Falls Board of Education for a token $1. Before the property changed hands, the corporation sealed the canal with a clay cap, which, according to prevailing engineering standards, would keep the chemicals dumped there from leaking out.

The school board built a school and houses on the site. Families moved in. The next 20 years passed peacefully.

The peace began to erode in 1976. Exceptionally heavy rains and snows in the mid-1970s seeped into the chemical grave, eventually pushing an oily black brew up through the clay seal into the neighborhood's lawns and basements. Scientists called in to investigate found traces of the once-interred chemicals in the air, water, and soil of Love Canal.

Concerned residents petitioned the state of New York for relief, and the state agreed in August 1978 to buy up the property bordering the canal and to relocate 239 families. The school was closed and a six-block area surrounding it fenced off.

However, the chemicals continued to move through the soil. They migrated beyond the evacuation line, and reports of disease among the remaining residents increased.

A survey commissioned by the Love Canal Homeowners Association found that the highest disease levels in the area occurred where chemical concentration was greatest. A study conducted for the Environmental Protection Agency (EPA) showed genetic damage in 11 of 36 residents tested. However, a panel of scientists appointed by New York Governor Hugh L. Carey ruled that both studies were inadequate.

These studies were nonetheless instrumental in President Carter's decision to issue the emergency declaration and to allot $5 million to evacuate 710 families. Yet few of these families have left, primarily because they cannot afford to leave until they sell their homes – and there are few offers to buy.

The homeowners hope to receive some compensation from Hooker, now known as Hooker Chemicals and Plastics Corporation, a subsidiary of the Occidental Petroleum Corporation. Some 1,300 individuals as well as the EPA and New York state have filed suits against the firm seeking more than $11 billion in damages. Hooker counters that it used the best disposal methods known in the 1950s and gave the school board written warnings of possible hazards and disclaimers of future liability when it turned over the property.

Whatever the courts decide, one thing is certain: the Love Canal case will not have a happy ending. In fact, it may be only the first in a series of such tragedies. A surgeon general's report issued on September 11 concluded that chemicals seeping into the environment will continue to pose a "major and growing health problem" for years to come, because Love Canal is just one of 50,000 toxic-waste disposal sites in the United States. **Beverly Merz**

A sign of the times

had been made by the environmental movement in the 1970s and recognizing that many new challenges lie ahead.

Environmental leaders attending an Environmental Decade Conference on April 14 said they were shifting their focus from pollution to energy as the primary issue for the 1980s. Such a shift, they said, is crucial to harnessing the public support necessary to continue the environmental campaigns of the 1970s. Many environmentalists agreed that the conservation movement should be aware of the need to make trade-offs and understand that a risk-free society is impossible if it is to avoid a collision course with other national priorities in the 1980s.

Critical Minerals. U.S. dependence on other countries for more than half of its critical minerals may leave the nation more vulnerable than its need for imported oil, according to a congressional committee report issued on September 22. Russia and South Africa dominate production of many minerals having vital military and industrial uses, including chromium, manganese, and vanadium. Many experts believe that U.S. reliance on foreign sources for minerals needed for industry is dangerous and could be used by Russia for a "resource war."

One hopeful sign was that the United Nations Conference on the Law of the Sea appeared to be ready to agree on a treaty in 1981. The treaty would provide for a 36-nation council to control seabed mining. See OCEAN.

The Deep Seabed Hard Minerals Resource Act was signed by President Carter on June 28. The act reaffirms the U.S. commitment to a law of the sea treaty and to orderly development of its own ocean-mining capability. Mining companies had pressed for the legislation, which would allow them to scoop up mineral-bearing nodules, or rock particles, from the deep ocean floor. Licenses for exploration will not be issued before July 1, 1981 — by which time, it was expected, the Law of the Sea Conference will have completed its work.

Acid Rain. The United States and Canada signed an agreement on August 5, attempting to solve the problem of pollution-laden acid rain drifting across their common border. Canada lodged a sharp protest with U.S. officials on April 18 against the potential impact of increased sulfur emissions that are anticipated from proposals to get oil-fired U.S. utilities to switch to coal. Canadian officials declared that acid rain is the most serious environmental problem that country faces and that at least half the acid rain falling in Canada originates in the United States.

The Environmental Protection Agency (EPA) on June 18 ordered two Ohio power plants to cut their sulfur dioxide output by 10,000 short tons (9,000 metric tons). The action was seen as a victory for environmentalists and others in the Northeastern states, which are especially affected by acid rain.

Many environmentalists believe that the increasing cost of oil will make it possible to equip older coal-burning plants not exempt from federal regulations to reduce the pollution-causing gases they emit and still keep the cost below that of oil-burning plants. They also urge legislation that would allow utilities to find the most cost-effective way to reduce acid-generating pollutants.

Three Mile Island. The Nuclear Regulatory Commission (NRC) reported on August 14 that existing methods can be used to clean up radioactive materials at the Three Mile Island nuclear power plant near Harrisburg, Pa., where a major accident occurred on March 28, 1979. The NRC rejected the idea that the plant would have to be permanently closed. Radioactive krypton-85 gas was vented into the air from one of the Three Mile Island reactors in June and July 1980.

Oil Well Capped. A nine-month fight against the world's worst oil spill ended on March 24 when engineers plugged Ixtoc I, a well in the Gulf of Mexico. The Mexican well blew out on June 3, 1979, and lost more than 3.1 million barrels of oil before it was capped. The largest previous oil spill was the 1.6 million barrels lost by the tanker *Amoco Cadiz* off the Brittany coast of France in March 1978. The United States and Mexico announced an agreement on July 24 to combat oil and hazardous-waste spills that could threaten their waters.

Toxic Substances. A surgeon general's report on September 11 concluded that toxic chemicals discarded in the environment pose "a major and growing public health problem." Love Canal, the neighborhood in Niagara Falls, N.Y., that discovered it was built on a toxic chemical dump, received emergency aid on May 21 to permit the evacuation of 710 families to temporary housing. See Close-Up.

A new federal law controlling disposal of toxic wastes, passed by Congress in 1976, became effective on November 19. The law, administered by the EPA, provides strict controls on disposal techniques and sites. Companies that manufacture or process chemicals must supply the EPA with records of who buys the chemicals, so that the substances can be traced through the manufacturing process and the waste-disposal process. The EPA and local officials across the United States in the 1970s had noted an upswing in illicit nighttime dumping — considerably cheaper than environmentally safe methods of disposal — that frequently rendered the water supply suspect or completely unfit.   Andrew L. Newman

See also CONSERVATION. In WORLD BOOK, see ENVIRONMENT; ENVIRONMENTAL POLLUTION.

EQUATORIAL GUINEA. See AFRICA.

ETHIOPIA. See AFRICA.

EUROPE

The European Community (EC or Common Market) began 1980 with a bitter struggle over Great Britain's demand for cuts in its contribution to the 1980-1981 budget and a constitutional wrangle between the European Parliament and the nine EC countries over the budget's size and composition. Before the EC resolved these issues, the invasion of Afghanistan hardened European attitudes toward Russia, even though France and West Germany tried to preserve détente.

United States President Jimmy Carter's call to boycott the Summer Olympic Games in Moscow received a mixed response in Europe. The North Atlantic Treaty Organization (NATO) considered building up its forces in Europe because of the Russian threat in the Middle East and the Warsaw Pact countries' increased superiority in weapons.

Europe's bloodiest terrorist incident since World War II occurred at the Bologna, Italy, railway station on August 2. A bomb planted by neo-Fascists killed 80 persons. See ITALY.

Budget Deadlock. Prime Minister Margaret Thatcher of Great Britain stuck grimly to the demand that she made in 1979 to close the $2.3-billion gap between what that country pays to the

Leaders of Canada, France, Great Britain, Italy, Japan, the United States, and West Germany hold an economic conference in June in Venice, Italy.

demands before Britain would agree to solutions of such disputes as lamb, fisheries, and farm prices.

The foreign ministers worked out a further compromise on May 30 that reduced Britain's 1980 contribution to $865 million and its 1981 total to $1.03 billion. They also proposed restructuring the budget over the next two years "to prevent the recurrence of unacceptable situations." Britain's Cabinet accepted the compromise on June 2.

Late Budget. The European Parliament approved the EC's $26.5-billion budget for 1980 on July 9, seven months late. The next day, Parliament received a $30.5-billion preliminary budget for 1981. Drafters of the 1981 budget assumed that the Common Market's biggest expenditure, support for 8 million farmers, would grow no more than 12.6 per cent, or barely half the average increase in recent years. Parliament endorsed the 1981 budget on June 27.

The EC agreed on December 2 to extend for two years the European Monetary System (EMS), under which all EC nations except Great Britain maintain fixed exchange rates among their currencies. The EMS helps these countries fight off speculative attacks on their money.

Farm Crisis. The EC's Common Agriculture Policy was in disarray during the first half of 1980. Farmers demanded a 7.9 per cent price hike to offset production costs, but surpluses of butter, tomatoes, peaches, and olive oil built up.

The farm crisis was worsened by France's refusal to accept British lamb exports, despite the European Court's ruling. But the lamb war ended on September 30. Great Britain withdrew its claim against France, and the French market was opened to British lamb on October 20. Agreement on other issues enabled the EC to fix a 5 per cent farm-price increase for 1980.

Détente in Danger. France and West Germany reacted to Russia's invasion of Afghanistan much more softly than did Great Britain and their other neighbors. President Valéry Giscard D'Estaing and Chancellor Helmut Schmidt moved up a summit meeting planned for February 4 by 24 hours to discuss how to continue a policy of détente. Nevertheless, they condemned the Soviet action in the strongest terms. The EC Council of Ministers took a harder attitude, declaring on February 5 that Russia had "destroyed the conditions which ought to prevail for the holding of the Olympic Games in Moscow in July." The EC proposed on February 19 that Afghanistan be neutralized under international guarantee and that Russia withdraw its troops. But Russia turned down that proposal.

EC and what it receives from the EC budget. She threatened to end all British budget contributions unless her demands were met. But settlement was delayed because the European Parliament had thrown out the EC's budget proposals at the end of 1979 and because the Council of Ministers could not agree on 1980 farm-price supports.

Thatcher further angered other EC members on April 28 when she turned down their proposal to cut Great Britain's budget contribution by two-thirds, to $754 million for 1979 and $1.1 billion for 1981. Roy H. Jenkins, president of the EC's executive commission, said it was "the most tantalizingly disappointing summit" he had ever attended. Thatcher said that the EC would have to meet her

Poland's Workers Erupt

Seething discontent among Polish workers weary of tightening their belts erupted in the last half of 1980 and profoundly changed that nation's political landscape, though perhaps not for long. Meat-price increases announced on July 2 provoked some 17,000 workers in a tractor factory near Warsaw to strike for wage hikes to make up for the added cost of meat. The tractor strike and several others that broke out in the Warsaw area were settled quickly.

But the settlements, which boosted wages by up to 10 per cent, encouraged workers elsewhere. By July 8, workers had struck in automobile, aircraft, and electrical-apparatus factories; and by July 16, strikes involving 80,000 workers had paralyzed the factories and the transportation and food-distribution systems in the eastern city of Lublin. As the summer went on, reports of wage increases led to strikes in other factories. Warsaw garbage collectors went on strike on August 8 and bus drivers struck on August 11.

On August 14, some 17,000 workers at the Lenin Shipyard in Gdańsk went on strike and took over the shipyard. Strikes soon spread throughout the Baltic region. Communist Party First Secretary Edward Gierek promised on August 18 that the government would import more meat, stabilize food prices, increase family allowances, and form a committee to investigate workers' grievances. But the strikes continued.

Talks opened in Gdańsk on August 23 between a government committee led by Deputy Prime Minister Mieczyslaw Jagielski and a workers' committee headed by Lech Walesa, an electrician who had often been unemployed because of his dissident activities. Similar talks took place in the Baltic city of Szczecin. Meanwhile, the strikes spread further. On August 29, miners struck in the southwestern region of Silesia.

The strikes in Gdańsk, Szczecin, and Silesia were settled by September 3. The government granted the strikers the right to establish independent, self-governing trade unions and promised a new censorship law by the end of the year, radio broadcasts of Sunday Mass, and release of political prisoners.

The government issued regulations for independent unions on September 15. Most of the unions that belonged to the state-controlled board of trade unions left it and registered, as required, with the Warsaw district court. Also registering was a nationwide federation of trade unions called Solidarity, led by Walesa and claiming a membership of 8 to 10 million.

When the court delayed processing Solidarity's registration, the powerful union staged a one-hour national strike on October 3. The court finally approved the charter on October 24, but not before adding clauses that acknowledged the Communist Party's leading role and limited the union's right to strike. Solidarity appealed to Poland's Supreme Court to restore the charter's original wording and threatened to call a general strike. The court granted Solidarity's appeal on November 10.

A fresh dispute flared up late in November when police arrested two union activists for copying a secret document. The union demanded reorganization of the state security system and an inquiry into its abuses.

But militant Warsaw unionists dropped plans for a general strike to support their demands because a shadow had fallen across Poland's political landscape. Poland's unrest had aroused Russia and other members of the Warsaw Pact. These nations had been urging Poland's government and workers to solve their problems by themselves. However, Warsaw Pact leaders held a meeting in Moscow on December 5 and said Poland could count on their "fraternal solidarity and support."

Western officials saw various reasons for the gathering, but its purpose seemed simple – and ominous – to Solidarity. The union immediately issued a statement condemning "irresponsible strikes" and claiming that they planned no further action. As 1980 closed, Poland's workers could still reflect joyously on their new freedoms – unless they were distracted by thoughts of what the neighbors might think.　　Chris Cviic

Lech Walesa

All the Common Market countries except West Germany had athletes in the Summer Olympics in Moscow, but the athletes abstained from activities that might have had political or propaganda significance. See OLYMPIC GAMES.

Iran Sanctions. The United States asked the EC to impose trade sanctions against Iran for holding U.S. hostages. France firmly opposed such a move. But the nine nations agreed by the end of April to impose full trade and economic sanctions unless "decisive progress" toward release of the hostages was made by May 17. When the ultimatum date passed, the EC imposed a partial embargo.

Middle East Initiative. EC heads of government, meeting in Venice, Italy, on June 13, changed their attitude toward the Middle East conflict by stating for the first time that the Palestine Liberation Organization (PLO) must be included in peace negotiations. They also recognized the "right to self-determination" of the Palestinian people. This decision angered Israel. Council of Ministers Chairman Gaston Thorn led a mission to the Middle East on July 31 for talks with Israeli and Arab leaders.

Poland Crisis. Schmidt planned to meet East Germany's Communist Party Secretary General Erich Honecker in East Germany on August 28 and 29. This would have been the first meeting between German heads of government in a decade. But strikes in Poland prompted Schmidt to cancel the talks. The Polish crisis began when the government raised meat prices on July 1 and protesting workers demanded pay raises. The strikes spread but were settled quickly.

But trouble broke out again in August. Workers took over the Gdańsk shipyards on August 14, and the unrest quickly spread. Premier Edward Babiuch was ousted on August 24 in a Communist Party shakeup after the workers won major concessions. But soon the strike involved more than 300,000 workers. The strikers went back to work on September 3 after winning most of their demands, including the right to strike and to form free, independent trade unions. Communist Party First Secretary Edward Gierek was replaced by Stanislaw Kania three days after the strike ended. Leaders of the Warsaw Pact nations held a meeting on December 5 in Moscow as they mobilized their armies. See Close-Up; KANIA, STANISLAW.

NATO Dilemma. The Afghanistan invasion and repressive rule in Iran confronted NATO with difficult policy problems. NATO needed to strengthen itself against Eastern bloc pressures and to keep the United States and European allies from becoming divided. European leaders recognized that Western Europe could not defend itself against Russia, so it had to retain 200,000 U.S. troops on its soil. But this knowledge did not prevent moves, especially by France, to strengthen national forces.

West Germany's desire to maintain détente made arms-limitation proposals more urgent, but 1980 saw little progress. A two-day meeting of NATO nuclear planners in Bodø, Norway, ended on June 4 with a warning that Russia had accelerated its nuclear missile build-up in the previous six months. British Defense Secretary Francis Pym said that Soviet three-headed SS20 missiles were being produced at the rate of one every five days, instead of one every six days as they were earlier. NATO called on Russia to accept NATO's December 1979 offer to negotiate missile controls.

NATO offered to discuss European troop cuts with Russia but received little response. Warsaw Pact countries said on April 4 that they were pulling 20,000 troops out of East Germany, but NATO said this withdrawal had nothing to do with the deadlocked 19-nation Vienna negotiations on military manpower in central Europe.

U.S. Secretary of State Edmund S. Muskie met Greek and Turkish ministers in Ankara, Turkey, on June 24 to discuss reintegrating Greece's armed forces with NATO forces. Greece maintained that reintegration was necessary for the United States to keep its bases in Greece, but Turkey opposed Greece's return to an unconditional membership. The Iran situation made NATO chiefs especially eager to strengthen their forces in the Aegean Sea

Medium tanks from Warsaw Pact armies rumble across an East German field near the Polish border during maneuvers in early September.

Facts in Brief on the European Countries

Country	Population	Government	Monetary Unit*	Foreign Trade (million U.S. $)	
				Exports†	Imports†
Albania	2,933,000	Communist Party First Secretary Enver Hoxha; People's Assembly Presidium Chairman Haxhi Lleshi; Prime Minister Mehmet Shehu	lek (7 = $1)	151	173
Andorra	27,000	The bishop of Urgel, Spain, and the president of France	French franc & Spanish peseta	no statistics available	
Austria	7,578,000	President Rudolf Kirchschlaeger; Chancellor Bruno Kreisky	schilling (13.7 = $1)	15,483	20,254
Belgium	10,091,000	King Baudouin I; Prime Minister Wilfried Martens	franc (31.1 = $1)	56,258 (includes Luxembourg)	60,410
Bulgaria	8,981,000	Communist Party First Secretary & State Council Chairman Todor Zhivkov; Prime Minister Stanko Todorov	lev (1 = $1.17)	8,879	8,447
Czechoslovakia	15,456,000	Communist Party General Secretary & President Gustav Husak; Prime Minister Lubomir Strougal	koruna (10.4 = $1)	13,198	14,262
Denmark	5,191,000	Queen Margrethe II; Prime Minister Anker Henrik Jorgensen	krone (6 = $1)	14,506	18,450
Finland	4,813,000	President Urho Kekkonen; Prime Minister Mauno Koivisto	markka (3.8 = $1)	11,175	11,400
France	54,250,000	President Valéry Giscard d'Estaing; Prime Minister Raymond Barre	franc (4.5 = $1)	98,059	106,994
Germany, East	16,631,000	Communist Party Secretary General & State Council Chairman Erich Honecker; Prime Minister Willi Stoph	mark (1.8 = $1)	15,063	16,214
Germany, West	61,888,000	President Karl Carstens; Chancellor Helmut Schmidt	Deutsche mark (1.9 = $1)	171,540	157,747
Great Britain	56,100,000	Queen Elizabeth II; Prime Minister Margaret Thatcher	pound (1 = $2.35)	91,030	102,969
Greece	9,585,000	President Constantine Caramanlis; Prime Minister George Rallis	drachma (46.1 = $1)	3,855	9,640
Hungary	10,819,000	Communist Party First Secretary Janos Kadar; President Pal Losonczi; Prime Minister Gyorgy Lazar	forint (19.1 = $1)	7,938	8,674
Iceland	233,000	President Vigdis Finnbogadottir; Prime Minister Gunnar Thoroddsen	krona (526 = $1)	781	824
Ireland	3,467,000	President Patrick J. Hillery; Prime Minister Charles J. Haughey	pound (1 = $1.94)	7,180	9,837
Italy	58,043,000	President Alessandro Pertini; Prime Minister Arnaldo Forlani	lira (920 = $1)	72,242	77,970
Liechtenstein	26,000	Prince Franz Josef II; Prime Minister Hans Brunhart	Swiss franc	no statistics available	
Luxembourg	366,000	Grand Duke Jean; Prime Minister Pierre Werner	franc (31.1 = $1)	56,258 (includes Belgium)	60,410
Malta	336,000	President Anton Buttigieg; Prime Minister Dom Mintoff	pound (1 = $2.95)	424	759
Monaco	26,000	Prince Rainier III	French franc	no statistics available	
Netherlands	14,358,000	Queen Beatrix; Prime Minister Andreas A. M. van Agt	guilder (2.1 = $1)	63,667	67,284
Norway	4,140,000	King Olav V; Prime Minister Odvar Nordli	krone (5.1 = $1)	13,271	13,818
Poland	35,964,000	Communist Party First Secretary Stanislaw Kania; President Henryk Jablonski; Council of Ministers Chairman Jozef Pinkowski	zloty (33.2 = $1)	16,233	17,488
Portugal	9,971,000	President Antonio dos Santos Ramalho Eanes; Prime Minister Francisco Pinto Balsemao	escudo (52.7 = $1)	3,468	6,085
Romania	22,537,000	Communist Party General Secretary & President Nicolae Ceausescu; Prime Minister Ilie Verdet	leu (4.5 = $1)	9,731	10,917
Russia	268,380,000	Communist Party General Secretary & Supreme Soviet Presidium Chairman Leonid Ilich Brezhnev; Council of Ministers Chairman Nikolay Aleksandrovich Tikhonov	ruble (1 = $1.56)	64,762	57,773
San Marino	22,000	2 captains regent appointed by Grand Council every 6 months	Italian lira	no statistics available	
Spain	37,977,000	King Juan Carlos I; President Adolfo Suarez Gonzalez	peseta (77.7 = $1)	17,903	25,432
Sweden	8,388,000	King Carl XVI Gustaf; Prime Minister Thorbjorn Falldin	krona (4.4 = $1)	27,240	28,488
Switzerland	6,403,000	President Kurt Furgler	franc (1.8 = $1)	26,507	29,354
Turkey	46,073,000	Head of State Kenan Evren; Prime Minister Bulend Ulusu	lira (84.8 = $1)	2,261	4,946
Yugoslavia	22,510,000	President Cvijetin Mijatovic; Prime Minister Veselin Djuranovic	dinar (26.6 = $1)	6,491	12,862

*Exchange rates as of Dec. 1, 1980. †Latest available data.

and the southern Mediterranean Sea. The parties finally reached an agreement in October. Turkey said that Greece's return would strengthen NATO and was in Turkey's interest.

Economic Recession struck Europe with 6.7 million unemployed in EC countries, inflation, and severe balance-of-trade deficits in 1980. On June 23, the leaders of Canada, France, Great Britain, Italy, Japan, the United States, and West Germany, meeting in Venice, pledged to cut their dependence on oil and to fight inflation. They also decided to step up their campaign to persuade oil producers to play a bigger role in helping poorer countries that faced serious problems because of oil-price hikes. The leaders decided that fiscal and monetary restraint was necessary to slow inflation, and that they would have to shift financial resources from government spending to the private sector and from consumption to investment.

Anti-Pollution Treaty. Eleven Mediterranean coastal nations and EC representatives signed a treaty in Athens, Greece, on May 17 to move toward a healthier and more balanced environment, cleaner beaches, and safer seafood. The treaty is expected to benefit 44 million inhabitants of coastal cities and many tourists each year by ending pollution from land-based sources. It provides for a program that will take 10 to 15 years to yield tangible results.

New Leaders. Gaston Thorn, foreign minister and former prime minister of Luxembourg, was chosen to become European Community Commission president when Roy H. Jenkins' four-year term of office ended on Jan. 1, 1981. Gunnar Thoroddsen became Iceland's prime minister on February 8, ending a crisis that began when a center-left coalition collapsed in October 1979. Thoroddsen deserted his own right-of-center Independence Party to form the government with the centrist Progressive Party, the Communist People's Alliance, and two minor parties. On June 30, Iceland elected Vigdís Finnbogadóttir president. She is Europe's first democratically elected woman head of state. Finnbogadóttir, 50, director of the Reykjavík Theater, won 33.6 per cent of the vote. She has opposed the U.S. air base at Keflavik.

East-West Talks. The Communist bloc's Council for Mutual Economic Assistance (COMECON) decided in June to resume talks with the EC. Negotiations have dragged on for several years, but they have made little progress because of differing viewpoints. COMECON has sought a global trade agreement with the EC, but the Community insists on a separate pact with each country. Kenneth Brown

See also the various European country articles. In WORLD BOOK, see EUROPE; EUROPEAN COMMUNITY; NORTH ATLANTIC TREATY ORGANIZATION (NATO).

EXPLOSION. See DISASTERS.

FARM AND FARMING. Agriculture in the United States did not have a good year in 1980. Net farm income dropped nearly 25 per cent, plumbing the depths of farmers' disappointment and lowering their boiling points. Farmers grew increasingly restive under current government policies. Instability and uncertainty haunted them.

The year started off strongly for them, but then they were buffeted by the general economic problems of inflation and recession, gyrating prices for both farm products and farm inputs, and erratic weather in the United States and several other regions. In addition, they were uncertain about U.S. farm policies in 1981, when a host of farm laws would terminate and be reconsidered. Among the problems that particularly enraged farmers were scarce, high-priced credit and the high cost of transportation and energy.

World Agriculture also suffered. Cold, wet weather caused a second consecutive poor grain harvest in Russia. Canadian wheat farmers were hurt by the same drought that plagued U.S. farmers in the northern Great Plains. Prolonged drought in Australia and continued low food productivity in Africa also caused concern.

The world food situation materially worsened. After the 1976-1979 period of relatively ample world supplies of grains, oilseed, sugar, cotton, and

By permission of Bill Mauldin
and Wil-Jo Associates, Inc.

even animal products, the specter of shortage of these commodities now loomed.

In March, a blue-ribbon Presidential Commission on World Hunger predicted long-term food problems and urged the United States to pay much more attention to global hunger. A world panel headed by West Germany's former Chancellor Willy Brandt echoed this concern, calling it the core issue in relationships between have and have-not countries. The panel appealed for responsible people throughout the world to tackle the hunger problem.

As a new decade started, American farmers were expected to get higher product prices and increase their incomes. World demand for their products

appeared strong for some time. But the possibility that the world was depending too much on U.S. farm production worried farmers and was of even greater concern to others, such as conservationists and U.S. consumers.

U.S. natural resources showed signs of being strained. Higher consumer food prices seemed assured. At the same time, a look back showed remarkable changes in American agriculture. In the 1970s, U.S. farm acreage increased 66 million acres (27 million hectares), or 2.3 per cent annually; farm production expenses went up 11.5 per cent annually, and much of that was for energy. The farm labor force dropped about 17,000 annually. Farmland values rose an astonishing 23 per cent annually; and the value of farm exports increased more than 18 per cent per year.

Production and Prices. Total farm production in 1980 was down 5 per cent. Overall livestock output was up 1 per cent, but total crops output was down more than 10 per cent. Some crops showed increases — rice, 11 per cent; wheat, 10 per cent; and tobacco, 11 per cent. But there were decreases in corn, 17 per cent; sorghum, 32 per cent; oats, 16 per cent; soybeans, 23 per cent; and cotton, 21 per cent. The major livestock groupings of meat animals, dairy, and poultry and eggs were each up about 3 per cent, led by increases of 7 per cent in pork and 6 per cent in turkeys.

Farm Prices continued the upward movement that started in 1978. Overall, farm prices were up 11 per cent in October, compared with those of the previous October. In general, farm prices sagged somewhat early in the year but the deteriorating crop forecasts pushed them higher as the year went on, so that prices averaged higher for the year. Compared with the previous year, prices for the 1979-1980 marketing year were up 28 per cent for wheat, 11 per cent for corn, 30 per cent for rice, and 7 per cent for cotton; soybean prices were down 7 per cent. Livestock prices were 7 per cent higher in October than in October 1979. However, prices that were paid by farmers in 1980 were 12 per cent higher, and many, if not most, farmers saw their financial situation deteriorating throughout the year.

The farm work force was 3.8 million in October 1980, down 4 per cent from 1979. Family labor made up 65 per cent of it. Wage rates for hired farm labor averaged $3.85 per hour, up 28 cents.

Agricultural Trade. Sharp gains in both export volume and value carried U.S. farm exports in fiscal 1980 to their 11th straight record — $40.5-billion, up about 27 per cent. U.S. agricultural imports in 1980 rose by 7 per cent to $17.3 billion, primarily as a result of sharp increases in sugar and coffee prices. The resulting positive trade balance hit a record $23.2 billion, helping offset the large negative showing in nonagricultural trade.

Agricultural Statistics, 1980

World Crop Production
(million units)

Crop	Units	1979	1980*	% U.S.
Corn	Metric tons	412.4	379.2	43.3
Wheat	Metric tons	419.9	431.1	14.9
Rice (milled)	Metric tons	251.0	264.2	1.8
Barley	Metric tons	160.1	167.6	4.5
Oats	Metric tons	45.2	45.4	14.3
Rye	Metric tons	21.8	24.8	1.6
Soybeans	Metric tons	94.0	81.6	59.2
Cotton	Bales**	65.6	63.5	17.0
Coffee	Bags***	80.1	80.1	0.2
Sugar (centrifugal)	Metric tons	84.6	87.1	6.1

*Preliminary
**480 lbs. (217.7 kilograms) net
***132.276 lbs. (60 kilograms)

Output of Major U.S. Crops
(millions of bushels)

Crop	1962–66*	1979	1980**
Corn	3,876	7,764	6,461
Sorghum	595	814	551
Oats	912	534	451
Wheat	1,229	2,142	2,362
Soybeans	769	2,268	1,775
Rice (rough) (a)	742	1,316	1,461
Potatoes (b)	275	343	297
Cotton (c)	140	146	109
Tobacco (d)	2,126	1,527	1,781

*Average; **Preliminary
(a) 100,000 cwt. (4.54 million kilograms)
(b) 1 million cwt. (45.4 million kilograms)
(c) 100,000 bales (50 million lbs.) (22.7 million kilograms)
(d) 1 million lbs. (454,000 kilograms)

U.S. Production of Animal Products
(millions of pounds)

	1957–59*	1979	1980**
Beef	13,704	21,261	21,377
Veal	1,240	410	365
Lamb & Mutton	711	284	299
Pork	10,957	15,270	16,306
Eggs (a)	5,475	5,769	5,771
Turkey	1,382	2,182	2,322
Total Milk (b)	123	124	128
Broilers	4,430	10,915	11,074

*Average; **Preliminary
(a) 1 million dozens
(b) Billions of lbs. (454 million kilograms)

Wheat and flour exports were up 15 per cent in fiscal 1980. Feed grains exports were up 20 per cent; rice, up 23 per cent; soybeans, up 18 per cent; protein meal, up 21 per cent; and cotton, up 48 per cent. Japan remained the number-one outlet for the United States, but the Netherlands replaced Russia as second, and Mexico shot from ninth in 1979 to third. China was close on its heels in fourth.

World Production. World grain production was estimated at 1.45 billion metric tons (1.6 billion short tons) of wheat, coarse grains, and rough rice, virtually unchanged from the 1979 harvest but considerably below the 1978 record. Increased production in Europe, India, and Canada and projected increases for Argentina's spring-planted grains offset the worst year-to-year setback in U.S. grain output in six years, smaller crops in Australia and China, and the second straight disappointing Russian harvest. World production of individual crops varied from 1979 as follows: wheat, up 3 per cent; rice, up 5 per cent; barley, up 5 per cent; rye, up 14 per cent; and sugar, up 3 per cent; while corn was down 8 per cent; soybeans were down 13 per cent; cotton was down 3 per cent; and coffee and oats were unchanged.

World meat production in 1980 was up for all products except veal.

U.S. Farm Finances. Net farm income dropped about 25 per cent from $31 billion in 1979. A 13 per cent increase in crop receipts and a slight increase in livestock receipts contributed to a 3 per cent rise in gross income. But an 11 per cent surge in production expenses — led by energy, short-term interest costs, and fertilizer — erased these income gains. The farmers' actual cash flow was down only about 10 per cent because much of the net income decline was the result of adjustment for the large farm inventories left from record 1979 crops.

The total value of farm assets at the end of 1980 stood at $999.3 billion, up 9 per cent. Farm real estate made up 73 per cent of that total. Farm debt outstanding at the end of the year was up 15 per cent, with farm real estate making up 53 per cent of that.

Agricultural Policy. Probably the most dramatic farm policy announcement was made by President Jimmy Carter on January 4, when he curtailed grain exports to Russia because of the Soviet invasion of Afghanistan. Adjustments were made throughout the year to try to prevent an unfair burden of the cost of this action from falling on U.S. farmers. These efforts and increasing exports elsewhere offset some of the effect on the farmer. Despite this, U.S. farmers felt that they, along with athletes who were not allowed to compete in the Olympic Summer Games in Moscow because of the Russian invasion, paid an unfair part of the cost of U.S. foreign policy.

A Texas farmer examines ears from his cornfield, ruined by the drought and the relentless heat that struck parts of the Midwest and Southwest.

Program Changes. Several policy changes were made in March. There were to be no paid land-diversion programs for 1980 crops of wheat, corn, or other grains; no extensions of outstanding Commodity Credit Corporation (CCC) nonrecourse loans on upland cotton; and no set-aside acreage or diversion payments for rice. The government also implemented the Agricultural Adjustment Act of 1980, which set target prices for wheat and corn; a new disaster payments program for producers of wheat, feed grains, upland cotton, and rice; an emergency loan program for farmers unable to get credit; and assistance to corn producers unable to get storage in order to participate in the farmer-owned reserve program.

A "noncompliers" law became effective on April 11 to allow farmers who did not comply with the 1979 set-aside program to put crops into the farmer-owned grain reserve. Secretary of Agriculture Bob Bergland signed the International Food Aid Convention of 1980 on April 29, pledging a minimum of 4.47 million short tons (4.05 million metric tons) of U.S. grain for developing countries. On July 28, President Carter announced higher loan, release, call, and CCC sales prices for major U.S. crops. A new credit export program to develop and expand foreign markets for U.S. farm products went into effect on September 26. An Office of Consumer Affairs was established in the

U.S. Department of Agriculture (USDA). The support price for manufacturing milk was set at 80 per cent of parity on October 1.

Congressional Acts. Congress passed a number of pieces of legislation directly affecting the agricultural sector. The Energy Security Act of 1980 aimed at reducing U.S. dependence on foreign oil by establishing a U.S. Synthetic Fuels Corporation to promote the production of synthetic fuels by private industry; the Motor Carrier Act of 1980 updated the statutes governing federal regulation of the motor-carrier industry; and the New Rural Development Policy Act was designed to improve government rural development efforts.

The Agricultural Subterminal Facilities Act of 1980 authorizes up to $3.3 million in government loans for each fiscal year from 1981 to 1983 for the construction and improvement of subterminal storage and transportation facilities for bulk agricultural commodities. The National Aquaculture Act of 1980 directs the government to develop a national program promoting commercial production of fish and shellfish. The United States Grain Standards Act eliminates the mandatory federal weighing of grain moved into export elevators by rails or truck, grain shipped from export elevators to internal U.S. points, and any grain reaching such an elevator as an intracompany transaction. The Federal Crop Insurance Act of 1980 phases in a new crop-insurance program during the 1981 crop year.

The Food and Agricultural Act of 1977 expires with the harvest of the 1981 crops. More than just a "farm bill," it contains 19 broad titles encompassing most major public farm and food programs. These include the farm-commodity programs (wheat, feed grains, cotton, soybeans, rice, peanuts, sugar, dairy, wool, and mohair); Food for Peace foreign-aid programs; the food-stamp program; and rural development and conservation programs. Also, agricultural research, extension, and teaching funding that expires in 1982 may be reconsidered. Thus, the year ended with farmers much concerned about the public policy issues to be considered in 1981.

Outlook for 1981 Brighter. In December, the USDA predicted that 1981 will be a much better year for American farmers. In part, the improvement will be due to the hot and dry weather that reduced the 1980 grain crop and to economic problems that caused many livestock producers to liquidate their stock. These factors will mean smaller supplies of meat and grain in 1981, forcing prices up. The brighter forecast is based on an assumption that 1981's weather will provide normal growing conditions and that interest rates, important to farmers, will be lowered. Steve Gabriel of the USDA's Economics and Statistics Service said that interest rates will remain high in 1981, but at a lower level than in 1980.

If the USDA's assumptions hold true, farmers' net income in 1981 should total between $26 billion and $33 billion, compared with $23 billion to $25-billion in 1980, according to USDA.

Farm Technology went forward as energy research took the spotlight. Widespread efforts included a federal gasohol program with a production goal of 400 million gallons (1.5 billion liters) by 1981. Research centers were established at Peoria, Ill.; Tifton, Ga.; and Madison, Wis. Public and private technology research cooperated in joint ventures, such as a pilot gasification plant run by the University of California, Davis, with help from Diamond/Sunsweet, Incorporated, and the California State Printing Plant.

Energy research advances included improvements in nitrogen fixation to save on the amount of fertilizer spread. For example, researchers announced a new alfalfa strain with 70 per cent more nitrogen, and vetch plants that provided nitrogen for rice. Another development was wind-powered irrigation pumps that promise to save over half the fossil fuel now used for irrigation in the Great Plains. An infrared thermometer gun was developed to take the temperature of crops so that they can be more efficiently irrigated. Researchers also developed eucalyptus trees that are capable of supplying up to 22 metric tons (24 short tons) of biomass per hectare (2.5 acres) annually.

Animal Disease Technology was important, especially in view of outbreaks of African swine fever in Brazil, the Dominican Republic, Haiti, and Cuba. The continued threat of this disease – as well as the more contagious foot-and-mouth disease – being brought to the North American continent alarmed Congress, U.S. livestock farmers, and scientists at USDA's Plum Island Animal Disease Center on Long Island, N.Y. USDA scientists were experimenting with new genetic manipulation technology to fight foot-and-mouth disease.

Another Northern Hemisphere animal problem was declared almost solved in 1980. The federally sponsored screwworm-eradication program has eliminated this livestock pest from the Southeastern and Southwestern United States and drastically reduced it in northern Mexico.

The use of satellite data materially improved crop-production estimates throughout the world in 1980. Also, satellites helped develop world soil surveys and provided new information on solar radiation of the earth's surface. The extensive satellite program was the result of cooperation among many federal agencies, such as USDA, the Department of Commerce, and the Department of the Interior, and many universities and other organizations.   Charles E. French

See also FOOD. In WORLD BOOK, see AGRICULTURE; FARM AND FARMING.

FARM MACHINERY. See MANUFACTURING.

FASHION. What people wear to protect or decorate their bodies has been a reflection of their culture throughout history, and future generations looking back on 1980 will see a paradox. The year's fashion reflected political unrest, energy and economic problems, international trade agreements, changing social values and living conditions, and uncertainty about the future.

Women's clothing and accessories ran the gamut from conservative traditionalism to opulent fantasy. Many influential high-fashion designers in Europe and the United States reached back in history for inspiration for contemporary dressing. They looked to the Middle Ages, the reign of the Hapsburgs, the Renaissance, the Victorian era, the Nordic peasants, and the Peruvian Indians for something "new." A few daring avant-garde designers took their cues from futurism and designed garb that looked like uniforms for interplanetary space travel. The jump suits and other costumes they produced were part of a wave of "adventure dressing" that focused on rugged survival gear and turn-of-the-century English colonialism.

Classic, tailored separates, including a major revival of the classic "preppie" look that began in New England preparatory schools and colleges in the 1940s and 1950s, became a refuge for the growing number of women who preferred versatili-

Fashions by American designer Perry Ellis recall the miniskirt era, to the delight of at least some spectators at a fall showing.

ty and durability to high fashion. Children's clothing reflected the dressing habits of their parents.

International Fashion was more influenced by American sportswear in 1980 than at any time since the blue jeans generation of the 1960s crossed the Atlantic Ocean in their denims and introduced European young people to Levi's. Western garb grew in popularity in the U.S. along with the trend in entertainment toward country music and saloons, and America's cowboy and Indian clothes were the rage in Europe.

China Pact. The People's Republic of China, striving to develop industry, signed a three-year bilateral textile agreement with the United States in September.

China also saw its first American fashion show in September, when designer Halston presented a large collection of his high-priced finery on 12 models whom he had brought to Shanghai with him. Chinese reaction to Halston's plunging necklines and transparent fabrics reportedly ranged from "polite admiration to outright dismay."

Variety of Options. Designers tried to please women with many choices. Hemlines bounced like a yoyo. Some climbed above the knee, others dropped low on the leg, and still others stopped just below the knee. There was no prescribed length, day or night. Shapes ranged from tube-slim to extremely full, and blousons returned. This variety of lengths and shapes existed in every category of clothing. It was a banner year for many styles of pants, with knee-lengths for winter looking newest. Low-heeled shoes vied with high heels day and night in fashion importance for the first time in a decade.

Daytime clothing styles went into night in dressier fabrics, a casual approach in direct contrast with the year's opulent fantasy. Velvet was popular around the clock, and women wore lace with tweeds and leather. The color story included every color in the spectrum, with emphasis on blocks and asymmetrical bands of two or more colors. More opaque-colored hosiery appeared than at any time since the miniskirt heyday of the 1960s.

Men's Dressing Habits changed little from the previous two years, when a new tide of traditionalism put conservative styles back into the front rank of fashion after more than a decade of being labeled "square." Italy's Giorgio Armani remained the darling of high-fashion menswear, with an approach best described as traditional ease. The most significant change in the United States in 1980 was a subtle, continuing one. More men were allowed to wear sportscoats and slacks to business in areas where suits were required previously. Experimentation in men's fashion was largely confined to off-duty dressing, where bright color was an escape from the drabness of business dress.   Patricia Shelton

In WORLD BOOK, see FASHION.

FIELD, SALLY (1946-   ), won the Academy of Motion Picture Arts and Sciences Oscar for best actress in 1980. She was honored for her dramatic role as a union organizer in *Norma Rae*. The part contrasted vividly with the light role that first brought her fame, Sister Bertrille in the television series "The Flying Nun."

Sally Field was born on Nov. 6, 1946, in Pasadena, Calif. Her father owned a drugstore, and her mother, Margaret Field, was an actress who, after divorce and remarriage, acted under the name Maggie Mahoney.

After being graduated from high school in 1964, Field studied acting at the Columbia Pictures Workshop. While still a student, she won the starring role in the television series "Gidget," which lasted only one season but earned her critical praise.

She achieved stardom with "The Flying Nun," which premièred in 1967. In 1973, she starred in the less successful series "The Girl With Something Extra," which dealt in a light fashion with extrasensory perception.

Field made her motion-picture debut in 1967 in *The Way West*. Other film credits include *Stay Hungry* (1976) and *Smokey and the Bandit* (1977).

Divorced, Field is the mother of two sons. Her romance with *Smokey* co-star Burt Reynolds has been publicized extensively.   Patricia Dragisic

FINLAND. An economic boom led by export sales forced the government to revise its 1980 growth estimates upward several times. In February, the Bank of Finland predicted a 4.5 per cent growth, but by March it had increased its estimate to 7 per cent, equal to the 1979 rate.

Wage settlements in the spring were moderate for a boom year, averaging slightly more than 10 per cent. But the favorable situation brought financial worries. Finland's monetary unit, the markka, devalued by 2.3 per cent in 1979 to slow inflation and avoid a serious trade imbalance, was devalued another 2 per cent in March 1980.

Détente between Finland and its eastern neighbor, Russia, continued in spite of a worsening international situation. President Urho Kekkonen appealed for full European détente when the *Eduskunta* (parliament) session opened on February 5. He hinted that the Finns should not allow their feelings to influence their conduct toward Russia.

In February, Russia increased the price of the crude oil that it sells to Finland to the level of Organization of Petroleum Exporting Countries (OPEC) prices. Russia supplies two-thirds of Finland's oil.   Kenneth Brown

See also EUROPE (Facts in Brief Table). In WORLD BOOK, see FINLAND; KEKKONEN, URHO KALEVA.

FIRE. See DISASTERS.

FISHING. Sports-fishing organizations in the United States threw their support behind a proposed 3 per cent tax on the sale of power boats in testimony before the House of Representatives Merchant Marine Fisheries Subcommittee on March 18, 1980. The sports fishermen said a bill that would expand the 30-year-old Dingell-Johnson fisheries tax, now limited to a 10 per cent levy on fishing tackle, to include a tax on power boats would help federal and state fish-management programs.

Edwin Morgens, president of the American League of Anglers, said the power-boat tax could raise $80 million a year to support sports fishing. The proposal drew heavy fire from the outboard motor industry, dooming the legislation in 1980.

Australia announced on June 5 that it would ban all longline fishing in an extensive area off North Queensland, effective on Oct. 31, 1980. The International Game Fish Association hailed the decision as a victory for recreational fishermen.

Raymond D. Easley of Fullerton, Calif., landed the biggest largemouth bass on record in 48 years on March 4. His catch, a lunker weighing 21 pounds 3 ounces (9.6 kilograms), was taken at Lake Casitas, Oak View, Calif. On April 22, Keith Haines boated a 103-pound 12-ounce (47.1-kilograms) cobia off Destin, Fla.   Andrew L. Newman

In WORLD BOOK, see FISHING.

Michael Marinkovich of Milwaukee holds a 30-pound (14-kilogram) northern pike he took while ice fishing in neighboring Pike Lake.

FISHING INDUSTRY. The dispute between Canada and the United States over fishing quotas in the rich Georges Bank fishing area off Cape Cod continued to escalate in 1980. The neighboring countries signed two treaties in March 1979 that attempted to provide an orderly system for allocating fish catches within the 200-nautical-mile fishing zones both nations had adopted. But when U.S. fishermen protested that the allocations were unfair, senators from New England states delayed approving the treaties by proposing amendments that Carter Administration officials said would kill the pacts.

New Legislation. To bolster the U.S. fishing industry, the House of Representatives approved legislation on September 23 designed to phase out foreign fishing in the U.S. territorial zone. The House acted on the legislation after the Carter Administration, which had earlier opposed the proposal, agreed to a compromise version. No deadline was set for barring foreign fishermen; the date would be keyed to U.S. fishermen's ability to harvest their allotment. The Senate, however, did not act on the legislation.

The Senate unanimously approved legislation on May 5 authorizing $162.5 million in fisheries aid. Some funds were to be used to increase salmon and steelhead runs by developing new hatcheries. The rest of the money was to go for a buy-back program to reduce the size of the non-Indian commercial salmon-fishing fleet in the state of Washington.

The U.S. Department of Commerce in October set a limit of 20,500 on the number of porpoises that can be killed by tuna fishermen in the five years starting Jan. 1, 1981. Tuna fishermen prefer not to kill porpoises; they say they have no choice because porpoises become entangled in tuna nets.

French Fishermen blockaded most French ports in August to protest against the economic problems faced by their weakened industry. Heading their list of complaints was the cost of diesel fuel, which rose 30 cents a gallon (3.8 liters) in France in 1980. Fish have been harder to find in French waters, forcing fishermen to make more costly trips. More than 80 per cent of their catch is now found in foreign waters, and imports account for almost half of French fish consumption.

It was reported early in 1980 that the world's total fish catch in 1978 was 72,379,500 metric tons (79,784,700 short tons), only a 1.6 per cent gain over the 71,212,900 metric tons (78,498,800 short tons) caught in 1977. United States commercial landings in 1979 increased a record 4 per cent to 6.3 billion pounds (2.9 billion kilograms), valued at a record $2.2 billion.   Andrew L. Newman

In WORLD BOOK, see FISHING INDUSTRY.

FLOOD. See DISASTERS.

FLORIDA. See STATE GOVERNMENT.

FLOWER. See GARDENING.

FOOD. Abundant supplies resulting from record-setting production of United States farm commodities a year earlier dampened food price increases for consumers somewhat through the first half of 1980. But higher transportation, labor, energy, and other costs in the food-processing and distribution chain continued their upward push. By midyear, however, grocery prices were just 7 per cent higher than a year earlier — less than half the average price rise for nonfood items. This reflected generally lower farm commodity prices.

The Hot, Dry Summer began to take its toll on crops and pastures in widespread portions of the South and Midwest in July and August. At the same time, continued strong export demand for grains and oilseeds, along with prospects for reduced world sugar output, contributed to price increases for these commodities in world markets. Meanwhile, U.S. hog and poultry producers had begun to scale back their operations because of the unprofitable cost-price situation they were facing.

Higher Farm Prices that resulted, coupled with continued increases for processing and distribution costs, set the stage for higher retail food prices during the second half of 1980 and into 1981. The U.S. Department of Agriculture (USDA) estimated in October that 1980 retail food prices would average about 9 per cent above 1979 prices, compared with increases of 10 per cent and 11 per cent for 1978 and 1979, respectively. USDA also estimated that food prices could rise 10 to 15 per cent in 1981. Liberal supplies held U.S. per capita food consumption at relatively high levels, though the composition changed from the preceding year. Beef and veal consumption declined about 1.5 pounds (0.68 kilogram) per person. Cattlemen were rebuilding herds in nondrought areas, and this contributed to a reduced supply of beef going to market. The decline in beef consumption was more than offset by a 4-pound (1.8-kilogram) per-person increase for pork, part of which can be attributed to producers reducing the size of their herds by sending more hogs to market. Chicken consumption was down slightly, after four consecutive years of increasing production and consumption.

Among crop products, potato consumption was down, reflecting smaller crops in 1980. Large supplies of fruit resulted in increased consumption of both citrus and noncitrus products. Sugar consumption was lower as processors and consumers responded to sharply higher sugar prices.

World Food Supply prospects improved, based on early indications for major grain crops. While U.S. crops suffered from summer heat and drought, grain crops production outside the United States generally appeared to be larger than in 1979. Production increases for wheat and rice more than offset a small decline for coarse grains. Crops in the developing countries were generally larger

Per Capita U.S. Food Consumption, 1979-1980	1979		1980	
	Pounds (Kilograms)			
Milk and cream	283.0	(128.4)	279.0	(126.6)
Wheat flour (in all products)	120.0	(54.4)	120.0	(54.4)
Fresh vegetables	94.6	(42.9)	93.7	(42.5)
Sugar	91.1	(41.3)	88.2	(40.0)
Fresh fruits	81.3	(36.9)	85.5	(38.8)
Beef	79.6	(36.1)	78.3	(35.5)
Potatoes	75.9	(34.4)	71.2	(32.3)
Pork	65.0	(29.5)	69.7	(31.6)
Canned vegetables	55.7	(25.3)	57.5	(26.1)
Chicken	51.5	(23.4)	50.9	(23.1)
Eggs	35.8	(16.2)	36.3	(16.5)
Canned fruit	19.4	(8.8)	18.8	(8.5)
Cheese	17.6	(8.0)	17.2	(7.8)
Ice cream	17.5	(7.9)	17.2	(7.8)
Frozen fruits and fruit juices	12.3	(5.6)	13.9	(6.3)
Fish	13.3	(6.0)	13.2	(6.0)
Margarine	11.5	(5.2)	11.5	(5.2)
Frozen vegetables	11.1	(5.0)	11.0	(5.0)
Turkey	10.1	(4.6)	10.8	(4.9)
Coffee	8.6	(3.9)	8.8	(4.0)
Butter	4.6	(2.1)	4.5	(2.0)
Lamb and mutton	1.4	(0.6)	1.5	(0.7)
Veal	1.6	(0.7)	1.4	(0.6)
Tea	0.7	(0.3)	0.8	(0.4)

Source: U.S. Department of Agriculture

and should contribute to increased direct use of grain in human food. However, grain use in livestock feeding will probably be lower.

Aggregate world food production fell nearly 2.5 per cent in 1979, the first decline in seven years. Given world population growth, estimated at 1.8 per cent annually, this production shortfall reduced global food availabilities for 1980 by more than 4 per cent on a per capita basis. Much of the decline resulted from crop shortfalls in Africa, Russia, and South Asia. Declines in Africa and South Asia continued the trend toward lower per capita food production in both regions throughout the 1970s, in contrast to the upward trend exhibited by most other regions.

Sodium Nitrite has been used to cure foods — especially meats — for thousands of years. In the United States, nitrite is added in the processing of such traditional foods as bacon, ham, and hot dogs and other sausages. Nitrite has been used primarily because of its unique preservative qualities and particularly because it protects against the growth of organisms that cause botulism poisoning. However, the safety of nitrite has been the center of controversy since a 1978 report suggested that nitrite causes cancer in animals.

After a thorough review of that study by independent scientists, the USDA and the Food and Drug Administration determined that there was

insufficient evidence to support that conclusion. A joint statement issued by the two agencies in August 1980 stated that there is no reason to remove nitrite from foods at this time.

Nevertheless, nitrite has not been given a completely clean bill of health. The problem of nitrosamines still exists. These compounds, which may cause cancer, can form when nitrites combine with other substances during cooking or digestion. Testing will continue to determine the conditions under which nitrosamines are formed and to find alternative meat-curing methods that work as well as nitrites but without the potential hazards.

Soft Freeze. A process for freezing foods that does not harden foods and beverages was introduced in June by Rich Products Corporation of Buffalo, N.Y. Spokesmen called it the most important development in the industry since Clarence Birdseye popularized frozen foods in the 1930s.

The new process isolates the water in food and binds it to other substances in the food so that it does not crystallize at freezing temperatures. This prevents the food from hardening. "Soft-frozen" foods do not need to be thawed, and this should cut frozen-food wastage, according to the company, which will license its process for use by other food manufacturers.   Larry V. Summers

See also FARM AND FARMING. In WORLD BOOK, see FOOD; FOOD SUPPLY.

FOOTBALL. The Philadelphia Eagles and the surprising Oakland Raiders, both noted for defense, won the 1980 National Football League (NFL) conference championships. The University of Georgia, the only major team to win all its games, was chosen as the college champion.

The Eagles continued their improvement under Coach Dick Vermeil, and their defense, especially from the linebackers, often was awesome. Wilbert Montgomery, a relatively small running back, and Ron Jaworski, an underrated passer, led the Philadelphia offense.

The Raiders hardly figured to be a winning team, especially after Dan Pastorini, their newly acquired quarterback, broke his right leg in the fifth game of the season. Jim Plunkett replaced him and led the Raiders to an 11-5 regular-season record and a wild-card berth in the play-offs. Until then, the 32-year-old Plunkett, once a star with the New England Patriots, had languished on the bench and had thrown only 15 passes in 1979.

But Super Bowl XV climaxed a thrilling comeback year for the Raiders and Plunkett. The veteran quarterback threw three touchdown passes as the Raiders whipped the Eagles 27-10 in New Orleans on Jan. 25, 1981. One of Plunkett's passes, to halfback Kenny King, went for an 80-yard touchdown, the longest in Super Bowl history. Oakland's Rod Martin intercepted three passes.

The NFL's 28 teams played 16 games each during the regular season from September to December. One unexpected result was the demise of the Pittsburgh Steelers, who finished with a 9-7 record and failed to qualify for the play-offs. The Steelers had been in the play-offs the eight previous seasons and won four Super Bowls, including the last two.

With one week remaining in the season, five of the 10 play-off berths were unfilled. At season's end, the Eagles, the Dallas Cowboys, and the Atlanta Falcons, all from the National Football Conference (NFC), had the best records, all 12-4. At 11-5 were one team (the Los Angeles Rams) from the NFC and five (Oakland, the San Diego Chargers, the Cleveland Browns, the Buffalo Bills, and the Houston Oilers) from the American Football Conference (AFC). Those nine teams made the play-offs with the Minnesota Vikings (9-7).

The Play-Offs. In the AFC wild-card games on December 28 in Oakland, the Raiders beat Houston, 27-7, stopping Kenny Stabler's passing with seven sacks and two interceptions. Stabler had been Oakland's quarterback for 10 years until the Raiders traded him to Houston during the off-season for Pastorini. Oail Andrew (Bum) Phillips, the Houston coach who engineered that and other trades, was fired three days after the play-off defeat.

The Chargers defeated Buffalo, 20-14, on Jan. 3, 1981, in San Diego, on Dan Fouts's 50-yard touchdown pass with 2 minutes 8 seconds remaining. On January 4, Oakland upset the Browns, 14-12, on a freezing day in Cleveland, intercepting a pass in the end zone with 41 seconds left. The Raiders upset the Chargers, 34-27, in the AFC championship game on January 11 in San Diego, as Plunkett passed for two touchdowns and ran for one.

Dallas opened the NFC play-offs by beating Los Angeles, 34-13, on Dec. 28, 1980, in Irving, Tex., as Tony Dorsett ran for 160 yards. The Eagles eliminated Minnesota, 31-16, on Jan. 3, 1981, in Philadelphia, as the Vikings lost five interceptions and three fumbles. The next day Dallas upset the Falcons, 30-27, in Atlanta on two touchdown passes from Danny White to Drew Pearson in the last 3 minutes 40 seconds. In the NFC championship game on January 11 in Philadelphia, the Eagles stifled the Dallas offense and won, 20-7. Montgomery led the Eagles, carrying the ball 26 times for 194 yards.

Brian Sipe of Cleveland and Jaworski became the conference passing leaders, and Fouts passed for 4,715 yards, breaking his all-time one-season record. Earl Campbell of Houston rushed for 1,934 yards and led the league for the third time in his three-year career. Walter Payton of the Chicago Bears, with 1,460 yards, led NFC rushers for the fifth straight season. Billy Sims of the Detroit Lions, a rookie, rushed for 1,303 yards and led the

1980 College Conference Champions

Conference	School
Atlantic Coast	North Carolina
Big Eight	Oklahoma
Big Sky	Boise State
Big Ten	Michigan
Ivy League	Yale
Mid-American	Central Michigan
Missouri Valley	Tulsa
Ohio Valley	Western Kentucky
Pacific Coast	Long Beach State
Pacific Ten	Washington
Southeastern	Georgia
Southern	Furman
Southland	McNeese State
Southwest	Baylor
Southwestern	Jackson State
Western Athletic	Brigham Young
Yankee	Boston U.

The Bowl Games

Bowl	Winner	Loser
Amos Alonzo Stagg (Div. III)	Dayton 63	Ithaca 0
Bluebonnet	North Carolina 16	Texas 7
Blue-Gray	Blue 24	Gray 23
Camellia (Div. 1AA)	Boise State 31	Eastern Kentucky 29
Cotton	Alabama 30	Baylor 2
Fiesta	Penn State 31	Ohio State 19
Garden State	Houston 35	Navy 0
Gator	Pittsburgh 37	South Carolina 9
Hall of Fame	Arkansas 34	Tulane 15
Holiday	Brigham Young 46	Southern Methodist 45
Hula	West 24	East 17
Independence	Southern Mississippi 16	McNeese State 14
Japan	West 25	East 13
Liberty	Purdue 28	Missouri 25
Orange	Oklahoma 18	Florida State 17
Peach	Miami (Fla.) 20	Virginia Tech 10
Rose	Michigan 23	Washington 6
Senior	North 23	South 10
Shrine	East 21	West 3
Sugar	Georgia 17	Notre Dame 10
Sun	Nebraska 31	Mississippi State 17
Tangerine	Florida 35	Maryland 20
Zia (Div. II)	Cal Poly 21	Eastern Illinois 13
NAIA Division I	Elon 17	Northeast Oklahoma 10
NAIA Division II	Pacific Lutheran 38	Wilmington 10

All-America Team (as picked by UPI)

Offense
Wide receiver—Ken Margerum, Stanford
Tight end—Dave Young, Purdue
Tackles—Keith Van Horne, Southern California; Mark May, Pittsburgh
Guards—Randy Schleusener, Nebraska; Roy Foster, Southern California
Center—John Scully, Notre Dame
Quarterback—Mark Herrmann, Purdue
Running backs—George Rogers, South Carolina; Herschel Walker, Georgia; Jarvis Redwine, Nebraska
Place kicker—Rex Robinson, Georgia

Defense
Ends—Hugh Green, Pittsburgh; E. J. Junior, Alabama
Tackles—Kenneth Sims, Texas; Leonard Mitchell, Houston
Middle guard—Ron Simmons, Florida State
Linebackers—Mike Singletary, Baylor; Bob Crable, Notre Dame; Lawrence Taylor, North Carolina
Defensive backs—Scott Woerner, Georgia; Ronnie Lott, Southern California; Ken Easley, UCLA
Punter—Rohn Stark, Florida State

Player Awards

Heisman Trophy—George Rogers, South Carolina
Lombardi Award—Hugh Green, Pittsburgh
Maxwell Trophy—Hugh Green, Pittsburgh
Outland Award—Mark May, Pittsburgh

league by scoring 16 touchdowns. The best defensive players were tackle Randy White of Dallas, free safety Nolan Cromwell of Los Angeles, and linebacker Ted Hendricks and cornerback Lester Hayes of Oakland.

Raiders Suit. The NFL was shaken by a bitter struggle pitting the Raiders against Commissioner Pete Rozelle and the other club owners. Before the 1980 season, the Los Angeles Rams moved 30 miles (48 kilometers) south to Anaheim, Calif., to play in Anaheim Stadium. Al Davis, the Oakland Raiders managing general partner, tried to move his team more than 400 miles (640 kilometers) south to play in the Memorial Coliseum in Los Angeles.

The Oakland public, which had provided sellout crowds for almost every home game in the 1970s, objected to the move. So did Rozelle, who said NFL bylaws prohibited it without approval of three-fourths of the club owners. Davis said permission was not required, and on March 1 he signed an agreement with Los Angeles officials to move. NFL club owners voted 22-0 on March 10 to bar the move. Davis then sued the NFL, charging antitrust violations, in an attempt to move in time for the 1981 season.

The Professional Football Hall of Fame in Canton, Ohio, added four players from the 1960s and 1970s — defensive end David (Deacon) Jones, defensive tackle Bob Lilly, center Jim Otto, and defensive back Herb Adderley.

Standings in American Football Conference

Eastern Division

	W.	L.	T.	Pct.
Buffalo	11	5	0	.688
New England	10	6	0	.625
Miami	8	8	0	.500
Baltimore	7	9	0	.438
New York Jets	4	12	0	.250

Central Division

	W.	L.	T.	Pct.
Cleveland	11	5	0	.688
Houston	11	5	0	.688
Pittsburgh	9	7	0	.563
Cincinnati	6	10	0	.375

Western Division

	W.	L.	T.	Pct.
San Diego	11	5	0	.688
Oakland	11	5	0	.688
Denver	8	8	0	.500
Kansas City	8	8	0	.500
Seattle	4	12	0	.250

American Conference Individual Statistics

Scoring

	TDs.	E.P.	F.G.	Pts.
Smith, New England	0	51	26	129
Benirschke, San Diego	0	46	24	118
Steinfort, Denver	0	32	26	110
Bahr, Oakland	0	41	19	98
Lowery, Kansas City	0	37	20	97

Passing

	Att.	Comp.	Pct.	Yds.	TDs.
Sipe, Cleveland	554	337	60.8	4,132	30
Fouts, San Diego	589	348	59.1	4,715	30
Morton, Denver	301	183	60.8	2,150	12
Fuller, Kansas City	320	193	60.3	2,250	10
Jones, Baltimore	446	248	55.6	3,134	23

Receiving

	No. Caught	Total Yds.	Avg. Gain	TDs.
Winslow, San Diego	89	1,290	14.5	9
Jefferson, San Diego	82	1,340	16.3	13
Joiner, San Diego	71	1,132	15.9	4
Largent, Seattle	66	1,064	16.1	6
M. Pruitt, Cleveland	63	471	7.5	0

Rushing

	Att.	Yds.	Avg. Gain	TDs.
Campbell, Houston	373	1,934	5.2	13
Cribbs, Buffalo	306	1,185	3.9	11
M. Pruitt, Cleveland	249	1,034	4.2	6
Van Eeghen, Oakland	222	838	3.8	5
Muncie, San Diego	175	827	4.7	6

Punting

	No.	Yds.	Avg.	Longest
Prestridge, Denver	70	3,075	43.9	57
Guy, Oakland	71	3,099	43.6	66
Roberts, Miami	77	3,279	42.6	71
Ramsey, N.Y. Jets	73	3,096	42.4	59
Weaver, Seattle	67	2,798	41.8	62

Punt Returns

	No.	Yds.	Avg.	TDs.
Smith, Kansas City	40	581	14.5	2
James, New England	33	331	10.0	1
Bell, Pittsburgh	34	339	10.0	0
Fuller, San Diego	30	298	9.9	0
Upchurch, Denver	37	353	9.5	0

Standings in National Football Conference

Eastern Division

	W.	L.	T.	Pct.
Philadelphia	12	4	0	.750
Dallas	12	4	0	.750
Washington	6	10	0	.375
St. Louis	5	11	0	.313
New York Giants	4	12	0	.250

Central Division

	W.	L.	T.	Pct.
Minnesota	9	7	0	.563
Detroit	9	7	0	.563
Chicago	7	9	0	.438
Tampa Bay	5	10	1	.344
Green Bay	5	10	1	.344

Western Division

	W.	L.	T.	Pct.
Atlanta	12	4	0	.750
Los Angeles	11	5	0	.688
San Francisco	6	10	0	.375
New Orleans	1	15	0	.063

National Conference Individual Statistics

Scoring

	TDs.	E.P.	F.G.	Pts.
Murray, Detroit	0	35	27	116
Mazzetti, Atlanta	0	46	19	103
Corral, Los Angeles	0	51	16	99
Sims, Detroit	16	0	0	96
Franklin, Philadelphia	0	48	16	96

Passing

	Att.	Comp.	Pct.	Yds.	TDs.
Jaworski, Philadelphia	451	257	57.0	3,529	27
Ferragamo, Los Angeles	404	240	59.4	3,199	30
Bartkowski, Atlanta	463	257	55.5	3,544	31
Montana, San Francisco	273	176	64.5	1,795	15
Danielson, Detroit	417	244	58.5	3,223	13

Receiving

	No. Caught	Total Yds.	Avg. Gain	TDs.
Cooper, San Francisco	83	567	6.8	4
Clark, San Francisco	82	991	12.1	8
Lofton, Green Bay	71	1,226	17.3	4
Rashad, Minnesota	69	1,095	15.9	5
Tilley, St. Louis	68	966	14.2	6

Rushing

	Att.	Yds.	Avg. Gain	TDs.
W. Payton, Chicago	317	1,460	4.6	6
Anderson, St. Louis	301	1,352	4.5	9
Andrews, Atlanta	265	1,308	4.9	4
Sims, Detroit	313	1,303	4.2	13
Dorsett, Dallas	278	1,185	4.3	11

Punting

	No.	Yds.	Avg.	Longest
Jennings, N.Y. Giants	94	4,211	44.8	63
Blanchard, Tampa Bay	88	3,722	42.3	62
Skladany, Detroit	72	3,036	42.2	67
Swider, St. Louis	99	4,111	41.5	66
Miller, San Francisco	77	3,152	40.9	65

Punt Returns

	No.	Yds.	Avg.	TDs.
Johnson, Atlanta	23	281	12.2	0
Solomon, San Francisco	27	298	11.0	2
Green, St. Louis	16	168	10.5	1
J. Jones, Dallas	54	548	10.1	0
Nelms, Washington	48	487	10.1	0

Canadian Football. The Edmonton Eskimos (13-3) and the Hamilton Tiger-Cats (8-7-1) won the division titles in the nine-team Canadian Football League. They survived the play-offs and met on November 23 in Toronto for the Grey Cup. Edmonton won, 48-10, for its third straight Canadian title, as Warren Moon passed for three touchdowns. Quarterback Dieter Brock of the Winnipeg Blue Bombers was the league's outstanding player.

College Football. The regular season ended with Georgia sporting an 11-0 record; Brigham Young with 11-1; Florida State, Pittsburgh, Baylor, and North Carolina with 10-1; Notre Dame with 9-1-1; Oklahoma, Nebraska, Michigan, Ohio State, Alabama, Mississippi State, UCLA, Washington, and Penn State, 9-2; and Southern California, 8-2-1.

Georgia had to win the Sugar Bowl game on Jan. 1, 1981, to assure itself of the unofficial national title, and it did. It beat Notre Dame, 17-10, as Herschel Walker ran for 150 yards in 36 carries. Two days later, the final polls of the Associated Press and United Press International placed Georgia first, Pittsburgh second, Oklahoma third, Michigan fourth, and Florida State fifth.

Walker, an 18-year-old freshman, was perhaps the year's most spectacular player. In the Heisman Trophy voting to determine the outstanding college player, he finished third.   Frank Litsky

In WORLD BOOK, see FOOTBALL.

The former President cautiously descends a ladder after inspecting work on the Gerald R. Ford Presidential Museum in Grand Rapids, Mich.

FORD, GERALD RUDOLPH (1913-   ), 38th President of the United States, flirted with becoming the Republican Party's vice-presidential candidate in 1980. In three days of negotiations during the Republican convention in July, Ford and presidential nominee Ronald Reagan discussed what role Ford might play in a Reagan Administration. On July 16, in a televised interview with Walter Cronkite of CBS Inc. at the Republican convention, Ford admitted that he might accept the vice-presidential nomination, and he repeated that statement a few minutes later in an American Broadcasting Company (ABC) interview with Barbara Walters.

Just before midnight, however, Ford finally refused Reagan's offer of the vice-presidential spot on the ticket, appearing before the convention with Reagan shortly thereafter to say that he could help his party more in the role of campaigner than as a vice-presidential candidate.

The Would-Be Candidate. Ford had declared on March 1 that Ronald Reagan could not win the presidency and said that "if there was an honest-to-goodness, bona fide urging by a broad-based group in my party, I would respond." But although Florida supporters had formed a Draft Ford Committee on March 6 and former Secretary of State Henry A. Kissinger had urged Ford to run, discussions with his staff and with high-ranking Republi-cans convinced the former President that he lacked the necessary support to win the nomination. Ford announced on March 15 what he termed "the toughest decision in my life" – his "final and certain" decision not to enter the 1980 presidential race so as not to "further divide my party."

When George H. W. Bush released his delegates to Reagan on May 26, assuring Reagan the nomination, Ford was among the first to congratulate Reagan. Meeting with Reagan at Ford's home in Rancho Mirage, Calif., on June 5, he promised to campaign for Republican candidates. Ford spent almost two months on the campaign circuit, making some 300 appearances in 30 states. He often referred to Reagan as an "able, dedicated, and responsible person" and sharply criticized President Jimmy Carter's foreign and domestic record. Ford conferred with Reagan in Middleburg, Va., before Reagan's debate with President Carter on October 27.

Personal Notes. Ford was elected to directorships of GK Technologies; Shearson Loeb Rhodes, Incorporated, a brokerage house; and Tiger International, Incorporated, an airline-freight and insurance firm, in 1980. On August 15, daughter Susan Ford Vance gave birth to the Fords' second grandchild, Tyne Mary Vance.   Carol L. Thompson

See also REPUBLICAN PARTY. In WORLD BOOK, see FORD, GERALD RUDOLPH.

FOREST AND FOREST PRODUCTS. The timber industry in the Pacific Northwest slumped severely early in 1980, creating one of the area's worst lumber recessions. A decline in housing starts, a mainstay of the industry, led lumber companies to curb sawmill operations and to ship more logs to Japan. Unemployment was expected to ease in 1981 with an increase in housing starts, but the long-term outlook was grim.

An acute shortage of timber ready for cutting in the Northwest has led major forest companies to look to the Southeast for new supplies. United States Forest Service experts predicted a decline of up to 45 per cent in wood-products employment in Washington and Oregon over the next 20 years.

Federal Forests. With the wood supply from private forests in the area expected to be reduced until the 1990s, timber companies urged the U.S. government to permit increased harvesting on federal lands. Environmentalists responded that the Forest Service is required by law to manage its lands under multiple-use policies to protect water and wildlife resources and for recreation.

President Jimmy Carter announced on June 20 that he was asking the Forest Service to reach annual supply goals of between 11 billion and 12.5 billion board feet (26 million and 29 million cubic meters) for timber by 1985 by relaxing long-standing sustained-yield policies under which only as much timber is cut as is grown to replace it. The National Forest Products Association welcomed this aspect of the President's policy, but noted that since the projected harvest for 1980 was 12.2 billion board feet (29 million cubic meters), the changed policy will have no immediate significance. John B. Crowell, Jr., of the Louisiana-Pacific Corporation, a major lumber company, said, "There is no timber shortage in this country, and there isn't going to be one. But there could be a wood-products shortage if we don't start cutting and managing federal lands properly." Forest Service chief R. Max Peterson said reforestation aid to state and private foresters will double replanting by 1985.

Forest Fires. Drought, high temperatures, and volcanic ash from the eruption of Mount Saint Helens all contributed to a difficult fire-fighting season in the Western states (see GEOLOGY [Close-Up]). During July and August, brush fires broke out in Arizona, California, Utah, and Wyoming. In Montana, the volcanic ash created haze that hid the smoke, making it difficult to detect new fires. The Bureau of Land Management reported on August 21 that brush fires during the summer had charred about 33,000 acres (13,330 hectares) of desert, the most ever recorded. Andrew L. Newman

In the Special Reports section, see PONDERING THE FATE OF THE FORESTS. In WORLD BOOK, see FOREST; FOREST PRODUCTS; FORESTRY.

FORLANI, ARNALDO (1925-   ), became prime minister of Italy on Oct. 18, 1980, heading a coalition of Christian Democrats, Socialists, Social Democrats, and Republicans. He was president of the Christian Democrat Party's National Council. Forlani succeeded fellow Christian Democrat Francesco Cossiga, whose government fell on September 27 when Parliament rejected his economic program. See COSSIGA, FRANCESCO; ITALY.

Arnaldo Forlani was born on Dec. 8, 1925, in Pesaro, a city on the Adriatic Sea in northern Italy. He holds a degree in law. Forlani was elected secretary of the Christian Democrat Party for Pesaro province at age 23. He was elected to the party's National Council in 1952 and to its Central Political Office in 1954. He has served with both groups ever since.

Forlani was elected to Italy's Chamber of Deputies – the lower house of Parliament – in 1958 and was re-elected in 1963, 1968, and 1972. He was national secretary of the party from 1969 until 1973 and was elected president of the National Council in 1979.

Forlani's first government post, in 1969, was minister for public holdings and agencies. He was minister for United Nations affairs in 1969 and 1970, defense minister from 1974 until 1976, then foreign minister until 1979. Jay Myers

FOUR-H CLUBS. See YOUTH ORGANIZATIONS.

FRANCE. The bombing of a Jewish synagogue in Paris on Oct. 3, 1980, in which four persons died and 12 were injured, climaxed a year of unrest at home and discord with France's neighbors. Thousands of French citizens marched in demonstrations after the bombing to protest this and other recent anti-Semitic attacks.

President Valéry Giscard d'Estaing and his government came under attack after the violence. Israel's Foreign Minister Yitzhak Shamir blamed France's support of the Palestine Liberation Organization. French Jewish leaders charged that the government had failed to take the neo-Nazi threat seriously. Giscard expressed solidarity with the Jews "in the name of the whole French people."

But anti-Semitism was not France's only problem. The government and the people were deeply divided on key issues. Rebellious farmers and fishermen opposed the government and angered neighboring countries, particularly Great Britain. Strikes by doctors against new health-service plans and by electrical workers seeking more pay and fewer hours, plus environmentalists' dissatisfaction with plans for nuclear power, disrupted production and made life in the cities difficult.

Lamb War. For the second time, European Commissioner for Agriculture Finn Gundelach announced on January 14 that he would take France to the European Court of Justice for refusing to

Hundreds of tourists are stranded at the French port of Cherbourg
in August when striking fishermen block English Channel ferries.

remove import controls on British lamb. France's policy was contrary to the rules of the European Community (EC or Common Market). Great Britain claimed $65 million damages from France, but the court's advocate-general ruled on March 25 that emergency legal action against France was not justified. The situation eased in October when the EC adopted a new system of price supports for sheep farmers. France also angered West Germany and the Netherlands in June by cutting lamb imports to 70 per cent of the tonnage imported in May. The French claimed that lamb originating in Eastern Europe had flooded the market. Hundreds of Spanish truckdrivers blocked the French border for 20 hours on June 17 in retaliation for the hijacking and burning of nine Spanish fruit and vegetable trucks. The roadblocks caused huge traffic jams.

Ports Blockaded. Angry fishermen blockaded ports in August in protest because the government was offering only $10 million in aid to the industry. In addition, the government ordered trawler owners to cut costs by reducing wages and the size of crews. The workers refused to accept wage cuts. Meanwhile, coastal fishermen blamed low fish prices and high fuel costs for their own difficulties.

Fishermen blocked all channel ports on August 13 to cargo boats, small cruisers, and ferries. Ferries taking thousands of vacationers to and from France could not dock, though one or two broke through the chains that the blockaders had placed across harbors. Some fighting broke out between vacationers and fishermen, and some ferries were rerouted to Belgian ports. About 7,000 British vacationers were stranded at Cherbourg for three days with inadequate sanitary and medical facilities, so the blockade was lifted for 24 hours on August 19.

Revenue Losses. The effect on the economy was serious. Cargo ships and oil tankers also were locked out, and revenue losses at the port of Le Havre were estimated at $1.25 million a day. The French Navy used water cannons on August 21 to open the Mediterranean port of Fos-sur-Mer, where nearly half of France's imported oil is unloaded. Boulogne-sur-Mer was hit the worst when truckdrivers joined the blockade and put the town in a state of siege. The fishermen lifted the blockade at several ports on August 23 and 24, but reimposed it on August 25. The blockade eased on September 3 when fleet owners and fishermen agreed to new crew sizes for trawlers. Kenneth Brown

See also EUROPE (Facts in Brief Table). In WORLD BOOK, see FRANCE.

FUTURE FARMERS OF AMERICA (FFA). See YOUTH ORGANIZATIONS.

GABON. See AFRICA.

GAMBIA. See AFRICA.

GAMES, MODELS, AND TOYS

GAMES, MODELS, AND TOYS. The toy industry in the United States held its own in 1980 despite the recession. Credit went to three predominant trends — increased year-round sales, a resurgence of basic toy purchases, and more home entertainment. Consumers became more value conscious and bought playthings with repeat play appeal such as games, dolls, stuffed toys, and craft and hobby kits.

Game Sales, traditionally strong, were bolstered by the year-round popularity of new adventure games and electronic-computer games. Because they challenge the player's intellect, adventure games including war games as well as strategy games dealing with sports, science fiction, and fantasy themes, appealed to a wide audience.

Sales of electronic games accounted for about 10 per cent of all toy sales in 1980. Newer, more sophisticated computer games, in which a microprocessor is programmed to challenge a human opponent in games such as chess, were developed through research with large computers. Many of these new games employed computer-synthesized voices that commented on the player's performance. New versions of programmable video-game systems that utilized a television screen for sports and strategy games were introduced, as were home computers capable of helping with homework and preparing tax returns.

Two toy companies exhibited solar-powered playthings at the 1980 American Toy Fair in February in New York City. Some engineers heralded solar power as a technological advance equivalent to the development of low-cost plastics and electronics — each of which introduced a new toy manufacturing era.

Doll Revival. The continued popularity of baby and fashion dolls, and a growing interest in collector dolls, allowed doll sales to make an impressive comeback in 1980, after a two-year decline. A doll electronically programmed to simulate infant babble was introduced in 1980, joining a wide array of baby dolls that can walk, drink, eat, cry, and wet. The continued popularity of fashion dolls and action figures, with a myriad of outfits and accessories, modeled after popular movie and TV characters, reflected the increasing variety of activities in which women are engaged today. Antique fanciers bought exquisitely designed new dolls, as well as vinyl reproductions of porcelain originals.

Lines of toys licensed to portray characters from motion pictures, television programs, and comic strips enjoyed continued popularity. Some manufacturers extended lines of licensed products to include toys, puppets, games, dolls, playsets, and puzzles.　　　　　　　　　　　Donna M. Datre

In WORLD BOOK, see DOLL; GAME; MODEL MAKING; TOY.

GANDHI, INDIRA PRIYADARSHINI

GANDHI, INDIRA PRIYADARSHINI (1917-   ), became prime minister of India for the second time in her stormy political career when her Congress-I Party won two elections in January 1980. She previously served as prime minister from 1966 to 1977. Attempting a comeback in 1978, she won a seat in Parliament. However, Parliament voted to take away the seat and jailed her for a week on contempt charges. See INDIA.

Despite her triumphant return to power, Gandhi had a difficult year in 1980. She narrowly escaped an assassination attempt in April — the first against an Indian prime minister while in office, and the third in her career as a public figure. Then her son Sanjay, 33, probably the most powerful politician in India after her, was killed in a plane crash in June. His death ended any hopes she might have had of continuing the political dynasty started by her father.

Indira Gandhi was the only child of the late Jawaharlal Nehru, India's first prime minister. She was born in Allahabad and attended Santiniketan University in India and Oxford University in England. In 1942, she married Feroze Gandhi, who died in 1960. They had two sons.

Indira Gandhi started her political career as an adviser to her father. She also served as the minister of information and broadcasting from 1964 to 1966.　　　　　　　　　　　Patricia Dragisic

A collector displays the original Barbie, right, and the latest model at a New York City party celebrating the popular doll's 21st birthday.

GARDENING. Lawn problems were bad enough in many parts of the United States because of 1980's summer drought and heat, but two new turf insects added to the difficulties. The new pests caused wilting that was easily confused with that resulting from dryness or heat. The Department of Agriculture's Science and Education Administration reported that the black turfgrass *Ataenius,* a black beetle less than a quarter-inch (6 millimeters) long, badly damages lawns during its white grub stage when it feeds on grass roots. The other pest, the greenbug, a yellow-green aphid with green stripes, attacks Kentucky bluegrass. Although it cannot survive winter in the North, it migrates and can complete a generation every seven days, enough time to harm a lawn by midsummer. Both pests can be controlled with Sevin or diazinon.

U.S. Wild Flowers seldom make it into gardens in their own country, though many — such as goldenrod (*Solidago*) and sneezeweed (*Helenium*) — are popular in Europe. Others, such as Russell Lupines, have re-entered their native hemisphere disguised as European-bred forms. Currently, some North American species of *Clematis,* small-flowered cousins of the garden *Clematis,* are coming home. One such species, *C. texensis,* with bell-shaped, 1-inch (2.5-centimeter), bright-red blossoms, is returning glamorized in such varieties as deep-pink Duchess of Albany and ruby-red Gravetye Beauty.

New Plants. All-America Selections included one silver and four bronze medals for four ornamental plants and one vegetable in 1980. All were distinguished for their compact form, allowing them to fit neatly into today's small home gardens. The silver medal winner, Peter Pan Flame Zinnia, displays 3-inch (7.6-centimeter), crimson blooms on 12-inch (30-centimeter) plants.

Dwarf French Marigold Janie is early, yellow-flowered, and about 8 inches (20 centimeters) tall. Verbena Sangria is a creeping plant with flat clusters of wine-red blooms. Ornamental Pepper Holiday Time can be grown as a low edging plant in the garden or as an indoor potted plant. Its yellow, turning red, fruit provides color — and very hot seasoning. Zucchini Squash Gold Rush requires only about 4 square feet (0.37 square meter) of garden space and will yield long, golden zucchini-type squash.

All-America Rose Selections for 1981 include a white grandiflora, White Lightnin', developed by Herbert C. Swim of southern California; a luminous red-orange hybrid tea, Bing Crosby, produced by Ollie Weeks of Ontario, Calif.; and a nonfading coral floribunda, Marina, hybridized by Reimer Kordes of Sparrieshoop, West Germany.

David Burpee, 87, of Doylestown, Pa., died on June 24. The retired president of the W. Atlee Burpee Company, which he headed for 55 years, he was widely known for his interest in marigolds and

Hydroponics — growing plants in water — is increasingly popular among gardeners, who claim larger crops and shorter growing times.

for his campaign to name the marigold the national flower of the United States.

The Flowering Plant Index of Illustration and Information, compiled by Richard T. Isaacson, was published in 1980 by the Garden Center of Greater Cleveland. Each of its 55,000 entries, arranged alphabetically by botanical name and cross-referenced by common name, lists author and title of the indexed work, and indicates its type of flower or fruit. About 400 works are indexed, and most are popular books published since 1930 that are most likely to be available in public libraries.

A new honey melon is, quite literally, one of the fruits of renewed diplomatic relations with the People's Republic of China. The *hami gua* (honey melon) is popular in China for its sweet flavor, crisp texture, and long-keeping quality, according to E. V. Wann of the Science and Education Administration of the Department of Agriculture, who in 1980 led a seven-member team of scientists to China. The visitors returned with more than 120 varieties of plants new to U.S. horticulture. The new forms may prove useful in improving yields, flavor, nutritive values, and disease resistance in American crops.   Phil Clark

In WORLD BOOK, see FLOWER; GARDENING; PLANT.

GAS AND GASOLINE. See ENERGY; PETROLEUM AND GAS.

GEOLOGY. The repeated eruption of Mount Saint Helens in Washington was the biggest geologic event of 1980. But in a sense, it was no surprise to geologists. Mount Saint Helens is part of the Cascade Range, a chain of volcanoes that extends from Lassen Peak and Mount Shasta in northern California to Mount Baker in northern Washington. Geologists have long known that all of these are *active* volcanoes — likely to erupt again. They know the average time between eruptions of any volcano is well over 200 years, the period for which records are available for the Pacific Northwest. Because record keeping in the Cascades is still relatively new, many maps list most Cascade volcanoes as dormant or inactive.

But the driving force behind the Cascade volcanoes has been very steady through several thousand years — recent geologic time. The theory of plate tectonics holds that the earth's crust is made up of about 20 giant plates. Since the 1960s, geophysicists have noted increased plate movement caused by the production of new oceanic crust at the Juan de Fuca Ridge off Oregon and Washington, at the edge of the Pacific Plate. The pushing of that crust beneath the coast of North America to produce the Cascade volcanoes has been equally steady. The resulting plate movements produced an eruption. See Close-Up.

Saint Helens Singled Out. Years before the eruptions, Mount Saint Helens had been singled out by scientists as especially dangerous. The beautiful symmetry of its cone was a hint that most of the cone had been built after the Ice Age glaciers retreated about 10,000 years ago. Other peaks in the Cascades, including Mount Hood, Mount Shasta, and Mount Rainer, have been partially carved up by glaciers, giving them less regular shapes. This visible contrast suggested that Mount Saint Helens had erupted more frequently than its neighbors.

A more explicit warning was sounded in 1975. Carbon-14 dating of charcoal buried by earlier lava flows and ash falls showed that Mount Saint Helens had been erupting every few hundred years.

Unusual Ash. Geologists were surprised when they examined the ash from the cataclysmic eruption of May 18. The ash appeared to contain only some crystals and many opaque grains, not the familiar shattered bubble walls. But a scanning electron microscope showed tiny bubbles. They were tiny because the May 18 explosion began on a time scale of less than one minute, in contrast to typical ash-producing eruptions, which occur over two or three days.   Kenneth S. Deffeyes

In WORLD BOOK, see GEOLOGY; VOLCANO.
GEORGIA. See STATE GOVERNMENT.

In an awesome display of power, Mount Saint Helens hurls billowing cloud of ash and steam 60,000 feet (18,000 meters) into the sky in May 18 blast.

Mount St. Helens Erupts

The peaceful beauty of the Cascade Mountains in the northwestern United States was shattered on May 18, 1980, when Mount Saint Helens in Washington erupted. A massive blast — the most serious of a number during the year — blew away more than 1,000 feet (300 meters) of the mountaintop and killed at least 34 persons. The volcano's eruption showered mud in the immediate area and ash over several states and changed the environment for years to come.

The blast, which was clearly heard 135 miles (215 kilometers) away, equaled the force of 10 million short tons (9 million metric tons) of TNT. It was about 500 times as powerful as the atomic bomb dropped on Hiroshima, Japan, in 1945, and it destroyed all life in an area of about 155 square miles (400 square kilometers). The eruption snapped off all the giant trees within 15 miles (24 kilometers) of the summit. It clogged rivers and streams with debris, causing some $2.7 billion in damage.

Mount Saint Helens had been inactive from 1857 until March 27, 1980, when it began to shake with localized earthquakes. The 1980 eruptions were the first in the continental United States outside Alaska since 1921, when Lassen Peak in California erupted.

A volcano is an opening in the earth through which ash, rock, and hot gases burst when magma, or melted rock, builds up just below the earth's surface. The magma accumulates near the surface, where it is under great pressure from the surrounding rock and from gases trapped with the magma. Eventually, the magma erupts, spouting a shower of intensely hot material.

Most volcanoes, including Mount Saint Helens, are found along a belt called the *Ring of Fire* that encircles the Pacific Ocean. According to the plate tectonics theory, the earth's outer shell is divided into about 20 giant plates that slide slowly over a layer of partly melted rock. Most volcanoes form when two of these plates collide and one slides under the other. The edges of the lower plate melt because of friction and the earth's heat, and the melted material rises into a peak, producing a volcano.

Plate movement is complex, and stresses between plates are relieved by earth movements as well as by eruptions. By monitoring earth tremors, two geologists predicted in 1978 that Mount Saint Helens was the likeliest candidate in the Cascades for a major destructive eruption.

Fortunately, Mount Saint Helens' earlier rumblings prompted authorities to evacuate residents from towns in the Toutle River Valley on the mountain's slope before the devastating May 18 eruption. However, those listed as missing after the mountain blew up included Harry Truman (no relation to the late President), 84, who refused to leave, saying he would never abandon his home at Spirit Lake, near the summit.

Biologists predicted that the complete recovery of plants and wildlife in the area would take many years. Large game animals such as deer, they said, would not return in great numbers for years, because they need the cover of the trees destroyed in May. Still, by September, scientists found a few deer tracks on the mountain's upper slopes. Smaller animals were returning, but they require insects for food. Insects, although they reproduce rapidly, must adapt to the changed plant environment — fewer and younger plants.

Millions of salmon and trout were killed outright by the hot mud that clogged the Columbia, Cowlitz, and Toutle rivers. And many spawning grounds where new generations of fish are hatched were filled with mud.

Scientists say it will take several years to determine how the dust sent into the atmosphere from Mount Saint Helens is influencing the weather. British scientists blamed Great Britain's cold, rainy summer on fallout from the May eruption.

A lava dome plugged the unsightly hole in Mount Saint Helens in August. Tourists began returning to the area then, and carted home souvenir packages of ash and bumper stickers like "St. Helens forgot her earth control pill."   Patricia Dragisic

Devastated trees

GERMANY, EAST, increased its industrial output by 5.9 per cent in the first six months of "the 1980 plan." The government invested $12 billion in industry, most of it in new technology. Exports increased by 16 per cent, with sales to Russia up 14 per cent. But East Germans were dissatisfied with the lack of variety in consumer goods, so the government tried to compensate by strengthening health and social welfare services.

The 1980 plan stipulated that 90 per cent of the increase in labor productivity must come from scientific and technological improvements. Workers were urged to do even better in 1981. On August 27, Communist Party Secretary General and State Council Chairman Erich Honecker mentioned a growth rate of 8.8 per cent for factory output. Meanwhile, rents and food prices increased sharply, largely because of imports of oil, raw materials, and capital goods.

Détente. East Germany sought reassurances from Russia and West Germany that détente could continue despite a worsening international climate after Russia's invasion of Afghanistan. East and West Germany signed a $282-million agreement on April 30 in Bonn to improve road, rail, and canal links between West Berlin and West Germany. Russia's approval of this relatively minor document signified its eagerness to continue détente.

West German Chancellor Helmut Schmidt and East German economic planner Günter Mittag agreed at an April 17 meeting in Bonn to expand trade between the two countries. But Schmidt cancelled a summit meeting with Honecker scheduled for August 28 and 29 because of the international situation and widespread strikes in Poland.

Trade Pacts. East Germany agreed in May to increase its economic cooperation and trade with Algeria and Madagascar. In April, France and East Germany restated their intent to implement a five-year plan for developing economic, industrial, and technical relations.

In June, East Germany and Poland reimposed currency restrictions on travelers between the two nations. Food and gasoline shortages and large differences in prices had spawned a black market. Poles crossed the border to buy relatively cheap gasoline, while East Germans exchanged their currency in Poland at nearly twice the official rate. The restrictions had been dropped in 1972.

In October, East Germany increased the amount of hard currency that visitors must exchange for East German marks from $7.20 to $13.85 per day and removed the special rate of $3.60 per day for visitors to East Berlin. West Berlin's Mayor Dietrich Stobbe called the move a "slap in the face of détente." About 8 million West Germans visit East Germany yearly.   Kenneth Brown

See also EUROPE (Facts in Brief Table). In WORLD BOOK, see GERMANY.

GERMANY, WEST. Chancellor Helmut Schmidt's coalition government of Social Democrats and Free Democrats increased its majority in the *Bundestag* (lower house of parliament) from 10 to 45 seats in elections held on Oct. 5, 1980. Schmidt's party, the Social Democrats, captured 218 seats, a gain of 4, while the Free Democrats picked up 14 seats for a total of 53. The opposition Christian Democrats and their Bavarian affiliate, the Christian Social Union, won 226 seats, a loss of 17. An antinuclear, environmentalist party, the Greens, won only 1.5 per cent of the popular vote, far short of the 5 per cent required for Bundestag membership.

Threats to Détente. For the first time in its 30-year history, West Germany did not see eye to eye with its closest Western ally, the United States. West Germans feared that the strong U.S. reaction to Iran's holding U.S. hostages and to Russia's invasion of Afghanistan would undermine their efforts at détente. The Germans dreaded a return to the Cold War atmosphere, and recalled the gradual easing of relations with East Germany in the past decade. Schmidt visited Moscow on June 30 and July 1 and urged Supreme Soviet Presidium Chairman Leonid I. Brezhnev and other leaders to withdraw Soviet troops from Afghanistan.

West Germany's National Olympic Committee voted on May 15 to boycott the Olympic Games in Moscow in July under pressure from the government, parliament, and President Karl Carstens. Schmidt regarded the decision as a demonstration of solidarity with the United States.

Russia was eager to maintain the momentum of détente. On August 11, the 10th anniversary of the Soviet-West German Treaty renouncing the use of force, Brezhnev and Council of Ministers Chairman Aleksey N. Kosygin sent a message to Bonn pointing out that the treaty had ushered in a period of good relations. They said that the treaty had laid the basis for an overall improvement in European relations, and that détente was "a decisive factor" for stability. In a return message, Schmidt said that he hoped Russia and West Germany would continue to keep their relations stable "even in difficult times."

Defense Contributions. Events in Afghanistan prompted the government to increase defense spending by 3 per cent in 1980. The government had resisted pressure from the United States and the North Atlantic Treaty Organization (NATO) to increase defense spending by more than 2 per cent, but it approved a $1-billion supplementary budget on May 1. Some of the money was earmarked for heating and fuel costs, munitions, and wage increases for military personnel. But a key part was to go to Turkey as part of West Germany's contribution to strengthening NATO.

In Local Elections on March 16, the Greens polled 5.3 per cent of the votes in Baden-

In July, West German Chancellor Helmut Schmidt, front row, center, pays first visit to Russia by a Western leader since Soviets invaded Afghanistan.

Württemberg, giving them six seats in the state parliament and raising hopes that they might win seats in the Bundestag in the October elections. The ruling Christian Democrats lost heavily in Saar elections on April 27, and the Social Democrats gained. The Christian Democrats lost again on May 11 in the North Rhine-Westphalia poll when the Social Democrats won an absolute majority in the state parliament.

Economic Slowdown. The government had hoped in January that the gross national product would increase by 2.5 per cent during 1980, with inflation around 4.5 per cent and unemployment between 3.5 and 4 per cent. But the hopes faded as the recession took effect. IFO, a research institute in Munich, warned in February that West Germany's recent strong growth could give way to stagnation and decline by the end of 1980. The Organization for Economic Cooperation and Development (OECD) reinforced this prediction on June 22, forecasting only a 2 per cent increase in gross national product in 1980. The OECD – a group of 24 nations, most of them in Western Europe – praised trade unions for settling for moderate wage increases, but warned against reversing the downward trend of unemployment.   Kenneth Brown

See also EUROPE (Facts in Brief Table). In WORLD BOOK, see GERMANY.

GHANA. See AFRICA.

GHOTBZADEH, SADEGH (1937?-   ), a close associate of Iran's spiritual leader, Ayatollah Ruhollah Khomeini, proved a powerful and controversial figure in the ongoing Iranian revolution in 1980. He began the year as foreign minister, having been appointed by the ruling Revolutionary Council in November 1979 when Abol Hasan Bani-Sadr was ousted from that post. He made a disastrous run for the presidency in January, polling only 0.3 per cent of the vote. He remained foreign minister until a new Cabinet was formed under Prime Minister Mohammed Ali Rajai in September.

Ghotbzadeh was jailed briefly in November for saying that the state radio and television service, which he directed briefly in 1979, was so dull that Iranians were turning to foreign broadcasts. His imprisonment was quickly ended by Khomeini's personal intervention. Little is known of Ghotbzadeh's previous career. He was a student at Georgetown University in Washington, D.C., in 1959 and left the U.S. in 1962. His Iranian passport was revoked in 1963, presumably because of his revolutionary tendencies, and thereafter he traveled on a Syrian passport. He became a follower of Khomeini and a roving ambassador for the ayatollah's brand of revolution.   Edward G. Nash

See also IRAN; RAJAI, MOHAMMED ALI.

GIRL SCOUTS. See YOUTH ORGANIZATIONS.

GIRLS CLUBS. See YOUTH ORGANIZATIONS.

329

GOLF. Tom Watson and Jack Nicklaus, who between them had dominated men's competition for the last two decades, were the outstanding golfers of 1980. The Professional Golfers' Association (PGA) named Watson as Player of the Year for an unprecedented fourth straight year.

The 30-year-old Watson entered 23 tournaments and won seven – the British Open, Tournament of Champions, World Series of Golf, Byron Nelson Classic, and the San Diego, Los Angeles, and New Orleans opens. He finished in the top 10 in nine other tournaments. Watson earned $530,808 on the tour, breaking his 1979 record of $462,636. Lee Trevino ranked second in earnings with $385,814 and had the best scoring average per round (69.73 to 69.95 for second-place Watson).

Nicklaus' Year. Nicklaus, at age 40, won two of the sport's four major professional championships – the United States Open with a record score and the PGA title by a record margin. He ranked only 13th in earnings with $172,386, little concern to him because he played in few tournaments and used most of them to prepare for the major championships. His last tournament was in August.

Nicklaus had not won a tournament in two years, and he was devoting more time to family and business than to golf. He spent the winter and spring reshaping his game, and was undismayed

Jack Nicklaus happily acknowledges gallery's cheers after a birdie on the final hole clinches his fourth U.S. Open title in June.

when he finished 53rd in the Jackie Gleason Inverrary Classic, tied for 43rd in the Byron Nelson Classic, and failed to qualify for the final 36 holes of the Atlanta Open.

When the big championships came, Nicklaus was ready. In the United States Open, held from June 12 to 15 in Springfield, N.J., his 72-hole score of 272 beat Isao Aoki of Japan by two strokes. In the PGA championship, held from August 7 to 10 in Rochester, N.Y., his 274 beat Andy Bean by seven strokes. Only Gene Sarazen in 1922 and Ben Hogan in 1948 had captured those two titles in the same year.

The victories gave Nicklaus a record 19 major titles – 5 PGAs, 5 Masters, 4 United States Opens, 3 British Opens, and 2 United States Amateurs. Next in the all-time standing are the late Bobby Jones with 13 major titles (7 open, 6 amateur) and the late Walter Hagen with 11 (all open).

In the British Open, held from July 17 to 20 in Muirfield, Scotland, Watson's 271 beat Trevino by four strokes. It was Watson's third British Open title in six years.

The other major championship was the Masters, held from April 10 to 13 in Augusta, Ga. Severiano Ballesteros, a dashing, 23-year-old Spaniard who had never taken a golf lesson, carded 274 and won by four strokes from Gibby Gilbert and Jack Newton. Ballesteros spurned a PGA offer to compete full time on its tour, preferring to concentrate on the 20-tournament, $3.5-million European tour. He said he found too little enjoyment in the American game.

The Women's Tour. The PGA and Ladies PGA tournament circuits ran from January to November. Both carried record prize money, the men playing in 45 tournaments for $13 million and the women in 38 tournaments for $5 million.

Donna Caponi Young won six women's tournaments; JoAnne Carner, five; Amy Alcott, four; Beth Daniel, four; and Nancy Lopez-Melton, three. The leading money winners were the 23-year-old Daniel with $231,000, Young with $220,619, Alcott with $219,887, and Lopez-Melton with $209,078. All bettered Lopez-Melton's 1979 record of $197,488.

The 35-year-old Young won the richest women's tournament in history, the $305,000 Colgate-Dinah Shore Winners Circle, held from April 3 to 6 in Rancho Mirage, Calif. Alcott won the women's United States Open; Sally Little, the Ladies PGA championship; and Daniel, the World Series of Women's Golf.

Daniel, the Rookie of the Year in 1979, was named Player of the Year in 1980. In her 27 tournaments, she placed in the top five 19 times, including her last 10 tournaments.   Frank Litsky

In WORLD BOOK, see GOLF.

GOVERNORS, U.S. See STATE GOVERNMENT.

GREAT BRITAIN. One phrase more than any other was on the lips of British political pundits in 1980 – "U-turn." It referred to the question of whether Prime Minister Margaret Thatcher's Conservative government would be forced to shift its policy and abandon the economic programs on which it had won the general election in 1979, or whether the "Iron Lady" would live up to her gritty reputation and remain impervious to the doubters rising even within her own Cabinet.

The question was intriguing because the government's economic policy was taking it into uncharted waters. In reaction against what they perceived as the previous Labour government's policy of encouraging inefficient working practices, voters had elected Thatcher because she promised severe cuts in government spending and less government interference in industry. The Tories decided to pursue a *monetarist* economic policy, which maintains that inflation will fall if the amount of money in circulation is strictly controlled. But unemployment rose to more than 2 million by autumn of 1980, the highest since the 1930s. Inflation remained above 15 per cent, though a few signs that it might drop appeared. But the worst damage seemed to be caused by extremely high interest rates, which were blamed for cutbacks in industrial production and a large number of factory closings. The government even appeared unable to limit the increase in the money supply to 11 per cent; a rise of 14 per cent was expected for fiscal 1980-1981.

The Opposition. The Labour Party accused Thatcher of being prepared to destroy Great Britain's economic base in pursuit of an economic theory. But criticism was not confined to her political opponents. Some ministers in the Cabinet favored *reflation* (restoring business conditions to prerecession levels) and a wage-control policy. Known as the "wets," or moderates, they included some powerful figures. Among them were the foreign secretary, Lord Carrington; the employment minister, James Prior; the agriculture minister, Peter Walker; and the minister of state at the Foreign Office, Sir Ian Gilmour.

In addition, industrialists and the press were alarmed. The Confederation of British Industry, which normally supported the Tories, in September demanded an early reduction in the 16 per cent minimum lending rate, and *The Times* of London editorialized that the government's economic policy was not working. But Prime Minister Thatcher announced at the Conservative Party's annual conference on October 10 that she was sticking to her guns. To roars of applause from the party faithful she said, "You turn if you want to, but this lady is not for turning."

However, fierce struggles continued inside the Cabinet as Treasury ministers tried to wring more cutbacks from the ministers in charge of spending

Robert A. K. Runcie, archbishop of Canterbury, greets Queen Elizabeth, the Queen Mother, as she celebrates her 80th birthday August 4.

departments, and as it appeared that the government would overspend by about $4.7 billion in 1980. One of the most dramatic rows was over defense spending. Confidential documents leaked to the press disclosed that the Treasury was seeking defense cuts of $1.2 billion and that military commanders were complaining that Great Britain's commitment to the North Atlantic Treaty Organization (NATO) would be jeopardized. The government announced that it would try to hold pay increases for civil servants and local government workers to 6 per cent in 1981, and so appeared set for another collision with the unions.

Economic Legislation. The government pushed legislation aimed at putting into practice the Thatcher political philosophy of encouraging more competition and individual effort. A Competition Bill abolishing the Price Commission, which had required companies to get government approval for price increases, became law on April 3. The new legislation strengthened the powers of the director general of fair trading and of the Monopolies and Mergers Commission to investigate anticompetitive practices in the public and private sectors. An Education Bill also became law on April 3. It contained a controversial provision for an "assisted places" scheme, by which the government would pay the private school fees of a selected number of children. The bill also proposed that local authorities be allowed to charge fares for school buses if they wished. But this clause was defeated in the House of Lords after an extraordinary revolt organized by the Duke of Norfolk, Great Britain's leading Roman Catholic aristocrat. He said that if the provision were adopted, it would destroy many of the religious-based schools in rural areas to which children were entitled to be bused free. After his protest, the government dropped the clause.

A Transport Bill enacted on June 30 removed restrictions on operators of bus and trucking services, opening up bus services to free competition. It put the National Freight Corporation, the nationalized road-haulage organization, into private hands. An Industry Bill that became law on June 30 substantially reduced the powers of the National Enterprise Board (NEB) established by Labour in 1975 to extend public ownership into profitable areas of manufacturing industry. It also reversed the NEB's role, redefining it as being to promote "the private ownership of interests in industrial undertakings by the disposal of securities and other property held by them."

Defense. After NATO's decision in December 1979 to modernize its nuclear weapons, British Defense Minister Francis Pym told the House of Commons on June 17 that 160 ground-launched

Prime Minister Margaret Thatcher, accustomed to steering the ship of state, takes the helm of a lifeboat given to the city of Holyhead.

cruise missiles would be stored in Great Britain at Greenham Common in Berkshire, a United States Air Force (USAF) base, and at Molesworth in Cambridgeshire, an airfield used for storage by the USAF. The first missiles were scheduled to be deployed in 1983.

The government announced on July 15, 1980, that it would continue Great Britain's independent nuclear deterrent policy by buying U.S. Trident I missiles, equipment, and supporting services, including four or five submarines, to replace four aging Polaris submarines. The purchases would cost $14 billion. At its annual conference, the Labour Party voted on October 2 to oppose the Tridents, the cruise missiles, and all U.S. nuclear warheads currently based in Great Britain, and stopped just short of voting to take Great Britain out of NATO.

Labour Struggles. Meanwhile, Labour had become engulfed in the fiercest internal war in more than 25 years. The struggle between left wing and right wing members was over the party's constitution as well as its policies. The left wing sought radical reforms in the party structure that would produce permanent left wing dominance. The Labour Party leader, 68-year-old James Callaghan, announced his retirement on October 15, and the question of electing a successor proved to be no simple matter.

Amid bitter scenes at the party's annual conference, the left wing, aided by some trade union votes, got the party to give grass-roots party workers in the constituencies and trade unions a voice in selecting the party leader. Traditionally, Labour members of Parliament (MP's) elected the party leader. But the conference could not agree on a precise formula and decided to refer the matter to a special conference to be held in January 1981. In view of this uncertainty, left wing MP's, led by Anthony Wedgwood Benn, who was regarded as the left wing's main contender for the party leadership, argued that Labour MP's should wait for the January conference and not proceed with an election. But they were outvoted by the right wing, led by a group of former ministers known as the "gang of three" – David Owen, the former foreign secretary; Shirley Williams, the former education minister; and William Rodgers, a junior defense minister. The right wing opposed the idea of an electoral college. They argued that Labour MP's might find themselves saddled with a leader they could not follow because many of the local constituency parties and some trade unions were in the hands of Trotskyites and others with extreme views. Moreover, such a leader would stand little chance of winning a general election.

On the first ballot, on November 4, former Chancellor of the Exchequer Denis Healey, an outspoken right winger, led the field against three other candidates, but did not receive an outright majority. On the second ballot, on November 10, with only two candidates, Deputy Leader Michael Foot, 67, a leading left winger, won with 139 votes to Healey's 129. Foot, a brilliant orator and journalist, fought his campaign on the basis of reuniting the party. He advocated nuclear disarmament and opposed British membership in the European Community (EC or Common Market), but did not urge committing withdrawal. Benn did not stand for election.

The leadership struggle was not the only battleground between Labour's left and right wings. The left also wanted to make it obligatory that the party's election platform be decided by the conference without later changes by the leadership. It also wanted to compel all Labour MP's to submit themselves for reselection by their local party groups between general elections, to ensure that they would vote for policies approved by their local party activists. Callaghan had fought to prevent any of these changes, but had been unable to muster enough union-bloc votes. As a result, the Labour Party's ruling body, the National Executive, also became dominated by the left wing. Many rightists talked about forming a new Social Democrat, or Centre, Party.   Ian Mather

See also EUROPE (Facts in Brief Table). In WORLD BOOK, see GREAT BRITAIN.

GREECE faced three major foreign policy problems in 1980. These concerns were its differences with Turkey, its role in the North Atlantic Treaty Organization (NATO), and the status of United States bases on Greek soil. Greece's military link with NATO received urgent attention after Russia invaded Afghanistan in December 1979 and Yugoslavia's President Josip Broz Tito died in May 1980.

The West tried to overcome Turkey's objections to the unconditional return of Greece to NATO's integrated military structure. On March 16, Greece rejected a measure proposed by NATO's Supreme Allied Commander, U.S. Army General Bernard Rogers, to designate a buffer zone between Greece and Turkey in the eastern Aegean Sea. Rogers believed that the zone would answer Turkey's objection to a return to the arrangement that existed before Greece withdrew from military participation in 1974. At that time, Greece had control of both the air and naval defense of the Aegean. Greece also reacted strongly against a huge military aid package that the United States and NATO allies promised Turkey. On October 18, Greece accepted a compromise offer from Rogers, and NATO ratified Greece's return on October 20.

New President. After failing to win the required 200 votes in two ballots on April 23 and 29, Constantine Caramanlis, prime minister for six years, was elected president on May 5. The main opposition party, the Pan Hellenic Socialist Movement, abstained from voting, claiming that Parliament did not represent the views of the people. Former Foreign Minister George Rallis succeeded Caramanlis as prime minister and leader of the majority New Democracy Party on May 10. His government won its first confidence vote 13 days later by 180 votes to 115. The debate centered on Rallis' policy statement that showed his concern to improve relations with Turkey. See CARAMANLIS, CONSTANTINE; RALLIS, GEORGE.

Joining the Market. Greece tried to balance its economy in time for its entry as the 10th member of the European Community (Common Market) on Jan. 1, 1981. Greece tightened restrictions on imports, and increased taxes on retail sales to 25 per cent. The government hoped to reduce inflation from 24 to 15 per cent.   Kenneth Brown

See also EUROPE (Facts in Brief Table). In WORLD BOOK, see GREECE; NORTH ATLANTIC TREATY ORGANIZATION (NATO).

GRENADA. See LATIN AMERICA (Facts in Brief Table); WEST INDIES.

GUATEMALA. See LATIN AMERICA.

GUINEA. See AFRICA.

GUINEA-BISSAU. See AFRICA.

GUYANA. See LATIN AMERICA.

HAITI. See LATIN AMERICA (Facts in Brief Table).

HANDICAPPED. Services for the handicapped in the United States continued to be controversial in 1980. Government officials attempted to unravel the many complications presented by Section 504 of the Rehabilitation Act of 1973, which prohibits discrimination against handicapped individuals in any federally funded or assisted project.

The U.S. House of Representatives Public Works Committee approved a bill in May that would have exempted cities from making costly changes in mass transit systems as long as they provided personalized service for the disabled. The House passed the bill in December, then sent it to the Senate, which failed to act on it before Congress adjourned. The Senate had passed a similar measure in June.

Compliance Is Costly. Local government officials voiced alarm as the financial implications of complying fully with Section 504 became clear. The Metropolitan Transportation Authority (MTA) of New York City voted in September not to comply with federal laws that require all transit systems in the United States to provide special access for the handicapped. MTA officials said compliance would cost at least $1.5 billion initially.

The vote was the first outright rejection by any such agency in the country. But in October, MTA asked for a six-month delay in meeting the federal

Blind and partially blind people can use a recorded edition of THE WORLD BOOK ENCYCLOPEDIA, which has a cassette player and tapes and two indexes.

requirements. Noncompliance could have cost New York City all federal transportation aid, which amounted to $435 million in 1980.

Gains Cited. On the other hand, lobbyists for the handicapped think that the May 1980 transit bill is an unreasonable barrier to their full equality. Despite these controversies, the handicapped have made significant political gains. People in wheelchairs now see more slopes in curbs, ramps in public buildings, and accessible doors in restaurants. In many school systems, deaf children now study in regular classrooms.

The U.S. Department of Labor announced in March that it had won a record $225,000 in back pay for 85 persons denied jobs with a Texas company because they were handicapped. Labor Secretary F. Ray Marshall said that the men and women who sought work at Varo, Incorporated, an electronics plant in Garland, Tex., from 1975 to 1978 would receive interest in addition to the $225,000 total.

Varo had defense contracts in 1978 totaling $53-million to produce electronic systems and equipment for the U.S. government. The 1973 Rehabilitation Act requires companies that do business with the government to take affirmative action to employ qualified handicapped people.

Communications. THE WORLD BOOK ENCYCLOPEDIA in 1980 became the first encyclopedia to be reproduced as a voice recording. The recorded edition – on cassettes, complete with cassette player and braille and large-type indexes – provides reference material for the blind and partially blind.

Deaf people can now partake of about 20 hours of television programs per week. The Public Broadcasting Service and two commercial networks began airing programs with special captions in March. A special adapter called Telecaption is attached to the TV set to reproduce the captions.

People in the News. Margaret Giannini of Pelham Manor, N.Y., became the first director of the National Institute of Handicapped Research (NIHR) in March. The NIHR was created in 1978 to handle data on needs of the handicapped.

Curtis Brewer of New York City was named Handicapped American of the Year in March by the President's Committee on Employment of the Handicapped. Brewer, who is paralyzed, founded an organization called Untapped Resources in 1964 to help disabled people cut through red tape.

Recognition çame to disabled people in the arts. Producer Ira Wohl won an Oscar in April for the feature documentary film *Best Boy*, a memoir of Wohl's retarded cousin. In June, Phyllis Frelich received the Tony Award for best actress for her performance in the Broadway play *Children of a Lesser God*. Frelich is deaf.   Virginia E. Anderson

In WORLD BOOK, see HANDICAPPED.

HARNESS RACING. See HORSE RACING.

HAUGHEY, CHARLES JAMES (1925-   ), the new prime minister of Ireland, declared in his first major policy statement on Feb. 16, 1980, that Great Britain should begin to withdraw from Northern Ireland. He said that Northern Ireland, "as a political entity, has failed." See IRELAND.

Haughey became prime minister on Dec. 7, 1979, succeeding Jack Lynch, who resigned. Both men are members of the ruling Fianna Fáil (Soldiers of Destiny) party. Lynch had de-emphasized nationalism; Haughey is an ardent nationalist.

Haughey was born on Sept. 16, 1925, in Castlebar, County Mayo. His father was an officer in the Irish Republican Army (IRA) and in the Irish Free State army. Haughey studied law and accounting at University College in Dublin, and was elected to Parliament in 1957. He became minister of justice in 1961, minister of agriculture in 1964, and minister of finance in 1966. In 1970, he was charged with conspiring to smuggle arms into Northern Ireland for the IRA. He was acquitted, but resigned as finance minister. Haughey became chairman of Parliament's committee on the European Community (Common Market) in 1973 and minister of health and social welfare in 1977. In 1951, Haughey married Maureen Lemass, daughter of Sean Lemass, who later became prime minister.   Jay Myers

HAWAII. See STATE GOVERNMENT.

HEALTH AND DISEASE. National organizations, United States government advisers, and physicians' groups disagreed sharply in 1980 in their recommendations about how to stay healthy and prevent disease. The American Cancer Society suggested in March that most people do not need annual chest X rays, Pap smears, and other screening tests for cancer. The society noted that risks are involved and that fewer tests would save billions of dollars each year. Radiologists, gynecologists, and other specialists protested the new guidelines.

The National Research Council (NRC) reported in May that healthy adults do not need to cut down on cholesterol to prevent heart disease. The NRC placed greater emphasis on restricting excess calories and salt consumption. The report evoked protest, especially from the American Heart Association (see MEDICINE; NUTRITION).

A Report on Exercise noted that regular, vigorous physical activity helps a person to dissolve blood clots, thus reducing the possibility of heart diseases. Physicians at Duke University in Durham, N.C., reported in May on their study of 69 healthy adults.

A February report on the largest test ever done on aspirin as a means of preventing heart attacks – conducted by the National Heart, Blood, and Lung Institute – said that aspirin does not prevent heart attacks in men and women who have already

335

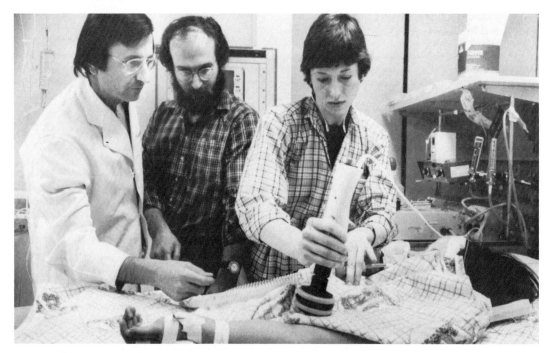

Philadelphia doctors treat a child with Reye's syndrome; since 1977, its mortality rate has dropped from 33 per cent to 10 per cent of cases.

had one. The three-year study looked at the progress of 4,021 men and 503 women who had suffered heart attacks and found a slightly higher rate of fatal attacks among those who were taking aspirin. However, even before the final report was issued, other researchers criticized the test, saying that the dosage was too high and that better results are obtained with fewer aspirin. In the Special Reports section, see CAN AN ASPIRIN A DAY HELP KEEP THE DOCTOR AWAY?

Baffling Diseases. The U.S. Centers for Disease Control in Atlanta, Ga., reported more than 300 cases, including more than a dozen fatal ones, of a bacterial infection called toxic-shock syndrome. The mysterious illness struck women, most often those under 30 years of age, during or just after a menstrual period, and was linked with the use of tampons. Symptoms of the ailment, which apparently is caused by *Staphylococcus aureus* bacteria, include sudden high fever, vomiting, diarrhea, a rapid drop in blood pressure often resulting in shock, and a sunburnlike rash.

The manufacturers of Rely tampons, a relatively new superabsorbent product that had been linked to toxic shock by federal researchers, recalled the product on September 22. Other brands of superabsorbent tampons were also implicated in the disease. The American College of Obstetricians and Gynecologists in October advised women of all ages to avoid the newer superabsorbent-type tampons, to alternate using tampons and napkins when possible, and to change tampons frequently.

Kawasaki disease, another puzzling illness, hit 46 children in Massachusetts between April and June. More than 600 cases of the disease have been reported in the United States between 1976 and 1980. The disease, first diagnosed in Japan in 1967, most often affects children under 5. Symptoms include high fever for five or more days, congested blood vessels in the eyes, skin rashes, and peeling of the skin from fingers and toes.

FDA Reports. In June, the Food and Drug Administration (FDA) licensed a new vaccine for rabies that is safer, less painful, and more effective than previous treatments. The vaccine, available only at major medical centers in 1980, had a 98 per cent success rate in early trials. Only five injections in the arm are required.

The FDA revised its stand on sodium nitrite, a preservative widely used in meat, poultry, and fish. In a joint statement with the U.S. Department of Agriculture, the FDA said in August that there is insufficient evidence of danger to humans from eating nitrites. See FOOD.

Saccharin. A Harvard University research team reported on March 6 that users of the artificial sweetener saccharin "have little or no excess risk of cancer of the lower urinary tract." Other studies by the American Health Foundation and the National Cancer Institute confirmed this.

Tobacco and Alcohol. Researchers at the University of California, San Diego, in March published the first scientific evidence that breathing other people's cigarette smoke is harmful for healthy nonsmokers. Examining the effects of smoking on more than 2,000 persons, the scientists found that nonsmokers who worked in smoke-free environments performed best on tests of the lungs' ability to hold and expel air. Those who had smoked more than a pack of cigarettes a day for more than 20 years performed the worst. Nonsmokers who had worked for more than 20 years in smoke-filled areas had test scores similar to those of light smokers who did not inhale or smoked fewer than 11 cigarettes per day.

A new study confirms a theory gaining strength among researchers in recent years—that alcoholism may be caused by heredity, not environment. University of Iowa psychiatrists reported in June that children of alcoholics have a high incidence of alcoholism, even when adopted and raised by nonalcoholics.   Dianne Hales

See also Drugs; Medicine; Public Health. In World Book, see Cancer; Health.

HIGHWAY. See Building and Construction; Transportation.

HOBBIES. Americans' interest in collectibles—everyday and frequently mass-produced articles from earlier periods—continued to grow in 1980. Widely sought items included furniture, wind-up toys, fountain pens, and juke boxes.

Industrialist Armand Hammer bought the Leonardo da Vinci notebook *Of the Nature, Weight and Movement of Water* for $5,126,000 on December 12. It was the highest price ever paid at auction for a manuscript. A new price record for a single piece of American furniture was set on May 24 at Cambridge, Md., when a 220-year-old Edmund Townsend desk sold for $250,000 at the Edward and Bernice Chrysler Garbisch estate auction. A Duncan Phyfe glass-door cabinet, made about 1800, sold for $39,000 at a New York City auction.

Collectors avidly sought pre-World War II coin-operated gambling machines. Twenty-nine states now allow ownership of these machines if they are not used for gambling purposes. At a March auction conducted by PB-44, the uptown New York City annex of Sotheby Parke Bernet, two one-wheel slot machines sold for $9,000 and $7,000. A Bally Reliance 5-cent dice machine brought $5,750, a world record for any Bally machine, and a Wurlitzer juke box sold for $5,250.

Other Purchases. John Grisanti of Memphis, Tenn., paid a record $31,000 for what he called

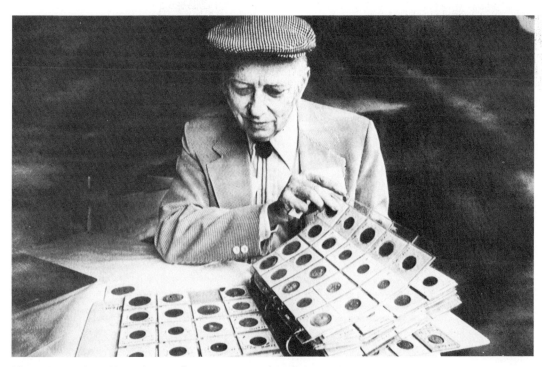

Mine scrip, once issued by coal companies as payment to miners but worthless as tender since 1840, has great value to token collectors.

"the finest bottle of wine in the world," an 1824 Chateau Lafite. Grisanti made the purchase at the 12th annual Heublein rare wine auction on May 28 in San Francisco.

Auction prices for Oriental textiles rose dramatically. At a New York City auction in January, a 19th-century embroidered Japanese fabric piece, expected to sell for about $250, went for $11,000 — a world record for an Oriental textile.

Carter Autograph. The first presidential autograph of United States President Jimmy Carter to be sold at public auction brought $500 in New York City in August. A membership card for a Ronald Reagan fan club, signed by Reagan, sold for $400. An autographed paperback copy of a 1976 Carter campaign biography, *Why Not the Best?*, sold for $225, and an inscribed photograph of Reagan, for $120.

An autographed photograph of Mohammad Reza Pahlavi, shah of Iran, sold for $475 at a New York City auction in June. In the same auction, autographed photographs of American Presidents commanded varying prices. A Carter photograph sold for $75; one of Gerald R. Ford for $60; a photograph of Lyndon B. Johnson for $100; and a Calvin Coolidge photo for $50.   Theodore M. O'Leary

See also COIN COLLECTING; STAMP COLLECTING. In WORLD BOOK, see HOBBY.

HOCKEY. The Montreal Canadiens, who always seemed to win the Stanley Cup, failed to do that in 1980. The New York Islanders, an eight-year expansion team, finally won their first cup.

The National Hockey League (NHL) played the regular season with 21 teams, including four from the defunct World Hockey Association (WHA) — the Winnipeg Jets, Quebec Nordiques, Edmonton Oilers, and Hartford Whalers.

The Philadelphia Flyers, Chicago Black Hawks, Buffalo Sabres, and Canadiens won division titles. The Islanders finished with only the fifth-best overall record and were among the 16 teams that qualified for the Stanley Cup play-offs. But the Islanders breezed through the play-offs. They beat the Los Angeles Kings in four games, the Boston Bruins in five, Buffalo in six, and the Flyers in six.

Bryan Trottier, the Islander center, set a play-off record with 29 points in 21 games and won the Conn Smythe Trophy as Most Valuable Player in the play-offs. It was a frustrating finish for the Flyers, a team that once won with brawn. Coach Pat Quinn had changed the team's style, emphasizing speed. He was so successful that from October 14 to January 6, the Flyers played 35 straight games without a loss (25 victories and 10 ties). That bettered the record of 28 that was set by the 1976-1977 Canadiens.

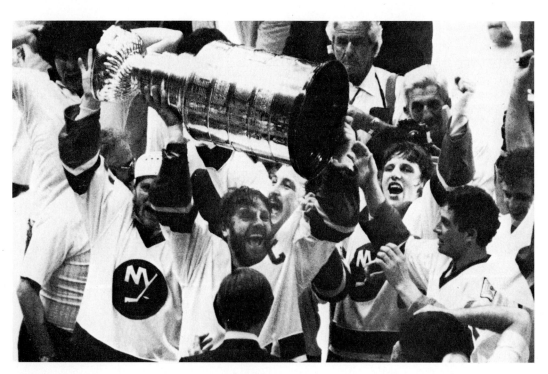

Happy members of the New York Islanders hoist the Stanley Cup in triumph after beating Philadelphia Flyers in play-off finals.

Montreal's Demise. The Canadiens had won the cup the four previous years and 15 times in 24 years. The Minnesota North Stars eliminated them in seven games in the quarterfinals, winning three of the four games on Montreal ice. While the outcome was surprising, the Canadiens had endured a troubled year. They had lost key people when Coach Scotty Bowman became general manager at Buffalo, center Jacques Lemaire became a player-coach in Switzerland, and goalie Ken Dryden retired.

The new coach was Bernie (Boom Boom) Geoffrion, once a star at right wing for the Canadiens. He quit in mid-December, though the team had a winning record, because the players did not respond to him. Claude Ruel replaced Geoffrion, and the team's losing streak reached six games before matters straightened out.

Under Ruel, the Canadien record was 32 victories, 11 defeats, and 7 ties. The team had the best record in the NHL for the second half of the season, but injuries proved costly in the play-offs.

Individual Honors. Two centers—28-year-old Marcel Dionne of Los Angeles and 19-year-old Wayne Gretzky of Edmonton, Canada—dominated scoring and postseason awards. They tied for first in scoring with 139 points each, but Dionne won the title and the Art Ross Trophy because he had outscored Gretzky in goals, 53 to 51.

Dionne also won the new Lester Pearson Trophy, voted by the players to the one who had contributed the most to hockey during the season. Dionne's employers added a reward, a new six-year contract for a reported salary of $600,000 a year. Gretzky did not leave empty-handed. He won the Hart Trophy as the league's Most Valuable Player, the Lady Byng Trophy for sportsmanship, and the Charlie Conacher Trophy for humanitarian work.

The James Norris Trophy for best defenseman went to Larry Robinson of Montreal, the Frank Selke Trophy for best defensive forward to Bob Gainey of Montreal for the third straight year, the Calder Trophy for Rookie of the Year to Ray Bourque of Boston, and the Vezina Trophy for goaltending to Don Edwards and Bob Sauve of Buffalo. The all-star team had Tony Esposito of Chicago in goal, Robinson and Bourque on defense, Dionne at center, and Guy Lafleur of Montreal and Charlie Simmer of Los Angeles on wing.

Gordie Howe of Hartford, the highest scorer in history, retired after the season at age 52. He had played 32 seasons of major-league hockey over five decades. In his last season, he achieved a dream by playing on the same NHL unit with his sons, Mark and Marty. For the last six weeks of the season, another teammate was 41-year-old Bobby Hull, also an all-time NHL scoring leader. Frank Litsky

See also OLYMPIC GAMES. In WORLD BOOK, see HOCKEY.

Standings in National Hockey League

Clarence Campbell Conference

Lester Patrick Division	W.	L.	T.	Pts.
Philadelphia	48	12	20	116
New York Islanders	39	28	13	91
New York Rangers	38	32	10	86
Atlanta	35	32	13	83
Washington	27	40	13	67

Conn Smythe Division				
Chicago	34	27	19	87
St. Louis	34	34	12	80
Vancouver	27	37	16	70
Edmonton	28	39	13	69
Winnipeg	20	49	11	51
Colorado	19	48	13	51

Prince of Wales Conference

Charles F. Adams Division	W.	L.	T.	Pts.
Buffalo	47	17	16	110
Boston	46	21	13	105
Minnesota	36	28	16	88
Toronto	35	40	5	75
Quebec	25	44	11	61

James Norris Division				
Montreal	47	20	13	107
Los Angeles	30	36	14	74
Pittsburgh	30	37	13	73
Hartford	27	34	19	73
Detroit	26	43	11	63

Scoring Leaders	Games	Goals	Assists	Points
Marcel Dionne, Los Angeles	80	53	84	137
Wayne Gretzky, Edmonton	79	51	86	137
Guy Lafleur, Montreal	74	50	75	125
Gil Perreault, Buffalo	80	40	66	106
Mike Rogers, Hartford	80	44	61	105
Bryan Trottier, N.Y. Islanders	78	42	62	104
Charlie Simmer, Los Angeles	64	56	45	101
Blaine Stoughton, Hartford	80	56	44	100
Darryl Sittler, Toronto	73	40	57	97
Blair MacDonald, Edmonton	80	46	48	94
Bernie Federko, St. Louis	79	38	56	94

Leading Goalies	Games	Goals against	Avg.
Bob Sauve, Buffalo	32	74	2.36
Don Edwards, Buffalo	49	125	2.57
Buffalo Totals	80	201	2.51
Gilles Gilbert, Boston	33	88	2.73
Gerry Cheevers, Boston	42	116	2.81
Marco Baron, Boston	1	2	3.00
Yves Belanger, Boston	8	19	3.48
Jim Stewart, Boston	1	5	15.00
Boston Totals	80	234	2.93

Awards

Calder Trophy (best rookie)—Ray Bourque, Boston
Hart Trophy (most valuable player)—Wayne Gretzky, Edmonton
Lady Byng Trophy (sportsmanship)—Wayne Gretzky, Edmonton
Norris Trophy (best defenseman)—Larry Robinson, Montreal
Ross Trophy (leading scorer)—Marcel Dionne, Los Angeles
Selke Trophy (best defensive forward)—Bob Gainey, Montreal
Smythe Trophy (most valuable in Stanley Cup)—
  Bryan Trottier, N.Y. Islanders
Vezina Trophy (leading goalie)—Don Edwards, Bob Sauve,
  Buffalo

HOFFMAN, DUSTIN (1937-), received the Academy of Motion Pictures Arts and Sciences Award for best actor on April 14, 1980. He won the Oscar for his performance as a rising New York City advertising man who is suddenly faced with raising his young son alone when his wife leaves, in *Kramer vs. Kramer*. He had twice previously been nominated for the award, for his roles in *The Graduate* (1967) and *Midnight Cowboy* (1969).

Dustin Hoffman was born on Aug. 8, 1937, in Los Angeles, the son of Harry and Lillian Gold Hoffman. He attended Santa Monica City College for a year and studied acting at the Pasadena Playhouse in California for two years. Hoffman moved to New York City in 1958. He supported himself by a succession of odd jobs and minor dramatic roles as he struggled to establish himself as an actor.

He achieved national recognition for his film performance as Benjamin, the disillusioned young romantic in *The Graduate*. The films that followed— including *Midnight Cowboy*, *Straw Dogs* (1972), and *Marathon Man* (1976) — established him as one of the most skilled and versatile film actors.

Hoffman and Anne Byrne married in 1969 and divorced in 1980. They have a daughter. He married Lisa Gottsegan in October 1980. **Edward G. Nash**

HONDURAS. See LATIN AMERICA.

HORSE RACING. Spectacular Bid, a 4-year-old, became the biggest money-earner in the history of thoroughbred racing and was syndicated for stud on March 11, 1980, at a world-record $22 million before his career ended in anticlimactic fashion. On May 3, Genuine Risk became only the second filly to win the Kentucky Derby. Mrs. Bertram Firestone's filly then finished second in both the Preakness and Belmont Stakes, the other two Triple Crown races.

Champion 2- and 3-year-old of the past two years, Spectacular Bid won nine straight stakes in 1980. Victory in the Californian at Hollywood Park on June 8 put his earnings at $2,394,268, breaking Affirmed's world record of $2,393,818.

Spectacular Bid was retired with $2,781,607 in earnings after being withdrawn, an hour before post time because of an ankle ailment, from the $549,000 Jockey Club Gold Cup on October 4 at Belmont Park in New York, the richest thoroughbred race ever run in the United States. His previous race, the Woodward Stakes at the same track, also disappointed fans because no rivals ran against him, causing the first *walkover* (uncontested race) in thoroughbred racing since 1949.

Ben Nevis won the Grand National Steeplechase at Aintree, in Liverpool, England, on March 29 over three rivals. Only four of the 30 starters

Genuine Risk wins the Kentucky Derby, first filly to do so since 1915. She then finished second in both the Preakness and the Belmont Stakes.

Major Horse Races of 1980

Race	Winner	Value to Winner
Belmont Stakes	Temperence Hill	$176,220
Benson & Hedges Gold Cup (England)	Master Willie	198,785
Californian Stakes	Spectacular Bid	184,450
Canadian International Championship	Great Neck	120,000
Epsom Derby (England)	Henbit	385,685
Grand National Steeplechase (England)	Ben Nevis	100,309
Irish Sweeps Derby	Tyrnavos	294,344
Jockey Club Gold Cup	Temperence Hill	329,400
Kentucky Derby	Genuine Risk	250,550
King George VI & Queen Elizabeth Diamond Stakes (England)	Ela-Mana-Mou	286,800
Marlboro Cup Handicap	Winter's Tale	180,000
Preakness	Codex	180,600
Prix de l'Arc de Triomphe (France)	Detroit	285,000
Prix du Jockey-Club (France)	Policeman	219,000
Santa Anita Handicap	Spectacular Bid	190,000
Washington D. C. Int'l	Argument	150,000
Woodward Stakes	Spectacular Bid	73,300

Major U.S. Harness Races of 1980

Race	Winner	Value to Winner
Cane Pace	Niatross	$112,478
Hambletonian	Burgomeister	146,785
Little Brown Jug	Niatross	104,717
Meadowlands Pace	Niatross	505,500
Messenger Stakes	Niatross	86,761
Roosevelt International	Classical Way	125,000
Woodrow Wilson Memorial Pace	Land Grant	1,005,500

finished the race. The horse is owned by Redmond C. Stewart, Jr., and was ridden by Charles Fenwick, Jr., both from Maryland.

The scandal in New York racing climaxed with the conviction on May 19 of former jockey Con Errico for conspiring to fix nine races in 1974 and 1975 at Saratoga and Aqueduct race tracks.

Harness Racing. Niatross set impressive records in the standardbred sport, including pacing a mile in 1 minute 49⅕ seconds in a time trial at the Red Mile in Lexington, Ky., on October 1. He broke Steady Star's world record of 1 minute 52 seconds.

Syndicated for stud for a standardbred record of $10 million, he is the leading money-winner in his sport and holds the record for one-year earnings.

Longshot Land Grant won the $2,011,000 Woodrow Wilson Memorial, richest horse race ever, on August 6 at the Meadowlands in New Jersey. The pacer paid $141.80 for a $2 wager.

Burgomeister won the Hambletonian on August 30, its final running at Du Quoin, Ill. The race will be run at the Meadowlands in 1981.

Quarter Horse Racing. Higheasterjet earned $440,000 by winning the $1.2-million All-American Futurity at Ruidoso Downs, N. Mex., on September 1. The 13-year-old champion sire Easy Jet was syndicated for $30 million.   Jane Goldstein

In WORLD BOOK, see HARNESS RACING; HORSE RACING.

HOSPITAL costs remained the most important and vexing issue in the United States health-care industry in 1980. More than $60 billion – about 9 per cent of the gross national product and nearly 40 per cent of the amount spent for all types of health care – went for patient care in American hospitals in 1980.

The Voluntary Effort cost-control program initiated by the American Hospital Association (AHA) and other groups in 1978 was less successful in 1980 than in previous years. Final figures showed that the voluntary program reduced the annual increase in hospital expenditures to 12.8 per cent in 1979. But hospital costs rose more than 13 per cent in 1980.

Another approach to cost containment – mandatory rate controls set by the states – has been more successful in holding down hospital costs, according to a study published in September by the Johns Hopkins Center for Hospital Finance and Management. Six states with such controls – Connecticut, Maryland, Massachusetts, New Jersey, New York, and Washington – saved a total of $3.1 billion over a three-year period and had lower rates of increases in patient-care costs than in the other states. But most of the savings were in just one state, New York, with $2.3 billion, leading cost-control critics to question whether state controls had general applicability.

The Administration of President Jimmy Carter, which advocated federal mandatory controls on hospital costs but could not get congressional support for its proposal, tried other strategies to slow the hospital cost spiral. It proposed mandatory federal review and approval of capital expenditures for hospital construction and expansion and an end to federal subsidies in "overbedded" areas, except for specific needs. The Administration guideline would be four hospital beds per 1,000 persons. According to Administration estimates, the United States was paying $4 billion annually – including $1.1 billion in federal funds – for unneeded hospital beds.

Patient Study. University of Chicago sociologists surveyed 7,787 persons, including 490 patients who had been hospitalized within the previous year, and reported that the patients greatly preferred small hospitals. As hospital size increased, so did the proportion of patients dissatisfied with their care, particularly with the courtesy – or lack of it – on the part of physicians and nurses.

Hospitals throughout the United States felt the pinch of a nationwide shortage of 100,000 nurses, according to the AHA. A severe shortage of staff nurses forced some hospitals to close beds or units and spend more money on recruiting nurses, or pay more for temporary nurses.   Dianne Hales

See also HEALTH AND DISEASE; MEDICINE. In WORLD BOOK, see HOSPITAL.

HOUSING

HOUSING. The worst slump in recent decades hit the housing industry in the United States in 1980. Inflation, recession, and high interest rates combined to push the price of new homes beyond the reach of most U.S. families. New housing starts during the year were expected to reach about 1.22 million, down 28.9 per cent from the 1.75 million houses started in 1979.

Housing starts dropped 22 per cent in March, the biggest monthly decline in 20 years, and continued to decline through May, bottoming out at an annually adjusted rate of 920,000 units. Sales of new, single-family homes fell to an annually adjusted total of 364,000 units – a 14-year low – in April.

Home Selling Prices. The median price of new, single-family homes was $65,700 in October. Regional variations ranged from a high of $74,900 in the West to a low of $59,100 in the South. San Francisco, with a median cost of $90,000, was rated the most expensive U.S. city in which to buy a home.

A study released by the United States League of Savings Associations on June 4 reported that double-digit inflation has made Americans in the market for their first home an "endangered species," and was responsible for making two-income families the majority among home buyers. A spokesman for the National Association of Home Builders reported in March that only 5 per cent of U.S. families could afford the median-priced new home.

Flexible Rates. A new, flexible-rate mortgage plan was approved by the Federal Home Loan Bank Board on April 3. Under the plan, available for immediate use by savings and loan associations, the interest rate on a home mortgage could be renegotiated up or down every three to five years, with changes limited to one-half of a percentage point per year, and a maximum variance of five percentage points over the life of the mortgage.

Interest rates on home mortgages rose to a nationally adjusted average of 16.5 per cent in April, a record monthly increase from the 14.72 per cent reached in March. Local rates ranged as high as 18 to 20 per cent in some communities. A decline in interest rates in late spring brought renewed activity to the industry, and housing starts increased each month throughout the summer, reaching a September level of 1.46 million units. Federal Home Loan Bank Board Chairman Jay Janis predicted on October 22 that increased mortgage interest rates in the fall would result in a housing industry decline for the rest of the year.

High interest rates also spelled trouble for the home-mortgage lending institutions in 1980. Savings deposits in savings and loan institutions fell sharply early in the year and failed to recover

High construction costs and soaring interest rates produced a severe home-building slump in 1980 as housing starts dropped almost 30 per cent.

sufficiently during the summer to improve the climate for home mortgages. By June, increases in savings remained 57 per cent below the mid-1979 level, and they declined still further in early fall.

Housing Facilities. A survey released on September 23 by the Federal Trade Commission and the Department of Housing and Urban Development (HUD) revealed that the average new home had defects that would cost nearly $1,000 to correct. The study said buyers with no warranty protection are the ones most likely to have problems.

Data released by the Environmental Protection Agency on June 5 suggested that energy-efficient homes can present health hazards by preventing airborne pollutants from escaping. As many as 20,000 deaths per year could be attributed to inadequate airflow in well-insulated buildings.

Federal agencies as well as the National Tenants' Union, which was formed in Cleveland on June 22, investigated discrimination and other unfair practices in rental housing. HUD reported on July 11 that "no children" rental policies were on the rise, with about 1 out of 4 rental units excluding youngsters. The U.S. Department of Justice reported on January 27 that it was studying suburban zoning laws that restrict the size of residential lots to see whether these statutes exclude most minorities from buying homes.   James M. Banovetz

In WORLD BOOK, see HOUSE; HOUSING.

HOUSTON. The U.S. Department of Justice filed a suit on May 15, 1980, seeking the integration of Houston's public school system with 22 suburban school districts. It was the first time the federal government had sought cross-district school desegregation in a major urban area. The Houston school system, sixth largest in the nation, contained 225 schools with a total of about 177,000 students. The suburban school districts were added to a desegregation suit against Houston schools that had been pending for 23 years.

The Justice Department charged in the suit that the city, the state of Texas, the Harris County Department of Education, and the Texas Education Agency had deliberately fostered a racially segregated school system. The suit pinpointed four factors responsible for continued school segregation – a student-transfer system in use in the metropolitan school district; the city's refusal to approve low-income housing outside minority neighborhoods; the state's encouragement of racial discrimination in the housing market; and the state's refusal to allow the school system to expand.

Almost 46 per cent of the Houston students are black, 28 per cent Hispanic. Of the 310,000 suburban pupils affected, about 10.9 per cent are Hispanic, and 10.7 per cent are black.

New City Council. Houston's expanded and restructured City Council was sworn into office on January 2. The new council consisted of nine members elected from geographic districts and five elected at-large. Eight of the members were new, including three blacks, the council's first two women, and its first Mexican American. Previously, all council members were elected at-large. The council was restructured in accordance with a 1978 Justice Department order in an effort to provide greater minority representation.

Growing Pains. In his inauguration address, Mayor Jim McConn advocated reducing the city's growth rate by slowing annexations, the city's primary form of expansion. The city had used annexation to increase its tax base, while maintaining a notoriously low tax rate. As a result, city services such as street construction and garbage collection had not kept pace with expansion. McConn called for a tax increase to boost services. However, voters on August 11 rejected proposed pay increases for city employees that would have resulted in a 26 per cent property tax increase.

The city's population was reported to be about 1.5 million – 300,000 more than in 1970 – making it the fifth largest city in the United States. With its rapid growth rate, Houston and surrounding Harris County experienced the highest rate of new housing starts for any U.S. city – more than 500,000 – each year since 1975.   James M. Banovetz

See also CITY. In WORLD BOOK, see HOUSTON.

HUNGARY continued to reform its economic system in 1980. The government echoed Russian statements on major issues, but without enthusiasm. Foreign Minister Frigyes Puja called off his January visit to West Germany in response to Western criticism of Russia's invasion of Afghanistan, but the visit took place in September. Hungary's press reported on Polish strike issues more fully than did the mass media of other Communist-bloc countries, and the Communist Party leadership took a moderate attitude toward the Polish situation.

Vatican Secretary of State Agostino Cardinal Casaroli visited Budapest in September and was received by Communist Party First Secretary Janos Kadar and President Pal Losonczi. Losonczi visited four African nations in September and signed friendship treaties with Ethiopia and Mozambique, both of which have Marxist, pro-Russian regimes.

Party Meeting. The 12th Congress of the Hungarian Socialist Workers' Party, Hungary's Communist party, in March concentrated on economic problems. The economy had grown by only 1.5 per cent in 1979, half of the planned rate. Industrial output had been 2.5 per cent higher than in 1978, rather than the planned 4 per cent. Furthermore, prices had increased by more than 9 per cent in 1979, Hungary's highest price rise since 1946.

343

Janos Kadar, first secretary of the Hungarian Socialist Workers' (Communist) Party, votes in local and parliamentary elections in August.

Prime Minister Gyorgy Lazar announced economic reforms, including phasing out enterprises that were losing money and encouraging small businesses and private farmers. Kadar was reelected for another five years, but five of the 15 persons in the Politburo, the party's policymaking body, were replaced.

In June, Finance Minister Lajos Faluvegi replaced Istvan Huszar, deputy prime minister and president of the national planning office. The government also appointed new ministers of finance, interior, and agriculture and merged the ministries of education and culture.

Industrial Production declined by 1.8 per cent in the first half of 1980, because of the government's squeeze on unsuccessful enterprises. The value of investments in the economy was down 11.5 per cent, but labor productivity increased by 1 per cent. Exports to non-Communist countries grew by 21.7 per cent, 11 per cent more than planned, but imports dipped by 1.4 per cent. The government increased prices in the first half of 1980 but slowed the pace of such increases during the remainder of the year.

Hungary disbanded its wine, sugar, tobacco, and confectionery trusts in July in order to create more competition. Chris Cviic

See also EUROPE (Facts in Brief Table). In WORLD BOOK, see HUNGARY.

HUNTING. Portions of 27 states in all four migratory waterfowl flyways were designated "steel shot zones" for the 1980-1981 waterfowl hunting season by the U.S. Fish and Wildlife Service on June 5, 1980. The service contends that lead shot should be banned to reduce the number of waterfowl — estimated at 2 million — which die of lead poisoning after eating spent lead shot.

Congress again passed legislation prohibiting the service from enforcing steel shot regulations in any state unless the state wildlife agency approves. State legislatures in Louisiana, Missouri, Wisconsin, Illinois, and Maryland did not approve enforcement of the regulations in all or part of the designated areas in 1980. An effort also began in Congress to prevent the U.S. Fish and Wildlife Service from barring the use of lead pellets on federal wildlife refuges.

The service warned hunters on August 29 that plugs that allow hunters to adjust the shell capacity of tube-fed shotguns in the field are illegal for taking migratory game birds. Federal regulations allow only shotguns with three or fewer shells.

The spring and summer drought that hit U.S. and Canadian waterfowl nesting areas reduced the size of the 1980 duck crop. About 18 million ducks are shot by hunters throughout the United States each year. Andrew L. Newman

In WORLD BOOK, see AMMUNITION; HUNTING.

ICE SKATING. Eric Heiden of Madison, Wis., dominated speed skating in 1980 for the fourth consecutive year. The 21-year-old Heiden won all five men's gold medals in the Winter Olympic Games in February in Lake Placid, N.Y. He took the world sprint championship for the fourth straight year. He finished second in the world overall championships after having won that title three straight years. And he broke the world record at three distances for men.

The world sprint championships for men and women were held at West Allis, Wis., on February 9 and 10. Heiden won three of the four men's races. His 20-year-old sister, Beth, finished third among the women behind Karin Enke of East Germany and the defender, Leah Poulos Mueller of Dousman, Wis. An injured ankle hampered Beth Heiden and limited her to one Olympic bronze medal.

After the Olympics, Eric Heiden skated in the world overall championships for men on March 2 and 3 in Heerenveen, the Netherlands. He finished first in the 500 meters, second in the 1,500, and sixth in both the 5,000 and 10,000, and he lost the title to Hilbert van der Duim of the Netherlands.

In 1979, Beth Heiden swept the four races in the women's overall championships. This time, in the January competition in Hamar, Norway, Natalia Petruseva of Russia won three of the four races en route to the title. Beth placed second overall.

Figure Skating. Robin Cousins of Great Britain, Anett Poetzsch of East Germany (for the fourth straight year), and the Russian husband-wife pair of Alexander Zaitsev and Irina Rodnina won European championships in January in Sweden.

The U.S. championships in January in Atlanta, Ga., also served as Olympic trials. The winners were Charles Tickner of Littleton, Colo., in men's singles for the fourth straight year; Linda Fratianne of Northridge, Calif., in women's singles for the fourth straight year; and Randy Gardner of Los Angeles and Tai Babilonia of Mission Hills, Calif., in pairs for the fifth straight year.

All those American champions were potential Olympic champions, but none came close. Tickner finished third, and Fratianne finished second. Gardner and Babilonia could not compete because of a groin injury to Gardner.

The injury did not heal in time for Gardner and Babilonia to defend their world championship in March in West Germany. Zaitsev and Rodnina regained that title, and Poetzsch and Jan Hoffmann of East Germany won the singles.   Frank Litsky

See also OLYMPIC GAMES. In WORLD BOOK, see ICE SKATING.

ICELAND. See EUROPE.

IDAHO. See STATE GOVERNMENT.

ILLINOIS. See CHICAGO; STATE GOVERNMENT.

IMMIGRATION. An extraordinary group of refugees arrived in the United States in 1980, sailing in a "freedom flotilla" from Cuba to Key West, Fla. From April 21 through early August, an estimated 125,000 Cubans made the 110-mile (180-kilometer) ocean trip with the permission of Cuban President Fidel Castro, who allowed them to board boats at Mariel on Cuba's north coast. See CUBA.

United States President Jimmy Carter said on May 5 that the nation would welcome the Cubans with "an open heart and open arms." As the number of refugees exceeded 46,000, however, Carter on May 14 ordered a reversal in U.S. policy and tried to restrict the inflow. The U.S. Coast Guard was ordered to intercept American boats bound for Cuba and to warn boat owners that their vessels would be seized and that they could be fined up to $1,000 for each Cuban they brought to the United States.

Still, the flood of Cubans continued, passing 110,000 about June 1. At that time, immigration officials reported, about 23,000 had been resettled and were living with relatives or other American sponsors. The others were sent to camps at Eglin Air Force Base in Florida, Fort Chaffee in Arkansas, Fort Indiantown Gap in Pennsylvania, and Fort McCoy in Wisconsin for processing and subsequent resettlement.

An airplane hangar at Eglin Air Force Base provides a temporary home for some of the thousands of Cuban refugees entering Florida in the spring.

Haitian Immigration. The Cuban influx was preceded by a wave of Haitian immigrants that began late in 1979. An estimated 25,000 Haitians sailed to south Florida in small boats seeking to escape poverty and the allegedly repressive rule of President Jean-Claude Duvalier. They were classified as illegal aliens and denied work permits and welfare aid until they requested political asylum.

President Carter on June 20 gave a six-month reprieve from deportation to some 114,000 Cubans and 15,000 Haitians. On October 10 he signed a bill providing federal grants of from $90 million to $127 million for education and $100 million for social services for Cuban, Haitian, and Indochinese refugee children. By providing equal benefits for the Cuban and Haitian refugees, Carter answered criticism from the Congressional Black Caucus and other groups charging that U.S. policy favored the predominantly white Cuban refugees over the mostly black Haitians.

On July 7, the U.S. government released 270 commercial fishing vessels and 430 private boats that had been seized because they ferried Cubans to the United States, under the condition they would not do so again.

There were many other problems associated with the rapid influx of Cubans. Riots and escapes occurred at all four resettlement camps. By June 30, a total of 1,395 Cubans had been found to have committed serious crimes and were placed in U.S. prisons. Immigration officials announced on July 7 that another 2,000 Cubans were self-professed homosexuals and, under existing statutes, not legally eligible to enter the U.S. However, they were admitted on a "deferred inspection" basis.

Other Developments. President Carter on March 17 signed the Refugee Act of 1979, setting up new procedures for the admission of refugees and immigrants. It raised the annual ceiling for immigrants from 290,000 to 320,000 and lifted the refugee ceiling from 17,400 to 50,000. However, on September 19 Carter announced a reduction in the 1981 immigrant quota to 217,000, primarily to balance the heavy influx in 1980.

Carter nominated Matias W. Garcia, a San Antonio lawyer, to be commissioner of the Immigration and Naturalization Service (INS).

In Chicago, 12-year-old Walter Polovchak was granted political asylum after he refused to return to Russia with his parents. See CIVIL RIGHTS.

A U.S. Census Bureau study released on February 4 reported that the number of illegal aliens in the United States had never exceeded 6 million and might not have exceeded 3.5 million. This was far below past INS estimates, which placed the number as high as 12 million.   William J. Eaton

In WORLD BOOK, see IMMIGRATION AND EMIGRATION; REFUGEE.

INCOME TAX. See TAXATION.

INDIA. Indira Gandhi pulled off what many regarded as a political miracle in 1980. After being beaten decisively in a 1977 general election, she regained power as prime minister in a landslide election victory on Jan. 3 and 6, 1980. Her Congress-I (I for Indira) Party won 351 of the 542 seats in the new *Lok Sabha*, the lower house of parliament.

Her triumph was as much due to her political skills as to the mismanagement and internal feuding by the Janata Party coalition, which in 1977 drove her from power. India's voters were distressed by the shortages of kerosene, electricity, salt, and sugar; a 22 per cent inflation rate; and soaring crime rates.

In February, Gandhi dismissed hostile governments in nine states and ordered elections. She won a sweeping victory in eight of these in late May, with her son Sanjay, 33, handpicking many of the Congress-I candidates.

Disorder, Violence. But the victories did not bring the firm and purposeful government that Gandhi promised. The effort to consolidate her party's gains took time and effort. Equally time-consuming was the dissident movement in Assam state in northwest India, where a student-led coalition was trying to drive out at least 3.5 million "foreigners," most of them Bengali immigrants from neighboring Bangladesh.

India's Prime Minister Indira Gandhi, center, joins folk dancers celebrating the nation's Republic Day on January 31 in New Delhi.

The Assamese resented the competition for jobs and services, as well as the growing political power of the outsiders. In a confrontation with New Delhi, the students – who had in effect taken over the government of the state – staged a general strike beginning in May. They disrupted government operations, rail transport, and the flow of oil to India. In June, the army was called in, but the violence spread to other northeast states.

Sanjay's Death. The situation deteriorated after Sanjay Gandhi was killed on June 23. Gandhi and his flying instructor took off in Sanjay's small plane, and the craft crashed 12 minutes later in the heart of New Delhi, killing both men. A heavy emotional blow to Prime Minister Gandhi, her son's death was also a major political loss. Sanjay, widely regarded as arrogant and ruthless, also represented a new, young breed on a political stage dominated by old-timers. He had long been a power through the party's Youth Wing, whose candidates he had been installing in key positions. His death left them without a strong patron.

Sanjay's death also left Prime Minister Gandhi without a trusted adviser. She turned to her older son, Rajiv, a 37-year-old commercial pilot, who was reluctant to go into politics. Rajiv was nevertheless expected to answer his mother's call.

Religious Riots began on August 13 in Moradabad, triggered by a rumor that police had allowed a pig – an unclean animal to Muslims – to wander around the grounds of a Muslim mosque. Fighting broke out among Muslims, Hindus, and the police. In the next 24 hours, 86 lives were lost, and in the days that followed, the trouble spread to other northern cities. Before the turmoil quieted, at least 150 persons were dead and thousands had been arrested. A new national security law proclaimed on September 22 gave Gandhi the power to jail anyone for a year without trial. The law was said to be needed to halt minority and regional unrest.

The Economy remained in the doldrums. After the worst drought in 60 years in 1979, the 1980 harvest was expected to be excellent. But industry remained stagnant, and $2 of every $3 earned by exports went to pay for imported oil. In mid-September, economists forecast a trade deficit of at least $4 billion in 1980-1981. The gross national product – the sum of the goods and services produced – dropped in 1979-1980 by 3 per cent, and the slump continued in 1980-1981. India stepped up the search for oil and pressed for nuclear power. In late September, the Congress of the United States approved the controversial sale of 38 short tons (34 metric tons) of enriched uranium to India for its nuclear-power program. On July 18, India became the sixth country to launch a space satellite.　　　　Mark Gayn

See also ASIA (Facts in Brief Table); GANDHI, INDIRA. In WORLD BOOK, see INDIA.

INDIAN, AMERICAN. The Supreme Court of the United States ruled 8 to 1 on June 30, 1980, that the federal government must pay seven tribes of Sioux Indians $17.5 million for the government's illegal seizure of 7 million acres (3 million hectares) of Indian lands in the Black Hills of South Dakota in 1877. The decision also provided for interest payments calculated at 5 per cent annually for 103 years, amounting to $105 million. The $122.5-million award was the largest in history to compensate American Indians for land seizures.

The decision upheld a 1979 award by the U.S. Court of Claims. In arguing the case, Department of Justice attorneys told the Supreme Court that the Court of Claims decision "creates a precedent that may well embarrass future litigation at very substantial cost to the national treasury." Government officials feared it might open the door for awards of similar size to other Indian tribes.

The Oglala Sioux filed suit in federal court on July 18 asking for $11 billion in damages and restoration of the Black Hills to the tribe. The Black Hills cover 6,000 square miles (15,500 square kilometers) in southwestern South Dakota and northeastern Wyoming.

The Oglala tribe argued it was not among the tribes represented in the $122.5-million Supreme Court award and said they wanted the land returned to them. Tribal attorney Mario Gonzalez said on August 13, "The land is very sacred to the tribe and it may be lost forever. The Black Hills are not for sale." U.S. District Judge Albert G. Schaltz dismissed the suit on September 11, but the Oglala Sioux said they would appeal.

The Black Hills were taken from the Indians in 1877, and litigation for settlement of the claim has been in the courts since 1922. Oglala officials said on July 24 that they expected it to take from two to four years to reach a final settlement.

Maine Claim Settled. President Jimmy Carter signed legislation on October 10 authorizing payment of $81.5 million to settle a claim by three Maine Indian tribes to more than 12 million acres (5 million hectares) of land. The Passamaquoddy, Penobscot, and Maliseet tribes contended that the land had been taken from them in violation of the Trade and Non-Intercourse Act of 1790, which required congressional approval of all transfers of Indian land.

Under the 1980 legislation, the federal government allotted the three tribes $54.5 million to buy about 300,000 acres (120,000 hectares) of land and a $27-million trust fund for social programs to benefit the Indians that would be administered by the Department of the Interior.

The Maine Indian claim was the largest of 17 such claims by Eastern Indian tribes. The House of Representatives rejected on March 18 a negotiated settlement of a claim by the Cayuga Indians to

American Indians attending beatification rites in Rome for an Indian woman, Kateri Tekawitha, visit with Pope John Paul II after ceremony.

64,000 acres (26,000 hectares) in central New York state. The settlement had awarded the Indians $8-million and 5,500 acres (2,200 hectares) of land.

Other Claims. The U.S. Court of Appeals for the Eighth Circuit ruled on January 15 that the Omaha Indian tribe owned 2,900 acres (1,200 hectares) of land along the Iowa side of the Missouri River near Blackbird Bend, Iowa. An 1854 treaty had established the area as a reservation site, but several individuals claimed the land when the river shifted its course, changing the state boundary, and relocating the area from Nebraska to Iowa.

President Carter on March 27 approved legislation that gives Indian tribes until Dec. 31, 1982, to begin legal action over claims based on alleged wrongs prior to 1966. This was the third extension exempting Indian claims from the statute of limitations that would otherwise bar such suits.

Thomas Fredericks, a member of the Mandan-Hidatsa tribe of North Dakota and a former associate solicitor of the Department of the Interior, was nominated to be assistant secretary of the interior for Indian affairs on June 18. He succeeded Forrest Gerard, a member of the Blackfoot tribe and the first person to serve in the highest-level Indian position in the federal government. Andrew L. Newman

In WORLD BOOK, see INDIAN, AMERICAN.
INDIANA. See STATE GOVERNMENT.

INDONESIA could count many pluses in 1980, at least on the surface. After the largest harvest in history, Indonesia's bins were packed with home-grown and imported rice. Thanks to soaring world prices, Indonesia's income from oil and gas exports exceeded $10 billion, or nearly 60 per cent of the nation's foreign-exchange earnings.

There was also a boom in oil and gas exploration, with the government claiming some promising discoveries that could halt a decline in oil production and bring it up to about 1.8 million barrels per day by 1985. The inflation rate dropped to about 20 per cent.

Reports of Corruption. An opinion poll in August reported that middle-class people thought they were better off financially and that official corruption was the greatest danger facing the nation. This belief was fueled by a series of scandals seemingly involving the elite, from the presidential family on down.

Several damaging disclosures were made in a court fight for $35 million deposited in the Singapore branch of a Japanese bank, part of the estate of Haji Thahir. Thahir was a $9,000-a-year official of the huge state-owned Pertamina oil company, which in 1975 triggered a national crisis by defaulting on its debts – eventually revealed to exceed $10 billion. A July statement by Thahir's widow implicated the wife of President Suharto and one of Suharto's financial advisers in a kick-back scheme. A retired army deputy chief of staff also charged that Suharto and his wife used questionable means to acquire a large cattle ranch.

The rumors reached such a point that the president, at a meeting of army officers in April, thought it necessary to deny that his wife was taking kickbacks on industrial contracts or deciding which contract bidder was to win. Vice-President Adam Malik was accused in United States Securities and Exchange Commission documents of having taken sizable kickbacks from a U.S. firm that won a Pertamina contract. Malik denied the charge.

Fifty Dissenters. Suharto also kept the political pot boiling by his moves to ensure victory in the 1982 parliamentary election and the 1983 presidential election, in which he would seek his fourth 5-year term. He argued at two military meetings that he and the official Golkar Party best represented the nation's ideals and that it was the army's duty to support him against critics. The speeches led 50 national figures, including two former prime ministers and nine former generals, to present a petition to Parliament demanding that Suharto explain his appeal to the military to intervene in politics. Mark Gayn

See also ASIA (Facts in Brief Table). In WORLD BOOK, see INDONESIA.

INSURANCE. Property and liability insurance companies in the United States projected an underwriting loss of nearly $3 billion for 1980 based on available data and discernible trends. By September, the recorded underwriting loss was $2.28-billion, a good deal larger than the $1.38 billion for the same period in 1979. For the full year of 1979, the loss reached $1.65 billion.

However, investment earnings more than offset underwriting losses. For the same period of 1980, the investment gain of $7.82 billion gave insurers an overall $5.09 billion in total earnings after taxes. Investment income was expected to exceed $10 billion by year-end – almost 40 per cent above the final 1979 investment income of $7.3 billion.

Written premiums for insurers went above $67.8-billion for the first nine months of 1980, a 7.4 per cent increase over the $63.1 billion for the same period of 1979. For the full year of 1979, premiums totaled $84 billion. Estimates indicated that 1980 premiums would reach $90 billion.

Private passenger and commercial automobile insurance continued to cause most underwriting losses, even though a trend toward lowered accident frequency and severity, as reflected by the average cost per claim, appeared by mid-1980. But nearly all lines, with the exception of workers' compensation and physical car damage, showed up

Brokers and underwriters get set to handle unusual commercial risks as the New York Insurance Exchange, similar to Lloyd's of London, opens on March 31.

poorly in 1980. In personal lines of coverage, rates did not keep pace with inflation. In the commercial lines, where rates are not generally subject to approval by state insurance supervisors, a rate-slashing contest fueled by reliance on investment gains adversely affected the underwriting picture.

Catastrophe Losses moderated in 1980 after setting a record in 1979. The potentially destructive Hurricane Allen, which did substantial offshore damage, lost its punch when it reached Texas cities along the Gulf of Mexico in August. Insured losses, not including federal flood claims, came to $57.9-million. The Mount Saint Helens volcanic eruptions, which started on May 18, resulted in about $14 million in insured losses, counting cars, houses and their contents, and some commercial structures. Money paid to clean up ash from the eruptions added to the loss. Problems resulting from the continuing eruptions brought a demand to insurers from Washington State Insurance Commissioner Richard Marquardt for a clarification of volcanic-eruption insurance and a mandatory deductible amount, so as to avoid a lot of small or nuisance claims (see GEOLOGY [Close-Up]). Rioting in the Liberty City area of Miami, Fla. which lasted for several days in May, caused more than $65 million in insured losses.

Metzenbaum Bill. Senator Howard M. Metzenbaum (D., Ohio) in March introduced his long-expected Insurance Competition Act. The bill was designed to repeal exemptions from federal anti-trust acts that insurance companies have enjoyed since 1945 under the McCarran-Ferguson Act. Almost universally opposed by the insurance industry and state regulators, the bill would set federal minimum standards to regulate rates in the auto and homeowner business under state control. However, the bill did not move out of committee.

Insurance Exchange. The New York Insurance Exchange, which is considered to be the first U.S. rival to Lloyd's of London, opened for business on March 31. By year-end, its premium volume was about $25 million, largely in reinsurance risks. Exchanges proposed for Illinois and Florida made no progress in 1980.

Consumer advocate Ralph Nader and a former head of the Federal Insurance Administration, Robert Hunter, formed the National Insurance Consumer Organization, which they called "the first major public interest group" dealing with insurance, in September. The group charged that Americans are paying $4 billion too much for car insurance. President Jimmy Carter on September 30 signed a bill that will enlarge the federal crop insurance program to cover all crops and all risks in all sections of the U.S. However, private insurers won the right to continue to offer hail and fire coverage for crops. Emanuel Levy

In WORLD BOOK, see INSURANCE.

INTERNATIONAL TRADE AND FINANCE. Pervasive inflation and sluggish growth characterized the world economy in 1980. While disasters such as mass unemployment in the industrial countries and widespread debt default among the poorer countries were avoided, United States Secretary of the Treasury G. William Miller summarized a common view when he said in September that "the international economy is in a critically difficult period, easily as dangerous as any since the second World War."

The inflation rate among the industrial countries as a group was about 12 per cent, with the United States near the average. The picture was far worse for the developing countries, where inflation averaged more than 30 per cent. Worsening inflation was explained in good part by the doubling of world oil prices during 1979; oil prices did not rise much higher in 1980.

Sluggish Growth. The International Monetary Fund (IMF) estimated that the gross national product — total production of goods and services — in the industrial countries of North America, Western Europe, and Japan grew by a meager 1 per cent in 1980, compared with an average of almost 4 per cent in the preceding three years. There were outright recessions in the United States, Great Britain, and Canada, while growth virtually ceased in West Germany and Italy. Japan's economy continued to grow, but at a slower rate.

Unemployment rose in many countries, though the increase was moderate in most cases. The chief exception was Great Britain, where a tough anti-inflation policy brought on a slump and pushed unemployment over the 2-million mark for the first time since the Great Depression of the 1930s (see GREAT BRITAIN).

After the disappointing growth of 1980, the outlook for 1981 was for more of the same. Because of high inflation rates, most countries were reluctant to stimulate their economies.

Trade Slow. As a natural consequence of the sluggishness of national economies, the growth of world trade slowed markedly, though it continued to show at least moderate expansion. After increasing in volume by 6.5 per cent in 1979, trade probably rose only 2 to 3 per cent in 1980, far below the average of the past 20 years — growth of trade had been 12 per cent as recently as 1976.

The slowdown did not reflect a new wave of "protectionism," though a few countries raised new trade barriers to protect severely pressed industries and workers. Rather, the slow growth of imports reflected the correspondingly weak expansion of domestic demand and production in each country. With the world still digesting the successful conclusion in 1978 and 1979 of the lengthy "Tokyo round" of negotiations aimed at reducing some barriers and providing new trade rules in

Bullion Goes Berserk

All that glittered was not gold in 1980; silver had a matching glow. Never in modern times had either precious metal become so valuable in so short a period of time. Never had buyers been so willing to pay such sky-high prices; never had sellers been so eager to dispose of their treasures for what the traffic would bear. Age, size, and shape of the two ores meant nothing; it was the content that counted.

Gold had long been pegged at $35 per troy ounce (31.1 grams). Silver had been pegged at $4 to $5 per ounce between 1974 and 1978. Suddenly, early in 1979, the pegs broke. Slowly at first, then faster, the prices began to rise until they were escalating by the hour. In January, gold stood at $200 per ounce; by July, it had doubled to $400 and by December 1979, it had reached $500.

Metal dealers were astounded as much by the price as by the continuing demand. Most dealers believed the boom would continue, though not a few predicted that the price of gold had reached its maximum. But the rise continued. By early January 1980, gold had reached $610 per ounce, and by month's end, it had soared an incredible 34 per cent, closing out the month at $808 in New York City, $823 in Hong Kong, and $835 in London and Zurich. Silver enjoyed the same spectacular leap from $5 to $48 per ounce. For the rest of the year, prices seesawed up and down.

Why did gold and silver soar so high in 1980? Most Americans believed they were good hedges against inflation; in Europe, uncertainty about Russia's intentions – in Poland, Yugoslavia, and elsewhere – provoked a stampede. But the metals fever was especially acute in the Persian Gulf area, where petroleum profits were pouring in at the rate of $50 million a day. There, the gold and silver rush was a classic case of panic: It reflected intense concern over the revolution in Iran, the war between Iran and Iraq, the Soviet invasion of Afghanistan, and unrest in Saudi Arabia and Kuwait. It was a case of too many riyals and dinars chasing too little gold and silver.

By mid-1980, gold fever had become a worldwide affliction. In New York, London, Chicago, Los Angeles, Rome, and Paris, metal dealers were besieged by thousands of sellers carrying shopping bags, suitcases, or even newspaper-wrapped parcels containing personal treasures carefully hoarded for a lifetime. There were filigreed candlesticks, ornate tea sets, gold rings, gold watchcases and silver spoons, bracelets, brooches, and even silver teething rings and gold dental inlays.

Most of the objects had only a basic value, but some were priceless antiques. Most dealers unhesitatingly heaved all of their haul pell-mell into the melting pot. Treasures of the jewelers' art or the silversmiths' skills were lost forever. But a few of the more discerning dealers recognized the pieces for what they were – irreplaceable treasures – and withheld them from the fiery crucibles.

Not all sellers disposed of their personal treasures out of greed or avarice. As gold and silver escalated in value, insurance costs went up, too. Some owners sold to avoid these higher premiums. Many, too, feared robbery, which had increased as gold and silver prices rose. Incidents were reported of burglars breaking into churches to steal chalices.

Ultimately, even governments got into the bullion act. The United States, which holds about 8,600 short tons (7,800 metric tons) of gold, reckoned its horde was worth $220 billion by current prices. In July, the U.S. Treasury began selling 1-ounce and half-ounce gold medallions.

At year's end, gold remained at about $528 per ounce and silver at $14. Whether or not they would ever fall back to their former pegged levels remained to be seen, but it was doubtful. "Gold," said Charles de Gaulle, "never changes; it can be shaped into ingots, bars, coins, and rings which not only have no nationality but are eternally and universally accepted as the one unalterable fiduciary value." In 1980, silver, too, demonstrated that it should have been included in De Gaulle's assessment.

Paul C. Tullier

Gold and silver treasure

Traders in precious metals had a hectic year on the metals exchanges as world inflation drove prices up, spurring speculators and investors alike.

such areas as subsidies and government procurement, there were no important international trade negotiations in 1980.

In the United States, the most dramatic trade case involving an important individual product in many years arose from a petition by the United Automobile Workers and the Ford Motor Company to the International Trade Commission (ITC) to restrict automobile imports from Japan. The ITC rejected the petition on November 10, blaming not the imports, but the economic downturn and a shift in consumer tastes toward smaller cars for Detroit's auto sales slump. The United States reinstituted the "trigger price mechanism," a system of import restraints on low-priced foreign steel, on September 30, but this drew no major objections from Europe and Japan. See AUTOMOBILE; STEEL INDUSTRY.

Rising Debts. The world's preoccupying monetary problem was the rising international payments deficits and corresponding debts of the less developed countries. Among the industrial countries there were no crises or other major developments in the foreign-exchange markets. The dollar continued to float against the other major currencies, rising strongly at year-end as high U.S. interest rates attracted foreign capital. The Japanese yen grew stronger in the last half of the year, largely because of an inflow of foreign investment in

Japanese banks and securities, much of it from the rich oil-producing countries. The British pound was also strong, reflecting the high British interest rates that were a key part of its anti-inflation program. But, in general, currency markets were unusually calm.

For many of the developing countries the situation was more ominous. Their economies, staggering under the oil price increases, suffered from weak export growth as the industrial nations imposed their own anti-inflation policies. As a result, balance-of-payments deficits grew alarmingly.

The stronger, or "middle-income," developing countries have been able to borrow extensively, mainly from private banks in the United States and other industrial countries, to cover their balance-of-payments deficits. But the debts have become a serious burden. The World Bank's annual report estimated that the total debt of all the less developed countries rose from $64 billion in 1970 to $376 billion in 1979 and that annual *debt service* (payment of interest and principal) in 1980 approached almost $70 billion a year.

While there were no outright debt defaults in 1980, a major international rescue operation was needed to avert a default by Turkey (see TURKEY). In addition, several other countries, such as Jamaica, Bolivia, and Sudan, were in precarious condition. Meeting in New Orleans at a monetary conference in June, private bankers from the industrial countries expressed strong doubts that they could continue to finance the deficits of the poorer countries on the scale of the past.

A major response to this growing problem came in more liberal IMF lending terms and a growth in the volume of its loans. In the first nine months of 1980, the fund loaned about $7.7 billion, nearly all to developing countries, compared with $5.6-billion in all of 1979.

Members were authorized to borrow larger amounts, and repayment terms were stretched out over a longer period in some cases. If the expanded pace of lending is to continue, however, the fund itself will soon have to borrow, either from its richer members or, for the first time, from the private markets.

A setback to IMF plans occurred in late 1980 when several oil-exporting countries, including Saudi Arabia and Kuwait, declined to make additional loans to the IMF because the Palestine Liberation Organization had been denied observer status at the IMF's annual meeting, though the permanence of this decision was unclear as the year ended.   Edwin L. Dale, Jr.

See also ECONOMICS. In WORLD BOOK, see INTERNATIONAL TRADE.

IOWA. See STATE GOVERNMENT.

IRAN. Despite war, international isolation, internal unrest, and a tattered economy, the revolutionary religious regime dominated by Ayatollah Ruhollah Khomeini made some progress toward its goal of a viable Islamic republic in Iran in 1980. Former Finance Minister and Khomeini protegé Abol Hasan Bani-Sadr was elected president in January by a 4-to-1 margin over his rivals (see BANI-SADR, ABOL HASAN).

The presidential election was followed by the two-stage election of a 270-member *Majlis* (parliament), as prescribed by the 1979 Constitution. Representatives of Ayatollah Mohammed Beheshti's Islamic Republican Party (IRP), presented to the electorate as the "Party of God," won 75 per cent of the seats.

Bani-Sadr encountered strong opposition in the Majlis over his nomination of a prime minister. Several of his choices were rejected, and the IRP challenged him with its own choice. A compromise was finally reached in August, with Majlis approval of Provisional Education Minister Mohammed Ali Rajai as prime minister (see RAJAI, MOHAMMED ALI).

A new Cabinet, the first in 10 months of revolutionary upheaval, was formed in September. It included several U.S.-educated ministers. As the new Constitution provided, the Revolutionary

Iranian officials and army officers inspect the wreckage of U.S. military equipment left in the desert after the abortive hostage-rescue mission.

Council that had governed Iran since the shah's overthrow in January 1979 dissolved itself and transferred its functions to a "supreme leader" — Ayatollah Khomeini.

Ethnic Troubles. In addition to the political polarization of religious fundamentalists and those supporting a secular government, the government faced strong resistance from Kurdish and other ethnic minorities seeking greater autonomy. A cease-fire between government forces and Kurdish guerrillas negotiated late in 1979 collapsed in April. Iranian Army units recaptured the provincial capital, Sanandaj, in May, but they were unable to pin down the guerrillas. The army, decimated by dismissals, defections, and executions, did not begin to give an effective performance until Iraqi forces invaded Iran's western Khuzistan province in September. See Close-Up.

Until the Iraqi attack, Iran continued to pump oil at a reduced rate — 1.8 million barrels per day. A shortfall of $10 billion in revenues for the $38.5-billion budget, plus the United States trade embargo, prompted Iran to sign treaty agreements with several Communist countries for direct or indirect purchases of essential imports.

The American Hostages remained prisoners in Iran, except for Vice-Consul Richard I. Queen, who was released for medical reasons in July. The United States, despairing that the hostage issue would be easily resolved, broke diplomatic relations with Iran on April 7 and instituted an economic boycott. Some Iranian diplomats and Iranian students were expelled or deported from the United States. Iranian assets in the United States were frozen and various aid and trade agreements halted. An abortive rescue mission by U.S. commandos on April 25 foundered in the Iranian desert (see ARMED FORCES).

The death of Shah Mohammad Reza Pahlavi — whose extradition was one of the conditions set by the militants — produced no change in the hostage issue. The shah left Panama for another home in Egypt in March, and died on July 27. See PANAMA.

The need for U.S. spare parts for its battered army, which might have spurred a hostage release, was largely dissipated as Iran obtained replacement material from various sources, notably Libya (as a conduit for Russia) and North Korea. But an overriding Iranian concern, as the two countries stumbled toward a solution, was Iran's extreme international isolation and the suspicion that maximum mileage had been extracted from the hostages, and that their continued detention interfered with the completion of the revolution.

Iran Sets a Price. Early in November, the Majlis announced four conditions for the hostages' re-

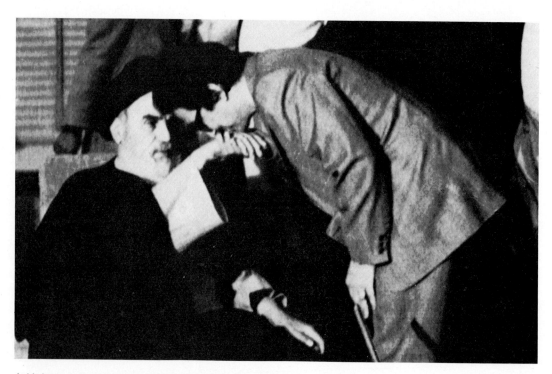

At his inauguration, Abol Hasan Bani-Sadr, the first president of Iran, kisses the hand of the Ayatollah Khomeini, Iran's spiritual leader.

Mideast Family Feud

The war had been brewing for months, the feud for centuries. When Iraq invaded Iran in September 1980, after weeks of border skirmishes, both countries called on long racial and religious memories to rouse their people.

The Iraqis remembered the battle of Qadisiyah in A.D. 637, when the Arabs — Iraq is Arab — defeated the Persians — who are not Arabs — and brought Islam to Persia (now Iran). The Iranians remembered their wars with the Ottoman Turks, who ruled Iraq from the 1500s until World War I. Underneath these ethnic quarrels ran the religious hostility of an Islamic rift between the Shiite Muslims and the Sunni Muslims that dates back to the A.D. 600s. Iran is Shiite; Iraq is ruled by Sunni Muslims, though more than half of the population is Shiite.

For all the historic propaganda, however, the 1980 war was basically an attempt by Iraqi President Saddam Hussein to take advantage of an Iran weakened by revolutionary turmoil in order to strengthen his own domestic situation and dominate the Persian Gulf area. The Iraqis saw an opportunity to regain full control of the Shatt al Arab estuary that separates the two countries at the head of the gulf. Some Iraqi control over the waterway had been bartered away in a 1975 treaty with Iran's Shah Mohammad Reza Pahlavi in return for his withdrawal of support for the Kurdish revolt in Iraq.

The Iraqis invaded Iran's Khuzistan province, which they call "Arabistan" because most of its people are Arabs, on September 22, confident of popular support and expecting the Iranian regime to collapse quickly. Iraqi planes left the huge oil refinery at Abadan in ruins, and ground forces moved on the key Iranian cities of Ahvaz, Dezful, and Khorramshahr.

But Iraqi expectations of rapid success were dashed by the failure of the Khuzistan Arabs to turn on their government, and by the unexpectedly stiff resistance of the Iranian army and auxiliary Revolutionary Guards. Iran's air force, flying low-level sorties under Iraqi radar, heavily damaged Iraqi ports, oil installations, and industrial targets. Iraq's oil exports through the Strait of Hormuz were cut off, hurting such major oil purchasers as Japan and Brazil.

On the ground, Iraqi forces captured only Khorramshahr, though Abadan was under siege. By mid-November, the war was stalemated.

Economically, the war was hard on both oil-rich countries. Fuel rationing appeared early in Iran's capital, Teheran. Iraqi gas rationing began in mid-December. Military equipment losses were high.

Politically, the war seemed to hold short-term benefits for both regimes. In Iran, the people's cultural and national identity was heightened by the struggle, though Iran's war propaganda was almost invariably cast in a religious mold, viewing the war as one against the "Iraqi infidel."

By attacking the "racist Persian regime," the Iraqis hoped to undercut whatever support Iraq's Shiite Muslims had for Iran's religious leader, Ayatollah Ruhollah Khomeini, who had spent 14 years in exile in Iraq until he was expelled in 1978.

The war split the Middle East into sometimes contradictory camps. Pro-Western monarchies Jordan and Saudi Arabia supported Russia's sometime client state Iraq. Syria and Libya, both recipients of much Russian aid, supported the fundamentalist, anti-Communist Islamic Republic of Iran. Feelings ran high enough that Syria and the other pro-Iranian Arab nations boycotted a November meeting of the Arab League held at Amman, Jordan, and Syria briefly threatened Jordan.

The conflict also gave Russia and the United States another lesson in the complexities of Middle Eastern politics. Neither seemed able to turn the situation to its advantage, though both played behind-the-scenes roles. Any superpower tilt toward one or the other combatant seemed certain to backfire.

As 1981 dawned, the war dragged on. Despite the racial and religious differences, the war appeared to many non-Islamic eyes to resemble a family fight, in which outsiders meddle at their own risk.   William Spencer

Iraqi tanks

lease: a U.S. commitment not to interfere in Iran's internal affairs; unfreezing of Iranian assets held in the U.S.; cancellation of claims by U.S. firms against Iran for contract breaches and confiscation of property; and return of the shah's wealth. The first condition was easy to accept, but the others faced enormous legal obstacles in the U.S.

The legal problem included claims against Iran filed by 270 banks, corporations, and individuals for recovery of more than $6.5 billion, against $8-billion in frozen Iranian assets. These claims were temporarily stayed by a U.S. judge on November 13, to ease negotiations. Damage suits by hostages who had already been released posed another headache for U.S. negotiators. The question of the shah's wealth rested on its actual value and location – which were unknown – and the fact that the shah's son, Crown Prince Reza Pahlavi, had declared himself the new ruler of Iran.

A U.S. delegation was sent to Algiers, Algeria, on November 3 to present the American response to the Majlis conditions. Negotiations continued in December, as the Algerians transmitted U.S. clarifications to the Iranian government, but it was still not known who would speak for Iran and finally order the hostages released.   William Spencer

See also MIDDLE EAST (Facts in Brief Table). In WORLD BOOK, see IRAN.

IRAQ sent its military forces into Iran on Sept. 22, 1980. The outbreak of war climaxed steadily increasing tension between Iraq's Baathist government and Iran's Khomeini regime, as each sought to overthrow the other. Before the attack, President Saddam Hussein on September 17 unilaterally canceled the 1975 agreement that gave Iran half of the Shatt al Arab waterway between the two countries in return for Iran's dropping its support for Kurdish rebels in Iraq.

After reoccupying border areas given up in the 1975 treaty, Iraqi troops struck deep into Khuzistan province and attacked the Iranian cities of Khorramshahr, Ahvaz, and Dezful. Iraqi airplanes bombed Iranian airfields, cities, and oil installations, leaving the Abadan refinery in ruins.

Invasion Stalls. But Iraqi expectations of a quick victory faded before fierce resistance by the supposedly weak Iranian Army. Iranian jets knocked out Iraqi oil installations around Kirkuk and Mosul in the north, and Basra in the south. They also bombed the capital, Baghdad. Iraqi offers of a cease-fire were rejected by Iran, and by November the war had become a stalemate, with Iraqi forces unable to capture key Iranian cities or knock out Iran's army and air force. See IRAN (Close-Up).

Despite the deadlock, the war proved an advantage to Hussein's Baathist regime in mobilizing

Iran and Iraq at War

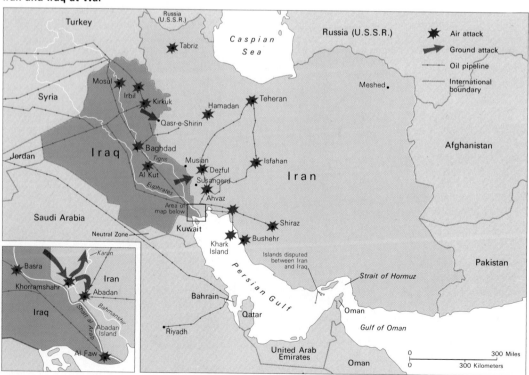

popular support and demonstrating the emergence of Iraq as a power in the Persian Gulf region. On February 8, the 17th anniversary of the first Baathist seizure of power, Hussein issued an eight-point "Arab Charter" that would prohibit non-Arab bases on Arab soil, ban the use of force in resolving inter-Arab disputes, and establish a joint Arab defense force. The charter was accepted by 15 Arab states as well as the Palestine Liberation Organization. Syria and Egypt rejected it.

Little Internal Opposition to Baathist rule surfaced during the year, though one cause of the Iraqi invasion of Iran was the attempt by Iran's Khomeini regime to overthrow the Iraqi regime through Iraq's Shiite Muslims, who form a majority of the population. A Shiite subversive organization, *al Dawa al Islamiya*, was uncovered in April and prominent Shiite leaders, including the chief *imam* (religious leader), were executed as spies.

With the regime firmly in power and the economy booming, elections were held on June 20 for a parliamentary assembly, the first since the 1958 overthrow of the monarchy. Voters elected a 250-member assembly, and Baath candidates won 75 per cent of the seats. At the same time, the Kurds elected a 50-member legislative council for the autonomous Kurdistan region.   William Spencer

See also MIDDLE EAST (Facts in Brief Table). In WORLD BOOK, see IRAQ.

IRELAND moved no nearer to a settlement with Northern Ireland in 1980, despite the fact that Prime Minister Charles J. Haughey had declared that to be his primary objective when he took office in December 1979. Domestic problems dominated the political scene during the year.

In his first major policy address, on February 16, Haughey called on the British and Irish governments to work together toward solving the Northern Ireland question. Haughey said that a declaration affirming Great Britain's interest in encouraging the unity of Ireland "would open the way towards an entirely new situation in which peace – real lasting peace – would become an attainable reality." He urged the British government to begin withdrawing from the province, and added that he would seek the aid of member nations of the European Community (EC) and of the United States in trying to settle the northern problem. Haughey's suggestions were greeted first with silence by the British government, then with a flat rejection. Humphrey Atkins, Britain's secretary of state for Northern Ireland, emphatically ruled out a summit meeting of leaders from Dublin, Belfast, and London. See HAUGHEY, CHARLES J.

With the initiative toward healing the country's long-time breach stalled, splits began to reappear in the Fianna Fáil leadership. Former Defense Minister James Gibbons, who had testified against Haughey on a gun-running charge in 1970, toured Ireland, sniping at Haughey in speeches.

Economic Problems lay behind the Irish people's growing disenchantment with their prime minister. Because Haughey is a self-made millionaire with a reputation as a "fixer," many people believed when he took office that he would be able to work economic miracles. However, as a consequence of the previous government's financial policies, Haughey had to impose a severe credit squeeze that allowed for no real increase in personal income and no industrial growth. Inflation rose to 18 per cent, and a rash of strikes protested a government attempt to impose a 13 per cent ceiling on salary raises.

A Buried Treasure Irish archaeologists called "the find of the century" turned up in the village of Killenaule in County Tipperary just in time for Saint Patrick's Day. A weekend explorer discovered a communion set dating from the 700s buried just under the ground surface. Breandain O Riordain, director of the National Museum of Ireland in Dublin, said in March that the set, which includes a gold and silver chalice, is the finest set of altar furnishings yet found.   Ian Mather

See also GREAT BRITAIN; NORTHERN IRELAND. In WORLD BOOK, see IRELAND.

IRON AND STEEL. See STEEL INDUSTRY.

Prime Minister Charles J. Haughey of Ireland visits France in March to discuss European affairs and the Northern Ireland situation.

ISRAEL

ISRAEL ended 30 years of isolation from its Arab neighbors when it established formal diplomatic relations with Egypt on Feb. 26, 1980. The Israeli ambassador took up his post in Cairo, and President Yitzhak Navon, arriving in Egypt in October, became the first Israeli head of state in history to pay an official visit to any Arab state.

But the government's rigid position on the questions of self-determination and statehood for Palestinians blocked further progress toward a final peace settlement. Egypt continued to insist on Palestinian self-government and Israeli compliance with United Nations (UN) Resolution 242, which specified Israel's withdrawal from occupied Arab territories. The government of Prime Minister Menachem Begin, under international pressure to abandon or modify its policy on Jewish settlements in the West Bank, was also under heavy pressure from many Israelis to maintain it.

The high point in Israeli resistance on the Palestinian question was reached on July 30, when the *Knesset* (parliament) approved a bill designating Jerusalem as the country's "eternal and indivisible" capital. Begin announced plans to move his offices to Jerusalem. The action aroused a storm of international protest, and the UN Security Council censured Israel in August by a 14-0 vote. About a dozen nations, most of them from Latin America,

moved their embassies from Jerusalem to Tel Aviv-Yafo. Turkey closed its embassy in December.

Government Losses. The Jerusalem bill and continued expansion of Jewish settlements in Arab areas not only isolated Israel internationally, but also divided the Begin government. Defense Minister Ezer Weizman resigned on May 25 to protest the settlements policy. He was followed by Justice Minister Shmuel Tamir in July. In June, two members withdrew from the ruling Likud Party coalition in the Knesset, reducing the government majority to 63 of the 120 seats. A further embarrassment was the arraignment in October of the minister of religious affairs on bribery charges. A Knesset move to topple the Likud coalition failed by only three votes in November, and on November 23, the Herut Party ousted Weizman for voting against the government.

Although no new Jewish settlements were started in the West Bank, 29 Jewish "industrial villages" were completed in September in Galilee, where 72 per cent of the population is Arab. Located on hilltop sites between Nazareth and the Lebanese border, the villages are intended to serve as security outposts and centers of high-technology industry.

The West Bank of the Jordan River became the center of Arab-Jewish tension as Jewish extremists of the Gush Emunim (Faithful Bloc), who believe

A mounted policeman struggles with an angry Israeli farmer during a violent demonstration in Jerusalem against government farm policy.

Left to right, Prime Minister Menachim Begin, his deputy Yigael Yadin, and Foreign Minister Yitzhak Shamir vote to make Jerusalem Israel's capital.

with Begin in the right of Jews to all of Biblical Israel, pressed their claims to settlement on expropriated Arab land. The Elon Moreh settlement near Nablus was moved to a new site on Mount Kabir outside the Arab town under a 1979 Israeli Supreme Court order. The government then seized additional land as "belonging to the state" to enlarge the settlement. A master plan to allocate 740 acres (300 hectares) more in Jerusalem for Jewish housing projects was unveiled in August.

Jewish-Arab Tensions erupted in violence in February when a Jewish student from the Qiryat Arba settlement was murdered in Hebron. Qiryat Arba residents swore revenge, beating up Arabs and looting Arab shops. In May, Arab gunmen shot up the settlement during a parade, killing six Jews. Israeli military authorities ordered a crackdown. A curfew was imposed on Hebron, and the mayors of Hebron and Halhoul along with Hebron's chief Muslim judge were deported to Lebanon, though they denied any connection with the shootings. The Israeli Supreme Court refused on August 19 to annul the deportation order, but it criticized military authorities for not permitting an appeal of the order, as required by Israeli law.

Violence escalated in June. The mayors of Ramallah and Nablus, both outspoken critics of the government's West Bank policy, were seriously injured by car bombs, allegedly the work of Jewish extremists. The Arab National Guidance Council, composed of West Bank mayors and leaders, called a region-wide strike in protest. Playing no favorites, Israeli authorities arrested Rabbi Meir Kahane, head of the Jewish Defense League, on charges of organizing a secret army to attack Arabs; closed all West Bank universities and Arab newspapers; and banished several Arab families to "exile" in the abandoned Palestinian refugee camp near Jericho.

The Economy. Israel's foreign debts reached $19.2 billion in July, one-third of it owed to the United States. With military spending taking up 15 per cent of the gross national product, inflation at an annual rate of 134 per cent in October, and large foreign debt repayments scheduled for early 1981, the country needed a respite from internal as well as international problems. The budget of $13.5 billion presented to the Knesset in June set off another crisis. Finance Minister Yigael Hurvitz threatened to resign if the budget was not reduced by $315 million. After Begin appealed to all Israelis to donate a day's pay and all ministry budgets were slashed by 1.25 per cent, a budget of $12.3-billion was approved.

In February, Israel replaced its monetary unit, the pound, with a new unit called the shekel that was worth 10 of the old pounds.   William Spencer

See also MIDDLE EAST (Facts in Brief Table). In WORLD BOOK, see ISRAEL.

ITALY suffered Europe's worst earthquake since 1915 on Nov. 23, 1980. The quake's initial shock, centered about 45 miles (72 kilometers) east of Naples, registered 6.8 on the Richter scale. Tremors were felt from Sicily to the northern Alps. The quake and sharp aftershocks killed about 3,000 persons and left an estimated 250,000 homeless.

Bad weather hampered relief efforts. Rain muddied the tent cities, and harsh winds chilled their miserable inhabitants. Looting and public disturbances and child kidnappings were reported in the devastated areas. The government was unable to persuade homeless survivors to accept evacuation to luxury hotels on the Mediterranean coast. The survivors did not want to leave while their dead lay buried under the ruins.

Station Explosion. Italy also suffered Europe's bloodiest terrorist incident since World War II. On August 2, a bomb blast killed 80 persons, many of them vacationers, at the Bologna railway station. A neo-Fascist group, the Armed Revolutionary Nuclei, was responsible. Neo-Fascist guerrillas claimed to have killed 132 of the 250 victims of terrorism in Italy in the last 11 years.

Cossiga Resigns. Prime Minister Francesco Cossiga's government was endangered when the Socialist Party withdrew its support on February 27. A March 19 debate in Parliament showed that his coalition no longer had a majority, so Cossiga resigned without insisting on a vote of confidence. Cossiga then formed a center-left coalition of his Christian Democrats plus Socialists, Liberals, and Republicans. Firmly in opposition were Social Democrats, left Independents, the Radicals, Communists, and the right wing Social Movement. The new government was sworn in on April 4.

But Cossiga resigned again on September 27 after Parliament defeated his economic proposals by one vote. Cossiga had proposed measures to reinforce the value of the currency, support failing industries, and combat Italy's 22 per cent inflation rate. Arnaldo Forlani, head of the Christian Democrats, then assembled a coalition of Christian Democrats, Socialists, Social Democrats, and Republicans that took office on October 18. The Socialists and Social Democrats eased Forlani's task by ending their long, bitter rivalry and deciding to work together in Parliament. Their new spirit of cooperation gave Prime Minister Forlani a 90-seat majority in the 630-member Chamber of Deputies.   Kenneth Brown

See also COSSIGA, FRANCESCO; EUROPE (Facts in Brief Table); FORLANI, ARNALDO. In WORLD BOOK, see ITALY.

IVORY COAST. See AFRICA.

JAMAICA. See WEST INDIES.

Workers clear away rubble after a bomb blasted the Bologna, Italy, train station on August 2. Right wing terrorists claimed responsibility.

JAPAN. Intraparty strife nearly unseated the governing Liberal-Democratic Party (LDP) in 1980. The trouble began on May 16 when 69 dissident LDP members, unhappy after a 1979 party leadership struggle, withheld their support and the LDP suffered a stunning defeat on a no-confidence motion in the House of Representatives. Prime Minister Masayoshi Ohira immediately dissolved the House and called for a new general election. In the midst of the election campaign, Ohira suffered a heart attack, apparently induced by fatigue. He died on June 12 at age 70.

In the general election on June 22, the LDP won decisively, reversing a decline that had begun in the early 1960s. The LDP won 284 seats, up 26 from the 1979 election; the Japan Socialist Party (JSP) still held 107; Komeito (Clean Government Party), with 33, was down 24; the Democratic Socialist Party dropped to 32, a loss of 3; the Japan Communist Party held 29, down 10; the New Liberal Club, with 12, was up 8. Minor parties with independents won 14 seats (down 7). The LDP thus won a comfortable majority of the 511 seats, compared with its one-seat margin eight months earlier. Ohira's death apparently gained some sympathy votes for the LDP.

A House of Councillors election was held simultaneously, for the first time in history, to fill 126 of the 252 seats. The LDP won 69 of the seats being contested, bringing its total in the upper house to 135. The next largest party was the JSP, with 47 seats. For the first time in years, the LDP held a majority in both houses.

Zenko Suzuki was elected LDP president to succeed Ohira on July 15 and on July 17 was elected the 15th postwar prime minister. Regarded as a master of political compromise, Suzuki helped found the LDP, has been a party leader for years, and has also served as a Cabinet minister. In his first major speech, Suzuki pledged in August to maintain close ties with the United States. He also reaffirmed Ohira's promise to increase Japan's military spending. See SUZUKI, ZENKO.

The Economy. Japan achieved an estimated 1980 economic growth rate of slightly under 5 per cent, compared with 6 per cent in 1979. The unemployment rate was about 2 per cent, roughly the same as in 1979.

Japan's 1978 trade surplus of $14.3 billion changed dramatically to a deficit of $13.4 billion in 1979, according to 1980 figures. Exports were $107-billion, up 8.1 per cent over those for 1978, but imports rose to $120 billion, up 42.3 per cent, mainly because of an oil price increase of about 66 per cent. However, the volume of oil imports was kept to a modest 0.2 per cent increase. Japan's

Just elected Japan's prime minister, Zenko Suzuki rises to acknowledge the round of applause from fellow *Diet* (parliament) members in July.

annual oil-import bill in 1980 averaged about $512 per person. By August, Japan had built up a trade surplus of about $880 million, a significant improvement over the 1979 figure. Automobiles and steel were the principal sources of export income.

The "Automobile War" continued to dominate Japan's export trade. In July, Japan's automobile production exceeded 1 million units per month for the first time. Resistance to Japanese automobile and truck imports increased in the United States and Europe. Japan attempted to protect its exports by developing joint ventures with foreign companies and building plants in countries that imported large numbers of its autos.

Japan's trade surplus with the United States continued to be a major issue in relations between the two countries. The United States increased its demands for greater access to Japan's markets.

Prime Minister Ohira met with President Carter in Washington, D.C., on May 1. Ohira reaffirmed support for any peaceful measures that would ensure the return of the U.S. hostages from Iran. He also opposed Russia's invasion of Afghanistan and supported the U.S. call for a boycott of the Summer Olympic Games in Moscow. Japan's Olympic Committee later voted not to send athletes to Moscow.

Other Events. Prime Minister Hua Kuo-feng (Hua Guofeng) of China made a formal state visit to Japan from May 27 to June 1, the first ever by a Chinese head of state. The two prime ministers discussed international problems and relations, particularly economic, involving their countries.

A Japanese group financed by Ryoichi Sasagawa, a wealthy right wing businessman and political figure, announced in September that it had succeeded in bringing to the surface part of an estimated $3.7 billion in treasure from a Russian battleship sunk off the Japanese coast in the 1904-1905 Russo-Japanese War. Sasagawa later offered to turn over the treasure to Russia if the Soviet government would return the Kuril Islands, which have been occupied by Russia since World War II, to Japan. Russia claimed ownership of both the ship and the treasure.

A Soviet nuclear submarine was disabled off the Japanese coast by a mysterious fire in August. The Japanese government, fearing a possible radiation leak, at first refused to allow the submarine to be towed through Japanese waters, but later gave in.

Prince Naruhito (Hiro), grandson of Emperor Hirohito and eldest son of Crown Prince Akihito, celebrated his coming of age – 20 years old – on February 23 in a six-hour ceremony televised to the nation. This was the first time that a reigning emperor witnessed the coming-of-age ceremony of a grandson.   John M. Maki

See also ASIA (Facts in Brief Table). In WORLD BOOK, see AKIHITO; HIROHITO; JAPAN.

JEWS AND JUDAISM. United States President Jimmy Carter met with leading Hasidic rabbis at the White House in May 1980, the first meeting of its kind. Most American Jews were keenly interested in the U.S. presidential election and how it might affect U.S. policy toward Israel.

When Ronald Reagan won the election in November, Jews noted that he had run on a Republican Party platform pledged to "honor our nation's commitment [to Israel] through political, diplomatic, and military aid." It also affirmed that "Jerusalem should remain undivided with . . . unimpeded access to all." The Democratic Party had pledged to maintain peace in the Middle East through the Camp David accords.

Many Jewish leaders protested U.S. actions in the United Nations (UN) regarding Israel. On March 1, the UN Security Council, of which the United States is a permanent member, voted unanimously to censure Israel for settling Jews in the West Bank and Gaza Strip areas. Two days later, President Carter issued a statement disavowing the U.S. vote against Israel, claiming that communications had broken down between the White House and the U.S. delegation to the UN. Despite this unusual statement, many Jewish voters felt unsure of Carter's support for Israel. Senator Edward M. Kennedy (D., Mass.), who criticized Carter's actions on the UN vote and expressed unflagging support for Israel, won the New York Democratic primary on March 25 by a wide margin.

Peace Now. A group of 56 prominent American Jews signed a newspaper advertisement in June supporting the moderate Peace Now movement in Israel. They stated that they strongly support the nation of Israel, but not the policies of Prime Minister Menachem Begin. This proved controversial because Zionists place a premium on unity.

About 2,600 leaders from the United States and Canada attended the 48th General Assembly of the Council of Jewish Federations in Montreal, Canada, in March to discuss issues affecting the needs of Jewish communities at home and abroad – especially in Israel, Russia, and Ethiopia. Despite great controversy, the Rabbinical Assembly in May endorsed the ordination of women as rabbis.

The assembly and other Jewish organizations have been concerned about the increase in assaults on Jewish institutions, cemeteries, synagogues, and personal property. Violence against Jews in France was a particular problem. Four persons were killed when a synagogue in Paris was bombed in October. Several French cities reported vandals' attacks – some involving machine-gun fire – on Jewish-owned businesses. To protest this new wave of anti-Semitism, about 150,000 persons demonstrated in Paris in October. Many of the protestors carried signs accusing the French government of being too passive in dealing with terrorism.

About 150,000 persons demonstrate in Paris in October to protest anti-Semitic violence in France, including a bombing at a synagogue.

In Russia. Nearly 70 per cent of the Jews who leave the Soviet Union choose destinations other than Israel, and some controversy arose over whether this "dropout" group endangered the basic movement to ensure the rights of Soviet Jews. Some leaders have suggested curtailing help to emigrants who go to a country other than Israel.

In Iran. Jews continued to flee Iran in fear of persecution by the Muslim government. As many as half of the country's 80,000 Jews left Iran between January 1979 – when the Ayatollah Ruhollah Khomeini overthrew the government of Shah Mohammad Reza Pahlavi and established a religious state – and March 1980. An Iranian Jew charged with spying for Israel was executed on June 5. Iran's parliament voted in August to expel its only Jewish member, accusing him of supporting Shah Mohammad Reza Pahlavi, working with Israel, and failing to support the taking of the American hostages in 1979.

War Crimes. The U.S. Department of Justice set a one-year deadline in January for disposing of cases pending against 250 alleged Nazi war criminals living in the United States. Many of the cases have been on file since World War II ended. The U.S. Department of Justice said that the deadline would not apply to any new cases.   Arnold G. Kaiman

See also ISRAEL; MIDDLE EAST. In WORLD BOOK, see JEWS; JUDAISM.

JORDAN resumed its traditional friendly relationship with the United States in 1980. King Hussein I visited the U.S. in June, ending a rift that began in September 1978 with the Camp David agreements and the U.S.-supported Egyptian-Israeli peace treaty. For his fence-mending, Hussein received a commitment for 100 M-60 tanks valued at $150 million to upgrade Jordan's armed forces. But he remained committed to the Palestinian cause.

Hussein also gave all-out support to Iraq in October in its war with Iran. That move was motivated in part by the earlier receipt of $247-million from Iraq, which replaced Saudi Arabia as Jordan's principal financial support. Jordan offered sanctuary to Iraq's aircraft threatened by Iranian airstrikes, and reportedly funneled military aid through its seaport on the Gulf of Aqaba.

Governmental Changes dominated Jordanian internal affairs. The changes brought some liberalization, though the long-promised restoration of parliamentary government remained unfulfilled. A new Cabinet headed by Prime Minister Sharif Abdul Hamid Sharaf introduced a Citizens Complaint Bureau in January.

Relations with Syria deteriorated thoroughly in November, when Syria accused Jordan of harboring members of the Muslim Brotherhood, a militantly conservative Islamic group bent on overthrowing the regime of Syrian President Hafiz

King Hussein I of Jordan speaks to the press after his June meeting
with President Jimmy Carter and Secretary of State Edmund Muskie.

al-Assad. Assad massed troops and tanks on the
Jordanian border and Hussein responded in kind.
Saudi Arabian diplomats defused the situation in
December and Syria began to step down from its
threatening border posture.

Prime Minister Sharaf, 41, died unexpectedly of
a heart attack on July 3, and Hussein named a
Palestinian, Kassem al-Rimawi, as his interim
successor. On August 28, Mudhar Badran, who
had served as prime minister from 1976 to 1979,
assumed the post again. Badran's 21-member Cabinet included seven ministers of Palestinian origin,
a record number. A Ministry of Occupied Territories Affairs was created.

The Economy. Discovery of high-grade phosphate deposits near Maan in January promised to
increase Jordan's major resource significantly. The
5 million short tons (4.5 million metric tons) of
phosphates produced in 1980 represented 21 per
cent of the world market. With inflation averaging
13 per cent annually and a population growth rate
of 4.85 per cent, rapid development of such export-
earning natural resources was critical. William Spencer

See also MIDDLE EAST (Facts in Brief Table). In
WORLD BOOK, see JORDAN.

JUDAISM. See JEWS AND JUDAISM.

JUNIOR ACHIEVEMENT (JA). See YOUTH ORGANI-
ZATIONS.

KAMPUCHEA. See CAMBODIA.

KANIA, STANISLAW (1927-   ), replaced Edward Gierek as first secretary of the Polish United
Workers' Party (PZPR), the Communist Party of
Poland, on Sept. 6, 1980. Gierek had resigned
following a series of strikes in northern Poland (see
POLAND). Kania had supervised the police, army,
and security since 1971 and had supervised the
trade union federation since August 1980.

Kania was born to farmer parents on March 8,
1927, in Wrocanka, in southeastern Poland. He
was apprenticed to a blacksmith during World War
II and joined the PZPR in 1945. Kania graduated
from the school operated by the PZPR's Central
Committee in 1952 and became director of the
PZPR youth movement. He was named director of
the PZPR's agriculture department for Warszawa
province in 1958.

Kania was elected an alternate member of the
Central Committee in 1964 and a full member in
1968. He directed the PZPR headquarters' administrative department from 1968 until 1971, when he
became an alternate member of the Politburo. He
gained full membership in 1975.   Jay Myers

KANSAS. See STATE GOVERNMENT.

KENTUCKY. See STATE GOVERNMENT.

KENYA. See AFRICA.

KIRIBATI. See WORLD BOOK SUPPLEMENT section.

KIWANIS INTERNATIONAL. See COMMUNITY OR-
GANIZATIONS.

KOREA, NORTH. The Korean Workers' Party, the nation's ruling Communist organization, held its first congress in 10 years in Pyongyang in October 1980. At the congress, Kim Chong-il was promoted to the second-highest position in the party secretariat, ranking only after his father, President Kim Il-song, the party leader.

Kim Chong-il, 39, was also named the fourth-ranking member of a newly created five-member standing committee of the Politburo, the party's political committee, and third on the party's important military affairs committee. These appointments put him in position to succeed his father in the Communist world's first family dynasty.

Kim Il-song repeated to the congress appeals for creation of a federal republic with South Korea as the "way to reunify the Korean peninsula." But his terms remained unacceptable to the South Korean government. Talks were held at Panmunjom on February 19 and March 4 to arrange a prime ministers' meeting on unification, but delegates could not agree on terms for the meeting.

The first visit by an elected official of the United States to North Korea since the Korean War in the 1950s was made by U.S. Congressman Stephen J. Solarz (D., N.Y.). He met Kim Il-song for several hours on July 18. Henry S. Bradsher

See also Asia (Facts in Brief Table). In WORLD BOOK, see KOREA.

KOREA, SOUTH. Chun Doo Hwan became president on Sept. 1, 1980. After the assassination of President Chung Hee Park on Oct. 26, 1979, Chun, a major general who was head of the Defense Security Command, eliminated other generals and civilian political leaders from power. Thus, South Korea returned to the kind of dictatorial rule based on control of the army that Park had established two decades earlier. See CHUN DOO HWAN.

Chun used his control of the army to influence the civilian government of President Kyu Ha Choi, Park's successor. Choi had promised liberalization, but instead Chun tightened control.

On April 14, Chun took the additional job of head of the Korean Central Intelligence Agency (KCIA), which Park had used to suppress dissent. Chun succeeded Jae Kyu Kim, who assassinated Park because of disagreement over repressive measures. Kim and four accomplices were hanged on May 24.

A Special Committee for National Security Measures was created on May 31 to advise Choi following unrest in Kwangju. Chun was chairman of the committee, and 15 of its 25 members were military officers. Fourteen subcommittees overshadowed the Cabinet and exercised the real governmental power. Chun strengthened his hold on the government with such moves as closing down 172 periodicals in July. Choi resigned the presi-

South Korean officials display a tunnel under the demilitarized border with North Korea as evidence that the latter plans an invasion.

South Korean dissident Dae Jung Kim, second from right, is tried for sedition at a court martial in August. He was later sentenced to death.

dency on August 16. Chun gave up his KCIA post on July 14 and resigned from the army on August 22 to qualify for president as a civilian. He was elected by the National Conference of Unification, an electoral college, with no popular vote.

Arrests and Unrest. Chun named as prime minister Nam Duck Woo, a former finance minister and deputy premier who had been educated in the United States. Chun said that "martial law will be lifted once the political situation has stabilized." He also said that he believed in social justice, but that "national security should be our country's top priority." In October, the regime announced that more than 46,000 persons had been arrested for "antisocial behavior" in the first two months of Chun's presidency.

On February 29, during Choi's liberalizing period, the civil rights of 687 political dissidents were restored. The amnesty included Dae Jung Kim, a leading opposition politician. But labor unrest by miners in April, and rioting by university students in May against Chun's increasing power, resulted in tighter martial law on May 18.

By May 21, the government had lost control of Kwangju. Army troops recaptured it on May 27, but 144 civilians, 22 soldiers, and four policemen were killed there. Dae Jung Kim was arrested on May 31 for having "manipulated and agitated" Kwangju students to revolt. He was sentenced to death in September on charges of sedition, despite his denials of guilt and a legal case against him that U.S. observers found weak.

Political Purge. Former Prime Minister Jong Pil Kim, a leader of Park's governing party – the other main political threat to Chun – was charged with corruption on June 18. He agreed to leave politics and surrender his wealth in return for immunity.

In a referendum on October 22, 92 per cent of the voters approved a new Constitution. It limited the president to one 7-year term and made it possible to dissolve political parties and disqualify most politicians from future political activity. Chun promised indirect elections by March 1981. But he used the new Constitution in November to ban 811 persons from politics for eight years.

The United States continued its military protection of South Korea. But it made clear its disapproval of these political trends, and pleaded with Chun not to execute Dae Jung Kim.

Rising oil prices and other problems hit the nation's growing but vulnerable economy. The currency was devalued 16.51 per cent in January. The foreign trade deficit soared to about $6 billion, well over the level considered safe by the World Bank.   Henry S. Bradsher

See also ASIA (Facts in Brief Table). In WORLD BOOK, see KOREA.

KUWAIT. See MIDDLE EAST.

LABOR. A sharp rise in unemployment in the United States coupled with continued double-digit inflation made life harder for the American worker in 1980. The jobless rate, as determined by the Bureau of Labor Statistics (BLS), soared from 6.0 per cent in February to 7.8 per cent in May, and then leveled off at an average 7.2 per cent through November. The jobless rate was 7.5 per cent, with some 7.9 million persons out of work in November, compared with 6.1 million in December 1979. Total employment stood at 97.4 million in November, down from 97.9 million in December 1979.

Inflation leaped to the virtually unprecedented annual rate of 18 per cent in the first quarter of 1980. Although efforts to stem inflation, including a sharp increase in interest rates, slowed the spiral, they also contributed to the decline.

The BLS Consumer Price Index (CPI) for all urban consumers (CPI-U) rose at a seasonally adjusted rate of 18.1 per cent in the first quarter of 1980, 11.6 per cent in the second quarter, and 7.0 per cent in the third quarter. During the year ending in October, both the CPI-U and the Index for Urban Wage Earners and Clerical Workers (CPI-W) rose 12.6 per cent.

These price rises, coupled with generally lower real earnings, resulted in a decline in purchasing power. For the year ending in October, real average weekly earnings dropped 5.1 per cent, as a 1.4 per cent drop in average weekly hours and the 12.6 per cent increase in the CPI-W wiped out an 8.4 per cent increase in average hourly earnings. In the Special Reports section, see THE INFLATION RATE, THE COST OF LIVING . . . AND YOU.

BLS estimates of major employment changes are summarized below:

	1979	1980*
	(in thousands)	
Total labor force	**104,996**	**106,757**
Armed forces	2,088	2,096
Civilian labor force	102,908	104,661
Total employment	96,945	97,256
Unemployed	5,963	7,405
Unemployment rate	5.8%	7.1%
Change in real weekly earnings (Worker with 3 dependents — private nonfarm sector)	−5.3%	−5.9%†
Change in output per man-hour	−0.8%	−0.5%††

*January to September average, seasonally adjusted except for armed forces data.
†For 12-month period ending Sept. 30, 1980.
††Third quarter of 1980, compared with third quarter of 1979.

Major Collective Bargaining settlements through the first nine months of 1980 provided average first-year wage adjustments of 9.7 per cent, compared with a 7.4 per cent average for 1979. When averaged over the life of the contracts, wages rose 7.3 per cent, compared with 6.0 per cent in 1979.

Most of the settlements with automatic cost-of-living-adjustment (COLA) clauses allowed for lower raises than did agreements where workers had no such protection. First-year negotiated wage adjustments in contracts with COLA provisions averaged 8.2 per cent, compared with 11.9 per cent for contracts without COLA clauses. COLA clauses provided pay gains averaging 6.1 per cent, accounting for 70 per cent of the increase in the CPI-W during the first nine months of the year.

Steel Bargaining. Soaring prices and continued lay-off threats influenced collective bargaining in the steel industry. Negotiating under the Experimental Negotiating Agreement of 1973 (ENA), which guaranteed a minimum wage in exchange for a pledge not to strike, the United Steelworkers of America and nine steel companies reached a three-year contract settlement on April 15.

Focusing on the erosion of prior retirees' pensions, the Steelworkers won a provision raising the pensions of those who retired in the previous three years by 10 per cent, or an average of $52 a month; and the pensions of those who retired before July 31, 1966, by 70 per cent, an average of $182 a month. Pensions for future retirees were also raised — to $17.50, $19, or $20.50 per month for each year's service, from a previous rate of $13.50 to $16.50 per month.

Actors display their talents on picket lines in August and September during a strike that postponed the beginning of the new TV season.

Labor Voice Is Silenced

Organized labor in the United States lost its strongest voice when George Meany, 85, died on Jan. 10, 1980 — exactly 63 years from the day the Plumbers and Pipefitters Local 2 in New York City issued his first union card. The man who was known as "Mr. Labor" spent his entire career promoting the economic welfare of American workers.

Meany won a reputation as a blunt and powerful fighter for trade unionists' rights, but he could also use tact and political persuasion to further his aims. Soon after becoming president of the American Federation of Labor (AFL) in 1952, he set about merging the group with Walter P. Reuther's Congress of Industrial Organizations (CIO). After three years of delicate negotiations, they formed the combined AFL-CIO, an umbrella organization that at one time covered 121 unions and 17 million workers. Meany served as the AFL-CIO president until November 1979. Then, 85 years old and ailing, he reluctantly handed the reins to Lane Kirkland, his chosen successor.

The 24 years that Meany served in what he called his "number-one job . . . holding the boys together," capped a career that seemed destined from the cradle. Born in New York City in 1894 to Irish Catholic parents, young William George early acquired the staunch morality and devotion to his fellows that set the course of his life. Meany's father was a plumber who headed his local union and dabbled in Democratic Party politics.

Starting as a plumber's helper when he was 16 years old, young Meany quickly learned that the union man on the rostrum wields more power than the one behind the wrench. By 1922, Meany had become business agent for his local. The next year, he was named secretary-treasurer of the New York Building Trades Council, and in 1934, he became president of the New York State Federation of Labor.

For five influential years as a lobbyist in Albany, N.Y., Meany worked to achieve what became his lifelong goals — the best possible pay rate and fringe benefits for workers. During his first legislative session, he persuaded state lawmakers to enact 72 measures he favored, including such innovations as unemployment compensation and a 48-hour workweek for women.

Meany's often-quoted approach to lobbying — "Never threaten, never be intimidated, tell the truth" — set the standard for all his activities. After he moved to Washington, D.C., in 1940 as secretary-treasurer of the AFL — a post he held until he became AFL president in 1952 — the burly, brash, cigar-chomping union chief gained national prominence.

Though Meany was unquestionably the leader of organized labor in the United States for a quarter century, two strong unions resisted his authority. In 1957, he expelled the Teamsters Union from the AFL-CIO because its leaders refused to eradicate corruption. Ten years later, because of a conflict in philosophy with Meany, Reuther led his United Auto Workers out of the federation.

Meany's AFL-CIO headquarters were directly across the street from the White House. Meany once told a young visitor that his office was thus situated "because the people of the country need me to watch over whoever is living there." He watched over seven occupants of the Oval Office and never hesitated to offer them all what one President admiringly called "his straightforward counsel."

Job opportunity — the right to work and to reap the fruits of labor guaranteed by a system of free collective bargaining and signed contracts — was what George Meany believed in all his life. He fought for legislation that would ensure higher minimum wages, health care, and the right to organize.

The workers cheered Meany as one of their own, but the "bosses" also recognized his achievements. In 1963, he received the Presidential Medal of Freedom. A few months before he died, he received a tribute he may have valued even more. Pope John Paul II told the doughty labor pioneer, "You do good work for your people."

Marsha F. Goldsmith

George Meany (1894-1980)

Most of the 285,000 steelworkers covered received hourly pay-rate increases of from 25 to 57 cents on May 1, 1980; 20 to 52 cents on Aug. 1, 1981; and 15 to 47 cents in the final year. Under ENA provisions, steelworkers employed on August 1 got a $150 bonus for their assurance that they would not walk out over economic issues in 1980.

The settlement contained a COLA clause, but the union waived the final COLA payment under the previous agreement to help the companies finance the pension raises for prior retirees. The new contracts also contained provisions for improved health insurance, supplemental unemployment benefits, and an extended vacation plan, as well as a provision requiring steel producers to give a 90-day notice of planned plant closings.

Aluminum and Copper settlements, negotiated by the Steelworkers in conjunction with other unions, also produced three-year contracts with similar wage increases. The Steelworkers and the Aluminum Workers of America, representing some 50,000 workers, reached a basic contract agreement with the aluminum industry on May 30. Under its terms, the COLA formula provides a 1-cent adjustment for each 0.26 percentage point change in the CPI-W in the third year – up from 1 cent per 0.3 point in the first two years.

Copper pacts, negotiated by the Steelworkers

and 22 other unions representing 40,000 workers, were preceded by walkouts against 11 companies. The first settlement, with Kennecott Corporation on August 27, followed a two-month strike.

Bell System Workers benefited from a three-year settlement reached on August 10, averting a nationwide strike against the American Telephone and Telegraph Company (A.T. & T.). Contracts covered 700,000 workers represented by the Communications Workers of America, the International Brotherhood of Electrical Workers, and the Telecommunications International Union.

Communications Workers President Glen Watts estimated that the pact provided a 34.9 per cent increase in total compensation over the term. It included provisions that increased vacation time and "excused workdays"; protected 15-year employees downgraded due to technological changes against pay reductions; and barred A.T. & T. from contracting out "traditional" work, leading to "layoffs or part-timing of employees."

Other Settlements. Some 60,000 members of the Oil, Chemical and Atomic Workers International Union struck against petroleum refiners for 11 weeks before reaching settlements with Gulf Oil and Cities Service Company. The longest major strike in the history of the United Automobile Workers (UAW), a 172-day walkout by 35,000

AFL-CIO President Lane Kirkland makes a gesture of farewell to his mentor and predecessor, George Meany, at funeral services for the labor leader.

A Russian container ship, boycotted by dockworkers protesting the invasion of Afghanistan, stands loaded in the Philadelphia harbor in January.

workers at the International Harvester Company, ended on April 20 after the company abandoned its demands to compel employees to work overtime and accept job transfers.

Additional contracts involved 45,000 members of the International Longshoremen's Association at Atlantic and Gulf Coast ports; 100,000 aerospace workers represented by the International Association of Machinists and Aerospace Workers; 75,000 workers in the Pacific Northwest timber industry; and 80,000 members of the Amalgamated Clothing and Textile Workers Union.

New York City and a union coalition representing 215,000 workers on June 19 signed a two-year agreement providing wage increases of 8 per cent on July 1 in 1980 and 1981. A July 3 settlement with 42,000 New York City uniformed employees and an April 12 settlement with 33,000 transit workers each provided 17 per cent raises over the same term. Chicago transit employees benefited from a May arbitration award ending a dispute that led to a four-day walkout just before Christmas 1979. Lengthy strikes ended in new contracts for teachers in Cleveland and Philadelphia.

Federal employees also received pay increases in 1980. Some 1.4 million U.S. government white-collar workers received a 9.1 per cent pay raise on October 1. About 2.1 million active servicemen and women got a larger raise – 11.7 per cent.

Anti-Inflation Measures. In response to recommendations of the tripartite Pay Advisory Committee, President Jimmy Carter announced on March 14 that the existing 7 per cent annual pay-increase guideline would be raised to 7.5 to 9.5 per cent. The Council on Wage and Price Stability extended the wage guidelines for one year past their scheduled September 30 expiration date, stipulating that they were mandatory "through the end of 1980."

Workers at all levels accepted pay cuts or raise deferrals to aid beleaguered employers. The UAW on February 1 agreed to additional contract concessions, worth a reported $243 million, to help Chrysler Corporation obtain federal backing for loans, bringing UAW's total concessions to Chrysler to $446 million – or $4,000 per employee.

Another financially troubled automobile manufacturer, Ford Motor Company, announced the termination of merit raises for its 70,000 salaried employees through 1980. Similarly, United States Steel Corporation revealed that management personnel would not receive pay raises in 1980, and Firestone Tire and Rubber Company announced it would end COLA payments for 20,000 nonunion salaried workers. Production workers at Wheeling-Pittsburgh Steel Corporation and Uniroyal, Incorporated, agreed to reductions in compensation.

J. P. Stevens Unionized. The Amalgamated Clothing and Textile Workers Union made a major breakthrough on October 19 after 17 years of effort when it announced its first collective bargaining agreement with J. P. Stevens and Company. The agreement with the giant textile firm affected 3,500 workers at 10 plants. However, Stevens also agreed to offer the contract provisions to workers who may unionize any of its 150 other plants within 18 months. The contract provided an 8.5 per cent raise immediately, with a 10 per cent raise retroactive to July 1979.

Changes and Mergers. George Meany died on January 10 at the age of 85. He had retired in November 1979 as president of the American Federation of Labor and Congress of Industrial Organizations (AFL-CIO), the post he had held since the merger of the AFL and the CIO in 1955. See Close-Up.

The 35-member AFL-CIO Executive Council on August 21 named Joyce D. Miller as its first female member. Miller is a vice-president of the Amalgamated Clothing and Textile Workers Union and heads the Coalition of Labor Union Women.

Two major unions had new leaders in 1980. Seafarers International Union President Paul Hall died on June 22 at the age of 65. He was succeeded by Frank Drozak, who headed the union's organizing activities. Moe Biller became president of the Postal Workers Union.

The ranks of three unions were increased by mergers. The 35,000-member Barbers and Beauticians union merged into the 1.3-million-member Retail Clerks and Meat Cutters union; the 10,000-member Jewelry Workers Union was taken into the 625,000-member Service Employees union; and the 8,000-member Railway and Airway Supervisors union became part of the 200,000-member Railway, Airline and Steamship Clerks.

Safety Measures. The Department of Labor's Occupational Safety and Health Administration (OSHA) in January outlined a new policy formulated to control cancer-producing substances frequently found in workplaces. The new policy established two categories for 500 substances suspected of causing cancer — "category 1" for substances found to pose a "grave" danger, and "category 2" for those that show "suggestive evidence" of a cancer risk. Employers would be required to reduce worker exposure to substances in category 1 to the "lowest feasible level." Substances in category 2 would be subject to more testing.

In another development, the Supreme Court of the United States ruled on July 2 that OSHA's 1977 standard for worker exposure to benzene was invalid because the agency did not prove that the substance presented a "significant risk." The decision upheld a lower court ruling.   Leon Bornstein

See also CHEMICAL INDUSTRY; CITY; ECONOMICS; STEEL INDUSTRY. In WORLD BOOK, see LABOR; LABOR FORCE.

LANSING, SHERRY (1944-   ), became president of Twentieth Century-Fox Productions in January 1980, at 35 the first woman to head a major motion-picture studio in Hollywood. She achieved prominence in the film industry as production executive on *China Syndrome* (1979) and *Kramer vs. Kramer* (1979). Both films were critically acclaimed box-office hits.

Lansing was born on July 31, 1944, in Chicago. She received a bachelor's degree from Northwestern University in Evanston, Ill., with a major in theater. However, she did not begin her career in the performing arts; instead, she taught high school mathematics in Los Angeles for three years.

After working as a model for television commercials, Lansing acted in two motion pictures, *Loving* (1970) and *Rio Lobo* (1970). She then became a story editor for an independent producer.

Lansing joined Metro-Goldwyn-Mayer (MGM) as executive story editor in 1975 and was promoted to vice-president for creative affairs at MGM two years later. She switched to Columbia Pictures in November 1977 as vice-president of production, and later became senior vice-president of production. It was at Columbia that she made *China Syndrome* and *Kramer vs. Kramer*.

Lansing is divorced. She frequently enjoys a busman's holiday in her spare time — going to the movies.   Patricia Dragisic

LAOS remained on a military footing in 1980, five years after the Communist victory. Militia forces had been beefed up, Laotian units were stationed alongside Vietnamese troops on the Chinese border, and there were sporadic clashes with Thai gunboats on the Mekong River. After a skirmish at a Laotian river village in which a Thai officer was killed, Thailand closed its border on June 16 and two months later reopened only one of the four main crossings. The closing of the Thai border produced a shortage of staples, including rice.

The continuing flight of Laotians to Thailand magnified the country's woes. With an estimated 40,000 escapees in 1980, the figure for the five years exceeded 300,000 — almost 9 per cent of the nation's population. The exodus left Laos without the civil servants and professionals it desperately needed. An estimated 5,000 to 10,000 former officials and soldiers were being held in the north in "seminars," where they did hard labor as roadbuilders for Highway Nine, which will link Laos with Vietnam.

About 40,000 Vietnamese troops and 5,000 civilian advisers were still stationed in the country. So denunciations of China were frequent. Thousands of Laotians journeyed to Hanoi for indoctrination and professional training.   Mark Gayn

See also ASIA (Facts in Brief Table). In WORLD BOOK, see LAOS.

LATIN
AMERICA

Dramatic events focused worldwide attention on Latin America in 1980. Some were tragic, like the mass exodus starting in April of about 125,000 Cuban refugees aboard a fleet of small vessels bound for Florida. Earlier, in February, the fate of 70 persons taken hostage by Colombian Marxist militants while attending a diplomatic function in Bogotá commanded international headlines and aroused grave concern until they were freed unharmed on April 27.

There were moments of pageantry, too, especially during the historic first visit of a reigning Roman Catholic pope to Brazil, the world's most populous Catholic country. Pope John Paul II arrived in Brazil on June 30 and traveled 17,500 miles (28,000 kilometers) to visit 13 Brazilian cities in 12 days.

Political Shifts. Peru's first election in more than a decade – on May 18 – was widely hailed; democracy was restored as the nation's left-of-center military leaders relinquished control and returned to the barracks. In Jamaica, a conservative candidate emerged triumphant in a murderous campaign that resembled gangland warfare and left 700 dead. Edward Seaga beat Prime Minister Michael N. Manley, promising that law and order would be restored and the country's Cuban connection would be severed (see SEAGA, EDWARD).

On tiny Dominica, another conservative candidate won, this time a woman who became the first female chief of state of a Caribbean country. Honduras held elections, too, and peacefully transferred power to a political party that had been out of office for 20 years.

Elsewhere in Latin America, political change occurred by force. A military coup d'état in Bolivia on July 17 shocked the democratic sensibilities of its partners in the Andean Pact. In Surinam, the former Dutch colony on mainland South America, a group of disgruntled army sergeants seized power in February, irked by the government's failure to take seriously their complaints about low pay, lack of advancement, and poor morale. A military countercoup followed in August after two members of the ruling junta were accused of planning a Cuban-backed takeover of the government.

Brazilian workers preparing for visit of Roman Catholic Pope John Paul II scrub huge Christ the Redeemer statue overlooking Rio de Janeiro.

Unrest prevailed in Guatemala, where dozens of persons died in fighting between leftists and rightists. But the most widely publicized assassinations were committed in El Salvador and Paraguay. In El Salvador, a widely respected Roman Catholic archbishop was killed on March 24 by a bullet through the heart while presiding at a celebration of the Mass in San Salvador. Anastasio Somoza Debayle, the ousted Nicaraguan strongman who had been denied permanent refuge in the United States, was killed in a blaze of bazooka and machine-gun fire on a street in Asunción, Paraguay, on September 17.

Among the politically charged events that attracted attention were the troubles of another exile, the ailing Shah Mohammad Reza Pahlavi of Iran. The shah had sought refuge in Panama late in 1979 after having been denied re-entry to Mexico. He stayed in Panama until March 23, before going off to die in Egypt.

Regional Blocs. Within South America, alignments were firmed up within two increasingly distinct power blocs. One comprised the democracies of Colombia, Ecuador, Peru, and Venezuela — politically moderate nations with a common ambition to create a common Andean market. Bolivia, a fifth member, announced in September that it was withdrawing from the group. A military coup in mid-1980 not only had set back its timetable for achieving democracy, but also had been condemned by the other Andean Pact countries.

Consequently, Bolivia fitted into the continent's second power bloc with Argentina, Brazil, Chile, Paraguay, and Uruguay, nations ruled by authoritarian governments and — all except Paraguay — by military dictatorships that seized power forcibly. Ironically, in light of the way they seized power, the four military dictatorships avowedly pursued a policy of eventually restoring some form of democracy. In a national plebiscite denounced as a "fraud" by opponents of its military regime, Chile set the stage on September 11 for the adoption of a new constitution and future elections. The three other military-run nations of the Andean Pact group — Argentina, Brazil, and Uruguay — took somewhat similar steps.

Collectively, the nations of the authoritarian bloc worked to develop the huge Río de la Plata Basin in east-central South America for mutual advantage. They collaborated extensively to realize the area's hydroelectric potential. Construction was rushed on the Itaipú hydroelectric power complex on the Upper Paraná River, where it flows along the Brazil-Paraguay border. Scheduled for completion in the late 1980s, the complex was expected to become the world's largest single source of electricity.

Mexican Policy. Mexico's President Jose Lopez Portillo courted Cuba's Fidel Castro during the year, and thus put distance between himself and a U.S. electorate disgusted with Castro's actions during the Cuban refugee exodus. Nor did Mexico seem to share in the U.S. government's concern with Cuban activities — as Russia's representative — in providing arms, training, and even troops for uprisings in Africa and the Middle East. Washington, D.C., worried about Cuba's meddling in the Caribbean.

Inter-American Cooperation. There was some rejuggling of groups promoting regional interests, and a tendency to strengthen those whose membership was exclusively Latin American. In June, the Latin American Free Trade Association, a hemisphere-wide entity designed to spur economic integration through methods judged as overly simplistic, was abolished. A new Latin American Integration Association, which will emphasize both bilateral and general preference trade agreements, and which will more fully take into account economic differences among Latin American countries, will be created to replace it. In late October, eight South American nations with territory within the Amazon Basin pledged themselves to preserve the region's ecology, while developing its potentially enormous resources. In the Special Reports section, see Pondering the Fate of the Forests.

The Inter-American Development Bank (IADB) marked its 20th anniversary in Rio de Janeiro, Brazil, in April. It reported that with the $16-billion it had provided over a 20-year period, the Latin American countries — which had themselves invested $48 billion — had accomplished impressive gains. Some 160 million acres (64 million hectares) of land had been brought into agricultural production, and a source of fresh and pure drinking water had been provided to about 135 million persons. Latin America's hydroelectric output had been increased by 500 per cent through IADB-supported projects. Per capita income stood at $1,200 annually, compared with half that figure in real terms 20 years ago.

As it entered the 1980s, Latin America was manufacturing about two-thirds of the products it consumes, compared with one-third when the IADB began. The bank membership constituted something of a manifesto of confidence in Latin America's future prospects. Originally set up by 20 Western Hemisphere countries, the IADB now has 41 members and includes as donors many countries in Western Europe, as well as Israel and Japan.

In assessing the hemisphere outlook, Antonio Ortiz Mena of Mexico, the IADB's president, cautioned that Latin America's agricultural productivity still fails to keep abreast of the region's population growth. Making matters worse, the youthfulness of the population — 60 per cent under 25 — places a tremendous burden on taxpayers to provide schools and other facilities, while simultaneously creating a dilemma for planners attempting to create enough jobs for all. Headlong urbanization also complicates the area's population problem. The number of people living in 11 capital cities – plus Rio de Janeiro and São Paulo, Brazil – is expected to double before the year 2000, when they will contain among them 125 million persons.

U.S. Relations. President Jimmy Carter's Administration was surprised to see such old and reliable allies as Argentina and Brazil choosing not to cooperate with the United States when the latter, protesting Russia's invasion of Afghanistan, called for a grain embargo against the Soviet Union. One reason for this was anger over the United States imposition of human rights criteria in allocating its foreign aid, including military assistance. Another irritant was the outspoken United States opposition to their development of nuclear power.

In an election year, the Congress of the United States – sensing rising voter resistance to foreign aid – failed to appropriate pledged U.S. contributions to such international agencies as the IADB and the World Bank. The U.S. Congress also rejected legislation that would have established new international agreements on coffee and sugar in order to stabilize prices and benefit both producers and consumers. And on one issue of increasing importance – illegal immigration into the United

Facts in Brief on Latin American Political Units

Country	Population	Government	Monetary Unit*	Foreign Trade (million U.S. $) Exports†	Imports†
Argentina	27,437,000	President Jorge Rafael Videla	peso (1,953 = $1)	6,400	3,834
Bahamas	253,000	Governor General Sir Gerald C. Cash; Prime Minister Lynden O. Pindling	dollar (1 = $1)	2,105	2,453
Barbados	264,000	Governor General Sir Deighton Harcourt Lisle Ward; Prime Minister J. M. G. Adams	dollar (1.9 = $1)	151	424
Belize	168,000	Governor James Patrick Ivan Hennessy; Premier George Price	dollar (2 = $1)	62	90
Bolivia	5,310,000	President Luis Garcia Meza Tejada	peso (21.7 = $1)	777	1,011
Brazil	129,312,000	President Joao Baptista de Oliveira Figueiredo	cruzeiro (61.1 = $1)	15,244	19,804
Chile	11,489,000	President Augusto Pinochet Ugarte	peso (39 = $1)	3,763	4,218
Colombia	28,082,000	President Julio Cesar Turbay Ayala	peso (49.7 = $1)	3,381	4,437
Costa Rica	2,295,000	President Rodrigo Carazo Odio	colón (8.4 = $1)	923	1,409
Cuba	10,270,000	President Fidel Castro Ruz	peso (1 = $1.43)	4,456	4,687
Dominica	86,000	President Aurelius Marie; Prime Minister Mary Eugenia Charles	dollar (2.7 = $1)	10	18
Dominican Republic	5,581,000	President Silvestre Antonio Guzman Fernandez	peso (1 = $1)	869	1,055
Ecuador	8,637,000	President Jaime Roldos Aguilera	sucre (25.1 = $1)	1,494	1,951
El Salvador	4,795,000	President Jose Napoleon Duarte	colón (2.4 = $1)	848	1,028
Grenada	99,000	Governor General Sir Paul Godwin Scoon; Prime Minister Maurice Bishop	dollar (2.7 = $1)	17	36
Guatemala	7,216,000	President Fernando Romeo Lucas Garcia	quetzal (1 = $1)	1,089	1,286
Guyana	909,000	President Forbes Burnham; Prime Minister Ptolemy A. Reid	dollar (2.4 = $1)	291	279
Haiti	5,080,000	President Jean-Claude Duvalier	gourde (5 = $1)	155	212
Honduras	3,314,000	President Policarpo Paz Garcia	lempira (2 = $1)	732	832
Jamaica	2,222,000	Governor General Florizel Glasspole; Prime Minister Edward Seaga	dollar (1.7 = $1)	744	874
Mexico	74,123,000	President Jose Lopez Portillo	peso (23.1 = $1)	8,768	12,004
Nicaragua	2,643,000	5-member Government of National Reconstruction Junta	córdoba (10 = $1)	774	848
Panama	2,024,000	President Aristides Royo; National Guard Commander Omar Torrijos Herrera	balboa (1 = $1)	288	942
Paraguay	3,341,000	President Alfredo Stroessner	guaraní (125 = $1)	305	432
Peru	18,593,000	President Fernando Belaunde Terry; Prime Minister Manuel Ulloa Elias	sol (323 = $1)	3,533	2,022
Puerto Rico	3,689,000	Governor Carlos Romero Barcelo	U.S. $	5,123	6,918
St. Lucia	119,000	Acting Governor General Boswell Williams; Prime Minister Allan Fitzgerald Laurent Louisy	dollar (2.7 = $1)	27	59
St. Vincent and the Grenadines	133,000	Governor General Sir Sydney Gunn-Munro; Prime Minister R. Milton Cato	dollar (2.7 = $1)	9	24
Surinam	498,000	President & Prime Minister Henk R. Chin A Sen	guilder (1.7 = $1)	308	396
Trinidad and Tobago	1,160,000	President Ellis Emmanuel Innocent Clarke; Prime Minister Eric E. Williams	dollar (2.3 = $1)	2,476	1,946
Uruguay	2,929,000	President Aparicio Mendez Manfredini	peso (9.7 = $1)	795	1,172
Venezuela	15,484,000	President Luis Herrera Campins	bolivar (4.3 = $1)	13,111	10,614

*Exchange rates as of Dec. 1, 1980. †Latest available data.

Victims of gunfire are carried from public square after violence disrupted the funeral services of El Salvador's Archbishop Oscar Arnulfo Romero.

the late José Posada, Mexico's greatest printmaker, at the U.S. Library of Congress. Posada's prints evoke various aspects of Mexico's 1910 Revolution.

For archaeologists, there was the amazing discovery, made through use of an aerial radar survey, of an elaborate network of ancient canals built in what is now Guatemala by Mayan Indians between 250 B.C. and A.D. 900. The canals give indication of a highly advanced state of agriculture under the Mayas, and explain how they managed to feed 2 to 3 million persons from agriculturally poor lands. See ARCHAEOLOGY.

Finally, *Evita*, a musical that took as its controversial theme the life of María Eva Duarte de Perón (1919-1952), was a smash hit in London, New York City, and elsewhere. The musical's heroine had been the second wife of Argentina's late dictator Juan Domingo Perón. Ironically, Perón's third wife, María Estela (Isabel) Martínez de Perón, who succeeded him as Argentina's president from 1974 to 1976, languished under house arrest in Argentina, awaiting trial on charges of malfeasance while in office.   Nathan A. Haverstock

See also articles on the various Latin American countries; WEST INDIES. In WORLD BOOK, see LATIN AMERICA and articles on the individual countries.

LAW. See CIVIL RIGHTS; COURTS AND LAWS; CRIME; SUPREME COURT OF THE UNITED STATES.

LEBANON. The Christian Falange Party's militia completely crushed the forces of its chief Christian rival, the National Liberal Party (NLP), in fierce fighting on July 7 and 8, 1980. The battle climaxed the intermittent fighting among various Christian and Muslim factions that oppose one another as violently as they do the central government.

The Falangist leaders, including Bashir Gemayel, who had escaped an attempted assassination by NLP gunmen in February, on July 9 formed a Lebanese Christian Front responsible for administration of all Christian-held areas in and around Beirut. With south Lebanon effectively controlled by the rebel Christian army of Major Saad Haddad, and feudal chiefs in control of other sections, President Elias Sarkis' government faced an unenviable task in restoring order.

Government Weakness was underscored by periodic Cabinet crises and by continued sectarian divisions in the armed forces. Although increased in numbers to 23,000 by newly trained recruits and strengthened with the arrival in February of United States artillery equipment, the army was still no match for the combined militias of the various factions, let alone the well-equipped Palestinian guerrillas. The withdrawal in February of Syrian units of the Arab peacekeeping force from areas near Beirut to prepared positions in the Bekaa Valley in eastern Lebanon, and their refusal to

States, particularly from job-short Mexico — the U.S. Congress failed to act at all.

Changing Fads. The wearing of blue jeans became universal among youngsters of the rising middle class in Latin America's cities. Also popular among them was military-style clothing, with markings as diverse as those of performers in an operetta. Roller skating assumed fad proportions, particularly in the more cosmopolitan cities. Disco music — and the score of *Saturday Night Fever* in particular — swept the continent.

On July 9, Vinicius de Moraes, a Brazilian poet who had been vaulted to fame by his lyric for "The Girl from Ipanema," died at age 75 of a lung disorder. The song had spearheaded the international popularity of the bossa nova dance craze in the early 1960s. There was a spontaneous outpouring of grief in Ipanema, now a very "in" section of Rio de Janeiro, following his death; people and musical combos took to the streets to dance and sing to some of De Moraes' works.

In the United States, Latin American artists past and present came into their own. An exhibit of paintings by Fernando Botero, a 47-year-old Colombian whose canvases depicting puffy, rotund people satirize society's foibles and poke fun at religion, politics, and morality, drew large crowds to Washington, D.C.'s Smithsonian Institution. There was a well-attended exhibit of the works of intervene in factional conflicts until all Christian commanders were removed from the army, deprived the Sarkis government of its only effective stabilizing force.

A Cabinet crisis resulted when Prime Minister Salim Ahmad al-Huss resigned for health reasons in June. Sarkis named elder statesman Takieddin Solh to succeed al-Huss, but Solh resigned on August 9 after Christian leaders rejected his appeal for a government of "national reconciliation" and gunmen shot up his motorcade in Beirut. Al-Huss then returned to office until October 25, when Shafiq al-Wazzan, a 55-year-old lawyer, formed a new 22-member Cabinet.

Economic Recovery. Despite the political chaos and casualties averaging 100 per month from the factional violence, the economy continued its slow recovery from the devastation of civil war. The first Beirut International Trade Fair since 1975 attracted 300 foreign exhibitors in February. Some 1,800 ships used the port of Beirut during the year, unloading 1.94 million short tons (1.76 million metric tons) of cargo for transshipment. Beirut also resumed its function as a Middle East banking center, with nine new banks chartered and deposits up 15 per cent by June. William Spencer

See also MIDDLE EAST (Facts in Brief Table). In WORLD BOOK, see LEBANON.

LESOTHO. See AFRICA.

LIBERIA. William R. Tolbert, Jr., president of Liberia since 1971, was assassinated and his government overthrown on April 12, 1980. His party, the True Whig Party, had been in control of Liberia's government for more than 100 years.

The military coup d'état was carried out by 17 noncommissioned officers, led by Master Sergeant Samuel K. Doe (see DOE, SAMUEL K.). They imprisoned about 200 officers of the rank of major and above as well as 95 civilian officials.

Doe suspended the nation's Constitution and declared martial law on April 25. His troubled government was faced with a $700-million foreign debt and demands at home for higher wages. In April, Doe raised the minimum monthly pay for civil servants from $100 to $200 and for soldiers, from $100 to $250.

The Coup was supported by many Liberians because the ousted leaders were Americo-Liberians, members of a privileged minority – the descendants of freed slaves who migrated to Liberia from America in the early 1800s. Liberia's wealthiest ethnic group, they comprise less than 5 per cent of the population.

Under the Tolbert government, unemployment and inflation rose steadily, often provoking riots and unrest. Some 40 persons were killed and 600 injured in the capital city, Monrovia, in April 1979 after the government increased food prices.

Master Sergeant Samuel K. Doe became Liberia's head of state after his forces assassinated that nation's long-time leader, William R. Tolbert, Jr., on April 12.

The New Government established by Doe consisted of a 17-member People's Redemptive Council (PRC), composed entirely of enlisted military personnel, and a five-member military and civilian Cabinet, which reports to the PRC. Doe was named chairman of the PRC and head of state.

The PRC executed 13 former officials of the Tolbert government on April 22 after a trial by a five-man military tribunal that had recommended the death penalty for only four of them. They were not allowed defense counsel, nor did they receive details of the charges against them.

Many African nations deplored the executions. In protest, Nigeria's government refused the new Liberian foreign minister, Gabriel Baccus Matthews, permission to enter Nigeria to attend an April 25 meeting of the Organization of African Unity. On May 28, Doe was denied admission to another inter-African conference – a meeting of the West African Economic Community in Togo.

The United States, long an important source of economic and military aid to Liberia, responded to the coup by suspending aid. However, U.S. Assistant Secretary of State for African Affairs Richard M. Moose visited Monrovia in June, and the Congress of the United States approved $5.5 million in economic aid in August. J. Dixon Esseks

See also AFRICA (Facts in Brief Table). In WORLD BOOK, see LIBERIA.

LIBRARY. The economic recession threatened financial support for many libraries in the United States in 1980. Some were able to garner local support, however. Alabama legislators raised the library aid budget by 12 per cent. Ohio voters turned down four funding issues, but the citizens of Cleveland renewed a second five-year tax levy supporting the Cleveland Public Library. "Keep Libraries Alive," a high-powered campaign by the Berkeley, Calif., Public Library, helped create a new tax to boost the library's depleted budget.

State officials announced plans for a new $7,653,000 building to house the Kentucky Department of Library and Archives at Frankfort. A $12-million renovation at the University of Oklahoma Library will provide a 2.3-million-volume stack capacity and increased study area.

Grants and Librarians. Columbia University in New York City received a $1-million donation from the Cornelius Vander Starr Foundation to expand and renovate its East Asian Library. The National Endowment for the Humanities awarded 101 matching grants for the expansion and renovation of various institutions, ranging from $13,980 to the Boston Medical Library to $600,000 to the Union Theological Seminary of New York City.

An attempt by Governor Edward J. King of Massachusetts to oust State Librarian A. Hunter Rineer from office in early 1980 and replace him with a political appointee aroused the Massachusetts library community. King unsuccessfully proposed replacing Rineer with Gasper Caso, Jr., a library employee who had been active in King's 1978 gubernatorial campaign.

Alphonse Trezza was named to head a Library of Congress study on the role of federal libraries in the national library network. Until July 1, Trezza had been executive director of the National Commission on Libraries and Information Science, which is funding the study. Lee T. Handley was appointed director of SOLINET, an Atlanta-based organization serving libraries in 10 Southeastern states.

Library Meetings. The Canadian Library Association's annual conference was held in Vancouver, B.C., from June 11 to 17. The 99th annual conference of the American Library Association was held in New York City from June 29 to July 5. A record 14,566 persons registered for the conference.

For Further Reading. After Mount Saint Helens spread ash and dust over much of the Pacific Northwest, Spokane librarian Charlotte Jones placed the novels *True Grit* and *Love Among the Ruins* on the recommended reading list.   Robert J. Shaw

See also AMERICAN LIBRARY ASSOCIATION; CANADIAN LIBRARY ASSOCIATION. In WORLD BOOK, see LIBRARY.

One of the New York Public Library's marble lions is shrouded in black by demonstrators protesting against cut in library funds.

LIBYA and Syria agreed on Sept. 2, 1980, to merge. The projected union was the latest in a series of efforts by Leader of the Revolution Muammar Muhammad al-Qadhafi to unite the Arab world under his leadership. After a few nonproductive meetings, however, prospects for an actual political merger seemed dim at year's end.

The mercurial Libyan leader suffered a string of other foreign policy failures during the year. His attempt to spark a revolution in Tunisia with a Libyan-trained commando raid on Qafsah in January backfired as Tunisians united behind President Habib Bourguiba. Egypt closed its border with Libya in February after the arrest in Alexandria on sabotage charges of 200 Egyptians recruited from the expatriate labor force in Libya and infiltrated into Egypt. In August, Malta expelled 50 Libyan military advisers in a dispute over offshore oil rights. Senegal and the Central African Republic broke diplomatic relations with Libya over alleged interference in their internal affairs. In September, Libya was one of the few Arab states to support non-Arab Iran in the war with Iraq.

Libya's touchy relations with the United States suffered when it was revealed that Billy Carter, the brother of U.S. President Jimmy Carter, had business dealings with the Libyan government in 1978 and 1979. See CARTER, JAMES EARL, JR.

Qadhafi's Popularity in Libya remained high, but there was growing discontent with the government. The discontent focused on economic shortages, corruption, and bureaucratic waste, as well as heavy-handed police action against critics of the regime. In April, the government launched a sweeping purge, arresting some 2,000 persons on various charges, notably corruption and disloyalty to the popular revolution. Those arrested included high government and business leaders, army commanders, and intellectuals.

Overseas Murders. The Libyan leader also initiated a purge of Libyan exiles. After Qadhafi warned exiles to return home to face trial, Libyan "death squads" gunned down dissident leaders in several European capitals. Ten were killed before Qadhafi withdrew his liquidation order.

A number of Libyan embassies were also occupied by militants and renamed People's Bureaus. The seizure of the Washington, D.C., embassy in April created a diplomatic problem. The four persons who occupied it were expelled in May, but the embassy remained "officially" a People's Bureau.   William Spencer

See also MIDDLE EAST (Facts in Brief Table). In WORLD BOOK, see LIBYA.

LIECHTENSTEIN. See EUROPE.

LIONS INTERNATIONAL. See COMMUNITY ORGANIZATIONS.

LITERATURE. Even as the weak U.S. economy caused profound changes in the publishing industry to accelerate in 1980, so durable literature was threatened on several fronts. There was a sharp dip in bookstore sales; a drought in auctions of the paperback rights that often make the difference between profit and loss on a hard-cover book; and a decision by the Supreme Court of the United States that endangered *backlists* — slower-selling volumes that can make money over a period of years. All these factors caused publishers to cut back the numbers of books they issued, rejecting high-quality but marginally profitable volumes in favor of shallow, short-lived best sellers.

The most obvious victim of this trend was the *first novel* of literary merit, a work of quality but low sales potential by an unknown author. Very few were published in 1980 and, except for one literary phenomenon, none was memorable.

The exception was the posthumously published *A Confederacy of Dunces*, a rollicking Falstaffian farce set in New Orleans. The author, John Kennedy Toole, had committed suicide in 1969. Louisiana State University Press published the book 11 years after its author's death — and sold 40,000 copies before the year closed.

Walker Percy wrote the finest novel of a year in which few major American authors published. His *Second Coming* was notable for its author's shift from

Libya's Muammar al-Qadhafi, left, and Syria's President Hafiz al-Assad meet in Tripoli to discuss the merger of their two nations.

Author P. D. James holds a copy of her new novel, *Innocent Blood*, which earned about $1 million in U.S. subsidiary rights before going on sale.

the despair of Angst – a deeply felt anxiety or fear – to a new optimism.

E. L. Doctorow solidified his reputation with *Loon Lake*, a dazzling novel of mirrors. John Gardner's *Freddy's Book* was an enchanting fable-within-a-novel. Thomas Berger finally lived up to his early promise with *Neighbors*, a brilliant comedy of domestic guerrilla warfare. The prolific Joyce Carol Oates's *Bellefleur* ambitiously transmuted the Gothic form into art.

Several younger writers added to their laurels, especially Ann Beattie, whose *Falling in Place* explored the malaise of young people in the 1970s, and Marge Piercy, whose sixth novel, *Vida*, told of youth caught up in radical political change.

Foreign Authors publishing in America found 1980 to be a relatively weak year. Among English-speaking countries, Great Britain contributed Graham Greene's *Doctor Fischer of Geneva, or the Bomb Party*, a dark novel of atheism and pride; Margaret Drabble's ninth novel, *The Middle Ground;* John Berger's *Pig Earth;* Angus Wilson's *Setting the World on Fire;* and Doris Lessing's *The Marriages Between Zones Three, Four, and Five*. A best seller in the entertainment category was British novelist P. D. James's *Innocent Blood*. From Canada came Margaret Atwood's finest novel, *Life Before Man*, and Mordecai Richler's *Joshua Then and Now*. The Australian author Thomas Keneally wrote an excellent

novel of the American Civil War, *Confederates*, and South Africa's Nadine Gordimer and Andre Brink were represented by *A Soldier's Romance* and *A Dry White Season*, respectively.

From south of the border came the Mexican Carlos Fuentes' short-story collection *Burnt Water*, the Brazilian Marcio Souza's picaresque novel *The Emperor of the Amazon*, and the Argentine Julio Cortazar's *A Change of Light and Other Stories*.

Two important books came from Italy: Alberto Moravia's 21st novel, *Time of Desecration*, and Italo Calvino's fine retelling of *Italian Folktales*.

Biography. It was an exceptionally strong year for literary lives, especially of American authors. Justin Kaplan won laurels for his new interpretation of the "Good Gray Poet," *Walt Whitman*. Townsend Ludington published the first major biography of novelist *John Dos Passos*. James R. Mellow's *Nathaniel Hawthorne In His Times* and Addison Gayle's *Richard Wright: Ordeal of a Native Son* also were contenders for prizes, as was Ronald Steel's *Walter Lippmann and the American Century*.

Monica Furlong's comprehensive *Merton* and Elena Malits' *The Solitary Explorers* were harbingers of a forthcoming avalanche of studies on Thomas Merton, the poet and Trappist monk.

There were few significant lives of British authors. Two were on the same subject: Antony Alpers' *The Life of Katherine Mansfield* and Jeffrey Meyers' *Katherine Mansfield*. Ted Morgan's clumsy, massive, but definitive *Maugham* and Peter Stansky and William Abrahams' crisp *Orwell: The Transformation* rounded out the offerings.

The life of the French poet Jules Laforgue was ably explored in David Arkell's *Looking for Laforgue; An Informal Biography of Jules Laforgue;* his controversial countryman received a balanced assessment in Merlin Thomas' *Louis-Ferdinand Céline*. Arthur Gold and Robert Fizdale's *Misia*, the life of Misia Sert, chronicled a Russian-born woman who was an arbiter of taste in Paris at the beginning of the 20th century.

The only political biographies of note were William L. Shirer's *Gandhi: A Memoir* and Merle Miller's *Lyndon: An Oral Biography*, a popular collection of anecdotes about President Lyndon B. Johnson. Of interest as a historical footnote was Doris Faber's gossipy *The Life of Lorena Hickok*, an intimate friend of Eleanor Roosevelt.

Ronald W. Clark's *Freud: The Man and the Cause*, and Frank J. Sulloway's *Freud, Biologist of the Mind* were outstanding additions to the Freud shelf.

Joseph Lash's enormous *Helen and Teacher*, a warts-and-all dual biography of Helen Keller and Anne Sullivan Macy, revealed their human sides without impugning their achievements.

Autobiography, Memoirs, and Letters. Near the end of her life, many observers considered Jean Rhys to be England's finest living author, but *Smile*

Please: An Unfinished Autobiography dwells on decades of obscurity and neglect. Her countryman Christopher Isherwood's *My Guru and His Disciple* was a fascinating portrait of Isherwood's devotions with the Vedantist Swami Prabhavananda.

Ever stalking controversy, Alexander Solzhenitsyn fueled the fires with *The Oak and the Calf: Sketches of Literary Life in the Soviet Union*, which some critics attacked as slanderous to Russian authors and editors. Malcolm Cowley's *The Dream of the Golden Mountains: Remembering the 1930s* relived literary life during the Great Depression.

There were two powerful memoirs of combat in World War II: the fine Canadian essayist and novelist Farley Mowat's *And No Birds Sang* and the American Elmer Bendiner's *The Fall of Fortresses*, about the air war over Europe.

Anne Morrow Lindbergh took her distinguished memoirs through the war years with *War Within and Without: Diaries and Letters, 1939-1944*. Vol. VII, 1966-1974.

There was a dearth of books devoted to literary letters, but those that were published were excellent. These included *The Letters of Gustave Flaubert, 1830-1857*, edited by Francis Steegmuller; *Byron's Letters and Journals, Vol. 10: 1822-1823*, edited by Leslie A. Marchand; *The Letters of Evelyn Waugh*, edited by Mark Amory; *Arna Bontemps-Langston Hughes Letters 1925-1967*, edited by Charles H. Nichols; and the sixth and last volume of *The Letters of Virginia Woolf: 1936-1941*, edited by Nigel Nicolson and Joanne Trautman.

Criticism. The first volume of Ian Watt's *Conrad in the Nineteenth Century*, immediately acclaimed as one of the great critical studies of our time, worked out many mysteries in the novels of Joseph Conrad.

Paul Fussells' highly entertaining *Abroad: British Literary Traveling Between the Wars* explored an almost lost art, travel writing, in this case of English authors between World Wars I and II. Another charming book was Vladimir Nabokov's idiosyncratic *Lectures on Literature*, collected from his years as a professor of English at Cornell University. Leon Edel collected and edited a second volume of Edmund Wilson's papers, *The Thirties*.

Pauline Kael's volume of film criticism, *When the Lights Go Down*, became a cause célèbre when it was savagely attacked in the *New York Review of Books* by Renata Adler, a fellow writer on *The New Yorker* magazine.

Susan Sontag's third collection of essays and criticism, *Under the Sign of Saturn*, cemented her reputation as America's widest-ranging intellectual critic. Janet Malcolm's *Diana and Nikon* studied the aesthetics of photography.

History. Only a handful of significant books were published in this category in 1980. Carl E. Schorske's *Fin-de-Siècle Vienna* was a profound study of the crisis of the bourgeoisie.

Two other intellectual studies were Robert Nisbet's *History of the Idea of Progress* and Isaiah Berlin's *Against the Current: Essays in the History of Ideas.*

Maxine Hong Kingston's *China Men* chronicled the emigration of Chinese to the United States. The young historian Michael R. Beschloss' *Kennedy and Roosevelt: The Uneasy Alliance* explored the relationship between Franklin D. Roosevelt and his ambassador to Britain, Joseph Kennedy. Richard Lingeman's *Small-Town America* was a fine study of the village from 1620 to the present.

The story of the French resistance during World War II was ably and excitingly related by David Schoenbrun in *Soldiers of the Night.*

A genuine publishing event was *The Plan of St. Gall*, by Walter Horn and Ernest Born, a massive three-volume study of the plan for a medieval Swiss monastery that was an exemplar of the bookmaker's art as well as a splendid cultural history.

Contemporary Affairs. Events in the Middle East gave impetus to several books. Edward Said's *The Question of Palestine* explored the issues of Israel from the point of view of its Arab inhabitants. Amin Saikal's *The Rise and Fall of the Shah* and William H. Farbis' *Fall of the Peacock Throne* were the two best studies of recent Iranian history, and G. H. Jansen's *Militant Islam* reviewed the resurgence of that religion in affairs of state.

American novelist Walker Percy displayed his usual skilled craftsmanship in *Second Coming*, a narrative of life and death in the South.

Writer Truman Capote's *Music for Chameleons,* a group of literary pieces published in 1980, received mixed praise from book reviewers.

The Nobel laureate economist Milton Friedman and his wife, Rose, wrote *Free To Choose,* a runaway best seller championing the idea of the free market.

The uprooting of populations in Europe after World War II was the subject of two books: Ann Cornelisen's *Strangers and Pilgrims,* which explored Italian migrant labor; and Jane Kramer's *Unsettling Europe.*

David S. Broder thoughtfully discussed the transference of power and leadership in America in *The Changing of the Guard.* Victor Navasky's *Naming Names* was a cogent study of the anti-Communist witch hunt in Hollywood, and Studs Terkel's finest oral history, *American Dreams: Lost and Found,* became an immediate best seller.

Science and Social Science. Increasing interest in the history of the family resulted in two fine studies: the Frenchman Jacques Donzelot's *The Policing of Families* and Carl N. Degler's *At Odds.* Stephen Jay Gould offered another volume of elegant essays on natural history, *The Panda's Thumb,* and the perceptive naturalist George Schaller's *Stones of Silence* told of his search for sheep and goats in the Himalaya. Horace Freeland Judson's *The Search for Solutions* was a landmark book on the taxonomy of science.

Miscellaneous. With the publication in 1980 of *The Collected Stories of Eudora Welty,* the Southern writer became the subject of several celebratory

volumes: *Eudora Welty: A Form of Thanks,* edited by Louis Dollarhide and Ann J. Abadle; *Eudora Welty: Critical Essays,* edited by Peggy Whitman Prenshaw; and *Eudora Welty's Achievement of Order,* by Michael Kreyling. Truman Capote, another Southern writer, published *Music for Chameleons* in the fall.

Paperbacks. The 10 top-selling paperbacks of 1980, all novels, were *Petals on the Wind,* an original commercial paperback by V. C. Andrews; *The Americans,* by John Jakes, also an original; *The Stand,* by Stephen King; *Memories of Another Day,* by Harold Robbins; *Dead Zone,* by Stephen King; *The Piercing,* by John Coyne; *A Necessary Woman,* by Helen Van Slyke; *A Woman of Substance,* by Barbara Bradford Taylor; *The Island,* by Peter Benchley; and *Sophie's Choice,* by William Styron.

Hard Cover Best Sellers. The year's three most popular entertainments were Sidney Sheldon's *Rage of Angels,* Stephen King's *Firestarter,* and Judith Krantz's *Princess Daisy.* As the year ended, James Michener's *The Covenant* drew abreast of them.   Henry Kisor

See also AWARDS AND PRIZES (Literature Awards); CANADIAN LITERATURE; LITERATURE FOR CHILDREN; POETRY; PUBLISHING. In WORLD BOOK, see LITERATURE.

LITERATURE, CANADIAN. See CANADIAN LIBRARY ASSOCIATION; CANADIAN LITERATURE.

LITERATURE FOR CHILDREN. It is a rare occasion when an author's first book succeeds in claiming two of the most prestigious awards in the field of children's literature, the Newbery Medal and the American Book Award for Children's Literature. But that is what *A Gathering of Days: A New England Girl's Journal, 1830–32,* by Joan W. Blos (Scribners) did in 1980.

Written in the style a 13-year-old might have used in the 1830s, the novel follows the main character as she helps a runaway slave, adjusts to a new stepmother, and suffers the death of her dearest friend. Suggested for ages 11 to 13, *A Gathering of Days* is quite different from many of the books being written today for the 12-year-old child — no profanities, obscenities, or sex. As more explicit sex creeps into books for this age group, at least one reprint publisher has felt the need for asterisks in its catalog to indicate books that, because of language or incidents, suggest a need for parental awareness or guidance.

The recent upsurge in interest in the United States in ballet dancing is reflected in the number of books published that deal with some aspect of the subject. Fantasy and science fiction remain popular reading topics. Some outstanding books of 1980 were:

Picture Books

Poofy Loves Company, by Nancy Winslow Parker

(Dodd). Poofy, a large dog of vaguely sheepdog ancestry, turns out to have his own enthusiastic way of entertaining company. Ages 4 to 8.

Paddy's New Hat, by John S. Goodall (McElderry/Atheneum). Told entirely in delightful full-color pictures, this shows Paddy Pork again involved in a series of adventures and misadventures that begin when his new hat gets blown away. Ages 3 to 8.

Truck, by Donald Crews (Greenwillow). Striking graphics with enough detail to please the most avid young truck lover show the journey of a truck through city and highway traffic. Ages 3 to 8.

Mrs. Tortino's Return to the Sun, by Shirley and Pat Murphy, pictures by Susan Russo (Lothrop). Mrs. Tortino's family home is surrounded by tall buildings as the city grows up around it. A unique solution proves completely satisfying. Ages 4 to 8.

Dame Wiggins of Lee and Her Seven Wonderful Cats, illustrated by Patience Brewster (Crowell). Delightful line drawings add humor to this 19th-century rhyme as they show the remarkable cats doing some very unusual things. Ages 3 to 8.

If You Say So, Claude, by Joan Lowery Nixon, drawings by Lorinda Bryan Cauley (Warne). Shirley and Claude are riding in their covered wagon looking for a place to settle when a series of mishaps proves to them both that Shirley's choice is obviously the right one. Ages 4 to 9.

Two, Four, Six, Eight, A Book About Legs, by Ethel and Leonard Kessler (Dodd). Lively illustrations of people, birds, animals, and insects animate the pages of this introduction to a few numbers and a variety of creatures. Ages 4 to 8.

Bear Hunt, by Anthony Browne (Atheneum). Stylized color illustrations show the dangers Bear encounters as hunters chase him and also show his own ingenious solutions as he escapes them — with the aid of his pencil. Ages 3 to 7.

The Devil Take You, Barnabas Beane! by Mary Blount Christian, drawings by Anne Burgess (Crowell). The title comes from the reply of cold, hungry orphan John when miser Beane refuses to help him. Later, when he finds tiny hoofprints around his house, Barnabas is afraid the curse will come true, but ingenious John helps him find a solution the reader will enjoy. Ages 7 to 10.

A Salmon for Simon, by Betty Waterton, illustrated by Ann Blades (McElderry/Atheneum). More than anything, Simon wanted to catch a salmon, until one day an unusual accident gives him an opportunity, and he changes his mind. Ages 5 to 8.

The Green Man, by Gail E. Haley (Scribners). Using the tradition of the existence of a kindly man of the forest who helps people, this award-winning artist creates a charming and believable explanation of this tradition and puts it in a beautiful medieval setting. Ages 6 to 9.

Super Bowl, by Leonard Kessler (Greenwillow/Read-Alone). The big game between the Animal Champs and the Super Birds is described, complete with introductions to players, coaches, cheerleaders, and cheers. This should be fun for the sports enthusiast who is just beginning to read.

Hattie, Tom and The Chicken Witch (a play and a story), by Dick Gackenbach (Harper/I Can Read). At first it seems Hattie won't have a part in the play, but she does and the reader has a chance to see the funny play about the Easter Eggs and the Chicken Witch. For the beginning reader.

Fun to Read and Do

Custard and Company, poems by Ogden Nash, selected and illustrated by Quentin Blake (Little). Blake's funny line drawings add the perfect touch to Nash's humor — fun for the whole family. Ages 8 and up.

A Person From Britain Whose Head Was the Shape of a Mitten, and Other Limericks, by N. M. Bodecker (McElderry/Atheneum). A delightful collection of nonsense verse made even funnier by the drawings that accompany them. Ages 8 and up.

Animal Snackers, by Betsy Lewin (Dodd). Photographs of delightful creatures made from bread dough illustrate the sprightly rhymes in this book. Ages 4 to 10.

Kaleidoscopic Designs and How to Create Them, by Norma Yvette Finkel, text by Leslie G. Finkel (Dover). Including 37 plates for coloring, this unusual paperback book gives detailed instructions for creating kaleidoscopic designs and could inspire an interesting art project for classes or individuals. Ages 8 and up.

The Magic Mirror, An Antique Optical Toy (Dover). A reproduction of a McLoughlin Brothers toy, this has 24 *anamorphic* (distorted) pictures and a reflecting device that transforms each distorted picture into a normal one. Ages 4 to 8.

Kites For Kids, by Burton and Rita Marks, illustrated by Lisa Campbell Ernst (Lothrop). Besides having clear, detailed information on how to build numerous kinds of kites, this book also explains why kites are made as they are, gives safety rules, lists suppliers, and even throws in "amazing moments in kite history." Ages 8 and up.

Bet You Can't! Science Impossibilities to Fool You, by Vicki Cobb and Kathy Darling, illustrated by Martha Weston (Lothrop). A fascinating book, this will make a reluctant learner want to stump his friends with these science "tricks," most of which require little or no equipment and seem so easy — though impossible — that the reader finds himself jumping up in the middle of a paragraph to try them out. Fun! Ages 10 and up.

People, Places, and Animals

An Edwardian Season, by John S. Goodall (McElderry/Atheneum). Although there is a list of events depicted, this book is entirely a pictorial representation of the height of the social season near the turn of the century, providing an interesting, accu-

Barbara Cooney's illustrations for *Ox Cart Man,*
by Donald Hall, won the 1980 Caldecott Medal
for the best U.S. picture book for children.

rate, artistic, and painless excursion into English
social history. All ages.

Count on Your Fingers African Style, by Claudia
Zaslavsky, illustrated by Jerry Pinkney (Crowell).
Pencil drawings depict an African market place
and illustrate various kinds of finger counting used
by different tribes, often showing how the words for
the numbers relate to this counting. Ages 4 to 8.

Strange Footprints on the Land: Vikings in America, by
Constance Irwin (Harper). A fascinating historical
mystery unfolds as the author investigates the
proofs and clues to Viking explorations and possible settlements in America long before Columbus
landed. Ages 10 to 14.

All Times, All Peoples: A World History of Slavery,
by Milton Meltzer, illustrated by Leonard Everett
Fisher (Harper). Slavery has been a fact of life for
many human beings almost since the beginning of
recorded history. This book shows how whites have
enslaved whites and blacks have enslaved blacks,
and stresses the evils of slavery, pointing out that it
still exists in some parts of the world and asking
what is to be done about it. Ages 10 to 14.

Horses as I See Them, pictures by Ugo Mochi, text
by Dorcas MacClintock (Scribners). Remarkable
silhouette illustrations, each cut from a single sheet
of black paper, make this book a special one. It includes information on the history of horses, breeds,
and sports involving horses. Ages 10 and up.

*Gigi: A Baby Whale Borrowed for Science and Re-
turned to the Sea,* by Eleanor Coerr and William E.
Evans (Putnam). The reader follows with interest
the scientific expedition from its beginning hunt for
a baby whale until the whale is released months
later, and rejoices with the scientists when news of
its successful survival in the open sea with its own
species is received. Ages 9 and up.

Giraffes, by Louise C. Brown, photographs by
Audrey Ross (Dodd). Through interesting text and
photographs, this book informs the reader of many
facts about the giraffe and indicates it is well fitted
for survival, though humanity is often a thought-
less and deadly enemy. Ages 7 to 10.

Unbuilding, by David Macaulay (Houghton). In
1989, Prince Ali Smith makes arrangements to buy
the Empire State Building, have it taken down,
then rebuilt in the Arabian desert. Ages 10 and up.

The Marathoners, by Hal Higdon (Putnam). This
book presents the stories of three great marathon
runners — Frank Shorter, Bill Rodgers, and Garry
Bjorkland — and describes their backgrounds,
training, and races. It also gives brief glimpses of
other runners, including some women. It is illustrated with photographs. Ages 10 and up.

Oh, Boy! Babies! by Alison Cragin Herzig and
Jane Lawrence Mali, photographs by Katrina
Thomas (Little). This funny and delightful book is
enlivened by actual quotes from the fifth- and sixth-
grade boys who took this unique elective course in
infant care. Ages 9 and up.

Fiction

The Frog Band Books (*The Frog Band and the Onion
Seller; The Frog Band and Durrington Dormouse; The
Frog Band and the Mystery of Lion Castle*), by Jim
Smith (Little). Originally published in Great Britain, these wildly adventurous tales, told with perfect seriousness, have large, sophisticated, and
humorous full-color pictures of dressed animals
shown in castles, dungeons, and automobiles. The
series offers an original approach to humor and
adventure. Ages 8 to 12.

Part-Time Boy, by Elizabeth T. Billington, illustrated by Diane de Groat (Warne). Jamie, youngest of three boys, makes a friend who keeps animals
"part time" and decides he wants to be her "part-
time boy" for the summer. Ages 8 to 10.

McBroom and the Great Race, by Sid Fleischman,
illustrated by Walter Lorraine (Atlantic/Little).
Another humorous tall tale by this author, the
book tells how McBroom manages to outwit Heck
Jones, a shifty customer who is trying to get the
McBroom farm and its astonishingly rich soil. Ages
8 to 12.

Finders Weepers, by Miriam Chaikin, drawings by
Richard Egielski (Harper). Molly is happy when
she finds a ring, but later feels guilty when she
learns the identity of the owner and cannot get the
ring off her finger to return it. This story of growing

up in a Jewish family in Brooklyn in the 1930s not only conveys childlike feelings, but also gives a sense of family warmth and love. Ages 8 to 11.

Butter on Both Sides, by Lucille Watkins Ellison, illustrated by Judith Gwyn Brown (Scribners). Though lacking the narrative pull of the Laura Ingalls Wilder books, this recreation of the author's childhood has the similar appeal of another period seen through the eyes of a child – this time in Alabama around 1900. Ages 8 to 12.

Kitty in the Summer, by Judy Delton, illustrated by Charles Robinson (Houghton). Kitty, a member of a devout Roman Catholic family, goes to visit her aunt, helps at the church bazaar where she tries to win a dog being raffled, and goes on a visit to the country. Ages 7 to 10.

The Fallen Spaceman, by Lee Harding, pictures by John and Ian Schoenherr (Harper). Tyro finds himself thrown to the alien earth in his giant robot-like spacesuit, and for a few tense hours his fate is linked with that of an earth child who becomes trapped in the spacesuit. Ages 8 to 12.

Arthur, for the Very First Time, by Patricia MacLachlan, illustrated by Lloyd Bloom (Harper). Ten-year-old Arthur's mother is expecting a baby. No one has told him, but he knows and is unhappy. He visits his aunt and uncle for the summer, and there, on the farm, begins to find out things about himself, the world, and loving people. Ages 9 to 12.

Pearl in the Egg, by Dorothy Van Woerkom, illustrated by Joe Lasker (Crowell). In this tale of 13th-century life, the names of the two women minstrels are historical and gave the author the idea for her story, an exciting and authentic one of a small runaway serf and her adventures with a troupe of entertainers. Ages 9 to 12.

The Magicians of Caprona, by Dianna Wynne Jones (Greenwillow). Humor, excitement, magic, and realistic characters and places – this book has all of these in a story telling how Tonino, youngest of a large clan of magicians, helps to save his city and end a family feud as well. Ages 10 and up.

That's One Ornery Orphan, by Patricia Beatty (Morrow). When Hallie Lee Baker, age 13, comes to the orphanage in Blanco County, Texas, she brings her own special verve and gumption, making another sprightly and humorous tale of the late 1800s. Ages 10 to 14.

Country of Broken Stone, by Nancy Bond (McElderry/Atheneum). Strong characterizations and a tangible sense of place make a memorable book of this story about 14-year-old Penelope and her reactions to the adjustments required by the acquisition of a stepmother (a professional archaeologist), two younger brothers, and a sister. The setting is near the Roman Wall in Great Britain. Ages 13 and up.

A Star for the Latecomer, by Bonnie Zindel and Paul Zindel (Harper). A very powerful account of 16-year-old Brooke's terrible year as her beloved mother slowly dies of cancer and Brooke – who has always been her mother's alter ego and her only hope for stardom – realizes she doesn't want to be a dancer. Ages 14 and up.

Awards in 1980 included:

American Library Association/Association for Library Service to Children Awards: *The Newbery Medal* for "the most distinguished contribution to American Literature for children," was awarded to Joan W. Blos for *A Gathering of Days: A New England Girl's Journal, 1830–32.* The *Caldecott Medal* for "the most distinguished American picture book for children" went to illustrator Barbara Cooney for *Ox Cart Man,* written by Donald Hall. The *Mildred L. Batchelder Award* cited E. P. Dutton for publication of *The Sound of the Dragon's Feet,* by Aliki Zei, translated from the Greek by Edward Fenton. *The Laura Ingalls Wilder Award,* presented every five years "to an author or illustrator whose books, published in the United States over a period of years, have made a substantial and lasting contribution to literature for children," was given to Dr. Seuss (Theodor Seuss Geisel).   Lynn de Grummond Delaune

See also CANADIAN LITERATURE; LITERATURE; POETRY. In WORLD BOOK, see CALDECOTT MEDAL; LITERATURE FOR CHILDREN; NEWBERY MEDAL; SEUSS, DR.; WILDER, LAURA INGALLS.

LIVESTOCK. See FARM AND FARMING.

LOS ANGELES instituted a court-ordered busing program designed to desegregate the nation's second-largest school system on Sept. 16, 1980. More than 25,000 students in 150 of the system's 497 elementary and junior high schools were involved in the program. The plan was ordered by Superior Court Judge Paul Egly on May 19 and upheld on September 12 when the Supreme Court of the United States refused to interfere.

Egly's plan, made final on August 25, established six "court areas," each containing clusters of schools. By confining busing to schools within clusters, no child had to be bused more than 10 miles (16 kilometers) from his or her neighborhood school. The desegregation plan, which was hotly contested by minority groups and civil rights groups as inadequate, and by antibusing factions as unnecessary, stemmed from a suit filed in 1963 by the American Civil Liberties Union.

Strike Problems. The second municipal employees' strike in the city's history began on November 13 when 5,438 workers defied a court order and walked off the job. Garbage piled up at the rate of 5,000 short tons (4,500 metric tons) per day, but other services were not immediately affected. The strikers included engineers, traffic controllers, maintenance workers, park and recreation employees, library and harbor staffs, mechanics, and computer operators in addition to sanitation work-

Actress Cheryl Ladd feeds Los Angeles Mayor Thomas A. Bradley a piece of the city's bicentennial cake to launch a two-year celebration in September.

ers. A one-percentage-point difference in pay scales was the key issue. Workers returned to their jobs on November 19, agreeing to resume work while "meaningful negotiations" continued.

Two strikes affected Los Angeles during the summer. A weeklong strike of dockworkers, settled on July 10, cost Los Angeles and Long Beach harbors and shippers an estimated $5 million per day in lost revenues. Mayor Thomas A. Bradley appealed to city residents on August 23 to conserve electricity in the face of a strike by power plant workers. Some 25 workers at two of the area's four power plants left their jobs on August 20. Management personnel operated the plants during the walkout, but not at full power. The workers returned to their jobs on August 25.

Court and Council Rulings. The City Council on January 31 approved an ordinance outlawing housing discrimination on the basis of age, pregnancy, or parenthood. The ordinance, in effect, banned the rental of housing "for adults only."

The U.S. Supreme Court on October 6 ordered Los Angeles International Airport to pay $86,800 in damages to 41 adjacent homeowners. The settlement was to provide compensation for noise pollution by jet aircraft. James M. Banovetz

In WORLD BOOK, see LOS ANGELES.

LOUISIANA. See STATE GOVERNMENT.

LUMBER. See FOREST AND FOREST PRODUCTS.

LUXEMBOURG. The January decision of the European Parliament, advisory body of the European Community (EC), to hold all its full sessions in Strasbourg, France, in 1980 – and probably indefinitely – dismayed those who had hoped that Luxembourg would at least share the title of "democratic capital of Europe." Parliament had previously held alternate sessions in Strasbourg and Brussels, Belgium. Luxembourg, as Parliament's administrative center, had hoped also to be a host country.

Luxembourg's main concern in 1980 was its declining steel industry. Arbed, its largest company, faced its worst crisis since 1975 as steel prices fell following the world slump. Prime Minister Pierre Werner sought diversification, looking particularly to a new heavy engineering industry.

Former Prime Minister Gaston Thorn, 51, was chosen in July to take over in 1981 as president of the EC's executive commission, succeeding Roy H. Jenkins of Great Britain, who was due to retire. Thorn, who favors eventual political unification of the nine EC nations, was appointed despite strong opposition from France's President Valéry Giscard d'Estaing, an opponent of Thorn's European federalist views. Kenneth Brown

See also EUROPE (Facts in Brief Table). In WORLD BOOK, see LUXEMBOURG.

MADAGASCAR. See AFRICA.

MAGAZINE advertising revenues in the United States approached $3 billion in 1980. This was an increase of about 9 per cent over a record 1979, with the number of ad pages also showing a slight increase. These gains capped a 100 per cent increase in ad revenues from 1975 through 1979.

The Audit Bureau of Circulations reported that combined paid circulation for the leading 100 magazines totaled more than 215 million for the first six months of 1980, up from 214 million for the same period in 1979.

To combat ever-increasing postal delivery costs, publishers continued to turn to private companies for delivery. Private carriers delivered more than 18 million copies of magazines in 1980.

New Magazines. Among the 140 new magazines introduced in 1980 was *Discover,* a monthly science publication, which premièred in October. Published by Time Incorporated, it is directed at an educated audience interested in how science affects everyday life. A bimonthly magazine, *Next,* a product of The Litton Publishing Group, went on sale in February. Subtitled "The Magazine of the Future," it forecasts breakthroughs and discoveries in science and technology.

Test copies of *Families,* the first new magazine to be published by *The Reader's Digest* since its debut in February 1922, hit the newsstands in September, bearing a record number of advertising pages for a new publication. A second issue was scheduled for the spring of 1981, and the magazine was to be a monthly by autumn 1981.

The Dial debuted in September. It is a monthly television magazine and program guide owned jointly by Public Broadcasting Service (PBS) affiliates in Washington, D.C.; New York City; Chicago; and Los Angeles; and it is sent to PBS station subscribers.

Major Business Ventures. Publishers of *Harper's*, the 130-year-old literary magazine, announced on June 17 that it would cease publication after its August issue. However, the John D. and Catherine T. MacArthur Foundation of Chicago purchased the magazine on July 9 for an undisclosed amount from the Minneapolis Star and Tribune Company, vowing to continue publication on schedule. The Atlantic Richfield Foundation will share operating costs.

Two other venerable journals changed hands in 1980. Macro Communications Incorporated, publisher of *Financial World*, purchased *Saturday Review* on May 20, and *The Atlantic Monthly*, the 123-year-old journal of literature and public affairs, was sold in March to Mortimer B. Zuckerman of Boston.

United Marine Publishing sold three of its properties during the year. *Marine Business* was sold to Whitney Communications Corporation; *Motor-boat* went to Ziff-Davis Publishing Company; and *Sail* was purchased by Meredith Corporation. *Us* magazine, a photo-feature publication started in 1977 by The New York Times Company, was sold to Macfadden Group Incorporated.

Australian publisher Rupert Murdoch purchased *Cue* magazine from the North American Publishing Company for $5 million in a transaction announced on March 3, and merged the publication with *New York* magazine. In August, Murdoch sold *New West* to Mediatex Communications Corporation, owner of *Texas Monthly*, for $3.2 million in cash and securities.

Awards. George H. Allen, senior vice-president of CBS Publications, was named by the Magazine Publishers Association as the 1980 recipient of the Henry Johnson Fisher Award, the industry's most prestigious honor. National Magazine Awards, sponsored by the American Society of Magazine Editors, were presented in April to *Antaeus* for fiction; *GEO* for design; *IEEE Spectrum* for specialized journalism; *Mother Jones* for reporting; *Natural History* for essays and criticism; *Saturday Review* for service to the individual; *Scientific American* for a single-topic issue; and *Texas Monthly* for public service.   Gloria Ricks Dixon

In WORLD BOOK, see MAGAZINE.

MAINE. See STATE GOVERNMENT.

MALAWI. See AFRICA.

MALAYSIA emerged from the economic storms of 1980 in far better shape than most of its neighbors, with its rate of economic growth exceeding 7 per cent. A United States Embassy report in August said that even if the situation deteriorated, "The effect . . . will be essentially to reduce Malaysia from an embarrassment of riches to simple prosperity." The secret of this success lay in the recently discovered oil, which became the country's biggest export – worth about $3 billion.

Malays First. The government had launched a 20-year program in 1970 to wrest economic power from the Chinese, who make up about 35 per cent of the population. At the plan's halfway point in 1980, the Malay share of corporate capital had gone up from 2 to 14 per cent. However, most of this was held "in trust" by the government to be resold to Malays when they acquired enough cash.

The national government feared that poor Malay peasants might fall under the sway of the fundamentalist Party Islam. In October, 15 Muslim zealots armed with swords raided a police station in a southern town and wounded 23 persons before they were captured or killed.   Mark Gayn

See also ASIA (Facts in Brief Table). In World Book, see MALAYSIA.

MALDIVES. See AFRICA.

MALI. See AFRICA.

MALTA. See EUROPE.

Panorama, a slick four-color magazine directed at the selective television viewer, was launched in January by the publishers of *TV Guide*.

MANITOBA, faced with too many hydropower generators in its northern area of rivers and lakes, continued a freeze on new projects in 1980. Premier Sterling R. Lyon's Progressive Conservative administration created an energy authority charged with negotiating export contracts to sell excess power before completing facilities such as the Limestone station on the Nelson River. The five-year freeze on hydro rates was continued, and the use of gasohol, especially on farms, was encouraged through tax incentives.

The legislature adjourned on July 30 after sitting for 112 days, the longest session on record, and passing 98 bills. A bill to give Manitoba bilingual statutes was passed on July 8, following a Supreme Court of Canada ruling in 1979 that an 1890 Manitoba law limiting the use of French was unconstitutional, as was Quebec's 1977 act restricting the official use of English.

Premier Lyon protested to the United States government on June 26 against the appropriation of more funds for the Garrison irrigation project in North Dakota. He asserted that the waters redirected into Canada would bring foreign fish species and pollutants to Manitoba rivers. The U.S. Senate on June 27 appropriated $9.7 million but included a guarantee that polluting waters would not reach Manitoba. David M. L. Farr

In WORLD BOOK, see MANITOBA.

MANUFACTURING in the United States suffered severe setbacks in 1980. At the beginning of the year, industry resisted the Federal Reserve Board's late-1979 effort to tighten credit, and the board's seasonally adjusted industrial production index dropped only 0.4 points in the first quarter of 1980. However, it began a slide in April that did not end until July. At the start of 1980, the index was at 152.6 per cent of the 1967 level, and by July, it was down to 140.1.

President Jimmy Carter had resolutely announced in April that the recession would be "mild and short. . . . " He said, "We cannot reduce interest rates and we cannot make jobs secure until we get the inflation rate down." Later, economists generally agreed that the short, one-quarter recession was "policy-induced," but they noted that the policy had not achieved its goal of reducing inflation. This was true even though the stern monetary policy caused the runaway 16.8 per cent annual inflation rate, as measured by the Consumer Price Index, that prevailed the first two months of 1980 to fall to 12.4 per cent by October. Industrial production also surged upward 1.6 points in October, the sharpest advance in 2½ years. The coincidence led William B. Franklin, a reporter for *Business Week* magazine, to write in the publication's November 17 issue that "the economic recovery is in trouble. The immediate threat . . . is

the startling alacrity with which prices and interest rates are accelerating."

From the July low, industrial production rose 4 points through October, powered by increases in the steel and auto industries and more government spending for defense. But by December, new car sales had sagged again, and slow sales were predicted for the spring of 1981. This was a sharp blow to car manufacturers. Chrysler Corporation had hoped for rescue by its new K cars, and the Ford Motor Company saw its new World Car series as fuel-efficient rivals to compact imports.

The Productivity Rate, which had declined over six previous quarters, reversed that trend in the last quarter of 1980. The productivity rate measures the amount of goods and services produced in one hour of paid working time. A first estimate by the Department of Labor posted an encouraging rise of 1.4 per cent in the rate on an annual basis, but this was later revised downward to 0.3 per cent, adding further doubt about the possibility of a real recovery.

Factory Utilization declined in the course of the recession, but began to rise in August and reached 77.6 per cent of capacity in October, according to the Federal Reserve Board. While that figure was far below the 92.6 per cent peak posted in 1973, it was well above the 69.4 per cent registered in the 1975 recession.

Unemployment rose from 6.2 per cent in January to 7.8 per cent, its worst point, in May, then dropped to 7.6 per cent in November and finished the year at a steady 7.5 per cent. Average unemployment throughout 1980 ran two percentage points higher than in 1979.

First-Year Wage Increases in new labor contracts ran at a five-year high of 8.5 per cent, according to an August report from the Department of Labor. First-year wage settlements were highest in the construction industry, where increases averaged 12.4 per cent. They averaged 6.8 per cent in manufacturing, down slightly from a year earlier. See LABOR.

New Technology. Manufacturing companies turned increasingly to industrial robots to raise productivity and make them competitive with foreign plants, especially those of Japan's Toyota Motor Company and Nissan Motor Corporation. The remarkable new robots can spot-weld, paint body parts, pluck hot objects out of ovens, pick parts off a conveyor belt and chuck them into a lathe, and even run quality-control tests at high speeds. Japan had about 7,000 industrial robots working in 1980; Western Europe, about 4,000; and the United States, about 5,000. A consortium of the Japanese government and 20 major Japanese companies announced that, by 1985, Japan expected to be able to construct products with up to 300 parts by automatic means, including robots. And in the United States, a spokesman for the International Harvester Company said that it was one of several major firms that would soon use robots to lower the cost of assembling trucks, tractors, and plows.

Gulf and Western Industries Incorporated disclosed in June that it had developed a zinc-chloride battery for electric cars that promised 150 miles (240 kilometers) between recharges, speeds of more than 60 miles (97 kilometers) per hour, and a service life of 150,000 miles (241,000 kilometers). That performance was short of the potential of the molten metal batteries being developed elsewhere. Manufacturers of these claimed they compared even more favorably with the driving ranges of cars equipped with conventional batteries. But the zinc-chloride battery was expected to appear on the market first because it had the fewest technological problems. In 1979, the General Motors Corporation had reported developing a zinc-nickel battery capable of a range of 100 miles (160 kilometers) at speeds up to 50 miles (80 kilometers) per hour. Industry sources looked for large-scale electric car production as early as 1984, and expected that by 1990, 10 per cent of all cars produced would be electric.

Researchers at the University of Rochester in New York announced in September that they had developed an ultraviolet laser. They said their product would advance the development of nuclear fusion power, because it offered 80 to 90 per cent efficiency in heating the hydrogen fuel pellets required by that process, compared with about 30 per cent achieved by the infrared lasers previously in use. The researchers said the new laser might cut three to four years from the ongoing program aimed at eventually generating power from nuclear fusion.

Other advances included fiber optics to replace lenses and mirrors in copying machines; progress toward marketing computerized machines that "talk"; new word-processing equipment from the International Business Machines Corporation (IBM) to compete against other text-editing equipment that led the field; a new IBM 3081 computer with twice the computational power of its forerunner; the start of production on 65,536-bit computer memory chips; energy-saving electronic ballasts for fluorescent lights; energy-saving electric motor controls; and the increasing use of plastic composites to replace metals in springs and other active components of cars, planes, and helicopters.

Textiles and Paper. Textile industry man-hours fell eight percentage points from May to June. Contributing factors were the recession and levels of apparel imports as high as those in 1978, which

Honda Motor Company President Kiyoshi Kawashima and Ohio Governor James A. Rhodes inspect a motorcycle engine at a new plant in Marysville, Ohio.

An inspector checks economical, low-maintenance fiberglass chimney liners to be used for the first time in a power plant being built in Merom, Ind.

were the highest ever. With the dip in textile output, there was a consequent fall in the production of apparel and textile-related home furnishings. Textile exports showed an upturn in poundage of 28 per cent, however. By the third quarter, industry figures showed that mill earnings and capacity utilization were down, along with profit margins, which approached zero after taxes. The high point for the industry in 1980 was the contract J. P. Stevens and Company signed with the Amalgamated Clothing and Textile Workers Union after a 17-year battle, part of which inspired the film *Norma Rae*. See LABOR.

Paper production followed the economy downward from January to August, then picked up in the third quarter. The downtrend was lessened by unprecedented orders from the People's Republic of China for 275,000 short tons (249,000 metric tons) of paperboard and 125,000 short tons (113,000 metric tons) of paper. For the first nine months, total production rose 1.8 per cent over the same 1979 period, according to the American Paper Institute. Net sales of 23 paper companies comprising about 55 per cent of the industry ran 9 per cent or $24.1 billion higher, though comparable earnings were lower by 9.5 per cent or $1.3-billion. Despite the uncertain economic picture, the Mead Corporation announced a $270-million expansion of its Escanaba, Mich., plant.

Electrical Equipment manufacturing fared better than most U.S. industries in 1980. The giants of the industry, the General Electric Company and Westinghouse Electric Corporation, both posted earnings increases for the third quarter, though the industry as a whole scored a 4.1 per cent real decline. The only absolute increase was in medical-equipment sales, which rose 4.7 per cent. The National Electrical Manufacturers Association projected a rise of 3.3 per cent in sales for 1981 for products in all categories.

Machine Tool Orders continued firm with a $5.5-billion order backlog despite a drop from August through October. Wholesale revamping of factories in several major industries, which will demand new computer-assisted machinery to achieve productivity rates competitive with foreign industry, accounted for optimism at the September industry trade show. A spokesman for the National Machine Tool Builders Association said that the industry will increase its capacity 50 per cent by the end of 1982 to meet the demand. Technologically, the industry backtracked from direct numerical control, in which all machines are controlled by a central computer, toward computer numerical control, in which smaller computers are interfaced with individual machines.

The Bendix Corporation introduced a small manual data-input system that enables smaller machine shops to do their own programming, as did several other companies. Imports continued to make inroads, with Japanese and West German machines accounting for an estimated 30 per cent of the machinery purchased, up from 22 per cent in 1979 and about 10 per cent in 1970.

Tire Production fell with lagging auto sales. Firestone Tire and Rubber Company was the hardest hit, with five tire plants closed in the United States and Canada. Uniroyal Incorporated took the highly unusual step of persuading its workers to accept a 12.9 per cent pay reduction in 1980 and another 6.5 per cent cut in 1981. The industry was hurt by the turn toward smaller cars using smaller tires that are less profitable, lighter cars that cause less wear on tires, and radial-ply tires that last longer and delay replacement sales. Akron, Ohio, long known as the tire city, had only one operating tire plant in 1980 – that of the General Tire Company. Akron's rubber industry, which employed some 50,000 persons in 1950, employed fewer than 22,000 in 1980.   George J. Berkwitt

In WORLD BOOK, see MANUFACTURING.

MARINE CORPS, U.S. See ARMED FORCES.

MARYLAND. See STATE GOVERNMENT.

MASSACHUSETTS. See STATE GOVERNMENT.

MAURITANIA. See AFRICA.

MAURITIUS. See AFRICA.

MAYOR. See CITY.

MEDICINE. The world's fourth "test-tube" baby – Candice Elizabeth Reed, born on June 23, 1980, in Melbourne, Australia – was the first to be born by normal vaginal delivery. Louise Brown, the first baby conceived in a test tube, was delivered by a Caesarean (abdominal) section in 1978, as were the following two test-tube infants.

The first U.S. test-tube-baby clinic opened under the auspices of the Eastern Virginia Medical School in Norfolk in January. Although the program triggered some controversy, thousands of women sought to participate in the research. Physicians at the clinic attempted to implant fertilized eggs into the wombs of women who were unable to conceive naturally, but no births were reported in 1980.

Cancer Report. The American Cancer Society (ACS) and the National Cancer Institute reported in 1980 that the rate of cancer in the United States began to rise for the first time in 25 years, with a 9 per cent increase among white males and a 14 per cent increase among white females. But they also reported that more people diagnosed as having cancer were surviving for longer periods and that 2 million Americans had lived for five years or more after diagnosis. Survival rates improved substantially for patients with seven of the 10 major forms of cancer: bladder, breast, uterine cervix, colon, endometrium, prostate, and rectum.

Preliminary reports showed that interferon, a natural antiviral agent being tested by the ACS, is effective in treating various cancers in the United States, but not to the extent reported in Sweden. European and American researchers announced in January that they had used gene-splicing techniques to synthesize human interferon. This advance would make available large amounts of interferon, which has been expensive and difficult to obtain, should it prove effective against cancer.

Four major medical centers began trials of Laetrile, an apricot-pit derivative used as a controversial cancer remedy, under the supervision of the National Institutes of Health. Laetrile was to be given to 200 cancer patients "for whom no other treatment has been effective."

The Food and Drug Administration on September 10 approved the use by cancer patients of an active ingredient in marijuana, delta-9-tetra-hydrocannabinol (THC). THC relieves the nausea and vomiting that often accompany chemotherapy.

Physicians at three Boston hospitals and the Harvard University Medical School reported in August that acute myelogenous leukemia, a blood cancer, had yielded to treatment with a combination of powerful drugs and either removal of the spleen, a blood-producing organ, or injection of leukemia cells from other patients. Although few

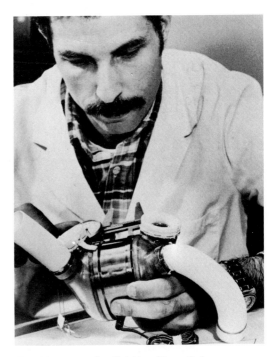

Electricity-powered artificial heart is readied for its first test on a calf. A similar device may be implanted in a human patient by 1990.

Physician Jack Moncrief of Austin, Tex., demonstrates the portable dialysis system he helped develop for kidney patients.

victims survived in the past, researchers estimated that as many as one-third of patients might be saved because of the new treatments.

Heart Disease. Medical technology and research produced a new device that may save the lives of thousands of heart patients who would otherwise die suddenly because of cardiac arrest. In such cases, an internal electrical disorder usually triggers ventricular fibrillation, a fluttering that cuts off blood flow to the brain. In August, a team of physicians in Baltimore unveiled a miniaturized defibrillator that responds to severe changes in the heartbeat by administering a shock that restores normal beating. The device, as big as a cigarette pack, is implanted under the skin on the abdomen. It proved effective in treating six patients, but still is considered experimental.

The role of diet in heart disease was hotly debated during the year. A report issued by the Food and Nutrition Board of the National Research Council (NRC) in May 1980 stated that reduced cholesterol levels in the diet do not significantly reduce the chances of developing atherosclerosis, or hardening of the arteries, which can lead to death by heart failure when the heart cannot receive enough nourishment. Medical wisdom has long prescribed a low-cholesterol diet as a means of avoiding heart attacks. The NRC is influential because it sets the Recommended Daily Allowances for nutritive substances such as vitamins. But the American Heart Association and other groups took sharp issue with the NRC report. To fend off heart disease, it is necessary to limit cholesterol intake, keep weight down, and limit or eliminate alcohol and tobacco consumption, they declared.

Transplant Surgery. The International Congress of the Transplant Society hailed the 1980s as a decade when more kidneys, pancreases, hearts, and bone marrow cells would be transplanted than ever before—and with far better results. One reason for the optimism is cyclosporin A, a new drug that has been shown to be a powerful suppressor of the body's natural urge to reject a transplanted organ.

Researchers at the University of California, San Francisco, reported in April another method of improving the success rate for kidney transplants—first giving the patient blood transfusions from the person donating the kidney. The transfusions desensitized the recipient's immune system and led to long-term acceptance of donated kidneys in all but one of the patients in the first trial of the procedure.

Eye Surgery. The U.S. National Advisory Eye Council urged "restraint on the part of patients and eye surgeons" regarding operations on the cornea to improve vision. Soviet surgeons have developed a technique called radial keratotomy involving more than a dozen cuts into the cornea, extending from the outer edge toward the center, to flatten the cornea and cure *myopia* (near-sightedness).

Professional Issues. For the first time in 23 years, the American Medical Association (AMA) voted in July to change its code of ethics. The AMA voted to drop a long-standing ban on physician advertising (a move ordered by the Federal Trade Commission) and strengthened the confidentiality of the physician-patient relationship. The delegates also took a stand against the use of physicians to administer drug injections for capital punishment, noting that the profession is "dedicated to preserving life when there is hope of doing so."

Federal agencies in April predicted an oversupply of doctors by 1990, but they disagreed about how many. The Congressional Office of Technology Assessment estimated 185,000 too many. But the Department of Health and Human Services – formerly the Department of Health, Education, and Welfare – estimated about 5,000.

Scientists at the Massachusetts Institute of Technology reported they had successfully used different types of "test-tube" skin on patients with burns and wounds. They cultured skin cells from the patients' healthy tissue in the laboratory and then grafted the lab-grown tissue as if it were transplanted skin. Dianne Hales

See also HEALTH AND DISEASE; PUBLIC HEALTH. In WORLD BOOK, see MEDICINE.

MENTAL HEALTH. President Jimmy Carter signed into law on Oct. 7, 1980, the Mental Health Systems Act. The new law initiates a major reorganization of federal aid programs for mental health services. It is designed to shift mental health care from institutionalizing patients in large hospitals to treating them as outpatients in community-based programs. It identifies the population groups deemed to be in greatest need of care and gives the states more flexibility in providing grants to serve those groups. The act provides for special treatment programs to aid children and adolescents, chronically ill mental patients who are not hospitalized, and older people.

The American Psychiatric Association (APA) published the third edition of the *Diagnostic and Statistical Manual of Mental Disorders (DSM III)*, the standard source for evaluating mental problems. Unlike previous editions, *DSM III* puts psychiatry on the same diagnostic footing as other medical specialties and classifies psychiatric disorders according to their symptoms. It was developed to ensure more precise and uniform diagnosis.

Positron emission transaxial tomography (PETT), a radiology technique that spots regions of abnormal brain activity, showed promise as a diagnostic tool in tests at several medical centers. PETT monitors a chemical with radioactive atoms as it passes through the brain, thereby revealing biochemical changes in the brain, including abnormalities characteristic of such serious mental illnesses as schizophrenia and manic depression. Still experimental, PETT may help psychiatrists confirm a diagnosis, particularly when the symptoms of two or more disorders overlap.

Patients' Rights. In several decisions, the Supreme Court of the United States clarified some issues related to involuntary commitment to a mental institution. The high court ruled in March that prisoners have the same constitutional protections as other citizens when an attempt is made to commit them to mental hospitals – specifically, the right to a formal hearing prior to commitment. The Supreme Court also ruled that involuntary commitment is legal on the basis of a psychiatrist's professional evaluation, but that there must be "clear and convincing" evidence of the need for institutionalization.

A federal district court in Boston ruled that committed and voluntary mental patients have a constitutional right to refuse psychoactive drugs prescribed for them. The decision was appealed by the psychiatrists involved, who argued that mental patients are not competent to decide on their own therapies.

Research on Depression. Mental health professionals reported new insights into depression, a problem so widespread that it is often termed "the common cold of mental health." In clinical trials in the United States and elsewhere, trazadone, a new antidepressant drug, yielded promising results. It provided therapeutic benefits more quickly than current medications and with fewer side effects.

Researchers reported at the APA meeting in May that altered sleep patterns can reveal the severity of depression. Depressed patients enter rapid eye movement (REM) sleep, the stage when dreaming occurs, much faster after falling asleep than healthy people do. The shorter the period between sleep onset and REM, the more severe the problem may be. By monitoring this period after treatment is begun, physicians may get an indication of whether an antidepressant drug is working.

There also was a resurgence of interest in electroconvulsive shock therapy (ECT) as a treatment for depression. A New York study, reported at the APA meeting, showed that – contrary to widespread belief – ECT is not used most frequently on poor and minority patients in public institutions. On the contrary, its recipients tend to be middle-class patients treated privately. Psychiatrists reported that because of improvements in technique and equipment, ECT is much safer than it was several decades ago and that it may help up to 80 per cent of those patients who do not respond to other treatments. Dianne Hales

See also DRUGS; HEALTH AND DISEASE. In WORLD BOOK, see MENTAL HEALTH.

Mexican President Jose Lopez Portillo, attended by Prime Minister Pierre Trudeau, addresses a joint session of the Canadian Parliament in May.

MEXICO. Using its vast new-found oil resources as a lever, Mexico in 1980 sought to establish itself in world affairs as a power to be reckoned with while simultaneously formulating a foreign policy based on self-interest and expressing Mexico's independence of the United States.

President Jose Lopez Portillo had been criticized in the past for aligning his administration too closely with U.S. economic interests. In 1980 alone, U.S. corporations had invested more than $1 billion in Mexican enterprises. Now, President Lopez Portillo was clearly trying to set Mexico on its own course as an economic and political entity. The main thrust of Mexico's new policy became apparent during a visit by Japanese Prime Minister Masayoshi Ohira from May 2 to 4. Ohira hoped to persuade Mexico to increase its oil exports to Japan by 100,000 barrels per day by the end of 1980. In return, Mexico extracted a guarantee of $204.5 million in financial aid over three years.

Economic Pacts. On May 28, Lopez Portillo completed a 12-day journey to France, West Germany, Sweden, and Canada. At each stop, he made it clear that in return for an increase in Mexican oil exports to each of the countries, Mexico expected reciprocal concessions. Its trading partners were expected to cooperate in joint ventures in Mexico and thus help convert the country's oil earnings into industrial development.

France was reportedly ready to help in refurbishing Mexico's ports, extending Mexico City's subway, and participating in constructing a railroad across the Isthmus of Tehuantepec. West Germany expressed willingness to build a plastics plant in Mexico, with a majority interest to be held by Mexicans. In Sweden, details were worked out for joint industrial projects in Mexico involving steel, mining, petrochemical, and pulp and paper manufacturing, as well as electric power production. Canada promised to supply Mexico with $430-million in credit to purchase capital equipment.

On July 27, Lopez Portillo began visits to several Western Hemisphere countries. In Brazil, he urged that Latin American countries work together to improve their future because of the slowness with which the superpowers respond to their development needs. Brazil's President Joao Baptista de Oliveira Figueiredo promised increased trade in exchange for more Mexican oil for his rapidly industrializing country.

In Costa Rica, Lopez Portillo joined with Venezuelan President Luis Herrera Campins in a pledge to supply Central American and Caribbean nations – hard hit by high oil prices – with more than 160,000 barrels of oil per day under a bargain arrangement. These countries would have the option of five-year loans at 4 per cent interest on 30 per cent of this oil. If they subsequently developed alternative sources of energy, and thus were able to help conserve world oil supplies, the loans could be converted into 20-year loans at 2 per cent interest.

U.S. Relations. Mexico's relations with the United States, which had been strained by Mexico's refusal in 1979 to permit the ailing Shah Mohammad Reza Pahlavi of Iran to re-enter Mexico from the United States, remained cool. There were other causes as well. Mexico rejected membership in the General Agreement on Tariffs and Trade – an international measure strongly backed by the United States and aimed at reducing barriers to the free flow of trade.

There were intermittent threats to "Mexicanize" or force U.S. corporations active in food processing and pharmaceutical production to divest themselves of majority interests in Mexican operations. Mexico itself did little to stem the tide of its citizens who were illegally entering the United States in search of jobs (see IMMIGRATION).

In his annual address to the Mexican people on September 1, President Lopez Portillo vowed to fight inflation, reduce government spending, and reduce income taxes for lower-paid workers. During 1980, Mexico's proven oil reserves rose to 60.1 billion barrels, and the country became the world's fifth-largest oil producer. Nathan A. Haverstock

See also LATIN AMERICA (Facts in Brief Table). In WORLD BOOK, see MEXICO.

MICHIGAN. See DETROIT; STATE GOVERNMENT.

MIDDLE EAST

The black smoke of war rises from Abadan,
Iran, to frame a lone Iraqi soldier on the
battleground of an ancient Mideast feud.

War between Iran and Iraq, coming on the heels of Russia's invasion of Afghanistan, brought more turmoil in 1980 to an area already divided by Egyptian-Israeli peace negotiations and unsettled by the revolutionary Islamic ferment in Iran. Higher oil prices, along with a reduction in Middle East oil production due to the war, underlined the region's critical importance in world affairs, both as a focus of major power interests and as a factor in the global economy.

The war with Iraq, though marked by a rise in Iranian patriotic feeling, further isolated the regime of Ayatollah Ruhollah Khomeini internationally and was an important factor in Iran's long-delayed decision to begin serious negotiations for the release of 52 American hostages held since November 1979 in Iran (see IRAN). But President Jimmy Carter's failure to gain the release of the hostages, along with apparent ineptness in dealing with Iran — as symbolized by the failure of the

U.S. Air Force F-4E jet fighters fly past the pyramids after arriving in Cairo for joint training exercises with Egyptian forces.

military rescue mission in April — contributed to his defeat in the November presidential election (see ARMED FORCES).

Ironically, Russia was no more able than the United States to advance its interests in the region, either before or as a result of the Iran-Iraq war. Russia found its options limited because of its heavy involvement in Afghanistan, which was strongly opposed by almost all Middle Eastern nations. The United States was hampered by the hostage issue and its inability to pressure Israel effectively to settle the Palestinian rights question as defined broadly in the 1978 Camp David agreements. As a result, a new balance of global forces began to emerge in the Middle East, one in which regional states could initiate actions independent of superpower influence.

Afghan Adventure. The steady Russian military build-up in Afghanistan drew heavy criticism from Islamic as well as Western nations. Russia justified its invasion under a Soviet-Afghan mutual defense treaty signed on April 5, claiming that Soviet troops were in Afghanistan to aid a legitimate government under attack by "counterrevolutionaries" backed by outside powers. Few countries outside the Soviet bloc agreed, and in November even Communist Romania publicly condemned the Russian invasion. The foreign ministers of the Islamic states, meeting in Pakistan in May, de-manded the immediate withdrawal of Soviet troops and declared the Afghan government of Revolutionary Council President and Prime Minister Babrak Karmal "illegal." But despite casualties and determined resistance from Afghan *mujahideen* (fighters for Islam) opposed to a hated atheistic regime, the Russians dug in firmly for a long stay.

American Strike Force. The U.S. need to ensure oil shipments from the region and counter Soviet influence led to new agreements during the year with Egypt, Oman, Somalia, and Kenya for bases to supplement the existing U.S. naval base at Bahrain. The U.S. began to develop a Rapid Deployment Strike Force to mount emergency military operations in the Middle East, and the first units were airlifted to Egypt in November to begin joint maneuvers with Egyptian forces. The action was intended to back up Carter's declaration that the Persian Gulf was an area of vital U.S. national interest.

French Moves. With both major powers hamstrung by their own policies and by circumstances, France and other European countries moved into the vacuum. With fine impartiality, France provided arms to Iran and Iraq, and in October concluded an agreement with Saudi Arabia for $3.4 billion in warships, missiles, and other weapons.

Another and potentially more dangerous aspect of French policy emerged in August with the delivery of enriched uranium ore – originally from Niger and Morocco – to the Iraqi nuclear research center at Tammuz, near Baghdad. A French-Iraqi nuclear pact also provided that France would furnish the services of 70 French technicians and a completed reactor. After an air strike on Tammuz – presumably by Iranian planes – on September 30, the French technicians were evacuated. However, Iraq's capability to separate the uranium ore to produce a bomb remained.

Inter-Arab Relations. Although it pitted the Arab Iraqis against non-Arab Iranians, the war further divided the Arab states into competing blocs. Ironically, the monarchies of Morocco, Jordan, and Saudi Arabia, normally opposed to the Baathist Socialist government of President Saddam Hussein, backed Iraq. Libya, Syria, and Yemen (Aden), though politically aligned with Iraq, opposed the war as contrary to Arab interests and Islamic solidarity. Iraq broke diplomatic relations with Libya and Syria on October 11 and accused them of supplying arms to Iran. Saudi Arabia broke relations with Libya.

Morocco sent medical teams to Iraq. King Hussein I of Jordan opened the port of Al Aqabah for shipments of French and Russian military equipment after the Iraqi port of Umm Qasr was put out of commission by Iranian air attacks. The materiel was trucked overland in Jordanian vehicles.

In a further complication of the muddled situation, Syria began massing troops on its Jordanian border in November. The move coincided with a meeting of the Arab League in Amman, which Syria and its allies boycotted, thus preventing united Arab support for Iraq. As its border build-up approached 35,000 troops and 1,200 tanks, Syria accused Jordan of harboring members of the militant Muslim Brotherhood, dedicated to the overthrow of Syrian President Hafiz al-Assad.

Hussein responded by massing Jordanian troops and tanks. An international mediation effort, led by Saudi Arabia, cooled the crisis.

The Saharan Struggle. The alignment of Morocco's King Hassan II with other Arab monarchs behind Iraq brought Morocco some advantages in its struggle to control the Western Sahara. In May, Saudi Arabia contributed $232 million toward the cost of U.S. F-5 jets and helicopter gunships released by the Congress of the United States to upgrade Morocco's military hardware. The new equipment enabled the Moroccan Army to shut off supply routes into Algeria used by the Polisario guerrillas fighting for an independent Sahara Arab Democratic Republic (SADR), and to drive the guerrillas from mountain hideouts.

But Morocco's military success was not matched in the political arena. In July, a drive led by Algeria, Libya, and several other Arab-African states at the Organization of African Unity (OAU) conference came within three votes of electing SADR to full membership as a sovereign state.

Under Leader of the Revolution Muammar Muhammad al-Qadhafi's vigorous if controversial leadership, Libya pursued active foreign policy efforts in other areas. A purge of antigovernment exiles abroad, ordered by the Libyan leader, resulted in the June assassination of several Qadhafi foes. After the murders, the French, British, and Italian governments deported Libyan diplomats.

In November, Libyan forces invaded northern Chad, supposedly in support of Chad's President Goukouni Weddeye against his chief rival, former Defense Minister – and Libyan protegé – Hissen Habre. The OAU was called into emergency session. In December, 2,000 Libyan soldiers supported by air power reached N'Djamena, the capital, and forced a cease-fire. See CHAD.

The Gulf States. Fallout from the Iran-Iraq war and related regional instability reached the normally tranquil oil-rich states of the Arabian Peninsula. Early in the year, Emir Jabir Al-Ahmad Al-Sabah of Kuwait issued a decree calling for general elections for a new National Assembly, but the vote was canceled after the war broke out.

A decree issued in September prohibited foreign contracting firms from hiring workers from other countries. Kuwait wanted to limit its large and potentially subversive foreign-labor force. Student demonstrations protesting high gasoline prices in the seven-member United Arab Emirates (UAE) in February forced a further delay in ratification of a new UAE constitution.

Government Changes. With three exceptions, the various regimes of the region survived the year relatively intact. The major change was in Turkey, where the army high command seized power on September 12. The action forestalled a complete breakdown in law and order brought about by the inability of Prime Minister Suleyman Demirel's government to deal with political terrorism and economic problems. Parliamentary freedoms were suspended and an interim Cabinet of officers and technicians was formed to govern under the overall authority of a National Security Council of senior military commanders.

By November, some 11,500 persons had been arrested, including leaders of several political parties and deputies of the Grand National Assembly. Most of them were soon released, however. Military leaders declared they acted to save the nation and intended to restore civilian parliamentary government as soon as possible. See TURKEY.

A smooth transition of power took place in Tunisia as Education Minister Mohamed Mzali was named in April by President Habib Bourguiba to succeed the aging Prime Minister Heidi Nouira, who was incapacitated by a stroke. The new leader's main problem was to restore public confidence in the ruling Destour Socialist Party and encourage wider political participation within the limits of the single-party state. See TUNISIA.

In Yemen (Aden), Supreme People's Council Presidium Chairman Abd al-Fatah Ismail resigned in April and went into exile in Moscow. He was succeeded by Council of Ministers Chairman Ali Nasir Muhammad. The Marxist-Leninist Aden regime's strong attachment to Russia continued, but the new head of state also went to such former adversaries as Saudi Arabia and the UAE in search of aid for Yemen's depressed oil-less economy.

Arab-Israeli Conflict. The border between Egypt and Israel was formally opened on January 26. Other far-reaching changes resulting from the 1979 Egyptian-Israeli peace treaty included the exchange of ambassadors, and civil aviation and tourism agreements. By September, some 6,000 Israeli tourists had visited Egypt. But the hoped-for exchanges of agricultural and technical experts and business leaders were slow to develop.

The unresolved issue of Palestinian self-determination remained the main obstacle to full observance of the peace treaty. Although ostracized by most of the other Arab countries for his contacts with Israel, Egypt's Anwar el-Sadat continued to support Palestinian autonomy and Israeli withdrawal from occupied Arab territories.

Israeli Prime Minister Menachem Begin's government was equally adamant, defending the es-

Facts in Brief on the Middle East Countries

Country	Population	Government	Monetary Unit*	Foreign Trade (million U.S. $)	
				Exports†	Imports†
Bahrain	302,000	Amir Isa bin Salman Al-Khalifa; Prime Minister Khalifa bin Salman Al-Khalifa	dinar (1 = $2.65)	2,416	2,046
Cyprus	661,000	President Spyros Kyprianou	pound (1 = $2.90)	456	1,001
Egypt	42,636,000	President & Prime Minister Anwar el-Sadat; Vice-President Mohamed Hosni Moubarek	pound (1 = $1.45)	1,840	3,837
Iran	37,989,000	President Abol Hasan Bani-Sadr; Prime Minister Mohammad Ali Rajai	rial (70.4 = $1)	19,307	7,261
Iraq	13,611,000	President Saddam Hussein	dinar (1 = $3.41)	11,064	4,213
Israel	3,996,000	President Yitzhak Navon; Prime Minister Menachem Begin	shekel (7 = $1)	4,553	7,471
Jordan	3,253,000	King Hussein I; Prime Minister Mudhar Badran	dinar (1 = $3.25)	402	1,949
Kuwait	1,431,000	Emir Jabir Al-Ahmad Al-Sabah; Crown Prince & Prime Minister Saad Al-Abdullah Al-Sabah	dinar (1 = $3.67)	17,748	5,352
Lebanon	2,687,000	President Elias Sarkis; Prime Minister Shafiq al-Wazzan	pound (3.6 = $1)	626	1,400
Oman	927,000	Sultan Qaboos bin Said	rial (1 = $2.90)	2,284	1,387
Qatar	176,000	Amir & Prime Minister Khalifa bin Hamad Al-Thani	riyal (3.6 = $1)	3,598	1,425
Saudi Arabia	8,487,000	King & Prime Minister Khalid ibn Abd al-Aziz Al Saud	riyal (3.3 = $1)	59,359	20,424
Sudan	19,152,000	President & Prime Minister Gaafar Mohamed Nimeiri	pound (1 = $2.02)	533	1,198
Syria	8,933,000	President Hafiz al-Assad; Prime Minister Abd al Ra'uf al-Kassem	pound (3.9 = $1)	1,634	3,301
Turkey	46,073,000	Head of State Kenan Evren; Prime Minister Bulend Ulusu	lira (84.8 = $1)	2,261	4,946
United Arab Emirates	1,041,000	President Zayid bin Sultan Al-Nahayyan; Prime Minister Rashid ibn Said al-Maktum	dirham (3.7 = $1)	12,793	5,874
Yemen (Aden)	2,031,000	Supreme People's Council Presidium Chairman & Council of Ministers Chairman Ali Nasir Muhammad	dinar (1 = $2.89)	221	544
Yemen (Sana)	6,070,000	President Ali Abdallah Salih; Prime Minister Abdul Karim al-Iryani	rial (4.4 = $1)	7	1,283

*Exchange rates as of Dec. 1, 1980. †Latest available data.

tablishment of Jewish settlements in the West Bank as necessary to Israel's security and refusing to deal with the Palestine Liberation Organization. A further problem developed in July as the government acquiesced in a resolution by the Israeli *Knesset* (parliament) making all of Jerusalem Israel's permanent capital. In November, the Knesset proposed to annex part of the Golan Heights, Syrian territory occupied in the 1967 Arab-Israeli war. See ISRAEL.

Israel's hard line caused Sadat to suspend the autonomy negotiations three times, the last time in July after the Knesset declaration on Jerusalem. Although the negotiations were resumed in September with U.S. help, the talks were deadlocked.

The United Nations tried to play an active role in the various Middle East crises, but with only minor effect. It adopted a resolution on January 14 censuring Russia for its Afghan intervention. The Security Council on March 1 approved Resolution 465 declaring that Israel's policies in establishing settlements in occupied Arab territories since 1967 were illegal, and the General Assembly voted 112-7 for Israel to begin withdrawing from the West Bank and Jerusalem by November 15. See UNITED NATIONS. William Spencer

In WORLD BOOK, see MIDDLE EAST and individual country articles.

MINING. Geologists with the United States Bureau of Mines reported in July 1980 that they may have uncovered evidence of a vast mineral belt that may stretch for miles along the rugged north slope of the Brooks Range in Alaska. They discovered deposits of lead, zinc, and silver in three different parts of the region, which is about 200 miles (320 kilometers) northeast of Kotzebue and 120 miles (190 kilometers) north of the Arctic Circle. The bureau's analysis of material taken from surface and stream sediments found some of the mineral deposits to be high grade.

Strategic Resources. Members of the House Subcommittee on Mines and Mining returned in August from a three-week investigation in southern Africa to warn that the United States could become involved in a "mineral war" over that region's rich deposits of such key resources as manganese, cobalt, chromium, and platinum. The United States imports virtually all of its supply of these critical materials. The subcommittee found that a supply disruption due to political instability or Russian intervention in southern Africa would cause serious defense and social problems for the United States and its allies. Yet, Subcommittee Chairman James Santini (D., Nev.) said, the United States is doing little politically to protect its interests in southern Africa.

A newly developed computer simulator trains workers to operate the continuous mining machines that now handle most underground mining.

William J. Perry, undersecretary of defense for research and engineering, told the subcommittee in April that Congress should rebuild the national defense stockpile of strategic minerals. Supplies of 93 key minerals kept in the stockpile now average about 50 per cent below government goals. The stockpile is supposed to contain sufficient raw materials for the United States to wage a three-year conventional war, even though cut off from foreign sources of supply. However, it now contains only an 18-month supply, valued at $13 billion. An additional $6 billion would be needed to restore critical materials to capacity.

Too Much Molybdenum? A potential oversupply of molybdenum was forecast in 1980. The once-scarce metal is used to strengthen stainless, tool, and other alloy steels and is expected to be a key ingredient in the high-temperature alloys needed to build America's synthetic fuels industry. Production of molybdenum had remained virtually static for several years at about 200 million pounds (90 million kilograms) per year in non-Communist countries.

Standard Oil Company of Indiana, for example, revealed a $300-million project to produce about 18 million pounds (8 million kilograms) per year in Custer County, Idaho. The mine will be fully operational by the mid-1980s. Five other firms said they would expand present capacity or open new molybdenum mines, adding another 80 million pounds (36 million kilograms) of production by 1983. Still other projects were under consideration in Alaska, Colorado, Washington, and Chile.

Uranium Surpluses plagued the domestic and world uranium-mining industry, as well. The Commodities Research Unit, a British consulting firm that specializes in minerals, said that intense prospecting during the mid-1970s led to discovery of many new uranium mines that are ready to begin production — just when demand from the nuclear power industry has slowed. If all the currently available mines were brought into production, the annual world uranium supply could reach almost 300 million pounds (140 million kilograms) by 1990. Demand for uranium in 1990, in contrast, is expected to range between 140 million and 200 million pounds (65 million and 90 million kilograms) per year.

A cable on an elevator car snapped on March 27 at the Vaal Reefs gold mine in Orkney, South Africa, killing 31 miners who plunged about 1.2 miles (2 kilometers) to the bottom of a shaft. The mine, about 100 miles (160 kilometers) southwest of Johannesburg, is the world's largest. Michael Woods

See also COAL. In WORLD BOOK, see MINING.

MINNESOTA. See STATE GOVERNMENT.

MISSISSIPPI. See STATE GOVERNMENT.

MISSOURI. See STATE GOVERNMENT.

MONACO. See EUROPE (Facts in Brief Table).

MONDALE, WALTER FREDERICK (1928-   ), 42nd Vice-President of the United States, traveled extensively on state and political business during 1980. Mondale acted as President Jimmy Carter's chief policy spokesman at home and abroad early in the year. Later, he campaigned widely for the unsuccessful Carter-Mondale ticket (see ELECTIONS).

While President Carter remained in Washington, D.C., to deal with the problem of the Americans held hostage in Iran, Mondale headed the U.S. delegation to the funeral of President Josip Broz Tito in Belgrade, Yugoslavia, on May 8. He toured western Africa from July 17 to July 23, signing an agreement with Vice-President Alex Ekwueme of Nigeria to increase trade and investments between the two countries.

Policy Spokesman. The Vice-President made more than 100 speeches and held some 200 news conferences and receptions during the first three months of the year. He announced on January 7 that the United States government would buy up some $2.25 billion in grain contracts that American farmers had negotiated with Russia before the Carter Administration ordered an embargo on grain shipments to that country. The embargo was imposed to express U.S. disapproval of the Soviet invasion of Afghanistan in December 1979. As an additional protest against the Russian invasion, Mondale suggested on January 10 that the 1980 Summer Olympic Games be moved from Moscow.

Mondale was also a frequent spokesman for United States policy on Israel. On March 4, he defended as an honest mistake the U.S. vote in favor of a United Nations Security Council resolution calling upon Israel to dismantle its settlements in the West Bank and Gaza Strip. President Carter had disavowed the vote on March 3. On October 15, Mondale announced a U.S.-Israeli agreement by which the United States would guarantee Israel's oil supply in times of shortage or soaring prices.

Mondale met with President Carter and Lane Kirkland, president of the American Federation of Labor and Congress of Industrial Organizations, on May 2 to discuss economic topics. He traveled to Detroit on July 7 to lay the groundwork for President Carter's conference with industry and labor officials on the nation's ailing auto industry.

Campaign Travels. Delegates to the Democratic Party's National Convention on August 14 confirmed President Carter's selection of Mondale as his running mate. During the course of the election campaign, Mondale often made four or more appearances a day. Despite his defeat on November 4, Mondale was mentioned as a 1984 Democratic presidential contender. Carol L. Thompson

In WORLD BOOK, see VICE-PRESIDENT OF THE UNITED STATES.

MONGOLIA. See ASIA.

MONTANA. See STATE GOVERNMENT.

MOROCCO. The Moroccan Army gradually won control of the Western Sahara from Algerian-backed Polisario guerrillas during 1980. The army's effort was aided by new military equipment bought from the United States, including $232.5-million worth of F-5 fighter-bombers and helicopter gunships. In May, after a series of reverses, tank units relieved the besieged garrison at Zag, near the Algerian border. An all-out campaign brought the key Ouarkiz mountain range under Moroccan control, with guerrillas forced out of their mountain strongholds into the open desert.

Vigorous prosecution of the war assured King Hassan II of continued popular support. A national solidarity tax to pay war costs was over-subscribed. In July, Hassan released 100 political prisoners as a further move toward national unity.

In May, voters approved a constitutional amendment lowering the age of majority to 16. Another new amendment provides that if a king dies and the future king is not yet 16, a regency council will rule until he is of legal age.

Phosphate exports reached a record 20 million short tons (18 million metric tons), but the continued shutdown of Saharan mines hampered Morocco's economic development.   William Spencer

See also AFRICA (Facts in Brief Table). In WORLD BOOK, see MOROCCO.

MOTION PICTURES. The motion-picture industry experienced a disappointing year in 1980, and the various economic and aesthetic developments did not hold great promise for the coming decade. Although the early 1970s had marked an end to the industry's 25-year economic decline, with revenues increasing steadily from 1971 through 1978, it now seemed that this upward trend was reversing itself.

Attendance and production were on the decline throughout the world, and in some instances, drastically so. Italy, for example, had suffered a 35 per cent decrease in ticket sales over three years and a 40 per cent decrease in the number of domestically made features. The situation was almost as bleak in Great Britain and France. The major exceptions to the rule were West Germany, where admissions in 1980 were 5 per cent ahead of those for 1979, and Australia, where film production certainly was thriving if the box office was not.

Over a single decade, the Australian film industry had grown from one or two productions a year to about 20. Australia had also begun to emerge as a significant force on the international film scene and, together with West Germany, was the source of the year's most acclaimed and popular foreign imports in the United States.

Australian Success. The most successful of these Australian films was *My Brilliant Career*, an adapta-

The character Oskar drums his protest against life in Germany in the 1930s in the Oscar-winning film *The Tin Drum,* based on a novel by Günter Grass.

Just before his life falls apart, Tommie Lewis
as Jimmie brings home a bride in
Australia's *The Chant of Jimmie Blacksmith.*

tion of an autobiographical 1904 novel concerning
a spirited young woman's choice of career over
marriage, which earned about $2 million at the
U.S. box office. Put together by an almost exclusively female crew, the film had a strong feminist
edge that, more than its quaint atmosphere and
delightful star Judy Davis, seemed a key to its
popularity. Similarly adapted from an autobiographical turn-of-the century novel about a gifted
young woman was Bruce Beresford's *The Getting of
Wisdom*, but it lacked the charm and thematic
relevance of *My Brilliant Career.* Making considerably more impact was Fred Schepisi's *The Chant of
Jimmie Blacksmith*, a powerful adaptation of Thomas
Kenneally's novel dealing with an Aborigine's
violent war with the white society around him.

Far and away the most popular West German
import was Volker Schlondorff's *The Tin Drum*, an
accomplished adaptation of Günter Grass's novel,
a disturbing allegory focusing on a boy named
Oskar who deals with the rise of Nazism in Germany in the 1930s by refusing to grow. Like *My
Brilliant Career*, *The Tin Drum* garnered some $2-
million in U.S. box-office receipts. More important, perhaps, it won the Academy of Motion
Picture Arts and Sciences Oscar for Best Foreign
Film, the first German work to be so honored.

Much more controversial was Hans Juergen
Syberberg's *Our Hitler*, a highly stylized seven-hour

film that was necessarily programmed in the United States as a special event. Also from West
Germany, where Swedish director Ingmar Berg-
man now resides, was his *From the Life of the
Marionettes*, which ranked among his lesser efforts.

Reviews were mixed for Akira Kurosawa's *Kagemusha*, a pictorially stunning but dramatically dull
epic from Japan, and Jean-Luc Godard's Swiss-
made *Every Man for Himself*, a black comedy. Still,
as this important New Wave director's first feature
in many years, *Every Man* received considerable
attention, as did another French-language feature,
Alain Resnais' *Mon Oncle d'Amerique*, an attempt to
explore the workings of the human psyche.

Hollywood's Offerings. The interest generated
by these imports—intermittent as it may have
been—at least helped to make up for the lackluster
quality of American productions. During the first
half of the year, only two U.S. films of any distinction were released: *Coal Miner's Daughter*, a biography of country singer Loretta Lynn featuring an
exceptional performance by Sissy Spacek, and
Fame, a musical celebration of New York City's
High School of Performing Arts. The box office
suffered accordingly, dropping 10 per cent below
1979 levels in the spring and 15 per cent during the
usually thriving summer months.

What made the economic picture seem even
worse was that 25 per cent of all summer receipts
were for a single film—*The Empire Strikes Back*—
which, despite its mixed critical reception, was, as
a sequel to *Star Wars*, assured of audience interest.
The only other summer box-office winners were
The Blue Lagoon, a glossy exploration of teen-agers
discovering sex on a deserted island, and two
low-budget productions: *Airplane*, a spoof on disaster pictures that grossed about $75 million against
its $2 million cost; and *Friday the 13th*, a tasteless
horror film that earned $42 million against a
$1.5-million outlay.

Otherwise, one commercial disappointment followed another, including many films featuring
high-priced stars whose presence had hitherto
signaled sure-fire box office. These included: *Bronco
Billy*, starring Clint Eastwood; *Rough Cut*, starring
Burt Reynolds; *Brubaker*, starring Robert Redford;
and *Urban Cowboy*, featuring John Travolta. Also
box office disasters, when costs were counted, were
those films whose music and stars were clearly
designed to attract the teen-age audience, such as
The Blues Brothers, with John Belushi and Dan
Ackroyd, and *Can't Stop the Music* with the Village
People and Valerie Perrine.

Analyzing the Box Office. Faced with all this failure, industry analysts began to speculate on the
reasons for it. They suggested the recession, inflated ticket prices, a release pattern in which too
many films were opened at once, and poor advertising campaigns. But none seemed quite so per-

suasive as the fact that nearly all of the films released early in 1980 were of inferior quality. However, from late August through December, quite a number of films of considerable interest were released, and the box office picked up.

Brian De Palma's Hitchcock-influenced *Dressed to Kill* was criticized by many for its violence and careless plotting, but was hailed by others as a genuinely effective thriller. *The Big Red One*, Sam Fuller's seriocomic exploration of World War II, was praised highly by critics, though it made a poor showing at the box office. Tony Bill directed *My Bodyguard*, a film about city high school students that earned praise. Also well-received was *Ordinary People*, actor Robert Redford's first effort as director. Based on Judith Guest's best seller about the emotional tensions within an upper-middle-class suburban family, the film starred popular television actress Mary Tyler Moore, Donald Sutherland, and Timothy Hutton.

Less successful with audiences but even more celebrated by critics were Jonathan Demme's *Melvin and Howard*, a comedy focusing on Melvin Dummar (played by Paul Le Mat), the gas-station attendant named heir to a fortune by eccentric billionaire Howard Hughes (very well portrayed by Jason Robards); and Richard Rush's playful study of illusion and reality, *The Stunt Man*, featur-

ing Peter O'Toole in an inspired performance as a genius movie director.

Also noteworthy was *The Elephant Man*, another retelling, distinct from the Broadway play, of the story of tragically disfigured John Merrick in Victorian England. Martin Scorsese's *Raging Bull* was dismissed by some critics for its extreme violence but applauded by others for its intensity and fine characterization. Detractors and admirers alike agreed, however, on the brilliance of Robert De Niro's performance as Jake La Motta, one-time middleweight boxing champion.

Despite the relative success of these films, the year was still more memorable for its problems and disappointments than for its achievements. Brilliant director Stanley Kubrick had, with his adaptation of Stephen King's best-selling thriller, *The Shining*, come up with his most unsatisfactory work to date; and the same was true of Woody Allen, whose *Stardust Memories*, a blatantly autobiographical and self-conscious lament over the director's creative agonies, was also a disappointment. The most significant failure, however, was *Heaven's Gate*, Michael Cimino's $40-million Western epic, which proved so incoherent that it was taken out of circulation for re-editing immediately after its New York City première.

Unnerving the entire industry, the withdrawal of

The Empire Strikes Back, sequel to *Star Wars*, continues the adventures in space of such popular characters as Han Solo, right, and Princess Leia.

Chris Makepeace, in front, and Adam Baldwin
stand ready to face the bullies in
their Chicago high school in *My Bodyguard.*

Heaven's Gate was a historical first; it was also a sadly appropriate capstone to the generally dismal year. Despite the gains made in the early fall, it seemed clear that the year's total gross in the United States would run about $40 million behind 1979's, without any adjustment for inflation. More telling, the number of admissions dropped an estimated 7 per cent in 1980. Aggravating the situation was the skyrocketing cost of motion-picture production—which was up some 15 per cent from 1979 and a startling 65 per cent from 1978—with the average film costing about $10-million and thus requiring a gross of about $40-million to recoup its investment.

Television's Shadow. With costs so high and the box office so unsteady, it was evident that the industry would have to find other sources of revenue for its productions. The trend had begun already, with more and more films depending on secondary markets to ensure their profits. These included book and record tie-ins, fees from video-cassette and tape sales, and, above all, sales to network television. These subsidiary markets were encouraging to those concerned with films as commerce, but deeply disturbing to those concerned with film as art.   Joy Gould Boyum

See also AWARDS AND PRIZES (Arts Awards); FIELD, SALLY; HOFFMAN, DUSTIN; LANSING, SHERRY. In WORLD BOOK, see MOTION PICTURE.

MOZAMBIQUE. President Samora Moises Machel announced on March 18, 1980, that his government would reduce its role in the nation's economy and revive private industry, inviting foreign business to invest. He pledged to return small businesses to private hands and to see that nationalized businesses turned a profit. Under his plan, the state would retain some control over major industries and housing, health, and education programs.

The new program, a reversal of the nation's socialist policy, signaled an attempt to halt the economic decline that began when Mozambique became independent from Portugal in 1975. Some 250,000 Portuguese, many of them businessmen and professionals, fled the country then. Machel invited the Portuguese to return and, as evidence of his conciliatory attitude, appointed five whites to his Cabinet.

A serious drought hindered the nation's economic recovery. In late August, the Ministry of Agriculture made an emergency appeal to foreign governments for food and medicine.

The government announced on July 10 that the army had attacked a camp of rebel soldiers, killing 272 and capturing more than 300. The rebels were identified as members of a counterrevolutionary group of about 4,000 formed in 1975.   J. Dixon Esseks

See also AFRICA (Facts in Brief Table). In WORLD BOOK, see MOZAMBIQUE.

MUGABE, ROBERT GABRIEL (1924-   ), became prime minister of Zimbabwe on April 18, 1980, the day that nation, formerly called Rhodesia, gained independence from Great Britain. Mugabe's party won a landslide victory over eight other political factions in February parliamentary elections. A black and an avowed Marxist, Mugabe brought whites into his government and vowed not to interfere with personal property. See ZIMBABWE.

Mugabe was born on Feb. 21, 1924, in the village of Kutama in northern Rhodesia. He received his early education from Roman Catholic missionaries and attended the University of Fort Hare in South Africa and University of South Africa. He taught school in Rhodesia and Ghana during the 1950s.

He became publicity secretary of the National Democratic Party, an organization devoted to gaining civil rights for blacks in white-ruled Rhodesia, in 1960. As a result of his party activities he served a 10-year prison sentence.

Following his release from prison in 1974, Mugabe recruited a guerrilla force to fight against the Rhodesian government. With an estimated 18,000 troops based in Mozambique, he conducted raids that helped to force the white majority government to relinquish much of its power.

Mugabe is married to Sarah Hayfron, a former Ghanaian schoolteacher.   Beverly Merz

MUSEUM. Political and natural events took their toll on museums during 1980. The United States Department of State, expressing national displeasure with the Russian invasion of Afghanistan, refused on January 21 to grant the customary "waiver of judicial seizure" to a major traveling exhibit, "Art from the Hermitage Museum in Leningrad." The waiver would have protected the Russian state-owned art treasures from seizure in U.S. courts. As a result, Russia canceled the exhibit, which was to open at the National Gallery of Art in Washington, D.C., in May.

Ash from the eruptions of Mount Saint Helens in Washington that began in May endangered precious specimens in many museums in the Pacific Northwest. Many museums sealed their windows and upgraded their ventilation systems to filter the ash, which was high in silica, adding to the danger of abrasion. The Yakima Valley Museum closed for 10 days while crews cleared the area. A November earthquake forced Italian officials to close the ancient Roman ruins of Pompeii to the public.

The Institute of Museum Services (IMS), founded by the Congress of the United States in 1976, reported on its survey of U.S. museums in October. Its survey showed that about 74 per cent of the almost 5,500 museums in the U.S. are small, with annual operating budgets under $100,000.

IMS found that nearly half of all U.S. museums were founded after 1960. Nearly half are private, nonprofit organizations, and 35 per cent are run by state or local governments. About 50 per cent of U.S. museums are history museums.

On September 7, the Department of Education announced that IMS grants totaling $10.5 million had been given to 405 U.S. museums during fiscal 1980. About $9.5 million of this was used for operating expenses; the rest, for special projects.

Budget Troubles. The fiscal 1981 budget submitted to Congress by President Jimmy Carter in January had a number of increases scheduled for museum services, including a 27 per cent increase in the National Endowment for the Arts Museum Program. But executive and congressional budget trimming later cut many museum appropriations.

New Exhibits. The American Wing of New York City's Metropolitan Museum of Art, with period rooms portraying life in America and examples of American painting, opened in June. In Great Britain, "Man's Place in Evolution" opened in May at the British Museum (Natural History), and a new London Transport Museum, depicting the history of one of the oldest transit systems in the world, opened in March.   Edward G. Nash

See also VISUAL ARTS. In WORLD BOOK, see MUSEUM.

The 1824 facade of the United States Branch Bank adorns one end of the new American Wing of New York City's Metropolitan Museum of Art.

MUSIC, CLASSICAL

The 1980 musicians' contract dispute at New York City's Metropolitan Opera highlighted a growing problem in the music world: How can musicians better their status, pay, and working conditions at a time when deficit-burdened managements increasingly resist all change in order to keep their organizations solvent?

The pressure has been building for years. Artists, with unions to back them, have sought to improve their financial position, to reduce the pressures of their demanding schedules, and to capture an esteem enjoyed by members of other professions, such as doctors, lawyers, and university professors. The battle was waged with less publicity in other cities. It was fought in Chicago early in 1980 when the Lyric Opera faced unhappy orchestra players. Their argument over working conditions lasted so long that the fall season had to be shortened.

Virtuosos of the Cleveland Orchestra went on strike for a better contract and got it. So did the North Carolina Symphony. The New Jersey Symphony and the Kansas City Philharmonic were shut down for extended periods. The Denver orchestra's season was canceled on November 4 after musicians turned down an offer involving improved salary and work schedules. The season was reinstated in December when the issues were resolved.

The Metropolitan Opera situation, however, focused attention on the problem. Serious trouble in an establishment of international repute brings with it the international press coverage that results in broader public involvement and a careful watch by managers of orchestras and opera and ballet companies elsewhere.

The immediate result, however, was the cancellation of the Met season on September 29. For millions of radio listeners, the weekly Met broadcasts were stilled and for thousands of New Yorkers and tourists, the Metropolitan was dark.

President Jimmy Carter expressed concern, urging the American Federation of Musicians and the Met management to solve their differences. He dispatched a federal mediator to move the combatants toward settlement. Even such highly placed external pressure did not work.

The Stumbling Block was the workweek. Orchestra members wanted parity with a handful of the most prestigious symphonies in the United States — four performances per week instead of five. Since an opera house such as the Met normally gives more operas per week than an orchestra gives concerts, management argued that such a reduction would force them to hire extra musicians, creating an expense beyond their ability to pay.

A compromise was reached. It involved fewer performances but additional rehearsal hours. No one was completely satisfied, but there was joy in the thought that the agreement made possible the reinstatement of the Met season.

Then came another snag. The Met management had expected its 16 other unions to agree quickly to their own contracts, and most did — even the sometimes temperamental stagehands. But the members of the hard-working chorus decided to seek equality of pay with the orchestral players and to get their workweek shortened. Their union, the usually more pliable American Guild of Musical Artists, took a hard line. Pressure from the unions that had settled finally forced the choristers to say yes on November 13, and the Met season opened on December 10 with, not an opera, but Gustav Mahler's *Symphony No. 2,* "Resurrection."

Musical Imports. Music critic Irving Kolodin highlighted another aspect of status for musicians at the annual gathering of the American Symphony Orchestra League in June. He charged that U.S. conductors are being denied job opportunities in their own country. Kolodin noted that recently named conductors in Denver (Gaetano Delogu); Cincinnati, Ohio (Michael Gielen); Minneapolis, Minn. (Neville Marriner); and Philadelphia (Riccardo Muti) are all from Europe. "To put it bluntly," Kolodin said, "Americans have to work as hard, concentrate as much as their European opposites, and then pray for someone to get sick in order to have the kind of opportunity that came to Leonard Bernstein in New York."

The import trend continued with the naming of Varujian Kojian to the Utah Symphony podium and Akira Endo to head the Louisville Orchestra. Kojian was born in Lebanon and Endo in Taiwan.

Muti's appointment in Philadelphia, the most important change of the year, gained attention for another reason. He succeeded Eugene Ormandy, who had led that orchestra for 44 years.

Special Anniversaries. Other people and companies marked noteworthy anniversaries. Revered American composer Aaron Copland celebrated his 80th birthday. In numerous cities, orchestras and dance companies feted him by performing his works. At New York City's Carnegie Hall in November, Copland and Bernstein shared the podium for an all-Copland program by the American Symphony Orchestra. Composers Samuel Barber

New and dazzling, Louise M. Davies Symphony Hall will house the San Francisco Symphony and visiting musical groups and concert artists.

and William Schuman marked their 70th birthdays, and violinist Isaac Stern celebrated his 60th year with special events highlighted by his appearance with the New York Philharmonic with his protégés Itzhak Perlman and Pinchas Zukerman.

Washington's National Symphony celebrated its 50th year; the Baltimore Opera marked its 30th; and the Houston Opera, its 25th. The Boston and St. Louis symphonies commemorated their 100th anniversaries.

But the anniversary that topped them all belonged to Los Angeles – not the orchestra but the city itself, which celebrated its 200th birthday. For that occasion, another city – West Berlin – sent dozens of musicians and musical groups as well as William Dieter Siebert's opera, *The Sinking of the Titanic*, which had its American debut in November. Far from being a routine production, this work required that the opera house – in this case a theater on the University of California, Los Angeles, campus – be turned into a ship and that the audience become the passengers who must flee.

Hail and Farewell. It was Luciano Pavarotti's year. The Italian tenor became a national idol in the United States and something of an industry, as well. People wore "Pavarotti for President" buttons. They gathered 150,000 strong for a summer concert in New York City's Central Park. They cheered him far more than they did the marching presidential candidates Jimmy Carter and Ronald Reagan when he played Columbus on horseback in New York City's Columbus Day parade in October. And Hollywood beckoned to Pavarotti. He signed a contract to make a film, a romantic comedy called *Yes, Giorgio*.

For Beverly Sills, the year marked a milestone. The soprano was honored with a farewell gala at the New York City Opera in late October. She would sing no more, she said – at least in public – and would give full attention to her new duties as director of the New York City Opera. But before she sang that farewell, she teamed for the first time with another famed soprano, Australia's Dame Joan Sutherland, in a San Diego Opera production of Johann Strauss's *Die Fledermaus*.

Tours were made by the National Symphony (to South America) and the Los Angeles Philharmonic (to Europe). For the San Francisco Symphony and for the city whose name it bears, there was a new home for music; the Louise M. Davies Symphony Hall opened in September with a series of special concerts, the first featuring the world première of David del Tredici's *Happy Voices*.

New Musical Sounds were heard elsewhere. World premières by major symphony orchestras included Jacob Druckman's *Prism* (Baltimore); *Fanfare* by Bernstein (Boston); Richard Manners' *Concerto for Violin and Orchestra* (Chicago); *Discantus II/Favola Boccaccosca* by R. X. Rodriguez (Dallas);

New Boston Pops Director John Williams applauds android C3PO after the mostly metal conductor led the Pops in the theme from *Star Wars*.

Ned Rorem's *Double Concerto for Piano and Cello* (Cincinnati); Matthias Bamert's *Keepsake for Orchestra* (Cleveland); *Akhenaten* by Gene Gutchë (Milwaukee); Krzysztof Penderecki's *Symphony Number 2* and Schuman's *French Horn Fantasy* (New York City); Del Tredici's *In Memory of a Summer Day*, for which the composer won the Pulitzer Prize (St. Louis); and *The Gift of Thanksgiving* by Norman Symonds (Toronto, Canada).

Among the new works for the operatic stage in 1980 were John Eaton's *The Cry of Clytaemnestra* (University of Indiana in March); and *Rosina* by Hiram Titus (Minnesota Opera in April), which continued the story told in Gioacchino Antonio Rossini's *Barber of Seville* and Wolfgang Amadeus Mozart's *Marriage of Figaro*. Jean-Michel Damase's *L'Héritière*, an operatic version of *The Heiress*, the well-known dramatization of Henry James's novel *Washington Square*, was introduced in Paris in September. The New York City Opera premièred three works on one October evening; *An American Trilogy* includes *Madame Adare* by Stanley Silverman, *Before Breakfast* by Thomas Pasatieri, and *The Student from Salamanca* by Jan Bach.

Important U.S. premières included Arnold Schoenberg's *Von Heute auf Morgen* by the Santa Fe Opera and Antonio Vivaldi's *Orlando Furioso* by the Dallas Civic Opera.   Peter P. Jacobi

In WORLD BOOK, see MUSIC.

MUSIC, POPULAR. John Lennon, 40, who helped found the Beatles, one of the most successful musical groups in history, was shot to death on a New York City street on Dec. 8, 1980. Lennon, a rock guitarist and composer, had just resumed his career with a new album, "Double Fantasy," after five years in retirement. See Close-Up.

Vocal duets, many of them by couples with diverse backgrounds, became best sellers in the United States during 1980. A hit record by Kenny Rogers and Kim Carnes, "Don't Fall in Love with a Dreamer," led to an avalanche of records by such couples as Barbra Streisand and Barry Gibb, Roy Orbison and Emmylou Harris, Billy Preston and Syreeta, Neil Sedaka and his daughter Dara, Glen Campbell and Rita Coolidge, and Glen Campbell and Tanya Tucker.

After the throbbing sound of disco gave way briefly to the hard-driving rhythms of new-wave rock, the motion picture *Urban Cowboy* created a new phenomenon. Discos throughout the United States began to drop the rock sounds in favor of country-flavored songs. Country discos complete with mechanical bulls or horses became the rage in such urban centers as Chicago, as well as in the South and West. The film also revitalized the career of Mickey Gilley as a country singer. His nightclub was used in *Urban Cowboy.*

The music of Minnie Riperton, a singer who died of cancer in 1979, was the subject of a unique experiment. Twenty months after her death, the backgrounds were erased from the tape for an unreleased Riperton album. New rhythms and vocalists were substituted, featuring such artists as Stevie Wonder, Michael Jackson, Peabo Bryson, George Benson, Tom Scott, and Hubert Laws. The result was a best-selling album.

Comedian George Burns made his disk debut at 84 and scored a big hit with "I Wish I Was 18 Again." Frank Sinatra ended his long absence from the recording studios and completed a three-record set, "Trilogy," from which one song, "Theme from New York, New York," climbed up the charts.

Motion-Picture Music, which had enjoyed a peak of popularity in the 1950s and 1960s, showed renewed strength, with scores from *Urban Cowboy, Xanadu, One-Trick Pony, Roadie, The Blues Brothers, Honeysuckle Rose, The Empire Strikes Back, Fame, Caddyshack,* and a punk-rock score, *Times Square.*

Pink Floyd, the venerable British rock band, established a record when its LP "Dark Side of the Moon," first released in 1973, stayed on the charts for more than 302 consecutive weeks, surpassing Carole King's "Tapestry." Elton John gave a free concert in September in New York City's Central Park, attracting 400,000 fans.

New Artists arose from various schools of music — new-wave performers Pat Benatar and the B-52s, soft-rock specialists Robbie Dupree and Christo-

pher Cross, melodic rockers Air Supply, and soul singer Irene Cara, who was helped by an appearance in the film *Fame.* Gospel music began to move into the secular field. Bob Dylan's "Saved" blended rock with an evangelical feeling; the Commodores included a pure gospel tune in an album; and such major record companies as CBS, Warner Brothers, and MCA, Incorporated, entered the field and sought such contemporary gospel artists as Andrae Crouch and James Cleveland. The latter at one time had eight albums among the top 35, including one with Albertina Walker and one with Aretha Franklin.

In the popular instrumental field, the appearance of flügelhorn and keyboard soloist Chuck Mangione at the Olympic Winter Games, televised on ABC-TV, helped publicize his theme song, "Give It All You've Got." The number was heard every evening on television and was released as a commercial disk.

Striking Musicians, members of the American Federation of Musicians, halted television and motion-picture production on July 21 (see TELEVISION). Several record companies went to West Germany, the Netherlands, and other countries, where local musicians did the work the striking Americans refused to do. Most overseas musicians agreed not to allow U.S. projects in their countries.

Singer Johnny Cash reached two milestones in 1980 – 25 years of music making and his admission to the Country Music Hall of Fame.

Death of a Poet

John Lennon (1940-1980)

Assassination is a term usually reserved for the act that puts a swift and violent end to the life of a head of state. When a confused young man with a pistol assassinated John Lennon on Dec. 8, 1980, he killed the head of a state of mind.

The worldwide outpouring of grief that followed Lennon's tragic murder focused on the fact that he articulated the aspirations and frustrations of a generation. Lennon was the "brain" of the Beatles, the remarkable rock music group that took the world by storm after a Feb. 8, 1964, appearance on the Ed Sullivan television show. He composed songs that fundamentally affected the attitudes of adolescents. Along with fellow Beatles Paul McCartney (his collaborator on most of the songs), Ringo Starr, and George Harrison, Lennon was a prime mover in what came to be called the "counterculture." The long-haired, barefoot "flower children" who seemingly arose spontaneously all over the world gave form to the freewheeling fantasies of the lads from Liverpool.

John Winston Lennon was born in Liverpool, England, on Oct. 9, 1940, to Julia and Alfred Lennon. A creative child who wrote and illustrated his own stories, Lennon learned to play the guitar and formed his first rock group, the Quarrymen, in 1956. By 1960, it became the Beatles.

Lennon married Cynthia Powell in 1962 and in 1963 they had a son, Julian. After a divorce, he wed Yoko Ono in 1969. They had a son, Sean, in 1975.

As Lennon and his generation grew up and the world changed, many of his songs became classics. "Yesterday" was very far away on December 14 when all the lonely people paid a final silent tribute to the man who told them that "All You Need Is Love."   Marsha F. Goldsmith

Pop singers Linda Ronstadt and Rex Smith make their operetta debuts in Gilbert and Sullivan's *The Pirates of Penzance* in New York City.

Changes. Kiss, the rock band whose members cover their faces with makeup, lost drummer Peter Criss, who organized his own group. But Kiss found a replacement and managed to keep its personality intact.

Led Zeppelin, which had planned its first U.S. tour since 1977, was struck by tragedy on September 24 when drummer John Bonham, 32, was found dead in England. The group postponed the tour and announced in December that it would disband.

Two of music's most talented songwriter-producers, the husband-and-wife team of Nick Ashford and Valerie Simpson, moved out of the recording studios long enough to show their skills as concert performers. The couple continued writing and recording their own albums while writing and producing for other artists.

Many of the more mature popular singers who rose to fame in the 1950s and 1960s found themselves virtually shut out of the mainstream of recording. With rare exceptions, such as Frank Sinatra, they relied on personal appearances, but were conspicuously absent from the recording studios. Some of them continued to earn five-figure weekly salaries at Nevada casinos. Among them were Shirley Bassey, Tony Bennett, Vic Damone, Billy Eckstine, Eydie Gorme, Engelbert Humperdinck, Frankie Laine, Steve Lawrence, Andy Williams, and Lena Horne, who announced her retirement in 1980.

Jazz continued its upward trend in the United States and elsewhere, in concert halls, at festivals, and on records — virtually everywhere except commercial television, where jazz artists were seldom seen. Jazz singer Angela Bofill, a newcomer, enjoyed great successes at the Playboy Jazz Festival and other jazz events, though critics questioned her credentials. Bofill, like many young jazz vocalists and instrumentalists, was considered part of the jazz-rock fusion world, which gained an ever-stronger foothold during 1980. Such figures as pianist-composer Bob James and trumpeter Tom Browne crossed over into the popular music charts.

Avant-garde artists enjoyed an upsurge in popularity at such events as the Newport Jazz Festival, though their record sales were tiny by comparison. Violinist Leroy Jenkins and a group known as the World Saxophone Quartet, who played without a rhythm background, made a strong impact. The Art Ensemble of Chicago gained enough fame through its records to earn a tour of Australia in January. Mainstream and other jazz forms were represented in a series of summer concerts at the Hollywood Bowl.   Leonard Feather and Eliot Tiegel

See also AWARDS AND PRIZES (ARTS AWARDS); RECORDINGS. In WORLD BOOK, see HORNE, LENA; JAZZ; POPULAR MUSIC; ROCK MUSIC.

MUSKIE, EDMUND SIXTUS (1914-   ), was named secretary of state by President Jimmy Carter on April 19, 1980. Muskie succeeded Cyrus R. Vance, who resigned in opposition to Carter's decision to attempt a military rescue of U.S. hostages in Iran. A leader in the Democratic Party, Muskie served 22 years in the United States Senate. See CABINET, UNITED STATES.

Edmund Muskie was born in Rumford, Me., on March 28, 1914. His father, a tailor, emigrated from Poland and changed the family name from Marcizewski. Muskie graduated from Bates College in Lewiston, Me., in 1936 and from Cornell University Law School in 1939. After serving in World War II, Muskie established a law practice.

In 1946, Muskie became one of the few Democrats elected to the Maine House of Representatives. He was elected governor of that heavily Republican state in 1954, was re-elected in 1956, and in 1958 became Maine's first popularly elected Democratic senator. He was the Democratic candidate for Vice-President in 1968 and campaigned unsuccessfully for the Democratic presidential nomination in 1972.

Among his former Senate colleagues, Muskie is regarded as something of a paradox — a moderate man with a hair-trigger temper.

Muskie married Jane Gray in 1948. They have five grown children.   Beverly Merz

NAMIBIA, Africa's last remaining colonial territory, moved haltingly toward independence in 1980. It has been the subject of a United Nations (UN) independence plan since 1978.

Negotiations early in the year whittled away at a major obstacle to the UN independence plan — regulation of a cease-fire between Namibian black nationalist guerrillas, known as the South West Africa People's Organization (SWAPO), and South African security forces. Both sides agreed to a demilitarized zone 31 miles (50 kilometers) wide on either side of Namibia's borders with Angola and Zambia, two nations in which SWAPO forces have bases. SWAPO forces were prevented from crossing the zone, and South Africa was assigned bases inside Namibia to monitor the cease-fire.

However, South Africa objected on August 29 to UN supervision of the cease-fire and subsequent elections on the grounds that the UN was likely to favor SWAPO. Brian E. Urquhart, a UN under-secretary-general, flew to South Africa in October to convince its government of UN impartiality, and established a cease-fire beginning March 1981. As the war between black nationalists and South Africa continued, an estimated 823 guerrillas and 73 South African soldiers were killed in the first nine months of the year.   J. Dixon Esseks

See also AFRICA (Facts in Brief Table). In WORLD BOOK, see NAMIBIA.

NATIONAL PTA (NATIONAL CONGRESS OF PARENTS AND TEACHERS) in 1980 presented its first television awards to the producers of 10 shows. The programs honored were "Little House on the Prairie," "Prime Time Saturday," "60 Minutes," "The Waltons," "20/20," "Eight Is Enough," "Quincy," "Salvage-1," "White Shadow," and CBS Specials.

A five-year PTA project to increase public awareness of the need for comprehensive school-community health education resulted in four Student Health Education Forums planned and run by students.

The Urban Education Action Plan entered its second phase with attention focused on financing public education, parental and community participation in schools, and youth unemployment. The PTA hopes to establish coalitions among groups and individuals in urban areas to address these problems. At the 1980 National PTA Convention held in Honolulu, Hawaii, in June, plans were made to study the problem of maintaining discipline in the schools.   Virginia E. Anderson

In WORLD BOOK, see NATIONAL CONGRESS OF PARENTS AND TEACHERS; PARENT-TEACHER ORGANIZATIONS.

NAVY. See ARMED FORCES.

NEBRASKA. See STATE GOVERNMENT.

NEPAL. See ASIA.

Princess Beatrix becomes the queen of the Netherlands on April 30, the 71st birthday of her mother, Queen Juliana, who abdicated.

NETHERLANDS. Queen Juliana abdicated her throne on April 30, 1980, her 71st birthday, after ruling for 31 years. Her daughter, Crown Princess Beatrix, 42, succeeded her (see BEATRIX). Beatrix' investiture on April 30 was marred by a skirmish between police and stone-throwing youths protesting a housing shortage. Areas of central Amsterdam became a battleground as police used batons and tear gas; about 100 persons were injured.

The rioting was typical of Amsterdam throughout 1980. On March 3, some 1,100 police used tanks to clear blazing barricades, and on September 8, squatters and their supporters fought police. About 10,000 squatters lived in Amsterdam, most of them in abandoned office buildings near the city's center. Amsterdam also had about 55,000 persons listed as homeless, but any action to remove squatters provoked immediate violence.

Government Survives. Prime Minister Andreas A. M. Van Agt's shaky coalition government barely survived two crises. Finance Minister Frans Andriessen resigned suddenly on February 20 because of a disagreement on public spending cuts. Andriessen's resignation threatened to wreck the Cabinet, but Van Agt held to his position and prevented the collapse. On June 27, the coalition defeated by two votes a censure motion brought against it for refusing to impose a unilateral oil embargo against South Africa. The government claimed that the embargo would have been disastrous for landlocked Zimbabwe, which uses oil that South Africa imports.

Wages Policy. A government proposal to extend a wage freeze that was due to end on March 10 provoked a nationwide strike of 500,000 persons on March 4. Transportation, telephone service, and the mail were disrupted. But despite union opposition, the lower house of Parliament passed a bill on March 6 enabling the government to freeze wages until January 1982 and cut $1.6 billion from the 1980 budget. On September 16, however, Queen Beatrix used the words "incomes moderation" rather than "income freeze" in the Speech from the Throne, a policy speech traditionally written by the prime minister and read by the monarch.

Pope John Paul II summoned the seven Dutch bishops of the Roman Catholic Church to the Vatican on January 14 to discuss limits of theological research, the celibacy of the clergy, and other issues that had caused a gradual drift of the Dutch Roman Catholic Church from Rome. The bishops agreed to accept the provisions of a 22-page document that bound the church to strict principles. The pope appealed to Dutch Catholics on January 31 to support this agreement. Kenneth Brown

See also EUROPE (Facts in Brief Table). In WORLD BOOK, see NETHERLANDS.

NEVADA. See STATE GOVERNMENT.

NEW BRUNSWICK. The leadership of Premier Richard B. Hatfield, who has headed a Progressive Conservative (PC) administration since 1970, was called into question in 1980 after a three-month trial involving an allegedly corrupt fund-raising scheme. The case began when a Fredericton lawyer was convicted of having planted an employee in a government department in order to gain information about companies bidding on provincial contracts. It was suggested that these companies were later approached for contributions by PC officials. Despite the conviction, the lawyer was given an absolute discharge on August 1 because the judge said that he did not entirely believe testimony given by a number of key witnesses at the trial, including Hatfield.

The legislature adjourned on July 17 after approving 84 bills, one of which gave its members a 33 per cent salary increase. The budget presented on March 25 called for a 14 per cent increase in spending and totaled $1.78 billion. New Brunswick's economic growth in 1980 was estimated at 2 per cent. David M. L. Farr

See also CANADA. In WORLD BOOK, see NEW BRUNSWICK.

NEW HAMPSHIRE. See STATE GOVERNMENT.

NEW JERSEY. See STATE GOVERNMENT.

NEW MEXICO. See STATE GOVERNMENT.

NEW YORK. See NEW YORK CITY; STATE GOV'T.

NEW YORK CITY progressed steadily in 1980 toward a full economic recovery from its near-bankruptcy in 1975. City officials announced on November 23 that the city was almost certain to have a budget surplus estimated at from $100-million to $300 million for the fiscal year that began on July 1.

The projected surplus was attributed to higher tax revenues – particularly from sales and income taxes – than expected when the budget was presented in July. These tax revenues increased as inflation accelerated. The city's major expense – employee salaries – did not increase as rapidly as revenues because union contracts had fixed most wages below the inflation rate.

The size of the surplus also depended upon how much of the $170 million in state and federal aid, already budgeted as income, would actually be forthcoming. However, the city was assured $300-million in federal loan guarantees.

Wage Settlements. An 11-day strike of city transit workers, which shut down the bus and subway system, was settled on April 11. The resulting contract provided wage and cost-of-living increases totaling more than 20 per cent over two years.

The city also negotiated two-year contracts with 242,000 municipal employees, effective on July 1. A June 19 settlement with a coalition of unions allowed a wage increase of 16 per cent for teachers,

Rush-hour traffic takes on a different look as pedestrians and cyclists jam the Brooklyn Bridge during an 11-day transit workers strike in April.

413

office workers, and other nonuniformed personnel over the life of the contract, and a July 3 settlement gave uniformed workers a 17 per cent increase.

The New York City Board of Education approved a $251-million budget for the coming school year on August 27. It entailed cutbacks of $124.8 million, requiring layoffs of at least 2,200 teachers – the first such reduction to take place since the mid-1970s.

City construction director Charles M. Smith, Jr., reported in November that spending on construction and repair of streets, sewers, and bridges had increased 46 per cent since 1979. Mayor Edward I. Koch announced plans on July 17 to build a waterfront community of stores, offices, restaurants, theaters, apartments, and a marina on the East River between 16th and 18th streets.

Census Settlement. U.S. District Judge Henry F. Werker ruled on October 6 that the 1980 census figures can be statistically adjusted to accommodate an undercount of some 800,000 New York City residents. Preliminary census estimates showed a population loss of 1 million since 1970, and city officials feared the low count would result in the loss of more than $1 billion in federal aid and as many as four congressional seats. Werker's ruling was set aside on December 30.   James M. Banovetz

See also CITY. In WORLD BOOK, see NEW YORK CITY.

NEW ZEALAND continued to struggle with economic difficulties in 1980, though prospects looked brighter because of energy- and forestry-industry expansion. Export prices for agricultural products improved, with a combined total for meat, wool, dairy, and other animal products of $3.2 billion. The government concluded long-term arrangements with the European Community (EC) for the sale of dairy products and sheep meats. Forest product exports brought in $455 million.

The loss of population, mainly to Australia through emigration, declined from a 1979 peak of 40,000 to about 15,000 persons, and 1979's net population loss was not repeated. However, unemployment rose steeply to 60,000 persons, or about 2 per cent of the population, its highest level since the 1930s, though still low by world standards. Inflation remained at a high 16.3 per cent at the end of September, and real output declined slightly.

Economic Strategy. The government eased controls on imports, foreign investment, and prices; enacted new export incentives; and moved toward a closer trading relationship with Australia. It also undertook a major analysis of the textile industry. The 1980 budget raised sales taxes on many goods and services and gave some income tax concessions. It was expected that government expenditure in fiscal 1980-1981 would increase by 18 per cent to stimulate economic activity.

Energy projects approved in 1980 emphasized the domestic production of liquid fuels, based largely on domestic natural gas resources, to replace imports and to provide export income. A major plant to produce methanol was planned.

The merger of three of the country's largest corporations – the Challenge, Fletcher, and Tasman groups – created New Zealand's largest business enterprise. The new conglomerate has interests in manufacturing, forestry, and construction.

Political Dissatisfaction with Prime Minister Robert D. Muldoon led to an unsuccessful attempt to remove him from the leadership of his center-right National Party. It also resulted in the Social Credit Party scoring an upset by-election victory in a previously safe National Party seat, and so increased its representation in Parliament to two seats. The government appointed a Royal Commission of Inquiry to investigate allegations of favoritism in the granting of a Marginal Lands Board loan to the family of Minister of Agriculture Duncan MacIntyre. A similar commission probed the evidence used to convict Arthur Allan Thomas, who was found guilty in two trials of a 1970 double murder but was subsequently pardoned by the government. In November, the commission awarded Thomas more than $1 million.   David A. Shand

See also ASIA (Facts in Brief Table). In WORLD BOOK, see NEW ZEALAND.

NEWFOUNDLAND waited in 1980 for confirmation that the Hibernia exploratory well on the Grand Banks could unlock the largest oil reserves in Canada. The drillers estimated that the field might contain 10 billion barrels of oil and probably could produce more than 20,000 barrels per day. Development of the field awaited resolution of the constitutional quarrel between Newfoundland and the federal government over its ownership.

A five-week strike of inshore fishermen ended on August 22 with a tentative agreement on new catch prices. A commission was set up to investigate the processing companies' alleged inability to pay more for fish. Each year, 12,000 fishermen in 500 coastal ports take part in the fishing.

The legislature adopted a provincial flag on May 26. Newfoundland artist Christopher Pratt designed the flag, which consists of six triangles and an arrow in red, blue, and gold on white.

The Viking settlement of L'Anse aux Meadows on Newfoundland's northern tip, a Canadian national park since 1978, became the first World Heritage Site on July 11. Occupied 1,000 years ago, the site represents the first point of contact between Europeans and North American native people and the first place in North America at which iron was worked.   David M. L. Farr

See also CANADA. In WORLD BOOK, see NEWFOUNDLAND.

NEWSPAPER companies in the United States scrambled for television cable franchises and other new communication outlets during 1980 as electronic news delivery became a reality. Knight-Ridder Newspapers began distributing information via teletext in July to some 200 families in Coral Gables, Fla.

In March, the New York Times Company bought two contiguous cable systems with 55 franchises in New Jersey, reportedly for more than $110 million, and Dow Jones & Company, publishers of *The Wall Street Journal*, discussed plans to provide two-way news-retrieval service to two Dallas suburbs. In this service, subscribers can use their home computer terminals to respond to newspaper advertisements. In July, Associated Press, the *Columbus* (Ohio) *Dispatch*, and several other metropolitan dailies agreed to distribute news through CompuServe, an Ohio computer firm.

Business Transactions occupied many newspapers' agendas throughout the year. The Times Mirror Company of Los Angeles agreed to pay $95 million for the *Denver Post* on October 22; industrialist Joseph E. Cole purchased *The Cleveland Press* for a reported $20 million on October 31; and Thomson Newspapers Limited of Toronto, Canada, bought a controlling interest in F. P. Publications Limited for $130 million in January.

Pressmen check copies of *The Ottawa Journal* as the last issue comes off the press. Financial losses forced the paper to close in August.

Thomson also bought five Michigan papers owned by Panax Corporation for $21.5 million in August.

Deaths and Births. In Canada, *The Ottawa Journal* and *The Winnipeg Tribune* published their last editions on August 27. In England, London's afternoon dailies – *The Evening Standard* and *The Evening News* – merged in October. Other newspapers to cease publication in 1980 included two Kansas publications – *The Topeka State Journal* on September 2, and *The Wichita Beacon* on October 1 – and *The Oklahoma Journal* on November 1.

The New York Times introduced a scaled-down Midwest edition on August 18. The paper is printed in Chicago from page layouts transmitted by satellite from New York City. In New York City, newspaper competition grew fierce when the evening *New York Post* introduced a morning paper on July 21. The morning *New York Daily News* on August 18 countered with an evening edition.

The press scored two First Amendment victories in 1980. The Supreme Court of the United States ruled on July 2 that both the public and the press have a constitutional right to attend criminal trials. The decision overturned a 1979 opinion stating that a judge acted legally in barring reporters from covering a Virginia murder trial. In October, President Jimmy Carter signed a bill prohibiting the surprise search of newsrooms.   Celeste Huenergard

In WORLD BOOK, see JOURNALISM; NEWSPAPER.

NICARAGUA. There were serious doubts both inside and outside Nicaragua in 1980 about the country's future political direction. The doubts persisted despite assurances by revolutionary leaders that they would steer a middle-of-the-road course and avoid pressures to move either to the right or to the left. Nowhere were doubts stronger than among members of the Congress of the United States, which on May 19 voted by a slim margin of only nine votes after a heated secret debate to grant $75 million in economic aid to Nicaragua.

Nicaraguan conservatives, too, were wary of the revolutionary regime. In March, the regime announced that an accord had been reached with Russia under which the Soviets would send technical experts to help develop Nicaragua's agriculture, transport, power engineering, and communications industries. The accord had been signed after a six-day visit to Russia by a Nicaraguan delegation headed by Moises Hassan Morales, a member of the ruling junta. The delegation also signed an accord calling for cooperation between Russia's Communist Party and the Sandinista National Liberation Front.

Castro Visits. Conservative fears were further strengthened in mid-July when Cuba's Prime Minister Fidel Castro, who has been described as Russia's stand-in in Latin America, toured Nicaragua during ceremonies commemorating the first

Cuba's President Fidel Castro, right, arrives in Managua in July for celebration of the first anniversary of the Nicaraguan revolution.

anniversary of Nicaragua's revolution. The presence in Nicaragua of thousands of Cuban teachers also alarmed those who hoped the country would not take Cuba's Communist path.

Most irksome to moderate Nicaraguans were the neighborhood "Defense Committees," established by the military junta and modeled on those in Cuba. The committees controlled everything from issuing driver's licenses to permitting travel abroad.

Debts Rescheduled. Internationally, a consensus developed in support of United States Nicaraguan policy, to the effect that Nicaraguans should be allowed time to work out their own problems. Consequently, about 120 banks in Canada, Europe, the United States, and Japan were liberal in rescheduling Nicaragua's international debts — which amounted to about $600 million. Most of the debt had been accumulated during the long rule of former President Anastasio Somoza Debayle, who was ousted in 1979.

The assassination of Somoza in Paraguay on September 17 touched off a wave of jubilation in Nicaragua. The Sandinista government made September 18 a day of nationwide celebration. See PARAGUAY. 			Nathan A. Haverstock

See also LATIN AMERICA (Facts in Brief Table). In WORLD BOOK, see NICARAGUA.
NIGER. See AFRICA.

NIGERIA, Africa's most prosperous nation and the second-largest supplier of foreign oil to the United States, cut oil production by about one-third in September 1980 in response to a worldwide surplus of petroleum. Nigerian oil output dropped from about 2.2 million barrels per day in August to 1.5 million barrels per day in September, cutting earnings by $450 million.

Oil Revenue Safeguards. Although oil production rose to 1.9 million barrels per day in October, the government decided late in that month to reorganize the Nigerian National Petroleum Corporation (NNPC), the state-owned oil company, to prevent or at least soften earnings slumps. Nigeria depends on oil for 90 per cent of its foreign exchange and more than 80 per cent of government revenues.

The NNPC had been rocked by scandal in April, when a government audit revealed that $4.6 billion in revenues from foreign oil sales had never been recorded. The investigation also revealed that the NNPC had not taken all the crude oil available to it from 1975 through 1978 under Nigerian oil-depletion laws. The government asked Gulf Oil Corporation, Mobil Oil Corporation, and Royal Dutch Shell Group to help make up this deficit.

U.S. Relations. Nigeria provides about 16 per cent of U.S. imported oil. In early October, while visting the United States, President Shehu Shagari threatened to use the United States dependence on Nigerian oil to influence American policy toward South Africa. Speaking in New York City on October 3, he said that his country would "use any means at our disposal, including oil" to persuade the United States to oppose *apartheid*, the system of separate development of the races imposed by South Africa's white minority government.

On October 7, Shagari met with President Jimmy Carter, who assured him of the U.S. commitment to majority rule and interracial cooperation in the South African colony of Namibia. The Nigerian leader also showed interest in acquiring American trade and technology.

Domestic Affairs. Revenue sharing among Nigeria's 19 state governments was a highly divisive issue during 1980. A special study recommended that 55 per cent of revenues collected be retained by the federal administration, 34.5 per cent shared among the states, and the remainder divided between local governments and a special fund for the new federal capital being built at Abuja. The oil-producing states in southern Nigeria opposed this allocation formula. They contended that they should be favored in revenue sharing because they produce most of the tax revenues.   J. Dixon Esseks

See also AFRICA (Facts in Brief Table). In WORLD BOOK, see NIGERIA.

NIXON, RICHARD MILHOUS (1913-   ), 37th President of the United States, completed his move to his four-story, 12-room, $750,000 town house on Manhattan's stylish Upper East Side on Feb. 14, 1980. Nixon, his wife, Pat, and daughter Tricia Cox arrived by limousine, escorted by five security cars. Because the New York City residence has inadequate facilities for inspecting and sorting a former President's mail, the Nixons' mail is shipped to the United States Coast Guard station near the Nixons' former residence in San Clemente, Calif.

Although he was eager to make public appearances and win acceptance as an elder statesman, Nixon's legal difficulties continued. On May 19, the Supreme Court of the United States agreed to review an appeals court decision that Nixon and his senior aides, including former Secretary of State Henry A. Kissinger, were liable for damages in the $1.26-million suit brought by a former Kissinger aide, Morton Halperin, for illegal wiretaps on his phone in 1969 and 1970. The case was not argued before the court by year-end.

Trial Witness. Nixon made his first courtroom appearance since he left the presidency when he appeared on October 29 as a rebuttal witness for the prosecution in the trial of W. Mark Felt and Edward S. Miller, two former Federal Bureau of Investigation (FBI) officials. The defendants were

United States Vice-President Walter F. Mondale receives a carved gourd from a Nigerian state governor during his visit to that nation in July.

Richard Nixon and his wife, Pat, greet passersby from a window of their new Manhattan town house. The Nixons moved to New York City in February.

NOBEL PRIZES in peace, literature, economics, and various sciences were awarded in 1980 by the Norwegian *Storting* (parliament) and the Royal Academy of Science, the Caroline Institute, and the Swedish Academy of Literature, all in Stockholm, Sweden.

Peace Prize. Adolfo Pérez Esquivel, 48, secretary general of the Service for Peace and Justice in Latin America, a human-rights organization based in Buenos Aires, Argentina, was named the 1980 prizewinner. A former sculptor and professor of architecture, Pérez Esquivel was jailed by the Argentine government in April 1977 after he condemned the ruling junta for its treatment of the estimated 10,000 to 20,000 persons who have "disappeared" at the hands of the state security forces. He was released from jail more than a year later without having been charged.

Literature Prize was awarded to Czeslaw Milosz, 69, a Lithuanian-born Polish poet and novelist who is now a United States citizen teaching at the University of California, Berkeley. Milosz was active in the Polish resistance movement against Germany during World War II. He served for four years as a diplomat, but fled to Paris in 1951 and to the United States in 1960. He writes in Polish, often translating his own work into English, and has published eight books in English.

found guilty on November 6 of conspiring to violate the constitutional rights of citizens by authorizing FBI agents to break into private homes and offices without a warrant in 1972 and 1973 in search of radical fugitives. Testifying for 45 minutes, the former President defended such searches on the grounds that, at the time, radical violence was endangering the security of the United States.

Nixon's long fight to suppress the tapes used as evidence in the Watergate trials ended on May 28 when they became available for public listening at the National Archives in Washington, D.C. The tapes released covered only 12½ hours of some 6,000 hours of White House conversations secretly recorded during the Nixon Administration.

Nixon's New Book, *The Real War,* was published by Warner Books in June. In the 341-page volume, Nixon offered his personal views on power politics and the proper role of the United States in the world. The book made the best-seller list in *The New York Times Book Review* on July 13.

Nixon and his wife, Pat, celebrated their 40th wedding anniversary on June 21 while vacationing in Europe. The former President attended the funeral of Iran's exiled Shah Mohammad Reza Pahlavi in Cairo, Egypt, on July 29, terming U.S. treatment of the shah "shameful." Carol L. Thompson

In WORLD BOOK, see NIXON, RICHARD MILHOUS.

Human rights advocate Adolfo Pérez Esquivel of Argentina holds the cable informing him that he has won 1980 Nobel Prize for Peace.

Polish-born writer Czeslaw Milosz, who now teaches at the University of California, Berkeley, won the Nobel Prize for Literature.

regard to recombinant DNA," Gilbert and Sanger "for their contributions concerning the determination of base sequences in nucleic acids."

Physics Prize was shared by James W. Cronin, 49, professor of physics at the University of Chicago, and Val L. Fitch, 57, professor of physics at Princeton University. Working together at Princeton in the 1960s, they demonstrated that a seemingly fixed law governing the behavior of subatomic particles is sometimes variable. The Nobel committee asserted that this work, in demonstrating the asymmetry in subatomic particles, contributed to an explanation of how matter came to exist in the universe.

Physiology or Medicine Prize was shared by three immunology researchers – two Americans and a Frenchman. Cited for discoveries that help explain the role of cell structures in disease and organ transplants were Baruj Benacerraf, 59, chairman of the pathology department of Harvard Medical School; George D. Snell, 76, senior scientist at Jackson Laboratory in Bar Harbor, Me.; and Jean Dausset, 64, head of the immunology department, University of Paris in France.   Foster Stockwell

In WORLD BOOK, see NOBEL PRIZES.

NORTH ATLANTIC TREATY ORGANIZATION (NATO). See EUROPE.

NORTH CAROLINA. See STATE GOVERNMENT.

NORTH DAKOTA. See STATE GOVERNMENT.

Economics Prize was given to Lawrence R. Klein, 60, a University of Pennsylvania economics professor, noted for work in *econometrics*, the development of mathematical models for forecasting economic trends and designing policies to deal with them. Klein was honored for his writings and research guidance, which have stimulated research on econometric forecasting models and on the possibilities of using such models for practical analysis of economic policies.

Chemistry Prize was shared by two Americans and an Englishman for developing techniques that made it possible to understand in detail the structure and function of deoxyribonucleic acid (DNA), the chemical that controls the activities of living cells. Paul Berg, 54, professor of biochemistry at Stanford University, Palo Alto, Calif., received half the $210,000 prize. Walter Gilbert, 48, professor of molecular biology at Harvard University, Cambridge, Mass., and Frederick Sanger, 62, professor of molecular biology at Cambridge University in England, shared the other half. Sanger, winner of the 1958 chemistry prize for discovering the structure of the insulin molecule, is the second person to win twice in the same category. John Bardeen of the University of Illinois won the physics prize in 1956 and 1972.

Berg was cited "for his fundamental studies of the biochemistry of nucleic acids, with particular

NORTHERN IRELAND. Patient diplomacy on the part of Humphrey Atkins, Great Britain's secretary of state for Northern Ireland, characterized most of 1980 as the British government searched for a formula that would set the province on the path to *devolution* (limited home rule). Immediately after winning the British general election in May 1979, the Conservative government announced its intention of ending nearly eight years of direct rule by the British Parliament. But the search for an acceptable formula proved elusive. The Protestant political parties, representing two-thirds of Northern Ireland's population, remained opposed to sharing power with the Roman Catholic minority.

In an attempt to negotiate a solution, Atkins convened a constitutional conference in Belfast on January 7. It was attended by representatives from the extreme Protestant Democratic Unionist Party (DUP), the Catholic Social Democratic and Labour Party (SDLP), and the moderate, bisectarian Alliance Party. Unfortunately, the Official Unionist Party (OUP), Northern Ireland's largest with five members of Parliament, boycotted the conference. Atkins suspended the conference on March 24 because the parties could reach no agreement.

White Paper. Despite the lack of agreement, the British government produced a *white paper*, or policy statement, on Northern Ireland on July 2. This plan provided that governing power would be

British soldier salutes hearse carrying body of Anne Maguire in Belfast in January. Death of her children in 1976 sparked Ulster peace movement.

given to a new single chamber of about 80 members to be elected by proportional representation. Two alternative schemes provided for forming a Cabinet-style executive, backed by a council with delaying or blocking powers. In the first model, any party winning a designated share of the popular vote would be guaranteed a certain number of executive seats. This plan, which would lead to power-sharing between the Protestant and Catholic communities, found favor with the SDLP. In the second proposal, an executive would be formed by the majority party or parties elected to the assembly. Probably because this plan offered no guarantee of representation to the minority parties, it was somewhat acceptable to DUP leader Ian Paisley. Both models were rejected outright by unionist James Molyneaux, who described the white paper as a "recipe for disaster."

Violence by both factions continued in 1980. A further threat kept Northern Ireland on tenterhooks near year-end, when seven prisoners at the Maze Prison in Belfast stretched a hunger strike from October 27 to December 18, demanding special political status. Even though 33 others joined them on December 1, the British refused to accede to their demands, and the prisoners finally gave in and began to eat.   Ian Mather

See also GREAT BRITAIN; IRELAND. In WORLD BOOK, see NORTHERN IRELAND.

NORTHWEST TERRITORIES. A ceremony on July 31, 1980, marking the 100th anniversary of Great Britain's transfer of the Arctic islands to Canada was marked by an eloquent *Inuit* (Eskimo) plea for a separate province in the Eastern Arctic. Speaking at Frobisher Bay, Simon Awa, a Baffin Island Inuit, said being Canadian meant having "the right to be represented by a duly elected provincial government." Former Cabinet Minister Charles M. Drury, the federal government's adviser on the future of the North, had recommended in a March 6 report against dividing the territories. However, he advocated turning over health, labor, justice, and land-resource management to the 22-member elected Territorial Council, and he emphasized the vital importance of settling native land claims.

The territorial government pledged support for the Eskimo Dog Research Foundation after the foundation announced that it would have to destroy 120 Eskimo dogs because it lacked funds.

For the first time, 21 female members of the Canadian Armed Forces were posted to alert on the tip of Ellesmere Island in September and October. During their six-month tour of duty 500 miles (800 kilometers) from the North Pole, the women maintained radio communications and weather equipment.   David M. L. Farr

See also CANADA. In WORLD BOOK, see NORTHWEST TERRITORIES.

NORWAY gave top priority to paying off its $22.6-billion foreign debt in 1980. The Organization for Economic Cooperation and Development (OECD) estimated that Norway would need until 1985 to retire just 25 per cent of the debt. The government wanted to apply its share of Norway's increasing oil revenue against the debt, despite pressures for wage hikes and tax cuts. But an agreement in the spring increased all wages by $298 million.

Petroleum studies conducted in 1980 were to be submitted to the *Storting* (parliament) early in 1981, in order to help it decide on the future of Norway's vast oil and gas resources. One study proposed piping gas from the Statfjord field in the North Sea to the Norwegian coast in order to meet the growing demands of other Scandinavian countries and the European Community. This plan also would boost Norway's petrochemical industry. Norway expected to get one-fourth of its gross national product and half its exports from oil by 1990. Total oil and gas output was expected to reach 50 million metric tons (55 million short tons) in 1980, an increase of 20 per cent from 1979, and 90 million metric tons (100 million short tons) by the mid-1980s.

More Government Control. Taxes on North Sea oil and gas yielded $226 million in 1980. A government report showed in February that state control over oil and gas production would increase as new fields began producing. Recent license allocations gave the state oil company at least a 50 per cent interest in each area to be drilled. Some 2,000 offshore oil workers struck for higher wages on July 10. They agreed to return to work on August 14 while a seven-member arbitration board appointed by the labor unions and drilling companies worked out a pay accord.

Oil Rig Disaster. A floating platform, the *Alexander L. Keilland*, capsized when one of its five steel legs snapped in a North Sea gale on March 27, killing 123 of some 200 oil workers on board. The disaster caused serious concern in the government. Prime Minister Odvar Nordli said that Norway could not afford to pay such a high price in human lives for its oil venture.

Arctic Venture. Norway started drilling exploratory oil wells in June in waters 50 miles (80 kilometers) northwest of Hammerfest. The location is important strategically, because Russia's northern fleet must pass through those waters to get from its Murmansk base to major Western seas. Norway's decision to drill north of the 62nd parallel prompted Russia to reopen negotiations with Norway over territorial rights, but five days of talks in March were inconclusive. Kenneth Brown

See also EUROPE (Facts in Brief Table). In WORLD BOOK, see NORWAY.

Floating dormitory for North Sea oil workers accidentally tilts 20 degrees while at anchor in Norway in April and must be evacuated.

NOVA SCOTIA. The Canadian and Nova Scotian treasuries approved grants on June 7, 1980, enabling Michelin Tires (Canada) Limited to establish a third plant in the province. The plant will be built at Waterville in the heart of the Annapolis River Valley apple country and will employ 1,500 persons, bringing Michelin's total work force in the province to 5,300. The move followed the Nova Scotia legislature's passage on Dec. 28, 1979, of a controversial bill that forced unions to organize all centrally owned "interdependent" plants if they wished to represent workers at any of them.

Premier John Buchanan's Conservative government, holding 33 seats of the legislature's 52, passed legislation on May 23, 1980, enabling Nova Scotia to claim offshore oil resources as far as the middle of the Atlantic Ocean. The action resulted from Prime Minister Pierre Elliott Trudeau's withdrawal of a 1979 Conservative offer to turn over ownership of these resources to Canada's Atlantic Provinces.

Premier Buchanan officiated at ceremonies on June 21 to inaugurate tapping the mammoth tides of the Bay of Fundy for electric power. The project, to be completed in 1983, is located at the mouth of the Annapolis River. David M. L. Farr

See also CANADA. In WORLD BOOK, see NOVA SCOTIA.

NUCLEAR ENERGY. See ENERGY.

NUTRITION

NUTRITION. The relationship between diet and such diseases as atherosclerosis and cancer was questioned in May 1980 by the Food and Nutrition Board of the National Research Council (NRC). The board advises the United States federal government on dietary matters and also sets the Recommended Dietary Allowance (RDA) for essential nutrients.

One of the board's major findings in a report called "Toward Healthful Diets" was that a link between high-cholesterol diets and the development of atherosclerosis has not been established. This conclusion drew protests from many nutritionists and medical researchers.

Atherosclerosis – the accumulation in arteries of fat deposits that can choke off blood flow and lead to heart disease and stroke – is the leading contributing factor in deaths in the United States. Many nutritionists have believed that a high dietary intake of foods containing cholesterol leads to atherosclerosis by raising the levels of the fatty substance in the blood.

Changing Attitudes. Based on studies of research on how low-cholesterol diets affect the incidence of heart disease, the American Heart Association and a U.S. Senate committee on nutrition recommended in 1977 that American adults reduce their cholesterol intake by one-third. In December 1979,

Anthropologist Robert Corruccini of Southern Illinois University claims that diet causes the crooked teeth that many Americans have.

the American Society of Clinical Nutrition supported the view that dietary cholesterol and heart disease were linked.

The NRC board, reviewing the scientific literature, found little link between dietary cholesterol and the incidence of heart disease. It recommended that fat intake be adjusted to an individual's needs. The American Medical Association and such industry groups as the National Dairy Council and the National Livestock and Meat Board agreed.

The heart association and government departments, such as the Department of Agriculture and the Department of Health and Human Services, maintained their anticholesterol stands. Several critics pointed out that the board had no heart specialists or epidemiologists, who are familiar with disease patterns, to evaluate research.

Diet and Cancer. The NRC board also found little evidence that any specific nutrient could be implicated as a cause of cancer, though some studies have linked colon cancer with high-fat, low-fiber diets. Overall caloric intake, said the board, might be related to some cancers.

In other recommendations, the NRC board called for proper diet and exercise as the best way to combat obesity, which many experts believe is the most common form of malnutrition in the developed world. The same regimen is best to control adult-onset diabetes mellitus, said the board.

The furor over the report reached Congress in June, and several scientists testified at hearings of the House Subcommittee on Domestic Marketing, Consumer Relations, and Nutrition. Most attacked the report for its recommendation on cholesterol. Representative Henry A. Waxman (D., Calif.) called the report "dangerously misleading" and charged that the NRC board had ignored "an enormous body of scientific research."

A Second Major Report shook the nutrition world in June. Epidemiologist Stephen B. Hulley and three colleagues at the University of California, San Francisco, questioned the theory that coronary heart disease was associated with not only blood cholesterol, but also blood triglycerides. Triglycerides are the normal form of fat storage in the body, but doctors often prescribe drugs or diet changes to treat high levels of blood triglyceride. The report by Hulley and his co-workers admitted that there is a statistical association between heart disease and blood triglyceride levels. But the investigators sought to determine whether the fat levels caused the disease, were caused by the disease, or varied with some other factor. They concluded that the triglyceride level varied with a third factor – probably a form of blood cholesterol – and thus is not in itself responsible for the disease. Paul E. Araujo

See also FOOD. In WORLD BOOK, see DIET; FOOD; NUTRITION.

OCEAN. Negotiators at the United Nations (UN) Law of the Sea Conference agreed unanimously that the five-week session that began on July 28, 1980, in Geneva, Switzerland, produced the breakthrough that had eluded them for six years. "It is now all but certain that the text of a convention on the Law of the Sea will be ready for signature in 1981," said the chief United States delegate, Elliot L. Richardson. The treaty, more than 300 articles long, would give coastal nations exclusive economic rights within 200 nautical miles of shore. But developing and landlocked countries would get a share of the profits made from mining under more distant waters. The session's most important result was a system of voting on the mining of minerals from the deep ocean floor, the area in which all nations share.

Two Major New Programs for the 1980s dominated the marine science budget submitted to the Congress of the United States in January 1980. The Ocean Margin Drilling (OMD) program is expected to cost $700 million over the decade, with the oil industry and the government sharing the cost equally. During the first year, eight to 10 oil companies are expected to match the initial federal appropriation of $5 million. The proposed National Oceanic Satellite System, priced at $800 million, will be financed jointly by the Department of Defense, the National Aeronautics and Space Administration, and the National Oceanic and Atmospheric Administration.

Two Mysteries. An international team of scientists on the Deep Sea Drilling Project (DSDP) found direct evidence that the mysterious extinction of certain marine surface-dwelling plants and animals that occurred about 65 million years ago coincided with, or preceded by 500,000 years, the equally mysterious extinction of the dinosaurs. Scientists on the drilling ship *Glomar Challenger* found a nearly complete record of the marine extinction in drill cores of sediment that was buried between layers of volcanic ash on the flanks of a 70-million-year-old ridge in the southwestern Atlantic Ocean near South Africa.

Ecological Treaty. Some 15 nations signed a convention on the Conservation of Antarctic Marine Living Resources in Canberra, Australia, in September. The treaty is unique in that it is based on the idea of managing an ecosystem rather than specific resources.

President Jimmy Carter signed the Deep Seabed Hard Minerals Act on June 28, ending a legislative struggle that began in the early 1970s. The act establishes laws for deep-sea mining. But UN laws will supersede these laws if the UN conference is successful. President Carter also signed major bills that support ocean thermal energy conversion (OTEC) research. OTEC uses the difference in energy between warm surface water and deep, cold

Volunteers in a pressure tank at Duke University set a record of 2,132 feet (650 meters) for a simulated dive in March.

water to drive a turbogenerator that produces electricity.

Sea Disaster. The Norwegian-owned *Alexander L. Keilland*, a floating platform that served as a dormitory for North Sea oil workers, collapsed during a gale on March 27, killing 123 persons.

A new Texas firm, Titanic 80, searched during the summer of 1980 for the wreck of the luxury liner *Titanic*. A sonar device aboard the research vessel *H. J. W. Fay* detected an object that the project leaders said was the *Titanic*, but bad weather and shortages of food and fuel thwarted efforts to take confirming photographs. The group hopes to return to the site in the summer of 1981. The *Titanic* hit an iceberg on its maiden voyage in 1912 and sank about 300 miles (480 kilometers) southeast of Newfoundland in water ranging from 12,300 to 14,300 feet (3,700 to 4,300 meters) deep.

The Mexican national oil company, Pemex, announced on March 24 that the runaway Ixtoc I well in the Gulf of Mexico had finally been capped. No precise measure exists of the amount of oil that began to spill in June 1979, but estimates range as high as 3 million barrels.   Arthur G. Alexiou

In WORLD BOOK, see DEEP SEA DRILLING PROJECT; OCEAN; TITANIC.

OHIO. See STATE GOVERNMENT.

OKLAHOMA. See STATE GOVERNMENT.

OLD AGE. See SOCIAL SECURITY.

Figure skater Anett Poetzsch of East Germany, American speed skater Eric Heiden, and the U.S. hockey team were stars of the Winter Games in Lake Placid, N.Y. In Moscow, where image of Misha, Russian Olympic mascot, greeted athletes in Lenin Stadium, Cuban heavyweight boxer Teofilo Stevenson won his third gold medal.

OLYMPIC GAMES

The XXII Olympic Summer Games and the XIII Winter Games in 1980 will be remembered as much for nonparticipation as for participation. The broadest boycott in Olympic history, led by the United States to protest Russian military intervention in Afghanistan, marred the Summer Olympics held from July 19 to August 3 in Mos-

cow. Of 145 nations eligible to take part, only 81 did. Of the 64 that did not, a number were part of the boycott movement. The 81 nations that competed contrasted with 88 in 1976 (when 27 African nations boycotted), 122 in 1972, and 113 in 1968, years in which the International Olympic Committee (IOC) had fewer members.

Russia and East Germany won the greatest number of medals, which assuredly would have happened in any case. However, the quality of competition suffered without Canada, the United States, West Germany, and other boycotting nations. About 6,000 athletes competed. Before the boycott was announced, about 10,000 were expected to take part.

Olympics be canceled or postponed unless Russia removed its troops. Barring that, he said, the Olympics should be moved. The IOC, which jealously guards its autonomy, refused any change and insisted that politics had no place in the Olympics.

The United States government sought boycott support from other nations, but most were reluctant to act until the United States formally acted. The power to decide whether the American team would boycott rested with the United States Olympic Committee (USOC).

Most American athletes opposed a boycott, though many older ones eventually favored one. President Carter summoned 150 athletes to the White House on March 21 for what was described as a briefing on the boycott situation, but the briefing became a lecture on why American athletes would not be allowed to go to Moscow.

"He closed the door," Willie Davenport, the 1968 Olympic high-hurdles champion, said of the President. "And not only did he close it, but he locked it and threw the key away."

The President put heavy pressure on the USOC to vote for a boycott. He said he would take legal action, if necessary, to keep American athletes out of the first Olympics to be held in a Communist nation. He urged corporations to withhold financial support from the USOC until it approved a boycott. White House aides privately threatened the USOC with loss of autonomy.

On April 12, the USOC voted by a 2-1 margin to boycott, a decision that brought tears to many athletes who voted. The boycott movement eventually embraced West Germany, China, Japan, Canada, Kenya, and other nations. It was also supported by the governments of Australia, New Zealand, Great Britain, France, Italy, and some other Western European nations, but their national Olympic committees decided to participate anyway. The committees contended that an Olympic boycott was not an appropriate measure.

Sixteen nations protested the Russian aggression in Afghanistan in a different way. Their athletes competed, but their national anthems and flags were replaced in ceremonies by the Olympic anthem and flag. Ten of the 16 did not allow their athletes to take part in the opening ceremonies.

"I've read some of the statements from Washington about how an Olympic boycott is the strongest weapon we can use against the Soviets," said Julian K. Roosevelt of Oyster Bay, N.Y., a member of the IOC. "If that's the strongest thing we can do, we have no Washington."

"What is wrong with the boycott," said Cornelis Kerdel of the Netherlands, another IOC member, "is that not enough other sanctions were fully brought to bear. It is unjust to make athletes bear the conscience of the world."

Russia and East Germany also won the most gold medals (10 and nine, respectively) in the Winter Olympics, held from February 12 to 24 in Lake Placid, N.Y. The United States was next with six, and they became the major stories of the competition. Five of the six were won by one athlete, 21-year-old Eric Heiden of Madison, Wis., who swept every title in men's speed skating. The sixth was won by the unheralded U.S. hockey team, which upset Russia's world and defending Olympic champions and unleashed unbelievable excitement in the United States.

The Boycott. After Russia sent troops into Afghanistan in December 1979, President Jimmy Carter proposed in January 1980 that the Moscow

Official Results of the 1980 Olympic Games

Winners of the Winter Olympics in Lake Placid, N.Y., in February

Event	Winner	Country	Mark
Men's Skiing			
Downhill	Leonhard Stock	Austria	1:45.50
Giant slalom	Ingemar Stenmark	Sweden	2:40.74
Slalom	Ingemar Stenmark	Sweden	1:44.26
15-kilometer cross-country	Thomas Wassberg	Sweden	41:57.63
30-kilometer cross-country	Nikolai Zimatov	Russia	1:17.02.80
50-kilometer cross-country	Nikolai Zimatov	Russia	2:27.24.60
40-kilometer cross-country relay	Vasili Rochev Nikolai Bazhukov, Evgeny Beliaev, Nikolai Zimatov	Russia	1:57.08.46
70-meter jump	Anton Innauer	Austria	266.30 pts.
90-meter jump	Jouko Tormanen	Finland	271 pts.
Nordic combined	Ulrich Wehling	E. Germany	432.200 pts.
Women's Skiing			
Downhill	Annemarie Moser	Austria	1:37.52
Slalom	Hanni Wenzel	Liechtenstein	1:25.09
Giant slalom	Hanni Wenzel	Liechtenstein	2:41.66
5-kilometer cross-country	Raisa Smetanina	Russia	15:06.92
10-kilometer cross-country	Barbara Petzold	E. Germany	30:31.54
20-kilometer cross-country relay	Marlies Rostock, Carola Anding, Veronika Hesse, Barbara Petzold	E. Germany	1:02.11.10
Ice Hockey			
		U.S.A.	5 pts.
Men's Speed Skating			
500 meters	Eric Heiden	U.S.A.	38.03*
1,000 meters	Eric Heiden	U.S.A.	1:15.18*
1,500 meters	Eric Heiden	U.S.A.	1:55.44*
5,000 meters	Eric Heiden	U.S.A.	7:02.29*
10,000 meters	Eric Heiden	U.S.A.	14:28.13*

Event	Winner	Country	Mark
Women's Speed Skating			
500 meters	Karin Enke	E. Germany	41.78*
1,000 meters	Natalia Petruseva	Russia	1:24.10*
1,500 meters	Annie Borckink	Netherlands	2:10.95*
3,000 meters	Bjoerg-Eva Jensen	Norway	4:32.13*
Biathlon			
10-kilometer event	Frank Ullrich	E. Germany	32.10.69
20-kilometer event	Anatoli Aljabiev	Russia	1:08.16.31
30-kilometer relay	Vladimir Alikin, Alexander Tikhonov, Vladimir Barnaschov, Anatoli Aljabiev	Russia	1:34.03.27
Bobsledding			
Two-man	Erich Schaerer, Josef Benz	Switzerland	4:09.36
Four-man	Meinhard Neimer, Bosdan Musiol, Bernhard Germeshausen, Hans Jurgen Gerhardt	E. Germany	3:59.92
Figure Skating			
Men's singles	Robin Cousins	Great Britain	189.48
Women's singles	Anett Poetzsch	E. Germany	189.00
Pairs	Irina Rodnina, Alexandr Zaitsev	Russia	147.26
Ice dancing	Natalia Linichuk, Gennadi Karponosov	Russia	205.48
Men's Luge			
Singles	Bernhard Glass	E. Germany	2:54.796
Doubles	Hans Rinn, Norbert Hahn	E. Germany	1:19.331
Women's Luge			
Singles	Vera Zozulia	Russia	2:36.537

Winners of the Summer Olympics in Moscow, Russia, in July and August

Event	Winner	Country	Mark
Archery			
Men	Tomi Poikolainen	Finland	2,455 pts.
Women	Keto Losaberidze	Russia	2,491 pts.
Boxing			
Light-flyweight	Shamil Sabyrov	Russia	
Flyweight	Peter Lessov	Bulgaria	
Bantamweight	Juan Hernandez	Cuba	
Featherweight	Rudi Fink	E. Germany	
Lightweight	Angel Herrera	Cuba	
Light-welterweight	Patrizio Oliva	Italy	
Welterweight	Andres Aldama	Cuba	
Light-middleweight	Armando Martinez	Cuba	
Middleweight	Jose Gomez	Cuba	
Light-heavyweight	Slbodan Kacar	Yugoslavia	
Heavyweight	Teofilo Stevenson	Cuba	
Canoeing, Men			
500-meter kayak singles	Vladimir Partenovich	Russia	1:43.43
500-meter kayak tandems	Partenovich, Chukhrai	Russia	1:32.38
500-meter Canadian singles	Sergei Postrekhin	Russia	1:53.37
500-meter Canadian tandems	Poltan, Vaskuti	Hungary	1:43.39
1,000-meter kayak singles	Rudiger Helm	E. Germany	3:48.77
1,000-meter kayak tandems	Partenovich, Chukhrai	Russia	3:26.72

Event	Winner	Country	Mark
1,000-meter kayak fours	Helm, Olbricht, Marg, Duvigneau	E. Germany	3:13.76
1,000-meter Canadian singles	Lubenov	Bulgaria	4:12.38
1,000-meter Canadian tandems	Oitzaucgub, Simionov	Romania	3:47.65
Canoeing, Women			
500-meter kayak singles	Birgit Fischer	E. Germany	1:57.96
500-meter kayak tandems	Genauss, Bischof	E. Germany	1:43.88
Cycling			
Individual road race	Sergei Sukhoruchenkov	Russia	4:48.2
Team road race	Kashirin, Logvin, Shelpak, Yarkin	Russia	2:01:21.7
Individual sprint	Lutz Hesslich	E. Germany	2:02:53.2
1,000-meter time trial	Lothar Thomas	E. Germany	1:02:9.55
4,000-meter individual pursuit	Robert Dill-Bundi	Switzerland	4:35:6.60
4,000-meter team pursuit	Manakov, Movchan, Osokin, Patrakov	Russia	4:15.70
Equestrian			
Three-day event, individual	Frederico Euro Roman	Italy	108.60 pts.
Three-day event, team	Blinov, Salnikov, Volkov	Russia	457.00 pts.

(*) Indicates new Olympic record; (†) new world record; (#) ties world record.

Event	Winner	Country	Mark
Dressage, individual	Elisabeth Theurer	Austria	1,370.0 pts.
Dressage, team	Kovshov, Ugryumov, Misevich, Plot	Russia	4,383 pts.
Show-jumping, team	Chukanov, Gepatit, Poganovsky, Topky	Russia	20.25 pts.
Show-jumping, individual	Jan Kowaiczyk	Poland	8 pts.

Fencing, Men

Event	Winner	Country	Mark
Individual foil	Vladimir Smirnov	Russia	
Team foil	Flament, Jolyot, Boscherie, Bonnin	France	
Individual épée	John Harmenberg	Sweden	
Team épée	Roboud, Picot, Gardas, Boisse	France	
Individual saber	Viktor Krovopuskov	Russia	
Team saber	Burtsev, Krovopuskov, Sidyak, Nazlymov	Russia	

Fencing, Women

Event	Winner	Country	Mark
Individual foil	Pascale Trinquet	France	
Team foil	Trinquet, Brigitte, Latri-Gaudin, Boeri-Begard, Brouquier	France	

Gymnastics, Men

Event	Winner	Country	Mark
All-around	Alexandr Ditiatin	Russia	118.650 pts.
Vault	Nikolai Andrianov	Russia	19.825 pts.
Floor exercise	Roland Bruckner	E. Germany	19.750 pts.
Pommel horse	Zoltan Magyar	Hungary	19.925 pts.
Rings	Alexandr Ditiatin	Russia	19.875 pts.
Horizontal bar	Stoyan Deltchev	Bulgaria	19.825 pts.
Parallel bars	Alexander Tkachyov	Russia	19.770 pts.
Team	Andrianov, Azarian, Ditiatin, Makuts, Markolov, Tkachyov	Russia	589.60 pts.

Gymnastics, Women

Event	Winner	Country	Mark
All-around	Yelena Davydova	Russia	79.150 pts.
Vault	Natalia Shaposhnikova	Russia	19.725 pts.
Floor exercise	Nelli Kim, Nadia Comaneci (tie)	Russia, Romania	19.875 pts.
Uneven parallel bars	Maxi Gnauck	E. Germany	19.875 pts.
Balance beam	Nadia Comaneci	Romania	19.800 pts.
Team	Davydova, Filatova, Kim, Naimoushina, Shaposhnikova, Zakharova	Russia	394.90 pts.

Judo

Event	Winner	Country	Mark
132 lbs. (60 kg.)	Thierry Rey	France	
143 lbs. (65 kg.)	Nikolay Solodukhin	Russia	
157 lbs. (71 kg.)	Ezio Gamba	Italy	
172 lbs. (78 kg.)	Shota Khabareli	Russia	
190 lbs. (86 kg.)	Juerg Roethlisberger	Switzerland	
209 lbs. (95 kg.)	Robert Van De Walle	Belgium	
Over 209 lbs. (95 kg.)	Angelo Parisi	France	
Open Class	Dietmar Lorenz	E. Germany	

Modern Pentathlon

Event	Winner	Country	Mark
Individual	Anatoly Starostin	Russia	
Team		Russia	

Rowing, Men (all distances 2,000 meters)

Event	Winner	Country	Mark
Single sculls	Pertti Karppinen	Finland	7:09.6
Double sculls	Dreipke, Kroppelien	E. Germany	6:24.33
Quadruple sculls	Dundr, Bunk, Heppner, Winter	E. Germany	5:49.81
Pairs without coxswain	Berndt Landvoigt, Jorg Landvoigt	E. Germany	6:48.01
Pairs with coxswain	Jahrling, Ulrich, Spohr	E. Germany	7:02.54
Four without coxswain	Thiele, Decker, Semmler, Brietzke	E. Germany	6:08.17
Four with coxswain	Wendisch, Gregor, Dohn, U. Diessner, W. Diessner	E. Germany	6:14.51
Eights with coxswain	Krauss, Kope, Kons, Friedrich, Doberschulz, Karnatz, Duhring, Hoing, Ludwig	E. Germany	5:49.05

Rowing, Women (all races 1,000 meters)

Event	Winner	Country	Mark
Single sculls	Sanda Toma	Romania	3:40.69
Double sculls	Khloptseva, Popova	Russia	3:16.27
Quadruple Sculls with coxswain	Reinhardt, Ploch, Lau, Zobelt, Buhr	E. Germany	3:15.32
Pairs without coxswain	Steindorf, Klier	E. Germany	3:30.49
Four with coxswain	Kapheim, Frohlich, Noack, Saalfeld, Wenzel	E. Germany	3:19.27
Eights with coxswain	Boesler, Neisser, Kopke, Schutz, Kuhn, Richter, Sandig, Metze, Wilke	E. Germany	3:03.32

Shooting

Event	Winner	Country	Mark
Skeetshooting	Hans K. Rasmussen	Denmark	196 pts.
Trapshooting	Luciano Giovannetti	Italy	198 pts.
Small bore rifle, prone	Karoly Varga	Hungary	599 pts.#
Small bore rifle, three positions	Viktor Vlasov	Russia	1,173 pts. †
Rifle, running game target	Igor Sokolov	Russia	589 pts. †
Free pistol	Alexander Melentev	Russia	581 pts. †
Rapid-fire pistol	Corneliu Ion	Romania	596 pts.

Swimming and Diving, Men

Event	Winner	Country	Mark
100-meter free-style	Jorg Woithe	E. Germany	50.40
200-meter free-style	Sergei Kopliakov	Russia	1:49.8 *
400-meter free-style	Vladimir Salnikov	Russia	3:51.31 *
1,500-meter free-style	Vladimir Salnikov	Russia	14:58.27 †
100-meter backstroke	Bengt Baron	Sweden	56.53
200-meter backstroke	Sandor Wlador	Hungary	2:10.90
100-meter breaststroke	Duncan Goodhew	Great Britain	1:03.34
200-meter breaststroke	Robertas Zulpa	Russia	2:15.85
100-meter butterfly	Par Arvidsson	Sweden	54.92
200-meter butterfly	Sergei Fesenko	Russia	1:59.76
400-meter individual medley	Aleksandr Sidorenko	Russia	4:22.89 *
400-meter medley relay	Kerry, Evans, Tonelli, Brooks	Australia	3:45.70
800-meter free-style relay	Kopilakov, Salnikov, Stukolkin, Krylov	Russia	7:23.50
Platform diving	Falk Hoffman	E. Germany	835.65 pts.
Springboard diving	Aleksandr Portnov	Russia	905.02 pts.

Swimming and Diving, Women

Event	Winner	Country	Mark
100-meter free-style	Barbara Krause	E. Germany	54.79 †
200-meter free-style	Barbara Krause	E. Germany	1:58.33 *
400-meter free-style	Ines Diers	E. Germany	4:08.76 *
800-meter free-style	Michelle Ford	Australia	8:28.90
100-meter backstroke	Rica Reinisch	E. Germany	1:00.86 †
200-meter backstroke	Rica Reinisch	E. Germany	2:11.77 †
100-meter breaststroke	Ute Geweniger	E. Germany	1:10.22

Event	Winner	Country	Mark
200-meter breaststroke	Lina Kachushite	Russia	2:29.54 *
100-meter butterfly	Caren Metschuck	E. Germany	1:00.42
200-meter butterfly	Ines Geissler	E. Germany	2:10.44 *
400-meter individual medley	Petra Schneider	E. Germany	4:36.29 †
400-meter free-style relay	Krause, Metschuck, Kiers, Hulsenback	E. Germany	3:42.71 †
400-meter medley relay	Reinisch, Geweniger, Pollack, Metschuck	E. Germany	4:06.67 †
Platform diving	Martina Jaschke	E. Germany	596.25 pts.
Springboard diving	Irina Kalinina	Russia	725.91 pts.

Track and Field, Men

Event	Winner	Country	Mark
100 meters	Allan Wells	Great Britain	10.25
200 meters	Pietro Mennea	Italy	20.19
400 meters	Viktor Markin	Russia	44.60
800 meters	Steve Ovett	Gr. Britain	1:45.4
1,500 meters	Sebastian Coe	Gr. Britain	3:38.4
5,000 meters	Miruts Yifter	Ethiopia	13:21.0
10,000 meters	Miruts Yifter	Ethiopia	27:42.7
Marathon	Waldemar Cierpinski	E. Germany	2:11.3
20-kilometer walk	Maurizio Damilano	Italy	1:23:35.5
50-kilometer walk	Hartwig Gauder	E. Germany	3:49.24
400-meter relay	Muravyov, Sidorov, Aksinin, Prokofev	Russia	38.26
1,600-meter relay	Valiulis, Linge, Chernetsky, Markin	Russia	3:01.1
110-meter hurdles	Thomas Munkelt	E. Germany	13.39
400-meter hurdles	Volker Beck	E. Germany	48.70
3,000-meter steeplechase	Bronislaw Malinowski	Poland	8:09.7
Decathlon	Daley Thompson	Great Britain	8,495 pts.
Long jump	Lutz Dombrowski	E. Germany	28 ft. ¼ in. (8.54 m.)
Triple jump	Jaak Uudmae	Russia	56 ft. 11 in. (17.35 m.)
High jump	Gerd Wessig	E. Germany	7 ft. 8¾ in. (2.36 m.) †
Pole vault	Wladyslaw Kozakiewicz	Poland	18 ft. 11½ in. (5.78 m.)
Shot-put	Vladimir Kiselyov	Russia	70 ft. ½ in. * (21.35 m.)
Discus throw	Viktor Rasshchupkin	Russia	218 ft. 7 in. (66.62 m.)
Javelin throw	Dainis Kula	Russia	299 ft. 2 in. (91.20 m.)
Hammer throw	Yuri Sedykh	Russia	268 ft. 4 in. † (81.79 m.)

Track and Field, Women

Event	Winner	Country	Mark
100 meters	Ludmila Kondrateva	Russia	11.06
200 meters	Barbel Eckert Woeckel	E. Germany	22.03 *
400 meters	Marita Koch	E. Germany	48.88 *
800 meters	Nadezhda Olizarenko	Russia	1:53.5 †
1,500 meters	Tatyana Kazankina	Russia	3:56.6 *
400-meter relay	Muller, Wockel, Auerswald, Gohr	E. Germany	41.60 †
1,600-meter relay	Prorochenko, Goistchik, Zyuskova, Nazarova	Russia	3:20.2
100-meter hurdles	Vera Komisova	Russia	12.56 *
Pentathlon	Nadezhda Tkachenko	Russia	5,083 pts. *
Long jump	Tatiana Kolpakova	Russia	23 ft. 2 in. * (7.06 m.)
High jump	Sara Simeoni	Italy	6 ft. 5½ in. * (1.97 m.)
Shot-put	Ilona Slupianek	E. Germany	73 ft. 6¼ in. * (22.41 m.)
Discus throw	Evelin Jahl	E. Germany	229 ft. 6 in. * (69.95 m.)
Javelin throw	Maria Colon	Cuba	224 ft. 5 in. (68.90 m.)

Weight Lifting

Event	Winner	Country	Mark
Flyweight	Kanybek Osmanoliev	Russia	540 lbs. * (245 kgs.)
Bantamweight	Daniel Nunez	Cuba	606 lbs. † (275 kgs.)
Featherweight	Viktor Mazin	Russia	639 lbs. † (290 kgs.)
Lightweight	Yanko Roussev	Bulgaria	755 lbs. † (343 kgs.)
Middleweight	Assen Zlatev	Bulgaria	794 lbs. † (360 kgs.)
Light-heavyweight	Yurik Vardanyan	Russia	882 lbs. † (400 kgs.)
Middle-heavyweight	Peter Baczako	Hungary	832 lbs. (377 kgs.)
First heavyweight	Ota Zaremba	Czecho-slovakia	871 lbs. * (395 kgs.)
Second heavyweight	Leonid Taranenko	Russia	931 lbs. † (422 kgs.)
Super-heavyweight	Sultan Rakhmanov	Russia	970 lbs.# (440 kgs.)

Wrestling (Free Style)

Event	Winner	Country
Paperweight (105.5 lbs.)	Claudio Pollio	Italy
Flyweight (115 lbs.)	Anatoly Beloglazov	Russia
Bantamweight (126 lbs.)	Sergei Beloglazov	Russia
Featherweight (137 lbs.)	Magomedgasan Abushev	Russia
Lightweight (150 lbs.)	Saipulla Absaidov	Russia
Welterweight (163 lbs.)	Valentin Raitchev	Bulgaria
Middleweight (180 lbs.)	Ismail Abilov	Bulgaria
Light-heavyweight (198 lbs.)	Sanasar Oganesyan	Russia
Heavyweight (220 lbs.)	Ilya Mate	Russia
Super-heavyweight (over 220 lbs.)	Soslan Andiev	Russia

Wrestling (Greco-Roman)

Event	Winner	Country
Paperweight	Zaksylik Ushkempirov	Russia
Flyweight	Vakhtang Blagidze	Russia
Bantamweight	Shamil Serikov	Russia
Featherweight	Stilianos Migiakis	Greece
Lightweight	Stefan Rusu	Romania
Welterweight	Ferenc Kocsis	Hungary
Middleweight	Gennady Korban	Russia
Light-heavyweight	Norbert Nottny	Hungary
Heavyweight	Gheorghi Raikov	Bulgaria
Super-heavyweight	Alexandr Kolchinsky	Russia

Yachting

Event	Winner	Country	Mark
Finn class	Esko Rechardt	Finland	36.70 pts.
Soling class	Richard, Jensen	Denmark	23.00 pts.
Flying Dutchman	Abascal, Naguer	Spain	19.00 pts.
470 class	Soares, Penido	Brazil	36.40 pts.
Tornado class	Welter, Bjorkstrom	Brazil	21.40 pts.
Star class	Mankin, Muzychenko	Russia	24.70 pts.

Team Sports

Event	Country
Basketball (men)	Yugoslavia
Basketball (women)	Russia
Field hockey (men)	India
Field hockey (women)	Zimbabwe
Soccer	Czechoslovakia
Handball (men)	E. Germany
Handball (women)	Russia
Volleyball (men)	Russia
Volleyball (women)	Russia
Water polo	Russia

Alternative Olympics were promised by the White House for the athletes who did not go to Moscow. U. S. Olympic teams were chosen and international competitions were created or expanded for them, but that was no substitute for the Olympics.

In swimming, the Olympics trials were combined with the national outdoor championships, and the winning times were faster than the Olympic winning times in 10 of the 22 individual events for men and women. But the comparison was invalid, said Ambrose (Rowdy) Gaines IV of Winter Haven, Fla., who might have won four gold medals in the Olympics. "My time in the 200-meter free-style would have won the silver medal in Moscow," he said. "I know that if I was there, I would have won the gold. I'm not bragging. I just know that."

Indeed, Gaines and the other Americans probably would have dominated Olympic men's swimming, men's basketball, and archery, and Americans would have scored strongly in men's track and field, women's swimming, men's gymnastics, boxing, diving, water polo, and modern pentathlon. Instead, the Russians scored well in all these sports, though they were outdone by East Germans in rowing and women's swimming and by Cubans in boxing. Unaccountably, the Russians finished third to Yugoslavia and Italy in men's basketball.

The Russians won 80 gold medals, and the East Germans 47 (the previous record was Russia's 50 in 1972). Russians won a total of 197 medals, and East Germans won 126 (the record was Russia's 125 in 1976). No other country was close; the next four in total medals – Bulgaria, Hungary, Poland, and Romania – were Eastern-bloc nations.

Two highlights of the competition were the confrontations between Great Britain's Sebastian Coe and Steve Ovett, two world-record-holding middle-distance runners. Ovett won Coe's best event, the 800 meters, in 1 minute 45.4 seconds. Coe then won Ovett's best event, the 1,500 meters, in 3 minutes 38.4 seconds.

There were world records by Wladyslaw Kozakiewicz of Poland in the pole vault (5.78 meters, or 18 feet 11½ inches); Gerd Wessig of East Germany in the men's high jump (2.36 meters, or 7 feet 8¾ inches); Vladimir Salnikov in men's 1,500-meter free-style swimming (14 minutes 58.27 seconds); and East German women in six swimming events (see accompanying table).

More Controversy. Gymnastics again provided Olympian drama. Alexandr Ditiatin of Russia included the men's all-around title in his haul of eight medals, the most by any Olympian in any year. Nadia Comaneci of Romania, winner of three gold medals in 1976, returned as a young woman of 18 and won two more, though she lost her all-around title after a scoring controversy. Romania's

Vladimir Salnikov of Russia spots his winning time in 1,500-meter free-style swim: 14 minutes 58.27 seconds, which set a new world record.

coach charged that an East German official lowered Comaneci's score on the balance beam to ensure a Russian victory.

The greatest controversies came in men's track and field, where Russian officials were accused of aiding Russian athletes illegally in the pole vault, triple jump, discus throw, and javelin throw. The International Amateur Athletic Federation, the sports world's governing body, failed to react at first, then assumed control of the officials.

Moscow had expected 500,000 Olympic visitors, including 300,000 from other nations. The boycott reduced that number severely. The 100,000 foreign tourists included about 1,000 Americans rather than the anticipated 20,000, and Americans who had expected to watch 152½ hours of Olympic television at home had to settle for a few minutes a day.

The Moscow Olympics were efficiently organized. Transportation was good because private vehicles had been barred from Olympic traffic areas. Many athletes complained of boredom, and almost all visitors mentioned the incessant security checks. But the absence of athletes from the boycotting nations left voids in several areas.

Lord Killanin of Ireland, the outgoing president of the IOC, was bitter and sad, saying, "I only grieve for those who were not able to participate." At the closing ceremonies, he said, "I would ask

Nadia Comaneci, the darling of the 1976 Olympic Games, wins two gold medals in 1980 but loses her all-around title after a scoring dispute.

the sportsmen of the world to unite in peace before a holocaust descends."

Winter Games. When Franklin D. Roosevelt, then governor of New York, formally opened the III Winter Olympics in Lake Placid in 1932, life was simpler. Seventeen nations competed, an impressive figure considering the worldwide economic depression. The entire budget was $1.1 million, and the little town in the Adirondack Mountains suffered a deficit of $52,468.

Everything was on a grander scale this time. There were 1,283 athletes from 37 nations; the number of nations represented is significantly lower in Winter Games than in Summer Games because most nations do not compete in winter sports. The budget exceeded $150 million, most of that coming from the U.S. federal and state governments, and the deficit was $4.3 million.

Horror stories from Lake Placid left the impression that thousands of people were freezing to death waiting for buses. It was not that bad, but some spectators waited for hours in subfreezing temperatures for buses to take them to the competitions. The problems eased within a week when New York state officials took charge of the transportation and brought in more buses.

Medal Leaders. Between them, the Russians and East Germans won half of the 38 gold medals. Among them, the East Germans (23), Russians (22), and Americans (12) won almost half of the 115 total medals. There were few real surprises in any sport except for hockey.

The Olympic hockey teams of Russia, Czechoslovakia, Sweden, Finland, and other European nations play and train for 10 or 11 months each year. The United States had always put together a patchwork team at the last moment. Such an American team won the gold medal in 1960, but similar heroics seemed impossible in this day.

This time, the Americans spent six months training. They played 60 exhibition games, and learned a new, aggressive style of hockey from Herb Brooks, who had left his coaching job at the University of Minnesota to undertake the Olympic task. His 20-man team included 16 Midwesterners, eight of them from his college team. The four other players were from Boston University.

The Americans tied Sweden, 2-2, in their first game, a surprisingly good showing. They beat Czechoslovakia, 7-3, in their second game, a major upset. They won their next three games, qualifying them for the dubious honor of playing Russia.

Scalpers sold tickets for $500 a pair, and their supply ran out. With an astonishing performance, the Americans won, 4-3, and the spectators stormed out of the arena onto Main Street and sang and danced and chanted, "USA, USA." Two days later, the Americans beat Finland, 4-2, and won the gold medal.

Heiden was the first athlete to win five gold medals in any Winter Olympics. He won the 500, 1,000, 1,500, 5,000, and 10,000 meters against rivals who generally concentrated on two or three races, not five. Heiden was favored in each race, but this five-race parlay was a startling demonstration of virtuosity as a sprinter and distance skater.

Robin Cousins of Great Britain won the men's figure skating with dazzling free skating. Among the women, Linda Fratianne of Northridge, Calif., earned a silver medal with an exciting free-skating routine. Anett Poetzsch of East Germany won the gold medal. Randy Gardner and Tai Babilonia, the Californians who held the world pairs championship, lost a chance to try for the Olympic title because of a last-minute injury to Gardner. Irina Rodnina and her husband Alexander Zaitsev, the Soviet husband and wife team, won the gold.

Hanni Wenzel of tiny Liechtenstein won two gold medals and a silver in the three Alpine skiing events for women. Ingemar Stenmark of Sweden won two gold medals for men, with Phil Mahre of White Pass, Wash., taking the silver medal behind him in the special slalom. Eleven months before, Mahre suffered a four-part fracture of his left ankle on the same hill. Frank Litsky

See SAMARANCH, JUAN ANTONIO. In WORLD BOOK, see OLYMPIC GAMES.

OMAN. See MIDDLE EAST.

ONTARIO experienced its worst summer of forest fires since 1923, with more than 1,600 fires ranging over 1.4 million acres (567,000 hectares) in 1980. Fires started by lightning caused timber losses of as much as $200 million.

The Progressive Conservative administration of William G. Davis continued its minority role. It held 58 seats in the 125-member legislature, outnumbered by the combined weight of 34 Liberals and 33 New Democratic Party representatives. A three-month session ended on June 19 with 36 of 53 government bills approved. Provincial Treasurer Frank Miller introduced his second budget on April 22, with no tax increase for the first time in 10 years. A "minibudget" on November 13 removed the 7 per cent sales tax on furniture, appliances, and building materials.

The federal government announced on April 25 that a new nuclear refinery would be built at Blind River, north of Lake Huron and close to northern Ontario's uranium deposits, rather than at Port Hope, in southern Ontario, as originally proposed. Nuclear wastes would be disposed of in cavities drilled into the extremely stable pre-Cambrian rock of the Canadian Shield.   David M. L. Farr

See also CANADA. In WORLD BOOK, see ONTARIO.

OPERA. See MUSIC, CLASSICAL.

OREGON. See STATE GOVERNMENT.

PACIFIC ISLANDS. The troubled birth of the new republic of Vanuatu, formerly the New Hebrides, overshadowed all other events in the Pacific Islands in 1980. The republic, which came into being on July 30 with Walter Lini, an Anglican priest, as prime minister, comprises a group of fertile volcanic islands some 1,000 miles (1,600 kilometers) northeast of Queensland, Australia. It has a population of about 120,000, most of them Melanesians. The United States was represented at the independence ceremony by author James A. Michener, who based *Tales of the South Pacific* on his World War II experiences on one island, Espiritu Santo.

For the previous 74 years, the islands were ruled jointly by France and Great Britain. When independence was declared, much of the island of Espiritu Santo had been in the hands of rebels armed with bows and arrows for two months.

The Rebellion began on May 28 when islanders led by Jimmy Stevens, a local man, seized the main police station, took several officials hostage, and demanded political autonomy. More than 1,000 Melanesians from other islands and about 100 Australians and New Zealanders were evacuated.

After the Australian government publicly rebuked Britain and France for failing to put down the rebellion, British and French troops were sent to Espiritu Santo in mid-June. But they did nothing other than ensure that the Vanuatu flag could

Citizens of Vanuatu, formerly the New Hebrides, raise their national flag on July 30, marking the end of 74 years of British and French rule.

be raised on Independence Day. The rebels held out for nearly six weeks after independence, until they were overcome by a military force from Papua New Guinea that arrived on August 18. In 17 days, these troops quashed the rebellion with only one death. Stevens and others arrested were later jailed for up to 14 years.

Other Changes. Gaston Flosse, leader of the majority Conservative Party in French Polynesia's Territorial Assembly, reversed his party's position in March and demanded self-government for his country in a loose association with France. Flosse's reversal brought his party into line with all the other political groups in French Polynesia that have long struggled for autonomy.

The government of Michael Thomas Somare, prime minister of Papua New Guinea since independence in 1975, lost a vote of confidence on March 11 and was put out of office. Sir Julius Chan, a former deputy prime minister and treasurer, succeeded Somare. Prime Minister Peter Kenilorea was re-elected in the Solomon Islands in August.

Self-Rule Plan. The Marshall Islands, Federated States of Micronesia, and Palau Islands initialed agreements in late 1980 providing for their future self-government in "free association" with the U.S. The U.S., which has administered them since 1947, will retain responsibility for defense and

**Newest Pacific
Nation**

★ National capital

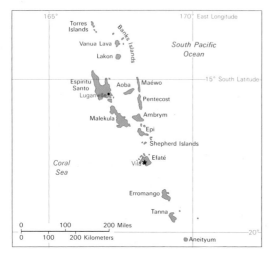

security. The three island groups are now part of the United Nations Trust Territory of the Pacific Islands. The trusteeship is expected to end in 1981. The Palau Islands became the republic of Belau on Jan. 1, 1981.

After 33 years of exile, the people of Enewetak Atoll, Marshall Islands, returned home on April 8, 1980. In 1947, the U.S. government removed 143 residents to use the atoll for nuclear tests. The islanders now number more than 450. Their return came after a three-year, $100-million cleanup program to rid the atoll of radioactivity.

Diplomats. When Commonwealth of Nations heads of government met in New Delhi, India, in September, Australia offered to allow diplomats of the Pacific Islands to be attached to Australian embassies and trade missions. The offer followed complaints by the prime ministers of Fiji and Vanuatu about the high cost of posting representatives overseas to keep abreast of economic developments.

The Sydney-based news magazine *Pacific Islands Monthly*, one of the Pacific area's best-known institutions, received many warm tributes from Pacific Islands leaders at its 50th-anniversary celebration in August.   Robert Langdon

In the WORLD BOOK SUPPLEMENT section, see KIRIBATI. In WORLD BOOK, see PACIFIC ISLANDS.
PAINTING. See VISUAL ARTS.

PAKISTAN suffered peril from without and deep unease at home in 1980. With about 85,000 Russian troops in Afghanistan, Russia had become Pakistan's immediate, and hostile, neighbor. By September, about 1 million Afghan refugees were crammed into border camps in Pakistan, adding to the pressures on the nation's lean resources.

Many of the refugees were civilians fleeing the continuing guerrilla fighting in Afghanistan, but others were armed rebels who—in one way or another—brought violence to Pakistan. About 9,000 armed Afghan rebels based on Pakistan's borders crossed into their homeland to join intensified fighting against the Russians. Rival Afghan rebel leaders fought each other in Peshawar in August. Pakistan reported on September 26 that six armed Afghan helicopters had attacked a border outpost near the Khyber Pass, killing two Pakistani soldiers. See AFGHANISTAN (Close-Up).

Internal Tensions were largely the product of the heavy-handed regime of President Mohammad Zia-ul-Haq, the general who seized power in a July 1977 coup d'état that unseated Prime Minister Zulfikar Ali Bhutto. Although Zia promised "free and fair" elections immediately after the coup, the pledge was not kept. Political parties and activities were still banned, and thousands of persons remained in prison, many of them mistreated.

Despite army threats, there were strikes, with lawyers leading the protests. Some legal strikes followed Zia's amendment of the Constitution in May to deny civilian courts the power to review decisions of the military courts, which handle not only military hearings, but also all matters coming under the nation's harsh martial law.

Shiite Muslims, who make up about one-third of Pakistan's population and draw their inspiration from Iran's Ayatollah Ruhollah Khomeini, demonstrated in Islamabad, the capital, in July. About 25,000 persons protested two new religious taxes. Violence broke out during the two days of demonstrations, but it was ended by police and the army.

The Wheat Harvest was excellent, exceeding 10 million short tons (9 million metric tons), and grain exports continued to rise. These were the only bright spots in an economic picture made bleak by soaring oil prices and a global recession. Western economists put the inflation rate at 20 per cent, about twice the official estimate.

After the Soviet invasion of Afghanistan, the United States offered Pakistan $400 million in aid, but Zia rejected it as "peanuts." He had asked the United States for "several billions" to help build up his armed forces. The United States was unwilling to increase its aid until Zia gave up the "Islamic A-bomb" he has been building just outside of Islamabad with Libyan aid.   Mark Gayn

See also ASIA (Facts in Brief Table). In WORLD BOOK, see PAKISTAN.

PALEONTOLOGY. Scientists offered new and important evidence in 1980 to support a surprising explanation for why dinosaurs, along with 70 per cent of all animal and plant species, became extinct at the end of the Cretaceous Period 65 million years ago. A giant meteorite, or asteroid, may have struck the earth, raising a dust cloud that enveloped the earth in almost total darkness for years, preventing plant growth and starving animal life.

The idea that a meteorite caused the mass extinction is not new, but until recently most geologists discounted it. Then in 1979, Luis W. Alvarez, a physicist at Lawrence Berkeley Laboratory (LBL), and his son Walter Alvarez, a geologist at the University of California, Berkeley, announced they had found greatly increased concentrations of the precious metal iridium in sediments dating from the time when the Cretaceous Period was changing to the Tertiary Period, the next geologic period in the earth's history. They published a full report on the meteorite theory in June 1980 with co-authors Frank Asaro and Helen V. Michel, also of LBL.

The scientists measured the concentration of iridium in seabed rock from Denmark, Italy, and New Zealand. The concentrations were from 20 to 160 times the expected level. Because iridium is much more abundant in extraterrestrial material such as meteorites than in the earth's crust, the Alvarez group concluded that the increased iridium came from a giant meteorite that disintegrated when it struck the earth. Iridium-rich dust was then thrown into the atmosphere and slowly settled to become ocean sediment.

The Scientists Estimated the size of the meteorite on the basis of the amount of iridium in meteorites and in today's sediments and concluded that it was about 6 miles (10 kilometers) in diameter. Astronomers have estimated that a meteorite of this size strikes the earth only once in about 100 million years. Because paleontologists have found evidence for five mass extinctions of life in the last 570 million years, the Alvarez group suggests that all five were caused by meteorite impacts.

The scientists estimate that the meteorite probably created 1,000 times more dust than issued from the eruption of the volcano Krakatoa in 1883, one of the world's major disasters. This dust, the Alvarez group speculate, would have turned day into night for several years. Photosynthesis, the process plants use to grow, would cease immediately, and most of the tiny, single-celled ocean plants would become extinct because few had reproductive spores able to survive in the dark for years. Land plants, with their roots and seeds, would have a better chance to survive. Most animals in the oceans and on land would quickly become extinct as plant growth ceased. But small animals that could eat decaying plants, roots,

Although *Argentavis magnificens* looks like a prop for a horror film, it is a re-creation of what the world's largest bird looked like.

seeds, and organic material in the mud would have the best chance of making it through the crisis.

Another Study of the Cretaceous-Tertiary boundary sediments, published in August 1980, supported the meteorite theory. Ramachanbran Ganapathy of the J. R. Baker Chemical Company in Phillipsburg, N.J., measured the concentrations of nine precious metals in the boundary clay from Denmark. He reasoned that if iridium found by the Alvarez group had come from a meteorite, related metals – osmium, gold, platinum, rhenium, ruthenium, palladium, nickel, and cobalt – should also be concentrated in the boundary sediments because they are 100 to 10,000 times more abundant in meteorites than in the earth's crust. Ganapathy found that the concentrations of these metals were close to what would be expected if they came from the disintegration of a large meteorite.

Monster Bird. The discovery of fossils that represent the world's largest flying bird was announced in September. Paleontologists Eduardo P. Tonni and Rosendo Pascual of the La Plata Museum in Argentina discovered the bird, which they say stood 6 feet (1.8 meters) tall and had a wingspan of 25 feet (7.5 meters). They named it *Argentavis magnificens* and said that the bird, which is related to living condors, lived about 5 million to 8 million years ago.   Ida Thompson

In WORLD BOOK, see FOSSIL; PALEONTOLOGY.

PANAMA. In a carefully orchestrated election held on Sept. 28, 1980, the progovernment Democratic Revolutionary Party (DRP) won 12 of the 19 new seats at stake in the executive council of the National Assembly. It was the first election in which political parties have been allowed to take part since a military coup d'état in 1968. Although 35 to 40 per cent of Panama's electorate stayed home, the government had left little to chance; 37 other seats in the legislature were filled by progovernment appointees selected by the National Assembly.

Anti-Shah Protests. The presence of the ailing exiled Shah Mohammad Reza Pahlavi of Iran caused unrest in Panama. The shah ended his stay at Lackland Air Force Base in Texas on Dec. 15, 1979, and by prearrangement between U.S. and Panamanian authorities flew to Contadora Island off Panama's Pacific coast. Students and left wing groups demonstrated against his presence. In one incident, 150 students stoned the United States Embassy in Panama City before being dispersed by the National Guard. Further aggravating the situation was a move by the Iranian government to submit a formal request for his extradition.

A major high-level complication was the need for an expert diagnosis of the shah's worsening physical condition and an expected need for highly skilled surgeons to remove his cancerous spleen. U.S. authorities had insisted any medical tests or surgery should be performed by an American doctor in a U.S. military hospital in Panama. Panama insisted the operation be carried out under Panamanian control. The shah ended the near-impasse by accepting permanent asylum in Egypt. He departed from Panama on March 23 and on March 26 was hospitalized in Cairo, where he died on July 27. See EGYPT.

Panama's Economy was buoyed by U.S. payments received as part of the transfer arrangements on the Panama Canal. The government used some of the funding to expand health and education programs. Foreign investment increased owing to the stability that was expected to follow the successful implementation of the canal treaties. Plans were made to mine rich copper deposits at Cerro Colorado, thought by some to constitute the country's most important economic asset.

President Aristides Royo worked out an agreement in March whereby Japan would undertake a feasibility study for a second canal across the isthmus that could more efficiently serve today's fleets, including supertankers. Japan also pledged to provide half of $133 million needed to modernize the Atlantic Ocean port of Colón and expand a free-trade zone there.   Nathan A. Haverstock

See also LATIN AMERICA (Facts in Brief Table). In WORLD BOOK, see PANAMA.

PAPUA NEW GUINEA. See ASIA; PACIFIC ISLANDS.

PARAGUAY. The construction of hydroelectric power plants along the Paraná River provided a sharp upward thrust to the Paraguayan economy in 1980. Three plants are being built on the Paraná, at places called Itaipú, Yacyretá, and Corpus, with financing provided by the World Bank, the Inter-American Development Bank, and Paraguay's neighbors Brazil and Argentina.

Nearest to completion is the gigantic power plant at Itaipú, a joint Brazil-Paraguay undertaking. When completed, the Itaipú plant will be the world's largest single source of electricity, with an installed capacity of 12.6 million kilowatts. The plant will increase 40-fold the power-generating capacity of Paraguay and make the nation the potential exporter of an estimated $500 million worth of power annually to neighboring Brazil.

The Itaipú Dam rises like a great cathedral on the upper Paraná River. A force of 24,000 persons, working 24 hours a day, was building it during 1980. The work has generated a sharply rising demand for wood and other locally available construction materials, and housing for a sizable construction population together with supporting services. Since construction began at Itaipú in 1976, the towns on either side of the river have become cities. President Alfredo Stroessner, longtime Paraguayan strongman, was reportedly awaiting completion of the first stage of construction in 1983 before retiring.

Stroessner has ruled Paraguay for 26 years. The nation's Constitution was amended in 1977 so he could serve indefinitely as president. The usual international charges of repression and police brutality were brought against his authoritarian government in 1980. These allegations grew in intensity after Stroessner's embrace of Nicaragua's ousted strongman Anastasio Somoza Debayle, who was hard put to find a nation willing to provide him exile after the United States discouraged his efforts.

Somoza was assassinated in Asunción on September 17 by terrorists who attacked his car with a bazooka blast and machine-gun fire barely 300 yards (275 meters) from Stroessner's residence. None of the assassins was wounded or captured.

Paraguay's Economy did well during 1980, with the large inflow of capital for the hydroelectric plants. Housing construction boomed in Asunción, the capital. Planning went forward, too, on how to use the new sources of energy in bringing into production the four-fifths of Paraguay's farmland that is not being fully utilized.   Nathan A. Haverstock

See also LATIN AMERICA (Facts in Brief Table). In WORLD BOOK, see PARAGUAY.

PARENTS AND TEACHERS, NATIONAL CONGRESS OF. See NATIONAL PTA (NATIONAL CONGRESS OF PARENTS AND TEACHERS).

PENNSYLVANIA. See PHILADELPHIA; STATE GOVERNMENT.

PERSONALITIES OF 1980 included the following:

Adams, Harriet Stratemeyer, 87, disclosed the secret of literary longevity to 500 guests at a party on August 16. Writing under the name of Carolyn Keene, she was at work on her 59th Nancy Drew mystery. The party celebrated her heroine's 50th anniversary, even though the dauntless girl detective had aged only two years — from 16 to 18 — between 1930 and 1980. The author said she kept the stories up to date by asking advice from her children and grandchildren.

Anderson, Maxie L., 45, a businessman from Albuquerque, N. Mex., and his son Kris, 23, completed the first nonstop balloon trip across the North American continent on May 12. For four perilous days, they floated in the helium-filled *Kitty Hawk* from San Francisco to Gaspé Peninsula in Canada, covering 3,100 miles (5,000 kilometers). Echoing the stalwart spirit that in 1978 took him and two companions across the Atlantic Ocean in the *Double Eagle II,* Maxie Anderson said, "I think it tests your mettle . . . it was an adventure."

Astaire, Fred, 81, did not dance on the ceiling or even down the center aisle, but he did appear to be walking on air in June when he married Robyn Smith, 35, at his home in Beverly Hills, Calif. The romantic and still agile octogenarian declined to don "white tie, top hat, and tails," but the bride wore a dress — not the racing silks she customarily sports as one of the best-known female jockeys.

Bosket, William, 38, was presented with a key on March 15, but it would not unlock his cell at the United States Penitentiary in Leavenworth, Kans. Bosket's "key" was the symbol of his membership in Phi Beta Kappa. He was the first prison inmate ever inducted into the honorary scholarship society. Bosket, serving a term for bank robbery, earned a bachelor's degree from the University of Kansas with a 3.97 grade-point average out of a possible 4.

Christian, Glynn, 38, of London, a great-great-great-great grandson of Fletcher Christian — leader of the mutineers on the British ship, the *Bounty* — in April took command of *Taiyo,* a 94-foot (29-meter) vessel, planning to retrace his ancestor's 1789 South Pacific voyage. Another descendant, airline pilot Arthur Munro Christian, 53, of San Francisco, historian of the H.M.S. *Bounty* Society, attended a bon voyage party on *Taiyo* and agreed with Glynn that Fletcher Christian's antagonist, the infamous Captain William Bligh, was not really a cruel man. They believe that the two men simply did not get along.

Clark, Edward, 50, Libertarian Party candidate for President, became the first independent presidential candidate to win a place on the ballot in all 50 states and the District of Columbia. In contrast

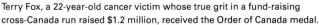
Terry Fox, a 22-year-old cancer victim whose true grit in a fund-raising cross-Canada run raised $1.2 million, received the Order of Canada medal.

with other political hopefuls who vied with each other in making generous campaign promises, Clark and his running mate, lawyer David Koch of New York City, stressed that government exists solely to protect individual freedom. Clark received more than 880,000 votes on November 4.

Commoner, Barry, 63, an environmental scientist at Washington University in St. Louis, in April organized the Citizens' Party and became its candidate for President of the United States. Running with LaDonna Harris, Commoner told his supporters that if the established political parties could not solve the nation's problems, "our answer to them is to move over, we'll do it." Commoner got about 220,000 votes on November 4.

Fox, Terry, 22, became the youngest Companion of the Order of Canada in September. Fox ran a 3,200-mile (5,150-kilometer) "Marathon of Hope" to raise funds for cancer research – despite having lost his right leg to the disease three years earlier. In presenting the award, which recognizes Canadians' accomplishments in the field of human endeavor, Governor General Edward R. Schreyer said Fox's feat had "succeeded in helping to build a better country."

Gatica, Pedro Alejandro, 45, arrived in New York City in May on a "grand tour" that was also a grand gesture. The Argentine house painter took eight months to reach the Big Apple from his hometown of Chivilcoy near Buenos Aires – but he covered the 11,500 miles (18,500 kilometers) on a bicycle. Gatica had dreamed for years of making the journey "to symbolize the joining of America." Pedaling through 14 countries along the way, the determined dreamer collected hundreds of messages of good will and support.

Gelinas, John, Jr., 18, found the water near his Scarsdale, N.Y., home too cold for water-skiing last spring, so he went to Florida. Why? Because John wanted to earn his last – and 121st – Boy Scout merit badge, the largest number possible. Eagle Scout Gelinas, one of few Scouts to achieve that record, said, "I guess I have to set a new goal now."

Henderson, Daphne, a hotelkeeper in Looe, England, would never carry coals to Newcastle, but she knew what to do with a 29-pound (12-kilogram) sturgeon caught off the coast – present it to the palace. A rarely invoked statute proclaimed by King Edward II in 1324 decreed that "the King shall have whales and sturgeons taken in the sea and elsewhere within the realm." So when Henderson's fishmonger sold her a super sturgeon for $300, she offered it to Queen Elizabeth II. Assuming that only token notice would be taken, Henderson then planned a charity banquet featuring the fish. However, the queen gladly accepted, and instead of starring at a local dinner, Henderson's proffered piscine prize wound up smoked for the royal breakfast table.

Mickey Mouse meets House Speaker Thomas P. (Tip) O'Neill, Jr., during a lobbying effort for a presidential proclamation honoring Walt Disney.

Hoffman, Abbie, 44, who gained notoriety as a radical Yippie leader in the 1960s, emerged after six years "underground" in September and revealed some startling facts about his interim activities. After he jumped bail in 1974 on a drug charge in New York City, Hoffman changed his face (through plastic surgery); his name (to Barry Freed); and his game (to environmental activist). He spoke at businessmen's clubs, testified before a U.S. Senate subcommittee, and was praised by New York Governor Hugh L. Carey for his "keen public spirit." Keen he is; Freed became Hoffman again just in time to publicize his autobiography, titled *Soon to Be a Major Motion Picture* – and movie rights were sold to Universal Pictures.

McLuhan, Marshall, 68, in June got the message that his teaching medium, the Center for Culture and Technology at Canada's University of Toronto, would be closed and he would have to retire. The man who proclaimed "the medium is the message" in the 1960s was recovering from a stroke. In spite of his illness, he completed a new book, *Laws of the Media,* before he died on the morning of December 31.

Restivo, James, 42, a New York City detective, refused to close a murder file and finally got his man in February – even though the case took all his off-duty hours for four months. Deeply affected by the senseless slaying of an immigrant who had recently realized his lifelong dream of owning his own restaurant, Restivo pieced together evidence from endless small clues. "It's not like television where cops solve a crime in one hour, with three commercials in-between," he remarked.

Russell, Harold, 66, never studied acting, but he won an Academy of Motion Pictures Arts and Sciences Award on his first try as best supporting actor in the 1946 film, *The Best Years of Our Lives.* The World War II veteran depicted a young man much like himself – a soldier who lost his hands in combat. Russell then packed up his Oscar, left Hollywood, and went into business. He returned in February 1980 to make his second movie, *Inside Moves.* He plays one of several handicapped persons who meet in a bar and decide to help one another. "I love this part," he said. "This picture is going to show that handicapped people can have dreams that come true. My own have come true. But I want this movie to give hope to others."

Scott Cowper, David, 28, a land surveyor from Newcastle upon Tyne, England, went to sea and set a record. He guided the 40-foot (12-meter) sailboat *Ocean Bound* into Plymouth Harbor on April 23 after 225 days of actual sailing time on a round-the-world voyage – one day faster than the record set by Sir Francis Chichester in 1967. Scott Cowper, who among other adversities survived a near-capsizing and endured gales and arctic temperatures between South Africa and Australia on his 30,000-mile (48,000-kilometer) voyage, remarked dryly, "I thoroughly enjoyed the whole trip."

Stewart, James, 71, still spry and evoking smiles as he did so often during his acting career, cheerfully accepted the American Film Institute's eighth life-achievement award on February 28. Cited for his performances in such films as *Mr. Smith Goes to Washington* (1939) and *Harvey* (1950), Stewart called himself "a remarkably fortunate fellow."

Truax, Robert, 63, a retired U.S. Navy captain from Fremont, Calif., who worked on developing the Polaris missile, carried a do-it-yourself project to a sky-high climax in June. Using four surplus Atlas steering rocket engines that cost $115 each at a scrapyard instead of their original $70,000 per unit, Truax built and successfully test-fired a 25-foot (8-meter) rocket he calls the X-3. He and 38 investors in Project Private Enterprise plan to hire an astronaut and launch the first privately sponsored suborbital flight late in 1981 to prove that inexpensive, reusable rockets are practical.

Urban, Matt, 60, of Holland, Mich., a retired U.S. Army lieutenant colonel, wept as he received the Medal of Honor, the nation's highest award for military valor, from President Jimmy Carter on July 19. A soldier who fought against the German Army in France under Colonel Urban recommended him for the award – in 1944. But no action was taken until a search for the letter of recommenda-

At first nobody believed him, but New York City eighth-grader Michael Morris did interview former President Nixon for a school assignment.

tion was begun in 1978. Two years later, with members of Colonel Urban's Ninth Infantry Division in attendance, President Carter cited him for "bold, courageous, inspired, and heroic action."

Virtue, David, in 1980 took over the position of public relations spokesman for a national organization from John Duguid (pronounced do-good), who became the group's special secretary for literature. It would be hard to find two more appropriately named executives – their employer is the American Bible Society.

Youngman, Henny, 73, was a bit over-age for a bar mitzvah, but he joyfully celebrated his coming of age according to the Jewish ceremony on January 12. He always regretted missing out on the big day when he was 13 because of a death in the family. Coached for the ritual by an old friend, tenor Jan Peerce, Youngman could not resist cracking one of his trademark one-liners: "I'm being bar mitzvahed now," he said, "because it took me 60 years to memorize the speech."

Yourcenar, Marguerite, 77, a novelist who lives in Northeast Harbor, Me., won a novel place in the history of literature on March 6. She became the first woman elected to the prestigious French Academy since it was founded in 1635. The author, born in France and a citizen of the United States for more than 30 years, had her French nationality restored in 1979.

Marsha F. Goldsmith

437

PERU celebrated its return to democratic government in 1980. On July 28, Fernando Belaunde Terry – who had been deposed in a military coup d'état in 1968 – took the oath of office as Peru's 85th president. Belaunde had captured 43 per cent of the popular vote in elections held May 18, winning decisively over other candidates. His victory reflected the nation's deep disenchantment with the left wing military rule that had increasingly isolated Peru from its neighbors and left the nation's economy in a shambles.

Rosalynn Carter, the wife of United States President Jimmy Carter, attended Belaunde's inauguration ceremony. The chiefs of state of several other democracies, including Colombia, Costa Rica, Spain, and Venezuela, also attended.

Belaunde said at his inauguration that Peru's return to constitutional rule guaranteed the "full exercise, from this moment, of human rights and freedom of the press." On his first full day in office, the new leader returned to their rightful owners seven newspapers that had been expropriated six years earlier. Belaunde also vowed to fight corruption and discontinue wasteful outlays for armaments, previously justified by the military because of border disputes with Chile and Bolivia. Belaunde also announced immediate administrative reform of the government's major ministries and state-run enterprises, which had become centers of petty corruption and bureaucratic overstaffing.

The problems the new president inherited from his predecessors were scarcely encouraging. Unemployment was extremely high, and the number of people working at less than the minimum wage, or less than 35 hours per week, was estimated at nearly 50 per cent of Peru's working force. Inflation was running at 70 per cent annually. Because of political instability, investment in the nation's all-important mining sector had all but dried up.

As the year progressed, Belaunde sought to encourage foreign investment with which to expand mining, fishing, and petroleum production. Large-scale public works construction programs were started to put people to work. Plans were laid to increase governmental support for the revitalization of Peru's agricultural sector. Low-interest credit was made available for housing construction as well as modernization programs to improve farm production methods. Almost all of the funds needed to carry out the programs were expected to derive from a $2-billion loan from the World Bank and other multilateral credit agencies and major international banks.   Nathan A. Haverstock

See also LATIN AMERICA (Facts in Brief Table). In WORLD BOOK, see PERU.

PET. See CAT; DOG. In the Special Reports section, see WHAT IS YOUR PET TRYING TO TELL YOU?

PETROLEUM AND GAS. The war between Iraq and Iran that broke out in September 1980 extensively damaged petroleum refineries, pipelines, and other installations in both countries, halting oil exports that had been averaging about 3.7 million barrels per day (bpd). Iranian bombers inflicted severe damage on key Iraqi refineries at Kirkuk, Basra, Baghdad, and Mosul. Iraq's major crude-oil loading sites on the Persian Gulf also were damaged. Prior to the conflict, Iraq was second only to Saudi Arabia as the leading oil exporter in the Organization of Petroleum Exporting Countries (OPEC). Its exports averaged about 3 million bpd.

Iran's important oil refinery at Abadan, one of the world's largest, also suffered serious damage. The country's main petroleum export terminal at Kharg Island also was severely damaged. Iran had been exporting about 700,000 bpd.

Saudi Arabia and other members of OPEC moved to increase their oil production to offset losses from Iraq and Iran. The conflict sent France, India, Brazil, and other countries scrambling to find new sources of petroleum. But the war occurred during a world oil surplus estimated at as much as 2.5 million bpd. So the estimated 40 countries supplied by Iraq and Iran were able to find alternative sources. As countries affected by the cutoff sought new sources of oil, prices on the spot market – where petroleum not committed to

Rosalynn Carter, wife of U.S. President Carter, congratulates Peru's new President Fernando Belaunde Terry after his inauguration in July.

After signing his long-sought bill to tax "windfall" oil profits, President
Jimmy Carter receives the applause of federal legislators and officials.

long-term contracts is sold – rose from $31 per
barrel to more than $40.

The World Oil Surplus occurred as a result of
higher oil prices, conservation measures, and an
economic slowdown that reduced demand for oil in
the United States and other countries. U.S. petroleum imports fell to their lowest levels in five years
by autumn, and oil stockpiles bulged to record
levels. By December, imports of crude oil and
refined petroleum products averaged 6.7 million
bpd, down 19.4 per cent from 1979.

United States oil inventories stood at 385.3
million barrels by December, 12 per cent above the
amount held in storage a year earlier. There was
plenty of gasoline throughout the year, with unleaded gas selling for a nationwide average of
$1.269 per gallon (3.8 liters) during peak summer
driving months.

Drilling for Oil and Natural Gas reached the highest levels in the United States in almost 25 years, as
drillers rushed to capitalize on higher prices. The
Natural Gas Supply Association said that there
were 3,069 rotary drilling rigs in operation around
the country on August 25, the highest level of
drilling activity since Dec. 19, 1955, when 3,137
rigs were in operation. *Oil & Gas Journal,* the
authoritative industry publication, estimated that
59,107 domestic wells would be completed during
1980, breaking a 24-year-old record that petroleum

analysts thought could never even be approached
again. The previous record was 58,160 wells drilled
in 1956.

Hectic drilling activity was partially responsible
for a pause in the long-term downward trend of
domestic petroleum production. U.S. production
was up about 0.7 per cent for the first 11 months of
the year. Production averaged 8.6 million bpd,
compared with 8.5 million bpd in 1979. Most of the
rise resulted from production increases in the
North Slope oil fields of Alaska.

Proven Reserves of domestic crude oil and natural gas continued their decline during 1979, the
last year for which complete data are available. But
the American Petroleum Institute said in May that
the decline in oil reserves was the smallest in nine
years. And the American Gas Association reported
that more gas was added to reserves from the
contiguous 48 states in 1979 than in any year since
1967. Proven crude oil reserves stood at about 27
billion barrels at the start of 1980, a decline of 752
million barrels from the 27.8 billion barrels that
existed at the start of 1979. More oil – 239 million
barrels – was added to reserves through the discovery of new fields than in any year since 1970, when
Alaska's Prudhoe Bay fields were added.

Much of the increase was due to the decontrol of
U.S. domestic oil prices in 1979, which made
formerly uneconomic fields more valuable. On

April 2, President Jimmy Carter signed the Crude Oil Windfall Profit Tax Act of 1980, designed to complement decontrol. The law was expected to produce $227 billion in government revenues from the earnings of domestic oil producers by 1990.

Total proven natural gas reserves stood at 194.9 trillion cubic feet (5.52 trillion cubic meters), down from 200.3 trillion cubic feet (5.6 trillion cubic meters) a year earlier. Total additions to reserves in the contiguous 48 states were 13.7 trillion cubic feet (388 billion cubic meters), a 12-year high. Another 600 billion cubic feet (17 billion cubic meters) were added from Alaska.

Pipeline Start. Construction began on July 29 on the first segment of the Alaska Natural Gas Transportation System, a 4,787-mile (7,704-kilometer) pipeline that eventually will carry more than 2 billion cubic feet (57 million cubic meters) of gas each day from Prudhoe Bay to the lower United States. The pipeline is being built in two stages. First to be completed will be a 1,500-mile (2,400-kilometer) section originating in the rich Canadian gas fields of Alberta, and split into an eastern and a western leg as it travels south into the United States. The eastern leg will carry up to 800 million cubic feet (23 million cubic meters) of gas per day to markets in the Midwest, South, and East. The western leg will carry up to 300 million cubic feet

(8.5 million cubic meters) per day to southern California.

New Developments. On August 26, the U.S. Department of the Interior lifted a 15-year moratorium on tar sands leasing on federal land in Utah. There are an estimated 30 billion barrels of tar sands oil in the United States. About 2 billion barrels can be recovered with existing technology.

The Continental Oil Company unveiled a "major advance" in deep-sea oil-drilling technology on January 16. The company's new "tension-leg" drilling platform, under development for five years, will permit the production of oil from seabed deposits lying under as much as 2,000 feet (610 meters) of water — roughly twice the depth at which drilling can now be done.

More for Mexico. Mexican President Jose Lopez Portillo announced a 20 per cent increase in the country's proven hydrocarbon reserves during his annual State of the Nation address on September 1. Mexico now has reserves equivalent to 60 billion barrels of crude oil, up from the previous estimate of 50 billion barrels. Pemex, the Mexican national oil company, announced plans to double domestic oil-refining capacity to meet growing demands for gasoline.

Russian Reduction. A study of world oil-production trends by the U.S. Central Intelligence Agen-

A 936-foot (285-meter) liquid natural gas (LNG) tanker undergoes sea tests. Its five insulated spheres will hold the LNG at subzero temperatures.

cy (CIA) said that Russia's oil production peaked in 1980 and would begin to decline in 1981. CIA Director Stansfield Turner warned that the decline will transform Russia and its allies from oil exporters to importers within the next several years. The result will be a "vicious struggle" among the world's nations for oil, and chronic oil shortages. The study concluded that Russian oil production would peak at about 11.9 million bpd during 1980, and then decline steadily to 9 million bpd by 1985. A Swedish report of a gigantic new Russian oil find, amounting to as much as 4.5 trillion barrels, rattled oil stock prices briefly in December, but was quickly discounted by experts.

North Sea Oil production in the British sector reached 1.65 million bpd by midyear, and was expected to rise to 1.8 million or 1.9 million bpd by year's end. This would be enough oil to meet virtually all of Great Britain's domestic needs. A group of oil companies drilling in the North Sea in July, about 70 miles (110 kilometers) off the coast of Norway, found what may be one of the world's largest natural gas fields. Estimates of possible reserves in the field, which lies beneath about 1,100 feet (335 meters) of water, ranged between 50 trillion and 70 trillion cubic feet (1.4 trillion and 2 trillion cubic meters).   Michael Woods

See also ENERGY. In WORLD BOOK, see PETROLEUM; GAS (Fuel).

Philadelphia police and fire fighters surround City Hall in February to protest announced budget-cutting layoffs in their departments.

PHILADELPHIA. Three City Council leaders were indicted on May 22, 1980, for accepting bribes from a Federal Bureau of Investigation (FBI) agent posing as an Arab millionaire in the so-called Abscam scandal. George X. Schwartz resigned as City Council president following his indictment, then resigned from the council following his September 16 conviction for conspiracy to commit bribery. He was replaced by Joseph E. Coleman, the first black to be elected City Council president. Council majority leader Harry P. Jannotti was also convicted of conspiracy charges on September 16, and Councilman Louis C. Johanson was convicted of similar charges on August 31. The convictions of Schwartz and Jannotti were overturned by U.S. District Court Judge John P. Fullam on November 26. He ruled that the FBI had entrapped the defendants.

Two Democratic congressmen from Philadelphia — Michael Myers and Raymond F. Lederer — were also indicted in the Abscam scandal. Myers was convicted of bribery charges on August 31 and expelled from the U.S. House of Representatives. See CONGRESS OF THE UNITED STATES.

Fiscal Problems. Mayor William J. Green projected a $28-million budget deficit for fiscal 1980 in his State of the City address on February 4, and called for layoffs of city employees, increased taxes, and departmental budget tightening. On March 4,

Green announced a "10-point tax-enforcement crackdown" on 100,000 persons and corporations who owed the city more than $138 million in taxes.

Police and fire-fighter union leaders threatened to strike in response to Green's plan to cut 738 police- and 256 fire-department jobs. Police staged a "sick-in" on February 9 and snarled traffic around City Hall during a February 11 demonstration. Philadelphia fire fighters signed a two-year contract on May 11 with a pay freeze the first year and a 10 per cent increase the second.

A U.S. District Court on July 15 ordered the Police Department to fill 30 per cent of the next 2,670 positions on the force and the next 16 detective and 17 sergeant positions with women. The order came as a settlement of a sex-discrimination suit brought against the department in 1974.

Philadelphia's 23,000 schoolteachers went on strike on September 1 to protest wage rates and the layoff of 2,300 school district employees in an effort to balance the district's $757-million budget. The strike ended on September 23 with an agreement that froze wages but rehired 2,000 teachers.

Law and Order. Three nights of violence in north Philadelphia followed the August 24 shooting of a black teen-ager by a white police officer, John Ziegler. Ziegler was charged with murder on August 29.   James M. Banovetz

In WORLD BOOK, see PHILADELPHIA.

PHILIPPINES. Pressure to restore democratic rule increased on President Ferdinand E. Marcos in August 1980 as the nation neared the end of eight years of martial law. A series of terrorist bombings rocked buildings in and around Manila on August 22, and a previously unknown group said it set the blasts. On August 29, eight opposition political groups issued a joint "Covenant for Freedom."

Nine bombs exploded on August 22 in government and private offices and banks in Manila without causing serious injury. However, the bombing of nine buildings in Manila on September 12 killed an American tourist and injured 33 other persons. Bombings on October 12 also caused injuries, and a convention of the American Society of Travel Agents was bombed on October 19 in an effort to discourage tourists. The April 6 Liberation Movement, which took its name from anti-Marcos demonstrations staged in the spring of 1978, claimed responsibility for the attacks.

Defense Minister Juan Ponce Enrile attributed the bombings to a faction of a Roman Catholic and Protestant opposition group known as Social Democrats. He called the organization a "potent and dangerous group" because of its broad scope, with members ranging from professional people to workers, and because there was "a moral quality to their movement." Other officials implied that former Senator Benigno S. Aquino, Jr., was involved, but they offered no proof, and Aquino denied it.

Aquino, whom the terrorists said "can be a rallying point for our people," was released after almost eight years in prison on May 8 so he could fly to Dallas for heart surgery. In a speech in New York on August 4, Aquino warned that rural insurgency would escalate in the Philippines unless martial law were lifted.

The Covenant for Freedom was signed by 72 persons, including several who were political leaders before Marcos assumed total power in 1972. It called for an immediate end to Marcos' dictatorship, the abolition of martial law, free elections, and other changes in government.

The first nationwide series of local elections under martial law was held on January 30. Marcos' New Society Movement won, but he said there had been fraud by both supporters and opponents. Two supporters quit the movement in protest.

Defense Minister Enrile reported that the New People's Army, a Communist guerrilla group with scattered pockets of strength, had increased its armed forces from 3,000 to 5,400 in recent years. The Moro National Liberation Front staged terrorist attacks in the southern islands sporadically throughout the year. The group sought autonomy or independence for Muslims.   Henry S. Bradsher

See also ASIA (Facts in Brief Table). In WORLD BOOK, see PHILIPPINES.

PHONOGRAPH. See RECORDINGS.

PHOTOGRAPHY. Stereo (three-dimensional) and video photography made news in 1980, along with lenses that focus automatically and can be interchanged between one camera and another. The four-lensed, handheld Nimslo camera produces pictures that can be printed to give the illusion of three dimensions to show depth. It uses ordinary 35-millimeter (mm) film that is specially processed and will appear on the market in 1981.

Videotape recorders, as well as small, hand-sized video cameras and video-disk players, continued to be announced for early delivery, though manufacturers have not settled on a standard system of reproduction. Sony Corporation demonstrated a prototype movie-camera-sized, battery-operated, TV color camera and recorder they expect to perfect within five years. Although they are still expensive, electronic cameras and recorders are expected eventually to replace home-movie equipment for hobbyists. They can be played back instantly through a TV set, and the tapes can be erased and used again.

Single-Lens Models. Camera designers continued to stress improved single-lens reflex (SLR) models. Several professional-level SLR's appeared, including the Nikon F3 and the Pentax LX. Both are system cameras backed by many lenses and accessories, and each measures exposures automat-

The only known photograph of naturalist John James Audubon, made by photographer Matthew Brady in 1847, was found in Cincinnati in 1980.

A fire fighter hoses down thousands of charred cans of irreplaceable movie film after fire destroyed a museum warehouse near Paris in August.

ically at the film plane. The Minolta CLE, a compact range-finder camera with automatic exposure and focal-plane exposure metering, also appeared.

The Ricoh Camera Company showed a prototype camera with a battery system that is recharged by sunlight or bright artificial light. One of the camera's two batteries is recharged by solar power; the second is recharged by the first and, in turn, powers camera operation.

New camera designs in the 110 format were few. A Minolta 110 SLR camera appeared with a 25- to 67-mm zoom lens. Pentax offered a 70-mm and a 20- to 40-mm zoom lens for its year-old 110 SLR.

Trends to Zoom Lenses continued. Lighter-weight, smaller lenses with better correction were presented by many manufacturers, especially in the wide-angle range. Also popular were medium-long zooms with a close-focusing range such as 70- to 150-mm and 80- to 200-mm.

Two companies showed prototypes of auto-focusing lenses that can be interchanged on any SLR cameras with a proper mount. Canon's model was an auto-focus version of their 35- to 70-mm zoom. Ricoh's was an auto-focusing 50-mm zoom.

"Instant" Photography stayed popular, but few exciting developments appeared. Polaroid Corporation's new "Time Zero," an improved color film that develops in about 60 seconds, was introduced.

And Kodak hinted at a future print material to make home-darkroom enlargements from both slides and color negatives. Processing would be done in a single solution, and development time would be short.

Although home movie cameras are being challenged by home video recorders, many improved models stressing auto-focusing, stereo sound, and higher-fidelity sound were introduced. In recognition of the arrival of home video systems, Super 8 film-to-videotape transfer systems were offered.

Versatile flash units designed for use only with specific camera models – so-called dedicated flash – continued as a trend in lighting. New flash units for general use also appeared in quantity.

High silver prices and increased costs of other photo materials combined with a general business recession caused a fall-off in 1980 photo business. Nevertheless, the popularity of the hobby continued to broaden. Collectors of photographic prints paid record prices for both 19th and 20th century examples – but only for the very best examples.

Prominent photographers who died in 1980 included John W. Doscher and Adolph Fassbender, both well known as teachers; Sir Cecil Beaton, the British theater and celebrity photographer; and Ben Rose, an innovative commercial and illustrative photographer.   Kenneth Poli

In WORLD BOOK, see CAMERA; PHOTOGRAPHY.

443

PHYSICS

PHYSICS. Discoveries announced in 1980 made it the "Year of the Neutrino." Experiments on this tiny elementary particle, if confirmed, will have a profound effect on theories of fundamental forces, nuclear reactions in the sun, and the history of the universe.

Three forms of neutrinos and antineutrinos seem to exist, though one of the forms has never been observed. These particles almost never interact directly with other forms of matter, because the force that attracts them to other particles is extremely weak. A single free neutrino could pass through trillions of miles of solid lead before matter in the lead would react with it, absorbing it.

Frederick Reines and Clyde L. Cowan, Jr., at Los Alamos Scientific Laboratory in New Mexico made the first observation of direct neutrino interactions in 1959. In April 1980, Reines and his colleagues Henry W. Sobel and Elaine Pasierb, now at the University of California, Irvine, announced experimental results indicating that a neutrino or antineutrino continually changes its form — that there is one type of neutrino or antineutrino that oscillates between two forms, assuming each form in turn, rather than two types of neutrino or antineutrino that have one form each.

Oscillations. Reines and his colleagues performed both experiments in the intense flow of antineutrinos produced by the Savannah River nuclear reactor in South Carolina. Their apparatus contained electronic detectors that were sensitive to neutrons produced by antineutrino reactions in the reactor. When they compared interaction rates that they observed with rates predicted by conventional theories about neutrinos and antineutrinos, they found a serious difference. This difference could be explained only if the antineutrinos had changed form as they traveled from the reactor core to the experimental apparatus.

Some scientists question Reines's results because the experiment was difficult and the calculations subtle. Furthermore, physicists from France, the United States, and West Germany reported in late June that data from a similar experiment at the Laue-Langevin Institute in Grenoble, France, showed no clear sign of antineutrino oscillations.

Question of Mass. Well-established physical laws indicate that the neutrino and antineutrino of the same apparent type have exactly the same mass. But oscillations between two types can take place only if the particles have different masses. Until 1980 there was no real evidence that the neutrino and antineutrino had any mass. But Reines's results can be interpreted as evidence that at least one type of neutrino and antineutrino has a small mass.

Further support for massive neutrinos came from a 1980 experiment by V. A. Lyubimov and his colleagues at the Institute of Theoretical and

Physicist Edward H. Thorndike of Cornell University in July reported finding a fifth quark, a fundamental particle of matter.

Experimental Physics in Moscow. Some nuclei undergo *beta decay*, in which a neutron decays to a proton, electron, and electron antineutrino. If the antineutrino has no mass, the electron and recoiling nucleus can share all of the available decay energy. Otherwise, a small amount of energy must be used to create the antineutrino's mass. At the subatomic level, energy is frequently converted to mass and vice versa. The Russian scientists studied the energy of electrons emitted in beta decay, particularly the more energetic electrons. They found amounts of energy that did not quite account for the energy they knew was available. The energy difference was indirect but powerful evidence of antineutrino and, presumably, neutrino mass.

Confirmation of Reines's neutrino results is extremely important. New theories that seek to unify our understanding of nature's basic forces must account for neutrino mass. Neutrino oscillation could explain the low flow of neutrinos from nuclear reactions in the sun that have puzzled physicists for more than a decade. Finally, if the universe originated in a big bang — a cosmic explosion of hydrogen — there should be about 100 million times as many neutrinos as heavier particles left over. So even if a neutrino has only a tiny mass, all of them taken together could constitute the dominant mass in the universe. Thomas O. White

In WORLD BOOK, see PHYSICS; RADIOACTIVITY.

PINKOWSKI, JOZEF (1929-   ), became chairman of Poland's Council of Ministers on Aug. 24, 1980. He succeeded Edward Babiuch, who was dismissed in a government shakeup following labor unrest in the northern part of the country (see POLAND). Babiuch had been in office only since February 18. He had succeeded Piotr Jaroszewicz, who resigned after being criticized for Poland's poor economy. Pinkowski had been secretary of the Central Committee of the Polish United Workers' Party (PZPR), the Communist party of Poland.

Jozef Pinkowski was born on April 17, 1929, in Siedlce, in eastern Poland. He graduated from business college and studied economics at Poznań, then served as an army officer. He held posts in the Ministry of Trade and the Ministry of Agriculture from 1956 until 1958, when he became secretary of the Council of Science and Economy in Warszawa province. Pinkowski was named deputy chairman of the People's Provincial Council in Warszawa in 1956 and was promoted to chairman in 1965. In October 1971, he was appointed first deputy chairman of the State Planning Council.

Pinkowski joined the PZPR Central Committee in 1971 and was named its secretary in 1974. He became an alternate member of the Politburo, the PZPR's policymaking body, in 1980. Pinkowski is a member of the national legislature.   Jay Myers

POETRY. In a year that brought an abundance of new works from promising and established poets, the selection of little-known Polish poet Czeslaw Milosz as winner of the 1980 Nobel Prize for Literature came as a surprise. The award citation praised Milosz as a writer who "voices man's exposed condition in the world of severe conflicts." See NOBEL PRIZES.

Evidence of poetry's increasing popularity in the United States achieved concrete form on January 3. President Jimmy Carter and his wife, Rosalynn, played host to 150 American poets at the first major White House function solely in honor of poets. This "Salute to Poetry and American Poets" was described by *The Washington Post* as "one of the most enjoyable White House parties."

Donald R. Justice won a Pulitzer Prize for Poetry with his *Selected Poems*, a generous book of self-realization. Two collections from Philip Levine, *Ashes* and *7 Years from Somewhere*, focused on the human struggle. British poet Basil Bunting's *Collected Poems* embraced 50 years of visionary writing. *Being Here* by Robert Penn Warren provided fresh perspectives on time and nature. James Merrill concluded a major narrative verse trilogy with *Scripts for the Pageant*.

Other New Books from proven talents included Laurence Lieberman's *God's Measurements*, fine and

Josephine Jacobsen reads to some of the 500 guests at an unprecedented White House "Salute to Poetry and American Poets" held on January 3.

intricate verse set in Japan. *As We Know* by John Ashbery delivered complex meditations on the cosmos. Howard Moss's *Notes from the Castle* offered dramatic reflections of heart and mind. *The Morning of the Poem* from James Schuyler was a unique blend of autobiography and aesthetics. Frederick Seidel's *Sunrise*, winner of the Lamont Prize, examined the joys and anguish of American life.

David Ray's humanizing *Tramp's Cup* won the W. C. Williams Prize for an outstanding small-press poetry book. William Virgil Davis addressed divergences of public and private lives in *One Way to Reconstruct the Scene*, which was the Yale Younger Poets' selection.

Also Notable were Dave Smith's *Goshawk, Antelope; Venetian Vespers* by Anthony Hecht; Galway Kinnell's *Mortal Acts, Mortal Words*; and *Blue Wine* from John Hollander. The first five entries in the new National Poetry Series came from Joseph Langland, Ronald Perry, Sterling A. Brown, Wendy Salinger, and Roberta Spears.

Leading Translations were *Selected Poems of Zbigniew Herbert* by John and Bogdana Carpenter; Saralyn Daly's rendering of the medieval Spanish of Juan Ruiz' *The Book of True Love*; and Edmund Keeley's *Ritsos in Parentheses*, a version of works by Greek poet Yannis Ritsos.   G. E. Murray

In WORLD BOOK, see POETRY.

POLAND went through a series of surprising strikes that brought important government concessions and four government shakeups in 1980. The government was forced to recognize a new trade union, and several leading officials, including Edward Gierek, first secretary of the Polish United Workers' Party (PZPR), the Communist party of Poland, were ousted. In November, Russia reportedly massed troops along the Polish border, raising fears that the Soviets would intervene militarily to prevent the changes in Poland from going too far.

The trouble began shortly after the party congress in February. The congress had re-elected Gierek to another five-year term, but dismissed Piotr Jaroszewicz, prime minister since 1970. Edward Babiuch, a close associate of Gierek's, replaced Jaroszewicz. The PZPR also removed two prominent critics of government economic policies, Stefan Olszowski and Jozef Tejchma, from the Politburo, the PZPR's policymaking body.

Two weeks after the congress, the Roman Catholic Church appealed for greater individual freedom including the right to form independent organizations. The appeal was ignored, but in May the government brought back into the social security system 6,000 priests who had been excluded from it and declared that young men studying for the priesthood would not have to join the armed forces.

Striking workers and their supporters gather outside the gates of the Lenin Shipyard in Gdańsk, Poland, during a Mass in August.

The Strike. Factory workers in Warsaw, Tczew, and Łódź struck on July 2 to protest against price increases of up to 90 per cent for the meat that high-priced commercial shops sold. These shops sold 20 per cent of the meat available in Poland. Wage hikes of up to 15 per cent failed to stop the strikes from spreading and becoming political protests. See EUROPE (Close-Up).

Deputy Prime Minister Mieczyslaw Jagielski opened talks with strike committees in Gdańsk on August 23. A government shakeup followed. Jozef Pinkowski replaced Babiuch as Council of Ministers chairman, Poland's highest government official, on August 24 (see PINKOWSKI, JOZEF). Three Politburo members responsible for economic planning, trade unions, and propaganda were fired. Olszowski regained his Politburo membership and replaced Pinkowski as secretary of the PZPR Central Committee.

Jagielski signed an agreement on August 31 that granted the Gdańsk workers several concessions, including the right to form a free trade union and to strike. And the government was shaken up again. Gierek was replaced on September 6 by Stanislaw Kania, who had been supervisor of the police, army, and internal security (see KANIA, STANISLAW). Gierek was said to have heart trouble.

Solidarity Recognized. On October 24, a Warsaw court recognized Solidarity, the new trade union, but wrote a clause into its charter that asserted the PZPR's leading role. The union leaders said that the charter should be nonpolitical and threatened to strike on November 12. However, the Supreme Court ruled on November 10 that the controversial clause could be part of a *charter annex*, a document separate from the union statutes, so the union called off the strike.

Kania strengthened his position in the third shakeup, which affected PZPR first secretaries in the provinces, including the party leaders in most major cities. The government replaced at least 18 of these officials by November 22. And on December 2, the Central Committee dismissed four members of the Politburo and returned to that body former Interior Minister Mieczyslaw Moczar, who had favored working closely with Solidarity.

Finance Minister Marian Krzak said on December 19 that Poland's foreign debt had risen to $23-billion and that 1981 would bring the nation's first budget deficit since World War II. Krzak also announced that Poland would ration meat and butter in the first three months of 1981, cut 5,000 persons from government payrolls, reduce by 25 per cent the number of automobiles used by the state, and slash investment spending.   Chris Cviic

See also EUROPE (Facts in Brief Table). In WORLD BOOK, see POLAND.

POLLUTION. See ENVIRONMENT.

POPULAR MUSIC. See MUSIC, POPULAR.

POPULATION. There were indications in 1980 that the global population explosion might be losing some of its momentum. A report issued in June by the United Nations (UN) Fund for Population Activities forecast a noticeable decline in world birth rates through the 1980s. In the past five years, the report stated, the annual level was 28.9 births for every 1,000 persons; this was expected to fall to 27.1 per 1,000 between 1985 and 1990. A continuation of the trend would outweigh the effects of longer life-expectancy rates.

However, the report warned that despite the drop, this would still mean a rise in total world population from 4.4 billion in 1980 to 6.2 billion by the year 2000. The biggest gains would continue to take place in the poorest nations, thus causing "explosive growth in the already crowded cities of the Third World."

Demographers outside the UN warned, however, that long-range forecasts are hazardous because the number of people in the world, particularly those in the large developing nations, is extremely uncertain. "The margin of error in the world population total is plus or minus at least 5 per cent – possibly twice that," according to Robert C. Cook, former president of the Population Reference Bureau and a consultant to the Environmental Fund of Washington, D.C. "This is because most of the developing countries have sketchy statistics."

Highs and Lows. The African continent, with a population of 477.6 million, had an overall birth rate of 46 per 1,000 population and a death rate of 19 per 1,000 in 1980. Its annual rate of growth – the world's highest – was 2.8 per cent. Latin America's total population of 363.6 million was also increasing at an annual rate of 2.8 per cent. The birth rate was 36 per 1,000 and the death rate, 9 per 1,000. The lowest annual rate of increase was in Europe, whose total population of 484.3 million was increasing at the rate of 0.4 per cent per year. The annual birth rate was 14 per 1,000 population and the death rate, 10 per 1,000.

In other areas, Asia, with a total population of 2 billion, had an annual growth rate of 2 per cent. Russia's population of 265.8 million was increasing by 0.8 per cent annually. Oceania, including Australia, New Zealand, and the Pacific Islands, had a population of 22.7 million and an annual growth rate of 1.2 per cent. North America, which includes the United States and Canada, was increasing its total population of 252.4 million at an annual rate of 0.7 per cent. The birth rate was 15 per 1,000, and the death rate was 8 per 1,000.

Birth Control. Religious restraints remained the principal obstacle to the spread of family planning, according to a study made in 41 developing and 20 developed countries by researchers of the International Statistical Institute.   Paul C. Tullier

In WORLD BOOK, see POPULATION.

PORTUGAL plunged into a political crisis when Prime Minister Francisco Sa Carneiro and his defense minister died in an airplane crash on Dec. 4, 1980. Deputy Prime Minister Diogo Freitas do Amaral became acting head of government. On December 13, the Social Democratic Party, which dominates the coalition, chose Minister of State Francisco Pinto Balsemao to replace Sa Carneiro.

Sa Carneiro's Democratic Alliance had won a 10-seat majority in parliamentary elections on October 5, and Sa Carneiro had withstood a strong campaign to bring down his government in August. The Socialists and Communists had demanded that the permanent commission of Parliament call an emergency session of that body to debate Sa Carneiro's business activities after the 1974 revolution that toppled the dictatorship of Prime Minister Marcello Caetano. The two parties maintained that Sa Carneiro had used his political influence in 1975 to discharge a bank debt and that he still owed the national banking system $575,000. He denied the accusation on August 14.

But more pressure for a public debate came from opposition parties and officers of the Revolutionary Council, the military advisory body that had been supervising Portugal's transition to civilian rule. On August 26, the commission rejected the demand for an emergency session of Parliament.

Clash with President. Sa Carneiro's bad relationship with President Antonio dos Santos Ramalho Eanes worsened when the government decided in March to stop sending military men on foreign assignments normally regarded as foreign-office missions. But Eanes denied on March 5 that there was a military plot to overthrow Sa Carneiro's government. On April 11, the Democratic Alliance chose anti-Communist General Antonio Soares Carneiro, no relation to Sa Carneiro, to run against Eanes in the December 7 presidential election. But Eanes captured 57 per cent of the vote to Soares Carneiro's 40 per cent. The Socialists, Communists, and some independents supported Eanes.

Prime Minister Sa Carneiro toured European capitals in 1980 seeking support for Portuguese membership in the European Community (EC) by 1983. Sa Carneiro claimed when he returned to Portugal that Denmark, Great Britain, Luxembourg, the Netherlands, and West Germany supported Portugal's entry.

Taxes Eased. The government announced tax cuts and increases in public purchasing power on April 2. The 1980 deficit would increase by 16.7 per cent, while inflation ran at 22 per cent. But there were also some tax increases.   Kenneth Brown

See also EUROPE (Facts in Brief Table). In WORLD BOOK, see PORTUGAL.

President Jimmy Carter places a wreath at the tomb of explorer Vasco da Gama in a Lisbon monastery during a brief visit to Portugal in June.

POSTAL SERVICE, UNITED STATES, asked the independent Postal Rate Commission on April 21, 1980, for a 28 per cent rate increase. The proposed hike would provide the Postal Service, which is beset by rising payroll and transportation costs, with an additional $5 billion per year in revenue. It would raise the cost of mailing a first-class letter from 15 cents to 20 cents, and of mailing a post card from 10 cents to 13 cents early in 1981.

Postmaster General William F. Bolger also recommended increases for most newspapers and magazines as well as for bulk mail. He also requested lower rates for such second-class mail as rural newspapers and nonprofit publications. In July, the Postal Service's board of governors voted to accept Bolger's proposal, and later it set June 1, 1981, as the effective date for higher second-class rates.

Bolger said the increases were needed because the average postal worker's pay and benefits rose to almost $22,000 a year in 1980, and because costs of gasoline for delivery trucks have risen sharply. Without the increase, the Postal Service said, it would have a budget deficit of $593 million in fiscal year 1980.

Six-Day Delivery of mail was threatened in 1980 by a congressional economy drive. In an effort to balance the federal budget, the United States Senate and House of Representatives approved a cut of $500 million in postal appropriations. The only way to absorb such a large reduction, postal officials said, was to cut back mail service to five days. However, a postal service task force later concluded that eliminating six-day service would not be in the best interests of the postal system or its customers.

Electronic Mail. The Postal Rate Commission on April 8 approved a one-year trial for a limited form of electronic mail service for businesses, and the Postal Service board of governors agreed under protest to begin the program on Jan. 4, 1982. Electronic computer-originated mail, known as E-COM, would allow business firms to transmit electronic messages, such as monthly bills, to participating post offices. At that point, the message would be printed, then delivered like regular mail. Controversy arose because no decision was made on how fully the Postal Service should compete with private telecommunications carriers.

Nine-Digit Zip Codes were scheduled to replace the five-digit codes in mid-July 1981. The use of the new codes, which are designed to route mail to an individual carrier or building and so be faster than the old routing to a postal station, would be voluntary. However, the Postal Service expected large-volume mailers to cooperate in order to speed service.   Willliam J. Eaton

In WORLD BOOK, see POST OFFICE; POSTAL SERVICE, UNITED STATES.

PREM TINSULANONDA (1920-   ) was elected premier of Thailand on March 3, 1980, by the nation's parliament. He replaced Kriangsak Chamanan, who resigned. A career soldier, General Prem served as defense minister and army chief in Kriangsak's last Cabinet.

Although he had little experience in civilian government, Prem had a reputation for being incorruptible, and he promoted understanding between the military and the general public during his brilliant military career. He pledged, as his country's premier, to seek new solutions to Thailand's economic problems, especially inflation (see THAILAND).

Prem was born on Aug. 26, 1920, in Songkhla, Thailand. He attended Suan Kularb College and graduated from Chulachomkhiao Royal Military Academy in 1941. He then entered the army.

He served as commander of a cavalry center at Lop Buri, commander of Lop Buri military province, and commanding general of the Second Army region in northeastern Thailand. Prem became assistant army chief in 1977 and army chief in 1978. In his first civilian post, he served as deputy interior minister in Kriangsak's first Cabinet in 1977. Kriangsak appointed him defense minister in his second and third Cabinets.

Premier Prem is a bachelor and has stated that he is "married to the army."   Patricia Dragisic

PRESIDENT OF THE UNITED STATES. Jimmy Carter suffered a decisive defeat on Nov. 4, 1980, when he lost his bid for re-election to Republican Ronald Reagan. Not since Herbert Hoover was defeated by Franklin D. Roosevelt in 1932 had an elected incumbent President seeking a second term failed to win it.

During his four years, President Carter chalked up some solid accomplishments – the negotiation of an Egyptian-Israeli peace treaty in 1978; the Panama Canal treaties of 1978; negotiations on the Strategic Arms Limitation Treaty (SALT II); an energy program; and deregulation of much of the nation's transportation system. But his accomplishments were overshadowed by what many persons saw as his weaknesses or personal failures – a vacillating policy toward Russia and Israel; an ambivalent attitude toward defense spending; failure to secure the release of the American hostages in Iran; and, above all, an inability to curb inflation, balance the federal budget, and reduce unemployment. Much of the American electorate came to judge him as a less than competent President.

The President's relations with a Congress controlled by his own party also worsened in 1980. For the first time in 28 years, a Democratic Congress twice overrode a Democratic President's veto.

The Russian Invasion of Afghanistan that began on Dec. 27, 1979, and consequently placed Soviet troops next to the troubled Middle East's oil fields came as a shock to the President. He immediately instituted economic measures designed to force Soviet withdrawal. Carter asked the Senate on January 2 to delay consideration of SALT II and recalled Ambassador Thomas J. Watson, Jr., from Moscow. On January 4, he curtailed grain sales to the Soviet Union; and, on January 9, he suspended exports of machinery and technology.

To emphasize his firm stance against Russian aggression, Carter on February 13 ordered a Marine battalion to the Arabian Sea area as a show of American strength. On March 14, he warned Moscow that he might renounce SALT II.

In his State of the Union address to Congress on January 23, President Carter declared that the U.S. would "use any means necessary, including force," to repel an attack on the Persian Gulf region. He also said that the United States would not take part in the 1980 Olympic Summer Games in Moscow unless the Soviet Union withdrew from Afghanistan by February 20. The U.S. Olympic Committee ratified the boycott, which had been approved by Congress on April 12. However, many Western European nations refused to go along with the United States. Moreover, the boycott may have irritated Americans eager to participate in the Olympics more than it dismayed the Soviet Union.

President Carter smilingly applauds Prime Minister Robert Mugabe of Zimbabwe during a White House reception for the African leader in August.

As his term came to an end, President Carter dealt with another threat of Russian aggression. The White House announced on December 7 that, according to National Security Council reports, Russia was preparing for military intervention in Poland to combat labor unrest there. The President briefed leaders of Congress, but added that there would be no U.S. military involvement.

Israeli Relations. When, on March 1, the United States cast its vote with 14 other nations in the United Nations (UN) Security Council to "deplore" the establishment of Israeli settlements in the West Bank, the President undermined much of the good will he had engendered with Israel and Jewish Americans. Then, on March 3, Carter disavowed the vote, pleading a failure in communications. Nonetheless, the President termed Israel's settlement policy "detrimental" to the autonomy talks between Egypt and Israel. The President's critics saw the UN episode as a sign of ineptitude. Friends of Israel saw it as an indication that the Administration was growing less friendly to Israel.

The Hostage Issue. In the first four months of 1980 especially, the President and his advisers tried unsuccessfully to persuade Iran to release the Americans seized by Iranian militants at the U.S. Embassy in Teheran in November 1979. Carter announced on April 7 that the United States was breaking diplomatic relations with Iran, ordered Iranian diplomats to leave the United States, invalidated all visas to Iranians for future use, and imposed an embargo on U.S. exports to Iran. On April 8, the Department of State said American allies had been asked to take similar action.

President Carter on April 13 held an unprecedented news conference that was carried on European cable television, in which he asked Western Europe to sever all relations with Iran by mid-May if the hostages were not released. In a speech on April 17, asking for a ban on Iranian imports and American travel in Iran, the President mentioned the possibility of "some sort of military action." Shortly thereafter, without consulting Congress, he ordered a military rescue attempt.

On April 25, he told surprised Americans that a rescue mission had been aborted in the Iranian desert the night before, and that eight American servicemen had died in an accident. Carter assumed full responsibility for the mission and for its failure. See ARMED FORCES.

The aborted mission triggered unfavorable reactions at home and abroad. Western allies severely criticized the President for not consulting them. Members of Congress were offended because few of them had been informed in advance. Iran announced angrily that the hostages were being dispersed to prevent any further U.S. rescue attempts, and Secretary of State Cyrus R. Vance resigned in protest against the mission.

A stern President Carter outlines the details of his new anti-inflation program of "pain and discipline" during a press conference in March.

On November 2, two days before the presidential election, the Iranian parliament issued an ultimatum listing conditions for the release of the hostages and demanding an immediate answer through the news media. President Carter refused to discuss the ultimatum in the media, and the State Department began detailed consideration of the Iranian proposal. The hostages entered their second year of captivity on election day.

The Outbreak of War between Iran and Iraq in September threatened to involve the superpowers and to cut off vital oil supplies to American allies. President Carter declared on September 18 that the United States would not become involved in the conflict. On September 30, the White House announced that the United States was sending four Airborne Warning and Control System radar planes and their ground crews to Saudi Arabia, but the President later refused a Saudi request for equipment that would allow Saudi planes to undertake long-range offensive flights. Carter revealed on October 6 that he had contacted Soviet Presidium Chairman Leonid I. Brezhnev in a mutual effort to avoid involvement.

Refugee Problem. The flood of refugees from Cuba and Haiti also troubled President Carter. When Cuba's President Fidel Castro began to allow Cubans to leave by boat in early April, the President welcomed them, announcing on April 24 that the United States would admit 3,500 Cubans under emergency authority granted by the Refugee Act of 1980. On May 5, he said that the United States was offering "open arms" to "literally thousands" of Cubans.

However, after some 46,000 Cubans – including criminals and mental patients – had poured into Florida, he ordered the Coast Guard on May 14 to intercept boats operating in the informal Cuban sea lift. Critics chided President Carter's change of policy as well as Administration efforts to settle in camps the refugees who failed to find sponsors. See CUBA; IMMIGRATION.

International Relations. The President spent most of the spring in the White House, explaining that he did not want to travel while the hostage situation was unresolved. His decision not to attend the funeral of President Josip Broz Tito of Yugoslavia on May 8 was regarded as a diplomatic blunder, particularly since he had announced that he was ending his self-imposed seclusion on April 30 to resume his campaign travels. President Carter made a five-nation visit to Europe from June 19 to June 26, attending an economic summit meeting in Venice, Italy, during that time. He visited Belgrade, Yugoslavia, on June 24 to assure the new government of U.S. support, and on June 25, in Madrid, Spain, he expressed the hope that Spain would join the North Atlantic Treaty Organization.

451

Relations with Japan and the People's Republic of China remained cordial. President Carter and Japan's Prime Minister Masayoshi Ohira signed a five-year agreement on May 1 for scientific research collaboration. On July 9, the President attended Ohira's funeral in Tokyo, conferring there with Chairman Hua Kuo-feng (Hua Guofeng) of the People's Republic of China on July 10. On September 17, the President and Chinese Vice-Chairman Bo Yibo signed agreements on textile trade, civil aviation, and shipping.

The U.S. Economy was President Carter's major domestic headache. His economic policy, designed to counter inflation, seemingly produced only recession and unemployment. The President proposed a program of "pain and discipline" to fight inflation on March 14, suggesting a $13-billion cut in federal spending to balance the fiscal 1981 budget. He urged the Federal Reserve Board to curb consumer credit and asked for a voluntary ceiling on pay increases of 7.5 to 9.5 per cent.

With unemployment on the rise, the President announced a $96-million job program on June 30 for 31 cities plagued by the deepening recession. On July 28, he ordered increased price supports for grain farmers.

In an economic message on August 28, the President outlined a "revitalization" program that would not "re-ignite inflation," asking Congress to extend unemployment benefits an additional 13 weeks; to appropriate an extra $1 billion to help spur local economic development; and to consider new tax incentives for industry and income tax reductions to offset the increase in Social Security taxes scheduled to take effect on Jan. 1, 1981. However, congressional response to the President's economic program was lukewarm at best – those measures that passed were pared significantly.

The President continued his efforts to deregulate the nation's transportation industry. The Motor Carrier Act signed by the President on July 1 ended 45 years of strict federal regulation of interstate trucking (see TRUCK AND TRUCKING). On October 22, he signed legislation ending federal control of railroad rates (see RAILROAD). Airline fares had been deregulated in 1978.

Energy Program. President Carter won congressional approval in 1980 for most planks of his energy program, which was designed to end United States dependence on foreign oil and to find new, renewable sources of energy (see ENERGY). Nonetheless, Congress and the courts refused to allow him to impose a fee of $4.62 a barrel on imported oil.

President Carter places a flower on an altar in Tokyo during a memorial service for Japanese Prime Minister Masayoshi Ohira, who died in June.

On July 31, the President signed a $1.4-billion agreement with West Germany and Japan to establish in West Virginia the world's first commercial-size facility to process oil from coal. The U.S., Japan, and West Germany, as well as private industries in these nations, will share expenses.

Defense and the Draft. President Carter on February 12 sent a proposal to Congress asking for $45-million to revive the Selective Service System and suggested that both men and women register. However, the House of Representatives on April 22 banned the use of Selective Service funds for registering women. On July 2, President Carter signed a proclamation ordering the 4 million men born in 1960 and 1961 to register. Registration began on July 21.

Presidential Directive 59, issued on August 5, outlined a changing nuclear strategy for the United States. It gave priority to attacking military targets in the Soviet Union in response to Soviet aggression, rather than mounting an all-out war.

After his defeat in the November election, the President kept a low profile, promising an orderly transition of power.   Carol L. Thompson

See also CARTER, JAMES EARL, JR.; CONGRESS OF THE UNITED STATES; DEMOCRATIC PARTY; ELECTIONS; UNITED STATES, GOVERNMENT OF THE. In WORLD BOOK, see CARTER, JAMES EARL, JR.; PRESIDENT OF THE UNITED STATES.

PRINCE EDWARD ISLAND, Canada's smallest and most energy-poor province, in 1980 made plans to cancel a 1978 agreement to buy electricity from nearby New Brunswick's Point Lepreau nuclear power plant. The plan was opposed by the Progressive Conservatives under Premier Angus MacLean in the 1979 election campaign because of uncertainty regarding the plant's completion date and the future cost of its power. Prince Edward Island paid $100,000 compensation for legal expenses to annul the agreement. The federal government currently pays Prince Edward Island residents $80 million per year to subsidize the high cost of imported oil.

The MacLean government stressed the importance of private enterprise in strengthening the island's economy. It advocated greater attention to forestry and to using wood fuel for home heating. The budget introduced on February 28 proposed higher personal income taxes and an increase in the sales tax to 9 per cent, a rate exceeded in Canada only by Newfoundland's 11 per cent. A surplus of $776,400 was predicted on expenditures of $306 million. Nevertheless, Prince Edward Island joined the other three Atlantic provinces in borrowing $29 million from the Alberta Heritage Savings Trust Fund.   David M. L. Farr

See also CANADA. In WORLD BOOK, see PRINCE EDWARD ISLAND.

PRISON

PRISON. The most savage riot in the history of United States prisons ripped through New Mexico's overcrowded state penitentiary in Santa Fe on Feb. 2 and 3, 1980, leaving 33 inmates dead and 89 guards and inmates hospitalized. Prisoners wrecked an estimated $40 million in property in 36 hours of looting, destruction, and burning, making the uprising also the costliest in United States history. Many buildings were destroyed by fire.

The riot began when a group of prisoners carried out a planned attack, overpowering four dormitory guards. Soon, prisoners were fighting one another. The death toll was lower than the 43 deaths in the Attica, N.Y., prison take-over in 1971, but the violence, fueled by drugs stolen from the dispensary, almost defied description.

Prisoners Killed. Apparently selected because of their race or because they were suspected informers, many inmates were killed in a hideous manner. They were thrown from buildings, beheaded, splashed with gasoline and set afire, axed, and tortured to death with blowtorches.

The prisoners took 14 hostages, but eight had been freed through negotiations by the time 250 state police and National Guard men retook the prison without firing a shot. Investigators said that the state legislature had long ignored signs of trouble at the prison.

Other serious riots occurred in Attica, N.Y., in January and in Essex County, New Jersey, in March. A September 4 disturbance in a Monroe, Wash., prison left one inmate dead and 23 injured. Five days later, one prisoner was killed and five were wounded in a gang fight at a Stillwater, Minn., prison.

More Prisoners. The number of inmates in state prisons continued to rise during 1980, while the population of federal prisons dropped. The federal Bureau of Justice Statistics reported a record 314,083 prisoners in penal institutions at the start of 1980, a 2.3 per cent increase from 1979. Some 26,233 of them (a 12.3 per cent reduction) were under federal supervision, and 12,927 were women.

The Council of State Governments released a study showing that distrust of judicial leniency and a lack of faith in parole authorities had prompted 35 states to adopt measures tending to lengthen prison terms and increase inmate populations. On December 16, Attorney General Benjamin R. Civiletti issued the first federal standards for prisons and jails. They include specifications for cells, health care, and security.   David C. Beckwith

In WORLD BOOK, see PRISON.

PRIZES. See AWARDS AND PRIZES; CANADIAN LIBRARY ASSN.; CANADIAN LITERATURE; NOBEL PRIZES.

A guard sifts through rubble left after a two-day rampage by inmates at the New Mexico State Penitentiary in Santa Fe in early February.

Moral Majority leader Jerry Falwell addresses an "I Love America" rally of 2,000 persons at the New Jersey State House in Trenton on November 10.

PROTESTANTISM. The three major candidates in the 1980 United States presidential election race were all Protestants, and all three belonged to at least moderately conservative branches or congregations of their churches. Independent John B. Anderson found his position on abortion repudiated by his Evangelical Free Church and evidently received little formal Evangelical church support. Early polls showed that a majority of Americans who considered themselves Evangelical, or born-again, Christians continued to support incumbent President Jimmy Carter, a Democrat and Southern Baptist. But Carter's failure to appoint many Evangelicals to office or to support the positions of what was called the New Christian Right led some to back Republican Ronald Reagan, a Presbyterian who during his campaign took pains to identify with some Christian-right positions.

Protestants who blended conservative religion with conservative politics dominated U.S. church news. Many fundamentalists had long shunned political involvements, but they became very public in their 1980 political stands.

Mobilizing Forces. Many conservatives, particularly the slightly more moderate group of Evangelicals, did not join the new political-action groups, such as the Moral Majority, Religious Roundtable, and Christian Voice. But others did, and — in localities where fundamentalists were numerous —

the organized New Christian Right held the balance of power in many close elections. Led by television evangelists such as Jerry Falwell, a minister from Lynchburg, Va., and several public officeholders, the rightists effectively used TV and direct-mail services to gather their forces.

Most conservative Christian groups judged candidates by how they had voted or promised to vote on selected issues, including the Equal Rights Amendment, homosexual-rights legislation, and legalized abortion. The Protestant conservatives also supported a constitutional amendment to permit voluntary prayer in public schools and backed various measures to ensure that a literal Biblical approach to the world's creation be taught along with the scientific theory of evolution.

Others who shared those political convictions set out to raise funds for conversion activities. A notable fund-raising event in Houston in May was hosted by investor Nelson Bunker Hunt. Hunt personally gave $10 million to the Campus Crusade for Christ International, a group headed by Bill Bright, a minister from San Bernardino, Calif., who is seeking to raise $1 billion for vigorous evangelizing efforts. At the Houston meeting, Hunt asked for pledges of $1 million per person, and announced $170 million in pledges up to that time.

Washington Rally. Many conservative Protestant leaders united to stage a "Washington for Jesus"

Evangelist Robert H. Schuller proudly shows off the Crystal Cathedral, his new $18-million church, at a benefit in May in Garden Grove, Calif.

rally in April. About 200,000 persons went to the nation's capital for a day of prayer and preaching. However, advance criticism caused leaders to mute the political aspects of the day. Moral Majority movements caused a backlash in some communities during the year, and Protestants from many denominations who did not agree with their political stands spoke up in opposition.

Conservatives made their voices heard also within some of the denominations. The Southern Baptist Convention (SBC) at its national meeting in June elected Bailey Smith, a fundamentalist minister from Del City, Okla., president – to lead continued efforts to enforce their view that the Bible is completely *inerrant* (free from error). Smith made news for a controversial statement at a religious rally in Houston in June. He claimed that in American political life, it seems necessary to have a Jew pray alongside a Christian, but that "God Almighty does not hear the prayer of a Jew." Many other SBC leaders immediately criticized Smith and pointed out that they had long worked for good relations with Jews.

Mormon Controversy. Although the Church of Jesus Christ of Latter-day Saints (Mormons) does not regard itself as Protestant, the church is linked to Protestants sociologically – and through common controversies over such issues as feminism. Sonia Johnson of Sterling, Va., excommunicated

from the Mormon church in December 1979 for her support of the Equal Rights Amendment (ERA), learned in June that her final appeal of the excommunication had failed. In announcing the appeal verdict, church leaders repeated that Johnson was expelled because of her criticism of church officials – not her feminism.

Other Controversy. The National Council of Churches (NCC), a largely main-line Protestant and Eastern Orthodox council, issued a controversial position paper on the Middle East in November. The NCC's 266-member governing board wrestled with the issue of Palestinian rights to "national self-determination" and endorsed the formation of a sovereign Palestinian state. The NCC statement also urged recognition of the Palestine Liberation Organization (PLO), claiming that the PLO is "the only organized voice of the Palestinian people." This position was highly offensive to most American Jews, and it threatened continued Jewish-Protestant cooperation and dialogue.

The United Methodist Church, the second-largest Protestant body, at its general conference in April passed a controversial message to the leaders of Iran. The message expressed Methodist sympathy for "cries for freedom" in Iran, but asked for the release of the American hostages held since Nov. 4, 1979. On another complex subject, the conference upheld civil rights for homosexuals, but reaffirmed that homosexuality is "incompatible with Christian teaching."

The United Presbyterian Church in the U.S.A., at a June meeting of its national assembly, voted to affirm that local church property is held in trust for the entire denomination. During the previous year, 28 congregations had left the church, claiming that it was too liberal. Church officials hoped that this vote would discourage further local withdrawals.

The Lutheran churches, which form one of the largest Protestant groupings, celebrated their 450th anniversary – marking the signing of the Augsburg Confession in 1530 in Germany. In their efforts at reconciliation, Roman Catholics and Lutherans held joint services, study groups, and dialogues throughout North America.

In Great Britain, Robert A. K. Runcie was enthroned as the 102nd archbishop of Canterbury on March 25. He thus became the spiritual leader of the world's Anglican Communion, which includes the Episcopalian Church. The Anglican Communion published its new Alternative Service Book in November, a collection of prayers and services to update the Book of Common Prayer – published in 1662 and long acclaimed for its beautiful language. Church leaders proclaimed publication of the new book, in work for more than 20 years, as a "major event." But many clergy and members of the Church of England found the book too modern and sterile and vowed a campaign to continue using the Book of Common Prayer. In the United States, the Episcopalian Church has already adopted a modernized prayer book.

Protestant Unity. The Consultation on Church Union (COCU), which since 1962 has been working toward unity for 10 Protestant denominations, in January approved a policy stating that their projected new Church of Christ Uniting would have bishops. Five of the 10 denominations that have delegates at COCU do not have bishops now. The new church would have clergy called presbyters, along with deacons and lay ministers. Despite the agreement on clergy, full union for COCU members seemed far in the future – with estimates ranging from 10 to 40 years. About one-third of America's Protestants, most of them characterized as "main-line," belong to COCU churches.

After years of general church building doldrums, evangelist Robert H. Schuller made news by dedicating the $18-million Crystal Cathedral in Garden Grove, Calif., in September. The church, which was designed by the noted architect Philip Johnson, drew praise from architectural critics and criticism from some churchmen, who questioned the use of so much money for such an ostentatious purpose.   Martin E. Marty

See also RELIGION. In WORLD BOOK, see PROTESTANTISM and articles on Protestant denominations.

PSYCHOLOGY. Several landmark publications marked the growing acceptance of an important trend in psychology in 1980. *Behaviorism* has dominated psychology since the 1930s with its emphasis on observable behavior, but is now giving way to *cognitive* perspectives that emphasize mental processes, such as perceiving, and problem-solving.

Herbert A. Simon, professor of computer science and psychology at Carnegie-Mellon University in Pittsburgh, Pa., winner of the 1978 Nobel Prize for Economics, is one of psychology's most original thinkers. He wrote in the 1980 centennial issue of *Science*, "Over the past quarter-century, no development in the social sciences has been more radical than the revolution – often referred to as the information processing revolution – in our way of understanding the processes of human thinking."

Simon and a team of psychologists and computer scientists at Carnegie-Mellon provided a good example of this new approach with their July report on "Expert and Novice Performance in Solving Physics Problems." They studied computer simulations of complex activities such as playing chess, as well as "thinking-aloud protocols" – reports of working discussions – from subjects trying to solve physics problems. The researchers found that experts in a particular field are sensitive to a large number of specific patterns of information. Each pattern guides the expert quickly to relevant knowledge in his or her memory.

This knowledge is highly organized in *schemata* (general memory structures), which guide the person in solving problems. The researchers concluded that no magic formula for producing "effortless learning" or "instant experts" will ever be found. Expertise results from amassing an enormous body of knowledge and then using it over a long period of time.

The Unconscious. In another offshoot of the cognitive revolution, the concept of "the unconscious," once scorned by psychologists as something too vague to be studied, is achieving new respectability. Psychiatrists Howard Shevrin and Scott Dickman of the University of Michigan Medical Center, writing in the May issue of *American Psychologist*, cited the evidence of sophisticated unconscious processing revealed by cognitive scientists in recent years. They argued that "no psychological theory can do without the assumption of a psychological unconscious."

Psychologist Ernest R. Hilgard of Stanford University reported in the 1980 *Annual Review of Psychology* that conscious and unconscious processes are receiving increased attention from experimenters and clinicians alike. He proposed three types of unconscious processes: subconscious processes, those that can be brought out by special techniques such as hypnosis; unconscious processes, those that remain hidden but can be inferred from psychological effects, such as the symbols in dreams; and nonconscious processes, such as biological regulatory activity, which do not affect perception or awareness directly but form a necessary underpinning for mental activity.

Right or Left? A popular assumption holds that the right hemisphere of the brain is responsible for unconscious or intuitive processes. Psychologist Michael C. Corballis of the University of Auckland in New Zealand attacked this assumption in a report published in March. Corballis pointed to the long history of human fascination with differences between left and right. He proposed that "the symbolic potency of right and left originates in the phenomenon of handedness." He also said, "Interpretations . . . that emphasize a fundamental duality in cognitive processing between the two sides of the brain, or that locate consciousness on the left side only, are probably modern manifestations of the age-old mythology of left and right."

Corballis thus contradicted such popular writers as Thomas R. Blakeslee, whose book *The Right Brain: A New Understanding of the Unconscious Mind and Its Creative Power* was published in 1980. Blakeslee depicted the right hemisphere as a "silent partner" responsible for dreams, intuition, and unconscious thoughts.   Russell A. Dewey

In WORLD BOOK, see PSYCHOLOGY.

PUBLIC HEALTH. A large-scale trial of a new vaccine for hepatitis B showed remarkable success in 1980. Hepatitis B is a viral liver infection that can cause disabling symptoms and may lead to other serious diseases. The test, reported on October 9 by epidemiologist Wolf Szmuness, director of the New York Blood Center's epidemiology laboratory, involved 1,083 homosexual men – who are about 10 times more likely to develop hepatitis B than the general population.

Half of the men received the vaccine, and half were given a placebo. Only 11 cases of hepatitis B occurred in 21 months in the vaccinated group, compared with 60 in the control placebo group. Hepatitis B annually strikes 100,000 to 200,000 Americans and leaves about 10 per cent chronic carriers. The infection may be linked to liver cancer. The importance of such a vaccine was underscored by the U.S. Surgeon General's report that at least 10 million Americans are affected by a sexually transmitted disease, including hepatitis B, gonorrhea, syphilis, and herpes simplex.

Conquering Measles. The U.S. Centers for Disease Control (CDC) in Atlanta, Ga., reported steady progress to eliminate measles by 1982. Although 25,000 cases still are reported each year, the CDC hopes to add measles to the list of diseases that have become so rare that physicians seldom see

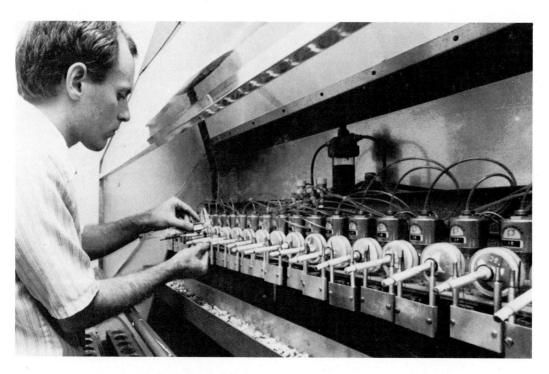

New machine smokes cigarettes to help the Federal Trade Commission determine how much carbon monoxide, in addition to tar and nicotine, each brand contains.

a case. Because of immunization with live-virus vaccine, the 1970s had no measles epidemic.

The National Research Council reported on July 29 that human cancer risks from X rays and other low-level ionizing radiation are only about half as great as had been estimated. The panel, using sophisticated methods of calculating risks, estimated that one-time exposure to 10 rads of low-level ionizing radiation would cause from 750 to 2,300 additional cancer deaths – above the normally expected 165,000 cancer deaths – over the lifetime of 1 million persons. The typical American is exposed to about one-fifth rad of low-level radiation per year, mostly from natural sources and X rays.

Birth Control Pills. An October report sponsored by the National Institute of Child Health and Human Development said that the risks from taking birth control pills appear to be negligible, at least for the young, white, middle-class females studied at the Kaiser-Permanente Medical Center in Walnut Creek, Calif. In a 10-year evaluation of more than 16,000 women, physicians found that oral contraceptive users do not increase their risk of developing cancers of the breast, ovary, or uterus. However, final data were not available on the association of pill use and skin cancer, high blood pressure, and chronic heart disease.   Dianne Hales

See also HEALTH AND DISEASE; MEDICINE. In WORLD BOOK, see HEPATITIS; PUBLIC HEALTH.

Artist Louise Nevelson displays the wall relief sculpture that she was commissioned to create for the winners of the American Book Awards.

PUBLISHING houses reacted unfavorably to two United States government rulings in 1980. The Supreme Court of the United States ruled on February 19 that the Central Intelligence Agency (CIA) had the right to prohibit the unauthorized publication of manuscripts written by current or former employees. The court ruled that former CIA agent Frank W. Snepp III violated his contractual obligations by not submitting his book, *Decent Interval*, to the agency for prepublication review. Snepp was ordered to forfeit his profits from that book to the U.S. government.

An Internal Revenue Service ruling that took effect on September 15 forced publishers to reduce the price of warehoused books or to destroy them in order to meet new criteria for inventory depreciation allowances. The ruling was expected to result in publishers' general reluctance to accept books that are unlikely to be rapid sellers.

Sales and Mergers. Several publishing houses changed hands during 1980, though merger transactions for the first six months were down 31 per cent from the same period in 1979.

In February, Newhouse Publications, a newspaper chain, agreed to buy Random House from RCA Corporation for between $65 million and $70 million. Houghton Mifflin Company acquired J. P. Tarcher Incorporated of Los Angeles for an undisclosed amount in January and in October purchased Rand McNally's elementary, high school, and college textbook lines for about $11.6 million. Bertelsmann Publishing AG of West Germany, which bought a 51 per cent interest in Bantam Books Incorporated in 1977, purchased the remaining 49 per cent interest from IFI International in May. One of Canada's leading publishers, MacMillan Company Ltd., merged with Gage Publishing Limited of Toronto.

Two International Agreements. Bertelsmann and World Book–Childcraft International, Incorporated, of Chicago embarked on a joint U.S. book club venture patterned after Bertelsmann's door-to-door and field-force sales operation in Europe. Richard Marek Publishers, Incorporated, on April 4 became the first U.S. publisher to sign a trade-book agreement with the People's Republic of China. Marek will publish a book of 180 photographs of Chinese art treasures.

A jury in a U.S. District Court in Springfield, Mass., on September 4 ordered Rand McNally to pay $155,000 to two former junior high school students who were burned while conducting an experiment described in a science textbook. It is believed to be the first time that a U.S. textbook publisher has been found negligent. Celeste Huenergard

See also CANADIAN LITERATURE; LITERATURE; MAGAZINE; NEWSPAPER; POETRY. In WORLD BOOK, see BOOKS; PUBLISHING.

PUERTO RICO. In a gubernatorial election held on Nov. 4, 1980, Governor Carlos Romero Barcelo won re-election by a razor-thin margin. His opponent, Rafael Hernandez Colon, favored continuance of the island's special United States commonwealth status. Romero Barcelo heads the New Progressive Party, which plans to move Puerto Rico toward statehood.

New System. Voting took place under a new system developed over a three-year period. For the first time, voters received registration cards with their photographs on them. They could vote any time in the six-hour period the polls were open. Results were reported by computer. Under the old system, all voters were required to gather at their local school at the same time on election day, to be locked inside until everyone had cast a ballot. The measure was adopted to prevent anyone from voting twice, and preliminary results were reported by telephone.

Earlier in the year, Puerto Ricans participated in another "first": the U.S. presidential primaries. In the Republican Party primary held on February 17, islanders overwhelmingly chose George H. W. Bush. Voters in the Democratic Party primary held on March 16 chose President Jimmy Carter.

The gubernatorial and primary elections were overshadowed by sporadic violence. On March 13, a Puerto Rican terrorist group ambushed a car carrying two U.S. Army officers and a sergeant. No one was seriously injured. Responsibility was claimed by terrorists advocating independence. However, no group took credit for predawn explosions on July 15 that demolished three aerial navigation stations and a U.S. Coast Guard navigation beacon in San Juan Harbor.

Resettlement Plan. A U.S. plan to resettle in Puerto Rico many Cuban refugees who had fled to Florida and adjacent Gulf Coast States was announced on September 18. It immediately drew strong protests from the Puerto Rican government as well as private citizens who feared that the influx would strain the country's weak economy. Under increasing pressure, the U.S. government announced on November 26 that it was abandoning the plan. See IMMIGRATION.

Eight members of the Armed Forces of National Liberation, a Puerto Rican revolutionary group, were convicted on July 30 in Chicago of conspiring to commit armed robbery and illegal possession of weapons. The eight were sentenced on August 26 to eight years in prison. On December 11, a federal grand jury indicted them and charged them with seditious conspiracy in connection with 28 bombings in the United States.   Nathan A. Haverstock

See also LATIN AMERICA (Facts in Brief Table). In WORLD BOOK, see PUERTO RICO.

PULITZER PRIZES. See AWARDS AND PRIZES.

QATAR. See MIDDLE EAST.

QUEBEC. Premier René Lévesque, after losing the independence referendum on May 20, decided not to call a provincial election in 1980 (see CANADA [Close-Up]). His separatist Parti Québécois (PQ) government, in power since Nov. 15, 1976, decided to go beyond the normal four-year term of Canadian governments. Instead, the premier held four by-elections on Nov. 17, 1980.

The party standings after the elections were: PQ, 68 seats; Liberals, 34; Union Nationale, 5; Independent, 3. The Liberals have now won 11 straight by-elections since 1976.

A politically popular budget was introduced by Finance Minister Jacques Parizeau on March 25. It cut income taxes by 3 per cent and increased personal exemptions. Furniture and textiles were added to the list of Quebec-made goods exempt from the 8 per cent sales tax. The $17.1-billion budget represented a 14 per cent increase.

Montreal Strike. Back-to-work legislation passed by the National Assembly ended on March 24 a 41-day strike by Montreal municipal workers that had resulted in icy and snow-clogged streets. It was the third time the PQ government had been forced to use this power to end labor disputes.

Echoes of the 1976 Olympic Summer Games in Montreal were heard in the June 5 report of the commission headed by Judge Albert Malouf, which

Quebec Premier René Lévesque adds his ballot to an avalanche of votes at the May referendum in which the province decided against sovereignty.

studied the dramatic cost overrun of the games. The Summer Games cost 11 times as much as estimated and incurred a $1-billion deficit. The blame was distributed among several key figures. Montreal's Mayor Jean Drapeau and architect Roger Taillibert of Paris, along with civic officials and contractors, were criticized, and fraud charges were laid against several persons.

Other Events. Eight miners, trapped on May 20 in a gold mine at Val d'Or, 220 miles (360 kilometers) northwest of Montreal, died as a wave of mud and water swept through the mine.

The land settlement signed in 1975 between the Cree Indians of northern Quebec and the provincial government, which gave the Indians $136-million in compensation for the loss of traditional lands and aboriginal rights, was considered a model for the resolution of native claims in Canada. But on Sept. 12, 1980, the Cree filed a $64-million lawsuit against the province, alleging that it failed to provide adequate health care in Cree villages. The Indians claimed that Quebec had not lived up to the agreement and requested that the federal government resume jurisdiction over health services.   David M. L. Farr

In WORLD BOOK, see QUEBEC.

RACING. See AUTOMOBILE RACING; BOATING; HORSE RACING; OLYMPIC GAMES; SWIMMING; TRACK AND FIELD.

RADIO. Network radio in the United States continued on the comeback trail in 1980, chalking up record commercial sales. National radio sales to sponsors during the first six months were an estimated 30 per cent higher than during the same period in 1979, and local radio advertising sales were running about 10 per cent ahead. The increase was in part attributed to the recession, which made radio, with its relatively low commercial costs, a more attractive buy than television.

Network Programming continued to feature musical specials. The four American Broadcasting Companies, Incorporated (ABC), radio networks, with a total of 1,732 affiliates, carried 32 specials in 1980, compared with 11 in 1979. One of ABC's most ambitious presentations was a 10-hour review of music of the 1970s, aired by its Contemporary Network on January 1. In September, The Source, the National Broadcasting Company (NBC) network aimed at young adults, drew an audience of 4.1 million for a live concert by the rock group Yes.

RKO Radio, the Mutual Broadcasting System (MBS), and National Public Radio (NPR) all utilized satellite hookups in 1980. NPR put the last of its 17 receivers in place on May 9 to become the first network entirely interconnected by satellite.

NPR's most popular entertainment program was "Jazz Alive," hosted by pianist Billy Taylor. Its top news series was the award-winning "All Things Considered." Other impressive NPR shows included the 13-part series "A Question of Place"; "Sound Portraits of 20th-Century Humanists"; "Invisible Men: Life in Baseball's Negro Leagues," hosted by James Earl Jones; "The Mind's Eye"; and the five-part "Vanished Voices: New Yorkers in the Thirties."

Popularity Sweepstakes. For the second year in a row, FM radio attracted a larger share of the radio audience – 55 per cent of all listeners – than AM. FM had a 50.5 per cent share in 1979.

Many radio stations dropped teen-oriented rock music in 1980 in favor of softer contemporary programming aimed at audiences from ages 18 to 34. "Modified" contemporary rock and "beautiful music" were the most popular radio formats in 1980, but country music programming increased dramatically in several major outlets. Among the stations "going country" were KHJ-AM, Los Angeles, and WRUR-FM, New York City.

On May 29, the Federal Communications Commission cut back on interference protection for 25 clear-channel AM stations by approving a plan that would permit up to 125 new nighttime AM outlets. Clear-channel stations are allowed to broadcast on a certain frequency 24 hours a day, while stations on neighboring channels must stop transmitting at night.   June Bundy Csida

In WORLD BOOK, see RADIO.

RAILROAD systems in the United States increased their profits in 1980 as brisk coal and grain hauling offset the recession's effect on other freight. The merger movement gathered momentum, and President Jimmy Carter signed a major railroad deregulation measure into law on October 14, beginning a period of reduced Interstate Commerce Commission (ICC) control over the industry. The law freed companies to raise or lower freight rates, sign contracts, and conduct other business more on their own.

The Association of American Railroads said that U.S. railroad companies earned $613.1 million in the first nine months of 1980, up from a profit of $554.9 million in the same 1979 period. Operating revenues were $20.7 billion, 12 per cent ahead of a year earlier. Third-quarter earnings were $156.1-million, 157 per cent higher than in the 1979 third quarter, on 9 per cent greater revenues. Freight traffic increased 0.2 per cent by December. The ICC approved rate increases of more than 11 per cent by September.

Merger Plans. Railroads moved along with merger plans. Union Pacific Corporation said in January that it would buy both the Missouri Pacific Corporation and the Western Pacific Railroad. In June, the Southern Railway System and the Norfolk and Western Railway Company proposed to merge. They had discussed a merger in

The Road Railer, a combination railroad car and truck trailer, might help railroads recover freight business that they have lost to truckers.

1979, but had abandoned the idea. The ICC approved the merger of Burlington Northern, Incorporated, and the St. Louis-San Francisco Railway on April 17 and the consolidation of the Chessie System, Incorporated, and Seaboard Coast Line Industries, Incorporated, on September 24.

Major cutbacks in the Chicago, Rock Island and Pacific and Chicago, Milwaukee, St. Paul and Pacific railroad systems also moved ahead. A federal judge ordered the Rock Island to begin liquidation by March 2.

Conrail Plan. Consolidated Rail Corporation (Conrail) issued a new five-year plan on July 16, calling for at least $900 million in federal financing through 1985, in addition to the $3.3 billion that the Congress of the United States had already authorized. Freight traffic sagged during the business slump, so Conrail's loss for the first nine months of 1980 increased to $203.2 million from $129.7 million a year earlier.

Congress in May approved another $750 million for work on the Boston-Washington, D.C., Northeast passenger-train corridor, and $38 million to study renovation of 13 other such corridors in the United States. National Railroad Passenger Corporation (Amtrak) ridership in the first nine months was off 1.7 per cent from 1979. Albert R. Karr

In WORLD BOOK, see RAILROAD.

RAJAI, MOHAMMED ALI (1934?-   ), became the first prime minister of the Islamic Republic of Iran on Aug. 11, 1980. The *Majlis* (parliament) approved Rajai by a 153 to 24 vote in a secret ballot after rejecting President Abol Hasan Bani-Sadr's first choice for the office. See IRAN.

Although Rajai insisted that he was not a member of the Islamic Republican Party, the fundamentalist religious party dominated by Islamic clerics that controls the Majlis, he received the strong support of that party. Rajai previously served 10 months as education minister beginning in February 1979.

Mohammed Ali Rajai was born in Qazvin, in northwest Iran, probably in 1934. He earned a mathematics degree at a college there and taught school.

After joining the revolutionary movement, Rajai was jailed several times for political activism, but, unlike other revolutionaries, he never went into exile during the reign of Shah Mohammad Reza Pahlavi. Thus, he has not acquired the Western ways and ideas that moderate the views of some other Iranian revolutionaries. He is a devout follower of the Ayatollah Ruhollah Khomeini.

Rajai's relationship with President Bani-Sadr, who is also close to Khomeini, has been difficult. Bani-Sadr reportedly considers Rajai inexperienced and politically unsophisticated. Edward G. Nash

RALLIS, GEORGE (1918-   ), was elected prime minister of Greece on May 8, 1980, by the members of Parliament who belonged to the ruling New Democracy Party. He succeeded Constantine Caramanlis, who was elected president on May 5. Rallis, foreign minister since 1977, favored Greek entry into the European Community (Common Market), which the country was scheduled to join in January 1981. A May 23 vote of confidence in Parliament supported his platform of close ties with the West. See CARAMANLIS, CONSTANTINE; GREECE.

Rallis was born in Athens on Dec. 26, 1918. He received a Doctor of Laws degree at the University of Athens in 1940 and began practicing law. His career was interrupted, however, when he was drafted into the Greek Army to fight against Italy in World War II. After Germany and Italy defeated Greece, Rallis' father became prime minister.

Rallis was drafted again in 1948 to fight in the civil war against Communist rebels. He was elected to Parliament in 1950 and held his seat until a military junta seized control of Greece in 1967. Rallis strongly opposed the junta, which ruled the country until 1974. He was arrested three times and spent six months in exile. Rallis was elected to Parliament when democracy was restored and was re-elected in 1977.

He married Helene Voultsos in 1950.   Jay Myers

RATHER, DAN (1931-   ), a veteran broadcast reporter, was named on Feb. 15, 1980, by CBS Inc. to succeed Walter Cronkite in 1981 as anchorman and managing editor of "The CBS Evening News." Rather appeared on the television program "60 Minutes" from October 1975 until 1981.

Dan Rather was born on Oct. 31, 1931, in Wharton, Tex., and grew up in Houston. Rather received his B.A. degree in journalism in 1953 from Sam Houston State College in Huntsville, Tex. He also attended the University of Houston and the South Texas School of Law.

While in college, Rather was a reporter for the Associated Press and United Press. He later worked at radio and television stations in Houston before joining CBS News in 1962 as chief of the Southwest Bureau in Dallas.

Rather served from 1964 to 1974 as CBS White House correspondent. President Richard M. Nixon's aides John D. Ehrlichman and H. R. Haldeman accused Rather in April 1971 of biased reporting and urged his reassignment. Later, Rather published *The Palace Guard* (1974), a study of the Nixon presidency.

Rather has won numerous awards for reporting, including five Emmys. He is married to Jean Goebel; they have two children.   Marsha F. Goldsmith

In the Special Reports section, see WALTER CRONKITE WRAPS IT UP.

REAGAN, RONALD WILSON (1911-   ), a former motion-picture actor and two-term governor of California, was elected President of the United States on Nov. 4, 1980. He defeated the incumbent, Democratic President Jimmy Carter, with 489 electoral votes to Carter's 49. See ELECTIONS.

Ronald Reagan was born in Tampico, Ill., on Feb. 6, 1911. He graduated from Eureka College in Illinois after winning letters in football, track, and swimming. He was a radio sports announcer in Des Moines, Iowa, during the 1930s.

Reagan played the part of a radio announcer in his first motion picture, *Love Is on the Air* (1937). He went on to appear in more than 50 films, notably *Kings Row* (1942) and *Storm Warning* (1950). During the 1940s and 1950s, Reagan served as president of the Screen Actors Guild. From 1954 to 1965, he was host of two television programs, "General Electric Theater" and "Death Valley Days."

An effective speaker and campaigner, Reagan was elected governor of California in 1966 and re-elected in 1970. He campaigned for the Republican presidential nomination in 1968 and 1976.

Reagan's first marriage to actress Jane Wyman ended in divorce. He has been married to the former Nancy Davis since 1952. He has two children from each marriage.   Beverly Merz

In the WORLD BOOK SUPPLEMENT section, see REAGAN, RONALD WILSON.

RECORDINGS. Recording industry sales in the United States continued their downward slide in 1980, partly because of the economic recession. Another reason was the tendency of listeners to copy records played on the radio onto their cassette recorders, instead of buying the disks.

Several record companies issued cut-rate albums that sold for $5.98 instead of the customary $8.98. At the other extreme, RCA Corporation celebrated the 25th anniversary of Elvis Presley's signing with the company by issuing an eight-album set entitled "Elvis Aaron Presley," priced at $69.95. The album included 65 previously unreleased numbers. Prestige Records issued a 12-record set by Miles Davis, "Chronicle," at a list price of $120. It contained all Davis' Prestige recordings from 1951 through 1956.

A major problem facing the recording industry was that of returns. Companies supplied dealers with enough records to claim a gold (500,000 records sold) or platinum (1 million) seller, but returns ran as high as 40 per cent of shipments. Returns entitled dealers to credits against the purchase of later releases, so some companies limited the number of records that dealers could return.

Counterfeit Recording continued. In February, a federal grand jury indicted the Sam Goody chain of record stores, claiming that they sold some coun-

The Doobie Brothers won four Grammy awards at the National Academy of Recording Arts and Sciences ceremony in Los Angeles in February.

Under tight security, RCA ships eight-record sets of "Elvis Aaron Presley," commemorating the 25th anniversary of Presley's signing with the company.

terfeit records and tapes and shipped others to their distributor for credit.

In an effort to discourage copying from radio, some leading popular artists such as Herb Alpert and Gordon Lightfoot began to record in the noise-free digital system, which provides quality that no other system can match. CBS Inc. became the first company to issue a series of albums for use on exceptionally good stereo systems. First to be featured in the Mastersound Audiophile series were Leonard Bernstein, Lorin Maazel, Zubin Mehta, Barbra Streisand, Bruce Springsteen, Billy Joel, and the percussionist Max Roach. The albums sold for $14.98.

Awards. Michael McDonald, the 28-year-old lead singer with the Doobie Brothers, won, individually or as a member of the group, four Grammy awards, among them record of the year and song of the year for "What A Fool Believes." Rickie Lee Jones won as best new artist. A new category, jazz fusion performance, brought victory to Weather Report. See AWARDS AND PRIZES (Arts Awards).

Four-time Grammy winner Bill Evans, who was considered a symbol of a tranquil, subtle brand of jazz piano, died in September. He had recorded 90 albums over 20 years.   Leonard Feather and Eliot Tiegel

See also MUSIC, CLASSICAL; MUSIC, POPULAR. In WORLD BOOK, see PHONOGRAPH.

RED CROSS. See COMMUNITY ORGANIZATIONS.

RELIGION remained an agent of conflict throughout the world in 1980. In some countries, violence erupted; in others, religion marked the divisions between people in more subtle ways.

In Iran, for example, the Shiite sect of Islam — which has been in control of the government since January 1979 — moved against various religious minorities, including members of the Bahá'í Faith, which claims 500,000 members in Iran. The new Islamic Constitution does not protect this faith, or even recognize it. The government closed Bahá'í schools and clinics. Bahá'í members were harassed and arrested without charges. Faramarz (Sam) Samandari, a Bahá'í leader, was convicted on July 11 of corruption, promoting Zionism, and spying for the United States and was executed the same day. Samandari had taken refuge in Canada when Iran's new regime began moving against the Bahá'í, but he had returned to Iran to plead for his imprisoned colleagues.

The Shiites see the Bahá'í Faith as perverse Islamic heresy. The Bahá'í recognize Muhammad, the founder of Islam, as a prophet — but as only one of many. Bahá'ís in the United States, 100,000 strong according to their own reports, sought international support for their fellow believers in Iran. The European Parliament, meeting in September, unanimously voted to ask Iran to stop persecuting the Bahá'í.

In Afghanistan, the Russian invaders became entangled with rebels, many of whom are Shiite Muslims fighting to perpetuate tribal religious ways. Soviet and Afghan security forces responded to a general strike in February in Kabul, Afghanistan's capital, with mass arrests of Shiite Muslim shopkeepers and others. Afghanistan's Shiites share the traditionalist values of Iran's ruling Muslims.

Lebanon remained another hot spot of religious conflict. Rival Christian factions fought each other and Syrian troops in northern Lebanon in February, killing about 60 villagers. At least 12 persons died when Christians clashed again in May. Serious fighting erupted repeatedly between Lebanon's rival Muslim groups — Shiites battling left wing Palestine Liberation Organization Muslims, in a reflection of the war between these groups in Iran and Iraq (see LEBANON; MIDDLE EAST).

In India, serious fighting erupted once again between Hindus and Muslims. Muslims worshiping in a mosque in Moradabad on August 13 heard a rumor that police allowed pigs — unclean animals according to Muslim teachings — to wander near the mosque. Muslims began battling police, then their religious rivals the Hindus. The fighting spread throughout the state of Uttar Pradesh, and at least 142 deaths were reported by August 17. Fighting broke out again in September, when journalists were arrested in connection with the August riots, and 10 more persons died.

U.S. Church Membership Reported for Bodies with 150,000 or More Members*

African Methodist Episcopal Church	1,970,000
African Methodist Episcopal Zion Church	1,125,176
American Baptist Association	1,500,000
American Baptist Churches in the U.S.A.	1,271,688
The American Lutheran Church	2,362,685
The Antiochian Orthodox Christian Archdiocese of North America	152,000
Armenian Church of America, Diocese of the (including Diocese of California)	450,000
Assemblies of God	1,629,014
Baptist Missionary Association of America	226,290
Christian and Missionary Alliance	173,986
Christian Church (Disciples of Christ)	1,213,061
Christian Churches and Churches of Christ	1,054,266
Christian Methodist Episcopal Church	466,718
Christian Reformed Church in North America	212,700
Church of God (Anderson, Ind.)	175,113
Church of God (Cleveland, Tenn.)	411,385
Church of God in Christ	425,000
Church of God in Christ, International	501,000
Church of God of Prophecy	227,850
The Church of Jesus Christ of Latter-day Saints	2,706,000
Church of the Brethren	172,115
Church of the Nazarene	474,820
Churches of Christ	1,600,000
Community Churches, National Council of	190,000
Conservative Baptist Association of America	225,000
The Episcopal Church	2,841,350
Free Will Baptists	231,167
General Association of Regular Baptist Churches	244,000
Greek Orthodox Archdiocese of North and South America	1,950,000
Jehovah's Witnesses	526,961
Jewish Congregations	5,860,900
Lutheran Church in America	2,921,090
The Lutheran Church—Missouri Synod	2,623,181
National Baptist Convention of America	2,688,799
National Baptist Convention, U.S.A., Inc.	5,500,000
National Primitive Baptist Convention	250,000
Orthodox Church in America	1,000,000
Polish National Catholic Church in America	282,411
Presbyterian Church in the United States	852,711
Progressive National Baptist Convention	521,692
Reformed Church in America	348,417
Reorganized Church of Jesus Christ of Latter Day Saints	188,580
The Roman Catholic Church	49,812,178
The Salvation Army	414,659
Seventh-day Adventists	553,089
Southern Baptist Convention	13,372,757
United Church of Christ	1,745,533
The United Methodist Church	9,653,711
United Pentecostal Church, International	465,000
The United Presbyterian Church in the U.S.A.	2,477,364
Wisconsin Evangelical Lutheran Synod	404,564

*Majority of the figures are for the years 1979 and 1980.
Source: National Council of Churches, *Yearbook of American and Canadian Churches* for 1981.

Queen Elizabeth II of Great Britain and her husband, Prince Philip,
receive an audience with Pope John Paul II in the Vatican on October 17.

Change in China. More positive news came from China, where the Communist regime was reportedly loosening its restrictions against religion. About 200 Chinese Roman Catholics attended a national synod in Peking (Beijing) in May, the country's first such meeting since 1962. The government granted China's Protestants permission to publish an edition of the Bible and to reopen a theological seminary in Nanking (Nanjing).

Religious news of an unexpected variety came from the South Pacific, where a cult may have been involved in an uprising in the New Hebrides. Jimmy Stevens, a plantation owner on Espiritu Santo, the largest island in Vanuatu (New Hebrides), led the revolt in May. Stevens and his followers apparently belong to a "cargo cult," a religious group that began during World War II. Cargo cultists have developed myths that explain their poverty and promise a utopian future — usually through the arrival of cargo dropped from airplanes or brought by ships, as occurred during the war. But the uprising may not have been entirely religious. Some New Hebrides officials said a group based in the United States might also be involved. See PACIFIC ISLANDS.   Martin E. Marty

See also EASTERN ORTHODOX CHURCHES; JEWS AND JUDAISM; PROTESTANTISM; ROMAN CATHOLIC CHURCH. In WORLD BOOK, see ISLAM; RELIGION; and articles on religions.

REPUBLICAN PARTY. Republicans swept to victory across the United States on Nov. 4, 1980, recapturing the White House, winning control of the Senate for the first time since 1954, gaining 33 seats in the U.S. House of Representatives, and swelling the ranks of Republican governors and state legislators. The election revived hopes of a lasting Republican majority, and some party leaders predicted that 1980 would be a turning point for their party just as the 1932 election was for the Democrats.

The Road to Victory for Ronald Reagan began in November 1979 when he declared his candidacy. He immediately assumed the front-runner's position in a crowded field that include Senator Howard H. Baker, Jr., of Tennessee, George H. W. Bush, U.S. Representative John B. Anderson of Illinois, former Texas Governor John B. Connally, and Senator Robert J. Dole of Kansas. Reagan won the first important primary of the season in New Hampshire decisively, and from then on he encountered serious opposition only from Bush and Anderson, a dark-horse contender who withdrew from the race on April 21 to mount an Independent candidacy. Bush withdrew on May 26, after Reagan had enough delegates to win the nomination.

The GOP Convention, which convened in Detroit from July 14 to July 17, adopted the longest platform in U.S. political history, a 40,000-word document in which the party proclaimed its commitments to cutting taxes, achieving military superiority, and solving the energy problem. It also called for a constitutional ban on abortion and dropped support of the equal rights amendment.

Former President Gerald R. Ford shared the spotlight with Reagan briefly as the two discussed Ford's possible role in a Reagan Administration. On July 16, Ford said that he might accept the vice-presidential nomination. But just before midnight that evening, Ford refused Reagan's offer and told the convention that he visualized his role as a campaigner rather than as a candidate. Reagan then named Bush as his running mate.

The Presidential Race. Throughout the campaign, the public-opinion polls showed Reagan in the lead – sometimes by a sizable margin, sometimes by only a percentage point. But election-eve polls showed Reagan and Carter running neck and neck. Because of this, Reagan's margin of victory over Carter came as a surprise. The final tally gave Reagan 51 per cent of the vote to Carter's 41 per cent, with 7 per cent going to Independent candidate Anderson. Winning 44 states, Reagan piled up 489 electoral votes to 49 for Carter, who carried only six states and the District of Columbia. It was the first time an elected incumbent President had been defeated since Franklin D. Roosevelt ousted Republican Herbert Hoover in 1932.

Reagan's victory invited comparison with Richard M. Nixon's crushing defeat of Senator George S. McGovern (D., S. Dak.) in 1972. In contrast to Nixon's triumph, which left both houses of Congress under Democratic control, Reagan appeared to help many other Republicans win their races. In both the Senate and House, well-known Democrats lost to Republican challengers while nearly all GOP incumbents kept their seats.

In the Senate, Republicans picked up 12 seats to take control of that body for the first time since 1954. The Senate in the 97th Congress will have 53 Republicans, 46 Democrats, and 1 Independent – Harry F. Byrd, Jr., of Virginia. Liberal Democrats, including McGovern, Frank Church of Idaho, Birch Bayh of Indiana, and Gaylord Nelson of Wisconsin, were the chief election victims.

Republicans also toppled two other venerable Democratic incumbents – six-term Senator Warren G. Magnuson of Washington and Herman E. Talmadge of Georgia. In Florida, Republican Paula Hawkins, a public service commissioner, was elected to the Senate, becoming its second current woman member. Alabamans elected Republican Jeremiah Denton, a former prisoner of war in Vietnam.

One liberal Republican, Senator Jacob K. Javits of New York, lost the Republican nomination to

Ronald Reagan is joined by running mate George Bush and former President Gerald R. Ford as he accepts the Republican presidential nomination.

Representative John B. Anderson of Illinois withdrew as a candidate for the Republican presidential nomination to run as an Independent.

Alphonse M. D'Amato. Javits then ran on the Liberal Party ticket, but D'Amato won.

In the House, Republicans sharply reduced the Democratic majority, producing a line-up of 242 Democrats, 192 Republicans, and 1 Independent for the 97th Congress, compared with 276 Democrats and 159 Republicans as the 96th Congress began. The GOP fell 26 seats short of winning control of the House but, because many of the newly elected Republicans were conservatives replacing liberal Democrats, observers predicted a decided shift to the right in the House.

In Governors' Races, Republicans won seven of 13 contests, putting the new line-up at 27 Democrats and 23 Republicans, compared with the pre-election count of 31 Democrats and 19 Republicans. GOP candidates defeated Democratic governors in Arkansas, Missouri, North Dakota, and Washington and held on to statehouses in Delaware, Indiana, and Vermont.

Republicans also won some 200 additional seats in state legislatures to gain control of four legislative chambers. They now control 30 of the 98 partisan state legislative chambers.   William J. Eaton

See also ELECTIONS. In WORLD BOOK, see REPUBLICAN PARTY.

RESEARCH. See SCIENCE AND RESEARCH.

RHODE ISLAND. See STATE GOVERNMENT.

RHODESIA. See ZIMBABWE.

ROMAN CATHOLIC CHURCH. Pope John Paul II in 1980 continued the pilgrim travels he initiated in 1979. He was well received by crowds in six African nations, France, West Germany, and Brazil.

In May, the pope made an 11-day visit to Zaire, the Congo, Kenya, Ghana, Upper Volta, and the Ivory Coast – in all of which considerable numbers of Roman Catholics turned out to greet him. At many stops on his African tour, the pope was greeted by tribal dancers and officials in native dress. Although he appeared to delight in such encounters with African culture, the pope declined to attend a Zairian-rite Mass that incorporates some tribal features such as dancing and drums.

About 1.5 million persons attended an outdoor Mass celebrated by the pope in Kinshasa, Zaire, on May 4, and nine persons were trampled to death in the crush. In all six African states, the pope preached peace and urged citizens to maintain the independence of their governments.

In a four-day visit to France beginning on May 30, the pontiff attempted to deal with the "spiritual fatigue" of French Catholics. Many people baptized as Catholics in France do not practice their faith, and the country ordained only 118 priests in 1978. France's President Valéry Giscard d'Estaing greeted the pope, noting that this was the first papal visit to France in 166 years. The pope said he hoped to inspire the "joy of the apostles" in French Catholics – and to banish "resignation, repudiation, or abandonment."

In Brazil, John Paul toured 13 cities beginning on June 30. He touched on the controversial issues of poverty, human rights, and the church's role in society throughout Latin America. Earlier in the year, on March 24, Archbishop Oscar Arnulfo Romero y Galdamez of El Salvador was assassinated by gunfire as he celebrated Mass. Archbishop Romero had been a leading proponent of "liberation theology" – the church's taking an active role in fighting injustice and poverty. About 30 persons were killed when gunshots and bombs stampeded the crowd of about 75,000 at Archbishop Romero's funeral on March 30.

In Brasília, his first stop in Brazil, the pope proclaimed "God's wish that Brazil construct an exemplary society, overcoming imbalances and inequalities with justice and harmony." Many Brazilian clergy, committed to liberation theology, applauded his stand. But at all stops on his tour, the pope emphasized that he could not sanction violence or Marxist materialism.

About half of Brazil's population is under 25 years of age. At Belo Horizonte, the Pope agreed that Brazil's youth must be liberated from misery, oppression, and degradation – but said that liberation should be in line with Christian concepts.

In a talk to workers at São Paulo, the pope condemned the situation confronting the poor:

"Factories discharge their waste, deform and pollute the environment; the air becomes unbreathable. Waves of migrants pile up in indecent shacks; many lose hope and live in misery."

In a moving gesture on July 2 in Rio de Janeiro, the pope gave his gold ring of office to a Brazilian church official – to be used to benefit the nearly 2 million persons who inhabit Rio's slums. But again he stressed that the church "denounces the incitation to any form of violence."

Three persons were trampled to death in Fortaleza, Brazil, in a crush of people trying to enter a soccer stadium to see the pope. At Fortaleza, he spoke about the plight of farmers forced to migrate by drought and poverty.

Pope John Paul II signs a document pledging church renewal that was issued at the close of the Dutch Bishops' Synod in January.

The Ecumenical Movement. The pope delivered several talks during the year on the ecumenical movement and asserted that the church unity movement is "irreversible" in direction. His efforts were focused especially on the return of the Orthodox Christians to Christian unity.

He also concentrated on Roman Catholic-Lutheran dialogues. The Lutheran Church in 1980 celebrated the 450th anniversary of the Augsburg Confession, the basic statement of faith of the

Lutheran Church. John Paul commented: "The intense and long-standing dialogue with the Lutheran Church has enabled us to discover how great and solid are the common foundations of our Christian faith. Catholic theology holds with the Lutheran tradition that the consecrated eucharistic elements do not exist as mere bread and wine but become the body and blood of Christ." The pontiff sought to improve relations with Jews and Protestants during a November visit to West Germany.

During his trip to Zaire in May, the pope met with Robert A. K. Runcie, recently enthroned as the 102nd archbishop of Canterbury, also on a pilgrimage to Africa. It was their first meeting. The pope gave an audience to Queen Elizabeth II in the Vatican in October.

The Küng Controversy. Catholics in many countries protested the Vatican's treatment of liberal theologian Hans Küng, a priest and professor at Tübingen University in West Germany. The Vatican Congregation on Doctrine declared on Dec. 27, 1979, that Küng has departed from the integral truth of the Catholic faith in his writings, and therefore cannot be considered a Catholic theologian. The congregation specifically criticized his views on infallibility. The Vatican at first stated that Küng would not be allowed to teach. However, under a compromise announced in April, he was allowed to continue teaching at Tübingen but not to examine candidates for the priesthood.

The Society of Jesus, a Catholic order, in May directed Congressman Robert F. Drinan (D., Mass.), a Jesuit priest, not to run for another term in the U.S. Congress. Drinan dropped out of the race with regret. The Vatican later said that no priest should hold public office.

Boston Catholics were stirred by a controversy over abortion. Humberto Cardinal Medeiros, Catholic archbishop of Boston, circulated a letter two days before the city's primary election in September that was read from many Catholic pulpits. The letter urged Catholic voters not to support candidates who favored abortion. Some Catholics felt that the Cardinal was using the pulpit to intimidate; others contended that he was exercising freedom of speech. Despite the cardinal's statement and the large number of Catholics in Boston, two candidates for the House of Representatives who supported public funding of abortions for the poor won nomination.

Married Priests. The National Conference of Catholic Bishops (NCCB) in August announced a plan to allow Anglican priests – including Episcopalians – to become Roman Catholic priests and still use some Anglican forms of worship. Married Anglican clergy could become priests of the Latin rite without renouncing their marriage vows.

Bishops' Meeting. Archbishop John R. Quinn, president of the NCCB, told the World Synod of Bishops in Rome on September 29 that nearly 80 per cent of married U.S. Catholics use contraceptives and only 29 per cent of American priests consider contraception "intrinsically wrong." He asked the bishops to make a new "honest examination" of the issue.

Other bishops raised the possibility of admitting to the sacraments Catholics who have been divorced. But at the close of the meeting, the pope reaffirmed the church's teaching against birth control and divorce. A furor later arose when, during a discussion of family life, the pope said that a married man who "lusts" after his wife commits adultery in the eyes of the church. The pontiff later clarified his remark by saying he recognized sex as an integral feature of Christian marriage.

Membership. According to the *Official Catholic Directory,* there were 81,968 converts to Catholicism in the United States in 1980, up from 77,205 in 1979. The total Catholic population in 1980 was 49,660,577, up from 49,602,035 in 1979. The number of priests in 1980 was 58,621, up from 58,430 in 1979. There were 126,517 nuns in 1980, compared with 128,378 in 1979. Catholic high school enrollment was 846,559 in 1980, down from 853,606 in 1979. Students in Catholic elementary schools totaled 2,317,200 in 1980, down from 2,379,816 in 1979.   John B. Sheerin

In WORLD BOOK, see ROMAN CATHOLIC CHURCH.

ROMANIA remained independent of Russia in foreign affairs during 1980, but edged closer to it economically. Romania was the only Warsaw Pact nation not to congratulate Afghanistan's Revolutionary Council President and Prime Minister Babrak Karmal when he assumed power in December 1979 and to abstain from a United Nations vote on the Russian invasion. In addition, Romania refused to endorse Russia's position on Afghanistan when Soviet Foreign Minister Andrei A. Gromyko visited Bucharest in January and February. Romania finally congratulated Karmal in April, but Communist Party General Secretary and President Nicolae Ceausescu said in a November interview with a Western newspaper that Russia should withdraw from Afghanistan.

In the Middle. Romania continued trying to mediate in the Arab-Israeli conflict and the Afghanistan struggle. Ceausescu sent an envoy, Vasile Pungan, to Afghanistan and Pakistan in August.

China's Communist Party Chairman Hua Kuofeng (Hua Guofeng) visited Bucharest after attending the funeral of Yugoslavia's President Josip Broz Tito in May, but Romania refused to endorse Hua's extreme anti-Russian remarks. Romania and East Germany signed a five-year trade agreement when East Germany's Communist Party Secretary General and State Council Chairman Erich Honecker visited Romania in June.

Twenty Romanians fled to Austria in July in a crop-duster plane designed for only 14 persons. It flew only 150 feet (46 meters) above the ground.

At the beginning of the summer, Romania announced that foreign visitors would be permitted to use Romanian money to buy gasoline in Romania. A 1979 law required payment in hard currencies.

Russia supplied Romania with 3 million short tons (2.7 million metric tons) of oil in 1980. Romania and the Soviet Union agreed in August to build a nuclear power station in Russia's Ukraine.

Western Trade. On July 28, Romania became the first nation in the Russian bloc's Council for Mutual Economic Assistance (COMECON) to sign a trade agreement with the European Community (EC). The EC agreed to lift import tariffs on 30 Romanian products and ease import quotas for the remaining goods by 20 per cent. A Romanian-EC committee was to draw up future agreements on industrial and economic cooperation and on fishing and agriculture.

Romania announced a plan in September to develop small industrial enterprises, especially consumer-goods producers. The government also said in September that it would cut military spending by 16 per cent in 1981.   Chris Cviic

See also EUROPE (Facts in Brief Table). In WORLD BOOK, see ROMANIA.

ROTARY INTERNATIONAL. See COMMUNITY ORGANIZATIONS.

ROWING. See OLYMPIC GAMES; SPORTS.

RUBBER. See MANUFACTURING.

RUSSIA faced major crises in bordering nations and a deteriorating economic situation at home in 1980. The Soviet media acknowledged for the first time that Russian troops were in Afghanistan at the end of February, two months after they had begun their invasion (see AFGHANISTAN [Close-Up]). Russia and Afghanistan signed a treaty in April on the "temporary stay" of Soviet troops there. Meanwhile, unrest and strikes in Poland caused Russia to mass troops along that border in December (see POLAND).

The most vigorous Western reaction to the Afghanistan invasion came from the United States. By January 9, President Jimmy Carter had asked the U.S. Senate to delay indefinitely considering the Strategic Arms Limitation Treaty (SALT II) with Russia, cut back on grain shipments to Russia, banned sales of high-technology and other strategic goods, restricted the rights of Russian ships to fish in U.S. waters, and curtailed economic and cultural contacts. West German Chancellor Helmut Schmidt and French President Valéry Giscard d'Estaing said détente between East and West "could not withstand another such blow."

Russia tried to soften the Western reaction by organizing a meeting between Communist Party General Secretary and Supreme Soviet Presidium Chairman Leonid I. Brezhnev and Giscard d'Estaing in Warsaw in May and by inviting Schmidt to

From *Herblock on All Fronts*. New American Library, 1980.

Moscow in July. Neither meeting produced a fresh proposal on Afghanistan. Schmidt's remark in a Moscow speech that those "who care for the peace of the world must refrain from forcing their own political, social, and economic ideas" on other countries received unusually hostile treatment in the Russian press. Russia announced in June that "some Soviet troops" had been withdrawn from Afghanistan, but the West dismissed this statement as propaganda.

U.S. Boycott. The United States tried, but failed, to organize an effective boycott of the Olympic Summer Games in Moscow. The only major Western countries that did not send teams were Canada, the United States, and West Germany. Athletes from Great Britain and Australia participated, against the advice of their governments.

Only 100,000 foreign guests went to Moscow instead of the 300,000 expected to watch the games, which lasted from July 19 to August 3. Most Western ambassadors stayed away from the games to express their governments' opposition to the Afghanistan invasion. See OLYMPIC GAMES.

The Diplomatic Front. In October, Russia concluded a treaty with Syria shortly after the outbreak of the war between Iraq and Iran. The treaty included clauses on military cooperation. Relations with Iran continued cool despite Russian attempts to ingratiate themselves with Ayatollah Ruhollah

Khomeini. Russia denied in October that it had offered arms to Iran.

Russia denounced Pakistan for helping Afghan insurgents, but praised India's detached attitude toward the invasion. In May, India signed a $1.6-billion arms deal with Russia, the biggest it had ever made. India promised to pay Russia over a 17-year period at 2.5 per cent interest.

A Nicaraguan delegation visited Moscow and signed a series of agreements calling for trade and cooperation. Russia also tried to befriend Mexico. Deputy Minister of Defense General Ivan Pavlovsky visited that nation in September. Deputy Minister of Defense and Admiral of the Soviet Fleet Sergei Gorshkov visited Ethiopia in July to discuss Russia's new naval base there.

Poland's Problems. Russian media mentioned Poland's labor unrest for the first time on August 19, six weeks after the first strikes. The next day, Russia resumed jamming broadcasts to the Soviet Union by the Voice of America, the British Broadcasting Corporation, and the West German *Deutsche Welle*. Russia had stopped jamming Western broadcasts almost exactly seven years earlier. The Russian Communist Party newspaper *Pravda* published three major statements concerning Poland in September. *Pravda* said that "real Socialism" and free trade unions not controlled by the Communist Party were incompatible.

Some 30,000 Russian troops took part in Warsaw Pact military exercises in East Germany in September. Other exercises took place in Hungary in August and in Poland in October.

Warsaw Pact foreign ministers met in Warsaw in October to discuss the Polish situation. They also planned the tactics that they would follow at the 35-nation European Security Conference in Madrid, Spain, in November, called to discuss progress in applying the 1975 Helsinki Agreement, which includes a section on human rights. All European countries except Albania and Andorra had signed the agreement, as had the United States, Canada, and Cyprus.

Brezhnev and other Russian leaders talked with Poland's Communist Party First Secretary Stanislaw Kania and Council of Ministers Chairman Jozef Pinkowski in Moscow on October 30. After the visit, the Polish authorities hardened their line toward demands for further liberalization. After new confrontations, Russia hinted on November 30 of Warsaw Pact action if trouble continued. Warsaw Pact leaders declared at a meeting in Moscow on December 5 that "the Polish people can firmly count on the fraternal solidarity and support of the Warsaw Treaty countries." A White House official charged on December 7 that Russia had completed preparations for military intervention.

Russia's relations with the Italian Communist Party remained strained because the Italians had

A Jamaican cyclist is stopped at one of the security checkpoints that Russian police set up around the Olympic Village in Moscow.

criticized Russian policies, especially in Afghanistan. But relations with Yugoslavia and Romania improved. Russia and Yugoslavia agreed in September to increase mutual trade from $11 billion during the previous five years to $26 billion from 1981 through 1985. Russia also placed a large order for Yugoslav ships.

Shortages and Shortfalls. *Pravda* admitted on February 15 that Moscow retail stores were short of grain and flour products, meat, cheese, salt, and sunflower oil. The Western press reported in June that 250,000 auto workers at a factory near Kuybyshev and at Gorki had struck to protest shortages of food. Russian authorities denied the reports.

Russia announced in October that its 1980 grain harvest was 181 million metric tons (199 million short tons), off 54 million metric tons (59 million short tons) from the production target and only 2 million metric tons (2.2 million short tons) above the poor 1979 harvest. On October 21, Brezhnev called attention to the "extraordinary importance" of solving the country's food-supply problem. The cotton harvest exceeded the record 9.2 million metric tons (10.1 million short tons) produced in 1979, but industrial growth fell short of target.

Kosygin Dies. Council of Ministers Chairman Aleksey N. Kosygin's health deteriorated during the summer. The 76-year-old leader made his final public appearance on August 2 and asked later to be relieved of his duties. Brezhnev announced at the October meeting of the Supreme Soviet that Kosygin had resigned because of illness. He was replaced by Nikolay Tikhonov, 75 (see TIKHONOV, NIKOLAY). Kosygin died of a heart attack on December 18. At the same October meeting, Mikhail Gorbachov, 49, secretary of the central committee for agricultural affairs, was made a full member of the Politburo.

Dissident Andrei D. Sakharov on January 2 called for a Soviet withdrawal from Afghanistan. Sakharov was exiled on January 22 to Gorki, a city out of bounds to Western visitors. Gleb Yakunin, a Russian Orthodox priest who led a group of dissident Christians, was sentenced to five years in prison and five years of internal exile on August 28 for anti-Soviet agitation and propaganda. Mathematician Tatyana Velikanova, a former member of an unofficial group that monitored Russian compliance with the Helsinki Agreement, was sentenced to four years in a labor camp and five years of internal exile. Several other religious activists were also imprisoned. Three feminists were expelled from Russia in July for suggesting that women should try to persuade their male relatives and husbands not to fight in Afghanistan.   Chris Cviic

See also EUROPE (Facts in Brief Table). In WORLD BOOK, see RUSSIA.
RWANDA. See AFRICA.

SAFETY

SAFETY. More drivers than ever before were slowing down in the United States in 1980 and obeying the speed limit of 55 miles (89 kilometers) per hour, according to the Highway Users Federation, a nonprofit group that produced a study in June for the federal government. The federation said that California had the highest percentage of speeders and Maryland the lowest. It estimated from reports that 51.6 per cent of all motor vehicles traveling on U.S. roads posted at 55 mph exceeded the limit during the first six months of the year. The 1979 average violation rate was 56 per cent.

Auto Safety. The U.S. Department of Transportation in August reported mounting evidence that most small economy cars fail to protect passengers in crash tests at 35 miles (56 kilometers) per hour and that foreign-made cars fail more often than domestic cars do. In crash tests of a dozen 1980-model small cars against stationary barriers, only the Chevrolet Chevette and Fiat Strada passed. All the others — two West German cars and eight Japanese entries — failed.

Joan Claybrook, administrator of the National Highway Traffic Safety Administration, said in January that current safety standards are inadequate for the protection of motorists involved in side-impact crashes, which account for 1 of every 3 U.S. traffic deaths. Claybrook said that the automobile industry had a prime opportunity to work on this problem because auto manufacturers are now making lighter and more fuel-efficient cars.

"Right on Red" Hazardous. The Insurance Institute for Highway Safety estimated in December that traffic laws allowing a right turn on a red light are responsible for increasing accidents at intersections by about 20 per cent. The institute studied police accident reports from New Jersey, Oklahoma, South Carolina, Tennessee, Virginia, and Wisconsin. From those reports, they estimated an additional 20,000 accidents occur each year, chiefly because drivers ignore the fact that they are supposed to yield the right of way to pedestrians and cars with a "green" signal. All 50 states now have right-turn-on-red laws, required by Congress if a state wishes to receive energy-conservation aid.

Nuclear Safety. The Federal Emergency Management Agency released a gloomy report on August 9 on the status of federal and state preparedness for another major accident similar to the one at the Three Mile Island nuclear power plant near Harrisburg, Pa., in March 1979. The report said that "little of the needed support facilities . . . are actually in place" for the emergency evacuation of the 3.3 million persons who live within a 10-mile (16-kilometer) radius of the nation's 73 operating nuclear plants.

Worker Safety Rules. In January, Secretary of Labor F. Ray Marshall announced the federal government's first comprehensive rules to protect workers from exposure to cancer-causing substances on the job. Under these rules, the Department of Labor will publish a list of 500 substances that are strongly suspected of causing cancer in workers. The agency will also require employers to take steps to protect workers from such substances.

The Department of Labor announced new workplace fire-protection standards in September. The agency claimed that the new rules will safeguard workers more effectively and simplify compliance for employers. The new rules include safety and training requirements for employee fire-fighting brigades. An estimated 141,000 to 165,000 workplace fires occurred in 1977, killing 124 persons.

The Environmental Protection Agency proposed a new rule in September that would require all public and private elementary and secondary schools in the United States to identify asbestos-containing materials in school buildings and take measures to protect students from the risk of inhaling asbestos dust. The rule was expected to be made final in February 1981.   Foster Stockwell

In WORLD BOOK, see SAFETY.

SAILING. See BOATING.

SAINT VINCENT AND THE GRENADINES. See WORLD BOOK SUPPLEMENT section.

SALVATION ARMY. See COMMUNITY ORGANIZATIONS.

Motorcycle Helmets and the Death Rate

Fatalities per 10,000 motorcycles

40 states enact helmet laws, 1966-1969

27 states repeal, weaken laws, 1976-1980

Source: National Highway Traffic Safety Administration

SAMARANCH, JUAN ANTONIO (1920-   ), Spain's ambassador to Russia, was elected president of the International Olympic Committee (IOC) on July 16, 1980. He succeeded Lord Killanin of Ireland, whose eight-year term ended when the 1980 Summer Olympics concluded in Moscow on August 3.

Juan Samaranch was born in Barcelona on July 17, 1920. He attended Barcelona schools, and received a degree in business there.

Samaranch was formerly president of the Provincial Savings Bank of Barcelona. He also served on the board of directors of several business and banking firms and was president of the Provincial Committee of Barcelona. He has been awarded the Grand Cross by Spain for civil, naval, military, aeronautical, and agricultural merit.

The new IOC president was a good boxer and hockey player as a youth. He now skis, plays golf, and enjoys sailing and horseback riding. He speaks English, French, German, and Russian.

Samaranch did not agree with the decision of the United States and other countries to boycott the 1980 Moscow Olympic Games (see OLYMPIC GAMES). However, he favors staging the 1984 Olympic Games in Los Angeles. Samaranch and his wife, the former Maria Teresa Salisachs, have a daughter and a son.   Joseph P. Spohn

SAN MARINO. See EUROPE.

SÃO TOMÉ AND PRÍNCIPE. See AFRICA.

SASKATCHEWAN witnessed the advent of a new political movement on March 11, 1980, when Richard Collver, leader of the province's Progressive Conservative Party until 1979, announced that he intended to promote the union of western Canada with the United States. He claimed that the February 18 federal election showed a refusal on the part of the rest of Canada to recognize the aspirations of western Canada. Collver was joined on April 25 by Dennis Ham, another Conservative legislator, in forming the Unionist Party. The defection left party standings as New Democratic Party, 44; Conservatives, 15; and Unionists, 2.

Eldorado Nuclear Limited, the federally owned uranium company, suffered a severe setback on August 6 when a federal environment-assessment panel rejected a plan to build Canada's third uranium refinery at Warman, 19 miles (30 kilometers) north of Saskatoon. The panel had told Eldorado to furnish information on the plant's possible negative impact on the religious beliefs of the largely rural Mennonite community. The company responded that it was impossible to predict.

A tragic highway crash near Swift Current claimed the lives of 22 railway workers on May 28. Ten were seasonal workers from Newfoundland who were upgrading track.   David M. L. Farr

See also CANADA. In WORLD BOOK, see SASKATCHEWAN.

SAUDI ARABIA. The government initiated certain reforms in 1980, prompted by fears of unrest or revolution after the occupation of the Great Mosque of Mecca by Islamic zealots in November 1979. Some of the changes were designed to bring the benefits of modernization to previously excluded groups, such as the Shiite religious minority and the rural poor. Other changes enforced Islamic law more strictly to preserve the support of religious leaders and defuse the fundamentalist unrest that may have been reflected in the Mecca raid.

But there was no political or social fallout from the Mecca debacle, and the country remained stable. Sixty-three zealots, including their leader, a self-proclaimed *Mahdi*, or messiah, were publicly beheaded for treason on January 9. The leadership of the armed forces was tightened up after the Mecca incident.

Political Reform. King and Prime Minister Khalid ibn Abd al-Aziz Al Saud announced the formation of a Consultative Council in May that was to prepare a constitution for the country based on Koranic law. The king also enlarged the Council of Ministers to include a number of religious leaders, who would now play a part in the nation's decision-making process.

Social progress continued, despite publicity from the television film *Death of a Princess* whose showing

Prince Fahd of Saudi Arabia attends the November Arab League summit conference in Amman, Jordan, to discuss the Iran-Iraq war.

on British and United States television raised Saudi hackles by depicting the harshness of Saudi social laws. The first bank for women opened in Riyadh in January and a second women's bank, sponsored by New York City's Citibank, opened in July.

The Economy continued to overheat, and the greatest Saudi need was for skilled workers, not money. The five-year plan approved in May set total expenditures at $235 billion, with $74 billion earmarked for fiscal 1980-1981 and a $5-billion surplus. Some $5.9 billion, a 55 per cent increase, was allocated to municipal and rural development and $6.8 billion to training workers.

In September, only days before the Iran-Iraq war broke out, a 755-mile (1,215-kilometer) pipeline was completed across the Arabian Peninsula to carry oil from eastern oilfields to Red Sea refineries, away from the dangerous Persian Gulf area. The Saudis watched the war nervously, supporting their long-time rivals in Iraq against their one-time Iranian friends. On September 26, they requested — and got — four U.S. AWACS (Airborne Warning and Control Systems) planes to strengthen their air defenses. The government also stepped up oil production to make up for some of the output lost in Iran and Iraq.   William Spencer

See MIDDLE EAST (Facts in Brief Table). In WORLD BOOK, see SAUDI ARABIA.

SAUVÉ, JEANNE (1922-   ), journalist and Liberal politician, became speaker of Canada's House of Commons on Feb. 29, 1980. She is the first woman to hold that post.

Sauvé was born Jeanne Benoit in Prud'homme, Sask., on April 26, 1922. She was national president of the Young Catholic Students Group from 1942 until 1947. She taught French and studied economics in London from 1948 to 1950. She received a degree in French civilization from the University of Paris in 1952.

From 1952 until 1972, Sauvé worked as a journalist and broadcaster for the Canadian Broadcasting Corporation. In 1964, she was elected president of the Canadian Institute on Public Affairs. She was general secretary of the Federation of Authors and Artists of Canada from 1966 to 1972.

Sauvé was first elected to Parliament in 1972. She became minister of state in charge of science and technology that year, minister of the environment in 1974, and minister of communications in 1975. In 1978, Sauvé was appointed the adviser to the secretary of state for external affairs on relations with the French-speaking world.

She married Maurice Sauvé, who later became a member of Parliament and a Cabinet minister, in 1948. They have one son.   Jay Myers

See also CANADA.

SCHOOL. See CIVIL RIGHTS; EDUCATION.

SCHREYER, EDWARD RICHARD (1935-   ), Canada's 22nd governor general, carried out a busy schedule as the queen's representative in 1980, despite emergency intestinal surgery in February. Schreyer awarded the country's highest decoration, the Order of Canada, to three men of remarkable accomplishments. They were Sir William Stephenson, "the man called Intrepid," a top-level intelligence coordinator for Great Britain, Canada, and the United States during World War II; Terry Fox, a 22-year-old student who, despite losing a leg to cancer, ran halfway across Canada to raise more than $12 million for cancer research; and Kenneth Taylor, Canada's ambassador to Teheran, Iran, who organized the evacuation of six U.S. diplomats from Iran after Iranian militants seized the U.S. Embassy in November 1979.

In addition to traveling throughout Canada, Schreyer led the Canadian delegation to the funeral of President Josip Broz Tito of Yugoslavia in Belgrade on May 8 and attended the ceremony at which Princess Beatrix became queen of the Netherlands on April 30. He also entertained several members of the British royal family and welcomed President Jose Lopez Portillo of Mexico on a state visit in May. Schreyer and his wife, Lily, for the first time asked anyone who cared to come to their annual summer garden party.   David M. L. Farr

See also CANADA.

SCIENCE AND RESEARCH. The Congress of the United States passed a law in September 1980 calling for the development of a fusion power plant by the year 2000, stating a commitment reminiscent of President John F. Kennedy's pledge in the early 1960s to put a man on the moon. The Magnetic Fusion Energy Engineering Act, signed by President Jimmy Carter in October, outlined objectives estimated to cost about $20 billion.

The goal of such magnetic-confinement fusion research is to enclose a hot, fully ionized gas of light nuclei, such as deuterium and tritium, within a "magnetic bottle" until the nuclei collide and fuse, thereby liberating energy. Recent research developments convinced lawmakers that the conditions needed to attain sustained and controlled fusion are now achievable.

Science Boycott. Several U.S. science organizations canceled cooperative exchanges with their Russian counterparts after the Soviet government ordered physicist Andrei D. Sakharov into internal exile in the Russian city of Gorki. For example, the prestigious National Academy of Sciences (NAS) in February suspended all bilateral meetings, symposiums, and workshops with the Russian Academy of Sciences for six months. The ban was extended in August. Members of the NAS Council approved a statement in July that read in part: "We remain deeply concerned by [Sakharov's]

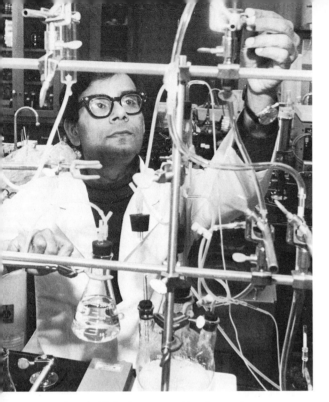

Ananda Chakrabarty won a historic suit when
the Supreme Court of the United States
allowed a patent on a bacterium he developed.

continuing exile. Our concern is not an indication of agreement or disagreement with his expressed opinions of political issues. It is rather a concern for his rights as a scientist and as a human being and, in particular, for his freedom to pursue scientific work."

Nuclear Power. Maine voters in September turned down a referendum that would have closed the Maine Yankee nuclear power plant near Wiscasset, the state's only such plant. This was the first popular vote on nuclear power plant issues since the major accident at the Three Mile Island nuclear power plant near Harrisburg, Pa., in March 1979. A report prepared for the Nuclear Regulatory Commission (NRC) in January stated that the NRC, as currently organized by the federal government, is not equipped "adequately to ensure the public health and safety."

Animal Migration. Zoologists tracing the migratory habits of a 212-pound (95-kilogram) loggerhead turtle encountered an unusual problem. They tracked signals from a transmitter strapped to the animal's back from Gulfport, Miss., along the coastline of Louisiana, and then onto the beach near Brownsville, Tex. The signals then migrated inland to Kansas. They were beamed via the National Oceanic and Atmospheric Administration's *Nimbus 6* satellite to the Goddard Space Flight Center in Maryland, where the scientists recorded them. The scientists concluded that something must be wrong, because no sea turtle had ever migrated naturally to Kansas. Investigators eventually found that the $5,000 transmitter had slipped off the turtle's back and been picked up in Texas by a fisherman, who took it to Kansas.

In another migration study, scientists found that dolphins may get their bearings from magnetic material in their heads, as pigeons do. Geophysicist Michael D. Fuller of the University of California, Santa Barbara, and his associates used sensitive magnetometers to examine 1-inch (2.5-centimeter) cross-section samples from the heads of five dolphins that had been stranded and died. The scientists measured magnetism 20 times stronger than that of the earth's magnetic field in some head tissue. Under a microscope, the samples were found to contain many opaque particles with the thermal properties of magnetite, a strongly magnetic mineral containing iron. If dolphins use the particles for navigation, Fuller suggests that it may be possible to wire fishing nets so that the animals can avoid capture.

Ancient Blood. Intact red and white blood cells of an extinct woolly mammoth that lived about 44,000 years ago have been found in tissues taken from a mammoth discovered frozen in Siberia in 1977. The cells are the oldest body cells to be examined in so natural a state. When Marion Barnhart of the Wayne State University School of Medicine in Detroit analyzed the dried tissue on a scanning electron microscope, she saw the red and white blood cells in blood vessels and capillaries. The blood cells resemble those of modern elephants, Barnhart says, but the mammoth's white blood cells were larger.

Alcohol and the Brain. Long-term alcohol use, even without the malnutrition that often accompanies it, can destroy brain cells, according to a study published in August. Neuroscience investigator Don W. Walker and his colleagues at the Veterans Administration Medical Center and the University of Florida College of Medicine in Gainesville have demonstrated that cell destruction is caused by heavy alcohol use, not by the malnutrition that frequently accompanies such use. They found that alcohol destroys brain neurons in rats.

In another study, J. N. Nestoros of McGill University in Montreal, Canada, reported in August that long-term alcohol use destroys the neurotransmitter that helps fight anxiety and thus encourages alcoholics to drink more and more to quell their anxiety. Nestoros' research suggests that alcohol relieves anxiety by acting on gamma-aminobutyric acid in the brain. Foster Stockwell

See also the various science articles. In WORLD BOOK, see RESEARCH; SCIENCE.

SCOTLAND. See GREAT BRITAIN.

SCULPTURE. See VISUAL ARTS.

SEAGA, EDWARD (1930-   ), leader of the Jamaica Labor Party, was elected prime minister of Jamaica on Oct. 30, 1980. He defeated Prime Minister Michael N. Manley, leader of the People's National Party, whom the voters blamed for Jamaica's economic problems. See WEST INDIES.

Seaga was born in Boston, Mass., on May 28, 1930, of Jamaican parents whose forebears were Scottish, Lebanese, and Jamaican. Seaga's father was a travel agent. Seaga attended Harvard University on a scholarship, graduating with a degree in sociology in 1952. He returned to Jamaica shortly thereafter and for the next several years lived in rural parts of Jamaica studying child development as well as the island's revivalist cults.

In 1959, Seaga began his political career as a member of the upper house of the Jamaican legislature. At 29, he was the youngest member in that body's history. Subsequently, he helped draft the Constitution under which Jamaica achieved its independence in 1962. He also held Cabinet posts in the Labor governments that ruled from 1962 to 1972. He became leader of his party in 1974.

Seaga and his wife, Marie Elizabeth (Mitsy) Constantine, live in Kingston. They have two sons and a daughter.   Paul C. Tullier

SENEGAL. See AFRICA.
SEYCHELLES. See AFRICA.

SHIP AND SHIPPING. Vessel demand showed some signs of improvement in 1980. Lloyd's Register of Shipping reported that 1,763 merchant ships were under construction throughout the world on June 30, down 6 per cent. But orders, including ships being built, rose from 2,967 to 3,111. Tonnage of vessels on order increased to 32.5 million gross tons, up 28 per cent.

The burden of laid-up tonnage eased as the oil-tanker surplus continued to shrink. But fuel costs climbed, replacing crew expenses as the largest merchant-ship cost, so ship operators accelerated their changeover from steam to diesel fuel. Diesels use less fuel. Severe congestion at United States ports hampered the industry's ability to handle the rising demand for exported coal.

New Construction. U.S. shipbuilders held orders of about $11.65 billion. The Maritime Administration said that commercial-ship orders were valued at $2.7 billion on September 1, down from $3.1-billion a year earlier. Some 48 ships were scheduled for completion by 1984, two fewer than on Sept. 1, 1979. However, the shipyards began to benefit from an increasing demand for tankers to haul petroleum products and liquefied natural gas (LNG). In October, General Dynamics Corporation signed a contract to build three 125,000-cubic-meter LNG tankers for Zapata Western LNG

The new Japanese tanker *Shin Aitoku Maru* can shut down engines and hoist sails when winds rise. It can make a speed of 12 knots under wind power.

Incorporated, a unit of the Zapata Corporation, for more than $500 million. Zapata will use the tankers to carry LNG from Indonesia to the United States. Oil tankers were needed mainly to carry Alaskan oil to other parts of the United States. The Shipbuilders Council of America estimated that U.S. Navy orders amounted to $8.95 billion at the end of 1979.

Agreement with China. The United States signed a maritime agreement with China on September 17 guaranteeing that U.S. vessels will carry at least one-third of the U.S.-China ocean trade and that Chinese ships will carry at least one-third. Chinese ships received access to 55 U.S. ports on four days' notice, and to most others on seven days' notice; U.S. vessels gained entry to 20 Chinese ports with seven days' notice. President Jimmy Carter imposed an embargo on grain shipments to Russia in January to protest the Soviet invasion of Afghanistan. The International Longshoremen's Association – a dockworkers' union – then boycotted all ocean freight bound for Russia. Albert R. Karr

See also TRANSPORTATION. In WORLD BOOK, see SHIP.

SHOOTING. See HUNTING; OLYMPIC GAMES; SPORTS.

SIERRA LEONE. See AFRICA.

SINGAPORE. See ASIA.

SKATING. See HOCKEY; ICE SKATING.

SKIING. Hanni and Andreas Wenzel, sister and brother, of Liechtenstein and Ingemar Stenmark of Sweden won the major skiing honors in 1980. The Wenzels became the first skiers from one nation, let alone one family, to take the World Cup overall titles in the same year. Hanni Wenzel and Stenmark dominated skiing in the Olympic Winter Games held in February in Lake Placid, N.Y. See OLYMPIC GAMES.

World Cup competition ran from December 1979 to March 1980 in the United States, Canada, and seven European nations. There were 27 events for men and 28 for women. The 23-year-old Hanni Wenzel totaled 311 points to 259 for second-place Annemarie Proell Moser of Austria, reversing the 1979 women's finish. Cindy Nelson of Lutsen, Minn., finished 10th overall with 94 points. In the Olympics, Wenzel won the slalom and giant slalom and finished second to Moser in the downhill.

Liechtenstein, a tiny principality in the Alps, has only 24,000 residents, 6,000 of them skiers. The best were Hanni and 22-year-old Andreas. He narrowly won the World Cup men's title with 204 points to 200 for Stenmark and 132 for Phil Mahre of White Pass, Wash. Ken Read of Calgary, Canada, won major downhill races in January in Kitzbühel, Austria, and Wengen, Switzerland.

Stenmark, 23, captured six of the eight World Cup giant slaloms and five of the eight slaloms, and

Hanni Wenzel of Liechtenstein wins the women's giant slalom, one of two skiing events in which she won gold medals in the Winter Olympics.

he took both gold medals in the Olympics. But because he had shunned all downhill races, he could not get enough points to win the World Cup overall title. He had been so dominant while winning three consecutive overall titles from 1976 to 1978 that the rules were changed to favor all-around skiers rather than specialists.

In the Olympics, Mahre won the silver medal behind Stenmark in the men's slalom and gained the unofficial combined title. The best finish by an American woman was fourth in the downhill by Heidi Preuss of Lakeport, N.H.

In all, it was a disappointing year for the American skiers, who said a change in team leadership had left them disorganized and demoralized. The U.S. Nordic skiers also fell below expectations in the Winter Olympics, with only an eighth by Jim Denney of Duluth, Minn., in the 90-meter jump.

Professional. The men's circuit consisted of 14 meets in the United States, Canada, Japan, Austria, and Switzerland, with almost $650,000 in prizes. André Arnold of Austria, the overall champion for the third straight year, earned $80,000 in prize money and $120,000 from sponsors.

Jocelyne Perrillat of France was the women's circuit point leader. She finished second in earnings with $27,078 to $30,725 for Toril Forland of Norway, the 1978 and 1979 champion. Frank Litsky

In WORLD BOOK, see SKIING.

SOCCER. The North American Soccer League (NASL) struggled to make progress in 1980. National television ratings were poor, attendance climbed only 2 per cent, and all clubs – 21 in the United States, three in Canada – lost money. But for the first time in its 14-year history, the league had the same teams in the same cities as in the previous season, and the quality of play was the best yet.

Each team played 32 regular-season games from March to August. Each had to have at least three North American citizens – up from two in 1979 – on the field at all times, part of a long-range plan to Americanize the game.

The best 1980 regular-season records were 25-7 by the Seattle Sounders and 24-8 by the Cosmos, who played in suburban East Rutherford, N.J. The Cosmos gained the play-off final by beating the Tulsa Roughnecks in two games, the Dallas Tornado in three (including a mini-game play-off), and the Los Angeles Aztecs in two. Then, in the Soccer Bowl on September 21 in Washington, D.C., they shut out the Fort Lauderdale Strikers, 3-0.

The Cosmos were led by Giorgio Chinaglia, a former Italian international player who had become a naturalized U.S. citizen. The 33-year-old striker became the leading scorer in NASL history on May 16 in Anaheim, Calif., when his two goals against the California Surf gave him 102 in 109 games in five years. Chinaglia scored seven goals on August 31 at East Rutherford, in an 8-1 victory over Tulsa.

The American Soccer League fired Bob Cousy, its commissioner since 1974, in December 1979 because, as one club owner said of the former basketball star, "He hasn't got soccer in his blood." The Pennsylvania Stoners won the championship of the eight-team league by beating the Sacramento Spirit, 2-1, on September 18.

Indoor Soccer. Two 10-team leagues played indoor soccer from November 1979 to March 1980 – the Major Indoor Soccer League (MISL) in its second season and an NASL league in its first. The New York Arrows won their second straight MISL title, and the Tampa Bay Rowdies triumphed in the new league. The high-scoring game featured six-player teams on artificial turf in indoor arenas.

In Europe, West Germany won the European Nations Cup, Nottingham Forest of England its second straight European Cup, Valencia of Spain the European Cup Winners Cup, West Ham United the English Football Association Cup, and Liverpool the English League first division. In an exhausting pairing, Arsenal beat Liverpool, 1-0, in the English Football Association Cup semifinals in four matches lasting seven hours.   Frank Litsky

In WORLD BOOK, see SOCCER.

Giorgio Chinaglia, left, and Julio Romero celebrate New York Cosmos' 3-0 victory over Fort Lauderdale Strikers in Soccer Bowl 80.

SOCIAL SECURITY. The United States Social Security Administration observed its 45th anniversary on Aug. 14, 1980. Patricia Roberts Harris, secretary of the Department of Health and Human Services (HHS) – formerly Health, Education, and Welfare (HEW) – celebrated the anniversary with a statement that the Social Security Act, signed in 1935, has proved to be one of the most effective programs in American history. The challenge, she said, is to make the system more equitable for women, guarantee that benefits are adequate, and strengthen the system's financial base.

In 1980, Social Security paid benefits every month to more than 35 million persons. In 1979, the total cost of old age and survivor's pensions was $104 billion, with 1 American in 7 benefiting.

Financial problems have been increasing in the last few years, and some predictions held that money in the old-age insurance fund would run out in 1981. The Congress of the United States passed legislation to make sure that the fund has enough money to pay old-age benefits through 1981.

Long-Range Solutions were proposed in a report by the Advisory Council on Social Security set up in 1979. The council concluded that the system is secure, but it recommended that the Social Security payroll tax be reduced and that Medicare hospital insurance be financed by individual and corporate taxes, instead of a payroll tax. It also recommended that Americans who work most of their lives be guaranteed retirement benefits that will keep them from poverty and that half of all Social Security benefits be taxed as income.

President Jimmy Carter signed the Social Security Disability Insurance Amendment into law on June 9. It cuts Social Security disability benefits an average of 14 per cent for families going on the rolls after July 1, 1980.

Going Up. Social Security recipients were granted a 14.3 per cent cost-of-living increase effective in July. This was the largest annual adjustment since 1975, when cash benefits were first linked to increases in the Consumer Price Index. Maximum individual monthly benefits for a worker retiring at age 65 rose to $653.80, an increase of $81.80. The minimum for workers retiring at 65 became $153.10 per month, up $19.20. The increase will raise the average retired worker's monthly check to $330 from $289. The annual amount that beneficiaries may earn without losing benefits increased from $5,000 to $5,500 on Jan. 1, 1981, for those aged 65 to 71. The amount of income subject to Social Security payroll tax rose to $29,700 on that date, an increase of $3,800.   Virginia E. Anderson

In the Special Reports section, see THE INFLATION RATE, THE COST OF LIVING . . . AND YOU. In WORLD BOOK, see SOCIAL SECURITY.

SOCIAL WELFARE. See WELFARE.

SOMALIA agreed on Aug. 21, 1980, to give the United States access to military bases at Mogadiscio on the Indian Ocean, and at the port city of Berbera, strategically located on the Gulf of Aden, in exchange for $5 million in economic aid and $40-million in military assistance. Under this pact, the United States would be able to use naval docking and refueling facilities and an airfield with a 15,000-foot (4,500-meter) runway, long enough for the largest U.S. aircraft. The bases at Berbera had been developed by Russia, which had to relinquish them in 1977 when the Soviets sided with Ethiopia in Somalia's war against that country.

Conflict with Ethiopia. Throughout 1980, Somalia's armed forces continued to aid a separatist movement of ethnic Somalis in the Ogaden region of neighboring Ethiopia, where rebels were fighting to detach their territory from Ethiopia and join it to Somalia. In August, elements of three Somali battalions were thought to be operating in the Ogaden, and from 300 to 1,000 other Somali regulars were believed to be serving with insurgent units. In addition, the rebels were allowed to have bases in Somalia and were provided with supplies. Ethiopia retaliated by bombing areas in Somalia suspected of harboring insurgents.

United States congressmen were concerned that the August 21 agreement would embroil the United States in the Ethiopian-Somali conflict. Ethio-pia protested the aid agreement, charging on October 7 that it represented "a direct threat to our independence." However, the U.S. Department of State insisted that the agreement limited Somalia to U.S. "defensive" arms and equipment, including antiaircraft weapons systems, communications gear, and trucks.

Refugee Problem. Somalia also sought foreign assistance to deal with its severe refugee problem. On October 1, more than 840,000 persons were estimated to be in refugee camps in Somalia, almost all of them having fled the war and drought in the Ogaden.

The United Nations and other relief agencies budgeted more than $120 million in aid for Somali refugees in 1980. However, relief operations were hampered by the scarcity of vehicle fuel, which prevented delivery of food and other supplies to 32 refugee camps. Somalia imports all of its fuel and it lacked the funds to ensure a steady supply.

The refugee crisis and the Ogaden war caused President Mohamed Siad Barre to declare a state of emergency on October 21. He revived the Supreme Revolutionary Council, a military group that ruled the country from 1969 to 1976, and also made each one of the existing civilian ministers members of the council.   J. Dixon Esseks

See also AFRICA (Facts in Brief Table). In WORLD BOOK, see SOMALIA.

SOUTH AFRICA. The nation's Parliament established a multiracial President's Council on Oct. 6, 1980, to advise the government on constitutional changes. Prime Minister Pieter Willem Botha appointed 54 persons, including whites, *Coloreds* (people of mixed race), Indians, and Asians, to sit on the council, which replaced the upper house of Parliament. Botha announced plans to establish a separate advisory council representing blacks, but abandoned the idea because of opposition from black leaders.

Although only advisory, the council constitutes a significant departure from the government's philosophy of *apartheid* (separate development). In the past, nonwhites were consulted only on issues affecting their particular race, but the council provides an official forum for nonwhites to debate constitutional issues affecting the entire nation.

Education for Blacks. Education Minister Ferdinand Hartzenberg announced on November 11 that the government would institute a policy of compulsory education for all black children on Jan. 1, 1981. Under previous policy, white, Colored, and Asian – but not black – children were required to attend school until they were 16. As a result, about 80 per cent of the nation's black children enrolled in school with half dropping out by age 10.

This policy change followed strong unrest in the public school system and months of intermittent boycotts by nonwhites. On April 29, riot police arrested about 600 of some 2,000 mixed-race students who were conducting a protest rally in a suburb of Johannesburg.

Black Rights. In another attempt to deal with black grievances, South Africa's white government on October 31 proposed legislation for liberalizing laws that apply to blacks living in urban areas. The proposed statutes, which will be presented to Parliament in 1981, would ease the conditions under which blacks move from city to city in search of work and permit the children of blacks legally residing in an urban area to live in the same area instead of in a rural tribal reserve.

South Africa was hit by a serious drought in 1980, resulting in crop failure and cattle losses. The most severe economic losses occurred in the black-occupied Ciskei and Kwazulu areas. Despite these losses and an overwhelming economic reliance on South Africa, Ciskeians voted on December 4 to become the fourth of 10 tribal areas or "homelands" to gain independence.   J. Dixon Esseks

See also AFRICA (Facts in Brief Table). In WORLD BOOK, see SOUTH AFRICA.

SOUTH AMERICA. See LATIN AMERICA and articles on Latin American countries.

SOUTH CAROLINA. See STATE GOVERNMENT.

SOUTH DAKOTA. See STATE GOVERNMENT.

SOUTH WEST AFRICA. See NAMIBIA.

SPACE EXPLORATION. Russian cosmonauts Valery Ryumin and Leonid Popov established a new space-endurance record on Oct. 11, 1980, when they returned to Earth after 185 days in space. They passed the previous mark of 175 days, set by Ryumin and Vladimir Lyakhov on Aug. 19, 1979. Both crews docked their spacecraft with the *Salyut 6* space station, where they spent their time in orbit.

Veteran Russian cosmonaut Valery N. Kubasov and Hungarian Bertalan Farkas left Earth on May 26 and docked their *Soyuz 36* spacecraft with the *Salyut 6* about 25 hours later. They returned on June 3 in the *Soyuz 35* craft used by Ryumin and Popov when they began their mission on April 9. Russian Viktor V. Gorbatko and Vietnamese Pham Tuan brought a fresh commuter spaceship and supplies to Ryumin and Popov on July 24 and returned to Earth on July 31. Yuri V. Romanenko and Arnaldo Tamayo Mendez, a Cuban, rocketed into space on September 18, joined *Salyut 6* the following day, and returned to Russia on September 26.

The European Space Agency (ESA) launched its first *Ariane* rocket from French Guiana on Dec. 24, 1979. A second test flight failed on May 23 when the French-built rocket plunged into the sea. When tests are completed, ESA plans to transfer *Ariane* to a private commercial organization that will use it for launching large communication, weather, and other satellites.

Shuttle Problems. The United States National Aeronautics and Space Administration (NASA) rescheduled the space shuttle's first orbital flight for March 1981. Problems with the main engines and heat shield prevented NASA from meeting its original launch date of March 1979. The engine problems appeared to be solved after the last of the three main engines completed individual test firings on June 16. However, a fire damaged one engine when NASA tested them as one unit in July.

The heat shield consists of about 31,000 ceramic tiles designed to protect the shuttle from the destructive high temperatures that it would encounter on its plunge into Earth's atmosphere during re-entry. Engineers had trouble bonding the tiles to the craft's metal skin. About 100 tiles fell off when a modified Boeing 747 jet carried the shuttle *Columbia* from California to the John F. Kennedy Space Center in Cape Canaveral, Florida. After all engine and heat shield repairs were made, NASA moved the *Columbia* and its booster rockets to a launch pad on December 29.

NASA selected 19 new astronaut candidates for space shuttle missions on May 29. Eight are pilots and 11 are mission specialists who would do scientific and technical work on the flights. The group, which includes one black, one Hispanic, and two women, reported to the Lyndon B. John-

Russian cosmonauts Valery Ryumin, left, and Leonid Popov relax on Earth in October after setting a space-flight record of 185 days.

son Space Center near Houston on July 7 to begin one year of training. They were joined by Claude Nicollier, a Swiss astronomer, and Wubbo Ockels, a Dutch physicist, nominated by ESA to fly as specialists on shuttle missions.

U.S. Satellites continued to study and monitor the Earth in 1980. *Magsat* made the most accurate maps of the Earth's magnetic field yet obtained from its launch on Oct. 9, 1979, until its re-entry in June. Launch of the environmental monitoring satellite *NOAA-B* failed on May 29, but the weather satellite *GOES-4* reached orbit after a successful launch on September 9. The Solar Maximum Mission Observatory satellite carried instruments aloft on February 14 to record events on the Sun during sunspot activity in 1980 and 1981.

Voyager 1 began sending photographs of Saturn to Earth in August as it headed for a November 12 encounter with the ringed planet. Launched in 1977, *Voyager 1* and *Voyager 2* provided scientists with a close-up look at Jupiter in 1979. On November 11, *Voyager 1* passed within 4,000 kilometers (2,500 miles) of Titan, Saturn's largest moon. It then crossed the plane of the rings, flew underneath them, and passed about 123,000 kilometers (76,000 miles) from Saturn's southern hemisphere. See ASTRONOMY. William J. Cromie

In WORLD BOOK, see SATURN; SPACE TRAVEL.

SPAIN suffered from murders and bombings in 1980, as political violence continued at a much higher level than in the years of Francisco Franco's dictatorship. In January alone, Basque separatists shot a provincial police chief, gunned down four persons in a Bilbao bar, and blew up nuclear power equipment at Vitoria.

The extremist Basque Homeland and Liberty Organization (ETA) threatened to disrupt tourism by exploding bombs at "an important number of places" along Spain's coasts during the summer unless the government freed imprisoned ETA activists and fired a prison governor. Bomb-disposal crews and frogmen searched beaches and police patrolled hotels, but ETA succeeded in exploding bombs in coastal resorts. No one was seriously injured, however.

Censure Move. Terrorism, judicial limitations on constitutional freedoms, and a severe recession brought increasing criticism of Prime Minister Adolfo Suarez Gonzalez. The Socialists introduced a censure motion against Suarez in the *Cortes* (parliament) in May. The parliamentary debate degenerated into personal accusations and bitter exchanges, but the motion failed.

Spain conducted a home-rule referendum in Andalusia, the vast southern region, on February 29, but voters in two Andalusian provinces rejected

The body of Spain's King Alfonso XIII begins a homeward journey from an Italian church. Alfonso left Spain in 1931 and died in Rome in 1941.

the proposal, so it failed. About 700 adults and children in the Andalusian village of Marinaleda went on a hunger strike on August 14 to try to persuade the national government to create more jobs in the area. The strike ended on August 22, when the government agreed to transfer $13.8-million from the Ministry of Agriculture to the Labor Ministry for public works in Andalusia.

March Elections. In the Basque region, Basque nationalist parties won 42 of the 60 seats in that area's first parliament in 40 years. In Catalonia regional elections, the rightist Democratic Convergence Party won 43 of the 135 seats. Spain's ruling Union of the Democratic Center won 18 seats; the Socialists, 33; and the Communists, 25. The Basque country and Catalonia became autonomous regions within Spain on January 11.

Voters in Galicia, the region in Spain's northwestern corner, approved home rule in a December 21 referendum. Less than one-third of the eligible voters cast ballots.

The Organization for Economic Cooperation and Development described the outlook in April as "uncertain." Spain's trade surplus had become a $2.7-billion deficit, inflation was rising, and the unemployment rate was 10 per cent.   Kenneth Brown

See also EUROPE (Facts in Brief Table). In WORLD BOOK, see BASQUE; SPAIN.

SPORTS. Financial problems hurt collegiate sports in the United States in 1980, and few colleges escaped without cash problems. At many colleges with strong football teams, football revenues once paid for entire sports programs. But increasing costs, especially for travel, reduced such profits and left many programs with deficits.

In the largest colleges, only football, basketball, and sometimes hockey or another sport provided revenues. Most of the smaller colleges realized little, if any, revenue from any sports.

In addition, the requirement to establish and finance athletic programs for women affected almost every college. Under the federal regulation known as Title IX, any college that failed to provide equal opportunity for women in many endeavors, including sports, could lose federal funds. The National Collegiate Athletic Association said men's and women's athletic programs grew, especially at major colleges. But there were many losses.

The University of Colorado eliminated four men's and three women's sports, including men's baseball, and offered the baseball caps to alumni for $7.50 each. The University of Tulsa, a College World Series finalist in 1969, reduced varsity baseball to a club sport. Yale did the same to two men's and two women's sports, saving $41,000 a year.

Nearly 5,000 cross-country skiers start the Birkebeiner, a 34-mile (55-kilometer) race from Cable, Wis., to Hayward, in February.

The American Council on Education (ACE) urged college presidents to reduce costs by trimming athletic scholarships, recruiting, and coaching staffs. The ACE said that only 5 per cent of college students participated in intercollegiate athletics at an annual cost of $500 million.

In professional sports, however, the money flowed more abundantly than ever. Sugar Ray Leonard collected $15.5 million for two fights. Nolan Ryan in baseball and Kareem Abdul-Jabbar in basketball collected million-dollar salaries. The best golfers and tennis players earned half a million dollars in tournaments.

Among the Winners in 1980 were:

Fencing. Russia won three gold, three silver, and two bronze medals in the eight Olympic events. In the United States, Peter Westbrook of New York City captured the national saber title for the second straight year.

Gymnastics. Russians took nine of the 16 gold medals in the Olympics and provided the all-around champions in the Olympics (Alexandr Ditiatin and Yelena Davidova) and the World Cup (Bogdan Makuts and Stella Zakharova). Bart Conner of Morton Grove, Ill., and 13-year-old Tracee Talavera of Walnut Creek, Calif., starred in the United States Olympic trials. Kurt Thomas of Mesa, Ariz., winner of two world titles in 1979, won the Sullivan Award in February as America's outstanding amateur athlete, then retired in June.

Rowing. East Germany won medals, including 11 gold, in all 14 Olympic events for men and women. The United States Olympic eight, competing as the Charles River Rowing Association of Boston, won the major prize in the Henley Royal Regatta in England, and the U. S. Olympic women's eight upset East Germany in a 31-nation regatta in Lucerne, Switzerland.

Shooting. Russia and East Germany took 11 of the 21 medals in the Olympics. Lones Wigger of Fort Benning, Ga., America's best rifleman for almost two decades, won the small-bore competition in the U.S. Olympic trials, the national championships at Camp Perry, Ohio, and the international championships at Phoenix, Ariz.

Weight Lifting. Russia captured five of the 10 gold medals in the Olympics and six of the 10 in the European championships. Sultan Rakhmanov of Russia became super-heavyweight champion in both competitions. Mark Cameron of Middletown, R.I., the best American lifter, recovered from illness to win his sixth national title.

Wrestling. Russia won seven of the 10 free-style and five of the 10 Greco-Roman titles in the Olympics. Four months before, the United States upset Russia, 7-3, in the World Cup final in Toledo, Ohio, its first victory over the Russians since the nations started competing in 1959. The 360-pound (163-kilogram) Jimmy Jackson of Stillwater, Okla., won his fourth straight World Cup title and Lee Kemp of Madison, Wis., his third straight.

Other Champions. *Archery,* U.S. champions: men, Rich McKinney, Glendale, Ariz.; women, Luann Ryon, Riverside, Calif. *Badminton,* world champions: men, Rudy Hartono, Indonesia; women, Wiharjo Verawaty, Indonesia. *Biathlon,* U.S. champions: 10-kilometer, Ken Alligood, Anchorage, Alaska; 20-kilometer, Don Nielsen, South Stratford, Vt. *Billiards,* world pocket champions: men, Nick Varner, Owensboro, Ky.; women, Jean Balukas, Brooklyn, N.Y. *Bobsledding,* U.S. champions: four-man, Bob Hickey, Keene, N.Y.; two-man, Brent Rushlaw, Saranac Lake, N.Y. *Canoeing,* U.S. 500-meter champions: canoe, Barry Merritt, Washington, D.C.; men's kayak, Greg Barton, Homer, Mich.; women's kayak, Ann Turner, St. Charles, Ill. *Casting,* U.S. all-around champion: Steve Rajeff, San Francisco. *Court tennis,* U.S. open champion: Chris Ronaldson, England. *Croquet,* U.S. champion: Archie Peck, Palm Beach, Fla. *Cross-country,* world champions: men, Craig Virgin, St. Louis; women, Grete Waitz, Norway. *Curling,* world champions: men, Saskatoon, Canada; women, Regina, Canada. *Cycling,* world champions: women's road, Beth Heiden, Madison, Wis.; women's sprint, Sue Novarra Reber, Flint, Mich.; motocross, Bob Woods, Van Nuys, Calif. *Darts,* world champion: Stefan Lord, Sweden. *Equestrian events,* World Cup jumping champion: Conrad Homfeld, Pinehurst, N.C. *Field hockey,* Champions Trophy: Pakistan. *Frisbee,* world champions: men, Scott Zimmerman, McLean, Va.; women, Cyndi Birch, Santa Barbara, Calif. *Handball,* USHA four-wall champion: Naty Alvarado, Hesperia, Calif. *Hang gliding,* American Cup: United States. *Horseshoe pitching,* world champions: men, Walter Ray Williams, Chino, Calif.; women, Opal Reno, Lucasville, Ohio. *Iceboating,* DN Class world champion: Matti Kleman, Russia. *Judo,* U.S. open champions: men, Dewey Mitchell, Seven Springs, Fla.; women, Margie Castro, New York City. *Karate,* U.S. advanced champions: men, Albert Pena, Haverstraw, N.Y.; women, Vicki Johnson, Dunlap, Ill. *Lacrosse,* U.S. champions: club, Long Island Athletic Club; college, Johns Hopkins. *Lawn bowling,* U.S. champions: men, Richard Folkins, Mission Viejo, Calif.; women, Harriett Bauer, Seattle. *Luge,* world champions: men, Erich Graber, Italy; women, Delia Vaudin, Italy. *Modern pentathlon,* U.S. champion: John Fitzgerald, Skokie, Ill. *Motorcycling,* world 500-cc champion: Kenny Roberts, Modesto, Calif. *Paddle tennis,* U.S. champion: Nels Van Patten, Santa Monica, Calif. *Paddleball,* U.S. champion: Dick Jury, Williamston, Mich. *Parachute jumping,* U.S. overall champions: men, Matt O'Gwynn, Langley AFB, Va.; women, Cheryl Stearns, Fort Bragg, N.C. *Polo,* Cup of the Americas: Argentina. *Racquetball,* U.S. pro champions: men, Marty Hogan, San Diego; women, Heather McKay, Toronto, Canada. *Racquets,* U.S. open champion: John Prenn, England. *Rodeo,* U.S. all-around champion: Paul Tierney, Rapid City, S. Dak. *Roller skating,* U.S. artistic champions: men, Michael Glatz, Lemon Grove, Calif.; women, Kathleen O'Brien Di Felice, Langhorne, Pa. *Roque,* U.S. champion: C.B. Smith, Decatur, Ill. *Rugby,* U.S. champion: Old Blues, Berkeley, Calif. *Sambo,* U.S. heavyweight champion: Carl Dambman, Philadelphia. *Shuffleboard,* U.S. open champions: men, Hans Streib, St. Petersburg, Fla.; women, Mae Hall, St. Petersburg. *Skateboarding,* world freestyle pro champion: Rodney Mullin, Gainesville, Fla. *Sled dog racing,* world champion: Debbie Molburg, Center Harbor, N.H. *Snowmobile racing,* world champion: Jacques Villeneuve, St. Cuthbert, Canada. *Softball,* world men's fast-pitch champion: Home Savings, Aurora, Ill. *Sports acrobatics,* U.S. tumbling champions: men, Jerry Hardy, Detroit; women, Julie Beatty, Roy, Utah. *Squash racquets,* U.S. champions: men, Michael Desaulniers, Montreal, Canada; women, Barbara Maltby, Philadelphia. *Squash tennis,* U.S. champion: Pedro Bacallao, Miami, Fla. *Synchronized swimming,* U.S. outdoor champion: Linda Shelley, Santa Clara, Calif. *Table tennis,* U.S. champions: men, Mikael Appelgren, Sweden; women, Kayoko Kawahigashi, Japan. *Tae kwon do,* U.S. heavyweight champions: men, Tom Seabourne, Allentown, Pa.; women, Lynnette Love, Detroit. *Team handball,* U.S. champions: men, Blick's All-Stars, Colorado Springs, Colo; women, Midwest Orange. *Volleyball,* U.S. champions: men, San Francisco Olympic Club; women, ANVA, Fountain Valley, Calif. *Water polo,* U.S. men's outdoor champion: Concord, Calif. *Water skiing,* U.S. overall champions: men, Carl Roberge, Orlando, Fla.; women, Karin Roberge, Orlando, Fla.   Frank Litsky

See also OLYMPIC GAMES and articles on the various sports. In WORLD BOOK, see OLYMPIC GAMES.

SRI LANKA. Militant union workers swept through the streets of Colombo, the capital, on Aug. 8, 1980, throwing stones and homemade bombs, smashing buses, and attacking the Central Bank and the offices of the state-owned Air Lanka. The army was called out and quickly ended the riot. The demonstration was a by-product of a general strike that began on July 10. The striking workers demanded pay boosts to compensate for an inflation rate of more than 30 per cent and demanded restoration of price subsidies on essential goods.

The United National Party government of President J. R. Jayewardene was prepared for trouble. It had the police and military forces ready. It declared a state of emergency on July 16 that outlawed strikes in "essential" services. Under these ordinances, the 40,000 state employees who went on strike were fired, and some unions were closed and their funds seized. It was these jobless people who went out into the streets in August to protest.

Sabotage Plot? Jayewardene regarded the strikes as attempts to sabotage the "economic miracle" he had initiated in 1977 after his overwhelming defeat of Prime Minister Sirimavo Bandaranaike's Freedom Party and its allies. He also saw the July labor turmoil as a conspiracy by Bandaranaike's coalition to regain on the labor front what it lost at the ballot box. At least 30 union and political leaders were arrested. The state of emergency was allowed to lapse on August 16, then was reinstated on October 14 in the face of continued unrest. Within a week, Parliament expelled Bandaranaike and took away her civil rights for seven years for offenses allegedly committed when she was in power. She therefore could not run in the next election.

The Economy. The labor unrest was less a political plot than a reflection of the nation's economic problems. Inefficient planning and deficit spending were blamed at least in part. But Sri Lanka, like so many other nations, was most hurt by soaring import costs—especially that of oil, which rose from $120 million in 1977 to nearly $540 million in 1980. The price of tea, the main export item, declined at the same time. The nation's finance minister gave another explanation for the weakness of the economy—overambitious investment plans, which he proposed to cut by 40 per cent. The only major scheme that would survive the pruning was the $1.6-billion Mahaweli power and irrigation project, on which the government pinned its hopes for economic progress. Monthly living costs for a family of three had risen to just under $80—more than twice the earnings of half the labor force—mainly because the government had begun withdrawing price subsidies on basic food items in 1979. In a nation of 15 million persons, more than 1 million were out of work in 1980. Mark Gayn

See also ASIA (Facts in Brief Table). In WORLD BOOK, see SRI LANKA.

STAMP COLLECTING. The United States Postal Service on Feb. 7, 1980, introduced an innovative $3 booklet containing five different 15-cent stamps depicting windmills from the states of Illinois, Massachusetts, Rhode Island, Texas, and Virginia. Each booklet contains two panes of 10 stamps arranged in a double row of five.

Fifteen-cent U.S. commemoratives issued in 1980 included those honoring black scientist Benjamin Banneker; novelist Edith Wharton; Frances Perkins, former U.S. secretary of labor; and Bernardo de Gálvez, a Spanish soldier who aided the American Revolution. Blocks of four 15-cent stamps depicted coral reefs, Northwest Indian masks, and the Olympic Winter Games.

United States stamps and post cards commemorating the Olympic Summer Games in Moscow were withdrawn from sale at U.S. post offices on March 11 by Postmaster General William F. Bolger. The Postal Service withdrew the commemoratives as part of the U.S. Olympic boycott protesting the Russian invasion of Afghanistan. Predictably, sales of Olympic material were resumed after the Moscow games ended. Olympic issues were made available from the Philatelic Sales Division in Washington, D.C., between August 4 and December 31, and the division's normal service charges and minimum purchase requirements were

Britain's General Post Office issued a 50-pence stamp in honor of the International Stamp Exhibition, which took place in London in May.

waived. Although large quantities of the stamps were sold prior to the ban, some impatient collectors paid inflated prices for the commemoratives during the ban.

New Stamps. The United Nations (UN) began an ambitious series of stamps depicting the flags of all its member nations. Sixteen flags, selected by random drawing and the first in the projected 10-year series, were released on September 26. The initial format consisted of four different minisheets of 16 stamps in four designs, each arranged in four blocks. This unusual format allows a sheet to be divided into various combinations. The wide choice of desirable philatelic elements may entice the collector to purchase entire sheets, rather than singles. For this reason, the UN issue garnered an American Philatelic Society (APS) Black Blot for high total face value (in sheets) and intentional oddity of design and format.

The 50th anniversary of the *Graf Zeppelin*'s 1930 Pan-American flight was a popular subject for commemorative cancellations and envelopes bearing *cachets* — souvenir slogans, designs, or emblems. The flight — from Germany to Brazil to the United States and back to Germany — was commemorated originally by the popular 1930 U.S. three-value Zeppelin set. Interestingly, the 50th anniversary of the U.S. Zeppelin stamp set was also honored in cachet designs.

Major Sales. The famous and unique British Guiana 1-cent magenta of 1856 was sold for a new high of $850,000 to an unidentified collector in New York City at a Robert A. Siegel Auction Galleries' sale in April. On November 18, an unidentified collector paid $230,000 for a Hawaiian "missionary" 2-cent stamp at Sotheby Park Bernet Galleries in New York City — a record price for a single U.S. stamp. An extremely fine unused four-margined copy of Canada's 12-pence black Queen Victoria issue of 1851 brought $126,500 — much more than the catalog estimate of $40,000 — at a Greg Manning Auctions' sale held on May 10 in London. A plate block of six of the U.S. $5 Columbian Exposition commemorative of 1893 brought a record $220,000 during the Manning firm's September 27 sale in New York City. Fewer than 10 such blocks are believed to exist.

Studying Stamps. The APS and Pennsylvania State University conducted their first Philatelic Seminar on the Penn State campus at State College from July 7 to 11. United States and Canadian participants, ranging in age from 15 to 73, attended lectures and workshops on such topics as counterfeits, aerophilately, and topical collecting. "Philately: Beginning Stamp Collecting," the first APS-Penn State correspondence course in a planned philately series, became available in both youth and adult versions from the university. Paul A. Larsen

In WORLD BOOK, see STAMP COLLECTING.

STATE GOVERNMENT. A volcanic eruption and an eruption of human emotion proved costly to two state governments in 1980. Meanwhile, others struggled with the continuing problems of the ailing automobile industry, taxation, education, fuel costs, and separation of church and state. In the November 4 general election, the Republicans increased their control of legislatures and statehouses.

The May 18 eruption of Mount Saint Helens killed more than 30 persons and damaged billions of dollars' worth of property in Washington state (see GEOLOGY). Continued eruptions contributed to a decline in tourism in that area. Governor Dixy Lee Ray agreed in May to have the state pay 25 per cent of the cost of the disaster in order to qualify for immediate federal aid. This was a new rate. Previously, a state could qualify for federal aid by paying only 10 per cent.

A February 2 and 3 riot at the New Mexico State Penitentiary in Santa Fe left 33 inmates dead and an estimated $40 million worth of property damage. The legislature held a special session to approve some $90 million in bonds and funds for repairs and a new prison. Illinois Attorney General William J. Scott resigned on July 29 after being sentenced to a year in prison for income tax fraud. The Supreme Court of the United States on April 14 refused to review the mail-fraud conviction of former Maryland Governor Marvin Mandel, so he began serving a prison term in May. Former Tennessee Governor Ray Blanton was indicted on charges of selling state liquor licenses.

Money Problems. Hard times for the United States auto industry caused budget problems in Michigan, where Governor William G. Milliken proposed budget cuts of $1 billion. Delaware, Illinois, Indiana, and Michigan authorized state loans to Chrysler Corporation in order to qualify that financially stricken firm for federal aid. Oregon's legislature held a special session to offset a budget deficit. Other states cut back spending and imposed hiring freezes to avoid deficits.

Some 16 states passed $850 million worth of tax increases. Gasoline-tax hikes in Alabama, Indiana, Kentucky, Massachusetts, Minnesota, Nebraska, New Mexico, South Carolina, South Dakota, Virginia, and Wisconsin netted $395 million. Indiana, Kentucky, Massachusetts, and Nebraska changed from taxing gasoline by the gallon to collecting a percentage of the price to make up for the declining growth of road funds. Connecticut and South Dakota raised sales taxes. Cigarette taxes went up in Alabama and Maryland.

Tax Relief in seven states amounted to $430-million. Alaska passed the year's biggest tax decrease in April. The legislature repealed the 31-year-old income tax, and Governor Jay S. Hammond signed the measure on April 15 for a revenue

Selected Statistics on State Governments

State	Resident population (a)	Governor	Legislature (b) House (D)	(R)	Senate (D)	(R)	State tax revenue (c)	Tax revenue per capita (d)	Public school enrollment 1979-80 (e)	Public school expenditures per pupil in average daily attendance 1979-80 (f)
Alabama	3,890	Forrest H. James, Jr. (D)	100	4(j)	35	0	$ 1,747	$ 464	754	$ n/a
Alaska	400	Jay S. Hammond (R)	22	16(k)	10	10	817	2,012	89	4,587
Arizona	2,718	Bruce E. Babbitt (D)	17	43	14	16	1,516	619	509	n/a
Arkansas	2,286	Frank White (R)*	93	7	34	1	995	456	453	n/a
California	23,669	Edmund G. Brown, Jr. (D)	47	33	23	17	16,352	720	4,048	2,173
Colorado	2,889	Richard D. Lamm (D)	26	39	13	22	1,441	520	551	2,409
Connecticut	3,108	William A. O'Neill (D)*	83	68	23	13	1,718	552	567	2,403
Delaware	595	Pierre S. du Pont IV (R)	16	25	12	9	492	845	104	2,327
Florida	9,740	D. Robert Graham (D)	81	39	27	13	4,291	484	1,508	n/a
Georgia	5,464	George D. Busbee (D)	157	23	51	5	2,448	478	1,078	n/a
Hawaii	965	George R. Ariyoshi (D)	39	12	17	8	876	957	169	1,695
Idaho	944	John V. Evans (D)	14	56	13	22	466	515	203	1,535
Illinois	11,418	James R. Thompson (R)	86	91	30	29	6,323	563	2,043	2,041
Indiana	5,490	Robert D. Orr (R)*	37	63	15	35	2,669	494	1,084	1,724
Iowa	2,913	Robert D. Ray (R)	42	58	21	29	1,569	541	548	2,430
Kansas	2,363	John W. Carlin (D)	53	72	16	24	1,188	501	423	2,372
Kentucky	3,661	John Y. Brown, Jr. (D)	75	25	29	9	2,076	589	677	1,293
Louisiana	4,204	David C. Treen (R)	95	10	39	0	2,240	556	800	1,797
Maine	1,125	Joseph E. Brennan (D)	84	67	16	17	554	505	228	1,859
Maryland	4,216	Harry R. Hughes (D)	125	16	40	7	2,647	638	778	2,248
Massachusetts	5,737	Edward J. King (D)	127	32(g)	32	7(g)	3,616	627	1,032	2,607
Michigan	9,258	William G. Milliken (R)	64	46	24	14	6,018	654	1,860	2,170
Minnesota	4,077	Albert H. Quie (R)	70	64	45	22	3,134	772	778	2,208
Mississippi	2,521	William F. Winter (D)	116	4(h)	48	4	1,196	497	482	1,419
Missouri	4,917	Christopher Bond (R)*	111	52	23	11	2,170	446	873	1,811
Montana	787	Ted Schwinden (D)*	43	57	22	28	401	510	158	n/a
Nebraska	1,570	Charles Thone (R)	49(i)(unicameral)				743	472	287	1,852
Nevada	799	Robert F. List (R)	26	14	15	5	463	659	148	2,019
New Hampshire	921	Hugh J. Gallen (D)	160	240	10	14	264	298	171	1,809
New Jersey	7,364	Brendan T. Byrne (D)	44	36	27	13	3,729	509	1,288	2,616
New Mexico	1,300	Bruce King (D)	40	29	22	20	845	681	276	1,935
New York	17,557	Hugh L. Carey (D)	86	64	25	35	11,688	662	2,969	3,197
North Carolina	5,874	James B. Hunt, Jr. (D)	96	24	40	10	2,915	520	1,150	1,800
North Dakota	653	Allen I. Olson (R)*	26	74	9	41	325	494	118	2,006
Ohio	10,797	James A. Rhodes (R)	56	43	15	18	4,620	431	2,025	1,918
Oklahoma	3,025	George P. Nigh (D)	73	28	37	11	1,516	524	583	1,872
Oregon	2,633	Victor G. Atiyeh (R)	33	27	22	8	1,384	548	467	2,459
Pennsylvania	11,867	Richard L. Thornburgh (R)	100	103	24	26	6,782	578	1,969	2,567
Rhode Island	947	J. Joseph Garrahy (D)	82	16	43	7	538	579	154	2,304
South Carolina	3,119	Richard W. Riley (D)	107	17	41	5	1,523	519	625	1,353
South Dakota	690	William J. Janklow (R)	21	49	10	25	246	356	133	1,943
Tennessee	4,591	Lamar Alexander (R)	58	39(h)	12	11	1,844	421	866	1,306
Texas	14,228	William P. Clements, Jr. (R)	114	36	24	7	5,738	429	2,873	n/a
Utah	1,461	Scott M. Matheson (D)	18	57	7	22	695	508	333	1,609
Vermont	511	Richard A. Snelling (R)	65	85	14	16	267	543	98	1,771
Virginia	5,346	John N. Dalton (R)	74	25(g)	31	9	2,564	493	1,031	1,802
Washington	4,130	John Spellman (R)*	42	56	25	24	2,718	692	765	2,373
West Virginia	1,950	John D. Rockefeller IV (D)	79	21	27	7	1,150	612	388	1,509
Wisconsin	4,705	Lee S. Dreyfus (R)	60	39	19	13(j)	3,260	691	858	2,433
Wyoming	471	Ed Herschler (D)	23	39	11	19	343	762	96	2,429

(a) Number in thousands, 1980 census (Bureau of the Census)
(b) As of December 2, 1980
(c) 1979 preliminary figures in millions (Bureau of the Census)
(d) 1979 preliminary figures (Bureau of the Census)
(e) Numbers in thousands, fall, 1979 (U.S. Office of Education)
(f) 1979-1980 (U.S. Office of Education)
(g) 1 Independent
(h) 2 Independents
(i) Nonpartisan
(j) 1 Vacancy
(k) 2 Libertarians
* Took office January 1981

loss of $116 million. But on September 5, the U.S. Supreme Court stayed a plan to distribute the state's oil wealth to its citizens, with the amount they would receive based on how long they had lived in Alaska.

Colorado, Illinois, and Louisiana approved other major tax-relief programs. Arizona exempted food from its sales tax, and Illinois reduced its sales tax on food and drugs. By the end of 1980, 41 of the 45 states that had sales taxes had exemptions or lower rates for food or drugs.

Proposition 13-type property-tax rollbacks lost in five states on November 4. Only in Massachusetts – called Taxachusetts by many – did a major tax reduction win approval. Howard Jarvis, author of California's successful Proposition 13 that started the 1978 tax revolt, saw his initiative to cut that state's income taxes in half lose in the June primary. Moderate tax relief measures succeeded on ballots in Arizona, Arkansas, Georgia, Louisiana, New Jersey, Ohio, Oregon, Virginia, and West Virginia elections.

Tax Caps. The tax revolt shifted from reducing taxes to controlling spending. Delaware, Hawaii, Missouri, and South Carolina limited spending growth in 1980. Arizona put its spending cap into its Constitution. Nine states now index personal income taxes to inflation, with the addition of Montana and South Carolina in 1980.

Summing Up. The Tax Foundation, a private, nonprofit organization, said that state tax collections rose $12 billion, or 10.3 per cent, to $125-billion in fiscal 1979, ending June 30, 1980. This was the lowest rate of gain since 1975.

California had a $2.6-billion surplus on July 1, 1979, and predicted an $828-million surplus in 1981. Expenditures for the fiscal year ending on June 30, 1981, were expected to amount to $24.6-billion there. New York's Governor Hugh Carey vetoed more than $240 million worth of appropriations before approving a $14.9-billion budget.

Fuel Taxes. A new form of tax on oil companies lost in the courts as Connecticut and New York tried to forbid such firms from passing taxes on their gross earnings along to consumers. North Dakota hiked its oil-production tax, New Mexico raised severance taxes, and Oregon earmarked future oil and natural gas taxes for education. Montana's heavy severance tax on coal came under fire in Congress and in the courts. The Montana Supreme Court upheld the tax, so Midwestern utility companies asked the U.S. Supreme Court to intervene. By the end of 1980, four states had joined the utilities in urging Supreme Court review.

Gasohol, a blend of 10 per cent alcohol and unleaded gasoline, continued to be a legislative favorite. Nearly 30 states now grant tax reductions on its sale or production.

Nevada Governor Robert F. List, right, chats with a miner about how the proposed M-X mobile missile system might affect mining.

Michigan and Ohio reduced their sales taxes on certain automobiles for a short time to boost new car sales. New Jersey restricted state purchases of imported cars.

Bond Issues. Voters approved $2.3 billion in state and local bond issues, 80 per cent of the $2.9-billion sought, according to the *Daily Bond Buyer,* a trade newspaper. State bond issues were approved on November 4 in Alaska, Maine, New Jersey, Rhode Island, and Washington. California approved $750 million in bonds for veterans' loans in its June 3 primary.

Education. The Illinois Supreme Court upheld a law that established an authority to issue $500-million in bonds to bail out Chicago's debt-ridden public school system. A U.S. district court ordered Ohio to help pay Cleveland's desegregation costs. Texas expected increased education costs as a result of a July 21 federal district court decision that compels its public schools to admit children of illegal aliens. New York established a daily lottery, with the proceeds to go to education.

Church and State. The U.S. Supreme Court on November 17 declared unconstitutional a Kentucky law that required the Ten Commandments to be posted in the public schools. A federal judge voided a similar requirement in North Dakota. Massachusetts' voluntary school prayer law was voided by that state's highest court on March 13.

First all-woman class of New Jersey State Police recruits sharpens handgun skills in March during a 20-week training program.

Oklahoma approved a voluntary prayer law in 1980. The U.S. Supreme Court on February 20 affirmed a 1974 New York law that allows the state to reimburse private schools for certain costs. The 50 states appropriated nearly $21 billion for annual operating expenses of higher education for fiscal 1980-1981, for a two-year gain of 23 per cent.

Law and Order. The U.S. Supreme Court struck down Alabama's death-penalty law on June 20. The court also overturned death sentences in Georgia and Texas. The Massachusetts Supreme Court voided that state's death penalty on October 28, but the California and Tennessee Supreme Courts upheld death statutes.

A dozen states passed laws attempting to crack down on *head shops,* stores that sell drug paraphernalia, but most were immediately challenged in court. Angel dust (phencyclidine, or PCP) was the subject of tougher laws in California and Massachusetts.

Florida and Rhode Island raised their drinking age to 19, and Nebraska increased its drinking age to 20. New York passed a law that requires a one-year jail term for carrying an unlicensed, loaded handgun in public.

Health and Welfare. The U.S. Supreme Court ruled on June 30 that the federal and state governments need not finance most abortions for poor women. Meanwhile, Louisiana, Rhode Island, and

South Dakota passed laws that required the *informed consent* of abortion patients—that is, the patient must receive certain information about the embryo or fetus and the abortion procedure before having the operation. However, a federal court voided the Louisiana law. Alabama's mental health facilities were placed in the hands of the governor as an outgrowth of a court case dating to 1972. Connecticut adopted so-called *workfare* legislation that allows cities and towns to put able-bodied general welfare recipients to work on public projects.

Other Developments. Most states raised their interest rate ceilings as banks raised their prime rates—the interest that banks charge their most creditworthy customers. Among them, New York raised its ceiling on credit-card loans in November, too late to prevent Citicorp from moving its credit-card center earlier in the year to South Dakota, where rates on loans were more favorable.

The furor over nuclear power stemming from the 1979 accident at Three Mile Island near Harrisburg, Pa., appeared to be dying down, as three states rejected bans on nuclear power. However, Oregon voted restrictions on new plants and Washington banned accepting out-of-state nonmedical nuclear waste for storage.   Elaine Knapp

In WORLD BOOK, see STATE GOVERNMENT and articles on the individual states.

STEEL INDUSTRY. The world steel situation in this decade was listed as the topic of an international symposium held in Paris in February 1980. However, those taking part were more concerned with the alleged dumping of European steel in the United States. American representatives at the symposium, which was sponsored by the Organization for Economic Cooperation and Development, threatened to sue the European steelmakers, complaining that Europe's low prices were backed by government subsidies. The threats were made good in March when United States Steel Corporation filed antidumping complaints against seven European steel producers.

President Jimmy Carter announced a government assistance program for the U.S. steel industry on September 30. The program was to reinstate "trigger prices" to provide limited protection against low-priced imports by setting minimum prices for foreign steel and allowing domestic steel companies to delay reducing air and water pollution. The President promised to ask Congress to authorize the Environmental Protection Agency to permit case-by-case delays in meeting clean-air standards. In exchange for the program, U.S. Steel agreed to withdraw its dumping complaints.

Exports Rise. Mexico was a major market for United States steel in the first seven months of 1980, with exports rising 47.1 per cent over the

A sign emphasizing corporate opposition to the growing amount of imported steel enlists worker support at a U.S. Steel plant in Pennsylvania.

STOCKS AND BONDS. The recession that began in the United States in January 1980 gave way to sluggish growth by the end of the summer. The stock market seemed unaffected, however. The Standard and Poor's (S&P) index of 500 common stocks began the year at 105.76, rose to 118.44 on February 10, hit a low point at 98.22 on March 27, and then rose for much of the rest of the year to finish at 135.76. The S&P index covers only stocks on the New York Stock Exchange (NYSE).

The Media General Composite Stock Index—which tracks all stocks traded on the NYSE, the American Stock Exchange (Amex), and many over-the-counter (O-T-C) stocks using Jan. 2, 1970, prices as a base of 100—opened the year at 123.4. It rose to 138.0 on February 13, fell to a low of 111.7 on March 27, and then began a sustained rise to end the year at 158.88. An investor far-sighted or lucky enough to buy a portfolio of many stocks in March would have made money at a rate far in excess of the inflation rate.

Stock Volume. The volume of new stock financing rose and fell with the market. In January, corporations issued $1.4 billion of new common stock. The total rose to $1.6 billion in February and March, and then fell to $900 million in April. New issues remained above $1.5 billion per month for the rest of the year.

Volume of trading on the exchanges increased as the market rose. On the NYSE, 50-million-share days became common. The NYSE set a record of 84,080,000 shares traded on November 5, the day after Ronald Reagan's election to the presidency. Mutual funds did very well, with positive net sales in every month from April on.

Internationally, the United States stock market lagged far behind the Hong Kong and Italian markets, where prices more than doubled, but did about as well as the roughly 35 per cent increase in world share prices.

The Bond Market was not nearly as cheerful a place in 1980 as the stock market. Aa-rated utility bond rates rose from about 12 per cent yields in January to more than 14 per cent through March. When bond yields rise, bond prices fall, and this rise of two percentage points in yields meant an 11 per cent fall in the price of a bond with 20 years left until maturity. Wide swings in bond prices are unusual, and the bond market attracts investors who want less risk than the stock market presents.

The volume of publicly offered bonds fell from $2.8 billion in January to $1.4 billion in February, and the ratio of short-term debt to long-term debt—which had been rising since 1976—peaked at about 40 per cent in March. Bond rates peaked at 14.6 per cent in the third week of March, and fell to under 12 per cent at the beginning of May. The volume of new issues rose to $6.2 billion in May and $7.3 billion in June.

same period in 1979, according to the American Iron and Steel Institute (AISI). Steel exports for the year were expected to total about 4.2 million short tons (3.8 million metric tons). For the year through August, the AISI reported, imports slipped to 11.6 million short tons (10.6 million metric tons) from 12 million short tons (11 million metric tons) a year earlier.

The U.S. industry used 70.9 per cent of capacity through September, compared with 89.8 per cent a year earlier. Output was 81.2 million short tons (73.7 million metric tons), down 22.1 per cent.

Late Upturn. In September, America's major steelmakers began gradually to restart some of the blast furnaces that had been shut down earlier in the year because of a decline in steel orders. Service centers, which buy about 20 per cent of the steel from domestic mills and then resell it, showed a 12 per cent increase in August shipments.

A bid for a share in the world steel market was made by South Korea, which announced that it had spent $1.2 billion to increase the annual capacity of the state-run Pohang Iron and Steel Company in an expansion program scheduled to be completed in June 1981. The former capacity of 2.6 million metric tons (2.9 million short tons) was more than doubled to 6.5 million metric tons (7.1 million short tons).   Mary E. Jessup

In WORLD BOOK, see IRON AND STEEL.

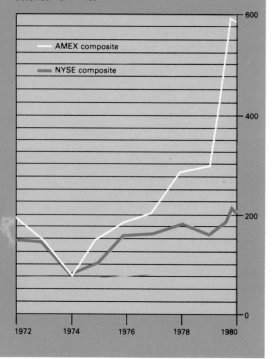

For the rest of the year, interest rates continued to rise, to more than 15 per cent again early in October, and the volume of bond financing fell to below $3 billion per month.

Tax-exempt bond rates rose and fell with corporate bond rates, but were lower, of course. The Bond Buyer Index of tax exempts began the year at about 7 per cent, peaked at just over 9 per cent at the end of March, and fell back to 7 per cent in the first week in May. Rates rose for the rest of the year, passing 10 per cent again in December.

The Silver Bubble. Winter saw a dramatic rise in the price of silver, which hit a high of $50.35 an ounce on January 21. Silver-trading regulations were promptly tightened by the metals exchanges.

The silver market collapsed in March, dropping to $10.80 per troy ounce (31.1 grams) on March 27 and causing enormous losses to speculators. The collapse came amid charges that some speculators, in particular Texas billionaire Nelson Bunker Hunt and his associates, had attempted to corner the market. To meet margin calls for hundreds of millions of dollars in additional cash to cover their position in silver, the Hunt group was forced to sell off large holdings in other areas. In the following months, congressional investigators probed the muddled affair inconclusively.   Donald W. Swanton

In WORLD BOOK, see BOND; CORNERING THE MARKET; INVESTMENT; STOCK, CAPITAL.

SUDAN signed an agreement with Ethiopia on March 7, 1980, ending a three-year dispute between the two neighbors over Sudan's support for Muslim Eritrean guerrillas fighting for secession from Christian Ethiopia. The border was reopened and joint patrols set up to intercept and imprison the guerrillas. Besides the restored border stability, President and Prime Minister Gaafar Mohamed Nimeiri benefited from internal peace.

Reorganizing the Country. In February, the Sudanese Socialist Union, the only legal political party, approved a plan to reorganize the country into five autonomous regions plus the already autonomous southern region. Khartoum would remain the national capital and headquarters of the federal government. The People's Assembly (parliament) was dissolved, and elections were held in June for six regional people's assemblies and a new National Assembly. The new regional assemblies are responsible for all regional legislation and government. Nimeiri named a new Internal Affairs Ministry to coordinate domestic affairs.

The government's support for peace negotiations between Egypt and Israel generated some opposition, particularly among university students. On February 26, police broke up student demonstrations at Khartoum University protesting the exchange of ambassadors by Egypt and Israel. The university was closed indefinitely on March 19 after a week of strikes and a student boycott.

The Economy. The Kenana Sugar Refinery, the world's largest, went into full production in late March after two years of bureaucratic delays and under new management by a United States firm. The previous management had been British. With production of 240,000 short tons (220,000 metric tons) for 1980-1981 and 330,000 short tons (300,000 metric tons) annually thereafter, the refinery would meet domestic needs with a surplus for export.

Another encouraging development came in April with the discovery by the Chevron Oil Company of a second producing oil well near Khartoum. The discovery lifted Sudanese oil production to 11,500 barrels per day and brought hope to an economy dependent on expensive imported oil.

The presence of some 500,000 refugees from Chad, Ethiopia, Uganda, and Zaire continued to cause economic and social problems for Sudan. The country receives only about $12 million per year from other nations and from the United Nations to help the refugees. A government-sponsored international conference on the problem, held in Khartoum in June, drew delegations from 27 nations and 58 voluntary agencies. The meeting's result – $6 million in pledged aid – was disappointing.   William Spencer

See also AFRICA (Facts in Brief Table). In WORLD BOOK, see SUDAN.

SUPREME COURT OF THE UNITED STATES, badly split on key issues and lacking internal leadership, drifted through a relatively uneventful term that ended in July 1980. It retreated from previous pronouncements on some issues and, according to critics, failed to articulate decisive principles on major, unsettled areas of the law. Of 129 opinions issued during the term, 34 were decided by 5 to 4 votes.

One major turnabout came in a case testing the right of trial judges to close criminal courtrooms to the press and the public. A 1979 high court ruling found that the Sixth Amendment guarantee to a "speedy and public trial" protected only the defendant and conferred no access rights upon spectators. But by a 7 to 1 margin in *Richmond Newspapers Inc. v. Virginia,* the justices decided on July 2 that First Amendment considerations of free speech and press demand that a judge find "an overriding interest" or extraordinary circumstances before closing any trial to outsiders.

The court also clarified previous decisions on two controversial topics – abortion and affirmative action. A 5 to 4 vote on June 30 upheld the constitutionality of the Hyde Amendment, which bans the use of federal Medicaid funds for abortions unless the pregnancy involves rape, incest, or danger to the mother's life.

Discrimination Decisions. For the third consecutive year, the court issued a nondefinitive ruling on measures to help minorities overcome the effects of past discrimination. In *Fullilove v. Klutznick,* the court ruled 6 to 3 on July 2 that the U.S. government could constitutionally set quotas for minority participation in awarding government contracts. This marked the first time the court had specifically endorsed awarding federal funds on the basis of the recipient's race.

In an important ruling that some observers believe could revolutionize or destroy the U.S. political patronage system, the court ruled that private political affiliation could not be the sole basis for discharging a public employee. The March 31 decision, also based on First Amendment grounds, dealt specifically with two assistant public defenders in Rockland County, New York.

The court also issued three rulings that dramatically expand the liability of municipalities and of state and local officials for their actions. One decision, an 8 to 0 ruling on June 2, was especially startling: It made members of the Virginia Supreme Court potentially liable for attorneys' fees in a case filed against them for actions taken while they were acting in an enforcement capacity.

The Occupational Safety and Health Commission, target of vociferous corporate complaints in recent years, split two high court decisions, but lost the more important one. The court on February 26 unanimously upheld OSHA regulations allowing employees to walk away from extremely unsafe working conditions, but by a 5 to 4 vote on July 2 voided the agency's key standard for benzene exposure in the workplace, saying the standard was not based on scientific proof.

Criminal Justice Rulings are often the basis upon which courts are judged as liberal or conservative, but the 1980 Supreme Court defied classification. Several decisions supported police and prosecutors. For example, the justices upheld a life sentence dealt a third-time offender under Texas' recidivist statute covering habitual criminals, even though the convict's total take was only $229.11. Of six knotty search-and-seizure cases decided late in the term, the criminal defendants won only one. Yet the court also threw out another capital punishment statute in Georgia on technical grounds and ruled that an offender could not receive consecutive life sentences for two charges arising from the same crime. And in a minor landmark decision, the justices ruled by 6 to 3 on April 15 that police must have a warrant in order to arrest a suspect in the privacy of his own dwelling.

Other Key Decisions included:

- A 9 to 0 ruling, on February 27, throwing out the traditional spousal privilege rule that prohibited one marriage partner from testifying against the other. The new rule allows the potential witness to decide whether to give testimony.

- A 5 to 4 ruling, on June 16, that human-created living microorganisms can be patented. The U.S. government had argued strenuously against the result, suggesting that encouragement of genetic research could spread pollution and disease, diminish genetic diversity, and depreciate the value of human life. See BIOLOGY.

- A 6 to 3 ruling, on February 19, that essentially granted the government all profits from a book written by a former Central Intelligence Agency (CIA) agent without the agency's permission. Former CIA agent Frank W. Snepp III had violated a pre-employment agreement in which he promised to submit any manuscript arising from his experiences for prior censorship.

The Bench. By year's end, five of nine justices – Harry Blackmun, William Brennan, Warren Burger, Thurgood Marshall, and Lewis Powell – were 70 years of age or older. This circumstance led to speculation that the next presidential term would bring multiple appointments and a possible realignment of the divided court. With Ronald Reagan's election victory, President Jimmy Carter became the first full-term President in U.S. history (and the fourth overall) who failed to make a single high court appointment.   David C. Beckwith

See also COURTS AND LAWS. In WORLD BOOK, see SUPREME COURT OF THE UNITED STATES.

SURGERY. See MEDICINE.

SURINAM. See LATIN AMERICA.

SUZUKI, ZENKO (1911-   ), was elected prime minister of Japan on July 17, 1980. He was chosen to run by the ruling Liberal Democratic Party (LDP) after Prime Minister Masayoshi Ohira died on June 12. See JAPAN.

Suzuki was born on Jan. 11, 1911, in Yamada on the northern end of Honshu island. His father was a powerful figure in the area's fishing industry. Accordingly, Zenko studied at a fisheries' training institute in the 1930s instead of attending a college or university. After working as a fisherman, he organized a nationwide union for fishery workers. Suzuki then was elected to the *Diet* (parliament) as a Socialist in 1947.

Two years later, however, Suzuki switched to the Liberal Party. That party merged in 1955 with the Democratic Party to form the powerful ruling LDP, and he is considered one of the founders of the LDP. His first Cabinet post was minister of postal services in 1960. He also held the ministries of welfare and agriculture. When Ohira died, Suzuki was chairman of the LDP's executive council. But he had never held one of the top Cabinet posts and was thought to be a compromise candidate for prime minister.

Married, Suzuki is the father of four children. He is a pleasant negotiator and behind-the-scenes mediator known as "Mr. Fish."   Patricia Dragisic

SWAZILAND. See AFRICA.

SWEDEN voted to expand its use of nuclear power in a national referendum on March 23, 1980. About 58 per cent of the voters favored either operating up to 12 reactors for 25 years and then phasing out nuclear power, or operating the reactors for 25 years without specifying the next step in Sweden's energy program. Prime Minister Thorbjorn Falldin, an opponent of nuclear power, accepted the people's decision.

Sweden had needed an energy policy urgently. The nation's half-completed nuclear program had been delayed for four years. Sweden has no oil and little coal, and oil imports had pushed the budget deficit up to a record $13.3 billion in 1980.

Industrial Chaos. Sweden's reliance on uninterrupted industrial progress received a severe jolt in 1980 – the country's biggest labor conflict since 1909. Selective strikes began on April 25 and soon paralyzed key industries. Trade unions demanded an 11.3 per cent wage increase over two years, but employers offered only 0.5 per cent. The employers increased their offer to 2.3 per cent, but by May 1 some 100,000 workers were on strike. Airlines, trucks, and subways came to a halt and oil refineries closed. Seamen joined the strike on May 6, cutting ferry and cargo links between Sweden and other Western European nations. Almost 25 per cent of the country's work force stayed home and hoarded dwindling supplies of food and gasoline.

Sweden's King Carl XVI Gustaf and Queen Silvia pound rice for cakes in traditional manner during an April visit to Japan.

The conflict ended on May 11, when employers responded to Falldin's urging by agreeing to a 6.8 per cent pay hike that a government mediation board had recommended. Employers ended a lockout of 770,000 workers in the private sector and unions called back the strikers. Schools reopened, radio and television stations went back on the air, and airports and seaports resumed business.

Higher Taxes. Falldin's non-Socialist coalition, with a majority of one in the *Riksdag* (parliament), raised alcohol and tobacco taxes on August 26. The opposition Social Democrats and Communists did not challenge the increases. As the economy worsened in September, Falldin raised the value-added tax (VAT), a kind of sales tax, from 20.63 per cent to 23.46 per cent. The increase made Sweden's VAT the highest in Europe.

Falldin said that Sweden could not continue to consume at a rate that was out of line with its production and export capacities. Unemployment was running at a low 1.9 per cent, but inflation was rising from 9 per cent at the beginning of 1980.

On October 22, the government survived Sweden's first no-confidence vote, 175 votes to 174. The Social Democrats and Communists forced the vote because they objected to Falldin's economic policies.   Kenneth Brown

See also EUROPE (Facts in Brief Table). In WORLD BOOK, see SWEDEN.

SWIMMING. For United States swimmers, 1980 was a year that might have been. Had they competed in the Olympic Games, they probably would have won two-thirds of the gold medals for men and one-third of the gold medals for women. As it was, the Russian men and East German women took most of the Olympic glory, and the Americans, lacking motivation and strong summer opposition, did well, but not as well as they might have. See OLYMPIC GAMES.

World records were broken by 15-year-old Mary T. Meagher of Louisville, Ky., in the women's 100-meter and 200-meter butterfly (59.26 seconds and 2 minutes 6.37 seconds); Craig Beardsley of Harrington Park, N.J., in the men's 200-meter butterfly (1:58.21); Bill Barrett of Cincinnati in the men's 200-meter individual medley (2:03.20); and Ambrose (Rowdy) Gaines IV of Winter Haven, Fla., in the men's 200-meter free-style (1:49.16).

Meagher won the two national butterfly titles for women both indoors and outdoors. She broke the world record for 200 meters for the fourth time in 13 months.

Beardsley's record led to his first national title, and his father had an unusual analysis. "He's never really swum to his potential before," said Sterling Beardsley. "I don't think he was ever motivated to win. Instead, I think he was motivated not to lose."

Gaines won the national titles indoors and outdoors in the 100-meter and 200-meter free-styles and the college titles in the 100-yard and 200-yard free-styles.

Mike Bruner of Mesa, Ariz., who lost his world record in the men's 200-meter butterfly to Beardsley, excelled in distance free-style races. He won the high-point awards in both national championships. Tracy Caulkins of Nashville, Tenn., won both high-point awards for women.

World records were broken in 6 of the 16 events for men and 10 of the 15 for women. Eight world records fell to East German women, two each to Petra Schneider in individual medley and Rica Reinisch in backstroke. The most impressive record for men was Vladimir Salnikov's 14:58.27 for the 1,500-meter free-style as the Russian became the first to better 15 minutes. Peter Szmidt of Edmonton, Canada, set a world record of 3:50.49 in the men's 400-meter free-style.

Diving. Greg Louganis of El Cajon, Calif., won five of the six national titles and the Olympic trials in springboard and platform. In a sport in which few competitors ever get even one perfect score of 10, Louganis, in national 3-meter springboard competitions, received seven 10s for a reverse 1½ somersault in layout position, six 10s for a forward 3½ somersault pike, and six 10s for a reverse 2½ somersault pike.   Frank Litsky

In WORLD BOOK, see SWIMMING.

SWITZERLAND experienced in 1980 a phenomenon familiar to the rest of Europe – riots by youths who wanted to change the old order. Demonstrators in Zurich fought with police on May 31 and June 1 over a plan to spend $38 million on renovating and enlarging an opera house. The police made several arrests. On July 13, groups of youths demanded that police free those persons who had been arrested in earlier riots. Disorder broke out again and lasted all night. The police arrested 124 rioters.

Citizens petitioned President Georges-André Chevallaz to send troops to help subdue the protesters, but rioting broke out again on September 4, when police raided a factory being used as a youth center. The police used water cannons and tear gas to break up the crowds.

In a national referendum on March 2, Swiss voters approved by 1,116,353 votes to 181,264 a measure that gave the government the power to ensure essential supplies in times of international crisis without the approval of the Federal Assembly. On the same day, they voted by a 10 to 3 margin to preserve the status quo in church-state relations.

Economic activity revived in 1980. Inflation fell to 5 per cent, but the rising cost of oil added $1.2-billion to the import bill.   Kenneth Brown

See also EUROPE (Facts in Brief Table). In WORLD BOOK, see SWITZERLAND.

SYRIA and Libya agreed on Sept. 2, 1980, to merge into a single Arab country. Their move marked the latest in a long – and so far unsuccessful – series of efforts to achieve Arab unity. Although the geographic separation of the two countries made merger difficult, the move gained Syria an important Arab ally in its efforts to organize a regional coalition against Israel and oppose the Egyptian-Israeli peace treaty. An immediate benefit was Libya's contribution of $1.6 billion to pay off Syria's debts to Russia for arms and provide $600-million for additional weapons.

Iraq Feud Revived. The merger plan followed a nearly complete breakdown in Syria's often-troubled relations with neighboring Iraq. In August, Iraq expelled Syria's ambassador for allegedly fomenting dissension in the Shiite Muslim community. Syria then expelled Iraq's diplomatic staff.

The natural sympathy of President Hafiz al-Assad's ruling Alawi minority regime with fellow Shiites in Iran led to further tension after the Iran-Iraq war broke out in September. Iraq closed the border and massed troops near it while Syria denounced Iraqi war actions.

In November, coinciding with a meeting in Amman, Jordan, of the Arab League, which Syria boycotted, Assad picked a quarrel with neighboring Jordan. Accusing Jordan of harboring members of the Muslim Brotherhood, a fundamentalist

495

group dedicated to his overthrow, Assad massed troops and tanks on the Syria-Jordan border. Jordan responded in kind. Saudi Arabian diplomacy, with some help from the United States and Russia, smoothed the crisis over in December.

Internal Unrest plagued Assad's government despite a sometimes ruthless campaign to suppress opposition. The Muslim Brotherhood continued to be the main threat to the regime. Sabotage, bomb attacks, and assassinations of government leaders and prominent members of the Alawi community continued throughout the year. In June, Assad narrowly escaped death when a soldier threw a grenade at him at a reception. The attempt coincided with the murder by a gunman in Paris of exiled former Prime Minister Salah al-Din Bitar.

Economic Ills compounded the nation's problems. Inflation, a swollen bureaucracy, inefficient management, and the cost of maintaining a peacekeeping force in Lebanon contributed to economic uncertainty. Lack of qualified technicians for the industrial development program was another problem. The country's first modern paper mill, for example, planned as the showcase for the disadvantaged northeast region, opened in January in Dayr az Zawr. It closed in April because of a shortage of skilled workers.   William Spencer

See also MIDDLE EAST (Facts in Brief Table). In WORLD BOOK, see SYRIA.

TAIWAN held a series of trials during 1980 arising from a rally held on Dec. 10, 1979, at Kaohsiung, a southern port city. The rally was sponsored by staffers of *Formosa* magazine, who advocated confrontational tactics in pressing claims by the nation's Taiwanese majority for greater political power. Since 1949, Taiwan has been ruled by members of the Kuomintang political party who retreated there from mainland China.

Violence erupted at the rally. The government reported that about 180 police officers were injured. More than 200 persons were arrested. Eight *Formosa* staffers were found guilty on April 18 of plotting the forcible overthrow of the government and of having the "seditious intent" of making Taiwan independent and separate from the Republic of China. The defendants denied these accusations, saying they wanted to replace one-party rule with multiparty democracy. Shih Ming-teh, the magazine's manager, was sentenced to life imprisonment, and the others were sentenced to 12 to 14 years in prison. In later trials, only one of 43 defendants was acquitted.

Foreign observers saw the case as ending two years of relative liberalization and raising new questions about Taiwan's stability. However, the island remained calm. As expected, the Kuomintang won the parliamentary elections in December that had been postponed in 1978 because the

United States broke diplomatic relations. But provincial elections were again postponed.

The United States took two steps during 1980 to keep close contacts with Taiwan. Both angered the People's Republic of China. On January 3, the Administration of President Jimmy Carter said it would sell armaments worth $291.7 million to Taiwan under a policy of providing "carefully selected defensive weapons." These arms included antiaircraft and antitank missiles. While keeping a ban on selling long-range warplanes able to strike into China from Taiwan, the United States relaxed restrictions on its rule against U.S. manufacturers selling short-range warplanes to Taiwan. The second step was an agreement by the United States and Taiwan to grant each other's official representatives most rights granted to diplomats.

Mainland Relations. Trade and other contacts with China increased, despite the lack of official ties. China announced on April 7 that it would allow mainland goods to be exported to Taiwan without customs duties. It also began importing more manufactured goods from the island. Trade through Hong Kong, valued at $79 million in 1979, exceeded $200 million in 1980.   Henry S. Bradsher

See also ASIA (Facts in Brief Table); CHINA. In WORLD BOOK, see TAIWAN.

TANZANIA. See AFRICA.

TAPE RECORDER. See RECORDINGS.

TAXATION. The United States taxpayer shouldered an increasingly heavy tax burden in 1980. Inflation pushed wages and salaries to higher income levels and thus into higher tax brackets, resulting in "bracket creep." In the five years before 1980, individual income taxes rose 63 per cent, and Social Security taxes rose 79.5 per cent. In 1971, the average taxpayer paid some 16.1 per cent of annual income in federal, state, local, and Social Security taxes. In 1979, the figure was about 18.5 per cent.

Social Security taxes rose to a maximum of $1,587.67 in 1980; the maximum Social Security tax paid by an individual will total $1,975.05 per year in 1981, with the tax rising from 6.13 per cent to 6.65 per cent on an individual's first $29,700 in earnings. The tax rise for the self-employed is steeper, from 8.1 per cent to 9.3 per cent of earnings.

With the cost of living rising steadily, U.S. voters were increasingly responsive to efforts to cut taxes and government spending and to balance the federal budget. But such "uncontrollable" federal budget items as Social Security payments, Medicare, veterans' benefits, and interest on the national debt cannot easily be reduced. More than two-thirds of all federal spending in 1981 went to such uncontrollables, many of which are benefit programs mandated by previous Congresses.

"You cannot deduct last year's taxes as a bad investment!"

President Jimmy Carter's original "prudent and responsible" budget for fiscal 1981 (Oct. 1, 1980, to Sept. 30, 1981), sent to Congress in January, called for reduced federal spending – except for defense – of $615.8 billion, with a projected deficit of $15.8-billion. As a means of curbing inflation, in March the President sent Congress a pared-down budget totaling $611.5 billion, projecting a surplus of $16.5 billion. But the projected surplus vanished as federal costs rose.

No tax cut was approved by the second session of the 96th Congress, but the outlook for a tax cut in 1981 was brighter. Republican presidential candidate Ronald Reagan promised to trim federal spending, balance the budget, and reduce federal income taxes. These promises had broad appeal and were said to contribute to his victory. Nonetheless, his original campaign proposal to cut federal income taxes 30 per cent over a three-year period was regarded by many economists as impractical and likely to be modified.

Windfall Profits Tax. Despite intensive special-interest lobbying, Congress on March 27 passed a bill taxing the "windfall" profits that oil companies realize because of the decontrol of oil prices. The largest tax ever imposed on a single U.S. industry was expected to yield about $227.3 billion in revenue over a 10-year period. The larger oil companies were expected to pay $204.8 billion of

the total; the smaller independent producers, $22.5-billion. The tax was effective retroactive to March 1, 1980. A rider on the bill gave taxpayers a break, increasing the exemption on income from dividends and interest to $200 ($400 for a joint return).

The Underground Economy, an exchange of goods and services on which no taxes are paid, was estimated at about $700 billion in 1980. (Goods and services that are officially reported and taxed total about $2.5 trillion a year, and the Internal Revenue Service collects more than $519 billion annually, including $360 billion in individual and corporate income taxes.)

Federal Tax Receipts totaled $519.4 billion in the fiscal year ending on Sept. 30, 1980. Individual income and employment tax receipts totaled $415.9 billion; corporation taxes, $72.4 billion; estate and gift taxes, $6.5 billion; and excise taxes, $24.6 billion.

State Taxes. Several states voted on tax-cutting proposals in the November elections. Massachusetts voters approved Proposition 2½, which limits homeowners' property taxes to 2.5 per cent of the property's full market value. Proposition 2½ also calls for cuts of 62 per cent in vehicle excise taxes and allows renters to subtract 50 per cent of their yearly rent total from state income tax. Many state officials, teachers, and labor leaders feared that schools and public safety would suffer.

TELEVISION

Ohio voters approved new methods of assessing property taxes on homes and farms. In Missouri, all state tax increases are to be tied to the federal Consumer Price Index, and Illinois voters reduced the size of the state legislature to save money on salaries and overhead. But California voters, who approved the pioneering tax-cutting measure Proposition 13 in 1978, failed to adopt Proposition 9, a more radical tax-cutting bill, in June.

Alaska's Governor Jay S. Hammond signed bills in April and September abolishing the state's income tax, unneeded because the state is so rich in oil wealth and sports a budget surplus of almost $2-billion. Depending on the outcome of a legal challenge, the 400,000 Alaskan residents may enjoy an annual share-the-wealth program, awarding them $50 each for every year they have lived in Alaska since it became a state in 1959.

Eight states collected more than half of all state revenue in fiscal 1980. California again headed the list; the next seven, in order, were New York, Pennsylvania, Illinois, Texas, Michigan, Florida, and Ohio.

Total state tax collections for fiscal 1980 came to $136.9 billion, up 9.6 per cent. The largest sources of state revenue were sales and gross receipts taxes at $67.7 billion. Forty-four states collected $37.1-billion in income taxes. Carol L. Thompson

In WORLD BOOK, see TAXATION.

TELEVISION in the United States in 1980 was highlighted by two events—the miniseries "Shō-gun" and the shooting of J. R. Ewing on "Dallas" — and a nonevent—the nonopening of the new fall season because of a strike. "Shogun," a $22-million miniseries, starred Richard Chamberlain as an Elizabethan seaman in feudal Japan. Despite the fact that much of the dialogue was in uncaptioned Japanese, the 12-hour epic captured the attention of an estimated 125 million persons during its five-night run in September. The adaptation of James Clavell's novel was the second-highest-rated miniseries in history. Only "Roots" in 1977 drew a larger audience.

Who Shot J. R.? The prime-time soap opera "Dallas" became one of the most-talked-about series of the year, especially after the evil oil tycoon J. R. Ewing, played by Larry Hagman, was shot during the final episode of the 1979-1980 season.

"Who shot J. R.?" was a much-asked question during the summer rerun period and as the new season—during which his assailant was to be unveiled—was delayed. The November 21 episode of "Dallas," which revealed that Kristin Shepard, his sister-in-law and former mistress, had shot J. R., was the highest-rated entertainment program in TV history with 83 million U.S. viewers.

The Screen Actors Guild (SAG) and the American Federation of Television and Radio Artists

J. R. Ewing, the evil oil tycoon, recovers from gunshot wounds on "Dallas." The episode revealing his assailant's identity broke TV ratings records.

(AFTRA) called their first strike in 20 years on July 21, halting production of all network TV shows except information and variety programs for almost 10 weeks. In a settlement with television and film producers reached on September 25, the actors were granted a 32 per cent increase in pay-scale minimums over the new three-year contract period. As a result of the strike, the three networks—the American Broadcasting Companies, Inc. (ABC); CBS Inc.; and the National Broadcasting Company (NBC)—were forced to delay traditional September premières of their new fall programs, filling their schedules with reruns, movies, news, and "reality" features.

So-called reality series, which relied heavily on "slice-of-life" features, invaded the small screen in force. Inspired by the success of "Real People" in 1979, the networks added "That's Incredible!," "Games People Play," "Those Amazing Animals," and "Speak Up, America."

The New Series were introduced over a period of months from late October 1980 through January 1981, and tended to favor situation-comedy formats featuring scantily clad young women and sex-oriented humor. "It's a Living," "I'm a Big Girl Now," "Bosom Buddies," "Too Close for Comfort," and "Ladies' Man" were representative of this genre. However, these new weekly programs made little impact in the ratings. The most-watched shows in 1980 continued to be the oldies — "60 Minutes," "Three's Company," "The Jeffersons," "Alice," "M*A*S*H," "Dukes of Hazzard," "Archie Bunker's Place," "The Love Boat," and "Dallas."

Biographical Specials were more prevalent than ever. Among them were *Father Damien: The Leper Priest; Gauguin the Savage; The Ordeal of Dr. Mudd; F.D.R.: The Last Years; The Jayne Mansfield Story;* and *Sophia Loren: Her Own Story,* in which the Italian star played both herself and her mother. There were also dramas about Humphrey Bogart (*Bogie*) and Margaret Sullivan (*Haywire*), and three on the life of Marilyn Monroe.

The most controversial television biography of 1980 was *Playing for Time,* a moving three-hour adaptation by playwright Arthur Miller of the Fania Fenelon memoir about life in the Nazi concentration camp Auschwitz. Fenelon and others protested the casting of anti-Zionist Vanessa Redgrave in the lead role. Other memorable specials of 1980 included the dramas *Amber Waves, The Day Christ Died, Off the Minnesota Strip,* and *A Private Battle,* and two Henry Fonda vehicles, *Gideon's Trumpet* and *The Oldest Living Graduate.*

Among the musical and variety programs were *Baryshnikov on Broadway, The Shirley MacLaine Show, A Musical Tribute to Toscanini,* and a nostalgic six-hour retrospective of comedian Bob Hope's 31 years entertaining U.S. servicemen. Best-selling books provided the basis for some of the miniseries, including Judith Krantz's *Scruples;* Lonnie Coleman's *Beulah Land;* and Garson Kanin's *Moviola.*

Sports and Politics. The sixth and final game between the Philadelphia Phillies and the Kansas City Royals on October 21 became the highest-rated World Series game in television history. The game drew 60 per cent of the United States TV audience. The February 23 telecast of the women's figure-skating championship at Lake Placid, N.Y., was the highest-rated Winter Olympics event.

Some 120 million persons watched the debate between President Jimmy Carter and Republican presidential candidate Ronald Reagan on October 28. During the campaign, the presidential candidates spent an estimated $45 million for TV commercial time, while the networks incurred combined costs of more than $7 million for election-night coverage.

Public Broadcasting System (PBS) ratings were up again in 1980, with overnight ratings for the film *Death of a Princess,* a dramatization of the 1977 execution of a Saudi Arabian princess, the highest in PBS history. The film aired on May 12, despite heated protests from the Saudi Arabian government. The most popular regularly scheduled PBS

"Shōgun," starring Richard Chamberlain as an Elizabethan seaman in feudal Japan, became the second-highest-rated miniseries in television history.

Vanessa Redgrave, left, starred in *Playing for Time,* a highly
acclaimed drama of life in the Nazi concentration camp Auschwitz.

series, "The MacNeil/Lehrer Report," had a week-ly audience of 8 million, up 100 per cent since 1978.

The PBS offered a fine six-hour adaptation of John le Carré's convoluted spy novel *Tinker, Tailor, Soldier, Spy,* a British Broadcasting Corporation (BBC) production. Sir Alec Guinness was superb as master spy George Smiley.

"Masterpiece Theatre" featured two British miniseries – Jane Austen's "Pride and Prejudice" and Fyodor Dostoevsky's "Crime and Punishment." Other distinguished miniseries imports on the PBS schedule were "The Voyage of Charles Darwin," "The Life of Molière," "Disraeli: Portrait of a Romantic," and "Rumpole of the Bailey."

"The Body in Question," 13 irreverent anatomy lectures by physician-performer Jonathan Miller, was the prime BBC contribution to the PBS science agenda, but the most-talked-about PBS science show was the extraordinary $8.5-million series "Cosmos," with astronomer Carl Sagan. Other commendable home-grown PBS science series were "The Search for Solutions"; "Odyssey"; the Children's Television Workshop's new "3-2-1 Contact"; and "Nova."

Musical highlights on PBS included a tribute to Fred Astaire and two remarkable "Live from Lincoln Center" concerts, one starring Luciano Pavarotti and the other, violinists Isaac Stern, Itzhak Perlman, and Pinchas Zukerman.

Cable-TV growth continued to accelerate in 1980. By midyear, there were some 4,200 cable systems and about 17 million subscribers. The Federal Communications Commission (FCC) on July 22 struck down its rules limiting the number of TV signals and programs that cable-TV operators could import from other cities.

The Cable News Network (CNN), the first 24-hour cable-news service, began operation on June 1. By midsummer, CNN programming was beamed, via satellite, to 227 cable systems with a total of 2.5 million subscribers.

Westinghouse Electric Corporation paid a record $646 million for the Teleprompter Corporation, the industry's largest multiple-system TV-cable company, in October. The merger had to be approved by the FCC, Teleprompter stockholders, and the Securities and Exchange Commission.

Citing "improper actions" by RKO General Incorporated, and its parent company, General Tire and Rubber Company, the FCC on January 24 refused to renew the licenses of three RKO stations – WNAC-TV, Boston; WOR-TV, New York City; and KHJ-TV, Los Angeles. Broadcasters called it one of the harshest decisions in FCC history. June Bundy Csida

See also AWARDS AND PRIZES. In WORLD BOOK, see TELEVISION.

TENNESSEE. See STATE GOVERNMENT.

TENNIS. Bjorn Borg and John McEnroe won major tennis honors in 1980 and beat each other in the year's two most important tournament finals. Chris Evert Lloyd, refreshed by a three-month layoff, became the leading women's winner.

More prize money was offered than ever before. The Grand Prix circuit for men comprised 90 tournaments in 20 nations and $11 million in purses. The women played the Avon 11-tournament, $1.8-million American circuit from January to March, then the Colgate series of 37 tournaments in 11 nations for $5.4 million. The United States Open offered $684,082 in prize money, Wimbledon $628,320, and the French Open $617,000.

The Men. Borg, a 24-year-old Swede, won his fifth straight Wimbledon title in England. In the memorable final on July 5, he outlasted the 21-year-old McEnroe of Douglaston, N.Y., 1-6, 7-5, 6-3, 6-7, 8-6, in an exciting and well-played match. McEnroe saved seven match points in the fourth set, five in a dramatic 34-point tiebreaker.

McEnroe alienated linesmen and spectators all year with chronic complaining and outbursts of temperament. In the Wimbledon semifinals, he beat Jimmy Connors in four sets on July 4 and provided his own fireworks. Once, when McEnroe disputed a service call, Connors shook a finger at him and said, "Keep your mouth shut out here."

McEnroe avenged his Wimbledon loss by beating Borg, 7-6, 6-1, 6-7, 5-7, 6-4, in the United States Open final on September 7 in Flushing Meadows, N.Y. The match lasted 4 hours 13 minutes. McEnroe, the defending champion, had to go 4 hours 16 minutes to defeat Connors in the semifinals two nights before.

Borg won his fifth French Open, a record, plus the $150,000 first prize in the Pepsi Grand Slam and the $100,000 first prize in the Colgate Grand Prix Masters. McEnroe won the United States indoor title and others, but he seemed worn down from playing with seldom a week off. Connors won the U.S. professional indoor title and the World Championship Tennis final.

Arthur Ashe, the first black male to win a major championship (1968 U.S. Open and 1975 Wimbledon), retired at 36, less than a year after a heart attack and by-pass surgery. He was named captain of the 1981 United States Davis Cup team. Argentina eliminated the U.S., 4-1, in the 1980 Davis Cup competition, held from March 7 to 9 in Buenos Aires. Czechoslovakia beat Italy in the final.

The Women. The 25-year-old Lloyd, from Fort Lauderdale, Fla., had dominated women's tennis from 1974 to 1978. In 1979, she married John Lloyd, a British tournament player, and her tennis intensity waned as Martina Navratilova and Tracy Austin won the big tournaments. After three losses to Austin in 11 days, Lloyd took an "indefinite

Coming back after three months "retirement," Chris Evert Lloyd beat Hana Mandlikova to win the U.S. Open women's singles title.

Bjorn Borg exults after beating John McEnroe in their exciting finals match to win his fifth consecutive Wimbledon singles title.

leave" from tennis on Feb. 1, 1980, and joined her husband. On May 5, she returned to competition and played better than ever for the rest of the year.

In the first tournament on her return, she beat Virginia Ruzici of Romania, 6-0, 6-3, for her fourth French Open title. She lost to Evonne Goolagong Cawley of Australia, 6-1, 7-6, in the Wimbledon final. Then she won her fifth U.S. Open in six years, beating defending champion Austin, 4-6, 6-1, 6-1, in the semifinals, and Hana Mandlikova of Czechoslovakia, 5-7, 6-1, 6-1, in the final.

The 28-year-old Cawley, of Hilton Head Island, South Carolina, won the 1971 Wimbledon title and lost in three subsequent finals there. Her game was as graceful and efficient as ever as she became the first mother in 66 years to win at Wimbledon. A chronic back ailment kept her out of the United States Open.

Lloyd also won the Italian and Canadian opens and her sixth straight United States clay-court title. Navratilova, from Dallas, dominated the winter tour, then played erratically.

Austin, from Rolling Hills, Calif., won the Clairol tournament (first prize $100,000), the Family Circle Cup, the Avon championship, and the U.S. indoor title. At 17, she became the youngest player to earn $1 million in tournaments.   Frank Litsky

In WORLD BOOK, see TENNIS.

TEXAS. See HOUSTON; STATE GOVERNMENT.

THAILAND changed governments when Prime Minister Kriangsak Chamanan resigned on Feb. 29, 1980. He was succeeded on March 3 by General Prem Tinsulanonda, the army commander in chief. Kriangsak had reduced subsidies on petroleum products on February 10, thus raising prices. Inflation generally was growing. Earlier in February, he reshuffled his Cabinet. Frustrated by parliamentary maneuvers against him, Kriangsak quit unexpectedly and criticized other politicians' failure to support positive economic policies or to deal with hard problems.

Prem brought to the office a reputation for personal honesty. He also had avoided involvement in earlier military coups. However, he caused political controversy by arranging the amendment of a law that would have required him to retire from command of the army when he became 60 years old in 1980. Critics said this upset the balance between the army and civilian government. See PREM TINSULANONDA.

Continuing Strife. Relations with Thailand's neighbors were mostly troubled. Vietnamese troops that had been fighting Khmer Rouge resistance forces in Cambodia struck into Thailand on June 23, attacking Cambodian refugee camps used by some resistance fighters. The Thai government called the two-day attacks premeditated and denounced them, but Vietnam denied that its troops had crossed the border. China said on June 25 that it would "resolutely support" Thailand against Vietnam. On July 1, United States President Jimmy Carter ordered an emergency airlift of weapons to Thailand in an effort to improve its defenses.

A Thai officer on a boat patrolling the Mekong River border with Laos was killed by gunfire on June 15. When Laos refused to accept responsibility, Thailand closed the border on July 6, cutting off Laos' main access to the outside world. The border was reopened on August 29, but relations remained poor.

The Thai Communist Party, which had waged guerrilla warfare against the government since the early 1960s, lost strength in 1980. It had been supported by both the People's Republic of China and Vietnam. But in the conflict between those two Communist countries, the Thai Communist Party sided with China, thus losing Hanoi's support. Chinese aid to the party was cut anyway, reportedly in a deal with the Thai government to permit China to supply the Cambodian resistance movement through Thailand. As the year ended, the Thai government was seeking an alternative to continued backing for the Khmer Rouge, along with a new solution for the continuing problem of Cambodian refugees.   Henry S. Bradsher

See also ASIA (Facts in Brief Table); CAMBODIA. In WORLD BOOK, see THAILAND.

THEATER

An election victory party is celebrated on the stage as P. T. Barnum is elected to the U.S. Senate in the smash musical *Barnum*.

Drama on Broadway in 1980 focused on the family. The Pulitzer Prize went to *Talley's Folly*, the beginning of a family saga by Lanford Wilson. The symbolic title refers literally to a decaying Victorian boathouse – 1944 scene of the improbable courtship of tradition-bound, spinsterish Sally Talley by an outsider. Judd Hirsch gave a consummate performance as Matt, the appealing Jewish refugee whose resourcefulness breaks down Sally's defenses. The sequel, *Fifth of July*, is set on that day in 1977, and brings together at the family farmhouse in Lebanon, Mo., Sally, now a feisty widow; the embittered Talley heir Kenny, a paraplegic Vietnam War veteran who plans to sell the homestead; and the would-be purchasers, a rich and ambitious rock star and her husband who were Kenny's classmates at the University of California, Berkeley, in the revolutionary 1960s. Wilson finds hope for the Talleys and the country in the humanity of his offbeat characters.

Phyllis Frelich, a deaf actress playing a deaf woman in *Children of a Lesser God,* communicates with her teacher, played by John Rubinstein.

In Mark Medoff's perceptive, award-winning *Children of a Lesser God,* Phyllis Frelich, who is herself deaf, created a moving portrayal of a lively and gifted deaf woman who has been an impossible child and an oversexed teen-ager, and is now a rebellious student in a school for the deaf. She refuses to learn speech, which she considers a betrayal of those who inhabit the world of the deaf. Her attempt to join the hearing world on her own terms by marrying her sympathetic teacher, impressively played by John Rubinstein, intensifies both her accomplishments and her isolation.

Arthur Miller returned to Broadway with *The American Clock,* inspired by *Hard Times,* Studs Terkel's oral history of the Great Depression, and by Miller's own family's experiences during that time. With warmth, humor, and lyricism, the play centers on an aspiring young writer and his views of some 44 characters — family, friends, relatives, and strangers — who touch the lives of the Baum family when the father's prosperous business fails.

Home, produced by the Negro Ensemble Company, presents Samm-Art Williams' poetic and warmhearted account of a storyteller who, from his Carolina armchair, spins yarns of his various homes — on a farm, in the big city, and in jail. In Neil Simon's comedy *I Ought To Be in Pictures,* a struggling Hollywood writer is surprised by a visit from his 19-year-old daughter, whom he deserted when she was 3. Bright with Simon one-liners, the comedy reaches its expected conclusion when the daughter achieves the ambition voiced by the play's title.

Revivals of family dramas also proved popular. Paul Osborn's 1939 *Morning's at Seven* boasted a stellar cast, with Nancy Marchand, Elizabeth Wilson, Maureen O'Sullivan, and Teresa Wright as the Gibbs "girls," elderly sisters in a Midwestern town in 1922. Set in the adjoining backyards of two of the sisters' huge, frame, turn-of-the-century houses, the action involves a nephew who, after years of courtship, brings his fiancée home for family approval.

Plays from Abroad included British playwright Harold Pinter's *Betrayal,* a piercing look at selfishness in the family relationship. Beginning with the end of an extramarital affair, the play works back in time through polite encounters and evasions, as the characters peel off layers of pretense to arrive at the truths of their various betrayals — of husband by wife and best friend, of lovers by each other, and of the husband who betrays himself by ignoring the affair he knows exists.

Nagged by his family, forgotten by his friends, unemployed and dejected, Sanya, the nondescript hero of Russian playwright Nikolai Erdman's *The Suicide,* announces he will shoot himself. He becomes an overnight celebrity, and a procession of persons comes to his home, each with a grievance

Maggie Smith plays the actress Arkadina,
and Brian Bedford her lover, in Chekhov's
The Seagull at Canada's Stratford Festival.

nounced that Gower Champion, the musical's director-choreographer, had died of cancer that afternoon. The dazzling *42nd Street* is a tribute to the talent of Champion, whose past work includes *Carnival* and *Hello, Dolly!* The minimal book, described as "lead-ins and crossovers," follows in song and story the Warner Brothers landmark film about a jaded director, played by Warner Baxter (played, in turn, by Jerry Orbach on stage) and the chorus girl, played by Ruby Keeler (Wanda Richert), who becomes an overnight star. Champion captured the essence of Busby Berkeley's 1930s routines in the precision tapping of chorus girls in mirrored multiplicity and patterned formations.

While *42nd Street* outdid Hollywood musicals, *A Day in Hollywood/A Night in the Ukraine*, directed by Tommy Tune, satirized them. In the bright first-half revue, eight players cavort as 1930s movie ushers, recreating in one imaginative number the dancing feet of famous stars, from Fred Astaire and Ginger Rogers to Mickey and Minnie Mouse. The second half is a zany version of Anton Chekhov's *The Bear* as a Marx Brothers movie. A successful revue substituted imagination for opulence; in *Tintypes*, a talented cast of five portrayed familiar types against a background of social change from 1890 to 1920.   Alice Griffin

See also AWARDS AND PRIZES (Arts Awards). In WORLD BOOK, see DRAMA; THEATER.

against the state and each imploring Sanya to declare this grievance the cause of his suicide.

Brilliantly enacted by Derek Jacobi, Sanya is transformed from a cipher to a man who realizes that if his death is so important, his life can have meaning, too. The anti-Stalinist comedy was never produced in Russia, but in the United States in 1980 it was seen not only on Broadway, but also in Chicago and at Yale University.

On the Musical Scene, three major works lit up the Broadway sky. *Barnum,* based on the life of P. T. Barnum and exploding with energy and talent, had more goings-on than a three-ring circus. Award-winning Jim Dale as a singing, dancing, and acrobatic Barnum did the legendary master of humbug and theatricality proud, while Joe Layton's staging created an imaginative and artistic circus world that reflected the real world outside.

Evita swept the 1980 Antoinette Perry (Tony) and Drama Critics Circle musical awards for its talented writers Andrew Lloyd Webber and Tim Rice, director Harold Prince, and actress-singer Patti LuPone, whose Eva Perón has the dynamism, "star quality," and ruthlessness of the original.

The August opening-night curtain speech by the producer of the musical *42nd Street* could have been drawn from the 1933 movie on which the show is based. Unhappily for the American theater, however, David Merrick spoke the truth. He an-

TIKHONOV, NIKOLAY A. (1905-), became chairman of Russia's Council of Ministers on Oct. 23, 1980, succeeding Aleksey N. Kosygin, who resigned because of ill health and died on December 18. See RUSSIA.

Nikolay Aleksandrovich Tikhonov was born in Kharkov, the Ukraine, on May 1, 1905. Tikhonov graduated from the Metallurgical Institute in Dnepropetrovsk, the Ukraine, in 1930. He went to work as an engineer and was promoted to chief engineer and, in 1947, to plant manager. From 1950 until 1957, he held positions in the Ministry of Ferrous Metallurgy.

Tikhonov was named director of the Dnepropetrovsk Economic Council in 1957. He returned to Moscow in 1960 as deputy chairman of the State Economic Council with the rank of minister. In 1963, he became a deputy chairman of the State Planning Committee. He was appointed deputy chairman of the Council of Ministers in 1965 and promoted to first deputy chairman in 1976.

Tikhonov became an alternate member of the Politburo, the policymaking body of the Communist Party Central Committee, in 1978 and a full member in 1979.   Jay Myers

TIMOR. See ASIA.

TOGO. See AFRICA.

TORNADO. See DISASTERS; WEATHER.

TOYS. See GAMES, MODELS, AND TOYS.

TRACK AND FIELD. Just as Sebastian Coe of Great Britain dominated middle-distance running in 1979, Steve Ovett of Great Britain did in 1980. In a six-week span in 1979, Coe broke the world records for 800 meters, 1,500 meters, and 1 mile. Later in 1979, Ovett came close to the 1,500-meter and 1-mile records, and in 1980 he broke them.

There were world records set all year, 13 by Europeans in May alone. Many did not survive the year.

Through all this, United States athletes were uncharacteristically silent. The only Americans who bettered world records were Edwin Moses of Mission Viejo, Calif., in the 400-meter hurdles (47.13 seconds) and Mary Decker of Eugene, Ore., in the women's mile (4 minutes 21.7 seconds).

The Olympic Games boycott by the United States seemed to reduce the level of American performances, though Moses, Decker, Stanley Floyd, Renaldo Nehemiah, and other Americans did well in European meets before and after the Moscow Olympics. With such track powers as the United States, West Germany, and Kenya boycotting, Russia and East Germany won two-thirds of the Olympic gold medals. See OLYMPIC GAMES.

Ovett and Coe won Olympic gold medals, each defeating the other. In the 800-meter final on July 26, Coe did not respond when Ovett made his move, and Ovett won in 1:45.4, with Coe second. Coe was depressed and Ovett was elated. He said, "The 1,500 is the one I'm really preparing for."

But in the 1,500-meter final on August 1, Coe broke away and won in 3:38.4, with Ovett third. Until then, Ovett had won 45 races at 1,500 meters or 1 mile since 1977.

World Records. Ovett's first world record of the year came on July 1 at Oslo, Norway, when his time of 3:48.8 trimmed two-tenths of a second off Coe's mile record. Ovett returned to Oslo on July 15 and ran 1,500 meters in 3:32.1, equaling Coe's record. On August 27, at Koblenz, West Germany, Ovett got the 1,500-meter record by running 3:31.4. Less than an hour before Ovett's record mile, Coe set a world record of 2:13.4 for 1,000 meters on the same Oslo track.

Ovett and Coe were an odd couple. Coe was friendly, Ovett irritable. Neither had special affection or small talk for the other. Ovett derided Coe's mental and physical preparation. "He's programmed, from getting up in the morning to going to bed," said Ovett. "I'm the opposite. I make up my mind at the last minute . . . ."

Ovett and Coe raced against each other only in the Olympics. Each raced in many other meets, too, but there was so much post-Olympic competition that no one seemed to know who would race

World Track and Field Records Established in 1980

Event	Holder	Country	Where made	Date	Record
Men					
1,000 meters	Sebastian Coe	Great Britain	Oslo, Norway	July 1	2:13.4
1,500 meters	Steve Ovett	Great Britain	Koblenz, W. Ger.	August 27	3:31.36
1 mile	Steve Ovett	Great Britain	Oslo, Norway	July 1	3:48.8
400-meter hurdles	Edwin Moses	U.S.A.	Milan, Italy	July 3	:47.13
High jump	Gerd Wessig	E. Ger.	Moscow	August 1	7 ft. 8¾ in. (2.36 m.)
Pole vault	Wladyslaw Kozakiewicz	Poland	Moscow	July 30	18 ft. 11½ in. (5.78 m.)
Hammer throw	Yuri Sedykh	Russia	Moscow	July 31	268 ft. 4 in. (81.80 m.)
Javelin throw	Ferenc Paragi	Hungary	Tata, Hungary	April 23	317 ft. 4 in. (96.72 m.)
Decathlon	Guido Kratschmer	W. Ger.	Bernhausen, W. Ger.	June 13–14	8,649 points
Women					
800 meters	Nadezhda Olizarenko	Russia	Moscow	July 27	1:53.5
1,500 meters	Tatyana Kazankina	Russia	Zurich, Switzerland	August 13	3:52.47
1 mile	Mary Decker	U.S.A.	Auckland, New Zealand	January 26	4:21.68
100-meter hurdles	Grazyna Rabsztyn	Poland	Warsaw, Poland	June 13	:12.36
400-meter hurdles	Karin Rossley	E. Ger.	Jena, E. Ger.	May 17	:54.28
Shot-put	Ilona Slupianek	E. Ger.	Potsdam, E. Ger.	May 11	73 ft. 8 in. (22.45 m.)
Discus throw	Maria Vergova	Bulgaria	Sofia, Bulgaria	July 13	235 ft. 7 in. (71.80 m.)
Javelin throw	Tatyana Biryulina	Russia	Podolsk, Russia	July 12	229 ft. 11 in. (70.08 m.)
Pentathlon	Nadezhda Tkachenko	Russia	Moscow	July 24	5,083 points
400-meter relay	Muller, Wockel, Auerswald, Gohr	E. Ger.	Moscow	August 1	:41.60
800-meter relay	Gohr, Muller, Wockel, Koch	E. Ger.	Jena, E. Ger.	August 9	1:28.15
*Marathon	Grete Waitz	Norway	New York City	October 26	2:25:42

m. = meters; *unofficial record.

where. That especially frustrated Don Paige of Baldwinsville, N.Y., America's best 800-meter runner, who wanted to race Ovett and Coe. He finally raced Coe on August 14 in Viareggio, Italy, and beat him in 1:45.04.

Field Events. Pole-vaulters had a good year. From May to July, Dave Roberts' 1976 world record of 18 feet 8½ inches (5.70 meters) was raised to 18 feet 9¼ inches (5.72 meters) by Wladyslaw Kozakiewicz of Poland; 18 feet 10¼ inches (5.75 meters) twice by Thierry Vigneron of France; 18 feet 11 inches (5.77 meters) by Philippe Houvion of France; and 18 feet 11½ inches (5.78 meters) by Kozakiewicz.

The men's high-jump record took a beating, too. On May 25 in Heilbronn, West Germany, Jacek Wszola of Poland raised Vladimir Yashchenko's record of 7 feet 8 inches (2.34 meters) to 7 feet 8½ inches (2.35 meters). Eighteen-year-old Dietmar Moegenburg of West Germany, who finished second at 7 feet 6¼ inches (2.29 meters), was so distraught with his performance that he slept poorly.

The next day, at Rehlingen, West Germany, Moegenburg arrived at the track, lifted his spirits with a cold shower, and matched Wszola's record. In the Olympics, Gerd Wessig of East Germany, who trained for the decathlon, improved the record to 7 feet 8¾ inches (2.36 meters).   Frank Litsky

In WORLD BOOK, see TRACK AND FIELD.

Passengers board a train at a subway stop beneath Rome's Trinità dei Monti church. The new Metropolitana subway opened in February.

TRANSIT systems in United States cities retained most of the patronage in 1980 that they had built up during the previous year's gasoline shortage, despite a surge of fare increases. The American Public Transit Association (APTA) said that urban mass-transit systems carried 6.88 billion passengers in the first 10 months of 1980, up 1.4 per cent from the same period in 1979. However, an 11-day transit strike in New York City in April pulled U.S. patronage down 4.6 per cent from April 1979, breaking a string of 32 consecutive month-to-month ridership increases. The APTA estimated that the nationwide transit operating deficit reached about $3.15 billion in 1980, compared with a $2.78-billion loss in 1979.

Through October 1980, New York City ridership was off 6.2 per cent from the first 10 months of 1979, and Chicago transit trips fell 3.9 per cent. But ridership rose 24.9 per cent in Atlanta, Ga.; 10.7 per cent in Washington, D.C.; 12.2 per cent in Miami, Fla.; 7.3 per cent in Indianapolis, Ind.; 0.3 per cent in Philadelphia; and 14.9 per cent in Los Angeles.

Transit Projects. Cities moved along with transit work and planned new projects. Houston, Los Angeles, and Pittsburgh considered new subways, while Baltimore and Miami continued construction. Denver; Detroit; Portland, Ore.; and Sacramento, Calif., planned *light rail* (trolley) lines. San Diego forged ahead, without federal money, on a 16-mile (26-kilometer) light rail line to Mexico. The United States Department of Transportation (DOT) granted Washington, D.C.'s Metro system $285.3 million in June and October for subway and other improvements. A $16.1-million grant in October enabled Los Angeles to enter the final design and construction phase of its downtown *people mover,* an automatic, short-trip service.

On November 28, the Supreme Judicial Court of Massachusetts ordered the Boston-area mass transit system to close on December 5 unless it could get more money from the state legislature. The system shut down on December 6, but restored limited service a day later after an emergency $41-million bailout.

Handicapped Service. On June 25, the U.S. Senate approved $24.8 billion in transit assistance over five years. The bill gives such transit-oriented cities as New York City a bigger share of federal aid and allows communities to develop their own special services for handicapped people. Similar legislation passed by the House in December would have rolled back a 1979 DOT ruling that required transit systems to equip main-line buses and many subway stations to handle handicapped people. A filibuster blocked Senate consideration of the bill, which died when Congress adjourned. A federal judge had ruled that DOT had issued its ruling properly. The New York Metropolitan Transportation Authority said on September 19 that it would defy the ruling, though its defiance would cost it $375 million per year in federal funds. But in October, it asked instead for a six-month delay in meeting the requirement.

Fare Hikes. After years of wooing riders with low fares, transit operators began to escalate trip charges, in the face of climbing wage and fuel costs. Lawsuits delayed some fare boosts. A superior court judge lifted an order restraining a Los Angeles area fare rise from 55 cents to 65 cents. Court action delayed a Philadelphia-area increase from 50 cents to 65 cents. The Metropolitan Atlanta Rapid Transit Authority doubled its 25-cent fare in July, after a lawsuit filed by the city held it up.

James R. Maloney, executive director of the Port Authority of Allegheny County, said that Pittsburgh needed higher fares because of "inadequate funding" by governmental agencies "in utter disregard" of inflation's continuing impact on transit operating budgets." The Dallas Public Transit board of directors recommended 16 per cent higher fares, because of a reduced city subsidy, more demand for transit services, and rising operating expenses. Albert R. Karr

See also Transportation. In World Book, see Transportation.

TRANSKEI. See Africa.

TRANSPORTATION industries in the United States suffered from the economic slump and inflation in 1980. Airline profits disappeared as traffic eased and fuel costs rose, so carriers imposed hefty fare hikes. But surging demand for coal and grain offset revenue declines in many other railroad freight categories and boosted earnings. Truckers' business and profits sagged, but both began to come back in late 1980.

The Transportation Association of America (TAA) estimated United States transportation revenues at $510 billion for 1980, up 3 per cent from 1979 revenues of $499 billion. The increase reflected higher prices, fares, and rates. But mainland intercity freight declined 4.8 per cent; truck freight and traffic on the Great Lakes, rivers, and canals were all down 10 per cent. Railroad freight traffic was off 1.5 per cent; air freight was unchanged; and pipelines were off 5 per cent. Intercity passenger traffic was down 2.3 per cent, and air travel was off 4.5 per cent. Automobile travel decreased 2 per cent, as motorists again cut their driving because of rising gasoline prices. Railroad passenger traffic was off 2 per cent, and bus travel held even.

Deregulation Spreads. Trucking and railroad deregulation laws were passed. The truck industry had opposed rolling back Interstate Commerce Commission (ICC) regulatory powers, but Congress adopted a measure on June 20 that was designed to make it easier for new companies to enter the trucking industry and give companies more freedom in raising or lowering their rates. The ICC then moved to carry out the law's provisions, even going beyond the law, in the view of the American Trucking Associations, Incorporated. Railroads, on the other hand, wanted deregulation legislation and finally got it in October. Deregulation gave them more freedom to raise and cut freight rates, abandon unwanted services, and conduct business with less ICC monitoring. Airlines, meanwhile, cut back some service and boosted fares sharply.

The intercity bus industry seemed to be the next candidate for decontrol. ICC Chairman Darius W. Gaskins, Jr., said on October 2 that the commission staff advocated partial bus-industry deregulation, including making it easier to enter the industry, giving more leeway to boost or trim fares, making it easier to abandon routes, and reducing joint fare-setting powers for bus concerns.

Safety Problems. The National Highway Traffic Safety Administration took a step toward what would be the largest auto recall in history on June 11. It found tentatively that a defect in certain 1970-1979 model Ford Motor Company car and light-truck transmissions made them tend to jump from parking gear into reverse gear. Ford fought the ruling at a public hearing in August, and prepared to oppose any final ruling in court. The U.S. Department of Transportation announced on December 31 that Ford had agreed to send information about the transmission problem to the vehicle owners and to provide warning labels to attach to the dashboard or sunvisor.

The Safety Administration said in February and August that crash tests conducted at 35 miles (56 kilometers) per hour – somewhat faster than the speed used to check automobiles against federal safety requirements – showed that most 1979 and 1980 model small cars could not protect occupants from death or serious injury. Foreign models were the most dangerous, the agency said.

General Motors Corporation in June dropped plans to offer automatically inflating airbags in 1982-model large cars, but said that it would make them optional on some 1983 models. Conferees from the two houses of the Congress of the United States voted on July 31 to put the federal rule requiring passive restraints – air bags or automatically fastening belts – into effect in 1983 instead of 1982. But the conferees also required that large-volume automakers offer airbags on one product line beginning in 1983. The Senate approved this, but the plan lost in the House. Albert R. Karr

See also Automobile; Aviation; Railroad; Ship and Shipping; Transit; Truck and Trucking. In World Book, see Transportation.

TRAVEL. For the first time since records have been kept, there were more overseas visitors to the United States in 1980 than U.S. travelers overseas, according to the United States Travel Service. There were 22.6 million foreign arrivals and 21.6 million U.S. citizen departures. Travel spending abroad was down to $1.8 billion, reducing the U.S. travel balance of payments by 30 per cent.

Canada again provided the United States with the largest number of visitors, 10.5 million – down 6.8 per cent. Mexico was second with 2.7 million, down 1.6 per cent. The United States also welcomed 1.3 million visitors from Great Britain; 1.75 million from Japan; 705,000 from West Germany; and 400,000 from France. Australia sent 233,500; 490,000 came from Venezuela, and 128,000 came from Brazil.

Total world travel expenditures reached nearly $520 billion, including about $75 billion for international transportation. The continued drop in value of the U.S. dollar against several strong foreign currencies, lower prices for goods and services in the United States, and a relatively lower rate of inflation stimulated the upswing in foreign travel to the United States.

Air Profits Down. Strong volume growth but a continuing erosion of profits characterized the airline industry. Deregulation allowed carriers to introduce low promotional fares, based on the purchase of a round-trip ticket, of as little as $129 from New York City to California and $204 from New York City to London. These competitive fares reduced charter-flight volume by 2.5 million passengers. Conversely, passengers carried on scheduled airlines jumped by 16 per cent to 15.9 million.

The increase in passengers and revenue was not enough to compensate for skyrocketing costs, however. U.S. scheduled airlines lost nearly $200 million in 1980, and sharp fare increases were announced late in the year to partially offset operating costs. On average, domestic air fares rose 30 per cent during the year. See AVIATION.

Cruise Passengers in 1980 numbered about 1.25 million – up 1 per cent – providing a gross income of $2.8 billion. Passengers could choose trips ranging from weekends to "nowhere" to round-the-world cruises.

A major sea tragedy was narrowly averted in October when some 400 passengers, most of them elderly, were rescued from the Holland America luxury vessel the S.S. *Prinsendam*. The ship caught fire and burned in Alaskan waters while on a 30-day cruise to the Orient.

Automobile travel piled up about 1.5 billion miles (2.4 billion kilometers) in 1980. These figures include travel by private car, truck, and recreational vehicle.

The 1980 Olympic Winter Games were held at Lake Placid, N.Y., from February 12 to 24 and

Even China has private enterprise. For only $1.50 a sitting, a tourist can pose armed and in costume on a camel near China's Great Wall.

attracted more than 150,000 persons. A shortage of bus transportation forced thousands of ticketholders to wait in subzero temperatures for several hours during the early days of the games.

In retaliation for Russia's invasion of Afghanistan in December 1979, President Jimmy Carter imposed a U.S. boycott on the Moscow Summer Games. Only about 100,000 of an expected 300,000 foreign visitors journeyed to Moscow for the games.

Other Developments. Japan Air Lines (JAL) and Pan American World Airways (PanAm) announced new tour programs to China in January. PanAm scheduled 50 departures and JAL, 56. JAL was allocated 2,200 visas for the year, and PanAm was granted 5,000. Tours averaged 12 to 15 days in China, 3 in Tokyo, and 2 in Hong Kong. Cost per person ranged from $1,750 to $1,850.

The Subcommittee on Transportation and Commerce of the U.S. House of Representatives in September received a bill to implement a national U.S. tourism policy. The measure provides for a new corporation to replace the United States Travel Service. However, many important points, such as structure and funding, remained to be worked out between the House and the Senate, and no action had been taken as the 96th Congress adjourned in December. The first World Tourism Conference in 25 years was held in Manila, the

Philippines, in September under the auspices of the World Tourism Organization.

New Hotels. Two major U.S. hotel chains with international operations, Hilton and Intercontinental, opened new properties in 1980. Hilton opened establishments in Switzerland, Venezuela, and New York City's World Trade Center. Intercontinental opened hotels in the United Arab Emirates and Bahrain.

In the United States, the number of hotel and motel rooms remained at about 260,000. Interest in urban hotels was strong, however, and new ones were under construction in Houston, Boston, Dallas, and New York City. Two luxury hotels opened in New York City in September: the 1,400-room Grand Hyatt (formerly the Commodore) on September 1; and the 1,100-room Helmsley Palace on September 15. Room rates ranged from $120 per night to $1,600.

Two hotel fires spurred interest in fire-safety regulations for hotels and other commercial buildings. Fire in the MGM Grand Hotel in Las Vegas killed 84 persons on November 21, and a flash fire in Stouffer's Inn in White Plains, N.Y., killed 26 persons on December 4.   Lynn Beaumont

In WORLD BOOK, see TRANSPORTATION.

TRINIDAD AND TOBAGO. See LATIN AMERICA (Facts in Brief Table); WEST INDIES.

TRUCK AND TRUCKING. A major deregulation law enacted in 1980 eased entry into the trucking business and new trucking markets, and gave truckers more freedom to change freight rates. The industry had opposed substantial decontrol, preferring the regulatory shield from competition.

The recession and rising fuel prices hit many companies hard, and some went out of business. The American Trucking Associations, Incorporated (ATA), estimated that freight hauled declined about 18 per cent to 825 million short tons (750 million metric tons), but motor-carrier revenues rose 5 per cent to $43.3 billion. Earnings before special write-offs fell 9 per cent from the 1979 profit of $820 million, to $750 million. Many truck concerns began to write off the value of their operating-rights certificates, because deregulation's free-entry provisions would make them worthless. The ATA said in November that 1980 net income after write-offs might fall to $400-million.

Rate hikes helped prevent a further profit drop. The Interstate Commerce Commission (ICC) approved boosts of up to 7.2 per cent effective on April 1 and up to 4 per cent on October 1.

Deregulation Arrives. President Jimmy Carter signed the deregulation bill into law on July 1. The law made it easier for new firms to enter the

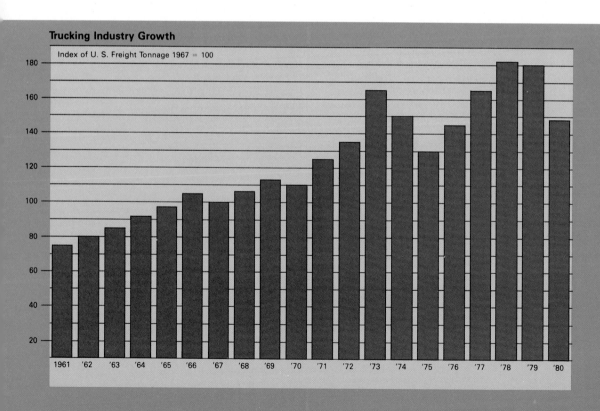

Trucking Industry Growth

Index of U. S. Freight Tonnage 1967 = 100

trucking business and for existing companies to expand. For example, it made it more difficult for existing firms to oppose new-service applications. The law also removed many route and commodity-hauling restrictions, relaxed food-hauling restrictions, and permitted truck companies to raise or lower rates by up to 20 per cent per year for two years.

The law trimmed the powers of regional rate-setting groups. Truckers will not be allowed to raise many rates jointly after Jan. 1, 1984.

Interim Deregulation Rules that could give way to permanent regulations later were issued by the ICC on July 2. They cut restrictions on the entry of new companies, accelerated the handling of operating-authority petitions, broadened the definition of commodity categories and geographic authority for which truckers can apply, eased conditions for trucking goods between corporate affiliates, and ended a ban on any truck company holding both common, or general, authority and authority to serve specific shippers under contract.

The ICC adopted rules that gave truck firms greater rate freedom on August 22, but said that it might restrict the activity of trucker regional rate-setting groups. The ATA said that some ICC moves went beyond the law. Albert R. Karr

See also TRANSPORTATION. In WORLD BOOK, see TRUCK.

TRUDEAU, PIERRE ELLIOTT (1919-   ), Canada's prime minister from 1968 to 1979, dramatically returned to power after the defeat of Prime Minister Charles Joseph (Joe) Clark's nine-month Progressive Conservative government in the general election on Feb. 18, 1980. Now 61 years old, Trudeau resumed office with an unchallenged position. The national election gave him a decisive majority in Parliament; his view of one Canada was upheld in the May 20 independence referendum in Quebec; and the danger of Quebec separatism seemed dispelled (see CANADA [Close-Up]). Thus, the events of 1980 gave Trudeau freedom to set his own priorities.

After failing to win agreement from the 10 provincial premiers on a revision of the constitution, Trudeau pressed ahead with changes that embodied his deepest convictions: Canada should have its own constitution, amendable in Canada rather than in Great Britain; it should ensure uniform language and civil rights in every region; and it should have a central government strong enough to pursue the country's general interest over the objectives of particular areas. In taking steps to secure these aims, Trudeau embarked on the greatest test of his career. Success would ensure his place in history as the architect of a more durable Canadian federalism. David M. L. Farr

In WORLD BOOK, see TRUDEAU, PIERRE E.

TUNISIA. Commandos of the Tunisian Resistance Army raided the southern oasis-town of Qafsah on Jan. 27, 1980, and threatened briefly to undermine the stability of President Habib Bourguiba's government. The 50 commandos, allegedly trained in Libya, entered Tunisia from Algeria. Tunisian army units assigned to protect Bourguiba, who was vacationing nearby, recaptured Qafsah after sharp fighting that left 44 Tunisians dead and more than 100 wounded. The anti-Bourguiba popular revolt expected by the raiders failed to materialize. In March, 59 persons were tried for the attack. In April, 13 commandos, among them Ezzedine Cherif, convicted as the leader of the rebel group, were executed for treason.

The Leadership Crisis was a major factor in the January raid. The crisis deepened in February when Prime Minister Hedi Nouira suffered a stroke. The 77-year-old Bourguiba, despite his age and ill health, resumed active control of the government. In April, he named Minister of Education Mohamed Mzali to succeed Nouira. This meant that Mzali, rather than the aging and infirm Nouira, would automatically become president in the event that President Bourguiba died or became incapacitated.

The new prime minister moved cautiously but firmly to restore public confidence in the ruling Destour Socialist Party government. He lifted suspensions of a number of former Cabinet ministers who had broken with Bourguiba in opposition to his authoritarianism. They included former Interior Minister Ahmad Mestiri and Defense Minister Hassib ben Ammar, founders of the opposition Movement for Socialist Democracy. The movement was permitted to solicit members openly and to publish two newspapers — in Arabic and French — with editorials critical of government policy. Two union members jailed since January 1978, when a one-day general strike by the General Union of Tunisian Workers flared into riots, were released from prison on August 1.

Economic Woes. The return of public confidence would come none too soon for Tunisia's hard-pressed economy. Inflation that included a 3 per cent increase in government-controlled basic food prices added to the general unrest. In May, the National Assembly approved emergency wage increases for all workers, with a 10 per cent increase in the minimum daily wage and the extension of pension and medical benefits to agricultural workers. Two bright spots in the bleak economic picture were an increase in olive oil production to 85,000 short tons (77,000 metric tons) and an agreement to sell Iran 100,000 short tons (90,000 metric tons) of Tunisian phosphates annually. William Spencer

See also AFRICA (Facts in Brief Table). In WORLD BOOK, see TUNISIA.

TUNNEL. See BUILDING AND CONSTRUCTION.

TURKEY. As they had done 20 years earlier under similar circumstances, Turkish military forces reluctantly seized power from a tottering, nearly paralyzed civil government in a bloodless coup on Sept. 12, 1980. About 100 persons were arrested, including Prime Minister Suleyman Demirel; his chief political opponent Bulend Ecevit; leaders of the Justice Party (JP) and Republican People's Party (RPP), the two major parties; minority party leaders; and officials and legislators. The Grand National Assembly, Turkey's parliament, was suspended.

A National Security Council headed by Chief of Staff General Kenan Evren as chairman was given overall government authority. An interim Cabinet of officers and technical experts headed by retired Admiral Bulend Ulusu was made responsible for day-to-day operations.

The Military Government acted swiftly to restore law and order and end the political violence that had claimed perhaps 2,000 victims in nine months. Striking workers were ordered back to work and awarded a 70 per cent bonus to meet their pay grievances. All bank assets were nationalized to forestall massive savings withdrawals.

The first death sentences for terrorism that had been imposed since 1972 were carried out in October, when four terrorists were executed.

A tank guards the approaches to a city square near Istanbul's famous Blue Mosque after the September military take-over in Turkey.

Demirel, Ecevit, and about 60 government officials were released on October 11.

The Civil Governments, both RPP and JP, had depended on minority-party support and could not solve Turkey's urgent economic problems or establish political consensus. In April, the political crisis prevented the appointment of a new president to succeed Fahri S. Koruturk when his seven-year term expired. The widespread violence, which claimed such prominent victims as former Prime Minister Nihat Erim, cast doubt on the Demirel government's ability to carry out the drastic reforms needed for financially beleaguered Turkey to qualify for large-scale foreign aid.

Some reforms were finally undertaken in June. The Turkish lira was devalued again. State subsidies for public-works projects were ended, and government credit spending was curbed. As a result, the European Community (Common Market) agreed to lend Turkey $852 million over a five-year period plus $106 million as a nonrefundable loan for technical aid. Major creditors agreed in July to reschedule $3 billion in foreign exchange debts over a 10-year period. The military government agreed to honor the commitments and announced a program for return to democratic rule, though it set no timetable. William Spencer

See also MIDDLE EAST (Facts in Brief Table). In WORLD BOOK, see TURKEY.

UGANDA. Apollo Milton Obote, who was overthrown as president by Idi Amin Dada in 1971, won the office for the second time on Dec. 13, 1980. Obote's government, installed on December 15, was the third to hold office in 1980. Rebel military leaders had overthrown the government of Godfrey L. Binaisa on May 11. Binaisa was installed as president in June 1979 by the Uganda National Liberation Front, a coalition of parties that assumed leadership in Uganda following the April 1979 overthrow of Amin's regime.

The May 1980 coup d'état was precipitated by Binaisa's dismissal of the army chief of staff, Brigadier General David Oyite Ojok, on May 10. Ojok refused to relinquish his command and become Uganda's ambassador to Algeria, and ordered his forces to take over government facilities and place Binaisa under house arrest.

State of the Nation. Paulo Muwanga, chairman of a six-member Military Commission, headed Uganda's government following the coup. His government faced serious economic and social problems. A spring drought in northern Uganda resulted in a severe famine, killing thousands. Production of coffee, Uganda's major export, was low, leaving the nation with little money to import oil and other essentials. The poor economy and a climate of general lawlessness remaining from the Amin regime produced high crime rates.

Tanzanian troops, stationed in Uganda to keep law and order and to ward off invasions from rebel forces, patrol the streets of Kampala.

Some 10,000 troops from neighboring Tanzania, stationed in Uganda to maintain law and order, helped to repel an October invasion by about 3,000 soldiers who had served in Amin's army.

The Elections. Muwanga's government pledged to hold elections on September 30, but postponed them until December so election authorities could complete voters' rolls and draw district boundaries. Four political parties ran candidates in the election – the Uganda People's Congress, led by Obote, Uganda's president from 1966 until 1971; the Democratic Party; the Uganda Patriotic Movement; and the new Conservative Party.

In mid-November, the Democratic Party and the Uganda Patriotic Movement threatened to boycott the elections, protesting that balloting and vote-counting procedures selected by Military Commission members – Obote's political allies – would favor Obote's party. However, the boycott was called off under an agreement to invite observers from Great Britain, Nigeria, and other countries to monitor the elections. Obote's party won 66 of 126 parliamentary seats.   J. Dixon Esseks

See also AFRICA (Facts in Brief Table). In WORLD BOOK, see UGANDA.

UNEMPLOYMENT. See ECONOMICS; LABOR.

UNION OF SOVIET SOCIALIST REPUBLICS (U.S.S.R.). See RUSSIA.

UNITED ARAB EMIRATES (UAE). See MIDDLE EAST.

UNITED NATIONS (UN) faced a series of crises in western Asia and the Middle East in 1980. The UN Security Council grappled with Russia's December 1979 invasion of Afghanistan; the holding of United States citizens as hostages in Iran since Nov. 4, 1979; open warfare between Iran and Iraq; and the continuing Arab-Israeli conflict.

Afghanistan's future was debated at a Security Council meeting that began on Jan. 5, 1980, at the request of 50 countries (see AFGHANISTAN [Close-Up]). Bangladesh, Jamaica, Niger, the Philippines, Tunisia, and Zambia introduced a resolution deploring "the recent armed intervention in Afghanistan" and calling for "the immediate and unconditional withdrawal of all foreign troops." Russia vetoed the resolution on January 7, and East Germany also voted against it.

Emergency Session. On January 9, Mexico and the Philippines pushed through by a 13-2 vote a resolution that called an emergency special session of the General Assembly, the sixth such session in UN history. A 1950 "Uniting for Peace" resolution permits nine Security Council members to call such a session when a veto prevents the Council from taking peace action. The session was held from January 10 through 14.

Afghan Foreign Minister Shah Mohammad Dost, the first speaker, termed the session "flagrant interference" in his country's internal affairs. He said that Afghanistan had invited a "limited" Russian military force to help foil "aggression from abroad." The next day, Russia's Ambassador Oleg A. Troyanovsky said that Afghan rebels were training in Pakistan. But Pakistan's Foreign Minister Agha Shahi denied this. He said there was an "entirely internal" uprising in Afghanistan against "massive military intervention . . . by a powerful neighbor."

The Assembly adopted a 24-nation resolution on January 14 deploring the intervention and calling for withdrawal of foreign troops. The vote was 104 to 18 with 18 abstentions and 12 nations absent.

At the request of 32 UN members, the Assembly debated the Afghanistan situation again from November 18 through 20 at its regular session. It adopted a 41-nation Third World resolution that called for "the immediate withdrawal of the foreign troops from Afghanistan." The vote was 111-22, with 12 abstentions.

U.S. Hostages. The Security Council on Dec. 31, 1979, called again on Iran to free the U.S. hostages. Russia, Czechoslovakia, Bangladesh, and Kuwait abstained from voting on the resolution, which also asked UN Secretary-General Kurt Waldheim to try to get the hostages out and to report his progress to the Council by January 7. Waldheim visited Iran from January 1 to 3. He reported that Iran would not release the hostages, but wanted an international commission to investi-

Iran's Prime Minister Mohammad Ali Rajai tells the Security Council
in October that his country has been the victim of Iraqi aggression.

gate human-rights violations under Shah Mohammad Reza Pahlavi, who left Iran in January 1979.

The United States proposed a Council resolution on January 11 that would have declared the
detention of the hostages a threat to international
peace and ordered UN members to stop trading
with Iran until that country freed the hostages.
Two days later, Russia vetoed the resolution. East
Germany also voted against it, Bangladesh and
Mexico abstained, and China did not participate.

Waldheim named a commission of inquiry on
February 20 to go to Iran, hear Iran's grievances,
and arrange for the hostages' release. The commission took testimony in Teheran that human rights
had been violated under the shah. But, contrary to
prior agreement, commission members were not
allowed to see the hostages. The commission had
no prospect that its report would lead to the
hostages' release, so it suspended its work on
March 10 and returned to New York City.

Iran and Iraq went to war after Iraq's September
17 cancellation of a 1975 agreement that fixed the
boundary between the two countries along the
Shatt al Arab River, which flows into the Persian
Gulf. Iraq claimed all of the Shatt al Arab.

On September 22, Waldheim appealed to both
countries to stop the fighting and offered to help
them begin negotiations. At Waldheim's request,
Tunisian Ambassador Taieb Slim, Security Coun-

cil president for the month, consulted the Council
privately on September 23 and issued a cease-fire
appeal on its behalf.

After a two-day debate requested by Mexico and
Norway, the Council on September 28 unanimously adopted a resolution written by Norway and
sponsored by Mexico that called on Iran and Iraq
"to refrain from any further use of force and to
settle their dispute by peaceful means," and asked
Waldheim to keep trying to resolve the situation.

Iraq's President Saddam Hussein and President
Abol Hasan Bani-Sadr of Iran then sent letters to
Waldheim that he forwarded to the Council. Hussein said on September 29 that Iraq would cease
fire and negotiate if Iran did. But Bani-Sadr wrote
on October 1 that Iran would consider no peace
appeal until Iraq stopped its "war of aggression."

Iraqi Foreign Minister Saadun Hamadi said at
an October 15 Security Council meeting that his
country wanted to protect "the economic interests
of other nations" and avoid foreign intervention in
the area. At a Council meeting arranged for him on
October 17, Iran's Prime Minister Mohammad Ali
Rajai predicted that "with the help of God" Iran
would win the war.

After more meetings and private talks, Great
Britain's Sir Anthony Parsons, Council president
for November, disclosed on November 5 that
Waldheim was considering sending a representa-

tive to seek peace negotiations between Iran and Iraq. Waldheim named Olof Palme, Swedish Socialist leader and former prime minister, for that mission on November 11. Palme conferred with Waldheim at UN headquarters in New York City on November 14, visited the two countries, reported to Waldheim on November 25, and told reporters the next day that Iran and Iraq would permit the safe departure under Red Cross flags of 70 merchant ships from various countries stranded in the Shatt al Arab. Palme said he planned to return to Iran and Iraq.

Palestine Question. Middle East debate in the Security Council caused trouble for U.S. Ambassador Donald F. McHenry as it had for his predecessor, Andrew J. Young, Jr. At the request of Jordan and Morocco, the Council debated a report by its commission on Israeli-occupied Arab territories at five meetings between February 22 and March 1. Meanwhile, delegates privately negotiated a resolution deploring Israel's establishment of Jewish settlements in those territories and calling for dismantling them. McHenry voted for the resolution, and the Council adopted it unanimously on March 1. But on March 3, President Jimmy Carter said that the United States should have abstained. He said the favorable U.S. vote had been approved on the understanding that all references to Jerusalem would be deleted, but the final resolution contained six references to Israeli-occupied Arab territories "including Jerusalem."

Carter blamed a "failure to communicate" for the United States affirmative vote. U.S. State Department spokesman Hodding Carter III said on March 4 that Secretary of State Cyrus R. Vance "accepts responsibility for this foul-up." The episode brought criticism from U.S. Jewish groups.

On April 18, Mexican Ambassador Porfirio Munoz Ledo, Security Council president for April, issued a statement authorized by the Council that condemned the "cold-blooded" murder of two Irish soldiers of the UN Interim Force in Lebanon (UNIFIL) in southern Lebanon that day. The statement blamed Lebanese Christian Major Saad Haddad's irregular troops, who are friendly to Israel, for the murders.

The United States joined in the condemnation, but abstained from voting on an April 24 resolution that condemned Israel's April 6 strike into southern Lebanon and Haddad's shelling of the UNIFIL on April 12. The resolution passed, 12-0. McHenry called the resolution unbalanced in not mentioning a Palestinian guerrilla raid from Lebanon that had killed a child in an Israeli nursery. Russia and East Germany also abstained, saying the resolution was not strong enough.

By request of Senegal as chairman of the UN Palestinian Rights Committee, the Council held seven meetings on the Palestinian question be-

Peace Form One and the New York City park it stands in were dedicated in September to Ralph J. Bunche, the late UN official.

tween March 31 and April 30. Finally, on a 10-1 vote – with France, Great Britain, Norway, and Portugal abstaining – the United States vetoed a Tunisian resolution saying Israel should withdraw from "all the territories occupied since 1967, including Jerusalem"; the Palestinians should be allowed to establish an independent state; and the independence of all states in the area should be guaranteed. McHenry said that the Council should not try to change the basis for Middle East peace set out in 1967 and 1973 resolutions that do not mention Jerusalem or the Palestinians.

The United States abstained on May 8 and 20 from voting on resolutions that called on Israel to permit the return of expelled West Bank Palestinian leaders and on a June 2 resolution censuring Israel for its failure to protect other Palestinian leaders who had been the targets of terrorist booby-traps. All three resolutions passed, 14-0.

Pakistan, as chairman of the Islamic group of nations, asked the Council to discuss Jerusalem at eight meetings between June 24 and 30. The Council adopted, on another 14-0 vote with a U.S. abstention, a 39-nation resolution declaring invalid all Israeli measures changing Jerusalem's status. The action was prompted by a bill pending in Israel's *Knesset* (parliament) that declared all of Jerusalem, including the former Jordanian part, to be Israel's capital. The Knesset passed the bill, and the Security Council demanded on August 20 that countries with embassies in Jerusalem withdraw them. All the nations that had embassies in Jerusalem then moved them to Tel Aviv-Yafo.

Falilou Kane of Senegal, chairman of the Palestinian Rights Committee, asked in a July 1 letter to Waldheim for an emergency special session of the General Assembly on Palestine. He based his request on the April 30 U.S. veto of a Palestinian rights resolution in the Security Council and cited the 1950 "Uniting for Peace" resolution. A majority of UN members endorsed the request on July 21, and the session started on July 22. On July 29, the Assembly adopted a resolution backed by 52 Third World and Communist nations that advocated a Palestinian state and called on Israel to start withdrawing from all occupied Arab territories by November 15 or risk Security Council sanctions. The vote was 112-7 with 24 abstentions. Israel, the United States, Australia, Canada, the Dominican Republic, Guatemala, and Norway voted "No." All nine nations of the European Community (Common Market) abstained. The Assembly adjourned on July 29.

The General Assembly held its 11th special session, on the world economy, from August 25 to September 15. The Assembly agreed on an international development strategy for the 1980s, but failed to schedule a negotiating conference that the Third World wanted to hold in 1981 because Western nations feared that such a conference would have too much power. The Assembly on August 25 admitted the 153rd UN member, Zimbabwe, the former British colony of Rhodesia.

On September 16, the Assembly opened its three-month 35th annual regular session and admitted the 154th UN member, the Caribbean islands of St. Vincent and the Grenadines, another former British colony. The Assembly elected West German Ambassador Rudiger von Wechmar president, adopted a 122-item agenda, and in three weeks of debate heard 145 countries.

By a vote of 74-35 with 32 abstentions, the Assembly on October 13 rejected a Russian-Vietnamese challenge to the credentials of the delegation from the Cambodian government of Pol Pot. The UN still recognized that government, though the rival Heng Samrin regime held the capital city of Phnom Penh with the help of Vietnamese troops. On October 22, the Assembly voted 97-23 with 22 abstentions for a resolution calling for a 1981 international conference to negotiate the withdrawal of foreign troops from Cambodia and conduct a UN-supervised election there. On December 16, the Assembly adopted a resolution calling for an independent Palestinian state under leadership of the Palestine Liberation Organization. William N. Oatis

In WORLD BOOK, see UNITED NATIONS.

UNITED STATES, GOVERNMENT OF THE. Americans shared a sense of frustration in 1980 as their government failed to solve pressing domestic and foreign problems. Economic problems worsened as the cost of living soared, unemployment increased, interest rates rose, and U.S. industry seemed unable to meet the challenge of foreign competition.

Diplomatic uncertainties added to the uneasiness. The American hostages remained captive in Iran despite attempts to free them. Russia's invasion of Afghanistan raised questions of U.S. military preparedness, and a flood of Cuban and Haitian refugees forced officials to redefine immigration policy. See IMMIGRATION; PRESIDENT OF THE UNITED STATES.

Nor did the 1980 elections stir the public imagination. With only 54 per cent of the electorate voting on November 4, the Republican landslide was hard to interpret. Some observers regarded it as an indication that Americans had moved considerably to the right. Others saw it as an expression of the public's frustration. In any event, the size of the Republican victory came as a surprise to pollsters and voters alike. See THE YEAR IN FOCUS.

The Executive Branch. Senator Edmund S. Muskie (D., Me.) was sworn in on May 8, replacing Cyrus R. Vance as secretary of state. Vance had resigned to protest the aborted U.S. rescue mission in Iran. The Department of Health, Education,

Federal Spending

Estimated U.S. Budget for Fiscal 1981*

	Billions of dollars
National defense	146.2
International affairs†	9.6
Science and space research	6.4
Natural resources, environment, energy	20.9
Agriculture	2.8
Commerce, transportation, housing credit	20.9
Community and regional development	8.8
Education, employment, social services	32.0
Health	62.4
Income security	220.0
Veterans benefits and services	21.7
Law enforcement and justice	4.7
General government	4.9
Revenue sharing and federal aid	9.6
Interest	67.2
Allowances	2.6
Undistributed funds	-25.1
Total	615.8

*Preliminary budget submitted by
President Jimmy Carter on Jan. 23, 1980,
subject to later revision

†Includes foreign aid

U.S. Income and Outlays

Billions of dollars

Revenue receipts
Total outlays

Fiscal Year: 1977, 1978, 1979, 1980 Est, 1981 Est

Source: U.S. Office of Management and Budget

and Welfare (HEW) split into two departments—the Department of Health and Human Services and the Department of Education—on May 4. Shirley M. Hufstedler became the first secretary of education, and HEW Secretary Patricia Roberts Harris became secretary of health and human services. See CABINET, UNITED STATES.

Other important administrative appointments included: Matt Garcia to replace Leonel J. Castillo as commissioner of the Immigration and Naturalization Service; Albert Carnesale as chairman of the Nuclear Regulatory Commission; and Deputy Secretary of Energy John C. Sawhill as chairman of the board of directors of the newly created Synthetic Fuels Corporation (see ENERGY).

President Carter on June 11 named Jack H. Watson to replace Hamilton Jordan as White House chief of staff, while Jordan worked on the President's re-election campaign. On July 16, the President, concerned about continuing leaks of information to the press, reportedly asked his senior aides for affidavits declaring they had not made unauthorized disclosures of classified information.

After the disclosure in August of a $220,000 loan made to the President's brother, Billy, by the Libyan government and the admission that top-ranking Administration officials were also involved in Billy Carter's Libyan activities, the President barred employees of the executive branch from financial dealings with members of his family. A special Senate subcommittee reported that though the President and Administration officials had shown bad judgment, there was no illegal or unethical conduct. See CARTER, JAMES EARL, JR.

The Military. The North American Air Defense Command was alerted twice in June by false reports that Russia had launched nuclear missiles against the United States. In both cases, the mistake, a computer error, was discovered within three minutes. The failure of the April 24 mission to rescue the hostages in Iran also cast doubt on military efficiency (see ARMED FORCES).

In light of reports that the all-volunteer Army was poorly prepared for combat, Carter's order to all men born in 1960 and 1961 to register for possible military service won widespread support. By September 4, about 3.6 million of an estimated 3.9 million men had registered.

A Titan nuclear missile silo near Damascus, Ark., exploded on September 19, killing one person and injuring 21. The explosion was attributed to a falling tool that punctured a fuel tank. The slightly damaged, but unexploded, nuclear warhead was flown to Texas, where it was disassembled.

Defense Secretary Harold Brown revealed on August 20 "a major technological advance" in U.S. defenses—a "stealth" plane capable of evading radar detection.

Major Agencies and Bureaus of the U.S. Government*

Executive Office of the President
President, Jimmy Carter

Vice-President, Walter F. Mondale
White House Chief of Staff, Jack H. Watson, Jr.
Presidential Press Secretary, Jody Powell
Central Intelligence Agency–Stansfield Turner, Director
Council of Economic Advisers–Charles L. Schultze, Chairman
Council on Environmental Quality–Gus Speth, Chairman
Council on Wage and Price Stability–R. Robert Russell, Director
Domestic Policy Staff–Stuart E. Eizenstat, Executive Director
Office of Management and Budget–James T. McIntyre, Jr., Director
Office of Science and Technology Policy–Frank Press, Director

The Supreme Court of the United States
Chief Justice of the United States, Warren E. Burger

Associate Justices:

William J. Brennan, Jr.	Harry A. Blackmun
Potter Stewart	Lewis F. Powell, Jr.
Byron R. White	William H. Rehnquist
Thurgood Marshall	John Paul Stevens

State Department
Secretary of State, Edmund S. Muskie

U.S. Representative to the United Nations–Donald F. McHenry

Department of the Treasury
Secretary of the Treasury, G. William Miller

Bureau of Alcohol, Tobacco, and Firearms–G. R. Dickerson, Director
Bureau of Engraving and Printing–Harry R. Clements, Director
Bureau of the Mint Stella B. Hackel, Director
Comptroller of the Currency–John G. Heimann
Internal Revenue Service–(vacant)
Treasurer of the United States–Azie T. Morton
U.S. Customs Service–Robert E. Chasen, Commissioner
U.S. Secret Service–H. Stuart Knight, Director

Department of Defense
Secretary of Defense, Harold Brown

Joint Chiefs of Staff–General David C. Jones, Chairman
Secretary of the Air Force–Hans Mark
Secretary of the Army–Clifford L. Alexander, Jr.
Secretary of the Navy–Edward Hidalgo

Department of Justice
Attorney General, Benjamin R. Civiletti

Bureau of Prisons–Norman A. Carlson, Director
Drug Enforcement Administration–Peter Bensinger, Administrator
Federal Bureau of Investigation–William H. Webster, Director
Immigration and Naturalization Service–Matt Garcia, Commissioner
Office of Justice Assistance, Research, and Statistics–Henry S. Dogin, Director
Solicitor General–Wade H. McCree, Jr.

Department of the Interior
Secretary of the Interior, Cecil D. Andrus

Bureau of Indian Affairs–William E. Hallett, Commissioner
Bureau of Land Management–Frank Gregg, Director
Bureau of Mines–Lindsay D. Norman, Director
Geological Survey–H. William Menard, Director
National Park Service–Russell E. Dickenson, Director
Office of Territorial Affairs–Ruth Van Cleve, Director
U.S. Fish and Wildlife Service–Lynn A. Greenwalt, Director
Water and Power Resources Service–R. Keith Higginson, Commissioner

Department of Agriculture
Secretary of Agriculture, Bob Bergland

Agricultural Economics–Howard W. Hjort, Director
Agricultural Marketing Service–Barbara Lindemann Schlei, Administrator
Agricultural Stabilization and Conservation Service–Ray V. Fitzgerald, Administrator
Farmers Home Administration–Gordon Cavanaugh, Administrator
Federal Crop Insurance Corporation–James D. Deal, Manager
Food and Consumer Services–Carol Tucker Foreman, Administrator
Forest Service–R. Max Peterson, Chief
Rural Electrification Administration–Robert W. Feragen, Administrator

Science and Education Administration–Anson R. Bertrand, Director
Soil Conservation Service–Norman A. Berg, Chief

Department of Commerce
Secretary of Commerce, Philip M. Klutznick

Bureau of the Census–Vincent P. Barabba, Director
Economic Development Administration–Robert T. Hall, Administrator
National Bureau of Standards–Ernest Ambler, Director
National Oceanic and Atmospheric Administration–Richard A. Frank, Administrator
Minority Business Development Agency–Daniel P. Henson III, Director
Patent and Trademark Office–Sidney A. Diamond, Commissioner

Department of Labor
Secretary of Labor, Ray Marshall

Bureau of Labor Statistics–Janet L. Norwood, Commissioner
Employment and Training Administration–Ernest G. Green, Administrator
Employment Standards Administration–Donald E. Elisburg, Administrator
Labor-Management Services Administration–William P. Hobgood, Administrator
Mine Safety and Health Administration–Robert B. Lagather, Administrator
Occupational Safety and Health Administration–Eula Bingham, Administrator
Women's Bureau–Alexis M. Herman, Director

Department of Health and Human Services
Secretary of Health and Human Services, Patricia Roberts Harris

Administration for Children, Youth and Families–John A. Calhoun, Commissioner
Administration on Aging–Robert C. Benedict, Commissioner
Alcohol, Drug Abuse, and Mental Health Administration–Gerald L. Klerman, Administrator
Centers for Disease Control–William H. Foege, Director
Food and Drug Administration–Jere E. Goyan, Commissioner
Health Care Financing Administration–Leonard D. Schaeffer, Administrator
Health Resources Administration–Henry A. Foley, Administrator
Health Services Administration–George Lythcott, Administrator
National Institutes of Health–Donald S. Fredrickson, Director
Office of Consumer Affairs–Esther Peterson, Director
Public Health Service–Julius B. Richmond, Administrator
Social Security Administration–William J. Driver, Commissioner

Department of Housing and Urban Development
Secretary of Housing and Urban Development, Moon Landrieu

Community Planning and Development–Robert C. Embry, Administrator
Federal Housing Commissioner–Lawrence B. Simons
Government National Mortgage Association–Ronald P. Laurent, President
New Community Development Corporation–A. Russell Marane, General Manager

Department of Transportation
Secretary of Transportation, Neil Goldschmidt

Federal Aviation Administration–Langhorne M. Bond, Administrator
Federal Highway Administration–John S. Hassell, Jr., Administrator
Federal Railroad Administration–John M. Sullivan, Administrator
National Highway Traffic Safety Administration–Joan B. Claybrook, Administrator
U.S. Coast Guard–Admiral John B. Hayes, Commandant
Urban Mass Transportation Administration–Theodore C. Lutz, Administrator

Department of Energy
Secretary of Energy, Charles W. Duncan, Jr.

Economic Regulatory Administration–Hazel R. Rollins, Administrator
Energy Information Administration–Lincoln E. Moses, Administrator
Federal Energy Regulatory Commission–(vacant)
Office of Energy Research–Edward A. Frieman, Director

Department of Education
Secretary of Education, Shirley M. Hufstedler
  National Institute of Education–P. Michael Timpane, Director

Congressional Officials
President of the Senate pro tempore–Warren G. Magnuson
  Speaker of the House–Thomas P. O'Neill, Jr.
  Architect of the Capitol–George M. White
  Comptroller General of the U.S.–Elmer B. Staats
  Congressional Budget Office–Alice M. Rivlin, Director
  Librarian of Congress–Daniel J. Boorstin
  Office of Technology Assessment–John H. Gibbons, Director
  Public Printer of the U.S.–Gerald R. Dillon†

Independent Agencies
  ACTION–Sam Brown, Director
  Civil Aeronautics Board–Marvin S. Cohen, Chairman
  Commodity Futures Trading Commission–James M. Stone, Chairman
  Community Services Administration–Richard John Rios, Director
  Consumer Product Safety Commission–Susan B. King, Chairman
  Environmental Protection Agency–Douglas M. Costle, Administrator
  Equal Employment Opportunity Commission–Eleanor Holmes Norton, Chair
  Export-Import Bank–John L. Moore, President
  Farm Credit Administration–Donald E. Wilkinson, Governor
  Federal Communications Commission–Charles D. Ferris, Chairman
  Federal Deposit Insurance Corporation–Irvine Sprague, Chairman
  Federal Election Commission–John W. McGarry, Chairman
  Federal Emergency Management Agency–John W. Macy, Jr., Director
  Federal Home Loan Bank Board–(vacant)
  Federal Maritime Commission–Richard J. Daschbach, Chairman
  Federal Mediation and Conciliation Service–Wayne L. Horvitz, Director
  Federal Reserve System–Paul A. Volcker, Board of Governors Chairman
  Federal Trade Commission–Michael Pertschuk, Chairman
  General Services Administration–Rowland G. Freeman III, Administrator
  International Communication Agency–John E. Reinhardt, Director
  Interstate Commerce Commission–Darius Gaskins, Jr., Chairman
  National Aeronautics and Space Administration–Robert A. Frosch, Administrator
  National Credit Union Administration–Lawrence Connell, Chairman
  National Endowment for the Arts–Livingston L. Biddle, Jr., Chairman
  National Endowment for the Humanities–Joseph D. Duffey, Chairman
  National Labor Relations Board–John H. Fanning, Chairman
  National Mediation Board–Robert O. Harris, Chairman
  National Railroad Passenger Corporation (AMTRAK)–Alan S. Boyd, President
  National Science Foundation–John Brooks Slaughter, Director
  National Transportation Safety Board–James B. King, Chairman
  Nuclear Regulatory Commission–Albert Carnesale†, Chairman
  Occupational Safety and Health Review Commission–Timothy F. Cleary, Chairman
  Office of Personnel Management–(vacant)
  Panama Canal Commission–Dennis P. McAuliffe, Administrator
  Securities and Exchange Commission–Harold M. Williams, Chairman
  Small Business Administration–A. Vernon Weaver, Jr., Administrator
  Smithsonian Institution–S. Dillon Ripley, Secretary
  Synthetic Fuels Corporation–John C. Sawhill†, Chairman
  Tennessee Valley Authority–S. David Freeman, Chairman
  U.S. Arms Control and Disarmament Agency–Ralph Earle II, Director
  U.S. Commission on Civil Rights–Arthur S. Flemming, Chairman
  U.S. International Development Cooperation Agency–Thomas Ehrlich, Director
  U.S. International Trade Commission–Bill Alberger, Chairman
  U.S. Metric Board–Louis F. Polk, Chairman
  U.S. Postal Service–William F. Bolger, Postmaster General
  Veterans Administration–Max Cleland, Administrator

*As of Jan. 1, 1981. † nominated but not yet confirmed.

Abscam was the code name for an investigation in which a Federal Bureau of Investigation (FBI) agent posed as a wealthy Arab "willing to pay American officials well" for special favors. Videotaped evidence was used to gain indictments against several congressmen and state and local officials. At year-end, some had been convicted of bribery and lesser charges and others were being tried, or awaiting trial.

Census. In 1980, the U.S. Bureau of the Census sent out 180 million forms and employed 300,000 workers to find out how many people were living in the United States and where they were located (see CENSUS). Because congressional representation and the allotment of federal funds are based on population figures, the preliminary results, which showed many of the older cities losing population, were challenged. In one such challenge, a U.S. district court in Detroit ruled on September 25 that the 1980 census had undercounted blacks and Hispanic Americans. The ruling, extended to apply to other cities, was appealed on October 3 by Census Bureau Director Vincent P. Barabba.

Census figures released on December 31 showed that there were some 226.5 million persons living in the United States. They also showed that a population shift to the South and West will result in the reallocation of 17 congressional seats.

The Legislative Branch of the U.S. government clashed repeatedly with the Administration in 1980, though both houses were controlled by the President's own Democratic Party. Because it could not agree on government spending, Congress did not adopt a final budget for fiscal 1981 in its regular session. Instead it relied on a series of "continuing resolutions" to allow federal agencies to operate at their 1980 rate of spending. The lame duck session that reconvened on November 12 approved a final budget of $632.4 billion on November 20.

Congress approved several major sections of the President's energy program, including a windfall oil profit tax; the establishment of a Synthetic Fuels Corporation; and the establishment of a National Center for Fusion Engineering. But in June, Congress overrode President Carter's veto of a bill to repeal his proposed fee on imported oil.

Two acts passed in 1980 deregulated sectors of the nation's transportation industry. One law gave the railroads rate-fixing flexibility, and the other eliminated some "senseless overregulation" of interstate trucking. Another law allowed savings banks to raise their interest rates.

In other action, Congress reinstated Selective Service registration; established wilderness areas in Idaho and Alaska; expanded Department of Housing and Urban Development programs; funded college-student loans and grants; appropriated funds to expand public school programs; prohibit-

519

ed surprise searches of newsrooms and the offices of authors and scholars; appropriated $1.6 billion for toxic-waste cleanup; agreed to $8.3 billion in spending cuts and revenue-raising measures; and appropriated $9.8 billion for the departments of State, Commerce, and Justice. See CONGRESS OF THE UNITED STATES.

The Supreme Court handed down still another ruling on the controversial abortion issue. On June 30, it ruled 5 to 4 that the so-called Hyde amendment was constitutional and that states and the federal government may refuse to fund abortions for women on welfare.

The court, in other major decisions, ruled that the press and the public have a constitutional right of access to civil and criminal trials; that patent protection may be extended into the field of genetic engineering; that police must obtain a warrant to enter a suspect's home to make an arrest; and that a Kentucky law requiring the posting of the Ten Commandments in every public school classroom in the state was unconstitutional. See CIVIL RIGHTS; SUPREME COURT OF THE UNITED STATES.   Carol L. Thompson

In WORLD BOOK, see UNITED STATES, GOVERNMENT OF THE.

UNITED STATES CONSTITUTION. See CONSTITUTION OF THE UNITED STATES.

UPPER VOLTA. See AFRICA.

URUGUAY. On June 10, 1980, the military regime that had seized power and dissolved parliament in 1973, announced it had drawn up a new constitution as part of a gradual return to elective government. In a referendum held November 30, however, the voters overwhelmingly rejected it, thereby extending indefinitely direct military rule.

There was increasing political unrest in Uruguay, whose high standard of living as well as its public education and welfare systems make it the envy of most other Latin American countries. In July, the government somewhat eased the ban on political activity that had existed since 1973.

Jorge Battle, who heads the most important faction in one of Uruguay's two major political parties, called upon the government in July to allow political parties to function openly. Battle, a respected leader and the son of a former president, was promptly detained along with three of his colleagues. All were later released.

Pressures mounted for easing government controls. In one widely circulated report, a defector from the nation's intelligence service alleged that he had taken part in training sessions on the techniques of torture. Exiled Uruguayans living in New York City formed a committee to press for the restoration of democracy. In a countermove to improve its image, the government allowed the International Red Cross to visit political prisoners

in the nation's prisons for the first time in four years.

The Economy benefited from the efforts of neighboring Brazil and Argentina to build hydroelectric plants and other projects in the large Río de la Plata Basin. Uruguay joined with Argentina to develop a hydroelectric power plant. São Paulo in Brazil and Buenos Aires in Argentina continued to absorb young Uruguayans whose education had prepared them for higher-paying jobs in these industrial areas than they could get in Uruguay.

Agricultural production, which accounts for 75 per cent of the nation's export earnings, was good. Earnings from agriculture, which employs 20 per cent of the nation's work force, have a strong effect on the nation's economy.

Owing to a favorable currency-exchange rate, Argentine tourists flocked to Uruguay looking for bargains in consumer goods and real estate. They had invested an estimated $500 million in property around the famed seaside resort of Punta del Este over the past four years.   Nathan A. Haverstock

See also LATIN AMERICA (Facts in Brief Table). In WORLD BOOK, see URUGUAY.

UTAH. See STATE GOVERNMENT.

UTILITIES. See COMMUNICATIONS; ENERGY; PETROLEUM AND GAS.

VANUATU. See PACIFIC ISLANDS.

VENDA. See AFRICA.

VENEZUELA. The administration of President Luis Herrera Campins faced problems in 1980 as it attempted to curb the rampant inflation caused by high oil earnings and to uproot corruption in the overgrown bureaucracy. Public works projects undertaken by the previous administration languished, including programs to boost production in such key industries as steel and aluminum. The Herrera government's efforts to cope with deteriorating public services, an upsurge in crime, and various complaints in overcrowded Caracas and other major cities had little or no impact.

Traffic congestion and pollution in Caracas were both annoyingly frequent and potentially dangerous. The construction of a subway system to relieve the congestion slowed. Bureaucratic apathy apparently affected everything, including the Central Office of Statistics and Information, where delays made it necessary to postpone for a year a national census scheduled for 1980.

Meanwhile, great public and government attention went to finding scapegoats, with the focus directed at the previous administration – the Democratic Action Party. There was vitriolic public debate over a scandal involving the *Sierra Nevada*, a refrigerated freighter bought in 1977 by the government for $20 million. The money was paid to a Swiss company, which then paid the Norwegian owners their original asking price of only $11.9-

Venezuelan President Luis Herrera Campins
waves to crowds in Caracas as he walks to
Congress to deliver his annual message.

VIETNAM failed in 1980 to fulfill the goals of its 1976-1980 economic development plan. Major reasons were the strain of maintaining control over Cambodia and Laos, where occupying Vietnamese troops met guerrilla resistance, and facing the armed hostility of the People's Republic of China. Domestic failures increased Vietnam's dependency on Russia, which – according to some estimates – provided between $2 million and $3.5 million per day in aid. This dependency worsened relations with China.

Le Duan, leader of Vietnam's Communist Party, was increasingly praised amid signs that a new constitution under consideration would add governmental powers to his party leadership. He told a Communist Party meeting on February 2 that many party members were unqualified for their jobs and others "are guilty of misappropriation, bribery, maltreatment of the masses, and other grave offenses." The National Assembly announced in December that it had approved a new collective form for the nation's presidency, and the party was expected to play a major role in this. In a speech on September 2, Prime Minister Pham Van Dong said the government had failed to satisfy public needs.

Corruption Increased as official machinery was unable to cope with economic hardships. In a work

million. The whereabouts of the other $8.1 million became the subject of heated congressional debate. On May 8, the National Congress censured former President Carlos Andres Perez for the overpayment, which, it said, had been distributed to corrupt officials during his tenure. President Herrera Campins charged that the scandal typified the wastefulness and mismanagement of the previous regime.

The government, in looking for scapegoats, resurrected back-tax claims against 50 foreign oil corporations. In a moralistic pronouncement, it acted to eliminate violence, triviality, and unbridled consumerism on television. It also banned alcohol and cigarette advertising, presumably because all were contributing to laxity in public morals.

In midyear, the administration announced that it would try to register illegal aliens, many of whom had been drawn to the oil-rich country by the lure of higher-paying jobs. The influx into Caracas, it implied, had heavily contributed to problems of unplanned growth.   Nathan A. Haverstock

See also LATIN AMERICA (Facts in Brief Table). In WORLD BOOK, see VENEZUELA.

VERMONT. See STATE GOVERNMENT.

VETERANS. See COMMUNITY ORGANIZATIONS.

VICE-PRESIDENT OF THE UNITED STATES. See MONDALE, WALTER FREDERICK.

Vietnam's Prime Minister Pham Van Dong, right, greets UN Secretary-General Kurt Waldheim, in Asia for Thailand-Cambodia border talks.

force of 23 million, an estimated 3 million were unemployed. Also, food rations were lower than during the Vietnam War, and shortages were widespread. Food production was down, in part because the third devastating hurricane in three years damaged crops in August.

Russian Naval and air units made greater use of Vietnam's Cam Ranh Bay. Pham Tuan, a lieutenant colonel in Vietnam's air force, became Asia's first space traveler with a trip in July on board Russia's *Soyuz 37* spacecraft with a Soviet cosmonaut. They visited the *Salyut 6* space station.

Vo Nguyen Giap, who is credited with Vietnamese defeats of France and the United States, gave up the post of defense minister on February 7 to his deputy, General Van Tien Dung. Pham Hung, who commanded Communist forces in South Vietnam during the war, became the interior minister.

Talks with China, intended to make peace after their 1979 war, broke down. Border clashes continued, intensifying in July. So did the flight of "boat people" refugees. Since the Vietnam War ended in 1975, more than 600,000 persons had fled the country.   Henry S. Bradsher

See also ASIA (Facts in Brief Table); CAMBODIA; THAILAND. In WORLD BOOK, see INDOCHINA; VIETNAM.

VIRGINIA. See STATE GOVERNMENT.

VISUAL ARTS. Both large and small art museums in the United States continued hectic exhibition schedules and hopeful expansion plans in 1980. Trustees of the new Museum of Modern Art in Los Angeles gave the museum $2 million toward its $10-million endowment fund. The Ahmanson Foundation gave the Los Angeles County Museum of Art $4.5 million to fund additional gallery construction.

A great deal more money was promised by voters in Dallas, who established $24.8 million as the public share of their new $40-million museum building. The Daniel J. Terra Museum of American Art, named for its founder, opened in Evanston, Ill., in May after Terra donated a building and 70 pieces of art from the late 19th and early 20th centuries.

In the East, the International Museum of Photography at the George Eastman House in Rochester, N.Y., began its first nationwide funding drive, in order to enlarge its quarters. And in Pittsburgh, Pa., the Carnegie Institute received $4 million from the Mellon Foundation, which also gave $5-million to the National Gallery of Art in Washington, D. C.

"Superexhibitions" continued to draw crowds. An important example of such shows in 1980 was a compendium of early Norse art and artifacts called

The largest collection of Pablo Picasso's work ever assembled was in New York City in 1980. Here the artist's widow, Jacqueline, views *Guernica*.

"The Vikings," the largest such display ever mounted, which the Metropolitan Museum conducted from October through December in conjunction with the British Museum. Other major archaeological shows included "The Great Bronze Age of China," which toured the U.S. It was the first instance of scholarly interaction between researchers and museum personnel in the United States and the People's Republic of China. "The Search for Alexander," at the National Gallery of Art, presented sculpture and metalwork from the 300s B.C., borrowed from Greek museums.

Anniversaries. One of the premier "jewel-box" museums in the United States, the Clark Art Institute in Williamstown, Mass., celebrated its 25th anniversary in 1980. The Whitney Museum of American Art in New York City celebrated its 50th anniversary by mounting several important exhibitions. These included the first retrospective display of the paintings of American artist Marsden Hartley, and the large show "Edward Hopper: The Art and the Artist."

Visitors waited hours in line for a chance to view "Picasso: A Retrospective" at New York City's Museum of Modern Art from May 22 through September 16. Almost 1,000 works in every medium used by the prolific Spanish painter filled the museum.

Midwestern Museums organized shows of great interest. The Cleveland Museum of Art presented a major reassessment of a neglected style in "The Realist Tradition: French Painting and Drawing, 1830-1900." The museum combined its holdings with those of the Nelson Gallery-Atkins Museum in Kansas City, Mo., to produce "Eight Dynasties of Chinese Painting," the most comprehensive such exhibition ever seen in the U.S. The Detroit Institute of Arts offered both "Treasures of Ancient Nigeria," the largest art loan to the United States from an African nation, and "Gods, Saints, and Heroes: Dutch Painting in the Age of Rembrandt," which opened at the National Gallery of Art.

University Art Museums organized such fine exhibitions as "The Meiji Era: Arts of Imperial Japan," at the Johnson Museum of Art of Cornell University in Ithaca, N.Y. The 100th anniversary of the birth of German painter Franz Marc was noted with the first large U.S. exhibition of his work at the University of California's Berkeley Art Museum.

German Art was seen also at New York City's Guggenheim Museum, where a huge exhibition, organized jointly with the San Francisco Museum of Modern Art, was titled "Expressionism – A German Intuition, 1905-1920." The Minneapolis (Minn.) Institute of Arts presented "German Realism of the 20's: The Artist as Social Critic."

Politics impinged upon the art world in Minneapolis, also. The city's Institute of Arts had

An 800-year-old bronze horse from Venice, Italy, gazes at a visitor to the Metropolitan Museum of Art in New York City in February.

planned a large exhibition from Russia, "Art from the Hermitage Museum in Leningrad." Because of the Soviet invasion of Afghanistan, the U.S. Department of State refused to issue the customary "waiver of judicial seizure" that exempts Russian state-owned works from seizure by United States courts, and Soviet authorities refused to lend the works. The entire exhibition was funded by a business corporation, as occurs frequently, and the show's cancellation caused Control Data Corporation, a Minneapolis computer firm, to sue the U.S. government for $1 million indemnification for its losses.

Outdoor Sculpture, which has been considered for at least 20 years to be a necessary accessory for any urban plaza in the United States, was recognized in an exhibition at the National Collection of Fine Arts in Washington, D.C. A group of 95 models represented the 205 works commissioned by the General Services Administration since the start of the Art-in-Architecture program in 1962. Since then, the National Endowment for the Arts has commissioned 300 other sculptures through matching-grant programs, and countless more have been produced across the country through corporate and private support.

Auctions and Other Sales of art works continued to bring incredible prices. Although prices at private sales are usually kept secret, it was revealed that the Whitney Museum paid $1 million for *Three Flags,* a 1958 painting by the American painter Jasper Johns. This was the highest price ever paid for a work by a living artist.

Great Britain's National Gallery in London reportedly paid about $5 million in November for a 16th-century German painting, *Christ Taking Leave of His Mother,* by Albrecht Altdorfer. Although the National Gallery would not reveal the price, it was less than the record set in May, when an Argentine buyer paid $6.4 million for *Juliet and Her Nurse* by the British painter J. M. W. Turner.

Other expensive museum purchases – but not necessarily the most interesting works bought by art museums – included *Peasant in a Blue Blouse,* which set the record for works by French painter Paul Cézanne when the Kimbell Art Museum in Fort Worth, Tex., bought it for $3.9 million, and *The Resurrection of Christ,* a 15th-century painting by Flemish artist Dierick Bouts, for which the Norton Simon Museum in Pasadena, Calif., paid $3.7-million. As the works of great artists become scarcer, record prices will continue to be set. The National Gallery in London, using a $7-million government grant for the purchase of art work, bought *Samson and Delilah,* a 1610 painting by Flemish artist Peter Paul Rubens, for $5.4 million. The highest price ever paid for a work by Pablo Picasso was the $3 million given by the Bridgestone Museum in Tokyo, Japan, for the 1923 *Saltimbanque [Acrobat] Seated with Arms Crossed.* The record price for folk art was $270,000 paid for American painter Edward Hicks's *Peaceable Kingdom,* a Quaker preacher's gift to his congregation from the early 1800s. On December 12, industrialist Armand Hammer paid $5.1 million at auction for a Leonardo da Vinci notebook.

Art Activities Elsewhere included the Art Institute of Chicago's loan of 40 of its finest late 19th-century paintings to the Albi Museum in France. This reciprocated the precedent-setting loan of 40 works by Henri de Toulouse-Lautrec from the French museum to the Art Institute, for its 100th anniversary celebration in 1979.

The United States International Communication Agency, together with the National Endowment for the Arts and the National Endowment for the Humanities, chose a 12-member advisory panel on the visual arts. The group will choose six exhibitions to travel abroad under U.S. government sponsorship. A typical example was the exhibition "Video Art," from the Long Beach (Calif.) Museum of Art, which was seen at the Paris Biennale. Joshua B. Kind

In WORLD BOOK, see ART AND THE ARTS; PAINTING; SCULPTURE.

VITAL STATISTICS. See CENSUS; POPULATION.
WALES. See GREAT BRITAIN.
WASHINGTON. See STATE GOVERNMENT.

WASHINGTON, D.C., voters approved, by a 3-2 margin, a referendum on Nov. 4, 1980, calling for the nation's capital to become the 51st state. The proposal would limit the federal district to a small area surrounding the mall, the Capitol, and the White House, with the remainder of the district becoming the state of Columbia.

Statehood was seen as an alternative to the proposed constitutional amendment that would give the District of Columbia voting representation in the Congress of the United States. The amendment, passed by Congress in 1978, appeared to have little chance of ratification by the required number of states. See CONSTITUTION OF THE UNITED STATES.

To gain statehood, voters must elect delegates to draft a constitution and elect two senators and one representative who must then present a statehood bill to Congress. Both houses of Congress must approve the bill by a simple majority, and it must be signed by the President.

Fiscal Crisis. The statehood movement was designed to free the city from federal control, specifically from Congress' right to approve the city budget. Washington Mayor Marion S. Barry, Jr., reported on July 21 that $179 million of the city's $409-million deficit had accumulated before 1975, when Congress had exclusive control over the city's

Construction begins on the $99-million Washington Convention Center – the first major building to be erected in an area damaged by riots in 1968.

finances. Barry attributed the debt to a $125-million deficit in fiscal 1980 and a previously hidden deficit of $284 million.

He proposed a three-part program to pay off the deficit – the sale of $215 million in bonds to the Federal Financing Bank, an agency that holds the securities of government-operated enterprises; cutting 2,100 city jobs; and grants from Congress.

Barry planned to ask Congress to make some payment in lieu of the $550 million it saves annually on untaxed federal real estate, to pay off the $179-million in debts accrued while Congress controlled the district, and to appropriate funds to support the city's pension plans. Congress enacted the pension plans in the early 1900s but never provided funding for them.

Metro Funding. President Jimmy Carter on January 3 signed into law a bill authorizing $1.7 billion to complete the remaining 41 miles (66 kilometers) of the Metro subway system. The bill required Virginia, Maryland, and the District of Columbia to share the system's operating expenses. Maryland announced on February 27 that it would pay its Metro obligation from surplus state funds, and Virginia established a gasoline tax on July 1 for that purpose. The district planned to provide its share through sales taxes.   James M. Banovetz

See also CITY. In WORLD BOOK, see WASHINGTON, D.C.

Irrigation canals on large California farms may continue to carry federally subsidized water, the Supreme Court ruled in June.

WATER. A searing drought in July and August 1980 withered farmland from Canada to Mexico and reduced harvests of most major food and feed crops in the United States. Record heat waves accentuated the problem. The United States Department of Commerce reported on October 20 that the heat wave and drought took at least 1,265 lives and cost the United States nearly $20 billion.

Texas and Arkansas were the hardest-hit states. A severe drop in the water table in those states and in Oklahoma threatened industrial development and forced farmers to dry-farm acreage that they ordinarily irrigated.

Higher Limit. The U.S. House of Representatives Interior Committee on June 19 reported out legislation that would modify the acreage limitations of the Reclamation Act of 1902. The bill placed a 2,400-acre (970-hectare) limit on the amount of land a farmer could irrigate with water from federal irrigation projects. The 1902 act helped settle the West by authorizing the federal government to build irrigation projects subsidized by taxpayers and sell the irrigation water to settlers at bargain rates. It entitled one person to buy cheap water to irrigate 160 acres (65 hectares) and a man and wife to buy cheap water to irrigate 320 acres (130 hectares).

A federal district court judge had ruled in 1977 that the secretary of the interior must enforce the 160-acre limitation. But Western farmers argued that the limitation did not reflect modern farming practices, so the Senate rewrote the 1902 law in 1979 to increase the limit for receiving water subsidies to 1,280 acres (520 hectares) per family.

Secretary of the Interior Cecil D. Andrus urged on May 30 that "Congress act boldly to reconfirm the value of the family farm." He contended that 97 per cent of all farms in federal reclamation districts were smaller than the 960-acre (390-hectare) limit supported by President Jimmy Carter's Administration. The Interior Department was restrained from enforcing the 1902 law until it completed an environmental study, but enforcement was expected to begin in 1981 unless Congress amended the law.

Exemption. The Supreme Court of the United States ruled unanimously on June 16 that farms in California's Imperial Valley are not subject to the 160-acre limitation. The ruling cleared the way for continued federally subsidized irrigation of 424,000 acres (172,000 hectares) of farmland that produce an estimated $500 million in crops each year. About 233,000 acres (94,000 hectares) of Imperial Valley land are held by large landowners.

More Projects. President Jimmy Carter signed legislation on October 1 providing $12 billion for water projects, including several he had attempted to kill in 1977. Among them were the Orme Dam

A weather satellite photo clearly shows the size and intensity of Hurricane Allen, which struck the Gulf of Mexico area in August.

in Arizona, the Yatesville Dam in Kentucky, and the Columbia Dam in Tennessee, which received total appropriations of $650 million. Also included were $212 million for the controversial Tennessee-Tombigbee waterway in Mississippi and Alabama and $795 million for the proposed Dickey-Lincoln hydroelectric dam in Maine.

A coalition of conservationists had urged the President to veto the bill. Brent Blackwelder of the Environmental Policy Center said on September 26 that the bill was "a crucial test" of Carter's commitment to reform "pork-barrel water policy." But the conservation-group pressure to veto the legislation was offset by election-year politics and the fact that leaders of most environmental groups had endorsed Carter's candidacy. Carter called the bill a "constructive compromise," but said that he had a continuing interest in working with Congress to reform water policy.

Long Canal. California's Governor Edmund G. Brown, Jr., signed a bill on July 18 authorizing a huge project to move water from northern California to dry areas in the southern part of the state. The main feature of the project, estimated to cost $5 billion to $23 billion, is to be the 43-mile (69-kilometer) Peripheral Canal that will carry water from the Sacramento River to a water project intake west of Stockton.   Andrew L. Newman

In WORLD BOOK, see WATER.

WEATHER. A prolonged summer heat wave in the United States took at least 1,265 lives and caused losses of almost $20 billion in 1980. The greatest number of fatalities in a single state, 311, occurred in Missouri. Texas was also severely affected, as temperatures in the state reached or exceeded 100°F. (38°C) every day from June 23 through August 3. According to the National Oceanic and Atmospheric Administration (NOAA), 26 states were affected, with most deaths occurring among elderly or low-income people who did not have air conditioning in their homes. Electricity use was 5.5 per cent above normal, and severe water shortages occurred in many areas.

The heat wave damaged crops, especially corn, soybeans, and spring wheat – but winter wheat benefited from the hot, dry weather during harvesting. Livestock also suffered, because the drought destroyed grazing grasses in the Plains states. Poultry farmers lost millions of birds.

In February, flooding killed at least 24 persons in California, Arizona, and Mexico. Six days of rain forced many residents to evacuate their houses in the Los Angeles area.

Effect on Crops. The National Weather Service (NWS) reported in August that weather determines crop yields and the quality of the produce more than any other single factor. Weather factors also play a role in determining the potential threat of plant disease and insects. Other weather-related decisions involve irrigating – whether to do so, and how much – and tractor trips to the fields. Weather is also a consideration when planting or, more importantly, harvesting crops. Some crops can be harvested early before frost occurs, while others can be protected by smudge pots or other measures.

Agriculture accounts for 2 to 3 per cent of the total U.S. fuel consumption, according to a report by climatologist James E. Newman of Purdue University in West Lafayette, Ind. But, Newman said, U.S. farmers save $750 million each year in production costs by consulting weather forecasts.

Hail and Crop Losses. A three-year study by the Illinois State Water Survey (ISWS) to predict long-term temperature and rainfall patterns has produced a hail-prediction technique, too. Climatologists James C. Neill and Floyd A. Huff of the ISWS worked closely with the Crop-Hail Insurance Actuarial Association in Chicago on hail prediction. In the past, insurance companies raised their rates when a major hail loss occurred. Now, with greatly increased prediction capability, insurance companies may be able to base their rates on anticipated losses. As a result, rates may be more fairly adjusted, based on losses expected to occur. A new rate structure was being tested experimentally in 1980. In the meantime, the ISWS continued to study and refine hail predictions.

Middle East Study. An agreement to carry on a cooperative marine meteorological program was signed in Jidda, Saudi Arabia, on January 21 by representatives of Iran, Iraq, Kuwait, Oman, Qatar, and Saudi Arabia. The United Arab Emirates was expected to join the program. The program, which began only after three years of extensive preparatory work, was initiated by R. M. Romaih, Saudi Arabia's director-general of meteorology, with the cooperation of the World Meteorological Organization secretariat.

The program consists of marine meteorological research, training, and observing and a data-processing and telecommunications system – all designed to aid fishing, oil exploration, and the cleanup of oil spills. The program will also provide advice on offshore construction – such as oil rigs – and information to make navigation safer.

Volcanic Ash from the eruption of the Mount Saint Helens volcano in Washington on May 18 was carried by wind across the United States (see GEOLOGY [Close-Up]). A team of scientists led by climatologist J. Murray Mitchell of NOAA in Silver Spring, Md., reported in June that most of the ash was thrown into the *troposphere* (lower atmosphere), and then fell back to earth directly or as precipitation – rain or snow.

Fine ash that reached levels of at least 40,000 feet (12,200 meters) has not readily fallen back

to earth. Instead, it has formed a shield across the Northern Hemisphere that may stay there for months or years. Mitchell and the others predicted slightly cooler weather – probably only about 0.18°F. (0.1°C) cooler in the Northern Hemisphere – because of the Mount Saint Helens eruption. However, if new eruptions should occur of a magnitude similar to the May 18 explosion, either in Mount Saint Helens or other North American volcanoes, more profound effects could be expected.

Sunspot Activity peaked in early 1980. Sunspots are areas on the sun's surface displaying unusual magnetic fields. They occur in 11-year cycles. The current cycle was potentially the second strongest since the early 1600s. Scientists from 19 countries continued studying sunspots in the Solar Maximum Year – actually 19 months, from Aug. 1, 1979, to Feb. 28, 1981 – to take advantage of the peak activity. Some scientists have identified a 22-year cycle of climate trends, especially for drought, and are trying to link this trend with the sunspot cycles. Solar activity may also be responsible for short-term cold spells.

Several years after the peak in sunspot activity, the earth is likely to experience unusually severe magnetic storms. Power-transmission systems in the United States are ripe for a major disruption

A Texas longhorn steer lies dead on the plain, struck down by the prolonged heat wave that killed many people, plants, and animals.

caused by such storms, according to space scientist Howard H. Sargent III of NOAA's Space Environment Laboratory in Boulder, Colo. Considerable damage to power plants could result, because power systems in the United States are linked into grids. The system may react like a series of old-fashioned Christmas tree lights — when one fails, the rest go off at the same time.

Improved Satellite. The latest model in the Geostationary Operational Environmental Satellite (GOES) series was launched by NOAA from Cape Canaveral, Fla., on September 9. Like earlier models, *GOES 4* is stationed over the central United States — and sends back photographs of weather patterns. Unlike earlier models, *GOES 4* can also take moisture and temperature readings at several atmospheric levels while remaining in its fixed location. This provides much more promising information for weather forecasters than did previous satellites, because major storms develop high in the atmosphere. A sophisticated experimental ground system for processing the *GOES 4* readings is operated by the National Aeronautics and Space Administration's Goddard Space Flight Center in Greenbelt, Md., in conjunction with the University of Wisconsin.   Edward W. Pearl

See also DISASTERS; ENVIRONMENT. In WORLD BOOK, see METEOROLOGY; WEATHER.

WEIGHT LIFTING. See SPORTS.

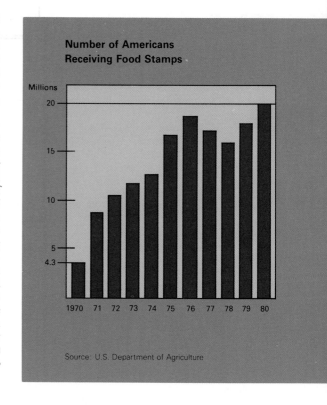

Number of Americans Receiving Food Stamps

Source: U.S. Department of Agriculture

WELFARE. Social welfare in 1980 became the target for proposed massive spending cuts aimed at a balanced United States federal budget for fiscal 1981 (Oct. 1, 1980, to Sept. 30, 1981). President Jimmy Carter's Administration and the United States Congress saw a balanced budget as a means of fighting inflation. A coalition of 147 organizations — including the National Council of Senior Citizens and labor, consumer, religious, and minority groups — announced a counteroffensive against the budget cuts endorsed by President Carter and some members of Congress. The coalition opposed "ruthless reductions" in programs that aid the poor, the handicapped, minorities, young people, and the elderly. "We do not oppose a balanced budget per se," the coalition's statement said. "We do oppose Administration and congressional proposals that place the burden of the battle against inflation on those least able to cope with the problems of our society."

Carter's earlier proposals for welfare reform received scant attention. Congress adjourned without enacting significant welfare reform legislation.

In the first budget resolution for fiscal 1981, approved in June 1980, defense spending was increased by 18 per cent, while nonmilitary spending was up only 5 per cent. Allowing for inflation and the decreasing value of the dollar, this meant that funding for social programs was actually cut.

Financing Welfare services was further complicated by the 1980 census. Several large cities complained that blacks, other minorities, and illegal aliens were not fully counted. Federal funds for many community services are allocated on the basis of census figures, so an undercount threatens reductions in federal funds. See CENSUS.

Food Stamps. For the second consecutive year, Congress enacted emergency legislation to prevent the food stamp program from ending in May. A revised ceiling of $9.49 billion was set for fiscal 1980, and $9.7 billion for fiscal 1981. The program helped feed about 21 million Americans in 1980.

Changes enacted by Congress provide that cost-of-living adjustments will be made only once a year, rather than twice a year. Also, about 200,000 persons — most of them college students — were dropped from the rolls as of October 1, when eligibility requirements were tightened.

Energy Assistance. Legislation to alleviate hardship due to the spiraling costs of heating fuels, passed in November 1979, provided $1.6 billion for fuel assistance in the winter of 1980. The money was divided among the Community Services Administration, for an existing program that began with weather stripping five years ago; block grants to states, for distribution to recipients of Aid to Families with Dependent Children; and energy-replacement costs and grants to individuals receiving Supplemental Security Income for the Aged, Blind, and Disabled (SSI). The SSI recipients received from $50 to $250, depending on the climate where they lived.

President Carter signed the Crude Oil Windfall Profits Tax Act of 1980 on April 2. It provides that 25 per cent of the revenues from the act be used to help the poor with increased energy costs. The act authorizes the program for fiscal 1981 only.

Family Theme. President Carter opened the first of three national White House Conferences on Families on June 5 in Baltimore, Md. The other conferences opened on June 19 in Minneapolis, Minn., and on July 10 in Los Angeles, Calif. Jim Guy Tucker, a former Democratic Congressman from Arkansas, chaired the conferences. Recommendations adopted by the conferences included one asking employers to be flexible about working hours and shared jobs and another urging aid to families of the handicapped.

A Conference on Aging was scheduled for 1981 to develop a comprehensive national policy for elderly Americans. President Carter appointed 81-year-old Sadie Alexander to chair it. She was the first black woman in the United States to receive a Ph.D. and earn a law degree from the University of Pennsylvania, and the first woman to practice law in Pennsylvania.   Virginia E. Anderson

In WORLD BOOK, see WELFARE.

WEST INDIES. Political and economic problems abounded in the West Indies in 1980. Until the emergence of several newly independent mini-nations in recent years, the Caribbean area — except for Cuba — had been mainly a placid colonial backwater. But during 1980 the economic future of some of the fledgling nations was of increasing concern to the United States. In April, U.S. President Jimmy Carter called upon international aid officials, Caribbean leaders, and volunteer agency leaders to establish a group called Caribbean-Central American Action. It was to focus on ways to increase productivity and to open U.S. markets to Caribbean products.

What particularly concerned the U.S. was the emergence of a Cuba-oriented government in tiny Grenada. There were fears that without some assistance, other small island countries might fall into the Russian sphere through relations with Communist Cuba. There was also mounting concern over the streams of refugees from Haiti, Cuba, and other Caribbean nations seeking to enter the U.S. See CUBA; IMMIGRATION.

Jamaica. Electioneering in Jamaica was marked by bloodshed and a tide of violence. By the time elections were held on October 30, some 700 Jamaicans had been killed and hundreds more wounded by militants of the left and right. The winner, in a landslide victory, was Harvard-

Crowd gathers under a revolutionary poster on soccer scoreboard to cheer on-field parade marking anniversary of Grenada's independence.

educated conservative Edward Seaga of the Jamaica Labor Party, who had to brave sniper fire at three locations while campaigning on election day. Seaga, whose party won 51 of the 60 seats in the nation's parliament, campaigned on a promise to develop close relations with the United States (see SEAGA, EDWARD). His opponent, Prime Minister Michael N. Manley of the People's National Party, had courted Cuba's Fidel Castro.

Dominica. The shift to conservatism was also evident in Dominica where voters gave Mary Eugenia Charles and her Freedom Party a landslide victory. In capturing 17 of the 21 seats in the bicameral parliament, Charles became the Caribbean's first woman head of state.

Grenada. On March 13, amid signs of a definite shift to socialism, the leftist New Jewel Movement of Prime Minister Maurice Bishop celebrated the first anniversary of the coup d'état that brought it to power. In May, Grenada signed a pact with Cuban Prime Minister Fidel Castro. Under it, Cuba was to provide Grenada with a fisheries training vessel and help in increasing its trade with Soviet-bloc nations.

Trinidad and Tobago. Revenues from its oil resources were a continuing boon to the economy in Trinidad and Tobago, which had a whopping $5-billion budget in 1980. Prime Minister Eric E. Williams offered to share part of his nation's new wealth with some of its less fortunate neighbors — including about $200 million in loans to its English-speaking neighbors of the Caribbean Community — at the low interest rate of 3 per cent. Williams, who has been in power for nearly 25 years, called for expanding the community to include Cuba and other Caribbean nations. Violence was on the rise, as opposition to Williams' rule increased. In Tobago's parliamentary elections on November 25, the Democratic Action Congress Party (DACP) captured 54 per cent of the vote and eight of the 12 seats at stake. Prime Minister Williams' People's National Movement won 45 per cent and four seats.

Barbados. The economy took a turn for the better with increased tourism and good prices for the island's sugar. Stable government and an absence of terrorism meant Barbados could attract a larger share of vacationers.   Nathan A. Haverstock

See also LATIN AMERICA (Facts in Brief Table). In WORLD BOOK, see WEST INDIES.

WEST VIRGINIA. See STATE GOVERNMENT.
WISCONSIN. See STATE GOVERNMENT.
WYOMING. See STATE GOVERNMENT.
YEMEN (ADEN). See MIDDLE EAST.
YEMEN (SANA). See MIDDLE EAST.
YOUNG MEN'S CHRISTIAN ASSOCIATION (YMCA). See COMMUNITY ORGANIZATIONS.
YOUNG WOMEN'S CHRISTIAN ASSOCIATION (YWCA) See COMMUNITY ORGANIZATIONS.

YOUTH ORGANIZATIONS. The Boy Scouts of America (BSA) celebrated the 50th anniversary of Cub Scouting in 1980 with special activities highlighting the Cub Scout program. The 30-millionth Cub Scout since 1930 was registered in March. Thomas C. MacAvoy, president and chief operating officer of Corning Glass Works, was named BSA president in May at the national meeting in New Orleans.

The Max C. Fleischmann Foundation of Nevada made a gift of $2.1 million to the BSA. The funds will be used to improve facilities at four national high-adventure bases that allow young people 14 years or older to explore wilderness areas.

Jeff Shimer, 19, of Clearwater, Fla., was elected president of the nation's 401,000 Explorers — young men and women aged 14 through 20 — at the 10th annual National Explorer Presidents' Congress in Phoenix in May. More than 2,000 Explorers took part in the sixth National Explorer Olympics in July at Colorado State University in Fort Collins.

Boys Clubs of America (BCA), in the third year of its National Health Project, provided 1,800 disadvantaged youngsters with comprehensive health examinations, compiled their health histories, and conducted thousands of hearing, vision, and dental screening tests.

Jace L. Smith, 16, a member of the Massillon, Ohio, Boys Club, was installed as National Boy of the Year in a special meeting with President Jimmy Carter in the White House on September 17. As Boy of the Year, Smith represents the more than 1 million young persons served by BCA.

Camp Fire. Program revision began in 1980 to reflect the recent inclusion of both girls and boys in the Camp Fire program. Three books were introduced at the Blue Bird, or primary, level: the *What, When, Why Book for Blue Bird Leaders;* the *Handbook to Starbird;* and the *Who Bird Handbook.* A Reader's Digest Foundation grant contributed to the research and development of a Discovery Club junior high program. *Helps, Hints & Hopes for Discovery Advisors* and the new *Outdoor Book* were completed.

4-H Clubs. The National 4-H Conference marked its 50th anniversary in April. 4-H programs reached more than 5 million young rural and urban Americans under the guidance of 566,000 4-H adult and teen volunteer leaders, contributing to energy conservation, environmental improvement, community service, and food production. During National 4-H Week in October, President Carter pointed out, "As your theme indicates, 4-H is 'expanding horizons' for young Americans — both rural and urban — from all social and economic backgrounds. 4-H represents unchanging American values in a changing world. You are proving how effectively young Americans can meet the challenges of the '80s."

The Boy Scouts of America introduced new winter, left, and summer, center, Cub Scout uniforms, and a new Webelos outfit, right.

Future Farmers of America (FFA) dedicated the first exhibits of the $600,000 FFA National Hall of Achievement at the National FFA Center in Alexandria, Va., in July. The exhibits record the history of the 500,000-member organization. Byron Rawls, national FFA adviser, co-chaired the National Agricultural Education Seminar in July, which discussed the direction of agricultural education in the 1980s.

FFA's 53rd annual convention took place in Kansas City, Mo., from November 12 to 14. During the convention, members competed in contests ranging from floriculture to extemporaneous speaking.

Girls Clubs of America (GCA) began building a national resource center for girls in Indianapolis in July. Funded by the Max C. Fleischmann Foundation, the facility will provide youth service professionals from government, education, and the private sector with data and other resources to develop programs for today's girls.

GCA received a major grant from the United States Department of Labor for Teen Women Employability Programs in 17 member clubs. The trial program seeks to raise the employment skills, aspirations, and prospects of nearly 1,000 girls.

Girl Scouts of the United States of America (GSUSA). New GSUSA materials for teens and younger girls were previewed in June at the White

House by the honorary Girl Scout president, Rosalynn Carter. Mrs. Carter was presented with a framed set of the 76 new Junior Girl Scout proficiency badges covering such topics as aeronautics, computer science, business, communication arts, and energy.

Girl Scouting's focus on career education and awareness for girls from 6 to 17 was expanded through a 19-month pilot project called Girl Scout Career Education in Schools. Career materials developed by GSUSA are being offered to school districts in 16 states during the project.

Junior Achievement (JA). During the 1979-1980 academic year, 30,388 volunteer adult JA advisers helped 192,065 students to establish and run their own businesses. A record 8,247 JA companies produced goods and services as the student company members got firsthand education and experience in the U.S. business system.

The sixth annual Junior Achievement National Business Leadership Conference and Business Hall of Fame induction ceremony in April attracted 1,977 leading U.S. decision-makers to Los Angeles. Among those honored at the ceremony were DeWitt Wallace and his wife, Lila Achison Wallace of Mount Kisco, N.Y., founders of the *Reader's Digest* magazine.   Virginia E. Anderson

In WORLD BOOK, see entries on the individual organizations.

YUGOSLAVIA maintained its independence and internal stability after President Josip Broz Tito died on May 4, 1980 (see DEATHS OF NOTABLE PERSONS [Close-Up]). Some observers had predicted that Tito's death might weaken Yugoslavia seriously because the six republics, including two self-governing provinces, that make up the country would not be able to agree on a new leader.

Tito had anticipated this problem, however, and had created a council called the *Presidency* to rule Yugoslavia after he died. Leadership of this group was to rotate annually among its eight members — one from each of these republics and provinces. Accordingly, the council vice-president, Lazar Kolisevski, a Macedonian, became president when Tito died. However, Kolisevski's term had only two weeks to run, so he stepped down on May 15. Cvijetin Mijatovic, a Serb from the republic of Bosnia and Hercegovina, then began a one-year term as president.

Stevan Doronjski, a Serb from the self-governing province of Vojvodina, became president of the League of Communists of Yugoslavia, the country's Communist party, when Tito died. His term expired in October and Lazar Mojsov, a Macedonian, succeeded him for a one-year term.

Political Dissidents were treated harshly in Yugoslavia in 1980. A law passed in January allowed the republic of Serbia to fire seven Marxist phi-

An elderly Yugoslav pauses in Ljubljana park before a statue of President Josip Broz Tito, who died in May after a lingering illness.

losophers at the University of Belgrade for criticizing the regime. Two Roman Catholic friars in Bosnia and Hercegovina received six-year prison sentences for possessing literature that criticized the government. Seven persons were sentenced in Zagreb in June to 5- to 15-year prison terms for plotting sabotage. Some 50 young Albanians in Kosovo province received prison sentences.

Foreign Relations. In September, Yugoslavia and Russia signed an agreement that would increase trade between the two countries from a total of $11 billion during the years 1976 through 1980 to $26 billion for 1981 through 1985. Russia ordered 98 ships worth $11.3 billion from Yugoslav shipyards.

In April, Yugoslavia signed an agreement with the European Community (EC) that granted Yugoslavia duty-free access to EC markets for a wide range of its products. About 30 per cent of Yugoslavia's exports remained subject to EC tariffs, most of them textiles, steel products, ferrous metals, and alloys. The EC granted Yugoslavia a $280-million credit for a highway between Austria and Greece.

Yugoslavia devalued its currency by 30 per cent in June. It removed some price controls in October. Yugoslavia's inflation rate was nearly 30 per cent throughout 1980.   Chris Cviic

See also EUROPE (Facts in Brief Table). In WORLD BOOK, see YUGOSLAVIA.

YUKON TERRITORY. The disposition of land claims proceeded slowly in 1980, hampering economic development and stiffening political discussion in the federal territory. The Council for Yukon Indians, representing 5,000 Indians and *métis* (persons of mixed white and Indian descent) in the Yukon, was reorganized, and it revised its original 1974 claim for $670 million in compensation and 70 per cent of the land area of the Yukon several times.

A tentative settlement reached by the *Inuit* (Eskimos) of the western Arctic in 1978 protected their right to use traditional hunting grounds and gave them exclusive hunting rights in a national wilderness park to be created by the federal government in the northern third of the territory. However, the plan came under fire from the Yukon government, which suggested a corridor through the park to gain access to the resource-rich Beaufort Sea.

Another dispute with the federal government arose over the Yukon's desire to be represented at the constitutional talks held in September in Ottawa, Ont. When the Yukon administration asked to present its views, Prime Minister Pierre Elliott Trudeau offered the territory observer status at the meeting but no chance to speak. Yukon Conservative leader Christopher Pearson declined to attend the meeting on Trudeau's terms.   David M. L. Farr

See also CANADA. In WORLD BOOK, see YUKON TERRITORY.

ZAIRE. President Mobutu Sese Seko's government tried in 1980 to deal with the country's severe economic problems. Among these were high unemployment, heavy foreign debts, and runaway inflation. Zaire devalued its currency by 30 per cent in February in an effort to reduce foreign debts by encouraging exports and discouraging imports.

Zaire reached an agreement with 130 foreign banks on April 23 to reschedule $400 million in debts over a 10-year period. Zaire's total foreign debt at the time was almost $4 billion, and the nation had failed to meet conditions to draw the second part of a $150-million loan from the International Monetary Fund. The government expressed hope that the new economic measures would keep the inflation rate below the 1979 rate of 100 per cent.

Some 8,000 university students in Kinshasa, the capital, boycotted classes and rioted in April against poor economic conditions and alleged government corruption. Mobutu closed the university and inducted all first-year students into the army.

Mobutu changed his government twice during 1980. On January 18 he fired 13 ministers, and on August 27 he named Foreign Minister Nguza Karl-I-Bond prime minister.   J. Dixon Esseks

See also AFRICA (Facts in Brief Table). In WORLD BOOK, see ZAIRE.

ZAMBIA. See AFRICA.

ZHAO ZIYANG (1919-   ) became premier of China on Sept. 10, 1980. He replaced Hua Kuo-feng (Hua Guofeng), who resigned but kept his post as chairman of the Communist Party. See CHINA.

Zhao was a surprising choice to many Western-ers. He was appointed a deputy premier in April, giving him only a few months of experience in the central government. Before that, he had headed the Sichuan (Szechwan) provincial government and Communist Party since 1975.

He did not appear to have close ties to Deputy Premier Teng Hsiao-p'ing (Deng Xiaoping), though Teng selected him for the premier's post.

Zhao (Chao Tzu-yang in the Wade-Giles system of spelling) was born in 1919 in Honan (Henan) Province. His father was a grain dealer and land-lord. Zhao joined the Young Communist League in 1932 and the Communist Party in 1938. He held a provincial party post in the 1940s. After the revolu-tion, he began working in Kwangtung (Guang-dong) Province, becoming first secretary of the provincial party in 1965.

Because of his wealthy family and his liberal ideas on agriculture, Zhao was purged during the Cultural Revolution in 1967. In 1971, he returned to power as an official of the Inner Mongolia (Nei Monggol) Party.   Patricia Dragisic

ZIMBABWE became Africa's 51st independent country on April 18, 1980. As Rhodesia, the nation had declared its independence from Great Britain in 1965. At that time, the government was con-trolled by the nation's white minority — about 4 per cent of the total population — and black national-ists within the country as well as most foreign governments refused to accept white rule. Black guerrillas began armed opposition in 1972.

The nationalist forces agreed in December 1979 to a cease-fire and temporary resumption of British rule. Under the agreement, the interim governor, Lord Christopher Soames, supervised the truce and conducted pre-independence elections.

Election Victors. The Zimbabwe African Nation-al Union-Patriotic Front (ZANU), led by Robert Mugabe, captured 57 of the 100 Parliament seats in the elections held from February 27 to 29. ZANU's nearest rivals, the Zimbabwe African People's Union (ZAPU), led by Joshua Nkomo, and the Rhodesian Front representing the white minority, led by former prime minister Ian D. Smith, won only 20 seats each. Under the cease-fire agreements, whites were guaranteed 20 seats in the 100-member parliament.

Mugabe, an avowed Marxist, was not popular among white voters, and Smith tried to persuade the British administration to nullify the election

Voters travel by boat to cast ballots at a mobile polling place moored in Lake Kariba during Zimbabwe's pre-independence elections in February.

results on the grounds that African voters had been massively intimidated. Nkomo also asked for a new election. However, an 11-nation group of monitors ruled that the elections had been fair.

New Government. Mugabe was appointed prime minister on March 11 and immediately announced his 23-member Cabinet. He assigned two posts to whites from the Rhodesian Front and four to ZAPU members, naming Nkomo minister of home affairs.

Mugabe tried to assure the whites that fears for their safety and personal property were unfounded and that they were welcome in Zimbabwe. Nonetheless, whites left the country at a rate of more than 1,000 per month. The December 8 conviction of Cabinet Minister Edgar Z. Tekere for the murder of a white farm manager and the September 15 dismissal of the white military commander, Lieutenant General Peter Walls, fueled tensions among blacks and whites. Tekere was subsequently freed in December.

Mugabe worked to strengthen economic ties with Western nations, visiting Washington, D.C., in August to ask United States officials for economic assistance. By late September, Great Britain, the U.S., and other Western countries had pledged more than $300 million in aid.   J. Dixon Esseks

See also AFRICA (Facts in Brief Table); MUGABE, ROBERT G. In WORLD BOOK, see RHODESIA.

ZOOLOGY. Researchers revealed new evidence in March 1980 on how the male narwhal, an Arctic toothed whale, uses its long, pointed tusk. Zoologists have long speculated about it. Some have suggested it is used to stir mud in search of prey, impale prey, pierce ice to make breathing holes, cool the body, and transmit sound.

In March, zoologists H. B. Silverman and Maxwell J. Dunbar of the Marine Sciences Center at McGill University in Montreal, Canada, reported that tusk crossing is part of mating behavior and that male narwhals use their tusks when they fight during the mating season. Silverman and Dunbar observed narwhals near northern Baffin Island in the eastern Canadian Arctic Ocean from June to October in 1976, 1977, and 1978.

The narwhals' mating season takes place from about March to May, so the researchers did not directly observe mating or tusk crossing in adult males. But they observed young males crossing tusks in the summer and concluded that the pups were imitating tusk-crossing behavior they had seen during the mating season.

In addition to their observations of live whales, Silverman and Dunbar made measurements on hunted specimens and counted scars visible on the heads. These measurements supported their theory, because they found many more scars on male adult heads than on adult female heads. Large numbers of scars occurred only on males big enough to be sexually mature. Also, the tusks of many sexually mature males were broken, and one male had the tusk of another male embedded in its upper jaw.

Reproduction and Crowding. Zoologists have often observed that rodents living in crowded conditions undergo puberty later than others and thus have a lower reproductive rate. A chemical cue in the urine has been suspected as a cause of the puberty delay. Zoologists Adrianne Massey and John G. Vandenbergh of North Carolina State University in Raleigh in August reported evidence to support this idea. They trapped mice from two groups – a high-density population and a low-density population – living in two different areas near highway cloverleafs and collected urine from mice on filter paper left in the traps. They then exposed laboratory mice to urine samples from the more crowded group. These lab mice had their first *estrus* (heat) period later than normal. Laboratory mice that were exposed to urine from the mice living in the low-density area followed a normal cycle. Scientists hope to isolate the chemical that slows the reproductive process in mice, and use it to control rodent pests.   Barbara N. Benson

See also BIOLOGY; BOTANY; CONSERVATION; ZOOS AND AQUARIUMS. In WORLD BOOK, see ESTROUS CYCLE; NARWHAL; ZOOLOGY.

ZOOS AND AQUARIUMS. Zoo officials in the United States and Canada committed themselves in 1980 to the development of a "species survival plan" to coordinate their conservation efforts for rare and endangered species. Providing the resources and space needed for each species will involve greater cooperation among zoos and require additional funds, as appropriate conservation plans are developed. Officials at the American Association of Zoological Parks and Aquariums meeting in Chicago in September proposed to develop banks for frozen sperm, eggs, and other cells as one way of keeping varied gene pools.

Breeding News. Among first-time achievements was the birth of a lowland gorilla conceived through artificial insemination at the Memphis (Tenn.) Zoo in August. The mother was on loan from Chicago's Brookfield Zoo, and the sperm sample came from a male at the Yerkes Primate Research Center in Atlanta, Ga. Unfortunately, the baby gorilla died of pneumonia when it was 5 days old.

Another accomplishment was the use of domestic cows as surrogate mothers to fertilized eggs from a gaur, a large species of wild ox found in tropical Asia, at New York City's Bronx Zoo. This work and a similar experiment with Barbados sheep at the San Diego Zoo demonstrated a promising means of reproducing some endangered species.

Veterinary medicine has spawned some unusual techniques – an employee of
the Milwaukee (Wis.) Zoo ropes a fleet-footed camel so it can be treated.

Other Events of note included the hatching of three emperor penguin chicks in a research colony at Sea World in San Diego; the hatching of Texas blind salamander eggs on three occasions at the Cincinnati (Ohio) Zoo; and the return of aquarium-reared salmon to spawn in an artificial fish ladder at the Seattle (Wash.) Aquarium.

Reintroduction of species to natural areas is a primary objective of some captive-breeding programs. One such program for the Arabian oryx began 20 years ago, and several thriving groups are now in U.S. and European zoos. Five animals were shipped in March from the San Diego Wild Animal Park to the Jiddat al Harasis Reserve in Oman as the first step toward re-establishing a wild population in the desert.

Declining numbers of cheetahs in South Africa may be offset by a remarkably productive program in a research center of the National Zoo near Pretoria. Curator Ann Van Dyk creates maximum interest in breeding by separating males and females for most of the year, then allowing them to choose mates. She reports that more than 180 cubs have been born at the facility in the five years, and some have been released in nature reserves.

A program aimed at saving the California condor through a captive-breeding program foundered in June when a large chick died in the nest. The California Department of Fish and Game tempo-rarily halted the cooperative project, which is being led by the Audubon Society and the U.S. Fish and Wildlife Service. However, success with a close relative, the Andean condor, indicates that the project should be workable. Andean condors hatched at the Bronx Zoo were placed in an appropriate habitat in Peru and soon joined wild condors.

Difficulties with giant pandas continued to make news around the world. The first panda cub born outside of China was produced at the Chapultepec Zoo in Mexico City, Mexico, in August. When it was 8 days old, the 5-ounce (140-gram) cub was accidentally crushed to death by its 6-year-old, 260-pound (122-kilogram) mother, Ying-Ying.

Scientists at the National Zoological Park in Washington, D.C., unsuccessfully tried artificial insemination in May with a pair of pandas. The World Wildlife Fund began collaborating with China in a project to help sustain giant panda populations in the wild.

New Exhibits in the naturalistic mode were widespread. Oklahoma City, Okla., now has a Galapagos Islands exhibit, featuring giant tortoises and flamingos, and relating naturalist Charles R. Darwin's findings about the islands. Grizzly bears, a wolf pack, and moose are featured in new areas of Canada's Calgary Zoo.   George B. Rabb

In WORLD BOOK, see AQUARIUM; ZOO.

1975
1976
1977
1978
1979
1980

World Book Supplement

To help WORLD BOOK owners keep their
encyclopedia up to date, the following new
or revised articles are reprinted from the 1981
edition of the encyclopedia.

See ''Petroleum,'' page 559.

Computers Have Many Uses and Come in a Variety of Sizes. A handheld computer game provides entertainment, *upper left.* A desk-top computer helps librarians check out reading materials, *lower left.* A large-scale computer directs the operations of a telephone switching system, *right.*

COMPUTER

COMPUTER is an electronic device that performs calculations and processes information. It can handle vast amounts of facts and figures and solve complicated problems at incredibly high speeds. The fastest computers are able to process millions of pieces of information in seconds.

A computer can process many kinds of information, from book titles and customer account numbers to chemical formulas and words from ancient Greek texts. It handles all such data in the form of numbers. A computer is able to solve problems involving words by changing them into problems dealing with numbers.

The ability of a computer to do so many tasks makes it useful for a wide variety of purposes. Many stores rely on computers to bill customers and to keep track of the amount of merchandise in stock. Industrial plants use computers to control machines that produce bakery goods, chemicals, steel products, and numerous other items. Computers are used as a navigation aid on airplanes, ships, and spacecraft. They also enable scientists to analyze data returned by space probes. Computers can be used as teaching machines. They even provide entertainment in the form of computerized games.

Although a computer can do many things, it cannot

George Epstein, the contributor of this article, is Professor of Computer Science at Indiana University.

think. A human operator has to instruct the computer in exactly what to do with the data it receives. Such instructions are called a *program.* Also, the operator must frequently check the performance of the computer and, in many cases, interpret the results of the performance.

Computers differ greatly in size. The biggest ones have enough equipment to fill a large room. The smallest computers can be held in a person's hand. No matter what their size, however, all computers have certain basic parts.

The typical computer has an *input* device, such as an electronic keyboard, through which the operator enters instructions and data. A *storage unit*, also called a *memory*, receives this information from the input device and holds it until it is needed. A *control unit* selects the instructions from the memory in their proper sequence and directs the operations of an *arithmetic/logic unit.* (The word *arithmetic* is pronounced *AR ihth MEHT ihk.*) The arithmetic/logic unit processes the data by means of mathematical calculations and operations involving logic. An *output* device then translates the processed data into a form meaningful to the operator. Typical output equipment includes automatic typewriters, high-speed printers, and visual displays that resemble television screens.

Computers and calculating machines share certain features, but they differ in major ways. The fastest electronic calculators cannot do the enormous number of computations performed in seconds by computers. Also, most computers can store a much larger amount of data

Bit, which comes from the term *binary digit,* is the basic unit of information in a digital computing system. It may be either the digit 0 or 1.

Central Processing Unit, or CPU, is the section of a digital computer that manipulates data according to a set of stored instructions.

Data Base is a collection of information stored in a computer. The data are recorded on a magnetic disk unit or other direct-access storage device.

Hardware refers to the physical parts, such as the electronic, magnetic, and mechanical devices, that make up a computer system.

Interface is any input or output device. An interface serves as a communication link between a computer and its human operator or a machine controlled by the computer.

Logic Circuit is an electronic circuit that enables a digital computer to compare, select, and perform other logic operations.

Microprocessor is a miniature electronic device consisting of thousands of transistors and related circuitry on a silicon chip. The device is often called a "computer on a chip" because it has all the elements of a central processing unit.

Network is a system consisting of two or more computers connected by high-speed communication lines.

Program is a set of instructions to be carried out by a computer to solve a problem.

Simulation is the representation or imitation of a particular situation, operation, or system by a computer. The purpose is to predict and analyze what is likely to occur under various conditions.

Software refers to the programs used by a computer to perform a desired task.

Terminal is any device connected to a computer for remote input or output of data.

---

and instructions than even the most advanced programmable calculators can. As a result, computers have the ability to solve a far greater variety of complicated problems than calculators.

Uses of the Computer

Computers play an increasingly important role in society, particularly in industrially developed countries. More than a million computers are in use in the United States and Canada alone, where they affect nearly every aspect of daily life. This section gives only a small sampling of their many and varied uses.

In Business and Industry. Businesses depend on computers to handle all kinds of accounting and bookkeeping jobs. Most large companies have computers calculate their employees' wages and print payroll checks. Banks use computers to record the amount of money deposited or withdrawn by customers. Many supermarkets have a computerized checkout system, which eliminates the need to ring up the price of each item by hand. Computers help airlines make reservations quickly by enabling each ticket agent to check hundreds of flights for available seating. Telephone and electric power companies use computers to help operate their facilities. Many book, magazine, and newspaper publishers have a computerized typesetting system.

Numerous factories use computers to control machines that make products. A computer turns the machines on and off and adjusts their operations when necessary. In most major industries, computers help researchers and executives make important decisions.

For example, oil companies use computer analyses of economic and geologic data to select drilling sites where petroleum is most likely to be recovered at lowest cost. An automaker's decision to expand the production of a certain model of car may hinge on a computer analysis of consumer demands and other market conditions.

In Government and Law Enforcement. The computer has great value to government and law enforcement agencies because it can store large amounts of data and then rapidly recover specific information from storage. The United States Bureau of the Census relies on this feature of the computer to update population figures. The Internal Revenue Service (IRS) uses computers to check more than 120 million tax returns each year for errors in arithmetic and other mistakes. The IRS computers also check whether such items as interest and dividends reported by a taxpayer match the amounts reported by banks and other institutions.

The Federal Bureau of Investigation (FBI) uses computers to store more than 20,000 fingerprints daily. FBI agents and other law enforcement officers can compare the fingerprints of a suspect with those in a computer *data base* (information file) and make a positive identification. Area crime statistics, license numbers of stolen cars, and daily police reports also can be stored in a computer data base.

In various large U.S. cities, the police keep track of patrol cars with computerized vehicle-monitoring systems. With such a system, police dispatchers can locate a squad car nearest an accident or crime within 15 seconds and automatically relay an emergency call to it.

In the Military. Computers form a vital part of the radar defense systems that guard the United States and Canada against surprise attacks from enemy planes or

WORLD BOOK photo

A Computerized Grocery Checkout System eliminates the need to ring up the price of each item by hand. It has an *optical scanner* that senses price codes printed on the grocery items.

missiles. Computers make effective *signal processors* for radar units. They can quickly analyze radar sightings and make identification of hostile aircraft possible at long distances. Also, jet fighters sent to shoot down enemy aircraft can pinpoint their targets by means of a computer-controlled guidance system.

Computers help military leaders plan troop maneuvers and solve difficult supply problems. Computers can even be used to *simulate* (duplicate) battle situations and so enable military personnel to predict the effectiveness of various tactics and weapons.

In Engineering. Without computers, it would be impossible for engineers to perform the enormous number of calculations needed to solve many advanced technological problems. For example, any project of the U.S. space program requires so many computations that not even a team of hundreds of experts could do them fast enough by hand. Computers help in the building of spacecraft, and they assist flight engineers in launching, controlling, and tracking the vehicles. Computers also are used to develop equipment for exploring the moon and planets.

Computers enable architectural and civil engineers to design complicated bridges and other structures with relative ease. In such projects, a computer analyzes factors ranging from the strength and weight of each structural part to its cost and availability. In addition, the computer can estimate the worth of any design changes that might be considered. Similar operations are performed by computers in the designing of more efficient cars, planes, and nuclear power plants.

In the Sciences. Computers have been of tremendous help to researchers in the biological, physical, and social sciences. They also have a major role in the field of *information science*. Information science deals with how information is collected, processed, and transmitted. It brings together knowledge from many fields of study. See LIBRARY (Information Science).

Researchers use computers in various ways to solve problems in the biological and physical sciences. One method used for certain problems provides exact solutions in the form of mathematical equations. A comput-er can be programmed to work out such equations.

Many scientific problems are so difficult that exact solutions are impossible. For such problems, the *Monte Carlo method* can be used to obtain an approximate solution through numerous trials. Scientists may be able to reach a solution after a few experiments. But they know that it is risky to draw conclusions from only a small number of observations. They thus use a computer to simulate the conditions of their experiment many times over. The larger the number of trials, the greater is the likelihood that the conclusions are close to the correct solution. The Monte Carlo method involves the element of chance. For this reason, it is named after the famous Monte Carlo gambling resort in Monaco.

In many scientific fields, researchers use computers to construct *mathematical models* of devices, systems, and theories that they wish to understand better or to evaluate. The models consist of equations that describe the possible relations between the parts or processes of a subject. Computers have helped scientists develop models of such complicated systems as underground petroleum reserves and worldwide weather patterns.

Chemists and physicists rely heavily on computers to control and check sensitive laboratory instruments and to analyze experimental data. Astronomers use computers to guide telescopes and to process photographic images of planets and other objects in space.

Computers provide an efficient means of storing and locating scientific research data for reference purposes. They store records of thousands of articles and reports published each year, giving specialists quick access to the latest developments in their field.

Computers assist physicians in special ways. At some hospitals, for example, physicians can consult a computer for the case histories of patients and the latest findings on various major illnesses. Computers have also been programmed to help doctors diagnose brain tumors and certain other disorders. They also control many kinds of hospital equipment used to treat patients.

In the Fine Arts. Computers can be used to compose music, write poems, and produce drawings and paintings. A work generated by a computer may resemble that of a certain artist in both style and form, or it may appear abstract or random. In either case, however, any

Goddard Space Flight Center

Computers Can Convert Data into various forms. For example, a computer used Census Bureau statistics to produce this map showing the schooling of people throughout the United States.

Dan McCoy, Rainbow

Law Enforcement Agencies Use Computers to store information about people who have a criminal record. This data may include photographs, fingerprints, and records of arrests.

A Computer-Processed Photograph of Mars reveals the planet's surface in considerable detail. A part of the equipment of the U.S. *Viking I* space probe appears at the lower right.

creativity in the work is basically that of the person who programmed the computer.

Computers are also used in the study of the fine arts, particularly literature. For example, scholars can recover various kinds of information from a computer data base to help them analyze a work of poetry. In many cases, biographical records, dictionaries, and lists of previous studies on the subject are computerized for easy reference. In addition, computers are sometimes used to determine whether a literary work by an unknown author was actually written by more than one person. Computers have also been programmed to help scholars identify paintings and sculptures from ancient civilizations.

In Education. A growing number of schools from the elementary through the college level use computers as a teaching aid. This method, called *computer-assisted instruction* (CAI), can reduce learning time and improve the performance of many students. CAI systems can teach biology, history, foreign languages, mathematics, and numerous other subjects.

In a typical CAI system, each student sits at a computer *terminal*, which consists of a TV-like screen and keyboard. The computer presents instructions and lessons on the screen and through prerecorded sound messages. The student responds by typing answers on the keyboard or by marking on the screen with a special *light pen*. The computer takes the student through a lesson step by step until the subject matter has been mastered. In doing so, the computer can drill, tutor, or carry on a "dialogue" in which the student makes up problems and has the machine solve them. At the end of the lesson, the computer judges the student's performance according to predetermined standards.

In the Home. Computers and computer-controlled devices have become fairly common in American homes. Computer games, especially electronic video games used with TV sets, are popular with both children and adults. Backgammon, chess, football, and table tennis are a few of the many games available in computerized form. Small computer-aided teaching machines have also been developed for use in the home.

More and more families own microwave ovens, sewing machines, and other appliances equipped with a miniature computing device. Some families have desktop or handheld computers designed for general-purpose use. They use these devices, called *personal computers*, to keep account of household expenses, to store income tax information, and to record addresses and telephone numbers. Some personal computers can be programmed to control home lighting, heating, and security systems.

Kinds of Computers

Computers are frequently divided into two groups according to the jobs they perform. These groups are *general-purpose computers* and *special-purpose computers*. A general-purpose computer can handle many kinds of jobs and is not restricted to any particular user. For example, it can be used as effectively by hospitals and libraries as by banks and stores. On the other hand, a special-purpose computer is designed to do one specific job for a particular user. An example is a navigational computer on an airplane. It can be used only to guide a plane.

Computers differ in the way they work as well as in what they can do. On this basis, they can be classified into three general types: (1) digital computers, (2) analog computers, and (3) hybrid computers. Digital computers are by far the most common type.

Digital Computers solve problems and do other tasks

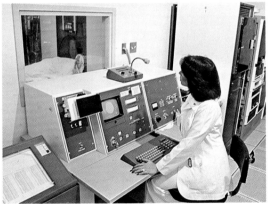

Computerized Axial Tomography, or *CAT scan*, helps doctors diagnose disorders. In this technique, a computer uses X-ray data to construct an image of a body part on a screen, *center*.

A Computer Can Produce Drawings of high quality, making it a useful tool for animation artists. An animated film may consist of computer-generated drawings like the one above.

COMPUTER

Milt and Joan Mann

Computer-Assisted Instruction enables students to interact closely with the "teacher." In the system above, the computer puts lessons on a screen, and students type their answers.

by counting, comparing, and rearranging digits in the arithmetic/logic unit. All the data, whether in the form of numbers, letters, or symbols, are represented by digits.

Digital computers use the digits of the *binary numeration system* (see NUMERATION SYSTEMS [The Binary System]). Unlike the familiar decimal number system, which uses 10 digits, the binary system uses only two digits: 0 and 1. These binary digits, called *bits*, can be easily represented by the thousands of tiny electronic circuits of a digital computer. The circuits operate much like an ordinary electric switch. When the switch is off, it corresponds to the binary digit 0. When the switch is on, it corresponds to the digit 1.

An electronic digital computer is able to perform all the basic arithmetic operations because binary digits, like decimal numbers, can be added, subtracted, multiplied, and divided. To solve a problem, it carries out these operations automatically one after the other according to the program stored in its memory.

Most digital computers are general-purpose computers. They can be programmed to handle all sorts of complicated, multistep tasks. These computers are so widely used that the word *computer* often means a general-purpose digital computer.

Analog Computers work directly with a physical quantity, such as weight, voltage, or speed, rather than with digits that represent the quantity. The computers solve problems by measuring the quantity in terms of another quantity. In a problem involving water pressure and water flow, for example, electrical voltage might serve as an *analogue* (likeness) for the water pressure, and electric current for the water flow. Many familiar devices, including speedometers, thermometers, and thermostats, operate on the same basic principle as analog computers. For example, a thermometer measures temperature in terms of the length of a thin line of liquid in a tube. An analog computer presents output data in a continuous form, often as a position on a scale. In some cases, the data are displayed as electrical signals on an instrument called an *oscilloscope*.

Analog computers are not as accurate as digital computers mainly because they work with continuous, varying quantities that cannot be measured exactly. Howev-

er, they can solve certain types of problems faster than digital computers. Analog computers also may be more convenient to use. They do not require the preparation of detailed programs. An operator "tells" an analog computer how to solve a problem by simply connecting its electronic circuits or mechanical parts in a particular way.

Most analog computers are special-purpose computers. They solve engineering and scientific problems that can be described as systems of *differential equations*. These mathematical equations are expressions of natural laws that describe the rates of change of quantities. Electronic analog computers are especially well suited for designing and analyzing electrical networks. They also control *simulators* for airplanes, space vehicles, and oceangoing ships. These simulators reproduce the conditions under which such craft must operate. They are used either to check the performance of a craft or to train its crew in operating procedures.

Hybrid Computers combine the features of analog and digital computers. They are as fast as analog computers in solving problems involving differential equations and as accurate as digital computers.

A typical hybrid computer has many of the same kinds of parts as an analog computer. But like a digital computer, it processes data by manipulating digits. It has a device called an *analog-to-digital converter*, which changes input data in the form of analog quantities into binary digits. A hybrid computer also has a *digital-to-analog converter*, which changes digitally computed data back to an analog quantity. This conversion makes the processed data easier to interpret.

Hybrid computers are basically special-purpose com-

Digital Computers and the Binary Number System

All data handled by digital computers, including words, are in the form of digits. But the computers use only the two digits of the binary number system—that is, 0 and 1. Different combinations of 0's and 1's represent letters and the various decimal numerals. The binary system is well suited for digital computers because their circuits have only two possible states and operate much like an ordinary light switch. When the switch is off, it corresponds to 0. When the switch is on, it stands for 1. The illustration below shows how different combinations of the binary digits represent the decimal numerals 1 through 4.

WORLD BOOK illustration by Steven Liska

	Binary digits 0 0 0 1 = Decimal numeral 1
	Binary digits 0 0 1 0 = Decimal numeral 2
	Binary digits 0 0 1 1 = Decimal numeral 3
	Binary digits 0 1 0 0 = Decimal numeral 4

An input device sends data and instructions to the main memory of a computer. The control unit then directs the data to the arithmetic/logic unit for processing. Finally, the control unit routes the processed data to an output device or an auxiliary storage unit, or back to the main memory.

WORLD BOOK illustration by Steven Liska

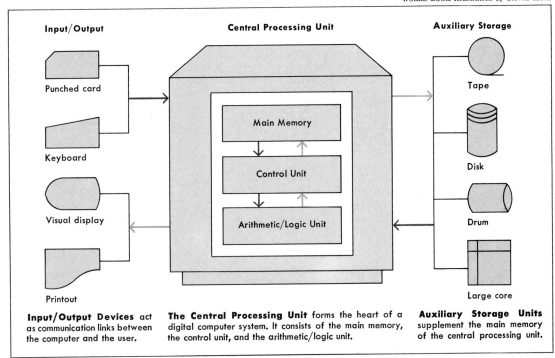

Input/Output

Punched card

Keyboard

Visual display

Printout

Central Processing Unit

Main Memory

Control Unit

Arithmetic/Logic Unit

Auxiliary Storage

Tape

Disk

Drum

Large core

Input/Output Devices act as communication links between the computer and the user.

The Central Processing Unit forms the heart of a digital computer system. It consists of the main memory, the control unit, and the arithmetic/logic unit.

Auxiliary Storage Units supplement the main memory of the central processing unit.

puters. They are used chiefly in simulation projects and in *feedback systems* for automated equipment (see AUTO-MATION [Feedback]).

Parts of a Digital Computer

Digital computers vary widely in size. The size of a computer partly determines the jobs it can do. However, the performance of smaller computers is not necessarily limited. For example, a computer that can be held in the hand may be able to translate thousands of words from one language into another. This type of pocket-sized computer is called a *microcomputer*. A larger machine, the *minicomputer*, may be only about the size of a TV set. However, it can handle all the data-processing needs of community libraries and many business firms. The largest computer, a *mainframe*, has so much equipment that it may fill a huge room. Such a large device can control a telephone switching network or serve as a data base for a major government agency.

Although digital computers differ greatly in size, they all have five basic parts. These parts consist of (1) the input equipment, (2) the main memory, (3) the control unit, (4) the arithmetic/logic unit, and (5) the output equipment.

In a mainframe, the main memory, control unit, and arithmetic/logic unit form a single unit called the *central processing unit* (CPU). Some mainframes have more than one CPU, which allows a number of operations to be performed at one time. At the other extreme, a microcomputer has a single CPU made up of one *large-scale integrated circuit* (LSI). This miniature electronic device, commonly called a *microprocessor*, contains thousands of

transistors and other circuitry but is so small that it can fit in the palm of the hand. See INTEGRATED CIRCUIT.

Input and output equipment functions as an *interface* between the CPU and the user—that is, it enables the machine and the human operator to communicate efficiently with each other. Such equipment, known as *peripheral equipment*, may be connected with a CPU or work independently of it. If the peripheral equipment is connected with a CPU, it is said to be *on-line*. If the equipment operates independently, it is *off-line*. Radio signals or telephone lines may link a CPU in one city with peripheral equipment in another city. Such equipment provides *remote terminals* for the CPU.

The Input Equipment transforms instructions and data into a code understandable to a computer. This code consists of a pattern of electrical signals that correspond to the 0's and 1's of the binary system.

There are various kinds of input devices. One common device is a *card reader*, which takes input information from punched cards. The pattern of punches in the cards represents letters, numbers, and other symbols. A related device is the *paper tape reader*, which senses data from holes in a roll of paper tape.

Most computers have a keyboard that enables the operator to enter alphabetical characters and numerals directly into the computer. Many keyboard units have a visual display, which consists of a *cathode-ray tube* (CRT). A CRT is a vacuum tube with a screen like that of a TV set (see VACUUM TUBE). The CRT display makes it possible for the keyboard operator to check—and correct if necessary—the data being entered into the computer. Some keyboard terminals of this type have a

COMPUTER

built-in microcomputer that controls their basic operations independently of the main computer. Input units with CRT displays called *interactive graphic devices* enable the user to communicate with the main computer by drawing a diagram on the screen with a light pen.

Some computers use *optical scanners* to change input data into electrical signals. The scanners optically sense bar codes and marks printed on grocery items, identification cards, and certain documents. Other digital computers are connected to *touch-tone telephones*. By pressing the buttons on the phone, the user can enter data into the computer.

Certain types of equipment handle input information and also function as output devices and *auxiliary storage units*. Auxiliary storage units, or auxiliary memories, can store more information than a computer's main memory but do not operate as fast. The major types of auxiliary memories include (1) magnetic tape units, (2) magnetic disk units, (3) magnetic drum units, and (4) large-core storage units.

Magnetic Tape Units put information on tape similar to that used in tape recorders. The computer tape carries data in the form of tiny magnetic spots, or *cells*. More than 48,000 binary digits can be recorded and stored on 1 inch (2.54 centimeters) of magnetic tape.

Magnetic Disk Units record information by magnetizing cells on the surface of specially coated metal or plastic disks. The disks are stacked in a *disk pack* and held in a storage unit. Data and instructions recorded on disks can be retrieved more rapidly than information on tape. Locating data on tape may require unwinding the entire reel if the desired information is stored at the end of the tape. In contrast, the disk system provides direct access to a specific disk and the precise spot on that disk where the needed information is located. A unit consisting of small, flexible disks called *floppy disks* is widely used with minicomputers and microcomputers.

Magnetic Drum Units work much like disk units. However, they record information as magnetic spots on a rotating metal cylinder instead of on disks. The magnetic spots are arranged in a series of circular tracks along the surface of the drum. Information can be retrieved more quickly from drums than from either disks or tapes. But drums cannot hold as much data as disks or tapes.

Large-Core Storage Units consist of thousands of tiny, doughnut-shaped iron cores. Each core encircles an intersection of wires on a rectangular grid. A core can be magnetized in either a clockwise or counterclockwise direction by an electric current passing through the wires. When magnetized one way, a core represents 1. When magnetized the opposite way, it stands for 0. Information is stored by magnetizing a group of cores in a certain combination of 1's and 0's. Large-core storage units are faster than tape, disk, or drum units. They are used in computer systems for space missions and other projects that require extremely fast retrieval of data.

The Main Memory receives and stores data and instructions from an input device or an auxiliary storage unit. It also receives information from the control and arithmetic/logic units. The main memory stores only information that is currently needed by the CPU. After the CPU has finished with it, the information is transferred to auxiliary units for permanent storage or sent directly to an output device for immediate use.

The main memory consists of many memory cells. Each cell is a tiny device or electronic circuit capable of storing a binary digit. The cells are arranged into groups. Each group is assigned a number called an *address*, which makes it possible to locate specific bits of information quickly.

One type of memory used in many mainframes is the *magnetic core memory*. This memory closely resembles large-core auxiliary storage units. However, it has many more cores assembled on a larger wire grid, and the circuitry is more complex.

Mainframes designed for jobs that require extremely fast operating speeds use a *semiconductor memory*. This type of memory consists of integrated circuits, generally large-scale integrated circuits. A semiconductor memory is composed of one or more silicon chips. A chip only one-fourth the size of a postage stamp contains thousands of microscopic electronic circuits, each forming a memory cell for a binary digit. The compact size of a semiconductor memory makes it particularly suitable for minicomputers and microcomputers.

The Control Unit directs and coordinates the operations of the entire computer according to instructions in the main memory. It has to select the instructions in proper order because their sequence determines each step in the operations. The control unit interprets the instructions and relays the appropriate commands to the arithmetic/logic unit. Each set of instructions is expressed through an *operation code* in binary form that specifies exactly what must be done to complete a job. The operation code also provides the addresses that tell where data for the processing operations are stored in the memory.

The control unit regulates the flow of data between the memory and the arithmetic/logic unit and routes processed information to the output device. In some cases, the actions generated by the control unit result in the storage of new data and instructions in the main memory and auxiliary units.

The Arithmetic/Logic Unit, which is also called the *ALU*, manipulates data received from the main memory. It carries out all the arithmetic functions and logic processes required to solve a problem.

Data from the memory are held by the ALU temporarily in its own storage devices called *registers*. The registers consist of individual storage cells known as *flip-flops*. These miniature electronic circuits are connected to other circuits containing transistors and related switching devices. Three basic circuits, called the *AND-gate, OR-gate,* and *NOT-gate* or *inverter*, are combined in different ways to perform arithmetic and logic operations with electrical signals that represent binary digits. For example, one simple combination of these logic circuits performs addition. Another combination compares two numbers and then acts on the results of the comparison.

After an arithmetic or logic operation has been completed, the answer appears in the ALU's main register, which is known as the *accumulator*. The answer may be transferred from the accumulator to the memory for storage until it is needed for another operation, or it may be sent to the output device.

The Output Equipment, like the input equipment, serves as a communication link between the computer

Main Memory and Auxiliary Storage

The main memory inside a computer stores data and instructions for immediate use. An auxiliary unit outside the computer provides additional storage. It can hold more information than the main memory but operates at a slower speed. The two types of main memories are *magnetic core* and *semiconductor* memories. Commonly used auxiliary devices include *magnetic tape* and *magnetic disk* units.

WORLD BOOK illustrations by Steven Liska

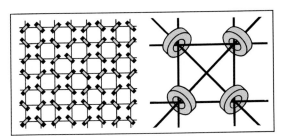

A Magnetic Core Memory has thousands of tiny rings. Each ring encircles an intersection of wires. A current passing through the wires magnetizes a ring, causing it to represent a binary digit.

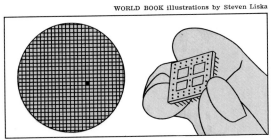

A Semiconductor Memory consists of one or more silicon chips that contain thousands of microscopic electronic circuits. Each of these circuits functions as a *memory cell* for a binary digit.

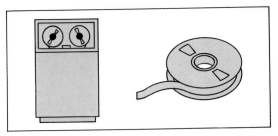

A Magnetic Tape Unit stores information on a reel of tape similar to that used in a tape recorder. The computer tape carries data and programs in the form of tiny magnetic spots.

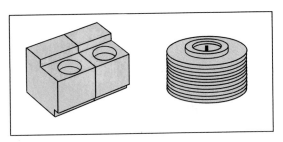

A Magnetic Disk Unit records data and instructions by magnetizing small areas on the surface of metal or plastic disks. The disks are stacked in a *disk pack* and held in a storage unit.

and the user. It translates the computer's electrical signals into a form comprehensible to the user. In some cases, the signals are altered so they can be used by machines that the computer operates.

Many computer systems have a CRT unit that displays output data as words, numbers, graphs, or pictures on a screen. Some of these units also can handle input material. Various computers use *automatic typewriters* or *line printers* to produce printed output data. Such output is called a *printout*. Automatic typewriters are used chiefly to print small amounts of data because they can type only one character at a time. Most line printers are high-speed devices that print a line of more than 100 letters and numbers at a time and from 60 to 2,000 lines a minute.

Other common output devices include *key punch machines*. These machines resemble typewriters and record data by punching patterns of holes in cards or paper tape. Output data presented in such a form or on magnetic tapes, disks, or drums can easily be put back into the computer when needed.

A few computer systems are equipped with *audio devices*, which transmit output information as spoken words through a type of telephone. The audio responses consist of words and phrases selected from a collection of human voice recordings.

Programming a Digital Computer

Programming involves the preparation and writing of detailed instructions for a computer. These instructions tell a computer exactly what data to use and what sequence of operations to perform with the data. Without such programs, a computer could not solve problems or deliver any other desired result.

In most cases, computer scientists and other computer specialists called *programmers* write the instructions. They refer to programs as *software* because the instructions have no physical parts. The term *hardware* is applied to the computer itself, including its electronic circuits and peripheral equipment.

Preparing a Program begins with a complete description of the job that the computer is to perform. This job description might be obtained from a business manager, an educator, an engineer, or a scientist. It explains what input data are required, what computing must be done, and what the output should be. Computer scientists or programmers use the job description to prepare diagrams and other pictorial aids that represent the steps needed to complete the task. They may also draw up a table listing all the variable conditions involved in the job. The computer specialists then produce a diagram that shows how all the major parts of the job fit together systematically. This diagram is called a *systems flow chart*.

In the case of a large or complicated project, the systems flow chart may be divided to break up the project into smaller jobs for which *subprograms* can be prepared. Different programmers work on the subprograms. A chief programmer writes the *main program*, which takes in all the subprograms.

The systems flow chart is often used to prepare another diagram, an *operations flow chart*. This kind of chart shows each step and instruction to create a clear picture

Producing a *World Book* Article with a Computer

The illustrations in this section show how the Computer article was prepared with a computer system. The text was keyed into the computer for storage in its memory. The computer was also used to plan the placement of illustrations. A computerized phototypesetting device used the text and layout data to set the type on photographic film, from which printing plates were made.

The pictures on this and the next page are WORLD BOOK photos.

An Editor reviewed the text of the article at a *video display terminal* (VDT). This device, equipped with an electronic keyboard and televisionlike screen, is connected with the computer for the input and output of text data.

Text Terminal Display

The Text of the article displayed on the terminal screen can be recorded as a *printout* by a high-speed printer.

An Editorial Artist prepared page layouts at another type of VDT. This terminal has various devices that enabled the layout artist to plot the position of the illustrations and accompanying caption material quickly.

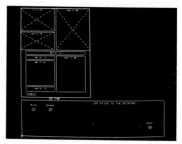

Layout Terminal Display

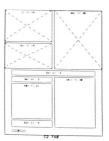

The Page Layout presented on the display can be reproduced in printed form just like the text.

The Computer Room contains the principal parts of *World Book*'s computer system, including the auxiliary storage units. All the information and instructions entered at the VDT's are processed and stored by this equipment.

Editorial Systems Computer Room

Phototypesetting. The text, captions, and layout data for each page of the article were transferred to computer tape. A computerized phototypesetting unit read the tape to set the type in its proper place on photographic film.

Computer Tape Drive

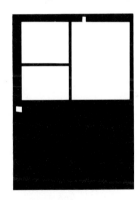

Computerized Phototypesetting Unit

The Elements of a Page consist of negatives of the type and illustration mask, both produced by the phototypesetter, plus *transparencies* (film copies of illustrations). The transparencies for the article were assembled as outlined by a set of illustration masks. The assembled transparencies were then sent to a photoengraver, who used them to produce negatives of the illustrations for the printer.

Negative of Type

Illustration Mask

Transparency Assembly

Producing the Printed Pages. The printer combined negatives of the text with negatives of the illustrations to produce final page film. The images on the combined negatives were then photographically transferred to printing plates. Finally, the pages were run off on the press.

Combining the Negatives

Printed Page

of every detail of a job. It helps programmers write their instructions and reduces the chance of introducing errors. After a program has been written, it is tested on the computer for mistakes. Computer experts refer to mistakes as "bugs" and the testing procedure as "debugging."

Programmers use various methods to enter programs into a computer. In one method, they write the instructions on forms called *coding sheets*. Key punch operators then put the instructions on punched cards, which are read by the computer's card reader. In a method called the *interactive mode*, programmers enter their instructions by means of a keyboard connected to a CRT display. All responses of the computer to the instructions appear on the screen immediately for the programmers to analyze. In most cases, programs resulting from this interaction between the computer and the programmers are recorded and stored on magnetic disks until needed.

Using Programming Languages. A programmer writes the instructions for a computer in a *programming language*. Such a language consists of letters, words, and symbols as well as rules for combining those elements. Some programming languages closely resemble the language of mathematics. Others enable programmers to write instructions in simple, everyday expressions, such as "READ," "ADD," and "STOP." Programming languages of this kind are called *high-level languages*.

The language that a programmer uses depends largely on the job to be done. If a task involves processing business data, the programmer would most likely use COBOL (*CO*mmon *B*usiness *O*riented *L*anguage). However, preparing a computer to solve complicated scientific problems might require the use of ALGOL (*ALGO*rithmic *L*anguage), which is a mathematically oriented programming language.

Some high-level languages can be used for business, technical, or scientific programming. Such languages include FORTRAN (*FOR*mula *TRAN*slation); APL (*A P*rogramming *L*anguage); and PL/1 (*P*rogramming *L*anguage *One*).

Another commonly used programming language is BASIC (*B*eginner's *A*ll-purpose *S*ymbolic *I*nstruction *C*ode). BASIC is well suited for writing relatively simple programs for minicomputers and microcomputers. Many high schools that offer a course in programming teach BASIC because it is both easy to learn and easy to use. Suppose that a computer is to print the sum of 2 and

4. A program for this operation written in BASIC would read:

```
10   PRINT 2 + 4
20   END
```

Each statement, or instruction, of a BASIC program begins with a line number, such as the 10 and 20 above. This number serves as the statement's label, identifying its exact position in the sequence of instructions. The word or phrase that appears after the line number instructs the computer what to do. PRINT tells it to print the sum of 2 plus 4. END stops the program. If this program were written in another high-level language, it would look quite different.

Some computer programs may be written in an *assembly language*. This kind of language is harder to use than a high-level language because it involves symbols as well as words. For example, an assembly language might use the symbols *AD* for *add* and *S* for *subtract*.

A computer cannot work directly with a program written in a high-level or assembly language. The instructions have to be translated into a *machine language* composed of binary digits that represent operation codes, memory addresses, and various symbols, such as plus and minus signs. Machine language is also known as *low-level language*. Special programs called *compilers* and *assemblers* translate high-level and assembly languages into machine language.

The Computer Industry

Commercial production of digital computers began in the mid-1950's. Since then, the computer industry has grown rapidly. It has become a major industry in the United States, which is the world's leading manufacturer and exporter of computer hardware and software. American computer companies employ more than 500,-000 workers, including manufacturing personnel, programmers, and technicians. The companies' sales total over $50 billion annually. A number of other countries, including Canada, France, Great Britain, Japan, and West Germany, also have a large computer industry.

This section deals chiefly with the computer industry in the United States. However, much of the information also applies to other countries. The computer industry can be divided into four branches: (1) research and development, (2) manufacturing, (3) sales, and (4) service and repair.

Research and Development. Most manufacturers of computers and computer equipment maintain research

An Operations Flow Chart is a kind of block diagram prepared by programmers to show the steps involved in a job. The example of a flow chart above gives the steps to be taken by a student arising in the morning and going to school. The symbols in the diagram are commonly used by programmers. For instance, a circle means stop or start. A diamond indicates a decision point.

laboratories. A number of universities, research institutions, and federal agencies also have computer research facilities. Computer engineers and scientists at these laboratories work on developing new high-speed switching devices, memories, and input and output devices. Other experts seek to improve the quality of programs or to devise new programming languages.

Manufacturing. Nearly 2,000 U.S. companies produce computer hardware and software. Many of the smaller firms specialize in input and output devices, microprocessors, or other computer parts. A number of these firms also specialize in microcomputers and minicomputers. The nation's largest computer and electronics companies produce chiefly mainframes. These companies include Burroughs, Control Data Corporation, Honeywell, and International Business Machines (IBM). Other large firms, such as INTEL Corporation, Texas Instruments, and Motorola, manufacture various kinds of computer equipment, particularly semiconductor devices.

Some manufacturers of computer systems provide their customers with programs suitable for a variety of purposes. However, programs for specific problems or special areas of application are generally supplied by software producers. Some customers prepare their own programs in such cases.

Sales. Manufacturers that make computer parts sell most of their goods to the producers of computer systems. Most producers of computer systems, in turn, sell directly to private businesses, federal agencies, educational institutions, and scientific research centers. Software producers also sell directly to users.

Some manufacturers of microcomputers, particularly personal computers and computer games, distribute their products to independent dealers and retail stores. These outlets then sell the products to the public. A few microcomputer and minicomputer manufacturers operate their own retail stores.

Service and Repair. Many manufacturers of computer systems have a staff of service engineers. These specialists repair and help maintain the equipment sold by their companies. A few independent dealers and stores also provide maintenance and repair service. Various government agencies and universities have their own staff for servicing computers.

The Development of the Computer

The inventions and ideas of many mathematicians and scientists led to the development of the computer. The first mechanical calculating machines were invented during the 1600's. One of the more notable of these devices was built in 1642 by the French mathematician and scientist Blaise Pascal. His machine added and subtracted by means of rotating toothed wheels.

During the 1830's, an English mathematician named Charles Babbage developed the idea of a mechanical digital computer. He tried to construct a machine called an *analytical engine*. The machine contained the basic elements of an automatic computer and was designed to perform complicated calculations according to a sequence of instructions. However, the technology of Babbage's time was not advanced enough to provide the precision parts needed to complete the machine.

Another important contribution to the development of the computer was made in the mid-1800's by George Boole, an English logician and mathematician. Boole devised a system of formulating logical statements symbolically so that they could be written and proved in a way similar to that of ordinary algebra. His system of mathematical logic, called *Boolean algebra*, later helped scientists design switching circuits for the arithmetic/logic unit of electronic computers.

The First Computers. In 1930, Vannevar Bush, an American electrical engineer, built the first reliable analog computer. He developed his machine, called a *differential analyzer*, to solve differential equations.

The first semielectronic digital computing device was constructed in 1939 by John V. Atanasoff, an American mathematician and physicist. In 1944, Howard Aiken, a Harvard University professor, built another early form of digital computer, which he called Mark I. The operations of this machine were controlled chiefly by electromechanical *relays* (switching devices). In 1946, J. Presper Eckert, Jr., and John W. Mauchly, two engineers at the University of Pennsylvania, built the first fully electronic digital computer. They called it ENIAC (*E*lectronic *N*umerical *I*ntegrator *A*nd *C*omputer). Vacuum tubes rather than relays controlled the computing operations of this machine. ENIAC worked about 1,000 times as fast as the Mark I and performed approximately 5,000 arithmetic operations a second.

During the 1940's, John Von Neumann, a Hungarian-born American mathematician, introduced an idea that greatly improved computer design. He proposed that programs could be coded as numbers and stored with data in a computer's memory. Von Neumann's idea was used in developing EDVAC (*E*lectronic *D*iscrete *V*ariable *A*utomatic *C*omputer), the first stored-program digital computer. EDVAC, which was completed in 1949, strongly influenced the design of later digital computers.

In 1951, the builders of ENIAC developed a more advanced electronic digital computer called UNIVAC I (*UNIV*ersal *A*utomatic *C*omputer). Within a few years, UNIVAC I was mass-produced and became the first commercially available computer. Unlike earlier computers, UNIVAC I handled both numbers and alphabetical characters equally well. It also was the first com-

University of Pennsylvania

ENIAC, completed in 1946, was the first fully electronic digital computer. Approximately 18,000 vacuum tubes controlled the computing operations of this enormous machine.

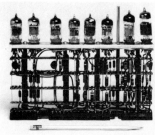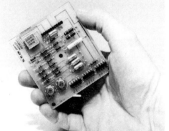

WORLD BOOK photo   WORLD BOOK photo   IBM

The Development of the Computer has been linked to technological advances. Mass production of vacuum tubes, *left*, made electronic digital computers possible. Transistors, *center*, resulted in faster, smaller computers. Miniaturization of circuits further reduced computer size. The multicircuited microprocessor, shown at right on a paper clip, led to pocket-sized microcomputers.

puter system in which the operations of the input and output equipment were separated from those of the computing unit. UNIVAC I used vacuum tubes for arithmetic and memory-switching functions. Machines that use vacuum tubes are often referred to as "first generation" computers.

Major Advances. The invention of the transistor in 1947 and of related solid-state devices during the 1950's and 1960's resulted in the production of faster and more reliable electronic computers. The new machines also were smaller and less expensive than earlier models. These "second generation" computers had logic circuits controlled by transistors and memory units composed of magnetic cores. They could process data in one-tenth the time it took computers that used vacuum tubes and magnetic drum memories.

The continued miniaturization of electronic equipment during the late 1960's and 1970's led to further advances in computer technology. The development of the integrated circuit enabled engineers to design both minicomputers and high-speed mainframes with tremendous memory capacities. Many of these "third generation" computers can carry out instructions at speeds measured in *nanoseconds* (billionths of a second).

The development of the microprocessor was another major breakthrough of the 1970's that benefited the computer industry. This large-scale integrated circuit made possible the production of inexpensive, pocket-sized microcomputers and portable terminals. The low cost of these devices has contributed to the increasing use of computers by small businesses and the public.

The widespread use of computers has promoted the development of *computer networks* on a local, national, and worldwide level. Such a network consists of two or more computers connected by high-speed communication lines. Network computers exchange data directly among one another. A network might also include terminals in banks, department stores, or schools.

Many computer networks have *time-sharing* capability, which allows several users to "share" a central computer at the same time. A computer can handle more than one job at a time because its CPU operates much faster than its peripheral equipment. The CPU works on one user's problem while the peripheral equipment handles input and output data for other users. This type of operation is sometimes called *multiprogramming*.

Computers of the Future. Researchers are seeking ways to improve computer memories and auxiliary stor-

age equipment. They expect to produce an efficient *magnetic bubble unit*, which is faster and cheaper to operate than mechanical tape or disk units. A magnetic bubble unit is a semiconductorlike chip that stores data in tiny, cylindrically shaped areas called *bubbles*. Up to a million bits of information can be stored in one bubble unit about the size of a matchbook.

Scientists are also working to increase computing speed by designing circuits that are even more densely packed and closer together. One proposed device, called a *very large-scale integrated circuit* (VLSI), would contain hundreds of thousands of transistors and other parts. Projects also are being undertaken to devise hardware and software that would enable a computer to understand ordinary speech. Such a system would simplify the preparation of written instructions to a certain degree.

Problems of the Computer Age. Vast amounts of personal, government, and business information are stored in computerized data bases maintained by government agencies and businesses. Many people fear that their right to privacy is threatened by the possible misuse or unauthorized disclosure of personal information in data bases. In addition, a major problem could result if someone obtained illegal access to top-secret information in government data bases. Business corporations face the possibility of industrial spies obtaining access to confidential material in their data bases.

Various attempts have been made to safeguard the information in data bases. For example, laws have been passed requiring better controls for managing and disclosing data. Also, computer designers have devised mathematical procedures for scrambling data so that it is comprehensible only to authorized personnel.

The growing reliance on computers has resulted in other problems besides those involving privacy and security. Computer breakdowns and faulty programming in business organizations delay transactions, disrupt work, and create inconveniences for consumers. An undetected computer malfunction at an air traffic control center could cause a collision. A computer failure at a national defense installation could have even far more serious consequences.

Careers

The use of computers in education, government, industry, science, and other fields is constantly increasing. As a result, career opportunities are excellent for computer specialists.

In most cases, a person needs thorough training in computer science or engineering to become a computer specialist. This training may begin with introductory computer courses in high school or college. It should also include considerable work in mathematics.

A college degree is desirable for many jobs in the computer field. College students study computer programming, computer systems, and information systems. They also take courses in such specialized areas as comparative programming languages, switching theory, and numerical and algorithmic analysis. Depending on the university or college, these courses may be offered by the department of computer science or by the departments of business, engineering, or mathematics. Some computer specialists continue their academic training after receiving a bachelor's degree.

Many employers provide training through an apprenticeship program or through courses offered by community colleges and vocational schools. Such on-the-job training takes several months and prepares a high school graduate for a lower-level position.

Jobs in the computer field can be divided into three major areas. They are (1) computer engineering, (2) computer science, and (3) computer operations.

Computer Engineering involves designing and servicing computer hardware. Design engineers develop new and better computers, peripheral equipment, and networks. Service engineers maintain and repair computers. Some service engineers work closely with design engineers to make certain that the features of a computer system are suited for a particular operation.

Computer Science. Occupations in the area of computer science include teaching, programming, systems analysis, and sales. Computer science teachers instruct students in how computers work and in how they are programmed. They may also serve as apprenticeship counselors. Computer science teachers work in high schools, training institutes, and colleges and universities. A large number of them have a master's or doctor's degree.

Many companies and government agencies employ programmers to write instructions for their particular computer operations. Software producers and computer manufacturers also hire programmers. Some programmers conduct research on programming languages and on computer operations and systems.

Systems analysts determine the most efficient use of a computer in any given situation. Analysts must have firsthand knowledge about the job, the equipment, and the skills of the people using the computer.

Computer companies sell their products or services through marketing and sales representatives. These representatives must have a background in computer science and engineering in addition to the necessary training in sales techniques.

Computer Operations are handled by a staff of various specialists. Computer operators control and monitor a computer and its peripheral equipment. They keep track of the jobs the computer does and may also schedule new jobs for it.

Other computer operations personnel include keyboard and key punch operators. A keyboard operator uses a data entry device that puts information directly into auxiliary storage units. A key punch operator prepares input data with a machine that punches holes in cards or paper tape.

A data-processing and operations manager directs the entire staff responsible for running a computer. The manager must have experience in using computers and be skilled in dealing with people.   GEORGE EPSTEIN

Questions

How does a computer solve problems involving words?

Why was the development of the large-scale integrated circuit important to computer technology?

WORLD BOOK photo

Programmers analyze a systems flow chart in planning instructions for a computer. Like many computer specialists, programmers need a college education or other advanced training.

RONALD REAGAN

FORD
38th President
1974—1977

CARTER
39th President
1977—1981

REAGAN, *RAY guhn,* **RONALD WILSON** (1911-   ), was elected President of the United States in 1980. Reagan, a Republican, previously had served two terms as governor of California. In the 1980 election, he defeated President Jimmy Carter, the Democratic candidate; and Representative John B. Anderson of Illinois, who ran as an independent. Before Reagan entered politics, he had been an actor nearly 30 years. He appeared in more than 50 movies and hosted two dramatic series on television.

When Reagan was elected President, the nation faced serious problems both in foreign affairs and in the economy. Relations between the United States and the Soviet Union had reached their worst point in several years following a Soviet invasion of Afghanistan in late 1979 and early 1980. In Iran, revolutionaries held hostage a group of Americans who had worked at the U.S. embassy in Teheran. The revolutionaries had seized the hostages in 1979 to protest American support for the deposed *shah* (king) of Iran. In the United States, the economy suffered from high unemployment and severe inflation.

During the presidential campaign, Reagan became known for his strongly conservative statements on many issues. He promised to increase military spending and to take a stronger stand against the Soviet Union and Iran. He called for less government regulation of business and the transfer of many federal welfare programs to state and local governments. He pledged to cut taxes and to balance the federal budget. Reagan also proposed to put a freeze on the hiring of federal employees and to dissolve the departments of Education and Energy, the two newest executive departments.

Reagan was a skillful campaigner and a gifted speaker. He stressed such traditional values as work, the family, patriotism, and self-reliance. Even his critics seldom questioned his sincerity.

At the age of 69, Reagan was the oldest man ever elected President. But he looked far younger than his years and was vigorous and athletic. He listed his chief interests as drama, politics, and sports. He especially enjoyed horseback riding at his weekend ranch, Rancho del Cielo, near Santa Barbara, Calif.

Early Life

Boyhood. Reagan was born on Feb. 6, 1911, in Tampico, Ill. His parents were John Edward Reagan, a shoe

Bill Boyarsky, the contributor of this article, is City-County Bureau Chief of the Los Angeles Times and the author of The Rise of Ronald Reagan.

salesman, and Nelle Wilson Reagan, a homemaker and occasional shop clerk. When Ronald was a baby, his father nicknamed him Dutch. The boy had one brother, John Neil (1909-   ), nicknamed Moon, now a retired advertising executive.

Nelle Reagan loved the theater and took part in many amateur productions. As a result, Dutch became interested in acting at an early age. During his boyhood, the Reagans lived in several small towns in western Illinois. Dutch's father moved the family from town to town as he searched for work. Reagan later wrote about his boyhood, "I realize now that we were poor, but I didn't know it at the time."

Education. When Dutch was 9 years old, he and his family settled in Dixon, Ill., where the boy finished elementary school and went to high school. In high school, he played football and basketball and took part in track and swimming meets. He appeared in several school plays and was elected president of the student council. During the summers, he worked as a lifeguard at a nearby resort.

In 1928, following graduation from high school, Reagan entered Eureka College in Eureka, Ill. He paid his college expenses with a partial scholarship, savings from the lifeguard job, and money he earned washing dishes at a fraternity house. In college, Dutch majored in economics and sociology. He played football, joined the track team, and served as captain of the swimming team. He had leading roles in many college plays and became president of the student body.

Acting Career

Motion-Picture Star. After Reagan graduated from Eureka College in 1932, he became a sports announcer for radio station WOC in Davenport, Iowa. That same year, he moved to station WHO in Des Moines, Iowa. At WHO, Reagan broadcast play-by-play accounts of major league baseball games, Big Ten football games, and other sports events.

In 1937, Reagan traveled to southern California to report on the spring training season of the Chicago Cubs baseball team. There, he made a screen test for Warner Brothers, one of the largest motion-picture studios. The studio signed him to an acting contract.

Reagan made his film debut in *Love Is On the Air* (1937), in which he played a radio announcer. He soon became a star and was known for his roles as a wholesome, likable young man. He portrayed Western heroes in such films as *Santa Fe Trail* (1940), *Law and Order* (1953), and *Tennessee's Partner* (1955). He also played American servicemen in many movies, including *International Squadron* (1941), *The Voice of the Turtle* (1947),

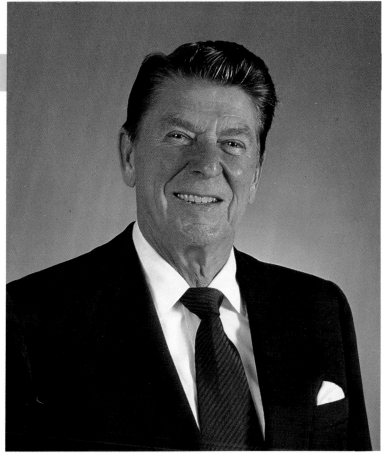

Michael Evans, Liaison

The United States flag had 50 stars when Ronald W. Reagan became President.

and *The Hasty Heart* (1949). In *Knute Rockne—All American* (1940), Reagan played one of his best-known roles, that of college football star George (the Gipper) Gipp. Reagan won praise from critics for his performance as a young man whose legs were amputated in *King's Row* (1942). In 1965, Reagan used a line he spoke in that film—"Where's the rest of me?"—as the title of his autobiography. Altogether, Reagan appeared in more than 50 feature films between 1937 and 1964, most of them for Warner Brothers.

Reagan entered the U.S. Army Air Forces in April 1942, during World War II. He was disqualified from combat duty because of poor eyesight. Instead, he spent most of the war in Hollywood, where he helped make

---

IMPORTANT DATES IN REAGAN'S LIFE

1911 (Feb. 6) Born in Tampico, Ill.
1932 Graduated from Eureka College.
1937 Made film debut in *Love Is On the Air*.
1940 (Jan. 25) Married Jane Wyman.
1942-1945 Served in the U.S. Army Air Forces.
1948 Divorced from Jane Wyman.
1952 (March 4) Married Nancy Davis.
1966 Elected governor of California.
1970 Reelected governor of California.
1980 Elected President of the United States.

---

training films. He was discharged in December 1945 as a captain.

Union Leader. In 1947, Reagan became president of the Screen Actors Guild (SAG), a union that represents film performers. He was elected to five consecutive terms, serving until 1952. During that time, which was a period of strong anti-Communist feeling in the United States, Reagan worked to remove suspected Communists from the movie industry. In 1949 and 1950, he served as chairman of the Motion Picture Industry Council, a public relations organization devoted to improving the public image of the film business.

Reagan served a sixth term as president of SAG in 1959 and 1960. During that period, he led a long and finally successful strike against the movie studios. The strike won payments to the actors for sales of their old films to television. Part of the money was used for a pension fund.

Family Life. Reagan met actress Jane Wyman while they both were appearing in Warner Brothers films. They were married on Jan. 25, 1940. The couple had a daughter, Maureen Elizabeth (1941-   ), and adopted a son, Michael Edward (1945-   ). The marriage ended in divorce in 1948.

In 1951, while Reagan was president of SAG, he met actress Nancy Davis (July 6, 1923-   ). Davis had complained to SAG that she was receiving unwanted

553

The Reagan Brothers are shown above at the ages of 3 and 1. John Neil is the boy at the left, and Ronald is the baby at the right.

Reagan's Birthplace, *left,* was an apartment above a bakery, later a bank, in this brick building. It stands on Main Street in Tampico, Ill.

Communist literature in the mail. She and Reagan were married on March 4, 1952. The couple had two children, Patricia Ann (1952-   ) and Ronald Prescott (1958-   ).

Television Star. From 1954 to 1962, Reagan hosted "The General Electric Theater," a weekly dramatic series on television. He also starred in several episodes in the series, which was sponsored by the General Electric Company, a leading manufacturer of electrical products. Between TV appearances, Reagan toured the country as a public relations representative for General Electric. He visited the company's plants and made speeches before chambers of commerce and other civic groups. In his talks, Reagan stressed such conservative

ideas as the importance of free enterprise and the dangers of too much government.

From 1962 to 1965, Reagan hosted and performed in a Western series called "Death Valley Days." He also made commercials for the sponsor, United States Borax & Chemical Corporation, a maker of cleaning products.

Political Career

Entry into Politics. Reagan had long taken an active interest in politics. At first, he held liberal views and belonged to the Democratic Party. In the 1948 presidential election, he campaigned for President Harry S. Truman, the Democratic candidate. During the 1950's, Reagan's views became more conservative. He cam-

The Reagan Family, *left,* posed for this portrait about 1913. From left to right are Ronald's father, John Edward Reagan, a shoe salesman; Ronald's brother, John Neil; young Ronald; and his mother, Nelle Wilson Reagan.

As a Teen-Ager, *right,* Reagan worked as a lifeguard at a resort near Dixon, Ill. He used his savings from the summer lifeguard job to help pay the costs of his education at Eureka College in Eureka, Ill.

Bettmann Archive

As a Sports Announcer, Reagan broadcast athletic events for Iowa radio stations during the 1930's.

Governor of California. Reagan first won public office in 1966, when he was elected governor of California. He defeated the state's Democratic governor, Edmund G. (Pat) Brown, by a landslide.

Reagan began his term as governor in January 1967. Once in office, he worked to slow the growth of government spending. He put a freeze on the hiring of state employees. He also persuaded state lawmakers to pass a welfare reform program. During his campaign, Reagan had criticized high taxes. Upon taking office, however, he found that there was a deficit in the state treasury. Reagan then sponsored three tax increases, one of them the largest in the state's history. But after the tax hikes had produced a surplus in the treasury, Reagan distributed much of the excess money to taxpayers.

Reagan was reelected governor in 1970 and served until 1975. As governor, he made major policy decisions himself but relied on others to handle the details.

Presidential Candidate. In 1968, Reagan had campaigned briefly for the Republican presidential nomination but did not win. In 1976, he tried again. He attracted much support among conservatives and won many delegates in the South and West. In an attempt to appeal to more liberal and Eastern delegates, he announced that his choice for Vice-President would be Senator Richard S. Schweiker of Pennsylvania. Schweiker was known for his liberal Senate record. But Reagan lost the nomination to President Gerald R. Ford by a narrow margin.

Reagan soon began to plan his campaign for the 1980 nomination. By November 1979, when he announced his candidacy, he had a huge lead in the polls over his Republican rivals. Six other Republicans sought the nomination. Reagan's chief opponents were Representative John B. Anderson of Illinois; George Bush, former U.S. ambassador to the United Nations (UN); and John B. Connally, former governor of Texas.

In February 1980, Reagan won the year's first presi-

paigned as a Democratic supporter of several Republican candidates, including presidential nominees Dwight D. Eisenhower in 1952 and 1956 and Richard M. Nixon in 1960. In 1962, Reagan became a Republican.

Reagan first gained nationwide political attention during the 1964 presidential campaign, when he made a stirring TV speech in behalf of the Republican candidate, Barry M. Goldwater. In the speech, Reagan attacked high taxes, wasteful government spending, the growth of government agencies, the rising crime rate, and soaring welfare costs. The speech drew record numbers of contributions for the Goldwater campaign.

Bettmann Archive

In *King's Row,* Reagan won praise from critics for his performance as a young man whose legs are amputated. Ann Sheridan appears with Reagan in this scene from the 1942 movie.

A Popular Movie Cowboy, Reagan starred in many Westerns. This scene is from *Tennessee's Partner* (1955). Reagan, playing a cowboy gold miner, holds his gun on a claim jumper.

As President of the Screen Actors Guild, a union representing film performers, Reagan, *right,* led a strike in 1960 that won payment to actors for TV sales of their old films.

As Governor of California, Reagan took part in a groundbreaking ceremony for an urban renewal project in Sacramento.

dential primary election in New Hampshire. His popularity continued to grow during the spring. In March, he won important primary victories over Connally in South Carolina and over Anderson and Bush in Illinois. By the end of May, Reagan had won 20 of the 24 primaries so far held, and the other Republican candidates had withdrawn from the race. Anderson, however, decided to run as an independent.

In July 1980, Reagan easily won the nomination for President on the first ballot at the Republican National Convention in Detroit. At his request, Bush was nominated for Vice-President. The Democrats renominated President Jimmy Carter and Vice-President Walter F. Mondale. Anderson chose former Governor Patrick J. Lucey of Wisconsin as his running mate.

The 1980 Election. In the presidential campaign, Reagan charged that Carter had failed to deal effectively with inflation and unemployment. During the first half of 1980, the inflation rate was about 15 per cent, and about $7\frac{1}{2}$ per cent of the nation's workers had no jobs. Reagan called for a lowering of the minimum wage law in the case of teen-agers to reduce unemployment among young people. To stimulate the economy, he proposed to slash federal income taxes by up to 30 per

---

———— REAGAN'S ELECTION ————

Place of Nominating Convention	Detroit
Ballot on Which Nominated	1st
Opponents*	Jimmy Carter (Democratic Party)
	John B. Anderson (independent candidate)
Age at Inauguration	69

*The table in the article ELECTORAL COLLEGE gives the electoral vote by states.

Michael Evans, Liaison
Reagan and His Wife, Nancy, liked to spend weekends at their ranch, Rancho del Cielo, near Santa Barbara, Calif.

cent. He pledged to boost military spending and to reduce government regulation of business. He also promised to balance the federal budget, claiming that a tax cut would increase economic activity so much that tax revenues would rise, not fall.

Carter argued that Reagan's plans would lead to still more inflation. He also questioned whether Reagan could balance the budget, reduce taxes, and increase defense spending all at the same time. In the 1980 presidential election, Reagan defeated Carter and Anderson.   BILL BOYARSKY

Related Articles in WORLD BOOK include:

Bush, George H. W.   President of the United States
Carter, James E., Jr.   Republican Party

Outline

I. **Early Life**
  A. Boyhood   B. Education
II. **Acting Career**
  A. Motion-Picture Star   C. Family Life
  B. Union Leader   D. Television Star
III. **Political Career**
  A. Entry into Politics   C. Presidential Candidate
  B. Governor of   D. The 1980 Election
     California

Questions

What were some problems the nation faced when Reagan became President?

How did Reagan serve in World War II?

What was Reagan's career before he entered politics?

When was Reagan first elected to public office?

What services did Reagan perform for the General Electric Company from 1954 to 1962?

Why did Reagan choose Senator Richard S. Schweiker as his running mate in 1976?

Where did Reagan get the title of his autobiography, *Where's the Rest of Me?*

How did Reagan's political views change during the 1950's?

What were some of Reagan's best-known screen roles?

How did Reagan gain national political attention?

Steve Liss and Eric Smith, Gamma/Liaison
At the 1980 Republican Convention, Reagan won his party's nomination for President. Former President Gerald R. Ford is at the left. Reagan's running mate, George Bush, is at the right.

Most Petroleum comes from the earth as a liquid called *crude oil*. Different types of crude oil vary in color and thickness, ranging from a clear, thin fluid to a dark, tarlike substance. In some parts of the world, petroleum also occurs as a solid in certain sands and rocks.

PETROLEUM

PETROLEUM is one of the most valuable natural resources in the world. Some people call petroleum *black gold*, but it may be better described as the lifeblood of industrialized countries. Fuels made from petroleum provide power for automobiles, airplanes, factories, farm equipment, trucks, trains, and ships. Petroleum fuels also generate heat and electricity for many houses and business places. Altogether, petroleum provides nearly half the energy used in the world.

In addition to fuels, thousands of other products are made from petroleum. These products range from paving materials to drip-dry fabrics and from engine grease to cosmetics. Petroleum is used to make such common items in the home as aspirins, carpets, curtains, detergents, milk cartons, phonograph records, plastic toys, and toothpaste.

Although we use a huge variety of products made from petroleum, few people ever see the substance itself. Most of it comes from deep within the earth as a liquid called *crude oil*. Different types of crude oil vary in thickness and color, ranging from a thin, clear oil to a thick, tarlike substance. Petroleum is also found in solid form in certain rocks and sands.

The word petroleum comes from two Latin words— *petra*, meaning *rock*, and *oleum*, meaning *oil*. People gave

Dan M. Bass, the contributor of this article, is the Kerr McGee Professor of Petroleum Engineering at the Colorado School of Mines.

it this name because they first found it seeping up from the earth through cracks in surface rocks. Today, petroleum is often referred to simply as *oil*, and most of it is found in rocks far beneath the surface of the earth.

Human beings have used petroleum for thousands of years. But few people recognized the full value of petroleum until the 1800's, when the kerosene lamp and the automobile were invented. These inventions created an enormous demand for two petroleum fuels, kerosene and gasoline. Since about 1900, scientists have steadily increased the variety and improved the quality of petroleum products.

Petroleum, like other minerals, cannot be replaced after it has been used. People are using more and more petroleum each year, and the world's supply is rapidly running out. Some experts predict that the demand for petroleum may exceed the supply by 1990.

Most industrialized nations depend heavily on imported petroleum to meet their energy needs. As a result of this dependence, oil-exporting countries have been able to use petroleum as a political and economic weapon by restricting exports to some of these nations. Oil exporters have also strained the economies of a large number of countries, particularly the poorer ones, by drastically increasing the price of petroleum. Many nations, rich as well as poor, have suffered petroleum shortages since the early 1970's.

To prevent a full-scale energy shortage, scientists are experimenting with artificial forms of oil and with other sources of fuel. But even if new energy sources appear quickly, people will have to rely on petroleum for many years. Conservation of oil has thus become urgent for

Robert H. Glaze, Artstreet

Oilways, Exxon Company, U.S.A.

Derricks and Refineries are familiar symbols of the petroleum industry. A tall steel derrick, *left*, supports the equipment used to drill deep into the earth for petroleum. In a refinery, *right*, crude oil is processed into fuels and other valuable products.

every country. People now need to be just as inventive in finding ways to conserve petroleum as they have been in finding ways to use it.

The Uses of Petroleum

Petroleum has a greater variety of uses than perhaps any other substance in the world. The reason petroleum has so many uses lies in its complicated molecular struc-

ture. Crude oil is chiefly a mixture of many different *hydrocarbons*, which are molecules made up of the elements hydrogen and carbon. Some of these hydrocarbons are gaseous, and some are solid. Most of the hydrocarbons, however, form a liquid.

The mixtures of different hydrocarbons give special characteristics to the *fractions* (parts) of petroleum. Some fractions, such as gasoline and kerosene, are valu-

Petroleum Terms

Barrel is the standard unit used to measure crude oil and most petroleum products. One barrel (159 liters) equals 42 gallons in the United States or 35 imperial gallons in Canada.

Bituminous Sands, or *tar sands*, are grains of sand surrounded by a black, gluelike substance that can be processed into oil or gas.

Bringing in a Well means to start the oil flowing in a well.

Crude Oil is oil as it occurs naturally in a reservoir.

Derrick is a tall steel structure that holds the equipment used to drill an oil well.

Dry Hole is a well that fails to produce oil or gas in commercial quantities.

Enhanced Recovery is any method of adding energy to a reservoir to force oil to flow into a producing well.

Fraction is any of the groups of hydrocarbons that make up crude oil. Fractions are separated during refining.

Hydrocarbon is a chemical compound made up of the elements hydrogen and carbon.

Mineral Lease is an agreement between an oil company and a property owner. It gives the company the right to drill for, and to produce, oil on the property.

Offshore Wells are wells drilled in oceans, seas, or lakes.

Oil Field is an area that contains one or more reservoirs.

Oil Shale is a sedimentary rock containing *kerogen*, a substance that can be processed into oil.

Oil Trap is a nonporous, underground rock formation that blocks the movement of oil and so seals off a reservoir.

Petrochemicals are chemicals processed from oil and gas.

Primary Recovery is a method in which the natural energy in a reservoir is used to bring oil into a producing well.

Reservoir is an accumulation of petroleum below the earth's surface. It consists of tiny drops of oil that collect in the pores of such rocks as limestone and sandstone.

Rig consists of the derrick, hoisting machinery, and other equipment used in drilling an oil well.

Roughneck is a worker on a drilling crew.

Royalty is money paid to landowners for oil produced on their property. Most oil companies pay a royalty of one-eighth to one-sixth the value of each barrel of oil produced and sold. Landowners may also take royalties in oil.

Wildcat Well is a well drilled in an area where no oil or gas has been found.

PETROLEUM

able in their natural liquid state. Others must be converted from one state to another or combined with different substances before they can be used.

Various types of crude oil contain different amounts of certain fractions. *Light crudes* have large amounts of dissolved gases, gasoline, and other light fractions. Most *heavy crudes* have a high proportion of heavy oils and asphalt. All crude oil contains some substances in addition to hydrocarbons. These impurities, which include metallic compounds and sulfur, may make up as much as 10 per cent of some types of oil.

Petroleum refineries separate the various fractions and change them into useful products. Most crude oil is refined into gasoline, heating oil, and other fuels. The rest of the oil is converted chiefly into industrial raw materials and lubricants.

Petroleum as a Fuel. Petroleum fuels ignite and burn readily and produce a great amount of heat and power in relation to their weight. They are also easier to handle, store, and transport than such other fuels as coal and wood. Petroleum supplies about half the energy consumed in the United States. It is the source of nearly all the fuels used for transportation and of many fuels used to produce heat and electricity.

Fuels for Transportation include gasoline, diesel fuel, and jet fuel. About 45 per cent of all crude oil is refined into gasoline, about 7 per cent into diesel fuel, and about 7 per cent into jet fuel.

Gasoline is classified into regular, premium, and aviation grades, according to how smoothly it burns in an engine. Most motor vehicles and all piston-engine airplanes use gasoline. Diesel fuel requires less refining and is cheaper than gasoline. Nearly all trains, ships, and large trucks use diesel fuel. Jet airplanes burn jet fuel, which is either pure kerosene or a mixture of gasoline, kerosene, and other fuels.

Fuels for Heating and Energy Production account for about 26 per cent of all refined petroleum. Such fuels may be classed as *distillate oils* or *residual oils*. Distillate oils are lighter oils, most of which are used to heat houses and small business places. Residual oils are heavier, thicker oils. They provide power for electric utilities, factories, and large ships. Residual oils are also used to heat large buildings.

Many people who live on farms or in mobile homes use *liquefied petroleum gas* (LPG) for heating and cooking. LPG consists chiefly of butane and propane gases that have been converted under pressure into liquids. LPG is used in industry for cutting and welding metals and on farms for operating various kinds of equipment.

Petroleum as a Raw Material. About 13 per cent of petroleum fractions serve as raw materials in manufacturing. Many of these fractions are converted into *petrochemicals*, which make up more than a third of all the chemicals produced in the United States. Petrochemicals are used in manufacturing cosmetics, detergents, drugs, fertilizers, insecticides, plastics, synthetic fibers, and hundreds of other products.

By-products of petroleum refining are also used as raw materials in certain industries. These by-products include asphalt, the chief roadbuilding material, and wax, an essential ingredient in such products as candles, milk cartons, and furniture polish.

Other Uses of Petroleum. Such products as lubricants and specialized industrial oils account for about 2 per cent of petroleum production. Lubricants reduce friction between the moving parts of equipment. They range from the thin, clear oil used in scientific instruments to the heavy grease applied to aircraft landing gear. Specialized industrial oils include *cutting oils* and *electrical oils*, which are used in certain manufacturing processes.

Where Petroleum Is Found

Petroleum is found on every continent and beneath every ocean. But present-day techniques enable petroleum engineers to *recover* (bring to the surface) only about a third of the oil in most deposits. These recoverable amounts of petroleum are called *reserves*.

Petroleum experts estimate that the world's oil reserves total about 640 billion barrels. Some geologists predict that additional reserves will be discovered, particularly in China, on Canadian islands in the Arctic Ocean, and in offshore seabeds. However, many experts think that most of the major oil fields have already been found. They believe that world reserves are more likely to be increased by better methods of recovery than by new discoveries of oil.

The Middle East has about 56 per cent of the world's oil. Its reserves total about 362 billion barrels. Saudi Arabia has more than 160 billion barrels, or about a fourth of the world's reserves. Kuwait, with about 65 billion barrels, and Iran, with about 58 billion barrels, rank second and third in the region. Large reserves have

Some Uses of Petroleum Products

Fuels

For Transportation

Aviation gasoline	Jet fuel
Diesel fuel	Kerosene
Gasoline	

For Heating and Energy Production

Distillate oils	Residual oils
Liquefied petroleum gas (LPG)	

Raw Materials

Asphalt	Industrial hydrogen
Carbon black	Naphtha
Coke	Wax

Miscellaneous Oils

Lubricating oils and greases	Road oils
Medicinal oils	Technical oils

Petrochemicals

Alcohol	Gasoline additives
Ammonia	Ink
Cosmetics	Insecticides
Drugs	Paint
Dyes	Plastics
Explosives	Resins
Fertilizers	Solvents
Fibers	Synthetic rubber
Food additives	

also been found in other countries on the Persian Gulf.

Europe, including Asian Russia, has about 15 per cent of the world's oil supply. The Soviet Union has the largest reserves in the region. Most of Russia's approximately 67 billion barrels lie west of the Ural Mountains, though there are several large oil fields in Siberia. The only other major European reserves, which amount to about 22 billion barrels, are beneath the North Sea and belong chiefly to Great Britain and Norway.

Africa possesses about 58 billion barrels of oil, or about 9 per cent of the world's reserves. Most of the oil lies in Libya, Algeria, and other countries in northern Africa. Libya's reserves of more than 23 billion barrels rank among the world's largest. South of the Sahara, large amounts of oil have been found only in Nigeria, which has about 18 billion barrels.

Latin America has about 56 billion barrels of petroleum reserves, or about 9 per cent of the world's total. Mexico has the largest reserves in the region, about 31 billion barrels. Rich oil fields lie in the states of Chiapas, Tabasco, and Veracruz, and in the Bay of Campeche. Other large deposits are along the Pánuco River and on the Isthmus of Tehuantepec. Venezuela has the second largest reserves in Latin America, about 18 billion barrels. Its principal reservoir, which is in the Lake

Maracaibo Basin, has produced more oil than any other field in the world. Venezuela also has large deposits of heavy oil north of the Orinoco River. Latin America's other major oil reserves lie in Argentina, Ecuador, and Brazil.

Asia, excluding Asian Russia and the Middle East, has about 40 billion barrels of oil, or about 6 per cent of the world's reserves. About half these reserves lie in China. Its largest oil field is at Ta-ch'ing in northern Manchuria. Other major Chinese deposits have been found on the Shantung Peninsula and in the province of Sinkiang. Indonesia, with about 10 billion barrels, has the second largest reserves in the Far East.

The United States and Canada have about 33 billion barrels of oil, which amounts to about 5 per cent of the world total. The United States has slightly more than 26 billion barrels of petroleum. Most of these reserves lie in Texas, Louisiana, California, Oklahoma, and Alaska. In time, U.S. reserves may be increased by oil produced from *oil shale,* a type of rock that is plentiful in Colorado, Wyoming, and Utah. Oil shale contains *kerogen,* a waxy substance that yields oil when heated.

Most of Canada's 7 billion barrels of oil lie in the

Arabian American Oil Company

The Middle East has more than half the world's oil. About a fourth of the total reserves lie in Saudi Arabia alone. Many nations depend on Middle Eastern oil to meet their energy needs.

Gamma from Liaison

Offshore Wells provide more than 20 per cent of the oil produced in the world. The North Sea, which has some of the richest offshore deposits, is a major source of oil for Western Europe.

© Alan Orling, Black Star

Bituminous Sands, or *tar sands,* can be processed into petroleum. The world's largest deposits of these sands lie along the Athabasca River in the Canadian province of Alberta.

Steve Northup, Camera 5

Oil Shale contains a substance that yields oil when heated. Huge deposits of oil shale in Colorado, Wyoming, and Utah may someday provide more oil than the oil fields of the Middle East.

PETROLEUM

province of Alberta. Saskatchewan, British Columbia, and Manitoba also have oil fields. In addition, geologists believe that Canada has the world's largest deposits of *bituminous sands*, or *tar sands* (sands soaked with an oil-producing substance). These deposits, which are estimated to contain up to 300 billion barrels of oil, lie along the Athabasca River in Alberta. Production of oil from the sands began in 1967.

How Petroleum Was Formed

Most geologists believe that petroleum was formed from the remains of tiny marine plants and animals that died millions of years ago. This *organic theory* of petroleum formation is based on the presence of certain carbon-containing substances in oil. Such substances could have come only from once living organisms. The same process that produced petroleum also produced natural gas. Natural gas therefore is often found on top of oil deposits or dissolved in them.

According to the organic theory, water covered much more of the earth's surface millions of years ago than it does today. Masses of plants and animals drifted about on the ancient oceans. After these organisms died, their remains settled to the bottom of the oceans. *Sediments*, which are particles of mud, sand, and other substances, drifted down over the organic matter on the ocean floor. As the sediments piled up, their great weight pressed them into layers of *sedimentary rock*.

The formation of the sedimentary rock, together with other changes in the earth's crust, subjected the buried plant and animal materials to great pressure and heat. Bacteria may also have acted on these materials, breaking down some of the complex chemicals into hydrocarbons. Over several million years, these and perhaps other natural forces converted the organic materials into crude oil.

In time, the oil moved up from the ancient ocean floor into the layers of sedimentary rock. Geologists believe this movement may have been caused by the presence of water in the rock. Water, which is heavier than oil,

World Production and Consumption of Petroleum

This graph shows the amounts of petroleum produced and used in various regions of the world. The Middle East produces about 12 times as much petroleum as it consumes. However, most regions consume more oil than they produce.

WORLD BOOK graph

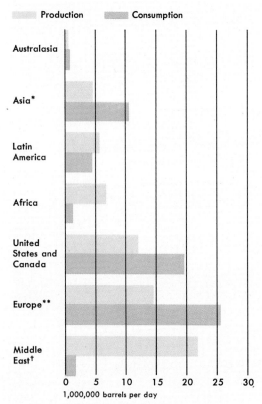

1,000,000 barrels per day

*Excludes Asian Russia and the Middle East.
**Includes Asian Russia.
†Excludes Egypt and the Sudan.

Source: *British Petroleum Statistical Review of the World Oil Industry 1979.*

Oil Regions of the World

- Oil field
- Oil sands
- Oil shale
- Major oil-producing region
- Possible oil-producing region

could have pushed the oil upward. Another possible cause was the weight of the overlying layers of rock, which would tend to squeeze the oil into holes and cracks in the rock.

Tiny drops of oil moved into a type of rock known as *reservoir rock*. Reservoir rock has two characteristics that enable fluids to move through it: (1) porosity and (2) permeability. Porosity is the presence of small openings called *pores*. Permeability means that some of these pores are connected by spaces through which fluids can move. The oil continued to migrate from pore to pore until it reached impermeable rock. In some cases, this rock sealed off the oil reservoir and formed a *trap*. Later, shifts in the earth's crust caused the oceans to draw back. Dry land then appeared over many reservoir rocks and traps.

The most common types of petroleum traps are *anticlines, faults, stratigraphic traps*, and *salt domes*. An anticline is an archlike formation of rock under which petroleum may collect. A fault is a fracture in the earth's crust, which can shift an impermeable layer of rock next

to a permeable one that contains oil. Most stratigraphic traps consist of layers of impermeable rock that surround oilbearing rocks. In a salt dome, a cylinder- or cone-shaped formation of salt pushes up through sedimentary rocks, causing the rocks to arch and fracture in its path. Petroleum may accumulate above or along the sides of such a formation.

Most reservoirs and traps lie deep beneath the surface of the earth. However, some reservoirs have formed near the surface, and others have been shifted upward by changes in the earth's crust. Oil from these shallow deposits may reach the surface as *seepages* (trickles) or springs. In some places, such as Venezuela and the island of Trinidad, enough oil has collected at the surface to form a lake.

Today, the organic matter in some sedimentary deposits is being subjected to conditions of pressure, heat, and bacterial action similar to those that formed oil ages ago. But it takes millions of years for useful amounts of

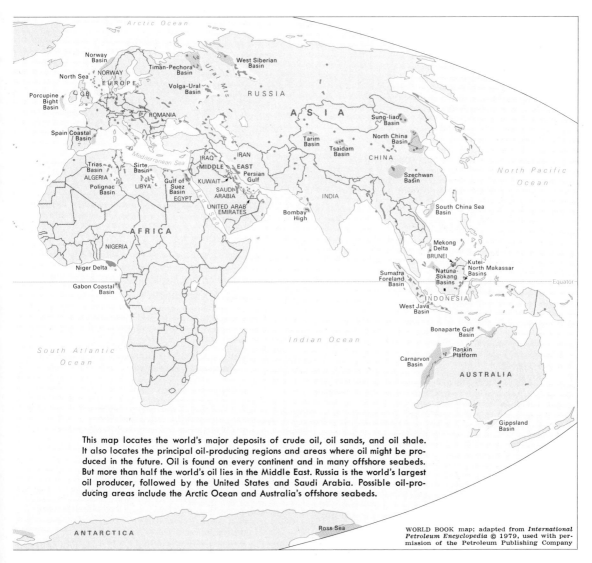

This map locates the world's major deposits of crude oil, oil sands, and oil shale. It also locates the principal oil-producing regions and areas where oil might be produced in the future. Oil is found on every continent and in many offshore seabeds. But more than half the world's oil lies in the Middle East. Russia is the world's largest oil producer, followed by the United States and Saudi Arabia. Possible oil-producing areas include the Arctic Ocean and Australia's offshore seabeds.

WORLD BOOK map; adapted from *International Petroleum Encyclopedia* © 1979, used with permission of the Petroleum Publishing Company

Most crude oil lies in underground formations called *traps*. In a trap, petroleum collects in the pores of certain kinds of rock. Gas and water are also present in most traps. The most common types of traps are *anticlines*, *faults*, *stratigraphic traps*, and *salt domes*.

WORLD BOOK illustrations by Robert Keys

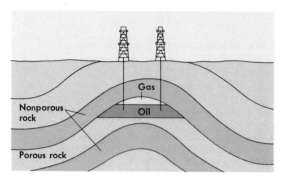

An Anticline Is an Archlike Formation.

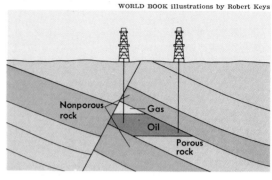

A Fault Is a Fracture in the Earth's Crust.

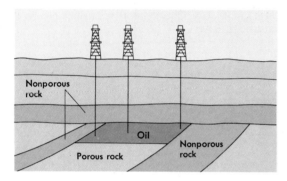

A Stratigraphic Trap Has Horizontal Layers of Rock.

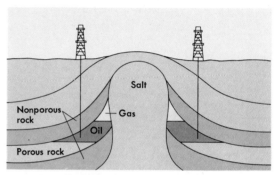

A Salt Dome Is Formed by a Large Mass of Salt.

oil to develop. People are consuming petroleum much faster than it is being formed.

Exploring for Petroleum

Before about 1900, petroleum prospectors could do little more than look for oil seepages and hope for luck. Their equipment consisted chiefly of a pick, a shovel, and possibly a *divining rod*, a forked stick that some people believed could magically locate oil or water. During the 1900's, however, petroleum exploration has developed into a science. Today's prospectors use a variety of complicated instruments and are likely to be *oil geologists* or *geophysicists*.

Geological Studies. Oil geologists study rock formations on and below the earth's surface to determine where petroleum might be found. They usually begin by selecting an area that seems favorable to the formation of petroleum, such as a sedimentary basin. Geologists then make a detailed map of the surface features of the area. They may use photographs taken from airplanes and satellites in addition to their ground-level observations, particularly if the area is difficult to cover on foot. The geologists study the map for signs of possible oil traps. For example, the appearance of a low bulge on an otherwise flat surface may indicate the presence of a salt dome, a common petroleum trap.

If the site looks promising, oil geologists may have holes drilled into the earth to obtain *cores*, which are cylindrical samples of the underground layers of rock.

The geologists analyze the cores for chemical composition, structure, and other factors that relate to the formation of petroleum.

Oil geologists also study *well logs*. A well log is a record of the rock formations encountered during the drilling of a well. Well logs describe such characteristics as the depth, porosity, and fluid content of the rocks. Oil geologists can use this information to estimate the location and size of possible deposits in the area surrounding the wells.

Geophysical Studies. Geophysicists provide oil geologists with detailed information about underground and underwater rock formations. Geophysicists can locate geological structures that may contain oil with the aid of special instruments. The most widely used instruments are (1) the gravimeter, (2) the magnetometer, and (3) the seismograph.

The Gravimeter (pronounced *gruh VIHM uh tuhr*), or gravity meter, measures the pull of gravity at the earth's surface. Different kinds of rocks have different effects on gravity. For example, nonporous rocks tend to increase gravitational pull, and porous rocks tend to decrease it. Low readings on a gravimeter may thus show the presence of possibly oilbearing, porous layers of rock. Gravimeters are particularly effective in detecting salt domes because salt decreases the pull of gravity more than most rocks do.

The Magnetometer (*MAG nuh TAHM uh tuhr*) records changes in the earth's magnetic field. The magnetic pull of the earth is affected by the types of rocks beneath its surface. Sedimentary rocks generally have lower magnetism than other types of rock, which may contain iron and other magnetic substances. This difference in magnetic pull enables geophysicists to identify layers of sedimentary rock that may contain oil. Magnetic pull is also affected by structural irregularities, such as anticlines and faults. Magnetometers may thus detect certain petroleum traps.

The Seismograph (SYZ muh graf) measures the speed of sound waves traveling beneath the earth's surface. This speed depends on the type of rock through which the sound waves move. Geophysicists can use the speeds recorded by a seismograph to determine the depth and structure of many rock formations.

In a seismographic survey, geophysicists may set off a small explosion at or just below the earth's surface. The sound waves generated by the explosion travel to underground layers of rock and bounce back to the surface. The seismograph records how long it takes the sound waves to reach the surface. Many geophysicists use a system called *vibroseis (vy BROH see ihs)* to eliminate the environmental risks of using explosives. In this system, sound waves are produced by a huge vibrator that repeatedly strikes the earth. The vibrator is mounted on a special truck called a *thumper truck.*

Geophysicists also conduct seismographic surveys of offshore areas. They send an electronic pulse or compressed-air discharge from a ship into the water. The resulting sound waves are reflected from underwater formations to seismographic equipment that is towed behind the ship.

By means of a technique called *bright spot technology,* geophysicists can use seismographs to detect the presence of fluids in underground and underwater rock formations. This technique involves the use of highly sensitive recorders that pick up changes in the *amplitude* (height) of sound waves. Sound waves change in amplitude when they are reflected from rocks that contain gas and other fluids. Such changes appear as irregularities, called *bright spots,* on the sound wave patterns recorded by the seismograph.

Drilling an Oil Well

Drilling for petroleum is nearly always an enormous gamble. Most geological and geophysical studies indicate the places where petroleum might have accumulated. But there is less than a 10 per cent chance that oil is actually present in those places. There is only a 2 per cent chance that it is present in commercially useful amounts. Many *dry holes* may be drilled before a producing well is finally *brought in* and the oil begins to flow.

Preparatory Measures take place both on and off the drilling site. These measures include (1) obtaining leases and permits, (2) preparing the site, and (3) rigging up.

Obtaining Leases and Permits. In the United States, oil companies must deal with the owner of a site—or with the government if the site is on public property—for permission to drill. Most companies obtain a *mineral lease,* which gives them the right to drill wells and to produce oil and gas on the site. In return, the owner generally receives *royalties* (shares of the income) from any oil and gas recovered.

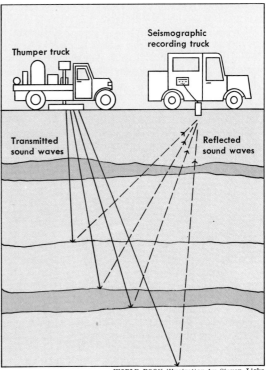

WORLD BOOK illustration by Steven Liska

Sound Waves Can Help Find Oil. A method called *vibroseis* operates on the principle that the speed of sound waves varies according to the type of rock through which they travel. Vibroseis thus enables geophysicists to locate rocks that may contain oil. In this method, a *thumper truck* produces sound waves. Another truck holds a *seismograph,* an instrument that records the time in which underground rocks reflect the waves to the surface.

After obtaining a mineral lease, an oil company must get drilling permits from the federal, state, and local governments. Before such permits are issued, a company has to meet certain requirements. In most cases, for example, a company must submit studies of the effect drilling will have on the environment. A company must also show how it intends to conserve natural resources and prevent waste.

In Canada, most of the mineral rights for land and offshore areas are owned by the federal or provincial governments. Oil companies therefore obtain most mineral leases from the government. The companies are then required by law to begin certain exploratory work on the leased area within a specified period.

Preparing the Site. A drilling site must be flat and free of trees and brush to make room for drilling operations. In most locations, bulldozers are used to clear and level the ground. If an area has rough terrain or a harsh climate, additional preparation may be required. On Alaska's North Slope, for example, drilling sites had to be reinforced with gravel and wood. If these measures had not been taken, the heat generated by the drilling equipment might have thawed the frozen soil and caused the wells to collapse.

Roads must be built to the drilling site. The site must also have a power plant and a water supply system. If the location is far from a city or town, living quarters may have to be set up for the crew.

After the drilling site has been prepared, the construction crew brings in the *rig*, which consists chiefly of drilling equipment and a derrick. The rig may be transported by truck, bulldozer, barge, or aircraft, depending on the location of the site.

Rigging Up is the process of setting up and connecting the various parts of the rig. First, the construction crew erects the derrick over the spot where the well is to be drilled. Derricks serve mainly to hold the hoisting machinery and other drilling equipment. The hoisting machinery, which includes pulleys, reels, and heavy wire, lowers the drill into the well hole and hoists it out. Derricks range in height from 80 to 200 feet (24 to 61 meters), depending on the estimated depth of the oil. Most construction crews use a *jackknife derrick*, which consists of two or more sections that can be easily transported and assembled.

Next, the crew installs the engines that power the drill and other machinery on the rig. The workers also assemble the various pipes, tanks, pumps, and other drilling equipment. After the drill is attached to the hoisting machinery, the well hole can be *spudded in* (started) by any of several methods of drilling.

Methods of Drilling. The first oil crews in the United States used a drilling technique called *cable-tool drilling*, which is still used for boring shallow holes in hard rock formations. Today, however, most American crews use a faster and more accurate method called *rotary drilling*. On sites where the well must be drilled at an angle, crews use a technique called *directional drilling*. In addition, petroleum engineers are testing a variety of methods to increase the depth of oil wells and reduce the cost of drilling operations.

Cable-Tool Drilling is a simple process. It works much as a chisel is used to cut wood or stone. In this method, a steel cable repeatedly drops and raises a heavy cutting tool called a *bit*. Bits may be as long as 8 feet (2.4 meters) and have a diameter of 4 to $12\frac{1}{2}$ inches (10 to 31.8 centimeters). Each time the bit drops, it drives deeper and deeper into the earth. The sharp edges of the bit break up the soil and rock into small particles. From time to time, the workers pull out the cable and drill bit and pour water into the hole. They then scoop up the water and particles at the bottom of the hole with a long steel pipe known as a *bailer*. The crew for cable-tool drilling generally consists of a *driller*, who operates the equipment on the rig, and a *tool dresser*, who sharpens the bit and does other jobs.

Rotary Drilling, like cable-tool drilling, works on a simple principle. The drill bores through the ground much as a carpenter's drill bores through wood. The bit on a rotary drill is attached to the end of a series of connected pipes called the *drill pipe*. The drill pipe is rotated by a turntable on the floor of the derrick. The pipe is lowered into the ground. As the pipe turns, the bit bores through layers of soil and rock. The drilling crew attaches additional lengths of pipe as the hole becomes deeper.

The drill pipe is lowered and raised by a hoisting mechanism called the *draw works*, which operates somewhat like a fishing rod. Steel cable is unwound

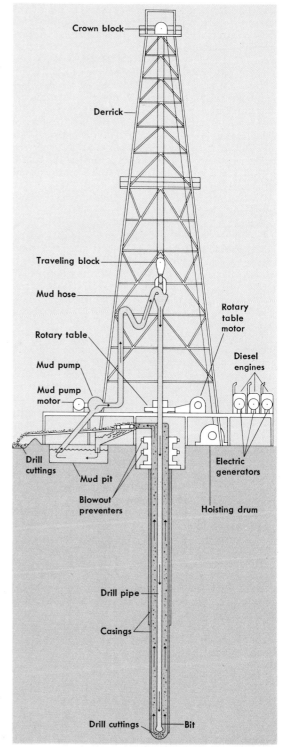

WORLD BOOK illustration by Robert Keys

A Rotary-Drilling Rig includes a derrick and the machinery that raises and lowers the drilling equipment. As the *drill pipe* is lowered into the ground, it is turned by a *rotary table*. The *bit* at the end of the drill pipe bores through the earth. A special type of mud is pumped through the well to clean the bit and bring *cuttings* (pieces of rock) to the surface.

from the *hoisting drum*, which is a kind of reel. The cable is then threaded through two *blocks* (sets of pulleys)—the *crown block*, at the top of the rig, and the *traveling block*, which hangs inside the derrick. The workers attach the upper end of the drill pipe to the traveling block with a giant hook. They can then lower the pipe into the hole or lift it out by turning the hoisting drum in one direction or the other.

During rotary drilling, a fluid called *drilling mud* is pumped down the drill pipe. It flows out of the openings in the bit and then back up between the pipe and the wall of the hole to just below the derrick floor. This constantly circulating fluid cools and cleans the bit and carries *cuttings* (pieces of soil and rock) to the surface. Thus, the crew can drill continuously without having to bail out the cuttings from the bottom of the well. The drilling mud also coats the sides of the hole, which helps prevent leaks and cave-ins. In addition, the pressure of the mud in the well reduces the risk of *blowouts* and *gushers*, which are caused by the sudden release of pressure in a reservoir. Blowouts and gushers may destroy the rig and waste much oil.

The drilling crew changes the bit when it becomes dull or if a different type of bit is needed. Different bits are used for hard and soft rocks. Each time the workers change the bit, they must pull out the entire drill pipe, which may be longer than 25,000 feet (7,620 meters). As the drill pipe is raised from the well, the crew disconnects the lengths of pipe and stacks them inside the derrick. After the new bit has been attached, the workers lower the pipe back into the hole.

Most rotary-drilling crews consist of a *driller*, one or more *derrickmen*, and several workers known as *roughnecks*. Crews work around the clock, rotating in 8- or 12-hour shifts called *tours* (pronounced *TOW uhrz*).

Directional Drilling. In cable-tool drilling and most rotary drilling, the well hole is drilled straight down from the derrick floor. In directional drilling, the hole is drilled at an angle. Drilling crews may use special devices called *turbodrills* and *electrodrills*. The motors that power these drills lie directly above the bit and rotate only the lower section of the drill pipe. Such drills enable drillers to guide the bit along a slanted path. Drillers may also use tools known as *whipstocks* to drill at an angle. A whipstock is a long steel wedge grooved like a shoehorn. The wedge is placed in the hole with the pointed end upward. The drilling path is slanted as the bit travels along the groove of the whipstock.

Many crews adopt directional drilling to drill more than one well at a site. The method is also used if a well cannot be drilled directly over a petroleum deposit. For example, oil was known to lie beneath the State Capitol in Oklahoma City. By means of directional drilling, the crew drilled a hole to the oil from a derrick 400 feet (120 meters) away.

Experimental Methods of Drilling include the use of electricity, intense cold, and high-frequency sound waves. Each of these methods is designed to shatter the rocks at the bottom of the hole. Petroleum engineers are also testing a drill that has a bit with a rotating surface. By means of remote control, drillers could rotate the bit to expose a new drilling surface. Such a bit would elimi-

© Dan Connolly, Sygma

Members of a Drilling Crew, called *roughnecks,* prepare to change the bit. As the drill pipe is raised, the workers disconnect the lengths of pipe and stack them in the derrick.

Continental Oil Company, American Petroleum Institute

The Bit is changed when it becomes dull or if a different type of bit is needed. A large-toothed bit, above, is used to drill through soft rock, such as limestone or sandstone.

PETROLEUM

Directional Drilling

In directional drilling, an oil well is drilled at an angle rather than straight down. Crews use such tools as *whipstocks* and *turbodrills* to guide the bit along a slanted path. This method is often used in offshore operations because many wells can be drilled directionally from one platform.

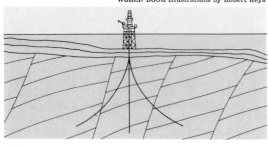

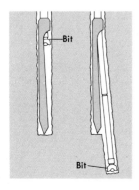

Whipstock

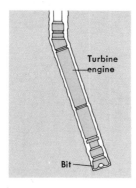

Turbodrill

Offshore Drilling Most exploratory offshore wells are drilled from *jack-up rigs, drill ships,* or *semisubmersible rigs.* A jack-up rig, which can be raised or lowered to various heights, has legs that rest on the ocean floor. A drill ship has drilling equipment mounted on its deck, and a special opening through which the drill pipe is lowered. A semisubmersible rig floats on cylindrical legs filled with air.

nate the need to pull the drill pipe out of the hole each time the bit is changed.

Offshore Drilling is much more expensive and dangerous than drilling on land. The average offshore rig costs 10 times more than a land rig. All the equipment and the crew must be brought to the site by helicopter or ship. In such waters as the Arctic Ocean and the North Sea, rigs may be damaged by storms or floating blocks of ice. But as the number of land reserves declines, the importance of offshore wells increasingly outweighs their higher costs and risks.

Drilling an offshore well is similar to drilling a well on land. The major difference in the two operations is in the type of rig. Offshore rigs require a drilling platform in addition to a derrick and drilling equipment. Exploratory wells are generally drilled from *jack-up rigs, drill ships,* or *semisubmersible rigs.* Most production wells are drilled from *fixed platforms.*

Jack-Up Rigs are commonly used in shallow water. The drilling platform is supported by steel legs that rest on the ocean floor. This platform, which holds the derrick and the drilling equipment, can be jacked up or lowered according to the depth of the water and the height of the waves.

Drill Ships are used for much of the drilling in deep water. The derrick and other equipment are mounted on the deck, and the drill pipe is lowered through a special opening in the bottom of the ship. Auxiliary engines and propellers, guided by computers, keep the ship over the drilling site.

Semisubmersible Rigs can be used in various depths of water. Such a rig has legs that are filled with air to enable it to float above the surface of the ocean. Anchors hold the drilling platform in place.

Fixed Platforms are the largest type of offshore rig. Most fixed platforms are used in shallow water, but some are used in water deeper than 700 feet (210 meters). The platforms may be built in two or more sections that are towed by ship to the drilling site. Workers sink the first section to the ocean floor. The top of this section is above the water and serves as the base for the rest of the platform. As many as 42 wells can be directionally drilled from a fixed platform.

Well Testing. Drilling crews try to determine as quickly as possible whether they are working on a productive site or a dry hole. During drilling, they continually examine the cuttings—the pieces of rock brought up by the drilling mud—for evidence of petroleum. When drilling reaches the depth of possible deposits, the crew may conduct several tests for oil. These tests include *coring, logging,* and *drill stem testing.*

In coring, the drill bit is replaced with a *coring bit.* This bit cuts out a cylindrical sample of soil and rock, which is brought to the surface for analysis. Logging involves lowering measuring instruments called *sondes* into the well hole. They transmit information about the composition, porosity, fluid content, and other characteristics of the underground rock. In the drill stem test, a device that takes samples of fluids and measures their pressure is lowered into the hole.

If the test results are negative, the drilling crew may plug the well with cement and abandon it. If the tests show evidence of petroleum, the crew reinforces the well hole with steel pipe called *casing.*

Casing is a kind of protective lining for the well hole. It consists of heavy steel pipe that ranges in diameter from $2\frac{7}{8}$ to 20 inches (7.3 to 51 centimeters). The lengths of pipe are held in place with cement. Casing helps prevent leaks and cave-ins during both the drilling stage and the production stage of the oil well. As an additional safeguard, nearly all drilling crews install one or more *blowout preventers* at the top of the casing. These devices consist of giant valves that close off the casing if pressure builds up in the well.

To install casing, drilling crews remove the drill pipe and lower the casing into the well hole. They then pump wet cement down the casing and cover the cement with a special plug that can be drilled through. Next, they pump mud into the casing. The mud pushes the plug down to the bottom of the casing. The cement is thus forced up into the space between the well hole and the outside of the casing from the bottom of the hole to the surface. After the cement hardens, the workers can continue to drill through the plug.

Completing the Well means bringing the well into production. This operation is carried out in several steps. First, the drilling crew lowers an instrument called a *perforator* into the casing to the depth of the oilbearing zone. The perforator fires special bullets or explosive charges into the casing, punching holes through which the oil can enter. The crew then installs the *tubing,* which is a string of smaller pipes that conducts oil to the surface. Tubing is used because the casing is generally too wide to maintain the fluid velocity necessary to keep the oil flowing upward. Tubing is also easier to repair and replace than casing.

One final step in completing a well is to assemble a group of control valves at the upper end of the casing and tubing. This valve system is known as a *Christmas tree* because of its many branchlike fittings. It controls the flow of oil to the surface.

In some wells, more than one oilbearing zone is

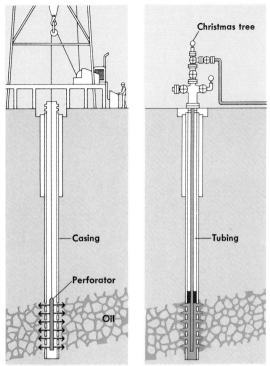

WORLD BOOK illustration by Robert Keys

Completing a Well. After lining the well hole with pipes called *casing,* the crew lowers an instrument called a *perforator* into the well. The perforator punches holes in the casing through which oil can enter, *left.* Then the crew installs the *tubing,* a string of smaller pipes that conducts the oil to the surface; and a *Christmas tree,* a set of valves that controls the flow of oil, *right.*

found. The drilling crew then installs separate tubing and control valves for each zone. Such operations are called *multiple completion wells.*

Recovering Petroleum

Petroleum is recovered in much the same way as underground water is obtained. Like certain types of water wells, some oil wells have sufficient natural energy to bring the fluid to the surface. Other oil wells have too little energy to produce oil efficiently, or they lose most of their energy after a period of production. In these wells, additional energy must be supplied by pumps or other artificial means. If natural pressure provides most of the energy, the recovery of petroleum is called *primary recovery.* If artificial means are used, the process is known as *enhanced recovery.*

Primary Recovery. The natural energy used in recovering petroleum comes chiefly from gas and water in reservoir rocks. The gas may be dissolved in the oil or separated at the top of it in the form of a gas cap. Water, which is heavier than oil, collects below the petroleum. Depending on the source, the energy in the reservoir is called (1) solution-gas drive, (2) gas-cap drive, or (3) water drive. Solution-gas drive brings only small amounts of oil to the surface. Most wells that have no natural energy other than solution-gas drive require supplementary forms of energy. Gas-cap drive and water drive, on the other hand, may result in the production of large quantities of petroleum.

How Oil Is Recovered   A tremendous amount of energy is needed to bring oil to the surface. This energy may come from the natural pressure in a reservoir or from various artificial means. Depending on the source of energy, the process is called (1) primary recovery, (2) secondary recovery, or (3) tertiary recovery.

WORLD BOOK illustrations by Robert Keys

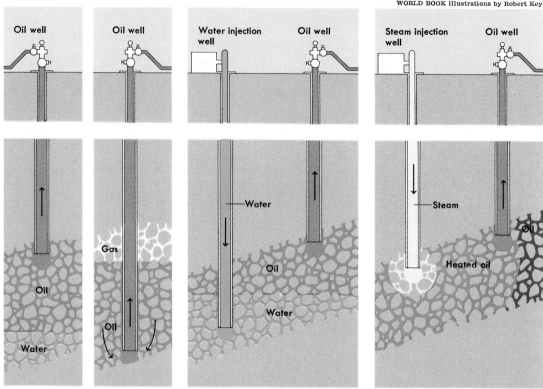

Primary Recovery depends chiefly on two types of natural energy in a reservoir, *water drive* and *gas drive*. If oil production reduces some of the pressure underground, water or gas in the reservoir may drive the oil into the well.

Secondary Recovery consists of replacing the natural energy in a reservoir. *Waterflooding*, one of the most widely used methods, involves injecting water into the reservoir. The water displaces the oil and causes it to flow into the well.

Tertiary Recovery includes a number of experimental methods of bringing oil to the surface. In one such method, steam is injected into the reservoir. The steam heats the oil and makes it thinner, enabling it to flow more freely into the well.

Solution-Gas Drive. The oil in nearly all reservoirs contains dissolved gas. The effect production has on this gas is similar to what happens when a bottle of champagne is opened. The gas expands and moves toward the opening, carrying some of the liquid with it.

Gas-Cap Drive. In many reservoirs, gas is trapped in a cap above the oil as well as dissolved in it. As oil is produced from the reservoir, the gas cap expands and drives the oil toward the well.

Water Drive. Like gas, water in a reservoir is held in place mainly by underground pressure. If the volume of water is sufficiently large, the reduction of pressure that occurs during oil production will cause the water to expand. The water will then displace the petroleum, forcing it to flow into the well.

Enhanced Recovery includes a variety of methods designed to increase the amount of oil that flows into a producing well. Depending on the stage of production in which they are used, these methods are generally classified as either *secondary recovery* or *tertiary* (third-level) *recovery*.

Secondary recovery, also called *pressure maintenance*, consists of replacing the natural drives in the reservoir. This form of recovery may involve injecting gas or water

into the reservoir from additional wells drilled near the producing well.

Although secondary recovery has nearly tripled the amount of recoverable oil, about two-thirds of the petroleum in most reservoirs remains below the surface after production. Petroleum engineers are testing techniques of tertiary recovery to bring more oil to the surface. One such technique uses heat to thin the oil and so make it flow more freely into the well. This heat may come from injections of steam or from burning some of the petroleum in the reservoir.

Transporting Petroleum

After crude oil reaches the surface, natural gas is separated from the oil. The gas is then sent to a processing plant or directly to consumers. Water and sediment are removed from the oil, which is then stored in tanks or sent to a refinery. From the refinery, petroleum products are delivered to markets.

In the United States, more than 10 million barrels of petroleum are transported daily. Petroleum is carried chiefly by pipeline, tanker, barge, tank truck, and railroad tank car.

Most petroleum moves through pipelines for at least

part of its journey. Pipelines transport crude oil from wells to storage tanks, to other carriers, or directly to refineries. Pipelines also carry petroleum products from refineries to markets. Some of the largest pipelines can carry more than a million barrels of oil daily. Pipelines can be built in almost any kind of terrain and climate. The Trans-Alaska Pipeline, for example, crosses 3 mountain ranges, more than 300 rivers and streams, and nearly 400 miles (640 kilometers) of frozen land. Pipelines cost much to build. But they are relatively cheap to operate and maintain and are generally the most efficient means of moving petroleum.

Tankers and barges transport oil on water. A tanker is a large oceangoing ship with compartments for liquid cargo. The largest tankers can hold more than a million barrels of petroleum. Tankers haul nearly all the oil imported by the United States. Barges, which can carry an average of 15,000 barrels of oil, are used mainly on rivers and canals.

Many petroleum products travel from refineries to markets by tank truck or railroad tank car. Tank trucks deliver gasoline to service stations and heating oil to houses. Such trucks can carry up to 300 barrels of fuel. Railroad tank cars range in capacity from about 100 to more than 1,500 barrels of oil. Some of these cars have

equipment to keep petroleum products at a certain temperature or level of pressure.

Refining Petroleum

From a distance, a petroleum refinery may appear to be a lifeless maze of towers, tanks, and pipes. But refineries hum with activity day and night. They can operate continuously for up to five years before being shut down for repairs. Refineries range in size from small plants that process about 150 barrels of crude oil a day to giant complexes with a daily capacity of more than 600,000 barrels.

The basic job of a refinery is to convert petroleum into useful products. Crude oil consists chiefly of combinations of hydrocarbons, as described in the section of this article called *The Uses of Petroleum*. Refineries separate the oil into various hydrocarbon groups, or fractions. The fractions are then chemically changed and treated with other substances. These refining processes may be classified as (1) separation, (2) conversion, and (3) chemical treatment.

Separation. The first stage in petroleum refining is *fractional distillation*, which is a process that separates

How Oil Is Transported
Petroleum is transported by a variety of methods during its journey from oil field to consumer. Nearly all oil moves through pipelines for at least part of the route. After crude oil is separated from natural gas, pipelines transport the oil to another carrier or directly to a refinery. Petroleum products travel from the refinery to market by tanker, truck, railroad tank car, or pipeline.

WORLD BOOK illustration by Robert Keys

571

PETROLEUM

crude oil into some of its fractions. Additional fractions may be separated from these fractions by the processes of *solvent extraction* and *crystallization*.

Fractional Distillation is based on the principle that different fractions *vaporize* (boil) at different temperatures. For example, gasoline vaporizes at about 75° F. (24° C), but some of the heavy fuel oils have boiling points higher than 600° F. (316° C). As vapors, such fractions also *condense* (cool and become liquid) at different temperatures.

In fractional distillation, crude oil is pumped through pipes inside a furnace and heated to temperatures as high as 725° F. (385° C). The resulting mixture of hot gases and liquids then passes into a vertical steel cylinder called a *fractionating tower* or a *bubble tower*. As the vaporized fractions rise in the tower, they condense at different levels. Heavy fuel oils condense in the lower section of the tower. Such light fractions as gasoline and kerosene condense in the middle and upper sections. The liquids collect in trays and are drawn off by pipes along the sides of the tower.

Some fractions do not cool enough to condense. They pass out of the top of the fractionating tower into a *vapor recovery unit*. Other fractions, which vaporize at temperatures higher than those in the furnace, remain as liquids or semisolids. These *residues* are recovered from the bottom of the tower and refined into such products as asphalt and lubricating oils.

The fractions produced by distillation are called *straight-run products*. Almost all these products must undergo conversion and chemical treatment before they can be used.

Solvent Extraction separates additional fractions from certain straight-run products. A chemical called a *solvent* either dissolves some of the fractions or causes them to separate out as solids. The principal solvents used include *benzene*, *furfural*, and *phenol*. Many refineries improve the quality of kerosene and lubricating oils by solvent extraction.

Crystallization is used chiefly to remove wax and other semisolid substances from heavy fractions. The fractions are cooled to a temperature at which they form crystals or solidify. They are then put through a filter that separates out the solid particles.

How Oil Is Refined   Refineries convert crude oil into useful products in three basic stages. The first stage, called *separation*, consists of separating the oil into its various *fractions* (parts). The main process in this stage is *fractional distillation*, which separates light, medium, and heavy fractions. In *conversion*, the second stage, less useful fractions are converted into more valuable ones. The third stage is *treatment*, which improves the quality and performance of petroleum products.

WORLD BOOK diagram by Leonard Morgan

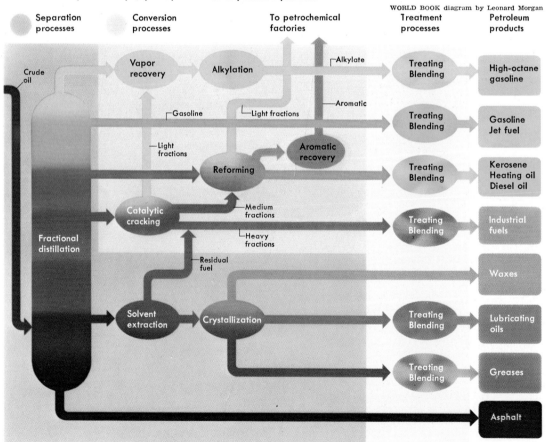

Conversion. Although nearly all petroleum can be refined into useful products, some fractions have much more value than others. Gasoline, for example, accounts for almost half the petroleum products used in the United States. But it makes up only about 10 per cent of the straight-run products. On the other hand, some fractions that are in less demand than gasoline make up a higher percentage of crude oil.

To increase the yield of desirable products from petroleum, scientists have developed several methods to convert less useful fractions into those that are in greater demand. These conversion methods fall into two main groups: (1) cracking processes and (2) combining processes. As a result of conversion processes, refiners are able to produce about half a barrel of gasoline from each barrel of crude oil.

Cracking Processes convert heavy fractions into lighter ones, mainly gasoline. These processes not only increase the quantity of gasoline obtained from oil but also improve the quality. Gasoline produced by cracking has a higher *octane number* than the straight-run product. Octane number is a measure of how smoothly fuel burns in an engine. See OCTANE NUMBER.

There are two principal types of cracking processes—*thermal cracking* and *catalytic cracking*. In thermal cracking, heavy fractions are subjected to intense heat and pressure in order to weaken the bonds that hold large, complex molecules together. The heat and pressure *crack* (break down) these molecules into the simpler ones that make up light fractions.

In catalytic cracking, a *catalyst* is used to accelerate the thermal cracking process. A catalyst is a substance that sets off or speeds up a chemical reaction without being changed by the reaction. In this form of cracking, the fractions are heated and then passed over minerals called *zeolites*, certain types of clay, or other catalysts. The combination of heat and catalytic action causes the heavy fractions to crack into lighter ones. Catalytic cracking is more widely used than thermal cracking because it requires less pressure and produces higher-octane gasoline.

During cracking, hydrogen may be added to the fractions. This procedure, known as *hydrogenation*, further increases the yield of useful products.

Combining Processes do the reverse of cracking. They combine or rearrange simple gaseous hydrocarbons to form more complex fractions. As a result of these processes, many of the gases produced by distillation and cracking are converted into high-octane liquid fuels and valuable chemicals. The major combining processes include *polymerization, alkylation,* and *reforming.*

In polymerization, gases are subjected to heat and pressure in the presence of a catalyst. The hydrocarbon molecules unite and form larger molecules known as *polymers.* Polymers are essential ingredients in high-octane gasoline. Alkylation is similar to polymerization. It produces a fraction called *alkylate*, which is used in both aviation fuel and gasoline. In reforming, the molecules in gases form different hydrocarbon groups after exposure to heat and a catalyst. Reforming produces high-octane fuels and *aromatics*, which are chemicals used in making explosives, synthetic rubber, food preservatives, and many other products.

Chemical Treatment. Nearly all fractions are chemically treated before they are sent to consumers. The

method of treatment depends on the type of crude oil and on the intended use of the petroleum product.

Many fractions are treated to remove impurities. The most common impurities are sulfur compounds, which can damage machinery and pollute the air when burned. Treatment with hydrogen is a widely used method of removing sulfur compounds. In this method, fractions are mixed with hydrogen, heated, and then exposed to a catalyst. The sulfur in the fractions combines with the hydrogen, forming hydrogen sulfide. The hydrogen sulfide is later removed by a solvent.

Some fractions perform better if they are blended or combined with other substances. For example, refineries blend various lubricating oils to obtain different degrees of *viscosity* (thickness). Gasoline is blended with chemicals called *additives*, which help it burn more smoothly and give it other special properties.

The Petroleum Industry

The petroleum industry is one of the world's largest industries. It has four major branches. The *production branch* explores for oil and brings it to the surface. The *transportation branch* sends crude oil to refineries and delivers the refined products to consumers. The *manufacturing branch* processes crude oil into useful products. The *marketing branch* sells and distributes the products to consumers. Gasoline service stations handle the largest share of these sales. Oil companies sell their petroleum products directly to factories, power plants, and transportation-related industries.

The petroleum industry plays a large role in the economy of many nations. In such developed countries as the United States and Canada, the industry provides jobs for a great many people. In addition, it is a major buyer of iron, steel, motor vehicles, and many other products. In certain developing but oil-rich countries, petroleum exports furnish most of the national income. Petroleum is also a source of political power for such countries because many other nations depend on them for fuel.

In the United States, the petroleum industry ranks as one of the largest private employers. The industry includes about 40,000 companies, most of which are small firms that specialize in one branch of the industry. The larger companies are active in all branches. The eight largest oil firms handle more than 50 per cent of the petroleum produced, refined, and sold in the United States. In addition to these companies, there are nearly 200,000 gasoline service stations, most of which are independently owned and operated. The petroleum industry employs a total of about $1\frac{1}{2}$ million workers and has an investment of more than $160 billion in plants, property, and machinery.

The United States is one of the world's leading producers and refiners of petroleum. American wells annually produce more than 3 billion barrels of crude oil. Only Russia and Saudi Arabia produce more petroleum. Refineries in the United States process more than 17 million barrels of petroleum daily, or about 22 per cent of the world total.

The United States is also the world's largest consumer of petroleum. In spite of the size of the U.S. oil industry, the nation's demand for petroleum products far exceeds

PETROLEUM

domestic production. As a result, the country imports about 40 per cent of the oil it uses.

The price of imported crude oil has soared since the early 1970's, leading the U.S. petroleum industry to look for ways to increase domestic oil production. The industry is researching methods of drilling in extremely harsh environments, such as the Arctic and underwater depths greater than 30,000 feet (9,100 meters). Researchers are also seeking more efficient techniques for recovering petroleum and for converting coal, oil shale, bituminous sands, and other plentiful hydrocarbons into synthetic oil and gas. In addition, researchers are studying such alternative sources of energy as the sun, wind, and internal heat of the earth.

In Canada, the petroleum industry is owned and run largely by private companies. Since 1975, however, a government corporation called Petro-Canada has been involved in exploring for new reserves and in developing synthetic forms of oil. The government also participates in the petroleum industry through its power to grant mineral leases to oil companies.

The petroleum industry in Canada began to expand rapidly in 1947, when prospectors made a great oil strike in Leduc, Alta. Annual production jumped from about 8 million barrels of oil in that year to a peak of about 650 million barrels in the mid-1970's. Canada was a leading exporter of oil to the United States until 1975. Since then, Canada's reserves and production have declined, and it has reduced oil exports to the United States. Canada produces about 540 million barrels of oil annually. The nation's refineries process about 1½ million barrels daily, which makes Canada one of the world's leading refiners.

More than 1,500 Canadian companies produce petroleum. However, the 20 largest firms account for about 80 per cent of Canada's oil production. About 64,000 persons work in the production and manufacturing branches of the oil industry, and many others have jobs in the transportation and marketing branches.

In Other Countries. During the early 1900's, foreign oil companies began to develop the petroleum industry in various countries in the Middle East, Africa, and other parts of the world. These firms, most of which were American or European, received ownership of the oil they discovered and produced. In return, they paid the host countries taxes and a share of the income from oil sales. Beginning in the 1950's, however, more and more host countries came to feel that they were not receiving a large enough share of the oil income. Today, many of these countries have acquired part or total control of the oil industry within their borders, either by negotiating with the foreign firms or by taking them over. In addition, a number of the countries belong to a powerful association called the Organization of Petroleum Exporting Countries (OPEC).

OPEC, which was formed in 1960, consists of 13 nations that depend heavily on oil exports for their income. These nations include Libya, Nigeria, Venezuela, and the major oil-producing countries of the Middle East. OPEC members provide about 60 per cent of all oil exports. Thus, the amount they produce and the prices they agree to charge largely determine the cost of oil throughout the world. Industrialized countries are so dependent on imported oil that OPEC can use petroleum as an economic and political weapon. Since 1973, OPEC has raised oil prices so drastically that its members have been able to increase their income from oil while restricting production.

Petroleum Conservation

The world's supply of petroleum is limited and will eventually run out. Some experts predict that if oil consumption continues to rise, existing petroleum reserves will be exhausted by the early 2000's. Conservation of oil has thus become urgent for all nations, but particularly for those that use the most energy. It is estimated that the United States, which consumes nearly 30 per cent of the petroleum produced in the world, could reduce its energy needs by half through an active program of conservation.

There are almost as many ways to conserve petroleum as there are to use its products. The petroleum industry has adopted many measures to maximize production and reduce waste at oil fields and refineries. Some of these measures have become law in the United States, Canada, and other countries. For consumers, conservation includes traveling less often by automobile, lowering furnace thermostats in winter, and raising air-

---

Leading Petroleum-Producing States and Provinces

Petroleum produced in 1978*

Texas	●●●●●●●●●●●●●●●●●● 1,074,000,000 barrels
Louisiana	●●●●●●●●● 534,737,000 barrels
Alaska	●●●●●●●(447,813,000 barrels
Alberta	●●●●●● 391,083,000 barrels
California	●●●●●(347,303,000 barrels
Oklahoma	●●(150,455,000 barrels
Wyoming	●● 136,798,000 barrels
New Mexico	●(83,134,000 barrels
Saskatchewan	● 60,700,000 barrels
Kansas	● 56,588,000 barrels

*In barrels of 42-gallon (159-liter) capacity.
Sources: U.S. Department of Energy; Statistics Canada.

Leading Petroleum-Producing Countries

Petroleum produced in 1978*

Russia	●●●●●●●●●●●●●●●● 4,161,000,000 barrels
United States	●●●●●●●●●●●●(3,160,900,000 barrels
Saudi Arabia	●●●●●●●●●●● 2,847,000,000 barrels
Iran	●●●●●●●(1,916,250,000 barrels
Iraq	●●●(912,500,000 barrels
Venezuela	●●● 784,750,000 barrels
Libya	●●(748,250,000 barrels
China	●●● 730,000,000 barrels
Kuwait	●●(693,500,000 barrels
Nigeria	●●(657,000,000 barrels

*In barrels of 42-gallon (159-liter) capacity.
Source: *Oil and Gas Journal*, Dec. 25, 1978.

conditioning thermostats in summer. Some measures of consumer conservation have also become law in a number of countries.

Conservation by the Oil Industry. Most of the oil-producing states in the United States and most such provinces in Canada have commissions that regulate oil companies. One function of these regulatory commissions is to ensure that oil companies recover petroleum efficiently. A commission may therefore restrict the number of wells drilled in an area and the rate at which wells are made to produce. Without such restrictions, the natural drives in oil fields would soon be exhausted, and much oil might be wasted.

The oil industry itself has developed a number of methods of conservation. Most of these methods are classed as either (1) oil-field conservation or (2) refinery conservation.

Oil-Field Conservation consists chiefly of methods to increase the amount of petroleum recovered. One of the most widely used measures of oil-field conservation is a pooling system called *unitization*. Under this system, two or more oil companies working in the same field agree to operate as a unit. Unitization enables the companies to make the most efficient use of natural and artificial energy in recovering oil.

Refinery Conservation is aimed mainly at reducing the amount of heat energy used in refining. Most refineries have devices called *heat exchangers*, which recycle excess heat from such processes as fractional distillation and thermal cracking. New catalysts are being developed to lower the energy requirements of the chemical reactions. Many plants use computers to maintain furnaces and heaters at the most efficient temperatures. Heat energy is also conserved by insulating pipes, tanks, and other refinery equipment.

Conservation by Consumers. Some of the most extensive conservation programs have been adopted by commercial consumers of petroleum. Many manufacturers have installed equipment to store energy and reduce fuel consumption in their plants. Such materials as aluminum and paper are reused in some factories because recycling waste products requires less energy than manufacturing new products.

Certain conservation measures originally adopted by some businesses and factories are now legally enforced. In the United States, for example, temperatures in most work areas cannot be cooled below 78° F. (26° C) in summer nor heated above 65° F. (18° C) in winter. American and Canadian automobile manufacturers are required by law to produce fuel-efficient cars.

In the home, common sense is often the best guide to saving energy. For example, people can take advantage of solar energy simply by opening their curtains during the day. They can further reduce fuel consumption by closing the curtains at night and by turning off the heat in rooms that are not being used. Homeowners who live in cold climates can conserve heat by installing storm windows, weather stripping, and other forms of insulation. The United States and Canadian governments offer loans and tax deductions for such energy-saving home improvements.

Most consumers can also conserve on fuel that they use outside the home. By keeping automobiles well tuned and by driving within speed limits, motorists can minimize gasoline consumption. They can save even more fuel by purchasing fuel-efficient cars, forming car pools, or switching to public transportation.

History of the Use of Petroleum

People have used petroleum for thousands of years. The Bible mentions that Noah used a solid form of petroleum called *pitch* in building the Ark. The ancient Egyptians coated mummies with pitch. About 600 B.C., King Nebuchadnezzar II used pitch to build the walls and pave the streets of Babylon.

In America, the Indians used crude oil for fuel and medicine hundreds of years before the first white settlers arrived. In the early 1600's, missionaries traveling through what is now Pennsylvania found Indians scooping up oil from surface pools. The remains of wells in the Eastern United States indicate that the Indians also obtained oil from underground deposits.

By 1750, the American colonists had found many oil seepages in New York, Pennsylvania, and what is now West Virginia. Some wells that were dug for salt produced oil. Salt makers regarded the oil as a nuisance, but other people found uses for it. About 1857, Samuel M. Kier, a Pittsburgh pharmacist, promoted oil as a cure for many ailments. The frontiersman Kit Carson sold oil as axle grease to pioneers.

A major breakthrough in the use of petroleum occurred in the 1840's, when a Canadian geologist named Abraham Gesner discovered kerosene. This fuel could be distilled from coal or oil. Kerosene became widely used for lighting lamps, and oil quickly rose in value.

Beginnings of the Oil Industry. Most historians trace the start of the oil industry on a large scale to 1859. That year, a retired railroad conductor named Edwin L. Drake drilled a well near Titusville, Pa. Drake used an old steam engine to power the drill. After Drake's well began to produce oil, other prospectors drilled wells nearby. Within three years, so much oil was being produced in the area that the price of a barrel dropped from $20 to 10 cents.

By the early 1860's, the oil boom had transformed western Pennsylvania. Forests of wooden derricks covered the hills, and thousands of prospectors crowded into the new boom towns. At first, wagons and river barges carried the oil to refineries on the Atlantic Coast. But the growing volume of oil soon required more efficient means of transportation. Railroads established branch lines to the fields and began to haul oil. In 1865, the first successful oil pipeline was built from an oil field near Titusville to a railroad station 5 miles (8 kilometers) away. Within 10 years, a 60-mile (97-kilometer) line ran from the oil region to Pittsburgh.

Prospectors discovered that other states had even larger oil deposits than Pennsylvania. By the 1880's, commercial production of oil had begun in Kentucky, Ohio, Illinois, and Indiana. In 1901, the opening of the Spindletop field in eastern Texas produced the first true gusher in North America. During the 1890's and early 1900's, California and Oklahoma joined Texas as the leading oil-producing states. Annual oil production in the United States rose from 2,000 barrels in 1859 to 64 million barrels in 1900.

Commercial oil production spread rapidly throughout the world. Italy began to produce oil in 1860. After

PETROLEUM

Italy, production began, in order, in Canada, Poland, Peru, Germany, Russia, Venezuela, India, Indonesia, Japan, Trinidad, Mexico, and Argentina. The first important oil discoveries in the Middle East occurred in Iran in 1908. Prospectors struck oil in Iraq in 1927 and in Saudi Arabia in 1938. Huge oil fields were later found in other states on the Persian Gulf.

Growth of the Oil Industry. During the 1800's, kerosene had been the chief product of the petroleum industry. Refiners considered gasoline a useless by-product and often dumped it into creeks and rivers. Then, about 1900, two events dramatically changed the situation—electric lights began to replace kerosene lamps, and the automobile rolled onto the American scene. The demand for kerosene thus declined just as an enormous market for gasoline opened up.

At that time, however, 100 barrels of crude oil produced only about 11 barrels of gasoline. As a result, petroleum refiners looked for ways to increase the output of gasoline without creating a surplus of kerosene and other less profitable products. The introduction of the thermal-cracking process in 1913 helped solve the problem. Within five years, refiners had more than doubled the amount of gasoline that they could produce from a barrel of crude oil.

World War I (1914-1918) created a tremendous demand for petroleum fuels to power tanks, ships, and airplanes. Fuels became as important to the war effort as

American Petroleum Institute

The First Gusher in North America blew in at the Spindletop field near Beaumont, Tex., in 1901. It sprayed more than 800,000 barrels of oil into the air until it was brought under control.

ammunition. After the war, the use of petroleum brought about big changes on farms. More and more farmers began to operate tractors and other equipment powered by oil. Agricultural productivity increased greatly as a result. In addition, gasoline taxes provided the money and asphalt furnished the raw material to build roads in rural areas. Farmers thereby gained better access to markets.

During World War II (1939-1945), the American oil industry proved its ability to increase production and develop specialized products quickly. Huge quantities of oil were produced and converted into fuels and lubricants. Such new refining processes as catalytic cracking and alkylation vastly increased the output of high-octane aviation gasoline. The United States supplied over 80 per cent of the aviation gasoline used by the Allies during the war. American refineries also manufactured *butadiene*, used in making synthetic rubber; *toluene*, an ingredient in TNT; medicinal oils to treat the wounded; and many other military necessities.

Postwar Developments. The demand for petroleum products became even greater after World War II. The petroleum used in the United States climbed from about $1\frac{3}{4}$ billion barrels in 1946 to almost $2\frac{1}{2}$ billion barrels in 1950. By the early 1950's, petroleum had replaced coal as the country's chief fuel. Some of the petroleum technology perfected during the war became the basis for peacetime industry. The petrochemical industry, for example, grew enormously as a result of the manufacture of synthetic rubber.

The United States was not alone in its rising level of petroleum consumption. Throughout the world, increased industrialization and rapid population growth created new and greater demands for oil. Control over the sources and transportation of oil soon became a vital issue in national and international politics.

In the United States, the issue of control over oil centered on the offshore deposits of Louisiana, Texas, and other states. These states claimed ownership of the *tidelands* (offshore areas within their traditional boundaries). The federal government, however, insisted that the tidelands belonged to the nation. The dispute delayed the development of new offshore wells because oil companies did not know whether the states or the federal government owned the territory. Finally, in 1953, Congress passed an act that granted jurisdiction of the tidelands to the states and so enabled them to lease offshore sites to oil companies. In 1975, the Supreme Court limited the tidelands of most states to areas within 3 nautical miles (5.6 kilometers) of their coastline.

On the international scene, the struggle for oil focused on the Middle East, which has more than half of the world's petroleum reserves. The petroleum industry in many Middle Eastern countries was owned or operated by American or European companies. In 1951, Iran became the first country to take over the holdings of such firms. By the mid-1970's, most nations in the Middle East either fully controlled or held a majority interest in their petroleum industry.

Recent Developments. The ever-increasing use of petroleum products, especially in developed countries, has helped raise the living standards of many people. But it has also resulted in some serious problems, which include (1) the energy shortage, (2) the rising cost of oil, and (3) environmental pollution.

The Energy Shortage. Discoveries of oil in northern Alaska and under the North Sea during the late 1960's added more than 30 billion barrels to world reserves. However, these gains were more than offset by rising levels of petroleum consumption, particularly among the industrialized nations. During the 1970's, the United States, Japan, and most countries in Western Europe steadily increased their oil imports.

At the same time, political instability in the Middle East continued to disrupt the flow of oil. During the Arab-Israeli wars of 1967 and 1973, the Arabs cut off or reduced petroleum exports to Japan and some Western nations. Other disruptions followed the Iranian revolution of 1979, during which oil production in Iran declined drastically.

People began to realize that oil would remain in short supply as exporters tried to conserve their limited reserves. Many nations that depended on imported oil started conservation programs of their own.

The Rising Cost of Oil. During the 1970's, the 13 member countries of OPEC increased their oil prices tremendously. The cost of a barrel of crude oil jumped from about $2.40 in 1973 to more than $30 in 1980. The countries were thus able to cut production and so conserve oil while still increasing their revenues.

The OPEC price increases severely strained the economies of many countries and worsened inflation throughout the world. Some of the poorer nations had to borrow heavily to pay for their petroleum imports. The United States, Great Britain, and other countries with petroleum reserves stepped up domestic production to help offset the higher-priced OPEC oil. But by 1980, OPEC members still controlled more than half the world petroleum market.

Environmental Pollution. The production, transportation, and use of petroleum have created serious environmental pollution problems. Tankers and offshore drilling accidents can cause oil spills that pollute the water, damage beaches, and destroy wildlife. Some people fear that hot oil flowing through the Trans-Alaska Pipeline will upset the ecological balance of the Arctic environment. Fuels burned by motor vehicles, power plants, and factories are the chief source of air pollution in most cities.

During the 1960's and 1970's, many laws were passed in the United States, Canada, and other countries to control environmental pollution. The petroleum industry itself has invested heavily in the development of techniques and products to minimize pollution. To reduce the pollutants in automobile exhaust, for example, oil companies cooperated with car manufacturers in the production of unleaded gasoline. However, rising levels of petroleum consumption have offset some of the gains against pollution.

The Future of the Petroleum Industry. Most experts predict that the worldwide demand for petroleum will continue to increase in the years ahead in spite of declining supplies and rising prices. To prevent a full-scale oil shortage, the petroleum industry is intensifying its exploration for new reserves and its research into better recovery and refining techniques.

However, the only long-range solution to the energy crisis is the introduction of alternative sources of fuel. Scientists have developed techniques to convert coal into oil and gas and to produce oil from bituminous

Oil Spills are generally caused by a damaged tanker, such as the one shown above, or by an offshore drilling accident. Spills pollute the water, damage beaches, and destroy wildlife.

sands and oil shale. These synthetic fuels are still too expensive to produce commercially on a large scale. But if oil prices continue to increase, such fuels eventually may be able to compete in cost with petroleum.

It will probably be many years before alternative fuel sources make a major contribution to the world's energy supply. Until then, oil companies and oil consumers will need to conserve existing reserves by using energy as efficiently and sparingly as possible.

Career Opportunities

The petroleum industry employs many kinds of workers, from unskilled laborers to highly trained scientists and engineers. Information on jobs in the industry can be obtained from the American Petroleum Institute, 2101 L Street NW, Washington, D.C. 20037.

Scientists and Engineers play a vital role in the petroleum industry. Geologists and geophysicists explore for oil. Other scientists, such as biologists and ecologists, study the environmental effects of the industry's operations. Petroleum engineers supervise well drilling and oil recovery. Oil companies also employ chemical, civil, electrical, and mechanical engineers. All these jobs require college training. Some universities offer degrees in petroleum engineering and specialized courses in geology and geophysics. High school students interested in such careers should study such subjects as mathematics, physics, and chemistry.

Oil-Field Workers include derrickmen, drillers, roughnecks, and *roustabouts* (production workers). These workers must have good physical coordination as well as mechanical ability. High school courses in sci-

PETROLEUM

ence and industrial arts help prepare students interested in becoming oil-field workers.

Machinists and Maintenance Workers include mechanics, welders, and electricians. Such jobs require good mechanical judgment and the ability to do precision work. Many workers in this field learn their skills through on-the-job training. Training is also provided by such courses as mathematics and shopwork.

Control Workers and Equipment Operators keep petroleum flowing efficiently through the various stages of production and refining. These workers read and maintain gauges, meters, and other instruments in oil fields, in refineries, and along pipelines. They also check all equipment to see that it runs properly. As computers take over many of these operations, oil companies are hiring increasing numbers of computer maintenance specialists. Except for such computer personnel, who must have special training, most of the workers in this field can be trained on the job.

Marketing Workers sell petroleum products and services. They include salespeople, service station attendants, and *jobbers* (middlemen). Jobs in this field require business judgment and personal qualities to attract and retain customers. Many oil companies offer training courses to their employees.

Clerical and Administrative Workers handle the business operations of the petroleum industry. Clerical jobs may require training in such subjects as bookkeeping and the operation of office machines. Most administrative jobs require college training in engineering, geology, or geophysics.   Dan M. Bass

Related Articles in World Book. See the *Economy* section of the articles on the various states, provinces, and countries mentioned in the *Where Petroleum Is Found* section of this article. See also the following articles:

Products

Asphalt	Kerosene	Naphtha
Benzine	Lubricant	Paraffin
Butane and Propane	Microcrystalline	Petrochemicals
Fuel	Wax	Petrolatum
Gas (fuel)	Mineral Oil	Petroleum Coke
Gasoline	Napalm	Plastics

Other Related Articles

Bituminous Sands	Octane Number
Conservation	Oil Shale
Distillation	Organization of Petroleum
Energy Supply	Exporting Countries
Environmental Pollution	Pipeline
Exxon Corporation	Rock
Hydrocarbon	Royal Dutch/Shell Group
Hydrogenation	Standard Oil Company
Magnetometer	

Outline

I. The Uses of Petroleum
    A. Petroleum as a Fuel   C. Other Uses of
    B. Petroleum as a Raw Material   Petroleum

II. Where Petroleum Is Found
    A. The Middle East   D. Latin America
    B. Europe   E. Asia
    C. Africa   F. The United States and
                         Canada

III. How Petroleum Was Formed

IV. Exploring for Petroleum
    A. Geological Studies
    B. Geophysical Studies

V. Drilling an Oil Well
    A. Preparatory Measures
    B. Methods of Drilling
    C. Offshore Drilling
    D. Well Testing
    E. Casing
    F. Completing the Well

VI. Recovering Petroleum
    A. Primary Recovery
    B. Enhanced Recovery

VII. Transporting Petroleum

VIII. Refining Petroleum
    A. Separation
    B. Conversion
    C. Chemical Treatment

IX. The Petroleum Industry
    A. In the United States
    B. In Canada
    C. In Other Countries

X. Petroleum Conservation
    A. Conservation by the Oil Industry
    B. Conservation by Consumers

XI. History of the Use of Petroleum

XII. Career Opportunities

Questions

What are some ways consumers can conserve petroleum?

How much oil can be recovered from most deposits?

What does petroleum consist of?

How do most scientists think oil and gas were formed?

What part did the automobile play in the development of the petroleum industry?

Why do oil crews sometimes inject water or gas into a producing well?

Which area of the world has the most oil?

Why is drilling for oil usually an enormous gamble?

Why is offshore drilling for oil more expensive and dangerous than drilling on land?

What is OPEC?

Books for Young Readers

Gans, Roma. *Oil: The Buried Treasure.* Harper, 1975.
Kraft, Betsy H. *Oil and Natural Gas.* Watts, 1978.
Lowery, Barbara. *Oil.* Watts, 1977.
Ridpath, Ian, ed. *Man and Materials: Oil.* Addison-Wesley, 1975.
Wade, Harlan. *Oil.* Rev. ed. Raintree, 1979.

Books for Older Readers

American Petroleum Institute. *Facts About Oil.* The Institute, 1980.
Berger, Bill D., and Anderson, K. E. *Modern Petroleum: A Basic Primer of the Industry.* Petroleum Publishing, 1978.
Eckbo, Paul L. *The Future of World Oil.* Harper, 1976.
Odell, Peter R. *Oil and World Power.* 5th ed. Penguin, 1979.
Oil and Gas Journal. A weekly publication; final issue of each year has worldwide survey of the petroleum industry.
Stokes, William L. *Essentials of Earth History: An Introduction to Historical Geology.* 3rd ed. Prentice-Hall, 1973.
Tiratsoo, Eric N. *Oilfields of the World.* 2nd ed. Gulf, 1976.
United States Bureau of Mines. *Mineral Facts and Problems.* 5th ed. U.S. Govt. Printing Office, 1975. *Minerals Yearbook: Vol. III, Area Reports—International.* Published annually.
Walton, Richard J. *The Power of Oil: Economic, Social, Political.* Seabury, 1977.
Wheeler, Robert R., and Whited, Maurine. *Oil, from Prospect to Pipeline.* 3rd ed. Gulf, 1975.

KIRIBATI, *KIHR ih bahs*, is a small island country in the southwest Pacific Ocean. It consists of 33 islands, including the 16 Gilbert Islands, Ocean Island (Banaba), the 8 Phoenix Islands, and 8 of the Line Islands. The islands of Kiribati are scattered over about 2 million square miles (5 million square kilometers) of ocean. For the location of Kiribati, see PACIFIC ISLANDS (map).

Kiribati has a total land area of 278 square miles (719 square kilometers) and a population of about 61,000. About 92 per cent of the people live in the Gilbert Islands. Tarawa, one of the Gilberts, is the nation's capital.

Great Britain ruled what is now Kiribati from the 1890's to 1979, when Kiribati became an independent nation. The country's basic unit of currency is the Australian dollar. Its national anthem is "Stand, Kiribati." For a picture of Kiribati's flag, see FLAG (Flags of Asia and the Pacific).

Government. Kiribati is a republic headed by a president. The president is elected by the people from among candidates nominated by the House of Assembly. The House, the nation's law-making body, consists of 36 members elected by the people to four-year terms. Most of Kiribati's inhabited islands have a local governing council.

People. Most of the people of Kiribati are Micronesians. The islanders call themselves *I-Kiribati*. Most of them live in rural villages of 10 to 170 houses that are clustered around a church and a meeting house. Many of the houses are made of wood and leaves from palm trees. The people grow most of their own food, which include bananas, breadfruit, papaya, and giant taro (called *babai* in Kiribati). The islanders also raise pigs and chickens and catch fish for food. The I-Kiribati wear light cotton clothing.

Norman Rosen, Miller Services Ltd.

The People of Kiribati live in houses made of wood and palm leaves. Most of the island families own a canoe for fishing.

The language of the islanders is Gilbertese, but most of them also speak some English. Kiribati has about 100 elementary schools and several high schools.

Land and Climate. Almost all the islands of Kiribati are coral reefs. Many are *atolls* (ring-shaped reefs that enclose a lagoon). Kiribati has a tropical climate, with temperatures of about 80° F. (27° C) the year around. The northern islands receive about 100 inches (254 centimeters) of rainfall annually. The other islands are drier, with a yearly rainfall of about 40 inches (100 centimeters).

Economy. Kiribati has only two important exports—phosphate from Ocean Island and *copra* (dried coconut meat). By 1980, all the major phosphate deposits had been used up, but small-scale mining continued. Most of the nation's commerce goes through Tarawa, which has an international airport and docks for ships. The government of Kiribati receives economic aid from Australia, Great Britain, and New Zealand. The government runs a radio station and publishes a weekly newspaper.

History. Most I-Kiribati are descended from Samoans who invaded the islands about 1400 and from people who had settled there earlier. In the 1500's, Spanish explorers became the first Europeans to sight the islands. During the 1890's, Great Britain took control of the Gilbert Islands and the neighboring Ellice Islands to the south. It gained control of Ocean Island in 1901. In 1916, the British made these islands the Gilbert and Ellice Islands Colony. Some of the Line Islands, and the Phoenix Islands, were later added to the colony. During World War II (1939-1945), Japanese troops occupied several of the islands. The United States Marines invaded Tarawa in 1943 and defeated the Japanese in one of the bloodiest battles of the war.

The Ellice Islands separated from the colony in 1975 and became the independent nation of Tuvalu in 1978. The remaining islands in the former Gilbert and Ellice Islands Colony gained independence as Kiribati on July 12, 1979.   ROBERT LANGDON

See also GILBERT ISLANDS; LINE ISLANDS; OCEAN ISLAND; TARAWA; WORLD WAR II (Island Hopping; picture: U.S. Marines).

TARAWA, *tah RAH wah* (pop. 20,000), is the capital of Kiribati, a country of many small islands in the southwest Pacific Ocean. Tarawa is an *atoll* (ring-shaped reef) composed of many coral islets that cover a total of 9 square miles (23 square kilometers).

The commercial and shipping center of Kiribati is Betio, a densely populated islet in the southwest area of Tarawa. Bairiki, east of Betio, is the government center. Bonriki, an islet in the southeast, has an international airport.

In 1788, the British explorer Captain Thomas Gilbert became the first European to sight Tarawa. The British took control of Tarawa in the 1890's. In 1942, during World War II, Japanese troops seized the atoll. American forces captured Tarawa from the Japanese in 1943 in one of the bloodiest battles of the war. Britain then ruled Tarawa until 1979, when it became part of the independent nation of Kiribati.   ROBERT LANGDON

See also KIRIBATI; WORLD WAR II (Tarawa; picture: U.S. Marines).

SAINT VINCENT AND THE GRENADINES

J. Alex Langley, DPI

St. Vincent and the Grenadines is a country in the Caribbean Sea. Its capital, Kingstown, has a beautiful harbor, above.

SAINT VINCENT AND THE GRENADINES is a small island country in the West Indies. It lies in the Caribbean Sea, about 200 miles (320 kilometers) north of Venezuela. For location, see WEST INDIES (map). The country consists of the island of St. Vincent and about 100 small islands of the Grenadine chain, including Bequia, Canouan, Mustique, and Union. It has a total land area of 150 square miles (388 square kilometers) and a population of about 133,000.

St. Vincent and the Grenadines became independent in 1979 after being ruled by Great Britain since 1783. Kingstown, on the southern coast of St. Vincent, is the capital and largest city. The basic unit of money is the East Caribbean dollar. For a picture of the nation's flag, see FLAG (flags of the Americas).

Government. St. Vincent and the Grenadines is a constitutional monarchy and a member of the Commonwealth of Nations (see COMMONWEALTH OF NATIONS). A prime minister runs the government, with the aid of a Cabinet. A one-house Parliament, which consists of 13 representatives and 6 senators, makes the country's laws. The people elect the representatives. The governor general, a symbolic official appointed by the British monarch, appoints the senators. The head of the political party with the most seats in Parliament serves as prime minister.

People. Most of the people of St. Vincent and the Grenadines are descendants of black African slaves. British and French settlers brought the slaves to the islands. More than 75 per cent of the people live in rural areas, and the rest live in urban localities.

English, the official language, is widely used, but a large number of the people also speak French. Many live in wood or concrete houses that have tile roofs. The main foods include bananas, fish, rice, and a special dish of baked breadfruit and fried fish.

Land and Climate. St. Vincent and the Grenadines is a mountainous country that was formed by volcanic eruptions. Tropical vegetation covers much of the land. Mount Soufrière, an active volcano on the northern end of St. Vincent, is the country's highest point. It rises 4,048 feet (1,234 meters).

Temperatures in the country seldom rise above 90° F. (32° C) or fall below 65° F. (18° C). The annual rainfall ranges from 60 inches (150 centimeters) on the southeast coast of St. Vincent to 150 inches (381 centimeters) in the island's central mountains.

Economy of St. Vincent and the Grenadines is based on agriculture. Most of the people work on farms. The main export crops include bananas, coconuts, and spices. The country is also one of the world's major suppliers of arrowroot, a plant whose roots are made into starch. Fishing, manufacturing, and tourism are minor economic activities.

History. Arawak Indians were the first inhabitants of what became St. Vincent and the Grenadines. They were conquered about 1300 by the Carib Indians of South America. The Carib, the British, and the French fought one another for the islands until 1783, when Great Britain took full control. During the period that the three groups struggled for possession, the British and French brought slaves from Africa to work on island plantations. The slaves were freed during the 1800's.

During the 1900's, St. Vincent and the Grenadines gradually gained more freedom from Britain. It became independent on Oct. 27, 1979. In December 1979, police put down a minor revolt on Union Island by a group that wanted more power in the country's new government. THOMAS G. MATHEWS

See also KINGSTOWN.

KINGSTOWN (pop. 29,831) is the capital and largest city of St. Vincent and the Grenadines, an island country in the Caribbean Sea. It lies in foothills on the southwest coast of St. Vincent Island.

Kingstown has a busy harbor whose import and export activities are the basis of the city's economy. The city has few other industries, and its unemployment rate is high. Most houses and other buildings in Kingstown are small and made of brick or wood. Near the city are an old British fort and a botanical garden.

Carib Indians lived in the Kingstown area, possibly as early as the 1300's. Beginning in the 1600's, France and Great Britain fought for control of St. Vincent Island. Britain governed the island from 1783 to 1979, when it became part of the independent country of St. Vincent and the Grenadines. THOMAS G. MATHEWS

Dictionary Supplement

1980

This section lists important words from the 1981 edition of THE WORLD BOOK DICTIONARY. This dictionary, first published in 1963, keeps abreast of our living language with a program of continuous editorial revision. The following supplement has been prepared under the direction of the editors of THE WORLD BOOK ENCYCLOPEDIA and Clarence L. Barnhart, editor in chief of THE WORLD BOOK DICTIONARY. It is presented as a service to owners of the dictionary and as an informative feature to subscribers to THE WORLD BOOK YEAR BOOK.

A a

ac|u|pres|sure (ak′yə presh′ər), *n.* a method of relieving pain, diagnosing illness, etc., by applying pressure where major nerves are close to the skin: *The advantages of diagnosis by way of acupressure are obvious, a probing finger on the outside of the body as compared, for example, to opening up the body to see what's wrong. One of the new alternative medical centers . . . reports considerable success in diagnosing otherwise inexplicable complaints with acupressure* (Stephen A. Applebaum). [< Latin *acus* needle + English *pressure*]

anx|i|o|lyt|ic (ang zī′ə lit′ik), *n., adj. —n.* a drug used to relieve anxiety; tranquilizer: *Physicians no less than patients . . . have always been, and still are, subject to fads and fashions in medicines, and the anxiolytics are today's "in" drugs* (New York Times Magazine).
—adj. used or tending to relieve anxiety; tranquilizing: *The doctors point out that big cash savings could be made by prescribing meditation rather than anxiolytic, hypotensive and antidepressant drugs* (London Times).
[< *anx*(iety) + *lytic*]

ASAT (ā′sat), *n.* a hunter-killer satellite able to destroy another satellite: *ASAT . . . has a parabolic "dish" antenna that homes in on the target satellite . . . where it detonates. The ASAT goes off like a super hand grenade* (Time). [< *A*nti-*Sat*ellite interceptor]

A|sia|dol|lar (ā′zhə dol′ər), *n.* a U.S. dollar deposited in Asian banks and used in various money markets of Asia: *U.S. companies flock to buy Asiadollar CDs* (Business Week).

B b

bi|gem|o|ny (bī′jem′ə nē), *n.* political domination by two states: *Bigemony . . . generally refers to the condominium exercised by the two superpowers, but inside the NATO camp, too, there are signs of a bigemony of sorts emerging, based on a Bonn-Washington axis* (David Rudnick). [< *bi*- two + (he)*gemony*]

bi|o|mass, 2 plant material or vegetation, especially as a source of fuel or energy: *The process by which vegetable material or "biomass" as it is technically known is transformed into alcohol fuel is simple* (Manchester Guardian Weekly).

blow|down (blō′doun′), *n.* rupture of a cooling pipe in a nuclear reactor, especially in a power plant: *In nuclear parlance, "blowdown" is synonymous with catastrophe, as it signifies loss of coolant with the nuclear reactor continuing to produce heat with nothing to carry it away* (New Scientist).

Bromp|ton / cocktail or **mixture** (brom′tən), a preparation of narcotics used to relieve pain and other symptoms of cancer: *The so-called Brompton cocktail, which can include both heroin and cocaine, is valuable in treating nausea* (New York Times). [< *Brompton* Chest Hospital, in London, England, where it was apparently first used]

bu|lim|a|rex|i|a (byŭ lim′ə rek′sē ə), *n.* a psychological disorder in which a person alternates between an abnormal craving for food and an aversion to it, found especially among young women: *The distinguishing feature of bulimarexia is its regu-lar binges, its orgies of eating followed by ritual purifications, over and over again* (Psychology Today). [< *bulim*(ia) + *a*(no)*rexia*]

C c

Chi|san|bop (chiz′ən bop, jē′sən-), *n. Trademark.* a system of calculating arithmetically with the fingers, invented by Sung Jin Pai, a Korean mathematician. It is used especially to teach elementary arithmetic. *With Chisanbop, the fingers are used to count to 99, with larger numbers being carried over by memory or written down. On the right hand the thumb stands for one unit with a place value of five, while each finger represents one additional unit. On the left hand the thumb stands for 50, with each finger representing 10* (Maclean's). [< Korean, literally, finger counting]

closed / caption, a television caption for the deaf and hard of hearing that is made visible by a special decoding device attached to or built into the television set: *The programs are to be encoded with what are called "closed" captions—subtitles that are invisible on all television sets except those specially equipped to make them appear* (New York Times).

D d

debit / card, a small plastic card with a code number enabling a bank customer to withdraw cash or make deposits by an automatic teller machine and to charge purchases directly to funds on deposit in the bank: *The debit card . . . is planned to replace the credit card of today. The debit card will be used to initiate a transaction at the bank itself, at a retail outlet, or at a remote unattended location where money can be deposited or withdrawn around the clock* (Rod N. Thorpe).

de|cruit (dē krüt′), *v.t. U.S.* to place (an older or unneeded employee) in another firm or in a lower-level position with his present employer: *Co-Op Denmark, which has department stores and supermarkets, . . . has started a policy of freezing promotions of top managers after age 50 and decruiting them at 60* (Time). [< *de*- + (re)*cruit*]

dis|in|form (dis′in fôrm′), *v.t.* to give distorted or false information to: *Advocates of the change say, in justifying it, that foreign intelligence services today are increasingly using so-called influencing agents for subverting, deceiving and disinforming French public opinion* (Manchester Guardian Weekly). [back formation from *disinformation*]

displaced / homemaker, *U.S.* a married woman who has lost her means of support by divorce, separation, or the death or disability of her husband: *The term displaced homemaker was invented by another Californian . . . who was divorced at 57 and "discovered I was part of an invisible problem, one of the women who had fallen through the cracks, too young for social security, too old to be hired, not eligible for unemployment insurance because homemaking is not considered work"* (Time).

E e

ecu or **ECU** (ā′kü; *sometimes* ē′sē′yü′), *n.* a money of account in the European Common Market, that is a standard in floating currencies within a narrow range: *The annexe suggested that ECUs would be . . . created against the deposits of a certain percentage of central bank gold and dollar reserves* (London Times). [< *E*(uropean) *C*(urrency) *U*(nit)]

en|do|per|ox|ide (en′dō pə rok′sīd), *n.* any one of a group of highly oxygenated compounds that are precursors of prostaglandins: *Prostaglandins can exert their biological action through these endoperoxides, which have been found to be released from a number of tissues. The endoperoxides are metabolized both to prostaglandins and to nonprostaglandin structures, and have unique biological actions on a number of different tissues* (Kenneth T. Kirton). [< *endo*- + *peroxide*]

F f

frac|tal (frak′təl), *n.* any one of a class of highly irregular and fragmented shapes or surfaces not represented in classical geometry: *Fractals arise in many parts of the scientific and mathematical world. Sets and curves with the discordant dimensional behavior of fractals were introduced . . . by Georg Cantor and Karl Weierstrass. Until now their use has been limited primarily to theoretical investigations in advanced mathematical analysis* (Science News). [< Latin *fractus*, past participle of *frangere* to break + English *-al*]

fuel|ish (fyü′lish), *adj.* using excessive fuel: *A word to the fuelish: Beginning Labor Day weekend, Canadians will again be bombarded by advertising campaign urging energy conservation* (Maclean's). [< *fuel* + *ish* as a pun on *foolish*] —**fu′el|ish|ly,** *adv.*

G g

grav|i|ti|no (grav′ə tē′nō), *n.* a hypothetical elementary particle with a spin of 3/2, postulated in the theory of supergravity: *Others are worried by the growing complexity of the theories and the proliferation of the supposedly "basic" building blocks of matter. There is talk of hundreds of them: quarks of different "colors" and "flavors," gluons that bind them inseparably, leptons, bosons and in one formulation that includes gravity, "gravitinos"* (New York Times). [< *gravit*(on) + *-ino* (as in *neutrino*)]

gray|mail (grā′māl′), *n. U.S.* a threat of possible public exposure of government secrets during prosecution in a trial: *Secret proceedings would not eliminate graymail. But the procedure would let all parties know where they stand and reduce the number of cases that cannot be prosecuted* (New York Times). [< *gray* + (black)*mail*]

grid / lock, a complete stoppage of all vehicular traffic on crossing streets in a given area of a city: *As most traffic-jammed New Yorkers found out . . . grid lock (a term used by traffic engineers) exists when traffic suffers paralysis and all vehicle movement stops* (New York Daily News).

H h

high-tech (hī′tek′), *n.* a style of design or interior decoration that uses or imitates objects normally found in factories, warehouses, restaurant kitchens, etc.: *Hightech . . . uses utilitarian industrial equipment and materials, out of context, as home furnishings* (New York Daily News). [< *high-style tech*(nology)]

hon|or / box, *U.S.* a newspaper vending machine which opens, trusting the customer to take a single copy: *The blue-and-white newspaper-vending machines that have been multiplying on city streets as newsstands approach extinction . . . are called "honor boxes"* (New Yorker).

hy|brid|o|ma (hī brə dō′mə), *n.* a cell formed by the fusion of two different cells: *Tissue typing . . . is the labour to which immunologists foresaw the end when they made the first antibody-secreting hybridoma: a hybrid between an ordinary mouse antibody-secreting cell, which has only a limited lifespan, and an immortal tumour cell from a mouse myeloma* (New Scientist). [< *hybrid* + *-oma*]

I i

in|fra|di|an (in frā′dē ən), *adj.* of or having to do with biological rhythms or cycles that recur less than once per day: *Neurobiologic rhythms are organized . . . in three frequency ranges: less than one per day* (infradian), *about one per day* (circadian) *and more than one per day* (ultradian) (J. Allan Hobson). [< *infra-* below + Latin *diēs* day + English *-an*]

ir|i|dol|o|gy (ir′ə dol′ə jē), *n.* a method of examining the iris of the eye as an aid in medical diagnosis: *Iridology can identify an organ that has degenerated enough to become cancerous. The basis for iridology is the neuro-optic reflex, an intimate marriage of the estimated half million nerve filaments of the iris with the cervical ganglia of the sympathetic nervous system* (Esquire). [< Greek *îris, îridos* iris + English *-logy*]
—**ir′i|dol′o|gist**, *n.*

J j

job / bank, a computerized job-placement service: *Job banks . . . produce periodic printout lists of available jobs* (New Scientist).

junk / bond, *U.S.* a high-risk, noncorporate bond that is bought at less than face value: *What they will also get is a piece of a fund that specializes in deep-discount bonds—sometimes known as "junk bonds" . . . Junk bonds, because they carry a much higher risk quotient than corporate bonds, typically offer a much higher return* (Richard Phalon).

K k

kneeling / bus, *U.S.* a bus with a pneumatic suspension system to lower its body to curb level so that passengers do not have to climb a step: *Pledging that his own administration would be "sensitive to the special needs of the aging," Mr. Koch promised, among other things, . . . the deployment of "kneeling" buses "on routes where they will serve the greatest number of people who need them"* (Charles Kaiser).

L l

liberation / theology, Christian theology viewing God as acting through histori-

cal processes to free mankind from oppression: *Some advocates of "liberation theology" have indeed embraced violence, joining guerrilla movements. But more have expressed their convictions peacefully* (New York Times).

lip|o|some (lip′ə sōm, lī′pə-), *n.* a tiny membranous capsule made by the action of ultrasonic vibrations on a suspension of fats in water: *Liposomes were successfully tested as an experimental form of cancer treatment, used to carry drugs selectively to the site of a tumour. They were also used for the first time to treat diseases caused by lack of essential enzymes. The liposomes were employed to carry the missing enzymes to the liver, where they were required. Liposomes were also used to make vaccines much more potent* (John Newell). [< Greek *lípos* fat + English *-some³*]
—**lip|o|so′mal**, *adj.*

M m

marriage / encounter, the meeting of a group of married couples to explore feelings between husbands and wives to improve their relationship: *Dialoguing is what Marriage Encounter is all about. It is a technique you will not learn . . . except during an encounter weekend, a form of communication that cannot be taught properly by one couple or through the printed word* (Kitty Hanson).

mon|o|clo|nal / antibody (mon′ə klō′nəl), a specific antibody produced in the laboratory by fusing genetically distinct cells and cloning resulting hybrids to produce the same antibody: *Active areas of research . . . include development of monoclonal antibodies that enhance organ transplants, that diagnose and monitor leukemia and that detect subtle changes in the nervous system* (Science News).

N n

ne|o|con|ser|va|tism (nē′ō kən sér′və tiz əm), *n. U.S.* conservatism that favors many social reforms while opposing big government and that often supports the interests of business on economic issues: *What is not often realized, however, is how much of the currently fashionable "neoconservatism" is made possible by the rapid exertions of government in the recent past to meet the real problems of this society* (Washington Post).

ne|o|mort (nē′ō môrt′), *n.* a body whose brain is dead but whose other organs keep functioning by artificial means: *The neomort by definition has no functioning nervous system* (Harper's). [< *neo-* new + Latin *mortuus* dead]

O o

O|klo / phenomenon (ō′klō), the occurrence of a series of natural nuclear chain reactions during the formation of a uranium deposit in geological times: *The "Oklo phenomenon" . . . is an occurrence of natural chain fission reactions which took place in a uranium deposit in Precambrian times, and which were moderated by groundwaters. Many of the resultant actinides and fission products are still

fixed in the host rocks in the reactor zones despite 1,800 million years of subsequent exposure to geological processes* (New Scientist). [< *Oklo*, a uranium mine in southeastern Gabon where the phenomenon was discovered]

OMA (ō′mə), *n. U.S.* Orderly Marketing Agreement (an agreement between governments that restricts imports of a product when it jeopardizes employment, production, and sales of the importing country's industry): *The Administration has negotiated an OMA limiting imports of Japanese color-TV sets to 41% of their 1976 level . . . Another OMA limits imports of shoes from Korea and Taiwan to 25% and 20%, respectively* (Time).

P p

(petro-) 3 of the oil-exporting countries: *Petropower- the power of oil-exporting countries. Part of sterling's strength may be its position as the "petrocurrency"* (Manchester Guardian Weekly).

pink-col|lar (pingk′kol′ər), *adj. U.S.* of or having to do with occupations in which women predominate: *Working women are still disproportionately herded into so-called pink-collar jobs—teaching, clerical and retail sales work* (Time).

Pin|yin (pin′yin′), *n.* a system for transliterating Chinese into Roman characters: *The adoption of the official system, known as Pinyin* (meaning simply "transcription"), *was announced . . . as a measure to standardize the spelling of Chinese words in English, French, German and other languages using the Roman alphabet* (Fox Butterfield).

pros|ta|cy|clin (pros′tə sī′klin), *n.* a substance produced by enzymes that inhibits the aggregation of blood platelets and dilates blood vessels: *Chemists have succeeded in synthesising a natural substance which it is hoped may lead to the prevention of heart attacks and strokes in people with atherosclerosis. The compound, prostacyclin . . . is thought to protect human beings from the formation of blood clots inside healthy blood vessels* (London Times). [< *prosta*(glandin) + *cycl*(e) + *-in²*]

psy|cho|bab|ble (sī′kō bab′əl), *n.* psychological jargon, especially the jargon of psychotherapy groups: *According to the practitioners of currently fashionable psychobabble, we live in the best of times because more and more people are "being upfront" about their feelings and "doing their own thing"* (William Colgan). [< *psycho-*(logical) + *babble;* coined by Richard D. Rosen, an American author]

Q q

quad⁴ (kwod), *n. U.S.* a unit of energy equal to one quadrillion British thermal units: *Without any new initiatives the need for imported oil will rise steadily from about 12 quads at present to more than 60 in the year 2000* (Scientific American). [< *quad*(rillion)]

Pronunciation Key: hat, āge, cãre, fär; let, ēqual, tèrm; it, īce; hot, ōpen, ôrder; oil, out; cup, pùt, rüle; child; long; thin; ᴛнen; zh, measure; ə represents **a** in about, **e** in taken, **i** in pencil, **o** in lemon, **u** in circus.

R r

ret|ro|vi|rus (ret′rō vī′rəs), *n.* any of a group of tumor-producing viruses that use RNA instead of DNA to encode genetic information: *The RNA tumor viruses, which produce animal cancers, use RNA instead of DNA to encode their genetic information. They are often called "retroviruses" because they reverse a step in one central dogma of biology: DNA makes RNA makes protein* (Science News).

S s

shi|at|su or **shi|at|zu** (shē ät′sü), *n.* a method of massaging parts of the body by finger pressure to relieve pain, fatigue, etc.: *Japanese shiatsu massage is available at several locations in addition to the Salon de Tokyo... The undisputed Sorbonne of shiatsu is the Shiatsu Education Center of America* (New York Sunday News). [< Japanese *shiatsu*]

silo / buster, *U.S. Slang.* a nuclear missile to destroy enemy missile silos: *The MX would be so accurate and powerful that it would fall into the first-strike category of "silo busters," especially in the eyes of the Soviets* (Washington Post).

singularity, *n.* **4** *Astronomy.* a hypothetical point in space at which an object becomes compressed to infinite density and infinitesimal volume: *A singularity is a mathematical point at which an object such as a burnt-out star that has collapsed under its own gravity is... effectively crushed out of existence, although its gravity continues to exert an influence on the surrounding space. In practice, a singularity is surrounded by a region of space so distorted by gravity that nothing can escape; it is this region that constitutes the black hole* (New Scientist).

sin|se|mil|la (sin′sə mil′yə), *n.* a highly cultivated strain of seedless marijuana: *THC, of course, is the active chemical ingredient in marijuana... Sinsemilla is loaded with THC* (Maclean's). [< Mexican Spanish, literally, without seed]

spa, *n.* **3** *U.S.* = hot tub: *Because of their small size, spas do not require as much energy or money to keep the water hot. In California, approximately $10 to $15 is required to heat a spa for an entire month* (Mark Lundahl).

status / offender, *U.S.* a child or adolescent placed under jurisdiction of a court because of incorrigible behavior, though not a delinquent: *PINS are called status offenders because it is their state of being... that brings them before the courts* (New Yorker).

su|per|grav|i|ty (sü′pər grav′ə tē), *n.* *Physics.* the gravitational force of supersymmetry: *Since supergravity incorporates standard general relativity in a very fundamental and unique way, it was hoped that the additional constraints imposed by the added symmetry would cause the unmanageable infinities to cancel each other* (Science News).

su|per|sym|me|try (sü′pər sim′ə trē), *n.* *Physics.* symmetry that relates the fermions and the bosons: *The symmetry operations of the hypothetical supersymmetry... assert that the fermions and bosons in a system of particles could be interchanged without substantially altering the system. Hence particles with integral spin and those with half-integral spin can be regarded as manifestations of a single underlying state of matter* (Scientific American).

T t

tau, *n.* **5** *Nuclear Physics.* a weakly interacting elementary particle with a mass about 3½ thousand times that of the electron: *The tau joins the lepton group of particles, which interact only through the forces of the weak nuclear interaction responsible for the radioactive decay of nuclei and electromagnetism. The electron is the best known member of the family* (New Scientist).

tech|ni|cism (tek′nə sizm), *n.* excessive emphasis on practical results or technical methods and procedures: *technicism which places central value on what can be measured* (New York Times). **—tech′ni|cist**, *n.*

tel|e|text (tel′ə tekst′), *n.* a communications system in which printed information transmitted over television channels is displayed on a television screen by a special encoder: *Viewdata and teletext, which allow a viewer to display a "page" of information from a choice of several hundred, will convert television sets into home terminals* (Raymond L. Boggs). [< tele(vision) + text]

throm|box|ane (throm bok′sān), *n.* a substance produced by enzymes in the blood platelets that stimulates the aggregation of blood platelets and constricts blood vessels: *A Swedish research team discovered that platelets can convert prostaglandins into previously unknown compounds, called thromboxanes, which not only encourage the platelets to stick to one another but also cause arteries to contract. That combined action can result in thrombosis and therefore needs to be suppressed. The mechanism of that suppression, it turns out, involves another new compound, probably a prostaglandin* (London Times). [< Greek *thrómbos* clot + English *ox*(ygen) + *-ane*]

U u

UDAG (yü′dag), *n.* Urban Development Action Grant (a U.S. government program granting federal funds for projects to revitalize and develop poor or older sections of a city): *Most UDAG projects have been initiated by city governments or agencies, but about one-fifth have been proposed by private developers, with lesser numbers proposed by nonprofit corporations, banks or financial institutions, and citizens' groups* (Cushing N. Dolbeare).

ul|tra|di|an (ul trā′dē ən), *adj.* of or having to do with biological rhythms or cycles that recur more than once per day: *It is... increasingly clear that a shorter cycle, occurring within mammalian sleep, is another manifestation of the tendency of living things to undergo regular fluctuations of functional level or state, or both, as a function of time; this ultradian clock organizes brain and body activity during mammalian sleep into alternating phases of activity and quiescence* (J. Allan Hobson). [< ultra- beyond + Latin *diēs* day + English *-an*]

V v

variable / rate / mortgage, *U.S.* a mortgage on which the interest rate rises or falls with the interest rate in the money market: *Variable rate mortgages (VRMs) are in use at savings and loan associations in about a dozen states. The VRM is usually offered at half a percentage point below the going interest rate, but after five years it fluctuates, depending on such factors as the long-term federal bond rate* (Ruth Rejnis).

view|da|ta (vyü′dā′tə, -dat′ə, -dä′tə), *n.* any system or network providing computerized information by linking television sets to a computer and displaying the printout on the television screen: *In education, Viewdata makes possible a sort of two-way Sesame Street for handicapped children who need individually paced instruction in the home; in politics, it offers a national poll on issues of the moment; and at income tax time, it can do everything from providing data on laws and procedures to making the calculations and delivering the returns to the revenue department* (David Thomas).

W w

wormhole, *n.* **2** *Astronomy.* a hypothetical passageway in space connecting a black hole and a white hole: *Particularly appealing to science-fiction writers is the concept of "wormholes," which tunnel through the contorted space-time geometry of black holes into other universes— or emerge into our own universe at some other time and place* (Walter Sullivan).

X x

xen|o|cur|ren|cy (zen′ō kėr′ən sē), *n.* currency circulating outside its country of origin: *West German Chancellor Helmut Schmidt and U.S. Treasury Secretary G. William Miller... made a point of referring to "xenocurrency" markets [and] argued that Eurodollars and Eurocurrency are misnomers when applied to billions of dollars and marks circulating in Hong Kong, Singapore, the Bahamas and other non-European money markets* (Newsweek).

Y y

YAVIS (yav′is), *n.* *U.S.* Young, Attractive, Verbal, Intelligent, and Successful: *As has been pointed out many times, psychotherapists prefer to work with people who have the YAVIS Syndrome... and psychotherapy has been found to work most effectively with such people* (Science News).

Z z

zebra, *n.* **2** *U.S. Slang.* an official in a sporting event who wears a striped shirt to distinguish his position as a referee, linesman, or the like: *This year's Super Bowl zebras will, as always, be an all-star cast, chosen by N.F.L. [National Football League] Supervisor of Officials Art McNally and his staff....* (Time).

1977
1977
1978
1979
1980

Index

How to Use the Index

This index covers the contents of the 1979, 1980, and 1981 editions of THE WORLD BOOK YEAR BOOK.

Each index entry is followed by the edition year (in *italics*) and the page number, as:

ADVERTISING, *81*-172, *80*-176, *79*-176

This means, for example, that information about Advertising begins on page 172 in the 1981 edition of THE YEAR BOOK.

An index entry that is the title of an article appearing in THE YEAR BOOK is printed in capital letters, as: **AUTOMOBILE.** An entry that is not an article title, but a subject discussed in an article of some other title, is printed: **Pollution.**

The various "See" and "See also" cross references in the index list are to other entries within the index. Clue words or phrases are used when two or more references to the same subject appear in the same edition of THE YEAR BOOK. These make it easy to locate the material on the page, since they refer to an article title or article subsection in which the reference appears, as:

Genetics: biochemistry, *81*-213, *80*-218, *79*-220; biology, *81*-214; health, *80*-346; *Focus, 79*-37; Supreme Court, *81*-493

The indication "*il.*" means that the reference is to an illustration only. An index entry in capital letters followed by "*WBE*" refers to a new or revised WORLD BOOK ENCYCLOPEDIA article in the supplement section, as:

PETROLEUM, *WBE, 81*-558

A

INDEX

Acknowledgments

The publishers acknowledge the following sources for illustrations. Credits read from top to bottom, left to right, on their respective pages. An asterisk (*) denotes illustrations created exclusively for THE YEAR BOOK. All maps, charts, and diagrams were prepared by THE YEAR BOOK staff unless otherwise noted.

3	Jet Propulsion Laboratory
9	© Henri Bureau, Sygma
10	© Andy Sacks, Black Star; © Dilip Mehta, Contact
11	© Steven E. Sutton, Duomo; © J. P. Laffont, Sygma; Montecino and Slaughter, Gamma/Liaison
12	© El Koussey, Sygma; Jacob Sutton, Gamma/Liaison; © P. Chauvel, Sygma
13	© Diego Goldberg, Sygma; Abbas, Gamma/Liaison; Jean-Claude Francolon, Gamma/Liaison; © ANP Foto
14	© James Mason, Black Star; © Susan Greenwood, Gamma/Liaison
15	© Dennis Brack, Black Star; Abril, Gamma/Liaison
16	Leif Skoogfors, Gamma/Liaison; © Arnold Zann, Black Star; © Sipa Press from Black Star; © Pana, Black Star
17	© Alain Keler, Sygma; © Dennis Brack, Black Star
18	© Henri Bureau, Sygma
19	© Paul J. Sutton, Duomo; Australian Consolidated News
20	© Tony Korody, Sygma; © Sygma; © Francois Lochon, Gamma/Liaison
21	© John Launois, Black Star
23	Steve Hale*
24	Steve Hale*; Steve Hale*; Steve Hale*; Steve Hale*; Dennis Brack, Black Star
25-27	Steve Hale*
28	Rick Bloom, Lensman
29	Rick Bloom, Lensman; John Lopinot, Black Star
30-31	Steve Hale*
32	Doug Wilson, Black Star
34	Steve Hale*
35	Fabian, Sygma
36	Steve Hale*
37	Abbas, Gamma/Liaison
39	Dennis Brack, Black Star
40	Andy Levin, Black Star
42	Herman J. Kokojan, Black Star
44	Wide World; WORLD BOOK photo*
46-47	Steve Hale*
48	Dave Harp, Lensman; Owen D.B., Black Star
49	Dirck Halstead, Gamma/Liaison
50	Steve Hale*
53	Dan Miller*
54	Steve Hale*
57	Bettmann Archive
60-67	Steve Hale*
69	CBS News
70	Steve Hale*
72-85	William Petersen*
88	© Nigel Smith, Earth Scenes
89	Nicholas de Vore III, Bruce Coleman Inc.
91	A. Devaney, Inc. from Marilyn Gartman Agency; Leon V. Kofod; Georgia-Pacific Corporation
92	Jim Holland, Stock, Boston; Robert H. Glaze, Artstreet
94	© Loren McIntyre, Cher Photography Agency
95	Lawrence S. Hamilton
96	Leon V. Kofod
97	© Loren McIntyre, Cher Photography Agency; Jay Lurie, Tom Stack & Assoc.
98	© Loren McIntyre, Cher Photography Agency
100	Lawrence S. Hamilton
101	© Loren McIntyre, Cher Photography Agency; Georgia-Pacific Corporation
102	Nancy Sefton; © Raymond A. Mendez, Animals Animals; Gerald L. French, The Photo File; © Zig Leszczynski, Animals Animals
103	Warren Garst, Tom Stack & Assoc.
106	Dan Miller*
110	Dan Miller*; Fred Leavitt, Atoz Images; Dan Miller*; Steve Hale*; WORLD BOOK photo*
111	Steve Hale*; Dan Miller*; Dan Miller*
112	WORLD BOOK photo*; Steve Hale*; Dan Miller*; Boy Scouts of Canada; Dan Miller*; WORLD BOOK photo*
114	Dan Miller*; Steve Hale*; WORLD BOOK photo*; WORLD BOOK photo*; WORLD BOOK photo*
115	© Joel W. Rogers, West Stock Inc.; Steve Hale*; Dan Miller*; Gerry Souter, Atoz Images; WORLD BOOK photo*
117	Steve Hale*; Herbst/Lazar Design Inc. (Steve Hale*); WORLD BOOK photo; Steve Hale*; Dan Miller*; L. L. T. Rhodes, Atoz Images
120	WORLD BOOK photo*
122	Camilla Fox
124	Michael W. Fox; Steve Harper, Atoz Images
125	Tracy Borland; Fred Leavitt, Atoz Images
126	Michael W. Fox
127	Steve Hale*
128	Michael W. Fox
129	Michael W. Fox; Michael W. Fox; Steve Hale*
130	© Ralph Hunt Williams, West Stock Inc.
131	Tom Buckhoe
132	Steve Hale*
133	Michael W. Fox; Steve Hale*
134	© Charles Glen Kirk, West Stock Inc.
136	Steve Hale*
139	Kinuko Craft*
141	Kinuko Craft*
142-143	Illustration by Kinuko Craft* adapted from photography by Bayer AG, Leverkusen, Germany
144	Monsanto Company; Walgreen Laboratories, Inc. (Steve Hale*); Walgreen Laboratories, Inc. (Steve Hale*)
145	Walgreen Laboratories, Inc. (Steve Hale*)
148	Kinuko Craft*
152	Steve Hale*
155	Leslie's Illustrated Weekly, The Newberry Library, Chicago
156-168	Leslie's Illustrated Weekly, The Newberry Library, Chicago Constructions by George Suyeoka. (Steve Hale*)
171	Keystone
172	United Press Int.
173	Wide World
174	Steve Wood, London Express
175	Wide World
176	Peter Jordan, Gamma/Liaison
180	United Press Int.
182	Wide World
183	Mario Ruiz
184	Steven Kimbrough, Duke University
186	Richard Gross
188-191	Wide World
193-194	United Press Int.
196	Sydney Morning Herald
198-200	Wide World
205	Michael T. Kaufman, NYT Pictures
206	Ted Mahieu
209-212	United Press Int.
214-215	Wide World
217	Phil Mascione, Chicago Tribune
218	© Camera Press Ltd.
219	Claus Meyer, Black Star
220	Wide World
221	Keystone
222	Mallet, Pourquoi Pas, Brussels from World Press Review
225-227	Wide World
228	United Press Int.
229	Wide World
232	Thomas Victor, People Weekly © 1980 Time Inc.
234	United Press Int.
235	Wide World
237	William E. Sauro, NYT Pictures
238	© Clarence Brown
240-242	United Press Int.
243-245	Wide World
246	United Press Int.
252	Wide World
254	United Press Int.
255	N. V. Philips' Gloeilampenfabrieken
256	Salvation Army
257	Wide World

A Preview of 1981

January

				1	2	3
4	5	6	7	8	9	10
11	12	13	14	15	16	17
18	19	20	21	22	23	24
25	26	27	28	29	30	31

1 **New Year's Day.**
St. Basil's Day, Eastern Orthodox feast day.

5 **97th Congress** convenes for first session.

6 **Epiphany,** 12th day of Christmas, celebrates visit of the Three Wise Men.

15 **Martin Luther King, Jr.'s Birthday,** celebrated in 17 states to honor the slain civil rights leader.

20 **Presidential Inauguration Day,** swearing-in of the 40th President of the United States.

28 **Australia Day** commemorates Captain Arthur Phillip's landing in 1788 at site where Sydney now stands.

February

1	2	3	4	5	6	7
8	9	10	11	12	13	14
15	16	17	18	19	20	21
22	23	24	25	26	27	28

2 **Ground-Hog Day.** Legend says six weeks of winter weather will follow if ground hog sees its shadow.

5 **Chinese New Year,** begins year 4679 of ancient Chinese calendar, the Year of the Cock.

8 **Boy Scouts of America Birthday Anniversary.**

12 **Abraham Lincoln's Birthday,** observed in most states.

14 **Saint Valentine's Day,** festival of romance and affection.

15 **Susan B. Anthony Day,** commemorates the birth of the suffragist leader.

16 **George Washington's Birthday,** according to law, is now legally celebrated by federal employees, the District of Columbia, and all 50 states on the third Monday in February. The actual anniversary is the 22nd.

March

1	2	3	4	5	6	7
8	9	10	11	12	13	14
15	16	17	18	19	20	21
22	23	24	25	26	27	28
29	30	31				

1 **Easter Seal Campaign** through April 19.
Red Cross Month through March 31.

3 **Mardi Gras,** last celebration before Lent, the penitential period that precedes Easter, observed in New Orleans and in many Roman Catholic countries.

4 **Ash Wednesday,** first day of Lent.

8 **Girl Scout Week,** through March 14, marks the organization's 69th birthday.

15 **Camp Fire Girls Birthday Week,** to March 21, marks 71st birthday of the organization.

17 **St. Patrick's Day,** honoring the patron saint of Ireland.

20 **First day of Spring,** 12:03 P.M., E.S.T.
Purim commemorates the saving of Jews through the death of the ancient Persian despot Haman.

April

			1	2	3	4
5	6	7	8	9	10	11
12	13	14	15	16	17	18
19	20	21	22	23	24	25
26	27	28	29	30		

1 **April Fool's Day.**
Cancer Crusade lasts through April 30.

5 **National Library Week** through April 11.

16 **Maundy Thursday,** celebrates Christ's injunction to love one another.

17 **Good Friday,** marks the death of Jesus on the cross. It is observed as a public holiday in 17 states.

19 **Easter Sunday,** commemorating the Resurrection of Jesus Christ.
National Boys' Club Week through April 25.
Passover, or Pesah, first day, starting the 15th day of the Hebrew month of Nisan. The eight-day festival celebrates the deliverance of the ancient Jews from bondage in Egypt.

30 **Walpurgis Night,** according to legend, the night of the witches' Sabbath gathering in Germany's Harz Mountains.

May

					1	2
3	4	5	6	7	8	9
10	11	12	13	14	15	16
17	18	19	20	21	22	23
24	25	26	27	28	29	30
31						

1 **May Day,** observed as a festival of spring in many countries.
Law Day, U.S.A.

2 **Kentucky Derby** at Churchill Downs, Louisville, Ky.

3 **National Family Week** through May 9.
National Music Week through May 10.

10 **Mother's Day.**

25 **Memorial Day,** by law, is the last Monday in May.

28 **Ascension Day,** or Holy Thursday, 40 days after Easter Sunday, commemorating the ascent of Jesus into heaven.

June

	1	2	3	4	5	6
7	8	9	10	11	12	13
14	15	16	17	18	19	20
21	22	23	24	25	26	27
28	29	30				

6 **D-Day,** commemorates the day the Allies landed to assault the German-held continent of Europe in 1944.

7 **Whitsunday,** or Pentecost, the seventh Sunday after Easter, commemorates the descent of the Holy Spirit upon Jesus' 12 apostles.

8 **Shabuot,** Jewish Feast of Weeks, marks the revealing of the Ten Commandments to Moses on Mount Sinai.
Stratford Festival, drama and music, Ontario, Canada, through October 31.

13 **Flag Day.**
Queen's Official Birthday, marked by trooping of the colors in London.

21 **Father's Day.**
First day of Summer, 6:45 A.M., E.S.T.

28 **Freedom Week** through July 4.

July

				1	2	3	4
5	6	7	8	9	10	11
12	13	14	15	16	17	18
19	20	21	22	23	24	25
26	27	28	29	30	31

1 **Dominion Day** (Canada) celebrates the confederation of the provinces in 1867.

3 **Ramadan,** the ninth month of the Muslim calendar, begins, observed by fasting.

4 **Independence Day,** marks Continental Congress' adoption of Declaration of Independence in 1776.

14 **Bastille Day** (France) commemorates popular uprising against Louis XVI in 1789 and seizure of the Bastille, the infamous French prison.

15 **Saint Swithin's Day.** According to legend, if it rains on this day, it will rain for 40 days.

20 **Moon Day,** the anniversary of man's first landing on the moon in 1969.

25 **National Farm Safety Week** through July 31.

August

						1
2	3	4	5	6	7	8
9	10	11	12	13	14	15
16	17	18	19	20	21	22
23	24	25	26	27	28	29
30	31

9 **Tishah B'ab,** Jewish fast day, on ninth day of Hebrew month of Ab, marking Babylonians' destruction of the First Temple in Jerusalem in 587 B.C.; Roman destruction of the Second Temple in A.D. 70; and Roman suppression of Jewish revolt in A.D. 135.

14 **V-J Day** (original) marks Allied victory over Japan in 1945.

15 **Feast of the Assumption,** Roman Catholic and Eastern Orthodox holy day, celebrates the ascent of the Virgin Mary into heaven.

16 **Edinburgh International Festival,** music, drama, and film, through September 8 in Scotland.

19 **National Aviation Day** commemorates the birthday of pioneer pilot Orville Wright.

26 **Women's Equality Day,** commemorating the ratification of the 19th Amendment giving women the vote.

September

	1	2	3	4	5
6	7	8	9	10	11	12
13	14	15	16	17	18	19
20	21	22	23	24	25	26
27	28	29	30

7 **Labor Day** in the United States and Canada.

13 **Harvest Moon,** the full moon nearest the autumnal equinox of the sun, shines with special brilliance for several days and helps farmers in the Northern Hemisphere to get more field work done after sunset.

22 **First day of Autumn,** 10:05 P.M., E.S.T.

29 **Rosh Hashanah,** or Jewish New Year, the year 5742 beginning at sunset. It falls on the first day of the Hebrew month of Tishri and lasts for two days.

October

				1	2	3
4	5	6	7	8	9	10
11	12	13	14	15	16	17
18	19	20	21	22	23	24
25	26	27	28	29	30	31

1 **Anniversary of the 1949 Chinese Communist Revolution,** China's national holiday.

4 **Fire Prevention Week** through October 10.
National 4-H Week through October 10.

8 **Yom Kippur,** or Day of Atonement, most solemn day in the Jewish calendar, marking the end of the period of penitence.

9 **Leif Ericson Day,** honoring early Norse explorer of North America.

11 **National Handicapped Awareness Week** through October 17.
National Y-Teen Week through October 17.

12 **Columbus Day,** commemorates Columbus' discovery of America in 1492.
Thanksgiving Day, Canada.

13 **Sukkot,** or Feast of Tabernacles, begins the nine-day Jewish observance, which originally celebrated the end of harvest season.

25 **National Cleaner Air Week** through October 31.

31 **Halloween,** or All Hallows' Eve.
Reformation Day, celebrated by Protestants, marks the day in 1517 when Martin Luther nailed his Ninety-Five Theses of protest to the door of a church in Wittenberg, Germany.
United Nations Children's Fund (UNICEF) Day.

November

1	2	3	4	5	6	7
8	9	10	11	12	13	14
15	16	17	18	19	20	21
22	23	24	25	26	27	28
29	30

1 **All Saints' Day,** observed by the Roman Catholic Church.

5 **Guy Fawkes Day** (Great Britain), marks the failure of a plot to blow up King James I and Parliament in 1605 with ceremonial burning of Guy Fawkes in effigy.

11 **Veterans Day.**

15 **American Education Week** through November 21.

26 **Thanksgiving Day,** United States.

29 **Advent** begins, first of the four Sundays in the season before Christmas.

December

	1	2	3	4	5
6	7	8	9	10	11	12
13	14	15	16	17	18	19
20	21	22	23	24	25	26
27	28	29	30	31

6 **Saint Nicholas Day,** when children in parts of Europe receive gifts.

10 **Nobel Prize Ceremony,** in Stockholm, Sweden, and Oslo, Norway.

15 **Bill of Rights Day,** marks the ratification of that document in 1791.

21 **Hanukkah,** or Feast of Lights, eight-day Jewish holiday beginning on the 25th day of the Hebrew month of Kislev that celebrates the Jewish defeat of the Syrian tyrant Antiochus IV in 165 B.C. and the rededication of the Temple in Jerusalem.
First day of Winter, 5:51 P.M., E.S.T.

25 **Christmas.**

26 **Boxing Day** in Canada and Great Britain.

31 **New Year's Eve.**

Cyclo-teacher® The easy-to-use learning system

Features hundreds of cycles from seven valuable learning areas

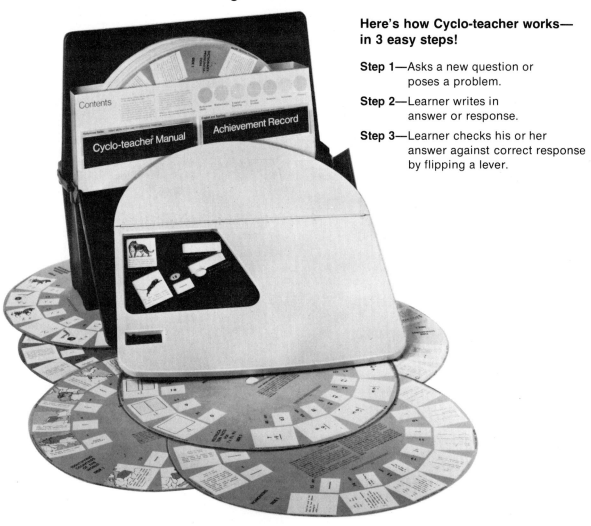

Here's how Cyclo-teacher works— in 3 easy steps!

Step 1—Asks a new question or poses a problem.

Step 2—Learner writes in answer or response.

Step 3—Learner checks his or her answer against correct response by flipping a lever.

Cyclo-teacher —the remarkable learning system based on the techniques of programmed instruction —comes right into your home to help stimulate and accelerate the learning of basic skills, concepts, and information. Housed in a specially designed file box are the Cyclo-teacher machine, Study Wheels, Answer Wheels, a Manual, a Contents and Instruction Card, and Achievement Record sheets.

Your child will find Cyclo-teacher to be a new and fascinating way to learn —much like playing a game. Only, Cyclo-teacher is much more than a game —it teaches new things

. . . reinforces learning . . . and challenges a youngster to go beyond!

Features hundreds of study cycles to meet the individual needs of students —your entire family —just as *Year Book* is a valuable learning aid. And, best of all, lets you track your own progress —advance at your own pace! Cyclo-teacher is available by writing us at the address below:

The World Book Year Book
Post Office Box 3564
Chicago, IL 60654

These beautiful bookstands–

specially designed to hold your entire program,
including your editions of *Year Book*.

Height: 26⅜″
with 4″ legs.
Width: 28¾″
Depth: 8³/₁₆″

Height: 9″
Width: 28½″
Depth: 8³/₁₆″

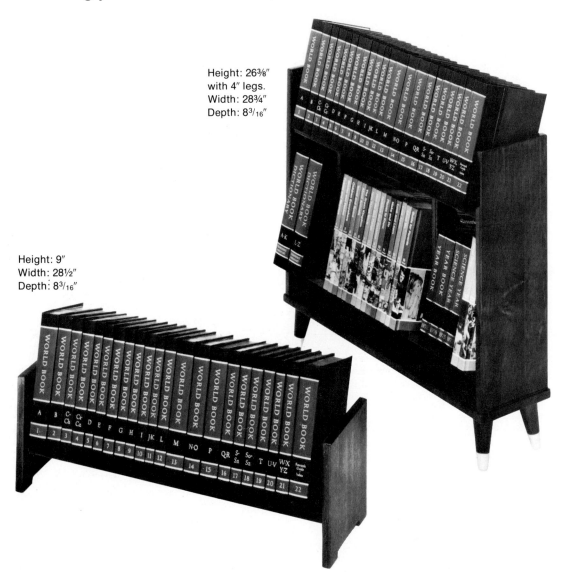

Most parents like having a convenient place to house their *Year Book* editions and their *World Book Encyclopedia*. A beautiful floor-model bookstand —constructed of solid hardwood —is available in either walnut or fruitwood finish.

You might prefer the attractive hardwood table racks, also available in either walnut or fruitwood finish. Let us know by writing us at the following address:

The World Book Year Book
Post Office Box 3564
Chicago, IL 60654